ORGANIZATION	INFORMATION PROVIDED
Major Industrial Accidents Council of Canada (MIACC) http://www.miacc.ca/MM.html	The MIACC is a not-for-profit organization that provides a forum for those who are interested in "prevention, preparedness and response" with regard to major accidents involving hazardous substances. One of the recent additions to this site is a "News Online" area that will bring practitioners up to date with key events and players in this specialized domain.
The Monster Board http://www.monster.ca/	For HR Professionals, The Monster Board offers a gathering place and an information resource. It includes several topic areas related to recruitment, including articles that describe effective recruitment practices, listings of job fairs, layoff notices, advertising agencies, and international recruiting organizations.
Ontario Ministry of Labour home page http://www.gov.on.ca/LAB/	Each province as well as the federal jurisdiction defines many legal entitlements or rights of employees through various pieces of legislation. Most jurisdictions have well-developed web sites that assist both employers and employees in learning about the legal parameters in employment standards, health and safety matters, and a number of other important aspects of the employment relationship. The Ontario Ministry of Labour web site provides a good illustration of the kind of information that can be accessed.
SHRM Gateway http://shrm.org/hrlinks/	This Web site is currently one of the most comprehensive access points to information dealing with human resources issues. It is part of the site for the Society for Human Resource Management, the major U.S. human resources professional association and includes linkages to many international (including Canadian) sites in addition to those oriented to a domestic audience.
Thunderbird School of International Management http://www.t-bird.edu/	This Web site provides access to Dom Pedro II International Studies Research Center, which is an outstanding source of international business and HR information. Thunderbird's home page provides links to files on more than 200 countries, as well as information on the European Union (EU) and the North American Free Trade Association (NAFTA). The sources of this information include economic reports, articles from international journals, and news clippings that pertain to business in many different countries and cultures.
The Training Net http://www.trainingnet.com/	The Training Net is an information resource for training professionals. It contains archives that can locate in-depth articles and books on training; it provides links to other Internet sites on specific training topics; and it includes a chat forum where training professionals can discuss various training topics such as computer training, just-in-time training, diversity training, and managing change in the workplace. The site also contains a jobs database and a training products database,
Transitions Newsletter http://www.murrayaxsmith.com/Publish.htm	This Web site offers a series of short, practical articles by legal and HR experts on various aspects of employment termination and outplacement. It is one of several sources offered by major consulting organizations as part of their larger Web sites.
Workflow and Reengineering International Association (WARIA) http://vvv.com/waria/	WARIA's Web site provides information in work flow and reengineering publications and conferences. It also identifies vendors of workflow software and has a list of consultants who provide reengineering services. Other Web sites on work flow and reengineering are also listed.

Managing Human Resources

Canadian Second Edition

Luis R. Gómez-Mejía
Arizona State University

David B. Balkin
University of Colorado, Boulder

Robert L. Cardy
Arizona State University

David E. Dimick
Schulich School of Business,
York University

Prentice Hall Canada Inc.
Scarborough, Ontario

Canadian Cataloguing in Publication Data

Main entry under title:

Managing human resources

Canadian 2nd ed.
Includes index.
ISBN 0-13-011447-2

1. Personnel management.   I. Gomez-Mejia, Luis R.

HF5549.M31349 2000   658.3   C98-932562-8

Prentice-Hall, Inc., Upper Saddle River, New Jersey
Prentice-Hall International (UK) Limited, London
Prentice-Hall of Australia, Pty. Limited, Sydney
Prentice-Hall Hispanoamericana, S.A., Mexico City
Prentice-Hall of India Private Limited, New Delhi
Prentice-Hall of Japan, Inc., Tokyo
Simon & Schuster Southeast Asia Private Limited, Singapore
Editora Prentice-Hall do Brasil, Ltda., Rio de Janeiro

ISBN 0-13-011447-2

Vice President and Publisher: Patrick Ferrier
Acquisitions Editor: Mike Ryan
Senior Developmental Editor: Lesley Mann
Senior Marketing Manager: Ann Byford
Production Editor: Andrew Winton
Copy Editor: Dianne Broad
Production Coordinator: Deborah Starks
Permissions/Photo Research: Susan Wallace-Cox
Art Director: Mary Opper
Cover and Interior Design: Lisa Lapointe
Cover Image: Steven Lyons
Page Layout: Joan M. Wilson

Original English Language edition published by Prentice-Hall, Inc., Upper Saddle River,
New Jersey. Copyright © 1998, 1995.

2 3 4 5   cc   04 03 02 01 00

Printed and bound in the United States of America.
An extension of this copyright page can be found on page 562.
Visit the Prentice Hall Canada Web site! Send us your comments, browse our
catalogues, and more at **www.phcanada.com**. Or reach us through e-mail at
phcinfo_pubcanada@prenhall.com.

To my wife, Diane, and my two sons,
Vince and Alex

—L.G.M.

To my parents, Daniel and Jeanne

— D.B.B.

To my parents, Ralph and Dorothy; my
wife, Laurel; and my two daughters,
Lara and Emery

—R.L.C.

To Charmaine, and to our daughter,
Sarah

—D.E.D.

Brief Contents

Contents

III   Staffing   142

V   Compensation   285

VI   Governance   382

Preface to the Canadian Second Edition

Formal organizations—businesses, governmental bodies, voluntary organizations—are indispensable in the work of a modern society. They are the vehicles we depend upon to get things done. The success of organizations increasingly rests on effective human resource management. What is becoming clear is that sustainable competitive advantage cannot depend as heavily as in the past on success factors such as a protected market, proprietary technology, or economies of scale. Increasingly global competition, accelerating technological change (particularly the nexus of computing and telecommunications), and social/demographic change have made human resource management not just important but essential.

Competition on price, service, quality, or innovation now comes from anywhere in the world. In more and more sectors of the economy, there is little choice but to use "world class" as the standard for organizational performance. The increasing dependence on "knowledge workers" and the decreasing leverage of other competitive factors together have created an implicit demand for excellence in human resource management.

We are moving through a period of major structural change in the Canadian economy. Natural resources, both renewable and non-renewable, have provided the engine that has driven the economy for much of the Canada's history. While resource industries are still very important, the increasingly open and competitive international economy of which Canada is a part dictates that "hewing wood and drawing water" must play a decreasing role, and that adding value—the application of human capital—must become more central.

Adding value implies a need for effectiveness in managing human resources. In simplest terms, if an organization manages human resources poorly, it is very difficult to sustain success. The qualities of an organization's employees, their enthusiasm and commitment to their work, and their sense of equitable treatment all have a significant impact on the organization's productivity, level of customer service, reputation, and survival.

This text treats human resource management as an integral part of management, not as a collection of activities assigned to a staff department. Human resource management—the management of the employment relationship—is a shared responsibility. Human resources specialists, supervisors and managers throughout the organization, and increasingly employees themselves all contribute to this shared responsibility. Any event or action that affects the employment relationship is an element of human resource management.

This managerial perspective has informed the organization and writing of this text. We offer sufficient detail on the technical issues of human resource management to provide a sound foundation for those who wish to pursue specialized study in human resources. However, the text is also written from the conviction that *all* students of management, regardless of their technical or professional specialization, need to understand the human resources role they will inevitably be asked to play in 21st century organizations. These principles are reflected in the following particulars:

◆ Rather than catalogue the technical details of HR procedures, emphasis is placed on how managers can use tools to solve human resource problems.

◆ Each chapter begins with a provocative situation, demonstrating the relevance of the material to be presented in pages that follow.

◆ Each chapter also includes HRM on the Web, an Internet website description that emphasizes the dynamic nature of HR issues and provides an example of one site that might be helpful with issues covered in that chapter.

◆ Entire chapters are devoted to important contemporary topics, including globalization, the legal framework of HR Management, and workforce diversity. However, such themes are not limited to separate chapters, but are also integrated throughout the text.

◆ Examples are taken from actual organizations. While many of them are Canadian, illustrations from the United States, Europe, and Asia are used liberally throughout the book.

◆ Cases, Minicases, and learning activities integrate the managerial and technical issues that are characteristic of contemporary human resource management.

■ Themes

In addition to the managerial perspective, we thread several themes throughout this book. These themes include:

◆ The need for proactive human resource management and cooperation between line managers and the HR department

◆ The importance of operating within the legal framework

◆ HRM in small businesses

◆ The effect of reorganization, outsourcing, and downsizing on HRM

◆ Workforce diversity as a source of competitive advantage in the global economy

◆ The changing forces of technology and their implications for HRM

■ Changes in the Canadian Second Edition

This Canadian second edition has undertaken several tasks, in addition to making the factual foundation as contemporary as possible.

◆ The book's overall length has been reduced from 19 chapters to 17. This reduction has been accomplished through reorganization and elimination of certain topics (most notably the material on Total Quality Management) that were judged to be somewhat peripheral to the essence of HRM. To emphasize the narrative line through the chapters, some redundant figures and illustrations have been removed, and the Endnotes have been moved from the end of each chapter to the end of the text.

◆ The first two chapters of the first edition have been combined and shortened, developing a sharpened case for the strategic relevance of human resource management.

◆ Organizational design, as reflected in work flows and job analysis, is dealt with in Chapter 3. Chapter 5 includes more extensive discussion of interviewing as part of the recruiting and selection process, as well as using human resource planning as an overall frame for the staffing and socializing processes.

◆ Time-sensitive data such as demographic information and changes to legislation and regulations have been updated. New developments have been noted at companies and organizations used as examples.

◆ Coverage of HRM resources on the Internet has been significantly expanded, reflecting the explosion over the last few years in the number of online references available. HRM on the Web is a new feature at the beginning of every chapter, and includes a topical web address with a short description outlining its relevance to HRM. (For example, Chapter 1 provides the website of the Canadian Council of Human Resources Associates; while Chapter 4 includes the website for the Canadian Human Rights Commission.) Other relevant sites for companies and topics discussed in each chapter appear as Weblinks in the margins of the book. All HRM on the Web sites and Weblinks are included and regularly updated in the "Destinations" area of the text's Companion Website, which is provided in the Take it to the Net box at the end of each chapter. The Companion Website also offers three Internet Exercises per chapter that can be submitted to instructors by e-mail for grading or self-graded by students against suggested answers.

◆ Issues and Applications boxes present additional examples and stories about HRM practices in Canada and around the globe, as well as information about current debates in HRM. For example, the Issues and Applications box in Chapter 2 asks "Are Jobs Obsolete?"

◆ Building Managerial Skills sections have been added to each chapter, providing perspectives and suggestions that will help students in the development of workplace skills.

◆ New opening vignettes, Manager's Notebook boxes, Minicases, Cases, CBC VideoCases, and discussion questions have been added throughout to update and improve the materials from the first edition.

■ Organization

Managing Human Resources, Canadian Second Edition, includes an introductory chapter, followed by another 16 chapters. The book is divided into seven parts.

Part One, a single chapter, provides an overview of the emerging challenges and strategic relevance of human resource management. These challenges—"change drivers," if you will—are distilled from the events that have filled the business press during the past decade. They are related to the basic framework of organizational strategies to provide an introduction to the role that human resource management plays. The overlap and differences between the HRM *process* and the role of the human resources *department* are introduced, portraying human resource management as a responsibility shared by managers in general as well as the HR department.

Part Two considers the contexts in which human resource management takes place. The contextual factors include work flows, the legal environment, and workforce diversity. The chapter on work flows (2) discusses how an organization can work to achieve its business objectives. The chapter on legal issues (3) addresses the legal challenges and constraints facing organizations. The last chapter in this part (4) explores the challenges of effectively managing an increasingly diverse workforce.

Part Three presents staffing issues and considers how organizations can effectively recruit, select, socialize, and phase out employees. The chapter on human resource planning and recruitment, selection, and socialization (5) examines the process by which organizations can attract human resources and then effectively select among the applicants. The chapter on employee separations and outplacement (6) explores the process of terminating the employee relationship, alternatives to layoffs, and different approaches to downsizing the workforce.

Part Four addresses the development of human resources. The chapter on appraising and managing performance (7) focuses on the manager as both a judge and a coach. The chapter on training (8) presents training as an ongoing process and as a critical part of maintaining human resource effectiveness. The chapter on career development (9) identifies the roles of the employee and the organization in the career development process.

Part Five examines compensation issues. The chapter on managing compensation (10) explains the important choices managers face when designing a compensation system and covers different approaches to salary management. The chapter on rewarding performance (11) examines the challenges of tying employees' pay to their performance. The benefits chapter (12) explains the significance of employee benefits programs and outlines how managers are containing costs in this area.

Part Six looks at the governance of the workplace and the employer/employee relationship. The employee relations chapter (13) looks at the ways managers can help the HR department to improve the quality of communications within the organization. The chapter on employee rights (14) examines the challenges of balancing those rights with the rights of managers. The chapter also offers guidelines for managing discipline and dealing with difficult employee problems such as chronic absenteeism and alcohol abuse. The organized labour chapter (15) examines why employees might seek to be represented by a union and how unions alter the employer/employee relationship. The workplace safety and health chapter (16) explains the regulations that govern health and safety in the workplace and emerging health and safety issues that pose challenges to managers.

Part Seven introduces the contemporary HR issues arising from the globalization of the economy, which is quickly becoming one of the defining attributes of the new century. By taking a close look at the emerging HR issues of global business, the book comes full circle to reiterate the importance of change and of change drivers, and to introduce new dimension of human resource management that will help to determine the success and failure of organizations as we enter the 21st century.

■ Features

Managing Human Resources contains a number of innovative pedagogical features. Each chapter contains a number of teaching tools:

◆ A set of learning objectives embodied as management challenges

◆ An opening vignette that draws students into the chapter

◆ A running marginal glossary of key terms, as well as Weblinks (Internet websites related to the topics and organizations discussed in the chapter)

◆ A Summary and Conclusions section

◆ A list of Key Terms and Concepts with page references (key terms are in bold throughout the text and key concepts are italicized, a convention that is also followed in the end-of-chapter list)

◆ A set of Discussion Questions

◆ Take it to the Net, an end-of-chapter reminder about resources available in the text's Companion Website

◆ Two Minicases based on the experiences of small, medium-sized, and large businesses, with discussion questions

◆ Two Cases with critical thinking questions and cooperative learning exercises

In addition, each chapter includes numerous examples of HRM practices at a wide variety of companies, from small, service-providing organizations to huge mega-corporations. References and indexes (Subject and Name) are provided at the end of the book.

Finally, each chapter features special elements that emphasize current issues and practices in HRM. They include:

HRM on the Web: In just a few years, the Internet has become an essential component of business courses. Each chapter of the Canadian second edition begins with a description of a World Wide Web site maintained or sponsored by an HRM-oriented organization. Students should visit these sites at some point while studying the chapter.

A Question of Ethics: Each chapter contains several questions aimed at generating classroom discussion of ethical issues. For example, an ethics feature in Chapter 5 asks students if they would write a positive letter of reference for a friend whom they knew to be unreliable. A Question of Ethics boxes are placed in the margins close to the text discussions of these issues.

Manager's Notebooks: To emphasize our managerial perspective, we've included at least one Manager's Notebook per chapter. These notebooks provide management tips on a variety of issues that managers confront daily, from reducing potential liability for sexual harassment, to managing telecommunications successfully, to conducting exit interviews. For example, Chapter 7 features a Manager's Notebook discussion of key steps in implementing 360-degree appraisal.

Issues and Applications: Students enjoy reading additional examples and stories about HRM practices both in Canada and around the globe. They also enjoy sinking their teeth into current debates. To provide more information on hot topics in

HRM, we've sprinkled Issues and Applications boxes throughout the text. For example, an Issues and Applications feature in Chapter 11 discusses incentive plans that backfired.

Building Managerial Skills: Because students want to take a set of skills into the workplace, each chapter includes a Building Managerial Skills section that provides detailed suggestions for the practice of HR management. For example, Chapter 13 provides suggestions for facilitating effective communications, and Chapter 15 provides guidelines for managing integrative bargaining in a union setting.

Take it to the Net: At the end of each chapter we provide a reminder about the online study materials and research resources available in the text's Companion Website.

Minicases: Each chapter includes two minicases based on the experiences of real-world companies. The discussion questions that accompany these brief exercises give students the opportunity to apply what they've learning in each chapter.

Cases with Critical Thinking Questions and Cooperative Learning Exercises: All chapters end with two case studies. We've developed these cases over the years and tested them in our classes, where they've generated excellent discussion. Critical thinking questions ask students to analyze the facts and situations presented in each case. Cooperative learning exercises ask students to work together, in pairs or in groups, to brainstorm ideas and arrive at solutions.

CBC ◉ **CBC Video Cases:** Each of the seven parts of the book concludes with a video case and discussion questions. The videos, from CBC programs such as *Venture* and *The National Magazine*, focus on current issues on the Canadian business scene, providing additional bridges between the concepts discussed in the text and ongoing events.

■ The Teaching and Learning Package

Companion Web Site with Online Study Guide: Our exciting new Website offers students a comprehensive online study guide with 20 multiple choice and 15 true/false review questions per chapter, experiential exercises, essay questions, Internet exercises, updated Internet destinations and search tools, CBC video case updates, and more. Instructors will be interested in our online syllabus builder and the password-protected Instructors area containing electronic versions of key supplements and updates to the text. (To obtain your password, please contact your Prentice Hall sales representative.)
See **www.prenticehall.ca/gomez** and explore!

www.prenticehall.ca/gomez

Instructor's Resource Manual and CBC Video Guide: The Canadian edition of this supplement has been prepared by David Dimick, the Canadian author of the text. For each chapter of the text the IRM includes a chapter overview/lecture launcher, an annotated outline (including all text features), answers to all questions developed for the chapter, and in-depth analysis of all discussion questions, cooperative learning exercises, minicases, and cases. The CBC Video Guide provides a brief synopsis of each video clip, with tie-in information and suggestions for using the video segment in class. (ISBN 0-13-012660-8)

Test Item File: Also revised for Canadian instructors by David Dimick, the Test Item File includes over 1700 questions. Each chapter includes Objective and Case questions in multiple-choice format, as well as true/false and essay questions. Answers, with page references, are given for all objective questions and suggested answers are provided for essay questions. All questions are rated by level of difficulty (easy, moderate, challenging). (ISBN 0-13-012671-3).

PH Test Manager: Utilizing our new Test Manager program, the computerized test bank for *Managing Human Resources* offers a comprehensive suite of tools for testing and assessment. Test Manager allows educators to easily create and distribute tests for their courses, either by printing and distributing through traditional methods or by on-line delivery via a Local Area Network (LAN) server. Once you have opened Test Manager, you'll advance effortlessly through a series of folders allowing you to quickly access all available areas of the program. Test Manager has removed the guesswork from your next move by incorporating Screen Wizards that assist you with such tasks as managing question content, managing a portfolio of tests, testing students, and analyzing test results. In addition, this all-new testing package is backed with full technical support, comprehensive on-line help files, a guided tour, and complete written documentation. Available as a CD-ROM for Windows 95. (ISBN 0-13-012672-1)

Transparency Resource Package with Electronic Transparencies: Over 300 transparencies in PowerPoint 7.0 have been created for the text, reproducing figures and illustrating important concepts. Detailed teaching notes with page references accompany each slide. (ISBN 0-13-012674-8)

Prentice Hall/CBC Video Library: In an exclusive partnership, the CBC and Prentice Hall Canada have worked together to develop an exciting video package. Segments from the prestigious business affairs series *Venture* and the *National Magazine* news program have been edited to create seven video cases. At an average of seven minutes in length, these segments show students how real Canadian individuals and companies are affected by current issues. Teaching notes are provided in *Instructor's Resource Manual and CBC Video Guide.* (Please contact your Prentice Hall sales representative for details. These videos are subject to availability and terms negotiated upon adoption of the text.)

■ Acknowledgments

My first obligation is to acknowledge the authors of the U.S. editions of this text. Professors Gómez-Mejía, Balkin, and Cardy wrote an excellent first edition, a book that stretched the envelope of conventional human resources texts in the right directions. Their understanding of human resource issues as being strategic and integral to organizational strategy and as integral to all managers' jobs is fundamental in setting this text apart. Their second edition, which sharpened and focused the presentation of the material in addition to updating factual content, has been useful to me as I have revised the Canadian edition. The paradox of their accomplishments in the U.S. editions is that a Canadian presentation has been more challenging to produce, not easier, because of their specificity and numerous examples. The United States and Canada are quite different in many particulars of HRM, despite the many homogenizing influences that exist in our economies and cultures. Some of the very qualities that have made the U.S. editions attractive are the ones that have made them inappropriate for Canadian readers. All chapters in this second Canadian edition been revised, in addition to the reorganization of content outlined earlier. While the differences between the U.S. editions and what follows in this volume are extensive, it still has been an inspiration to have works of such a high standard in front of me as I prepared the Canadian second edition.

I have benefitted significantly from the insights of the following reviewers:

G. Clifford Barrett, Kwantlen University College
Brian Bemmels, University of British Columbia
Edward G. Fisher, University of Alberta
Douglas Fletcher, Kwantlen University College
Jane Haddad, Seneca College
Eli Levanoni, Brock University
Dale McGory, College of the North Atlantic
M.L. Newell, Fanshawe College
Sudhir Saha, Memorial University of Newfoundland
A.V. Subbarao, University of Ottawa

I would also like to acknowledge the people at Prentice-Hall Canada who have played a role in this edition. Mike Ryan, as acquisitions editor, made the case for the project. Lesley Mann, as developmental editor on this edition as well as the first edition, was supportive and found the resources that were crucial to moving though the project in a timely fashion. The rest of the team at Prentice Hall—copyeditor Dianne Broad, production editor Andrew Winton, production co-ordinator Deborah Starks, photo researcher Susan Wallace-Cox, and designer Lisa Lapointe—were also professional and helpful as we dealt with tight timelines.

Finally, I would like acknowledge family, colleagues and friends for their support and encouragement.

David Dimick
Toronto, Ontario

This text has been approved by the Human Resources Professionals Association of Ontario and is listed as a recommended text in HRPAO's "Curriculum Summary".

The Prentice Hall Canada
companion Website...

Your Internet companion to the most exciting, state-of-the-art educational tools on the Web!

The Prentice Hall Canada Companion Website is easy to navigate and is organized to correspond to the chapters in this textbook. The Companion Website is comprised of four distinct, functional features:

1) **Customized Online Resources**

2) **Online Study Guide**

3) **Reference Material**

4) **Communication**

Explore the four areas in this Companion Website. Students and distance learners will discover resources for indepth study, research and communication, empowering them in their quest for greater knowledge and maximizing their potential for success in the course.

A NEW WAY TO DELIVER EDUCATIONAL CONTENT

1) Customized Online Resources

Our Companion Websites provide instructors and students with a range of options to access, view, and exchange content.

- **Syllabus Builder** provides *instructors* with the option to create online classes and construct an online syllabus linked to specific modules in the Companion Website.

- **Mailing lists** enable *instructors* and *students* to receive customized promotional literature.

- **Preferences** enable *students* to customize the sending of results to various recipients, and also to customize how the material is sent, e.g., as html, text, or as an attachment.

- **Help** includes an evaluation of the user's system and a tune-up area that makes updating browsers and plug-ins easier. This new feature will enhance the user's experience with Companion Websites.

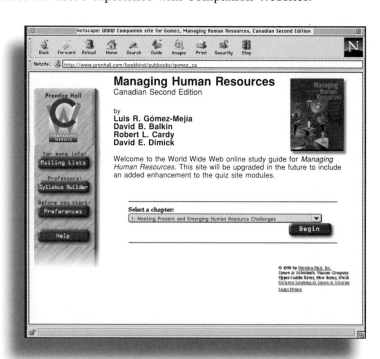

2) Online Study Guide

Interactive Study Guide modules form the core of the student learning experience in the Companion Website. These modules are categorized according to their functionality:

- True-False
- Multiple Choice
- Essay questions
- Experiential Exercises

The True-False, Multiple Choice, Essay and Experiential Exercise modules provide students with the ability to send answers to our grader and receive instant feedback on their progress through our Results Reporter. Coaching comments and references back to the textbook ensure that students take advantage of all resources available to enhance their learning experience.

3) Reference Material

Reference material broadens text coverage with up-to-date resources for learning. **Web Destinations** provides a directory of Web sites relevant to the subject matter in each chapter. **NetNews (Internet Newsgroups)** are a fundamental source of information about a discipline, containing a wealth of brief, opinionated postings. **NetSearch** simplifies key term search using Internet search engines.

4) Communication

Companion Websites contain the communication tools necessary to deliver courses in a **Distance Learning** environment. **Message Board** allows users to post messages and check back periodically for responses. **Live Chat** allows users to discuss course topics in real time, and enables professors to host on-line classes.

Communication facilities of Companion Websites provide a key element for distributed learning environments. There are two types of communication facilities currently in use in Companion Websites:

- **Message Board** – this module takes advantage of browser technology providing the users of each Companion Website with a national newsgroup to post and reply to relevant course topics.

- **Live Chat** – enables instructor-led group activities in real time. Using our chat client, instructors can display Website content while students participate in the discussion.

Companion Websites are currently available for:
- Starke: Contemporary Management in Canada
- Robbins: Organizational Behaviour
- Dessler: Human Resource Management in Canada
- **Note:** CW '99 content will vary slightly from site to site depending on discipline requirements.

PRENTICE HALL CANADA

1870 Birchmount Road
Scarborough, Ontario M1P 2J7

To order:
Call: 1-800-567-3800
Fax: 1-800-263-7733

For samples:
Call: 1-800-850-5813
Fax: (416) 299-2539
E-mail: phcinfo_pubcanada@prenhall.com

The Companion Websites can be found at:

About the Authors

Luis R. Gómez-Mejía is Professor of Management in the College of Business at Arizona State University. He received his Ph.D. and M.A. in industrial relations from the University of Minnesota and a B.A. in economics from the University of Minnesota. Prior to entering academia, Professor Gómez-Mejía worked for eight years in human resources for the City of Minneapolis and Control Data Corporation. He has served as consultant to numerous organizations since then. Prior to joining ASU, he taught at the University of Colorado and the University of Florida. He has served two terms on the editorial board of the *Academy of Management Journal* and is editor and co-founder of the *Journal of High Technology Management Research*. He has published over 60 articles appearing in the most prestigious management journals including the *Academy of Management Journal, Administrative Science Quarterly, Strategic Management Journal, Industrial Relations,* and *Personnel Psychology*. He has also written and edited a dozen management books published by Prentice Hall, Southwestern Press, JAI Press, and Grid. He was ranked one of the top nine in research productivity based on the number of publications in the *Academy of Management Journal*. He has received numerous awards including "best article" in the *Academy of Management Journal* (1992) and *Council of 100 Distinguished Scholars* at Arizona State University (1994). Professor Gómez-Mejía's research focuses on macro HR issues, international HR practices, and compensation.

David B. Balkin is Associate Professor of Management in the College of Business Administration at the University of Colorado at Boulder. He received his Ph.D. in industrial relations from the University of Minnesota. Prior to joining the University of Colorado, he served on the faculties of Louisiana State University and Northeastern University. He has published over 35 articles appearing in such journals as the *Academy of Management Journal, Strategic Management Journal, Industrial Relations, Personnel Psychology, Journal of Labor Research,* and *Academy of Management Executive*. One of his publications (co-authored with Luis Gómez-Mejía) was selected as the best article published in 1992 in the *Academy of Management Journal*. Professor Balkin has written or edited three books on HRM topics. He has consulted for a number of organizations, including U.S. West, Baxter Healthcare, Hydro Quebec, and The Commonwealth of Massachusetts. Professor Balkin's research focuses on the interaction between business strategy and HR policies, and the design and implementation of reward systems.

Robert L. Cardy is Professor of Management in the College of Business at Arizona State University. He received his Ph.D. in industrial/organizational psychology from Virginia Tech in 1982. He is an ad hoc reviewer for a variety of journals, including the *Academy of Management Journal* and the *Academy of Management Review*. He is editor and co-founder of the *Journal of Quality Management*. Professor Cardy has been recognized for this research, teaching, and service. He was ranked in the top 20 in research productivity for the decade 1980–89 based on the number of publications in the *Journal of Applied Psychology*. He was doctoral coordinator in ASU's management department for five years and received a University Mentor Award in 1993 for his work with doctoral students. He authors a regular column on current issues in HRM and received an Academy of Management certificate for outstanding service as a columnist for the HR division newsletter. Professor Cardy was a 1992 recipient of a certificate for significant contributions to the quality of life for students at ASU. His research focuses on performance appraisal and effective HRM practices in a quality-oriented organizational environment.

David E. Dimick is Associate Professor of Organizational Behaviour and Industrial Relations in the Schulich School of Business at York University in Toronto. He received his Ph.D. and M.A. in Industrial Relations from the University of Minnesota and his B.A. in economics and mathematics from St. Olaf College. His research has been published in a number of journals, including the *Academy of Management Review*, the *Academy of Management Journal, Management Science, Relations Industrielles,* and the *Canadian Journal of Sociology*. He has served for the past ten years as the Chair of the Board of Examiners for the Human Resources Professionals Association of Ontario (HRPAO) and is a Contributing Editor to *Human Resources Management in Canada*. He is currently Program Director of the BBA Program at the Schulich School of Business.

Meeting Present and Emerging Human Resource Challenges

After reading this chapter, you should be able to deal more effectively with the following challenges:

1 Explain how a firm's human resources influence its performance.

2 Describe how firms can use human resource initiatives to cope with workplace changes and trends such as a more diverse work force, the global economy, and new legislation.

3 Distinguish between the role of the human resources department and the role of the firm's managers in utilizing human resources effectively.

4 Indicate how members of the human resources department and managers within a company can establish a strong partnership.

5 Formulate and implement HR strategies that can help the firm achieve a sustained competitive advantage.

6 Identify HR strategies that fit corporate and business unit strategies.

The far-reaching effects of labour strikes.
For years, General Motors was known as a source of secure employment. However, in an attempt to reduce costs and operate more effectively in an increasingly competitive global marketplace, GM sought to outsource more of its part manufacturing. GM employees were understandably concerned about potential job losses. These challenges—and employee responses to employer actions—are among the most important facing managers today.

The strike that hit General Motors (GM) in the summer of 1998 started at a single plant in Flint, Michigan. Before it was resolved, however, the whole of GM's North American auto manufacturing operations had been shut down as needed parts from the Flint plant ran out as a result of a strike that lasted two months. The key issues that prompted the strike were contracting out work and moving work out of the plant in question. GM was attempting to reduce its costs. Industry analysts suggest that the cost per vehicle is higher and the profit per vehicle is lower than at Ford and Chrysler, the other two of the big three auto makers. GM clearly wants to outsource more of its parts manufacturing to reduce costs—a change from the strategy of the 1960s and 1970s, which emphasized in-house production and which accounts for much of the difference between GM's number of vehicles per employee (18.5) compared with Chrysler's (29) and Ford's (34).

This conflict at GM might appear to be a "zero-sum game," with either the unionized workers losing jobs or other benefits or the company being forced to compete with a higher cost structure than its major competitors. However, union leaders including Buzz Hargrove, president of the Canadian Auto Workers, made the point that it had been possible for management and unionized workers to find ways of dealing with these issues at the other companies, but that there often seemed to be greater difficulty when it came to GM.

The unavoidable implication of this dispute and of many other situations in virtually every sector of the economy is that human resource management *is* strategic. Getting the human resource relationships "right" is not a guarantee of organizational success, just as simply having a good product is no guarantee. But getting HR wrong or treating it as simply an administrative activity with no real strategic relevance exposes an organization to high risks of substandard performance or even outright failure.[1]

This book is about the people who work in an organization and their relationship with that organization. Different terms are used to describe these people: employees, associates (at Wal-Mart, for instance), personnel, human resources. None of these terms is better or worse than the others, and they often are used interchangeably. The term we have chosen for the title of this text, and which we will use heavily throughout, is **human resources (HR)**.* It has gained widespread acceptance over the last decade because it expresses the current belief in organizations that workers are a valuable, and sometimes irreplaceable, resource. Effective human resource management (HRM) is a major component of any manager's job.

A **human resource strategy** refers to a firm's deliberate use of human resources to help it gain or maintain an edge against its competitors in the marketplace.[2] It is the grand plan or general approach an organization adopts to ensure that it effectively uses its people to accomplish its mission. A **human resource tactic** is a particular policy or program that helps to advance a firm's strategic goal. Thus, an oil company wishing to use excellence among its petroleum geologists as an HR strategy may decide to select candidates from only a select set of schools or may decide to pay its geologists significantly more than other oil companies do. Either of these decisions or policies is a tactic.

human resources

People who are employed by an organization. In the past, the term *personnel* was frequently used.

human resource strategy

A firm's deliberate use of human resources to help it gain or maintain an edge against its competitors in the marketplace. The grand plan or general approach an organization adopts to ensure that it effectively uses its people to accomplish its mission.

In this chapter and the next, we focus on the general framework within which specific HR activities and programs fit. With the help of the company's human resources department (HR department, for short), managers implement the chosen HR strategies. In subsequent chapters, we move from the general to the specific and examine in detail the spectrum of HR strategies: (those regarding work design, staffing, performance appraisal, career planning, and compensation).[3]

human resource tactic

A particular HR policy or program that helps to advance a firm's strategic goal.

■ Human Resource Management: The Challenges

Before we take up the HR challenges that face managers, we need to define *manager* and indicate where human resources fit into the organization. **Managers** are people who are given the authority to direct the work of other people and are responsible for the timely and correct execution of actions that promote their units' successful performance. In this book we use the term *unit* in a broad sense: it may refer to a work team, a department, business unit, or division.

Often employees are differentiated into the categories "line" and "staff." **Line employees** are directly involved in producing the company's products or services. **Staff employees** are those whose work supports the line function(s). For example, people who work in the HR department are typically considered to be staff employees because their primary role is to support those parts of the organization involved in direct production of products or services to external consumers. This line-staff distinction is very useful in defining and focusing on those tasks that are central to an organization's mission. However, contemporary work arrangements such as self-managing teams often involve employees in both "line" and "staff" tasks; many jobs are neither strictly line nor strictly staff. The terms *junior* and *senior* are often used to characterize employees. The context in which they are used is crucial because "junior" or "senior" can refer to a person's age, to their length of service in the organization, or to their managerial rank.

Figure 1–1 summarizes the major human resource challenges facing managers in the late 1990s and beyond. Firms that meet these challenges are likely to outperform those that do not. These challenges may be categorized according to their primary focus: the environment, the organization, or the individual.

manager

A person who is in charge of others and is responsible for the timely and correct execution of actions that promote the successful performance of his or her unit.

line employees

Employees who are directly involved in producing the company's products or services.

staff employees

Employees whose work supports the line function.

Environment
- Rapid Change
- Workforce Diversity
- Globalization
- Legislation
- Evolving Work and Family Roles
- Skill Shortages

Organization
- Competitive Position: Cost, Quality, Distinctive Capabilities
- Flexibility
- Downsizing
- Organizational Restructuring
- Self-Managed Work Teams
- Small Businesses
- Organizational Culture
- Technology
- Unions

Individual
- Matching People and Organization
- Ethical Dilemmas
- Productivity
- Empowerment
- Brain Drain

Figure 1–1 Key Human Resource Challenges

■ Environmental Challenges

environmental challenges
Forces external to a firm that affect the firm's performance but are beyond the control of management.

Canadian Business
www.canbus.com

The Wall Street Journal
www.wsj.com

Environmental challenges are the forces external to the firm. They influence organizational performance but are largely beyond the control of management. Managers, therefore, need to monitor the external environment constantly for opportunities and threats. They must also react quickly to challenges. One common and effective method for monitoring the environment is to read the business press, including *Canadian Business, The National Post,* and *The Globe and Mail*'s *Report on Business,* as well as international publications such as *The Wall Street Journal, Fortune,* and *The Economist.* (The appendix to this book provides an annotated listing of both general business publications and more specialized publications on HR management and related topics.)

Six current and important environmental challenges are rapid change, work force diversity, globalization, legislation, evolving work and family roles, labour market changes such as skill shortages, and the rise of the service sector.

Rapid Change.   Many organizations face a volatile environment in which change is nearly constant. If they are to survive and prosper, they need to adapt to change quickly and effectively. Human resources are almost always at the heart of an effective response system. Here are a few examples of how human resource policies can help or hinder a firm grappling with external change:

A Question of Ethics

How much responsibility does an organization have to shield its employees from the effects of rapid change in the environment? What risks does this type of "shock absorber" approach to management entail?

◆ *Just-in-time hiring.* Hon Industries, Inc, an office furniture maker, faces unprecedented requirements for factory employees in its main production facility. Instead of waiting until the last minute to recruit, Hon has created a pool of "prequalified" candidates willing to wait for job opportunities. Out of 2,000 people seeking jobs, Hon prequalified 109, and offered 48 immediate employment with the remainder being brought on over the next several months.[4]

◆ *The benefits of redefining "work."* Chrysler Canada has dramatically reversed its fortunes. As recently as the early 1990s, sales were falling sharply and thousands of workers were being laid off. By the first quarter of 1994, Chrysler Canada had sold some 600,000 vehicles, more than any previous quarter in 69 years of operation. The turnaround was partly due to the popularity of the models assigned to the Canadian plants. But also crucial to the success was a change from the old "you give us loyalty and we give you job security" culture to "you give us creative effort and we'll give you the opportunity to use it.[5]   While there was resistance, management and unionized workers had come to realize that nobody functions with a completely fixed job description anymore. People now have tasks, processes they own and results they are accountable for. Although the word "job" is still used, it means something quite different than it did even as little as a decade ago. This reflects a thorough rethinking of how to engage people in the work of an organization.

Throughout this book we emphasize how HR practices can enable a firm to respond quickly and effectively to external changes.

Workforce Diversity.   Canadian organizations have perhaps the most diverse work forces of any industrialized country. Diversity has many dimensions; for example, Canada is the only G7 country with two official languages. Although most organizations function in a single language, many employers in both public and private sectors need the capability of serving their clientele in both French and English. While 12 percent of the national population were visible minorities in 1996 according to the Census of that year, the percentages for the major metropolitan areas were larger including Toronto at 32% and Vancouver at 31%.[6] Estimates indicate that by the year 2006, some 19% of the Canadian population will be "visible minorities."[7] This ethnic diversity is increasing because of immigration patterns. Between 1991 and 1996, fewer than one in four immigrants came from Europe or the United States.[8] Although immigration flows to all parts of Canada, recent immigrants tend to settle initially in the larger cities. Surveys indicate that 80% of Canadians say they live in neighbourhoods that include people of different ethnic backgrounds and almost two-thirds say they work with people of different backgrounds. Immigration from Asia and Africa accounts for almost two-thirds of immigrants to Canada in the 1990s.

The influx of women into the Canadian work force has been one of the most important human resource management change drivers. Labour force participation by women was as high as 33% during World War II but dropped to 23.5% in 1954.[9] Since then, a dramatic increase has occurred. The participation rate for women in 1996 was 59%, compared to 73% for men. Women constitute 45% of all paid workers in Canada. Perhaps one of the most important aspects of this change has been the increase in the number of working mothers. By 1994, 63% of women with children under the age of 16 were active in the labour force.[10]

The age composition of the labour force is also an important influence on human resource management. Until the early 1980s Canada typically had more younger workers than older workers. Between 1981 and 1994, the median age of the Canadian work force had increased from 32 to 36, a remarkable shift over a relatively short period.[11] A greying work force raises a number of HR issues, including health and safety, career management, and matching education and skills with the demands of an economy where knowledge-based work is increasingly important.

All these trends present both a challenge and a real opportunity for organizations, and they add an important dimension to managers' jobs. Employers that formulate HR strategies that capitalize on employee diversity are more likely to survive and prosper. Chapter 4 is devoted to the topic of managing diversity; employee diversity is also discussed in other chapters of this book.

Globalization.   One of the most dramatic challenges facing Canadian firms as they enter the 21st century is how to compete in an increasingly globalized marketplace. In the past decade, the forces that have led to the Free Trade Agreement (FTA) between the United States and Canada, and the North American Free Trade Agreement (NAFTA) that added Mexico to the arrangements, have combined with the continuing liberalization of trade under the multi-nation GATT (General Agreement on Tariffs and Trade) and the Multilateral Agreement on Investment (MAI) now being negotiated to establish a highly globalized economy. One prediction about the future is safe: Canada's economic success will depend on the ability of Canadian employers to meet international standards of productivity, quality, and creativity. This prediction obviously applies to Canadian organizations that sell products and services in international markets. Importantly, it also applies to organizations whose products or services are sold to a domestic market, where foreign competition is increasingly a factor. The international standard applies even to the greater *public sector* of the economy—government and publicly supported organizations such as health care and education. Not only are public sector organizations pressured by the alternative of privatization; they must also compete for executive and professional talent in an environment where the best and the brightest will find it increasingly easy to move to attractive alternatives in the United States, Europe, Asia, Latin America, or elsewhere.

Canada's situation contrasts with that of the United States, as globalization intensifies. The United States has always had a very large domestic market for the products of its industries. And although the United States is the home country for more large multinationals than any other single nation, relatively few (roughly 10%) U.S. companies are active exporters. This focus on internal markets contrasts sharply with Europe and the Pacific Rim,[12] countries where 80% of manufacturers export. The challenge for many U.S. employers is to overcome a parochial orientation to product markets.

The influence of large U.S. corporations has been an important factor for Canadian firms for some time. Canada's manufacturing industries were influenced by significant tariff and non-tariff barriers for many years. Foreign producers wishing to sell products in Canada were induced to set up manufacturing operations to produce for the Canadian market. Domestic Canadian companies also emerged, focussed primarily on the Canadian market. The small but protected Canadian market led to the presence of a branch-plant production process in a number of industries, with research and product development largely done elsewhere. In the past two decades, the combination of globalization and accelerating technological change has led to major restructuring. Canadian units of multinational companies are increasingly being given the function of producing for all of North America (for example, the automobile industry, with Chrysler minivans coming from Windsor or Toyota Corollas from Cambridge, Ontario) or being given world product mandates, as is the case with Xerox Canada (whose Oakville plant has the worldwide mandate for colour toner) and several products made by Canadian General Electric.

Over the years, Canadians have been more directly affected by the international economy than have their American neighbours. To begin with there is the presence of the world's largest national economy just to the south. This reality has been combined with the strong natural resource base in the Canadian economy, which requires external markets. Significant parts of the Canadian economy are still based on resource foundations.

Canada has also developed commercially viable expertise in a number of areas that derive from its geography and climate. Transportation, construction, and, particularly, telecommunications are all industries in which Canadian firms have established a significant international presence. Bombardier, Nortel, and SNC/Lavalin are examples of such companies.

We will examine the human resource implications of globalization in detail in Chapter 17. However, the central implication of global competition and global opportunities is clear: organizations must concentrate on adding value (through innovation, quality, and/or productivity) both to be able to compete, and to be able to provide good incomes for their employees. Adding value depends crucially on managing human resources effectively, because employees are the chief source of added value. We include international examples throughout this book to illustrate how human resources are managed in other national cultures.

Legislation.   Laws passed by federal and provincial parliaments and court decisions have triggered many of the significant changes in human resource management over the past several decades in Canada. These laws have prohibited certain actions by employers (such as discrimination on the basis of race, religion, or gender) and have required employers to meet certain obligations—for example, to pay at least the minimum wage, to meet health and safety standards, and to make various payments (such as Employment Insurance, Workers' Compensation, or Canada/Quebec Pension Plan contributions). To a much lesser extent, legislation has imposed obligations on employees (for example, no strikes during the term of a collective agreement).

Employment legislation has many specific purposes, but the common intent behind the legislation is establish employment relationships where employee and public interests are assured while providing a framework in which the employer can pursue its goals.

◆ In the case of *employment standards* legislation, the intent is to establish such standards as minimum wages, maximum hours, overtime provisions, minimum notice periods in the case of layoffs, and minimum vacation and holiday entitlements.

◆ *Workers' compensation* legislation substitutes a kind of "no-fault" insurance for an employee's right to sue employers if employees suffer disabling injury or illness because of their employment.

Xerox Canada
www.xerox.com

Bombardier
www.challenger.bombardier.com

A Question of Ethics

What is the ethical responsibility of an employer to employees who lack basic literacy and numeracy skills?

◆ *Labour relations* legislation legitimizes the option for workers to choose to be represented by a union in their relations with their employer, and regulates the relationship among the parties.

◆ *Human rights* codes, *employment equity* legislation, and *pay equity* legislation are all responses to the unequal circumstances (pay, promotion, job assignments, harassment or mistreatment) of different identifiable groups in the work force.

◆ *Health and safety* legislation has become more complex, reflecting the increased range of risks that can be encountered in the workplace. We are learning more about ergonomic factors that affect the chance that an employee may suffer such afflictions as repetitive strain injuries. We are are also faced with workplaces where exposure to increasing numbers of chemical agents requires specialized knowledge and procedures.

◆ Various *social programs* require payments by employers. Employment Insurance, Workers' Compensation, and the Canada/Quebec Pension Plan all reflect a single underlying factor: most people depend heavily on employment income for their economic viability. Interrupting that income stream is a serious financial problem for most households. Social programs are public policy attempts to replace a portion of regular earnings while at the same time sustaining levels of consumer buying power for people who are not in the work force, and dampening the "boom and bust" extremes of the business cycle.

The laws that govern employment in Canada are challenging for employers because of the range of issues covered and also because different jurisdictions legislate in different areas. Some areas, such as Employment Insurance and the Canada Pension Plan, have federal laws that apply to all employers in Canada. Other legislation varies from one jurisdiction to another. The *Canada Labour Code* (federal legislation) applies to sectors of the economy regulated by the federal government, including the federal public service and federal Crown corporations, the airlines and the chartered banks. In total, this is about 10% of the Canadian work force. Human rights codes, employment standards, labour relations acts, pay equity and workers' compensation legislation all vary, province by province.

Employment law is continually in flux. While employers often find complying with legislation to be an expensive aggravation, there is no doubt that the law will continue to be an important driver for change in human resources. There are virtually no significant areas of HR practice today that are not affected by legal or judicial influences.

Evolving Work and Family Roles.   The structure of Canadian households has always varied: adults living alone, couples with children, childless couples, single-parent families, blended families resulting from divorce or death followed by remarriage, and a range of other forms. The "traditional" household where there are children living at home with an employed father and a stay-at-home mother has dropped from being the case more than four times out of five to less than one in four, since 1958.[13] According to the 1996 Census, some 15% of Canadian families were headed by single parents, 70% of those women. Of those households in 1996 with children at home and two parents present, over 70% of the women were active in the labour force.[14] The dramatically increased presence of mothers with young children in the labour force has created a need to accommodate employees' desire to balance work and family responsibilities. Many employers have responded with such policies as flexible working hours, job sharing, telecommuting, and paid maternity leave. A few organizations have introduced on-site child-care arrangements or other innovative programs.

The Increasing Importance of the Service Sector.   The 20th century has seen a dramatic shift in employment from agriculture to manufacturing to the service sectors. As reflected in Figure 1-2, employment in agriculture, forestry, the fishery and resource industries during the last 30 years decreased from 15% to 5% of all

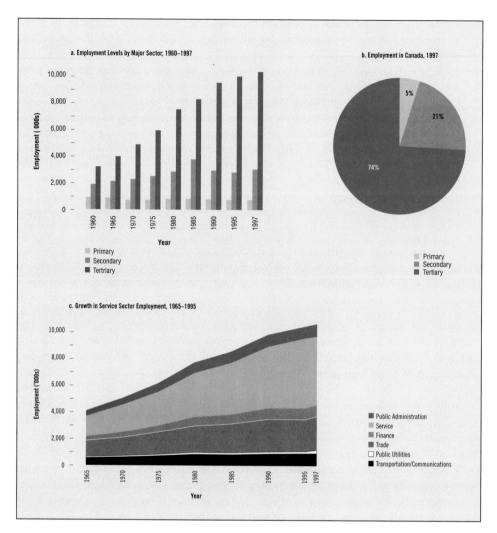

Figure 1–2 Changes in Employment Patterns
SOURCE: Statistics Canada, "Changes in Employment Patterns," adapted from "Labour Force Annual Averages, 1995" Catalogue No. 71–220, page A50; and Statistics Canada Webpage <www.statcan.ca>.

Canadian employment. During that period, employment in the secondary (manufacturing) sector increased in numbers (but not as a percentage of total employment) until 1985 after which it decreased some 20% into the late 1990s.

The tertiary or "service" sector has accounted for the most dramatic increases in employment. At present three of every four jobs exist with employers whose business is categorized as "service." Financial institutions, public utilities, trade, public service and administration, personal and professional services, transportation, and communications are the major elements of the service sector. Thus, the "service sector" is far more than the restaurants, hairdressers, and taxi drivers that the term often suggests.

Service-sector jobs have grown more rapidly than jobs in other sectors for at least two major reasons. The first reason is that technology—first in the form of automation and later in the form of information technologies—has reduced the demand for human involvement in physical production while increasing the need for people who will perform the knowledge-intensive work that supports the capital-intensive production processes that are increasingly dominant. The second reason is that service tasks are increasingly being contracted out so that the increase in the service sector may overstate the change in job content. If a manufacturing company contracts out its shipping and delivery activities, the jobs involved are no longer counted in the manufacturing sector but show up, instead, in the service sector.

Many dramatic shifts are taking place in the employment patterns in Canada. As a result, employers may face shortages of skilled people at the same time as substantial numbers of people are seeking employment and are unable to find it. Both appropriate public policy and appropriate actions on the part of individuals and employers will be required to meet employers' demand for contemporary skills as well as the need for employment opportunity.

◼ Organizational Challenges

Organizational challenges are concerns or problems internal to a firm. They are often a byproduct of environmental forces because no firm operates in a vacuum. Still, managers can usually exert much more control over organizational challenges than over environmental challenges. Effective managers identify organizational issues and deal with them before they become major problems. One of the themes of this text is *proactivity:* the need for firms to take action before problems get out of hand. This can only be done by managers who are well informed about important HR issues and organizational challenges. These challenges include the need for a competitive position and flexibility, the problems of downsizing and organizational restructuring, the use of self-managed work teams, small businesses, the need to create a strong corporate culture, the role of technology, and the presence of unions.

organizational challenges
Concerns or problems internal to a firm; often a byproduct of environmental forces.

Competitive Position: Cost, Quality, or Distinctive Capabilities. Human resources represent the single most important cost in many organizations. Organizational labour costs range from 36% in capital-intensive firms such as commercial airlines to 80% in labour-intensive firms like colleges and universities. How effectively a company uses its human resources can have a dramatic effect on its ability to compete (or even survive) in an increasingly competitive environment.

An organization will outperform its competitors if it effectively utilizes its work force's unique combination of skills and abilities to exploit environmental opportunities and neutralize threats. HR policies can influence an organization's competitive position by controlling costs, improving quality, and creating distinctive capabilities.

◆ *Controlling costs.* One way for a firm to gain a competitive advantage is to maintain low costs and a strong cash flow. A compensation system that uses innovative reward strategies to control labour costs can help the organization grow, as we discuss in Chapters 10 and 11. A well-designed compensation system rewards employees for behaviours that benefit the company.

Other factors besides compensation policies can enhance a firm's competitiveness by keeping labour costs under control. These include better employee selection so that workers are more likely to stay with the company and to perform better while they are there (Chapter 5); training employees to make them more efficient and productive (Chapter 8); attaining harmonious labour relations (Chapter 15); effectively managing health and safety issues in the workplace (Chapter 16); and structuring work to reduce the time and resources needed to design, produce, and deliver products or services (Chapter 2).

◆ *Improving quality.* The second way to gain a competitive advantage is to engage in continuous quality improvement. Many companies have implemented *total quality management (TQM)* initiatives, which are programs designed to improve the quality of all the processes that lead to a final product or service. In a TQM program, every aspect of the organization is oriented toward providing a quality product or service to its customers. Other chapters discuss how quality management should be integrated with specific human resource programs such as pay-for-performance plans (Chapter 11) and employee appraisal (Chapter 7).

◆ *Creating distinctive capabilities.* The third way to gain a competitive advantage is to utilize people with distinctive capabilities to create unsurpassed competence in a particular area (for example, Corel with graphics software or Bombardier in corporate aircraft). Chapter 5 (which discusses the recruitment and selection of employees), Chapter 8 (training), and Chapter 9 (the long-term grooming of employees within the firm) are particularly relevant to managers seeking to establish distinctive capabilities through the effective use of human resources.

Decentralization.   In the traditional organizational structure, most major decisions are made at the top and implemented at lower levels. It is not uncommon for these organizations to centralize major functions, such as human resources, marketing, and production, in a single location (typically corporate headquarters) that serves as the firm's command centre. Multiple layers of management are generally used to execute orders issued at the top and to control the lower ranks from above. Employees who are committed to the firm tend to move up the ranks over time in what some have called the *internal labour market.*[15] However, the traditional top-down form of organization is quickly becoming obsolete, both because it is costly to operate and because it is too inflexible to compete effectively. It is being replaced by **decentralization**, which transfers responsibility and decision-making from a central office to people and locations closer to the situation that demand attention.

HR strategies can play a crucial role in enhancing organizational flexibility by improving decision-making processes within the firm. The need for maintaining or creating organizational flexibility in HR strategies is addressed in several chapters of this book, including those dealing with work flows (Chapter 2), compensation (Chapters 10 and 11), training (Chapter 8), staffing (Chapter 5), and globalization (Chapter 17).

decentralization

Transferring responsibility and decision-making authority from a central office to people and locations closer to the situation that demands attention.

Downsizing.   Periodic reductions in a company's work force to improve its bottom line—often called **downsizing**—are becoming standard business practice, even among firms that were once legendary for their "no layoff" policies.

In addition to fostering a lack of emotional commitment,[16] transient employment relationships create a new set of challenges for firms and people competing in the labour market as well as for government agencies that must deal with the social problems associated with employment insecurity (including loss of insurance coverage and mental illness). However, the good news for laid-off employees is that the poor-performance stigma traditionally attached to being fired or laid off is fading.[17]

Chapter 6 of this book is devoted to downsizing and how to manage the process effectively. Other chapters of this book also shed light on this important issue, including the chapters on benefits (Chapter 12), the legal environment (Chapter 3), labour relations (Chapter 15), and employee relations and communications (Chapter 13).

downsizing

A reduction in a company's work force to improve its bottom line.

Organizational Restructuring.   The past two decades have witnessed a dramatic transformation in how firms are structured. Tall organizations that had many management levels are becoming flatter as companies reduce the number of people between the chief executive officer (CEO) and the lowest-ranking production employee in an effort to become more competitive.

This transformation has had enormous implications for the effective utilization of human resources. Since the late 1980s, many companies have instituted massive layoffs of middle managers, whose traditional role of planning, organizing, implementing, and controlling has come to be equated with the kind of cumbersome bureaucracy that prevents businesses from responding quickly to market forces. Other firms have been redeploying managers rather than terminating them. For example, Toyota reassigned 1,000 of its managers after going from 16 management levels to seven. This contrasts with 17 levels at Ford and 22 at General Motors.[18] The newly emerging flatter form of organization has been labelled the *horizontal corporation.* In this "delayered" corporate model, supervisors manage across, not up and down. Management guru and lecturer Tom Peters summarized the new order this way: "Big corporations are a thing of the past; crazy times call for crazy actions; and it takes only 48 hours to break down a corporate hierarchy."[19]

New relationships among firms are also fostering hybrid organizational structures and the blending of firms with diverse histories and labour forces. Mergers and acquisitions, in which formerly independent organizations come together as a single entity, represent important sources of restructuring. Such was the case when the very large German electronics company Siemens AG acquired Relcon, a Brampton, Ontario, manufacturer of speed controllers for electric motors. An entrepreneurial and informal culture gave way to formalization and control. Relcon, as a division within Siemens' Canadian operations, has become more of a high-volume manufacturing operation and less of a custom shop. But it also anticipates doubling its $50 million annual sales by the end of the decade through access to Siemens' worldwide operations.[20] Such transitions can pose challenges. For example, the recent pattern of major banks acquiring brokerage houses (e.g., CIBC and Wood Gundy) almost inevitably combines a conservative banking culture with the more volatile and freewheeling environment of the brokerage industry. While the strategic advantages are undeniable, the cultural tensions are unavoidable.

A newer and rapidly growing form of interorganizational bonding comes in the form of joint ventures, alliances and collaborations among firms that work together on specific products to spread costs and risks. Such complex arrangements are frequently seen in the electronics and automobile industries. They often involve some of the largest corporations in the world, although there are examples of major Canadian corporations being part of such networks, as illustrated by Figure 1–3. To be successful, organizational restructuring requires effective management of human resources. For instance, flattening the organization requires careful examination of staffing demands, work flows, communication channels, training needs, and so on. Likewise, mergers and other forms of interorganizational relations require the successful blending of dissimilar organizational structures, management practices, technical expertise, and so forth. Chapter 2 deals specifically with these issues. Other chapters that focus on related issues are Chapter 5 (staffing), Chapter 8 (training), Chapter 9 (career development), and Chapter 17 (international management).

Self-Managed Work Teams.   Another sweeping organizational change that has occurred in the 1990s is in the supervisor-worker relationship. The traditional system, in which individual employees report to a single boss (who typically oversees a group of three to seven subordinates), is being replaced in some organizations by the self-managed team system. In this system, employees are assigned to a group of peers and, together, they are responsible for a particular area or task.[21]

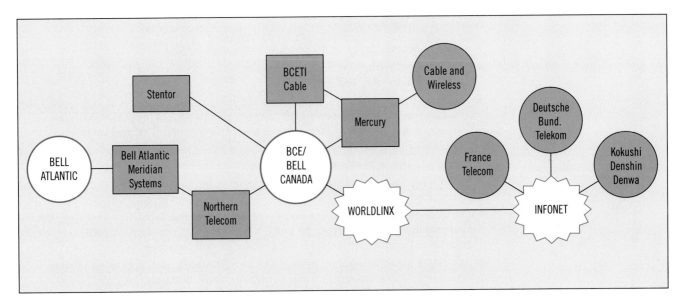

Figure 1–3 Examples of Alliances in the Telecommunications Industry

Conference Board of Canada
www.conferenceboard.ca

According to a recent Conference Board of Canada survey, over 40% of those responding indicated that team-based activity was widespread.[22] While self-managed teams involve a great deal of self-organizing and delegation of authority to the team and currently represent a smaller faction of all team applications, there are several companies in which the concept has taken hold. They include Xerox Canada,[23] Saskatoon Chemicals,[24] and the IS unit of London Life Insurance.[25]

According to two experts on self-managed work teams, "Today's competitive environment demands intense improvement in productivity, quality, and response time. Teams can deliver this improvement. Bosses can't. ... Just as dinosaurs once ruled the earth and faded into extinction, the days of bosses may be numbered."[26]

Very few rigorous scientific studies have been done on the effectiveness of self-managed work teams, mostly because the programs are so new. However, case studies do suggest that many firms that use teams enjoy impressive payoffs. For example, Electrohome was able to bring its Marquee video/data/graphics projector to market in half the regular development time by the use of "breakthrough management," a technique that was useful in overcoming departmental barriers by focussing interrelating groups' energies on turning development breakdowns into solutions (successes).[27]

Human resource issues concerning self-managed work teams are discussed in Chapter 2 (work flows), Chapter 10 (compensation), and Chapter 11 (rewarding performance).

The Growth of Small Businesses.   Small businesses, whether sole proprietorships, partnerships, or corporations, are a large and increasingly important, if often overlooked, part of the Canadian economy. Statistics Canada suggests that small businesses account for 98% of all enterprises and slightly less than one-fifth of all business revenue. Small businesses are generally characterized by ownership by an individual or a small group, and ownership involvement in the management of the company, with operations generally restricted to a particular geographical location (although customers may be geographically dispersed). About four of 10 private-sector employees work for small business.[28] The rapid growth in the service sector mentioned earlier in this chapter parallels the growth of the small-business sector during the past two or three decades. Large firms are continuing to downsize and outsource various activities, while the number of small businesses and employment levels in small business have grown.

Several factors underlie the proliferation of small businesses in recent years. Among these factors are[29]:

◆ The increasing number of two-income, two-career families.

◆ The growing recognition that larger organizations do not always fulfill people's basic needs for autonomy and security.

◆ The shift in women's roles in economic life along with a parallel shift in the belief that women can be entrepreneurs. The current growth rate of new ventures created by women is considerably higher than the rate of new ventures created by men.

◆ A desire by local government officials to avoid falling hostage to larger corporations that become a city or town's dominant employer.

◆ A growing appreciation that entrepreneurship is not just the province of a few superstars or celebrity entrepreneurs.

◆ An understanding that owning one's own business is one of the few pathways left for the middle and lower classes to build wealth in an increasingly tax-conscious society that often penalizes the achiever who works for someone else.

◆ A computer and information revolution that is presenting new opportunities while lowering entry costs and other startup barriers in many industries.

◆ The development of programs to study, teach, promote, and accelerate entrepreneurship in many nations around the world.

Unfortunately, small businesses face a high risk of failure. While small businesses have added net jobs to the economy at the rate of 26% per year, they have also eliminated them at the rate of 18% per year. While this is a net gain for the economy (compared with the 6% increase/7% decrease of companies with 500 or more employees), it still is a volatile situation for the nearly one in five small-business employees whose job disappears each year.[30] To survive and prosper, a small business needs to exercise extra care in managing its human resources effectively because the firm does not have the slack enjoyed by more mature, established firms. For example, a mediocre performance by one person in a 10-employee firm has a much greater impact than that of one person in a company with 1,000 employees.

Most chapters in this book incorporate small-business examples to show how the HR practices discussed in that chapter relate to the special needs of small firms.

Organizational Culture.   The term **organizational culture** refers to the basic assumptions and beliefs that are shared by members of an organization, that operate unconsciously, and that define in a basic "taken for granted" fashion an organization's view of itself and its environment.[31] The key elements of organizational culture are:[32]

1. *Observed behavioural regularities* when people interact, such as the language used and the rituals surrounding deference and demeanour.
2. The *norms* that evolve in working groups, such as the norm of a fair day's work for a fair day's pay.
3. The *dominant values espoused* by an organization, such as product quality or low prices.
4. The *philosophy* that guides an organization's policy toward employees and/or customers.
5. The *rules of the game* for getting along in the organization—"the ropes" that a newcomer must learn to become an accepted member.
6. The *feeling* or *climate* that is conveyed in an organization by the physical layout and the way in which members of the organization interact with one another, customers, or outsiders.

Often a firm's culture hits you between the eyes as soon as you walk into the company's building. In some firms a male "uniform" of white shirt, dark suit, and plain-colour tie is prevalent; such a uniform projects a conservative company philosophy that emphasizes conformity. Employees in other firms may wear a wide array of clothing: the very lack of a uniform projects a company philosophy of individuality, autonomy, and low dependence on superiors. Even within an industry, organizational culture may differ greatly. Figure 1–4 compares the organizational culture at two well-known U.S.-based computer firms, Hewlett-Packard and Apollo.

A company's organizational culture strongly influences its human resource practices. The ways managers treat their subordinates, which HRM practices are deemed appropriate for the organization, and communication and coordination processes within the firm reflect and help define the organization's culture.

Firms that make cultural adjustments to keep up with environmental changes are likely to outperform those whose culture is rigid and unresponsive to external jolts. IBM's bureaucratic culture—with its emphasis on hierarchy, centralization of decisions, permanent employment, and strict promotion-from-within policy—has played a large role in its recent difficulties.[33] In contrast, Hewlett-Packard, named one of the best-managed new companies more than a decade ago, has retained its strong position in the 1990s. Many attribute Hewlett-Packard's continued success to the fact that the corporation divided into smaller sections in the mid-1980s, making it more nimble and able to bring new products to market quickly.[34]

However, given the pervasiveness of this human resource challenge, we refer to organizational culture throughout the book—for instance, in discussing work design, performance appraisal, pay for performance, labour relations, and outplacement.

organizational culture
The basic assumptions and beliefs that are shared by members of an organization, that operate unconsciously, and that define in a basic taken-for-granted fashion an organization's view of itself and its environment.

Hewlett-Packard
www.hp.com

Cultural Element	Hewlett-Packard	Apollo
Behavioural regularities	• Planning and coordination • Professional orientation • People-minded style	• Crisis management • Entrepreneurial orientation • Rough-and-tumble style
Norms	• Carefully laid-out work	• Pushing your own agenda objectives
Dominant values	• Quality/reputation • Components company	• Time-to-market • Systems integrator
Philosophy	• Flexible bureaucracy • Functional/matrix structure	• "Ad-hoc-racy" • Functional/integrated structure
Rules of the game	• Problem solving • Specialize • Long tenure	• "Winning is everything" • Be a generalist • Job hoppers
Feeling or climate	• Strong engineering and marketing influence • Polite/congenial • Sing from the same hymnbook	• Strong R&D and engineering influence • Political/confrontational • Mixed bag/misfits

Figure 1–4 **Cultural Differences Between Hewlett-Packard and Apollo**

SOURCE: Adapted with permission from Mirvis, P., & Marks, M. L. (1992). The human side of merger planning: Assessing and analyzing fit. *Human Resource Planning, 15*(3), 77. Copyright 1992 by The Human Resource Planning Society.

Technology.   Technological advances are being introduced to organizations at an ever-increasing pace. Although technology is rapidly changing in many areas, such as robotics, one area in particular is revolutionizing human resources: information technology.[35] Computer systems that were state-of-the-art three years ago are now obsolete and being replaced by faster, cheaper, more versatile systems. The *telematics technologies*—a broad array of tools including microcomputers (PCs) and word processors, networking programs, telecommunications, and facsimile machines—are now available and affordable to businesses of every size, even one-person companies. These new technologies have had multiple impacts on the management of human resources in organizations, including:

◆ *The rise of telecommuting.* Because the new technology makes information easy to store, retrieve, and analyse, the number of company employees working at home (*telecommuters*) at least part time has been increasing by 15% annually. Because telecommuting arrangements are almost certain to grow in the future, they raise many important questions concerning such issues as performance monitoring, career planning, and overtime pay.

◆ *The ethics of proper data use.* Questions concerning data control, accuracy, right to privacy, and ethics are at the core of a growing controversy brought about by the new information technologies. Personal computers now make it possible to access huge databases containing information on credit files, work history, driving records, health reports, criminal convictions, and family makeup. It is tempting to access this type of data for personnel decisions such as hiring, promotions, international assignments, and the like. A critical observer notes: "The worst thing about this information blitzkrieg is that even though errors abound, what's said about us by computers is usually considered accurate, and significant decisions are made based on this information. Often those affected are unaware of the process and are given no chance to offer explanations."[36]

◆ *An increase in egalitarianism.* Because information is now available both instantaneously and broadly, organizational structures are becoming more *egalitarian,* meaning that power and authority are spread more evenly among all employees. In the words of noted HR consultant Randall Schuler, this means that "there is little need for layers of management between the top and first-line management. Automation also causes a significant change in organizational culture. It permits top management to bypass middle managers on their way to the first-line management."[37] In addition, groupware networks, which enable hundreds of workers to share information simultaneously, can give office workers intelligence previously available only to their bosses. They also enable the rank-and-file to join in online discussions with senior executives. In these kinds of interactions people are judged more by what they say than by their rank on the corporate ladder.[38]

◆ *The arrival of resource information systems.* Technology has also had an impact on the HR department itself. The advent of personal computers and sophisticated database software has dramatically increased the ability of managers to monitor the results of human resource policies and to manage HR issues such as compensation and benefits more effectively. The same technology allows HR information to be widely distributed to managers for their use. We discuss this technology in detail in Chapter 3.

◆ *The rise of the Internet.* The Internet started as a way for university scholars and government researchers to collaborate on projects and share research findings. Today the Net and its multimedia offshoot, the World Wide Web, are virtually everywhere. Companies typically set up Internet sites, creating organizational units and jobs that did not exist until the very recent past. The Internet contains a wealth of information for students (and managers) in all disciplines, including human resources. To acquaint you with some HRM-related sites, we begin each chapter with an "HRM on the Web" feature that refers you to a relevant site.

The challenges and implications of rapidly changing technologies, especially information technologies, for human resources are discussed in several chapters of this book, including Chapter 13 (employee relations).

Unions.   In many of the general trends that affect human resource management (technology, globalization, and so forth), there are parallels between Canada and its most important trading partner, the United States. In some areas, however, there are dramatic differences. The prevalence of union membership is one such area. In the United States, membership over the past 50 years has declined from 35% of the work force to about 16% today.[39] In Canada, union membership grew steadily during that period from less than 25% to (as of 1993) about 38% of the non-agricultural paid work force.[40] The major reason for this difference between Canada and the United States is the political culture of the two countries during this period. Much of the growth of the Canadian unionized work force is due to the right of both federal and provincial government employees to organize, the result of decisions in the 1960s. In both countries, the private sector's pattern of massive growth in service-sector organizations and the increasing importance of small business to overall employment have led to a decline in the dominance once exerted by the major manufacturing-based trade unions.

The recent emphasis on reducing governmental debts and deficits is setting the stage for challenging human resource management in the greater public sector. One illustration of that is the month-long 1996 strike by OPSEU, the union representing Ontario provincial government employees. The strike, the first for the union, was not about pay increases; rather, it was about how the thousands of provincial public servants who were about to be laid off or replaced by outsourcing should be treated. In Chapter 16, we discuss labour relations and how they have evolved in response to changing labour-management environments and a changing legal system.

OPSEU
www.opseu.org

■ Individual Challenges

Human resource issues at the individual level address the decisions most pertinent to specific employees. These **individual challenges** almost always reflect what is happening in the larger organization. For instance, technology affects individual productivity; it also has ethical ramifications in terms of how information is used to

individual challenges
Human resource issues that address the decisions most pertinent to individual employees.

make HR decisions (for example, use of credit or medical history data to decide whom to hire). How the company treats its individual employees is also likely to affect the organizational challenges we discussed earlier. For example, if many key employees leave the firm to join competitors, the organization's competitive position is likely to be affected. In other words, there is a two-way relationship between organizational and individual challenges. This is unlike the relationship between environmental and organizational challenges, in which the relationship goes only one way (refer to Figure 1–1 on page 3). Few organizations can have much impact on the environment. The most important individual challenges today involve matching people and organizations, ethics and social responsibility, productivity, empowerment, and brain drain.

Matching People and Organizations.   Research suggests that HR strategies contribute to firm performance most when these strategies are used to attract and retain the type of employee who best fits the firm's culture and overall business objectives. For example, one study showed that the competencies and personality characteristics of top executives can hamper or improve firm performance, depending on what the firm's business strategies are. Fast-growth firms perform better with managers who have a strong marketing and sales background, who are willing to take risks, and who have a high tolerance for ambiguity. However, these managerial traits actually reduce the performance of mature firms with an established product that are more interested in maintaining (rather than expanding) their market share.[41] Other research has shown that small high-tech firms benefit by hiring employees who are willing to work in an atmosphere of high uncertainty, low pay, rapid change in exchange for greater intrinsic satisfaction and the financial opportunities associated with a risky but potentially very lucrative product launch.[42]

Chapter 5 deals specifically with the attempt to achieve the right fit between employees and the organization to enhance performance.

Ethics and Social Responsibility.   People's expectations that their employers will behave ethically are increasing,[43] so much that many firms and professional organizations have introduced codes of ethics outlining principles and standards of personal conduct for their members. Figure 1–5 shows the Code of Ethics for the Hu-

Figure 1–5 Code of Ethics for the Human Resources Professionals Association of Ontario (HRPAO)

> Members of the Human Resources Professionals Association of Ontario strive for growth as human resources professionals and commit to the principles of the Code of Ethics to the best of their ability. A human resources professional shall:
>
> - continue professional growth in human resources management, in support and promotion of the goals, objectives and By-laws of the Association;
>
> - not knowingly violate or cause to be violated any legislated act, regulation or by-law which relates to the management of human resources;
>
> - demonstrate commitment to such values as respect for human dignity and human rights, and promote human development in the workplace, within the profession and society as a whole;
>
> - treat information obtained in the course of business as confidential; and avoid, or disclose any conflict of interest which might influence personal actions or judgements;
>
> - refrain from inappropriately using their position to secure special privileges, gain or benefit for themselves, their employers of the Association;
>
> - acknowledge an obligation to the employer community to encourage and foster generally accepted codes of moral behaviour; and,
>
> - practise respect and regard for other professional Associations.

man Resources Professional Association of Ontario. Codes of ethics in various professions attempt to articulate standards for behaviour that reflect how professional discretion is guided so that the interests of employers, clients, employees, and the general public are not compromised. Increasing use of ethics codes in many areas (such as marketing) is a response to growing concerns that managers do not consistently make decisions that are ethical.[44]

The widespread perceptions of unethical behaviour may be attributed to the fact that managerial decisions are rarely clear-cut. Except in a few blatant cases (such as willful misrepresentation), what is ethical or unethical is open to debate. Even the most detailed codes of ethics are still general enough to allow much room for discretion by managers. In other words, many specific decisions related to the management of human resources are subject to judgement calls. Often these judgement calls constitute a "Catch-22" because none of the alternatives is desirable.[45]

In recent years, the concept of social responsibility has been frequently discussed as a complement to ethics. A company that exercises *social responsibility* attempts to balance its commitments—not only to its investors, but also to its employees, its customers, other businesses, and the community or communities in which it operates. McDonald's, for example, established Ronald McDonald houses several years ago to provide lodging for families of sick children hospitalized away from home. Investment management firm Gluskin, Sheff and Associates donated $1 million to support the Barnes exhibit at the Art Gallery of Ontario, BPI Financial supports artists and performers, and many local merchants support local children's sports teams.

An entire chapter of this book is devoted to employee rights and responsibilities (Chapter 13); it addresses important ethical issues in employer-employee relations. However, because most of the topics discussed in this book have ethical implications, pertinent ethical questions for which there are no absolute answers are brought to the reader's attention throughout the various chapters.

Productivity.   A prominent business concern over the past 20 years or so is that Canadian productivity is rising at a lower rate than is found in many other industrialized nations. **Productivity** is a measure of how much value individual employees add to the goods or services that the organization produces. The greater the output per individual, the higher the organization's productivity. Two important factors that affect individual productivity are ability and motivation.

Employee **ability**, competence in performing a job, can be improved through a hiring and placement process that selects the best individuals for the job; Chapter 5 specifically deals with this process. It can also be improved through training and career development programs designed to sharpen employees' skills and prepare them for additional responsibilities; Chapters 8 and 9 discuss these issues.

Motivation refers to a person's desire to accomplish a task or achieve a goal. Motivation energizes, directs and sustains human behaviour. Motivation can be influenced by the full range of HR policies and practices. Often, strategic changes and key leaders have the effect of changing motivation for large groups of the work force. William Catucci, who took over as president and CEO of Unitel Communications (now AT&T Canada Long Distance Services) in January 1996 where he was the fifth CEO in as many years at a company (his predecessor had cut 950 jobs the year before) that was losing $1 million a day, did something unexpected— he announced a $150 bonus for every employee. Two years later he took the stage at a large employee gathering and was greeted with a long and enthusiastic applause. The $150 was clearly symbolic and was simply the first move in a turnaround that has seen the company move to profitability and a sense of having a future. But Catucci's management style and attention to HR issues is given much of the credit for the transformation.[46]

William Catucci

President/CEO of Unitel (now AT&T Canada)

productivity

A measure of how much value individual employees add to the goods or services that the organization produces.

ability

Competence in performing a job.

motivation

A person's desire to do the best possible job or to exert the maximum effort to perform assigned tasks.

Several key factors affecting employee motivation are discussed in this book, including work design (Chapter 2), matching of employee and job requirements (Chapter 5), rewards (Chapters 11 and 13), and due process (Chapter 14).

A growing number of companies recognize that employees are more likely to choose a firm and stay there if they believe that it offers a high **quality of work life (QWL)**. A high quality of work life is related to job satisfaction, which in turn is a strong predictor of absenteeism and turnover.[47] A firm's investments in improving the quality of work life also pay off in the form of better customer service.[48] We discuss issues covering job design and their effects on employee attitudes and behaviour in Chapter 2.

quality of work life (QWL)

A measure of how safe and satisfied employees feel with their jobs.

Empowerment.   In recent years many firms have reduced employee dependence on superiors and placed more emphasis on individual control over and responsibility for the work that needs to be done. This process has been labelled **empowerment** because it transfers direction from an external source (normally the immediate supervisor) to an internal source (the individual's own desire to do well). In essence, the process of empowerment entails providing workers with the skills and authority to make decisions that would traditionally be made by managers. The goal of empowerment is an organization consisting of enthusiastic, committed individuals who perform their work ably because they believe in it and enjoy doing it (internal control). This situation is in stark contrast to an organization that gets people to work as an act of compliance to avoid punishment (for example, being fired) or to qualify for a paycheque (external control).

empowerment

Providing workers with the skills and authority to make decisions that would traditionally be made by managers.

Human resource issues related to internal and external control of behaviour are discussed in Chapter 3 (work flows) and Chapter 19 (quality management).

Brain Drain.   With organizations' success more and more dependent on knowledge held by specific employees, companies are becoming increasingly vulnerable to what can be termed a "**brain drain**"—the loss of intellectual property and organizational memory when key people move from one firm to another (spontaneously, or as the result of "raiding"). Senior management opportunities in the United States can be particularly attractive. Compensation levels are often higher; this, combined with lower effective rates of income taxation and the differences in currency value, provides financial attraction. Often the responsibilities and potential for development are greater, as David Preston found when he moved from Gillette of Canada to the U.S. parent corporation, where one division had four times the sales of the entire Canadian operation, or when Jacques Boisvert moved from the presidency of Sterling-Winthrop (400 employees) to head another pharmaceutical operation in New York (3,000 employees).[49] It has become increasingly easy for Canadians to pursue careers across international boundaries, including work in the United States. There has been a marked increase—some 30% during the early 1990s—in the number of Canadian managers applying for U.S. work permits. While Canada has attracted both managerial and entrepreneurial talent from international sources, Canadian employers need to come to terms with the wide range of options available to highly qualified and talented employees.

brain drain

The loss of high-talent key personnel to competitors or startup ventures.

Issues concerning the brain drain and measures for dealing with it effectively are discussed in several chapters in this book, including Chapter 3 (the legal framework and employment equity), Chapter 4 (managing diversity), Chapter 6 (separations and outplacement), and Chapter 11 (rewarding performance).

■ Planning and Implementing Strategic HR Policies

To be successful, organizations must closely align their HR strategies and programs (or "tactics") with environmental opportunities, business strategies, and the organization's unique characteristics and distinctive competence. A firm with a poorly defined HR strategy or a business strategy that does not specifically incorporate human resources is likely to lose ground to its competitors. Similarly, a firm may have a well-articulated HR strategy, yet fail if its HR tactics/policies do not help implement its HR strategy effectively.

■ The Benefits of HR Planning

The process of formulating HR strategies and establishing programs or tactics to implement them is called **strategic human resource (HR) planning.** When done correctly, strategic HR planning provides many direct and indirect benefits for the company.

strategic human resource (HR) planning
The process of formulating HR strategies and establishing programs or tactics to implement

Encouragement of Proactive Rather Than Reactive Behaviour. Being *proactive* means looking ahead and developing a vision of where the company wants to be and how it can use human resources to get there. In contrast, being *reactive* means responding to problems as they arise. Companies that are reactive may lose sight of the long-term direction of their business.

Explicit Communication of Company Goals. Strategic HR planning can help a firm develop a focussed set of strategic objectives that capitalizes on its special talents and know-how. One company that has combined a clear sense of direction and an implicit human resources strategy is Bombardier Inc., a Montreal-based aerospace company. Laurent Beaudoin, the company's president, recently was named Flight International's "Personality of the Year" for his accomplishments of building a major aerospace company in less than seven years. Much of the growth was via acquisitions, including Learjet, Canadair, Short Brothers PLC (a British company), and the 1992 purchase of controlling interest in de Havilland Inc. from Boeing. The niche that Bombardier has selected and where it has prospered—regional airlines and executive jets—has avoided the less attractive defence and large-airliner segments of the aerospace industry. Through patience and negotiating attractive prices, Bombardier has not only acquired a valuable set of physical assets, but has also assembled a highly qualified work force that is aligned to its market strategy.[50]

Stimulation of Critical Thinking and Ongoing Examination of Assumptions. Managers often depend on their own personal views and experiences to solve problems and make business decisions. The assumptions on which they make their decisions can lead to success if they are appropriate to the environment in which the business operates. However, serious problems can arise when these assumptions no longer hold. For instance, IBM deemphasized sales of its personal computer in the 1980s because IBM managers were afraid that PC growth would occur at the expense of the firm's highly profitable main-frame products. This decision allowed competitors to move aggressively into the PC market, resulting in a serious setback for IBM.[51]

The strategic HR planning process can help a company critically re-examine its assumptions and determine whether the programs that follow from these assumptions should be modified or discontinued. But strategic HR planning can stimulate critical thinking and the development of new initiatives only if it is a continuing and flexible process rather than a rigid procedure with a discrete beginning and a specific deadline for completion. That is why many firms have formed an executive committee, which includes an HR professional and the CEO, to discuss strategic issues on an ongoing basis and periodically modify the company's overall HR strategies and supporting HR programs.

Identification of Gaps between Current Situation and Future Vision. Strategic HR planning can help a firm identify the difference between "where we are today" and "where we want to be." By forcing managers to think ahead, strategic planning can serve as the catalyst for change and mobilize the firm's resources to achieve or enhance a competitive edge in the future. Pepsi-Cola Canada has expanded from 150 employees to more than 3,000 over a five-year period as it changed from a marketing company to a manufacturing company. This change, including the shift from a predominantly white-collar employee population to a more diverse one and the inclusion of plants with varying benefits programs, was facilitated by the presence of a classic "core-plus" flexible benefits package.[52] National Rubber, a Toronto company involved in recycling rubber materials, concluded that in addition to improvements in costs and productivity, they needed to make major improvements in employee safety. A process of "future state visioning," involving wide participation among the work force and workshops, led over two years to a tenfold reduction in major injuries. The change was the result of clear identification of where they wanted to be, what impediments existed, and what courses of action would lead to the desired results.[53]

Encouragement of Line Managers' Participation.   Like most HR activities, strategic HR planning will be of little value unless line managers are actively involved in the process. Unfortunately, top management (including HR professionals) sometimes tends to see strategic planning as its domain, with line managers merely responsible for implementation of the plan. For HR strategy to be effective, line managers at all levels must buy into it. If they don't, it is likely to fail. For example, a large cosmetics manufacturing plant decided to introduce a reward program in which work teams would receive a large bonus (up to 20% of their annual salary) for turning out high-quality products. The bonus was part of a new strategic plan to foster greater cooperation among employees working in teams. But the plan, which had been developed by top executives in consultation with the HR department, backfired when managers and supervisors began hunting for individual employees responsible for errors. This created divisiveness within teams and conflict with supervisors. The plan was eventually dropped.

Identification of HR Constraints and Opportunities.   Human resources play a major role in the eventual success or failure of any strategic business plan. When overall business strategy planning is done in combination with HR strategic planning, firms can identify the potential problems and opportunities with respect to people expected to implement the business strategy.

Diversity (racial, gender, family status, etc.) is an increasingly prominent attribute of many companies' work forces. While some employers view diversity as a potential source of difficulties, an increasing number see diversity as a potential resource. Imperial Oil has identified four areas that, if addressed properly, release that potential: training, workplace policies, guidelines for bias-free employment practices, and special initiatives. Connaught Laboratories has also been a pace-setter, being recognized two years running by the Federal Contractors Program for employment equity initiatives.[54] The Bank of Montreal, ranked first in 1995 in the *Report on Business'* "Most Respected Corporations" for Human Resource Management, has achieved considerable recognition for its initiatives for advancing women to senior ranks and for initiating polices that make it possible for employees to balance their work, family and community commitments. BMO president Tony Comper explains that these actions are taking place because "... [this initiative] was the right thing, and the smart thing from the economic perspective of the bank and shareholders to make the most of the resources we have in the bank."[55]

Creation of Common Bonds.   A well-developed, strategic HR plan with involvement at all levels can help the firm create a sense of shared values and expectations. This is important because a substantial amount of research shows that, in the long run, organizations that have a strong sense of "who we are" tend to outperform those that don't. A strategic HR plan that reinforces, adjusts, or redirects the organization's present culture can foster such values as a customer focus, innovation, fast growth, and cooperation.

■ The Challenges of Strategic HR Planning

In developing an effective HR strategy, the organization faces several important challenges.

Maintaining a Competitive Advantage.   Any competitive advantage enjoyed by an organization tends to be short-lived because other companies are likely to imitate it. This is as true for human resource advantages as for technological and marketing advantages. For example, many high-tech firms have "borrowed" reward programs for key scientists and engineers from other successful high-tech firms.

The challenge from a human resource perspective is to develop strategies that offer the firm a sustained competitive advantage. For instance, a company may put in place programs that develop present employees' maximum potential through carefully developed career ladders (see Chapter 9) while at the same time rewarding them generously with company stock with strings attached (for example, a provision that they will forfeit a substantial amount of the stock if they quit the firm before a certain date).

Reinforcing Overall Business Strategy.   Developing HR strategies to support the firm's overall business strategy is a challenge for these reasons. First, top management may not always be able to enunciate clearly what the firm's overall business strategy is. Second, there may be much uncertainty or disagreement concerning which HR strategies should be used to support the overall business strategy. In other words, it is seldom obvious how particular HR strategies will contribute to the achievement of organizational strategies. For example, a bonus plan that pays executives for increasing firm growth may lead to undesirable mergers and acquisitions. A TQM program that encourages extensive employee participation may produce so many meetings that the productivity increases resulting from the program do not outweigh the hours lost. Third, large corporations may have different business units, each with its own business strategies. Ideally, each unit should be able to formulate the HR strategy that fits its business strategy best. For instance, a division that produces high-tech equipment may decide to pay its engineering staff well above average to attract and retain the best possible engineers, while the consumer products division, which operates with a lower profit margin, may decide to pay its engineers an average wage. Of course, such differential strategies may cause problems if the engineers from the two divisions have contact with one other. Thus diverse HR strategies may spur feelings of inequity and resentment.

Avoiding Excessive Concentration on Day-to-Day Problems.   Some managers devote most of their attention to urgent problems. They are so busy putting out fires that they have no time to focus on the long term. Nonetheless, a successful HR strategy demands a vision tied to the long-term direction of the business. Thus a major challenge of strategic HR planning is to prod people into stepping back to consider the big picture.

It takes considerable discipline to detach oneself from current events and past history and trace a master plan for the organization's future direction. This is particularly true in many small companies, whose staffs are often so absorbed in growing the business today that they seldom take a breath and pause to look at the big picture for tomorrow. Also, in companies with fewer than 50 employees, strategic HR planning is often synonymous with the whims of the company owner or founder, who may not take the time to formalize his or her plans.

Many companies today—both small and large—try to avoid excessive concentration on the present by creating a mission statement in which the company's purpose and goals are committed to paper. Alan Blazar, president of Blazing Graphics, a small graphics production company, feels that crafting a mission statement is "a very helpful process in that it makes you sit back and focus on things outside the day-to-day, filling-the-order kind of mentality."[56] Blazing Graphics' mission statement is reprinted in Figure 1–6.

Developing HR Strategies Suited to Unique Organizational Features. No two firms are exactly alike. Firms differ in history, culture, leadership style, technology, and so on. Firms differ in culture, leadership style, and technology. The chances are high that any ambitious HR strategy or program that is not moulded to organizational characteristics will fail.[57] Therein lies one of the central challenges in formulating HR strategies: creating a vision of the organization of the future that does not provoke a destructive clash with the organization of the present.

Coping with the Environment. Just as no two firms are exactly alike, no two firms operate in an identical environment. Some must deal with rapid change, as in the computer industry; others operate in a relatively stable market, as in the market for food processors. Some face a virtually guaranteed demand for their products or services (for example, medical providers); others must deal with turbulent demand (for example, fashion designers). Even within a very narrowly defined industry, some firms may be competing in a market where customer service is the key (IBM's traditional competitive advantage), while others are competing in a market driven by cost considerations (the competitive advantage offered by the many firms producing IBM clones). A major challenge in developing HR strategies is to craft strategies that will work in the unique environment in which the firm operates to give it a sustainable competitive advantage.

Securing Management Commitment. Many HR programs that originated within the HR department have failed because line managers were not involved in creating them. HR strategies that originate in the HR department will have little chance of succeeding unless managers at all levels—including top executives—support them completely. To ensure managers' commitment, HR professionals must work closely with them when formulating policies. This is a point we emphasize again and again throughout this book.

Figure 1–6 Blazing Graphics' Mission Statement

SOURCE: Nelton, S. (1994, February). Put your purpose in writing. *Nation's Business,* 61. Reprinted by permission. Copyright 1994, U.S. Chamber of Commerce.

Blazing Graphics will provide you with the most effective visual communication attainable. We will help you achieve all of your goals while providing you with the greatest value both seen and unseen.

Here at Blazing Graphics we will take the time to do things right. We do this by controlling the entire graphic arts process. This enables us to better coordinate each job while providing a higher level of service.

Our mission is to ensure exceptional quality by opening up communication between crafts normally separated and at times adverse to one another.

Here at Blazing Graphics we have committed ourselves and our resources to being on the forefront of technology.

Creative technical know-how is the single most critical determinant of economic competitiveness.

It's our real belief that together we can create an environment that will be both personally and professionally fulfilling for all the people who make up the Blazing Community.

Translating the Strategic Plan into Action.   Often a strategic plan that looks great on paper fails because of poor implementation. The acid test of any strategic plan is whether it makes a difference to practise. If the plan does not affect practice, it will be regarded by employees and managers alike as all talk and no action.

Cynicism regarding the strategic plan is practically guaranteed when a firm experiences frequent turnover at the top, with each new wave of high-level managers introducing their own freshly minted strategic plan. Perhaps the greatest challenge in strategic HR planning lies not in the formulation of strategy, but rather in the development of an appropriate set of programs or tactics that will make the strategy work.

Combining Intended and Emergent Strategies.   There is a continuing debate over whether strategies are *intended* or *emergent*—that is, whether they are proactive, rational, deliberate plans designed to attain predetermined objectives (intended) or general "fuzzy" patterns collectively moulded by the interplay of power, politics, improvisation, negotiation, and personalities within the organization (emergent).[58] Most people agree that organizations have intended *and* emergent strategies, that both are necessary, and that the challenge is to combine the best aspects of the two.

When based on a rigorous analysis of where the organization is at present and where it wishes to go in the future, intended strategies can provide a sense of purpose and a guide for the allocation of resources. Intended strategies are also highly useful for recognizing environmental opportunities and threats and mobilizing top management to respond to these in a deliberate and effective manner. On the downside, intended strategies may lead to a top-down strategic approach that squashes creativity and innovation and surrenders the potential gains that can come from widespread involvement in strategy development.[59]

Emergent strategies also have their advantages and disadvantages. Among their benefits: (1) they involve everyone in the organization, which fosters grass-roots support; (2) they develop gradually out of the organization's experiences, and thus can be less upsetting than intended strategies; and (3) they are more pragmatic than intended strategies because they evolve to deal with specific problems or issues facing the firm.[60] On the negative side, emergent strategies may lack the strong leadership and fail to infuse the organization with a creative vision.

Combining intended and emergent strategies effectively requires that managers blend the benefits of formal planning (to provide strong guidance and direction in setting priorities) with the untidy realities of dispersed employees who, through their unplanned activities, formulate emergent strategies throughout the firm.

Accommodating Change.   Strategic HR plans must be flexible enough to accommodate changes affecting the business. A firm with an inflexible strategic plan may find itself unable to respond to changes quickly because it is so committed to a particular course of action. This may lead the organization to continue to devote resources to an activity that is now of questionable value simply because so much has been invested in it already.[61] The challenge is to create a strategic vision and develop the plans to achieve it while staying flexible enough to adapt to change.

■ Strategic Human Resource Choices

A firm's **strategic HR choices** are the options it has available in designing its human resources system. Choices are strategic to the extent that they affect the firm's performance either favourably or unfavourably in the long run.

Figure 1–7 shows a sampling of strategic HR choices. At this point, it is important to keep three things in mind. First, the list of strategic HR choices in Figure 1–7 is not exhaustive. Second, many different HR programs or practices may

strategic HR choices
The options available to a firm in designing its human resources system.

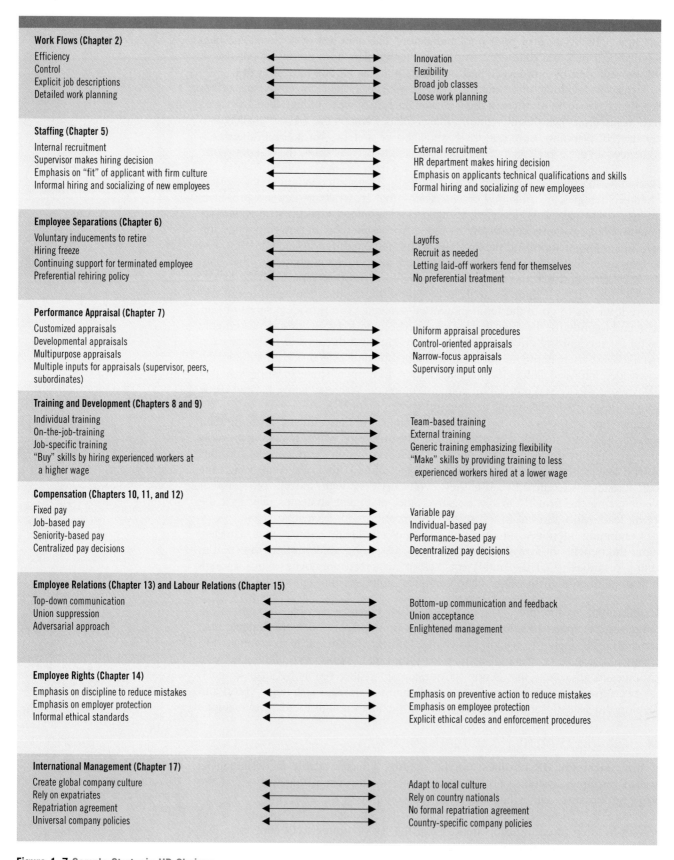

Work Flows (Chapter 2)

Efficiency	Innovation
Control	Flexibility
Explicit job descriptions	Broad job classes
Detailed work planning	Loose work planning

Staffing (Chapter 5)

Internal recruitment	External recruitment
Supervisor makes hiring decision	HR department makes hiring decision
Emphasis on "fit" of applicant with firm culture	Emphasis on applicants technical qualifications and skills
Informal hiring and socializing of new employees	Formal hiring and socializing of new employees

Employee Separations (Chapter 6)

Voluntary inducements to retire	Layoffs
Hiring freeze	Recruit as needed
Continuing support for terminated employee	Letting laid-off workers fend for themselves
Preferential rehiring policy	No preferential treatment

Performance Appraisal (Chapter 7)

Customized appraisals	Uniform appraisal procedures
Developmental appraisals	Control-oriented appraisals
Multipurpose appraisals	Narrow-focus appraisals
Multiple inputs for appraisals (supervisor, peers, subordinates)	Supervisory input only

Training and Development (Chapters 8 and 9)

Individual training	Team-based training
On-the-job-training	External training
Job-specific training	Generic training emphasizing flexibility
"Buy" skills by hiring experienced workers at a higher wage	"Make" skills by providing training to less experienced workers hired at a lower wage

Compensation (Chapters 10, 11, and 12)

Fixed pay	Variable pay
Job-based pay	Individual-based pay
Seniority-based pay	Performance-based pay
Centralized pay decisions	Decentralized pay decisions

Employee Relations (Chapter 13) and Labour Relations (Chapter 15)

Top-down communication	Bottom-up communication and feedback
Union suppression	Union acceptance
Adversarial approach	Enlightened management

Employee Rights (Chapter 14)

Emphasis on discipline to reduce mistakes	Emphasis on preventive action to reduce mistakes
Emphasis on employer protection	Emphasis on employee protection
Informal ethical standards	Explicit ethical codes and enforcement procedures

International Management (Chapter 17)

Create global company culture	Adapt to local culture
Rely on expatriates	Rely on country nationals
Repatriation agreement	No formal repatriation agreement
Universal company policies	Country-specific company policies

Figure 1–7 Sample Strategic HR Choices

be used separately or together to implement each of these choices. For example, if a firm chooses to base pay on performance, it can use many different programs to implement this decision, including cash awards, lump-sum annual bonuses to top performers, raises based on supervisory appraisals, and an employee of the month award. Third, the strategic HR choices listed in Figure 1–7 represent two opposite poles on a continuum. Very few organizations fall at these extremes. Some organizations will be closer to the right end, some closer to the left end, and others closer to the middle.

A brief description of the strategic HR choices shown in Figure 1–7 follows. We will examine these choices, and provide examples of companies' strategic decisions in these areas, in later chapters.

Work Flows.   Work flows refer to the ways tasks are organized to meet production or service goals. Organizations face several choices in what they emphasize as they structure work flows (Chapter 2). They can emphasize:

◆ efficiency (getting work done at minimum cost) or innovation (encouraging creativity, exploration, and new ways of doing things, even though this may increase production costs)

◆ control (establishing predetermined procedures) or flexibility (allowing room for exceptions and personal judgement)

◆ explicit job descriptions (in which the duties and requirements of each job are carefully spelled out) or broad job classes (in which employees are able to perform multiple tasks and are expected to fill different jobs as needed), and

◆ detailed work planning (in which processes, objectives, and schedules are laid out well in advance) or loose work planning (in which activities and schedules may be modified on relatively short notice, depending on changing needs).

Staffing.   Staffing encompasses the HR activities designed to secure the right employees at the right place at the right time (Chapter 5). Organizations face several strategic HR choices in recruiting, selecting, and socializing employees—all part of the staffing process. These include:

◆ promoting from within (*internal* recruitment) versus hiring from the outside (*external* recruitment)

◆ empowering immediate supervisors to make hiring decisions versus centralizing these decisions in the HR department

◆ emphasizing a good fit between the applicant and the firm versus hiring the most knowledgeable individual regardless of interpersonal considerations, and

◆ hiring and socializing new workers informally or choosing a more formal and systematic approach to hiring and socialization.

Employee Separations.   Employee separations occur when employees leave the firm, either voluntarily or involuntarily (Chapter 6). Some strategic HR choices available to the firm for handling employee separations are:

◆ use of voluntary inducements (such as early retirement packages) to downsize a work force versus use of layoffs

◆ imposing a hiring freeze to avoid laying off current employees versus recruiting employees as needed, even if this means laying off current employees

◆ providing continuing support to terminated employees (perhaps offering them assistance in securing another job) versus leaving laid-off employees to fend for themselves, and

◆ making a commitment to rehire terminated employees if conditions improve versus avoiding any type of preferential hiring treatment for ex-employees.

A Question of Ethics

Experts in career development note that in today's increasingly chaotic business and economic environment, individual employees need to prepare themselves for job and career changes. Does an employer have an ethical duty to help employees prepare for the change that is almost certain to come?

Performance Appraisal.   Managers assess how well employees are carrying out their assigned duties by conducting performance appraisals (Chapter 7). Some strategic HR choices concerning employee appraisals are:

◆ developing an appraisal system that is customized to the needs of various employee groups (for example, by designing a different appraisal form for each job family) versus using a standardized appraisal system throughout the organization

◆ using the appraisal data as a developmental tool to help employees improve their performance versus using appraisals as a control mechanism to weed out low producers

◆ designing the appraisal system with multiple objectives in mind (such as training, promotion, and selection decisions) versus designing it for a narrow purpose (such as pay decisions only), and

◆ developing an appraisal system that encourages the active participation of multiple employee groups (for example, supervisor, peers, and subordinates) versus developing one that asks solely for the input of each employee's supervisor.

Training and Career Development.   Training and career development activities are designed to help an organization meet its skill requirements and to help its employees realize their maximum potential (Chapters 8 and 9). Some of the strategic HR choices pertaining to these activities are:

◆ choosing whether to provide training to individuals or to teams of employees who work together as a group and who may come from diverse areas of the firm

◆ deciding whether to teach required skills on the job or rely on external sources for training

◆ choosing whether to emphasize job-specific training or generic training (which increases the firm's flexibility and may help it to respond rapidly to changing conditions), and

◆ deciding whether to hire at a high wage people from outside the firm who already have the required talents ("buy skills") or to invest resources in training the firm's own lower-wage employees in the necessary skills ("make skills").

Compensation.   Compensation is the payment that employees receive in exchange for their labour. Organizations vary widely in how they choose to compensate their employees (Chapters 10, 11, and 12). Some of the strategic HR choices related to pay are:

◆ providing employees with a fixed salary and benefits package that changes little from year to year (and therefore involves minimal risk) versus paying employees an amount subject to change

◆ paying employees on the basis of the job they hold versus paying them for their individual contributions to the firm

◆ rewarding employees for the time they've spent with the firm versus rewarding them for performance, and

◆ centralizing pay decisions in a single location (such as the HR department) versus empowering the supervisor or work team to make pay decisions.

Employee and Labour Relations.   Employee and labour relations (Chapters 13 and 15) refer to the interaction between workers (either as individuals or as represented by a union) and management. Some of the strategic HR choices facing the firm in these areas are:

◆ relying on "top-down" communication channels from managers to subordinates versus encouraging "bottom-up" feedback from employees to top managers

◆ actively trying to avoid or suppress union-organizing activity versus accepting unions as representatives of employees' interests, and

◆ adopting an adversarial approach to dealing with employees versus responding to employees' needs so that the incentive for unionization is removed.

Employee Rights.   Employee rights concern the relationship between the organization and individual employees (Chapter 14). Some of the strategic choices that the firm needs to make in this area are:

◆ emphasizing discipline as the mechanism for controlling employee behaviour versus proactively encouraging appropriate behaviour in the first place

◆ developing policies that emphasize protecting the employer's interests versus policies that emphasize protecting the employees' interests, and

◆ relying on informal ethical standards versus developing explicit standards and procedures to enforce those standards.

International Management.   Firms that operate outside domestic boundaries face a set of strategic HR options regarding how to manage human resources on a global basis (Chapter 17). Some of the key strategic HR choices involved in international management are:

◆ creating a common company culture to reduce intercountry cultural differences versus allowing foreign subsidiaries to adapt to the local culture

◆ sending expatriates (domestic employees) abroad to manage foreign subsidiaries versus hiring local people to manage them

◆ establishing a repatriation agreement with each employee going abroad (carefully stipulating what the expatriate can expect upon return in terms of career advancement, compensation, and the like) versus avoiding any type of commitment to expatriates, and

◆ establishing company policies that must be followed in all subsidiaries versus decentralizing policy formulation so that each local office can develop its own policies.

■ Building Managerial Skills: Selecting HR Strategies to Increase Firm Performance

No HR strategy is "good" or "bad" in and of itself. Rather, the success of HR strategies depends on the situation or context in which they are used. In other words, the effect of an HR strategy on firm performance is always dependent on how well it fits with some other factors. This fact leads to a simple yet powerful prediction for HR strategies that has been widely supported by research: Fit leads to better performance, and lack of fit creates inconsistencies that reduce performance.[62] *Fit* refers to the consistency or compatibility between HR strategies and other important aspects of the organization.

Figure 1–8 depicts the key factors that firms should consider in determining which HR strategies will have a positive impact on firm performance: organizational and business strategy, environment, organizational characteristics, and organizational capabilities. As the figure suggests, the relative contribution of an HR strategy to firm performance increases:

1. The greater the match between the HR strategy and the firm's overall organizational strategies.
2. The greater the extent to which the HR strategy is attuned to the environment in which the firm is operating.
3. The more the HR strategy is moulded to unique organizational features.
4. The more the HR strategy enables the firm to capitalize on its distinctive competencies.
5. The more the HR strategies are mutually consistent or reinforce each other.

■ Fit with Organizational Strategies

Depending on the firm's size and complexity, organizational strategies may be examined at two levels: corporate or business. A corporation may have multiple

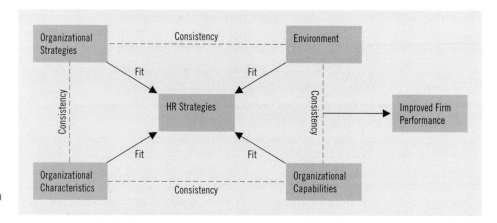

Figure 1–8

Effective HR Strategy Formulation and Implementation

corporate strategy

The mix of businesses a corporation decides to hold and the flow of resources among those businesses.

business unit strategy

The formulation and implementation of strategies by a firm that is relatively autonomous, even if it is part of a larger corporation.

businesses that are very similar to or completely different from one another. **Corporate strategy** refers to the mix of businesses a corporation decides to hold and the flow of resources among those businesses. The main strategic business decisions at the corporate level concern acquisition, divestment, diversification, and manner of growth. **Business unit strategies** refer to the formulation and implementation of strategies by firms that are relatively autonomous, even if they are part of a larger corporation. Companies such as Power Corporation, active in media and financial services industries, and Imasco, whose businesses include tobacco, fast food, financial services and retailing, require both business unit and corporate strategies.

Corporate Strategies. Corporations adopting an *evolutionary business strategy* engage in aggressive acquisitions of new businesses, even if these are totally unrelated to one another.[63] For example, Gulf + Western, before its reorganization, was nicknamed "Engulf and Devour" because of its extensive purchasing and divesting of businesses in diverse markets and industries, including oil, agriculture, tourist attractions, and the arts.[64]

In evolutionary firms, the management of change is crucial to survival. Entrepreneurship is encouraged and control is de-emphasized because each unit is relatively autonomous. Certain HR strategies fit best with an evolutionary strategy. HR strategies that foster flexibility, quick response, entrepreneurship, risk sharing, and decentralization are particularly appropriate. Because the evolutionary corporation is not committed to a particular business or industry, it may hire workers from the external market as needed and lay them off to reduce costs if necessary, with no promise of rehiring them. These HR strategies are appropriate because they "fit" with the organizational reality that change is the only constant.

At the other end of the spectrum, corporations adopting a *steady-state strategy* are very choosy about how they grow. They avoid acquiring firms outside their industry or even companies within the industry that are very different from them. Firms with a steady-state strategy have an inward focus. Top managers exercise a great deal of direct control over the company and prefer to promote employee dependence on supervisors rather than independent action or entrepreneurship. Internal development of new products and technologies and interunit coordination are very important to these firms.[65] This is the case at Rubbermaid, a company known for producing such mundane products as garbage cans and dustpans. Yet, Rubbermaid's record for innovation is anything but mundane. The company brings out new products at the rate of one a day.[66] The HR strategies most appropriate to steady-state firms emphasize efficiency, detailed work planning, internal grooming of employees for promotion and long-term career development, centralization, and a paternalistic attitude (reflected, for example, in preferential recall of laid-off employees when the economic environment improves).

Porter's Business Unit Strategies.   Two well-known business unit strategies were formulated by Porter[67] and Miles and Snow.[68] Both of these may be used to analyse which HR strategies represent the best fit with a firm's business strategy.

Porter's Business Strategies.   Porter has identified three types of business unit strategies that help a firm to cope with competitive forces and outperform other firms in the industry. For each of these strategies outlined in Figure 1–9, a certain set of HR strategies would fit best.[69]

The *overall cost leadership strategy* is aimed at gaining a competitive advantage through lower costs. Financial considerations and budgetary constraints play a critical role here in shaping HR strategies. Cost leadership requires efficient plant facilities (which requires sustained capital investment), intense supervision of labour, vigorous pursuit of cost reductions, and tight control of distribution costs and overhead.

Low-cost firms tend to emphasize structured tasks and responsibilities, products designed for easy manufacture, and the need to predict costs with minimal margin of error. The HR strategies that fit a low-cost orientation emphasize efficient, low-cost production; reinforce adherence to rational, highly structured procedures to minimize uncertainty; and discourage creativity and innovation (which may lead to costly experimentation and mistakes). Thus effective HR strategies include carefully spelling out the work that each employee needs to do, job-specific training, hiring workers with the necessary technical qualifications and skills, paying employees on the basis of job held, and relying on performance appraisals as a control tool to weed out low performers.

Business Strategy	Common Organizational Characteristics	HR Strategies
Overall cost leadership	• Sustained capital investment and access to capital • Intense supervision of labour • Low-cost distribution system • Tight cost control requiring frequent, detailed control reports • Structured organization and responsibilities • Products designed for ease in manufacture	• Efficient production • Explicit job descriptions • Detailed work planning • Emphasis on technical qualifications and skills • Emphasis on job-specific training • Emphasis on job-based pay • Use of performance appraisal as a control device
Differentiation	• Strong marketing abilities • Product engineering • Strong capability in basic research • Corporate reputation for quality or technological leadership • Amenities to attract highly skilled labour, scientists, or creative people	• Emphasis on innovation and flexibility • Broad job classes • Loose work planning • External recruitment • Team-based training • Emphasis on individual-based pay • Use of performance appraisal as developmental tool
Focus	• Combination of cost leadership and differentiation strategy directed at a particular strategic target.	• Combination of HR strategies above.

Figure 1–9 Selected HR Strategies That Fit Porter's Three Major Types of Business Strategy

SOURCE: Common organizational characteristics: Porter, M. E. (1980). *Competitive Strategy,* 40–41. New York: Free Press. HR Strategies: Prepared by the authors for this book.

A firm with a *differentiation business strategy* attempts to achieve a competitive advantage by creating a product or service that is perceived to be unique. Some common characteristics of such firms are strong marketing abilities, an emphasis on product engineering and basic research, a corporate reputation for quality products, and amenities that are attractive to highly skilled labour. Approaches to differentiating can take many forms, among them: design or brand image (Mercedes, Jaguar, Saturn, and others in the auto industry; Roots or Club Monaco in apparel); Canadian identity (*Maclean's* in magazine publishing; PetroCan and Canadian Tire in retailing), dealer networks (Caterpillar Tractor); good price/high value (President's Choice in grocery products); customer service (IBM in computers); and features (Jenn-Air in electric ranges).

Differentiation provides a competitive advantage because of the brand loyalty it fosters. Consumers who are brand loyal are less sensitive to changes in price. This enables the differentiator to enjoy higher profit margins, which, in turn, allow it to invest in activities that are costly and risky but that enhance the perceived superiority of its products or services. These activities include extensive research, experimentation with new ideas and product designs, catering to the needs of different customers, and supporting creative initiatives by managers and employees.

HR strategies that fit a business strategy of differentiation emphasize innovation, flexibility, renewal of the work force by attracting new talent from other firms, opportunities for mavericks, and reinforcement (rather than discouragement) of creative flair. The specific HR strategies that are likely to benefit differentiators include the use of broad job classes, loose work planning, external recruitment at all levels, team-based learning, emphasis on what the individual can do (rather than on the job title held) as a basis for pay, and reliance on performance appraisal as a developmental (rather than as a control) device.

The *focus strategy* relies on both a low-cost position and differentiation, with the objective of serving a narrow target market better than other firms that are competing more broadly. As a result, the firm achieves either differentiation from better meeting the needs of the particular target, or lower costs in serving this target, or both.[70] Firms that have used this strategy successfully include Illinois Tool Works (in the specialty market for fasteners), Gymboree (a national franchise providing creative activities and accessories for children under the age of five), Fort Howard Paper (manufacturer of specialized industrial grade papers), and Porter Paint (producer of paints for professional housepainters).

The HR strategies likely to fit the focus strategy would be somewhere in the middle of those described earlier for low-cost producers and differentiators. The plastics industry is one in which the focus strategy is often effective. MAC Closures of Waterloo, Quebec, increased sales by 50% over a four-year period as they emphasized quality, built on intensified on-the-job training and coaching combined with investments in supervisory knowledge through off-site technological education.[71] The quality emphasis has been taken further at Toronto Plastics, with their application for ISO 9002 certification. In time, key customers such as Nortel are expected to forgo their own quality audit of components from Toronto Plastics because of the ISO program.[72] Waltech Plastics, a custom injector and thermoset moulder, has a work force of some 230 at its Midland, Ontario, location. Employees coming to the company from other parts of Ontario have tended to leave after three to five years. The solution to retaining skilled operators for a longer period has been to recruit mechanically inclined local high school graduates and invest in their development, including collaboration with community colleges in the area.[73] In all these cases, the various techniques reflect a common strategic emphasis on a restricted range of products, high-quality standards and cost control.

Miles and Snow's Business Strategies.   Miles and Snow created a second well-known classification of business unit strategies.[74] They characterize successful businesses as primarily adopting either a defender or a prospector strategy.

Defenders are conservative business units that prefer to maintain a secure position in relatively stable product or service areas instead of looking to expand into uncharted territory. Defenders attempt to protect their market share from competitors rather than engage in new-product development. Firms that are defenders tend to be highly formalized and centralized, to emphasize cost control, and to operate in a stable environment. Many defenders develop an elaborate internal system for promoting, transferring, and rewarding workers that is relatively isolated from the uncertainties of the external labour market. In exchange for a long-term commitment to the firm, employees are rewarded with job security and the expectation of upward mobility through the ranks. Defenders discourage risk-taking behaviours because they prefer reliability to innovation.

The HR strategies that best fit defenders' needs, categorized according to six major strategic HR choices we discussed earlier, are summarized in Figure 1–10. These strategies include work flows emphasizing control and reliability, staffing and employee separation policies designed to foster long-term employee attachment to the firm, performance appraisals focussed on control and hierarchy, structured training programs, and compensation policies that emphasize job security.

Unlike defenders, whose success comes primarily from efficiently serving a stable market, the prospector's key objective is to find and exploit new product and market opportunities.[75] *Prospectors* emphasize growth and opportunities for growth through innovation, development of new products, and an eagerness to be the first players in new product or market areas, even if some of these efforts fail. The prospector's strategy is associated with flexible and decentralized organizational structures, complex products (such as computers and pharmaceuticals), and unstable environments that change rapidly.

The HR strategies that match the strategic orientation of prospectors, also summarized in Figure 1–10, involve work flows that foster creativity and adaptability; staffing and employee separation policies that focus on the external labour market; customized, participative employee appraisals used for multiple purposes (including employee development); training strategies targeting broad skills; and a decentralized compensation system that rewards risk taking and performance. The Issues and Applications entitled "Lincoln Electric and Hewlett-Packard: Defender and Prospector" discusses how these two firms have successfully used HR strategies to support their opposite business strategies.

▉ Fit with the Environment

In addition to reinforcing overall organizational strategies, HR strategies should help the organization better exploit environmental opportunities or cope with the unique environmental forces that affect it. The relevant environment can be examined in terms of four major dimensions: (1) *degree of uncertainty* (how much accurate information is available to make appropriate business decisions); (2) *volatility* (how often the environment changes); (3) *magnitude of change* (how drastic the changes are); and (4) *complexity* (how many different elements in the environment affect the firm, either individually or together). For example, much of the computer and high-tech industry is very high on all four of these dimensions:

◆ *Degree of uncertainty.* Compaq thought consumers would continue to pay a premium price for its high-performance computers. The company was proved wrong in the 1990s as low-cost competitors such as Dell, Packard Bell, and AST quickly cut into Compaq's market.

Strategic HR Area	Defender Strategy	Prospector Strategy
Work flows	• Efficient production • Control emphasis • Explicit job descriptions • Detailed work planning	• Innovation • Flexibility • Broad job classes • Loose work planning
Staffing	• Internal recruitment • HR department makes selection decision • Emphasis on technical qualifications and skills • Formal hiring and socialization process	• External recruitment • Supervisor makes selection decision • Emphasis on fit of applicant with culture • Informal hiring and socialization process of new employees
Employee separations	• Voluntary inducements • Hiring freeze • Continuing concern for terminated employee • Preferential rehiring policy	• Layoffs • Recruit as needed • Individual on his/her own • No preferential treatment for laid-off workers
Performance appraisal	• Uniform appraisal procedures • Used as control device • Narrow focus • High dependence on superior	• Customized appraisals • Used as developmental tool • Multipurpose appraisals • Multiple inputs for appraisals
Training	• Individual training • On-the-job training • Job-specific training • "Make" skills	• Team-based or cross-functional training • External training • Generic training emphasizing flexibility • "Buy" skills
Compensation	• Fixed pay • Job-based pay • Seniority-based pay • Centralized pay decisions	• Variable pay • Individual-based pay • Performance-based pay • Decentralized pay decisions

Figure 1–10 Selected HR Strategies That Fit Miles and Snow's Two Major Types of Business Strategy

SOURCE: Gómez-Mejía, L. R. (1994). Compensation strategies and Miles and Snow's business strategy taxonomy. Unpublished report. Management department, Arizona State University.

◆ *Volatility.* IBM paid dearly when demand for its main-frame computers declined drastically in the late 1980s and it was caught unprepared.

◆ *Magnitude of Change.* The advent of each successive new generation of computer microprocessor chips (for example, Intel's 386, 486, Pentium, Pentium II) has almost immediately rendered all previously sold machines obsolete.

◆ *Complexity.* The number and variety of competitors in the computer industry, both domestically and overseas, have grown dramatically in recent years. The life of a product seldom extends more than three years now, as new innovations drive previous equipment and soft-ware out of the market.

Before formulating and implementing HR strategies, a firm needs to examine how low or high it is on each of these environmental dimensions. As Figure 1–11 shows, firms that are high on these four dimensions are more likely to benefit from HR strategies that promote flexibility, adaptiveness, quick response, transferability of skills, the ability to secure external talent as needed, and risk sharing with employees through variable pay.

Environmental Dimension	Low	High
Degree of Uncertainty	• Detailed work planning • Job-specific training • Fixed pay • High dependence on superior	• Loose work planning • Generic training • Variable pay • Mulitple inputs for appraisals
Volatility	• Control emphasis • Efficient production • Job-specific training • Fixed pay	• Flexibility • Innovation • Generic training • Variable pay
Magnitude of Change	• Explicit job descriptions • Formal hiring and socialization of new employees • "Make" skills • Uniform appraisal procedures	• Broad job classes • Informal hiring and socialization of new employees • "Buy" skills • Customized appraisals
Complexity	• Control emphasis • Internal recruitment • Centralized pay decisions • High dependence on superior	• Flexibility • External recruitment • Decentralized pay decisions • Multiple inputs for appraisals

Figure 1–11 Selected HR Strategies for Firms Low and High on Different Environmental Characteristics

SOURCE: Based on Gómez-Mejía, L. R., & Balkin, D. B. (1992). *Compensation, organizational strategy, and firm performance.* Cincinnati, OH: Southwestern; Gómez-Mejía, L. R., Balkin, D. B., & Milkovich, G. T. (1990). Rethinking your rewards for technical employees. *Organizational Dynamics, 18*(4), 62–75; Gómez-Mejía, L. R. (1992). Structure and process of diversification, compensation strategy, and firm performance. *Strategic Management Journal, 13,* 381–397; and Gómez-Mejía, L. R. (1994). *Fostering a strategic partnership between operations and human resources.* Scarsdale, NY: Work in America Institute.

Conversely, firms facing environments that are low on uncertainty, volatility, magnitude of change, and complexity benefit from HR strategies that allow for an orderly, rational, and routine approach to dealing with a relatively predictable and stable environment. Bell Canada (before reduced regulatory controls and the appearance of competitors in their long-distance market), other regulated monopolies, the financial services industries (especially before changes to the *Bank Act*) and many government bureaucracies fall at the low end of these four dimensions. Figure 1–11 shows that HR strategies for firms operating under these conditions tend to be rather mechanistic: detailed work planning, job-specific training, fixed pay, explicit job descriptions, centralized pay plans, and the like.

▪ Fit with Organizational Characteristics

Every firm has a unique history and its own way of doing business and getting the work done. To be effective, HR strategies must be tailored to the organization's personality. The features of an organization's personality can be broken down into five major categories:

The production process for converting input into output. Firms with a relatively routine production process (such as large-volume steel mills, lumber mills, and automobile plants) tend to benefit from HR strategies that emphasize control, such as explicit job descriptions and job-specific training. The opposite is true for

Lincoln Electric and Hewlett-Packard: Defender and Prospector

To get a better idea of what it means for a company to be either a defender or a prospector, look at the activities of two companies: Lincoln Electric, a manufacturer of electrical products; and Hewlett-Packard, the electronics manufacturer that put Silicon Valley on the high-tech map back in 1939. These U.S.-based multinationals are frequently identified as classic examples of these two strategies.

Lincoln Electric

Lincoln Electric is a classic defender. Lincoln has carved out a niche in the electrical products industry (the manufacture of electric arc-welding generators, welding equipment, and supplies) and has "defended" it for over 70 years through continuous efforts to improve production processes and product quality, cut costs, lower prices, and provide outstanding customer service. Lincoln is best known for its incentive system that pays off for high-quantity, high-quality output with total wages and bonuses for employees that regularly average over twice the national average for comparable work classifications. Lincoln's HR strategies fit with the company's strategy because Lincoln has created a secure market share with moderate, steady growth. It relies heavily on internally developed human resources. Employees are carefully selected, placed, and trained, and they are expected to be with the company for much, if not all, of their careers—tied to the organization by guaranteed employment. ... Long-term personal development is rewarded by slow but relatively certain internal promotion.

The appropriate role for the human resources department at Lincoln is implied in the organization's description. Selection, placement, appraisal, and long-term training assistance are key services. In addition, the human resources department must constantly maintain the fit between job design and the incentive system. Lincoln is a tightly integrated company that requires predictable, planned human resources inputs and then only regular maintenance.

Hewlett-Packard

Hewlett-Packard (HP) began with the notion that high returns were possible from moving products as rapidly as possible from basic design to the market. It is a company well suited to the rapid expansion of a growing industry—a true prospector—with small, changing product divisions as its basic organizational building blocks (the company has over 60,000 employees worldwide in more than 60 divisions or units). A new product idea or offshoot is evolved, a self-contained division created, and a market pursued as long as HP has a distinctive design or technological advantage. When products reach the stage where successful competition turns primarily on cost, HP may move out of the arena and turn its attention to a new design or an entirely new product. ...

Human resources units at both the division and the corporate level have the constant task of starting new groups, and finding and deploying managerial and technical resources. ... In such a setting, human resources units perform an essentially entrepreneurial role, helping to identify and quickly develop (through rapid movement and alternative assignments) crucial human resources. At HP, key human resources are brought from the outside and invested in myriad units and divisions, as well as developed internally. Thus the overall human resources strategy at Hewlett-Packard can be characterized as acquiring human resources.

Dynamic Considerations

Overall strategies for successful corporations, including the human resources dimension, are executed in a changing environment. For HP, this meant amending a commitment to employment security when competitive pressures became intense. Making such changes has helped HP sustain its success. More recently, for Lincoln Electric, the defender strategy has created a something of a dilemma. Lincoln dominated its core business sector, but was slower than some rivals to develop new products. As Lincoln examined the international environment, it identified ESABAB of Sweden as a potential threat in the North American market. In response, between 1986 and 1992 Lincoln expanded manufacturing operations from four countries to 15. This overly costly expansion, combined with the recession of the early 1990s, created a substantial debt, which led to a intensified effort to install the "standard" package of Lincoln human resources polices in international operations. These policies have run into both employee resistance and employment legislation obstacles. The damage to profitability has undermined the profit-triggered bonuses and has shaken, if not derailed, the long-term prospects of Lincoln Electric's highly regarded human resources strategy.

The implication of these events is not that Lincoln's strategy was wrong, but rather that success can be a trap. Environments (markets, competitors, institutional/legal parameters) change. Strategies need to be reevaluated and amended regularly, in light of such changes. Past successes, particularly successes built on unusual strategies, are difficult to change because decision makers come to believe in them strongly. It should not be surprising that some of the most successful organizations can get into some of the greatest difficulties when they fail to respond to the need for strategic change.

SOURCES: Excerpted, by permission of publisher, from Miles, R. E., & Snow, C. C. (1984). Designing strategic human resources systems. *Organizational Dynamics* 13(1), 43–46. © 1984 American Management Association, New York. All rights reserved; Feder, B. (1994, September 13). Workers without wages. The *Globe and Mail*, B22.

firms with nonroutine production processes (such as advertising firms, custom printers, and biotechnology companies). These firms benefit from flexible HR strategies that support organizational adaptability, quick response to change, and creative decision making. These flexible strategies may include broad job classes, loose work planning, and generic training.

The firm's market posture.   Firms that experience a high rate of sales growth and that engage in product innovation destined for a wide market segment tend to benefit from HR strategies that support growth and entrepreneurial activities. These HR strategies include external recruitment ("buying" skills), decentralized pay decisions, and customized appraisals. The opposite is true for firms with low rates of growth and limited product innovation destined for a narrow market segment. These firms tend to benefit more from HR strategies that emphasize efficiency, control, and firm-specific knowledge. These HR strategies include internal recruitment ("making" skills), on-the-job training, and high dependence on superiors.

The firm's overall managerial philosophy.   Companies whose top executives are averse to risk, operate with an autocratic leadership style, establish a strong internal pecking order, and are inwardly rather than outwardly focussed may find that certain HR practices match this general outlook best. The HR strategies most often used in these kinds of firms include seniority-based pay, formal hiring and socializing of new employees, selection decisions made by the HR department, and use of top-down communication channels. The HR strategies that fit a managerial philosophy high on risk taking, participation, egalitarianism, and an external, proactive environmental orientation include variable pay, giving supervisors a major role in hiring decisions, up-and-down communication channels, and multiple inputs for performance appraisals.

The firm's organizational structure.   Some HR strategies fit very well with highly formalized organizations that are divided into functional areas (for example, marketing, finance, production, and so on) and that concentrate decision making at the top. The HR strategies appropriate for this type of firm include a control emphasis, centralized pay decisions, explicit job descriptions, and job-based pay. Firms whose organizational structures are less regimented will benefit from a different set of HR strategies, including informal hiring and socializing of new employees, decentralized pay decisions, broad job classes, and individual-based pay.

The firm's organizational culture.   Two important dimensions of a firm's culture should be considered when formulating and implementing HR strategies: entrepreneurial climate and moral commitment. Companies that foster an entrepreneurial climate benefit from such supporting HR strategies as loose work planning, informal hiring and socializing of new employees, and variable pay. Firms that discourage entrepreneurship generally prefer other HR strategies, such as a control emphasis, detailed work planning, formal hiring and socializing of new employees, and fixed pay.

A strong emphasis on moral commitment —the extent to which a firm tries to foster a long-term emotional attachment to the firm among its employees— is also associated with certain supporting HR strategies. These include an emphasis on preventive versus remedial disciplinary action to handle employee mistakes, employee protection, and explicit ethical codes to monitor and guide behaviour. Firms that are low on moral commitment usually rely on an authoritarian relationship between employee and company. HR strategies consistent with this orientation include an emphasis on discipline or punishment to reduce employee mistakes, employment at will (discussed in Chapters 3 and 14), and informal ethical standards.

■ Fit with Organizational Capabilities

distinctive competencies
The characteristics that give a firm a competitive edge.

A firm's organizational capabilities include its **distinctive competencies**—those characteristics such as technical ability, management systems, and reputation that give a firm the competitive edge. For instance, Mercedes-Benz automobiles are widely regarded as superior because of the quality of their design and engineering. Wal-Mart's success has been due, at least in part, to its ability to track products from supplier to consumer better than its competitors can. Lactantia has established a premium-quality image in dairy and related food products.

Following the fit logic, HR strategies make a greater contribution to firm performance the greater the extent to which

◆ They help the company exploit its specific advantages or strengths while avoiding weaknesses.

◆ They assist the firm in better utilizing its own unique blend of human resource skills and assets.

The following examples illustrate how one type of HR strategy—compensation strategy—may be aligned with organizational capabilities.[76]

◆ Firms known for excellence in customer service tend to pay their sales force only partially on commission, thereby reducing their sales employees' potential for abrasive behaviours and overselling.

◆ Smaller firms can use compensation to their advantage by paying low wages but being generous in stock offerings to employees. This strategy allows them to use more of their scarce cash to fuel future growth.

◆ Organizations may take advantage of their fixed costs to increase sales volumes by selling to their employees at a discount. Department stores and many other retail organizations thus make their products available to employees at below-retail prices. Organizations with excess capacity (such as airlines) allow employees to fly at a substantial discount, often under the condition that the travel be on an off-peak or stand-by basis.[77]

■ Choosing Consistent and Appropriate HR Tactics to Implement HR Strategies

As noted earlier, even the best-laid strategic HR plans may fail when specific HR programs are poorly chosen or implemented. In addition to fitting with each of the four factors just described (organizational strategy, environment, organizational characteristics, and organizational capabilities), a firm's HR strategies must be mutually consistent. That is, HR strategies are more likely to be effective if they reinforce one an-

---

Manager's Notebook

But Will It Work? Questions for Testing the Appropriateness of HR Programs Before Implementation

HR programs that look good on paper may turn out to be disasters when implemented because they conflict too much with company realities. To avoid this kind of unpleasant surprise, it's important to ask the following questions *before* implementing a new HR program.

✓**1. Are the HR Programs Effective Tools for Implementing HR Strategies?**
- Are the proposed HR programs the most appropriate ones for implementing the firm's HR strategies?
- Has an analysis been done of how each of the past, current, or planned HR programs contributes to or hinders the successful implementation of the firm's HR strategies?
- Can the proposed HR programs be easily changed or modified to meet new strategic considerations without violating either a "psychological" or a legal contract with employees?

✓2. Do the HR Programs Meet Resource Constraints?
- Does the organization have the capacity to implement the proposed HR programs? In other words, are the HR programs realistic?
- Are the proposed programs going to be introduced at a rate that can be easily absorbed, or will the timing and extent of changes lead to widespread confusion and strong employee resistance?

✓3. How Will the HR Programs Be Communicated?
- Are the proposed HR programs well understood by those who will implement them (for example, line supervisors) and employees?
- Does top management understand how the proposed programs are intended to affect the firm's strategic objectives?

✓4. Who Will Put the HR Programs in Motion?
- Is the HR department playing the role of an internal consultant to assist employees and managers responsible for carrying out the proposed HR programs?
- Is top management visibly and emphatically committed to the proposed programs?

other rather than work at cross-purposes. For instance, many organizations are currently trying to improve firm performance by structuring work by teams. However, these same organizations often continue to use their traditional performance appraisal system in which each employee is evaluated individually. The appraisal system needs to be overhauled to make it consistent with the emphasis on team performance.

Because it is not always possible to know beforehand if an HR program will meet its objectives, a periodic evaluation of HR programs is necessary. The Manager's Notebook entitled "But Will It Work?" lists a series of important questions that should be raised to examine the appropriateness of HR programs. These questions should be answered as new programs are being chosen and while they are in effect.

■ The HR Department and Managers: An Important Partnership

This book takes a managerial approach to human resources. All managers—regardless of their functional area, their position in the hierarchy, and the size of the firm for which they work—must effectively deal with HR issues because these issues are at the heart of being a good manager.

The role of a company's human resources department is to support, not to supplant, managers' HR responsibilities. For instance, the HR department may develop a form to help managers measure the performance of subordinates, but it is the managers who conduct the actual evaluation. Stated another way, the HR department is primarily responsible for helping the firm meet its business objectives by designing HR programs, but managers must carry out these programs. This means that every manager is a human resource manager.

There is widespread consensus that HR professionals need to know their organization's business thoroughly—not only in terms of people, but also in terms of the economic, financial, environmental, and technological forces affecting it.[78] Rather than playing a staff role, they should become internal consultants known for their expertise and ability to help solve the HR problems faced by line managers. They should also be able to merge HR activities effectively with the firm's business needs.[79]

For the sake of the firm, managers and the HR department need to work together closely. Unfortunately, lack of cooperation has traditionally been a problem, and even today it is not uncommon for managers and HR professionals to view each other negatively. These negative perceptions often create a communication gap and hinder the establishment of an effective partnership between the two groups.

Figure 1-12 lists five sets of competencies that HR professionals need to consider to become full strategic partners in the running of an organization.

Companies can take certain steps to foster an effective partnership between managers and the HR department.[80] Specifically, companies should:

♦ Analyse the people side of productivity rather than depend solely on technical solutions to problems. This requires that managers be trained in certain HR skills. It also requires encouraging managers to value human resources as a key element in organizational effectiveness and performance.

♦ View HR professionals as internal consultants who can provide valuable advice and support that improve the management of operations. In other words, rather than thinking of the HR department as a group responsible for enforcing bureaucratic procedures, view it as a source of expertise capable of assisting managers in solving personnel-related problems, planning for the future, and improving utilization of productive capacity.

Leadership

- Understand the nature and styles of leadership, and display appropriate leadership characteristics in performance of professional responsibilities.
- Demonstrate leadership at multiple performance levels:
- Individual
- Team
- Unit or organization

Knowledge of the Business

- Understand corporate business (structure, vision and values, goals, strategies, financial and performance characteristics).
- Understand the unit's business, including special knowledge of competitors, products, technology, and sources of competitive advantage.
- Understand internal and external customers.
- Understand the environment (external and internal) of corporation and individual businesses.
- Understand
  - Key business disciplines
  - Nature, scope, and HR implications of business globalization
  - Information technology as it affects competitiveness and business processes

HR Strategic Thinking

- Understand the strategic business planning process.
- Understand and be able to apply a systematic HR planning process.

- Be able to select, design, and integrate HR systems or practices to build organizational mindset, capability, and competitive advantage for the business.
- Be able to develop and integrate business unit HR strategies within framework of corporate HR strategies.

Process Skills

- All HR professionals should be competent in key corporate processes and understand management processes critical to particular business units.
- Understand key process skills such as consulting, problem solving, evaluation/diagnosis, workshop design, and facilitation.
- Understand the basic principles, methodologies, and processes of organizational change and development. Facilitate and manage organizational change.
- Balance, integrate, and manage under conditions of uncertainty and paradox.

HR Technologies

- All HR professionals should have a generalist perspective on HR systems and practices as they relate to achievement of business competitive advantage.
- Generalists are capable of designing, integrating, and implementing HR systems to build organizational capability and create business competitive advantage.
- Specialists are capable of designing/delivering leading-edge practices to meet competitive business needs.
- All HR professionals are capable of measuring effectiveness of HR systems and practices.

Figure 1–12 Competencies Required of HR Department to Become a Full Strategic Partner
SOURCE: Adapted with permission from Boroski, J.W. (1990). Putting it together: HR planning in "3D" at Eastman Kodak, *Human Resource Planning, 13*(1), 54. Copyright 1990 by The Human Resource Planning Society.

- ◆ Instill a shared sense of common fate in the firm rather than a win/lose perspective among individual departments and units. This means developing incentives for managers and HR professionals to work together to achieve common goals.
- ◆ Require some managerial experience as part of the training of HR professionals. This requirement should make HR staff more sensitive to and cognizant of the problems that managers face.
- ◆ Actively involve top corporate and divisional managers in formulating, implementing, and reviewing all HR plans and strategies in close collaboration with the HR department. This should increase top management's commitment to the effective implementation of these plans.
- ◆ Require senior HR executives to participate on an equal basis with other key managers from the various functional areas (marketing, finance) involved in charting the enterprise's strategic direction.

■ Specialization in Human Resource Management

Over the past three decades, the size of the typical HR department has increased considerably. This increase reflects both the growth and complexity of government regulations and a greater awareness that human resource issues are important to the achievement of business objectives.

Many universities and community colleges now offer specialized programs in human resources. The creation by the Ontario legislature in 1990 of a legally recognized designation, the Certified Human Resources Professional (CHRP), has precipitated similar legislation in other provinces. The CHRP comprises three requirements: (1) successful completion of an educational qualification, (2) a specified number of years in professional/managerial experience, and (3) adherence to a code of ethics (see Figure 1–5). The educational requirements of professional associations (such as Ontario's HRPAO) are used by many educational institutions in their curriculum design. Currently, a system for reciprocal professional recognition among provinces is being developed under the auspices of the Canadian Council of Human Resources Associations. In addition to local and provincial human resources associations, there are a number of other professional associations that relate to specific human resources responsibilities. Examples include The Association of Canadian Pension Management, The Industrial Accident Prevention Association, the Canadian Compensation Association, and the Canadian Association of Human Resource Systems Professionals.

Human resource management is an evolving field. Two trends appear to be particularly important. The first is the trend toward professionalism. There is an increasingly complex knowledge base that is required for effective human resource management, and on-the-job learning, while important in any career, is clearly inadequate as we enter the next century. The other trend is outsourcing. The specialized ("professional") competencies that organizations use are increasingly available from external vendors such as consultants or specialist services. Payroll, recruiting, training, and benefits administration are examples of activities that are being outsourced. If that trend continues to gain momentum, the configuration of human resource management may increasingly consist of a small group of professionals employed by the "host" organization, whose major tasks are sourcing specialized expertise and playing a much more strategic and integrative role within the organization.

There will continue to be a growing need for individuals with specialized expertise in human resources. However, whether that function is provided increasingly by external specialist organizations or by internal staff units is a question yet to be answered.

The Human Resource Planning Society
www.hrps.org/html/index1.htm

Links to various Web sites of interest to HR professionals
www.athabascau.ca/html/depts/eiros/indrel/hrmsites.htm

Summary and Conclusions

Human Resource Management: The Challenges. The major human resource challenges facing managers today can be divided into three categories: environmental challenges, organizational challenges, and individual challenges.

The environmental challenges are rapid change, work force diversity, economic globalization, legislation, evolving work and family roles, skill shortages, and rise of the service sector.

The organizational challenges are choosing a competitive position, decentralization, downsizing, organizational restructuring, the rise of self-managed work teams, the increased number of small businesses, organizational culture, advances in technology, and labour unions.

The individual challenges involve matching people with the organization, treating employees ethically and engaging in socially responsible behaviour, increasing individual productivity, deciding whether or not to empower employees, and taking steps to avoid brain drain.

Planning and Implementing Strategic HR Policies. Correctly done, strategic HR planning provides many direct and indirect benefits for the employer. These include the encouragement of proactive (rather than reactive) behaviour; explicit communication of organizational goals; stimulation of critical thinking and ongoing examination of assumptions; identification of gaps between the organization's current situation and its future vision; the encouragement of line managers' participation in the strategic planning process; the identification of HR constraints and opportunities; and the creation of common bonds within the organization.

In developing an effective HR strategy, an organization faces several challenges. These include implementing a strategy that creates and maintains competitive advantage for the organization and reinforces overall strategy; avoiding excessive concentration on day-to-day problems; developing strategies suited to unique organizational characteristics; coping with the environment in which the organization functions; securing management commitment; translating the strategic plan into action; combining intended and emergent strategies; and accommodating change.

An organization's strategic HR choices are the options available to it in designing its human resources systems. Employers must make strategic choices in many HR areas, including work flows, staffing, employee separations, performance appraisal, training and career development, compensation, employee rights, employee and labour relations, and international management.

The HR Department and Managers: An Important Partnership.   Responsibility for the effective utilization of human resources lies primarily with managers. Hence all managers are personnel managers. HR professionals' role is to act as internal consultants or experts, assisting managers to do their jobs better.

Over the past three decades, the size of the typical HR department has increased considerably. This increase reflects both the growth and complexity of government regulations and a greater awareness that HR issues are important to the achievement of business objectives.

Key Terms and Concepts

ability, 17
brain drain, 18
business unit strategy, 28
corporate strategy, 28
decentralization, 10
defender, 31
differentiation business strategy, 30
distinctive competencies, 36
downsizing, 10
egalitarian, 14
emergent strategies, 23
employment equity, 7
employment standards, 6
empowerment, 18
environmental challenges, 4
evolutionary business strategy, 28
focus strategy, 30

health and safety, 7
horizontal corporation, 10
human resource strategy, 2
human resource tactic, 3
human resources (HR), 2
human rights, 7
individual challenges, 15
intended strategies, 23
internal labour market, 10
labour relations, 7
line employees, 3
manager, 3
motivation, 17
organizational challenges, 9
organizational culture, 13
overall cost leadership strategy, 29
pay equity, 7

proactive, 19
productivity, 17
prospector, 31
quality of work life (QWL), 18
reactive, 19
social programs, 7
social responsibility, 17
staff employees, 3
steady-state strategy, 28
strategic human resource (HR) planning, 19
strategic HR choices, 23
telecommuters, 14
telematics technologies, 14
total quality management (TQM), 9
workers' compensation, 6

Discussion Questions

1. Can well-meaning human resource programs have negative effects on an employer? If so, how?

2. Which of the environmental, organizational, and individual challenges identified in this chapter are most important for human resource management in the 1990s, in your opinion? Which are least important? Use your own experiences in your answer.

3. In a recent national survey of HR executives in more than 400 companies, most respondents reported that the priorities of top management at their firms are to counter competition, cut costs, and improve performance. Yet only 12% of these HR executives said that their department had a major responsibility for improving productivity, quality, and customer service in their companies. What do you think are some of the reasons for this gap between top management's

priorities and the responsibility of the HR department? What are some of the consequences of this gap? Outline several ways in which HR departments can align themselves with their company's strategic goals. How do you think an HR department can gain top management's support for *its* programs and goals?

4. What type of background and training would you recommend for human resource professionals? Explain.

5. In 1995, the Bank of Montreal reported a sixth straight year of record profits. During the preceding year it had shed 1,400 workers. It joins a growing number of firms that are reducing employment during times of profitability, not only when profits have shrunk or business is declining. BMO, well regarded as an employer, explained its decision this way, according to

Canadian Press: "We say that's a good transformation from the 1980s but we're not sure the transformation is complete," says BMO chairman Matthew Barrett about the profits. With reference to the downsizing, he commented, "I think we're in a world of contin-

ual transformation. Change is the order of the day." In contrast with Nortel, IBM Canada and other companies that reduced their work forces in the face of financial adversity, what particular challenges does BMO's HR unit face in carrying out these layoffs?

Check out the Companion Website at: **www.prenticehall.ca/gomez** for a selection of self-study questions, key terms and concepts, updated Weblinks to related Internet sites, newgroups, CBC video updates, and more.

MiniCase 1

Flexible Employment and conventional Culture

When the Royal Bank created its Work-Family Life Program in 1990, it was considered one of the Canadian forerunners in addressing the issue of work and family life. By 1995, some 2,000 Royal Bank employees were working with flexible start and finish times (a quarter of them using satellite offices or working from home), another 1,000 were working compressed work weeks (the normal 37.5 hours completed in four or sometimes three days), and another 900 were involved in job sharing, where two individuals share a single full-time position. These arrangements have helped retain valuable employees who would otherwise have had difficulty meeting both personal and work commitments. Such arrangements also reduce absence, as employees can make small adjustments in their daily schedule to accommodate appointments or unexpected events.

Flexible scheduling success stories like the experience at Royal Bank (or Warner-Lambert Canada or Apple Canada) are fairly common. One frequent observation is that although flexibility policies are in place, many companies find that a relatively small fraction of eligible employees choose to use them.

What challenges await the growing number of companies that are initiating flexible work programs? HR experts say that in many companies, the corporate culture just hasn't caught up with the programs. For instance, the notion that produc-

tivity and loyalty can be measured by how many hours a day you work at the office is still strongly held. Appraisal systems, compensation systems, and career management systems often reinforce this attitude. Others say that companies need to make their new family-friendly policies formal. The fact that flexible work benefits are subject to managerial discretion in many cases remains one of the major stumbling blocks to employees' use of flexible programs.

Discussion Questions

1. In what type of organizational culture do flexible scheduling programs have the highest chance of success? What aspects of a company's culture might make it difficult for employees to take advantage of flexible benefits?

2. What do you think the HR department and top management can do to ensure that employees take advantage of—and benefit from—flexible schedules?

3. Suppose a company has initiated a flexible scheduling program, but has no formal policy regarding its use—it's left up to individual employees and their supervisors to determine whether their jobs lend themselves to part-time work or telecommuting. Do you think this arrangement would discourage employees from telecommuting?

SOURCE: Adapted from Solomon, C. M. (1994, May). Work/family's failing grade: Why today's initiatives aren't enough. *Personnel Journal*, 72–87; McCallum, T. (1995, June). The old "three to seven." *Human Resources Professional*, 12–14.

MiniCase 2

HR on the carpet

Milliken & Company once manufactured carpet tiles in Canada. By 1993, the company had shut down the Canadian operation and left 22 production employees out of work. That isn't a large number, in the larger ebb and flow of employment opportunity, but the story is not one of a poorly managed organization. The employer had done many of the "right" things from a human resources point of view. Workers were

empowered to make decisions and functioned in self-managed teams. When new employees were hired, team members did the interviewing. The plant was non-union (and therefore no contract provisions existed that might block innovation), and workers had a great deal of discretion in getting their jobs done. There were special awards for employees who devised creative ideas. Workers liked their jobs. These policies showed results. Milliken, having won the prestigious Baldrige Award for quality in its U.S. operations, set similar objectives for their Canadian operation. In 1990, the company placed a commendable third in the Canadian Award for Business Excellence competition.

Three years later, the operation was shut down, and Milliken was supplying its Canadian customers from U.S. production. The story of what happened is familiar to many Canadian companies: the increasing influence of international competition (in this case precipitated by the Free Trade Agreement) and a sharp recession, combined with a change in product design, made this effective and well-run operation uncompetitive.

Not all manufacturers succumb to these pressures. In fact, many thrive. But such changes require a new and different approach.

Discussion Questions

1. Why do you think that a large number of manufacturing jobs appear to have "migrated" to other countries?

2. To what extent can effective human resource management make Canadian operations competitive with other countries where wage rates may be lower or environmental regulations less stringent?

3. If manufacturing needs to become more efficient to compete, and that requires the use of increasing automation and high-technology applications, what implications are there for the kinds of jobs that will be available in manufacturing? What does this say about the kind of training that employers need to provide?

SOURCES: Pitts, Gordon. (1993, June 1). How good jobs can come to a bad end. *The Globe and Mail,* B24.

Case 1

Managers versus HR Professionals at Sands Corporation

Sands Corporation is a medium-sized company located in Alberta. It manufactures specialized computer equipment used in cars, serving as a subcontractor to several automobile manufacturers as well as to the military. Federal contracts are an important part of Sands' total sales. In 1965 the firm had 130 employees. At that time, the personnel department had a full-time director (who was a high school graduate) and a part-time clerk. The department was responsible for maintaining files, placing recruitment ads in the newspaper at management's request, processing employment applications and payroll, answering phones, and handling other routine administrative tasks. Managers and supervisors were responsible for most personnel matters, including whom to hire, whom to promote, whom to fire, and whom to train.

Today Sands employs 700 people. Personnel, now called the Human Resources Department, has a full-time director with a master's degree in Industrial Relations, three specialists (with appropriate degrees and certifications: one in compensation, one in staffing, and one in training and development), and four HR assistants. Sands' top management believes that a strong HR department with a highly qualified staff can do a better job of handling most personnel matters than line supervisors can. It is also convinced that a good HR department can keep line managers from inadvertently creating costly legal problems. One of Sands' competitors recently was found guilty of human rights violations and faces large financial penalties. This situation has only strengthened Sands' resolve to maintain a strong HR department.

Some of the key responsibilities the company assigns to its HR department are:

◆ *Hiring.* The HR department approves all ads, screens all applicants, tests and interviews candidates, and so forth. Supervisors are given a limited list of candidates (usually no more than three) per position from which to choose.

◆ *Workforce diversity.* The HR department ensures that the composition of Sands' work force meets the government's diversity guidelines for federal contractors.

◆ *Compensation.* The HR department sets the pay range for each job based on its own compensation studies and survey data of salaries at similar companies. The department must approve all pay decisions.

◆ *Employee appraisal.* The HR department requires all supervisors to complete annual appraisal forms on their subordinates. The department scrutinizes these appraisals of employee performance closely; it is not uncommon for supervisors to be called on the carpet to justify performance ratings that are unusually high or low.

◆ *Training.* The HR department conducts several training programs for employees, including programs in improving human relations, quality management, and the use of computer packages.

◆ *Attitude surveys.* The HR department conducts an in-depth attitude survey of all employees each year, asking them how they feel about various facets of their job, such as satisfaction with their supervisor and working conditions.

Over the past few weeks several supervisors have complained to top executives that the HR department has taken away many of their management rights. Some of their gripes are:

◆ The HR department ranks applicants based on test scores or other formal criteria (for example, years of experience). Often the people they pick don't fit well in the department and/or don't get along with the supervisor and co-workers.

➤

◆ Excellent performers are leaving because the HR department will not approve pay raises exceeding a fixed limit for the job title held, even when a person is able to perform duties beyond those specified in the job description.

◆ It takes so long to process the paperwork to hire new employees that the unit loses good candidates to competitors.

◆ Much of the training required of employees is not focussed on the job itself. These "canned" programs waste valuable employee time and provide few benefits to the company.

◆ Supervisors are afraid to be truthful in their performance ratings for fear of being investigated by the HR department.

◆ Attitude survey data are broken down by department. The HR department then scrutinizes departments with low scores. Some supervisors feel that the attitude survey has become a popularity contest that penalizes managers who are willing to make necessary (but unpopular) decisions.

The HR department director rejects all these accusations, arguing that supervisors "just want to do things their way, not taking into account what is best for the company."

Critical Thinking Questions

1. What seems to be the main source of conflict between supervisors and the HR department at Sands Corporation? Explain.
2. Do you believe that managers should be given more autonomy to make personnel decisions such as hiring, appraising, and compensating subordinates? If so, what are some potential drawbacks to granting them this authority? Explain.
3. How should Sands' top executives deal with the complaints expressed by supervisors? How should the director of the HR department deal with the situation? Explain.

Cooperative Learning Exercise

4. The CEO of Sands Corporation has called a meeting of four managers, all of whom have lodged some of the complaints noted in the case, and four members of the HR department (the director and three specialists). The instructor or a student acts as the CEO in that meeting. The exercise is carried out as follows: (a) Each side presents its case, with the CEO acting as moderator. (b) The two groups then try to agree on how Sands' HR department and managers can develop a closer working relationship in the future. The two groups and the CEO may conduct this exercise in separate groups or in front of the classroom.

Case 2

How Hampton Inn Guarantees "100% Satisfaction"

Hampton Inn, a hotel chain, recently introduced a "100% Satisfaction Guarantee" policy to help it gain a distinctive advantage in a highly competitive industry where customers have little allegiance to any particular hotel. When guests walk away from a hotel dissatisfied, chances are that they will relate their unhappy experience to friends and business associates, who might spread the story around even further. Thus are hotel reputations lost. Hampton Inn decided to take advantage of this informal communication chain with its new policy. The company believes that guests who go away impressed with the way Hampton Inn handled a problem will spread the word and generate additional business for the chain.

The guarantee is simple: Guests who are not completely satisfied with every aspect of their stay are not expected to pay. The guarantee allows every Hampton Inn employee to do whatever it takes to satisfy guests — including giving them their money back. Rhonda Thompson, one of Hampton Inn's employees, describes the 100% Satisfaction Guarantee policy in terms of its supporting HR strategies:

While working as a guest services representative at a Hampton Inn hotel, I overheard a guest at our complimentary continental breakfast complaining quite loudly that his favourite cereal was not available. Rather than dismiss the person as just another disgruntled guest, I looked at the situation and saw an opportunity to make this guest happy. I gave him his money back — not for the continental breakfast, but for the cost of one night's stay at our hotel. And I did it on the spot, without checking with my supervisor or the general manager of the hotel, and without making the guest fill out a long complaint form.

Some people might be surprised to hear this story, or they might not believe it could happen. After all, how could a front-desk employee give a guest his money back without getting permission from the boss? And why would the hotel support this action for something simple like a bowl of cereal?

Before the 100% Satisfaction Guarantee was introduced, my job was like most other jobs in the hotel industry. My responsibilities were outlined in my job description, and I was evaluated on how well I fulfilled those duties. There wasn't much room to express my own ideas, and I wasn't really expected to come up with any. Most people I worked with liked it this way because they knew what their jobs entailed and what to expect. When the 100% Satisfaction Guarantee policy was first announced, many employees thought this program would have very little effect on their jobs. But when we learned that every employee would go through a three-day training program, we knew that the guarantee was something special. It became more and more apparent that the new Hampton Inn guarantee would affect all of our jobs, and we would have to change the way we thought about performing our routine duties. The company scheduled a series of training sessions at every hotel, involving videos, classroom-style teaching, open discussions and role playing. Through this training, we learned what to do if a guest asks to invoke the guarantee. We also learned how to identify situations when we, as employees, should invoke the guarantee for guests before they even complain. This training reinforced the message that employees at every level should use this responsibility to make sure guests are satisfied.

Many employees—including myself—were skeptical at first. Although we were proud of our hotels and the service that we offered, we thought that guests might take advantage of the guarantee as a way to get something for free. But the training emphasized that, although any reason given by a guest is a valid reason to invoke the guarantee, most guests would not take

➤

advantage of us. Hampton Inn basically threw out its old job descriptions. Of course, a housekeeper's duties still include cleaning and preparing guest rooms. But the housekeeper's real job is to satisfy guests and this typically is accomplished by cleaning the room to perfection. For example, if a housekeeper sees a guest having a problem with the lock on her room door, the housekeeper has the authority to stop what he or she is doing and take whatever action is necessary to correct the situation. While the goal of the 100% Satisfaction Guarantee is to give every guest a satisfying stay, the guarantee has made employees' jobs more satisfying as well. When Hampton Inn tells employees that they can do whatever it takes to make a guest happy—without needing approval from a manager—they're telling employees that they trust them to do their jobs. Most employees have never worked for a company that will unconditionally back them up for refunding a guest's money, no matter how small the problem was to begin with.

This type of trust motivates employees to do a better job, and makes them try harder to deliver excellent customer service. Employees know that they don't have to wait for their once-a-year review to find out if they're doing a good job; they find out every day from guests staying at the hotel.

SOURCE: Adapted, by permission of publisher, from Thompson, R. (1993, July). An employee's view of empowerment. *HR Focus* (an American Management Association human resources publication), 14–15. © 1993 American Management Association, New York. All rights reserved.

Critical Thinking Questions

1. How would you describe the new HR strategy adopted by Hampton Inn? How does it compare with Hampton's previous HR strategy?

2. Distinguish between Hampton's HR strategy and the HR program used to implement it. Is the HR program Hampton chose an effective mechanism for implementing its HR strategy?

3. Does Hampton's new HR strategy fit with the hotel's business strategy? Explain.

4. How does Hampton's new HR strategy allow the hotel to deal with environmental threats more effectively?

5. What risks may Hampton Inn incur by adopting its new HR strategy? Explain.

Cooperative Learning Exercise

6. Students form groups of five and role-play the following situation: A major stockholder has complained that Hampton Inn's new HR strategy will lead to higher costs. According to this stockholder, customers will take advantage of the employees, who will be unable to protect the hotel's interests. This stockholder is calling for tighter controls to prevent abuses of the 100% Satisfaction Guarantee. Hampton's CEO has called a meeting in response to the stockholder's complaint. The meeting is attended by the complaining stockholder, two workers (who will provide the employee perspective of the situation), and the HR director (who will discuss the business rationale for the new HR strategy). Each of these parties presents its view of the situation to the CEO, who then makes a decision concerning the new HR strategy based on the arguments advanced in the meeting.

VideoCase

Human Resources: A Strategic Asset?

Any thoughtful person might be surprised with the broad assertion that human resources are "strategic assets" in today's economy. Regular reading of the newspapers has been enough to reveal a pattern of continual downsizing, layoffs, re-engineering, and slow wage growth that became pronounced during the recession of the early 1990s and that persisted even through the long period of economic expansion that dominated most of the rest of the decade. Maybe certain employee groups could be fairly described as strategic—groups such as senior managers or professionals or technology specialists. But many people in middle management, health care workers such as nurses, teachers, and large numbers of front-line workers in many sectors of the economy—have been treated not as assets to be nurtured and developed, but as commodities that are best secured from the cheapest source, hired as "contingent" workers, and replaced with technology (prototype: the automated tellers) wherever cost-benefit calculations suggest operating costs can be reduced.

It has been suggested that technology is a major force in creating two distinct kinds of knowledge workers: the fortunate few who use technology (computers, communications technology, and other applications of micro-electronic technology) to do challenging, interesting and varied tasks for good incomes, and the unfortunate many who, if they are not displaced by technology, become an extension of it, at relatively low incomes. (An example of the latter group are people who work in telephone call centres reading scripted appeals for donations or making cold-call sales pitches.)

Other observers suggest that it is international competition from lower wage economies that is driving the recent political emphasis on deregulation as well as the preoccupation of employers with controlling costs, especially employment costs.

Discussion Questions

1. Do you think human resources are strategic? If you think it is necessary to qualify a "yes" answer to that question, would you limit your "yes" to management employees, to professionals, to knowledge-intensive industries, to industries that are facing strong international competition, to industries where competition is based on being highly innovative, or to some other subset of employees or situations? Explain your views.

2. Do you think there are many jobs where high levels of employee commitment and involvement would be nice to have, but where having people who "show up and do what they're told" is quite sufficient? Explain.

Video Resource: "Service Ha!", *Venture* 533 (March 26, 1995).

Managing the Structure and Flow of Work

After reading this chapter, you should be able to deal more effectively with the following challenges:

1 Describe bureaucratic, flat, and boundaryless organizational structures and the business environments in which each is most appropriate.

2 Explain why managers use worker teams to produce products and services.

3 List the factors that influence worker motivation that are under managers' control.

4 Design jobs to maximize company performance.

5 Use job analysis as the first step in designing HR programs.

6 Apply flexible work designs to situations in which employees have conflicts between work and family or employers face uncertain demand for their products.

7 Develop policies and procedures to protect human resource information system data so that employees' privacy rights are maintained.

The benefits of a team effort. Nortel is an example of a high-tech company that has successfully used worker teams to improve quality and productivity and to reduce operating costs. Often members of worker teams are cross-trained on different tasks assigned to the team so that members can assume responsibility for all aspects of the task.

As the powerful forces of technology and global competition force managers to rethink all aspects of business, the way organizations structure work into jobs and larger units is undergoing a fundamental change. Work is in a state of constant flux as companies change basic work processes to focus more on customers' needs. Employees who were once located in functional units (marketing, manufacturing, research, quality control, and so forth) now find themselves working with people from different areas of specialization in groups with names like "order generation and fulfilment" (with employees from sales, manufacturing, and shipping and receiving), "commercialization of technology" (with employees from marketing, engineering, research, and manufacturing), and "customer support" (with employees from research, customer service, and advertising).

One important change in the way work is structured is the fairly recent practice of using work teams instead of individual workers as the basic unit of work. A recent comprehensive report on HMR practices in Canada indicated that three areas tended to distinguish the most successful manufacturing plants from the least successful. One of these three was the greater use of work teams (the other two were delegation of responsibility and training).[1]

◆ Teams are integral to the success of many organizational strategies. One such strategy, "concurrent engineering," reduces product development cycles by integrating outside information from customers and suppliers on a continual basis during the process of product development. Large companies such as Nortel and Pratt and Whitney, as well as small firms such as Raychem's Advanter plant in Richmond, British Columbia, have recorded impressive results. Nortel reduced the development time on its Norstar phone system from the normal two years to 18 months, gaining a first-to-market advantage that helped generate significant sales. Pratt and Whitney developed an engine design for a proposed business jet in just over 12 months rather than the normal 18 to 24 months, and Raychem was able to shorten the period for preparing documentation for new products from days to less than an hour, in some cases.[2]

◆ MacMillan Bloedel has found that team-based operations can substantially improve productivity in an industry where contentious employment relations are not uncommon. Their experience shows that commitment, changes in management style, and persistence are crucial to making such initiatives work.[3]

◆ Team-based systems and reward systems need to be compatible, so that the incentives offered to employees reinforce the team process rather than undermine it. One of the best distribution teams at Campbell Soup's Canadian operations has devised three monthly awards: "Exceptional Teamwork," "Total Team Incentive," and "King Damage" (a humorous award that employees earn for damaging the greatest number of cases during distribution—the point is *not* to get it!). The positive awards were carefully designed to reinforce the team nature of the work.[4]

◆ CircoCraft Co., Ltd., a circuit-board manufacturer based in Kirkland, Quebec, was the Canadian leader in its field during the late 1980s. A combination of international competition and complacency led to two consecutive money-losing years. A combination of reorganization (reducing the number of organizational levels) and an increased emphasis on teamwork, supported by extensive training and delegation of responsibility to groups, led to a return to profitability (some $3 million in 1992) as quality increased and costs savings were achieved.[5]

HRM on the Web

http://vvv.com/waria/

Workflow and Reengineering International Association (WARIA)

WARIA's Web site provides information in work flow and re-engineering publications and conferences. It also identifies vendors of workflow software and provides a list of consultants who offer re-engineering services. Other Web sites on work flow and re-engineering are also listed.

Like work teams, organizations are fundamentally groups of people. The relationships among these people can be structured in different ways. In this chapter we describe how top managers decide on the most appropriate structure for the organization as a whole and for the flow of work within the organization. While you may not be asked to redesign your organization, it is quite likely that your company will at some point undergo structural change because such change is necessary for survival. It is important to understand structural issues so that you can see the big picture and take an active role in implementing changes.

Work can be viewed from three different perspectives: that of the entire organization, that of work groups, and that of individual employees. We examine each of these perspectives in turn. We also discuss the use of contingent workers and alternative work schedules to create a flexible work force. We also discuss job analysis and the use of contingent workers and alternative work schedules to create a flexible work force. We conclude the chapter with a discussion of human resource information systems.

■ Work: The Organization Perspective

organizational structure

The formal or informal relationships between people in an organization.

work flow

The way work is organized to meet the organization's production or service goals.

Organizational structure refers to the formal or informal relationships between people in an organization. **Work flow** refers to the way work is organized to meet the organization's production or service goals. In this section we discuss the relationship between strategy and organizational structure, the three basic organizational structures, and the uses of work flow analysis.

■ Strategy and Organizational Structure

An organization develops a business strategy by establishing a set of long-term goals based on (1) an analysis of environmental opportunities and threats, and (2) a realistic appraisal of how the business can deploy its assets to compete most effectively. The business strategy selected by management determines the structure most appropriate to the organization.[6] Whenever management decides to change its business strategy, it should also reassess the structure of its organization.

Recall from Chapter 1 that a company would select a *defender strategy* when it is competing in a stable market and has a well-established product. For example, an electric utility company that does business in a fairly stable environment because it is government-regulated might adopt a defender strategy. Under a defender strategy, work can be efficiently organized into a structure based on an extensive division of labour, with hierarchies of jobs assigned to functional units such as customer service, power generation, and accounting. Management is centralized and top management is responsibile for making key decisions. Decisions are implemented from the top down via the chain of command. Workers are told what to do by supervisors, who in turn are handed directions from middle managers, who take orders from the company's top executives.

A company would select a *prospector strategy* when operating in uncertain business environments that require flexibility. Companies that are experiencing rapid growth and launching many new products into a dynamic market are likely to select a prospector strategy. Workers who are close to the customer are allowed to respond quickly to customers' needs without having to seek approval from supervisors.

Management selects HR strategies to fit and support its business strategies and organizational structure. Here are some examples of strategic HR choices regarding the structure and flow of work that companies have made to achieve strategic goals:

◆ Bell Canada's business environment has changed dramatically with changes in regulation and the emergence of new competitors. While Bell is in the midst of what might be termed a "rude awakening," it has the advantage of technological expertise and an established market presence as it sets out to remake itself.[7]

◆ CIBC, one of Canada's major banks, has reorganized its operations to reflect its strategic intention to become a major investment bank in the United States and to concentrate on its retail operations in Canada. These changes are reflected in the realignment of operating personnel and changing relationships between the bank and Wood Gundy, its brokerage unit.[8]

? A Question of Ethics

Implicit in this chapter is the view that organizational change is necessary for survival. However, organizational change often places individual employees under considerable stress, particularly the stress resulting from job loss. Is the organization ethically responsible for protecting employees from these stressful changes?

■ Designing the Organization

Designing an organization involves choosing an organizational structure that will enable the company to achieve its goals most effectively. Three basic types of organizational structure are currently in use: bureaucratic, flat, and boundaryless (Figure 2–1).

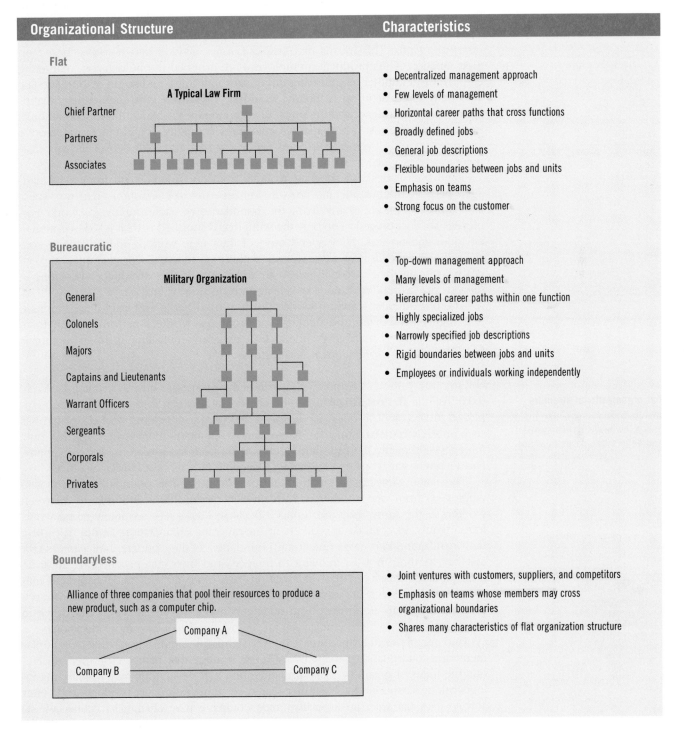

Organizational Structure	Characteristics
Flat **A Typical Law Firm** Chief Partner / Partners / Associates	• Decentralized management approach • Few levels of management • Horizontal career paths that cross functions • Broadly defined jobs • General job descriptions • Flexible boundaries between jobs and units • Emphasis on teams • Strong focus on the customer
Bureaucratic **Military Organization** General / Colonels / Majors / Captains and Lieutenants / Warrant Officers / Sergeants / Corporals / Privates	• Top-down management approach • Many levels of management • Hierarchical career paths within one function • Highly specialized jobs • Narrowly specified job descriptions • Rigid boundaries between jobs and units • Employees or individuals working independently
Boundaryless Alliance of three companies that pool their resources to produce a new product, such as a computer chip. Company A / Company B / Company C	• Joint ventures with customers, suppliers, and competitors • Emphasis on teams whose members may cross organizational boundaries • Shares many characteristics of flat organization structure

Figure 2–1 Organizational Structures

bureaucratic organizational structure

A pyramid-shaped organizational structure that consists of hierarchies with many levels of management.

Bureaucratic Organization.   Companies that adopt a defender business strategy are most likely to choose the **bureaucratic organizational structure.** This pyramid-shaped structure consists of hierarchies with many levels of management. It utilizes a top-down or "command and control" approach to management in which managers provide considerable direction to and have considerable control over their subordinates. The classic example of a bureaucratic organization is the military, which has a long pecking order of intermediate officers between the generals who initiate combat orders and the troops who do the fighting on the battlefield.

A bureaucratic organization is organized into units based on a *functional division of labour.* This means that employees are divided into divisions based on their function. Thus production employees are grouped in one division, marketing employees in another, engineering employees in a third, and so on. A bureaucratic auto-parts manufacturing company would be organized into engineering, manufacturing, sales, and accounting units. Rigid boundaries separate the functional units from one another. At a bureaucratic auto-parts company, for instance, automotive engineers would develop their plans for a new part and then deliver its specifications to the production workers.

Rigid boundaries also separate workers from one another and from their managers because the bureaucratic structure utilizes *work specialization*—narrowly specified job descriptions clearly mark the boundaries of each employee's work. Employees are encouraged to do only the work that is specified in their job description—no more and no less. They spend most of their time working individually at specialized tasks and usually advance only within one function. For example, employees who begin their career in sales can advance to higher and higher positions in sales or marketing, but cannot switch into production or finance.

The bureaucratic structure works best in a predictable and stable environment. It is highly centralized and depends on front-line workers performing repetitive tasks according to managers' orders. In a dynamic environment, this structure is less efficient, and sometimes it is disastrous.

flat organizational structure

An organizational structure that has only a few levels of management and emphasizes decentralization.

Flat Organization.   A company that selects the prospector business strategy is likely to choose the **flat organizational structure.** Flat organizations encourage high employee involvement in business decisions. Nucor, an innovative steel company, has such an organizational structure. Its work force numbers more than 5,000, but only three levels separate the front-line steel workers from the president of the company. Headquarters staff consists of roughly 30 people in a modest cluster of offices.[9]

The flat organizational structure reduces some of the boundaries that isolate employees from one another in bureaucratic organizations. Boundaries between workers at the same level are reduced because employees are likely to be working in teams. In contrast to workers at bureaucratic organizations, employees of a flat organization can cross functional boundaries as they pursue their careers (for instance, starting in sales, moving to finance, and then into production). In addition, job descriptions in flat organizations are more general and encourage employees to develop a broad range of skills (including management skills). Boundaries that separate employees from managers and supervisors also break down in flat organizations, where employees are empowered to make more decisions.

Flat organizational structures can be useful for organizations that are implementing a total quality management (TQM) strategy that makes customer satisfaction the focus of business goals. Implementing a TQM strategy may require changing work processes so that customers can receive higher-quality products and better service. For example, an auto insurance company may change its claims adjustment process to speed up reimbursement to customers. Rather than using 25 employees who take 14 days to process a claim, the company may create a claims adjustment team that works closely with the customer to take care of all the paperwork within three days.

The flat structure works best in rapidly changing environments because it enables management to create an entrepreneurial culture that fosters employee participation.

Boundaryless Organization.

A **boundaryless organizational structure** enables an organization to form relationships with customers, suppliers, and/or competitors, either to pool organizational resources for mutual benefit or to encourage cooperation in an uncertain environment. Such relationships often take the form of joint ventures, which let the companies share talented employees, intellectual property (such as a manufacturing process), marketing distribution channels (such as a direct sales force), or financial resources. Boundaryless organization structures are most often used by companies that select the prospector business strategy and operate in a volatile environment.

Boundaryless organizations share many of the characteristics of flat organizations. They break down boundaries between the organization and its suppliers, customers, or competitors. They also strongly emphasize teams, which are likely to include employees representing different companies in the joint venture. For example, a quality expert from an automobile manufacturing company may work closely with employees at one of the company's auto parts suppliers to train them in specific quality management processes.

Companies often use a boundaryless organization structure when they (1) are adopting a total quality management strategy, (2) are entering foreign markets that have entry barriers to foreign competitors, or (3) need to manage the risk of developing an expensive new technology. The boundaryless organization is appropriate in these situations because it open to change, facilitates the formation of joint ventures with foreign companies, and makes it easier for a company to pool resources with other companies so that the financial risk to any one organization is reduced. Here are some examples of companies that have boundaryless organization structures:

◆ Pratt and Whitney Canada is focussing on partnership arrangements with Asian and European counterparts. They say it is "trading technology for market presence," forging partnerships that will result in indigenous production of Pratt Canada's engines, making those engines affordable in some developing economies.[10]

◆ Air Canada and its partners in Texas invested in Continental Airlines, taking a substantial equity position. Continental had been contracting out maintenance, and Air Canada maintenance facilities were underutilized. As a result, Dorval (Montreal) and Winnipeg maintenance employees have found themselves working on Continental aircraft.[11]

◆ Japanese auto manufacturers have established their presence in Canada and are geographically concentrated in southern Ontario. CAMI Automotive Ltd. (Ingersoll, Ontario) was formed as a joint venture between General Motors of Canada and Suzuki Motor Corporation in 1989. Honda has built an assembly facility near Alliston and Toyota's is located near Cambridge. Toyota's plant has been cited by (independent) auto consultant J. D. Power for its quality levels and was the first Toyota plant outside Japan to win the corporate quality award. The synthesis of Japanese management and design with a Canadian work force has contributed to the success of these ventures.[12]

◆ Apple Computer, IBM, and Motorola formed a strategic alliance in 1991 to develop the Power PC microprocessor used in the Power Macintosh. The alliance links a supplier of integrated circuits (Motorola) with customers (Apple and IBM) that will use the circuits in the designs of their latest personal computers.[13]

■ Work Flow Analysis

We explained earlier that work flow is the way work is organized to meet the organization's production or service goals. Managers need to do **work flow analysis** to examine how work creates or adds value to the ongoing processes in a business. (*Processes* are value-adding, value-creating activities such as product development,

boundaryless organizational structure
An organizational structure that enables an organization to form relationships with customers, suppliers, and/or competitors, either to pool organizational resources for mutual benefit or to encourage cooperation in an uncertain environment.

Air Canada
www.aircanada.com

IBM Canada
www.can.ibm.com

work flow analysis
The process of examining how work creates or adds value to the ongoing processes in a business.

customer service, and order fulfilment.[14]) Work flow analysis looks at how work moves from the customer (who initiates the need for work) through the organization (where employees add value to the work in a series of value-creating steps) to the point at which the work leaves the organization as a product or service for the customer.

Each job in the organization should receive work as an input, add value to that work by doing something useful to it, and then move the work on to another worker. Work flow analysis usually reveals that some steps or jobs can be combined, simplified, or even eliminated. In some cases, it has resulted in the reorganization of work so that teams rather than individual workers are the source of value creation.

Work flow analysis can be used in TQM programs to tighten the alignment between employees' work and customers' needs. It can also help a company make major breakthroughs in performance through another program called business process re-engineering.

Business Process Re-engineering. The term "re-engineering" was coined by Michael Hammer and James Champy in their pioneering book *Reengineering the Corporation.* Hammer and Champy emphasize that re-engineering should not be confused with restructuring or simply laying off employees in an effort to eliminate layers of management.[15] **Business process re-engineering (BPR)** is not a quick fix but rather a fundamental rethinking and radical redesign of business processes to achieve dramatic improvements in cost, quality, service, and speed.[16] Re-engineering examines the way a company does its business by closely analysing the core processes involved in producing its product or delivering its service to the customer. By taking advantage of computer technology and different ways of organizing human resources, the company may be able to reinvent itself.[17]

BPR uses work flow analysis to identify jobs that can be eliminated or recombined to improve company performance. Figure 2–2 shows the steps involved in processing a loan application at IBM Credit Corporation before and after business process re-engineering. Before the BPR effort, work flow analysis showed that loan applications were processed in a series of five steps by five loan specialists, each of whom did something different to the loan application. The entire process took an average of six days to complete, which gave the customer the opportunity to look elsewhere for financing.[18] For much of that time, the application was either in transit between the loan specialists or sitting on someone's desk waiting to be processed.

business process re-engineering (BPR)

A fundamental rethinking and radical redesign of business processes to achieve dramatic improvements in cost, quality, service, and speed.

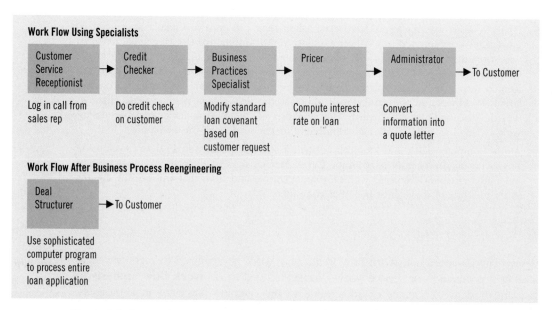

Figure 2–2 Processing a Loan Application Before and After Business Process Re-engineering

Using BPR, the jobs of the five loan specialists were reorganized into the job of just one generalist called the deal structurer. The deal structurer uses a new software program to print out a standardized loan contract, access different credit-checking databases, price the loan, and add boilerplate language to the contract to satisfy most of the customer's special needs for contract modifications. With the new process, loan applications can be completed for the customer in four hours instead of six days.[19]

Critics of re-engineering, however, claim that over half of re-engineering projects fail to meet their objectives while causing pain to companies and employees in the form of layoffs and disruptions in established working patterns.[20] However, a recent survey by CSC Index, a leading re-engineering consulting firm, reported that re-engineering is very popular in both the United States and Europe. The survey of 621 large European and North American companies found that over 70% are already

---

Issues and Applications

Roadblocks to Re-engineering in Europe

Re-engineering is a radical change—such changes are particularly difficult in societies where cultural resistance is strong. Canada and especially the U.S. value individualism and entrepreneurial initiative. In contrast, while the R-word is cropping up more frequently in Europe, the buzz has so far outstripped its bite. Some of the barriers to re-engineering in Europe are:

◆ *An abiding belief in social rights.* In its initial phase, re-engineering usually means heavy layoffs and substantial job reorganization. Member countries of the European Union that already have a high average unemployment rate are loath to do anything that will cost jobs in such alarming numbers. The opposition of organized labour is also a factor. Trade unions in Europe tend to be much stronger than in North America. Particularly in Germany, Holland, and Italy, they have a powerful voice in policy making.

◆ *Corporate culture.* The overall corporate culture in Europe is significantly different from that in North America. Consider Germany. According to Gunter Conrad, a partner at Andersen Consulting in Munich, pride in their craft keeps German workers from embracing radical change. Says Conrad, "When you used to be the best man-

ufacturers in the world, it is sometimes difficult to admit that other ways of doing things might be better."

◆ *Nationalism.* While 12 West European countries form a single market today, a residual nationalism keeps companies in those countries from reducing bureaucracy and eliminating costly duplication. Companies usually find it prudent to keep a few managers in each country in the European Union to untangle local laws and sweet-talk local politicians.

Still, the forces of ruthless competition and stubborn recession are pushing European firms to take the plunge into re-engineering. Companies that have already made significant strides range from Britain's Reuters Holdings and Rolls-Royce Motor Cars to Switzerland's Union Bank and Ciba Geigy. Rolls-Royce actually started redesigning itself in 1990, before the term "re-engineering" was coined. The company simplified its management structure, eliminated foremen and shop stewards, and handed decision-making responsibilities over to teams of workers.

SOURCES: *The Economist.* (1994, February 26). Re-engineering Europe, 63–64; Guterl, F. (1993, June 14). On the Continent, a new era is also dawning. *Business Week,* 61.

---

engaged in re-engineering and half of the remaining firms are considering the possibility of embarking on a re-engineering project.[21] For a further look at some of the barriers that Europe faces in re-engineering, see the Issues and Applications feature entitled "Roadblocks to Re-engineering Europe."

■ Work: The Group Perspective

We turn now to an examination of work from the perspective of employee groups. In the flat and boundaryless organizational structures, teamwork is an imperative. Indeed, as we've seen, teams are the basic building blocks of both types of structures.

What exactly is a team and how does it operate? A **team** is a small number of people with complementary skills who work toward common goals for which they hold themselves mutually accountable.[22] The size of most teams ranges from six to 18 employees.[23] Unlike *work groups,* which depend on a supervisor for direction, a team depends on its own members to provide leadership and direction.[24] Teams can also be organized as departments. For example, a company may have a product development team, a manufacturing team, and a sales team.

Several types of teams are used in organizations today. The type that is having the most impact in many companies is the self-managed team.

team

A small number of people with complementary skills who work toward common goals for which they hold themselves mutually accountable.

Five Common Misconceptions About Self-Managed Teams

1. Self-managed teams do not need leaders. The opposite is true. Teams definitely need some type of leader (who may be called a "coach" or "facilitator") to transfer what has traditionally been called leadership responsibility to team members. The role of the leader will vary from team to team, but leaders definitely have a role to play.

2. Leaders lose power in the transition to teams. Power is a flexible resource. Instead of exercising power within the group to control people, leaders of self-managed teams turn their power outward and use it to break down barriers in the organization that prevent the team from being effective.

3. Newly formed teams are automatically self-managing. Team development takes time. Describing new teams as self-managed by definition may establish unrealistic expectations.

4. Employees are eager to be empowered. Some consultants have estimated that 25% to 30% of people in the work force—regardless of their position in the organization—don't want to be empowered.

5. If you group employees in a team structure, they will function as a team, and the organization will reap the benefits of teamwork. Unfortunately, it doesn't always work that way. Groups must go through a developmental process before they can function successfully as teams.

SOURCE: Excerpt from Caudron, S. (1993, December). Are self-directed teams right for your company? *Personnel Journal*, 81. Copyright December 1993. Reprinted with the permission of *Personnel Journal*, ACC Communications, Inc., Costa Mesa, California; all rights reserved.

self-managed team (SMT)
A team responsible for producing an entire product, a component, or an ongoing service.

■ Self-Managed Teams

Organizations are implementing self-managed work teams primarily to improve quality and productivity and to reduce operating costs. **Self-managed teams (SMTs)** are responsible for producing an entire product, a component, or an ongoing service. The self-managed team is part of the organizational structure because employees in companies with SMTs do most of their work as team members. In most cases, SMT members are cross-trained on the different tasks assigned to the team. Some SMTs have members who cross functional boundaries that represent different complex skills—for example, scientists and engineers with training in different disciplines. Members of the SMT have many managerial duties, including work scheduling, selecting work methods, ordering materials, evaluating performance, and disciplining team members.[25]

In the early 1990s, a subsidiary of the well-known European multinational, Asea Brown Bovari Canada, Inc., applied its commitment to team-based processes when it designed a team-based factory. The goals of the design team were clear: to cut manufacturing time in half, to reduce headcount by 20%, to increase output from 280 to 400 units of the switchgear products—and to do all this within seven months. The careful selection and orchestration of the group process were essential to the company's success.[26]

HRM practices are likely to change in the following ways when SMTs are established:

♦ Peers, rather than a supervisor, are likely to evaluate the individual employee's performance.

♦ Pay practices are likely to shift from pay based on seniority or individual performance to pay focussed on team performance (for example, team bonuses).

♦ Rather than being based solely on input from managers and HR staff, selection practices may change to give team members a decisive amount of input in the hiring of new employees.

Self-managed teams have made some impressive contributions to the bottom lines of companies that have used them. For instance, Tremco, a Canadian building materials manufacturer, has used workshops run by KPMG to launch its transition to empowered groups, whereby decision processes can be "pushed downwards."[27] The Information Systems unit at London Life formed self-managed teams to create a model of a professional service firm and enhance its overall effectiveness. The result was a 22% increase in performance levels.[28] A self-managed team of Federal Express clerks solved a billing problem that was costing the company over $2 billion a year. Xerox Canada is using empowered groups and is experiencing success in increasing productivity, in terms of gross revenue per employee.[29]

Because team members often initially lack the skills necessary for the team to function successfully, it may take several years for a self-managed team to become fully operational. A company can hasten this evolution by using its HR department to train employees in the skills required of team members. Three areas are important:[30]

1. *Technical skills.* Team members must be cross-trained in new technical skills so that they can rotate among jobs as necessary. Team members who are cross-trained in multiple skills give the team greater flexibility and allow it to operate efficiently with fewer workers.

2. *Administrative skills.* Teams do much of the work done by supervisors in organizations that don't have teams. Therefore team members need training in such management/ administrative skills as budgeting, scheduling, monitoring and evaluating peers, and interviewing job applicants.

3. *Interpersonal skills.* Team members need good communication skills to form an effective team. They must be able to express themselves effectively in order to share information, deal with conflict, and give feedback to one another.

In addition to training employees in the skills needed for teamwork, companies would be wise to debunk some of the myths that managers commonly hold about SMTs and how they work. For more on this topic, see the Manager's Notebook entitled "Five Common Misconceptions About Self-Managed Teams."

Other Types of Teams

In addition to the SMT, businesses use two other types of teams: the problem-solving team and the special-purpose team.[31] The **problem-solving team** consists of volunteers from a unit or department who meet one or two hours per week to discuss quality improvement, cost reduction, or improvement in the work environment. The formation of problem-solving teams does not affect an organization's structure because these teams exist for only a limited period; they are usually disbanded after they have achieved their objectives. Problem-solving teams are often used when organizations decide to pursue a TQM effort; the teams focus on making improvements in the quality of a product or service.

The **special-purpose team** consists of members who span functional or organizational boundaries and whose purpose is to examine complex issues—for example, introducing a new technology, improving the quality of a work process, or encouraging cooperation between labour and management in a unionized setting. For example, Saskatoon Chemicals, a wholly owned subsidiary of Weyerhauser Canada Ltd. with some 150 employees, devised a co-management arrangement with the union (Communication, Energy and Paperworkers Union of Canada) representing its production employees. Management and the union, both dissatisfied with a history of constant confrontation, established a joint standing committee in the early 1990s and gave it the responsibility for improving relations. Both the quality of life and the effectiveness of operations have been dramatically improved as a new climate and culture was established.[32]

Work: The Individual Perspective

The third and final perspective from which we will examine the structure and flow of work is that of the individual employee and job. We look first at the various theories of what motivates employees to achieve higher levels of performance, and then at different ways jobs can be designed to maximize employee productivity. Next we look at job analysis, the gathering and organization of information concerning the tasks and duties of specific jobs. We conclude with a discussion of job descriptions, which are one of the primary results of job analysis.

Motivating Employees

Motivation can be defined as that which energizes, directs, and sustains human behaviour.[33] In HRM, the term refers to a person's desire to do the best possible job or to exert the maximum effort to perform assigned tasks. An important feature of motivation is that it is behaviour directed toward a goal.

problem-solving team
A team consisting of volunteers from a unit or department who meet one or two hours per week to discuss quality improvement, cost reduction, or improvement in the work environment.

special-purpose team
A team consisting of workers who span functional or organizational boundaries and whose purpose is to examine complex issues.

Communication, Energy and Paperworkers Union of Canada
www.cep.ca

motivation
That which energizes, directs, and sustains human behaviour. In HRM, a person's desire to do the best possible job or to exert the maximum effort to perform assigned tasks.

Motivation theory seeks to explain why employees are more motivated by and satisfied with one type of work than another. It is essential that managers have a basic understanding of work motivation because highly motivated employees are more likely to produce a superior-quality product or service than are employees who lack motivation.

Two-Factor Theory.   The *two-factor theory of motivation,* developed by Frederick Herzberg, attempts to identify and explain the factors that employees find satisfying and dissatisfying about their jobs.[34] The first set of factors, called *motivators,* are internal job factors that lead to job satisfaction and higher motivation. In the absence of motivators, employees will probably not be satisfied with their work and will not be motivated to perform up to their potential. Some examples of motivators are:

◆ The work itself   ◆ Responsibility

◆ Achievement   ◆ Opportunities for advancement

◆ Recognition

Notice that salary is not included in the motivator list. Herzberg contends that pay belongs among the second set of factors, which he calls *hygiene* or *maintenance factors.* Hygiene factors are external to the job; they are located in the work environment. The absence of a hygiene factor can lead to active dissatisfaction and demotivation and, in extreme situations, to avoidance of the work altogether. Hygiene factors include the following:

◆ Company policies   ◆ Employee benefits

◆ Working conditions   ◆ Relationships with supervisors and managers

◆ Job security   ◆ Relationships with co-workers

◆ Salary   ◆ Relationships with subordinates

According to Herzberg, if management provides the appropriate hygiene factors, employees will not be dissatisfied with their jobs, but neither will they be motivated to perform at their full potential. To motivate workers, management must provide some motivators.

The two-factor theory has two implications for job design:

◆ Jobs should be designed to provide as many motivators as possible.

◆ Making (external) changes in hygiene factors such as pay or working conditions is not likely to sustain improvements in employee motivation over the long run unless (internal) changes are also made in the work itself.

Work Adjustment Theory.   Every worker has unique needs and abilities. *Work adjustment theory* suggests that employees' motivation levels and job satisfaction depend on the fit between their needs and abilities and the characteristics of the job and the organization.[35] A poor fit between individual characteristics and the work environment may lead to reduced levels of motivation. Work adjustment theory proposes that:

◆ A job design that one employee finds challenging and motivating may not motivate another employee. For example, an employee with a cognitive disability may find a repetitive job at a fast-food restaurant highly motivating and challenging, but a college or university graduate may find the same job boring.

◆ Not all employees want to be involved in decision making. Employees with low needs for involvement may fit poorly on a self-managed team because they may resist managing other team members and taking responsibility for team decisions.

Goal-Setting Theory.   *Goal-setting theory,* developed by Edwin Locke, suggests that employees' goals help to explain motivation and job performance.[36] The reasoning is as follows: Since motivation is goal-directed behaviour, goals that are clear and challenging will result in higher levels of employee motivation than goals that are ambiguous and easy.

Because it suggests that managers can increase employee motivation by managing the goal-setting process, goal-setting theory has some important implications for managers:[37]

◆ Employees will be more motivated to perform when they have clear and specific goals. A store manager whose specific goal is to "increase store profitability by 20% in the next six months" will exert more effort than one who is told to "do the best you can" to increase profits.

◆ Employees will be more motivated to accomplish difficult goals than easy goals. Of course, the goals must be attainable; otherwise the employee is likely to become frustrated. For example, an inexperienced computer programmer may promise to deliver a program in an unrealistic amount of time that does not take into account the time needed for debugging the program. The programmer's manager may work with her to establish a more realistic, yet still challenging, deadline for delivering the program to the customer.

◆ In many (but not all) cases, goals that employees participate in creating for themselves are more motivating than goals that are simply assigned by managers. Managers may establish mutually agreed-upon goals with employees through a management-by-objectives (MBO) approach (discussed in Chapter 7) or by creating self-managed teams that accept responsibility for establishing their own goals.

◆ Employees who receive frequent feedback on their progress toward reaching their goals sustain higher levels of motivation and performance than employees who receive sporadic or no feedback. For example, a restaurant manager can motivate servers to provide better service by soliciting customer feedback on the quality of the service and then communicating this information to employees.

Job Characteristics Theory.   Developed by Richard Hackman and Greg Oldham, *job characteristics theory* states that employees will be more motivated to work and more satisfied with their jobs to the extent that jobs contain certain core characteristics.[38] These core job characteristics create the conditions that allow employees to experience critical psychological states that are related to beneficial work outcomes, including high work motivation. The strength of the linkage among job characteristics, psychological states, and work outcomes is determined by the intensity of the individual employee's need for growth (that is, how important the employee considers growth and development on the job).

There are five core job characteristics that activate three critical psychological states. The core job characteristics are:[39]

1. *Skill variety*. The degree to which the job requires the person to do different things and involves the use of a number of different skills, abilities, and talents.
2. *Task identity*. The degree to which a person can do the job from beginning to end with a visible outcome.
3. *Task significance*. The degree to which the job has a significant impact on others—both inside and outside the organization.
4. *Autonomy*. The amount of freedom, independence, and discretion the employee has in areas such as scheduling the work, making decisions, and determining how to do the job.
5. *Feedback*. The degree to which the job provides the employee with clear and direct information about job outcomes and performance.

The three critical psychological states affected by the core job characteristics are:[40]

1. *Experienced meaningfulness*. The extent to which the employee experiences the work as important, valuable, and worthwhile.
2. *Experienced responsibility*. The degree to which the employee feels personally responsible or accountable for the results of the work.
3. *Knowledge of results*. The degree to which the employee understands on a regular basis how effectively he or she is performing in the job.

Skill variety, task identity, and task significance are all linked to experienced meaningfulness of work, as Figure 2–3 shows. Autonomy is related to experienced responsibility and feedback to knowledge of results.

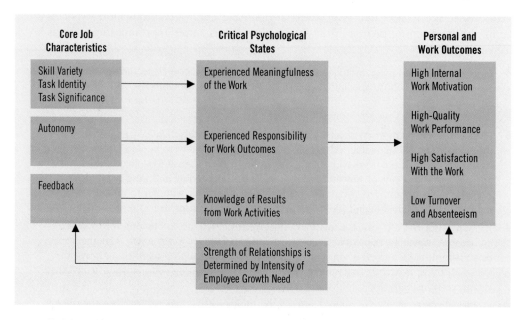

Figure 2–3 The Job Characteristics Theory of Work Motivation

A job with characteristics that allow an employee to experience all three critical psychological states provides internal rewards that sustain motivation. These rewards come from having a job where the person can learn (knowledge of results) that he or she has performed well on a task (experienced responsibility) that he or she cares about (experienced meaningfulness).[41] In addition, this situation results in certain outcomes that are beneficial to the employer: high-quality performance, higher employee satisfaction, and lower turnover and absenteeism. Job characteristics theory maintains that jobs can be designed to contain the characteristics that employees find rewarding and motivating.

■ Building Managerial Skills: Designing Jobs and Conducting Job Analysis

job design

The process of organizing work into the tasks that are required to perform a specific job.

All the theories of employee motivation suggest that jobs can be designed to increase motivation and performance. **Job design** is the process of organizing work into the tasks that are required to perform a specific job.

There are three important influences on job design. One is work flow analysis, which (you will recall) seeks to ensure that each job in the organization receives work as an input, does something useful to add value to that work, and then moves it on to another worker. The other two influences on job design are the strategy of the business and the organizational structure that best fits that strategy. For example, an emphasis on highly specialized jobs could be expected in a bureaucratic organizational structure because work in a bureaucratic organization is built around the division of labour.

We will examine five approaches to job design: work simplification, job enlargement and job rotation, job enrichment, and team-based job design.

Work Simplification.   *Work simplification* assumes that work can be broken down into simple, repetitive tasks that maximize efficiency. This approach to job design assigns most of the thinking aspects of work (such as planning and organizing) to managers and supervisors, while giving the employee a narrowly defined task to perform. Work simplification can utilize labour very effectively to produce a large amount of a standardized product. The automobile assembly line, where workers engage in highly repetitive tasks, exemplified the work simplification approach.

Work simplification can be efficient in a stable environment, but it is less effective in a changing environment where customers demand custom-built products of high quality. Moreover, management can expect high levels of employee turnover and low levels of employee satisfaction on simplified jobs. In fact, where work simplification is used, employees may feel the need to form unions to gain some control over their work. Finally higher-level professionals subjected to this approach may become so specialized in what they do that they are unable to see how their job affects the organization's overall product or service. The result can be employees doing work that has no value to the customer. This is a discovery that organizations suddenly made in the 1990s. Hence many professional employees in highly specialized jobs have become casualties of corporate restructurings in recent years.

Work simplification should not be confused with *work elimination*. Companies trying to eliminate work challenge every task, and every step within every task, to see if there is some better way of getting the work done. Even if parts of the work cannot be eliminated, some aspect of the work may be simplified or combined with another job. IBM Canada has gone through dramatic changes during the 1990s, with an emphasis on service, team orientation, empowered business units and substantial downsizing. As employee numbers decreased from 13,000 to 8,000, the company targeted improvement in information systems efficiency and consolidated its data centre operations. A team approach has drastically streamlined tasks; as a result, some work has been eliminated.[42] While similar to re-engineering, work elimination typically has a more specific focus.

Job Enlargement and Job Rotation.

Job enlargement and job rotation are used to redesign jobs to reduce fatigue and boredom among workers performing simplified and highly specialized work. **Job enlargement** expands a job's duties. For example, an auto worker whose specialized job is to install carpets on the floor of the car may have his job enlarged to include the extra duties of installing the car's seats and instrument panel.[43]

job enlargement
The process of expanding a job's duties.

job rotation
The process of rotating workers among different narrowly defined tasks without disrupting the flow of work.

Job rotation rotates workers among different narrowly defined tasks without disrupting the flow of work. On an auto assembly line, for example, a worker whose job is to install carpets would be rotated periodically to a second workstation where she would only install seats in the car. At a later time period she might be rotated to a third workstation, where her job would be to install only the car's instrument panels. During the course of a day on the assembly line, the worker might be shifted at two-hour intervals among all three workstations.

Both job enlargement and job rotation have limitations because these approaches focus mainly on eliminating the de-motivating aspect of work and thus improve only one of the five core job characteristics that motivate workers (skill variety).

Job Enrichment.

Job enrichment is an approach to job design that directly applies job characteristics theory (refer back to Figure 2–3) to make jobs more interesting and to improve employee motivation. *Job enrichment* puts specialized tasks back together again so that one person is responsible for producing a whole product or an entire service.[44]

Job enrichment expands both the horizontal dimension and the vertical dimension of a job. It is compatible with the concept of empowerment. The premise shared by both is that employee involvement will yield

Dirty, Dangerous, or Dull.
Many of the repetitive manufacturing tasks that were once done by workers on assembly lines are now done with fewer people, especially where monotony or aversive physical surroundings are a factor.

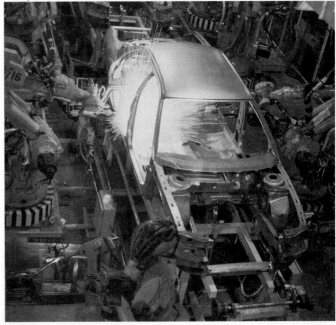

better decisions, better customer service, and more efficient operations. One large insurance company trained staff from four of its branches in problem-solving skills. By focussing them on customer needs and issues, the company was able to create a successful pilot project that many others in the organization wanted to share. Babcock and Wilcox, an industrial manufacturer, found that in addition to training people, it was important to recognize the efforts of these initiatives and celebrate success, on both an individual and a team basis.[45] In a manufacturing environment, enrichment often takes a much more pedestrian form, such as changing product assembly from hundreds of tasks done by many workers to one task that is done by one person or a small team. Such changes are often welcomed, but they can also meet resistance. In white-collar environments, shared knowledge and decision making offer implicit threats to the "turf" of people with specialized roles. People protect their turf by disrupting the flow of information, as Campbell Soup Company Ltd. found when trying to implement such change.[46] It has taken time and persistence to reduce the 31 steps in their customer management process to four, making it clear how Campbell's food products move "from the farmer's gate to the consumer's plate."

The successful implementation of job enrichment is limited by the technology available to make a product and the capabilities of the employees who produce the product or service. Some products are highly complex and require too many steps for one individual to produce them efficiently. Other products require the application of so many different skills that it is not feasible to train employees in all of them. For example, it could take an employee an entire lifetime to learn all the skills necessary to assemble a Dash-8 aircraft.

Campbell Soup Company Ltd.
www.campbellsoups.com

Team-Based Job Designs.   *Team-based job designs* focus on giving a team, rather than an individual, a whole and meaningful piece of work to do. Team members are empowered to decide among themselves how to accomplish the work.[47] Team members are cross-trained in different skills, then rotated to do different tasks within the team. Team-based job designs match best with flat and boundaryless organization structures.

One of the highest-profile initiatives using team-based job designs has been the General Motors Saturn division. Started as a completely new venture within GM, the process for assembling the Saturn car is accomplished by teams of eight to 15 workers. Each team is responsibile for managing itself. It reviews and hires new team members, manages its own budget, and receives reports on the amount of waste it generates so that it can develop plans to utilize its materials more effectively.[48]

■ Job Analysis

After a work flow analysis has been done and jobs have been designed, the employer's expectations for individual employees need to be defined and communicated. This is best done through **job analysis,** which is the systematic gathering and organization of information concerning jobs. Job analysis puts a job under the microscope to reveal important details about it. Specifically, it identifies the tasks, duties, and responsibilities of a particular job.

job analysis

The systematic process of collecting information used to make decisions about jobs. Job analysis identifies the tasks, duties, and responsibilities of a particular job.

◆ A *task* is a basic element of work that is a logical and necessary step in performing a job duty.

◆ A *duty* consists of one or more tasks that constitute a significant activity performed in a job.

◆ A *responsibility* is one or several duties that identify and describe the major purpose or reason for the job's existence.

Thus for the job of administrative assistant, a task might be completing a travel authorization form, which is part of the duty to keep track of the department's travel expenses, which is part of the responsibility to manage the departmental budget.

Job analysis provides information to answer the following questions: Where does the work come from? What machines and special equipment must be used? What knowledge, skills, and abilities (KSAs) does the job holder need to perform the job? How much supervision is necessary? Under what working conditions should this job be performed? What are the performance expectations for this job? On whom must the job holders depend to perform this job? With whom must they interact?

Who Performs Job Analysis?   Depending on the technique selected, job analysis is performed either by a member of the HR department or by the *job incumbent* (the person who is currently assigned to the job in question). In some businesses a manager may perform the job analysis.

Methods of Gathering Job Information.   Companies use several methods to gather job information: interviews, observation, diaries, and questionnaires. Factors such as cost and complexity will influence the choice of method.

◆ *Interviews*. The interviewer (usually a member of the HR department) uses a structured interview to interview a representative sample of job incumbents. The structured interview includes a series of job-related questions that are presented to each interviewee in the same order.

◆ *Observation*. An individual observes a job incumbent actually performing the work and records the core job characteristics. This method is used in cases where the job is fairly routine and the observer can identify the job essentials in a reasonable period of time. The observer may also videotape the job incumbent in order to study the job in greater detail.

◆ *Diaries*. Several job incumbents may be asked to keep diaries or logs of their daily job activities and record the amount of time spent on each activity. By analyzing these diaries over a representative period (perhaps several weeks), a job analyst is able to capture the job's essential characteristics.

◆ *Questionnaires*. The job incumbent fills completes a questionnaire that asks a series of questions about a job's duties, responsibilities, and knowledge, skill and ability requirements. Each question is associated with a quantitative scale that measures the importance of the job factor or frequency with which it occurs. A computer can then tally the scores on the questionnaires and create a printout summarizing the job's characteristics. The computerized method of gathering job information with questionnaires is the most expensive method.

The Uses of Job Analysis.   Job analysis measures job content and the relative importance of different job duties and responsibilities. Having this information helps companies comply with government regulations and defend their actions from legal challenges that allege unfairness or discrimination. As we will see in Chapter 3, the generic defence against a charge of discrimination is that the contested decision (to hire, to give a raise, to terminate) was made for job-related reasons. Job analysis provides the documentation for such a defence. For instance:

◆ Suppose a city requires firefighters to lift 30-kg objects. Job analysis can help the city defend itself against the charge of gender discrimination if it can show that the ability to perform heavy lifting is a legitimate job requirement that the female candidates were unable to meet.

◆ Human rights codes in many jurisdictions have the implicit effect of requiring employers to be careful in their job specifications. For example, requiring a sales representative to have a valid driver's licence may be a legitimate requirement if the employer can demonstrate that the ability to drive is an essential qualification for the job. However, if the company simply desires this criterion (e.g., to provide flexibility in unexpected and infrequent circumstances), the employer might be in violation of the human rights protection afforded to people with physical disabilities. If a requirement for hiring or promotion disadvantages a person protected by human rights legislation, the employer must be able to demonstrate that the requirement (in this case, a driver's licence) is a bona fide occupational requirement (BFOR) that cannot be mitigated by "reasonable accommodation."

◆ The owner of a fast-food restaurant who pays an assistant manager a weekly salary (with no provision for overtime pay) should be in a position to defend herself with a job analysis that demonstrates that the assistant manager's responsibilities truly meet the definition of managerial work. This would exempt the assistant manager's position from the maximum hours and overtime provisions stipulated in employment standards legislation.

In addition to establishing job relatedness for legal purposes, job analysis is also useful for the following HR activities:

◆ *Recruitment.* Job analysis can help the HR department generate a higher-quality pool of job applicants by making it easy to describe a job in a newspaper ad that can be targeted to qualified job applicants. It also helps on-campus recruiters screen job applicants because it tells them what tasks, duties, and responsibilities the job entails.

◆ *Selection.* Job analysis can be used to determine whether an applicant for a specific job should be required to take a personality test or some other test. For example, a personality test that measures extroversion (the degree to which someone is talkative, sociable, active, aggressive, or excitable) may be justified for selecting a life insurance sales representative. (Such a job is likely to emphasize customer contact, which includes making "cold calls" on potential new accounts.) Job analysis may also reveal that the personality test measuring extroversion has a weak relationship to the job content of other jobs (for example, lab technician) and should not be used as part of the selection process for those jobs.

◆ *Performance appraisal.* The performance standards used to judge employee performance for purposes of promotion, rewards, discipline, or layoff should be job related. A company may be required to defend its appraisal system against charges of discrimination and may need to prove the job relatedness of the performance criteria used in the appraisal.

◆ *Compensation.* Job analysis information can be used to compare the relative worth of the contributions made by each job to the company's overall performance. The value of each job's contribution is an important determinant of the job's pay level. In a typical pay structure, jobs that require mastery of more complex skills or that have greater levels of responsibility pay more than jobs that require only basic skills or have low amounts of responsibility.

◆ *Training and career development.* Job analysis is an important input for determining training needs. By comparing the knowledge, skills, and abilities that employees bring to the job with those that are identified by job analysis, managers can identify their employees' skill gaps. Training programs can then be put in place to improve job performance.

The Techniques of Job Analysis.   Figure 2-4 lists the major techniques of job analysis. Detailed descriptions of these techniques are beyond the scope of this book; however a brief description of four of them—task inventory analysis, critical incident technique, position analysis questionnaire, and functional job analysis —will provide a sense of what job analysis entails.

KSAs

The knowledge, skills, and abilities needed to perform a job successfully.

Task Inventory Analysis.   *Task inventory analysis* is used to determine the **knowledge, skills, and abilities (KSAs)** needed to perform a job successfully. The analysis involves three steps: (1) interview, (2) survey, and (3) generation of a task by KSA matrix.

The interview step focusses on developing lists of tasks that are part of the job. Interviews are conducted both with workers who currently hold the job and with their managers. The goal of the interviews is to generate specific descriptions of individual tasks that can be used in the task inventory survey.

The survey step involves generating and administering a survey consisting of task statements and rating scales. The survey might ask respondents—the current job holders—to rate each task on importance, frequency, and training time needed. Whether the survey is sent to a sample of the workers or to all of them will depend on the number of workers and the economic constraints on the job analysis.

The final step is the creation of a task by KSA matrix, which is used to rate the extent to which a variety of KSAs are important for the successful completion of each task rated. An abbreviated example of a KSA rating matrix is presented in Figure 2–5. Ratings in the matrix are usually determined by subject matter experts, who might include supervisors, managers, consultants, and job incumbents.

Technique	Employee Group Focussed On	Data-Collection Method	Analysis Results	Description
1. Task Inventory Analysis	Any—large number of workers needed	Questionnaire	Rating of tasks	Tasks are rated by job incumbent,* supervisor, or job analyst. Ratings may be on characteristics such as importance of task and time spent doing it.
2. Critical Incident Technique	Any	Interview	Behavioural description	Behavioural incidents representing poor through excellent performance are generated for each dimension of the job.
3. Methods Analysis (Motion Study)	Manufacturing	Observation	Time per unit of work	Systematic means for determining the standard time for various work tasks. Based on observation and timing of work tasks.
4. Position Analysis Questionnaire (PAQ)	Any	Questionnaire	Rating of 187 job elements	Elements are rated on 6 scales (for example, extent of use, importance to job). Ratings are analysed by computer.
5. Functional Job Analysis (FJA)	Any	Group interview/ Questionnaire	Rating of how job incumbent relates to people, data, and things	Originally designed to improve counselling and placement of people registered at local government employment offices. Task statements are generated and then presented to job incumbents to rate on such dimensions as frequency and importance.
6. Guidelines-Oriented Job Analysis	Any	Interview	Skills and knowledge required	Job incumbents identify duties as well as knowledge, skills, physical abilities, and other characteristics needed to perform the job.
7. Management Position Description Questionnaire (MPDQ)	Managerial	Questionnaire	Checklist of 197 items	Managers check items descriptive of their responsibilities.
8. Hay Plan	Managerial	Interview	Impact of job on organization	Managers are interviewed regarding such issues as their responsibilities and accountabilities. Responses are analysed according to four dimensions: objectives, dimensions, nature and scope, accountability.

*The term "job incumbent" refers to the people currently filling a particular job.

Figure 2–4 The Techniques of Job Analysis

Task inventory analysis has two major advantages. First, it is a systematic means for analysing the tasks in a particular situation. Second, it uses a tailor-made questionnaire rather than an already-prepared stock questionnaire. The technique can be used to develop job descriptions and performance appraisal forms, as well as to develop or identify appropriate selection tests.

| | | | | | | | | Rating Scale
Importance of characteristic for successful performance of task
1 Very Low   2 Low   3 Medium   4 High   5 Very High | |

	Worker Characteristics									
Job Tasks	Mathematical Reasoning	Analytical Ability	Ability to Follow Directions	Memory	Comprehension—Oral	Comprehension—Written	Expression—Oral	Expression—Written	Problem-Solving Ability	Clerical Accuracy
1. Reviews production schedules to determine correct job sequencing										
2. Identifies problem jobs and takes corrective action										
3. Determines need for and provides special work orders										
4. Maintains log book and makes required assignments										
5. Negotiates with foremen to determine critical dates for emergency situations										
6. Analyses material availability and performs order maintenance										
7. Prepares job packets										
8. Maintains customer order file										
9. Negotiates with Purchasing to ensure material availability										
10. Determines product availability for future customer orders										
11. Determines promise dates and provides to customers										
12. Determines adequacy of materials given document forecast										

Figure 2–5 Sample Task by KSA Matrix

Critical Incident Technique. The *critical incident technique (CIT)*[49] is used to develop behavioural descriptions of a job. In CIT, supervisors and workers generate behavioural incidents of job performance. The technique involves the following four steps: (1) generate dimensions, (2) generate incidents, (3) retranslate, and (4) assign effectiveness values. In the generating dimensions step, supervisors and workers identify the major dimensions of a job. "Dimensions" are simply aspects of performance. For example, interacting with customers, ordering stock, and balancing the cash drawer are the major dimensions of a retail job. Once they have agreed upon the job's major dimensions, supervisors and workers generate "critical incidents" of behaviour that represent high, moderate, and low levels of performance on each dimension. An example of a critical incident of high performance on the dimension "interacting with customers" might be:

When a customer complained to the clerk that she could not find a particular item, seeing no one else was in line, this clerk walked with the customer back to the shelves to find the item.

An example of low performance on that same dimension might be:

When a customer handed the clerk a large number of coupons, the clerk complained out loud to the bagger that he hated dealing with coupons.

The last two steps, retranslation and assigning effectiveness values, involve ensuring that the critical incidents generated in the first two steps are commonly viewed the same way by other employees.

The CIT provides a detailed behavioural description of jobs. It is often used as a basis for performance appraisal systems and training programs, as well as to develop behaviourally based selection interview questions. The appendix to Chapter 7 gives you the opportunity to develop critical incidents.

Position Analysis Questionnaire (PAQ).   The PAQ is a job analysis questionnaire that contains 194 different items. Using a five-point scale, the PAQ seeks to determine the degree to which different job elements are involved in a particular job.[50] The 194 items are organized into six sections:

1. *Information input.* Where and how a worker gets information needed to perform the job.
2. *Mental processes..* The reasoning, decision-making, planning, and information processing activated involved in performing the job.
3. *Work output.* The physical activities, tools, and devices used by the worker to perform the job.
4. *Relationships with other persons.* The relationships with other people required in performing the job.
5. *Job context.* The physical and social contexts in which the job is performed.
6. *Other characteristics.* The other activities, conditions, and characteristics relevant to the job.

A computer program is used to analyse the completed PAQ, generating a score for the job and a profile of its characteristics.

Functional Job Analysis.   Functional job analysis can be done by either interview or questionnaire. This technique collects information on the following aspects of the job:

1. What the job incumbent does to people, data or things.
2. The methods and techniques used by the incumbent to perform the job.
3. The machines, tools and equipment used by the job incumbent.
4. The materials, projects, or services produced by the job incumbent.

The results of functional job analysis are published in the *Canadian Classification and Dictionary of Occupations* (CCDO), which contains standard and comprehensive descriptions of many thousands of jobs. The CCDO descriptions are useful benchmarks when comparing jobs in one organization with those in another (for example, when conducting wage and salary surveys).

Canadian Classification and Dictionary of Occupations
www.hronline.com/lib/recruit/nocintro.html

Job Analysis, the Legal Environment, and Organizational Flexibility. Because job analysis can be the basis on which a firm wins or loses a lawsuit over how it selects or appraises employees, it is important that organizations carefully document their job-analysis efforts.

There are two important questions regarding job analysis. First: Which job-analysis method is best? Although there are many job-analysis techniques, there is no clear choice as to which is best. Some, like task inventory analysis, were initially developed to meet employment legislation in the United States. In most Canadian jurisdictions, there is little specific legal influence on the mode of job analysis. One exception to that is the implicit need for employers operating under Ontario law to be able to demonstrate that the job analysis provides the appropriate foundation for pay equity-required job evaluations.

As a general rule, the more concrete and observable the information, the better. Thus, job-analysis approaches that provide specific task or behavioural statements, such as task inventory analysis or CIT, may be preferable. Cost is another consideration. Some techniques, such as CIT, can be very expensive because of the time required of supervisors and workers.

Given the lack of a single best job-analysis technique, the choice of technique should, within economic constraints, be guided by the purpose of the analysis. For example, if the major purpose of the analysis is the redesign of jobs, then an analysis focussing on tasks would probably be best. But if the major purpose is the development of a training program, a behaviourally focussed technique would probably be best.

The second question regarding job analysis is: How does detailed job-analysis information fit into today's organizations, which need to be flexible and innovative to remain competitive?

Whatever technique is used, job analysis is a static view of the job as it currently exists, and a static view is not consistent with the current trend for organizations to emphasize flexibility and innovativeness in their operations. Even government, often thought to be one of the last places to find flexibility and innovation, has provided a number of demonstrations of just such qualities.[51] In the early 1990s, Ontario shifted the Registrar-General's office from Toronto to Thunder Bay. Art Daniels, the assistant deputy manager in charge, simplified an operation that previously had 14 layers of staff with 43 job descriptions for 23 categories of employees. Two levels of management hierarchy and seven clerical levels were eliminated; all employees are now called customer-service representatives. Rotation among 12 functional units further reduced the possibility of boredom. Recruiting new staff, many from employment equity categories, has improved productivity by 20 percent, sustained over a four-year period.

In an organizational environment of change and innovation, it is better to focus job analyses on *worker* characteristics than on *job* characteristics. The tasks involved in jobs may change, but such employee characteristics as innovativeness, team orientation, interpersonal skills, and communication skills will likely remain critical to organizational success. Unfortunately, most job-analysis techniques are not focussed on discovering worker characteristics not directly related to the immediate tasks. But, because the importance of fit with the organization is being increasingly recognized as a factor that should be considered in selection,[52] job analysis may become more focused on underlying employee factors.[53]

A small but growing number of employers have expanded the job analysis that provides the foundation for selection and recruiting. Rather than simply focus narrowly on the fit between the person and the technical demands of the first job, they broaden their analysis to examine the fit between the person and the organization. Companies such as Cadet Uniform Supply of Toronto and Manpower Services Ltd. are using peer assessment and extensive testing to determine an applicant's suitability.[54] Because jobs are broader and are changing more rapidly, this more inclusive assessment of a person's suitability can make a real contribution to hiring the right people.

Manpower Services Ltd.
www.manpower.com

■ Job Descriptions

A **job description** is a summary statement of the information collected in the job analysis process. It is a written document that identifies, defines, and describes a job in terms of its duties, responsibilities, working conditions, and specifications. There are two types of job descriptions: specific job descriptions and general job descriptions.

A *specific job description* is a detailed summary of a job's tasks, duties, and responsibilities. This type of job description is associated with work flow strategies that emphasize efficiency, control, and detailed work planning. It fits best with a bureaucratic organization structure with well-defined boundaries that separate functions and the different levels of management. Figure 2–6 shows an example of a specific job description for the job of service and safety supervisor. Note that this job description closely specifies the work that is unique to a person who will supervise safety employees. The specific job knowledge of safety regulations and first-aid procedures that are included in this job description make it inappropriate for any other type of supervisor (for example, a supervisor at a local supermarket).

The *general job description,* which is fairly new on the scene, is associated with work flow strategies that emphasize innovation, flexibility, and loose work planning. This type of job description fits best with a flat or boundaryless organization structure where there are few boundaries between functions and levels of management.

Only the most generic duties and responsibilities for a position are documented in the general job description. Figure 2–7 shows a general job description for the job of "supervisor." Note that all the job duties and responsibilities in Figure 2–7 apply to the job of any supervisor—one who supervises accountants, engineers, or even the safety employees managed by the service and safety supervisor in Figure 2–6.

The driving force behind a move to general job descriptions may be a TQM program or a re-engineering of a business process. For example, APS, a public utility, moved toward general job descriptions after discovering that it had 1,000 specific job descriptions for its 3,600 workers.[55] This massive number of job descriptions erected false barriers among work functions, stifled change, and prevented APS from providing high levels of customer service. By using general job descriptions, APS was able to reduce the number of job descriptions to 450.

An even more impressive application of job descriptions is seen at Nissan, the Japanese auto manufacturer. Nissan has only one job description for all its hourly wage production employees.[56] By comparison, some of the divisions of General Motors have hundreds of specific job descriptions for their hourly wage production force. Practices entrenched by years of collective bargaining are a partial explanation for this contrast.

Elements of a Job Description. Job descriptions have four key elements: identification information, job summary, job duties and responsibilities, and job specifications and minimum qualifications.[57] Figures 2–6 and 2–7 show how this information is organized on the job description.

To comply with human rights legislation, it is important that job descriptions document only the essential aspects of a job. Otherwise qualified women, minorities, and persons with disabilities may be unintentionally discriminated against for not meeting specified job requirements.

Identification information. The first part of the job description identifies the job title, location, and source of job analysis information; who wrote the job description; the dates of the job analysis and the verification of the job description; and whether the job is exempt from the overtime provisions of employment standards legislation. To ensure that the identification information ensures equal employment opportunities, HR staff should:

job description

A written document that identifies, describes, and defines a job in terms of its duties, responsibilities, working conditions, and specifications.

JOB TITLE:	SERVICE AND SAFETY SUPERVISOR	
DIVISION:	Plastics	
DEPARTMENT:	Manufacturing	
SOURCE(S):	John Doe	
JOB ANALYST:	John Smith	VERIFIED BY: Bill Johnson
DATE ANALYSED:	12/26/95	DATE VERIFIED: 1/5/96

JOB SUMMARY

The SERVICE AND SAFETY SUPERVISOR works under the direction of the IMPREGNATING & LAMINATING MANAGER: **schedules** labour pool employees; **supervises** the work of gardeners, cleaners, waste disposal and plant security personnel; **coordinates** plant safety programs; **maintains** daily records on personnel, equipment, and scrap.

JOB DUTIES AND RESPONSIBILITIES

1. **Schedules** labour employees to provide relief personnel for all manufacturing departments; **prepares** assignment schedules and **assigns** individuals to departments based on routine as well as special needs in order to maintain adequate labour levels through the plant; **notifies** Industrial Relations Department weekly about vacation and layoff status of labour pool employees, contractual disputes, and other employment-related developments.
2. **Supervises** the work of gardeners, cleaners, waste disposal and plant security personnel; **plans** yard, clean-up, and security activities based on weekly determination of needs; **assigns** tasks and responsibilities to employees on a daily basis; **monitors** progress or status of assigned tasks; **disciplines** employees, contractual disputes, and other employment-related developments.
3. **Coordinates** plant safety programs; **teaches** basic first-aid procedures to security, supervisory, and lease personnel in order to maintain adequate coverage of medical emergencies; **trains** employees in fire fighting and hazardous materials handling procedures; **verifies** plant compliance with new or changing legislated health and safety regulations; **represents** division during company-wide safety programs and meetings.
4. **Maintains** daily records on personnel, equipment, and scrap; **reports** amount of waste and scrap to cost accounting department; **updates** personnel records as necessary; **reviews** maintenance checklists for tow-motors.
5. **Performs** other miscellaneous duties as assigned.

JOB REQUIREMENTS

1. Ability to apply basic principles and techniques of supervision.
   a. Knowledge of principles and techniques of supervision.
   b. Ability to plan and organize the activities of others.
   c. Ability to get ideas accepted and to guide a group or individual to accomplish the task.
   d. Ability to modify leadership style and management approach to reach goal.
2. Ability to express ideas clearly both in written and oral communications.
3. Knowledge of current Red Cross first-aid operations.
4. Knowledge of health and safety regulations as they affect plant operations.
5. Knowledge of labour pool jobs, company policies, and labour contracts.

MINIMUM QUALIFICATIONS

Twelve years of general education or equivalent; and one year supervisory experience; and first-aid instructor's certification.

OR

Substitute 45 hours classroom supervisory training for supervisory experience.

Figure 2–6 Example of a Specific Job Description

SOURCE: Excerpt from Jones, M. A. (1984, May). Job descriptions made easy. *Personnel Journal*. Copyright May 1984. Reprinted with the permission of *Personnel Journal*, ACC Communications, Inc., Costa Mesa, California; all rights reserved.

◆ Make sure the job titles do not refer to a specific gender. For example, use the job title "sales representative" rather than "salesman."

◆ Make sure job descriptions are updated regularly so that the date on the job description is current. Job descriptions more than two years old have low credibility and may provide flawed information.

◆ Ensure that the supervisor of the job incumbent(s) verifies the job description. This is a good way to ensure that the job description does not misrepresent the actual job duties and responsibilities. (A manager who is familiar with the job may also be used to verify the description.)

JOB TITLE: SUPERVISOR
DIVISION: Plastics
DEPARTMENT: Manufacturing
SOURCE(S):   John Doe, S. Lee
JOB ANALYST: John Smith   VERIFIED BY: Bill Johnson
DATE ANALYSED: 12/26/95   DATE VERIFIED: 1/5/96

JOB SUMMARY

The SUPERVISOR works under the direction of the MANAGER: **plans** goals; **supervises** the work of employees; **develops** employees with feedback and coaching; **maintains** accurate records; **coordinates** with others to achieve optimal use of organization resources.

JOB DUTIES AND RESPONSIBILITIES

1. **Plans** goals and allocates resources to achieve them; **monitors** progress toward objectives and adjusts plans as necessary to reach them; **allocates** and **schedules** resources to assure their availability according to priority.
2. **Supervises** the work of employees; **provides** clear instructions and explanations to employees when giving assignments; **schedules** and assigns work among employees for maximum efficiency; **monitors** employees' performance in order to achieve assigned objectives.
3. **Develops** employees through direct performance feedback and job coaching; **conducts** performance appraisals with each employee on a regular basis; **provides** employees with praise and recognition when performance is excellent; **corrects** employees promptly when their performance fails to meet expected performance levels.
4. **Maintains** accurate records and documents actions; **processes** paperwork on a timely basis, and with close attention to details; **documents** important aspects of decisions and actions.
5. **Coordinates** with others to achieve the optimal use of organization resources; **maintains** good working relationships with colleagues in other organizational units; **represents** others in unit during division or corporate-wide meetings.

JOB REQUIREMENTS

1. Ability to apply basic principles and techniques of supervision.
   a. Knowledge of principles and techniques of supervision.
   b. Ability to plan and organize the activities of others.
   c. Ability to get ideas accepted and to guide a group or individual to accomplish the task.
   d. Ability to modify leadership style and management approach to reach goal.
2. Ability to express ideas clearly both in written and oral communications.

MINIMUM QUALIFICATIONS

Twelve years of general education or equivalent; and one year supervisory experience.
                                    OR
Substitute 45 hours classroom supervisory training for supervisory experience.

Figure 2–7 Example of a General Job Description

SOURCE: Excerpt from Jones, M. A. (1984, May). Job descriptions made easy. *Personnel Journal.* Copyright May 1984. Reprinted with the permission of *Personnel Journal*, ACC Communications, Inc., Costa Mesa, California; all rights reserved.

Job summary.   The job summary is a short statement that summarizes the job's duties, responsibilities, and position in the organizational structure.

Job duties and responsibilities.   Job duties and responsibilities explain what is done on the job, how it is done, and why it is done.[58]

Each job description typically lists the job's three to five most important responsibilities. Each responsibility statement begins with an action verb. For example, the job of supervisor in Figure 2–7 has five responsibilities that start with the following action verbs: plans, supervises, develops, maintains, and coordinates. Each responsibility is associated with one or more job duties, which also start with action verbs. For example, the supervisor job in Figure 2–7 has two job duties associated with the responsibility of "plans goals": (1) monitors progress toward objectives, and (2) allocates and schedules resources. The job duties and responsibilities statement is probably the most important section of the job description because it influences all the other parts of the job description. Therefore it must be comprehensive and accurate.

Job specifications and minimum qualifications. The *job specifications* section lists the worker characteristics needed to perform a job successfully. These characteristics are often called KSAs (knowledge, skills, and abilities). The KSAs represent the things that an employee who has mastered the job can do. As part of a training program some employees may be taught the necessary KSAs. An experienced job applicant may be able to perform all of the KSAs.

When documenting KSAs it is important to list only those that are related to successful job performance. It is inappropriate to list what a specific job incumbent knows that is not related to the job. For example, a current computer programmer may have mastered some programming languages that are not necessary for job performance. These should not be included in the job description.

The *minimum qualifications* are the basic standards a job applicant must have achieved to be considered for the job. These can be used to screen job applicants during the recruiting and selection process. Minimum requirements must be carefully specified to avoid discriminating against job applicants. Here are some things to watch for when documenting minimum qualifications:

◆ A college or university degree should be used as a minimum qualification only if it is related to the successful performance of the job. For example, an undergraduate degree may be a minimum qualification for a management training position in a large company, but it is unlikely to be necessary for the job of shift supervisor at a fast-food restaurant. The same logic applies to requirements for all other educational standards, including high school diplomas or graduate degrees.

◆ Work experience qualifications should be carefully specified so that they do not discriminate against visible minorities, women, people with disabilities, or other groups protected by human rights or employment equity. The job description in Figure 2–7 provides a substitute of 45 classroom hours of supervisory training for the one-year minimum work experience requirement. This provision allows people who have been excluded from employment opportunities in the past to be considered for the position. Such flexibility allows the company to consider diverse job applicants who are less likely to meet the work experience qualification.

■ The Flexible Work Force

One of the imperatives for many modern organizations is flexibility. We have seen how organizations can be structured and jobs designed to maximize this flexibility. In this section we examine two additional strategies for ensuring flexibility. First, we look at the practice of using contingent workers. Second, we examine flexible work schedules, which allow employees to balance the demands of family responsibilities, lifestyle choices, and personal interests with their willingness and ability to offer their services to an employer. Flexible work schedules let employers utilize talented employees who might otherwise be unavailable for employment.

■ Contingent Workers

core workers

An organization's full-time employees.

contingent workers

Workers hired to deal with temporary increases in an organization's workload or to do work that is not part of its core set of capabilities.

There are two types of workers: core workers and contingent workers. A company's **core workers** have full-time jobs and enjoy privileges not available to contingent workers. Many core workers expect a long-term relationship with the employer that includes a career in the organization, a full array of benefits, and job security. **Contingent workers** have a more tentative relationship with an employer than traditional full-time employees because the duration of the employment relationship is based on the convenience and efficiency needs of the employer. Firms hire contingent workers to help them deal with temporary increases in their workload or to do work that is not part of their core set of capabilities. Contingent workers are easily dismissed when an organization no longer needs their services. When the business cycle moves into a downturn, the contingent workers are the first employees to be discharged. They thus provide a buffer zone of protection for the core workers. For example, in some large Japanese corporations core

workers because these core workers' jobs are buffered by a large contingent work force that can be rapidly downsized when business conditions change.

Contingent workers include people working in a range of paid work situations. Statistics Canada has estimated that more than 30% of Canadians with paid jobs were engaged in "non-standard" work. This included self-employment, contracts, part-time work, or anything outside traditional, full-time employment.[59] Of these various groups, part-time workers form the largest component. Contingent workers hold a great diversity of jobs: they include secretaries, security guards, sales clerks, assembly-line workers, doctors, professors, engineers, managers, and even CEOs.[60]

Statistics Canada
www.statcan.ca

Temporary Employees.   Temporary employment agencies provide companies with *temporary employees* (or "temps") for short-term work assignments. Temps work for the temporary employment agency and are simply reassigned to another employer when their current job ends. Temporary employees are used to fill in for employees who are sick or on family leave. They can also be used to increase output when demand is high and to do work that is peripheral to the core employees' work.

Temporary employees provide employers with two major benefits:

◆ Temps may, on average, receive less compensation than core workers. Temporary employees are not likely to receive health insurance, retirement, or other optional benefits from the company that uses their services. They often do not receive these benefits from the temporary agency either.

◆ Temporary employees may be highly motivated workers since many employers choose full-time employees from the ranks of the top-performing temps. Since a temp can be screened for long-term career potential in an actual work setting and be easily dismissed if the company determines that he or she has low potential, hiring temps helps employers reduce the risk of selecting employees who prove to be a poor fit.

One of the new trends in the use of temporary employees in Canada is the increasing frequency with which highly skilled scientific and professional employees including lawyers and accountants are working in the mode.[61] What was once limited to clerical employees is being used with increasing regularity throughout the world. In France, one in five workers is a on a temporary or part-time contract, and in Britain, more than 30% of the work force is temporary or part-time. Almost 70% of the jobs created in Spain during one recent year were for temporary workers.[62]

Part-Time Employees.   *Part-time employees* work fewer hours than full-time core employees. Employers have the flexibility to schedule these people for work when they are needed. Part-time jobs offer far fewer employee benefits than full-time jobs, thus providing substantial savings to employers. Traditionally, part-timers have been employed by service businesses that have a high variance in demand between peak and off-peak times. For example, restaurants and retail stores hire many part-time employees to provide service to customers during peak hours (usually evenings and weekends).

Companies are finding many new applications for part-time workers. For example, United Parcel Service has created 25-hour-per-week part-time jobs for shipping clerks and supervisors who sort packages at its distribution centres. Companies that downsize their work forces to reduce payroll costs have been known to restructure full-time core jobs into part-time positions.

In a special type of part-time employment called *job sharing,* a full-time job is divided between two people to create two part-time jobs. The people in the job-sharing arrangement divide the job's responsibilities, hours, and benefits among themselves. Royal Bank, widely seen as a forerunner in alternative work arrangements, reports that job sharing is by far the most popular of it various work-week options. The majority of the over 900 people choosing job sharing are women with children. Some of these job-sharing teams have been so successful that they have been promoted to higher-level positions.[63]

Outsourcing/Subcontracting.   As we saw in Chapter 1, *outsourcing,* sometimes called *subcontracting,* is the process by which employers transfer routine or peripheral work to another organization that specializes in that work and can perform it more efficiently. Employers that outsource some of their non-essential work gain improved quality and cost savings. Outsourcing agreements may result in a long-term relationship between an employer and the subcontractor, though it is the employer who has the flexibility to renew or end the relationship at its convenience.

Outsourcing is the wave of the future as more and more companies look to the "virtual corporation" as an organizational model. A virtual company consists of a small core of permanent employees and a constantly shifting work force of contingent employees. A recent survey found that 32% of employers already outsource some or all of the administration of their human resources and benefit programs.

Establishing the right relationship with service vendors is of extreme importance for companies that decide to outsource. While some companies view their outsourced vendors as strategic partners, others caution that, ultimately, company and vendor do not have identical interests. One petroleum company that outsourced its entire information systems function in the late 1980s, for example, found itself paying $500,000 in excess fees the first month into the contract—a full 50% more than it expected—because the company managers had erroneously assumed that certain services were covered by the contract. This isn't to say that vendors are inherently opportunistic, but that they are looking out for their own bottom line first. The lesson is that it pays to communicate clearly and specifically with vendors from the beginning.[64]

One company that relies on outsourcing as a source of competitive advantage is Benetton, the Italian multinational corporation that makes clothing sold in 110 countries. Benetton views itself as a "clothing services" company rather than as a retailer or manufacturer.[65] The company outsources a large amount of clothes manufacturing to local suppliers but makes sure to provide its subcontractors with the clothes-making skills that Benetton views as crucial to maintaining quality and cost efficiency.[66, 67]

Contract Workers.   *Contract workers* are employees who develop work relationships directly with an employer (instead of with a subcontractor through an outsourcing arrangement) for a specific piece of work or time period.[68] Sometimes contract workers are referred to as *consultants* or *freelancers.* Because contract workers are not part of the company headcount, managers can rely on their services to get around company restrictions on staffing policies intended to avoid payroll costs.

Many professionals with specialized skills become contract workers. Hospitals use emergency room physicians on a contract basis. Universities use them as adjunct professors to teach basic courses when restrictions on the headcount of core faculty make it difficult to hire a full-time professor to teach courses that are in demand. Highly successful companies such as SNC/Lavalin, the Montreal-based design, construction and manufacturing company, achieve their success in part by being able to reduce their project-related work force when the need for those employees has ended.[69]

Contract workers can often be relied upon to be more productive and efficient than in-house employees because freelancers' time is usually not taken up with the inevitable company bureaucracy and meetings. They can also give companies a fresh outsider's perspective. However, for all the benefits of using contract workers, they do pose some administrative challenges. It's not always easy to motivate someone for whom you are one of several clients, each with urgent projects and pressing deadlines. The rise of outsourcing and contract workers has led some to predict the death of the traditional job. Such predictions seem extreme, but they do reflect the reality that the job market has changed greatly as a result of the contingent work force. For more details, see the Issues and Applications feature entitled "Are Jobs Obsolete?"

? A Question of Ethics

Many employees and union representatives complain bitterly about the practice of outsourcing work, particularly to foreign countries. Part of the complaint is that companies do this to avoid paying fair wages and providing employee benefits that Canadian workers expect. Is this an ethical issue? If so, on what basis should companies make outsourcing decisions?

College and University Co-op Programs.   One of the newest elements to make a major incursion into the contingency work force (as well as into recruiting and selection programs) is the use of "co-op" students (sometimes referred to as "interns"). The idea was pioneered in Canada nearly 40 years ago at the University of Waterloo in Ontario. The philosophy has spread rapidly: there are now more than 50,000 students in co-op programs in a wide range of disciplines at over 140 universities and institutes.[70] *Co-op students* are students enrolled in college or university programs who spend a period of time working in organizations (either part time or full time). Their co-op assignment is an integral part of their academic program, and gives them invaluable work ex-

Are Jobs Obsolete?

Not long ago, most people worked 40 hours a week, 50 weeks a year. But such traditional jobs are becoming increasingly scarce in an era of downsizing, re-engineering, outsourcing, and part-time employment.

Does the rise of a contingent work force mean that traditional jobs, in which workers can expect a long-term relationship with their employer, will soon be obsolete? Probably not, although there are likely to be many fewer traditional jobs than in the past. Rather, the trend toward a flexible work force is leading to a redefinition of the term *job*. Jobs are increasingly viewed as arrangements in which people sell their services to employers in a variety of ways, often starting as contingency workers and being promoted to full-time positions later on. For example, new entrants to the labour market may first work as temporary employees, then move into traditional jobs with clients who hired their services and were pleased with their work.

The evolution of the job requires a corresponding evolution in the employee's approach to work. Just as employers are transforming themselves to get closer to their market, employees must get closer to the reality of the labour market. Employees should think of themselves as entrepreneurs who own a bundle of skills and competencies that they can market to their "clients." Thus workers need to continuously update their skill bundles to remain attractive to employers. The best way to do this: look for work arrangements that offer good training opportunities and the opportunity to work with the latest equipment and technology.

SOURCE: Adapted from Bridges, W. (1994, September 19). The end of the job. *Fortune*, 62-74.

perience, exposing them to organizational environments and engaging them in real tasks. In addition to establishing a positive relationship with the schools that supply the newly educated work force, employers who hire interns also have the opportunity to assess and recruit potential full-time employees.

Co-op students are also used extensively by small companies that want to attract employees who will grow with the company. For example, at Seal Press, a small publishing company owned and operated by women, a woman who started as marketing intern went on to become marketing assistant and is now marketing director. For internships where the work is challenging, there are often long waiting lists of candidates.

▪ Flexible Work Schedules

Flexible work schedules alter the scheduling of work while leaving intact the job design and the employment relationship. Employers can use flexible work schedules to modify the traditional nine-to-five, Monday-through-Friday routine to provide advantages for both themselves and their employees. Employers may get higher levels of productivity and provide better service to clients and customers. Employees may be more satisfied with their job and may feel more strongly that they are trusted by management. This change has the potential to improve the quality of employee relations (see Chapter 13).[71]

The three most common types of flexible work schedules are flexible work hours, compressed work weeks, and telecommuting.

Flexible Work Hours.   **Flexible work hours** give employees control over the starting and ending time of their daily work schedule. Employees are required to put in their full 35 to 40 hours at their normal workplace, but have some control over the time they begin and end their work. Flexible work hours divide work schedules in "core" time during which all employees are expected to be at work and "**flextime**" (flexible hours), when employees can arrange work or personal activities.

flexible work hours

A work arrangement that gives employees control over the starting and ending times of their daily work schedules.

flextime

Time, under flexible work hours, when employees can choose whether to be at work.

core time

Time, under flexible work hours, when all employees are expected to be at work.

Companies that use flexible work hours vary in the flexibility of their programs. In many, employees must declare their preferences in advance to ensure that units are adequately staffed. In service units, it is not unusual for the period from 10:00 a.m. to 3:00 p.m. to be **core time**.[72] Meetings and any team-based activities take place around the core. Obviously, flexible hours are more feasible where tasks do not involve the need for employees to be at the same place at the same time. Manufacturing or other work processes that require physical proximity limit scheduling flexibility.

Compressed Workweeks.   *Compressed workweeks* alter the number of workdays per week by increasing the length of the workday, often to 10 or more hours. One type of compressed workweek schedule consists of four 10-hour workdays. Another consists of four 12-hour workdays in a four days on/four days off schedule, providing workers with roughly eight four-day blocks of time off every month.

Compressed workweeks provide employers with two main advantages. First, they create less potential for disruption to organizations that provide 24-hour-per-day services, such as hospitals and police forces. Second, they lower absenteeism and tardiness rates at work sites in remote locations that require long commuting trips.

Compressed workweeks offer both advantages and disadvantages to employees. The major advantage is that the longer blocks of time off increases their flexibility in scheduling personal activities. However, employees who work a compressed workweek may encounter increased fatigue and stress, as well as finding that they have significantly less time to be with young or school-aged children during the work period. The longer workday should be carefully evaluated before it is introduced.

Telecommuting.   *Telecommuting* provides flexibility in both hours and the location of work. Personal computers, modems, fax machines, e-mail, and the Internet have created the opportunity for large numbers of people to work out of a home office. Telecommuting allows employees to develop modes of working specific to their circumstances, while still working full time. Telecommuting does not need to be an "either/or" situation; many teleworkers work part of the time at home or at other off-site locations while also spending some of their work time at the employer's location.

Telecommuting gives employers the flexibility to hire candidates who might not otherwise be considered. For instance, telecommuting makes it possible for a parent of a young child who is away from home less than a full day to work from his or her home. Employers also can maintain smaller offices because fewer employees need to be accommodated. However, telecommuting does present several challenges to managers. We will examine these challenges in greater detail in Chapter 13.

■ Human Resource Information Systems

As we have seen, many organizations are choosing non-traditional structures, designing work to break down barriers among employees, and using a variety of techniques to ensure workforce flexibility. While these strategies are very potent for increasing organizational effectiveness, they can make it difficult to keep track of all the people who work for the organization. Fortunately, computer hardware and software have made it possible to keep track of human resources much more effectively.

human resource information system (HRIS)

Systems used to collect, record, store, analyse, and retrieve data concerning an organization's human resources.

Human resource information systems (HRIS) are systems used to collect, record, store, analyse, and retrieve data concerning an organization's human resources.[73] Most of today's HRIS are computerized, so we will focus on these. While it is beyond the scope of this book's managerial approach to discuss the technical details of the HRIS, it is worth briefly exploring two relevant issues: the applications of HRIS and the management of security and privacy issues related to HRIS.

▓ HRIS Applications

A computerized HRIS contains computer hardware and software applications that work together to help managers make HR decisions. The hardware may be a main-frame computer or a fairly inexpensive personal computer. The software may be a custom-designed program or an off-the-shelf (pre-packaged) applications program. (The latter is more likely to be used on personal computers.) Figure 2–8 shows some HRIS software applications currently available to business. These include:

◆ *Employee information.* An employee information program sets up a database that provides basic employee information: name, sex, address, phone number, date of birth, marital status, job title, and salary. Other applications programs can access the data in the employee information database for more specialized HR uses.

◆ *Applicant tracking.* An applicant tracking program can automate some of the labour-intensive activities associated with recruiting job applicants. These activities include storing job applicant information on a database so that multiple users can see it and evaluate the applicant, scheduling interviews with different managers, updating the status of the job applicant (such as whether the applicant has received other job offers generating correspondence (for example, a job offer or a rejection letter), and providing the basis for employment equity analyses.

◆ *Skills inventory.* A skills inventory keeps track of the supply of job skills in the employer's work force and searches for matches between skill supply and the organization's demand for job skills. The skills inventory can be used to support a company's policy of promotion from within.

◆ *Payroll.* A payroll applications program computes gross pay, income taxes, Canada/Quebec Pension Plan, Unemployment Insurance, other taxes, and net pay. It can also be programmed to make other deductions from the paycheque for such items as employee contributions to health insurance, employee contributions to a tax-deferred retirement plan, and union dues.

◆ *Benefits administration.* A benefits application program can automate benefits records keeping, which can consume a great deal of time if done manually. It can also be used to administer various benefit programs by status (identifying which employees are using child care benefits) and by intensity of utilization (pinpointing the heaviest users of the health insurance plan) or to provide advice about benefit choices (determining when an employee will have enough deferred compensation in her retirement fund to be able to consider early retirement). Benefits software can also provide an annual benefits statement for each employee.

- Applicant tracking
- Basic employee information
- Benefits administration
- Bonus and incentive management
- Career development/planning
- Compensation budgeting
- Employment history
- Health and safety
- Health insurance utilization
- HR planning and forecasting
- Job descriptions/analysis
- Job evaluation
- Job posting
- Labour relations planning
- Payroll
- Pension and retirement
- Performance management
- Short- and long-term disability
- Skills inventory
- Succession planning
- Time and attendance
- Turnover analysis

Figure 2–8 Selected Human Resource Information Systems Applications

SOURCE: Kavanagh, M., Gueutal, H., & Tannenbaum, S. (1990). *Human resource information systems: Development and application, 50.* Boston: PWS-Kent. Reproduced with the permission of South-Western College Publishing. Copyright 1990 by PWS-Kent. All rights reserved.

■ HRIS Security and Privacy

The HR department must develop policies and guidelines to protect the integrity and security of the HRIS so that private employee information does not fall into the wrong hands. Unauthorized users of HRIS who gain access to employee data can create havoc. In one case, an executive who worked for a brokerage house tapped into her company's HRIS to get employee names and addresses for her husband, a life insurance agent who used the information to mail solicitations to his wife's colleagues. The solicited employees brought a law suit against the company for invasion of privacy.[74] In another case, a computer programmer tapped into a computer company's HRIS, detected the salaries of a number of employees (including top managers and executives), and disclosed this information to other employees. The situation became very disruptive as angry employees demanded to know why large pay discrepancies existed.[75]

To maintain the security and privacy of HRIS records, companies should:

◆ Limit access to the HRIS by controlling access to the computer and its data files. Rooms that house computers and sensitive databases should be locked. Sometimes the data can be encoded so that they are not understandable to an unauthorized user.

◆ Permit access to different portions of the database with the use of passwords and special codes. For example, a manager may receive authorization and a special code to tap into the skills inventory database, but may not be granted permission to access sensitive medical information in the benefits database.

◆ Grant permission to access employee information only on a need-to-know basis.

◆ Develop policies and guidelines that govern the utilization of employee information and notify employees how this policy works.

◆ Allow employees to examine their personal records from time to time so they can verify their accuracy and make corrections if necessary.

Summary and Conclusions

Work: The Organizational Perspective.   A firm's business strategy determines how it structures its work. Under a defender strategy, work can be efficiently organized into a functional structure based on division of labour, with hierarchies of jobs assigned to functional units. Under a prospector strategy, decentralization and a low division of labour are more appropriate. The bureaucratic organizational structure is likely to be most effective when an organization is operating in a stable environment. The flat and the boundaryless organizational structures are more likely to be effective when organizations operate in uncertain environments that require flexibility.

Work flow analysis examines how work creates or adds value to ongoing processes in a business. It helps managers determine if work is being accomplished as efficiently as possible. Work flow analysis can be very useful in TQM programs and business process reengineering.

Work: The Group Perspective.   Flat and boundaryless organization structures are likely to emphasize the use of self-managed teams (SMTs), small work units (between six and 18 employees) that are responsible for producing an entire product, a component, or an ongoing

service. Businesses also use two other types of team designs. Problem-solving teams consist of volunteers from a unit or department who meet one or two hours per week to discuss quality improvement, cost reduction, or improvement in the work environment. Special-purpose teams consist of members who span functional or organizational boundaries and whose purpose is to examine complex issues.

Work: The Individual Perspective.   Motivation theory seeks to explain how different job designs can affect employee motivation. Four important work motivation theories are the two-factor, work adjustment, goal-setting, and job characteristics theories.

Designing Jobs and Conducting Job Analysis.   Job design is the process of organizing work into the tasks required to perform a specific job. Different approaches to job design are work simplification, job enlargement, job rotation, job enrichment, and team-based designs.

Job analysis is the systematic process of gathering and organizing information concerning the tasks, duties, and responsibilities of jobs. It is the basic building block of many important HR activities. Job analysis can be used for purposes of legal compliance, recruitment, selection, performance appraisal, compensation, and training and career development. Given the lack of a single best job-analysis techniques, the choice of technique should be guided by the purpose(s) of the analysis.

Job descriptions are statements of a job's essential duties and are derived from job analysis. Job descriptions, which can be general or specific, have four elements: identification information, job summary, job duties, and job specifications/minimum requirements.

The Flexible Work Force.   Flexible work designs help managers deal with unexpected jolts in the environment and accommodate the needs of a diverse work force. To maintain flexibility in the work force, employers can use contingent workers (e.g., temporary workers, part-time

workers, outsourced subcontractors, or university or community college co-op students). They can also alter work with flexible work schedules (flexible hours, compressed work weeks, and telecommuting).

Human Resource Information Systems.   Human resource information systems (HRIS) are systems used to collect, record, store, analyse, and retrieve relevant HR data. HRIS data matched with the appropriate computer software have many applications that support HR activities. These include applicant tracking, skills inventories, payroll management, and benefits administration. It is important that the HR department develop policies to protect the security of HR data so that employees' privacy rights are not violated.

Key Terms and Concepts

boundaryless organizational structure, 51
bureaucratic organizational structure, 50
business process re-engineering (BPR), 52
co-op students, 73
compressed workweek, 74
contingent workers, 70
contract workers/consultants/ freelancers, 72
core time, 74
core workers, 70
critical incident technique, 64
defender strategy, 48
duty, 60
flat organizational structure, 50
flexible work hours, 73
flextime, 73
functional division of labour, 50
general job description, 67
goal-setting theory, 56

human resource information system (HRIS), 74
hygiene factors, 56
job analysis, 60
job characteristics theory, 57
job description, 67
job design, 58
job enlargement, 59
job enrichment, 59
job incumbent, 61
job rotation, 59
job sharing, 71
job specifications, 70
KSAs, 62
maintenance factors, 56
minimum qualifications, 70
motivation, 55
motivators, 56
maintenance factors, 56
organizational structure, 48
outsourcing, 72
part-time employees, 71

problem-solving team, 55
prospector strategy, 48
responsibility, 60
self-managed team (SMT), 54
special-purpose team, 55
specific job description, 67
subcontracting, 72
task, 60
team, 53
team-based job designs, 60
telecommuting, 74
temporary employees, 71
two-factor theory of motivation, 56
work adjustment theory, 56
work elimination, 59
work flow, 48
work flow analysis, 51
work groups, 53
work simplification, 58
work specialization, 50

Discussion Questions

1. When a large greeting card and licensing company redesigned about 400 jobs in its creative division, it asked workers and managers to reapply for the new jobs. Everyone was guaranteed a position and no one took a pay cut. When the restructuring is complete, employees will develop products in teams instead of in assembly-line fashion, and they'll be free to transfer back and forth among teams that make different products instead of working on just one product line, as they have in the past. Give some reasons that you think this company, like many others, is restructuring its work to be performed in teams. Would its teams be considered self-managed work teams? Why or why not?

2. Why is it so difficult to predict whether a new employee will be a highly motivated employee? What factors can influence employee motivation?

3. Motivating employees saddled with routine work has become a significant challenge for information systems managers. In the 1970s IS jobs were very exciting because IS managers were creating systems. Today more and more companies are buying applications programs rather than developing them in-house. This means that between 70% and 75% of systems work is now maintenance. In addition, IS departments at many companies are still regarded as an expense rather than a strategic investment and receive little recognition for their efforts. What types of job-design strategies would you suggest to motivate underappreciated IS workers?

4. Are job descriptions really necessary? What would happen if a company decided not to use any job descriptions at all?

5. Are managers likely to question the work commitment of their contingent workers? What might be the consequences for management when the majority of a company's work force consists of temporary employees and contract workers?

6. What are the drawbacks to using flexible work hours from the organization's perspective? Compressed work weeks? Telecommuting? How should the HR department deal with these challenges?

Check out our companion Website at: **www.prenticehall.ca/gomez** for a selection of self-study questions, key terms and concepts, updated Weblinks to related Internet sites, newsgroups, CBC video updates, and more.

MiniCase 1 — *Food Lion, Inc., and Maids International: Working Smarter or Just Working Harder?*

Companies design jobs and work flow with many different goals in mind, from maximizing efficiency and profits to motivating employees to stay at the company longer. The following examples show how management ideas influence workers in a grocery chain and house-cleaning franchise—for better and for worse.

◆ Maids International, a franchised house-cleaning service, employs mainly female part-timers with young children. These women earn at or slightly above the minimum wage. To avoid high turnover rates, CEO Dan Bishop studied how his employees worked to see if the job could be redesigned to make it both more efficient and more satisfying. Now his maids wind a vacuum cord in 3 seconds (versus the previous 8) and bend over 30 times while cleaning the average house (versus the previous 72). The maids work in groups of four and rotate jobs. The maid who cleans the kitchen in one house does the bedroom in another. There's even a scheduled time to chat—during drives between customers' houses. Average length of employment at Maids International is nine months, compared to five months at places such as McDonald's.

◆ In the 1990s Food Lion, Inc. was a very fast-growing supermarket chain, partly because of a brainchild that CEO Patrick Smith called "effective scheduling." This system mandates the work each department should do in 40 hours, based on anticipated sales and on the number of items scanned at the cash register the week before. The result: baggers pack with two hands at once and stockers are expected to reload shelves at the rate of 50 cases an hour. Managers who run out of allocated hours have to pitch in themselves to meet the mandate. Smith's goal is to make sure there's "an hour's worth of work for an hour's worth of labour." Former employee Francis C. Carpenter routinely put in 60- to 70-hour weeks during his seven years at the non-unionized grocery chain in order to meet productivity goals. Yet he didn't see a penny of overtime pay.

Discussion Questions

1. The emphasis on "lean and mean" corporations in recent years has led to various efforts to speed up work to get costs down. How effective do you think the speeding up policies at Food Lion and at Maids International are in terms of motivating employees? How do these management initiatives differ?

2. Why do you think former Food Lion workers are supporting a drive to unionize the 730-store chain? What job design steps could Food Lion take to keep workers like Francis Carpenter from quitting or to convince current workers not to vote for unionization?

SOURCES: Stewart, T. (1990, October). Do you push your people too hard? Fortune, 121–128; Denton, D. K. (1994, January–February). !#*@#! I hate this job! *Business Horizons,* 46–52; and Konrad, W. (1991, September 23). Much more than a day's work—for just a day's pay? Business Week, 40.

MiniCase 2 — *No Job Descriptions: Prescriptions for Quality or Recipe for Disaster?*

At a recent HRM conference, the keynote speaker—a well-known consultant and HR professor—described a situation he had encountered in his consulting practise. The story went as follows:

Silica, Inc. (name disguised) is a computer components manufacturer in Silicon Valley, California. The electronic components manufactured by Silica require advanced technologies that change rapidly, and have short product life cycles before they become obsolete (about 18 months). The company does not use job descriptions and has no intentions of doing so. A high priority for the company is manufacturing quality parts that are as defect-free as possible. In speaking with Silica's general manager, the consultant noted that without job descriptions the company would find it difficult to defend its employment in a court of law. The general manager replied that he agreed with the consultant's observation, but implied that job descriptions would likely reduce the company's flexibility to deploy its human resources to their full potential in a highly competitive environment.

Discussion Questions

1. Are there some business situations in which it is better to not use any job descriptions? Do you think the situation described in this minicase is one such situation? If you were the consultant, what further advice would you give to the manager concerning the use of job descriptions?

2. Other than written job descriptions, are there alternative ways of finding out what people are doing on their jobs?

SOURCE: Author's files

Case 1

Temps on the Team?

Techno Toys, located in Regina, Saskatchewan, produces electronic toys for children between the ages of 6 and 12. The toy industry is a cyclical business with peak demand for its products during the Christmas season. Management at Techno Toys anticipates a strong demand for its toys this Christmas season and has added 50 temporary toy assemblers for its four-month peak production period (September through December). Techno management chose to hire these workers through temporary employment agencies rather than directly recruit full-time workers. It did so for two important reasons. First, the temps can be easily dismissed after the four-month peak production season ends. Second, given the seasonal time constraints, it is difficult to locate and hire 50 full-time assemblers from the Regina labour market, which currently has a very low unemployment rate of only 3.5%.

The 50 temporary toy assemblers were assigned to work side by side with the 50 full-time assemblers on self-managed work teams. Dave Smith, the plant manager, organized the assemblers into 10 teams. Each assembly team was assigned an equal number of temps and full-time employees. Each team must decide how to schedule its work, choose the appropriate methods and tools for assembling the toys, and control the quality of the toys that it produces.

After about a month of experience with the self-managed toy assembly teams, Dave Smith noticed a higher-than-acceptable rate of return from retailers with complaints about the toys' reliability and quality. These problems could be traced to the assembly process. After investigating, Dave discovered the following facts:

◆ The temporary employees were hired through two different temporary employment agencies, and each agency paid its temps a different rate. All the temps were paid lower wages than the full-time employees. The temps knew about these pay disparities.

◆ All the temporary employees anticipated being reassigned to work at a different company after the Christmas toy season. They knew they had no future at Techno Toys.

◆ The full-time employees on each team tended to act as supervisors to the temps, closely monitoring their work. The temps tended to comply with directions given by the full-timers but showed little initiative in doing their jobs.

After reviewing this information, Dave wondered whether he should recommend reorganizing the toy assembly operation and terminating all the temps or try to improve the teams' effectiveness by making some changes in the teams.

➤

Critical Thinking Questions

1. What do you think of the practice of mixing temporary employees with full-time employees on teams? Do you see any problems in how the temps are being used at Techno Toys?
2. Is there a better way to utilize temporary employees in the toy assembly process?
3. How can the HR department help Dave solve his problem of getting the self-managed teams to produce high-quality toys?

Cooperative Learning Exercise

4. In groups of five, rethink how Techno Toys can better manage its flexible work force. Should Dave terminate all the temps and start over with a totally new approach, or is there a way to improve the performance of the self-managed teams as they are now constituted? Each group should elect a spokesperson to provide a recommendation to the instructor.

Case 2

How Flexible Can a Manager Be?

Manager Barbara Reed has a big problem. Actually, four of the seven tellers at the branch of the medium-sized trust company she runs have the problems. Barbara has the headache of dealing with them.

One teller is on maternity leave. Nearly three months ago, she gave birth to a very premature baby. She's due back soon, but she is unwilling to leave her baby, who is still in an incubator in the neonatal unit of a big-city hospital more than an hour's drive away. She wants to extend her leave.

Another teller has just informed Barbara that his elderly mother, who has been living by herself in a distant town, fell and broke her hip. The teller, an only child, wants at least a month off to tend to his mother and find a new living arrangement for her.

A new teller has asked to cut back her hours slightly so that she can be home with her children after school. The next-door neighbour who had been caring for them will be moving soon, and the teller—who is new in town—can't find anyone she trusts to watch them.

Barbara's best teller, one who she thinks could be a manager someday, has just asked to pare her hours so she can begin taking courses for her MBA. Barbara sorely wants to grant this request because her own performance is judged in part by her skillfulness in developing and promoting women and minorities.

In the past, Barbara wouldn't have agonized over any of these decisions. She simply would have said no, instructed all her tellers to stay at their posts, and replaced any who didn't. But Barbara's company recently adopted a policy saying it would do whatever it could to accommodate employees who had conflicts between work and family responsibilities. Barbara is now supposed to be a flexible manager, which means that she has to try to satisfy her employees' requests. But how can she do that and still run the branch?

Barbara is considering an array of flexible work options, including regular part-time and temporary part-time work, flexible work hours, compressed work weeks, job sharing, leaves of absence, and telecommuting.

SOURCE: Adapted with permission from Geber, B. (1993, February). The bendable, flexible, open-minded manager. *Training*, 46–48. Copyright 1993. Lakewood Publications, Minneapolis, MN. All rights reserved. Not for resale.

Critical Thinking Questions

1. Do all these tellers have sufficient reasons to modify their work schedules? How can Barbara determine which tellers' requests should receive priority, which should be taken into consideration, and which should be turned down?
2. What might happen if Barbara tries to satisfy every employee's request for a modified work schedule?
3. What implementation guidelines should Barbara put in place so that the branch will operate smoothly without disruption of service to its customers? For example, how much flexibility in hours should the flex program provide? Who should be eligible for it? How much advance notice should a manager require to change an employee's work schedule?

Cooperative Learning Exercise

4. With a partner or small group, decide on some programs that would enable Barbara to respond to the four tellers' needs for modified work schedules from the array of flexible work options. Can Barbara satisfy all four of these requests simultaneously with the program(s) you have selected? If not, what should she do?

chapter 3

challenges

The Legal Environment and Issues of Fairness

After reading this chapter, you should be able to deal more effectively with the following challenges:

1 Explain why compliance with human resource law is an important part of doing business and why the human resource function is heavily regulated.

2 Anticipate and follow changes in HR law, regulation and, court decisions.

3 Manage within employment standards, human rights and equity laws, and understand the rationale and requirements for compliance.

4 Make managerial decisions that will reduce the likelihood of legal liability.

5 Know when legal and fairness issues require external expertise.

Equality under law. Federal and provincial laws regulate the practice of human resource management. Often the goal of the legal framework is to assure that employees do not face workplace-related discrimination on the basis of race, religion, national origin, age, or disability.

Robert Henderson applied for a job as a bus driver with B.C. Transit. He completed the first stages of the hiring process successfully. However, his medical history included the fact that he had a condition known as Crohn's disease. Upon learning this, the employers informed him that they did not hire as drivers people who had Crohn's disease, and included in his letter of rejection the observation that he did not meet the medical requirements for the position. Their judgement was based on the fact that people with Crohn's disease are prone to suffer from diarrhea and therefore have difficulty with the one-and-a-half- to two-hour stretches of work without a break.

They also indicated that such a candidate would likely have high levels of absence because of the disease and would be unable to deal with the stress involved in the job. At first glance, this decision appears to be unfortunate but justifiable. Was it?

Henderson filed a complaint of discrimination on the basis of disability, and the B.C. Council of Human Rights found that the employer had, in fact, illegally discriminated against him. The Council reasoned as follows. First, the employer failed to take account of Henderson's employment history. He had driven a tourist trolley bus on two-hour runs (with no breaks), and he had also driven trucks as an owner/operator of his own cartage and air freight business. Medication was successful in controlling his diarrhea. Second, in his previous employment, his absenteeism was considerably below the average experienced by B.C. Transit among its work force. Finally, B.C. Transit's standard 66-day probationary period would have been more than adequate to assess Henderson's ability to handle the job. He was awarded the first available driver's position, compensation for lost income, and a total of $3,500 for psychological impact.[1]

What inferences should we draw from the preceding account?

First, it is improper to assess individuals with a disability on the basis of stereotypes or generalizations about their condition. Sweeping policies that disqualify candidates because of one type of disability or another lead to ethically questionable decisions. Some sufferers from Crohn's disease may not be capable of doing a bus driver's job, but others such as Henderson should not be disqualified. Second and more generally, legal influences on employment are important, both in the framework they provide for decision making and for the shared value system they reflect.

■ Managing Human Resources: The Legal Context

The practice of managing human resources is extensively regulated by government at many levels. Which employees are selected, what minimum benefits and holidays they are entitled to, how they are to be treated when their children are born or adopted, their hours of work, their pay, and what is required when their employment is terminated are all subject to legal regulation.

In this chapter we examine the various aspects of human resource law and regulation. Part of our goal is to identify and discuss the laws themselves, but we are also interested in (1) why these laws exist and (2) how best to comply with legal requirements while doing what is best for the organization.

First, we look at why understanding the legal environment is important and explore the context in which the HR regulation occurs. Next, we look at the range of major employment legislation, selecting for this chapter those that are explicitly designed to establish "fairness" in the employment relationship. (Other laws will be taken up in the specialized chapters to which their content applies.) Employment standards laws establish the basic minimum elements for the employment relationship, while human rights and pay equity laws are targeted at reducing the effects of bias against various groups in society. Finally, we describe ways for an effective manager to avoid potential pitfalls in these areas.

One caveat: it is often said that a person who serves as his or her own lawyer has a fool for a client. This chapter is aimed at providing you with an introduction to the legal framework for human resource management. Because legislation and legal precedents change continually on a case-by-case basis, the information in this chapter is *not* adequate, in detail or in timeliness, for use as a definitive guide for specific legal questions. To assist you with policy formation, federal and provincial regulatory agencies offer employer's guides to the many acts and regulations. Various consulting organizations can assist in areas where an employer may not have expertise. Lawyers have the knowledge of legal procedure that is often essential in dealing with complex or contentious decisions. Our goal in this text is to provide you with a basic orientation to the legalities you will encounter in practice and a sensitivity to the values that are reflected in the law. Exposure to daily HR situations will expand your knowledge and help you to develop the judgement that will allow you to decide when to act—and when to secure professional assistance.

■ Why Understanding the Legal Environment Is Important

Understanding and complying with laws pertaining to human resource management is important for three reasons: it helps you do the right thing; it reinforces the view of human resource management shared by HR professionals and management; and it reduces both the expense and the public relations damage of being found in violation of the law.

■ Doing the Right Thing

What values should govern human resource management? What standards should be met? These are basic questions for everyone involved in human resource management. There are pressures on employers in both the public and private sectors to reduce costs and increase efficiency. One widely held view of publicly traded companies is that management has one overriding responsibility—to maximize shareholder value. Should such values be the *only* ones that shape decisions about who is hired, how much they are paid, and how they are treated on the job?

To put this issue in context, it is useful to remember that employers are embedded in a broader society. For example, the "Ltd." that follows the names of many corporations stands for "limited liability" and indicates that owners (shareholders) of that company risk only the money they have invested in it and not their other personal assets if the company incurs large debts that it cannot pay. This legal protection has allowed corporations to attract the capital on which their financial structures are based. Tax laws are also an important part of the financial framework of business. Patents and licences, as well as regulatory regimes, are crucial to competitive strategies in many industries, and such groups as physicians and lawyers are allowed under law to be self-regulating professions. Despite the trend toward deregulation in many aspects of the economy, it is clear that a modern, complex society must construct a legitimate (that is, legal) way to accommodate a wide range of interests. In a democracy this is accomplished through free

Human Resources Professional
Association of Ontario
www.hrpao.org

elections of governments that pass laws specifying what individuals and organizations are obliged to do, and what they are prohibited from doing.

Doing the right thing raises the question, "What is 'right'?" In human resource management, the right thing is more than simply obeying the law, although legal compliance is a basic requirement. You may find that you disagree with some employment laws or regulations that are discussed in these pages. That does not mean your views are inherently wrong. For example, a law does not always accomplish what was intended, or may have unintended side effects. Professional associations actively participate in the development of employment legislation. The Human Resources Professional Association of Ontario, for example, worked hard to oppose certain changes in labour relations law and to shape the employment equity legislation in Ontario that came forward from the NDP government in the early 1990s.[2] It is also true that a shift in the social or political consensus can change the law, as happened dramatically in Ontario after the 1995 election when the Conservatives' "Common Sense Revolution" changed the legal landscape for employment in that province in areas ranging from employment equity (the law was rescinded), to health and safety, to labour relations.

Efficiency and wealth creation are important value drivers for a dynamic economy. However, human resource management is obliged to place those objectives into a broader frame. Most employment laws have been enacted to establish and articulate what is required to ensure that employees are treated fairly. While a law is in effect, compliance is part of doing the right thing. And if employees believe that they are treated more fairly as a result, the resulting positive influence on motivation and morale is clearly to the employer's advantage.

■ Human Resource Management: A Shared Responsibility

An organization's HR department has considerable responsibilities with respect to human resources law. These include keeping records, setting and implementing appropriate HR policies, and monitoring the employer's HR decisions. However, if managers make poor decisions, the HR department is rarely in a position to prevent damage from being done. For example, unjustified favourable performance appraisals can undermine a legitimate attempt to terminate an employee for performance reasons. The experience of Ontario Hydro, which paid a former employee $400,000 to settle allegations of age discrimination, makes it clear that such matters often are not trivial. The employee, a 56-year-old lawyer, was terminated during a reorganization because of what Hydro claimed was poor performance, while the employee was able to produce several positive performance reviews to counter that claim.[3]

Ontario Hydro
www.hydro.on.ca

Many of the most important human resource decisions—hiring, performance review, recommendations for pay and promotion, and termination of employment—depend on major contributions from managers throughout the organization. HR managers and professionals often act as internal consultants, supporting managers and supervisors who make decisions that have legal implications. For example:

◆ A supervisor wants to discharge an employee for unexcused absences and consults the HR department to determine whether there is enough evidence to dismiss the employee "for cause." In such a case the HR department can help the manager and company determine whether they would be vulnerable to a suit for wrongful dismissal.

◆ A manager receives a phone call from a company inquiring about the qualifications of a former employee. The manager is not sure whether she should respond, and if so, what information can be released. Through consultation with the HR department and a considered response, the manager and the company can avoid liability for defamation (unwarranted damage to the former employee's reputation).

■ Limiting Potential Liability

Human resource management is a responsibility shared throughout the management group. When managerial decisions violate employment law or make an employer liable to successful lawsuits, employers may face significant costs. Recently, a warehouseworker employed by Nike in British Columbia was awarded more than $2 million after he drank eight beers provided by a company manager and subsequently suffered car accident injuries that left him a paraplegic. Although Nike's responsibility was assessed at 75 percent (the employee was judged to be 25 percent responsible), B.C. Supreme Court Justice Risa Levine determined that employers owed employees a higher standard of care than that required by tavern owners.[4] In a somewhat different situation, employers can be found liable for criminal acts of their employees if the criminal act falls within the individual's scope of employment. Just such an event arose in the B.C. Supreme Court, which found a children's foundation liable for sexual assaults of an employee upon one of the children in the organization's care.[5] Thus, it is clear that there are circumstances in which employers can incur costs, both in financial terms and in terms of damage to their reputation.

Nike
www.nike.com

Canadian experience differs from that in the United States when it comes to the expense of legal liability. Wrongful dismissal awards in Canada vary with circumstances; the amount awarded is usually the result of the length of notice required rather than an emphasis on punitive damages. The highest *punitive damage* award on record was $50,000 (not including pay in lieu of notice or legal fees) in the 1992 case of an employee of CIBC.[6] In Canada, illegal discrimination on the basis of age, race or sex is usually addressed via a human rights complaint. The *remedies* (court awards) can be expensive, but typically are more modest than in the United States where civil suits have led to substantial sums, such as those reported below (in U.S. dollars):

Age bias	$302,914
Sex bias	$255,734
Race bias	$176,578
Disability claims	$151,421[7]

Often the cost associated with blatant discrimination or other violations of the law comes by way of unfavourable publicity as well as financial penalties. In one case that attracted considerable local attention in the late 1980s, five employees of a Toronto-area consumer electronics retailer were awarded $300,000 for the harassment they suffered from the company's president when they resisted his orders that women and minorities be fired from the company. The Ontario Human Rights Commission, finding that the president had made "bigoted and racist remarks," also had ordered the company to hire qualified women and racial minorities in proportion to the percentage of applicants they receive from those groups, and that any advertisement that featured the company's employees include women and visible minorities.[8] It is clear that a retailer in this situation is vulnerable to significant loss of business because of adverse public reaction.

■ An Overview of the Legal Context

There are three basic legal modes of employment in Canada: individual bargaining, collective bargaining, and explicit (individual) employment contracts. Most employed Canadians work in the first mode. Although increasing numbers of employees have written contracts with their employers, verbal commitments from employers to employees are also legally binding. Verbal commitments also can be expensive if they are not honoured, as British Columbia Hazardous Waste Management discovered. Having offered employment to Margaret Nevin, they didn't accede to her request to put their verbal commitment to a three-year, eight-month term of employment in writing for what they referred to as "technical reasons." The B.C. Court of Appeal awarded Ms. Nevin, who was dismissed before the specified period expired, the balance of the term of her contract—some $300,000—on the strength of the verbal commitment made by a recruiter and the company president at the time of hiring.[9]

legal framework for employment

The combination of common law, constitutional law, legislation, and contract law that governs employment.

The **legal framework for employment** includes *common law* (the accumulation of judicial precedents that do not derive from specific pieces of legislation), *constitutional law* (in particular, the *Charter of Rights and Freedoms* that accompanied the patriation of the *British North America Act* in 1982), *acts of federal and provincial parliaments*, and *contract law* (governing individual employment contracts and collective agreements). Under the *British North America Act* of 1867, now patriated as the Canadian Constitution, the provinces were given jurisdiction over many areas of the economy, including employment relations. Thus there are 14 employment jurisdictions (10 provinces, three territories, and the federal jurisdiction) that pass laws regulating the employment relationship. People working in federally regulated industries are found in every province and territory, they are only one-tenth of the overall work force.

Major forms of the employment legislation reviewed in this chapter include:

1. *Employment standards legislation.* Present in every jurisdiction, these laws establish minimum entitlements (examples: wages, holidays and vacations, overtime pay) for employees and set maximum hours of work per day and/or per week. This chapter outlines the basic provisions of employment standards legislation, and identifies some of the major variations among jurisdictions.

2. *Human rights codes.* These laws also are common to every jurisdiction. They prohibit discrimination in hiring and other employment decisions on the basis of various characteristics, including race, national origin, and sex. There is some variability among jurisdictions as to the full list and definition of protected groups. However, human rights codes focus on actions an employer should *not* take. This focus differs from that in item (3) below, which identifies legislation that obliges employers to be proactive.

3. *Legislation to advance the employment circumstances of designated groups.* Human rights legislation makes it illegal to discriminate, even unintentionally ("systemic discrimination"), against various groups. Other laws have been passed that have the expressed intention of quickening the pace of change when it comes to certain groups that have been disadvantaged historically. These laws fall into two groups:

   a. Employment equity laws have identified four groups: women, visible minorities, aboriginals, and people with disabilities. These laws encourage employers to be proactive in hiring and promoting individuals from these groups.

   b. Pay equity has had a narrower focus, that of reducing the differences in pay earned by men and by women. The premise for these laws has been that an amount of the roughly 30 percent differential in pay cannot be attributed to differences in ability, qualifications, experience or other "legitimate" influences, but rather has reflected entrenched biases in organizational pay decisions.

Specific legislation affects various HR management processes. Particulars of these laws will be discussed in the context of dealing with those topics.

1. *Separation and outplacement* (Chapter 6) is directly influenced by statutory provisions having to do with required notice periods from employment standards and also by common law issues that define the legal concept of wrongful dismissal.

2. *Compensation practices* (Chapter 10) are affected by minimum wage laws as well as those directed to pay equity. Requirements of the Ontario Securities Commission with regard to executive compensation disclosure have brought increased attention to executive compensation issues (Chapter 112).

3. *Benefits* (Chapter 12) are affected by a wide range of legislation, including Employment Insurance, the Canada (or Quebec) Pension Plan, and the provisions of the *Income Tax Act*.

4. *Employee rights and legally appropriate discipline* (Chapter 14) are defined by both common law and specific statutes including those dealing with labour relations, human rights, and health and safety.

5. *Collective bargaining and the organization of unions* (Chapter 15) are regulated by the Canada Labour Code for federally regulated industries and by labour relations legislation specific to each province and territory for other industries.

6. *Management of health and safety in the workplace* (Chapter 16) is strongly affected by the law, including workers' compensation, omnibus health and safety laws, and a very wide range of laws and regulations that apply to specific industries or occupations.

■ Fairness: The Intended Purpose

The law reviewed in this chapter has been formed by a wide range of specific historical concerns, including child labour, inadequate wages, racial prejudice, and pay inequalities due to gender. The legal framework for fairness in employment is a combination of explicit legislation, common law, and constitutional principle. Although the statutes differ in particulars from one jurisdiction to the next, these laws represent society's attempt, through its legal system and elected representatives, to define what is essential to fairness in the employment relationship.

Employment legislation primarily focuses on the actions of employers, with some provisions directed at union organizations and officials, and relatively few legislated expectations for employees. However, that doesn't mean that employees have *no* legally enforceable obligations. One example of such an enforced obligation was a court ruling that Vancouver-based Lower Mainland Hearing Centres Inc. was entitled to a $10,000 award from a former employee because she had not provided appropriate notice of her resignation.[10] However, such incidents are rare. There are two underlying reasons for the emphasis on regulating employers while specifying few employee obligations: First, employers are the masters in the "master-servant" relationship, which means they have the legal authority to make decisions in employment matters. The individual employee's influence ultimately derives from his or her willingness to quit if the employer's actions are unacceptable. Second, the legal authority that employers have is usually reinforced with economic power. A free labour market is one mechanism that can discipline an employer who offers low pay or poor terms and conditions of employment, by making it difficult to attract and retain employees. However, the market by itself has proven inadequate. The result in Canada (and other democratic countries) has been the creation of an extensive legal framework that attempts to balance the legitimate interests of employers, employees, unions, and the general public.

The Canadian legal framework is complex, because the issues are numerous and changing, and because of the multiple legal jurisdictions within Canada. However, there are several major themes or concerns even though the specific details may vary extensively. Most employment law represents an ongoing attempt to determine and enforce standards that reflect the consensus on what it means to be fair (i.e., equitable) as an employer. While all employment laws generally share

On Appeal.
Although boards and commissions administer many laws pertaining to employment, their decisions are ultimately tested in and enforced by the courts.

that purpose, this chapter deals with legislation that is explicitly concerned with issues of fairness and equity.

■ Employment Standards: The Basic "Deal"

The history of employment practices since the industrial revolution of the 18th and 19th centuries is punctuated by controversies over such issues as child labour, length of the work week, reliability of wage payments, and entitlement of workers to holidays and vacations. In Canada the laws that govern such matters (and which also specify a "fair" minimum wage) have been consolidated into **employment standards** laws. The federal jurisdiction is governed by the *Canada Labour Code,* while the provincial legislation often bears the name *Employment* (or *Labour*) *Standards Act.*

Although there are numerous minor variations among clauses and provisions (see Figure 3–1), the following matters are regulated in all jurisdictions: minimum wage rates; maximum hours of work; paid holidays and vacations; leave for some mix of maternity, adoption, and bereavement; and payment upon termination of employment. The provisions of employment standards legislation are an attempt to guarantee that people who are employed have minimum terms and conditions for their employment.

employment standards

Omnibus (all-encompassing) legislation specifying basic obligations of employers, including wages, hours, and working conditions.

■ Major Provisions of Employment Standards Legislation

Assurance of Wage Payments.   Employment standards legislation makes timely payment of wages a legal requirement. Unlike creditors (such as suppliers or lenders) who need to resort to the courts if payments are not forthcoming, employees have another option. Failure by an employer to pay wages in accordance with the applicable employment standards legislation can lead to enforcement action. Employment standards legislation is enforced through various reporting requirements. Enforcement procedures can also be invoked by complaints. Employers can be required to turn over relevant records to investigating officers and, like the owner of a Timmins, Ontario, fuel company accused of non-payment of wages, can be fined for obstructing an employment standards investigation if they don't comply.[11] However, in the case of bankruptcy, employees owed wages are among the class of unsecured creditors and often receive nothing from the employer. In several jurisdictions there are public funds established to pay a certain portion of wages owed. Ontario's Employee Wage Protection Program will honour claims of up to $2,000 of gross wages.[12]

Employment of Children.   The employment of children under the age of 16 years (15 in Newfoundland) during school hours is not permitted in any Canadian jurisdiction. The minimum age for legal employment at other times varies considerably by province, by type of work, and by time of day. These regulations are the legacy, in part, of social reformers and labour activists. They also reflect the perceived risks that a young employee will encounter. Some forms of part-time employment are now allowed as early as age 14, while more dangerous forms of work (such as mining) may not be allowed until an individual reaches 18 years or more.

minimum wage

The lowest hourly rate that an employer can legally pay.

Minimum Wages.   Figure 3–1 reflects a wide range of **minimum wage** rates in different jurisdictions. Often, different rates apply to specific groups in the labour market such as students, agricultural workers, wait staff who work in licensed establishments, and so forth. The federal minimum wage has been set at the applicable rate of the province in which employment occurs. The existence of a minimum wage is generally accepted, but upward adjustments often prompt opposition from some employers and economists, who view minimum wages as an obstacle to competition in certain industries (for example, garment manufacturing, which

	Min. Wage	Overtime Rate	Paid Holidays	Annual Vacation	Leave Provisions	Termination Notice
Alberta	$5.00	1.5x after 8hrs/d or 44hrs/ wk	NY, GF, CN, LD, CH VIC, TH, REM, Alta	2 weeks [+]	Mat/Preg - 18w; Adopt - 8w	1w after 3m; 2w after 2y;... 8w after 10Y Deemed: layoff of 60d+
British Columbia	$7.15	1.5x after 8/d or 40/wk; 2x after 10/d, 48/wk	NY, GF, CN, LD, CH VIC, TH, REM, BCDay	2 weeks [+]	Mat./Preg. - 18w; Parent.- 12w, Breave.- 3d [+]	1w after 3m; 2w after 1y; ... 8w after 8y; Deemed: laid off 13w out of 20w
Manitoba	$5.40	1.5x after 8/d or 40/wk	NY, GF, CN, LD, CH VIC, TH	2 weeks [+]	Mat./Preg. - 17w; Parent. - 17 w.	1 pay period, after 30d Deemed: laid off 8+w out of 16w
New Brunswick	$5.50	1.5x after 44/wk	NY, GF, CN, LD, CH NBDay	2 weeks	Mat./Preg. - 17w. Adop - 12 w [+] Breave. - 3 d.	2w after 6m; ... 4w after 5y Deemed: laid off 6d+
Newfoundland	$5.25	1.5x min. wage after 40/wk	NY, GF, LD, CH MEM, REM (limited)	2 weeks	Mat./Preg. - 17w; Adopt - 17w; Parent. - 17w Bereave. - 1d + 2d (no $) Sickness - 5d (no $)	1w after 1m; 2w after y Deemed: laid off 13 out of 20
Nova Scotia	$5.50	1.5x min wage after 48/wk	NY, GF, CN, LD, CH REM	2 weeks	Mat./Preg. - 17 w; Parent. 17w; Breave. - 3d	1w after 3m; 2w after 2y; ... 8w after 10y Deemed: laid off 6 consecutive days
Ontario	$6.85	1.5x after 44hrs/wk	NY, GF, CN, LD, CH VIC, TH, BOX	2 weeks	Mat./Preg. - 17w; Parent. -18w	1w after 3m; 2w after 1y; ... 8w after 8y Deemed:laid of 13w out of 20, or 35w out of 52
PEI	$5.40	1.5x after 48/wk	NY, GF, CN, LD, CH	2 weeks	Mat./Preg. - 17w; Parent.- 17w, Bereave - 3d	2w after6m; 4w after 5y
Quebec	$6.80	1.5x after 43hrs/wk	NY, GF, CN, LD, CH VIC, TH, StJBab	2 weeks [+]	Mat./Preg. - 18w; Birth/Adopt - 5d; Parent- 34 w (2 parents, combined; Child care - 5d Other - 2d	1w after 3m; 2w after 1y ... 8w after 10y Deemed: layoff of six months
Saskatchewan	$5.60	1.5x after 8hrs/d or 40 hrs/wk	NY, GF, CN, LD, CH VIC, TH, REM, SaskDay	3 weeks [+]	Mat./Preg. - 18 w; Par./Adpt.- 12w/18w Bereave - 5d	2w after 3m; 4w after 1y; ... 14w after 11y
Federal	(provincial rates, adjusted to province)	1.5x after 8hrs/d or 40 hrs/wk	NY, GF, CN, LD, CJ VIC, TH, REM, BOX	2 weeks [+]	Mat./Preg. - 17w Child care - 24w; Sickness - 12d; Bereave. - 3d.	2w after 3m; Deemed: laid off 3 months+ Severance pay: 2d per complete year of service (5d minimum)'

Notes: Minimum wage: the rate applied to the largest group; Holidays: NY=New Year's Day, GF=Good Friday; CN=Canada Day; LD=Labour Day, CD=Christmas Day, VIC=Victoria Day; TH=Thanksgiving; REM=Remembrance Day, BOX=Boxing Day; Vacation: entitlement after a year, [+] = increasing entitlement with longer service; Leave provisions, unpaid: Mat.= Maternity, Preg.= Pregnancy; Parent.=Parental; Adopt. = Adoption, Bereave.= Bereavement; Termination: Deemed = length of layoff before termination benefits are mandated.

SOURCE: Adapted from Employment Standards Rapid Reference Chart, *Human Resources Management in Canada*, by permission of Carswell, a division of Thomson Canada Limited, Scarborough, Ontario, 1-800-387-5164.

Figure 3–1 Employment Standards in Canada, 1998: Selected Provisions

includes many low-wage jurisdictions). Some parties also argue that minimum wage requirements increase levels of unemployment among people who have difficulty competing for higher-paying jobs. Minimum wages create a "floor" not only for the lowest-paying job, but also for other jobs that have greater responsibility or require greater knowledge and skill than the lowest-paying job. Although $7 per hour as a minimum wage (the 1998 rate in British Columbia) may seem fairly high, a person earning that rate for a full year (2,000 hours) would have an annual income of only $14,000. The objective implied by employment standards legislation is that competitiveness and the pursuit of efficiency should not take the form of a downward spiral of wages and working conditions.

Hours of Work and Rest Days. All jurisdictions require that the standard work week have a maximum number of hours (typically 40, although Quebec, Ontario, and New Brunswick set the number at 43 or 44 hours, and Nova Scotia and Prince Edward Island at 48). Some also set a daily maximum before overtime pay is required. Hours worked beyond the maximum draw mandatory overtime premiums and are often accompanied by a requirement that the employer obtain a permit from the relevant employment standards authority. The minimum overtime rate is 1.5 times the normal hourly rate, except for Nova Scotia and Newfoundland, where it is 1.5 times the minimum wage. Not all employees are covered by hours or work limitations, with managers and professional employees often not subject to such provisions. Historically, weekly hours of work for full-time employees dropped from 60 hours or more a century ago to current levels, although changes during the past few decades have been small.

Employers are often willing to absorb overtime costs rather than hire additional workers. Not only does this give employers more flexibility; they also avoid a range of benefits and training costs associated with a larger work force.

Most jurisdictions require one full day off per week. Until the past few years, both law and custom dictated Sunday for most employees. However, with increasing religious diversity in the population and widespread Sunday retailing, the "one day in seven" is less likely to be a common day for all employees.

Vacations and Holidays. Employees are entitled to a certain minimum number of vacation days and paid holidays, although the provisions vary among jurisdictions. The number of statutory holidays range from five in Prince Edward Island to nine in Alberta, British Columbia, and Saskatchewan. Premium pay and/or time off compensation is mandated for employees who work on statutory holidays. An annual vacation entitlement of at least two weeks (after a certain minimum period of employment) is common. Saskatchewan's minimum begins at three weeks. In many jurisdictions, the minimum vacation increases after longer service. Vacation pay is payable even to many part-time employees, typically at the rate of four percent of earnings. As you will notice in our later discussion of employee benefits (Chapter 12), pay for time not worked represents a significant element of employment costs.

Leave Provisions. The large increase in labour force participation by women has had the effect of changing the way households with young children work. Apart from issues of child care, there is also the need to accommodate the physical reality of pregnancy and birth. Pregnancy leave of 17 or 18 weeks is required in all jurisdictions, after a certain minimum qualifying period of employment. This unpaid leave allows the employee to take time off in the later stages of pregnancy and just after the birth of the child, knowing that she will have a job to return to. Employment Insurance payments provide some income to women who are off work in these circumstances. Recognizing the increasing role of men in child rearing, several jurisdictions have instituted "parental leave" entitlements to allow male employees to take time away from work at the time of a child's birth. As with many specifics in employment standards, jurisdiction differences are many and detailed.

Bereavement due to the death of a close family member typically entitles an employee to three days of leave, although Manitoba, Ontario, and Quebec have no specific requirement. Mandatory court appearances and sickness are subject to explicit leave provisions in only a few jurisdictions.

Termination Notice.   Termination will be discussed in detail in Chapter 6. However, employment standards provide an important component of the legal obligations that employers are subject to when terminating the employment relationship. Employers are required by employment standards laws to provide a certain length of notice of termination (or pay in lieu of notice) when terminating an employee, unless that employee is dismissed for cause. The length of the required notice varies across jurisdictions, and increases with the length of service. The most common minimum notice is one week after at least three months of employment. For long-service employees, the greatest minimum notice varies from two weeks after one year in Newfoundland to 14 weeks after 11 years in Saskatchewan, the most frequent being eight weeks after eight years.

There are times when temporary layoffs effectively become terminations. Employers are subject to termination obligations when layoffs reach a certain stage. A layoff becomes a **deemed termination** when it has passed a certain threshold. In New Brunswick, that period is six days; in Quebec, it is six months; in several provinces, it is 13 weeks out of 20.

deemed termination
Layoff conditions so prolonged that the employer is considered to have laid off the employee.

The statutory requirements for the length of notice (or pay in lieu of notice) that an employer must provide when terminating employment are summarized in Figure 3–1. Normally, the application of this employment standards provision is straightforward. However, there have been some notable examples where such provisions have led to some dramatic outcomes.

◆ In Ontario, a Court of Appeal decision determined that TNT Canada Ltd., operating as Alltrans Express, owed its 1,251 employees termination pay under the *Canada Labour Code* requirement of "two days' wages for each year of continuous employment or five days' wages, whichever is greater." This is despite the fact that employees were on strike at the time. Compensation and penalties, yet to be determined by provincial court, will be substantial.[13]

◆ Termination pay, vacation pay, and back wages totalling $490,000 are owed by three directors of failed clothing manufacturer Lark Manufacturing, according to an Ontario Supreme Court ruling. Keith Lam, Raymond Lam, and Herbert Hui resigned their directorships just before the factory folded in 1988. By this finding, the court affirmed that officers, directors and agents of a corporation must be able to prove that they did not authorize, permit or acquiesce to a violation of the provincial *Employment Standards Act* if they wish to avoid personal liability.[14]

The Law and Discrimination

The term "discrimination" has taken on a negative connotation. When people say, "you are discriminating," they generally mean, "you are being unfair (even prejudiced)." But every time people make a choice—which running shoes to buy, which movie to see, which entrée to order from a restaurant's menu—they *are* discriminating. They make choices based on perceived differences.

The issue of discrimination in employment is not *whether* employers will make choices. After all, they must choose whom to hire, whom to promote, whom to train, how much to pay, how and when to terminate an employee. Thus employers *must* discriminate, in the broad sense of making distinctions. The legal issue is *how* such choices are to be made—that is, which criteria should *not* be allowed to influence these decisions. Such criteria are specified in the *Charter of Rights and Freedoms,* in human rights legislation, in employment equity legislation, and in laws aimed at providing pay equity between men and women.

? **A Question of Ethics**

Is it justified for the law to dictate the criteria people can and cannot use in making private or business decisions?

Developing Consensus: What Is Unfair Discrimination?

The definition of unfair discrimination has changed over time. The standard reflects a social consensus that has been filtered through the efforts of judges and elected legislators, and has been formulated as law. Some prohibitions, such as those against basing decisions on racial bias, are well entrenched. Others, such as gender equality, have been accepted, but the implications (e.g., how to deal with informal barriers within organizations) are still being worked out. Some issues, such as protection against discrimination based on sexual orientation, have gained acceptance in some jurisdictions but continue to be contentious in others.

Until the development of human rights legislation, employers were essentially free to use whatever criteria they wanted in employment decisions. More than a few employers deliberately and sometimes overtly excluded certain religious groups such as Jews or Catholics, visible minorities (effectively, individuals whose ancestry wasn't European), and aboriginals. Even where people with those attributes were hired, they were often subject to discriminatory treatment. Although overt bias against such groups is no longer common, it would be naive to think it has disappeared.

Women have become a much larger part of the workforce. The idea that they should not be discriminated against has gained general acceptance. This is a change from the once-common presumption that women didn't need to be paid as much because theirs was the second income in a household and was therefore less important. Still, many women find themselves concentrated in certain occupations, earning less (on average) than men and often hitting a **glass ceiling** when they aspire to promotion. More recently, employers' use of other characteristics (such as disabilities, sexual orientation, or age) as a basis for employment decisions has been called into question in society at large, as reflected in amended human rights and employment equity laws. In many Canadian jurisdictions, such attributes are now excluded as a basis for employment decisions.

The laws that make certain personal attributes off-limits do limit the freedom that employers otherwise have. For example, if an employer terminates a tall employee because of a preference for short people, the employee would have no recourse other than the normal wrongful dismissal procedures and payments (see Chapter 6). However, if the termination was based on the fact that the employer preferred not to have women or people of Asian ancestry or people who wear a prosthetic device (e.g., an artificial leg) as employees, it would also constitute a human rights violation, with additional legal sanctions.

■ Human Rights Legislation

■ Charter of Rights and Freedoms

The Canadian Constitution includes a ***Charter of Rights and Freedoms.*** Section 15 of the *Charter,* which came into effect in 1985, guarantees the right to "equal protection and equal benefit *of the law* without discrimination and, in particular, without discrimination based on race, national or ethnic origin, colour, religion, sex, age or mental or physical disability" [emphasis added]. The extent of the *Charter's* influence on employment is not yet clear. The court process in *Charter* cases takes time, and many decisions are required to define an overall pattern. The *Charter* is important because it takes precedence over other laws, so that legislation must meet *Charter* standards. There are two notable exceptions to this generalization. The *Charter* allows that laws infringing on *Charter* rights may be permissible if they can be demonstrably justified as reasonable limits in a "free and democratic society." For example, the prohibition against age discrimination in the *Charter* did not invalidate mandatory retirement when a case was taken to the Supreme Court. The other situation in which the *Charter* does not apply is when a legislative body invokes the "notwithstanding" provision, which allows the legislation to be exempted from *Charter* challenge. The *Charter* applies to all actions of all levels of government (federal, provincial, local) and of government's agents, including police. The *Charter* is *not* directly applicable to the actions of private individuals or organizations, but it does apply to the laws that govern their actions.

glass ceiling

The intangible barrier within the hierarchy of an organization that prevents female employees from rising to positions above a certain level.

Charter of Rights and Freedoms

Constitutional law forbidding discrimination. Applies to actions of government and to laws enacted in Canada.

For that reason, the impact of the *Charter* on private-sector employees, though indirect, will become increasingly important over time in areas ranging from collective bargaining to the extension of human rights.

■ Human Rights Codes

Although each Canadian jurisdiction has its own human rights legislation, there is consistency in the characteristics that are prohibited as a basis for discrimination. All jurisdictions prohibit discrimination based on race, colour, creed or religion, sex, marital status, and physical disability. All prohibit age-based discrimination (although the age groups protected differ), and all jurisdictions other than Alberta and Saskatchewan prohibit discrimination on the basis of mental handicap. Discrimination on other grounds (ethnic origin, criminal history, or sexual orientation) is prohibited in some, but not all jurisdictions. In an interesting development, the Supreme Court of Canada has upheld a trial judge who decided that the words "sexual orientation" must be read into Alberta's *Individual's Rights Protection Act* (IRPA), as a means of bringing Alberta's legislation in line with the *Chater of Rights and Freedoms*.[15] Harassment is perhaps one of the more interesting additions to the law, currently in effect in Newfoundland, Ontario, Quebec, the Yukon, and the federal jurisdiction. Figure 3–2 summarizes the major protected categories under human rights legislation in Canada.

■ The Canadian Human Rights Act

The **Canadian Human Rights Act** took effect in March 1978. The *Act* applies to all federal government departments, agencies, and Crown corporations. It also applies to organizations regulated by the federal government including airlines, banks, railways, and communications companies. The proportion of all Canadian employees covered by this law is about 10 percent; the remainder are covered under laws in the provincial or territorial jurisdiction in which they work. The Canadian Human Rights Commission (CHRC) investigates complaints lodged under the *Act*.

Canadian Human Rights Act
Federal legislation prohibiting discrimination and establishing the Canadian Human Rights Commission.

Prohibited Grounds of Discrimination	Federal	Alta.	B.C.	Man.	N.B.	Nfld.	N.S.	Ont.	PEI.	Que.	Sask.	N.W.T	Yukon
Race	◆	◆	◆	◆	◆	◆	◆	◆	◆	◆	◆	◆	◆
Colour	◆	◆	◆	◆	◆	◆	◆	◆	◆	◆	◆	◆	◆
Ethnic or national origin	◆			◆	◆	◆	◆	◆	◆				◆
Creed or religion	◆	◆	◆	◆	◆	◆	◆	◆	◆	◆	◆	◆	◆
Sex	◆	◆	◆	◆	◆	◆	◆	◆	◆	◆	◆	◆	◆
Marital status	◆	◆	◆	◆	◆	◆	◆	◆	◆	◆	◆	◆	◆
Age	◆	18+	45–65	◆	19+	19–65	40–65	18–65	◆	◆	18–65	◆	◆
Mental handicap	◆		◆	◆	◆	◆	◆	◆	◆	◆		◆	◆
Physical handicap	◆	◆	◆	◆	◆	◆	◆	◆	◆	◆	◆	◆	◆
Pardoned offence	◆									◆	◆		
Record of criminal conviction		◆						◆					◆
Harassment[1]	◆					◆		◆					◆
Sexual orientation			◆					◆		◆			◆
Language										◆			

[1]*The federal, Ontario, Quebec, and Yukon statutes ban harassment on all proscribed grounds. Manitoba prohibits sexual harassment.*

Figure 3–2 **Selected Prohibited Grounds of Discrimination in Employment by Jurisdiction**
SOURCE: Selected Prohibited Grounds of Discrimination in Employment by Jurisdiction, *Human Resources Management in Canada* (1998 edition). Toronto: Carswell Thomson Professional Publishing.

If the Commission finds that human rights have been infringed on, financial and other penalties can be imposed. Appeals to the courts are possible. Similar enforcement mechanisms are common in other jurisdictions.

What does this legislation mean for employers? There are *general* issues such as what the law includes as discriminatory practices, the situations under which an employer can legally discriminate against members of protected classes of people, and how much flexibility an employer has to show in accommodating individual employees. There are also *specific* issues of how to conduct HR activities, such as hiring and promotion, without violating human rights obligations. We'll turn to the general issues first.

■ Intentional and Systemic Discrimination

intentional discrimination

Deliberate use of race, religion or other prohibited criteria in employment decisions.

Intentional discrimination is often difficult to identify. Most employers are aware that discrimination based on prejudice toward a person's race, religion, sex (gender), or ethnic background is unacceptable. Even those employers who deliberately apply such criteria are unlikely to declare the fact publicly.

This is not to say that intentional discrimination is never detected. There are indications that some employers have attempted to buffer themselves by asking employment agencies to discriminate illegally on their behalf. The Recruiters Guild, in a confidential survey of over 650 recruiters and hiring managers, indicated that during the previous two years respondents had rejected a candidate based on physical disability (97%), age (95%), race (94%), or sex (81%). When asked how many of the last 10 people these recruiters and managers had hired for *supervisory* positions were a member of any of these groups, a total of *four* of 6,720 selections was obtained. All employment agencies contacted indicated they had received discriminatory hiring requests, and 94% indicated that they had complied with these requests, citing fear of reprisal or loss of business if they did not.[16] An employer's use of an employment agency to discriminate in no way reduces that employer's culpability. Intentional discrimination by individual managers or HR employees also is the employer's responsibility, even if it is done on the individual's own initiative, rather than under the explicit direction of someone in authority.

Intentional discrimination is clearly offensive; it rarely has any plausible connection to the effectiveness of the organization and is usually a reflection of the personal biases and prejudices of the decision makers.

systemic discrimination

Employment criteria that have the effect of discriminating on prohibited grounds but are not used with the intent to discriminate.

There is another form of illegal human rights discrimination, one that does not reflect any necessary bias on the part of the decision maker. **Systemic discrimination** (or, as it is called in the Ontario *Human Rights Code,* "constructive discrimination") is the result of employment policies that have an unintended, but unnecessary adverse effect on protected classes of people. The *Canadian Human Rights Act* as well as several provincial jurisdictions have adopted a definition based on case law from the U.S. Supreme Court. In 1970, that court found in the landmark *Griggs v. Duke Power Co.* that a company's educational and employment tests were discriminatory because of two elements:

1. There was no justification of the tests on the basis of business necessity, and the tests were not demonstrably related to job performance.

2. The procedures had an *adverse impact* on blacks in that a greater proportion of blacks than whites were disqualified.[17]

In Canada, this prohibition of systemic discrimination has been applied to protect such individuals as Sikh men, whose religion requires long hair, turbans and beards, from being discriminated against by an employer that required male employees to be clean shaven and have short hair and to protect women from discrimination implied by minimum height requirements (5'10") for employment as a police officer.[18] The height requirement, based partly on an undemonstrated premise that effective policing was more likely when the police officer was physically imposing, had the effect of disqualifying a disproportionate number of women. In both examples, the finding of discrimination was not based on the intentions of the employers' decisions. Rather, it depended on the *effects* of the employers' actions.

■ Bona Fide Occupational Requirements

Bona fide occupational requirements (BFORs) are employer requirements that can be clearly defended as intrinsically required by the task(s) an employee is being asked to perform, even though such requirements may violate human rights protection. A 1982 Supreme Court of Canada decision established that an age-60 mandatory retirement for firefighters in Etobicoke, Ontario, was *not* a BFOR, even though honestly imposed, because there was insufficient evidence that reaching that age established an inability to perform adequately.[19] A similar result occurred when the Canadian Coast Guard attempted to disqualify an applicant for officer cadet training who had complete hearing loss in one ear on the basis that his disability constituted a unacceptable safety risk. Although the applicant's hearing impairment was clearly demonstrated, the BFOR claim was denied because the evidence introduced by the employer to indicate a safety risk was not compelling.[20]

One setting in which a BFOR exception to human rights standards is easily understood is in theatrical productions. If directors need to select cast members to play an old person, a white middle-aged male, an Asian athlete and so forth, they can clearly justify using age, sex, or national origin as a basis for recruiting and selecting actors. Where the issue of BFORs get more complicated is when the occupational requirement is less transparent. There are cases where BFORs have been established. Sex has been found to be a legitimate requirement when selecting (male) nursing attendants to provide intimate care such as bathing for male patients (the hospital in question had numerous female nurses) and for the RCMP's requirement that guards be of the same sex as prisoners being guarded. However, sex has often *not* been allowed as a BFOR in what might seem plausible circumstances: customer preferences or employer strategies for service by only men or only women; a remote, male-dominated worksite; or lack of a women's washroom.[21]

■ Reasonable Accommodation

Employers who believe there is a BFOR for denying employment or assignment to a specific position may encounter the legal principle of **reasonable accommodation.** Manitoba, Ontario, and the Yukon incorporate this into their legislation. If an individual's inability to meet job requirements can be mitigated by the employer's making minor adjustments, such "reasonable accommodation" is required. Adjustments to schedules and redesign of work stations or lighting are examples of such adjustments.

In a well-known case (*O'Malley v. Simpson-Sears Ltd.*), the concepts of systemic discrimination, BFORs, and accommodation are implicitly drawn together. O'Malley, a sales clerk, had been working full time for the retailer for several years, during which time she had worked two out of three Saturdays. She joined the Seventh-Day Adventist Church, which observes as Sabbath the period from sunset Friday until sunset Saturday, and was no longer available for work Saturdays. The employer requested that she resign and, when O'Malley did not, subsequently cut her hours to the point where she became part time, losing benefits available to full-time employees. The Ontario Divisional Court and the Ontario Court of Appeal agreed with the employer that the human rights complaint on the basis of religious discrimination was not valid. However, in December 1985, the Supreme Court of Canada reversed the lower courts' position that the *intention* to discriminate was necessary to find the employer in breach of the law. Effectively, the Supreme Court found that the action was discriminatory and, by implication, that the (occupational) requirement for weekend hours was not sufficient reason in these circumstances not to accommodate this employee's religious beliefs.[22]

bona fide occupational requirement (BFOR)
A job requirement that legally overrides a human rights protection.

reasonable accommodation
Adjustments in job content and working conditions that an employer may be expected to make in order to accommodate a person protected by human rights provisions.

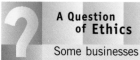

There are a number of specific human rights issues that deserve attention. Recruiting and selection procedures, as well as those that determine promotion, need to avoid techniques that may be discriminatory or that may expose an employer to the accusation of discrimination. The Appendix to Chapter 3 shows guidelines for employee screening and selection provided by the Canadian Human Rights Commission. Similar guidance is generally available from provincial commissions for employers, subject to their scrutiny. Some human rights issues are attracting considerable attention, even though they are not issues common to every jurisdiction. Sexual orientation and harassment are two such issues that are gaining prominence.

Sexual Orientation.   Sexual orientation (whether an individual is heterosexual or homosexual) has become one of the most contentious human rights issues in recent years. It has been included in the human rights codes of most provinces, and was added to the *Canadian Human Rights Code* in May 1996. However, the ultimate implications of this protection have yet to be worked out. In the workplace, certain issues become relatively straightforward. Hiring, promotions, wages and salaries, and termination decisions cannot legally be based on whether an individual is gay or straight. The more complicated issues attach to employee benefits such as insurance and pensions. Specifically, are the partners of gay men or lesbian women entitled to be treated as spouses? Common-law marriages between heterosexual men and women have legal standing if the partners have been together for at least a year's duration and the man and woman have publicly represented themselves as husband and wife. This means that the fact that homosexual partners have not been formally married does not in itself disqualify their relationship; rather, it is the fact that the partners are not of the opposite sex. In 1995, in a key decision about the provisions of the *Old Age Security Act,* the Supreme Court of Canada concluded that the distinction between heterosexual and homosexual couples was indeed discriminatory under the *Charter of Rights and Freedoms,* but that such infringement was "justifiable in a free and democratic society." Case law in one major jurisdiction (Ontario) now seems to indicate that the provincial human rights law combined with *Charter* provisions would *not* permit employers to have insurance or pension plans that do not extend spousal and dependent benefits to same-sex partners. One problem for employers who wish to extend such benefits is that registered pension plans and private health services plans could lose their preferred tax status if same-sex benefits are provided. For now, employers may need to provide same-sex benefits of these types through separate plans.[23]

Harassment.   In several Canadian jurisdictions, harassment on any of the prohibited grounds in the *Canadian Human Rights Code* is a violation. *Harassment* can include verbal abuse, threats, unwelcome comments, ridicule, taunting, display of offensive pictures, unnecessary physical contact, assault, or other acts that humiliate or embarrass an individual. The lack of a clear, simple definition bothers some commentators, but the Canadian Human Rights Commission's standard is that such acts constitute harassment "if a reasonable person ought to have known that the behaviour was unwelcome."[24]

Although harassment can occur on racial or ethnic lines, sexual harassment is probably its single most common form. Employers are responsible for harassment that employees experience. General Motors Canada had a sexual harassment policy, but was still assessed $120,000 in damages for wrongful dismissal of a security supervisor on the basis of his harassment of a female subordinate. The supervisor claimed that he had been fired without cause. What turned the case in his favour was that the harassment policy had not been adequately communicated or monitored, and that the employer had acted arbitrarily in his case because his behaviour was not substantially different from that of other people in the department. For harassment policies to work, clear communication and fair, equitable enforcement are required.[25] (See the "Manager's Notebook" for some guidelines for avoiding harassment incidents.)

General Motors Canada Ltd.
www.gmcanada.com

■ Human Rights Violations: Procedures and Penalties

Human rights laws are generally invoked by a complaint from an individual or individuals claiming illegal discrimination. This written submission is evaluated by the Human Rights Commission, and if there appears to be substance to the complaint, an investigation is undertaken. If the investigation supports a finding of discrimination and subsequent mediation does not lead to a mutually acceptable resolution between the parties, the Commission specifies a remedy or remedies. Decisions of the various human rights commissions and their appeals tribunals are ultimately subject to appeal in the courts, with some cases finding their way to the Supreme Court of Canada.

Remedies.   What are the remedies that can be imposed? The most common is compensation for lost wages. Further financial remedies can include compensation for general damages, for complainant's expenses, and for pain and humiliation. If a person has not been hired or has been dismissed for discriminatory reasons, employment or re-employment may be stipulated, and if there is a pattern of discriminatory action by the employer, such practices can be ordered to cease. Other remedies are symbolic but often important. They include requiring the employer to display the *Human Rights Code* prominently, to write letters of apology, and to attend designated human rights workshops.

Two characteristics of human rights investigations are notable and imply that employers should take human rights violations seriously as a practical matter. The first is that the Commission, once having accepted the legitimacy of a written complaint, assumes responsibility for pursuing the investigation and defending the decision reached. This means that those costs are borne by the Commission and not by the complainant, making the process accessible to individuals who may not otherwise be able to pursue a civil suit. Second, there are some occasions when a human rights commission may launch an investigation in the absence of a formal complaint. This procedure is invoked when there is reason to believe that an employer is exhibiting a pattern of discriminatory practice.

One of several things you will note in Figure 3–3, which summarizes the experience of employers over the recent past, is that the number of *inquiries* to the Canadian Human Rights Commission exceeds the number of complaints, but has dropped roughly one-third over the period 1992–95. The number of *complaints* has remained relatively stable. Sex-based complaints (which have increased steadily) and disability-based complaints together account for three of every five complaints. The final disposition of complaints indicates that, in many cases, informal mechanisms result in the complaint not reaching the stage of formal findings by the Commission. Data in the late 1990s suggest a sharp increase in the number of age-based complaints, jumping from an average of eight percent of all complaints during 1994-1996, but jumping sharply to 25% of all complaints in 1997.[26]

Manager's Notebook

Discipline Guidelines for Dealing with Sexual Harassment

Managers who want to balance the interests of avoiding human rights complaints against avoiding costly wrongful dismissal lawsuits can be guided by the following suggestions:

1. Avoid a "zero tolerance" approach. Every case should be decided on its own facts.

2. Have a clear Workplace Harassment Policy that specifically provides for the option of termination of employment where harassment is proven.

3. Provide training sessions to all managers and employees. Providing a copy of your Workplace Harassment Policy is a must, and mandatory attendance at sessions is recommended. Many employers are requiring that all employees sign a copy of the policy and return it to the employer.

4. Monitor the workplace. Supervisors and managers must be advised of their obligations with respect to monitoring the workplace to prevent a "poisoned atmosphere" from developing.

5. If a complaint is filed, conduct a proper investigation. It is imperative that the accused be given all the details of the complaint and be provided with an opportunity to respond to each allegation.

6. Consider all the relevant factors in determining whether dismissal is appropriate in the circumstances. For instance: the complainant's demands; the nature of the conduct; the frequency of the conduct; the position and length of service of the harassed; adverse effects to the business and the corporate culture.

SOURCE: MacKillop, Malcolm. (1996, April). Dismissal if necessary, not necessarily dismissal. *Human Resources Professional*, 24–25. Reproduced with permission of the Human Resources Professionals Association of Ontario (HRPAO).

Figure 3–3 Human Rights Cases in the Federal Jurisdiction

SOURCE: Canadian Human Rights Commission (1996). *Annual Report.*

Reproduced with the permission of the Minister of Supply and Services Canada.

A. Number of Inquiries During the Last 10 Years

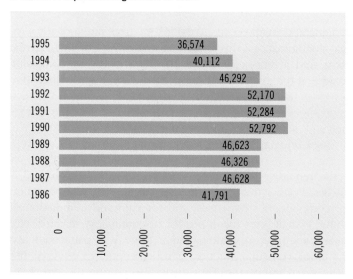

B. Distribution of Complaints, by Grounds of Discrimination, 1992–95

GROUND	1992		1993		1994		1995	
	No.	%	No.	%	No.	%	No.	%
Sex	316	24	304	25	373	27	299	30
Race/Colour	111	9	71	6	139	10	106	11
Disability	424	33	362	30	420	31	308	30
Family/Marital Status	134	11	109	9	82	6	52	5
Age	142	11	143	12	154	11	70	7
National/Ethnic Origin	143	11	101	8	99	7	96	10
Religion	10	1	22	2	37	3	23	2
Pardoned Criminal Conv.	2	0	2	0	4	0	3	0
Sexual Orientation	–	–	100	8	64	5	53	5
TOTAL	**1,282**	**100**	**1,214**	**100**	**1,372**	**100**	**1,010**	**100**

C. Disposition of Complaints, 1992–95

	1992	1993	1994	1995
Sent to tribunal	88	40	48	54
Sent to conciliation	209	189	164	118
Settlement approved[1]	135	126	149	142
Dismissed	322	293	273	277
Not dealt with[2]	37	50	26	18
No further proceedings[3]	220	375	316	394
To deal with	16	35	40	14
No tribunal	29	89	81	36
Stood down	115	159	141	265
Early resolution	177	173	144	96
Referrals	1345	265	488	410
TOTAL	**1,693**	**1,794**	**1,870**	**1,824**

[1] Settlement agreed to by the parties and approved by the Commission.
[2] The Commission decided not to investigate the complaint because it was out of time or, technically, without purpose.
[3] The Commission decided not to pursue the complaint because it was withdrawn or the matter was resolved.

■ Equity in the Workplace: Legal Initiatives

Human rights codes focus on prohibitions of various kinds of discrimination. They are an attempt to create a "level playing field" in the employment relationship. However, some identifiable groups in the work force appear to have been subject to pervasive patterns of differential treatment by employers. Such groups find themselves working in less well-paid jobs, being excluded (even if unintentionally) from attractive career opportunities, and/or suffering significantly higher levels of unemployment than the averages for the work force as a whole.

Figure 3–4 illustrates one aspect of this situation. The graph indicates the extent to which four groups are employed in federally regulated employment relative to their presence in the labour force. Women and visible minorities are the groups that are employed in federally regulated industries in proportion to the population. However their mere *presence* in the work force does not ensure that they are paid equitably. Aboriginals and people with mental and physical disabilities are dramatically underrepresented in federally regulated employment, holding only roughly 40 to 60 percent of the positions that one would expect based on their general labour force activity.

This situation has prompted a concern that simply levelling the playing field is insufficient to affect these patterns significantly, that patterns of conventional employer practices would effectively block disproportionate numbers of women, visible minorities, aboriginals, and people with disabilities from employment opportunities for which they were qualified. These concerns have led to the passage of two categories of legislation in several Canadian jurisdictions. The first category, employment equity, attempts to find mechanisms to increase these groups' opportunities for employment, for promotion, and for pay. The second legislative category, pay equity, focusses specifically on pay differences between men and women with the intention of creating mechanisms that will redress the imbalance.

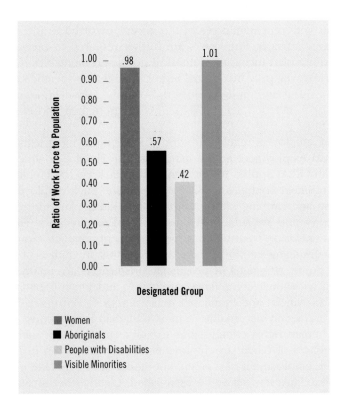

Figure 3–4 Ratio of People Employed in Federally Regulated Private-Sector Employment to Their Proportion in Labour Force, 1997

SOURCE: Derived from *Annual Report, Employment Equity Act* (1998).

■ Employment Equity

Employment equity is a term coined in Canada. In many respects, it refers to practices that have been termed "affirmative action" in the United States. Judge Rosalie Abella in her 1984 Royal Commission Report, *Equality in Employment,* suggested the term, indicating that "affirmative action" was often associated with quotas, which had become a divisive political issue.[27]

Employment equity is unavoidably controversial. Those who support it are convinced that there will be slow progress, at best, unless there *is* some kind of intervention to change patterns of past practice. Those who oppose equity legislation see it as leading to preferential treatment (sometimes called "reverse discrimination") favouring individuals who would not get the job or the promotion in a fair competition. Two elements heighten the tension around employment equity. One is the fact that some people who are persuaded that the *patterns* outlined in Figure 3–4 *are* unfair still have difficulty accepting solutions that in some cases appear to be unfair to individuals who are white or male or without a disability. The other factor making employment equity programs more controversial has been the flattening of organizational structures and the widespread downsizing of many organizations. A growing organization may allow hiring and promotion of designated groups to increase while not seeming to block progress for other employees. When layoffs occur and when there are very few promotions, equity-influenced decisions attract greater attention and potential resistance because more people perceive it as forcing a choice between applicants from a designated group or applicants who have the best qualifications.

Employment Equity Act

The 1986 federal law to improve the employment status of women, visible minorities, aboriginals, and people with disabilities.

Employment Equity Act
info.load-otea.hrdc-drhc.
gc.ca/~weeweb/lege.htm

The federal **Employment Equity Act** (**EEA**) came into effect in 1986. It applies to federal Crown corporations and federally regulated private-sector organizations with at least 100 employees. The *Act* requires that such employers file a report annually that indicates the representation of the four designated groups in a comprehensive set of 12 occupational categories, also providing comparative data on salary range, hiring, promotion and terminations. It also requires employers to meet with representatives of the groups involved to identify and eliminate employment barriers. Employers are further required to prepare an annual employment equity plan including numerical goals and timetables. Of these three requirements, however, only the annual report is subject to specific sanctions (with fines up to $50,000) if an employer does not comply. However, legislation before Parliament in 1995 included several measures to strengthen and extend the provisions of the EEA.

A number of employers regulated by provincial employment legislation are still subject to federal employment equity initiatives. The Federal Contractors Program, a provision of the EEA, applies to companies with at least 100 employees that bid on federal government contracts of $200,000 or more. Such employers must commit to designing and carrying out an employment equity plan addressing the four designated groups, and are subject to on-site compliance reviews. Failure to comply can lead to exclusion from bidding for subsequent contracts. Some 1.1 million workers were working for employers certified under this program as of March 1996.[28]

Mandatory equity programs in provincial jurisdictions are relatively rare, with Quebec having a contract compliance program[29] and Ontario having legislation that applies to provincial and municipal police forces.[30] *Voluntary* affirmative action programs are legally acceptable in most Canadian jurisdictions, often making provisions for human rights commissions to assist employers in such initiatives.

The effectiveness of Canadian employment equity legislation in redressing the imbalance in the employment of women, aboriginal people, visible minorities, and people with disabilities has yet to be established. Clearly, the imbalances are still substantial, but it would be premature to conclude that the law will fail to result in change. For affected employers, employment equity represents not only an obligation, but also an opportunity to identify capable and motivated employees whose progress may have been unintentionally blocked.

■ Pay and Equity

Estimates of women's pay compared with that of men indicate that, for men and women employed full time, women earn on average no more than 70 percent of what men earn. This pattern is partially attributable to differences in education, experience, and the occupational mix for men and women. However, roughly 20 percent of the differential (about six to seven percent of male earnings) cannot be attributed to such factors and is thought to indicate the extent to which pay discrimination is reflected in overall compensation. This pervasive pattern has resulted in **pay equity** legislation designed to reduce the effects of such discrimination.

Every Canadian jurisdiction has requires *equal pay for "the same or similar" work* within the employing organization. These laws, which in some cases are reflected in employment standards and sometimes in human rights codes, allow for differences based on performance, experience and other factors, but prohibit sex-based discrimination. These laws focus on comparisons of people doing the same work, although court decisions have defined "same" as broader than "identical." These laws are enforced on a complaint-trigger basis, and violations can result in fines.

"Equal pay for equal work" laws have been augmented by laws intended to ensure *equal pay for work of equal value* in the federal jurisdiction, Manitoba, Nova Scotia, Ontario, Prince Edward Island, Quebec, and the Yukon. Such laws require comparing the value of jobs with different content. Administratively, this is more complicated for an employer or a government agency to apply. It is no longer a matter of determining whether two people are doing essentially the same job, but rather whether jobs with dissimilar content have the same value. Job evaluation (see Chapter 10) becomes an important element because a common measurement of value is needed.

You might wonder why the "equal value" laws were developed, given the complexity in administering them. Equal pay for the same or similar work left many women unaffected. Historically, some 60 percent of all women work in 20 of some 500 occupational classifications, concentrated in clerical, non-commission sales, and service occupations.[31] For example, women in teaching represent 63 percent of that group, and some 86 percent of nurses are women.[32] This occupational segregation has often led to large numbers of women working in occupations that have poor levels of pay and are often undervalued. In many cases, there were no men doing the same or nearly the same jobs within an organization, and comparisons were therefore impossible. "Equal value" has been seen as a standard that can remove that obstruction.

The jurisdictions with the most comprehensive pay equity coverage are the federal jurisdiction, Quebec, and Ontario, where virtually all public and private employers are covered. Manitoba, Nova Scotia, Prince Edward Island, and the Yukon have laws that are restricted to the public sector. The only jurisdiction that requires proactive employer behaviour (as opposed to complaint-prompted responses or voluntary initiatives) is Ontario. The Ontario pay equity law has been amended several times since its initial passage in 1988 to include increasingly broader comparison techniques to increase the proportion of women whose jobs can be compared. The Ontario law focusses on comparing female-dominated job classes (those in which at least 60 percent of the incumbents are women) with male-dominated jobs (70 percent or more male), requiring that the comparisons be made on a gender-neutral composite assessment of required skill, effort, responsibility, and working conditions.

pay equity

Legislation designed to reduce the pattern of pay discrimination that women experience.

Manager's Notebook

Designing Flexible Work Areas to Adapt to Employees with Disabilities

By planning ahead when designing work areas, employers can easily accommodate employees with disabilities. Here are some tips for designing flexible work areas:

1. Use panel systems so that work spaces can be easily modified and work surface heights raised and lowered as needed.

2. Install electronically controlled work surfaces and tables.

3. Lower storage areas or install storage areas that are mobile.

4. Install adjustable keyboard pads that adjust easily with little hand pressure.

5. Install adjustable lighting with variable intensity that can add more or less light to the work space as needed.

SOURCE: Some quick tips to make workspaces more flexible. (1992, July). *HR Focus, 69*, 12–14. New York: American Management Association. Reprinted by permission of the publisher. All rights reserved.

Pay equity is most problematic for employers in cases in which the law is least precise. At the federal level, a July 1998 ruling by a tribunal established by the Canadian Human Rights Commission ruled that the federal government had underpaid workers in female-dominated jobs over the previous 13 years by an amount that totalled billions of dollars. While negotiations and appeals can amend such results, the implication for failing to establish equitable compensation can be very expensive.[33]

▊ A Snapshot of Equal Opportunity Law in the United States

"Equal opportunity" law in the United States is relevant to Canadian HR practitioners. The political and social dynamics at work there have also had an influence on Canadian political culture, although the resulting legal regime in the United States is different from that in Canada. As more Canadian employers have U.S. operations, and as the overall internationalization of business increases, a general familiarity with the similarities and differences between the United States and Canada is important.

U.S. employment standards and human rights are regulated by federal legislation and the U.S. Constitution with its *Bill of Rights*. Thus, the Canadian pattern of variability among provinces has no true counterpart in the United States. The federal laws most directly relevant to the issues of this chapter are:

◆ *The Equal Pay Act of 1963*. The statute is a pay equity law as defined in this chapter. It prohibits different pay for men and women doing the same job in the same organization. Merit pay and seniority are acceptable. The pay differential (women's pay as a fraction of men's pay) in the United States has increased from 59 percent in 1963 to 71 percent in 1992.[34] Some states, such as Washington and Illinois, have required civil service employees to be paid on the basis of comparable worth.[35]

◆ *Title VII of the Civil Rights Act of 1964*. This legislation, amended several times since initially passed, is the most important of the U.S. civil rights laws with respect to employment. It prohibits employers from basing employment decisions on a person's race, colour, religion, sex, or national origin, thus addressing the issues addressed by human rights codes in Canada. It includes prohibition of discrimination in the form of "disparate treatment" (intentional discrimination) as well as "adverse impact" (systemic) discrimination. The prohibition of sex-based discrimination has been interpreted by the courts to prohibit sexual harassment, whether it be "quid pro quo" harassment (where requests for sexual favours are involved) or "hostile work environment." The *Civil Rights Act of 1991* has added specific provisions that shift the burden of proof toward the employer in discrimination cases and allow punitive and compensatory damages, in addition to recovery of back pay.[36]

◆ *The Age Discrimination in Employment Act of 1967*. This law prohibits employment discrimination for people between age 40 and an upper limit that was initially 65, but now has been removed.

◆ *The Americans with Disabilities Act of 1990*. Title I of the *Act* applies to employment, identifying various physical or mental activities that may be impaired. The *Act* requires employers to distinguish between *essential* functions and *marginal* functions in a job and requires employment decisions to be made on the basis of essential functions only. Employers are expected to make reasonable accommodation for known disabilities.

The pursuit of equity.

The Public Service Alliance, having won a human rights claim to redress pay discrimination against female employees of the federal government, urges the government to comply with the decision.

Enforcement and compliance are the responsibility of two government agencies, the Equal Employment Opportunity Commission (EEOC), which was created by Title VII, and the Office of Federal Contract Compliance Programs. EEOC procedures are generally triggered by complaints, and the number of complaints has increased sharply in recent years.[37] If a plausible case for discrimination is found by the EEOC, a mediation process among the parties is attempted. If a satisfactory solution is not found, the EEOC can either sue on the employee's behalf (an expensive and infrequent choice) or can issue a right-to-sue letter to the complainant, who has the option to pursue the issue in court. The EEOC, unlike human rights commissions in Canada, cannot set penalties on its own authority, that power being reserved to the courts.

Summary and Conclusions

Why Understanding the Legal Environment Is Important.
Understanding and complying with the legal environment is important because (1) it is the right thing to do, (2) it underlines the importance of the shared responsibilities between HR professionals and the rest of management in complying with legal requirements, and (3) it helps limit the risk of financial liability and public relations problems associated with non-compliance.

An Overview of the Legal Context.
Employment in Canada occurs within a complex legal context. Many employment relationships are governed by provincial jurisdiction, so that there are 13 human rights codes (10 provinces, two territories, and the federal jurisdiction) and 13 differing acts establishing employment standards. The legal framework includes not only legislation, but also constitutional principles embedded in the *Charter of Rights and Freedoms*, the accumulated body of common law, and the specific provisions of contract law. This chapter examined employment standards legislation, human rights codes, and employment pay equity in some detail. Later chapters deal with legal influences such as wrongful dismissal principles, Employment Insurance, pension and taxation legislation, labour relations law, health and safety, and workers' compensation.

Fairness: The Intended Purpose.
Attempting to provide a legal framework that ensures an equitable or "fair" relationship between employer and employee is a central concern in much employment law. Recognizing that employers typically have more intrinsic power in employment relationships than individual employees, most employment law either obliges employers to do certain things (e.g., pay a minimum wage) or prohibits them from doing others (e.g., discriminating on the basis of race).

Employment Standards: The Basic "Deal."
Employment standards laws define a minimum set of obligations on the part of the employer, establish limits to the length of the work week, and stipulate employee entitlements to such benefits as statutory holidays, maternity and required other leaves or absences, and a definition of how much notice an employee must receive if he or she is to be terminated.

The Law and Discrimination.
Although the word "discrimination" is often associated with biased or prejudiced decisions, *any* choice involves discrimination. What the law attempts to forbid is *unfair* discrimination. The definition of unfair discrimination is the result of a political and social process of seeking a consensus. Some characteristics including race and sex are clearly seen as inappropriate as grounds for discrimination under the law. Others, such as sexual orientation, have gained legal protection in some jurisdictions, but not in others.

Human Rights Legislation.
Personal beliefs or cultural practices can influence managers and HR professionals in ways that are generally considered to be unfair. The *Charter of Rights and Freedoms*, part of the Canadian Constitution, applies to government and to laws passed by government, prohibiting discrimination on the basis of race, national or ethnic origin, colour, religion, sex, age, or cognitive or physical disability. Human rights codes now exist in every Canadian jurisdiction, prohibiting discrimination by employers on the basis of *Charter* stipulations.

Both intentional discrimination and systemic discrimination are illegal. Systemic discrimination occurs when employer decisions or policies have an adverse impact on groups protected by human rights legislation. An employer is allowed to discriminate against a member of a protected group if that decision is based on a bona fide occupation requirement (BFOR). However, the courts have developed the doctrine of "reasonable accommodation," which requires that an employer wishing to claim a BFOR must be able to demonstrate that accommodating the applicant was not possible with minor modifications to the job, the work environment, or the work rules that apply.

Human rights laws are generally enforced based on complaints received. Violations, if not resolved through a conciliation process, can be penalized both through financial assessment against employers and through requiring employers to take actions to restore or improve the human rights standards applied in their actions.

Equity in the Workplace: Legal Initiatives.   While human rights codes prohibit discriminatory behaviour, they are not proactive in trying to change the disadvantaged status of protected groups. In contrast, employment equity legislation is proactive. It identifies four groups: women, visible minorities, people with disabilities, and aboriginal people, and encourages employers affected by the law to take steps to employ more people from these groups and to remove the barriers to their advancement. The federal equity legislation is the single most important example, and the provisions of the Federal Contractors Program extend this initiative beyond the narrowly defined federal jurisdiction.

Pay equity is focussed on the most persistent employment discrepancies—for example, the difference in average pay for men and for women. Pay equity laws tend to focus on comparisons between male-dominated and female-dominated jobs, and are moving toward the standard of equal pay for work of equal value to increase the number of women whose jobs can be included.

A Snapshot of Equal Opportunity Laws in the United States.   The size and proximity of the United States, and the extensive economic connections between the U.S. and Canada, make their experience and practices relevant to Canadians. U.S. employment laws are more centralized than in Canada, with Title VII of the 1964 *Civil Rights Act* creating the Equal Employment Opportunity Commission (EEOC), which plays the major role in enforcement of the prohibition against discrimination on the basis of race, colour, religion, sex, or ethnic origin. Subsequent legislation has provided protection against discrimination on the basis of age (over 40) and disability.

Key Terms and Concepts

bona fide occupational requirement (BFOR), 95
Canadian Human Rights Act, 93
Charter of Rights and Freedoms, 92
common law, 86
constitutional law, 86
contract law, 86
deemed termination, 91

Employment Equity Act (EEA), 100
employment equity, 100
employment standards, 88
equal pay for "the same or similar" work, 101
equal pay for work of equal value, 101
glass ceiling, 92
harassment, 96
intentional discrimination, 94

legal framework for employment, 86
minimum wage, 88
pay equity, 101
punitive damage, 85
reasonable accommodation, 95
remedies, 85
systemic discrimination, 94

Discussion Questions

1. Why should managers be concerned with understanding human resource law instead of leaving it to experts?
2. Explain why human resource management is so heavily regulated. Based on your analysis of current social forces, what new laws or regulations do you think will be passed or issued in the next few years?
3. Suppose your boss tells you that she has reviewed the human rights code for your province and doesn't understand how sexual harassment is covered. How would you explain the legal basis of the prohibition of sexual harassment?
4. You own a construction business. One of your employees is 55 years old and had heart bypass surgery about six months ago. He wants to come back to work, but you are

concerned about his ability to handle some of the job's physical tasks. What do you think you are legally obliged to do? What are you legally prohibited from doing?

5. There has been some suggestion that the way to deal with chronically high unemployment is to reduce the maximum work week in employment standards legislation from 40 to 36 or even fewer hours, and/or sharply raise the overtime rates required, so that employers will be induced to spread the available work among more people. Evaluate this idea. Would it produce the desired effect?
6. Some human rights commissions in Canada have included substance dependence (alcohol and other drugs) as a disability/handicap. How does this affect the usefulness of drug testing as a selection procedure?

Check out our companion Website at: **www.prenticehall.ca/gomez** for a selection of self-study questions, key terms and concepts, updated Weblinks to related Internet sites, newsgroups, CBC video updates, and more.

MiniCase 1   *Spousal Identity*

Robert LeBlanc, a management employee with Canada Post Corporation, married a female employee of the Corporation who was employed in a unionized position. The general climate between the union and the employer at that time was tense and antagonistic. Upon returning to work after getting married, both received a rough reception including taunts, jeers, and harassing posters. LeBlanc's wife filed a human rights complaint because of the harassment and management's lack of response. LeBlanc was told by management that he and his wife had "gotten what they deserved," and that things would "blow over" if she dropped the complaint. LeBlanc's relationships with his unionized subordinates deteriorated, and pressure from the union led to his reassignment to a lower managerial position. The Canadian Human Rights Commission accepted LeBlanc's complaint that he had been discriminated against on the basis of marital status (which the Commission deemed to include "spousal identity"). The Commission found that management should have worked to alleviate the problems faced by LeBlanc and his wife rather than to be dismissive. LeBlanc was awarded $5,500 for hurt feelings and loss of income.

Discussion Questions

1. Why is harassment considered to be the responsibility of the employer? What might management have done in this case to reduce it?
2. How do you react to a human rights commission's expanding the concept of "marital status" (which usually means *whether* you are single, living common law, married, divorced, or widowed) to include "spousal identity" (that is, *who* your spouse is)? If employers received such an expanded interpretation, what recourse would they have?
3. Should an employer have an explicit policy on whether spouses are allowed to work in the same workplace? If so, are there any limits on the *work* relationships they are allowed to have?

SOURCE: Marital status discrimination. (1992, July). *Human Resources Management in Canada*. Report Bulletin 113 (p. 7). Toronto: Prentice Hall Canada.

MiniCase 2   *Racial Discrimination?*

John Lilley worked part time for a doughnut shop in British Columbia. He was fired because, according to his employer, he did not show up for a shift for which he was scheduled to work. He filed a human rights complaint and eventually won a settlement of $2,300 for lost wages and humiliation. Not showing up for scheduled work *can* be a legitimate basis for dismissal. However, the employer's case was compromised by two factors. First, there were no records to corroborate the schedule or work assignments, or to document attendance. Second, Lilley, an aboriginal Canadian, testified that he had heard his supervisor tell customers that he (Lilley) was being let go, indicating "...we don't want Indians hanging around here."

Discussion Questions

1. How much evidence of prejudice is necessary to make a compelling case? In this case, the statement of the complainant was the only direct evidence of the employer's intention. Should any further evidence be required?
2. If some customers or clients prefer not to deal with minorities (or women, or other groups protected under human rights legislation), should an employer be permitted to take that into account in selecting employees or in deciding which employees do which jobs?

SOURCE: Employer without records loses complaint. (1993, January). *Human Resources Management in Canada*. Report Bulletin 119 (p. 6). Toronto: Prentice Hall Canada.

Case 1

A Surprise Complaint

Several employees of Asian background in an electronics assembly and distribution facility have filed a human rights complaint because they feel the company's promotion patterns are racially biased.

Marcia Roberts, the plant manager, is surprised by the complaint. She was in charge when the current policy was put in place, and she knows that it was carefully designed to ensure fair treatment for all employees. Employees are chosen for a supervisory training program based on their supervisors' evaluations of them. The performance appraisal form on which these evaluations are recorded asks supervisors to rate each employee on each of the following 10 dimensions on a five-point scale from "outstanding" to "unsatisfactory:"

- knowledge of work
- dependability
- productivity
- safety
- quality of output
- cooperation
- initiative
- judgement
- relationships with others
- organizing and planning

The assumption behind the company's promotion policy—that supervisors are the most qualified people to decide whether a subordinate might make a good supervisor—has always seemed fair and reasonable to Roberts. However, she has to admit that very few of the plant's Asian-background employees have been selected under this policy to enter the training program.

Critical Thinking Questions

1. What type of discrimination is being alleged by the employees who are making the complaint?
2. If this case were to go before a human rights commission, what features of the promotion decision process would the commission be most likely to scrutinize?
3. How can the company defend itself in this case?

Cooperative Learning Exercise

4. Students form groups of six. Each group is given the task of suggesting ways to change the promotion decision process so that it is more legally defensible.

SOURCE: Ledvinka, J., & Scarpello, V. G. (1991). *Federal regulation of personnel and human resource management* (2nd ed.). Boston: PWS-Kent.

Case 2

Is This an Opportunity I Can Afford to Turn Down?

Shelagh McLeod is the human resource director for a medium-sized producer of sports and outdoor apparel: T-shirts, "sweats," rain gear, and the like. Most of the company's 400 employees work at sewing machines, but the firm also employs designers, engineers, buyers, warehouse personnel, and a diverse range of office and support personnel.

McLeod is concerned about her company's status in terms of accommodating people with disabilities. Although regulated by the provincial human rights code, the company also bids on contracts from the federal government, and needs to be in compliance with the employment equity requirements of the Federal Contractors Program. A local non-profit organization that offers vocational skill training for people with various disabilities has contacted her to see whether McLeod's firm would consider recruiting their "graduates." She is interested, but at the same time concerned. The factory is in an old building with awkward access from the street, and antiquated freight elevators provide the only mechanical access among the four floors. This firm, like many in the industry, has been dominated by conventional practices that include only rudimentary job descriptions. However, the business is very competitive and margins are thin, making it difficult to find substantial funds to do renovations or install sophisticated HR polices and systems. By opening the door to the new source of disabled recruits, McLeod wonders whether this approach is likely to create more problems than it solves.

Critical Thinking Questions

1. Are McLeod's concerns justified?
2. What steps would be necessary before McLeod is ready to recruit from this new source?

Cooperative Learning Exercises

3. Students form groups of five and role-play a task force put together by McLeod. This task force includes employees from each of the major departments. The task is to explore ways the organization can make reasonable accommodations that make the company more accessible to people with disabilities.
4. Students form pairs. One takes the role of McLeod, the other the director of the non-profit organization. McLeod expresses her interests as well as her concerns about recruiting from the training program. The director tries to alleviate those concerns, sharing her experience of dealing with human rights bodies at both provincial and federal levels. Role-play the discussion.

Appendix to Chapter 3

A GUIDE TO SCREENING AND SELECTION IN EMPLOYMENT

SUBJECT	AVOID ASKING	PREFERRED	COMMENT
Name	about name change: whether it was changed by court order, marriage, or other reason maiden name		ask after selection if needed to check on previously held jobs or educational credentials
Address	for addresses outside Canada	ask place and duaration of current or recent address	
Age	for birth certificates, baptismal records, or about age in general	ask applicants if they are eligible to work under Canadian laws regarding age restrictions	if precise age required for benefits plans or other legitimate purposes, it can be determined after selection
Sex	males or females to fill in different applications about pregnancy, child bearing plans, or child care arrangements	can ask applicant if the attendance requirements can be met	during the interview or after selection, the applicant, for purposes of courtesy, may be asked which of Mr/Mrs/Miss/Ms is preferred
Marital Status	whether applicant is single, married, divorced, engaged, separated, widowed, or living common law whether an applicant's spouse is subject to transfer about spouse's employment	if transfer or travel is part of the job, the applicant can be asked if he or she can meet these requirements ask whether there are any circumstances that might prevent completion of a minimum service commitment	information on dependents can be determined after selection if necessary
Family Status	number of children or dependents about child care arrangements	if the applicant would be able to work the required hours and, where applicable, overtime	contacts for emergencies and/or details on dependents can be determined after selection
National or Ethnic Origin	about birthplace, nationality of ancestors, spouse, or other relatives whether born in Canada for proof of citizenship	since those who are entitled to work in Canada must be citizens, permanent residents, or holders of valid work permits, applicants can be asked if they are legally entitled to work in Canada	documentation of eligibility to work (papers, visas, etc.) can be requested after selection
Military Service	about military service in other countries	inquiry about Canadian military service where employment preference is given to veterans by law	
Language	mother tongue where language skills obtained	ask if applicant understands, reads, writes, or speaks languages required for the job	testing or scoring applicants for language proficiency is not permitted unless job related
Race or Colour	any inquiry into race or colour, including colour of eyes, skin, or hair		
Photographs	for photo to be attached to applications or sent to interviewer before interview		photos for security passes or company files can be taken after selection
Religion	about religious affiliation, church membership, frequency of church attendance if applicant will work a specific religious holiday for references from clergy or religious leader	explain the required work shift, asking if such a schedule poses problems for the applicant	reasonable accommodation of an employee's religious beliefs is the employer's duty
Height and Weight			no inquiry unless there is evidence they are genuine occupational requirements
Disability	for listing of all disabilities, limitations, or health problems whether applicant drinks or uses drugs whether applicant has ever received psychiatric care or been hospitalized for emotional problems whether applicant has received workers' compensation	ask if applicant has any condition that could affect ability to do the job ask if applicant has any condition that should be considered in selection	a disability is only relevant to job ability if it: – threatens the safety or property of others – prevents the applicant from safe and adequate job performance even when reasonable efforts are made to accommodate the disability
Medical Information	if currently under physician's care name of family doctor if receiving counselling or therapy		medical exams should be conducted after selection and only if an employee's condition is related to job duties offers of employment can be made conditional on successful completion of a medical
Pardoned Conviction	whether an applicant has ever been convicted if an applicant has ever been arrested whether an applicant has a criminal record	if bonding is a job requirement ask if applicant is eligible	inquiries about criminal record/convictions are discouraged unless related to job duties
Sexual Orientation	any inquiry about the applicant's sexual orientation		contacts for emergencies and/or details on dependents can be determined after selection
References			the same restrictions that apply to questions asked of applicants apply when asking for employment references

SOURCE: Canadian Human Rights Commission (1995). *A Guide to Screening and Selection in Employment*. Ottawa: Minister of Supply and Services. Reproduced with permission of the Minister of Supply and Services Canada, 1993.

Managing Workforce Diversity

After reading this chapter, you should be able to deal more effectively with the following challenges:

1 Link employment equity programs to employee diversity programs to ensure that they support each other.

2 Identify the forces that contribute to the successful management of employee diversity within an organization.

3 Reduce potential conflict among employees resulting from cultural clashes and misunderstandings.

4 Draw a profile of employee groups that are less likely to be part of the corporate mainstream and develop policies specifically directed to these groups' needs.

5 Implement human resource systems that assist the organization in successfully managing employee diversity.

Celebrating diversity. The Canadian workforce grows more diverse with each passing year. Progressive and effective companies recognize that this diversity can be the source of greater creativity, better problem solving, and increased enthusiasm in the workplace. Such advantages can provide an organization with a powerful competitive advantage in the global marketplace.

The grade two teacher in an urban school posed what she thought was a very straightforward problem for her class. She said, "There are four blackbirds sitting in a tree. Someone shoots a stone with a slingshot and hits one of them. How many blackbirds are left?"

"Three," answered one of her attentive young students, who had lived a couple blocks from the school all his life.

"Zero," answered another keen seven-year-old. "If you shoot one blackbird, the others will fly away." This student's family had recently immigrated to Canada and had previously lived in a rural area.

The problem, it turns out, was not so simple. Which child answered correctly? That depends on the frame of reference you apply. For the first child, the birds represented a hypothetical situation (similar to others used to teach math skills) that required a computational answer. For the second seven-year-old, the question was understood to be about how birds behave, something that was quite familiar from experience.[1]

The blackbird story clearly illustrates something that is true of all people, not just of children: our life experiences shape our perception of what is going on and, therefore, which behaviour is called for. Human resource management has to accommodate the reality that people will behave on the basis of what they perceive, not necessarily on "objective reality." People's *cognitive structure*—the way they perceive and relate to the world around them—is shaped by both personal experiences (with family, peers, the school system) and by the socializing influences of the larger culture that has shaped their development. Managing workforce diversity in a way that both respects the employee and promotes a shared sense of corporate identity and vision is one of the greatest human resource challenges facing organizations today. In Canada, as elsewhere, the design and implementation of HR programs cannot ignore the diverse nature of the work force. By the end of this chapter, you should have a broader understanding of diversity issues and have some insights on how employers can handle them successfully.

▇ What Is Diversity?

Although definitions vary, **diversity** simply refers to human characteristics that make people different from one another. The English language has more than 23,000 words to describe personality[2] (such as "outgoing," "intelligent," "friendly," "loyal," "paranoid," and "nerdy"). The sources of individual variation are complex, but they can generally be grouped into two categories: those over which we have little or no control and those over which we have more control.[3]

Individual characteristics over which a person has little or no control include biologically determined characteristics such as race, sex, age, and certain physical attributes, as well as the family and society into which we are born. These factors exert a powerful influence on individual identity and directly affect how a person relates to other individuals and groups in general and at work.

HRM on the Web

http://www.ccla.org/news/index.shtml

Canadian Civil Liberties Association

The Canadian Civil Liberties Association (CCLA) is a member-supported non-profit organization that provides a "voice" for the interests of individuals when those liberties are seen to be unfairly threatened by public policy, government, or other forces or institutions in society. Often, members of disadvantaged groups are among those most likely to experience such treatment. By monitoring this Web site, it is possible to identify the groups and issues that are likely to move into high profile.

diversity
Human characteristics that make people different from one another.

In the second category are characteristics that people can adopt, drop, or modify during their lives through conscious choice and deliberate efforts. These include work background, income, marital status, political beliefs, geographic location, and education.

It is important to keep in mind the distinction between the sources of diversity and the diversity itself. Without this distinction, stereotyping tends to occur. For instance, the *Meyers-Briggs Type Indicator* has identified differences between men and women on "ways of deciding and evaluating." (On several other dimensions, there are no significant sex-associated differences.) One way of deciding and thinking is labelled "thinking," an approach that emphasizes logic and objective considerations using impersonal analysis and principles. The other way is "feeling," an approach that bases decisions on personal, subjective values including a concern for the impact of decisions on people, an emphasis on harmony, compassion, and accommodation. While virtually nobody is completely "thinking" or completely "feeling" in their approach, the Meyers-Briggs method determines which of the two is dominant for an individual. Men are more likely to be classified as "thinking" personalities and women as "feeling" personalities. However, this is only part of the story. Although more men are more likely to be "thinking," not all men are. In fact, only about 60% of men are "thinking" while 40% are "feeling." Similarly, roughly 40% of women use a predominantly "thinking" approach, while 60% use a "feeling" approach to deciding and evaluating.[4] Drawing a conclusion about whether a particular man or woman is likely to emphasize "thinking" or "feeling," based on this knowledge about men (or women) as a group, is risky. In both cases, you have only slightly better than a 50–50 chance of being correct.

If you take this example and substitute another personal attribute (e.g., age, level of education, socioeconomic status) and any human trait (e.g., aggressiveness, intellectual flexibility, authoritarianism), you will find in a majority of circumstances that the pattern in Figure 4–1 holds true. In fact, it is difficult to find any human attribute that does not have substantial overlap among various groups. The point to remember is that while employees do differ greatly, only a small amount of this diversity is explained by differences among groups.

As we proceed through this chapter, we will point out some characteristics that are typical of specific groups. Such depictions are both valuable and dangerous. They are valuable because they alert managers to diversity in their employees. But they are dangerous because it is very easy to fall into the trap of assuming that a group tendency is true of all individual employees. The effective manager sees his or her employees as individuals, not as members of a particular group. As we saw in Chapter 3, it is illegal to base employment decisions on certain group characteristics. The laws reviewed in that chapter merely codify an important principle of effective management: Treat people as individuals, not as representatives of a group.

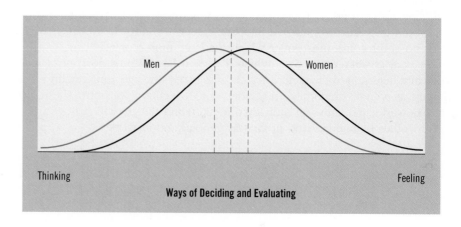

Figure 4–1 Group versus Individual Differences on Ways of Deciding and Evaluating

■ Why Manage Employee Diversity?

Unless effectively managed, the presence of diversity among employees may have a negative impact on work performance by creating misunderstandings, ill feelings, and a breakdown of productive teamwork. It may also result in overt or subtle discrimination by those who control organizational resources against those who do not fit the dominant group.

For several years, a dispute over uniform requirements in the RCMP provided a public forum that displayed the kind of issues involved. The specific issue revolved around the effect of requiring the Stetson as a mandatory part of the uniform on Sikhs who wished to join the RCMP. The Sikh religion requires male adherents to wear a turban, have uncut hair and facial hair, and wear a *kirpan*, a ceremonial dagger. Following some controversy, the RCMP revised its policy on uniforms in a way that accommodated Sikh religious requirements. Three former RCMP officers and a wife of a former officer challenged this policy in court, but received an unequivocal court ruling supporting the RCMP's accommodation policy. Among the Federal Court of Appeal's findings were that "[the RCMP] was not seeking to weaken the institution, but to strengthen it," that "the purpose of the change was ... to reflect the newer multicultural nature of Canada," and that "Other groups are in no way prejudiced by this policy allowing Sikhs an exception."[5]

While there was strong public feeling in some quarters that a Canadian "institution" shouldn't be altered and that religious symbols should not be allowed in policing, police have found that having officers from different racial and ethnic backgrounds, particularly when language skills are important, is crucial to effective policing among communities of recent immigrants.

Excluding certain people from full participation in an organization because of their group membership is not only illegal, it is counter-productive because it prevents capable and motivated people from making a contribution. To survive and prosper in an increasingly multicultural and diverse society, organizations must capitalize on employee diversity as a source of competitive advantage. Like the advantages gained by police forces, private-sector companies such as Levi Strauss find that promoting and valuing diversity not only makes good ethical sense; it makes good financial sense as well. Levi Strauss executives say it is easier to develop and design merchandise for markets when you understand them, and that understanding begins in the workplace.

RCMP Changes Dress Regulations.

RCMP uniform regulations have been changed to accommodate variations based on religious obligation.

RCMP
www.rcmp-grc.gc.ca

■ Employment Equity versus Managing Employee Diversity

Many people perceive "management of diversity" as another term for employment equity. In reality, these are two very distinct concepts. Affirmative action programs to increase employment equity are permitted in most Canadian jurisdictions, and often the human rights body with authority will review and advise an employer with respect to a program the employer may be considering to assure that the program does not infringe the human rights of other groups. **Management of diversity,** in contrast, recognizes that firms in which white male employees without disabilities form a majority are becoming a thing of the past. An emerging key factor shaping organizational performance is how well *non-traditional employees* such as women and visible minorities can be integrated and work effectively with one another and the traditional work force.

The push behind employee diversity originated and found its strongest advocates among private corporations in the 1980s. It has continued despite an apparent retreat from aggressive employment equity in some Canadian jurisdictions. Many corporations now see diversity management as a business necessity rather than a means to achieve public policy goals or meet government requirements. Several factors provide a rationale for active diversity management. These include demographic trends, the potential of diversity to be an asset, and marketing considerations.

management of diversity
The set of activities involved in integrating non-traditional employees into the work force and using their diversity to enhance the firm's effectiveness.

Demographic Trends.   Consider the following facts:

◆ Visible minorities represented slightly less than 10% of the Canadian population in 1991, but by 2001, projections indicate that the percentage will increase to over 17%.[6] In 1991, more than four million Canadian residents (or 15% of the population) had a first language other than French or English, an increase from roughly three million in 1981. Some 380,000 could speak neither official language, of which group 28% spoke Chinese as a first language, 15% Italian, and 11% Portuguese.[7]

◆ Although still a relatively small percentage (about 3% of the population), people identifying themselves of non-Christian Eastern religions (Islam, Buddhism, Hinduism, and others) increased at a dramatic rate (244%) between 1981 and 1991, during which the number of Canadians indicating "no religion" increased about 90%, to 3.3 million people.[8]

◆ Some 4.2 million Canadians, or 16% of the population, identify themselves as having disabilities; many of them (almost 60% of those between the ages of 35 and 54) are employed, and many others would like to be.[9]

◆ The population is getting older—the proportion of people below 14 years of age decreased from 27% in 1974 to 20.4% in 1994, while during the same period, the proportion over 65 increased from 8.3% to 11.9%, trends that are projected to continue.[10]

◆ Canada is a highly urbanized country and is becoming more so—in 1991, there were four metropolitan areas with a population in excess of one million people: Toronto (4,281,900), Montreal (3,344,400), Vancouver (1,774,700), and Ottawa/Hull (1,010,300). Five other metropolitan areas—Edmonton, Calgary, Quebec, Hamilton, and Winnipeg—had populations in excess of 500,000. These nine centres accounted for slightly less than 80% of Canada's total population.[11]

◆ Women are participating in the labour market at the highest level in history, with patterns approaching those of men in several age categories.

The brief sketch that these numbers provide suggests a changing, dynamic employment environment in Canada, one that looks markedly different from two or three decades ago. It is different because the racial and ethnic composition of the population is becoming more varied. It is also changing because groups that traditionally had very circumscribed roles in the work force (women, the disabled, and so forth) are now participating much more frequently and, in many cases, are aspiring to career options that were formerly unavailable. What Canada is and will increasingly become is an urban, multicultural country with generally high average levels of education and a work force in which barriers based on gender, disability, and age will become increasingly unacceptable. Human resource management needs to take account of these changes.

Together, all these demographic changes are making it imperative that employers plan for the central role that the management of diversity will play in the 21st century. The forces of international competition (discussed in Chapter 17) are creating increased pressure to produce higher-quality goods and services at competitive prices and to accelerate the rate of technological innovation. The Canadian record over the past few decades in many sectors of the economy, contrasted with that of foreign competition, has not always been impressive. Canadian employers can respond to these challenges by treating diversity as an asset and by capitalizing on the different strengths it brings to the work force.

Efficiency the Key.

One of the industries that has historically provided employment for a significant number of Canadians, including recent immigrants, is the needle trade. Garment manufacturing and related businesses currently face increasing global competition.

Diversity as an Asset.   Once, human diversity was understood to be a liability leading to garbled communications and disorganization. Today, many organizations realize that employee diversity can actually enhance organizational effectiveness. There are at least two main business-related arguments—beyond ethics and legal compliance—for pursuing employment equity: the globalization of world trade and the increasing ethnocultural diversity of Canadian markets.[12] There are also useful changes in internal decision processes. Employee diversity can improve organizational functioning by stimulating greater creativity, improving problem solving, and increasing the organization's flexibility.[13] Rosabeth Kanter, a well-known business consultant based at Harvard University, notes that most innovative firms purposely establish heterogeneous work groups "to create a marketplace of ideas, recognizing that a multiplicity of points of view need to be brought to bear on a problem."[14]

◆ *Greater creativity.* Employee diversity can stimulate consideration of less obvious alternatives. Consider the following story:

   Two female employees, one white and the other from a visible minority, were members of a task force advising a CEO on a proposed organizational downsizing. The recommendation of the majority of the task force was to reduce the work force by 10 percent through layoffs, a move that would have been devastating to morale. The majority, who were white males, initially felt that these two members were allowing their "soft hearts" to interfere with the need to make a hard-nosed business decision. Upon further consultation, the CEO decided not to lay off employees but, instead, opted for the plan proposed by these two women and seconded by the rest of the committee. The plan proposed to reduce labour costs through a combination of voluntary early retirement, unpaid vacations, and stock in the firm combined with a five percent salary cut. Most employees reacted very positively to the plan, with many reporting that it had increased their loyalty and commitment to the firm.[15]

◆ *Better problem solving.* Groups that are homogeneous are prone to a phenomenon called *groupthink,* in which all members quickly converge on a mistaken solution because they all share the same mindset and view the problem through the lens of uniformity.[16]

◆ *Greater system flexibility.* In today's rapidly changing business environments, flexibility is an important characteristic of successful firms. If properly managed, employee diversity can infuse more flexibility into the firm. The mere presence of diversity at different organizational levels generates openness to new ideas in general and greater tolerance for different ways of doing things.

Marketing Concerns.   Most members of visible minority groups in Canada live in large metropolitan areas. Their concentration in these areas means that there are significant markets for consumer products and services that may differ from other markets. And, although many members of visible minority groups will face some challenges not faced by mainstream employees, it is estimated that they will have a per capita Gross Domestic Product of $54,560 in 2001, compared with an overall Canadian average of $50,055. Thus, with about 18 percent of the population and 20 percent of the GDP by the beginning of the next century, visible minorities represent a very important part of the market.[17] Many organizations, including the Bank of Montreal, have undertaken programs that will ensure that their work force resembles their clientele. Such programs not only make clients more comfortable with the organizations they are dealing with, but they also provide an insight for the organization into differences in customer needs and preferences that might otherwise be overlooked.

■ Challenges in Managing Employee Diversity

Although employee diversity offers opportunities that can enhance organizational performance, it also presents managers with a new set of challenges. These challenges include appropriately valuing employee diversity, balancing individual needs with group fairness, dealing with resistance to change, ensuring group cohesiveness and open communication, avoiding employee resentment, retaining valued performers, and maximizing opportunity for all.

■ Valuing Employee Diversity

In some ways, the idea that diversity is good runs counter to the desire for cohesiveness within a company or a country. When group identification becomes a dominant issue for people, social cohesion beyond the group is almost impossible to sustain. In the political sphere, Michael Ignatieff's succinct observation about some of the most intractable group-based conflicts on the international scene (Bosnia, Northern Ireland, the Kurds' aspirations for political autonomy, and others) is that "what's different is dangerous."[18] Clearly, his examples are polarized cases. But the underlying point is clear: where there are tensions between groups, and group membership defines how individuals from one group relate to those from another, communication and cohesion between groups is seriously undermined. It is important to find common ground, and diversity should help accomplish that objective.

The challenge that arises from diversity in organizations is not simply that people from different backgrounds see the world differently. As well, some people perceive employees from "other" groups as different, and sometimes even as threatening. It is understandable that differences that society has flagged as significant—race, sex, religion, national background, etc.—will be noticed and will be part of the way any individual perceives other people: "How are they like me, and in what ways are they different from me?" What is crucial, from an employer's perspective, is to prevent such differences from becoming lines of division within the organization, or to reduce those differences where they have emerged. Employees (managers, professionals, and the rank-and-file) will be sensitive to such differences; it is the employer's responsibility to ensure that differences are accommodated as a reality and valued as a resource.

In recent years the *"difference as deficiency" perspective* (which assumes that assimilation to the culture of the dominant group should occur) has been joined and sometimes replaced by the *"difference as asset" perspective*. Initially, the unstated premise of employment equity was that the solution to inequity was to remove any sense of difference among groups—that is, to create a level playing field—but to make no changes in the established rules of the game. Women, visible minorities, and other groups would become equal players, but they were expected to assimilate the existing corporate culture rather than change it, adopting the behaviours, skills, and styles of the (predominantly white male) group already in place.

Many employers are beginning to recognize that the introduction of significant numbers of non-traditional employees changes the organization's culture. That can often be a real asset to the organization. However, this process of change can cause tensions and frictions to develop. Organizations often find themselves under pressure from both sides—the old guard that may accept increased diversity as long as it doesn't require them to change anything they're accustomed to doing or saying, and individuals from outside the dominant group who are willing to work hard to earn their positions but who resent the pressure they feel to submerge their personal identity. As one divisional manager of a major corporation puts it:

> I feel like as a company we are walking on eggshells all the time. No matter what we do, someone will find it offensive. If we use the term "diversity" some people accuse us of political correctness. If we don't openly celebrate diversity, others will accuse us of being sexists and racists.[19]

?

A Question of Ethics

Many organizations have policies requiring that members of certain demographic groups (such as women or visible minorities) sit on various committees or boards. Are there dangers to such policies? Could the potential benefits outweigh the potential costs?

Individual versus Group Fairness

An issue closely related to the "difference as deficiency/asset" debate is the extent to which HR policies should be tailored to various groups. We have already seen (Chapter 3) that human rights precedents have obliged employers to examine ways of making "reasonable accommodation" before concluding that there is a legitimate reason (BFOR) not to hire or promote an individual for reasons grounded in race, religion, gender, and so forth. Should an employer go beyond that standard? For example, should a company make the ability to speak Cantonese a requirement for first-line supervisors who manage units that include large numbers of first-generation Canadians from Hong Kong? Should a firm extend health care and other benefits to the partners of homosexual employees? Should an employer make adjustments in matters of punctuality and deadlines for employees who have come from cultures that are less time-sensitive? Should management amend dress codes for employees who view jackets and ties as cultural customs with which they are uncomfortable? Such questions are not strictly hypothetical; they are being seriously discussed in some companies.

The extent to which a **universal concept of management,** which leads to standardized practices, should be replaced by a **cultural relativity concept of management,** which calls for moulding management practices to different sets of values, beliefs, attitudes, and patterns of behaviours exhibited by a diverse work force, is a very complex question. Proponents of universalism believe that fitting management practices to a diverse work force sows the seeds for a permanent culture clash in which perceived inequities lead to intense workplace conflict. Conversely, proponents of relativity argue that failure to adapt HR practices to the needs of diverse groups within the population may alienate and marginalize people who otherwise could have made a significant contribution.

◼ Resistance to Change

Although employee diversity is a fact of life, the dominant groups in most organizations are still white males. Some argue that the long-established corporate culture is very resistant to change, and that this resistance is a major roadblock for women and minorities seeking to survive and prosper in a corporate setting.

Although employee diversity can lead to greater creativity and improved problem solving, it can also lead to open conflict and antagonism if there is mistrust and lack of respect among groups. This means that as organizations become more diverse, they face greater risks that employees will not be able to work together effectively.

◼ Segmented Communication Channels

Shared experiences are often strongly reinforced by *segmented communication channels* in the workplace. One study found that communication within organizations occurs between members of the same sex and race. This was found to be true across all professional categories, even at the top, where the number of women and visible minorities is very small.[20]

The presence of segmented communication poses three major problems to businesses. First, the organization cannot fully capitalize on the perspectives of diverse employees if they don't communicate across groups. Second, segmented communication makes it more difficult to establish common ground across various groups. Third, women and minorities often miss opportunities or are unintentionally penalized for not being part of the mainstream communication networks.

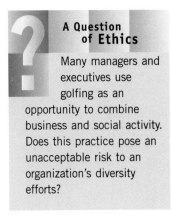

A Question of Ethics

Many managers and executives use golfing as an opportunity to combine business and social activity. Does this practice pose an unacceptable risk to an organization's diversity efforts?

universal concept of management

The management concept holding that managerial practices should not be adjusted by type or background of employee, but rather should be uniform.

cultural relativity concept of management

The management concept that managerial practices should be tailored to the different sets of values, beliefs, attitudes, and behaviours represented in the work force.

■ Resentment

The influence of government regulation and fiscal incentives on the employment policies and practices of private-sector employers is always a contested matter. Typically the tensions exist between employers and individual employees or between employers and unions. However, policies that attempt to improve the prospects of women, visible minorities, and other groups can increase tensions *among* employees.

If employers and the long-dominant employee group (white males) view the status quo as normal, and perhaps even "right," then anything done to systematically change the balance of who gets hired and promoted will be viewed as artificial and a distortion of proper practice. Employers often resist such changes because they are viewed as intrusions into how they run their business. Many white males see interventions such as employment equity as making it easier for women or visible minorities to get hired and promoted than it is for them. In both cases, it is easy to understand the source of resentment.

What many employers and white males need to understand is that the status quo often is not the level playing field they think it is. Sometimes the unfair discrimination is deliberate, but many times it is systemic—built into conventional practices and the shared assumptions of the larger culture. Senior management leadership is crucial to maintain the legitimacy of equity initiatives. In that regard, it is encouraging to note that, in the United States, 96% of CEOs polled by *Fortune* magazine indicated that they would not change their affirmative action efforts, even if the legal obligations that prompted them were abolished.[21]

■ Backlash

Some white males believe that they have been unfairly blamed for a wide range of social problems. They feel that this perception has put them at a disadvantage when it comes to promotions, salary adjustments, and job security. Such men might agree that, historically, groups such as women and visible minorities may have been treated unfairly. However, many would assert (1) that they as individuals do not discriminate and (2) that it is unfair not to apply exactly the same expectations to all candidates for a position or for determining who will be laid off if that is necessary. Thus, while women and minorities may view an employer's diversity policy as a commitment to help them gain equal standing in the organization, those who aren't part of this diversity often see it as a threat, and an unfair one. Phrases such as "reverse discrimination" are often used by those who feel threatened.

Clearly, firms face a major challenge in trying to grapple with backlash. As a group, men still have substantial advantages compared with non-traditional employees. For diversity programs to be successful, the antagonism between groups must be managed so that it does not undermine organizational performance.

■ Retention

The job satisfaction levels of women and other visible-minority employees are often lower than for the work force overall. The main complaint of these groups is the lack of career growth opportunities. The perception is that upward mobility is thwarted at higher levels as these groups encounter what has been termed the **glass ceiling,** so named because the promotional opportunities are visible, but invisible obstructions seem to block the way. This experience results in frustration and reduced job satisfaction, feelings that lead to reduced motivation and increased turnover. Although some progress is being made, the glass ceiling effect is still strong. A recent study of 776 Canadian companies surveyed indicated that women make up only 5.5% of the members of boards of directors, and only 7.5% of officers, and that 52% of the companies had no women on their boards.[22] Another survey, by *The Financial Post,* provided even more striking results: only 0.7% of the top jobs (CEOs and their direct reports) in corporate Canada were held by women.

A Question of Ethics

What ethical problems might arise from giving preferential treatment to certain employees based on their group membership?

---

glass ceiling

The intangible barrier within the hierarchy of an organization that prevents female and visible-minority employees from rising to senior levels of responsibility.

For women, representation in the work force is less of an issue than the jobs they work in. For aboriginal people and people with disabilities, both getting jobs and gaining advancement are areas of significant difficulty. The federal Human Rights Commission's report for 1997 indicated that aboriginal people represented about 3.0% of the available work force, and that only 1.2% of people employed in federally regulated employment were aboriginal. Aboriginal people were underrepresented in all regions, including areas with large aboriginal populations, as a result of low levels of hiring and disproportionately high termination rates. However, it is noteworthy that some employers that have undertaken significant recruiting and development programs have been able to achieve much better results with aboriginal employees.

Competition for Opportunities

As visible minorities grow in numbers (some projections suggest that by 2016 they will comprise 20 percent of the adult Canadian population), there is the potential for tensions to arise among groups. This potential is heightened by the trend toward downsizing, job insecurity, and chronically high levels of unemployment. The perception that a less qualified person is being hired or promoted needs to be met with a clear message that providing training or recruiting more widely to ensure that qualified individuals from various backgrounds are given consideration does not mean compromising standards of qualification.

There are no fail-proof techniques for effectively handling these challenges. There is, however, one principle that managers should constantly keep in mind: Treat employees as individuals, not as members of a group. With this principle as a guide, many of the issues become much more manageable.

We turn now to a discussion of concerns of specific employee groups. As you read the next section, remember that discussions such as this necessarily make generalizations that can be willfully or unintentionally used to characterize groups in a stereotypic way. Our purpose is quite the opposite. The following section, read as intended, will provide a sense of some of the more important dimensions of diversity and not lead to conclusions about a particular individual simply because of the group to which he or she belongs.

Accommodating people with disabilities.
Many employers have overestimated the costs of accommodating employees with disabilities. One report indicates that 31% of all accommodations cost nothing at all, and less than 1% cost more than $7000.

Diversity in Organizations

Employee diversity in such characteristics as race, ethnicity, and gender has important effects on how people relate to one another. In this section, we discuss the groups that are most likely to be left out of the corporate mainstream, or around whom issues of difference arise. However, it is important to emphasize that such attributes do not define an individual.

It is crucial to recognize that, for the most part, these categories of diversity are important not because of *intrinsic differences* between these groups and other people, but rather because of *attributed differences*. Culture and history give people a sense of what is "normal," assigning roles and status based on a wide range of personal attributes. Such cultural conventions—and every culture has its own set—are influential because they make it possible to navigate when dealing with other people.

However, the personal attributes that we use to make inferences about others are and have always been subject to ongoing change. The professional (and personal) challenge we all face today is dealing with rapid changes by applying largely unwritten rules over a wide range of issues. In matters that range from

trivial (is it polite or sexist for a man to open a door for a woman?) to funda-mental (are two people in a long-standing homosexual relationship as "married" as a heterosexual couple?), the generally accepted answers from 20 or 30 years ago no longer generate the same level of agreement. For some people, many of these "rule changes" are welcome because they hold the promise of ending in-equity or injustice. For others, the pattern and pace of change provokes anxiety and resistance, either because ideas and values they have internalized over the years are being challenged, or sometimes because they see their interests (i.e., their position or advantages) being threatened by people who previously were not a threat.

■ Types of Diversity: Emerging Groups and Visible Minorities

In Canada, diversity in the workplace deals with two broad categories of people: (1) *emerging groups* who have been part of the Canadian population for a long period of time but are claiming or aspiring to employment situations in which they have been underrepresented, and (2) *visible minorities*—people of non-European ancestry, an increased number of whom live in Canada as a result of immigration during the past 50 years. The emerging groups include women, homosexuals, people with disabilities, and older employees. These categories of people, histor-ically, have been subject to social conventions about their proper roles in society. A woman's "place" was in the home; homosexuality was regarded as a pathology; people with disabilities were seen as incapable of anything other than a few restricted occupations (e.g., tuning pianos, making handicrafts); and older people were generally seen as less efficient, more prone to absence, and slow to learn new skills or ideas. While not everybody has dropped these opinions, they are views that most individuals reject. Finally, there is the element of diversity that is quintessentially Canadian—our bilingual foundation.

The other broad class of people who are a source of diversity are the visible minorities. Even the term "visible minority" reflects a frame of reference. In Canada today, a person with darker skin pigmentation or with facial features appearing to reflect non-European ancestry is a member of a visible minority, particularly to Canadians of European ancestry. Visible minorities include people who trace their origins to Asia, Africa, the Caribbean, or Latin America. And although the aborig-inal peoples are truly the first North Americans, their employment circumstances are affected by the same mindset as affects the other visible minorities—they are perceptibly non-European. There are as many or more cultural differences *among* the various visible minority groups as there are between any one of them and Canadians of European ancestry. Thus, it often makes little intrinsic sense to group visible minorities together except for the fact that they are perceived as such—in essence, seen as "different" from the mainstream and therefore subject to similar employment-related situations.

The challenges facing employers with respect to the first class of diversity—the emerging groups—is to legitimize a change in the "rules" that have used gen-der, sexual orientation, disability, and age to determine a person's employment prospects. Although many of the "old rules" have deep emotional roots, such in-dividuals have a potential advantage, compared to visible minorities. They are the sons, daughters, wives, and long-term neighbours of the proverbial white middle-aged male. As society continues to work out the definition of "what is fair," these groups and their claims for better treatment appear to be gaining acceptance.

■ Women

As discussed throughout this book, it is difficult to overestimate the importance of changes in women's labour force behaviour over the past few decades. In 1975, women made up 37% of the labour force, while by 1996, they were 46%.

Even more dramatic is the increase in raw numbers, from 3,680,000 in 1975 to 6,800,000 in 1996, an increase of 85%.[23] Women work part time (33% of all employed women) more than men do (15%). Roughly two-thirds of these women have chosen part-time work, although fully one-third of those working part time—some wanted, but could not find full-time work.[24] Women are still concentrated in traditional occupations—some 70% in teaching, nursing, health-related occupations, clerical, sales and service occupations, but significant numbers are moving into professional employment, where they tend to earn more than women in other occupational categories, but not as much as the men who are their professional counterparts.[25] In terms of moving to the most senior positions, the glass ceiling still appears to be largely intact.

Biological Constraints and Social Roles.   Obviously, only women can become pregnant and give birth. Even after several decades of feminist initiatives, many women still encounter a fairly clear set of expectations regarding their appropriate roles and behaviour that extend far beyond their reproductive role. Most people live in family households; only 17 percent of Canadians do not live in families (see Figure 4–2). Although marriages today end much more frequently in separation and divorce than was the case a generation ago, the overall pattern shows seven of 10 households being headed by a couple (61% married plus 10% common-law partners). Only one family in ten is headed by a woman alone, and only one in 50 is headed by a lone male.

Women still are allocated primary responsibility for child care and household functions in most homes, especially where there are young children. Men in such households are much less likely to take on these roles, although the rise of the dual-earner household often means that both partners feel an obligation to make a significant contribution to household income. Women spend more of their total day in various tasks (and have less personal and free time) than do men.

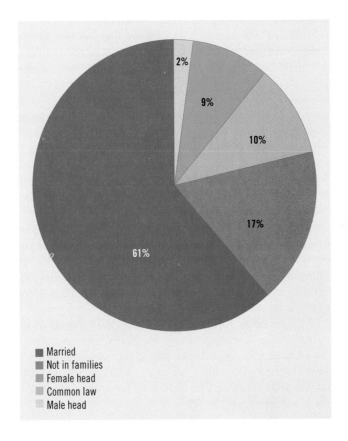

- ■ Married
- ■ Not in families
- ■ Female head
- ■ Common law
- ■ Male head

Figure 4–2 Family Characteristics, 1996

SOURCE: Statistics Canada, "Family Characteristics, 1996," adapted from "A Portrait of Families in Canada, 1993," Catalogue No. 89–253, page 13, Table 1.1.

Perhaps reflecting these societal norms, organizations have traditionally failed to be flexible enough to meet the needs of working women. (In addition to their role as mothers, an increasing number of women also find themselves becoming involved in the care of aging parents.) Only a tiny proportion of employers provide day care and other support options such as job sharing and flexible work hours for employees with young children. For this reason, many talented and highly educated young women find that they are forced to make decisions in their 20s and 30s between parenthood and being able to sustain a career. It is therefore not surprising that large proportions of top managers who are male are married and have children, while most of the few women at that level are single and childless. As one female VP in a *Fortune 500* company observes, "You can't have a career and a family. You make choices and you give things up."[26] For many women, this is a very high price to pay.

Fortune 500
cgi.pathfinder.com/fortune/
fortune500/500list.html

A Male-Dominated Corporate Culture.

Most women perceive male-dominated corporate culture as an obstacle to their success.[27] However, most inter-gender differences are not related to job performance, particularly in white-collar occupations where physical strength is not relevant.

A number of studies have shown that men emerge in leadership positions in North American culture because they are more likely to exhibit traits that are associated with the behaviour of authority figures. These traits include: (1) more aggressive behaviours and tendencies, (2) initiating more verbal interactions, (3) focussing on "output" rather than on "process" issues, (4) less willingness to reveal information and expose vulnerability, (5) a tendency to task orientation as opposed to social orientation, and (6) less sensitivity, presumably enabling them to make difficult choices with less distress.[28]

old boys' network

An informal social and business network of high-level male executives that typically does not include women or visible minorities. Access to the old boys' network is often an important factor in career advancement.

Exclusionary Networks.

Many women are hindered by lack of access to the **old boys' network,** the set of informal relationships that develop among male managers and executives. As we noted earlier in this chapter, most communication at work takes place within groups of members of the same sex. This happens even at the highest levels of the organization. With high-level positions held overwhelmingly by men, women are excluded from many of the conversations that are important to their male counterparts' understanding of the organization, and to getting ahead.[29]

Sexual Harassment.

Women have to deal with sexual harassment much more frequently than do men. Some women have had to forfeit promising careers with a particular employer because they were unwilling to accept the behaviour and sexual expectations of men in positions of power, but did not believe they had an alternative to leaving their position. Human rights codes in several Canadian jurisdictions protect employees not only from discrimination on the basis of sex, but also make harassment a human rights offence.

"Quid pro quo" harassment (i.e., the belief that "if you want to get ahead/keep your job/get a raise/get a choice assignment, you will provide sexual favours") is clearly offensive. It is an abuse of authority or power. With or without human rights legal pressure, employers should clearly indicate that such behaviour is unacceptable and thus subject to discipline, and make sure that there is a credible process to deal with such harassment.

Harassment can take other forms. Most people don't intend to harass anybody and therefore assume that the rules apply to others, not to them. However, behaviours such as teasing someone, especially if the joking is repetitive (e.g., "targetting" a fair-haired employee with a series of "blonde" jokes) can constitute harassment. Verbal remarks alone can be sufficient for a legal finding of harassment, particularly if they are persistent.[30]

Employers have been getting tougher on this issue in the 1990s by crafting stronger policies and setting up training sessions for employees. However, a 1994 survey by *Report on Business* magazine indicated that only 23 percent of companies surveyed had a policy for dealing with harassment in the workplace. Those that had policies also tended to provide supporting programs, including:[31]

◆ Training and/or seminars

◆ Publishing of pamphlets and inclusion of articles on harassment in newsletters and bulletins

◆ Formation of committees to establish complaint and investigation procedures and/or develop a communication plan

◆ Development and/or presentation of videos

These education efforts are particularly important since men and women often have different ideas of what constitutes harassment. (See Figure 4–3 for a look at how women and men view certain uninvited behaviours in supervisors and co-workers.) In addition to private consultants' services, educational materials are available from various governmental organizations. For example, the Ontario Women's Directorate released a booklet, *Workplace Harassment: An Action Guide for Women,*[32] and has previously produced other materials, including a video in which vignettes of various harassment situations are presented and examined.

(It should be noted that harassment on grounds other than sex is possible, does happen, is illegal in many jurisdictions, and should not be tolerated any more than sexual harassment. The Canadian Human Rights Commission has published a *Harassment Casebook,* which presents actual examples of harassment on the basis of marital and family status, religion, ethnic origin, and race.[33])

Ontario Women's Directorate
www.gov.on.ca/owd

■ Older Workers

The Canadian work force is aging. Figure 4–4 demonstrates current and future population distributions. Not only has the median age of Canadians increased from 32 in 1981 to 37 in 1995, but it will continue to rise. In 1994, there were more people in their 40s than in any other decade of life.[34] The employment issue of older workers is not simply one of their rights—it is also an increasingly important category of employees. Around the age of 40, but particularly after the age of 50, employees encounter a number of stereotypes that may interfere with their careers. Among the most common assumptions about older workers are that they are:

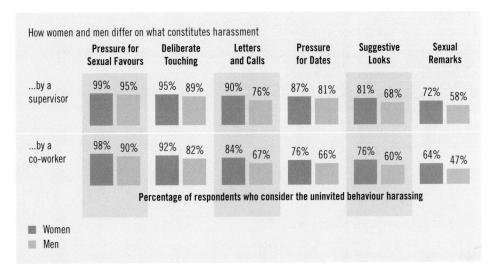

Figure 4–3 Male and Female Views of Sexual Harassment

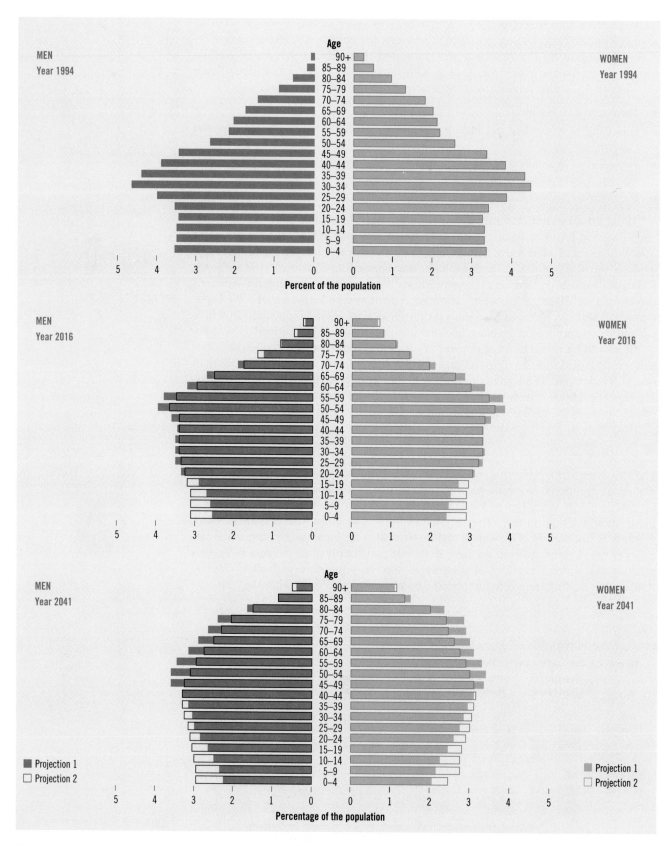

Figure 4–4 Population by Age Group and Sex, Canada—1994, 2016, and 2041

SOURCE: George, M. V, Norris, M. J., Nault, F., Loh, S., & Das, S. Y. (1994, November). *Population projections for Canada, provinces and territories: 1993–2016*. Ottawa: Statistics Canada Catalogue No. 91-520. Reproduced with authority of the Minister of Industry, 1996, Statistics Canada.

◆ Less motivated to work hard

◆ "Deadwood"

◆ Resistant to change; cannot learn new methods

◆ Plateaued after 40, buried after 50.[35]

These negative assumptions are not supported by research. For example, older workers have fewer on-the-job accidents than younger workers and have fewer avoidable absences from work. They tend to stay with employers considerably longer than younger employees, making the payback on training greater even though they are closer to retirement age. International studies of worker productivity indicate that decreases in productivity that occur with age are often so gradual that a worker in his or her 50s can be as productive as a worker under 30.

While age does have some effect on capacity and on learning styles, the important point is that as people age, they become more heterogeneous—more different from one another. Any employment decision based strictly on a person's age, therefore, becomes more *unreliable* the older the person is (not to mention that such a practice is illegal; see Chapter 3).

Second, *generational conflict* may arise from insecurities on the part of older workers who feel that their position and status are threatened by younger workers eager to push them out of the way so that the youngsters can receive faster advancement. This tension can negatively affect the cohesiveness of teams and work units. It can also affect relationships between bosses and subordinates.

Third, although many older workers are in good health, this group is slightly more susceptible to physical problems. Often they are forced to step down from their jobs because the firm cannot and/or will not find appropriate opportunities for them. When they have had senior responsibilities, either technically or managerially, being unable to construct career paths that allow them to remain with the organization can lead to the loss of judgement and knowledge that is important for decision making and as a source of mentoring and advice for younger managers.

■ Gays and Lesbians

Research suggests that 10 percent of the population is gay or lesbian.[36] Homosexuality has been an emotionally and politically inflammatory issue in recent years. Sexual orientation was added to the list of prohibited grounds for discrimination under the *Canadian Human Rights Code* in 1996, although it had previously been included in the majority of provincial jurisdictions. The matter was sufficiently contentious that the governing Liberal party, despite campaign promises to bring in this legislation, allowed a "free vote" (i.e., Liberal members were not obliged to vote for this measure) when the bill came to the floor.

It is difficult to understand why it should be allowable for an employer to discriminate against a person because of sexual orientation, a characteristic that has nothing to do with competence or suitability for the vast majority of jobs. However, the stigma that has historically been attached to being gay or lesbian does explain the opposition to gay rights that exists in some quarters. Homosexuality is understood by some people as a moral issue. Others see it as a deliberate lifestyle choice. Others understand it to be a form of emotional or mental illness. Treating homosexuality as one of many ways of being "normal"—the effective legal standard—does not sit well with people who hold such convictions.

Although much of the Canadian population may not be in complete agreement about how to regard homosexuality, the legal protections extended to homosexuals make it clear that employment decisions should not be based on this attribute. These Canadian laws also clearly differentiate Canada from the United States, where only six states (Connecticut, Hawaii, Massachusetts, Minnesota, New Jersey, and Wisconsin) have such laws. As mentioned in Chapter 3 (employment law), and as we will examine more closely in Chapter 12 (employee benefits), the main employment issues associated with homosexuality in Canada have to do with the status of the partners of gay or lesbian employees when it comes to such matters as health care insurance and pensions. However, the presence of openly homosexual employees creates a potential for friction among employees that diversity management needs to address.

Homosexuals face three major problems in the workplace. One is the outright refusal to hire or retain homosexual employees, a practice that is legally permissible in some Canadian jurisdictions. The second is intolerance from other employees or managers in companies that have not taken steps to articulate a non-discriminatory anti-harassment policy with respect to sexual orientation. Third, AIDS has become associated with homosexuality for many people, and that association adds fear to prejudice. It should also be noted that a person, gay or straight, who is HIV-positive (that is, has the virus that leads to AIDS) cannot be automatically disqualified from employment, in most Canadian jurisdictions.[37] These problems have a chilling effect that causes many gay people to deny or hide their sexual orientation, for fear of being ostracized or losing their job.

In most jobs sexual orientation is not likely to be relevant to job performance. Companies that legally or otherwise discriminate against homosexuals are denying themselves potentially valuable employees. However, employers cannot assume that simply hiring gays or lesbians will tap that potential. As with other groups that have been subject to prejudice and exclusion, employers need to establish a firm commitment to non-discriminatory treatment.

▓ People with Disabilities

World Health Organization
www.who.org

Some 16% of all Canadians are affected by a disability. Disability, according to the World Health Organization definition used by Statistics Canada, is "any restriction or lack (resulting from an impairment) of ability to perform an activity in a manner or within a range considered normal for a human being."[38] Disabilities vary in extent; mild disabilities were reported by 47% of adults with disabilities, 32% had moderate levels of disability, and some 22% had severe disabilities.

People with disabilities are at a disadvantage in employment settings, a fact that is reflected in a range of ways. Social acceptance of disabilities hasn't advanced much since the dark ages.[39] Many still view people with apparent disabilities with some discomfort, often feeling that the disabled should stay away from the work world and let "normal people" assume their duties.

Respondents to a Statistics Canada survey reported that during the preceding five years, they had been refused employment (8% of respondents), had been refused a promotion (4%), had been dismissed from their job (6%), or had been denied access to training (2%) because of their disabilities. As Figure 4–5 indicates, securing employment is more difficult when the level of disability is higher, and it is also more difficult for women than for men at any level of disability. Similarly, as reflected in Figure 4–6, employment income is lower for disabled men and women than for their same-gender counterparts at any age.

Part of the challenge in dealing with disabilities is determining what extent of accommodation is required in order to make employment (or promotion) plausible. Employer attitudes are far from the only impediment. Although many persons with disabilities have excellent abilities, they have lower average levels of education attainment than their fully able counterparts. There are also institutional impediments that inhibit their seeking employment. In almost 20% of cases, employment would result in reduction or loss of other income, and 12% indicate they would lose other supports. Family and friends discourage their seeking work (5%), and nearly 10% have family responsibilities that make employment implausible. Thus, employers have a role to play, but the issue of employment for people with disabilities is affected by a very wide range of influences.[40]

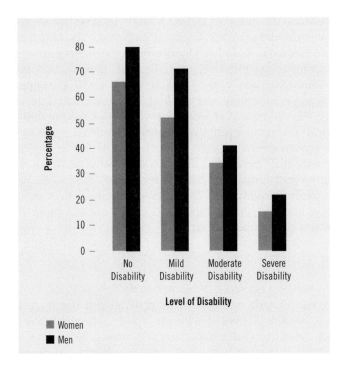

Figure 4–5 Percentage of People 15–64 Years Old Living in Households, Who Were Employed

SOURCE: *A Portrait of Persons with Disabilities.* (1995). Tables 6.1 and 6.2. Ottawa: Statistics Canada Catalogue No. 89-542E. Reproduced with authority of the Minister of Industry, 1996, Statistics Canada.

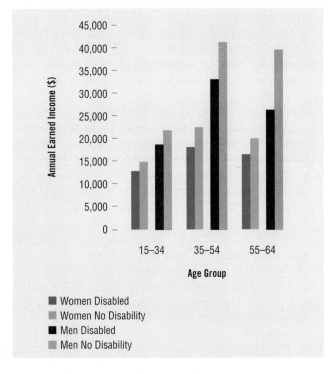

Figure 4–6 Average Employment Income of Persons Aged 15–64

SOURCE: *A Portrait of Persons with Disabilities.* (1995). Table 7.4. Ottawa: Statistics Canada Catalogue No. 89-542E. Reproduced with authority of the Minister of Industry, 1996, Statistics Canada.

▪ French and English

Canada's policy of two official languages is one of the country's defining characteristics. Official bilingualism has some implications for employers in general, although the greatest impact is on the federal government, which has committed to provide a wide range services in either official language. Although there has been past friction in the public-service sector over whether it was the anglophones who knew some French or the francophones who knew some English who were gaining unfair advantage for positions requiring bilingual skills, those disputes have ceased to grab public attention.

Olsten Corporation
www.olsten.com

Canadian bilingualism presents different kinds of diversity issues than most of the others discussed in this chapter. For most employers, the language issue is market driven. If an employer based in Quebec or in the francophone region of New Brunswick is going to be effective, the language of work will be French even though many employees may also have English facility. If a company is going to buy or sell across Canada, they will need at least some sales, service, and other employees who are bilingual. A recent survey by Olsten Corporation indicated that nearly three in 10 companies provide translated (French–English) work materials. (The language sensitivity spilled over into generally available English-as-a-second-language programs in 27 percent of the companies surveyed).[41] Rather than being a matter of employers taking down barriers for various groups, English/French language issues usually constitute an employer requirement that should be considered in selection, training, and compensation practices to ensure that employees have the skills sets that employers require.

■ Visible Minorities

Aside from the increased presence of women in the labour force, perhaps the greatest single change in Canada during the past generation is the sharp increase in the number and proportion of people who are visibly different from the European-derived majority. Although visible minorities vary among themselves, there are some common HR issues that arise with many of these groups. Appearance, language facility, religious difference, and other cultural dimensions are often found in combination. This means that it takes wisdom to differentiate between stated reasons for various issues. For example, if a female Filipino applicant is not hired to work at the pro shop of a golf club, was it a lack of job knowledge and appropriate experience, or were those "reasons" simply the hiring manager's way of excluding someone from a group that he or she didn't like or didn't feel comfortable with?

The Effects of Immigration.   During the 20th century, some 12 million immigrants will have come to Canada. People of French and British ancestry were 90% of the total population in 1881, 80% in 1931, and 67% in 1981. In 1986, two of five Canadians had at least one ancestor who was neither French nor British, and some 6.3% of Canadians were visible minorities. The proportion of non-European Canadians has risen and is expected to continue to rise. By 2001, 5.7 million people living in Canada—some 17.7% of the population—will be members of visible minorities.[42] This changing composition of the population is the result of changing patterns of immigration. If you look at the composition of the immigrant population to Canada, the shift from European and U.S. sources to non-traditional sources (Figures 4–7 and 4–8), is clear and quite dramatic. The ethnicity of visible-minority in Figure 4–9. By 2001, Chinese ancestry will pertain for 1.3 million people; and South Asians (East Indians, Pakistanis, Sri Lankans, and Bangladeshis) will number 1.1 million people, as will blacks.[43]

Urban Centres.   The largest metropolitan areas in Canada—Toronto, Montreal and Vancouver—have attracted the largest numbers of recent immigrants. Many of these immigrants are also visible minorities because recent immigration has been predominantly from sources other than Europe or the United States. Currently, half Toronto's population is visible minorities, as will be true for 40 percent of the population of Vancouver by 2001.[44]

Aboriginal People.   Aboriginal people, often referred to as "First Nations" people, include various North American Indian groups, Inuit people, and Metis. Although their circumstances vary widely in terms of treaty rights (or lack of them), lan-

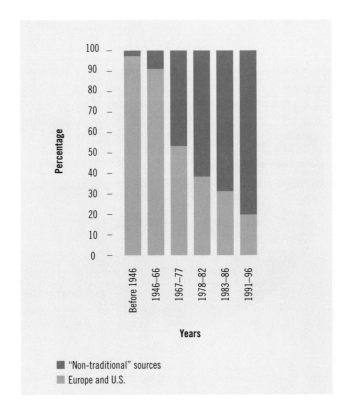

Figure 4–7 Composition of Immigrant Groups, for Selected Periods

SOURCES: DaSilva, A. (1992). *Earnings of immigrants: a comparative analysis.* Table 2-1. Ottawa: Economic Council of Canada; and Dumas, J., & Bélanger, A. (1994). *Report on the demographic situation in Canada, 1994.* Ottawa: Statistics Canada Catalogue No. 91-209E; 1996 Census, Catalogue No. 93 F0023XDB96005. Reproduced with authority of the Minister of Industry, 1996, Statistics Canada.

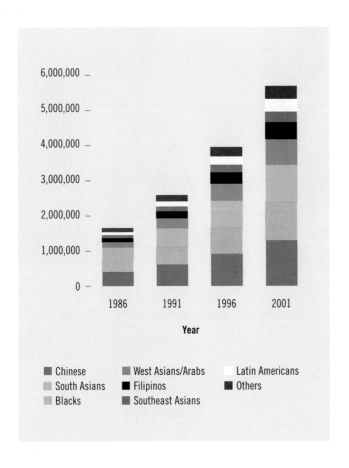

Figure 4–8 Projected Growth of Visible Minority Population, 1986–2001

SOURCE: From *Visible Minorities in Canada: A Projection* by Dr. T. John Samuel with permission to reprint from Canadian Advertising Foundation.

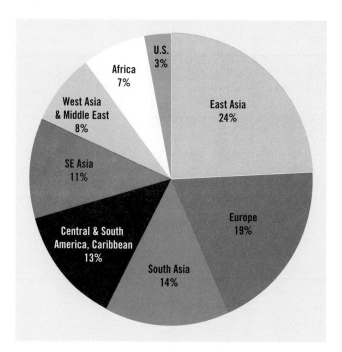

Figure 4–9 Immigrants to Canada, by Region of Origin 1991–1996

SOURCE: Statistics Canada, "Immigrants to Canada, by Region of Origin," adapted from "Report on the Demographic Situation in Canada, 1994," Catalogue No. 91–209, Table 27.

guage, and culture, their collective employment situation shows them to be a highly disadvantaged group. They are one of the four groups identified under federal employment equity legislation (along with women, visible minorities, and people with disabilities). To date, income and employment outcomes have not responded strongly to equity initiatives. Figure 4–10 illustrates the dramatic income disparities between the general population and aboriginal people in Canada, with incomes for Indians living on reserves being lower than the overall group that identified themselves in the census as aboriginal.

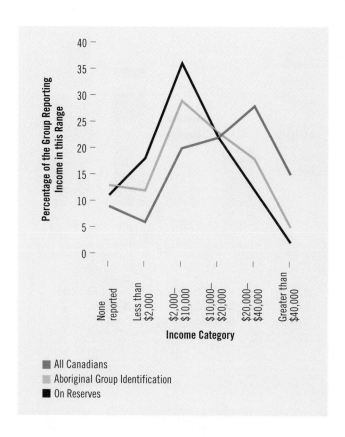

Figure 4–10 Income Profiles for Aboriginal People and Canadians in General

SOURCE: *Schooling, work, and related activities, income, expenses and mobility.* Highlights (pp. xi–xlix). Ottawa: Statistics Canada Catalogue No. 89-534. Reproduced with authority of the Minister of Industry, 1996, Statistics Canada.

Language Issues.   Census data indicate that 87 percent of recent immigrants to Canada were from non-English-speaking countries.[45] For a sense of which languages are most common and where in Canada these people live, refer to Figure 4–11. Of these top 10 groups, Chinese, Polish, Spanish, and Punjabi are the ones that have grown most dramatically in the last decade.

Thus, in many cases, visible differences combine with language skills to differentiate these groups from the mainstream population. One of the biggest obstacles for people who have not grown up speaking English (or French, for those who come to francophone areas of Canada) is language facility. For many jobs, varying degrees of English or French language facility are important. Jobs that require telephone conversations with customers or other people require clear speech.

Language skills or one's accent can also be a social marker. People with limited skills in English (or French, where it is the dominant language) face two problems. First, it is more difficult for them to gain acceptance from the people of the dominant language group with whom they have contact. Second, their lack of language skills in English or French limits their ability to learn about the Canadian environment, making them feel isolated or making them highly dependent on a social network that functions in their first language.

Combinations of Influences.   Several influences are frequently combined when visible minorities, the "outsider" group, seek fairness in employment. It is clear that racial prejudice can often be an element of the overall situation faced by outsider groups, not least in the case with aboriginal people in Canada. But there are a range of other factors beyond skin colour—accent being one—that play a role in defining a person as an outsider. Religious practices, dietary preferences, group-specific music and sports, clothing, hair style, and adornment combine with language to provide the sense of a group that is different.

Visible minorities typically have many fewer personal ties to the white male cohort than do members of the emerging group. As a result, the HR diversity issues are generally more challenging. First, managers have to identify the legitimate barriers for visible minorities (e.g., specific skills such as language facility)

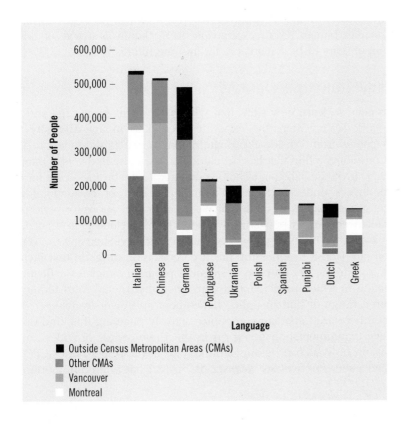

Figure 4–11 Mother Tongue Other Than English or French, by Location

SOURCE: Harrison, B., & Marmar, L. (1994). *Language in Canada.* Table 3.5. Ottawa: Statistics Canada Catalogue No. 96-313E. Reproduced with authority of the Minister of Industry, 1996, Statistics Canada.

and determine how to address or accommodate them. Second, managers need to provide leadership in establishing visible minorities as full members of the organization and to establish an organizational commitment to any individual's potential for any position within the organization. Finally, an employer needs to communicate clearly that any harassment or other antagonistic behaviour directed by anyone (manager or rank-and-file employee) toward an employee because he or she is a member of a visible minority group will not be tolerated.

■ Improving the Management of Diversity

Organizations that have made the greatest strides in successfully managing diversity tend to share a number of characteristics. These are commitment from top management to valuing diversity, diversity training programs, employee support groups, accommodating family needs, senior mentoring and apprenticeship programs, communication standards, diversity audits, and a policy of holding management responsible for the effectiveness of diversity efforts.

■ Top-Management Commitment to Valuing Diversity

It is unlikely that division managers, middle managers, supervisors, and others in positions of authority will become champions of diversity unless they believe that the chief executive officer and those reporting to the CEO are committed to valuing diversity. A Conference Board of Canada study published in April 1995 indicated that only six percent of companies surveyed included references to workforce diversity in their mission statements. Eighty-six percent of the 466 organizations surveyed indicated that responsibility for diversity issues was assigned to HR departments.[46]

It is clear that broader ownership of diversity concerns is growing. Employers recognized as leaders in this area demonstrate this fact. The Bank of Montreal has gained a reputation for its diversity programs (including winning the prestigious Catalyst Award) in no small measure because of senior management commitment.[47] Diversity programs are sometimes stimulated by legal prodding, but can and should be much more, to capture their full potential. As Rose James, Warner-Lambert Canada's human resources manager says, "Equity is a way of doing business—an opportunity to be remarkable far into the future."[48]

■ Diversity Training Programs

Supervisors need to learn new skills that will enable them to manage and motivate a diverse work force. Often, the expertise needed to mount **diversity training programs** comes from outside the organization. Renee Bazile-Jones, a partner in Omnibus Consulting, a firm that has developed an expertise in diversity training, says that employers invite Omnibus in to help communicate the business case for diversity, so that employees understand "the bottom-line impact of creating an equitable employment system, its link to valuing diversity, and ramifications for performance."[49] Other Canadian employers pursuing diversity training include Petro-Canada, British Columbia-based Ebco Industries, Du Pont Canada, and Levi Strauss & Co. (Canada).[50]

The Toronto Transit Commission has a core training program that includes extensive equity training. Its four-day residential program simulates a fictitious transit organization in which participants are assigned managerial roles requiring them to deal with a range of human rights, harassment and diversity issues.[51]

Although there are Canadian companies actively pursuing this kind of training, the extensive experimentation going on in the United Sates provides an interesting window on how such programs are likely to develop. Du Pont's CEO personally launched a series of five-day workshops.[52] AT&T has offered homophobia sem-

Warner-Lambert Canada
warner-lambert.com

diversity training programs
Programs designed to provide diversity awareness training and to educate employees on specific cultural and gender differences and how to respond to them in the workplace.

Dupont Canada
www.dupont.ca

PetroCanada
www.petro-canada.ca/index.html

inars designed to help heterosexual employees feel comfortable working alongside openly gay employees and to eliminate offensive jokes and insults from the workplace.[53] Corning has introduced a mandatory four-day awareness training program for some 7,000 salaried employees—a day and a half for gender awareness, two and a half days for ethnic awareness.[54] In one of the most creative programs of its kind, Ethicon, Inc., a subsidiary of Johnson & Johnson that makes sutures, requires each supervisor to assume the identity of an employee of different ethnicity or gender and to role-play accordingly.

Diversity training is also gaining a toehold in smaller companies, where managing diversity is not a "frill" or an "extra" but a survival tactic. Consider the case of Cardiac Concepts, an outpatient laboratory in which most of the 11 employees are women or visible minorities representing half a dozen different faiths. At one time, religious squabbles were common. Owner Emma Colquitt did what many large companies are doing: she hired a consultant to give her diverse workers a course on how to get along. The session with the consultant cost the company a little over $3,000. Large companies may pay 10 times as much, and more, for outside trainers.

Companies that are known for success at diversity management do not rely on one-shot workshops. Rather, they use these as part of an ongoing effort. "The biggest myth is that we [give] training, we hold hands and sing 'We are the World,' and things are all better—but that's not true," says Hattie Hill-Storks, a co-partner at the International Productivity Institute. "If the boss uses diversity training as a Band-Aid, the problems often recur."[55]

Aetna's Family-Friendly Executive.

Michelle Carpenter, pictured here with her sons Matthew and Peter, is proof that employees who ask for flexible hours can still get promotions. Recently promoted to manager of Aetna's Work/Family Strategies unit, Carpenter has helped Aetna set up a variety of programs designed to give working parents more time with their families. The result: Aetna estimates it saves $1 million per year in not having to train new workers.

■ Support Groups

Some employees perceive corporate life as coldly insensitive to their culture or background, perhaps explicitly hostile. The perception of an attitude that says, "you don't belong here," or "you are here because we need to comply with government regulations," is largely responsible for the often-high turnover among visible minorities in many organizations.

To counteract these feelings of alienation, top management in a number of firms have been setting up **support groups** that are designed to provide the nurturing climate for employees who may otherwise feel shut out. These groups also provide a way for employees who share the same background to find one another in larger organizations.

support group

A group established by an employer to provide a nurturing climate for employees who would otherwise feel isolated or alienated.

■ Accommodation of Family Needs

Firms can dramatically cut the turnover rate of their female employees if they are willing to help women handle a family and career simultaneously. A 1995 survey of Canadian employers by Watson Wyatt Wordwide indicated that 28 percent of the firms surveyed offered child care resource or referral programs, but that the percentage rose to 38 percent among those companies in which 75 percent or more of the employees were women.[56] The following examples demonstrate the range of options that employers have found useful.

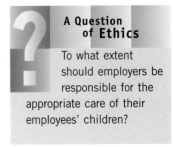

A Question of Ethics

To what extent should employers be responsible for the appropriate care of their employees' children?

Day Care.   Perhaps the best way to assist female employees in their efforts to meet both family and employment responsibilities is to assist them in securing appropriate care for their children while they are at work. In a small number of cases, employers have actually established day care centres on site. In other cases employers have solved day care concerns by providing information that helps employees to identify and select a facility that will meet their needs.

One of the more innovative aspects of child care assistance is helping the employee who may have an unexpected, occasional need. A child's normal day care provider may become ill, or a child may be ill and unable to go to school or the usual day care setting. VanCity Credit Union's head office in Vancouver has paired with a nearby community-based child care centre, purchasing one emergency child care position along with six priority positions for use by employees, picking up $25 of the $35 daily cost. A number of Ottawa-area employers have formed an emergency child care consortium. Although there are costs borne by the employer to pay for this service (provided in the child's home in nine of 10 cases), they often cost half or one-third the cost of replacing the employee for the day.

Absence levels cost Canadian employers an average of $1,750 annually per employee, and although absences for employee illness are down in the period from 1983–93, overall absences have risen from 8.3 days to 9.3 days per year because of the increase in absence owing to "personal reasons."[57] Many of these personal days off are the result of obligations due to child care (and, increasingly, elder care). It is clearly in an employer's best interests to provide alternative solutions to staying away from work.

Canadian public policy supports day care in several ways. In addition to income tax provisions for the cost of day care fees, various provincial and municipal programs of subsidies and licensing are directed to the issues of affordability and quality. For a sense of what several European countries are doing in this area, refer to the Issues and Applications feature, entitled "What European Countries do for Mum, *Maman, Mütter,* and More… ."

What European Countries Do for Mum, *Maman,* *Mütter,* and More …

When it comes to creating a family-friendly workplace, more than an ocean separates North American and European companies. Many European countries have made provisions for maternity leave, child care, and flexible schedules that are generous by North American standards—and they've had them in place for years. For example:

- Germany adopted its maternity leave law back in 1878. As of 1993, German women receive six weeks' prenatal leave at full pay and eight weeks' postnatal leave, also at full pay. After mothers return to work, they get time off to breast-feed. In addition, there is a three-year parental leave for all working parents, both male and female.

- Sweden was the first nation to broaden extended postnatal maternity leave to "parental leave," for either the mother or the father, or for both alternately. Today Swedish parents are guaranteed a one-year leave of absence after childbirth: The first half is reserved for the mother, who receives 90% of her salary from social security.

- Denmark, with the highest level of publicly funded services in Europe, offers women 18 weeks' maternity leave, 4 weeks before the birth and 14 weeks afterward. Men can take 10 days' leave after their baby is born, and parental leave policy allows either the mother or the father to take an additional 10 weeks off after the birth.

- France leads the pack in day care support. In addition to getting at least 16 weeks' maternity leave at 84% of their salaries, working mothers can bring their children to state-run day care centres called crèches, which are open 11 hours a day and cost between $5 and $25 daily.

- Some European companies, such as National Westminster Bank (NWB) in London, have career break policies that allow employees to take a multiyear leave following the birth of a child. During that period the employee remains in contact with the company, fills in for vacationing employees, and participates in training. At NWB, career breaks of six months to seven years are available to staff at all grades.

"What we tend to find in Europe," says a coordinator of Day Care Trust in London, "is that the more government involvement there is in these issues, the more likely there is to be involvement by employers." In North America it is up to individual companies to provide family-friendly programs. This creates some pockets of work-family innovation, but to the chagrin of many strapped and frazzled dual-earner families, there is no broad-based trend to provide these kinds of services.

SOURCES: *Time.* (1987, June 22). How public policy helps working women around the world, 45; Cook, A. H. (1989, January). Public policies to help dual-earner families meet the demands of the work world. *Industrial and Labor Relations Review, 42*(2), 201–215; and Mason, J. C. (1993, April). Looking across the Atlantic: Work-family initiatives in Europe. *Management Review,* 36–38.

Alternative Work Patterns.   Employers such as Royal Bank, Bell Canada, Warner-Lambert Canada, and Apple Canada have been willing to experiment with new ways to help women balance career goals and mothering, and thereby have retained the services of many excellent employees who may otherwise have had difficulty meeting all their obligations. As we saw in Chapter 2, these programs come in a variety of forms, including **flexible work hours**, **telecommuting**, and **job sharing**. Another option is *extended leave*. A rare benefit, **extended leave** allows an employee to take a sabbatical from the office with the assurance of a comparable position upon return. Some companies require leave-takers to be on call for part-time work during their sabbatical.[58]

These alternative work patterns are often collectively labelled the *mommy track*. The term had negative connotations when it was first coined to describe women who were thought to need extra consideration from employers in order to balance their family and work lives. These days the "mommy track" can be negative or positive, depending on how an employer views its female employees who need assistance in combining a career with motherhood. The less common term *daddy track* has arisen to describe the career paths of men who opt to spend some time raising their children. Although a relatively small number of men are currently doing this, a survey conducted by benefits consulting firm Robert Half International indicated that 74 percent of the men surveyed would accept slower career development in exchange for more time to spend with their families.[59]

◼ Senior Mentoring Programs

Some companies encourage **senior mentoring programs,** in which senior managers identify promising women (or visible-minority persons, or people with a disability) and play an important part in nurturing their career progress. Canadian National, for example, has initiated a bridging program where a woman moving toward managerial responsibilities learns the job under the guidance of a senior manager. At the end of a two-year period, a determination is made as to whether she will be given the job on a permanent basis.[60]

◼ Apprenticeships

Apprenticeships are in some ways similar to mentoring programs, except that they are usually applied to employees at more junior levels, and often involve working with prospective employees before they become full members of the organization. Xerox Canada partners with community colleges to design technical training programs, and works to restructure entry-level jobs so that they have fewer initial technical requirements. Warner-Lambert works with the Scarborough Board of Education's co-op program for students with disabilities. Hewlett Packard's Canadian operations work with high schools to provide co-op tracks to employment, with the result that over 80 percent of the students in their co-op program are in designated (equity) groups.[61]

◼ Communication Standards

Certain styles of communication that are inconsequential to some people may be offensive to others. This is particularly true if the style reflects traditional biases or status differences. Referring to managers in general as "he" and secretaries as "she" is one example. Failure to represent a broad range of the work force in terms of age, gender, race, and so forth in company publications is another. To avoid such problems, organizations should set communications

flexible work hours

An alternative work pattern in which employees create customized schedules for themselves and work at home part of the time.

telecommuting

An alternative work pattern that permits employees to work in their homes full time, maintaining their connection to the office through fax, phone, and computer.

job sharing

An alternative work pattern in which two or more employees split their hours in the office and share title, workload, salary, health benefits, and vacation time.

extended leave

A benefit that allows an employee to take a long-term leave from the office, while retaining benefits and the guarantee of a comparable job on returning.

senior mentoring program

A support program in which senior managers identify promising women (or other "diversity group" employees) and play an important role in nurturing their career progress.

apprenticeship

A program in which promising prospective employees are groomed before they are actually hired on a permanent basis. Company managers are encouraged to become actively involved in apprenticeships.

standards that take into account the sensibilities of a diverse employee group. It is important to realize that inclusive language and representation are important symbolic means to send the message that race, gender, and other similar attributes do not assign status or roles within an organization. Even the most progressive employers have not completed this transition, so deliberate sensitivity toward those who have been marginalized and excluded in the past is still important.

Diversity Audits

diversity audit

A review of the effectiveness of an organization's diversity management program.

Often the roots of an employee diversity problem (such as high turnover of minority employees) are not immediately evident. In these instances, research in the form of a **diversity audit** may be useful in uncovering the source and dimensions of the problem. The employment equity program of the federal government has required employers in their jurisdiction to do just that. Clearly, any human resource planning or information system that incorporates information about such characteristics will help an employer to diagnose the problem and evaluate potential solutions.

Management Responsibility and Accountability

Management of diversity will not be a high priority or a formal organizational objective unless managers and supervisors are held accountable for implementing diversity management. Sometimes it takes an external push for organizations to undertake these commitments. For example, it took a joint complaint from 13 organizations for the disabled to the Canadian Human Rights Commission to get firm targets established in the major banks, but the Royal Bank of Canada has now committed to making people with disabilities at least 12.5 percent of their hires during the last five years of the 1990s.[62] And at Xerox Canada, "equity goals are not seen as 'soft' targets. If these goals are not met, the president has to be satisfied there is a very good reason."[63]

Some Warnings

Two potential pitfalls must be avoided if diversity management programs are to be successful. These are (1) avoiding the appearance of reverse discrimination, and (2) avoiding the promotion of stereotypes.

Avoiding the Appearance of Reverse Discrimination

Disproving the accusation that managing diversity is just a polite phrase for providing opportunities for emerging groups and visible minorities at the expense of white males is crucial to successful diversity programs. Failure to deal effectively with that perception can increase resentment and friction among employees. The perception of white male disadvantage is unfounded, in the aggregate. Max Yalden, chief of the Canadian Human Rights Commission, indicated that white men without disabilities accounted for 55 percent of the people hired in the federal jurisdiction, although they made up only 45 percent of the total national labour market.[64]

Management needs to "frame" these programs in a context that is accepted as legitimate, including two elements: (1) diversity programs make sense for good business reasons, and (2) the purpose of the programs is not to exclude anybody but is rather to include as broad a range of the work force as possible so that people can contribute to the full extent of their potential. Other HR policies, such as compensation, can be used to reinforce the sense of common cause. One appliance manufacturing facility that had a large visible-minority population used plant-wide productivity and product improvement incentives that had the effect of breaking down barriers between groups. For some guidelines on what HR professionals and other managers can do to eliminate unnecessary resistance to diversity programs, see the Manager's Notebook entitled "Preventing Diversity Backlash."

■ Avoiding the Promotion of Stereotypes

As we discussed earlier, an inherent danger in diversity programs is the inadvertent reinforcement of the notion that one can draw conclusions about a particular person based simply on his or her group characteristics (e.g., race, gender, disability). That error, stereotyping, should be avoided. *Within* groups identified by a single characteristic, differences among individuals on almost any human dimension are much greater than the average difference *between* that group and another (for example, men and women). **Cultural determinism**—the idea that it is possible to infer an individual's motives, interests, values, and behavioural traits based on his or her group membership—robs employees of their individuality and reinforces an "us-versus-them" mindset that can be very divisive.

The challenge in cultural awareness programs is to alert and sensitize people to differences among various subcultures without overdramatizing those differences to the point that it is difficult to portray the variety that exists within every group. Generalizations about "women," about "visible minorities," about "white males," or about any group are clearly misleading if the message is that these people are all clones of one other. Such a message is misleading and offensive.

Every employee deserves to be treated as an individual who has a unique set of needs, motives, interests, capabilities, and experiences. With those people we know well, the two statements, "people are all alike," and "everybody is different," are not contradictory. They are a paradox that reflects the experience of everyday life. The purpose of diversity programs is to allow organizations to extend the range of people to whom those two statements are applied. To achieve that end, it may be necessary to discuss group differences. But such a discussion should not be the stopping point. Rather, it is a means to get beyond group differences to realize the full potential of all individuals.

cultural determinism
The idea that it is possible to infer an individual's motives, interests, values, and behavioural traits based on his or her group membership.

Manager's Notebook

Preventing Diversity Backlash

Many organizations that have instituted diversity and employment equity programs have experienced adverse reactions from employee groups, particularly white males. Here are some guidelines for human resource professionals and company managers who are attempting to create a program for managing diversity without adversity.

1. Adopt an inclusive definition of diversity that addresses all kinds of differences among employees, including, but not limited to, race and gender. A broader definition of diversity will invite participation and lower resistance.

2. Make sure that top management is not only committed to establishing a diversity program but also communicates that commitment directly to all employees. Top executives should also let managers know why diversity is important to the company's bottom line and global competitiveness.

3. Involve everyone, including white males, in designing the diversity program. White men will be less resistant to these programs if they are on the task forces, panels, and other groups the company sets up to look at diversity issues and decide how the company should handle them.

4. Avoid stereotyping groups of employees, such as white males, when explaining cultural or ethnic differences. While the airing of stereotypes is a common facet of diversity training workshops, trainers should direct trainees away from focusing on any group as "the culprit" and affirm the value of each person's individual experience and viewpoint.

5. Recognize and reward white males who are part of the solution rather than blaming men who are part of the problem. Many white men who have long been advocates for diversity feel they aren't getting recognized for it.

6. Avoid one-shot training efforts that stir up emotions without channelling them in productive directions. Use ongoing training that encompasses diversity as only one facet of needed change in the corporate culture.

SOURCES: Mobley, M. (1992, December). Backlash! The challenge to diversity training. *Training & Development*, 45–52; Nelton, S. (1992, September). Winning with diversity. *Nation's Business*, 18–24; Galen, M. (1994, January 31). Taking adversity out of diversity. *Business Week*, 54–55.

Summary and Conclusions

What Is Diversity? Diversity refers to human characteristics that make people different from one another. Today's labour force is highly diverse. If effectively managed, this diversity can provide an organization with a powerful competitive edge because it stimulates creativity, enhances problem solving by offering broader perspectives, and infuses flexibility into the firm.

Challenges in Managing Diversity. An organization confronts significant challenges in making employee diversity work to its advantage. These include: (1) genuinely valuing employee diversity, (2) balancing individual needs with group fairness, (3) coping with resistance to change, (4) promoting group cohesiveness, (5) ensuring open communication, (6) avoiding employee resentment, (7) avoiding employee resentment, (8) retaining valued performers, and (9) maximizing opportunity for all employees.

Diversity in Organizations. Some groups are more likely to be left out of the employment mainstream. Such people, described as "emerging groups" in this chapter, include women, homosexuals, persons with disabilities, and older employees. Women encounter male-dominated cultures that can exclude them, expose them to the potential for sexual harassment, and often create difficulties in balancing employment and family responsibilities. Older workers are subject to stereotyping. A person with a disability is often excluded or marginalized unnecessarily. Homosexuals encounter prejudice, a response that can be compounded by an absence of a clear corporate position on non-discrimination and the perceived association between homosexuality and AIDS. All these groups differ, but all have been present in the Canadian population for a long time. The barriers they face are the social conventions that have assigned them to subordinate or marginalized roles. As they act on their aspirations to participate fully in the Canadian work force, they will be involved in the process of helping society redefine what it means to be fair.

A significant and growing element in the Canadian work force is visible minorities. Many groups fall within this category, and they share only one key characteristic: they appear to be of other than European ancestry. Their rapid increase in the population stems largely from dramatically changing immigration patterns. Visible minorities often (but do not necessarily) share other characteristics, such as less facility in English or French, and difference in religious affiliation or elements of varied ethnic heritage, such as dress and diet. Aside from their rapid increase (to some 20 percent of the adult population by 2016), the most notable feature of this category is its diversity. Some visible-minority groups work mainly in lower-paying jobs. However, some projections indicate that the average per-capita GDP will be slightly greater for these groups than for the population in general by 2001, attributable to high average levels of education. It is with regard to visible minorities that employers will need to launch their most thorough diversity programs.

Improving the Management of Diversity. Organizations that have capitalized the most on their diverse human resources to gain a competitive advantage tend to have top management committed to valuing diversity; solid, ongoing diversity training programs; support groups that nurture non-traditional employees; and policies that accommodate employees' family needs. They also have senior mentoring and apprenticeship programs to encourage employees' career progress, set communication standards that discourage discrimination, celebrate diversity through organized activities, use diversity audits to uncover bias, and hold their managers responsible for effectively implementing diversity policies.

Some Warnings. There are two pitfalls in diversity management programs that managers must be careful to avoid: (1) giving the appearance of reverse discrimination, and (2) unintentionally promoting stereotypes.

Key Terms and Concepts

apprenticeship, 133
attributed differences, 117
cognitive structure, 109
cultural determinism, 135
cultural relativity concept of management, 115
daddy track, 133
"difference as asset" perspective, 114
"difference as deficiency" perspective, 114
diversity, 109

diversity audit, 134
diversity training programs, 130
emerging group, 118
extended leave, 133
flexible work hours, 133
generational conflict, 123
glass ceiling, 116
intrinsic differences, 117
job sharing, 133
management of diversity, 111
Meyers-Briggs Type Indicator, 110

mommy track, 133
non-traditional employees, 111
old boys' network, 120
segmented communication channels, 115
senior mentoring program, 133
support group, 131
telecommuting, 133
universal concept of management, 115
visible minorities, 118

Discussion Questions

1. Why is management of diversity acquiring such a central role in human resource management as we near the 21st century? Is this a temporary or a long-term phenomenon? Explain.

2. Explain how a firm could use employee diversity as a competitive advantage.

3. Women and minorities are often lumped together as a single class. What do these two groups have in common? What are the major differences between them? Explain.

4. "Visible minorities" is a category that is used in federal employment equity legislation. Human rights codes use categories such as "race" and "national" or "ethnic" origin. How would you recommend that an organization refer to this issue when trying to increase appreciation for and understanding of diversity?

5. Conflicts among minority groups may arise as they compete for what they perceive as a limited number of jobs and promotion opportunities. Is this perception accurate? What can firms do to avoid these kinds of conflict?

6. Some people still believe that the best way — and perhaps the only fair way — to manage is to treat all employees equally regardless of their sex, race, ethnicity, physical impairment, and other personal characteristics. Do you agree? Explain.

7. A major insurance company's diversity training program for managers was conducted by two external consultants. When introducing the program to non-management employees, however, the company opted to train internal trainers for the task. "We didn't anticipate the time it would take to train others to do this or how important it is that trainers first resolve their own prejudices," said the company's vice president of human resources. "The seven-day train-the-trainer program didn't deal with personal bias as much as it needed to." What are the potential benefits and drawbacks to using outside consultants to facilitate diversity programs? What potential problems do companies face in implementing diversity programs, and how can these problems be resolved?

8. When a long-time contract employee for a utility company was the first in his unit to be laid off, he claimed that others — an African-Canadian woman and a man of East Indian descent — had been kept on even though they were less qualified than he was because the company was intent on creating a more diverse workplace. "I feel like I'm losing out," this white male employee said. The company claimed his race and sex had nothing to do with his being laid off. What can companies do to keep white males from feeling victimized by diversity efforts and training programs instead of valued as "diverse" employees in their own right?

 Check out our Companion Website at: **www.prenticehall.ca/gomez** for a selection of self-study questions, key terms and concepts, updated Weblinks to related Internet sites, newsgroups, CBC video updates, and more.

MiniCase 1   *Taking a Joke*

Consider the following account, adapted from the *Canadian HR Reporter*:

In a British Columbia human rights case, a store owner engaged in behaviours that could be construed as teasing or as simply crude. Some of these behaviours included:

◆ Reference by the owner to photo processing machines as "female machines" because they "alarm and go off and make a lot of noise" and suffer from PMS (premenstrual syndrome).

◆ Reference to part of the photo process as being like "a little boy going wee."

◆ Statements that one employee had problems with the machine because her "arms were too short" while he gestured in a manner that indicated she had large breasts.

When told that these remarks were offensive, the owner, who was of British ancestry, said, "You Canadians are so backwards because nobody can take a joke."

Such comments were made frequently, and the complainant said she found them offensive.

Still, there is evidence to suggest that the store owner did not see himself as harassing. He asked that investigators speak with another female employee. This employee confirmed the allegations. She could tell the complainant was embarrassed by the owner's comments about her.

The complainant conceded that the owner was a good person and a good employer who probably didn't mean to offend to the degree that he did. He wanted the work environment to be "fun."

Discussion Questions

1. Do you think it is reasonable for an employer to be subject to legal sanctions for the kind of behaviour described above?

2. Do you think it is reasonable for an employee to be subject to such treatment, even if it is not meant to be offensive but just an expression of a sense of humour?

3. In a larger organization, what steps should be taken to minimize friction over this kind of behaviour?

SOURCE: Adapted from Weiner, N. (1996, March 25). "Teasing" can lead to harassment complaints. *Canadian HR Reporter*, 15–16. Used with permission of *Canadian HR Reporter*, MPL Communications Inc. Copyright 1996.

MiniCase 2   *On the Outside, Looking In*

The *Annual Reports* of the Canadian Human Rights Commission includes the following statement:

> We regret to report that the *Employment Equity Act* has done little to improve the situation of people with disabilities. Although their representation in the work force subject to the *Act* improved from 1.6% in 1987 to 2.7% in 1996, it remained well below the 6.5% availability estimate.

The same document reported significant progress for women and for visible minorities.

Discussion Questions

1. What are the barriers to employment for persons with disabilities?

2. Indications are that many disabilities can be accommodated at little or no cost. What other objections might employers have in cases where the costs are minor?

3. Is the prospect of working with people whose disabilities are obvious (e.g., wheelchairs, speech impediments) disturbing or upsetting to some employees? Why might this be so?

Case 1

Surprise under the Carpet at Northern Sigma

Northern Sigma, a hypothetical high-technology firm headquartered in the Ottawa area, develops and manufactures advanced electronic equipment. The company has plants across Canada and 3,200 employees, 300 of whom work at a single site in suburban Toronto that is responsible for research and development. About half of the employees at that facility are scientists and engineers. The other half are support personnel, managers, and market research personnel. Corporate executives are strongly committed to hiring women and visible minorities throughout the entire organization, but particularly at the Toronto site. The company has adopted this policy for two reasons: Women and visible minorities are severely underrepresented in the Toronto plant (making up only about 13% of the work force), and it is becoming increasingly difficult to find top-notch talent in the dwindling applicant pool of white men.

Phillip Wagner is the general manager of the Toronto plant. In his most recent performance evaluation he was severely criticized for not doing enough to retain women and minorities. For the past two years, the turnover rate for these groups

has been three times higher than that for other employees. Corporate executives estimate that this high turnover rate is costing at least $150,000 a year in training costs, lost production time, recruitment expenses, and so forth. In addition, more than 10 charges of discrimination have been filed with the Human Rights Commission against the Toronto plant during the past three years alone — a much higher number of complaints than would be expected given its size and demographic composition.

Wagner's first reaction to his performance evaluation was very defensive. He told his boss that it was unfair to hold him responsible for things beyond his control. He also pointed out that women and minority hiring at his plant is greater than it has ever been, and better than the average for other Northern Sigma plants. His boss's response: Getting to the root of the problem and doing something about it would be crucial to Wagner's future with the company.

Under pressure from headquarters, Wagner has targeted the turnover and discrimination problems as among his highest priorities for this year. As a first step, he has hired a con-

➤

sulting team to interview a representative sample of employees to find out (1) why the turnover rate among women and minorities is so high and (2) what is prompting so many complaints from people in these groups. The interviews were conducted in separate groups of 15 people each to facilitate candid comments. Each group consisted either of white men or a mix of women and minorities. A summary of the report prepared by the consultants is provided below.

Women and Minority Groups

A large proportion of women and minority employees expressed strong dissatisfaction with the company. Many felt they had been misled when they accepted employment at Northern Sigma. Among their most common complaints:

◆ Being left out of important task forces.

◆ Personal input not requested very often — and when requested, suggestions and ideas generally ignored.

◆ Contributions not taken very seriously by peers in team or group projects.

◆ Need to be "10 times better" than white male counterparts to be promoted.

◆ Lack of respect and lack of acknowledgement of work experience.

◆ A threatening, negative environment that discourages open discussion of alternatives.

◆ Supervisors often arrogant, insensitive, domineering, and patronizing.

◆ Frequent use of demeaning ethnic- or gender-related jokes.

◆ Minimal career support once hired.

White Male Groups

Most white males, particularly supervisors, strongly insisted that they were interested solely in performance and that neither race nor sex had anything to do with how they treated their staff members or fellow employees. They often used such terms as "equality," "fairness," "competence," and "colour-blindness" to describe their criteria for promotions, assignments, selection for team projects, and task force membership. Many of these men felt that, rather than being penalized, women and minorities were given "every conceivable break."

The consulting team asked this group specific questions concerning particular problems they may have encountered at work with women and the two largest minority groups in the plant (blacks, predominantly from Caribbean backgrounds, and Chinese Canadians). The most common comments regarding the white men's encounters with each of these groups are listed below.

Blacks

◆ Frequently overreact.

◆ Expect special treatment because of their race.

◆ Unwilling to blend in with the work group, even when white colleagues try to make them feel comfortable.

◆ Like to do things on their own terms and schedules.

◆ Do not respond well to supervision.

Chinese Canadians

◆ Difficult to figure out what they really think; very secretive.

◆ Passive-aggressive: One can never tell when they are upset, but they have their way of getting back at you when you least expect it.

◆ Very smart with numbers, but have problems verbalizing ideas.

◆ Stoic and cautious; will not challenge another person even when that person is blatantly wrong.

◆ Like to be left alone; don't want to become supervisors even if this means an increase in pay.

◆ Prone to express agreement or commitment to an idea or course of action, yet are uncommitted to it in their hearts.

Women

◆ Most are not very committed to work and are inclined to quit when things don't go their way.

◆ Often more focussed on interpersonal relationships than work performance.

◆ Respond too emotionally when frustrated by minor problems, thus unsuited for more responsibility.

◆ Sensitive and unpredictable.

◆ Moody.

◆ Often misinterpret chivalry as sexual overtures.

◆ Indecisive.

◆ Cannot keep things confidential and enjoy the rumour mill.

Phillip Wagner was shocked at many of these comments. He always thought of his plant as a friendly, easygoing, openminded, liberal, intellectual place because it has a highly educated work force (most employees have college or university degrees, and a significant proportion have advanced graduate degrees). He is now trying to figure out what to do next.

Critical Thinking Questions

1. Based on the information generated by the interviews with the two different groups and what you have learned in this chapter, what do you see as the major problems affecting this plant from a management-of-diversity perspective? What may have led to these problems? What consequences are likely to result from these problems? Explain your answers.

2. Do you agree that Wagner should be held responsible for these problems? Explain.

3. What specific recommendations would you offer Wagner to improve the management of diversity at the Toronto plant? Explain how each of your recommendations addresses the underlying problems identified under Question 1.

Cooperative Learning Exercise

4. The class divides into groups of three to five students. Each group should discuss what recommendations it would make to Wagner. After 10 to 15 minutes, each group should present its recommendations to the class. How different are the recommendations from group to group? What principles from the chapter were you able to apply to this problem?

Case 2

Advise and Percent

IBM has long had a reputation for being a progressive employer. As long ago as the early 1970s, IBM Canada identified women employees based on their potential and tracked them through a female resource program. Managers were given awareness education to identify female leaders for developmental opportunities, and individualized development plans were prepared. In 1973, women represented 19.5% of the IBM work force, 7% of the professional group, and only 3.8% of the management group. By 1989, the population was 25.8% female, and 24.4% of managers and professionals were female. It was a significant change, and a positive reflection on the early initiative of IBM Canada in this area.

However, a closer look at the numbers revealed that there was still work to be done. Within the managerial and professional group, the proportion of women decreased as the level of responsibility grew. The glass ceiling was still a factor because rather than eliminating it, it had effectively been raised a level or two. In 1992, building on the work at the Bank of Montreal's 1991 "Study of the Advancement of Women," IBM Canada renewed its drive for change in this area. Research indicated that IBM's female employees were as well-educated, experienced and capable as the males, yet were underrepresented in senior positions. One of the patterns seemed to be a breakdown between theory and practice. While some women had been identified early and were still highly regarded, management had not taken risks with them—as they had with men—by giving them particularly challenging assignments.

Of the things that have happened since, perhaps the single most important was the creation of IBM's Advisory Council on Women, comprising six women and two men with managerial responsibilities across a range of functional areas, and having CEO Bill Etherington as the Council's executive sponsor. Objectives included (a) understanding the issues and initiating solutions, (b) assisting the corporation in attaining proportional representation at senior levels, and (c) providing ongoing advice to senior management. Actions taken included:

◆ Communicating the aims and existence of the Council—that is, let people know the facts in order to build general support for action.

◆ Creating an on-line system that employees can use to identify job openings.

◆ Focussing on proportional representation as the standard to be used in executive resources reviews—not quotas, but a benchmark to assess the extent and sufficiency of change.

◆ Continuing to communicate flexible work arrangements that are of value to all employees, including those women who have work and family responsibilities to balance.

◆ Delivering diversity awareness training to all employees during the 1993–94 period.

Critical Thinking Questions

1. Do you think that this program will have the effect of increasing the proportion of senior managers who are women? Is there a qualitative difference between the nature of senior positions and those at lower levels that makes it more difficult to accommodate family and other obligations?

2. IBM Canada, like its parent company and a number of other companies that were very successful during the 1980s, found it necessary to reduce their work force sharply in the early 1990s. How do you think reorganization and layoffs are likely to affect an initiative such as the one described?

3. This initiative has been directed at women. Although there was some discussion during the formation of the Council to broaden its mandate to include other employee groups, the decision to limit the Council's mandate to women was made to keep the focus clear. What do you think of this strategy for change? What are its strengths? What are its potential problems?

Cooperative Learning Exercise

4. The class divides into groups of eight to 10. Each of these groups divides into two subgroups—one subgroup simulating the Advisory Council and the other a group of senior managers.

   a. As subgroups, the Council and the senior managers prepare for a meeting between them. The topic to be discussed is the notion of proportional representation as a standard for progress. The Council should make the case as convincingly as possible, and the senior managers should test this proposal to determine whether it is a workable idea (10–15 minutes).

   b. The two groups meet together to decide whether the proportional representation standard should be applied. (10–15 minutes).

   c. Class meets as "committee of the whole" and compares experiences, with one person from each of the groups serving as reporter to the class.

SOURCE: Odam, P. (1995, December 4). At IBM, equity means going the extra mile. *Canadian HR Reporter*, 19–20. Used with permission of *Canadian HR Reporter*, MPL Communications Inc. Copyright 1995.

VideoCase

Who *Do* They Want?

It is very easy to adopt a rather one-sided view of human resource management: the employer's side. Any manager and particularly any person working in the human resources function of the organization is continually faced with the reality of meeting the organization's human resource needs. The skill sets and attitudes that are needed to do the jobs at hand, the cost constraints that make untempered generosity in pay and benefits obvious "non-starters," the need for employee flexibility and willingness to take on new tasks or learn new skills as the organization grows and changes in response to in strategic direction and as it copes with a dynamic product market: all of these "realities" managers understand and accept.

What many managers and even human resource specialists fail to grasp is that in managing the employment relationship, there is another set of needs that have an influence on that relationship: what applicants and current employees are looking for in their work. If asked, many employers will acknowledge this need although it is still often difficult to get the employee perspective factored into management thinking. Some employers even resent the notion that employee views should play a role. The view of such managers is that they offer a job, with pay and some range of benefits, and employees should accept it as it is or go elsewhere.

It has always been true that essential or star performers can get the attention of an employer. They do have options elsewhere, and the risk of losing them is great. This is true whether you consider high-profile fund managers in the financial industry, professional athletes, or CEOs who have built a reputation of "turning around" companies that are in trouble. What is less automatic is whether employees in general receive any serious consideration, along the same lines.

Employers don't provide as much job security as they may have a generation ago. Many employees seem to demonstrate less loyalty and commitment to any one employer, being willing to change jobs with less consideration of how their departure will hurt the place they leave. These trends may or may not continue, but the lack of employee attachment to their employer seems to be a reality that employers will increasingly face.

Questions

1. Is it realistic to take careful consideration of employee aspirations and preferences into account when managing human resources? What are the costs of doing so? What are the costs of failing to do so? (Do you think that paying attention to employee preferences is 'coddling' or 'pampering' employees?)

2. What happens to an employer where pay, benefits, and working conditions are enough to attract enough people to meet requirements but where there is general dissatisfaction with management styles and career opportunities? If turnover is high in this kind of organization, what kind of a work force is likely to evolve over time?

3. How is the basic employment relationship changing, as we enter a new century? How are employers' expectations changing? Employees expectations?

Video Resource: "Keeping Them," *Venture* 682 (March 24, 1998).

Recruiting, Selecting, and Socializing Employees

After reading this chapter, you should be able to deal more effectively with the following challenges:

1 Understand the human resource planning process.

2 Weigh the advantages and disadvantages of internal and external recruiting.

3 Distinguish among the major methods of selection.

4 Make staffing decisions that minimize the hiring and promotion of the wrong people.

5 Provide reasonable job expectations to new recruits.

There's a Job in Your Future!

Career Expo. A great number of recruitment sources are available to organizations. These include current employees, referrals from employees, advertisements, employment and temporary-help agencies, and (pictured here) college career expositions.

Acme Publishing Company was looking to replace Jerry Rogers, a manager who left to accept a job with a competitor. After a few months of interviewing and testing, the HR department announced that a new manager, George Agros, had been hired.

However, George turned out to be a bit too gruff and distant for most of the workers. At first, they were relieved that a manager was finally in place, even if he wouldn't win any personality awards. But this relief soon changed to resentment. The workers disliked George's style and often disagreed with his decisions, which seemed to depend more on Acme's internal politics than on their clients' needs. Since George's past managerial experience was in another industry, they also doubted that he knew enough to make the best decisions for the unit.

Six months after taking over, George met with Acme's director of human resources. The director asked him how things were going and mentioned that he had heard a number of complaints from employees in George's unit. George couldn't believe what he was hearing. He had agreed to take this position in a new field at a very modest salary because he had been promised a promotion and a salary increase after two months. Both were four months overdue. He knew that he didn't fit into the unit's culture, he said, but it wasn't his fault. Acme had hired him and Acme should have known what it was getting. After the meeting, the director wondered whether George would have to be transferred or terminated, and George wondered whether he should quit and sue Acme for misrepresenting the job and his promotion and salary opportunities. The workers in George's unit wondered how they could survive another hiring process if George left or was forced out.

The experience of the Acme Publishing Company illustrates several important issues that firms face when hiring employees.

- ◆ Who should make hiring decisions?
- ◆ What sources should the company consult to recruit the best workers?
- ◆ How should applicants' "fit" with the firm's culture be considered in addition to their skills?
- ◆ How can a firm give applicants realistic expectations about a job so that new hires don't become disillusioned?
- ◆ What characteristics should the firm look at to determine whom to hire, and how should these characteristics be measured?

    The way these and other staffing questions are handled will directly affect the quality of the people hired and the retention rate of skilled workers. Hiring (and promoting) the right people is critical to effective operations and organizational potential. In addition, the barriers to terminating employees mean that it can be difficult and expensive to reverse a hiring mistake.

In this chapter we focus on staffing, perhaps one of the most important HR activities in which line managers are involved. First, we define and discuss the human resource planning process. Second, we examine the hiring process in detail. Third, we look at the major challenges that managers face in hiring and promoting. Fourth, we recommend a set of procedures for dealing with these challenges and avoiding potential problems. Finally, we describe and evaluate specific methods for making hiring decisions and briefly discuss some legal issues involved with staffing.

■ Human Resource Planning

human resource planning (HRP)

The process an organization uses to ensure that it has the right amount and the right kind of people to deliver a particular level of output or services in the future.

Human resource planning (HRP) is the process of an organization uses to ensure that it has the right number and the right kinds of people to deliver a particular level of output or services in the future. Firms that do not conduct HR planning may not be able to meet their future labour needs (a labour shortage) or may have to resort to layoffs (in the case of a labour surplus).

A failure to plan can lead to significant financial costs. For instance, firms that lay off large numbers of employees are required to provide extended notice periods in some provinces, while firms that ask their employees to work overtime are required to pay them a wage premium. In addition, firms sometimes need to do HR planning to satisfy legally mandated employment equity programs (see Chapter 3).

Line managers often do have control over certain HR decisions, such as choosing a particular approach for training their employees, and they may have considerable discretion over how employees are paid. Therefore they are in a position to make HR decisions that are strategic in nature. However, HR planning is usually done centrally in large organizations by specially trained HR staff. For this reason, we discuss only the basics of HR planning in this text so that you will be familiar with the process and purpose of such an analysis.

Figure 5-1 summarizes the HRP process. The first HRP activity entails forecasting *labour demand*, or how many workers the organization will need in the future.

Labour demand is likely to increase for the firm's product or services increases and to decrease as labour productivity increases (since more output can be produced with fewer workers, usually because of the introduction of new technology).

The second part of the HRP process entails estimating *labour supply*, or the availability of workers with the required skills to meet the firm's labour demand. The labour supply may come from existing employees (the internal labour market) or from outside the organization (the external labour market).

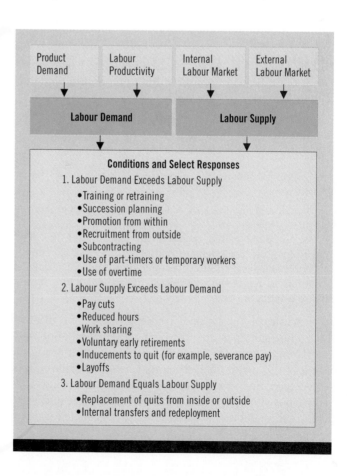

Figure 5–1 Human Resource Planning

After estimating labour demand and supply for a future period, a firm faces one of three conditions, each of which requires a different set of responses. In the first scenario, more workers will be needed than will be available. A variety of approaches can be used to increase the labour supply available to a specific firm. These include training or retraining existing workers, grooming current employees to take over vacant positions (succession planning), promoting from within, recruiting new employees from outside the firm, subcontracting part of the work to other firms, hiring part-timers or temporary workers, and paying overtime to existing employees to expand the number of hours worked. Which approach or approaches are appropriate will depend on their relative costs and how long the labour shortage is expected to last. For instance, if demand exceeds supply by only a small amount and this situation is deemed temporary, paying overtime may be less expensive than hiring new workers, which entails extra costs in terms of training and legally mandated benefits (such as workers' compensation insurance).

In the second scenario, labour supply is expected to exceed labour demand. This means that the firm will have more employees than it needs. Firms may use a variety of measures to deal with this situation. These include pay cuts, reducing the number of hours worked, and work sharing (all of which may save jobs). In addition, the firm may eliminate positions through a combination of tactics, including enticements to employees to retire early, severance pay, and outright layoffs. (We discuss these issues in detail in Chapter 6 and Chapter 13.) If the labour surplus is expected to be modest, the firm may be better off reducing the number of hours worked instead of terminating employees.

In the third and last scenario, labour demand is expected to match labour supply. The organization can deal with this situation by replacing employees who quit with people promoted from the inside or hired from the outside. The firm may also transfer or redeploy employees internally, with training and career development programs designed to support these moves.

■ A Simplified Example of Forecasting Labour Demand and Supply

Figure 5-2 shows an example of how a large national hotel chain with 25 units forecasts its labour demand for 16 key jobs three years ahead. Column A indicates the number of employees who currently hold each of these jobs. Column B calculates the present ratio of employees to hotels—that is, number of current employees divided by the current number of hotels (25). The hotel chain expects to add seven additional hotels by 2002 (for a total of 32). In column C, the expected number of employees for each job in 2002 is calculated by multiplying the current ratio of employees to hotels (column B) by 32. For instance, in 1999 there were nine resident managers for 25 hotels, or a ratio of 0.36 (9 divided by 25). When the number of hotels expands to 32 in 2002, it is forecasted that 12 resident managers will be needed (0.36 x 32 = 11.52, or 12.0 after rounding).

The same hotel chain's labour supply prediction is found in columns A-D of Figure 5-3. Column A shows the percentage of employees in each of the 16 key jobs who left the firm during the past three years (1996–1999). Multiplying this percentage by the number of present employees in each of these key jobs produces an estimate of how many current employees will have quit three years from now (by 2002). For example, 38% of general managers quit between 1996 and 1999. Since there are now 25 employees holding this job, it is forecasted that by 2002, 10 of them will have left the firm (0.38 x 25 = 9.5, rounded to 10). The projected turnover for each job is shown in column C. This means that by 2002, 15 of the current general managers (25 minus 10; see column D) will still be working for the company. Since the projected labour demand for general managers in 2002 is 32 (see Figure 5-2), 17 new general managers (32 minus 15) will have to be hired by 2001.

	A Number of Employees (1999)	B Ratio of Employees/Hotels (Calculated as Column A ÷ 25)	C Projected 2002 Labour Demand for 32 Hotels (Calculated as Column B × 32)*
Key Positions			
General Manager	25	1.00	32
Resident Manager	9	0.36	12
Food/Beverage Director	23	0.92	29
Controller	25	1.00	32
Assistant Controller	14	0.56	18
Chief Engineer	24	0.96	31
Director of Sales	25	1.00	32
Sales Manager	45	1.80	58
Convention Manager	14	0.56	18
Catering Director	19	0.76	24
Banquet Manager	19	0.76	24
Personnel Director	15	0.60	19
Restaurant Manager	49	1.96	63
Executive Chef	24	0.96	31
Sous Chef	24	0.96	31
Executive Housekeeper	25	1.00	32
Total	379		486

*These figures are rounded.

Figure 5–2 Example of Predicting Labour Demand for a Hotel Chain with 25 Hotels

■ Other Forecasting Techniques

There are two basic categories of forecasting techniques, quantitative and qualitative. The example we have just gone through is a highly simplified version of a *quantitative technique*. A variety of mathematically sophisticated quantitative techniques have been developed to estimate labour demand and supply.[1] Although used more often, quantitative forecasting models have two main limitations. First, most rely heavily on the past data or previous relationships between staffing levels and other variables, such as output or revenues. Relationships that held in the past may not hold in the future, and it may be better to change previous staffing practices than to perpetuate them. Second, most of these forecasting techniques were created during the 1950s, 1960s, and early 1970s, and were highly appropriate for the large firms of that era, which had stable environments and work forces. They are less appropriate in the 1990s, when firms are struggling with such destabilizing forces as rapid technological change and intense global competition. These forces are creating major organizational changes that are more difficult to predict from past data.

Unlike quantitative techniques, *qualitative* techniques rely on subjective estimates made by experts to forecast labour demand or supply. The expert may include top managers, whose involvement in and support of the HR planning process is a worthwhile objective in itself. One advantage of *qualitative techniques* is that they are flexible enough to incorporate whatever factors or conditions the expert feels should be considered in estimating future labour needs. In other words, unlike quantitative methods, qualitative techniques are not constrained by past relationships. However, a potential drawback of these techniques is that subjective judgements may be less accurate or lead to rougher estimates than those obtained through quantitative methods. The appendix to this chapter contains tables outlining both groups of techniques and their major advantages and disadvantages.

	Supply Analysis				Supply-Demand Comparison	
Key Positions	A % Quit* 1997–1999	B Number of Present Employees (See Figure 2–10, Column A)	C Projected Turnover by 2002* (Column A × Column B)	D Employees Left by 2002 (Column B – Column C)	E Projected Labour Demand in 2002 (See Figure 2–10, Column C)	F Projected New Hires in 2002 (Column E – Column D)
General Manager	38	25	10	15	32	17
Resident Manager	77	9	7	2	12	10
Food/Beverage Director	47	23	11	12	29	17
Controller	85	25	21	4	32	28
Assistant Controller	66	14	9	5	18	13
Chief Engineer	81	24	16	8	31	23
Director of Sales	34	25	9	16	32	16
Sales Manager	68	45	30	15	58	43
Convention Manager	90	14	13	1	18	17
Catering Director	74	19	14	5	24	19
Banquet Manager	60	19	12	7	24	17
Personnel Director	43	15	6	9	19	10
Restaurant Manager	89	49	44	5	63	58
Executive Chef	70	24	17	7	31	24
Sous Chef	92	24	22	2	31	29
Executive Housekeeper	63	25	16	9	32	23
Total Employees		379	257	122	486	364

*These figures are rounded.

Figure 5–3 Example of Predicting Labour Supply and Required New Hires for a Hotel Chain

◼ The Hiring Process

As Figure 5–4 shows, the hiring process has three components: recruitment, selection, and socialization.

Recruitment is the process of generating a pool of candidates for a particular job. The employer must announce the job's availability to the market and attract qualified candidates to apply. The market from which the firm attempts to draw job applicants can be internal, external, or a combination of the two. In other words, the employer may seek applicants from inside the organization, outside the organization, or both.

Selection is the process of making a "hire" or "no hire" decision regarding each applicant for a job. The process typically involves determining the characteristics required for effective performance on the job and then measuring applicants on those characteristics. The characteristics required for effective job performance are typically based on a job analysis, which is a systematic study and summary of a job (see Chapter 2). Depending on applicants' scores on various tests and/or the impressions they have made in interviews, managers determine who will and will not be offered a job. This selection process often involves the establishment of *cut scores;* applicants who score below these levels are considered unacceptable.

recruitment

The process of generating a pool of qualified candidates for a particular job; the first step in the hiring process.

selection

The process of making a "hire" or "no hire" decision regarding each applicant for a job; the second step in the hiring process.

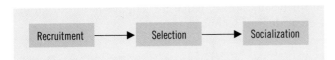

Figure 5–4 The Hiring Process

socialization

The process of orienting a new employee to the organization or the unit in which he or she will be working; the third step in the hiring process.

Socialization involves orienting new employees to the organization and to the units in which they will be working. It is important that new employees be familiarized with the company's policies and procedures and with performance expectations. Socialization can make the difference between a new worker's feeling like an outsider and feeling like a member of the team.

■ Challenges in the Hiring Process

Most people would agree that the best-qualified candidate should be hired or promoted. In the long run, hiring the best-qualified candidates makes a tremendous difference to the organization's effectiveness and bottom-line performance. Imagine, for example, the level of service and overall performance you would get in a retail organization whose workers are all average in job skills and abilities. Now imagine the service you would get in a retail organization whose workers are all 20 percent above average in job skills and abilities.

The potential negative consequences of poor hiring decisions are equally graphic. Poor hiring decisions are likely to cause problems from the outset. Unqualified or underqualified workers will probably require closer supervision and direction. They may require additional training, yet not reach the required performance standards. They may give customers or clients inaccurate information or poor service that prompts complaints or loss of business.

All of these issues underscore a simple point: if a company makes the right hiring decision to begin with, it will be far better off. For this reason, it is essential that line managers be involved in the hiring process. While the HR department has an active role in recruiting, selecting, and socializing new employees, managers also need to be active in this process. In the end, it is the managers who will be active supervising the new employee, and managers from operating units often have insights into their operations that the HR department may lack.

Despite the obvious importance of selecting the best from the available talent, the hiring process presents several challenges. The most important of these are:

◆ Determining which characteristics that differentiate people are most important to performance.

◆ Measuring those characteristics.

◆ Evaluating applicants' motivation levels.

◆ Deciding who should make the selection decision.

■ Determining the Characteristics Most Important to Performance

The characteristics a person needs to perform a job effectively are not necessarily obvious, for several reasons.

Several factors make determining the characteristics necessary for good job performance a challenge. First, the job itself is very often a moving target. For instance, the knowledge, skills, and abilities (KSAs—see Chapter 2) necessary to be a good computer programmer right now are almost certainly going to change over the next few years as both hardware and software continue evolving. Second, the culture of the organization may need to be taken into account. Sun Microsystems, a very fast-growing computer company, interviews up to 20 applicants between four and seven times each before it makes a hiring decision because it is very concerned that each new hire fit in with Sun's dynamic, growth-oriented culture.[2] Third, different people in the organization often want different characteristics in a new hire. For example, upper-level managers may want the new manager of an engineering group to be financially astute, while the engineers in the group may want a manager with a great deal of technical expertise.

■ Measuring the Characteristics That Determine Performance

Once a set of characteristics has been determined to be important for job performance, how are those characteristics to be measured? Say that mathematical ability is considered critical. You can't infer from looking at someone what level of mathematical ability he or she possesses. Rather, to find this out, you must administer some test or other measure of mathematical ability. Some measures are better than others, and they can vary widely in cost.

■ The Motivation Factor

Most of the measures used in hiring decisions focus on ability rather than motivation. There are countless tests of mathematical ability, verbal ability, and mechanical ability. But as the following equation makes clear, motivation is also critical to performance:

$$\text{Performance} = \text{Ability} \times \text{Motivation}$$

This equation shows that a high ability level can yield poor job performance if it is combined with low motivation. Likewise, a high level of motivation cannot offset a lack of ability. (We will discuss another influence on performance, system factors, in Chapter 7.)

Unfortunately, motivation is very difficult to measure. Many employers try to assess motivation during the employment interview, but as we will see later in this chapter, there are numerous problems with this method. In addition, motivation seems to be much more dependent on context than ability is. If you are a typical student, your motivation to work hard in a class depends to a large extent on whether you like the course content, how much you like and respect your instructor, and the way in which grades are determined. Your academic ability is fairly stable from course to course, but your motivation level is much more variable. Work situations are just as variable: how much you like your job responsibilities, how well you get along with your boss, and how you are compensated all affect your level of effort.

■ Who Should Make the Decision?

In many organizations, staffing decisions are routinely made by the HR department, particularly for entry-level jobs. There are two good reasons for letting the HR department run the staffing process. The first and more important one is that the organization must ensure that its employment practices comply with the legal requirements described in Chapter 3, and making the HR staff responsible for hiring decisions can help avoid problems in this area. The second reason is that since the HR staff is usually responsible for processing initial contacts with applicants, and is often the centralized repository of information about the applicants, many organizations find it easier to let the HR department follow through and make hiring decisions.

However, there is an obvious problem with having the HR department play the central role in hiring: This system leaves the line personnel out of a process that is critical to the operation's effectiveness. It is the line personnel, after all, who are intimately familiar with the line jobs and who must work with the candidates selected in the staffing process.

If an organization decides to involve line employees in hiring decisions, which ones should it consult? There are at least three separate groups. The first, and most obvious, are the managers who will be supervising the new hire. The second interested group consists of the new hire's co-workers. The third group, where applicable, is the new hire's subordinates. As we saw in the Acme Publishing case that opened the chapter, these groups do not necessarily share the same view of what characteristics are important in the new employee.

An interesting example of a company that heavily involves subordinates in hiring decisions is Semco, a Brazilian firm that manufactures everything from cooling units for air conditioners to entire cookie factories. Semco is well known for its egalitarian culture and policies. The company has no receptionists, secretaries, standard hierarchies, or executive privileges. It lets workers set their own hours and salary, and asks subordinates to help hire their own managers. In his book *Maverick,* Semler sets the scene for a group "grilling" of a Semco manager being considered for promotion to general manager of another unit:

> Anatoly Timoshenko was going into the arena, and the lions were hungry. Gathered in a meeting room at Santo Amaro was as antagonistic a group of people as he was likely to face in peacetime. If he was lucky, they would be his future subordinates.[3]

■ Building Managerial Skills: Meeting the Challenges of Effective Staffing

Choosing the right person for a job can make a tremendous positive difference in productivity and customer satisfaction. Choosing the wrong person can result in sluggish operations and lost business and customers. For these reasons it is important that each step of the staffing process—recruitment, selection, and socialization—be managed carefully. We discuss each of these steps in turn.

■ Recruitment

Recruitment aims to attract *qualified* job candidates. We stress the word "qualified" because attracting applicants who are unqualified for the job is a costly waste of time. Unqualified applicants need to be processed and perhaps even tested or interviewed before it can be determined that they are not qualified. To avoid these costs in time and money, the recruiting effort should be targeted solely at applicants who have the basic qualifications for the job.

Sources and Costs of Recruiting.   A great number of recruitment sources are available to an organization. The most prominent of these are:

◆ *Current employees.* Many companies have a policy of informing current employees about job openings before trying to recruit from other sources. The primary advantage of internal postings is that they give current employees the opportunity to move into the firm's more desirable jobs. The disadvantage is that the move creates another vacancy that needs to be filled.

◆ *Referrals from current employees.* Studies have often shown that employees hired through such referrals tend to stay with the organization longer and display greater loyalty and job satisfaction than employees who were recruited by other means.[4] However, a disadvantage of this source is that current employees tend to refer people who are demographically similar to themselves, which can create potential employment equity or human rights problems.

◆ *Former employees.* A firm may decide to recruit employees who formerly worked for the organization. Typically, these are people who were laid off or may have worked seasonally (e.g., summer employees or those who worked at Christmastime or during tax season). Because the employer already has experience with these people, they tend to have low failure rates.

◆ *Advertisements.* Advertisements can be used both for local recruitment efforts (newspapers) and for targeted regional, national, or international searches (trade or professional publications).

◆ *Employment agencies.* Many organizations use external contractors to recruit and screen applicants for a position. Typically, the employment agency is paid a fee based on the salary offered. Agencies can be particularly effective when an employer is looking for an employee with a specialized skill. Such agencies are also effective in identifying people who currently have jobs and are not actively looking for a new position. For an employer who is not equipped to handle large numbers of applications, private employment agencies provide a buffer between the applicant pool and the organization. Canada Employment Centres (CECs) are another way of making job openings known to a large number of applicants. Many employers find using their CEC a useful way of tapping into the local labour market at a fairly low cost.

◆ *Temporary help agencies.* An increasing number of organizations are turning to temporary workers as a source of employees. Temporary workers allow an organization to get through the ups and downs of the business cycle without adjusting the number of full-time employees.

◆ *University and college recruiting.* Your school probably has a job placement office that helps students make contacts with employers. Many larger employers have college or university programs that target various schools or various majors. Accounting, engineering and computer science majors at the undergraduate level and those with graduate degrees in business and law are often considered to be desirable sources for organizational recruiting.

Many major firms with well-established organizational cultures such as the chartered banks, IBM Canada, or Procter & Gamble are known to take considerable care to assess the fit between applicants and the organization. Many employers maintain a presence on preferred university campuses, even in years when they anticipate hiring fewer people than normal.[5]

In Japan, where lifetime employment is still practised at some large companies, college recruitment is practically the only way employers can bring in new blood. Competition among college students to gain access to the largest companies is fierce. For instance, college students routinely send "information request postcards" to prospective employers beginning in December of their junior year. A student may mail well over 1,000 cards to prospective employers, with 40 to 50 cards alone sent to an employer the student really wants to impress. The companies send the students information, including an invitation to come to the company's "information sessions." Companies also engage in fierce competition to skim the cream off the top of the hiring pool. Even though Nikkeiren, the Japan Federation of Employers' Associations, has stipulated that firms cannot initiate contact with students until July of their junior year, many companies jump the gun and start screening students earlier.[6]

◆ *Customers.* One innovative recruitment source is the organization's customers, who are already familiar with the organization and what it offers.[7] These people, who must be happy with the organization's product or service because they've remained customers, may bring more enthusiasm to the workplace than other applicants who are less familiar with the organization. Also, customers have been the recipients of the firm's product or service and therefore may well have valuable insights into how the organization could be improved.

The appropriateness of these sources depends on the type of job to be filled and the state of the economy. When the unemployment rate is high, companies find it easy to attract qualified applicants. When it is low, organizations need to be more resourceful in locating a reasonable pool of qualified applicants. For some years now, the unemployment rate has been higher than normal for the post–World War II period and companies have scaled back their on-campus recruiting efforts. Most college and university programs experienced fewer employers coming on campus during sharp recessionary periods, particularly during the early 1990s, when the recession was followed by a "jobless recovery." Although employment levels did increase, their growth was significantly less than the expansion in economic activity, as technology was deployed to help employers meet the pressures of increased international competition.[8]

Small companies often find it difficult to recruit qualified applicants, even in times when unemployment is relatively high. For example, a recent survey of such businesses indicated that finding qualified and motivated employees was among their top three business worries.[9] Hiring mistakes can be particularly difficult for smaller organizations to cope with because the options for reassigning a new employee are fewer.

Canada Employment Centre—Toronto
www.the-wire.com/hrdc/hrdc.html

Canada Employment Centre—Calgary Region
www.ffa.ucalgary.ca/hrdc

How does an employer evaluate the worth of different recruitment sources? One way is to look at how long employees recruited from different sources stay with the company. Studies show that employees who know more about the organization and have realistic expectations about the job tend to stay longer than other applicants.[10] For instance, potential flight attendants who are familiar with the job realize that the position's glamorous, jet-setting image is offset by its many not-so-attractive aspects: dealing with difficult passengers, flying the same route over and over again, living out of a suitcase, and working on odd schedules. The first three sources we discussed—current employees, employee referrals, and former employees—are likely to turn up applicants with realistic expectations of the job.

Another way of evaluating recruitment sources is by their cost. The organization should carefully consider what the most cost-effective recruiting method is in its particular situation. There are substantial cost differences between advertising and using cash awards to encourage employee referrals, and between hiring locally and hiring beyond the local area (which entails relocating the new employee). When it is necessary to go outside the local area to get the type of employee the company wants, it may make sense for company managers to travel to other cities and conduct employment interviews there rather than to pay transportation expenses for applicants to visit the company site.

Line managers can increase the effectiveness of the HR department by providing HR personnel with continuous feedback on the quality of the various recruitment sources. For example, managers can set up a simple spreadsheet with recruiting sources in the rows and effectiveness measures (say, a "1 to 10" scale) in the columns. Alternatively, other entries might be put in such a spreadsheet (measures such as number of employment offers, number of acceptances, turnover by year, and employee performance ratings after one year on the job. See Figure 5-5 below.

Managers themselves might update the grid periodically or (alternatively) delegate the task of interpreting the grid and providing recommendations to the HR department. (Some data such as performance appraisals may be confidential and appropriate only for management consideration.)

Laidlaw Inc.
www.laidlawcorp.com

External versus Internal Candidates.   *External* and *internal candidates* have both benefits and drawbacks. Hiring externally gives the firm the benefit of fresh perspectives and different approaches. Sometimes organizations deliberately go outside to create such change, to set a new direction. Donald Jackson, the president of Laidlaw, Inc., the Burlington, Ontario-based Waste Management Company,

Source	Number of employment offers	Number of acceptances	Total cost	Turnover after one year	Average performance rating at one year
Employee referrals					
Ads					
Agencies					
University recruiting					
Customer referrals					

Figure 5-5 Chart for Summarizing the Effectiveness of Recruiting Sources

resigned in 1993 and was replaced by James Bullock, who had previously been with Cadillac Fairview Corporation, Ltd. This change was not inexpensive, costing the employer well over $2 million in separation allowances and inducements to the new president, over and above the salaries involved.[11] Sometimes it also makes economic sense to search for external specialists rather than bear the expense of training current workers in a new process or technology. On the downside, externally recruited workers may be considered "rookies" by everyone in the system, and therefore their ideas and perspectives may be discounted by long-service employees. When this occurs, people brought in to rejuvenate the department for organizations will have only limited impact. Another disadvantage is that external workers need time to become familiar with the policies, practices, and culture of their new employer. It may take weeks before a new recruit is up and running, which could prove costly to the organization's effectiveness and productivity. Bringing in someone from the outside can also cause difficulties if current workers resent the recruit for filling a job they feel should have gone to a qualified worker within the firm. Finally, as you saw in the case of Acme Publishing Company, the outsider's style may clash with the work unit's culture.

Internal recruiting, usually in the form of promotions and transfers, also has its advantages and disadvantages. On the positive side, it is usually less costly than external recruiting. It also provides a clear signal to the current work force that the organization offers opportunities for advancement. Moreover, internal recruits are already familiar with the organization's policies, procedures, and customs.

Many large employers, including IBM Canada, 3M, and Imperial Oil, have sophisticated internal recruiting and career development systems. 3M, for example, has an information system that helps managers identify suitable candidates and helps employees identify skills that they need to prepare for different jobs. Some 98% of all jobs are listed on the posting system, and the result is that information sharing has improved throughout the company.[12]

One drawback of internal recruiting is that it reduces the likelihood of innovation and new perspectives. Another is that workers being promoted into a higher-level job may be undercut in their authority because they are so familiar to their subordinates. For example, former co-workers may expect special treatment from a supervisor or manager who used to be a colleague.

Recruiting and Legally Protected Groups.

There are two related concerns that employers must be aware of in recruiting: human rights codes and employment equity. (See Chapters 3 and 14.) Human rights codes exist in all Canadian employment jurisdictions. The specific groups identified as being explicitly protected by these codes differ. However, all jurisdictions effectively prohibit discrimination on the basis of religion, race/ethnicity, and sex, among other characteristics. Recruiting is an integral part of the staffing process, and staffing processes that have the effect of selecting disproportionately small numbers from protected groups when there is no demonstrable difference in their qualifications can be found to be discriminatory. Employers need to take care that their overall staffing process does not unintentionally penalize the various groups protected by human rights codes. Extensive use of employee referrals tends to replicate the mix of employees already employed; how and where an employer advertises vacancies will influence the applicant pool. The hiring decision is the one that is most likely to precipitate a human rights complaint, but recruiting is an integral part of the process; it sets the stage.

Employment equity legislation is in a state of flux in Canada. Employers regulated by the federal government are obliged to be proactive in their attempts to employ and advance women, visible minorities, people with disabilities, and aboriginal ("First Nations") people. The question of what posture an employer should take with respect to the great and increasing diversity of the Canadian population is important even though legal compliance is not a change driver for many employers. If a work-

Cadillac Fairview Corporation Ltd.
www.cadillacfairview.com/ cadfair1.htm

3M
www.mmm.com

Imperial Oil
www.imperialoil.com

force becomes more diverse, maintaining effective communications and the desired corporate culture may be more difficult than with the status quo. However, increased diversity can help employers (especially those with a great deal of consumer contact) seem more approachable to their clientele. Ensuring that artificial barriers are removed also assures employers of the best possible talent pool, and creates the additional resource of people who will understand cultures and who may know languages that are becoming increasingly important in a global economy.

A good rule of thumb for increasing diversity in applicant pools is to identify the media (newspapers, radio stations, associations, etc.) to which various underrepresented groups are likely to pay attention, but not to modify the content of the recruiting message. To overemphasize the fact that women, gays or lesbians, people with disabilities, or visible minorities are being singled out for attention can create the impression that someone may get a job because of his or her sex, colour, or some other such characteristic. This can create suspicion and resentment among other employees because it undermines the perception that the new employee got the job based on merit alone.[13]

The Planning Recruitment Effort.   To be effective, recruitment should be tied to human resource planning.[14] As we discussed earlier, human resource planning involves a comparison of present workforce capabilities with future demands. The process might involve sophisticated technical analysis or simply rely on the subjective judgement of managers. The analysis might indicate, for example, a need for 10 more staff personnel given the firm's expansion plans and anticipated market conditions. This information should play a key role in determining the level of the recruitment effort.

Once HRP has been performed, an important question remains: How many candidates should the recruitment effort attempt to attract for each job opening? The answer depends on *yield ratios,* which relate recruiting input to recruiting output. For example, if the firm finds that it has to make two job offers to get one acceptance, this offer-to-acceptance ratio indicates that approximately 200 offers will have to be extended to have 100 offers accepted. Perhaps the interview-to-offer ratio has been 3:1. This ratio would indicate that the firm will have to conduct at least 600 interviews to make 200 offers. Other ratios to consider are the number-of-invitations-to-interview ratio and the number-of-advertisements-or-contacts-to-applicant ratio. Each firm sets its own number-of-candidates-to-number-of-job-openings ratio. The desired level of recruitment effort may be higher if the firm wishes to be particularly selective in making employment offers.

■ Selection

Given the pool of candidates that results from the recruitment effort, selection is the mechanism that determines the overall quality of the human resources in an organization. To understand the impact of selection practices, consider what happens when the wrong person is hired or promoted. How do you, as a customer, like being served by someone who is slow and inept? How would you, as a line supervisor, like to deal with the problems caused by a worker who is unable to perform necessary tasks on a production line? These kinds off direct effects of poor selection practice are only the beginning. Hiring the wrong person can also cause friction among staff as other workers become resentful of having to pick up the slack for an inept employee. Inappropriate hires may even lead better employees to seek employment elsewhere. While job-specific knowledge, skills, and abilities are important, the overall "fit" between candidate and organization also has a bearing on the effectiveness of the staffing process (see Figure 5-6).

All these effects have economic ramifications.[15] In fact, the economic value of good selection procedures is higher than most people realize. For example, the U.S. federal government's use of ability testing for entry-level jobs has been estimated to save them over $15 billion per year.[16] This amazing figure is derived from

1. **Assess the Overall Work Environment**
   - Job analysis
   - Organizational analysis

2. **Infer the Type of Person Required**
   - Technical knowledge, skills, and abilities
   - Social skills
   - Personal needs, values, and interests
   - Personality traits

3. **Design "Rites of Passage" for Organizational Entry That Allow Both the Organization and the Applicant to Assess Fit**
   - Tests of cognitive, motor, and interpersonal abilities
   - Interviews by potential co-workers and others
   - Personality tests
   - Realistic job previews, including work samples

4. **Reinforce Employee-Organization Fit at Work**
   - Reinforce skills and knowledge through task design and training
   - Reinforce personal orientation through organization design

Figure 5–6 Hiring Process Designed to Produce Employee-Organization Fit

SOURCE: Bowen, D. E., Ledford, G. E., Jr., & Nathan, B. R. (1991, November). Hiring for the organization, not the job. *Academy of Management Executive,* 5 (4), 37.

the cumulative effects of modest job-performance increases by people who were hired because they scored better than average on the selection test. Continually hiring people who perform, say, 20 percent above average can make a tremendous difference to an organization that hires many workers. It can even make a dramatic difference when job performance over time is considered.

A variety of tools can be used in the selection process. Before we consider these techniques, though, it is important for you to be aware of two important concepts important to selection tools: reliability and validity.

Reliability and Validity.   **Reliability** refers to consistency of measurement, usually across time, but also across judges. Put differently, reliability depends upon how much error is present in a measure. There are many sources of error in measurement. Consider the typical employment interview. After the interview is over, the interviewer has an overall impression of the suitability of the job candidate. This overall impression is the measurement that results from the interview. It is hoped that the candidate's job-related qualifications have had a large impact on that measurement. But, almost certainly, other factors not related to the job have also influenced the measure. These other factors may include:

reliability
Consistency of measurement, usually across time but also across judges.

◆ *Comparison with other candidates:* If the other candidates the interviewer has seen have been pretty bad, a mediocre candidate will probably impress the interviewer as strong. The reverse also holds: if the other candidates have been exceptionally strong, a well-qualified candidate may seem merely mediocre.

◆ *Time pressures:* The interviewer may be distracted during the interview by other pressing job demands and therefore unable to evaluate accurately the candidate's strengths and weaknesses.

◆ *Impression management:* Some interviewees are skillful at creating a very positive first impression, but this favourable impression does not carry over to actual job performance. (Of course, some jobs, like sales, are probably best filled by people who are skilled at impression management.)

The job interview is supposed to measure job-related qualifications. The more factors such as those mentioned above influence the interview impression, the more errors there are likely to be in that particular measure. Reliability is an index of how much these errors have influenced the measure. To the extent that a measure lacks reliability, it limits its *potential* validity as a predictor.

validity

The extent to which scores on a test or interview correspond to actual job performance.

Validity is the extent to which scores on a test or interview correspond to actual job performance. Validity is at the heart of effective selection. It represents how well the technique being used to assess candidates for a certain job is related to performance in that job. A technique that lacks validity is useless. In fact, documentation of the validity of a selection technique is central to the legal defensibility of a selection procedure.

There are two important strategies for demonstrating the validity of selection methods: content validity and empirical validity. A *content validity* strategy assesses the degree to which the content of the selection method (say, an interview or a test) is representative of job content. For example, people who wish to drive large trucks require a specific kind of driver's licence. Job knowledge tests are often validated using content validation. The rules of the road and the regulations that apply to the operation of commercial trucks are examined by a written test; the validity of that testing is determined by the extent to which the candidate is knowledgeable in those areas. Passing this part of the examination, valid as it is, is not a guarantee that the individual can safely operate a large vehicle. For that, a test of actual driving performance is required.

An *empirical validity* strategy demonstrates the relationship between the selection method and job performance. Scores on the selection method (say, interview judgements or test scores) are compared to ratings of job performance. If applicants who receive higher scores on the selection method also turn out to be better job performers, then empirical validity has been established.

Before we proceed to examine specific methods of selection, we need to emphasize an important point concerning reliability and validity. Selection methods can be reliable, but not valid; however, selection methods that are not reliable cannot be valid. This fact has a great deal of practical significance. Whether someone has an MBA or not can be measured with perfect reliability. But if having an MBA is not associated with improved job performance, attainment of an MBA is not a valid selection criterion for that job. It seems clear that more highly motivated applicants make better employees, but if the selection method used to measure motivation is full of errors (not reliable), then it cannot be a valid indicator of job performance.

Selection Tools as Predictors of Job Performance.   In this section we look at the most commonly used methods of selection. Each approach has its limitations as well as its advantages. Each method attempts to reliably measure one or more personal characteristics that can predict future employee performance. Each approach has its limitations as well as its advantages. Usually, a hiring process uses several methods, in combination.

Letters of Recommendation.   In general, letters of recommendation are not highly related to job performance because most are highly positive.[17] This doesn't mean that *all* letters of recommendation are poor indicators of performance, however. A poor letter of recommendation may be very predictive and shouldn't be ignored.

A content approach to considering letters of recommendation can increase the validity of this selection tool. This approach focusses on the content of the letters rather than on the extent of their positivity.[18] Assessment is done in terms of the traits the letter writer ascribed to the job candidate.[19] For example, two candidates may produce equally positive letters, but the first candidate's letter may describe a detail-oriented person, while the second candidate's letter describes someone who is outgoing and helpful. The job to be filled may require one type of person rather than the other. For example, customer relations calls for an outgoing and helpful person, while clerical work requires someone who is detail oriented. Desired personal characteristics should be identified though job analysis prior to any recruitment efforts.

? A Question of Ethics

Suppose you are asked to write a recommendation letter for a friend whom you like but know to be unreliable. Would it be ethical for you to write a glowing reference even though you anticipate that your friend will not be a good employee? If not, would it be ethical for you to agree to write the letter knowing that you will not be very positive in your assessment of your friend's abilities?

Application Forms.   Organizations often use application forms as screening devices to determine if a candidate satisfies minimum job specifications, particularly for entry-level jobs. The forms typically ask for information regarding past jobs and present employment status.

A recent variation on the traditional application form is the *biodata form*.[20] This is essentially a more detailed version of the application form in which applicants respond to a series of questions about their background, experiences, and preferences. Responses to these questions are then scored. For instance, candidates might be asked how willing they are to travel on the job, what leisure activities they prefer, and how much experience they have had with computers. As with any selection tool, the biodata most relevant to the job should be identified before the application form is created. Biodata have been found to have moderate validity in predicting job performance.

Ability Tests.   Ability tests measure a wide range of abilities, from verbal and qualitative skills to perceptual speed. *Cognitive ability tests* measure a candidate's potential in a certain area, such as math, and are valid predictors of job performance when the abilities tested have been identified as relevant by job analysis.

A number of studies have examined the validity of *general cognitive ability (g)* as a predictor of job performance. General cognitive ability is typically measured by summing the scores on tests of verbal and quantitative ability. Essentially, g measures general intelligence. A higher level of g indicates a person who can learn more and faster and who can adapt quickly to changing conditions. People with higher levels of g have been found to be better job performers in a wide range of occupations, at least in part because few jobs are static today.[21]

Some more specific tests measure physical or mechanical abilities. For example, police and fire departments use physical ability tests to measure strength and endurance. The results of these tests are considered indicators of how productively and safely a person could perform the job's physical tasks. However, employers can often get a more direct measure of applicants' performance ability by observing how well they perform on actual job tasks. These types of direct performance tests, called work sample tests, ask applicants to perform the exact same tasks that they would be performing on the job. For example, Levi Strauss's work-sample test asks applicants for maintenance and repair positions to disassemble and reassemble a sewing machine component.[22]

Work-sample tests are widely viewed as fair and valid measures of job performance, as long as the work samples adequately capture the variety and complexity of tasks in the actual job. Work-sample tasks have even been used as criteria for assessing the validity of general mental ability selection measures.[23] However, physical ability measures have been found to screen out disproportionate numbers of men and certain minorities, a problem that can be minimized by physical preparation for the tests.[24]

Testing can be a source of illegal discrimination. While not intentionally discriminatory, testing can be a form of *systemic discrimination* if it disqualifies disproportionate numbers of a protected class (e.g., women, visible minorities) where there is no demonstrated difference in performance. An example of this occurred with CN Rail, where a particular test was found to discriminate unfairly against women.[25]

The Second Step.

After sending in a résumé or completing a qualifying test, qualified candidates are often called in for a face-to-face interview. Many candidates are chosen only after a series of interviews with managers and employers from across the company.

Personality Tests.   Personality tests assess *traits,* personal characteristics that tend to be consistent and enduring. Personality tests were widely used to make employee selection decisions in the 1940s and 1950s,[26] but today they are rarely used to predict job-related behaviours.[27] The arguments against using personality tests revolve around questions of reliability and validity. It has been argued that traits are subjective and unreliable,[28] unrelated to job performance,[29] and not legally acceptable.[30]

Perhaps the major reason personality tests fell out of favour is that there is no commonly agreed-upon set of trait measures. Many traits can be measured in a variety of ways, and this lack of consistency produces problems with reliability and validity. However, recent research on personality measurement has demonstrated that personality can be reliably measured[31] and summarized as being composed of five dimensions.[32] These "Big Five" factors, now widely accepted in the field of personality psychology, are:[33]

◆ Extroversion—the degree to which someone is talkative, sociable, active, aggressive, and excitable.

◆ Agreeableness—the degree to which someone is trusting, amiable, generous, tolerant, honest, cooperative, and flexible.

◆ Conscientiousness—the degree to which someone is dependable and organized and conforms and perseveres on tasks.

◆ Emotional stability—the degree to which someone is secure, calm, independent, and autonomous.

◆ Openness to experience—the degree to which someone is intellectual, philosophical, insightful, creative, artistic, and curious.

Of the five factors, conscientiousness appears to be most related to job performance.[34] It is hard to imagine a measure of job performance that would not require dependability or an organization that would not benefit from employing conscientious workers. Conscientiousness is thus the most generally valid personality predictor of job performance.

The validity of the other personality factors seems to be more job-specific, which brings us to two caveats about personality tests. First, whether personality characteristics are valid predictors of job performance depends on both the job and the criteria used to measure job performance. As in all selection techniques, a job analysis should be done first to identify the personality factors that enhance job performance. Second, personality may play little or no role in predicting performance on certain measures, such as the number of pieces produced on a factory line, which may largely depend on such factors as speed of the production line. Personality factors may, however, play a critical role in jobs that are less regimented and demand teamwork and flexibility.

The Meyers-Briggs Type Indicator, a popular personality test used by a number of large, progressive companies, has been used primarily in management development programs. As companies increase their efforts to determine how well applicants fit into the organization, however, this type of personality indicator is being used as a selection test as well.[35]

Meyers-Briggs Type Indicator
metalab.unc.edu/personality/
faq-mbti.html

Interviews.   Although the job interview is probably the most common selection tool, it has often been criticized for its poor reliability and low validity.[36] Countless studies have found that interviewers do not agree with one another on candidate assessments. Other criticisms include human judgement limitations and biases to which interviewers are subject. For example, one early study found that most interviewers make decisions about candidates in the first two or three minutes of the interview.[37] Snap decisions can adversely affect an interview's validity because they depend on very limited information. More recent research, however, indicates that interviewers may not consistently make such hasty decisions.[38]

Another criticism is that traditional interviews are conducted in such a way that the interview experience is very different from interviewee to interviewee. For instance, it is very common for the interviewer to open with the following question: "Tell me about yourself." The interview then proceeds in a haphazard fashion depending on the applicant's answer to that first question. Essentially, each applicant experiences a different selection method. Thus it is not surprising that traditional interviews have very low reliability. It is possible to increase the effectiveness of traditional, unstructured job interviews, however, by following the guidelines presented in the Manager's Notebook entitled "Unstructured Doesn't Mean Unprepared: Making the Most of the Hiring Interview."

Dissatisfaction with the traditional unstructured interview has led to an alternative approach called the structured interview.[39] The **structured interview** is based directly on a thorough job analysis. It applies a series of job-related questions with predetermined answers consistently across all interviews for a particular job.[40] Figure 5–7 gives examples of the three types of questions commonly used in structured interviews.[41]

♦ *Situational questions* try to elicit from candidates how they would respond to particular work situations. These questions can be developed from the critical incident technique of job analysis: supervisors and workers rewrite critical incidents of behaviour as situational interview questions, then generate and score possible answers. During the interview, candidates' answers to the situational questions are scored on the basis of the possible answers already generated.

♦ *Job knowledge questions* assess whether candidates have the basic knowledge needed to perform the job.

♦ *Worker-requirements questions* assess their willingness to perform under prevailing job conditions.

Manager's Notebook

Unstructured Doesn't Mean Unprepared: Making the Most of the Hiring Interview

Managers can increase the effectiveness of unstructured interviews by focussing on six simple tasks.

♦ **Be prepared.** The Boy Scouts' motto could just as well be the interviewer's. Lack of preparation is the most common, and costly, mistake interviewers make. At least a day in advance, use the interviewee's résumé and discussions with key personnel to create an interview agenda, and take at least 15 minutes to review this agenda before the appointment.

♦ **Put applicants at ease in the first few minutes.** Few things are more unsettling to an interviewee than being ushered into an office and watching his or her interviewer make business phone calls or have an impromptu meeting with a colleague. Take care of business before greeting interview-ees, and put them at ease with some pleasant small talk before rushing into the interview questions.

♦ **Don't be ruled by snap judgements or stereotypes.** Stereotyping is bad for the manager and bad for the company. Curb your tendency to rush to judgement and always keep in mind that you are dealing with an individual, not a type.

♦ **Ask results-oriented questions.** Ask questions that are designed to uncover not only what the job candidate has done but also what the results of the person's actions have been.

♦ **Don't underestimate the power of silence.** Many interviewers make the mistake of jumping in during any pause in the dialogue to discuss their own views on management and the company. Silences can be a time when the inter-viewee is absorbing information and forming a question or comment, and these are usually worth waiting for.

♦ **Close the interview with care.** Some interviewers let the session drift on until both parties begin to flounder about or lose interest. Others close an interview abruptly when interrupted by a phone call or a colleague. It's best to plan a time limit for the interview and to bring it to a natural close rather than let an outside event terminate the conversation prematurely.

SOURCE: Excerpted, with permission of the publisher, from Uris, A. (1988). *88 mistakes interviewers make and how to avoid them.* New York: Amacom Books. © 1988 AMACOM, a division of the American Management Association. All rights reserved.

Type	Example
Situational	You're packing things into your car and getting ready for your family vacation when it hits you that you promised to meet a client this morning. You didn't pencil the meeting into your calendar and it slipped your mind until just now. What do you do?
Job Knowledge	What is the correct procedure for determining the appropriate oven temperature when running a new batch of steel?
Worker Requirements	Some periods are extremely busy in our business. What are your feelings about working overtime?

structured interview
A job interview based on a thorough job analysis. It applies a series of job-related questions with predetermined answers that are consistent across all interviews for a particular job.

Figure 5–7 Examples of Structured Interview Questions

Structured interviews are quite valid predictors of job performance.[42] A number of factors are probably responsible for this high level of validity. First, the content of a structured interview is, by design, limited to job-related factors. Second, the questions that are asked are consistent across all interviewees. Third, all responses are scored the same way. Finally, a panel of interviewers is typically involved in conducting the structured interview; this limits the impact of individual interviewers' idiosyncrasies and biases.

Structured interviews have been used quite successfully in practice. One variant of the structured interview is the "behavioural sample" technique. The Edmonton police force has found it useful in assessing the assertiveness of candidates, to assess how persuasive a candidate can be without resorting to aggression or violence.[43] Structured interviews are sometimes combined with other techniques, such as panel interviews. Such a panel would typically include an HR manager, the hiring manager, perhaps the hiring manager's boss, and key people from other departments that would work closely with the new hire. Employers using this process often find it useful to interview all candidates for a position within a fairly short period so they can make accurate comparisons among the candidates. To maintain the value of independent assessors, some employers use written ratings immediately after the interview to facilitate the discussions where candidates are compared.[44]

If the structured interview is so effective, why is the traditional interview a much more popular selection tool? One reason is that the panel format typical of structured interviews is equated by many with a stress test. Perhaps the major reason that the structured interview has failed to replace the traditional unstructured interview, however, is that organizations find the traditional type of interview quite useful, probably because it serves more functions than just selection.[45] For example, it can be an effective public relations tool in which the interviewer gives a positive impression of the organization. Even a candidate who isn't hired may retain this positive impression. In addition, the unstructured interview may be a valid predictor of the degree to which a candidate will fit with the organization. While the concept of "fit" is somewhat ambiguous,[46] we are referring here to the match between the candidate's values and traits and the chemistry of the organization or work unit. A good fit helps make things run smoothly and efficiently. People who fit in well tend to feel a greater commitment to the organization. A good fit between the person and the organization is also related to job satisfaction and intention to stay with the organization.[47] Fit with the organization can be particularly important in team situations, which is why some organizations have begun to use team interviews. For more details, see the Issues and Applications feature entitled "Hiring for Teamwork: What to Look For."

Finally, unstructured interviews may be better than structured interviews at screening out unsuitable applicants.[48] Many times a candidate who seemed "fine" on paper reveals some disturbing qualities during an unstructured interview (see Figure 5–8). Human judgement may be subject to error and bias, but people can be quite good at assessing a candidate's fit with their organization.

From time to time, the "stress" interview is offered as a prescription for identifying weak candidates who might otherwise slip through the screening process. The interviewer behaves in an adversarial, abrasive manner. The applicant is assessed on whether he or she responds effectively, as defined by the interviewer, to this treatment. There are some anecdotal accounts that attribute great success to such tactics.[49] However, there is no general or systematic evidence along those lines. With the exception of certain jobs—perhaps salespeople who deal with high levels of resistance—the stress interview is not a very good sampler of behaviour required for good performance. This limited relevance, combined with interviewers whose diagnostic abilities are often uneven, and the public relations liabilities of treating applicants this way justify the following conclusion: Most employers should exclude the "stress'" interview from their recruiting and selection procedures.

Based on a nationwide survey of 200 executives conducted by Accountemps, the world's largest temporary personnel service for accounting, bookkeeping, and information technology, the interview behaviour of some jobseekers today can only be described as bizarre. Here are some of the more unusual behaviours respondents witnessed or heard of happening during a job interview:

- "Left his dry cleaner tag on his jacket and said he wanted to show he was a clean individual."
- "After a difficult question, she wanted to leave the room momentarily to meditate."
- "Applicant walked in and inquired why he was here."
- "Said that if I hired him, I'd soon learn to regret it."

- "Said if he was hired, he'd teach me ballroom dancing at no charge, and started demonstrating."
- "Arrived with a snake around her neck. Said she took her pet everywhere."
- "Woman brought in a large shopping bag of cancelled cheques and thumbed through them during the interview."
- "When asked about loyalty, showed a tattoo of his girlfriend's name."

- "Applicant indicated that if he wasn't hired, the future of the company would be jeopardized for confidential reasons."
- "Took three cellular phone calls. Said she had a similar business on the side."
- "She returned that afternoon asking if we could re-do the entire interview."

Figure 5–8 Unusual Job Interview Behaviours

SOURCE: Survey reveals unusual job interview behavior. *Human Resource Measurements* (a supplement to the September 1992 issue of *Personnel Journal*), 7.

Whether employers choose to use structured or unstructured interviews, they need to make sure their interview questions are not illegal. Companies that ask job applicants certain questions (for example, their race, religion/creed, sex, national origin, marital status, or number of children) either on application forms or in the interview process run the risk of violating of federal or provincial human rights codes. To comply with the law, interviewers should remember the nine don'ts of interviewing:[50]

1. Don't ask applicants if they have children, plan to have children, or what child care arrangements they have made.

2. Don't ask an applicant's age.

3. Don't ask whether the candidate has a physical or mental disability that would interfere with doing the job. The law allows employers to explore the subject of disabilities only *after* making a job offer that is conditional on satisfactory completion of a required physical, medical, or job-skills test.

4. Don't ask for such identifying characteristics as height or weight on an application.

Issues and Applications

Hiring for Teamwork: What to Look For

Teamwork situations require team members to communicate and work toward common goals. Specific technical skills, which are often the central concern when selecting people to work in individual jobs, may be relatively less important in team situations. What characteristics, then, should employers look for when hiring people who will work on a team? While much research remains to be done, preliminary findings indicate that effective team members should be able to:

◆ *Recognize and resolve conflict.* Conflict can destroy a team's effectiveness. Team members must have the ability to deal with and resolve the disagreements and clashes that will inevitably occur.

◆ *Participate and collaborate in problem solving.* Teams are often expected to solve their own problems rather than look to supervisors for answers.

◆ *Communicate openly and supportively.* Teams need open communication, and team members need to support one another. The inability to communicate, or a tendency to communicate negatively, could be very detrimental to team effectiveness.

◆ *Coordinate and synchronize activities.* Team operations require the cooperation of all team members and the coordination of various tasks.

In addition, effective team members usually have the following personality characteristics.

◆ *Conscientiousness.* Team members must be able to depend on one another. Someone who doesn't follow through can cause problems for the entire group effort.

◆ *Agreeableness.* Team members need to be flexible and tolerant if they are to meld into an effective unit.

Because current team members are often very sensitive to requirements for success on their team, a number of companies are now conducting "team interview" to determine whether job candidates possess the necessary skills and traits. such interviews are likely to become more popular as the emphasis on teamwork increases.

SOURCE: Cardy, R.L. and Stewart, G.L. (1997). Quality and teams: Implications fir HRM theory and research. In D.B. Fedor and S. Goshs (Eds.), *Advances in the Management of Organizational Quality,* 2. Greenwich, Connecticut: JAI press; Stevens, M.J and Campion M.A. (1994). The knowledge, skill, and ability requirements for teamwork: Implications for human resource management. *Journal of Management,* 20, 503-530.

5. Don't ask a female candidate for her maiden name. Some employers have asked this in order to ascertain marital status, another topic that is off-limits in interviewing both men and women.

6. Don't ask applicants about their citizenship.

7. Don't ask applicants about their arrest records. You are, however, allowed to ask whether the candidate has ever been convicted of a crime for which a pardon has been granted.

8. Don't ask if a candidate smokes. Because there are numerous federal, provincial, and local ordinances that restrict smoking in certain buildings, a more appropriate question is whether the applicant is aware of these regulations and is willing to comply with them.

9. Don't ask a job candidate if he or she has AIDS or is HIV-positive.

The key point to remember is not to ask questions that are peripheral to the work itself. Rather, interviewers should stay focussed on the objective of hiring someone who is qualified to perform the tasks the job requires.

assessment centre

A set of simulated tasks or exercises that candidates are asked to perform.

Assessment Centres. An **assessment centre** is a set of simulated tasks or exercises that candidates (usually for managerial positions) are asked to perform. Observers rate performance on the simulations and make inferences about a candidate's managerial skills and abilities. Major companies such as Nortel and IBM make use of assessment centres. So does the federal civil service.[51] In addition, there are consulting companies that run assessment centres, thus enabling smaller organizations that could not afford the costs of designing their own to gain the benefits of this sophisticated diagnostic technique.

While expensive, the assessment centre appears to be a valid predictor of managerial job performance.[52] Assessment centres are usually conducted off premises, last from one to three days, and may include up to six candidates at a time. Most assessment centres evaluate each candidate's abilities in four areas: organizing, planning, decision making, and leadership. However, there is considerable variability in what an assessment centre includes, how it is conducted, and how it is scored.[53]

The *in-basket exercise* is probably the exercise most widely associated with assessment centres. An in-basket exercise includes problems, messages, reports, and so on that might be found in a manager's in-basket. The candidates are asked to deal with these issues as they see fit, and then are assessed on how well they prioritized the issues, how creative and responsive they were in dealing with each one, the quality of their decisions, and other factors. Performance on an in-basket exercise can be highly revealing. Often it identifies the skills of a candidate who might otherwise have appeared average.[54]

Mercury Communications
www.mercury.net

Assessment centres have been used to help select front-line workers as well as managers. For instance, the British telecommunications firm Mercury Communications used assessment centres to recruit 1,000 customer service assistants for its new site near Manchester. The assessment centre activities involved simulated call-handling and decision-making exercises. Mercury's managers believe that these assessment centres are very effective in screening for skills that are important for customer service representatives to have—skills including listening, sensitivity to customers, and the ability to cope in a pressured environment.[55]

Drug Tests. The purpose of pre-employment drug testing, usually based on urinalysis, is to avoid hiring workers who pose unnecessary risks to themselves and others on the job, and who may be more frequently absent from work or performing below expectations.

Pre-employment drug testing is not a matter in which simple statements about what is legal or proper can be made. The legal ambiguity comes from the fact that employment-related drug testing is not directly legislated, but rather is affected by several laws and precedents. The legal limits to pre-employment drug testing stem primarily from human rights codes. The federal human rights code, for example, treats drug or alcohol dependence as a disability. To deny employment on the basis of a positive test could be construed as discriminating against someone on the basis of a disability.[56] A protracted case involving drug testing at the Toronto Dominion Bank permitted the bank's testing to continue for some time because employees could not be dismissed for drug dependence, only for refusing to agree to a legally acceptable company policy on drug testing.[57] Thus, testing with the subsequent action of supporting rehabilitation for those who test positive appears to be legal under federal legislation. The provinces vary in their posture (see MiniCase 1 for further exploration of this topic). It is not clear how aggressive an employer may be in pursuing the matter of drug testing without risk of protracted legal challenge.

Toronto Dominion Bank
www.tdbank.ca/tdbank/
indexjava.html

It is clear that employers can legally discipline employees for being impaired on the job. Such discipline can include sanctions up to and including discharge. It may then seem unreasonable that drug testing should be so contentious. The difficulties lie more with the usefulness of drug testing than with the understandable desire to run a safe, unimpaired operation. Here are a few of the problems:

◆ Urinalysis is not an indicator of whether the individual is impaired at the time the sample is provided. It may indicate use of a substance during some preceding period of days or weeks, but it does not indicate current impairment.

◆ Drug tests are not infallible. Some less expensive tests generate both false negative and false positive results. Some illegal substances do not register on commonly used tests. Further, the accuracy of the tests is influenced by the care and professionalism of those processing the samples.

◆ Some legal substances (e.g., foods such as poppy seeds) can sometimes trigger a false positive reading. Some legal prescription medications have ingredients that also will yield a false positive result.

◆ Sampling of urine is intrusive into individuals' privacy. Body fluids can indicate many things, depending on the analyses that are performed. There is little to stop an unscrupulous employer from performing other tests that might reveal something about an employee, for example, whether she is pregnant.

Employers do have a legitimate concern with maintaining a safe and productive organization. To the extent that impaired workers pose a threat, the following steps deserve consideration.

◆ Relatively simple tests that demonstrate the extent of impairment are being developed for both manual dexterity and hand-eye tasks, and for tasks of an intellectual nature. These are potentially much more effective in identifying impaired conditions than drug tests.[58]

◆ Human rights commissions are generally open to bona fide exceptions to the prohibition of testing; safety-sensitive positions (e.g., operating public transportation vehicles) can be treated as exceptional circumstances where the risks of being impaired are compelling, leading to allowable testing.

◆ A study of the causes of workplace accidents among 882 Ontario employers indicated that sleep disorders, not the use of illicit drugs, was the single most common factor contributing to or associated with workplace accidents.[59] Employers concerned with workplace safety need to apply a sense of proportion when trying to reduce overall risks.

◆ The central objection to widespread drug testing combines both the efficacy of and the motive for such tests. Bruce Feldthusen, a law professor at the University of Western Ontario, succinctly refers to such tests as "lifestyle control." "It has nothing to do with productivity or employer interests. ... None of these tests tell you anything about whether this person is impaired at work."[60]

In 1998, Canadian Human Rights Commission (CHRC) ruled on a case initiated by the Canadian Civil Liberties Association in 1991. The CHRC found that the policy of the Toronto-Dominion Bank to give recently hired employees a drug-screening test unnecessarily infringed on the privacy of the employees. The bank, they found, had not demonstrated the connection between the results of the drug test and employee performance, nor had they shown that there was evidence of a problem with drug-related crime.[61]

There is some evidence that some pre-employment drug testing done in the United States has been a moderately useful predictor of work-related shortcomings reflected in absence and terminations.[62] The general societal concern with substance abuse will likely continue because such abuse is associated with serious social problems such as crime and dysfunctions within the family. The statutes and the precedents of courts and commissions will certainly provide increasing clarity as to what employers are permitted to do. What employers need to ask themselves is what their objectives are in the area of drug testing, and how best to pursue those objectives. From what we know now, drug testing probably deserves no more than a minor and specialized role in the overall pursuit of a healthy, unimpaired work force and a safe working environment.

Honesty Tests. Each year businesses lose billions of dollars to employee theft. Limiting these losses has an obvious payoff for employers, and various ways have been tried to inhibit theft and to detect those who are responsible. The polygraph, popularly known as the lie detector, was used by some employers to screen prospective employees. Using physiological indicators (pulse, breathing rate, galvanic skin response [perspiration]), subjects were asked to respond to a range of questions; their physical reactions while they answered were observed and recorded. The technique's potential for error, combined with its intrusiveness, has led to a general prohibition of its use by employers in several jurisdictions. Paper-and-pencil honesty tests have proved to be an increasingly popular alternative. The typical test measures attitudes toward honesty, particularly whether the applicant believes that dishonest behaviour is normal and not criminal.[63] For example, the test might measure the applicant's tolerance for theft by other people and the extent to which the applicant believes that most people steal regularly.

A recent study by independent researchers appears to confirm the validity of honesty testing.[64] It found that scores on the honesty test taken by applicants for positions at a retail convenience store chain were moderately tied to actual incidences of theft. Specifically, those who scored more poorly on the honesty test were more likely to steal from their employer.

Nevertheless, honesty tests are controversial. Most of the arguments against integrity testing centre on the issue of false positives: people who are honest but score poorly on the tests. Typically, at least 40 percent of the test takers receive failing marks.[65] To see how you might score on such a test, answer the sample honesty test questions in the Issues and Applications feature entitled "Your Answers Could Win—or Cost—You Your Job."

Reference Checks. One of the best methods of predicting the future success of prospective employees is to look at the applicant's past employment record. Unfortunately, fear of defamation suits has caused many companies to keep mum about job-related information on former employees. However, checking employees' references is an employer's best tactic for avoiding negligent hiring suits, in which the employer is held liable for injuries inflicted by an employee on the job. What should companies do? It is generally accepted that employers—both former and prospective—are justified in discussing an employee's past performance. However, it is realistic to expect that previous employers may be rather cryptic in their comments, especially with regard to negative information. The potential for being accused of deliberate defamation will frequently limit the amount of information released. Many employers have policies that direct such inquiries from other employers to the Human Resources unit, from which the prospective employer is likely to get little more than a confirmation of dates of employment and position held.

graphology
The study of handwriting for the purpose of measuring personality or other individual traits.

Handwriting Analysis. **Graphology,** the study of handwriting for the purpose of measuring personality or other individual traits, is routinely used to screen job applicants in Europe, the birthplace of the technique. Analysis can involve assessment of over 300 aspects of handwriting, including the slope of the letters, the height at which the letter *t* is crossed, and the pressure of the writing. Although graphology is not as widely used in North America as it is in Europe, a significant number of companies use the procedure as part of their screening process. The important question, of course, is whether handwriting is a valid predictor of job performance. Research on this issue indicates that the answer is no.

One study collected handwriting samples from 115 real estate associates and gave them to 20 graphologists, who scored each sample on a variety of traits, such as confidence, sales drive, and decision making.[66] Later, these results were com-pared with the subject's actual performance ratings as well as with objective performance measures such as amount of sales. There was a fair amount of consistency across graphologists' judgements of the handwriting samples (reliability). However, none of the judgements made by the graphologists correlated with any of the performance measures, so graphology cannot be considered a valid measure. Thus it should not be used as an employment screening device.

Issues and Applications

Your Answers Could Win—or Cost—You Your Job

Selection usually focusses on knowledge, skill, and ability, as well as on the overall "fit" between a candidate and the organization. Some employers have at least one other important consideration that has little bearing on whether the person is competent or will fit in. Employees working in positions where theft of merchandise, tools, or supplies is plausible; employees who handle cash; and employees in a position with discretion to allocate organizational resources all represent potential threats.

Although prudent employers take security precautions, they still depend on employee honesty. It is simply too expensive to depend only on "policing" to control the costs of dishonesty. But how can department stores and other retail organizations control shrinkage? How can manufacturers keep tools and supplies from disappearing? One technique that is receiving increased attention is testing of applicants for "integrity." The following are typical questions used in integrity tests prepared by test publisher Reid Psychological Systems. Some of these questions are clearly "no-brainers" for test takers aware of the purpose of the test: *Of course* it's wrong to give other employees improper discounts. But other questions may be more grey than black and white.

◆ Do you believe a person who writes a cheque for which he knows there is no money in the bank should be refused a job in which honesty is important?

◆ Do you think a person should be fired by a company if it is found that she helped the employees cheat the company out of overtime once in a while?

◆ If you found $100 that was lost by a bank truck on the street yesterday, would you turn the money over to the bank, even though you knew for sure that there was no reward?

◆ Do you think it is all right for one employee to give another employee a discount even though the company does not allow it?

◆ Do you believe that an employee who regularly borrows small amounts of money from the place where he works without permission, but always pays it back, is honest?

◆ Do you think that the way a company is run is more responsible for employee theft than the attitudes and tendencies of employees themselves?

◆ On the 20th of each month, an old employee took company money to pay on his mortgage. On the 30th of each month—payday—he paid it back. After 15 years the man finally was seen by his boss putting the money back. No shortage was found, but the boss fired him anyway. Do you think the boss was right?

◆ Would you ever consider buying something from somebody if you knew the item had been stolen?

SOURCE: Adapted from Budman, M. (1993, November–December). Your answers could win — or cost—your job. *Across the Board*, 35.

Combining Predictors.   Organizations often use multiple methods to collect information about applicants. For instance, managers may be selected on the basis of past performance ratings, an assessment centre evaluation, and an interview with the manager to whom they will be reporting. How should these pieces of information be combined to make an effective selection decision? There are three basic strategies. The first requires making a preliminary selection decision following the administration of each method. This approach is called *multiple hurdle strategy* because an applicant has to clear each hurdle before moving on to the next one.

Both of the remaining approaches require collecting all the information before making any decision; the difference is in how that information is combined. In a *clinical strategy* the decision maker subjectively evaluates all of the information and comes to an overall judgement. In a *statistical strategy* the various pieces of information are combined according to some type of formula, and the job goes to the candidate with the highest score.

The multiple hurdle strategy is often the choice when a large number of applicants must be considered. Usually, the procedure is to use the less expensive methods first to screen out clearly unqualified applicants. Research studies indicate that a statistical strategy—where it can be used—is generally more reliable and valid than a clinical strategy,[67] but many people, and probably most organizations, prefer the latter.

◼ Socialization

The staffing process isn't, and shouldn't be, complete once applicants are hired or promoted. To retain and maximize the human resources who were so carefully selected, organizations must pay careful attention to socializing them.

Socialization is the process by which new employees are introduced to the organization, their work unit, and their job. This socialization is often informal, and, unfortunately, informal can mean poorly planned and haphazard. A thorough and systematic approach to socializing new employees is necessary if they are to become effective workers. Without a socialization program, new employees may misunderstand the company's mission and reporting relationships, and may get inaccurate views of how things work and why. Socializing new employees is too important to be left to chance.

The process of socialization can be divided into three phases: (1) anticipatory, (2) encounter, and (3) settling in.[68] At the *anticipatory stage,* applicants generally have a variety of expectations about the organization and job based on accounts provided by newspapers and other media, word of mouth, public relations, and so on. A number of these expectations may be unrealistic and, if unmet, can lead to dissatisfaction, poor performance, and high turnover.

realistic job preview (RJP)

Realistic information given to new hires about the demands of the job, the organization's expectations of the job holder, and the work environment.

A **realistic job preview (RJP)** is probably the best method of creating appropriate expectations about the job.[69] As its name indicates, an RJP presents realistic information about the demands of the job, the organization's expectations of the job holder, and the work environment. This presentation may be made either to applicants or to newly selected employees before they start work. For example, a person applying for a job selling life insurance should be told up front about the potentially negative parts of the job, such as the uncertain commission-based income and the need to try to sell insurance to personal acquaintances. Of course, the positive parts of the job, such as personal autonomy and high income potential, should also be mentioned. RJPs can be presented orally, in written form, on videotape, or, occasionally, in a full-blown work sample. Such processes work effectively in situations ranging from manufacturing, such as at Toyota's Cambridge, Ontario, plant, to selecting senior staff, as done by the Privy Council Office of the federal government.[70]

In the *encounter phase* of the socialization process, the new hire has started work and is facing the reality of the job. Even if an RJP was provided, new hires need information about policies and procedures, reporting relationships, rules, and so on. This type of information is helpful even for new employees who have had substantial experience elsewhere because often the organization or work unit does things somewhat differently than these employees are used to. In addition, providing systematic information about the organization and job can be a very positive signal to new workers that they are highly valued members of the organization. We discuss this *orientation period* for employees as a training opportunity in detail in Chapter 8.

During the *settling-in phase,* new workers begin to feel they are part of the organization. If the settling in is successful, the worker will feel comfortable with the job and his or her role in the work unit. If it is unsuccessful, the worker may feel distant from the work unit and fail to develop a sense of membership in the organization. An *employee mentoring program,* in which an established worker serves as an adviser to the new employee, may help ensure that settling in is a success.[71] (We discuss mentoring programs at length in Chapter 9.)

Even the most extensive socialization program won't make new hires feel at ease if their immediate supervisors are not supportive during the adjustment period. See the Manager's Notebook entitled "Building New Workers' Confidence" for a list of actions that managers can take to make new employees feel at home in the organization.

■ Legal Issues in Staffing

Legal issues can play a significant role in staffing. Human rights codes provide the major source of legal requirements. Employers should take these requirements seriously, because (1) there are important ethical and legal issues involved, (2) there can be significant penalties for violating the law, and (3) there are very few cost barriers to a complainant. If a person files a human rights complaint, the Human Rights Commission with jurisdiction typically will pursue the matter if there appears to be a plausible basis for it. Unlike a civil suit, the aggrieved party does not need deep pockets to pursue the complaint. The bases on which an employer can be charged with unlawful discrimination in all Canadian jurisdictions include the following: race, colour, religion/creed, sex, marital status, physical disability, and age (protected age categories vary among jurisdictions). In some jurisdictions, discrimination is also prohibited on the basis of mental disability, ethnic/national origin, harassment (on any of the proscribed grounds), criminal conviction or pardoned offence, family status, political beliefs, and sexual orientation.

Discriminatory actions in hiring can take two forms, intentional and unintentional (also referred to as systemic discrimination). To establish that the first kind of discrimination has occurred, there must be evidence that there was an intention to discriminate. Systemic discrimination, in contrast, simply requires the demonstration that the procedures and practices created an adverse impact on members of a particular group that is protected under the law. Practices that required male employees to be clean shaven and have short hair were found to be discriminatory against Sikh men (*Ishar Singh v. Security and Investigation,* 1977), as was a company policy that required workers to be available for work on Saturdays with reference to members of the Seventh-Day Adventist faith (*O'Malley v. Simpson-Sears Ltd.,* 1985).[72] Systemic discrimination during recruiting and selection can take place through use of recruitment channels that effectively exclude members of protected groups, advertising that discourages some groups from applying, application forms that ask for information about age, sex, marital status, etc., testing that has an adverse impact on protected groups where there is no demonstrated validity of the test, and requirements for Canadian experience, educational attainment, or height/weight requirements that are not grounded in explicit job requirements.

Manager's Notebook

Building New Workers' Confidence

Although there is no universally effective set of practices for helping new workers get into the swing of things, the following actions tend to work well with most people and in most situations.

1. Delegate non-critical tasks that are challenging yet achievable. Letting new people test their wings on a series of challenging tasks where mistakes can't do too much damage is always a good idea. As they experience success incrementally, their confidence will grow.

2. Sandwich criticism between praise. When something the new employee does causes things to go haywire, try not to blow the error out of proportion. Start by praising positive accomplishments, then discuss what needs correcting and close the conference on a note of praise.

3. Express confidence in the person's abilities. It's a real ego boost to hear someone say "I think you can do it."

4. Share early job experiences and self-doubts. Hearing about the boss's days as a new recruit makes employees realize that their anxiety is natural.

5. Acknowledge the value of previous experience. Ask new workers with previous experience to compare your company's systems and procedures with those of other employers.

6. Emphasize potential. Emphasizing potential encourages new workers to focus their energy on growth and development.

SOURCE: Adapted from Straub, J. T. (1993, May). Building new workers' confidence. *Supervising Management,* 10.

Mentoring.

Many people who settle into a job successfully have done so with the help of a mentor. Mentoring can be especially important for those who have not traditionally found positions in the upper echelons of management—specifically, women and members of ethnic and racial minority groups.

Many of the characteristics protected from discrimination can be discerned by looking at a person; for that reason, photographs should not be requested with application materials. Interviews are almost always part of the selection process. Avoiding illegal discrimination in interviewing should take two general forms. First, questions that directly or indirectly require an applicant to disclose information about prohibited criteria (e.g., age, marital status) should be avoided. Second, interviews should be designed so that the questions asked are grounded in an explicit job/organizational analysis and so that all candidates are treated in a similar fashion. For example, there should not be separate sets of questions for particular groups (e.g., young white males, women, visible minorities, older applicants).

For many employers, the attempt to function within human rights requirements may mean some changes in practice, and may feel awkward. For example, not asking applicants about their personal situation may strike someone who has often done so as strange and unreasonable. However, certain information needed for administrative or health and safety reasons can be collected at another, appropriate time. Where medical conditions may have a bearing on a person's suitability, such questions and examinations can take place after a conditional offer of employment has been extended. Only in the case of medical disqualification could the offer be withdrawn. Similarly, information on marital status and other personal data required for benefits plans administration should be collected after employment has been offered and accepted, not on applications or in interviews.

There is a limited range of circumstances under which members of protected groups can be rejected because of their age, sex, or other characteristics. These are generally referred to as bona fide occupational requirements (BFORs). If an employer acts in good faith and can demonstrate that a hiring standard is based on job requirements, they may escape the sanctions for illegal discrimination. For example, prisons may require guards to be of the same sex as the inmate population. Casting directors and advertising agencies can use age and sex in selecting models and actors. In general, the BFOR standard is quite stringent, and has been sustained that way by the legal doctrine of "reasonable accommodation." Under this doctrine, employers who could accommodate an applicant's religious holiday schedule or employ a person in a wheelchair with minor physical modifications to the workplace cannot claim BFOR as the reason for denying employment. If redesigning job duties, adjusting work schedules, or making minor changes to the physical/technological aspects of the workplace can be done at reasonable cost, employers in jurisdictions where reasonable accommodation is law are required to make such adjustments. Where an employer is found guilty of discrimination, the commission or court has a range of possible remedies, including:

♦ Prominent display of the appropriate human rights code.

♦ Required cessation of illegal practice(s), including improper selection tools and procedures.

♦ Compensation to the complainant for general damages, expenses, pain and humiliation.

♦ Reinstatement of employee.

♦ Required letter of apology.

♦ Offer of employment/promotion at next opening.

The federal *Employment Equity Act* of 1986 was passed to increase employment opportunities for four groups: women, aboriginal people, people with disabilities, and visible minorities. The *Act* applies to federal Crown corporations and federally regulated private sector employers with 100 or more employees, requiring them to file an annual report with the government documenting the status of their employee population. The Canadian Human Rights Commission has the authority to review these reports and can initiate complaints if it identifies systemic discrimination. The *Act* also requires employers to draft an annual equity plan, although this document does not have to be filed with the government. Other legislation having the purpose of advancing the employment status of designated groups includes the Federal Contractors Program, which requires employers doing business with the federal government and employing 100 or more employees to establish employee equity plans. Some 1,300 employers accounting for more than 1,100,000 employees are certified under this program.[73]

The *Public Service Reform Act* of 1992 had the effect of extending employment equity to the federal public service. Affirmative action programs of a voluntary nature are permissible in most Canadian jurisdictions; in some cases, human rights authorities are directed to advise and assist employers wishing to pursue affirmative action. Finally, equal pay legislation exists in all Canadian jurisdictions. Such laws affect hiring to the extent that men and women cannot be offered substantially different levels of pay for the same or similar work. Differences in relevant qualifications such as experience or education may play a legitimate role, but differences based on sex alone expose employers to liability.

Negligent Hiring.   A final legal concern is the possibility of wrongful or negligent hiring. Although the cumulative number of cases is still small, there are two ways in which an employer can encounter problems. First, failing to examine carefully the qualifications and background of an applicant who subsequently causes harm to others may legally implicate the employer. Second, seriously misrepresenting the nature of the position to the applicant opens the possibility that the employee can sue because of such misrepresentation.

The legal context for recruiting and selecting employees may appear to be tortuous. Intuition and traditional practices probably are not enough to keep the process on track. However, the legal framework largely reinforces practices that come from enlightened self-interest.

◆ Hiring should be based on a foundation of clear, up-to-date job analysis.

◆ Predictors, including tests, interviews, and all other devices should be constructed or chosen on their capability of accurately predicting the person's KSAs and demonstrated record of competence.

◆ Recruiting should not limit the probability of qualified candidates knowing about the position and becoming part of the applicant pool.

◆ Employers should be knowledgeable about the human rights legislation that applies, and should understand the requirements (if any) imposed by employment equity legislation. While involving some administrative expense, adhering to these requirements gives employers access to groups that have been excluded from many employment settings. Such people often constitute an underutilized resource.

◆ In issues such as employee honesty and substance abuse, employers should understand that the selection process is probably one of the least effective points at which to influence these matters. Care should be taken in reviewing employment histories and checking references. However, the validity of honesty tests and the ethics, legality, and predictive power of drug testing are unresolved questions.

Summary and Conclusions

Human Resource Planning.   HR planning is the process that an organization uses to ensure that it has the right numbers and right kinds of people to deliver a particular level of output or services at some point in the future. HR planning entails using a variety of qualitative and quantitative methods to forecast labour demand and labour supply, and then taking actions based on those estimates.

The Hiring Process.   The hiring process consists of three activities: recruitment, selection, and socialization.

Challenges in the Hiring Process.   The hiring process is filled with challenges. These are (1) determining which characteristics are most important to performance, (2) measuring these characteristics, (3) evaluating applicants' motivation, and (4) deciding who should make hiring decisions.

Meeting the Challenges of Effective Staffing.   Because choosing the right person for a job can make a tremendous positive difference to productivity and customer satisfaction, it is important that each step of the hiring process be managed carefully.

Recruiting should focus on attracting qualified candidates, internally, externally, or both. Recruiting efforts should be tied to the firm's human resource planning efforts. To ensure proper fit between hires and their jobs, and to avoid legal problems, firms should conduct job analyses.

Many selection tools are available. These include letters of recommendation, application forms, ability tests, personality tests, psychological tests, interviews, assessment centres, drug tests, honesty tests, reference checks, and handwriting analysis. The best (and most legally defensible) selection tools are both reliable and valid.

Socialization takes place in three stages: anticipatory, encounter, and settling in. Good socialization procedures ensure that new employees fit into the organization and work productively and effectively.

Legal Issues in Staffing.   Most of the legal influences on staffing are in the form of human rights code provisions, which differ slightly among Canadian jurisdictions. In addition to avoiding intentional and systemic discrimination on various grounds prohibited by human rights legislation, some Canadian employers also are subject to employment equity requirements designed to enhance the employment prospects of women, visible minorities, aboriginal people, and people with disabilities.

Key Terms and Concepts

anticipatory stage, 166
assessment centre, 162
biodata form, 157
clinical strategy, 165
cognitive ability test, 157
content validity, 156
cut score, 147
empirical validity, 156
employee mentoring program, 166
encounter phase, 166
external candidates, 152
general cognitive ability (g), 157

graphology, 164
human resource planning, 144
in-basket exercise, 162
internal candidates, 152
job-knowledge questions, 159
labour demand, 144
labour supply, 144
multiple hurdle strategy, 165
qualitative techniques, 146
quantitative techniques, 146
realistic job preview (RJP), 166
recruitment, 147

reliability, 155
selection, 147
settling-in phase, 166
situational questions, 159
socialization, 148
statistical strategy, 165
structured interview, 159
systemic discrimination, 157
traits, 158
worker-requirements questions, 159
yield ratios, 154
validity, 156

Discussion Questions

1. Smith and Nephew DonJoy is a small but fast-growing manufacturer of medical devices. Because of recent downsizing of large high-tech companies in the region where DonJoy is located, each job opening at DonJoy draws as many as five times as many applicants as it did just a few years ago. Although this seems like an ideal recruiting situation, many of the additional candidates were not necessarily well suited. What tools should DonJoy use to get the most qualified candidates from this large applicant pool, taking the costs of time and other expenses into consideration?

2. Should applicants be selected primarily on the basis of ability or on personality/fit? How can fit be assessed?

3. In 1995, Wayne Lynch tried to sign up for a computer upgrading course at Truro, Nova Scotia's federal employment centre. He recounts being told that unless he was an aboriginal, a woman, or a visible minority, there was no program available to help him. "Now, if that's not reverse discrimination, what is?" he said in an interview. Although this situation arose out of there being two funds for training—one from Employment Insurance funds and another dedicated to providing training for designated groups—it is not difficult to understand Lynch's question. What arguments would you advance to defend "earmarked" funding for groups such as those indicated? What criticisms would you lodge of such a policy?

4. Julie Watkins has worked in her new position writing software documentation for three months. At first, she was excited about joining the fast-paced, growing software industry, but now she's having doubts. She keeps hearing about how important her job is to the company, but she doesn't understand how her work contributes to the whole. Her exposure to the company is limited to her department colleagues (other technical writers), the employee cafeteria, and the payroll office. What should Watkins's company have done to make her see the whole picture and gain an understanding of and commitment to how the company works?

5. You work for a medium-sized high-tech company that faces intense competition in the product market. Change seems to be the only constant in your company and industry, and employee responsibilities shift from one project assignment to the next.

Suppose you have the major responsibility for filling the job openings that occur in your company. How would you go about recruiting and selecting the best people? How would you assess their ability to work effectively in your kind of environment?

Check out our Companion Website at: **www.prenticehall.ca/gomez** for a selection of self-study questions, key terms and concepts, updated Weblinks to related Internet sites, newsgroups, CBC video updates, and more.

MiniCase 1   *Unjustified Demotion*

In 1995, Imperial Oil was ordered by a human rights adjudicator to pay Martin Entrop $20,000, half in general damages and half for "mental anguish." This unprecedented sum revolved around events following the disclosure of a previous alcohol problem that Mr. Entrop made to his employer. The situation was labelled a "Catch-22" in an article published in the *Journal of the Addiction Research Foundation*. The policy required disclosure of past substance abuse problems (failure to disclose could potentially lead to discharge); yet, disclosure might well lead to demotion. Thus, Entrop claimed that the policy was unfair. Upon learning of it, he wrote to his employer indicating that he had previously had an alcohol abuse problem, but had been sober and abstinent for seven years. It was the length of his period of sobriety that made the company's action unjustified, in his view. He was immediately demoted from his position as a senior control room operator at the company's Sarnia, Ontario, refinery. The employer's actions, prior to reinstatement more than a year later, included conducting physical and psychiatric examinations, interviewing Entrop's wife, and compelling him to complete a lengthy personal questionnaire about such things as his sexual history, religious beliefs, childhood, and manner of dress. The employer denied that Entrop was subject to reprisals, suggesting rather that he was misreading the company's actions.

Discussion Questions

1. To what extent does an employer have a right to know the personal and lifestyle behaviour of an employee? Whether considering alcohol, prescription drugs, or illicit substances, how can an employer distinguish the point at which use becomes abuse?

2. Given that in the Exxon Valdez oil tanker's grounding and oil spill, alcohol abuse was identified as a contributing factor, are there some jobs where you would support more intrusive measures than for employees in general?

3. In general, how should employers deal with the risks associated with impairment on the job?

SOURCES: Employee wins unprecedented $20,000 after complaining about alcohol policy. *Canadian Press* Newswire (1995, August 16); and Catch-22. *Journal of the Addiction Research Foundation* (1994, November/December), 12ff.

MiniCase 2

Dial 1-800-U-Hire-Me: How Pic 'n Pay Picks Employees by Phone

When Pic 'n Pay Stores had a problem with turnover, the shoe retailer decided on a radical solution. It replaced its old hiring system, which relied on more than 900 store managers—many of whom lacked HR expertise—with a centralized electronic hiring process called HR Easy. Now the company interviews and hires people for all of its stores via telephone from its headquarters.

First, applicants complete an application in the store where they wish to work and submit it to the manager, who checks it for any obvious inconsistencies. If the application passes muster, the store manager gives the candidate an 800 number to call for an interview in which an electronic voice leads the candidate through a battery of yes/no questions about honesty, drug use, and personal habits. Answers are entered on a Touch-Tone phone and MCI computers record responses and response times. Then interviewers at corporate headquarters review the record and design questions for a follow-up live interview, in which applicants get a chance to explain their answers to interviewers who are trained by psychologists to interpret pauses, changes of tone, and speech patterns.

Local store managers can challenge central decisions, but so far, challenges have been rare. The company estimates that it has saved over $1 million through reduced turnover and theft since using HR Easy. What's more, it plans to market its new system to fast-food chains, convenience stores, and other high-turnover businesses.

Discussion Questions

1. Do you think Pic 'n Pay's hiring process is more reliable for recruiting qualified employees than unstructured interviews and paper-and-pencil honesty tests?
2. How would you feel about being interviewed by "voice mail"? Do you think qualified people might be passed over by such an electronic screening process? Why or why not?
3. Do you think electronic screening is better at ruling out bias and stereotyping in the selection process than the traditional person-to-person interview?
4. How does Pic 'n Pay's HR Easy hiring program change the role of local store managers? Do you think this change is for the better? Explain.

SOURCE: Adapted from Nhan, T. (1994, March 7). Turning a problem into profit. *The Charlotte Observer*, Section D, 1.

Case 1

Selecting for Survival at Future Horizons Foundry

Future Horizons (FH) is a foundry that produces parts for the automobile industry, including spindles, axles, and suspension components. To increase its competitiveness, FH executive managers have made a major investment in cutting-edge technology in the foundry business: they purchased a computerized foundry machine and placed it in the plant. The machine takes up storeys of space and includes remote-controlled cranes and a series of electric ovens to heat the steel. The heart of the system is a series of workstations through which the heated steel is moved by robotic steel fingers. Runs of different parts call for different grades of steel, different temperatures, and different specifications.

The computerized production requires a crew of three to four workers who set the specifications, then sample the product and compare it against standards. Much of the job consists of workers making adjustments to try to bring the product in line with specifications. Therein lies the major problem facing FH foundry.

The computerized system is down more often than not. Records indicate that the equipment is up and running good-quality parts only 34 percent of the time. It only takes a small amount of time to refit the machine to run a new part. Most of the crew's time is spent troubleshooting and making adjustments.

At least part of the problem is the quantity and complexity of the machine's settings and controls. With over 250 variables and settings that can affect product quality, the control station is so surrounded by dials, switches, and gauges that it resembles the cockpit of a jet fighter. One wrong setting can cause a problem with the product that can take hours — even whole shifts — to locate and fix. In addition, it is often difficult to diagnose the source of a problem. For example, a misshaped product could be due to the amount of steel used, the grade of steel, the temperature, or a combination of these factors.

FH managers are extremely frustrated. They had seen computerized equipment as the future of the operation because the computerized portion of the plant can produce at a rate 30 times faster than traditional foundry methods. But the computers are down two-thirds of the time. Top management has stated that the plant may have to close down unless the foundry's computerized portion is fixed so that it runs profitably.

Under this threat, the union at FH has agreed to the establishment of a selection program for placing workers in the computerized section of the foundry. Up until now, placement into the computerized section has been based solely on seniority.

Critical Thinking Questions

1. How would you go about developing a selection program for staffing the foundry's computerized section?
2. Do you think personality or fit issues should enter into FH's new selection system, or should abilities be the sole basis for staffing decisions? Explain your answer.
3. Should a job analysis be done in this case? If so, what kind would you recommend?
4. Do you think the selection program will be an improvement over the current seniority system? Why or why not?

Cooperative Learning Exercises

5. With your partner or group, identify the *first* thing you would do in trying to establish a selection program for FH.
6. How could you collect evidence for the validity, or lack of validity, of various predictors that could be used in FH's new selection program? Brainstorm the possibilities with your partner or team and present your best idea to the class.
7. Write down the worker characteristics that you think might be important to job performance in FH's computerized section. Share these possibilities with your partner or team and compile a composite list. Present your conclusions to the class.

Case 2

Wanted: Enthusiastic Employees to Grow with Growing Minds, Ltd.

Growing Minds, Ltd., is a national chain of retail outlets specializing in creative toys and innovative learning materials for children. The company caters to the upper end of the market and focusses on customer service for competitive advantage. It provides workshops for parents and children on such topics as learning with the computer and indoor gardening, and offers crafts classes ranging from papier mâché to pottery for children.

Growing Minds plans to expand and open five new retail outlets in the coming quarter. This may mean up to 200 new hires, and the executive team wants to make sure that the best people are hired and retained. It has issued a challenge to the retail management personnel to design a staffing process that will accomplish these goals.

The children's market in which Growing Minds operates demands service personnel who are endlessly patient; knowledgeable about children, toys, and learning; and, perhaps most important, sociable, enthusiastic, and engaging. Excellent customer service is the top priority at Growing Minds, and obtaining the desired performance from personnel has meant a major investment in training. Unfortunately, new workers often leave within a year of being hired. This means that the company barely gets an adequate return on the training it has invested in its new hires. Apparently, turnover is due, at least in part, to the demanding nature of the job.

Recently, Growing Minds has been emphasizing the establishment of work teams to improve the quality of its services, identify and fix any problems in service delivery, and brainstorm new opportunities. This approach has yielded better-than-anticipated results, so the team concept will be central to the new outlets.

Critical Thinking Questions

1. How can Growing Minds attract the best applicants for jobs at its new retail outlets? On what groups, if any, should the company's recruiting efforts focus? How should the recruiting be done?
2. How should Growing Minds select the best candidates? What type of characteristics and measures should be used? Why?
3. How might Growing Minds address its retention problem?

Cooperative Learning Exercises

4. Students who have worked in a retail setting, particularly one focussing on children and/or excellent customer service, should share with the class the worker characteristics they found most important in that experience.
5. Divide into groups of three or four to identify possible sources of Growing Minds' employee retention problem. What could be done in the staffing process to address this problem? Each person in the group should list at least one possibility. Compile the best ideas produced by your group and present them to the class.

Appendix to Chapter 5

QUANTITATIVE AND QUALITATIVE METHODS OF HR
FORECASTING

This appendix provides a summary of various methods that may be used to forecast labour demand and supply. These methods are divided into two major groups: those that rely on statistical formulas (quantitative) and those that rely on expert judgements (qualitative).

QUANTITATIVE METHODS OF FORECASTING HR DEMAND			
Method	**Description**	**Advantages**	**Disadvantages**
Moving Average	• Averages data about HR demand from recent periods and projects them into the future.	• Simplicity. • Data easily available.	• Seasonal or cyclical patterns may be ignored. • Relies on past data.
Exponential Smoothing	• Forecasters can vary weights for HR demand assigned to different past time periods used to project future HR demand.	• May be used to take into account factors ignored by the moving average method (for example, cyclical patterns).	• Mathematical complexity. • Choice of weights may be arbitrary. • Relies on past data.
Trends Projections	• Numbers of people hired or requested placed on one axis; time is placed on the other axis. A straight line is plotted from past to future to predict HR demand.	• Easily explained to managers. • Easily prepared by HR planners.	• Rough estimates. • Relies on past data.
Regression	• Mathematical formula used to relate staffing to several variables (for example, output, product mix, per capita productivity).	• Can include many variables. • Efficient use of all available data.	• Mathematical complexity. • Requires large sample sizes. • Relies on past data.
Linear Programming	• Assesses required staffing level that matches desired output levels, subject to certain constraints (for example, budget, cost).	• Assesses what should be in the future, not what probably will be.	• Managers are skeptical of highly sophisticated methodology. • Numerous assumptions must be made.
Actuarial Models	• Relate turnover to such factors as age and seniority.	• Reflect past.	• May not be accurate in individual cases.
Simulations	• Use scenarios to test the effect of various personnel policies.	• Useful for considering alternative HR programs.	• Accuracy varies.
Probability Matrices	• Define "states" in the organization—such as strategy levels, performance ratings. • Identify time period.	• Help identify career patterns. • Help perform turnover analysis.	• Require some mathematical sophistication. • Accuracy varies.

QUANTITATIVE METHODS OF FORECASTING HR DEMAND (continued)

Method	Description	Advantages	Disadvantages
First-Order Markov Model	• Multiply number of people in each job category by the probability of movement between job/position categories. Model assumes that current job/position category is the chief determinant of movement.	• Adequate for considering alternative effects of various HR strategies.	• Not adequate for long-term forecasts. • Requires mathematical sophistication.
Semi-Markov Model	• Same as first-order Markov model except that probability of movement is determined by (1) job/position category and (2) the individual's length of stay in the job class.	• More inclusive than a first-order Markov model.	• Not very useful for considering alternative effects of various HR strategies. • Requires mathematical sophistication.

QUALITATIVE METHODS OF FORECASTING HR DEMAND OR SUPPLY

Method	Description	Advantages	Disadvantages
Delphi Technique	• A group of experts exchanges several rounds of estimates of HR demand or supply, normally without meeting face to face. Feedback from other experts is used by each individual to "fine-tune" his/her independent estimate.	• Can involve key decision makers in process. • Can focus on what is expected or desired in future. • Not bound to the past.	• Highly subjective. • Judgements may not efficiently use objective data.
Nominal Group Technique	• A small group of experts meet face to face. Following a procedure that involves open discussion and private assessments, the group reaches a judgement concerning future HR demand or supply.	• Same as for Delphi technique. • Group discussions can facilitate exchange of ideas and greater acceptance of results by participants.	• Same as for Delphi technique. • Group pressure may lead to less accurate assessments than could be obtained through other means.

Source: Rothwell, W. J., & Kazanas, H. C. (1988). *Strategic human resources planning and management.* Englewood Cliffs, NJ: Prentice Hall.

chapter 6

Managing Employee Separations and Outplacement

After reading this chapter, you should be able to deal more effectively with the following challenges:

1 Identify the costs and benefits associated with employee separations.

2 Understand the differences between voluntary and involuntary separations.

3 Avoid problems in the design of early retirement policies.

4 Design HRM policies for downsizing the organization that are alternatives to a layoff; and, when all else fails, develop a layoff program that is effective and fair to the firm's stakeholders.

5 Understand the significance and value of outplacement programs.

Increasing global competition. As the economy becomes more globally competitive, companies have found themselves having to identify the most cost-effective environments in which to operate. Sometimes this has meant that companies relocate to other areas of the world. When companies move, downsize or close and employees lose their jobs, the surrounding community is negatively affected also.

Assume, for the moment, you are a senior manager in a Canadian aerospace company. The federal government's budget of March 1995 reduced the money available through the Defence Industry Productivity (DIP) Program from $144 million to $90 million in the following fiscal year and to $21.6 million in 1997–98. The effect on your company has been that much of the research that previously was plausible with higher levels of DIP funding can simply no longer be justified. A strategic planning meeting of your firm's executives has generated a plan for the company that requires you to develop a layoff policy and implement it immediately. In drafting the layoff policy, you are considering the following questions:

◆ **What criteria should we use to determine who will be laid off?** Should the determination be based on seniority? If so, would we lose some of the top-performing employees we recently hired? But if we base the layoff on merit, do we have an accurate system to measure performance? Will this system be defensible if angry employees challenge it in court?

◆ **How much notice should we give to employees who will be laid off?** Should we give them several years, as General Motors did in 1992 when it announced future plant closings (including the large St. Catharines, Ontario, plant) in advance? Or should we give no advance notification to avoid potential performance problems by employees who are searching for new jobs?

◆ **How will we provide security to our other employees and protect our business from sabotage or theft by employees who are losing their jobs?** Will we have to deal with a disgruntled former employee who becomes abusive or even violent, or who willfully corrupts computer systems? What costs do we incur when we protect other employees from such actions? Should we hire guards to escort our laid-off employees out of the building? What kind of message would that send to remaining employees and the media?

◆ **How should we communicate news of the layoff to the employees who will be let go?** Should we let them know about the layoff in a memo or let them read about it in the newspaper? Alternatively, should we hold a general meeting to inform the affected employees? Should each supervisor be responsible for telling his or her employees that they were selected for discharge?

◆ **When should we tell the media about the layoffs?** How do we control rumours that may appear in the media? How do we let our investors, our suppliers, and our customers know that we are committed to doing business with them and that the layoff will not hurt our relationship with them?

◆ **How will our remaining work force, the "survivors," feel about working for our company after the layoff?** Will they still be motivated to perform and be committed to our company? How should we deal with the anger and grief they will be feeling?

◆ **What kind of services can we provide to separated employees to help them find other jobs?** Should we retain a company that can supply these services? Can we extend the benefits of laid-off employees for a certain period of time to help ease the pain?

HRM on the Web

http://www.murrayaxsmith.
com/Publish.htm

Transitions Newsletter

This Web site offers a series of short, practical articles by legal and HR experts on various aspects of employment termination and outplacement. It is one of several sources offered by major consulting organizations as part of their larger Web sites.

These are just some of the questions that managers face in trying to implement a layoff effectively. While the previous chapter discussed aspects of managing the inflow of employees into an organization (HR planning, recruitment, selection, and placement), this chapter deals with the sometimes unpleasant task of managing an organization's outflow of human resources. This is a particularly pressing issue in today's business environment, where downsizing and layoffs are frequent occurrences.

Competent management of workforce reductions an essential skill in human resource management because reductions are sometimes necessary, and significant costs can be incurred if the process is poorly managed. It is not only the people who lose their jobs that are of concern; the impact of downsizing on the morale of survivors is also important. Downsizing often is disappointing in terms of its overall impact on costs and efficiency, and organizations are well advised to explore all options to cost reduction and over-capacity. In a fairly "Canadian" nutshell: downsizing if necessary, but not necessarily downsizing.

▮ What Are Employee Separations?

employee separation

The termination of an employee's membership in an organization.

turnover rate

The rate of employee separations in an organization.

An **employee separation** occurs when an employee ceases to be a member of an organization. The rate of employee separations in an organization, the **turnover rate,** is a measure of the rate at which employees leave the firm. Companies try to monitor and control their employees' turnover rate so that they can, in turn, monitor and control the costs of replacing employees. An excessively high turnover rate compared with the industry standard is often a symptom of problems within the organization. For example, excessive employee turnover may occur if a company pays a rate that is below the going rate in the industry. Figure 6–1 shows turnover rates and the costs of replacing employees in some specific job categories.

Employee separations can and should be managed. Before we discuss their management, however, it is beneficial to examine both the costs and the benefits of separations.

▮ The Costs of Employee Separations

The costs of employee separations depend on whether managers intend to eliminate the position or to replace the departed employee. By eliminating positions, the company can reduce costs in the long run. This is why many companies in the 1990s are downsizing their labour forces. However, even when positions are eliminated, the separation costs can be considerable. For example, IBM Canada's 1991 decision (in concert with other units of IBM) to reduce staff through early retirement has cost millions of dollars a year; for all of IBM, the cost is in the hundreds of millions.

Figure 6–2 shows some of the costs involved in replacing an employee. These costs can be categorized as *recruitment costs, selection costs, training costs,* and *separation costs.*

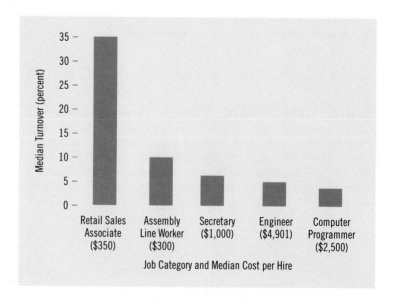

Figure 6–1 Turnover Rates and Costs for Specific Job Categories

SOURCE: Adapted with permission from *Journal of Accountancy* (1992, October), p. 18. Copyright © 1992 by American Institute of Certified Public Accountants, Inc.

Recruitment Costs	Selection Costs	Training Costs	Separation Costs
◆ Advertising	◆ Interviewing	◆ Orientation	◆ Separation pay
◆ Campus visits	◆ Testing	◆ Direct training costs	◆ Benefits
◆ Recruiter time	◆ Reference checks	◆ Trainers' time	◆ Employment Insurance costs
◆ Search firm fees	◆ Relocation	◆ Lost productivity during training	◆ Exit interview
			◆ Outplacement
			◆ Vacant position

Figure 6–2 Human Resource Replacement Costs

Recruitment Costs.   The costs associated with recruiting a replacement may include advertising the job vacancy and using a professional recruiter to travel to various locations (including college and university campuses) and generate a pool of job applicants. To fill top-level executive positions or technologically complex openings, it may be necessary to employ a search firm to locate qualified individuals, who most likely are already employed. A search firm typically charges the company a fee of about 30 percent of the employee's annual salary for its services.

Selection Costs.   Selection costs are associated with selecting, hiring, and placing a new employee in a job. Selection can involve interviewing the job applicant, which includes the costs associated with travel to the interview site and the productivity lost in organizing the interviews and arranging meetings to make selection decisions. Because many employees view selection decisions as important, it is common to involve many different people in the process. For example, a law firm's decision to hire a new associate may involve the participation of many junior lawyers as well as senior partners in the firm. Each of these lawyers may charge clients hundreds of dollars per hour for their time. If the selection decision results in several meetings after the interviews are completed, these lawyers may charge their clients for fewer hours.

Other selection costs involve testing the applicant and conducting reference checks to confirm that the applicant's qualifications are legitimate. Finally, the company may have to pay relocation costs, which include the costs of moving the employee's personal property, travel costs, and sometimes even housing costs if the employee is moving into a high-cost housing market such as Toronto or Vancouver. Housing costs may include the costs of selling one's previous house and the transaction costs of buying a house in a more expensive market.

Training Costs.   Organizations incur costs in providing new employees with the knowledge necessary to perform on the job. Most new employees need some specific training to do their job. For example, sales representatives need training on the company's line of products so that they can provide information to customers. Training costs include the costs associated with an orientation to the company's values and culture. Also important are the direct training costs—specifically, the cost of instruction, books, and materials for training courses. Finally, while new employees are being trained, they are not performing at the level of fully trained employees, so some productivity is lost until trainees master the skills required by the job. For example, new computer programmers may write fewer lines of code in a given amount of time and may need more supervision to check the quality of their work than experienced programmers do.

Separation Costs.   A company incurs separation costs for all employees who leave, whether or not they will be replaced. The largest cost of separation involves compensation for the job loss in terms of pay and benefits. Most companies provide *severance pay* (also called *separation pay*) for employees who are laid off through no fault of their own. Severance pay may add up to several months' salary for an experienced employee. Sometimes, severances are even more generous. The Ontario government, in an attempt to reduce its work force in 1995, offered severance packages that provided employees having as little as two years' service a full year's pay, and workers with 16 years' service 90 weeks (about 21 months') pay.[1] Less frequently, employees may continue to receive health benefits until they find a new job.

Other separation costs are associated with the administration of the separation itself. Administration often includes an **exit interview** to find out the reasons why the employee is leaving (if he or she is leaving voluntarily) or to provide counselling and/or assistance in finding a new job. It is common practice now in larger firms to provide departing employees with **outplacement assistance,** which helps them to find a job more rapidly by providing them with training in job-search skills. Finally, employers incur a cost if a position remains vacant because some of the former employee's work may not get done by others who have assumed additional workloads. The result may be a reduction in output or quality of service to the firm's clients or customers.

Conducting exit interviews is a challenge because it is often difficult to get departing employees to speak openly and frankly about their experiences in the company, often because they don't want to "burn their bridges behind them." The Manager's Notebook entitled "Excelling at Exit Interviews" gives some suggestions for eliciting truthful responses.

exit interview

An employee's final interview following separation. The purpose of the interview is to find out the reasons why the employee is leaving (if the separation is voluntary) or to provide counselling and/or assistance in finding a new job.

outplacement assistance

A program in which companies help their departing employees find jobs more rapidly by providing them with training in job-search skills.

Manager's Notebook

Excelling at Exit Interviews

Consulting firms offer the following advice for telling employees that they will be terminated or laid off.

1. Start with the assumption that open and honest responses will not be easily obtained.

2. Use skilled interviewers, preferably from the HR department. In very small or family-run companies where this is impossible, paper-and-pencil questionnaires can be mailed to an ex-employee's home. This may not be a disadvantage because these kinds of surveys tend to produce more candid answers.

3. Assure departing employees that any comments they make will be held confidential (except those that concern potential legal issues) and that their responses won't endanger their chances of getting a good job reference.

4. Start with routine departure basics, such as when benefits will end, before moving to the heart of the interview: why the employee is leaving.

5. Ask open-ended questions and avoid coming across as the company's interrogator or defender.

6. Before taking any action, make sure the feedback from exit interviews correlates with other available information.

7. Take action. People are more likely to feel their comments make a difference at companies that have a history of responding to ex-employees' perspectives.

SOURCE: Messmer, H. (1993, September). Parting words. *Small Business Reports,* 9–12; Pearl J. (1993 June). Exit interviews: Getting the truth. *Working Woman,* 16–17; and Drost, D. A. (1987, February). Exit interviews: Master the possibilities. *Personnel Administrator,* 104–110.

■ The Benefits of Employee Separations

Although separations are often thought of negatively, they have several benefits. When turnover rates are too low, few new employees will be hired and the number of opportunities for promotion is sharply curtailed. A persistently low turnover rate may have a negative effect on performance if the work force becomes complacent and fails to generate innovative ideas. A certain level of employee separations is a good and necessary part of doing business.

The benefits of employee separations to the organization may include the following: labour costs are reduced; poor performers are replaced; innovations are increased; and opportunities for greater diversity are enhanced.

Employees may receive some potential benefits from a separation too. An individual may escape from an unpleasant work situation and eventually find one that is less stressful or more personally and professionally satisfying.

Reduced Labour Costs.   An organization can reduce its total labour costs by reducing the size of its work force. Although separation costs in a layoff can be considerable, the salary savings resulting from the elimination of some jobs can easily outweigh the separation pay and other expenditures associated with a layoff.

Replacement of Poor Performers.   An integral part of management is identifying poor performers and helping them improve their performance. If an employee does not respond to coaching or feedback, then he or she may be advised to leave so that a new (and presumably more skilled) employee can be brought in. The separation of poor performers creates the opportunity to hire good performers in their place.

Increased Innovation.   Separations create opportunities for advancement as high-performing individuals can be rewarded with promotions. They also create opportunities for new entry-level positions as employees are promoted from within. An important source of innovation in companies is new people hired from the outside who can offer a fresh perspective. Such individuals may be entry-level university graduates armed with the latest research methods, or they may be experienced managers or engineers hired from leading research corporations.

The Opportunity for Greater Diversity.   Separations create opportunities to hire employees from diverse backgrounds and to redistribute the cultural and gender composition of the work force. This allows an organization all the advantages of a diverse work force and the ability to maintain control over its hiring practices while meeting diversity objectives and satisfying employment equity standards, where applicable.

Types of Employee Separations

Employee separations can be divided into two categories. Voluntary separations are initiated by the employee. Involuntary separations are initiated by the employer. When employees leave voluntarily, they are less likely to take their former employers to court for "wrongful dismissal." To protect themselves against legal challenges by former employees, employers must manage involuntary separations very carefully with a well-documented paper trail.

Voluntary Separations

Voluntary separations occur when an employee decides, for personal or professional reasons, to end the relationship with the employer. The decision could be based on the employee's obtaining a better job, changing careers, or requiring more time for family or leisure activities. Alternatively, the decision to leave could be based on the employee's finding the present job unattractive because of poor working conditions, low pay or benefits, a bad relationship with a supervisor, and so on. In most cases, the decision to leave is a combination of having attractive alternatives and being unhappy with aspects of the current job. There are two types of voluntary separations: quits and retirements.

voluntary separation
A separation that occurs when an employee decides, for personal or professional reasons, to end the relationship with the employer.

Quits.   The decision to *quit* depends on (1) the employee's level of dissatisfaction with the job and (2) the number of attractive alternatives the employee has outside the organization.[2] The employee can be dissatisfied with the job itself, the job environment, or both. For example, if the hours and location of a job are unattractive, an employee may look for a job with better hours and a location closer to home.

In recent years some employers have been using pay incentives to make it financially attractive for employees to quit voluntarily. Employers use these *voluntary severance plans,* or *buyouts,* when they want to reduce the size of their work force while avoiding the negative factors associated with a layoff. The pay incentive may amount to a lump-sum cash payment of six months to two years of an employee's salary, depending on the amount of time the employee has been with the company and the plan's design.

Retirements. *Retirement* is similar to quitting in that retirement is *not* the result of an employer's dissatisfaction with the employee. The initiative to retire may come from the employee or it may be the result of an employer's mandatory retirement policy. However, a retirement differs from a quit in a number of respects. First, while a retirement usually occurs at the end of an employee's career, a quit can occur at any time. Second, retirements usually result in the individual receiving retirement benefits from the organization. These may include a retirement income that may be supplemented with personal savings and government-funded benefits. Finally, the organization normally plans retirements in advance. HR staff can assist employees in planning their retirement, and managers can plan in advance to replace individuals by grooming current employees or recruiting new ones to fill the anticipated job vacancies. Quits are more difficult to plan for because the decision to quit is often influenced by the number of opportunities available in the labour market.

All Canadian jurisdictions have human rights provisions providing protection against discrimination on the basis of age, at least until the age of 65. To terminate employees because of their age or to force them to retire prior to age 65 would violate such protection. For example, the courts have upheld a human rights tribunal ruling that the Canadian Forces' policy of mandatory retirement at age 55 is illegal.[3] Many employers have found *early retirement incentives* to be an effective way to reduce their work force. Despite the costs involved, buyouts and early retirements often are used as alternatives to layoffs because they are less disruptive to organizational morale.

Although employers use voluntary early retirement as an option to reduce the work force, avoiding legal liability means ensuring that the program is, in fact, voluntary. Early retirement is becoming more common, and the average age of retirement, according to Statistics Canada,[4] is now closer to 61 than to 65. However, it is important to note that the variation in retirement age is increasing, with blue-collar workers more likely to be displaced from the work force.[5] Various government programs have also had an influence. Concern about the financial condition of the Canada/Quebec Pension Plan may lead to policy changes that will affect retirement choices for many people. We will discuss the management of early retirements in detail later in this chapter. In addition to pay, various benefits, such as drug plans, are not picked up by government programs until normal retirement age (See Chapter 12 for a detailed discussion of benefits plans.)

Many companies have found early retirement incentives to be an effective way to reduce their work force. These incentives make it financially attractive for senior employees to voluntarily retire early. Along with buyouts, they are used as alternatives to layoffs because they are viewed as a gentler way of downsizing a work force. We discuss the management of early retirements in detail later in this chapter.

■ Involuntary Separations

involuntary separation

A separation that occurs when an employer decides that it needs to terminate its relationship with an employee due to economic necessity or a poor fit between the employee and the organization.

An **involuntary separation** occurs when management decides that it needs to terminate its relationship with an employee due to (1) economic necessity or (2) a poor fit between the employee and the organization. Involuntary separations are the result of very serious and painful decisions that can have a profound impact on the *entire* organization, especially the employee who loses his or her job.

Although managers implement the decision to dismiss an employee, the HR staff makes sure that the dismissed employee receives "due process" and that the dismissal is performed within the letter and the spirit of company employment policy. Cooperation and teamwork between managers and HR staff are essential to effective management of the dismissal process. HR staff can act as valuable advisers to managers in this arena by helping them avoid mistakes that can lead to claims of wrongful dismissal. They can also help protect employees whose rights are violated by managers. There are two types of involuntary separations: the dismissal and the layoff.

Dismissal.   A *dismissal* takes place when management decides that there is a poor fit between an employee and the organization. The dismissal is a result either of poor performance or a failure by the employee to change some unacceptable behaviour that management has tried repeatedly to correct. Sometimes employees engage in serious misconduct, such as theft or dishonesty, which may result in immediate termination.

Managers who decide to dismiss an employee must make sure they follow the company's established discipline procedures. Most non-union companies and all unionized firms have a *progressive discipline procedure* designed to allow employees the opportunity to correct their behaviour before receiving a more serious punishment. For example, an employee who violates a safety rule may be given a verbal warning, followed by a written warning within a specified period of time. If the employee does not stop breaking the safety rule, the employer may have no choice but to dismiss the employee for failure to perform the job according to safety procedures. Managers must document the occurrences of the violation and provide evidence that the employee knew about the rule and was warned that its violation could lead to dismissal. In this way, managers can prove that the employee was dismissed for just cause. Chapter 14 details the criteria that managers can use to determine if a dismissal meets the standard of just cause.

Layoffs.   A *layoff* differs from a dismissal in several ways. In a layoff, employees lose their jobs because a change in a company's environment or strategy forces it to reduce the size of its work force. Global competition, reductions in product demand, changing technologies that reduce the need for workers, and mergers and acquisitions are the primary factors that influence managers to initiate a layoff. In contrast, a dismissed employee usually has been a direct cause of his or her separation.

Layoffs have a powerful impact on the organization. Layoffs can affect the morale of the organization's remaining employees, who may fear losing their jobs in the future. In addition, layoffs can affect the economic vitality of a community, including the merchants who depend on the patronage of the workers to support their business. When plants close due to layoffs, the entire community may suffer. This is particularly true when a variety of unrelated companies close, as happened with the Niagara Peninsula's manufacturing sector during the early 1990s, or when a single-industry town collapses after the mine, mill, or fish plant that sustained it disappears. Investors may be affected by layoffs as well. The investment community may interpret a layoff as a market signal that the company is having serious problems; this, in turn, may lower the price of the company's stock on the stock market. (Ironically, stock markets have recently appeared to "reward" layoffs as indicating aggressive cost control.) Finally, a company's image may be damaged by a layoff. Layoffs can hurt a company's standing as a good place to work and may make it difficult to recruit highly skilled employees who may choose among numerous employers.

> **A Question of Ethics**
> What can a company do to help a community when it decides to close a plant that is important to the community's economic prosperity?

Layoffs, Downsizing, and Rightsizing.   It is appropriate at this point to clarify the difference between a layoff and two concepts that are frequently associated with it: downsizing and rightsizing. A company that adopts a *downsizing* strategy reduces its scale (size) and scope of its business in order to improve its financial performance. When an organization decides to downsize, it may choose layoffs as one of several ways of reducing size and improving efficiency. In recent years many firms have done exactly this, but it is important to remember that such employers can take many measures other than layoffs to meet their objectives. Such measures are discussed later in this chapter.

Rightsizing.   Rightsizing involves reorganizing a company's employees to improve their efficiency. An organization needs to rightsize when it becomes bloated with too many management layers or overly bureaucratic work processes that do not add value to the products or services being produced. For example, companies that move to self-managed teams in operational areas may discover that they are overstaffed and can look to workforce reductions to take advantage of efficiencies created by the team structure. The result may be layoffs, but there are other ways of reducing the number of employees as rightsizing occurs.

Managing a layoff is an extremely complex process. Before we examine the specifics of managing a layoff, however, it is useful to look at an important alternative to reducing the size of a company's work force: early retirements.

■ Building Managerial Skills: Managing Early Retirements

When a company realizes that it needs to downsize its scale of operations, its first task is to examine alternatives to layoffs. One of the most popular of these methods, as we mentioned earlier, is early retirement. Some 40 percent of over 1,000 companies surveyed by consultant Murray Axsmith indicated that they had offered early retirement to employees during the previous year, and that roughly half the employees to whom it had been offered accepted.[6]

■ The Features of Early Retirement Policies

Early retirement policies consist of two features: (1) a package of financial incentives that make it attractive for senior employees to retire earlier than they planned and (2) an *open window* that restricts eligibility to a fairly short period of time. After the window is closed, the incentives are no longer available to senior employees.[7]

The financial incentives are usually based on a formula that accelerates senior employees' retirement eligibility and augments their pension income. It has not been unusual for companies to provide an additional one or two years' salary in a lump-sum payment as an incentive to leave. The continuation of health benefits is also a typical part of the package. However, as organizations go through recurring rounds of downsizing, the severance and retirement packages appear to be getting less generous. A survey done by Drake Beam Morin, Inc. indicated that severance benefits for middle managers had decreased steadily during the early 1990s. There were variations among industries—insurance and communications firms offered about seven months' benefits compared with five weeks offered by professional and transportation firms.[8]

Early retirement policies can reduce an organization's work force substantially. In 1995, budget cuts by the federal government led to attractive early retirement and severance arrangements that have effectively reduced the federal civil service by 5,000—over 10 percent of its 45,000 employees.[9]

Drake Beam Morin Inc.
www.dbm.com

Smooth Sailing.

Retirement means many things to people who are concluding a career as an employee. The fact that most people should anticipate living fifteen to twenty or more years after retirement means that personal financial planning is crucial.

■ Avoiding Problems with Early Retirements

Managing early retirement policies requires careful design, implementation, and administration. When not properly managed, early retirement policies can give rise to a host of problems. Too many employees may take early retirement, the wrong employees may leave, and employees may perceive that they are being forced to leave, which may result in age discrimination complaints.

Some organizations are surprised by the number of employees who opt for early retirement packages. Some 340 senior professors and support staff, including 14 of 32 professors in the civil engineering department at the University of Waterloo accepted an early retirement offer prompted by the University's attempts to slash $19 million from its budget. Although University administrators met their financial target, student leaders expressed concern over the effect of these changes on program availability and quality of instruction.[10] One way to avoid excess resignations is to restrict eligibility to divisions that have redundant employees with high levels of seniority (instead of making the policy available to all employees throughout the corporation). Another way is to survey senior employees and ask them how they would respond to a specific type of early retirement plan. The survey could then be used to predict the number of senior employees who would retire if the incentives were made available. If the survey shows that too many

---

Issues and Applications

Early Retirement: Closing Personal Doors ...

Veteran CBC announcer Frank Cameron will take early retirement next fall before budget cuts pose a real threat to his job. The anchor of the late Atlantic regional news and weatherman on Nova Scotia's supper-hour news show says he surprised himself as much as anyone else. "I didn't really approach them [about retiring] but I asked what the score was on buyouts," says 56-year-old Cameron. They gave me the picture and I thought, "Hmmmm, this doesn't sound too bad."

Preferring employees to jump rather than be pushed by budget cuts, the CBC is making this an especially sweet time for its older workers to leave the company.

Cameron's last CBC appearance will probably come in September or October, but he hopes to stay active and is already negotiating with a Halifax-area radio station. "It won't be full time, but just something to keep my hand in broadcasting," said Cameron, who has been on local radio and television airwaves for 36 years.

SOURCE: CBC veteran Frank Cameron takes golden handshake. (1995, May 17). *Canadian Press Newswire.*

... and Opening Windows of Opportunity

Gary Vollens and Tony Hajar see the downsizing of the federal civil service as a boon, at least for the present. Vollens, a 28-year veteran whose job required him to devise clever answers for his minister to offer reporters about events in the Hibernia oil field, was a few years from age 60 eligibility for early retirement and had resolved to tough it out. Then along came "this wonderful program" that classified him as age 60 for pension purposes, and let him go on his way. Vollens has since opened his own consulting business.

Tony Hajar, a labourer at the former Uplands defence base, was just a few weeks away from five years' service (which would have given him permanent employee status) when he learned his job was to disappear. However, the package offered him $35,000 for a job that had paid $28,000, and has allowed him a bit of a nest egg for the first time in his life — enough to allow Hajar to contemplate a return to school while being able to support his family.

SOURCE: Cashing in big on public service early retirement plan. (1995, November 26). *Canadian Press Newswire.*

---

would leave, the incentives could be fine-tuned so that a controlled number of employees take early retirement.

Sometimes the most marketable employees with the best skills can easily find another job and can "take the money and run." To avoid this problem and to keep its most valuable people, the employer can develop provisions to hire back, on a temporary or contractual basis, a retired employee with key skills. Colleges and universities are finding this both useful and necessary to balance their patterns of student demand and teaching resources. The featured Issues and Applications "Early Retirement: Closing Personal Doors ... and Opening Windows of Opportunity" presents examples in which unexpected departures have worked out well for individuals. There is no basis for assuming, however, that such situations are the norm. There are indications that people displaced from work are turning to options that indicate a certain amount of desperation. For example, disability claims to both the Canada and Quebec Pension Plans and to long-term disability (LTD) programs offered by employers are up disproportionately, particularly for conditions such as mental distress and back disorders, which are medically difficult to assess—suggesting to some experts that disability claims are becoming an unintended form of early retirement for some employees.[11]

Early retirement programs must be managed so that eligible employees do not perceive that they are being forced to retire and consequently file age discrimination charges. Situations that could be interpreted as coercive include the following:

◆ A long-time employee who has performed satisfactorily over many years suddenly receives an unsatisfactory performance evaluation.

◆ A manager indicates that senior employees who do not take early retirement may lose their jobs anyway because a layoff is likely in the near future.

◆ Senior employees notice that their most recent pay raises are quite a bit lower than those of other younger workers who are not eligible for early retirement.

An example from the business pages illustrates how an improperly implemented early retirement can result in serious consequences for an employer. A 1993 human rights award in excess of $250,000 in back pay plus benefits was given to a 57-year-old supervisory employee of Hayes-Dana Inc. who, perceiving (accurately, in the Human Rights Commission's view) that previous layoff patterns targeted older workers, chose an early retirement offer over financially much less attractive layoff alternatives. While the company claimed that those tabbed for the severance-or-early-retirement offers had been identified on the basis of a performance assessment by a senior foreman, notes left by a vice-president stating that the company "hoped to keep people with career potential" persuaded the Commission that age-based discrimination had influenced the decision.[12]

(Some basic facts underlie this human rights concern with the displacement of older workers: (1) workers over the age of 45 are more likely to be laid off and tend to have longer periods of unemployment; (2) between 1993 and 2015, the number of people in the labour force between age 15 and 24 will increase five percent, those between 45 and 54 will increase 155 percent, and those between 55 and 64 will increase 194 percent; and (3) Canadian experience is beginning to follow the European pattern, with disability pensions from the Canada and Quebec Pension Plans increasingly becoming an income support that bridges the period until people reach 65, when they can claim a retirement pension.[13])

Managers can avoid this situation by following a few simple guidelines. All managers with senior employees in their units should be aware of company policy and ensure that they do not treat senior employees any differently than other employees. HR staff members play an important role here by keeping managers aware of the letter and the spirit of the early retirement policy so that they do not (consciously or unconsciously) coerce senior employees during the open-window period.

■ Building Managerial Skills: Managing Layoffs

Typically, an organization will institute a layoff when it cannot reduce its labour costs by any other means. Figure 6–3, which presents a model of the layoff decision and its alternatives, shows that managers should first try to reduce their labour costs by using alternatives to layoffs, such as early retirements and other voluntary workforce reductions. After managers make the decision to implement a layoff, they must concern themselves with the outplacement of the former employees.

An important influence on the likelihood of a layoff is the business's HR strategy (see Chapter 1). Companies with a lifelong employment HR strategy are less likely to lay off employees because they have developed alternative policies to protect their permanent employees' job security. The best-known examples of firms that use lifelong employment policies are the large Japanese corporations, which employ about one-third of the Japanese work force. Until relatively recently, a number of Canadian companies such as Nova Corporation, Ontario Hydro, and many of the utility companies, as well as Canadian arms of multinationals, such as IBM, had strong although often de facto commitments to employment security. It is clear that such arrangements have been modified sharply by most employers. The strike by the CAW and other unions in 1995 against CN Rail, CP Rail, and Via Rail led to an arbitrator's decision to modify the contentious contractual lifetime employment security clause to a maximum of six years for then-current employees and to eliminate that provision for new employees.[14] This event, combined

Canadian Auto Workers
www.caw.ca

Via Rail
www.viarail.ca

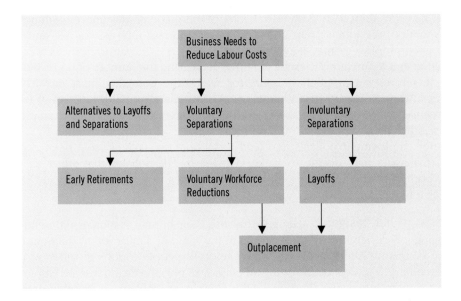

Figure 6–3 The Layoff Decision and Its Alternatives

with cutbacks throughout the broader public sector, in many ways punctuated the end of employment security as an accepted standard. Emphasis has shifted to employees being responsible for their own careers and for employers to pursue policies, such as training and development, that keep employees employable.

◼ Alternatives to Layoffs

Figure 6–4 shows alternatives to layoffs. These alternatives include employment policies, changes in job design, pay and benefits policies, and training. Managers can use these to reduce labour costs as well as to protect the jobs of full-time employees.

Employment Policies.   The first alternatives to the layoff that managers are likely to consider are those that are least intrusive to the day-to-day management of the business. These alternatives usually focus on adjustments to employment policies.

The least disruptive way to cut labour costs is through **attrition.** By not filling certain job vacancies that are created by turnover, improvements can be made to the bottom line. When greater cost reductions are needed, a **hiring freeze** is probably the next step to take. Many universities have used hiring freezes to balance their budgets in years of fiscal restraint. Next, temporary employees' work

attrition

An employment policy designed to reduce the size of the work force by not refilling job vacancies that are created by turnover.

hiring freeze

An employment policy designed to reduce the size of the work force by not hiring any new employees into the company.

Employment Policies	Changes in Job Design	Pay and Benefits Policies	Training
◆ Reduction through attrition	◆ Transfers	◆ Pay freeze	◆ Retraining
◆ Hiring freeze	◆ Relocations	◆ Cut overtime pay	
◆ Cut part-time employees	◆ Reduced work hours	◆ Use vacation and leave days	
◆ Cut internships or co-ops	◆ Job sharing	◆ Pay cuts	
◆ Give subcontracted work to in-house employees	◆ Demotions	◆ Profit sharing or variable pay	
◆ Voluntary time off			
◆ Leaves of absence			
◆ Reduced work hours			

Figure 6–4 The Alternatives to Layoffs

loads may be shifted to protect the jobs of permanent full-time employees. In this situation, the jobs of part-time employees, student interns, co-ops, and subcontracted employees may be eliminated.

Other employment policies are aimed at decreasing the number of hours worked and, therefore, the number of hours for which the company must pay its employees. Workers may be encouraged to take voluntary (unpaid) time off or leaves of absence, or they may be asked to put in a shorter work week (for example, 35 hours rather than 40).

After employment policies that lead to labour-cost savings have been considered, managers may decide to make changes in HR policies that affect all or a large portion of the company's employees. Changes in job design, pay and benefits, or training can be made.

Changes in Job Design.

Managers can use their human resources differently by changing job design, transferring people in the same or similar job to different units of the company. Alternatively, they may relocate people to jobs in different parts of the country. The cost of relocating an employee plus the fact that some employees do not want to move sometimes make this alternative problematic. Another practice, common in unionized companies, allows a senior employee whose job is eliminated to take a job in a different unit of the company from an employee with less seniority. This practice is called *bumping*. A reduction in work hours can also be used as a temporary way to cut labour costs. This method is popular in cyclical industries, such as the construction and clothing industries, where the amount of work available varies from month to month or season to season.

Employers can also use *job sharing* (which we discussed in Chapter 2) when it is possible to reconfigure one job into two part-time jobs. The challenge here lies in finding two people willing to cooperate with each other to share the job's hours and pay. Finally, as a last resort, highly paid workers may be demoted to lower-paying jobs.

Pay and Benefits Policies.

As one way of reducing costs, managers can enforce a *pay freeze* during which time no wages or salaries are increased. These can be augmented by reductions in overtime pay and policies that ask employees to use up their vacation and leave days. Unfortunately, pay freezes often cause some top-performing, highly marketable employees to leave the company.

A more radical and intrusive pay policy geared toward reducing labour costs is a *pay cut*. This action is potentially very disruptive to an organization, and works best when there is a general acceptance that such a step is necessary for the company's viability. Often, a pay cut is more acceptable if it is seen as a way of avoiding job losses. Fleet Aerospace, a Fort Erie, Ontario, manufacturer of airplane parts, rolled back pay 10 percent for all employees including executives in 1993, when the company was losing money.[15] This once-taboo alternative of wage reduction has become a real option for employers and unions facing difficult circumstances. For example, Air Canada's five percent wage rollback in the early 1990s made a significant difference in its turnaround efforts.[16] In Atlantic Canada, rollbacks of five to 15 percent were achieved in efforts to save pulp and paper mills that might otherwise be closed.[17]

A longer-term pay policy that may protect jobs from layoffs is structuring compensation so that profit sharing (sharing a portion of company profits with employees) or variable pay (setting aside some pay and making it contingent on meeting performance goals) makes up a significant portion of employees' total compensation (around 15 to 20 percent). When the business cycle hits a low point, the company can save up to 20 percent of payroll costs by not paying out the profit sharing or variable pay while still retaining its employees at their base wage or salary levels. Only a small (but growing) number of companies in Canada and the United States use this approach, although it is very common in Japan.

Training.   By retraining employees whose skills have become obsolete, a company may be able to match newly skilled workers with available job vacancies. In addition to cutting its work force through layoffs and other measures, Bell Canada's training institute has refocussed its programs to teach employees personal growth management and other "soft" skills, to enhance their ability to adapt to changing job demands and thereby sustain their employment.[18]

Non-traditional Alternatives to Layoff.   In their attempt to avoid layoffs, some employers have come up with innovative alternatives that involve changes in both employment policy and job design.

♦ The federal government, in designing the buyout packages it used to reduce the federal public service, allowed employees in areas slated for layoffs to swap jobs with others working in "safer" areas so that the more junior employees could continue working. In some cases, the unexpected response has been for people to attempt to get into positions that are going to be eliminated to qualify for the Early Departure Incentive, a pattern seen by some as indicative of low morale.[19]

♦ CIBC, knowing from customer feedback that a bank's employees have a greater influence than the product mix on customers' decisions to select and stay with a bank, developed a creative redeployment policy for people whose jobs were being eliminated. Begun in 1991, this "employment continuity program" provided satisfactory contributors with a three-stage program: (a) Three months' notice of the change, which (b) allows the employee, together with his or her immediate manager, to formulate a redeployment plan. If the plan is determined to be viable, (c) the employee may receive an additional six months for retraining and repositioning, based on plans made jointly by the employee, the immediate manager, and the receiving manager.[20]

CIBC
www.cibc.com

■ Implementing a Layoff

Once the layoff decision is made, managers must implement it carefully. A layoff can be a traumatic event that affects the lives of thousands of people. As the Issues and Applications "Layoffs at General Motors: Strictly an Exercise in Economic Rationality?" shows, General Motors' 1992 announcement that it was closing 21 plants had a major effect on all associated with the company.

The key issues that must be settled when implementing a layoff are notifying employees, developing layoff criteria, communicating to laid-off employees, coordinating media relations, maintaining security, and reassuring survivors of the layoff.

Notifying Employees.   Employment standards legislation in various provinces and in the federal jurisdiction requires that individual employees being laid off receive notice of various lengths, depending on length of service. (See Figure 6–5.) In addition, most jurisdictions also impose additional requirements when large groups of employees are being let go at the same time.

There are several arguments in favour of giving at least several weeks' notice prior to a layoff. It is socially and professionally correct to extend employees this courtesy. Also, this treatment is more acceptable to the employees who will remain with the company. But there are also arguments in favour of giving no notification. If the labour relations climate is poor prior to the layoff announcement, there is the potential for theft or sabotage to company equipment. In addition, the productivity of employees who are losing their jobs may decline.[21]

It is interesting to note that the requirements for layoff notification in European countries tend to be more restrictive than those in Canada. For example, in Sweden management must give at least 60 days' advance notice to five or more workers, while in France as few as two workers must get at least 45 days' notification.[22] Figure 6–6 lists advance notice requirements in several other European nations, as well as in the United States.

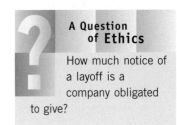

A Question of Ethics

How much notice of a layoff is a company obligated to give?

Issues and Applications

Layoffs at General Motors: Strictly an Exercise in Economic Rationality?

The following two articles appeared February 25, 1992:

DETROIT—General Motors Corp. reported a record $4.5 billion 1991 loss yesterday and identified some of the plants it will close to try to restore profits at the world's largest industrial corporation.

It was the worst annual loss for an American corporation in history.

GM Chairman Robert Stempel announced the closings of two assembly plants—one each in Michigan and New York—and the shuttering of operations in 10 of GM's supplier complexes, affecting 16,000 workers.

He also described a long-range plan to eliminate redundancies in nearly all areas of the company's operations, including vehicle design and marketing, technical research and support operations.

"We must accelerate the fundamental changes," Stempel told a news conference.

The details answered some of the questions left when the automaker announced a broad restructuring program last December. The overall plan calls for 21 plant closings and 74,000 job cuts by the middle of the decade.

Analysts have said slow vehicle development, generous labour contracts and the recession have combined to force GM to shrink. ...

Stempel is importing to GM's struggling North American car and truck operations some of the structural changes the company instituted in its European operations.

GM said that overseas operations earned $2.1 billion last year, much of it coming from Europe.

Prime among the European changes is workers opting for more flexible work rules that have boosted productivity.

"If you look at what we've been doing in Europe, one of the things we've done over there is used fixed facilities literally 24 hours a day," Stempel said.

"We know where we are and we know what's happening to our costs over there.

"Obviously it's the way we're going to have to go."

UAW [United Auto Workers] President Owen Bieber and Vice-President Stephen P. Yokich accused GM of "closing its eyes to the misery inflicted on its workers and their communities."

"They have failed to inform us of significant decisions, disregarded major cost-saving proposals on sourcing and employee efficiency and, contrary to their official rhetoric, pitted plant against plant and community against community," the labour leaders said in a statement.

OSHAWA—With much of the North American car industry on its knees, General Motors of Canada Ltd. announced yesterday that it has bucked the sorry trend by turning in a solid profit for 1991.

But the $323 million earned by the Canadian unit of General Motors Corp.—its best performance since 1988, a record year for car sales — is proving no defence against the plant closings and job losses being undertaken to get the parent company off the critical list.

The coupling yesterday of the profit numbers with word that 2,300 jobs will be lost at the company's St. Catharines, Ontario, plant between now and 1995 left GM workers and their union representatives bewildered and frustrated.

Canadian Auto Workers officials concluded that "it is not enough" for Canadians to manufacture top-quality, cost-competitive auto products—the jobs are still moving south.

"We have seen the prime example of that today," said CAW president Bob White after hearing details of GM's plans to close its St. Catharines engine lines this fall and a foundry operation in 1995. GM is trying to come to grips with excess manufacturing capacity in the North American car industry.

"We keep getting all this jargon that if we are competitive, cost competitive, and build a good-quality product, it will secure our futures," the visibly frustrated Mr. White said in an interview. "In fact, it does not guarantee that we are going to have the jobs."

The work being taken out of St. Catharines is to be shifted to larger U.S. plants. "It makes me feel vulnerable," said White. "But my feelings are nothing compared with the feelings of the workers today."

Reprinted with permission from Standish, F. (1992, February 25). *Denver Post,* 1C, 3C; and Pritchard, T., & Galt, V. (1992, February 25). *The Globe and Mail,* B1.

Bob White.

As president of the CAW and more recently as head of the Canadian Labour Congress, Bob White became a familiar spokesman for the view that workers are legitimate stakeholders whose needs should be considered in organizational decisions.

Jurisdiction	No. People to be Laid Off	Required Notice Period
Alberta	50 or more	4 weeks
British Columbia	50-100	8 weeks
	101-300	12 weeks
	301+	16 weeks
Manitoba	50+ w/in 4 weeks	10 weeks
	101–300	14 weeks
	300+	18 weeks
New Brunswick	25% or more w/in 4 weeks	6 weeks
Newfoundland	50-200	8 weeks
	200-500	12 weeks
	500+	16 weeks
Nova Scotia	10+ w/in 4 weeks	8 weeks
	100–299	12 weeks
	300+	16 weeks
Ontario	50-200	8 weeks
	200-500	12 weeks
	500+	16 weeks
Quebec	10–99 (w/in 2 months)	2 months
	100–299	3 months
	300+	4 months
Yukon	25–49 w/in 4 weeks	4 weeks
	50–99	8 weeks
	100–299	12 weeks
	300+	16 weeks
Federal jurisdiction	50+ w/in 4 weeks	16 weeks
NWT, PEI	no legislation	

Figure 6–5 Required Notice Period for Group Layoffs

SOURCE: *Human Resources Management in Canada,* by permission of Carswell, a division of Thomson Canada Limited, Scarborough, Ontario, 1-800-387-5164

Country	Notice Requirements
Belgium	30 days
Denmark	30 days
Germany	30 days
Greece	30 days
Ireland	30 days
Italy	22 to 32 days
Luxembourg	60 to 75 days
Netherlands	2 to 6 months
United Kingdom	30 to 90 days (if at least ten workers are involved)
United States	60 working days (if there are more than 50 employees)

Figure 6–6 Requirements of Advance Notice for Collective Dismissals in Selected Countries

SOURCE: Ehrenberg, R. G. and Jakubson, G. H., (1988). *Advance notice provisions in plant closing legislation.* Kalamazoo, MI: W. E. Upjohn Institute for Employment Research.

Developing Layoff Criteria.   In managing a layoff, it is essential that the criteria for dismissal be clear. When the criteria are clearly laid out, the managers responsible for determining who will be laid off can make consistent, fair decisions. The two most important criteria used as the basis for layoff decisions are seniority and employee performance.

seniority

The length of service of an employee with a particular employer.

Seniority, the length of service of an employee with a particular employer, is by far the most commonly used layoff criterion. It has two main advantages. First, seniority criteria are easily applied; managers simply examine all employees' dates of hire to determine the seniority of each (in years and days). Second, many employees see the seniority system as fair because (1) managers cannot play "favourites" under a seniority-based decision and (2) the most senior employees have the greatest investment in the company in terms of their job rights and privileges (they have accrued more vacation and leave days, and have more attractive work schedules, for example).

There are disadvantages to using the "last in, first out" method, however. The firm may lose some top performers, as well as a disproportionate amount of women and minorities—who are more likely to be recent hires in certain jobs. Despite these challenges, the courts have upheld seniority as the basis for layoff as long as all employees have equal opportunities to obtain seniority.

When the work force is unionized, layoff decisions are usually based on seniority because union members generally believe it is the most fair method. This provision is written into the labour contract. However, when the work force is non-union and especially when cuts must be made to professional and managerial employees, it is not unusual for management to base layoff decisions on performance criteria or a combination of performance and seniority. The advantage of using performance as the basis for layoffs is that it allows the company to retain its top performers in every work unit and eliminate its weakest performers. Unfortunately, performance levels are not always clearly documented, and the company may be exposed to wrongful dismissal lawsuits if the employee can prove that management discriminated or acted arbitrarily in judging performance. Further, an employer could risk human rights charges if the employee belongs to a protected group. Because of these legal risks, many companies avoid using performance as a basis for layoff.

If a company has taken the time to develop a valid performance appraisal that accurately measures performance, then there is no reason why appraisal data cannot be used as the basis for layoff. When basing layoffs on performance, managers should take the employee's total performance over a long period of time into account. Managers who focus on one low performance appraisal period and ignore other satisfactory or exceptional performance appraisals could be viewed as acting arbitrarily and unfairly. We discuss this topic in more detail in the next chapter.

Communicating to Laid-off Employees.

It is crucial to communicate with the employees who will be laid off as humanely and sensitively as possible. No employee likes being told he or she will be dismissed, and the way a manager handles this unpleasant task can affect how the employee and others in the organization accept the decision. Some general guidelines on how to lay off an employee are given in the Manager's Notebook.

Laid-off employees should first learn of their fate from their supervisor in a face-to-face private discussion. Employees who learn about their dismissal through a less personal form of communication (for example, a peer or a memo) are likely to be hurt and angry. The information session between supervisor and employee should be brief and to the point. The manager should express appreciation for what the employee has contributed, if appropriate, and explain how much severance pay and what benefits will be provided and for how long. This information can be repeated in greater detail at a group meeting of laid-off employees and should be documented in a written pamphlet to be handed out at the meeting.

The best time to hold the termination session is in the middle of the work week. It is better to avoid telling workers they are being laid off during their vacation or right before a weekend, when they have large blocks of time on their hands.[23]

One example of how *not* to communicate a layoff is provided by a petroleum company in which employees were brought together for a rather unsettling meeting. Each employee was given an envelope with the Letter A or B on it. The A's were told to stay put while the B's were ushered into an adjacent room. Then, en masse, the B's were told that they were being laid off.

Coordinating Media Relations.

Rumours of an impending layoff can be very dangerous to the work force's morale as well as to the organization's relations with customers, suppliers, and the surrounding community. Top managers, working with HR staff members, should develop a plan to provide accurate information about the layoff to both external clients (via the media) as well as the work force (via internal communications).[24] In this way, managers can control and put to rest rumours that may exaggerate the extent of the firm's downsizing efforts. It is also important that direct communication take place with the employees directly affected by the layoff *and* with the surviving employees and that all communication be coordinated with press releases to the media. In addition, HR staff must prepare to answer any questions that employees may have regarding outplacement, severance pay, or the continuation of benefits.

Manager's Notebook

The Dos and Don'ts of Terminating/Laying Off Employees

Consulting firms offer the following advice for telling employees that they will be terminated or laid off.

DOs
◆ Give as much warning as possible for mass layoffs.
◆ Sit down one-on-one with the individual, in a private office.
◆ Complete a firing session within 15 minutes.
◆ Provide written explanations of severance benefits.
◆ Provide outplacement services away from company headquarters.
◆ Be sure the employee hears about his or her termination from a manager, not a colleague.
◆ Express appreciation for what the employee has contributed, if appropriate.

DON'Ts
◆ Don't leave any room for confusion. Tell the individual in the first sentence he or she is terminated.
◆ Don't allow time for debate.
◆ Don't make personal comments; keep the conversation professional.
◆ Don't rush the employee off-site unless security is really an issue.
◆ Don't fire or lay people off on significant dates, like the twenty-fifth anniversary of their employment or the day their mother died.
◆ Don't fire employees when they are on vacation or have just returned.

SOURCE: Adapted with permission from Alexander, S. (1991, October 4). *The Wall Street Journal*, p. B1. © 1991 Dow Jones & Company, Inc. All Rights Reserved Worldwide.

Maintaining Security.

In some situations a layoff may threaten company property. Laid-off employees may find themselves ushered out of the building, escorted by guards, and their personal belongings delivered to them later in boxes. Such treatment is usually more harsh than is needed, although it may be necessary in certain industries (such as banking and computer software) where sabotage could result in substantial damage to the company. Security was given high priority when one newspaper discharged many employees. Employees indicated that the newspaper cut off their access to computers before they learned about their terminations so that they would not be able to sabotage the computer system.[25]

In most cases security precautions are probably unnecessary when implementing a layoff, and using guards and other heavy-handed tactics will lead only to hard feelings and resentment. Treating laid-off employees with dignity and respect generally reduces the potential for sabotage.

Reassuring Survivors of the Layoff.

A sometimes neglected aspect of layoff implementation is developing plans to deal with the layoff's survivors. An organization may lose the cost savings of a layoff if survivor productivity drops as a result of the layoff.[26] Survivors of a layoff can be expected initially to have low morale and to experience stress. Many will have lost important friendships in the layoff. Some may feel the same emotions experienced by survivors of tragedies: guilt ("Why not me?"), anger ("This is not fair"), and anxiety ("Am I next?").[27] The following reactions of layoff survivors express some of the feelings of anger and depression that are very common:

◆ "Stop telling us to work smarter. Show us how .. . Stop blaming us! We've been loyal to the company. We've worked hard and did everything we were told. We've moved for the company, we've travelled for the company; and we've taken extra work on for the company. And now you say we did wrong. You told us to do it. Management told us to do it! And the company did pretty well while we did it. Stop blaming us!"[28]

◆ "You see a lot of good people being let go and that's very demoralizing, to know that an excellent person is being let go. It affects your credibility with your company, and it also affects your productivity."

◆ "I don't go that extra step anymore, whereas I [used to take on more, on] my own initiative. Because when I would go that extra, I felt I owed the company that. [Now] I don't necessarily feel I owe the company."

◆ "They're padding their pockets. In the good times the bonuses and everything go to the top executives, and during the bad times the workers get cut out. The company hasn't shown me that they care as much about me."[29]

To cope with these feelings, the survivors may try to "escape." It is not unusual to see a sharp increase in absenteeism as well as in turnover of key people with critical skills who leave to work for another company. Problems of this type can be minimized through the development of special programs for survivors. Organizations that can see these difficulties can help their employees improve their coping skills with such programs as mandatory stress-counselling, employee assistance plans (EAP), and flexibility in responding to requests for time off for personal matters. Some ways to help survivors cope include holding small-group discussions with their supervisor, offering pep talks to larger groups from senior managers, and providing social events to help people re-establish their sense of community.

Finally, managers can work on the difficult matter of restoring open and trusting communication. The roots of the communication problem often lie in the stress of implementing downsizing. When a survey conducted by HR consultants Murray Axsmith and Associates asked respondents to identify the most stressful of a number of management tasks, seven of 10 chose firing.[30] Doug Anderson, vice-president of HR at Telemedia Inc., observed that one unsettling possibility is that "we will lose touch with the fact that we're dealing with real people and become desensitized."[31] It has been observed that after a major downsizing, executives tend to hide from their employees. This is particularly serious because surveys indicate that fully 25 percent of the work force didn't know the reasons for the change, that two of five employees didn't know the details of the change, and that three of five didn't know what was going to happen to them. Yet the lack of specifics doesn't indicate a lack of awareness that something is happening. As Mary Ann Prychoda, principal of Toronto-based Insider Communications, observes, "Employees usually already know what you're afraid to tell them, or they can sense that you're not telling them the whole story. Management credibility is always a huge issue because it's so difficult to build and so easily damaged."[32] The decline in productivity and morale that frequently follows a downsizing (because survivors are preoccupied with what the change means for them) can be minimized by treating subordinates as trusted adults, and by providing a clear picture of how the "new" organization will work.

Telemedia Inc.
www.telemedia.fr

■ Outplacement

As we mentioned at the beginning of this chapter, outplacement is a human resource program created to help separated employees deal with the emotional stress of job loss and provide assistance in finding a new job.[33] Outplacement activities are often handled by consulting firms retained by the organization, which pays a fee based on the number of employees who are outplaced. Companies are often willing to pay for outplacement because it can reduce some of the risks associated with layoffs, such as negative publicity or an increased likelihood that unions will attempt to organize the work force.[34] Employers who provide outplacement services tend to give the goal of social responsibility a high priority as part of their human resource strategy.

A 1995 survey of over 1,000 employers across Canada conducted by consulting firm Murray Axsmith indicated that during the preceding 12 months these firms, with an average of 550 employees, had dismissed (on average) 35 employees, and that slightly over half of these cases were for reasons of redundancy. Virtually all these firms offered re-employment counselling services, four out of five citing a desire to help former employees become re-employed as quickly as possible.[35]

■ The Goals of Outplacement

The goals of an outplacement program reflect the organization's need to control the disruption caused by layoffs and other employee separations so that they do not hurt productivity. The most important of these goals are (1) reducing the morale problems of employees, both those who are about to be laid off (so that they remain productive until they leave the firm), and also those who remain (so that they see their employer is trying to do the "right thing" in difficult circumstances), (2) minimizing the amount of litigation initiated by separated employees, and (3) assisting separated employees in finding comparable jobs as quickly as possible.[36]

■ Outplacement Services

The most common outplacement services provided to separated employees are emotional support and job-search assistance. These services are closely tied to the goals of outplacement.

Emotional Support.   Outplacement programs usually offer the services of trained counsellors to help employees deal with the emotions associated with job loss— shock, anger, denial, and lowered self-esteem. Because the family may suffer if the breadwinner becomes unemployed, sometimes family members are included in the counselling as well.[37] Counselling also benefits the employer because it helps to defuse some of the hostility that laid-off employees are feeling toward the company.

Job-Search Assistance.   Employees who are outplaced often do not know how to begin the search for a new job. In many cases, these individuals have not had to look for a job in many years.

An important aspect of this assistance is teaching separated employees the skills they need to find a new job. These skills include résumé writing, interviewing and job-search techniques, career planning, and negotiation skills.[38] Outplaced employees will receive instruction in these skills from either a member of the outplacement firm or the HR department. In addition, the former employer sometimes provides administrative support in the form of clerical support, phone answering, e-mail, and fax services.[39] These services allow laid-off employees to use computers to prepare résumés, copiers to copy them, and fax machines to send them out.

The use of outplacement has become a global management practice. Several large corporations in Great Britain have recently restructured their operations, eliminating thousands of jobs. British Telecom has announced plans to cut its work force by 40,000 jobs in the 1990s, and Midland Bank has eliminated 10,000 jobs over the past decade.[40] An important part of these downsizing strategies is the use of outplacement services to smooth the affected employees' transition to a new job. Similarly, Japanese corporations have started to use outplacement firms to find jobs for surplus workers. Foreign competition from Korea, Taiwan, and Brazil has increasingly led some Japanese corporations to do the formerly unthinkable—lay off Japanese workers in steel plants, coal mines, and shipyards, which have been vulnerable to competition in global markets.[41] The Issues and Applications feature entitled "Saving Face While Saving the Company" shows why Japanese firms are starting to adopt outplacement—which in Japan is viewed as a North American management practice.[42]

Saving Face While Saving the Company

These days, a layoff of a few dozen employees from a Canadian company wouldn't raise many reporters' eyebrows. However, when Japan's Pioneer Electronics announced a layoff of 35 workers in 1993, the news sparked headlines in Japan and abroad. In a culture famous for its lifetime employment policies, layoffs used to be avoided at all costs—even if it meant that Tokyo paid companies to retain redundant workers. Now, with an estimated one million "in-house unemployed" on company payrolls, surging manufacturing costs, and economic downturn, the threat of layoffs looms in many of Japan's largest companies.

To avoid the stigma of announcing layoffs, many Japanese companies are resorting to transfers and early retirement. And, to ease the transition for workers who get the dreaded *kata-tataki*, or tap on the shoulder, more Japanese firms are relying on North American-style outplacement firms to counsel workers and find new jobs for them. The sole North American-based outplacement firm in Japan, Drake Beam Morin Inc., grew fivefold between 1991 and 1993 and now serves 500 Japanese companies.

Yet few Japanese companies will admit publicly that they use outplacement firms. Most are embarrassed about being unable to honour the promise of lifetime employment. Some workers are optimistic, though, about hints of more freedom in the workplace. "The company isn't a god any more," says one software salesman who was advised by his company to start looking for a new job.

Sources: Based on Miller, K. L. (1993, January 11). Land of the rising jobless. *Business Week, 47.* Schlesinger, J. M. (1993, September 16). Japan begins to confront job insecurity. *The Wall Street Journal,* A10

Summary and Conclusions

What Are Employee Separations?   Employee separations occur when employees cease to be members of an organization. Separations and outplacement can be managed effectively. Managers should plan for the outflow of their human resources with thoughtful policies. Employee separations have both costs and benefits. The costs include (1) recruiting costs, (2) selection costs, (3) training costs, and (4) separation costs. The benefits are (1) reduced labour costs, (2) replacement of poor performers, (3) increased innovation, and (4) the opportunity for greater diversity.

Types of Employee Separations.   Employees may leave either voluntarily or involuntarily. Voluntary separations include quits and retirements. Involuntary separations include dismissals and layoffs. When an employee is forced to leave involuntarily, a much greater level of documentation is necessary to show that a manager's decision to terminate the employee was fair and consistent.

Managing Early Retirements.   When downsizing an organization, managers may elect to use early retirements or voluntary severance plans as an alternative to layoffs. Early retirement programs must be managed so that eligible employees do not perceive that they are being forced to retire.

Managing Layoffs.   Layoffs should be used as a last resort after all cost-cutting alternatives have been exhausted. Important considerations in developing a layoff policy include (1) notifying employees, (2) developing layoff criteria, (3) communicating to laid-off employees, (4) coordinating media relations, (5) maintaining security, and (6) reassuring survivors of the layoff.

Outplacement.   No matter what policy is used to reduce the work force, it is a good idea for the organization to use outplacement services to help separated employees cope with their emotions and minimize the amount of time they are unemployed.

Key Terms and Concepts

attrition, 187
bumping, 188
dismissal, 183
downsizing, 183
early retirement incentives, 182
employee separation, 178
exit interview, 180
hiring freeze, 187
involuntary separation, 182
job sharing, 188

layoff, 183
open window, 184
outplacement assistance, 180
pay cut, 188
pay freeze, 188
progressive discipline procedure, 183
quit, 181
recruitment costs, 178
retirement, 182
selection costs, 178

seniority, 192
separation costs, 178
severance/separation pay, 179
training costs, 178
turnover rate, 178
voluntary separation, 181
voluntary severance plan or buyout, 181

Discussion Questions

1. After eight years as marketing assistant for a Montreal office of a large French bank, Sarah Schiffler was told that her job, in a non-revenue-producing department, was being eliminated. Her choices: She could either be laid off, with eight months' severance pay, or stay on and train for the position of credit analyst, a career route she had turned down in the past. Nervous about making mortgage payments on her new condo, Sarah agreed to stay, but after six months of feeling miserable in her new position, she quit. Was her separation from the bank voluntary or involuntary? Can you think of situations in which a voluntary separation is really an involuntary separation? What are the managerial implications of such situations?

2. What are the advantages and disadvantages of using seniority as the basis for layoff? What alternatives to seniority are available as layoff criteria?

3. Would an employer ever want to increase the rate of employee turnover in a company? Why or why not?

4. What role does the HR department play in employee separations and outplacement?

5. In an age when more and more companies are downsizing, an increasingly trendy concept is "the virtual corporation." The idea is that a company should have a core of owners and managers, but that, to the greatest degree possible, workers should be contingent — temporary, part-time, or on short-term contracts. This gives the corporation maximum flexibility to shift vendors, cut costs, and avoid long-term labour commitments. What are the advantages and disadvantages of the virtual corporation from the point of view of both employers and workers?

6. Under what circumstances might a company's managers prefer to use a layoff instead of early retirements or voluntary severance plans as a way to downsize the work force?

7. Under what set of conditions should a company lay off employees without giving them advance notice?

8. "The people who actually have the face-to-face contact with the person who is being laid off aren't the ones who made the decision. They often didn't have any input into which of their people would go," says a technician at a firm that experienced large-scale layoffs. What role should managers—who have the "face-to-face" contact with employees—play in implementing a layoff? Do you think managers and HR staff members always agree on how employee separations should be handled? Why or why not?

Check out our companion Website at: **www.prenticehall.ca/gomez** for a selection of self-study questions, key terms and concepts, updated Weblinks to related Internet sites, newsgroups, CBC video updates, and more.

MiniCase 1   *Something New at Nova*

Nova Corporation of Alberta, a pipeline and petrochemical company, had a work force of some 6,000 employees in 1995, a number greater than economic and business conditions warranted. In June of that year, it ended the unspoken lifetime employment commitment that had been part of its culture. Nova introduced an Employment Transition and Continuity Program in an attempt to deal with the potential sense of betrayal such a change can prompt. "We wanted every employee leaving to have a range of options and feel well treated," said Sheila O'Brien, Senior VP for human resources.

These were the options open to people leaving Nova:

◆ To work for a non-profit charity for up to one year, collecting 50 percent of salary during that period.

◆ To go back to school, earning 50 percent of salary plus $5,000 per year in expenses.

◆ To start a business, with Nova providing $25,000 in start-up capital in addition to severance.

Discussion Questions

1. What do you think of these options? To which groups of employees do you think they would be attractive?
2. Assume you were in this position (say) 10 years from now. Which option do you think you'd choose? Why?
3. Sheila O'Brien also said, "We don't look at it as a productivity booster. We look at it as something we ought to do for people who've worked for us long term and earned some security." Do you think this is sufficient justification for a major expenditure? Explain.
4. Nova's pipelines earn a government-mandated return from natural gas shippers. Given this financial cushion, is it fair to use Nova as an example of what companies in unregulated sectors should do under similar circumstances?

SOURCE: Concerned capitalists: Nova takes care of its own, however briefly. (1995, June 26). *Western Report*, 16–17.

MiniCase 2   *Any Questions?*

David M. Noer, Vice-President for Training and Education for the Centre for Creative Leadership, has conducted extensive studies on the effects of layoffs on survivors and the organizations that employ them. "If I were to compile a composite of all the speeches I have heard executives present to layoff survivors," says Noer, "it would go like this":

Our ROI has eroded to the point where the security analysts have expressed concern over the value of our stock to the shareholders. As you may know, our gross margins have also been declining over the past six quarters and reached a point last quarter where we suffered a pre-tax loss. Based on recent market research, we have confirmed the fact that we are losing [domestic] market share ... and are facing increasingly stiff competition in Europe. The quality indicators we installed last year show that we are not making the gains we had planned and our revenue per employee has declined. We have no alternative but to implement a downsizing effort at this time if this organization is to remain a viable economic entity. It is a straightforward economic decision. Any questions?

Discussion Questions

1. Imagine you have just survived a layoff in which some of your co-workers have been let go. What is your reaction to this speech?
2. Put yourself in the employer's shoes and try to write a brief speech that addresses how survivors might be feeling.

SOURCE: Noer, David M. (1993). *Healing the wounds: Overcoming the trauma of layoffs and revitalizing downsized organizations.* San Francisco, CA: Jossey-Bass, pp. 103–104.

Case 1

Is the Layoff Justified?

Wilson Industrial is a small auto-parts manufacturer. It employs about 100 people and its work force is non-union. Owing to increased competition in the automobile industry, the company's managers anticipate a permanent reduction in the demand for Wilson Industrial's products. They have decided to lay off 15 production workers. The company has never experienced layoffs and at present has no policy that governs how a layoff should be conducted.

➤

Top managers have told Joe McGuire, the manager of the production department, to retain the best performers. McGuire examined the performance appraisals and production records of all 60 employees in his department and drew up a list of 15 employees to lay off. Many of the top performers have been working for Wilson Industrial for only one or two years.

Sam Kowalski has been employed as a lathe operator by Wilson Industrial for 20 years. Although McGuire has always given Kowalski good performance evaluations, he now informs Kowalski that he is on the layoff list and that his job performance is marginal. McGuire also explains that he gave good evaluations to Kowalski in the past only so that he could receive higher pay increases. Kowalski is very upset about los-

ing his job and is thinking about taking legal action against Wilson Industrial.

Critical Thinking Questions

1. Does Kowalski have good reason to take his case to court?
2. Did top management handle the layoff correctly?
3. What could Joe McGuire have done differently to avoid potential litigation?

Cooperative Learning Exercise

4. Students form pairs and take the roles of Kowalski and McGuire. The student with the McGuire role is to explain to Kowalski that he is about to be laid off. Kowalski reacts to this news. How could the HR department support McGuire in his unpleasant task?

Case 2

Outplacement at Rocky Mountain Oil

Rocky Mountain Oil has announced that it will reduce the scale of its Canadian operations and will need to eliminate several hundred administrative positions at its headquarters in Denver. The organization wants to provide outplacement assistance to the employees who will lose their jobs. However, it does not want to spend much money on outplacement.

The company has formed an outplacement committee consisting of top managers, most of whom come from the operations and financial units of the business. The committee has provided a recommendation for an outplacement program that has been accepted by Rocky Mountain's CEO, Barbara Robinson. This program consists of two parts. First, each laid-off employee's immediate supervisor will provide counselling and emotional support to his or her laid-off employees. All supervisors will receive an outplacement counselling packet that includes the recent article "Ten Easy Steps to Help Employees Deal With Losing Their Jobs." Trailers will be placed at the far end of the company parking lot to serve as temporary offices for former employees, who can use them while searching for jobs and receiving counselling from their former supervisors. The trailers are surplus equipment from domestic oil operations.

Second, the outplacement program will help former employees develop job-search skills. Each employee will be given a copy of the book *What Color Is Your Parachute?,* which pro-

vides tips on how to conduct a job search. In addition, each employee will be offered the opportunity to take a course at a nearby community college called "Introduction to Personnel Management," in which students learn to write a résumé, gain information about the labour market, and gather tips on how to interview. Rocky Mountain Oil will pick up the cost of tuition (about $100 per employee) for the course.

Shortly after the CEO approved the outplacement program, Rocky Mountain Oil's Director of Human Resources, Karen Sinclair, read a copy of the memo announcing the program. Sinclair had not been invited to be a member of the outplacement committee. After she finished reading the memo, Ms. Sinclair thought to herself, "That's what happens when you let accountants design a human resource program."

Critical Thinking Questions

1. Do you see any problems with the outplacement program at Rocky Mountain Oil?
2. What did Karen Sinclair mean by her statement?
3. What improvements to the design of the outplacement program do you think need to be made?

Cooperative Learning Exercise

4. Students form pairs, one role-playing Barbara Robinson and the other playing Karen Sinclair. Each tries to convince the other of the advantages of the outplacement program she prefers.

VideoCase

Recruiting in a Tight Labour Market

While all employees can potentially make an important contribution to an organization, from time to time certain groups of employees are almost indispensable. When this happens across a number of companies or industries at the same time, competition heats up. A recent example has been the demand for programmers who know the COBOL programming language, a language that is used less often than it was 10 or 20 years ago. The "Year 2000" (a.k.a. "Y2K") problem existed in many computing systems, causing serious errors in calculations based on two-digit dates where "99" means 1999 and "01" is intended to mean 2001 but is read by the computer as 1901. For the two years or so when this problem has been a major concern, the antiquated COBOL skills became a lucrative asset for those programmers who could help sort out the problem.

When there is a shortage of certain critical skills, it is not surprising that employers bid up the price to attract the people they need. However, attractive pay (salaries, bonuses, and benefits) is only one element of the package. The challenge for employers in tight markets is to devise a strategy to attract and hold critical employees.

Discussion Questions

1. How can an employer attract employees in a hot market without depending solely on simply raising pay levels to buy the talent they need? Are there any considerations that make it desirable to use *non*-pay factors to attract such employees?

2. Are the factors (pay, job content, etc.) that influence a person's decision to accept a particular job the same as those that make an individual open to moving to another employer? If you think they are generally the same, do you think the relative importance or "weight" given to various factors that shape the decision to leave a particular job the same weights that determine *which* job people are likely to accept when they do move?

3. The problem with underqualified employees (incompetence) is easy to anticipate. What risks are there, if any, of hiring the very best people (who may be overqualified for the job they are offered)? Can those risks be avoided, or at least tempered? How?

Video Resource: "Hiring Wars," *Venture* 661 (September 23, 1997).

Appraising and Managing Performance

After reading this chapter, you should be able to deal more effectively with the following challenges:

1 Explain why performance appraisal is important and describe its components.

2 Discuss the advantages and disadvantages of different performance rating systems.

3 Manage the impact of rating errors and bias on performance ratings.

4 Discuss the potential role of emotion in performance appraisal and how to manage its impact.

5 Identify the major legal requirements for appraisal.

6 Understand how to manage and develop employee performance proactively.

The Value of Feedback. Although some managers consider performance appraisal a time-consuming chore, many realize that periodic reviews can help employees improve their performance over time. The best managers both appraise their workers' performance and act as coaches, encouraging employees to learn new skills and expand their responsibilities.

Bob has just come out of his annual feedback session with his manager. He feels great. True, his manager did not give him the highest possible ratings. However, she spent time reviewing the areas in which he excelled as well as those in which he could improve his performance. Best of all, she gave him the opportunity to express his frustrations with the way his work is organized. He feels he can do a much better job if some fairly minor changes are made. He has the sense that his manager is "in his corner," sincerely hoping he will do a great job so that next year his ratings will be even higher.

*　　*　　*

At Joan's company, the annual appraisal period has just ended, and it has done so with the usual mix of worker anxieties and complaints. What a process! Managers had to conduct employees' performance reviews to satisfy legal requirements, and the process seemed rational and positive in the abstract. But the reality fell far short of the ideal. The appraisal, in fact, turned into a bureaucratic paper-shuffling exercise that took far too long and resulted in too many grievances.

Several issues came up this year. Many workers charged their supervisors with bias, complaining that performance ratings are a function of "how much a supervisor likes you." Others complained that their managers autocratically handed down annual ratings without providing any feedback on how they should improve their performance. Another prickly issue was the apparent conflict between the appraisal system and the organization's team structure. The team structure requires cooperativeness, Joan complained, but the appraisal system focusses on individual achievement. Managers overheard some workers say that they were going to "take care of number one" for the next appraisal period and not concern themselves so much with the team.

Supervisors raised another troublesome issue. They argued that jobs are so much in flux that by the time the appraisal period comes around, they are rating workers on things they are no longer doing. Performance appraisals aren't supposed to hinder progress, managers said, but that seemed to be exactly what was happening.

HRM on the Web

http://shrm.org/hrlinks/

SHRM Gateway

This Web site is currently one of the most comprehensive access points to information dealing with human resources issues. It is part of the site for the Society for Human Resource Management, the major U.S. human resources professional association and includes linkages to many international (including Canadian) sites in addition to those oriented to a domestic audience.

Which of these stories reflects most people's experience? Unfortunately, the second story seems more representative of what goes on in many organizations than the first. The measurement and management of performance are two of the most difficult issues a general manager faces.

It is widely thought that accurate measurement of employee performance is a necessary precondition for effective management. Our first goal in this chapter is to acquaint you with the foundation, design, and implementation of performance measurement systems. Our second is to describe the principles of effective performance management.

■ What Is Performance Appraisal?

Performance appraisal (see Figure 7-1) involves the *identification, measurement,* and *management* of human performance in organizations.[1]

performance appraisal
The identification, measurement, and management of human performance in organizations.

◆ *Identification* means determining what areas of work the manager should be examining when measuring performance. Rational and legally defensible identification requires a measurement system that is based on job analysis (Chapter 2). Thus the appraisal system should focus on performance that affects organizational success rather than performance-irrelevant characteristics such as race, age, or gender.

◆ *Measurement,* the centrepiece of the appraisal system, entails making managerial judgements of how "good" or "bad" observed employee performance was. Good performance measurement must be consistent throughout the organization. That is, all managers in the organization must maintain comparable rating standards.[2]

◆ *Management* is the overriding goal of any appraisal system. Appraisal should be more than a past-oriented activity that criticizes or praises workers for their performance in the preceding year. To facilitate performance management, appraisal must take a future-oriented view of what workers can do to achieve their potential in the organization. This requires managers to provide workers with feedback and coach them to higher levels of performance.

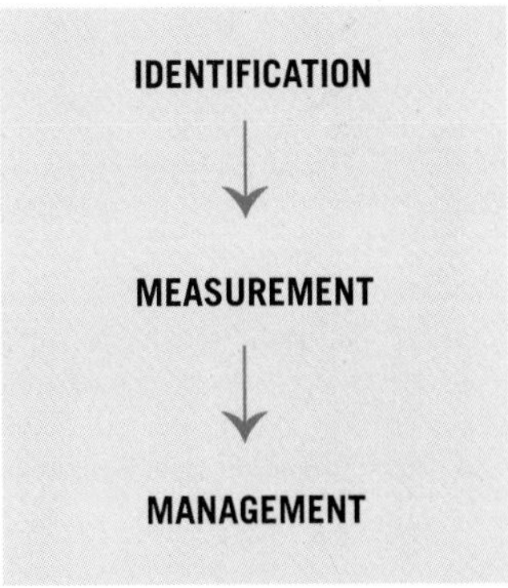

IDENTIFICATION

↓

MEASUREMENT

↓

MANAGEMENT

Figure 7–1 A Model of Performance Appraisal

■ The Uses of Performance Appraisal

Organizations usually conduct appraisals for administrative and/or developmental purposes.[3] Performance measurements are used administratively whenever they are the basis for a decision about the employee's work conditions, including promotions, termination, and rewards. Developmental uses of appraisal, which are geared toward improving employees' performance and strengthening their job skills, include counselling employees on effective work behaviours and sending them for training.

Appraisals are typically done once a year, and are usually based on supervisors' subjective judgements[4] rather than on objective indicators of performance, such as number of units produced. The subjective nature of most appraisals has led many to conclude that appraisals are full of errors. For example, annual appraisals can place an excessive burden on the memory of the person rating multiple workers. Also, supervisors' judgements may be influenced by stereotypes and other personal beliefs or perceptions. However, as we discuss later in this chapter, objective performance data are not necessarily better than subjective appraisal.[5]

For these and other reasons, dissatisfaction with appraisal is rampant. One survey found that most human resources professionals are dissatisfied with their current appraisal system.[6] Some companies have even decided to do away with the usual numerical ratings altogether. For example, some Cigna divisions have dropped numerical ratings in favour of coaching employees to focus more on verbal communications than on written appraisals.[7]

Nonetheless, formal appraisal remains an important activity in most organizations. The challenge is to manage the appraisal system to realize the ideals of performance improvement and worker development. In the next two sections, we explain the issues and challenges involved in the first two steps of performance appraisal: identification and measurement.

■ Identifying Performance Dimensions

We have said that the first step in the performance appraisal process (see Figure 7-1) is identifying what is to be measured. This process seems fairly simple at first glance. In practice, however, it can be quite complicated. Consider the following example:

Nancy manages a group of computer programmers. She needs to evaluate each of them to determine who should receive the largest raise. Before she can decide which programmer is most effective, she must identify the aspects, or **dimensions,** of performance that determine effective job performance. Whether the computer programs work well is one appropriate dimension. This aspect of performance

dimension
An aspect of performance that determines effective job performance.

might be labelled *quality of programs written*. But Nancy also realizes that David, one of the programmers, always does very good work—but takes three times as long to write a program as the other programmers. So she includes a dimension called *quantity of programs written* on her list of things to assess. Unfortunately, Ian, the programmer with the best mix of quantity and quality, also constantly berates his co-workers and refuses to work cooperatively on programs requiring more than one programmer. So Nancy adds a third dimension to her list labelled *interpersonal effectiveness*.

This process might continue until Nancy has identified eight or 10 dimensions. As you have probably realized, the process of identifying performance dimensions is very much like the job analysis process described in Chapter 2. In fact, job analysis is the mechanism by which performance dimensions should be identified.

Identification of performance dimensions is the very important first step in the appraisal process. If a significant dimension is missed, then employee morale is likely to suffer because employees who do well on that dimension will not be recognized or rewarded. If an irrelevant or trivial dimension is included, employees may perceive the whole appraisal process as meaningless.

■ Measuring Performance

Measuring employee performance involves assigning a number to reflect an employee's performance on the identified characteristics or dimensions.[8] (Technically, numbers are not mandatory. You might use labels such as "excellent," "good," "average," and "poor" instead. But these grades could just as well be numbered 1 through 4, and you would still need to decide what grade is appropriate for a given employee.)

It is often difficult to quantify performance dimensions. For example, "creativity" may be a very important part of an advertising copywriter's job. But how exactly does one measure creativity—by the number of ads written, by the winning of industry awards, by peer ratings, or by some other criterion? These are issues that managers face when evaluating an employee's performance.

■ Measurement Tools

Numerous techniques for measuring performance have been developed over the years. Today, managers have a wide array of appraisal formats from which to choose. Here we discuss the formats that are most common, legally defensible, and promising. These formats can be classified in two ways: (1) the type of judgement that is required (relative or absolute), and (2) the focus of the measure (trait, behaviour, or outcome).

Relative and Absolute Judgements.   Measures of employee performance can be classified on the basis of whether the type of judgement called for is relative or absolute.

relative judgement

An appraisal format that asks a supervisor to compare an employee's performance to the performance of other employees doing the same job.

Relative judgements.   Appraisal systems based on **relative judgement** ask the supervisor to compare an employee's performance to the performance of other employees doing the same job. Providing a *rank order* of workers from best to worst is an example of a relative approach. Another type of relative judgement format classifies employees into groups, such as top third, middle third, or lowest third.

Relative rating systems have the advantage of forcing supervisors to differentiate among their workers. Without such a system, many supervisors are inclined to rate everyone the same, which destroys the appraisal system's value. For example, one study that examined the distribution of performance ratings for more than 7,000 managerial and professional employees in two large manufacturing firms found that 95 percent of employees were crowded into just two rating categories.

Most HR specialists believe that the disadvantages of relative rating systems outweigh their advantages.[9] First, relative judgements (such as ranks) do not make clear how great or small the differences between employees are. Second, such systems do not provide any absolute information, so managers cannot determine how good or poor employees at the extreme rankings are. For example, relative ratings do not reveal whether the top-rated worker in one work team is better or worse than an average worker in another. The worst-rated worker in one team may be a better performer than the average-rated workers in another team that has a poorer overall level of performance. Under a relative system, the pay increases could be distributed to workers who are at the top of their own work groups but are poorer performers than some other workers in other, higher-performing groups. This problem is illustrated in Figure 7–2. Ali, Jill, and François are the highest-ranked performers in their respective work groups. However, Jill, François, and Gunther are actually the best overall performers.

Third, such systems force managers to identify differences among workers where none may exist.[10] This can cause conflict among workers if and when ratings are disclosed. Finally, relative systems typically require assessment of overall performance. The "big picture" nature of relative ratings makes performance feedback ambiguous and of questionable value to workers who would benefit by receiving specific information on the various dimensions of their performance.

Absolute judgements.   Unlike relative judgement appraisal formats, **absolute judgement** formats ask the supervisor to make judgements about an employee's performance based solely on performance standards. Comparisons to the performance levels of co-workers are not made. Typically, the dimensions of performance deemed relevant for the job are listed on the rating form, and the manager is asked to rate each one. An example of an absolute judgement rating scale is shown in Figure 7–3 on the next page.

Theoretically, absolute formats allow employees from different work groups, rated by different managers, to be compared to one another. If all employees are excellent workers, they all can receive excellent ratings. Also, because ratings are made on separate dimensions of performance, the feedback to the employee can be more specific and helpful.

Although often preferable to relative systems, absolute rating systems have their own drawbacks. One is that all workers in a group can receive the same evaluation if the supervisor is reluctant to differentiate among worker performance levels. Another is that different supervisors can have markedly different evaluation standards. Comparison of ratings across work groups in an organization then becomes invalid. For example, a rating of 6 from an "easy" supervisor may actually be lower in value than a rating of 4 from a more stringent supervisor. But when the organization is handing out promotions or pay increases, the worker who received the 6 rating would be rewarded.

absolute judgement

An appraisal format that asks a supervisor to make judgements about an employee's performance based solely on performance standards.

Actual Performance	Ranked Work Group 1	Ranked Work Group 2	Ranked Work Group 3
10 (High)		Jill (1)	François (1)
9			Gunther (2)
8		Tom (2)	Lisa (3)
7	Ali (1)	Su-Yin (3)	
6	Pam (2)		
5			
4	Joyce (3)	Greg (4)	
3	Mark (4)	Ken (5)	Cindy (4)
2	Richard (5)		Steve (5)
1 (Low)			

Figure 7–2 Rankings and Performance Levels across Work Groups

PERFORMANCE REVIEW

Three-month (H&S) ☐   Annual (H-Only) ☐
Six-month (H&S) ☐   Special (H&S) ☐

H = Hourly   S = Salaried

For probationary employee review: Do you recommend
that this employee be retained?   Yes   No
                                        ☐   ☐

Review period: From_____ To_____

Employee Name

☐☐☐☐☐☐☐☐☐☐☐   Hourly ☐   Salaried ☐

Employee I.D. #

Classification/Classification Hire Date

Department/Division

For each applicable performance area, mark the box that most closely reflects the employee's performance.
1= unacceptable;   2= needs improvement;   3= satisfactory;   4= above average;   5= outstanding.

Performance Area	1	2	3	4	5
Ability to make job-related decisions					
Accepts change					
Accepts direction					
Accepts responsibility					
Attendance					
Attitude					
Compliance with rules					
Cooperation					
Cost consciousness					
Dependability					

Performance Area	1	2	3	4	5
Effective under stress					
Initiative					
Knowledge of work					
Leadership					
Operation & care of equipment					
Planning & organizing					
Quality of work					
Quantity of acceptable work					
Safety practices					
SUPERVISOR'S OVERALL APPRAISAL					

For overall appraisals at the 1 or 2 level: Is the employee to remain and be placed on probationary status? Yes ☐ No ☐
If yes, what is the approximate date of next performance review? _____

JOB STRENGTHS AND SUPERIOR PERFORMANCE INCIDENTS: _____
_____
_____
_____

AREAS FOR IMPROVEMENT: _____
_____
_____
_____

PROGRESS ACHIEVED IN ATTAINING PREVIOUSLY SET GOALS: _____
_____
_____
_____
_____

SPECIFIC OBJECTIVES TO BE UNDERTAKEN PRIOR TO NEXT REVIEW FOR IMPROVED WORK PERFORMANCE: _____
_____
_____
_____
_____

SUPERVISOR COMMENTS: _____
_____
_____
_____

EMPLOYEE COMMENTS: _____
_____
_____
_____

_____ _____   _____   ☐☐☐☐☐☐☐☐☐☐   _____
Employee's Signature   Date   Rating Supervisor's Signature   Employee I.D. #   Date

_____   _____   _____   _____
Second Level Supervisor's Signature   Date   Department Head's Signature   Date

Figure 7–3 Sample of Absolute Judgement Rating Scale

Nonetheless, absolute systems do have one distinct advantage: They avoid directly creating conflict among workers. This, plus the fact that relative systems are generally harder to defend when legal issues arise, may account for the prevalence of absolute systems.

It is interesting to note, though, that most people *do* make comparative judgements among both people and things. That is, they tend to make evaluative judgements in relative rather than absolute terms. A political candidate is better or worse than opponents, not good or bad in an absolute sense. Your favourite band is better than others, not a 5.6 on some scale of band quality. If comparative judgements are actually the common and natural way of making judgements, it may be that supervisors can be more accurate when making relative ratings than when making absolute ratings.[11]

Trait, Behavioural, and Outcome Data.   In addition to relative and absolute judgements, performance measurement systems can be classified by the type of performance data they focus on: trait data, behavioural data, or outcome data.

Trait data.   **Trait appraisal instruments** ask the supervisor to make judgements about *traits,* worker characteristics that tend to be consistent and enduring. Figure 7–4 presents four traits that are typically found on trait-based rating scales: decisiveness, reliability, energy, and loyalty. While a number of organizations use trait ratings,[12] the weight of current opinion is against them. Trait ratings have been criticized for being much too ambiguous[13] as well as for leaving the door open for conscious or subconscious bias. In addition, trait ratings are less defensible in court than are other types of ratings, mostly because of their ambiguous nature.[14] Definitions of "decisiveness," for example, can differ dramatically across supervisors, and the courts can be sensitive to the "slippery" nature of traits as criteria. Another difficulty with trait formats is choosing, from among the hundreds of possible traits, those that should be included in the rating instrument.

Assessment of traits also focuses attention on the person rather than on the performance, which can create defensiveness in employees. Trait ratings imply that a performance deficit resides within the person and, therefore, are equivalent to ratings of the person's worth. From the limited research done in this area, it seems that this type of person-focussed approach is not conducive to performance development. Measurement approaches that focus more directly on performance, either by evaluating behaviours or results, are generally more acceptable to workers and more effective as development tools.

trait appraisal instrument
An appraisal tool that asks a supervisor to make judgements about worker characteristics that tend to be consistent and enduring.

Rate each worker using the scales below.						
Decisiveness:						
1	2	3	4	5	6	7
Very low			Moderate			Very high
Reliability:						
1	2	3	4	5	6	7
Very low			Moderate			Very high
Energy:						
1	2	3	4	5	6	7
Very low			Moderate			Very high
Loyalty:						
1	2	3	4	5	6	7
Very low			Moderate			Very high

Figure 7–4 Sample Trait Scales

Despite these problems, trait ratings may be more effective than many believe. Traits, after all, are simply a shorthand way of describing a set of behavioural tendencies. Thus trait judgements can have a concrete behavioural basis that makes them less error-laden than critics suggest. We routinely make trait judgements about others, and it is rare for someone to be described other than through his or her traits. If you doubt this, perform the following experiment:

Let's say a classmate has asked you what one of your professors is like. Let's also imagine that this professor does magic tricks to maintain class interest and to accentuate lecture points, sparks lively discussion, and is known for wearing outrageous costumes that go along with the class topic. Would your initial response to your classmate consist of a list of behaviours that you've seen the professor engage in? Not likely! You'd more likely use the words "lively," "wild," "entertaining," "engaging," "crazy"—all trait terms. You might follow up this assessment with some behavioural description, but probably more for the purpose of enjoyable storytelling than anything else. The point is that we routinely make trait judgements about others; they are a powerful way of describing people. Because we do it all the time, we also may be quite good at it.

behavioural appraisal instrument

An appraisal tool that asks managers to assess a worker's behaviours.

Behavioural data.   **Behavioural appraisal instruments** focus on assessing a worker's behaviours. That is, instead of ranking leadership ability (a trait), the rater is asked to assess whether an employee exhibits certain behaviours (for example, works well with co-workers, comes to meetings on time). In one type of behavioural instrument, Behavioural Observation Scales, supervisors record how frequently various behaviours listed on the form occurred.[15] However, ratings assessing the value rather than the frequency of specific behaviours are more commonly used in organizations. Probably the best-known behavioural scale is the Behaviourally Anchored Rating Scale (BARS). Figure 7–5 is an example of a BARS scale used to rate the effectiveness with which a department manager supervises his or her sales personnel.

The main advantage of a behavioural approach to performance measurement is that the performance standards are concrete. Unlike traits, which can have many facets, behaviours across the range of a dimension are included directly on the behavioural scale. This concreteness makes BARS and other behavioural instruments more legally defensible than trait scales, which often use such adjectives as "poor" and "excellent." Behavioural scales also provide employees with specific examples of the types of behaviours to engage in (and to avoid) if they want to do well in the organization. In addition, behavioural scales encourage supervisors to be specific in their performance feedback. Finally, both workers and supervisors can be involved in the process of generating behavioural scales,[16] which is likely to increase understanding and acceptance of the appraisal system.

Behavioural systems are not without disadvantages, however. Most notably, the development of behavioural scales can be very time-consuming, easily taking several months. Another disadvantage of behavioural systems is their specificity. The points, or *anchors,* on behavioural scales are clear and concrete, but they are only examples of behaviour a worker *may* exhibit. Employees may never exhibit some of these anchor behaviours, which can cause difficulty for supervisors at appraisal time. Also, significant organization changes can invalidate behavioural scales. For example, computerization of operations can dramatically alter the behaviours that workers must exhibit to be successful. Thus the behaviours painstakingly developed for the appraisal system could become useless or, worse, operate as a drag on organizational change and adaptation. Workers will be unwilling to make changes in their work behaviours as long as the criteria by which their performance is judged aren't changed as well.

Another potential difficulty with behavioural systems is many supervisors' belief that a behavioural focus is an unnatural way of thinking about and evaluating workers. As we discussed earlier, traits are a more natural way to organize infor-

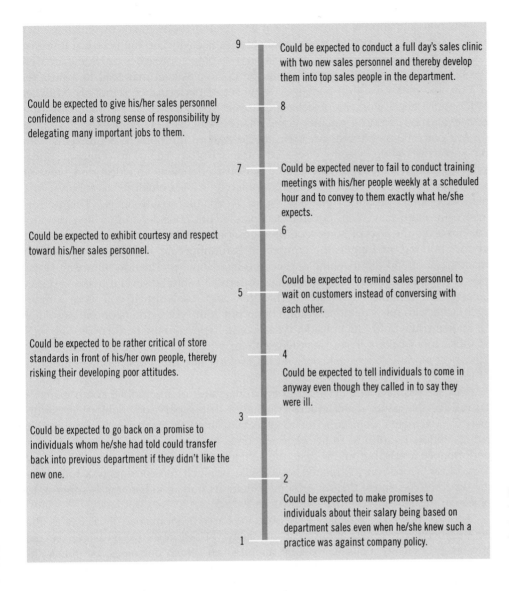

9 — Could be expected to conduct a full day's sales clinic with two new sales personnel and thereby develop them into top sales people in the department.

Could be expected to give his/her sales personnel confidence and a strong sense of responsibility by delegating many important jobs to them. — 8

7 — Could be expected never to fail to conduct training meetings with his/her people weekly at a scheduled hour and to convey to them exactly what he/she expects.

Could be expected to exhibit courtesy and respect toward his/her sales personnel. — 6

5 — Could be expected to remind sales personnel to wait on customers instead of conversing with each other.

Could be expected to be rather critical of store standards in front of his/her own people, thereby risking their developing poor attitudes. — 4

Could be expected to tell individuals to come in anyway even though they called in to say they were ill.

3 —

Could be expected to go back on a promise to individuals whom he/she had told could transfer back into previous department if they didn't like the new one. — 2

Could be expected to make promises to individuals about their salary being based on department sales even when he/she knew such a practice was against company policy.

1 —

Figure 7-5 Sample BARS Used to Rate a Sales Manager
SOURCE: Cascio, E. F. (1991). *Applied psychology in personnel management*, Englewood Cliffs, NJ: Prentice Hall.

mation about others. Supervisors required to make behaviourally based evaluations may merely translate their trait impressions into behavioural judgements. Thus although a behavioural approach seems less ambiguous, it may require mental gymnastics that can introduce additional error into ratings. No research has directly examined this issue, but one study has found a preference among both supervisors and workers for a trait-based system over a behaviourally based system.[17] The "unnaturalness" of a behavioural orientation may underlie this preference.

Outcome data.   **Outcome appraisal instruments** ask managers to assess the results achieved by workers, such as amount of sales or number of products produced. The most prevalent outcome approaches are **management by objectives**[18]**(MBO)** and naturally occurring outcome measures. MBO is a goal-directed approach in which workers and their supervisors set goals together for the upcoming evaluation period. The rating then consists of deciding to what extent the goals have been met. With *naturally occurring outcomes,* the performance measure isn't so much discussed and agreed to as it is handed to supervisors and workers. For example, a computerized production system used to manufacture cardboard boxes may automatically generate data regarding the number of pieces produced, the amount of waste, and the defect rate.

outcome appraisal instrument
An appraisal tool that asks managers to assess the results achieved by workers.

management by objectives (MBO)
A goal-directed approach to performance appraisal in which workers and their supervisors set goals together for the upcoming evaluation period.

The outcome approach provides clear and unambiguous criteria by which worker performance can be judged. It also eliminates subjectivity and the potential for error and bias that goes along with it. In addition, outcome approaches provide increased flexibility. For example, a change in the production system may lead to a new set of outcome measures and, perhaps, a new set of performance standards. With an MBO approach, a worker's objectives can easily be adjusted at the beginning of a new evaluation period if organizational changes call for new emphases.

Are outcome-based systems, then, the answer to the numerous problems with the subjective rating systems discussed earlier? Unfortunately, no. Outcome measures, although objective, may give a seriously deficient and distorted view of worker performance levels. Consider an outcome measure defined as follows: "the number of units produced that are within acceptable quality limits." This performance measure may seem fair and acceptable. But consider further that production involves the use of some complex equipment that not everyone is good at troubleshooting. As long as the equipment is running fine, even an inexperienced worker can attend the machine and accrue handsome production numbers. However, when the machine is not running properly, it can take several hours—sometimes an entire shift—to locate the problem and resolve it. If you were a manager faced with this situation, wouldn't you put your best workers on the problem? Of course you would. But consider what would happen to the performance records of those top workers if you reassigned them whenever equipment broke down. Your best workers could actually end up looking like the worst workers in terms of the amount of product produced.

This situation actually occurred at a manufacturer of automobile components.[19] To resolve the issue, management concluded that supervisors' subjective performance judgements were superior to objective outcome measures. The subjective ratings differed radically from what outcome measures indicated about worker performance levels, but in this case, the subjective ratings were found to be related to workers' scores on job-related tests while no such relationship was found for the outcome measures. Clearly, in some situations human judgement is superior to objective measures.

Another potential difficulty with outcome-based performance measures is the development of a "results at any cost" mentality.[20] Using objective measures has the advantage of clearly focusing workers' attention on certain outcomes, but this focus can have negative effects on other facets of performance. For example, an organization may use the number of units produced as a performance measure because it is fairly easy to quantify. Workers concentrating on quantity may neglect quality and follow-up service, to the long-term detriment of the organization. Although objective goals and other outcome measures are effective at increasing performance levels, these measures may not reflect the entire spectrum of performance.[21]

Measurement Tools: Summary and Conclusions.   Our discussion so far makes it clear that there is no single best appraisal format. Each approach has positive and negative aspects. Figure 7–6 summarizes the strengths and weaknesses of each approach in the areas of administration, development, and legal defensibility. The choice of appraisal system should rest largely on the appraisal's primary purpose.

Most of these systems were developed on the premise that rater errors could be reduced or eliminated by using the right format. However, rating formats make precious little difference in the actual ratings that are obtained. In fact, empirical evidence suggests that the type of tool doesn't make that much difference in the accuracy of ratings.[22]

If formats don't have much impact on ratings, what does? Not surprisingly, the supervisor. Characteristics such as the rater's intelligence, familiarity with the job,[23] and ability to separate important from unimportant information[24] influence rating quality. A number of studies indicate that raters' ability and motivation levels are the critical factors in rating employees effectively.

Criteria			
Appraisal Format	Administrative Use	Developmental Use	Legal Defensibility
Absolute	0	+	0
Relative	++	–	–
Trait	+	–	– –
Behaviour	0	+	++
Outcome	0	0	+

– – Very poor   – Poor   0 Unclear or mixed   + Good   ++ Very good

Figure 7–6 Evaluation of Major Appraisal Formats

That supervisors are more important than the format used should be no surprise. The user is more important than the system in many different contexts. For example, the computer adage "garbage in, garbage out" means that someone who puts poor information into a state-of-the-art computer will get poor results. Similarly, no amount of high-tech diagnostic equipment will guarantee that your car will be fixed or tuned up correctly if the mechanic is careless, incapable, or malicious. The same holds true in performance measurement. A careless, incapable, or malicious supervisor can produce inaccurate and biased evaluations even with the most sophisticated measurement system. However, a careful, capable, and unbiased supervisor can produce accurate ratings and meaningful performance feedback with relatively basic measuring instruments.

■ Challenges to Effective Measurement

How can the well-intentioned manager assure quality measurement of worker performance? The primary means is to understand the barriers that stand in the way. Managers confront five challenges in this area:

◆ Rater errors
◆ The influence of liking
◆ Organizational politics
◆ Whether to focus on the individual or the group
◆ Legal issues

Rater Errors.   **Rater errors** are errors in performance appraisals that reflect consistent biases on the part of raters. One of the most prominent rater errors is *halo error.*[25] the tendency to rate similarly across dimensions. For instance, if when buying a refrigerator you are most interested in one particular feature—say, the versatility of shelving arrangements—you would commit a halo error if you allowed the shelving versatility of a particular model to influence your ratings of its other features (appearance, energy efficiency, and so on). Similarly, raters commit halo errors in performance measurement when they allow the rating they give to one dimension of performance to influence the ratings they give to other dimensions. Despite the word's angelic connotations, "halo" can cause uniformly negative ratings as well as uniformly positive ones.

There are at least two causes of halo error:[26] (1) A supervisor may make an overall judgement about a worker and then conform all dimensional ratings to that judgement, and/or (2) a supervisor may make all ratings consistent with the worker's performance level on a dimension that is important to the supervisor. To return to the computer programmer example we used earlier: If Nancy rates Ian low on all three performance dimensions (quality of programs written, quantity of programs written, and interpersonal effectiveness) even though his performance on quality and quantity is high, then she has committed a halo error.

rater error
An error in performance appraisals that reflects consistent biases on the part of the rater.

Restriction of range error is another type of rater error. This type of error occurs when a manager restricts all of his or her ratings to a small portion of the rating scale. A supervisor who restricts ranges tends to rate all workers similarly. Three different forms of range restriction are common: *leniency errors,* or restricting ratings of all employees to the high portion of the scale; *central tendency errors,* or using only the middle points of the scale; and *severity errors,* or using only the low portion of the rating scale.

Suppose that you are a middle manager with responsibility for reviewing the performance ratings that the supervisors who report to you have given to their subordinates. The question is: How can you tell how accurate this rating is? In other words, how can you tell what type of rating error, if any, has coloured the ratings? The answer is that it is very difficult to tell. Let's say that a supervisor has given one of her subordinates the highest possible rating on each of five performance dimensions. There are at least three possible explanations. The employee may actually be very good on one of the dimensions and have been rated very high on all because of this (halo error). Or the rater may only use the top part of the scale (leniency error). Or the employee may be a very good all-around worker (accurate). Although a variety of sophisticated statistical techniques has been developed to investigate these possibilities, none is practical for most organizations or managers.

This problem is of more than academic interest. A major difficulty in performance measurement is ensuring comparability in ratings across raters.[27] **Comparability** refers to the degree to which the values of ratings given by various supervisors in an organization are similar. In essence, the comparability issue is concerned with whether supervisors use the same measurement yardsticks. What one supervisor considers excellent performance, another may view as only average.

Personal bias.

Personal bias may also be a problem. Consciously or subconsciously, a supervisor may systematically rate certain workers lower or higher than others on the basis of race, national origin, gender, age, or other factors. Conscious bias is extremely difficult, if not impossible, to eliminate. Subconscious bias, due to a subtle shifting of standards for various subgroups, can be overcome once it is brought to the rater's attention. For example, a supervisor might be subconsciously giving higher evaluations to employees who went to his alma mater. When made aware of this leaning, however, he may correct it.

One of the most effective ways to deal with errors and bias is to develop and communicate evaluation standards via **frame-of-reference (FOR) training,**[28] which uses fictitious examples of performance that a worker might exhibit. These performance examples are presented to supervisors for evaluation, either in writing or on videotape. After rating the performance of the person in the example, the supervisors are told what their ratings should have been. Discussion follows of which worker behaviours represent each performance dimension and why they are valued at the level they are. This process of rating, feedback, and discussion is succeeded by the presentation of another example. Again, rating, feedback, and discussion follow. The process continues until the supervisors develop a common frame of reference for performance evaluation.

FOR training is the only type of rater training that actually increases the accuracy of performance ratings.[29] Perhaps even more important, it develops common evaluation standards among supervisors. This makes comparability among various supervisors' ratings possible and is critical to lowering bias in ratings.

The FOR training procedure does have a number of drawbacks, though. One glaring problem is the expense, which can be prohibitive owing to the amount of time and number of people involved. (The Appendix to this chapter presents an abbreviated and less costly approach to the *critical incident technique,* a process that underlies training.) Another drawback of the FOR approach is that it can only be used with behaviourally based appraisal systems.

comparability

In performance ratings, the degree to which the values of ratings given by various supervisors are similar.

frame-of-reference (FOR) training

A type of training that presents supervisors with fictitious examples of worker performance (either in writing or on videotape), asks the supervisors to evaluate the workers in the examples, and then tells them what their ratings should have been.

The Influence of Liking.   *Liking* can cause errors in performance appraisals when raters allow their like or dislike of an individual to influence their assessment of that individual's performance. Liking plays a potent role in performance measurement because both liking and ratings are person-focussed. The two may be at odds, however. Liking is emotional and often subconscious, whereas formal ratings are —or should be—non-emotional and conscious. Because liking is subconscious, it seems to be established very quickly,[30] which may influence (bias) more conscious evaluations that occur later.

Although there is much to be learned in this area, one study found that liking may be a more important determinant of performance ratings than actual worker performance.[31] This provocative finding can be interpreted in two ways. One possibility is that performance ratings have little, if anything, to do with worker performance and instead are based largely on how much a supervisor likes the employee. The second possibility is that objective performance indicators are seriously deficient as indicators of worker performance. Objective measures may miss a number of important characteristics of job performance that supervisors pick up. Furthermore, good supervisors may tend to like good performers and dislike poor performers. Thus it would be no surprise to find performance ratings related to supervisory liking but not related to objective measures of worker performance.

The fundamental question, of course, is whether the relationship between liking and performance ratings is appropriate or biased.[32] It is appropriate if supervisors like good performers better than poor performers. It is biased if supervisors like or dislike employees for reasons other than their performance and allow these feelings to contaminate their ratings. It is often very difficult to separate these two possibilities.[33] Nonetheless, most workers appear to believe that their supervisor's liking for them influences the performance ratings they receive.[34] The perception of bias can cause communication problems between workers and supervisors and lower supervisors' effectiveness in managing performance.

Precautions.   Given the potentially biasing impact of liking on supervisors' appraisals, it is critical that supervisors manage their emotional reactions to their subordinates. The first step in managing these reactions is recognizing the presence of the emotion, so that they can counter its influence.

To ensure that they evaluate workers on performance rather than liking, managers should keep a performance diary on each worker.[35] This diary, which should consist of behavioural incidents observed by the supervisor, can serve as the basis for evaluation and other managerial actions. An external record of worker behaviours can dramatically reduce, if not eliminate, error and bias in ratings.

Record keeping should be done routinely—for example, daily or weekly. This may seem like a time-consuming task, but the time spent keeping such records may be less than anticipated and the benefits greater. In one field study of such record keeping, supervisors reported that the task took five minutes or less per week.[36] More important, after experience with the procedure, most supervisors reported that they would prefer to continue, rather than discontinue, the recording of behavioural incidents. This preference for additional paperwork may seem unusual until one considers the benefit that the supervisors derived from

How Do I Like My Employees? Let Me Count the Ways ...

While liking can be a source of bias in performance appraisals, it can also be the direct result of good performance. Managers tend to like employees who have a positive attitude, who get along well with their coworkers, and who perform consistently well.

the process. By compiling a record of observed worker behaviours week by week, they did not have to rely much on general impressions and possibly biased memories when conducting appraisals. In addition, the practice signalled workers that appraisal wasn't a personality contest. Finally, should a worker make a claim of bias, the supervisor could cull from the records concrete behavioural examples that justified the rating.

Two warnings are in order here. First, performance diaries are not guarantees against bias due to liking, for supervisors can be biased in the type of incidents they choose to record. However, short of intentional misrepresentation, the keeping of such records should go a long way toward reducing both actual bias and the perception of bias.

Second, some managers use performance diaries in place of intervention and discussion because it is less uncomfortable, initially, to record a performance problem than to discuss it with the employee. Documenting problems is fine, and even useful for creating a legally defensible case in the event that the manager must terminate the employee. However, it is unfair to keep a secret running list of "offences" and then suddenly unveil it to the employee when he or she commits an infraction that can't be overlooked. The likely result will be an explosive confrontation between manager and employee. The message for managers is simple: If an employee's behaviour warrants discussion, the discussion should take place immediately.[37]

Azteca Foods, Inc.
www.aztecafoods.com

The following is an example of how one company used performance diaries both to aid performance appraisal and to enhance employee coaching. In its drive to revamp its performance appraisal system, Azteca Foods, Inc., a 125-employee company, asked its 25 managers to begin keeping a daily log of each employee's performance. Every time an employee did something negative (such as arriving late to work or missing an assignment deadline) or something positive (such as making a notable contribution), the manager was expected to write it down and give immediate feedback. While this procedure may sound time-consuming, the company found the payback worth the extra effort. At appraisal time managers were able to bring up concrete examples of what an employee did instead of saying "You've done a good (or inadequate) job." The procedure also fosters communication between managers and subordinates on continually improving performance.[38]

Organizational Politics. Thus far we have used a *rational perspective* in discussing appraisal. In other words, we have assumed that the intention of the supervisor is to accurately measure the value of each subordinate's work. Unlike the rational approach, the *political perspective* reflects the situations in which the appraisal is conducted so that the results suit the supervisor's agenda. Sometimes this agenda is self-serving on the supervisor's part, such as when appraisals are manipulated to block promotions of valued subordinates, or to punish a subordinate who has irritated his or her boss. At other times, a supervisor may manipulate the results to secure a deserved promotion or raise for a subordinate. Whatever the supervisor's motives, a political approach to appraisal involves "working backwards" from the desired result to what the supervisor thinks needs to be on the appraisal to achieve that result. Consider the following quotation from an executive with extensive experience in evaluating his subordinates:

> As a manager, I will use the review process to do what is best for my people and the division ... I've got a lot of leeway—call it discretion—to use this process in that manner ... I've used it to get my people better raises in lean years, to kick a guy in the pants if he really needed it, to pick a guy up when he was down or even to tell him he was no longer welcome here ... I believe that most of us here at _____ operate this way regarding appraisals.[39]

The distinction between the rational and political approaches to appraisal may best be understood by examining how they differ on various facets of the performance appraisal process.

♦ The *goal* of the appraisal process from a rational perspective is accuracy. The goal for a political perspective is utility—the maximization of benefits over costs given political context and supervisor's goals. For example, a supervisor may give a very poor rating to a subordinate who seems uncommitted, in hopes of shocking the worker into adopting a higher standard of performance. Or a supervisor may give high ratings to subordinates with the goal of reducing complaints or conflict. The goal in these examples clearly is not accuracy.

♦ The *roles* played by supervisors and workers also differ in the rational and political approaches. The rational approach sees supervisors and workers largely as passive agents in the rating process: supervisors observe and evaluate what they observe. The obstacles to accurate evaluate are to be found in evaluation systems and supervisory skill in using the system. In contrast, the political approach includes the personal motives that both parties bring to the measurement process. Just as supervisors have their "agendas," subordinates also attempt to influence the process because of the personal outcomes (pay, opportunities for promotion, job security) that are frequently attached.

The various persuasion techniques that workers use to alter their supervisor's evaluation are a direct form of influence. For example, just as a student may tell a professor that she needs a higher grade to keep a scholarship, a worker might tell his boss that he needs a good raise to send his child to a "special needs" program. Influence attempts by workers can be indirect and can take any of the many ways in which people ingratiate themselves with others ... being pleasant, doing favours, paying compliments, expressing sympathy or admiration for the supervisor's situation and accomplishments, and so forth.

Appraisal in most organizations seems to be a political rather than a rational exercise.[40] It appears to be used as a tool for serving various and changing agendas; accurate assessment is seldom the real goal. But the rational approach should not be abandoned simply because appraisal is subject to political influences. Politically driven assessment may be a reality, and it cannot be completely eliminated. However, accuracy should still be the ideal behind appraisal processes.[41] What is important is to remove as many of the legitimate reasons for "political" appraisals, such as inequitable pay systems or inadequate career development, so that supervisors who want to do the right thing can concentrate on accuracy. Accurate assessment is necessary if feedback, development, and HR decisions are to be based on employees' actual performance levels. Basing feedback and development on managerial agendas can lead to unjust treatment of human resources. Careers have been ruined, self-esteem lost, and productivity degraded because of the political use of appraisal. Such costs are difficult to assess and to ascribe clearly to politics. Nonetheless, they are very real and important for workers. Distortion of evaluations should not be condoned. Although managers must influence subordinates to be effective, a loss of credibility can outweigh the gains from short-run persuasion or manipulation.

Individual or Group Focus. Just as we have assumed through this chapter that the performance measurement process is rational, we have also assumed that the appropriate focus is on the individual employee. This is largely a reflection of our Western culture. We value the rugged individual, the superstar, the person who stands out from the crowd. Our entire economic system is based on the

? A Question of Ethics

Is it right to give someone a higher (or lower) rating than you think that person deserves because you are trying to "send a message"? Or is this sort of behaviour simply lying and therefore wrong?

Playing Ball Without the Coach.

Recent innovations in organizational design have necessitated breaking away from traditional performance appraisal that depends on boss-subordinate dynamics. When work is assigned to groups, especially when the groups are self-organizing, only peers, clients, and others who have direct contact have the information needed to perform useful appraisals.

competition and survival of the fittest. However, in organizations, teamwork and cooperation are necessary for the achievement of common goals. Indeed, teamwork is becoming more common as companies strip layers of middle management from their organizations and managers have large groups of employees under their control. Performance appraisal that focuses solely on individual achievement can create serious morale problems among employees working in teams. One person may be an excellent team player who spends time helping her co-workers, only to get penalized at appraisal time for not reaching her individual objectives. W. Edwards Deming, a founder of the quality movement, went so far as to suggest that individually focused performance assessment is a "deadly management disease" that is killing organizations. He argued that performance reviews that focus on the individual tell only part of the story; if an individual's performance is not up to par, it may be because of problems that are part of the system. Deming went so far as to suggest performance appraisals be eliminated.

In practice, most companies have not followed this extreme advice.[42] (Figure 7-7 lists several reasons, from both employer's and employee's perspective, as to why appraisal is still valuable, despite the criticisms levelled against it.) However, many quality-oriented companies have changed their appraisal practices—such as adopting non-numerical appraisal formats—to make them more compatible with a quality environment. For example, workers and their peers may identify their relative strengths and weaknesses, then meet with team members to determine how they can improve their performance. By not using numbers on a rating form, which tends to create competition and divisiveness among employees, a cohesive team environment can be better sustained.

Two final points: first, experts recommend that individual performance be assessed in cultures (such as North America) in which individualism is a strongly held cultural value. Second, there is not consensus as to what type of appraisal instrument should be used for team evaluations. It may be useful to include both internal and external customers and have them evaluate both behaviours and results, as criteria.[43]

Figure 7–7 The Benefits of Performance Appraisal

Source: Cardy, R.L., and Carson, K.P. (1996). Total quality and the abandonment of performance appraisal: Taking a good thing too far? *Journal of Quality Management,* 193–206.

Employer Perspective

1. Despite imperfect measurement techniques, individual differences in performance can make a difference to company performance.
2. Documentation of performance appraisal and feedback may be needed for legal defense.
3. Appraisal provides a rational basis for constructing a bonus or merit system.
4. Appraisal dimensions and standards can help to implement strategic goals and clarify performance expectations.
5. Providing individual feedback is part of the performance management process.
6. Despite the traditional focus on the individual, appraisal criteria can include teamwork and the teams can be the focus of appraisal.

Employee Perspective

1. Performance feedback is needed and desired.
2. Improvement in performance requires assessment.
3. Fairness requires that differences in performance levels across workers be measured and have an effect on outcomes.
4. Assessment and recognition of performance levels can motivate workers to improve their performance.

Legal Issues.   Human rights codes and, in various Canadian jurisdictions, common law precedents with reference to employer actions such as reassignment or termination predicated on poor performance, suggest standards for performance appraisal—even though there are no specific statutory parameters. Human rights codes protect employees in various designated groups from discriminatory treatment not only in hiring, but also in other decisions made by employers. (See Chapter 3 for a more complete discussion.) Implicit in that protection is an obligation not to promote, transfer, or change compensation based on evaluations that can be shown to be unfair measures of the performance of (say) women or visible minorities or individuals who adhere to particular religious beliefs. The implied requirements are twofold: first, that the assessment procedure be fair, and second, that the individuals doing the evaluation be properly trained in the use of the procedure, to minimize the potential that their judgements will be biased.

An employer wishing to discharge an employee "for cause," where cause is poor job performance, has a substantial obligation to demonstrate that such poor performance has been identified and communicated to the employee in question. To avoid the obligation to make severance payments when discharging an employee for poor performance, the employer must be able to demonstrate via documentation that the poor performance has been identified and communicated, and that the employee has been given a chance to improve. If a given level of performance (even poor performance) has been tolerated for an extended period, an employer may be deemed to have condoned that level of performance. An employee suing for wrongful dismissal will usually be awarded damages if the employer cannot establish the pattern of poor performance. Employer and employee rights are discussed in greater detail in Chapter 14. With respect to performance appraisal, it is fair to say that good professional practice—honest, accurate, fair, and documented feedback that results from well-designed evaluations and well-trained evaluators—is the best protection from legal liability or potential lawsuits.

■ Building Managerial Skills: Managing Performance

The effective management of human performance in organizations requires more than formal reporting and annual ratings. A complete appraisal process includes informal day-to-day interactions between managers and workers as well as formal face-to-face interviews. Although ratings are important, even more critical is what managers do with them. In this section, we discuss the third and final component of performance appraisal, performance management.

■ Performance Diagnosis and Feedback

Upon completing the performance rating, the supervisor usually conducts an interview with the employee to provide feedback—one of the most important parts of the appraisal process. Many managers find performance appraisal interviews to be a difficult task, particularly if the employee is performing poorly. Human resources professionals can assist managers by training them in conducting interviews through such methods as role-playing, and by advising them on how to handle specific difficult issues.

There are two schools of thought on whether performance appraisal discussions should have both developmental ("coaching") and administrative (pay adjustments, promotability) issues covered together, or whether separate interviews should be held. Based on early research, the argument for two separate interviews was that employees are likely to be defensive rather than open in discussing problem areas, interfering with the coaching process. In Great Britain, this argument has been sufficiently persuasive that some 85% of employers surveyed used separate interviews. The preference for a single interview for both developmental and administrative uses has several foundations. The most persuasive is pragmatism: it is sufficiently difficult to get supervisors to do one cycle of performance reviews; expecting them to do two interviews with each subordinate increases the likelihood that those interviews will be superficial, or will not happen at all. There is also the notion that both managers and subordinates are more likely to take the process seriously if pay decisions are involved.

What is quite clear is that when the only discussion that managers and subordinates have about performance is an annual interview, coaching will not be very effective. Coaching and employee development needs to be an integral part of the ongoing manager-subordinate relationship if they are to be successful. Where this is true, the combined annual performance review is adequate "punctuation" for the feedback process.

■ Performance Improvement

Because formal appraisal interviews typically are conducted only once a year,[44] they may not always have substantial and lasting impact on worker performance.[45] Much more important is informal day-to-day performance management. Supervisors who manage performance effectively generally share four characteristics. They:

- ◆ Explore the causes of performance problems.
- ◆ Direct attention to the causes of problems.
- ◆ Empower workers to reach a solution.
- ◆ Direct communication at performance and emphasize non-threatening communication.[46]

Each of these characteristics is critical to achieving improved and sustained levels of performance.

Exploring the Causes of Performance Problems.
Exploring the causes of performance problems may sound like an easy task, but it is often quite challenging. Performance can be the result of many factors, some of which are beyond the worker's control. In most work situations, though, observers tend to attribute the causes to the worker.[47] That is, supervisors tend to blame the worker when they observe poor performance, while workers tend to blame external factors. This tendency is called *actor/observer bias*.[48] For example, when a basketball team is losing, players ("workers") point to external causes such as injuries or a tough road schedule. The coach ("supervisor") points to sloppy execution or perhaps a poor work ethic. The owner ("senior executive") tends to blame the coach for not getting the best out of the players.

Accurate determination of the causes of performance deficiencies is critical for three reasons. First, determination of causes can influence how performance is evaluated. For example, a manager is likely to evaluate an episode of poor performance very differently if she thinks it was due to low effort rather than poor materials provided to the worker. Second, causal determination can be an unspoken and underlying source of conflict between supervisors and their workers. Supervisors often act on what they believe are the causes of performance problems. This is only rational. But when the supervisor's perception significantly differs from the workers', the difference can cause tension. Third, defining the cause influences the type of remedy selected; what is

Sizing Up Situational Factors.

Managers must be careful to pinpoint the causes of performance problems accurately. A simple adjustment to a machine can increase a worker's output substantially.

thought to be the cause of a performance problem determines what is done about it. For instance, very different actions would be taken if poor performance was thought to be the result of inadequate ability rather than inadequacies in the raw materials.

How can the process of determining the causes of performance be improved? A starting point is to consider the possible causes of performance consciously and systematically. Traditionally, performance has been thought to be caused by two primary factors: ability and motivation.[49] A major problem with this view is that situational factors external to the worker, such as degree of management support, also affect worker performance.[50] A more inclusive version of the causes of performance embraces three factors: ability, motivation, and situational factors. The *ability* factor reflects the worker's talents and skills, including such characteristics as intelligence, interpersonal skills, and job knowledge. *Motivation* can be affected by a number of external factors (such as rewards and punishments) but is ultimately an internal decision. It is up to the worker to determine how much effort he or she will exert on any given task. **Situational factors** include a wide array of organizational characteristics that can positively or negatively influence performance. For example, quality of materials and quality of supervisor are situational factors that can dramatically influence performance.

Performance depends on all three factors. The presence of just one cause is not sufficient for high performance to occur; however, the absence or low value of one factor can result in poor performance. For example, making a strong effort will not result in high performance if the worker has neither the necessary job skills nor adequate support in the workplace. On the other hand, if the worker doesn't put forth any effort, low performance is inevitable, no matter how good that worker's skills and how much support is provided.

In determining the causes of performance problems, managers should carefully consider situational factors. Figure 7–8 presents some of the situational factors that managers need to consider.[51] These factors are only a starting point; they are too generic for use in some situations. For best results, supervisors should use this list as a basis for generating their own job-specific lists of factors. Involving workers in the generation of the list will not only produce examples supervisors may not have been aware of but will also send a signal that managers are serious about considering workers' input. The supervisor and worker (or work team) can go over the list together to isolate the causes of any performance difficulties.

Finally, supervisors should also consider using self-, peer-, and subordinate reviews on an annual or semiannual basis to determine the causes of performance. **Self-review,** in which workers rate themselves, allows them input into the appraisal process and can help them gain insight into the causes of performance problems. For example, there may be a substantial difference in opinion between a supervisor and an employee regarding one area of the employee's evaluation. Communication and possibly investigation would be warranted in such a case.

situational factors or system factors

A wide array of organizational characteristics that can positively or negatively influence performance.

self-review

A performance appraisal system in which workers rate themselves.

- Poor coordination of work activities among workers.
- Inadequate information or instructions needed to perform a job.
- Lack of necessary equipment.
- Inability to obtain raw materials, parts, or supplies.
- Inadequate financial resources.
- Uncooperative co-workers and/or poor relations among people.
- Inadequate training.
- Insufficient time to produce the quantity or quality of work required.
- A poor work environment (for example, cold, hot, noisy, frequent interruptions).
- Equipment breakdown.

Figure 7–8 Situational (System) Factors to Consider in Determining the Causes of Performance Problems

peer review

A performance appraisal system in which workers at the same level in the organization rate one another.

subordinate review

A performance appraisal system in which workers review their supervisors.

When a supervisor and a worker cannot resolve their disagreement, performance assessments from additional sources, such as peers and subordinates, may be useful. In a **peer review,** workers at the same level of the organization rate one another. In a **subordinate review,** workers review their supervisors. If peers' and subordinates' judgements converge with the supervisor's, then it is likely that the supervisor's judgement is correct. If peers' and subordinates' judgements do not match the supervisor's, it may be that the supervisor is not aware of or sensitive to the impact of certain factors on the worker's performance.

More and more companies are using peer review as a performance appraisal system in its own right. W. L. Gore & Associates, the company known by outdoors types for its Gore-Tex fabric, has used peer review ever since its founding over 30 years ago. At Gore, every employee is ranked by peers on the basis of his or her contributions to the company's goals. The peers in this case are committees of six to 10 co-workers. Because W. L. Gore limits the size of its 40-odd plants to fewer than 200 people, co-workers tend to be familiar with one another's work. The rankings, called "contribution lists," may be compiled several times a year. They begin at the team level, asking about each group, "Who is the most valuable contributor to this function? Who is the next most valuable?" and so on.

How does peer review work in practice? At Xerox Canada, there are technical service groups that have been organized as self-managed units. Units determine their own objectives and utilize a monthly within-group review shaped by criteria that have been set by prior agreement. These internal data will be combined with customer survey data to get an integrated assessment of processes and outcomes.[52]

360° feedback

The combination of peer, subordinate and self-review.

The combination of peer, subordinate, and self-reviews, termed **360° feedback,** is being used by increasing numbers of employers. One reason for the rise of 360° feedback is the trend to fewer layers of management. The increasing numbers of subordinates for each manager or supervisor mean that the supervisor will typically know less about any individual subordinate's work and will have more subordinates to manage. Upward feedback, part of the 360° concept, has been adopted by Atomic Energy of Canada, Ltd. (AECL) to stimulate discussion of leadership styles. Managers had indicated misgivings about the process because they were concerned that subordinates might use this anonymous process to attack them, but this has not happened. Another well-known company using 360° feedback is Consumers Gas. The 360° feedback process is also consistent with the concepts of empowerment and increased responsibility for individual employees.

The shift to a 360° systems can be a major change that requires careful planning to be successful. The Manager's Notebook entitled "Key Steps in Implementing 360° Appraisal" provides steps to follow that should result in an effective and acceptable system.

Collecting performance appraisals from multiple sources can be time consuming and expensive. For example, 400 employees each receiving feedback from 12 people where each appraisal took 30 minutes to complete would translate into 2400 employee hours, or 300 workdays, which is roughly 1.2 person-years. If the average rate of pay is $25 per hour, the cost would be $60,000.

Companies can significantly reduce the time needed for 360° appraisal by putting the appraisal system on-line. The time used to complete the forms can be reduced and the compilation of the results can be effectively streamlined.

Manager's Notebook

Key Steps in Implementing 360° Appraisal

Consulting firms offer the following advice for telling employees that they will be terminated or laid off:

1. Top management communicates the goals of and need for 360° appraisal
2. Employees and managers are involved in the development of the appraisal criteria and appraisal process.
3. Employees are trained in how to give and receive feedback.
4. Employees are informed of the nature of the 360° appraisal instrument and process.
5. The 360° system undergoes pilot testing in one part of the organizations.
6. Management continuously reinforces the goals of the 360° appraisal process, and is ready to change the process where necessary.

SOURCE: Adapted from Millman, J.F., Zawacki, R.A., Norman, C., Powell, L. and Kirskey, J. (1994) Companies evaluate employees from all perspectives. *Personnel Journal*, November, 99-103.

Customer Appraisals.   In addition to feedback from within the organization, companies are increasingly looking to customers as a valuable source of appraisal. Traditional top-down appraisal systems encourage employees to perform only those tasks that supervisors see or pay attention to. Thus, some behaviours that are critical to customer satisfaction may be ignored.

In fact, customers are often in a better position to evaluate the quality of a company's products and services than supervisors are. Figure 7-9 presents an example of a customer appraisal form.

Directing Attention to the Causes of Problems.   After the supervisor and worker have discussed and agreed on the causes of performance problems, the next step is to take measures to control them. If certain factors affect performance positively, managers should try to ensure that those factors are present as much as possible. In the more common case of constraining factors, managers should try to reduce or eliminate them. Depending on whether the cause of performance problems is related to ability, effort, or situational characteristics, very different tactics are called for. As Figure 7–10 makes clear, different remedies are required for different categories of performance shortfalls. Leaping to a remedy like training (a common reaction) will not fix a problem that is not ability-caused and will be a waste of the organization's resources.[53]

Name: _____

This survey asks your opinion about specific aspects of the products and services you received. Your individual responses will remain confidential and will be compiled with those of other customers to improve customer service. Please use the following scale to indicate the extent to which you agree with the statement. Circle one response for each item.

    1 = Strongly Disagree
    2 = Disagree
    3 = Neutral
    4 = Agree
    5 = Strongly Agree
    ? = Unsure

If you feel unable to adequately rate a specific item, please leave it blank.

QUALITY
_____

I had to wait an unreasonable amount of time for my requests to be met .... 1 2 3 4 5 ?

The products I have received have met my expectations.................... 1 2 3 4 5 ?

My requests were met on or before the agreed upon deadline................................. 1 2 3 4 5 ?

The products I have received have generally been error free............ 1 2 3 4 5 ?

SERVICE/ATTITUDE
_____

When serving me, this person:

Was helpful....................... 1 2 3 4 5 ?

Was cooperative in meeting my requests......... 1 2 3 4 5 ?

Communicated with me to understand my expectations for products......................... 1 2 3 4 5 ?

Was uncooperative when I asked for revisions/additional information...................... 1 2 3 4 5 ?

Told me when my requests would be filled................................. 1 2 3 4 5 ?

When necessary, sufficiently explained to me why my expectations could not be met................................... 1 2 3 4 5 ?

Kept me informed about the status of my request............................ 1 2 3 4 5 ?

CUSTOMER SATISFACTION
_____

How would you rate your overall level of satisfaction with the *service* you have received?

    1 = Very Dissatisfied
    2 = Dissatisfied
    3 = Neutral
    4 = Satisfied
    5 = Very Satisfied

What specifically could be done to make you more satisfied with the *service?*

_____
_____
_____

How would you rate your overall level of satisfaction with the *products* you have received?

    1 = Very Dissatisfied
    2 = Dissatisfied
    3 = Neutral
    4 = Satisfied
    5 = Very Satisfied

What specifically could be done to make you more satisfied with the *products?*

_____
_____
_____

Figure 7–9 Customer Appraisal Form

SOURCE: Cardy, R.L., and Dobbins, G.H. (1994). *Performance appraisal: Alternative perspectives.* Cincinnati, OH: South-Western

Cause	Questions to Ask	Possible Remedies
Ability	Has the worker ever been able to perform adequately? Can others perform the job adequately, but not this worker?	Train Transfer Redesign job Terminate
Effort	Is the worker's performance level declining? Is performance lower on all tasks?	Clarify linkage between performance and rewards Recognize good performance
Situation	Is performance erratic? Are performance problems showing up in all workers, even those who have adequate supplies and equipment?	Streamline work process Clarify needs to suppliers Change suppliers Eliminate conflicting signals or demands Provide adequate tools

Figure 7–10 How to Determine and Remedy Performance Shortfalls

Manager's Notebook

Providing Constructive Feedback

To maximize the effectiveness of the performance appraisal, managers should:

1. Conduct the appraisal in private and allow enough time for the employee to discuss issues important to him or her.

2. Present perceptions, reactions, and opinions as such and *not* as facts.

3. Refer to the relevant performance, behaviour, or outcomes, not to the individual as a person.

4. Provide feedback in terms of specific, observable behaviour, not general behaviour.

5. Talk in terms of established criteria, probable outcomes, or possible improvement, as opposed to such judgements as "good" or "bad."

6. Discuss performance and the specific behaviours that appear to be contributing to or limiting full effectiveness.

7. Suggest possible means of improving performance in discussing problem areas that contain technical or established procedures for achieving solutions.

8. Avoid loaded terms (for example, "crabby," "mess-up," "rip-off," or "stupid"), which produce emotional reactions and defensiveness.

9. Concentrate on those things over which an individual can exercise some control, and focus on ways that indicate how the employee can use the feedback to improve performance.

10. Deal with defensiveness or emotional reactions rather than trying to convince, reason, or supply additional information.

11. Give feedback in a manner that communicates acceptance of the appraisee as a worthwhile person and of that person's right to be an individual.

12. Keep in mind that feedback is intended to be helpful and, therefore, should be tied to specific development plans to capitalize on strengths and minimize performance weaknesses.

SOURCE: Adapted from Gómez-Mejía, L. R. (1990). Increasing productivity: Performance appraisal and reward systems. *Personnel Journal 19* (2).

As one company's director of marketing said:

My boss thinks nothing of sending me to a $3,000 seminar each winter. I think it eases his conscience since he so rarely gives me feedback, or talks to me about personal improvement, or my future. Is that too much to ask?[54]

It isn't!

Developing an Action Plan and Empowering Workers to Reach a Solution. Effective performance management requires empowering workers to improve their performance. The traditional management approach of supervisors giving orders and workers following them usually does not lead to maximum performance levels. A more contemporary approach requires supervisors to take on the role of coach rather than director and controller.[55] As in a sports team, the supervisor-as-coach assists workers in interpreting and reacting to the work situation. The role is not necessarily one of mentor, friend, or counsellor. It is, rather, that of enabler. The supervisor-as-coach works to ensure that the necessary resources are available to workers and carefully listens to employees to help them identify an action plan to solve performance problems. For example, the supervisor may suggest ways for the worker to eliminate, avoid, or get around situational obstacles to performance. In addition to creating a supportive, empowered work environment, coach/supervisors clarify performance expectations; provide immediate feedback; and strive to eliminate unnecessary rules, procedures, and other constraints.[56]

Directing Communication at Performance.   Communication between supervisor and worker is critical to effective performance management. Exactly what is communicated and how it is communicated can determine whether performance improves or declines. The Manager's Notebook entitled "Providing Constructive Feedback" provides 12 recommendations for communicating and maximizing the effectiveness of performance feedback.

It is important that communication regarding performance be directed at the performance and not at the person. For example, a worker should not be asked why he's such a jerk! It is usually much more effective to ask the worker why his performance has been ineffective lately. In the first communication, the supervisor is attacking the employee, which is likely to make him defensive. In the second communication, the supervisor is showing that he has an open mind regarding the cause of recent performance problems. Open-minded communication is more likely to uncover the real reason for a performance problem and thus pave the way for an effective solution and performance improvement.

Communication to workers regarding performance should be probing but non-evaluative to avoid evoking a defensive reaction. Figure 7–11 presents some examples of good and bad forms of supervisory coaching communications.

The communication approaches suggested here are designed to reduce ratee defensiveness. All of these approaches emphasize analysis rather than evaluation of employee problems.

I. Evaluation vs. Description

Rather than evaluate the employee's behaviour, try describing the problem so that you and the ratee can jointly arrive at a solution.

EXAMPLES

Evaluation	**Description**
1. You simply can't keep making these stupid mistakes.	1. We're still having a problem reducing the amount of waste produced.
2. You're tactless and undiplomatic.	2. Some people interpret your candour as hostility.
3. The accident was your fault.	3. This accident appears to involve some differences in interpreting the safety regulations.

II. Control vs. Problem Orientation

Control communications emphasize the supervisor's power over the ratee. Problem orientation conveys respect for the ratee's ability to solve the problem and is more likely to generate useful options.

EXAMPLES

Control	**Problem Orientation**
1. I'd like to see you doing X, Y, and Z over the next week.	1. What sort of things might we do here?
2. I think my suggestions are clear, so why don't you get back to work?	2. Let's both think about these possibilities and get back together next week to discuss them.
3. I've decided what you must do to reduce mistakes.	3. Have you thought about what we might do to reduce mistakes?

➤

Figure 7–11 Suggestions for Coaching Communications

III. Neutrality vs. Empathy

Employees often interpret a supervisor's neutrality as lack of interest in the problem and its impact on them. Empathy signals concern for the ratee and his or her situation.

EXAMPLES

Neutrality	**Empathy**
1. I really don't know what we can do about it.	1. At this point I can't think of anything, but I know where we might look for help.
2. Too bad, but we all go through that.	2. I think I know how you're feeling. I can remember a similar experience I had...
3. I didn't know that.	3. I wasn't aware of that. Let me make sure I understand.

IV. Superiority vs. Equality

Managers who emphasize their own superiority in their communications can keep a ratee at arm's length and stifle feedback. Equality-evoking communications can lead to ratee input into solving problems.

EXAMPLES

Superiority	**Equality**
1. I've worked with this problem for 10 years and I know what will work.	1. This idea has worked before. Do you think it might work in this case?
2. Look, I'm being paid to make these decisions, not you.	2. I'll have to make the final decision, but why don't you get your suggestions in to me as soon as possible?
3. The management staff has thought this policy through pretty thoroughly.	3. We've discussed this policy at the management meeting, but I'm interested in your thoughts since you're the one who has to deal with it on the front line.

Figure 7–11 Suggestions for Coaching Communications (continued)

SOURCE: Adapted, by permission of publisher, from Wallace, L. (1978). Nonevaluative approaches to performance appraisals. *Supervisory Management,* 23, 2–9. © 1978. American Management Association, New York, N.Y. All rights reserved.

Summary and Conclusions

What Is Performance Appraisal?   Performance appraisal is the identification, measurement, and management of human performance in organizations. Appraisal should be a future-oriented activity that provides workers with useful feedback and coaches them to higher levels of performance. Appraisal can be used developmentally or administratively.

Identifying Performance Dimensions.   Performance appraisal begins by identifying the dimensions of performance that determine effective job performance. Job analysis is the method by which performance dimensions should be identified.

Measuring Performance.   The methods used to measure employee performance can be classified in two ways: according to whether the type of judgement called for is relative or absolute, and according to whether the focus of the measure is on traits, behaviour, or outcomes. Each measure has its advantages and disadvantages. But it is clear that the quality of ratings is much more a function of the motivation and ability of the rater than of the type of instrument chosen.

Managers face five challenges in measuring performance: managing the impact of rater errors, or consistent biases like halo and restriction of range errors; liking, or allowing feelings about a subordinate to influence ratings; organizational politics, or using the appraisal system to further an agenda; deciding between an individual and a group focus; and legal issues (discrimination).

Managing Performance.   The primary goal of any appraisal system is managing performance. Approaches to improve performance include exploring the causes of performance problems, directing manager and employee attention to those causes, empowering workers to find solutions, and using performance-focused communication.

Key Terms and Concepts

absolute judgement, 205
actor/observer bias, 218
anchors, 208
behavioural appraisal instrument, 208
central tendency error, 212
comparability, 212
critical incident technique, 212
dimension, 203
frame-of-reference (FOR) training, 212
halo error, 211

identification, measurement, and management, 202
leniency error, 212
liking, 213
management by objectives (MBO), 209
naturally occurring outcomes, 209
outcome appraisal instrument, 209
peer review, 220
performance appraisal, 202
political perspective, 214
rank order, 204

rater error, 211
rational perspective, 214
relative judgement, 204
restriction of range error, 212
self-review, 219
severity error, 212
situational factors or system factors, 219
subordinate review, 220
360° feedback, 220
trait, 207
trait appraisal instrument, 207

Discussion Questions

1. At ARCO Transportation, employees are hired, promoted, and appraised according to how they fulfill the "performance dimensions" most valued by the company. For instance, one of the performance dimensions employees are reviewed on is "communication,"—specifically, such criteria as "listens and observes attentively, allowing an exchange of information," and "speaks and writes clearly and concisely, with an appropriate awareness of the intended audience." Would you say that ARCO appraises performance based on personality traits, job behaviour, or outcome achieved? On which of these three aspects of performance do you think workers should be appraised?

2. Superficially, it seems preferable to use objective performance data (such as productivity figures), when available, rather than subjective supervisory ratings to assess employees. Why might objective data be less effective performance measures than subjective ratings?

3. How important are rating formats to the quality of performance ratings? What is the most important influence on rating quality?

4. What is comparability? How can it be maximized in performance appraisal?

5. "Occasionally an employee comes along who needs to be reminded who the boss is, and the appraisal is an appropriate place for such a reminder." Would the manager quoted here be likely to use a rational or a political approach to appraisal? Contrast the rational and political approaches. To what extent is it possible to separate the two?

6. What criteria do you think should be used to measure team performance? What sources should be used for the appraisal? Should individual performance still be measured? Why or why not?

7. What steps can a supervisor take to be an effective coach?

8. You're the owner of a 25-employee company that has just had a fantastic year. Everyone pulled together and worked hard to achieve the boost in company profits. Unfortunately, you need to sink most of those profits into paying your suppliers. All you can afford to give your workers is a three percent pay raise across the board. At appraisal time, how would you communicate praise for a job well done coupled with your very limited ability to reward such outstanding performance? Now assume you can afford to hand out some handsome bonuses or raises. What would be the best way to evaluate employees when *everyone* has done exceptional work?

Take it to the Net

Check out our Companion Website at: **www.prenticehall.ca/gomez** for a selection of self-study questions, key terms and concepts, updated Weblinks to related Internet sites, newsgroups, CBC video updates, and more.

MiniCase 1   *Two approaches to 360° Appraisal*

A number of companies are turning to 360° appraisal systems as a means of providing performance information to employees and making them accountable to their customers. However, 360° appraisal can involve some difficult choices.

Johnson & Johnson Advanced Behavioural Technology uses a 360° approach that asks internal customers, external customers, and peers to rate each employee. Each Johnson & Johnson employee compiles a list of five to ten people who could serve as his or her raters. However, the supervisor has final authority over who will be selected as each employee's raters, and may choose to remove some people from the employee's list while adding others. The employee's supervisor is also responsible for summarizing the judgements and determining the final performance rating. Supervisors are encouraged to look for trends in the ratings, rather than overinterpret one rater's particularly positive or negative evaluation. After compiling the ratings, the supervisor conducts a formal performance review session with the employee. Johnson & Johnson also provides raters with the option of making ratings anonymously or providing the ratee with his or her identity.

Appraisal at Digital Equipment Corporation is very different. In Digital's 360° system, the employee has the primary responsibility for selecting raters. A random sample of the people nominated by each employee is then asked to serve as raters. The ratee is also responsible for summarizing his or her own feedback from the raters. Employees throw out the lowest and highest ratings to ensure the least biased set of judgements. Digital also has a rule that no rater can give negative feedback in the appraisal unless he or she has previously given that feedback directly to the ratee.

Discussion Questions

1. How do you think raters should be selected in a 360° appraisal system? Should the supervisor or the ratee have primary control over this factor? What are the advantages and disadvantages of each approach?

2. Should the ratee be trusted with the responsibility of summarizing his or her own feedback, or should the Johnson & Johnson approach of having supervisors do this task be followed? Why or why not? What are the advantages and disadvantages of each approach?

3. Should feedback from the various sources in a 360° appraisal system be anonymous? What problems or benefits might result from each approach?

SOURCE: Adapted from Milliman, J. F., Zawack, R. A., Norman, C., Powell, L., and Kirksey, J. (1994). Companies evaluate employees from all perspectives. *Personnel Journal*, November, 99-103.

MiniCase 2   *Internal Appraisal*

A ppraisal ratings from multiple sources can provide a rich source of feedback to employees. However, translating this feedback into concrete objectives that will guide and improve performance in the next appraisal period may be difficult. To improve its internal operations, Federal Express is shifting to a future-oriented approach and piloting a 360° "goal-setting system."

How does this system work? Departments at Federal Express assess how well other departments are providing needed inputs to their internal customers. Based on the ratings it receives, each department summarized the goals of its internal customers and then provides those customers with a service guarantee. For example, Fed Ex's HR department has provided the following guarantee to its internal customers:

◆ Timely response

◆ A 24-hour turnaround for feedback on important requests

◆ Two-hour response time to emergency calls

◆ Critical feedback on EEO and employee grievances

◆ Semi-annual training sessions on topical subjects

◆ Updates on employee relations issues

◆ Meetings with managers to review recruitment, plans, goals, and results

◆ Bimonthly meetings with employees.

These goals set a clear foundation for future customer assessment of how well HR employees are performing.

Discussion Questions

1. A potential with 360° goal setting is that various internal customers may have unrealistic and conflicting performance expectations. What actions could managers take to avoid this problem?

2. It is possible for a business to be overly concerned with satisfying customers. For example, giving away products for free might delight customers but would put the company out of business. How could a company use customer-driven goal setting to avoid this problem?

SOURCE: Adapted from Milliman, J. F., Zawacki, R. A., Schulz, B., Wiggins, S., and Norman, C. A. (1995). Customer service drives 360 degree goal setting. *Personnel Journal*, June, 136-141.

Case 1

New Boss, New Problems

Ron Moore has worked for Assessment Systems, Ltd., for five years. In his third year with the company, he was recognized as a top performer because of his outstanding enthusiasm and reliability, his team orientation, and his dedication to charitable activities on behalf of the company. Don McFarland, his manager, was very proud of Moore's performance and often held him up as a model employee to other workers and managers. A little over a year ago, McFarland left to direct the start-up of an overseas arm of Assessment Systems, Inc., and another manager, Paul Adams, took his place at Ron Moore's unit. Shortly afterward, Moore's performance began to decline.

When Adams arrived on the scene, he had already been informed by McFarland that Moore was an excellent performer. Adams met with Moore and told him that he felt fortunate to have such a good performer under his direction. He went on to say that he was counting on Moore to make sure things ran smoothly during the transition in management.

At first, things went well. Adams found he could even count on Moore to step in and take responsibility when Adams was called away for meetings and other duties. Then Adams started to notice a dip in Moore's performance. At first this consisted of avoiding responsibility in Adams' absence and responding to other employees' requests by telling them to wait for Adams to deal with the issue. Then Moore started calling in sick and showing up late for work. This pattern was unprecedented in Moore's work record, and Adams thought that Moore might be having some personal problems. He decided not to confront him about the change in his performance, but rather to cut him some slack so he could work out whatever problems he was having.

When the performance problems continued for more than a month, Adams felt compelled to confront Moore. The following conversation occurred at Moore's workstation after he arrived late yet again.

Adams: About time you rolled in, Ron. I've been waiting for you since 8 A.M., and it's now 12 minutes after. I don't have time for this and you, award-winning performer or not, have no business showing up here late.

Moore: Well, good morning, Paul. It's nice to see you.

Adams: Listen, don't give me that nonchalant stuff. Your whole attitude has become too nonchalant. It's time you turned things around.

Moore: Hey, what's the big deal? Other people come in late and don't have you jumping on them for it.

Adams: I know what you're capable of, Ron. You owe it to yourself and the company to perform to the best of your potential. I'm going to be watching you closely from now on, and another string of absences or late arrivals is going to get you a verbal warning.

Adams walked away. He hated making threats, and the confrontation had gone even worse than he had anticipated. But, he told himself, he couldn't just let things go on as they were. He hoped he would see Moore's performance jump back to what it had been when he first arrived at the unit.

Two weeks later, Adams was examining performance records and noticed that Moore was tardy only one day. "What an improvement," he thought. "I guess our little talk did some good after all." But his positive feeling soon disappeared when he noticed Moore's productivity. Although Moore had routinely performed at or near the top, he was now in the average range. Adams knew that some work procedures had changed, but he couldn't believe they had caused Moore's performance problems. Another talk with Moore was definitely in order.

Adams: Ron, your performance over the past few weeks hasn't been up to par. You can do better if you apply yourself. I know you can.

Moore: What do you mean, my performance hasn't been up to par?

Adams: It looks like you've licked the problem of getting here on time, but your productivity is off. You're only hitting the average for your group.

Moore: So, what's so bad about average?

Adams: You know the answer to that. You're capable of doing better. Let me give you some advice. I've had rough periods, too. The key is to just knuckle down and do it. When the going gets tough, the tough get going, and all that sort of thing. OK?

Moore: Yeah, I'll see what I can do.

Moore's performance problems continued and so did Adams' frustration. Every performance record gave Adams a reason to confront Moore. The confrontations accomplished nothing, and Adams was feeling increasingly frustrated. The annual appraisal was coming around, and Adams was considering giving Moore a low rating so that he would get the message that his performance was unacceptable.

Critical Thinking Questions

1. What is wrong with Adams' approach to managing Moore's performance problem?

2. What do you think might be causing Moore's performance difficulties? How should Adams go about identifying the cause(s)?

3. Once Adams has explored the causes, how should he approach the issue of improving Moore's performance?

4. Do you agree with Adams' decision to give Moore a low rating to send him a message? Why or why not?

Cooperative Learning Exercises

5. Form groups of three students each. One student in each group takes the role of Ron Moore and the other two play Ron's co-workers. The role-play begins with "Ron" describing his recent run-ins with Paul Adams, perhaps over lunch. The "co-workers" should react as they think co-workers would react in such a situation.

6. Form pairs of students. One student takes the role of Paul Adams, the second the role of Don McFarland. Paul has placed an overseas call to Ron Moore's former boss because he is very frustrated by his inability to reach Ron. Role-play the resulting phone conversation.

7. Form into groups of four students each. One student assumes the role of Ron and another plays Paul Adams. The situation is the performance review session that has followed the interactions described in the case. As the two students role-play that session, the other two students observe and then critique the interaction. What alternate approaches might Adams take?

Case 2

Changing the Appraisal System

The staff at Northern University has expressed a number of complaints regarding performance appraisal over the past couple of years. The system was put in place more than 12 years ago, and a number of people on staff feel that it is time for a change. Staff positions run the gamut from janitors and plumbers to secretaries. The staff has its own council and has appointed a committee to study the appraisal issue. One of the committee's more interesting findings was that the university is using more than a dozen different rating forms. This discovery has only added to employees' perceptions of inequitable appraisal, and soon there were a number of charges of discrimination in appraisal.

These problems attracted the attention of Northern University's president, who appointed a task force to study the issue and to recommend a new appraisal system. In the course of its study, the task force surveyed other universities' staff appraisal systems. It found every type of approach, ranging from the simple to the highly sophisticated. Some were based on traits, others on outcomes, still others on behaviours. There seemed to be no consistency across universities.

With the assistance of a management professor, the task force also conducted a survey of staff workers and their supervisors. Here are some of the major findings of this survey:

1. The majority of supervisors and staff (60%) view the purpose of the current system as administrative rather than developmental. The percentages are reversed (40/60) in regard to what staff would prefer the purpose of appraisal to be. A more developmental system seems to be desired.

2. Approximately two-thirds of the staff believe that supervisory liking influences performance appraisal. One-third of the supervisors concur.

3. Both supervisors and workers believe that situational factors place constraints on performance. For example, more than half of those surveyed indicated that budget constraints and equipment availability adversely affected performance.

4. Many workers believe that their supervisor does not provide adequate feedback. Overall, there seems to be dissatisfaction with supervision and a belief that favouritism and bias are commonplace.

The task force needs to make recommendations to the university president, and the chair of the task force is looking for direction.

Critical Thinking Questions

1. What kind of staff appraisal system would you recommend for Northern University? Why?

2. How can managers address the issues raised in the staff survey? Explain.

3. Describe how the new system should be implemented.

Cooperative Learning Exercises

4. orm pairs of students. Each pair spends five to 10 minutes discussing the recommendations they think the task force should make to the president and then writes down the three best recommendations. Recommendations are exchanged with a second group. All four students from both groups then present the reasoning behind their recommendations to the class, explaining why they chose the particular approach they did.

5. The entire class discusses recommendations until the students reach a consensus on four or five that the task force should present to the university president. Then students form groups of three. One student assumes the role of the task force chair, another that of the university president, and a third that of the management professor who assisted the committee. Role-play the meeting at which the task force informs the president of its recommendations.

Appendix to Chapter 7

THE CRITICAL INCIDENT TECHNIQUE: A METHOD FOR DEVELOPING A BEHAVIOURALLY BASED APPRAISAL INSTRUMENT

The critical incident technique (CIT) is one of many types of job-analysis procedures. The CIT is often used because it produces behavioural statements that make explicit to an employee what is required, and to a rater what the basis for an evaluation should be.

CIT Steps

The following steps are involved in a complete CIT procedure:

1. *Identify the major dimensions of job performance.*
   This can be done by asking a group of raters and ratees to brainstorm and generate dimensions relevant to job performance. Each person lists, say, three dimensions. The group members then combine their lists and eliminate redundancies.

2. *Generate "critical incidents" of performance.*
   For each dimension, the group members should list as many incidents as they can think of that represent effective, average, and ineffective performance levels. Each person should think back over the past six to 12 months for examples of performance-related behaviours that they have witnessed. Each incident should include the surrounding circumstances or situation.

   If you are having trouble generating incidents, you might want to think of the following situation:

   Suppose someone said that person A, whom you feel is the most effective person in the job, is a poor performer. What incidents of person A's behaviour would you cite to change the critic's opinion?

   Try to make sure that the incidents you list are observable *behaviours* and not *personality characteristics* (traits).

3. *Double-check that the incidents represent one dimension.*
   This step is called *retranslation*. Here you are trying to make sure there is clear agreement on which incidents represent which performance dimension. If there is substantial disagreement among group members, this incident may need to be clarified. Alternatively, another dimension may need to be added or some dimensions may need to be merged.

   In the retranslation process, each person in the group is asked to indicate what dimension each incident represents. If everyone agrees, the group moves on to the next incident. Any incidents on which there is disagreement are put to the side for further examination at the end of the process, when they may be discarded or rewritten.

4. *Assign effectiveness values to each incident.*
   Effectiveness values are assigned to all the incidents that survived retranslation. How much is incident "A" worth in our organization, on, say, an effectiveness scale of 1 (unacceptable) to 7 (excellent)? All group members should rate each incident. If there is substantial disagreement regarding the value of a certain behaviour, that behaviour should be discarded.

   NOTE: Disagreement on incident values indicates differences in valuative standards or lack of clarity in organizational policy. Differences in valuative standards can be a fundamental problem in appraisal. The CIT procedure can help to reduce these differences.

The next page includes some CIT worksheets for you to try. The dimensions included are a subset of those generated in a research project conducted for a hos-

---

*Goodale, J. G., & Burke, R. J. (1975). Behaviorally based rating scales need not be job specific. *Journal of Applied Psychology, 60*, 389–391.

pital that wanted a common evaluation tool for all non-nursing employees.* The jobs covered ranged from floor sweeper and clerical worker to laboratory technician and social worker. Of course, the behavioural standards for each dimension differed across jobs—an excellent floor sweeper behaviour would not be the same as an excellent lab technician behaviour. These dimensions appear fairly generic, though, and are probably applicable to jobs in most organizations. You may want to develop more specific dimensions, or other dimensions altogether.

Remember, after generating incidents, your group should determine agreement levels for the dimension and value for each incident. An easy way to do this is for one person to recite an incident and have everyone respond with dimension and value. This could be informal and verbal, or formal and written.

Critical Incidents Worksheet

Job Title:
Job Dimension: Knowledge of Job—Understanding the mission of the position held and of the job's policies, techniques, rules, materials, and manual skills.
Instructions: Provide at least one behavioural statement for each performance level.

1. Needs improvement:
2. Satisfactory:
3. Excellent:
4. Outstanding:

Critical Incidents Worksheet

Job Title:
Job Dimension: Personal Relations—Attitude and response to supervision, relationships with co-workers, flexibility in working as part of the organization.
Instructions: Provide at least one behavioural statement for each performance level.

1. Needs improvement:
2. Satisfactory:
3. Excellent:
4. Outstanding:

Critical Incidents Worksheet

Job Title:
Job Dimension: Initiative—The enthusiasm to get things done, energy exerted, willingness to accept and perform responsibilities and assignments; seeks better ways to achieve results.
Instructions: Provide at least one behavioural statement for each performance level.

1. Needs improvement:
2. Satisfactory:
3. Excellent:
4. Outstanding:

Critical Incidents Worksheet

Job Title:
Job Dimension: Dependability—Attention to responsibility without supervision, meeting of deadlines.
Instructions: Provide at least one behavioural statement for each performance level.

1. Needs improvement:
2. Satisfactory:
3. Excellent:
4. Outstanding:

Training the Workforce

After reading this chapter, you should be able to deal more effectively with the following challenges:

1 Determine when employees need training and the best type of training given a company's circumstances.

2 Recognize the characteristics that make training programs successful.

3 Weigh the costs and benefits of a computer-based training program.

4 Design job aids as complements or alternatives to training.

For most workers, an important part of the job involves training in the latest technology. At Motorola's Illinois learning center, trainees practice operating assembly lines on virtual-reality computer programs that let them "stop" production, troubleshoot, and restart when the problem is solved.

It's impossible to pick up a magazine or newspaper today without reading about virtual reality (VR), a computer-based technology that replicates the real world. Using special gloves and headsets, users of VR programs can interact with virtual worlds and manipulate objects in real time.

Many companies have been exploring the "fun side" of virtual reality, creating adventure games for adults. But virtual reality also holds promise in many other areas of business, particularly in training. Indeed, at high-tech companies like Motorola, the future of VR training is already here.[1]

Motorola manufactures a variety of communication and computer equipment, including pagers, semiconductors, and cellular telephones. The company employs approximately 60,800 manufacturing workers worldwide and uses cutting-edge robotic machinery in its many manufacturing plants. Of course, all of these employees must be trained to run and troubleshoot the robotic assembly lines effectively. Because technology advances so quickly, the need for training is ongoing.

In the past, Motorola trained its employees in a classroom setting. The company equipped each classroom with duplicates of the machinery found in its manufacturing sites. However, duplicating the ever-evolving equipment was both expensive and difficult. Sending workers for three-day training sessions was also costly and inefficient. Furthermore, continued company growth meant an ever-increasing demand for training—a demand that was becoming increasingly difficult to meet. The company needed a more efficient way of delivering the training while retaining the relevance of a hands-on environment.

To meet these challenges, Motorola decided to try VR technology to replicate its assembly-line equipment. While the cost of program development and equipment for the virtual reality training could range from $30,000 to over $100,000, Motorola's managers realized that the cost of duplicating manufacturing equipment was even higher. As a result, VR seemed worth a shot.

The results of early VR training efforts, based on a comparison of three separate training groups, have been stunning. One group was trained on real equipment, Motorola's traditional training method. Another group was given computer-based training using a computer screen and mouse. The third group was given virtual reality training. Following the training, trainees were asked to start, run, and shut down the actual equipment. Training managers tallied the number of errors made in each of these steps. The first two groups averaged six mistakes per step, whereas the group trained in three-dimensional virtual worlds averaged only one mistake per step!

Motorola's experience illustrates some of the important training issues facing today's organizations. Specifically:

◆ How can training keep pace with a changing organizational environment? Motorola confronted this challenge by using computer software that can be updated as manufacturing equipment and techniques change. However, the computerized approach may not be the answer for all organizations. For example, many companies operate in fast-paced service-oriented environments rather than assembly-line environments. Training in these situations might be better focused on improving employees' customer-service skills.

◆ Should training occur in a classroom setting or on the job? Classroom training may lack realism and may be less effective than training that occurs while on the job. However, on-the-job training can cause slowdowns that decrease production or irritate customers. Motorola's solution maximizes the relevance of classroom training by using virtual reality technology. However, this approach may not be applicable or cost-effective in other organizations. For example, virtual reality cannot be used to improve teamwork or people skills because VR training is, by its nature, an individual experience.

◆ How can training be effectively delivered worldwide? Many of today's organizations conduct operations around the world. Consistent quality of products or service is critical to organizational survival in today's competitive markets. Unfortunately, achieving uniformity worldwide can be difficult. Virtual reality training provides Motorola with a realistic and effective training tool that can easily be deployed worldwide. Solutions for companies that cannot afford VR training might include teleconference- or video-based training.

◆ How can training be delivered so that trainees are motivated to learn? Although lectures and workbooks may have outstanding content, they may be totally ineffective if they do not engage the trainees or motivate them to learn. Motorola's VR training appears to overcome this problem; in many cases, its trainees have decided to skip lunch rather than take a break from the training. Other engaging delivery mediums might include videos and multimedia displays.

We address these and other training challenges in this chapter. First, we distinguish between training and development. Then, we discuss the major challenges that managers face in trying to improve workers' performance through training. Next, we offer some suggestions on managing the three phases of the training process, explore selected types of training, and consider ways to maximize and evaluate the effectiveness of training. We close the chapter with a section on what is arguably the single most important training opportunity: the orientation of new employees.

◼ Training versus Development

Although training is often used in conjunction with development, the terms are not synonymous. **Training** typically focuses on providing employees with specific skills or helping them correct deficiencies in their performance.[2] For example, new equipment may require workers to learn new ways of doing the job, or some workers may have a deficient understanding of a work process. In both cases, training can be used to correct the skill deficit. In contrast, **development** is an effort to provide employees with the abilities that the organization will need in the future.

Figure 8–1 summarizes the differences between training and development. In training, the focus is solely on the current job; in development, the focus is on both the current job and jobs that employees will hold in the future. The scope of training is on individual employees, while the scope of development is on the entire work group or organization. That is, training is job specific and addresses particular performance deficits or problems, while development is concerned with the work force's skills and versatility.[3] Training tends to focus on immediate organizational needs, while development tends to focus on long-term requirements.

training
The process of providing employees with specific skills or helping them correct deficiencies in their performance.

development
An effort to provide employees with the abilities that the organization will need in the future.

	Training	Development
Focus	Current job	Current and future jobs
Scope	Individual employees	Work group or organization
Time Frame	Immediate	Long term
Goal	Fix current skill deficit	Prepare for future work demands

Figure 8–1 Training versus Development

The goal of training is a fairly quick improvement in workers' performance, while the goal of development is the overall enrichment of the organization's human resources by preparing employees for future work demands. Training strongly influences present performance levels, while development pays off in terms of more capable and flexible human resources in the long run.

It is essential to remember these differences when generating and evaluating training programs. For example, using a training approach to affect a long-range issue is likely to be futile. Similarly, taking a development approach to improve current job performance problems will probably prove ineffective. In this chapter we focus on training. Development is the subject of the next chapter.

■ Challenges in Training

The training process brings with it a number of questions that managers must answer. These are:

- Is training the solution to the problem?
- Are the goals of training clear and realistic?
- Is training a good investment?
- Will the training work?

■ Is Training the Solution?

A fundamental objective of training is the elimination or improvement of performance problems. However, not all performance problems call for training. Performance deficits can have several causes, many of which are beyond the worker's control and would therefore not be affected by training.[4] For example, unclear or conflicting requests, morale problems, and poor-quality materials cannot be improved through training.

Before choosing training as the solution, managers should carefully analyse the situation to determine if training is the appropriate response.

■ Are the Goals Clear and Realistic?

A Question of Ethics

Some companies reimburse the educational expenses of employees who take classes on their own. In an era when people can count less and less on a single employer to provide them with work over the course of their careers, do you think employers have a responsibility to encourage their employees to pursue educational opportunities? What benefits might an employer gain through this policy?

To be successful, a training program must have clearly stated and realistic goals that will both guide the program's content and determine the criteria by which its effectiveness will be judged. For example, management cannot realistically expect one training session to make everyone a computer expert. Such an expectation guarantees failure because the goal is unattainable.

Unless the goals are clearly articulated before training programs are set up, the organization is liable to find itself training employees for the wrong reasons and toward the wrong ends. A 1993 survey of 200 companies in Canada and the United States found that while most information systems (IS) managers have no trouble naming the challenges faced by their organization, few have training programs in place that address those challenges. Managers said that the most pressing skills needed by their staffs were non-technical skills such as communications, managing, and teamwork, but the survey found that the goals of current IS training programs were geared more toward improving technical skills such as programming and analysis.[5]

■ Is Training a Good Investment?

Training can be quite expensive, but there are indications that when money is spent wisely, training is definitely worth the investment. In manufacturing industries, a recent examination of what distinguished the most successful from the least successful plants identified three mutually supporting characteristics. First there was extensive use of work teams; second, there was extensive delegation of responsibility to production workers; and third, training was given strong emphasis.[6]

A survey of employers in a cross-section of sectors by the Conference Board of Canada indicated that the average spending per employee was slightly more than $650. (See Figure 8–2 for a breakdown of those results, by cost category.) Figure 8–3 presents an indication of the variability of training expenditures among industries. You will note that many of the more labour-intensive industries fall toward the bottom of this ranking, indicating both the higher costs of training with large employee populations and also the expectation that, in some industries such as education and health care, much of the training is accomplished through formal education.

These estimates of the amount spent on training are just that—estimates. A great deal of training within organizations is done by supervisors and peers of the employee, and does not show up as a discrete expenditure. However, it is fair to look at training expenditures as a rough index of the amount of the overall training being done. Bear in mind, however, that small companies currently account for a disproportionate amount of employment growth. Since very small companies are much less likely to have elaborate HR units with training specialists, assessing how much they invest in training is difficult.

In addition to the cost of delivering the training program, costs are associated with analysing and evaluating the program's effectiveness. In some cases, training may be appropriate but not cost effective. Before beginning a training program, managers must weigh how much the current problem costs against how much the training to eliminate it will cost. It could be that the training cure is more costly than the performance ailment—in which case alternatives to training must be considered.

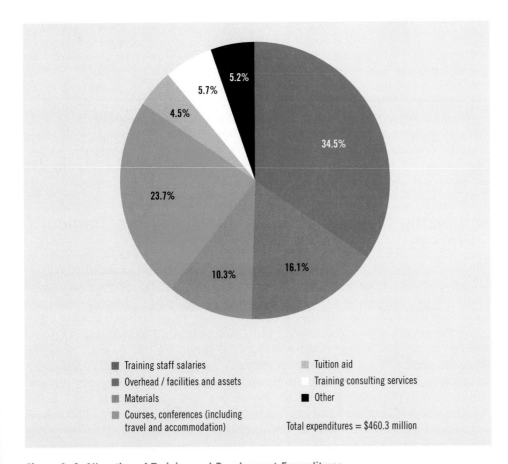

Figure 8–2 Allocation of Training and Development Expenditures
SOURCE: McIntyre, D. (1992). *Training and development 1991: Expenditures and policies* (p. 8). Ottawa: The Conference Board of Canada. Reproduced with permission.

Figure 8–3 Average Per-Capita Spending on Training by Industry

Oil and Gas	$1,158
Transportation, Communication and Public Utilities	945
Finance, Insurance and Real Estate	743
All Sectors	**659**
Manufacturing	576
Mining	525
Services	510
Retail	458
Health	293
Education	269
Construction	162
Accommodation and Food Services	131

SOURCE: McIntyre, D. (1992). *Training and development 1991: Expenditures and policies* (p. 10). Ottawa: The Conference Board of Canada. Reproduced with permission.

Determining whether training is a good investment requires measuring the training's potential benefits in dollars. Training that focuses on "hard" areas (such as the running and adjustment of machines) that have a fairly direct impact on outcomes (such as productivity) can often be easily translated into a dollar value. Estimating the economic benefits of training in softer areas—such as teamwork training—is much more challenging.

■ Will Training Work?

A variety of training programs are in widespread use. Some are computerized, others use simulations, and still others use the traditional lecture format. Some types of training are more effective than others for some purposes and in some situations. Designing effective training remains as much an art as a science, however, because no single type of training has proved most effective overall.

Beyond the type of training and its content, a number of contextual issues can determine a training program's effectiveness. For example, an organizational culture that supports change, learning, and improvement can be a more important determinant of a training program's effectiveness than any aspect of the program itself. Participants who view training solely as a day away from work are unlikely to benefit much from the experience. Further, if participants' managers do not endorse the content and purpose of the training, there is little likelihood that the training program will have any influence on work processes.

Some training programs are absolutely critical to organizational success. Canadian Airlines International engaged in a major training initiative prior to installing entirely new reservations, airport, cargo, and financial information systems to support their 1994 TQM initiative. The period of preparation and training took about 18 months. During that period, not only were employees utilized extensively to identify the many technical issues for which people would need to be prepared at the time of switching systems, but the employer also included a "dealing with change" module and made Employee Assistance counsellors available to help employees work through the personal upheaval that can be triggered by a major organizational change.[7]

Finally, training will not work unless it is related to organizational goals. A well-designed training program flows from the strategic goals of the company; a poorly designed one has no relationship to—or even worse, is at cross-purposes with—those goals. It is the manager's responsibility to ensure that training is linked with organizational goals.

■ Building Managerial Skills: Managing the Training Process

Effective training can raise performance, improve morale, and increase an organization's potential. Poor, inappropriate, or inadequate training can be a source of frustration for everyone involved. To maximize the benefits of training, managers must closely monitor the training process.

As Figure 8–4 shows, the training process consists of three phases: (1) needs assessment, (2) development and conduct of training, and (3) evaluation. In the *needs assessment phase,* the problems or needs that the training must address are determined. Too often organizations have implemented training programs because of their faddish popularity rather than because the organization needs them. In the *development and conduct phase,* the most appropriate type of training is designed and offered to the work force. In the *evaluation phase,* the effectiveness of the training program is assessed. In the pages that follow, we provide recommendations for maximizing the effectiveness of each of these phases.

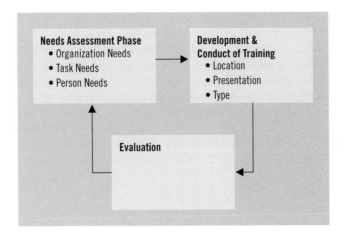

Figure 8–4 The Training Process

In large organizations, managers are very important for determining what training is needed (phase 1), but the actual training (phase 2) is usually provided by either the organization's own training department or an external resource (such as a consulting firm or a local university). After the training program is completed, managers are often called upon to provide the information necessary to determine whether the training has been useful (phase 3). In small businesses, the manager may be responsible for the entire process, although external sources of training may still be used.

The Assessment Phase

The overall purpose of the assessment phase is to determine if training is needed, and if so, to provide the information required to design the training program. Assessment consists of three levels of analysis: organization, task, and person.

The Levels of Assessment.   *Organizational analysis* examines such broad factors as the organization's culture, mission, business climate, long- and short-term goals, and structure. Its purpose is to identify both overall organizational needs and the level of support for training that exists in the organization. Perhaps the organization lacks the resources needed to support a formal training program, or perhaps the organization's strategy emphasizes innovation. In either case, the organizational analysis that reveals such information plays a major role in determining whether training will be offered and the type of training (or alternative to training) that would be most appropriate. If a lack of resources precludes formal training, a mentoring program might be used as an alternative. An innovative environment may call for a training program focussed on encouraging workers' creativity.

Task analysis is an examination of the job to be performed. It focusses on the duties and tasks of jobs throughout the organization to determine which jobs require training. A recent and carefully conducted job analysis should provide all the information needed to understand job requirements. These duties and tasks are then used to identify the knowledge, skills, and abilities (KSAs) required to perform the job adequately (see Chapter 2). Then the KSAs are used to determine the kinds of training needed for the job.

Person analysis determines which employees need training by examining how well employees are carrying out the tasks that make up their jobs.[8] Training is often necessary when there is a discrepancy between a worker's performance and the organization's expectations or standards. Often, a person analysis entails examining the worker performance ratings routinely collected by the organization, then identifying individual workers or groups of workers who are weak in certain skills.

The source of most performance ratings is the supervisor, but a more complete picture of workers' strengths and weaknesses may be obtained by expanding the sources to include self-assessment by the individual worker and performance assessments by a couple of the worker's peers.[9]

As noted earlier, performance problems can come from numerous sources, many of which would not be affected by training. The only source of a performance problem that can be addressed through training is a deficiency that is under the trainee's control.[10] Because training focusses on changing the worker, it can improve performance only when the worker is the source of a performance deficiency. For example, sales training will improve sales only if poor sales techniques are the source of the problem. If declining sales are due to a poor product, high prices, or a faltering economy, sales training will not help.

It is important to note that when we talk about the worker as the source of performance problems, we are not referring only to deficiencies in such hard areas as knowledge, skills, and abilities directly connected to the job. Sometimes the deficiencies occur in such soft areas as diversity, ethics, and AIDS awareness, and they, too, require training to correct. Sun Life of Canada has instituted a very successful and comprehensive AIDS education program in its U.S. head office. AIDS has come to be seen as not just another health issue. The disease affects large numbers of younger people, and at present cannot be cured. This can lead to fear and potential disruptions in the workplace. Sun Life's program used a knowledgeable, outside third party to provide the education program, and was pleased to note significant increases in willingness to work alongside a co-worker who has AIDS.[11] (AIDS awareness programs are discussed in more detail in Chapter 16.)

Training is not the only option available for responding to a worker deficiency. If, for example, it is determined that the training needed to bring workers up to desired levels would be too costly, transferring or terminating the deficient workers may be the more cost-effective course. Strict KSA requirements can then be used to select new employees and eliminate the performance gap. The obvious drawback of terminating or replacing employees deemed deficient is that these options are likely to harm commitment and morale in the work force. For this reason, managers should consider training as preferable to transfer or termination.

Clarifying the Objectives of Training.   The assessment phase should provide a set of objectives for any training program that might be developed following the assessment. Each objective should relate to one or more of the KSAs identified in the task analysis, and should be challenging, precise, achievable, and understood by all.[12]

Whenever possible, objectives should be stated in behavioural terms and the criteria by which the training program's effectiveness will be judged should flow directly from the behavioural objectives. Suppose the cause of a performance deficiency is poor interpersonal sensitivity. The overall objective of the training program designed to solve this problem, then, would be to increase interpersonal sensitivity. Increasing "interpersonal sensitivity" is a noble training goal, but the term is ambiguous and doesn't lead to specific content for a training program or to specific criteria by which the training's effectiveness can be judged. Stating this objective in behavioural terms requires determining what an employee will know, do, and not do after training—for example, the employee will greet customers and clients by name, refrain from sexual humour that could be perceived as harassing, and show up for all meetings on time.[13]

Figure 8–5 shows how the overall objective of training provides a starting point that can be broken down into dimensions (specific aspects of job performance) for which specific behavioural goals can then be developed. The overall objective in the figure is to increase the interpersonal sensitivity of supervisors in their relations with production employees. First, this overall objective is divided into two dimensions: listening and feedback skills. Then specific behaviours that are part of these dimensions are identified, both to guide the training effort and to help evaluate whether the training has been successful.

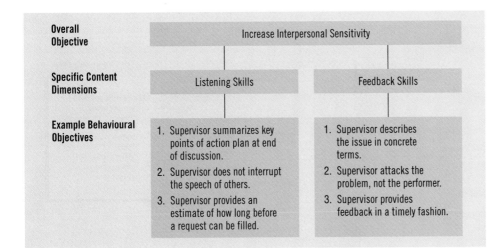

Figure 8–5 Example of Development of Behavioural Training Objectives

The Training and Conduct Phase

The training program that results from a thorough assessment should be a direct response to an organizational problem or need.

Training approaches vary by location, presentation, and type.

Location Options.   Training can be carried out either on the job or off the job. In the very common **on-the-job (OJT) training** approach, the trainee works in the actual work setting, usually under the guidance of an experienced worker, supervisor, or trainer. The Manager's Notebook on this page provides a list of the factors that HR professionals and managers need to consider when developing an OJT program.[14]

Job rotation, apprenticeships, and internships are all forms of OJT training.

♦ *Job rotation,* as we saw in Chapter 2, allows employees to gain experience at different kinds of narrowly defined jobs in the organization. It is often used to give future managers a broad background.

♦ *Apprenticeships,* OJT programs, typically associated with the skilled trades, derive from the medieval practice of having the young learn a trade from an experienced worker. In Europe, apprenticeships are still one of the major ways for young men and women to gain entry to skilled jobs. In Canada, apprenticeships are largely confined to adults looking to work in certain occupations. These apprenticeships generally last for four years, and the apprentice's pay starts at about half that of the more experienced "journey workers." Apprenticeship training requires that three different parties take a role: employers who sponsor apprentices, the apprentices themselves, and an authority to run the apprenticeships. Figure 8–6 indicates where apprenticeships fit into the overall flow of people from the school to the workplace. Close observers of Canadian educational systems frequently point out that while the average level of education in Canada is quite high, other countries such as

---

Manager's Notebook

A Checklist for Using OJT

The following checklist is useful for determining when OJT is appropriate and what it should cover.

Managers Should Select OJT When:

♦ Participatory learning is essential.

♦ One-on-one training is necessary.

♦ Five or fewer employees need training.

♦ Taking employees out of the work environment for training is not cost-effective.

♦ Classroom instruction is not appropriate.

♦ Equipment and safety restrictions make other training methods ineffective.

♦ Frequent changes in standard operating procedures allow minimal time for retraining.

♦ Work in progress cannot be interrupted.

♦ The task for which the training is designed is infrequently performed.

♦ Immediate changes are necessary to meet new safety requirements.

♦ A defined proficiency level or an individual performance test is required for certification or qualification.

What OJT Should Cover:

♦ Large or secured equipment.

♦ Delicate or calibrated instruments.

♦ Tools and equipment components of a complex system.

♦ Delicate or dangerous procedures.

♦ Classified information retained in a secured area.

Source: Mullaney, C. A., & Trask, L. D. (1992, October). Show them the ropes. *Technical & Skills Training,* 8–11. Copyright 1992 by American Society for Training and Development, 1640 King St., Box 1443, Alexandria, VA 22313.

---

on-the-job training
Training for which the employee remains in the actual work setting.

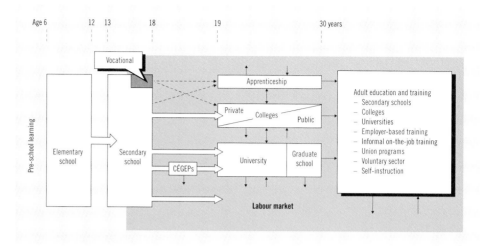

Figure 8–6 A Schematic Overview of the Education and Labour Market System in Canada

Source: A lot to learn: Education and training in Canada (p. 17). (1992). Ottawa: Economic Council of Canada. Reproduced with permission.

Japan and Germany provide a clearer indication to young people of how to move from education to employment in various occupations. There is also concern that many of the existing Canadian apprenticeship programs are geared toward the industrial mix of the 1960s rather than the high-tech industries of the present. The fact that apprenticeships in Canada are often unconnected to the formal education offered through secondary schools has led to their being much less frequently used than in countries where secondary schools and apprenticeships are integrated.

♦ Just as apprenticeships are a route to certain skilled blue-collar jobs, *internships* are a route to white-collar or managerial jobs in a variety of fields. Internships are opportunities for students to gain some real-world job experience, often during summer vacations from school. Although most internships offer low pay, student interns can often gain college or university credits and, possibly, the offer of a full-time job after graduation.

OJT has both benefits and drawbacks. This type of training is obviously relevant to the job because the tasks confronted and learned are generated by the job itself. Very little that is learned in the context of OJT would not transfer directly to the job. OJT also spares the organization the expense of taking employees out of the work environment for training and usually the cost of hiring outside trainers, since company employees generally are capable of doing the training. On the negative side, OJT can prove quite costly to the organization in lost business when on-the-job trainees cause customer frustration. (Have you ever been caught in a check-out line that moves like molasses because a trainee is operating the cash register?) Even if only a handful of customers switch to a competitor because of dissatisfaction with service provided by trainees, the cost to the organization can be substantial. Errors and damage to equipment that occur when a trainee is on the job may also prove costly. Another potential drawback is that trainers might be top-notch in terms of their skills but inadequate at transferring their knowledge to others. Often "best practice" is to use subject matter experts (SMEs) to plan and deliver OJT. However, in technical organizations, SMEs are usually technical specialists accustomed to working alone in a laboratory environment and writing up their research, so their general focus is on technical problems or abstract concepts rather than on people. To get full value from OJT, employers make sure to provide their in-company trainers with the skills and support they need to do a good job.

Off-the-job training is an effective alternative to OJT. Common examples of off-the-job training are formal courses, simulations, and role-playing exercises in a classroom setting. One of the advantages of off-the-job training is that it gives employees extended uninterrupted periods of study. Another is that a classroom setting may be more conducive to learning and retention because it avoids the distractions and interruptions that commonly occur in an OJT environment. The big disadvantage of off-the-job training is that what is learned may not transfer back to the job. A classroom, after all, is not the workplace, and the situations simulated in the training may not closely match those encountered on the job. Also, if employees view off-the-job training as an opportunity to enjoy some time away from work, not much learning is likely to take place.

Presentation Options.   A variety of presentation techniques can be employed in training. Many of these options can be used either at off-the-job locations or in training sessions that occur internally but not on the job. The most common presentation techniques are slides and videotapes, computers, simulations, virtual reality, and classroom instruction.

Slides and videotapes.   Slides and videotapes can be used either off-the-job or in special media rooms in an organization's facility. Slides and videotapes provide consistent information and, if done well, can be interesting and thought-provoking. However, these presentation media do not allow trainees to ask questions or receive further explanation (although new advances in videotape technology are permitting some interaction between the observer and the medium). Many companies prefer to use slides, film, or tapes to supplement a program led by a trainer, who can answer individuals' questions and flesh out explanations when necessary.

Teletraining.   Teletraining is a training option that is particularly useful when trainees are dispersed across various physical locations.[15] Satellites or other forms of transmission can be used to beam live training session to various locations. In addition to being able to hear the trainer, the link-up allows trainees in remote locations to ask questions of the instructors. Such technologies are becoming increasingly common in Executive MBA and other distance education settings offered by Canadian universities.

The "live" hook-up is still an expensive technology and, where organizations have employees working in a range of different time zones, the scheduling problems can become difficult. Various hybrid models are possible, such as using videotaped presentations (physically shipped to the various locations) combined with conference calls with the instructor at pre-arranged times for various groups of trainees.

Computers.   With the widespread availability of personal computers, it is often cost-effective to use this medium for training. Figure 8–7 summarizes some of the advantages of computer-based training, sometimes also referred to as *computer-assisted instruction (CAI)*. If a job requires extensive use of computers, then computer-based training is highly job related and provides for a high degree of transfer of training back to the job. Computers also have the advantage of allowing trainees to learn at a comfortable pace. As a trainer, the computer never becomes tired, bored, or short-tempered. Finally, advancing technology is making the computer a truly multimedia training option in which text can be combined with film, graphics, and audio components.

Indeed, many organizations are successfully using computer-based multimedia approaches to training. For example, a major gasoline retailer recently developed a multimedia training and evaluation program for new owner/operators of Texaco

> **OJT at AT&T.**
> AT&T began manufacturing telephones on Batam Island, an island close to Singapore, in 1985. "The operation has been successful beyond our wildest dreams," says the AT&T vice-president of manufacturing in Singapore. AT&T credits much of its success on Batam Island to the training it gives to local workers.

Content

1. Job-related   For jobs that involve computer duties, the training may match the work situation. For jobs that aren't computer intensive, the computer training medium can still closely match the actual work environment.

2. Flexible   Changes in procedure or equipment can be easily accommodated with a computer program. With training based on written materials, such changes may make the package obsolete.

Process

3. Self-paced   Trainees can learn at their own pace. Those who are slower and more methodical in their approach to learning won't be rushed and those who are faster won't be bored.

4. Easily distributed   Computer-based training can easily be distributed electronically over a network or on disks. It is easier and cheaper to distribute the training than it is to bring all the trainees to one location.

5. Standardized   Computer-based training means that the material is covered in a uniform way regardless of time, place, instructor, and so on.

6. Available   Trainees can start a computerized session whenever they want to.

7. Self-sufficient   Trainees control the learning process without direction from supervisors, peers, or others.

8. Individualized   Computerized training can be programmed so that trainees can skip sections that they have already mastered. This means training time should be maximally effective for each trainee.

Outcomes

9. Learning   Computer-based training has been found to result in levels of learning that are equal to or higher than more traditional approaches to training.

10. Costs   Computerized training costs more to develop but is much cheaper to deliver than traditional training (due mainly to reduced training time and the elimination of travel).

11. Time   Time savings of 40 to 60% are commonly reported with computerized training. The time savings are primarily due to tighter instructional design and the ability to focus on sections yet to be mastered.

Figure 8–7 Potential Advantages of Computer-Based Training

SOURCE: Adapted from Granger, R. E. (1989). Computer-based training improves job performance. *Personnel Journal, 68,* 116–123. Hall, B. (1996, March). Lessons in corporate training: Multimedia's big payoff. *NewMedia,* 40–45.

service stations.[16] The program covers all of the important aspects of running a gas station, including advertising, accounting, merchandising, and the handling of hazardous materials. The program includes graphics, audio, and video, and is distributed over a network from the company's mainframe. It takes new operators about three hours to complete the program and a final quiz. The quizzes are automatically scored and the scores are added to an operator database.

Computer-based training may pose disadvantages in some circumstances. The most obvious drawback is the fact that an adequate number of computers must be available for training. Otherwise the experience can be overshadowed with frustration as employees crowd around the available machines ready to take their turn. Also, although computers connote cutting-edge technology and precision, the quality of the medium is not necessarily an indicator of the quality of the training content. Whether utilizing computers or some other medium, the content of a training program requires careful preparation. Further, the learning of some areas—particularly complex and conceptual issues—may best be accomplished through interaction with peers or supervisors who have developed expertise through experience. Finally, using computers for training makes most sense when the trainee's job duties require interaction with a computer. When this is not the case, the computerization aspect may interfere with transference of what is learned back to the job.

simulation

A device or situation that replicates job demands at an off-the-job site.

Simulations.   Particularly effective in training are **simulations,** devices or situations that replicate job demands at an off-the-job site. Organizations often use simulations when the information to be mastered is complex, the equipment used on the job is expensive, and/or the cost of a wrong decision is quite high.

The airline industry has long used simulators to train pilots. Flight simulations often include motion in addition to visual and auditory realism. This aspect substantially increases the cost of simulation but makes the training even more realistic. CAE Ltd., with headquarters in Montreal, is a world leader in the design and manufacture of flight simulators. The development of a simulator for Boeing's 777 was accomplished parallel to the development of the aircraft itself, with a configuration team from CAE conferring on a regular basis with Boeing to ensure that the simulator accurately reflected any modifications or changes made as the aircraft was developed.[17] Another type of simulation confronts trainee doctors with an accident victim arriving at the emergency room. The trainees choose from a menu of options, with the patient "dying" if the decision is delayed too long or is incorrect.

Traditionally, simulators have been considered separate from computer-based training. With recent advances in multimedia computer technology, however, the distinctions between these two methods have blurred considerably. In fact, as the technology develops, the price of simulators is becoming more affordable, and hence accessible, for a wider range of organizations.

Few studies have been done on the effectiveness of simulations, but the limited data available indicate that this method of training does have a positive impact on job performance. For example, one study found that pilots who trained on simulators become proficient at flight manoeuvres nearly twice as fast as pilots who trained only in the air.[18] The importance of this difference is underscored by the fact that the cost of simulator training is only about 10 percent of the cost of using the real equipment to train pilots.

Simulating the Workplace.

Many newly hired pilots are instructed by seasoned professionals using a flight simulation program. The new pilots gain valuable experience while not putting anybody's life in danger.

Boeing Company
www.boeing.com

Virtual Reality.   **Virtual reality (VR)** uses a number of technologies to replicate the entire real-life working environment rather than just several aspects of it, as in simulations. Within these three-dimensional environments a user can interact with and manipulate objects in real time.

Tasks that are good candidates for VR training are those that require rehearsal and practice, working from a remote location, or visualizing objects and processes that are not usually accessible. VR training is also excellent for tasks in which there is a high potential for damage to equipment or danger to individuals. One such task is marshalling, an operational job in the armed forces in which a person on the ground uses hand and arm signals to assist a plane to land. Imagine the stress you'd feel the first time you rehearsed these manoeuvres with a multi-tonne aircraft approaching you at high speed! It's easy to see why VR training is used to prepare people to handle the real situation.[19]

Early studies have indicated a great deal of success with VR training. The immersion of the trainees in a virtual world may be the key to this success.[20] The VR experience provides a sense of self-location in a simulated environment in which objects appear solid and can be navigated around, touched, lifted, and so on. This sense of immersion is probably connected to the excitement and motivation often reported by VR trainees.

One drawback of VR training is that current technology is meant for one individual trainee at a time, not multiple participants. Thus, VR training has not applied to team training situations. Technology soon will be capable of simulating a

virtual reality (VR)

The use of a number of technologies to replicate the entire real-life working environment.

much more complex and interactive experience. The programming and design work will be sufficiently expensive that this will still be used for a limited number of situations where such investments are justified.

Classroom Instruction.   Classroom lectures are used in many organizations to impart information to trainees. Although widely viewed as "boring," classroom instruction can be brought to life if other presentation techniques are integrated with the lecture. For example, a videotape could complement the lecture by providing realistic examples of the lecture material. In-class case exercises and role-plays (both of which are found throughout this book) provide opportunities for trainees to apply what is being taught in the class and increase transfer back to the job. Solving and discussing case problems helps trainees learn technical material and content, and role-plays are an excellent way of applying the interpersonal skills being emphasized in the training. If done well, role-plays give trainees the opportunity to integrate new information with job behaviour.[21]

Types of Training.   As we noted earlier, there are many approaches to training. We focus here on the types of training that are commonly used in today's organizations: skills, retraining, cross-functional, team, creativity, and literacy training. In each section we consider the factors that influence the effectiveness of the training program.

Skills Training.   When we think of training, most of us probably envision a program that focusses on particular skill needs or deficits. Indeed, this type of training is probably the most common in organizations. The program is fairly simple: the need or deficit is identified via a thorough assessment. Specific training objectives are generated, and training content is developed to achieve those objectives. The criteria for assessing the effectiveness of the training are also based on the objectives identified in the assessment phase.

To understand how skills training programs are developed, let's examine a classic example of skills training. In one point in the early 1990s, 10% of all complaints to IBM's CEO stemmed from the handling of phone calls. Since customer service was a high priority for IBM, the CEO recognized that action was required. He appointed a project team composed of both line managers and trainers to investigate the situation. This arrangement was designed to ensure that line personnel would take the project team's recommendations and actions seriously. (Programs that simply appear from the HR department are sometimes not taken seriously by line managers.)

The project team did a careful assessment. Surveys of IBM customers revealed that 70 percent of customer contact was via telephone, and that shoddy phone handling was the biggest complaint.[22] As Figure 8–8 shows, analysis of the survey responses indicated that customers' most frequent complaints were that they could not reach a knowledgeable person and that their calls were not returned. The project team then conducted a survey of IBM employees and found that while over 75 percent knew how to put a customer on hold, less than five percent knew how to forward a call. The team also found that most professional employees felt that they didn't need telephone skills because calls from customers should be handled by the secretarial staff. Based on these survey results, the team categorized the telephone interaction problem into two broad categories: (1) not using phone features and (2) not treating customers with professional courtesy.

The team presented its findings and recommended a training strategy to senior management. The senior vice-president, who agreed that telephone interactions were a problem to be taken seriously, issued the stern memo reprinted in Figure 8–9. Any employee receiving this memo clearly got the message that telephone skills were now a major issue. The strong support of top management forced line employees to take the issue seriously and helped the project team obtain funds for the training program.

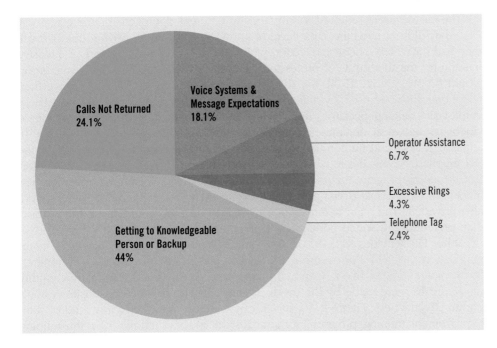

Figure 8–8 Sources of Customer Dissatisfaction with IBM Telephone Service

SOURCE: Estabrooke, R. M., & Foy, N. F. (1992). Answering the call of "tailored training," *Training*, 29, 85–88. Reprinted with permission from the October 1992 issue of *Training* magazine. Copyright 1992. Lakewood Publications, Minneapolis, MN. All rights reserved. Not for resale.

INTEROFFICE MEMO

Overall, the rating of our telephone service by customers and internal users is poor. Together, we are going to fix this problem, and fix it fast.

Figure 8–9 IBM Senior Vice-President's Memo to All Managers

SOURCE: Estabrooke, R. M., & Foy, N. F. (1992). Answering the call of "tailored training." *Training*, 29, 85–88. Reprinted with permission from the October 1992 issue of *Training* magazine. Copyright 1992. Lakewood Publications, Minneapolis, MN. All rights reserved. Not for resale.

The project team divided employees into two groups on the basis of how often they used the phone system and then tailored the training to each group. The "intensive" group was composed of such employees as secretaries and operators, the "casual" group of engineers, managers, and other professionals. The intensive group was relatively small in number but accounted for most of the phone interaction with customers. It was important that this group be both well acquainted with the phone system and trained to be courteous. The casual group needed only to understand the basics of the phone system, but also had to be trained in telephone etiquette.

Training for the intensive user group involved broad-based coverage of expected behaviours and instruction in the phone system's specific operational features. Among the training program's features: a videotape of good and poor role models of phone interaction shown to secretaries and switchboard operators, a computer-based training program that covered details of the phone system as well as courtesy skills, and pamphlets and other reference materials. Depending on their current levels of skill and knowledge, trainees took three to nine hours to complete the program.

The casual users required a substantially different approach for three reasons. First, they did not need the same level of knowledge as the intensive group because they had much less phone interaction with customers. Second, the cost of intensive training for the thousands of professional employees who fell into the casual group would be prohibitive. Third, the casual users were not motivated to improve their telephone skills because they didn't see a problem in their phone performance. These employees' training package, then, was designed to be brief and entertaining. A videotape shown at departmental meetings provided an overview of the topic. In addition, a brief and humorous audiotape that could be played in the car or on the job emphasized the desired behaviours. An abbreviated version of the computer-based training program focussing on only the key elements of phone operation was included in the casual users' package. Pamphlets and other reference sources were also provided. The team assumed that most casual users would select the product they preferred and spend perhaps an hour with the material.

Other HR activities focused on motivating employees to solve the phone communication problem. For example, the senior vice-president selected telephone effectiveness as one of five key annual performance measures. Additionally, monthly random calls were made by the product team's staff to assess each business unit's phone effectiveness. Figure 8–10, which can serve as a model for any kind of skill-improvement training program, summarizes the process followed by the training project team.

The program has been quite successful. After one year, customer satisfaction with telephone responsiveness increased by nearly 10 percent. The goal is 100 percent satisfaction, and it appears that this goal is within reach.

This skills improvement program offers several lessons:

◆ In some organizational settings, the most important step in building commitment to training may be the conscious inclusion of people who have a great deal of informal or political power in the organization. If someone is politically strong enough to torpedo an instructional effort, it may be best to include him or her in the design of the program from the outset.

◆ The idea of beginning with assessments at organizational, task, and personal levels may be more academic than realistic. In reality, problems often suddenly come to light in organizations, and something must be done about them fast if the organization is to remain competitive.

◆ Multiple forms of a training package may be needed for different groups of trainees. Some employee groups may need detailed knowledge and a high level of skills in a particular area, while others may need only broad familiarity and basic skills. Tailoring the training to each group of employees' skill requirements maximizes the training's effectiveness.

job aids

External sources of information, such as pamphlets and reference guides, that workers can access quickly when they need help in making a decision or performing a specific task.

◆ Providing trainees with materials such as pamphlets and reference guides can help to ensure that the training results in improved performance. These sorts of materials, **job aids,** are external sources of information that workers can access quickly when they need help in making a decision or performing a specific task.[23] Their use is growing rapidly for a few reasons. First, job aids reduce the need to memorize many details and therefore cut down on errors and bolster efficiency. Second, although job aids can't replace formal training programs, they can supplement training and help ensure that the training transfers back to the job. Third, they are relatively inexpensive and can be developed and delivered quickly.

1. Build in commitment
   • Gain support of management.
2. Thorough analysis of the problem
   • Is it important?
   • What is the real problem?
3. Gain line support

4. Develop training strategies
   • Is there more than one group of employees that needs training?
   • Design materials appropriate to each group's needs and motivation levels.
5. Develop motivational strategies
   • Take steps to heighten awareness of issue.
   • Signal importance of issue through measurement and recognition programs.

Figure 8–10 Steps to Skill Improvement

Retraining.   A subset of skills training, *retraining* focuses on giving employees the skills they need to keep pace with the changing requirements of their jobs. For instance, however proficient garment workers may be at a traditional skill such as sewing, they will need retraining when the company invests in computerized pattern-making equipment. Unfortunately, even though retraining is much cited in the media as an item at the top of the corporate agenda, many companies rush to upgrade their equipment or processes without taking comparable steps to upgrade their employees' skills. They erroneously believe that automation means a lower-skilled work force when, in fact, it often requires a more highly skilled one.

Bell Canada has utilized extensive retraining as part of its "Modernization of the Sales Team" program. Trained intensively on a range of computer applications featuring the use of modems and portable printers, the sales representatives have become proficient in the area of mobile computing. Other firms, such as Smith Kline Beecham, have adopted pen-based portable computers to provide sales representatives with ready access to the most recent data.[24]

Retraining has been a major part of public policy for some time, taking the forms of training programs offered by governmental agencies or by educational institutions under contract as well as a wide variety of subsidies and incentives to employers to encourage the continual retraining of the work force. While the federal and provincial governments continue to use retraining as a policy lever, the fiscal restraint that has characterized the 1990s has led to reductions and, in some cases, the elimination of programs.

Cross-Functional Training.   Traditionally, organizations have developed specialized work functions and detailed job descriptions. However, today's organizations are emphasizing versatility rather than specialization. For example, the experience of companies such as Nortel and Pratt and Whitney Canada has demonstrated that cross-functional training is one of the staple requirements for the process generically referred to as **concurrent engineering (CE),** the bringing together of product designers with other people involved in bringing an innovation to market.[25] Many companies need workers who can quickly change job assignments, help out where needed, and respond rapidly to changing conditions.[26] Training workers in multiple functions or disciplines is thus becoming increasingly popular.

Cross-functional training involves training employees to perform operations in areas other than their assigned job. There are many approaches to cross-functional training. For example:

◆ Job rotation can be used to provide a manager in one functional area with a broader perspective than he or she would otherwise have.

◆ Departments can trade personnel for periods of time so that each worker or set of workers develops an understanding of the other department's operation.

◆ **Peer trainers,** high-performing workers who double as internal on-the-job trainers, can be extraordinarily effective in helping employees develop skills in another area of operation.[27]

Peer trainers must be selected carefully. Aside from having top-notch skills, they must be patient and motivated to teach others. A simple and effective way to choose people with the right motivation is simply to ask workers if they would like to be a peer trainer and then select the best among the volunteers. Some organizations promote the peer-trainer role as an honour and offer a tangible reward to sweeten the added responsibility. At Disney theme parks, peer trainers are paid extra while they're instructing and bear a trainer designation on their name badges as they move around the park.

Volunteers often need to undergo a formal training program to become successful peer trainers. At T. J. Maxx, a retail chain, peer trainers receive five days of training at national headquarters. The course includes discussions of adult learning theory, questioning skills, facilitation skills, and the technical skills involved in running cash registers and managing inventory.[28]

Bell Canada
www.bell.ca

concurrent engineering (CE)
The bringing together of product designers with others involved in bringing an innovation to market.

cross-functional training
Training employees to perform operations in areas other than their assigned jobs.

peer trainers
High-performing workers who double as internal on-the-job trainers.

Team Training at Toyota.

Already recognized for its commitment to total quality, Toyota is also widely respected for the training it gives its worker teams. Here, teammates work together at Toyota's plant in Cambridge, Ontario.

Since some workers, and even some managers, balk at the idea of cross-functional training, it is important that they be instructed in the necessity for such training and the benefits it can provide. Among these benefits:

◆ The more adaptable workers are, the more valuable they become to the organization. Adaptability increases both workers' job security and the organization's "depth on the bench." The analogy to baseball is apt. If a baseball team does not have a trained replacement for a particular player, when that player is injured, the coach has a problem because there is no one on the bench who can effectively play that position. Similarly, an organization is in trouble if a worker who leaves, is promoted, or becomes ill cannot quickly be replaced with someone else who can do the job. Cross-functional training can provide the talent base that ensures operations will continue to run smoothly.

◆ Versatile employees can better engineer their own career paths.

◆ When promotions aren't available, broader exposure and responsibility can motivate workers.

◆ Training co-workers can clarify a worker's own job responsibilities.

◆ A broader perspective increases workers' understanding of the business and reduces the need for supervision.[29] This broader understanding allows workers to anticipate the effects of possible actions on the entire operation and to use cross-departmental ties to solve problems collectively.

◆ When workers can fill in for other workers who are absent, it is easier to use flexible scheduling, which is increasingly in demand as more employees want to spend more time with their families. Often the absence of one skilled worker can disrupt production and increase costs for the company. See the Issues and Applications feature entitled "Putting Cross-Training Across at Graphic Controls" for details on how one company is cross-training its workers to gain flexibility.[30]

Employees aged 50 years or older may be particularly valuable when it comes to cross-functional versatility.[31] Older workers have often performed a variety of jobs, which will have naturally provided them with a good amount of cross-functional training. They also tend to have a broader perspective on the organization's operations. For these reasons, older workers are often quick studies in a cross-functional training program and make effective peer trainers.

AFG Industries
www.afg.com

Team Training.   Many companies are organizing more and more of their work around teams. For instance, AFG Industries, a producer of glass products, built two new plants in the late 1980s that were designed to be run by employee teams.[32] For these types of organizations, it makes sense to train employees in how best to work in teams. But, surprisingly, little is known about how to do team training. The following initial findings can be used to guide team training efforts:

◆ Team members should be trained in communication skills (both speaking and listening) that encourage respect for all team members.

◆ Training should emphasize the interdependence of team members.

◆ Instruction should instill the recognition that team and individual goals are not always the same, and should provide strategies for dealing with conflicts that will inevitably arise between the two.

◆ Flexibility should be emphasized because teamwork almost always gives rise to unexpected situations.[33]

One type of training that has become increasingly popular for developing teamwork, particularly among managerial and supervisory employees, is outdoor experiential training. CIBC uses an intensive five-day Foundations for Leadership course offered at its own Leadership Development Centre to provide the impetus for organizational cultural change.[34] Eagle's Flight, of Guelph, Ontario, provides a different kind of experiential training. Sales people are formed into teams and given maps of the territory to be explored. Then they must decide collectively how to deal with a range of environmental threats while mining for gold and exchanging it at market rates to determine the winning team.[35]

Many experiential training programs have a physically rigorous dimension—similar to Outward Bound, except that the emphasis is often on mutual dependence among a team rather than individual self-sufficiency. Since the Project Excel course was installed at the Doral Arrowood Conference Centre and Resort, many groups from major corporations have participated in the program, at a cost of $30 to $100 a person,

Issues and Applications

Putting Cross-Training Across at Graphic Controls

At the headquarters of Graphic Controls Corporation (GCC), management is trying to create a flexible work force by cross-training manufacturing operators to perform the duties of at least one other position. In May 1990, GCC began a pilot project to cross-train workers for some highly skilled positions in its industrial chart manufacturing area. A brochure issued to workers proclaims that the goals of this "designated trainee program" are "to produce a well-trained and versatile work force *qualified and willing to work where the need arises,* and, at the same time, to provide individuals with cross-training, skills enhancement and job enrichment."

To achieve these goals, Graphic Controls developed four basic steps:

1. Managers review the work flow in their individual departments and establish their needs for additional or back-up coverage for particular months or the entire year.

2. For each position identified, the manager works with an HR specialist to develop a training curriculum and choose a trainer. The ideal trainer is a member of the work force who has demonstrated successful performance and has the potential to be a good teacher.

3. Once the curriculum has been formalized, the HR department posts the positions identified for training, much in the same way it posts regular job openings. The key concern is to make sure the job requirements are consistent with those for the regular posting for that job opportunity. Each position is posted for three to five days. Applicants go through the company's regular job-screening process. Once a candidate is accepted into the training program, an agreement is reached on what the higher hourly rate will be for the new position after the candidate completes the program.

4. The fully trained individual joins a pool of designated trainees. Whenever there is a need to fill a position on a temporary basis, the manager selects an individual from the pool. The selected individual is paid for the work at the agreed-upon higher rate of pay. When more than one person has been trained for a particular position, selection is made according to seniority and availability.

This program has obvious payoffs for both employees and management. Employees see it as a way to gain skills, with the possibility of higher pay. Managers see it as a way to reduce downtime and eliminate the need to hire skilled temporary help.

SOURCE: Adapted from Santora, J. E. (1992, June). Keep up production through cross-training. *Personnel Journal,* 162–166.

for anywhere from a half day to two days. Ryan Partnership, a small promotional marketing agency, put eight of its employees through Project Excel. The experience could be likened to a teamwork obstacle course. For instance, at one stage in the course, the group had to cross Mohawk Walk, a series of cables 20 to 45 cm off the ground supported by beams and posts. They were told that, as a team, they were to plan the best way to traverse the wires without touching the ground. Aside from the rush that came from negotiating a network of swaying cables and scaling three-metre-high walls, the most important feeling the Ryan participants gained from the experience was a sense of cooperation and support from co-workers. "Here, we're really a group," said Ryan Partnership's managing director. "If you fall, someone is always there to pick you up."[36]

Creativity Training.   As a means of tapping their workers' innovative potential, many organizations have been turning to creativity training. According to *Training* magazine, the number of U.S. organizations with 100 or more employees that offer creativity training doubled from 16 percent in 1986 to 32 percent in 1990.[37] In 1995, the figure was 35%.[38] Canadian employees of the packaging company Lawson Mardon Group Ltd. who were involved in the greenfield startup of a plant in New York State all went through a training process called the Starship Exercise, to facilitate the crafting of a new corporate culture.[39]

brainstorming

A creativity training technique in which participants are given the opportunity to generate ideas openly, without fear of judgement.

Creativity training is based on the assumption that creativity can be learned. There are several approaches to teaching creativity, all of which attempt to help people solve problems in new ways.[40] One common approach is the use of **brainstorming,** in which participants are given the opportunity to generate ideas as wild as they can come up with, without fear of judgement. Only after a good number of ideas have been generated are they individually submitted to rational judgement in terms of their cost and feasibility. Creativity is generally viewed as having two phases: imaginative and practical.[41] Brainstorming followed by rational consideration of the options it produces satisfies both of these phases. Figure 8-11 presents some other approaches to increasing creativity. Since people sometimes find it difficult to break out of their habitual ways of thinking, creativity trainers often provide exercises designed to help them see things in a new way.

Skeptics criticize creativity training, saying there is no way to measure its effectiveness. They also say that training in a soft skill like creativity might make people feel good but does not produce any lasting change in their work performance. It's true that documenting the bottom-line results of creativity training is nearly impossible. Yet some companies, including large American employers such as Frito-Lay and Du Pont, have observed impressive results.

Creativity training, of course, is not a magic solution to all problems. No training program is. And while a training program can help stimulate creativity, the more important factor in generating creative solutions is an organizational environment that supports creativity.[42]

A Question of Ethics

Are companies ethically responsible for providing literacy training for workers who lack basic skills? Why or why not?

Literacy Training.   The abilities to write, speak, and work well with others are critical in today's business environment. Unfortunately, as Figure 8–12 shows, many U.S. workers do not meet employer requirements in these areas. In Canada, it is estimated that 38 percent of those 16 years old or older cannot read well or at all.[43] In a recent survey of manufacturers, over half of the responding companies indicated serious worker deficiencies in such basic skills as math, reading, and problem solving. In the face of these problems, the need for literacy training is clear.

literacy

The mastery of basic skills (reading, writing, arithmetic, and their uses in problem solving).

Before proceeding further, it is important to clarify some definitions. The term **literacy** is generally used to mean the mastery of *basic skills*—that is, the subjects normally taught in elementary schools (reading, writing, arithmetic, and their uses in problem solving). It is important to distinguish between general literacy and functional literacy. *General literacy* is a person's general skill level, while *functional literacy* is a person's skill level in a particular content area. An employee is functionally literate if he or she can read and write well enough to perform important job duties (reading instruction manuals, understanding safety messages, filling out order slips). The most pressing issue for employers is not the general deficiencies in the work force. Rather, a business's foremost concern is its workers' ability to

---

Creativity can be learned and developed. The following techniques can be used to improve a trainee's skill in generating innovative ideas and solutions to problems.

1. **Analogies and Metaphors**—drawing comparisons or finding similarities can improve insight into a situation or problem.

2. **Free Association**—freely associating words to describe a problem can lead to unexpected solutions.

3. **Personal Analogy**—trying to see oneself as the problem can lead to fresh perspectives and, possibly, effective solutions.

4. **Mind Mapping**—generating topics and drawing lines to represent the relationships among them can help to identify all the issues and their linkages.

Figure 8–11 Techniques to Increase Creativity

SOURCE: Adapted from Higgins, J.M. (1994). *101 creative problem solving techniques: The handbook of new ideas for business.* Winter Park, FL: New Management Publishing Company.

Skills Area	All Industries	Percent of Companies Manufacturing	Service
Reading	16.0%	17.2%	16.0%
Basic mathematics	20.2	17.2	23.4
Written communication	22.7	21.9	24.5
Oral communication	14.7	6.3	21.3
Computer capability	10.4	9.4	11.7
Work readiness[1]	17.2	12.5	21.3

[1]Attendance, dress, cooperation, etc.

Figure 8–12 Basic Skill Deficits in Workers That Cause Difficulties for Employers
SOURCE: Lund, L., & McGuire, E. P. (1990). *Literacy in the work force.* New York: The Conference Board.

function effectively in their jobs. For example, a generally low level of reading ability may be cause for societal concern, but it is workers' inability to understand safety messages and work manuals or fill out order slips that is the immediate concern for business. Functional illiteracy can be a serious impediment to an organization's productivity and competitiveness.

While it is difficult to put a dollar figure on how much functional illiteracy costs, these are some of the consequences of illiteracy:

◆ Clerks send out instructions that contain typographical or factual errors. The instructions must be recalled and corrected.

◆ Accounting clerks bill customers incorrectly, and thousands of dollars in accounts receivable are lost.

◆ Production workers incorrectly measure raw materials because of an inability to read, and these errors result in production waste.

◆ Plant workers unable to read manuals maintain machinery inadequately, causing break-downs.

◆ Order clerks misinterpret customers' instructions and send the wrong product or incorrect amounts.[44]

Illiteracy is also a real threat to the safety of other workers. Evidence indicates that there is a direct correlation between illiteracy and some workplace accidents.

Functional literacy training programs focus on the basic skills required to perform a job adequately and capitalize on most workers' motivation to get help or advance in a particular job. These programs use materials drawn directly from the job. For example, unlike a reading comprehension course, which teaches general reading skills, functional training would teach employees to comprehend manuals and other reading materials they must use on the job.

Working in concert with unions, government agencies, and schools, companies have devised a number of programs to remedy deficiencies in basic skills. These programs generally fall into three basic categories:

◆ *Company in-house programs.* These programs are conducted solely or primarily for company employees. One of the earliest in-house programs in North America was begun in the 1960s at Polaroid Corporation. Polaroid's program focusses on a range of basic literacy and arithmetic skills. Employees are assessed by their supervisors and the human resources department, and those with reading skills below the Grade 4 level enter a tutorial program that takes four hours per week. Instruction is tailored to the individual's job. Companies that engage in literacy training must vigorously advertise and promote their programs in order to reach the employees who need them. Many firms do this through company newsletters or bulletin-board announcements.

◆ *Company/local schools programs.* One of the most common functional literacy approaches is for companies to join with a local high school or community college in a partnership aimed at improving workers' literacy. In these partnerships, companies and/or unions pay the tuition for workers to attend classes at local schools. Some companies allow workers up to six hours off per week to attend classes. Sometimes several companies are involved in the partnership.

◆ *Company/government programs.* In some areas, governments have supplied the major initiative for literacy programs.

Diversity Training.   Ensuring that the diverse groups of people working in a company get along and cooperate is vital to organizational success. As we saw in Chapter 4, *diversity training programs* are designed to educate employees on specific cultural and gender differences and how to respond to these differences in the workplace. Diversity training is particularly important when team structures are used.

Crisis Training.   Unfortunately, accidents, disasters, and violence are possibilities that organizations may need to deal with. Yet many employers are ill prepared to deal with tragedies and their aftermath. High-profile disasters such as the events surrounding a terrorist attack aboard an airliner illustrate the ways in which mistakes can compound the problem in crisis situations:

◆ The airline informed one family of their daughter's death by leaving a message on their answering machine.

◆ A family awaiting the arrival of their only child's body was told that their "shipment had arrived." At the local airport the family was met by a forklift operator at a building marked "livestock."

◆ A flight attendant who was supposed to work on the doomed flight was so upset that she asked to be excused from her next flight. She was told that if she didn't fly, she would be fired.

While the airline in question had practised responding to a mock crash just two months previous, the crisis-management training concentrated on the physical aspects to the virtual exclusion of many of the human factors. However, many airlines do have contingency plans that include emotional and logistic support for families and survivors. The organizational response to the crash of a Swiss Air flight just off Peggy's Cove in Nova Scotia illustrated how to deal with tragedy effectively.

In addition to after-the-fact crisis management, *crisis training* can also focus on prevention. For example, the potential problem of workplace violence can be reduced through a range of initiatives from stress management to supervisory training in identifying situations that represent high risk.

Customer Service Training.   Organizations are increasingly cognizant of the importance of meeting customer expectations. In addition to establishing philosophies, standards, and systems that support customer service, these companies provide training to give employees the skills they need to meet and exceed customer expectations. The customer service training program at Federal Express provides an example of an effective program. See the Issues and Applications feature entitled "Customer Service Training at Federal Express."

▥ The Evaluation Phase

In the evaluation phase of the training process, the effectiveness of the training program is assessed. Effectiveness can be measured in monetary or non-monetary terms. However it's measured, it is important that the criteria by which the training is judged reflect the needs that the training was designed to address. For example, a training program designed to increase workers' efficiency might justifiably be assessed in terms of its effects on productivity or costs, but not in terms of employee satisfaction.

All too often the evaluation phase of the training process is neglected. This is tantamount to making an investment without ever determining if you're receiving an adequate (or any) return on it. Granted, it is sometimes difficult to collect the necessary data and find the time to analyse and interpret training results. But at the very least, companies should estimate the costs and benefits of a training program if they cannot be directly measured. Without such information, the value of training cannot be demonstrated and upper management may feel there is no compelling reason to continue the training effort.

The evaluation process followed by Allied Signal's Garrett Engine Division provides an excellent illustration of how to measure the effectiveness of training. Personnel responsible for training at Garrett Engines assessed the effectiveness of training at the four levels presented in Figure 8–13. At level 1,

trainees rated the course and instructor at the time of training. At level 2, participants were given an after-training test. The results of these tests were compared against scores on a pretest and against the scores achieved by a group of workers who did not go through the training. At level 3, trainees' use of their new skills and knowledge back on the job were compared against the job performance of a control group that had not received training. At level 4, the evaluation team examined the critical issue of whether the training made a real difference to the company's bottom line.

In general, the outcomes of the first three levels of measurement were positive. At level 1, trainees gave high ratings to the course and instructor. The test at level 2 indicated that the performance of employees who had received training was higher than that of the employees who had not. The same result was achieved at level 3. Nonetheless, the big question remained: Did the training have a positive dollar impact on the company?

To answer this question, the Garrett training team measured performance before and after training for both trained and untrained groups of maintenance workers in terms of response time to job requests and job-completion time. It was assumed that if the maintenance teams were responding and completing jobs more quickly, the equipment would be down less time and Garrett Engine Division would save money. The maintenance department had already calculated the cost of equipment downtime, and this figure was used to translate downtime into dollar amounts. As Figure 8–14 shows, the after-training downtime for the

Federal Express
www.fedex.com

Level	Type of Measurement
1	Participants' reaction to the training at the time of the training.
2	Participants' learning of the content of the training.
3	Participants' use of their new skills and knowledge back on the job.
4	Company's return on the training investment.

Figure 8–13 Four Measurement Levels Employed by Garrett Engine Division

SOURCE: Pine, J., & Tingley, J. C. (1993). ROI of soft skills training. *Training*, 30, 55–60. Reprinted with permission from the February 1993 issue of *Training* magazine. Copyright 1993. Lakewood Publications, Minneapolis, MN. All rights reserved. Not for resale.

Figure 8–14 Performance Levels of Training and Control Groups at Garrett Engine Division

SOURCE: Pine, J., & Tingley, J. C. (1993). ROI of soft skills training. *Training*, 30, 55–60. Reprinted with permission from the February 1993 issue of *Training magazine.* Copyright 1993. Lakewood Publications, Minneapolis, MN. All rights reserved. Not for resale.

	Response Time	Completion Time	Total Down Time	Estimated Cost ($US)
Training Group				
Before training	4.8 hours	13.6 hours	18.4 hours	$1,341
After training	4.1 hours	11.7 hours	15.8 hours	$1,156
Control Group[1]				
Before training	4.4 hours	11.6 hours	16.0 hours	$1,165
After training	4.4 hours	11.7 hours	16.1 hours	$1,211

[1]The control group was not trained. The numbers cited here for the control group were compiled before and after the training group underwent training.

training group, at $1,156, was $55 less than that for the control group, at $1,211. This dollar value appears to be the monetary benefit of the training experience. While this may seem like a small amount, it represents the savings *per job,* and the team completed on average 55 jobs per week. The total cost of the team-building training was estimated at $5,355. A monthly return on investment (ROI) calculation using these figures is presented in Figure 8–15. While the training's long-term effectiveness is not yet known, in the short run the training certainly appears to be paying off.

orientation

The process of informing new employees about what is expected of them in the job and the organization and helping them cope with the stresses of transition.

$55 (average savings per job)

×   55 (jobs per week)

×   4 (number of weeks)

= $12,100 (benefits)

− $ 5,355 (cost of training)

_____

= $ 6,745 (net benefits)

$$\frac{6,745}{5,355} = 1.26 = \textbf{126 percent ROI}$$

Figure 8–15 ROI After Four Average Work Weeks at Garrett Engine Division

SOURCE: Pine, J., & Tingley, J. C. (1993). ROI of soft skills training. *Training*, 30, 55–60. Reprinted with permission from the February 1993 issue of *Training* magazine. Copyright 1993. Lakewood Publications, Minneapolis, MN. All rights reserved. Not for resale.

A Special Case: Employee Orientation

It is possible, though difficult to prove, that the most important training opportunity for many organizations occurs when employees start with the firm. At this time managers have the chance to set the tone for new employees through **orientation,** the process of informing new employees about what is expected of them in the job and helping them cope with the stresses of transition. Orientation is an important aspect of the socialization stage of the staffing process discussed in Chapter 5. Perhaps no organization accomplishes orientation quite as effectively as the armed forces. As soon as new recruits step off the bus at the base, they are confronted by the stereotypical "in your face" drill sergeant. The recruits know immediately who is in charge and that only absolute, unquestioning obedience is acceptable.

The point of this example is not to suggest that other organizations copy the armed forces and demand unquestioning obedience from new employees. The relevant "lesson" is that new recruits are informed immediately about what is expected of them, and that this expectation is consistent throughout their career with the armed forces. What other organizations can learn from the armed forces is that the optimal time to establish expectations about appropriate behaviour is right at the beginning of the employee's tenure with the organization. Metropolitan Property and Casualty Insurance Company has taken this lesson to heart with its Focus from the Start program. Figure 8–16 details what this MetLife division does to let new employees know about the company's expectations.[45]

Orientation is important not just for the firm, but also for the new employee. Several studies indicate that starting a new job is a very stressful event for many people.[46] Employees often start a new job around the time that other stressful events are occurring in their lives: loss of previous job, marriage, or moving into a new area. One important function of orientation is to provide the new workers with the tools to manage and control their own levels of stress. John Wanous sug-

Metropolitan Property and Casualty Insurance Company's Focus from the Start Program combines several elements to provide a high level of support to the new employee during his or her first six to nine months with the company. The key components of this intensive orientation program are:

- **Supervisor's role.** A four-page guide is given to each new employee's supervisor; it may be individualized for each employee. The guide includes topics for dialogue and a discussion of expectations, and encourages the supervisor to provide ongoing feedback to support the employee's adjustment and shorten the learning curve.

- **Mentor's role.** Each employee is assigned a mentor—a co-worker selected by the supervisor.

- **Partnership of peers.** The program sensitizes all employees to the needs of new associates by providing their co-workers with "A Guide for Peers."

- **Self-development.** The employee is responsible for working through an employee Orientation Workbook, which includes self-paced activities, discussion topics for the employee to pursue, a list of educational programs, and a six-month planner.

- **Feedback.** The system is intended to encourage ongoing informal dialogue and feedback. During the third month on the job, the employee completes a feedback form and meets with the supervisor.

- **Videos.** The new employee views two videos: Looking Back to See Ahead (a history of the parent company, MetLife) and Focus from the Start (which highlights teamwork and creativity).

- **Vision.** Each new employee receives a copy of the company vision statement, which discusses mission, philosophy, and goals.

- **Values.** Each new employee receives an employee handbook that covers key corporate policies and core values.

Figure 8–16 Orientation Program at Metropolitan Property and Casualty Insurance Company

SOURCE: Adapted from McCarthy, J. P. (1992, September). Focus from the start. *HR Magazine*, 77–83. Reprinted with the permission of HRMagazine (formerly *Personnel Administrator*). Published by the Society for Human Resource Management, Alexandria, VA.

gests that companies use an orientation approach referred to as Realistic Orientation Programs for new Employee Stress, or *ROPES*.[47] (The acronym is easy to remember because the program is applicable to employees who are "learning the ropes.") A good ROPES program does all of the following:

◆ *Provides realistic information.* Orientation should include realistic information about the job and the organization. While sugar-coated information may postpone stress for a little while, the stress will be magnified later on when employees' expectations are not met.

◆ *Gives general support and reassurance.* The orientation program should let new employees know that the stress they are experiencing is normal. Also, it should provide managers with training in how to give support to their new employees.

◆ *Demonstrates coping skills.* As part of an orientation program, new employees should be trained to cope with the stresses of the new job. For instance, the training situation might include a role-play in which a new employee asks his or her new manager for advice and guidance. Or the trainer might describe a stressful event and demonstrate by "thinking out loud" how new employees can control the stress by managing their own thoughts. In this type of training practice, called *behaviour modelling,* the trainees model, or copy, the behaviour demonstrated by the trainer.

◆ *Identifies specific potential stressors.* The organization should try to identify specific stressors that new employees might face. For instance, Texas Instruments found that its current employees tended to initiate new employees by telling them exaggerated horror stories from the company's past. To counteract this influence, the company included a segment warning of this behaviour in its new-employee orientation.

The ROPES approach to orientation helps new employees cope with the transition to a new job and reduces turnover, which saves the company both time and money.[48] We discuss more techniques for reducing employees' stress levels in Chapter 16.

Summary and Conclusions

Training versus Development. Though training and development often go hand in hand, the terms are not synonymous. Training typically focusses on providing employees with specific skills and helping them correct deficiencies in their performance. Development is an effort to provide employees with the abilities that the organization will need in the future.

Challenges in Training. Before embarking on a training program, managers must answer several important questions: (1) Is training the solution to the problem? (2) Are the goals of training clear and realistic? (3) Is training a good investment? and (4) Will the training work?

Managing the Training Process. The training process consists of three phases: assessment, development and conduct of training, and evaluation. In the assessment phase, organizational, task, and personal needs are identified and the goals of training are clarified. Several options are available during the training phase. Training can take place either on the job or off the job, and can be delivered through a variety of techniques (slides and videotapes, computers, simulations, virtual reality, and classroom instruction). The most appropriate type of training (for example, skills, retraining, cross-functional, team, creativity, or literacy) should be chosen to achieve the stated objectives. In the evaluation phase, the costs and benefits of the training program should be assessed to determine its effectiveness.

A Special Case: Employee Orientation. Organizations should pay particular attention to orientation, or informing new employees about what is expected of them in the job and the organization and helping them cope with the inevitable stresses of transition. The ROPES method of orientation can help companies orient employees successfully.

Key Terms and Concepts

apprenticeships, 239
basic skills, 250
behaviour modelling, 255
brainstorming, 250
computer-assisted instruction (CAI), 241
concurrent engineering (CE), 247
cross-functional training, 247
development, 233
development and conduct phase, 236

evaluation phase, 236
functional literacy, 250
general literacy, 250
internships, 240
job aids, 246
literacy, 250
needs assessment phase, 236
on-the-job training, 239
orientation, 254

organizational analysis, 237
peer trainers, 247
person analysis, 237
retraining, 247
ROPES, 255
simulation, 242
task analysis, 237
training, 233
virtual reality (VR), 243

Discussion Questions

1. Performance problems seem all too common in your workplace. People don't seem to be putting forth the needed effort, and interpersonal conflict on work teams seems to be a constant. Is training the answer? If so, what kind of training should be done? What other actions might be appropriate?

2. How effective do you think training can be in raising employee motivation?

3. An HR manager recalls a longtime employee who came to her in tears because she had heard a rumour that workers like her would soon be required to use new equipment with a video screen that provided information in text form. The worker knew her inability to read would be discovered and feared she would lose her job. Many workers who are illiterate would not be so forthright — partly out of embarrassment, partly out of fear. Another HR manager notes, "They will ask for directions many times, even though the instruction manual is alongside their machine. ... Some workers always seem to be having problems with their eyesight or their glasses. ... The truth is that they simply cannot read." How would you go about identifying workers who should receive literacy training? Discuss the differences between general illiteracy and functional illiteracy and how you would decide which of these issues a training program should address.

4. How important is it that the effectiveness of a training program be measured in dollar terms? Why is it important to measure training effectiveness in the first place?

5. Some elements within the labour movement oppose many of the new training programs auto companies are using to develop teamwork and increase productivity. These workers say that cross-training and job rotation are management tricks for getting more out of workers without raising their wages and are ways of making workers interchangeable. How would you design a cross-functional training program that counters these claims? Explain the benefits and disadvantages of cross-training for both workers and their employers.

6. Simuflite, an aviation training company, expected to whip the competition with FasTrak, its computer-based training (CBT) curriculum for corporate pilots. Instead, the new venture sent Simuflite into a nose dive. In traditional ground-school training, pilots ask questions and learn from "war stories" told by classmates and instructors. With FasTrak, they sat in front of a computer for hours absorbing information. Their only interaction was in tapping the computer screen to provide answers to questions, and that novelty wore off very quickly. Pilots grew bored with the CBT ground school, and, after a couple of visits, voted with their feet. What does Simuflite's experience suggest about the limitations of interactive media and CBT? In what situations is CBT most likely to be beneficial to trainees?

7. According to one survey, trainees list the following as some of the attributes of a successful trainer: knowledge of the subject, adaptability, sincerity, and a sense of humour. What other attributes do you think trainers need to be successful in a training situation?

Check out our Companion Website at: **www.prenticehall.ca/gomez** for a selection of self-study questions, key terms and concepts, updated Weblinks to related Internet sites, newsgroups, CBC video updates, and more.

MiniCase 1 ⟫ *Team Training at Coca-Cola*
Keeping a Classic on Top

For a long time, the corporate culture at Coca-Cola was largely driven by individualistic values. But today Coke is committed to shifting its culture toward a team orientation. The team training process developed at Coke's Syrup Operation is a good example of an effective approach to developing team skills simultaneously with other important job-related skills.

The syrup plant trains its employees in three skill areas: technical job skills, interpersonal skills, and team-action skills.

♦ The technical job skills training consists of training in the job-related knowledge and skills trainees need to be good performers. In addition, Coca-Cola encourages its associates to complete "four-deep training." Four-deep training means learning at least four different jobs. This depth of technical training provides flexibility and the ability to cover tasks when people are absent.

♦ Interpersonal skills training focuses on listening skills, handling conflict, and influencing and negotiating with internal and external customers. Trainees need these skills to be effective team members.

♦ Team-action skills training addresses such skills as team leadership, meeting management, team member roles and responsibilities, group dynamics, and problem solving. Team members need these skills to work together effectively.

The team focus seems to be working quite well at the syrup plant. Associates have participated in thousands of hours of training, and the majority have received training in areas outside their normal work duties. Productivity has increased. Employees are satisfied because they are finding that the team training gives them skills that widen their career choices.

Discussion Questions

1. Of the three categories of training at the syrup plant, do you think one is more important than the others? Why or why not?

2. Coca-Cola had to overcome an individualistic culture. How can resistance to a team orientation be reduced? What steps would you take to make sure teams become recognized as the best way of doing things? How can training help here?

SOURCE: Phillips, S.N. (1996). Team training puts fizz in Coke plant's future. *Personnel Journal*, 75, 87–92.

MiniCase 2   *Partners International:*
"Train Thy Neighbour"

Small companies face a common challenge: how to train employees without a training budget. After installing a new computer system for its 50 employees, Partners International, a small non-profit organization that provides counselling services for Protestant churches, found a way to get the right training to the right people without additional expense:

> Installing the system was one thing; using it effectively was another. Very few people knew how to operate a computer-based information system. Partners International got the equipment for a bargain, but the vendor contract didn't include much training. If people couldn't use the system, it obviously would be no bargain at all.
>
> As support services manager, [Diane] Mundy was responsible for training — though she had no previous experience in either computer systems or training. Fortunately, she had a few things going for her: a teachable spirit, a genuine interest in helping people succeed and the good sense to trust others with responsibility. ...
>
> "Before the computer system was installed," Mundy says, "I recruited a few key staff people to learn the system with me. At first we learned the basics and took all the training the vendor offered. When that was exhausted, we participated in training seminars outside the organization. Then the money ran out, so we continued learning through self-teaching and by collaborating on problems as they

arose." To gain the expertise the organization needed without waiting for everyone to keep up, Mundy assigned each staff member to learn a special application. In this way, every major functional area of the organization developed its own in-house expert. ... The purpose of involving those key staff members from the outset was, of course, to develop a team of amateur trainers. Through them every computer user in the organization had access to timely, well-informed help.

Discussion Questions

1. In Partners International's OJT of computer users there were no scheduled classes and no instructional materials. The computer manuals served as textbooks and the work to be done as the course outline. What do you think are the potential benefits and drawbacks of this type of approach?

2. Partners International is a small company without a training department. Do you think its unstructured approach to peer training could work in a larger company with, say, 500 employees? Why or why not?

SOURCE: Adapted from Rickett, D. (1993, February). Peer training: Not just a low-budget answer. *Training,* 70–72. Reprinted with permission from the February 1993 issue of *Training* magazine. Copyright 1993. Lakewood Publications, Minneapolis, MN. All rights reserved. Not for resale.

Case 1

Rough Edges at Central Lumber

Central Lumber Company is a retail lumber and home improvement operation that caters to both contractors and do-it-yourselfers. The company has outlets across the country, with each outlet under the direction of a general manager. One of the largest outlets, Lakeside Central, is located on the outskirts of a rapidly growing city and employs 22 salespeople. Head office wants to improve customer service and its outlets' sales performance, and intends to use Lakeside Central as a model operation.

Given these aspirations, Central's regional manager, Ann Henry, has been instructed to assess the current situation at Lakeside Central. To scope the place out, Ann sent some of her employees to Lakeside Central. These "spotters" were to pose as customers and provide her with reports on what they observed and experienced.

The reports did not make Ann happy. A central complaint was the salespeople's behaviour. They seemed to treat contractors much better than they treated do-it-yourselfers. Several of the spotters saw salespeople leave the service counter to carry on extended conversations with people who appeared to be their personal friends. In addition, salespeople were several times heard using crude and vulgar language in front of customers and displayed a noticeable disdain for organizational procedures.

Ann summarized these problems in a memo and sent it to Les Giacomo, Lakeside Central's general manager, along with a description of headquarters' plans for the operation. Shortly after, she paid a personal visit to Lakeside Central.

"Listen, Les," she said, "this is a second-rate operation and headquarters wants to move it up to world class. Frankly, I doubt that can be done with your current work force. I think you should seriously consider getting rid of most of your salespeople and bringing in higher quality."

"Oh, come on," responded Les. "You know that these guys know their stuff. They're just a little rough around the edges — same as the sales staff at all our outlets. It comes with the lumber territory. Besides, I could hire a new set of salespeople who have great manners but don't know the difference between a two-by-four and a one-by-two. Then where would we be?"

Ann knew Les was right. Nonetheless, something had to be done about the sales force's attitude toward customer service. "That may be true, Les, but we can't capitalize on the do-it-yourself market until we turn around the behaviour of our people. Lakeside Central isn't going to be a model of customer service and sales performance until we smooth out those rough edges. How you do it is up to you. Just do it! I'll check back with you in three months."

➤

Les was worried about the ultimatum. His salespeople weren't perfect, but they knew the lumber business, and some of them had been with the company for more than 10 years. What could he do?

Critical Thinking Questions

1. Do you think Lakeside Central's problem should be solved through training or replacement? Should an assessment phase be carried out? Why?
2. Describe the kind of training you think would be effective in this situation. How would you go about developing such a training program for the sales staff?

3. What criteria could be used to determine the effectiveness of a new training program at Lakeside Central?

Cooperative Learning Exercises

4. With your partner or group, identify the *first* thing you would do in trying to develop a training program for Lakeside Central. What objectives do you think the training should have? Share these ideas with your partner or team and compile a composite list of objectives. Hand in the list at the end of class.
5. What types of location and presentation options could be used for a training program at Lakeside Central? Brainstorm the possibilities with your partner or team and present your best idea to the class.

Case 2

Virtual Teams: A Special Case for Team Training?

Pulling together a diverse group of people from various functional and geographic areas sounds like the beginning of a great "virtual team." Indeed, many organizations are finding that much of their teamwork is taking place through telephone, fax, and computer connections, not through face-to-face contact. There is concern, however, over how to get everyone working together compatibly and productively because electronic communications may not always be efficient. Differences in time zones, telephone tag, and different work styles can all be sources of frustration to team members—especially when these people have never met face-to-face.

Most companies believe that a crucial step in making a geographically dispersed team work is to provide time for initial face-to-face interaction among team members. However, there is great variance across organizations in terms of how much introductory time is needed. For example, virtual teams at Price Waterhouse usually do not meet physically before being put on projects. In contrast, the research and education operation of Lotus Development Corporation always sponsors at least a one-day videoconference for team members to see and meet one another. Other companies bring remote team members together for weeks or months before they separate and become a virtual team.

Critical Thinking Questions

1. How important do you think initial face-to-face contact is to the effectiveness of virtual teams? What characteristics of an organization or team assignment may make "team bonding" more or less important?
2. What type(s) of training do you think virtual team members should be given? How would you go about delivering this training? What delivery formats would you use?

Cooperative Learning Exercises

3. With your partner or group, brainstorm the skills particularly important for virtual team members. Based on your list, suggest the types of training that would best provide those skills. Share the list and suggested training approaches with the rest of the class.
4. With your partner or group, survey local companies to get a sense of how often they use virtual teams. How do these companies approach bonding and training of virtual teams? Report your findings to the class.

SOURCE: Geber, B. (1995). Virtual teams. *Training*, 32, 36–40.

Developing Careers

After reading this chapter, you should be able to deal more effectively with the following challenges:

1 Establish a sound process for developing your employees' careers.

2 Understand how to develop your own career.

3 Identify the negative aspects of an overemphasis on career development and the importance of dual-career issues in career development.

4 Understand the importance of dual careers in career development.

5 Develop a skills inventory and a career path.

6 Establish an organizational culture that supports career development.

For most employees, career development is a priority—understandably so, because salaries increase as one climbs the corporate ladder. Progressive companies sponsor active career development programs for their employees, but in today's competitive environment workers must take responsibility for their own career advancement.

Steve, a technician at GCX for the past six years, was once an excellent performer. The first few years on the job, he was very happy to be working at GCX. Over the past couple of years, however, he has grown increasingly frustrated and disillusioned because he expected to move up in the company and it isn't happening.

When his department supervisor left the company last year, Steve thought that he would be promoted into the position. He told Natalie, the unit manager, of his interest in the management position, and she assured him that he would be given every consideration. The next thing Steve knew, the job was given to someone from outside the company.

Steve was disappointed and more than a little angry, and the lack of an explanation didn't help matters. He didn't understand why he had been passed over. He had consistently been a top performer in the department. He knew the technical end of the business as well as anyone, and he always achieved his performance objectives. What did he have to do to get into management?

Steve's disillusionment has been taking a toll on his job performance. At one time he couldn't understand those of his co-workers who simply showed up and did the minimum necessary to get their paycheque. But now he identifies with them! Why should he feel committed and loyal to a company that doesn't seem to care about his aspirations? If good performance doesn't help you move ahead, then what does?

After a couple of weeks of quietly seething, Steve decided to ask Natalie point blank why he had not gotten the supervisor's job and how he could increase his chances of promotion into a management position. Natalie seemed quite surprised at Steve's eagerness to be promoted. She told him that she had believed his interest in the supervisory position hadn't been very strong and that an outsider had been given the job simply because he had better credentials. She advised Steve that the best thing to do is to keep trying and that, sooner or later, something would open up.

While his meeting with Natalie had been very cordial, as the day wore on, Steve got angry all over again. He was no closer to understanding what he needed to do to get into management. When he got home that night, he made some phone calls about job openings he had seen advertised. Maybe he could advance faster somewhere else. Even if he didn't leave GCX, he thought, he sure wasn't going to go out of his way for the company anymore. He had some sick days coming and he planned on using them soon.

*　　*　　*

Barbara relaxed at home after a long, interesting two days. Her company, a large telecommunications firm, had sent her to an assessment centre for an evaluation of her strengths and weaknesses as a potential middle-level manager. Currently, she was the head of a sales office located in Winnipeg, and was responsible for the surrounding metropolitan area. She had started with the firm three years ago, after obtaining her bachelor's degree in management from the University of Manitoba.

Barbara had been a nervous wreck before attending the assessment centre because she knew her company leaned heavily on its evaluations when deciding which employees to put on the management fast track. But her experience could not have been better. After a day and a half of various activities, she had met with the consultants who operated the centre. They told her that she definitely had the characteristics her company was looking for in a future manager. She had a few weak areas—most notably, confidence in pushing her ideas in the face of opposition—but she already knew this and was working on overcoming her timidity. They told her that the report she received would also be given to her boss, as well as to the HR manager responsible for management development activities. She knew that while it might take a year or two for a position to open up, she was on her way up.

HRM on the Web

http://www.careermosaic.com/cm/gateway/

Career Mosaic

The Career Mosaic Web site contains a wealth of career and job information. This site also provides a career resource centre with tips of job hunting and resume writing, and links to major employers and professional trade associations. The gateway part of the career mosaic site provides access to the international career marketplace, relevant for both personal and professional reference.

Steve's experience,

unfortunately, is much more common than Barbara's. Workers often have goals and aspirations for themselves that their organizations do not know about. Whether these goals are reasonable or unrealistic, lack of progress toward them can have a very negative effect on performance.

An active career development program can lead to a win/win scenario for both the worker and the organization. In this chapter we consider the career development process. First, we define and discuss career development. Second, we explore some of the major managerial challenges connected with career development and offer some approaches that can help managers avoid problems in this area. We conclude the chapter by discussing three special issues in career development: managerial development, development through the life cycle, and self-development.

▓ What Is Career Development?

As we noted in the previous chapter, career development is different from training. Career development has a wider focus, longer time frame, and broader scope. The goal of training is improvement in performance; the goal of development is enriched and more capable workers. **Career development** is not a one-shot training program or career-planning workshop. Rather, it is an ongoing organized and formalized effort that recognizes people as a vital organizational resource.[1]

The field of career development is quite young—most career development programs were initiated only in the 1970s—but it has grown rapidly over the last two decades. The companies that have had the most success with career development are those that have integrated it with other HRM programs, such as performance appraisal and training.[2] The following companies are often seen as being exemplary in their career development activities, although they do differ in approach and techniques.

◆ The Bank of Montreal was the first-ranked company in the *Report on Business'* "most respected in human resources" list in 1995. Particularly central to that assessment were the accomplishments of the bank in career development for women. The previous year, BMO became the first non-U.S. company to win the Catalyst Award, presented annually to companies showing progress in the advancement of women.[3]

◆ The North York (Ontario) Board of Education has been cited as one of the 10 best employers for women in Canada, but as one author points out, to be on the "best 10" in terms of human resources means that all employees, male and female, are valued. One of the key ingredients in the Board's strategy is extensive use of mentoring to facilitate careers.[4]

◆ 3M has actively addressed the needs of its employees since the mid-1980s. While the company has historically focussed more on appraisal and HR planning, it is now trying, with its relatively new career resources department, to strike a better balance between organizational and employee needs. This department systematizes and coordinates career development through such programs as supervisor and employee workshops, career counselling, and partner relocations for dual-career couples.[5]

Initially, most organizations instituted career development programs to help meet organizational needs (such as preparing employees for anticipated management openings) rather than to meet the needs of employees.[6] More recently, career development has come to be seen as a means for meeting both organizational and employee needs. Figure 9–1 shows how organizational and individual career needs can be linked to create a successful career development program. Organizations now view career development as a way of preventing job burnout (see Chapter 16), providing career information to employees, improving the quality of employees' work lives, and meeting employment equity goals.[7] This change in emphasis has largely resulted from a combination of competitive pressures (such as downsizing and technological changes) and workers' demands for more opportunities for growth and skill development.[8] This combination has made career development a more difficult endeavour than it used to be. There is no longer a

---

career development

An ongoing and formalized effort that focusses on developing enriched and more capable workers.

Bank of Montreal
www.bmo.com

North York Board of Education
nybe.interlog.com

Organizational Needs

What are the organization's major strategic issues over the next two to three years?

• What are the most critical needs and challenges that the organization will face over the next two to three years?

• What critical skills, knowledge, and experience will be needed to meet these challenges?

• What staffing levels will be required?

• Does the organization have the strength necessary to meet the critical challenges?

Issue:

Are employees developing themselves in a way that links personal effectiveness and satisfaction with the achievement of the organization's strategic objectives?

Individual Career Needs

How do I find career opportunities within the organization that:

• Use my strengths?

• Address my developmental needs?

• Provide challenges?

• Match my interests?

• Match my values?

• Match my personal style?

Figure 9–1 *Career Development System: Linking Organizational Needs with Individual Career Needs*

SOURCE: Gutteridge, T. G., Leibowitz, Z. B., & Shore, J. E. (1993). *Organizational career development: Benchmarks for building a world-class workforce.* San Francisco: Jossey-Bass.

strict hierarchy of jobs from which a career path can easily be constructed. Career development today involves workers' active participation in thinking through the possible directions their careers can take.

An organization must make career development a key business strategy if it intends to survive in an increasingly competitive and global business environment.[9] In the information age, companies will compete more on their workers' knowledge, skill, and innovation levels than on the basis of labour costs or manufacturing capacity.[10] Because career development plays a central role in ensuring a competitive work force, it cannot be a low-priority program offered only in good economic times.

■ Challenges in Career Development

While most businesspeople today agree that their organizations should invest in career development, it is not always clear exactly what form this investment should take. Before putting a career development program in place, management needs to consider three major challenges.

■ Who Will Be Responsible?

The first challenge is deciding who will ultimately be responsible for career development activities. In traditional, bureaucratic organizations, development was seen as something that was done "for" individual employees. For instance, the organization might have an assessment centre to identify employees who have the characteristics necessary to hold middle- and upper-management positions. Once identified, these individuals would be groomed through a variety of programs: special-project assignments, positions in foreign divisions, executive training programs, and so on. The individual employee, while certainly not kept in the dark about the company's plans, would not actively participate in the development decisions.

In contrast, many modern organizations have concluded that employees have to take an active role in planning and implementing their own personal development plans. The mergers, acquisitions, and downsizings of the late 1980s and 1990s have led to layoffs in managerial ranks and the realization among managers that they cannot depend on their employers to plan their careers for them. Added to this economic turmoil is the empowerment movement, which shifts down responsibility for decisions in organizations. Both of these trends have led companies to encourage their employees to take responsibility for their own development. We will look at strategies for personal development at the end of this chapter.

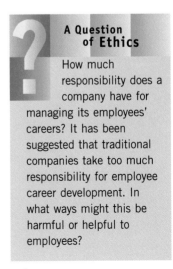

A Question of Ethics

How much responsibility does a company have for managing its employees' careers? It has been suggested that traditional companies take too much responsibility for employee career development. In what ways might this be harmful or helpful to employees?

BP Amoco
www.bpamoco.com

One company known for encouraging employees to develop their own careers is British Petroleum Exploration (BPX), the arm of British Petroleum that finds and develops oil and gas reserves.[11] BPX provides its employees with a personal development program that they can use to improve their skills, performance, and job satisfaction. Employees go through five phases in this do-it-yourself development process:

1. In the first phase, they complete self-assessment exercises that help them determine which skills, interests, and values they already have and which they need to develop.

2. In the second phase, they are encouraged to ask for feedback from their supervisors, peers, subordinates, family, and friends.

3. In the third phase, they establish goals both for their current jobs and for future positions. Employees may decide to improve their performance in their present job, take on new responsibilities, do something to enhance their core skills, or volunteer for lateral moves. They turn this blueprint into a real structure by specifying development and improvement actions, setting target dates for completing these actions, and identifying the resources required to complete them.

4. In the fourth phase of the do-it-yourself process, employees and supervisors agree on assessments, goals, and action plans. Together, they do a "reality check," asking such questions as: How can the employee reach this goal within BPX? and What job qualifications does the employee need to meet?

5. The process doesn't end when the employee and supervisor agree on a course of action. Personal development plans are updated as employees increase their skills and knowledge, as they complete items on their action plans, or as business needs change.[12]

It is probably a mistake for companies to take the employee responsibility perspective too far, though. Giving employees total responsibility for managing their own careers can create problems in today's flatter organizations, where opportunities to move up through a hierarchy of jobs are far fewer than in traditional bureaucratic organizations. Employees need at least general guidance regarding the steps they can take to develop their careers, both within and outside the company.

How Much Emphasis Is Appropriate?

So far, we have presented career development as a positive way for companies to invest in their human resources. However, too great an emphasis on career enhancement can be detrimental to organizational effectiveness.[13] Employees with an extreme career orientation can become more concerned about their image than their performance.

It is difficult to pinpoint where an employee's healthy concern for his or her career becomes excessive. However, there are certain warning signs that managers should be on the lookout for:

◆ Is the employee more interested in capitalizing on opportunities for advancement than in maintaining adequate performance?

◆ Does the employee devote more attention to managing the impressions that he or she makes on others than to reality?

◆ Does the employee emphasize networking, flattery, and being seen at social functions over job performance? In the short run, people who engage in these tactics often enjoy advancement. However, sooner or later they run into workplace duties or issues they are not equipped to deal with and that cannot be resolved with impression-management tactics.

Managers should also be aware that a career development program can have serious side effects—including employee dissatisfaction, poor performance, and turnover—if it fosters unrealistic expectations for advancement.

How Will the Needs of a Diverse Work Force Be Met?

To meet the career development needs of today's diverse work force, companies need to break down the barriers that some employees face in achieving advancement. Both anecdotal evidence and systematic studies have established that various groups within the work force are underrepresented not only in terms of the numbers who reach executive positions, but also in terms of the numbers who move into management or directorships. Women, visible minorities, aboriginal people, and people with disabilities are the focus of federal employment equity legislation because they are acknowledged to be the groups most likely to encounter a "glass ceiling" in their career. Although such frustrations are rarely the result of a deliberate management policy, the informal mechanisms such as networking, mentoring, and participation in ad hoc committees often exclude such employees. Human resource policies that tend to reinforce the barriers for women, visible minorities and others include word-of-mouth recruitment, failure to use training and other initiatives that sensitize managers to the problem, and a premature determination of who are high-potential employees.[14]

Because the barriers to advancement of women and minorities tend not to be obvious, they are difficult to identify and remove. Perhaps the best course a company can take to ensure that these groups have a fair shot at managerial and executive positions is to design a broad-based approach to employee development that is anchored in education and training. For instance, in an industry long dominated by men, the accounting firm Deloitte and Touche launched a long-term initiative intended to lower the rate of turnover among female managers and to encourage the promotion of more women to partnership ranks. The initiative, prompted by the company's Task Force on the Retention and Recruitment of Women, features companywide training in workplace gender dynamics along with structured career planning for women, succession planning, networking opportunities, and family-friendly work options.[15]

Another employee group that may need special consideration is **dual-career couples.** When both members of a couple have occupational responsibilities and career issues at stake, personal lives can complicate and become intertwined with occupational lives. A career opportunity for one member that demands making a geographic move can produce a crisis for both the couple and their organizations. Rather than waiting until they reach such a crisis point to resolve competing career issues, it would be better for the couple to plan their careers and discuss how they will proceed if certain options become available. This approach also reduces the possibility of abrupt personnel losses for organizations.

The most common organizational approaches to dealing with the needs of dual-career couples are flexible work schedules and telecommuting (both discussed in Chapter 4) and the offering of child care services (see Chapter 12). These practices are not prevalent, but they are increasing.

Some companies have also begun counselling couples in career management. These proactive programs, which involve both the employee and his or her spouse or significant other, are usually reserved for executives and others who are considered key personnel in the organization.[16] First, each partner individually comes up with his or her goals and action plans. Then the partners are brought together to share their agendas and work through any conflicts. Professional counsellors offer possible solutions and alternatives to the couple as they go through the process.[17] The result of the process—a joint career plan—is then provided to the organization. The employee and his or her partner benefit from this approach by formulating a mutually agreeable plan, and the organization benefits by increasing the probability of retaining key employees. While career management for couples is fairly new and costly, it is a very promising approach whose use is expected to increase. Indeed, recent findings underscore the importance and potential benefits of dual-career counselling and spousal support services.[18] The levels of work stress and job satisfaction experienced by dual-career workers are significantly influenced by the spouse's level of support; over the long term, lack of spousal support can have a negative effect on job performance and can even cause a worker to leave his or her job.

Deloitte and Touche
www.deloitte.com/cons_g.htm

dual-career couple
A couple whose members both have occupational responsibilities and career issues at stake.

▇Building Management Skills: Meeting the Challenges of Effective Development

Creating a development program will almost always consist of three phases: the assessment phase, the direction phase, and the development phase (Figure 9–2). Although presented separately in Figure 9–2, the phases of development often blend together in a real-life program.

▇The Assessment Phase

The *assessment phase* of career development involves activities ranging from self-assessment to organizationally provided assessment. The goal of assessment, whether performed by employees or by the organization, is to identify employees' strengths and weaknesses. This kind of clarification helps employees (1) to choose a career that is realistically obtainable and a good fit and (2) to determine the weaknesses they need to overcome to achieve their career goals. Figure 9–3 lists some tools that are commonly used for self-assessment and for organizational assessment.

Self-Assessment.   Self-assessment is increasingly important for companies like BPX that want to empower their employees to take control of their careers. The major tools used for self-assessment are workbooks and workshops.

Career workbooks have been very popular for decades. Generic workbooks were commonly used by organizations in the 1970s, but tailored workbooks gained in popularity in the 1980s.[19] In addition to the exercises included in a generic career workbook, tailored workbooks might contain a statement of the organization's policies and procedures regarding career issues as well as descriptions of the career paths and options available in the organization.

Career-planning workshops, which may be led either by the company's own HR department or by an external provider such as a consulting firm or local university, give employees the opportunity to obtain more information about career options in the organization. They may also be used to provide participants

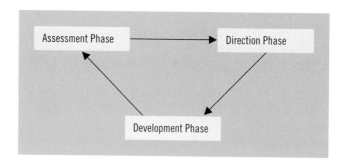

Figure 9–2 The Career Development Process

Self-Assessment	Organizational Assessment
Career workbooks	Assessment centres
Career-planning workshops	Psychological testing
	Performance appraisal
	Promotability forecasts
	Succession planning

Figure 9–3 Common Assessment Tools

with useful feedback on their career aspirations and strategy. Participation in most work-shops is voluntary, and some organizations hold these workshops on company time to demonstrate their commitment to their work force.

Whether done through workbooks or workshops, self-assessment usually involves doing skills assessment exercises, completing an interests inventory, and clarifying values.[20]

◆ As their name implies, *skills assessment exercises* are designed to identify the skills that an employee has exhibited. For example, a workbook exercise might ask the employee to compile a brief list of his or her accomplishments. Once the employee has generated a set of, say, five accomplishments, he or she must then identify the skills involved in making each accomplishment a reality. In a workshop situation, people might share their accomplishments in a group discussion, and then the entire group might help identify the skills underlying the accomplishments.

Another skills assessment exercise presents employees with a list of skills they must rate on two dimensions: their level of proficiency at that skill and the degree to which they enjoy using it. A total score is then generated for each skill area—for example, by multiplying the proficiency by the preference rating. Figure 9–4 shows an example of this approach to skills assessment. Scores below 6 indicate areas of weakness or dislike, while scores of 6 or above indicate areas of strength. The pattern of scores can guide employees regarding the type of career for which they are best suited.

◆ An *interest inventory* is a measure of a person's occupational interests. Numerous off-the-shelf inventories can give employees insight into what type of career will best fit their interests. One of the best-known of these inventories is the Strong Vocational Interest Inventory.[21] The interest inventory asks people to indicate how strong or weak an interest they have in such activities as dealing with very old people, making a speech, and raising money for charity. Responses to items on the inventory are then scored to identify the occupations in which the individual has the same interests as the professionals employed in those fields.

Use the scales below to rate yourself on each of the following skills. Rate each skill area both for your level of proficiency and for your preference.

Proficiency:

1	2	3
Still learning	OK— competent	Proficient

Preference:

1	2	3
Don't like to use this skill	OK— Don't particularly like or dislike using this skill	Really enjoy using this skill

Skill Area	Proficiency	×	Preference	=	Score
1. Problem solving	_____		_____		_____
2. Team presentation	_____		_____		_____
3. Leadership	_____		_____		_____
4. Inventory	_____		_____		_____
5. Negotiation	_____		_____		_____
6. Conflict management	_____		_____		_____
7. Scheduling	_____		_____		_____
8. Delegation	_____		_____		_____
9. Participative management	_____		_____		_____
10. Feedback	_____		_____		_____
11. Planning	_____		_____		_____
12. Computer	_____		_____		_____

Figure 9–4 Sample Skills Assessment Exercise

◆ *Values clarification* involves prioritizing personal values. The typical values clarification exercise presents employees with a list of values and asks them to rate how important each value is to them. For example, employees may be asked to prioritize security, power, money, and family in their lives. Knowing their priority values can help employees make satisfying career choices.

Organizational Assessment.   Some of the tools traditionally used by organizations in selection (see Chapter 5) are also valuable for career development. Among these are assessment centres, psychological testing, performance appraisal, promotability forecasts, and succession planning.

◆ *Assessment centres* are situational exercises—such as interviews, in-basket exercises, and business games—that can be used to identify managerial talent. They are most commonly used as a way of screening and evaluating current employees being considered for management positions, although some employers use them to screen external applicants, as well. The process is sufficiently elaborate that generally only larger employers can run in-house programs. However, there are consultants that can provide assessment centre screening for employers, where in-house programs are not available. Assessment centres can also provide participants with feedback on their strengths and weaknesses as uncovered in the exercises. The results thus can assist both the employer with selection and employees who are interested in identifying their own potential and also the areas in which they need to develop greater competence.

◆ Some organizations also use *psychological testing* to help employees better understand their skills and interests. Tests that measure personality and attitudes, as well as interest inventories, fall into this category.[22]

◆ Performance appraisal is another source of valuable career development information. Unfortunately, appraisals are frequently limited to assessment of past performance rather than oriented toward planning future performance improvements and directions. Future-oriented performance appraisal can give employees important insights into their strengths, their weaknesses, and the career paths available to them.

promotability forecast

A career development activity in which judgements are made by managers regarding the advancement potential of subordinates.

◆ **Promotability forecasts** are judgements made by managers regarding the advancement potential of their subordinates. These forecasts allow the organization to identify people who appear to have a high advancement potential.[23] The high-potential employees are then given developmental experiences, such as attending an executive training seminar, to help them achieve their advancement potential.

For example, a major telecommunications company has launched a companywide computerized program to track high-potential managers and equip them with the right experiences to face business challenges in the years ahead. The emphasis in this Leadership Continuity Program (LCP) is on development, not promotion in the near term. Participants accept assignments that will prepare them for increased responsibilities. Candidates are selected for LCP on the basis of three criteria: sustained strong performance, overall high standing in relation to peers, and a demonstrated potential to perform at least four salary levels above their current level.[24]

succession planning

A career development activity that focusses on preparing people to fill executive positions.

◆ **Succession planning** focuses on preparing people to fill executive positions. Formally, succession planning means examining development needs given a firm's strategic plans. Informally, it means high-level managers identifying and developing their own replacements.[25] Most succession planning is informal. The employees identified as having upper-management potential may then be given developmental experiences that will help prepare them for the executive ranks, such as workshops on the organization's values and mission. Succession planning can be particularly challenging when the business is closely held by an individual or a family. Although the formula for managing succession is not easily summarized, the absence of an adequate arrangement can lead to turmoil, such as that experienced by McCain's (a family-held company) in the early 1990s. Companies as diverse as CanWest Communications, Vickers and Benson Advertising (in Toronto), as well as the widely held Imperial Oil, are quite deliberate both in growing and in keeping the management talent that they need for long-term viability, a practice that increasingly will become a necessity rather than an option.[26] Succession planning is one of the trickiest challenges in the area of career development. Organizations have often been accused of discriminating against women and minorities when filling high-level positions. Rather than outright discrimination, it is usually the informality of much succession planning that makes companies unwittingly exclude these groups as candi-

McCain Foods Ltd.
www.mccain.com

dates. Formal succession planning programs, such as those in place at 3M and Westpac Banking Corporation (Australia's largest bank), can make the identification of high-potential employees and replacement candidates a more egalitarian procedure.[27]

What employee characteristics and experiences predict success at the managerial and executive levels? The earliest research was done by researchers at AT&T.[28] For example, one study examined the influence of various educational characteristics on managerial performance two decades later. The study found that the choice of college major and extent of extracurricular activities were significantly related to later management performance. Grades were found to predict managers' overall motivation levels, with grades themselves reflecting more the manager's work ethic than the degree of skill or knowledge obtained in various courses.

A more recent study examined the extent to which demographic, human capital, motivational, and organizational variables predict executive career success.[29] The researchers divided career success into objective (for example, pay level) and subjective (for example, job satisfaction) components. The researchers concluded that educational level, quality and prestige of university, and major were all related to pay levels of a sample of more than 1388 executives. Interestingly, ambition was negatively related to job satisfaction, with more ambitious executives indicating less satisfaction with their current positions.

Personality characteristics are also a determinant of success in higher-level management jobs. For example, one study examined the effects of both personality and cognitive abilities on the current earnings of managers, and concluded that such characteristics as creativity, sociability, self-reliance, and self-control are strongly related to managers' success as indicated by pay level.[30] Thus managers should consider these characteristics as well as level of technical knowledge when preparing their promotability forecasts and conducting succession planning.

In small companies succession planning is crucial since the sudden departure or illness of a key company player can set the business foundering. Yet just as some people shy away from the task of drafting a will for fear of recognizing their own mortality, some small-business owners shy away from succession planning for fear of recognizing that they won't always be in control of their business. Other small-business owners are too caught up in the daily pressures of running a business to plan for the future. In fact, a recent poll of 800 business owners revealed that only about one-fourth of small-business owners have a succession plan, and just half of those owners have formalized the plan by committing it to paper.[31]

In doing succession planning, small-business owners—whether aged 20 or 50—should consider whether they want to keep the business in the family, recruit an outside manager to run it, sell it to a key executive, or put it on the market. At Lavelle Company (a building materials company), founder George Lavelle used these considerations as a starting point for fleshing out a detailed succession plan. He wanted to involve all six of his sons who worked in the business in succession planning, so he took them to a succession program at The Centre for Family Business in Cleveland, Ohio, in 1980, 13 years before he retired in 1993. Shortly after, he also decided to hire and groom an outsider to serve as president when he retired. He made this move because he thought that none of his sons should be pressured to assume the top leadership role before he was ready. Lavelle also avoided the emotional task of choosing which son to appoint as successor. Instead he left the decision up to an executive committee, which includes the new president and several of Lavelle's sons. In praise of his father's deliberate planning, the eldest son acknowledges, "We are probably the envy of other companies in our position."[32]

The Direction Phase

The *direction phase* of career development involves determining the type of career that employees want and the steps they must take to make their career goals a reality. Appropriate direction requires an accurate understanding of one's current position. Unless the direction phase is based on a thorough assessment, the goals and steps

Making Career Development an Organizational Priority

1. Stress commitment to career growth and development in formal communications with employees.

2. Make career development a priority at all levels of the organization, starting at the top.

3. Provide managers with the people skills they need to develop their subordinates.

4. Emphasize that career development is a collaborative effort and that the employee must take primary responsibility for his or her own career.

5. Require managers to meet with their subordinates regularly to review personal career goals and objectives.

6. Ask managers to outline employee achievements and strengths when conducting an appraisal review session.

7. Encourage managers to collaborate with subordinates to develop a career vision.

8. Emphasize that part of the manager's job is helping employees develop career action plans.

9. Encourage employees to take advantage of continuing education and other development activities.

10. Require managers to develop collaborative rather than top-down, control-oriented working relationships with their subordinates.

SOURCE: Adapted from Koonce, R. (1991, January–February). Management development: An investment in people. *Credit Magazine*, 16–19.

identified may be inappropriate. The two major approaches to career direction are individual counselling and various information services.

Individual Career Counselling. *Individual career counselling* refers to one-on-one sessions with the goal of helping employees examine their career aspirations.[33] Topics of discussion might include the employee's current job responsibilities, interests, and career objectives. Although career counselling is frequently conducted by managers or HR staff members, some organizations use professional counsellors.[34] When it is the line manager who conducts the career counselling sessions, the HR department generally monitors the effectiveness of these sessions and provides assistance to the managers in the form of training, suggested counselling formats, and the like.

There are several advantages to having managers conduct career counselling sessions with their employees. First, managers are probably more aware of their employees' strengths and weaknesses than anyone else. Second, knowing that their manager understands their career development concerns can foster an environment of trust and greater employee commitment to the organization.

Unfortunately, simply assigning career counselling responsibility to managers does not guarantee that the task will be carried out carefully. As with performance appraisal and many other important HR activities, managers may treat employee career development simply as a paper-shuffling exercise unless top management signals its strong support for this activity. If managers only go through the motions, there is likely to be a negative impact on employee attitudes, productivity, and profits.

The Manager's Notebook entitled "Making Career Development an Organizational Priority" lists 10 actions that organizations and managers can take to ensure that employees see career development as an important activity. Together, these actions create an organizational culture that places a priority on development. The first step—emphasizing commitment to development in formal communications—can be a refreshing change for employees, many of whom are accustomed to formal communications that deal only with what is expected of them.

Information Services. Information services, as their name suggests, provide information to employees. Determining what to do with this information is largely the employee's responsibility. This approach makes sense given the diversity of interests and aspirations in today's organizations.

The most commonly provided information services are job-posting systems, skills inventories, career paths, and career resource centres.

job-posting system

A system in which an organization announces job openings to all employees on a bulletin board, in a company newsletter, or through a phone recording or computer system.

◆ **Job-posting systems** are a fairly easy and direct way of providing employees with information on job openings. The jobs available in an organization are announced ("posted") on a bulletin board, in a company newsletter, or through a phone recording or computer system. Whatever the media used for the posting, it is important that all employees have access to the list. All postings should include clear descriptions of both the job's specifications and the criteria that will be used to select among the applicants. Such information assists employees in determining whether they are qualified for the position. In addition, information on how the criteria will be applied to fill the position should be supplied. Doing so alleviates employees' fears that selection may be a political process.

Job-posting systems have the advantage of reinforcing the notion that the organization promotes from within.[35] This belief not only motivates employees to maintain and improve their performance but also tends to reduce turnover.

◆ **Skills inventories** are company-maintained records with such information as employees' abilities, skills, knowledge, and education.[36] The company can use this comprehensive, centralized information system to get an overall picture of the training and development needs of its work force as well as to identify existing talent in one department that may be more productively employed in another.

Skills inventories can prove valuable for employees as well. Feedback regarding how they stack up against other employees can encourage them to improve their skills or seek out other positions that better match their current skill levels.

In some cases, skill inventories are compiled within a professional community consisting of many small employers. Career paths are more likely to involve moving from one employer to another. An association devoted to cracking the glass ceiling for women in communications, Canadian Women in Communications, has been formed. Its core technology is a database containing (in 1995) the names and qualifications of more than 350 women a number that increased to over 1300 in 1998,[37] roughly two-thirds of whom are qualified for senior management or directorship positions. It has met with enthusiasm from many in the industry.[38]

◆ **Career paths** provide valuable information to employees regarding the possible directions and career opportunities available in an organization. A career path presents the steps in a possible career and a plausible timetable for accomplishing them. Just as a variety of paths may lead to the same job, so may starting from the same job lead to very different outcomes. Figure 9–5 provides an example of alternative career paths that someone who starts as a busperson in the hotel business might follow. Other optional steps along each of these paths may be possible.

To be realistic, career paths must specify the qualifications necessary to proceed to the next step and the minimum length of time an employee must spend at each step to obtain the necessary experience. This information could be generated by computer.

Figure 9–6 presents examples of two survey forms that might be used to collect career path information. Form A asks employees to indicate how important certain skills are for the performance of their job. The skills included on such a form can be determined by examining job analysis information and by interviewing individual employees. Employee responses can then be used to develop lists of critical and desirable skills for each job in the organization. The abbreviated list of skills in Form A is based on jobs in the hotel industry.

Form B asks employees to judge the extent to which experience in other jobs in the organization is needed to perform their current job adequately. The lowest-level jobs, which still involve the skill requirements uncovered with the use of Form A, would not require previous job experience within the organization. Higher-level or more complex jobs would likely require greater amounts of job experience.

◆ A **career resource centre** is a collection of career development materials such as workbooks, tapes, and texts. These resources might be maintained by the HR department, either in its offices or in an area that is readily accessible to employees. Companies with many locations might publicize the availability of these materials and mail them out on

skills inventory
A company-maintained record of employees' abilities, skills, knowledge, and education.

career path
A chart showing the possible directions and career opportunities available in an organization; it presents the steps in a possible career and a plausible timetable for accomplishing them.

career resource centre
A collection of career development materials such as workbooks, tapes, and texts.

Figure 9–5 Alternative Career Paths for a Hotel Employee
This is a generic example of alternative career paths. Actual career paths should specify a time frame for each job.

Form A: Skill Requirements in the Hospitality Industry (continued)

Instructions: A list of various skills that apply to various jobs is presented below. Use the scale provided to indicate the extent to which each skill is applicable to your current position.

Circle the Most Appropriate Number

Skills	Not applicable	Somewhat desirable/ useful at times	Very desirable but not essential	Critical— could not perform job without it
1. Determine daily/forecasted production and service equipment requirements.	1	2	3	4
2. Clean guest rooms.	1	2	3	4
3. Set up, break down, and change over function rooms.	1	2	3	4
4. Handle security problems.	1	2	3	4
5. Clean public areas/restrooms.	1	2	3	4
6. Assist in menu development.	1	2	3	4
7. Register/preregister guests into hotel.	1	2	3	4
8. Participate in the preparation of sauces, soups, stews, and special dishes.	1	2	3	4
9. Prepare and serve salads, fruit cocktails, fruits, juices, and so on.	1	2	3	4
10. Participate in the rating of meats and other dishes.	1	2	3	4
11. Care for, clean, and distribute laundry items.	1	2	3	4

Form B: Experience Requirements in the Hospitality Industry

Instructions: A list of work experience by job titles is presented below. Use the scale provided to indicate for each item: (a) how important previous experience in this work is for the successful performance of your current job duties; and (b) the amount of experience that constitutes adequate training or exposure so that you are able to function efficiently in your current position.

Circle the Most Appropriate Number

Work Experience	Importance of Requirement			Minimum Experience				
	Not very important	Very desirable but not essential	Critical— could not perform job without it	0–6 months	7–11 months	1–2 years	3–5 years	6+ years
1. Storeroom Clerk: Accurately compute daily food costs by assembling food invoices, totalling food requisitions, taking monthly inventory of food storeroom, and so on.	1	2	3	1	2	3	4	5
2. Liquor Storeroom Steward: Maintain adequate levels of alcoholic beverages and related supplies; properly receive, store, and issue them to user departments.	1	2	3	1	2	3	4	5

(continued)

Figure 9–6 Two Career Path Information Forms

Form B: Experience Requirements in the Hospitality Industry (continued)								

Instructions: A list of work experience by job titles is presented below. Use the scale provided to indicate for each item: (a) how important previous experience in this work is for the successful performance of your current job duties; and (b) the amount of experience that constitutes adequate training or exposure so that you are able to function efficiently in your current position.

Circle the Most Appropriate Number

Work Experience	Importance of Requirement			Minimum Experience				
	Not very important	Very desirable but not essential	Critical— could not perform job without it	0–6 months	7–11 months	1–2 years	3–5 years	6+ years
3. Pantry Worker: Prepare and serve to waiters salads, fruit cocktails, fruit juices, and so on.	1	2	3	1	2	3	4	5
4. Pastry Cook: Prepare mixes for baking cakes, pies, soufflés, and so on.	1	2	3	1	2	3	4	5
5. Short-Order Cook: Prepare short-order foods in assigned restaurant areas.	1	2	3	1	2	3	4	5
6. Sous-Chef: Assist Executive Chef in all areas of kitchen production; directly supervise the operations of the kitchen in his or her absence.	1	2	3	1	2	3	4	5
7. Waiter or Waitress: Take food and beverage orders from customers and serve them in a restaurant or lounge.	1	2	3	1	2	3	4	5
8. Beverage Manager: Supervise and schedule personnel as required and maintain budgeted liquor cost and supplies for the lounge and/or banquet functions.	1	2	3	1	2	3	4	5
9. Assistant Banquet Manager: Assist in the coordination and successful completion of all banquet functions, such as coordinating staffing requirements, ensuring that function room is properly set and tidied, and keeping banquet manager fully informed of all problems or unusual matters.	1	2	3	1	2	3	4	5

a loan basis to employees who express an interest in them. Some colleges and universities maintain career resource centres, and many consulting firms, particularly those specializing in employee outplacement, provide career development materials as well. Career resource centres can help people identify for themselves their strengths and weaknesses, career options, and educational and training opportunities.

■ The Development Phase

Meeting the requirements necessary to move up in an organization can require a great deal of growth and self-improvement. The *development phase,* which involves taking actions to create and increase skills to prepare for future job opportunities, is meant to foster this growth and self-improvement. The most common development programs offered by organizations are mentoring, coaching, job rotation, and tuition assistance.

Manager's Notebook

A Short Course in Mentoring Management

1. Establish a clear set of goals and objectives. Mentoring goals may emphasize vocational or educational outcomes and/or social outcomes such as working with a role model or receiving support.

2. Orient the participants. Discuss the roles, responsibilities, and qualifications of both the mentor and the protégé.

3. Evaluate and match mentor personal characteristics, skills, and goals with the characteristics and needs of the protégés.

4. To increase the immediate effectiveness and subsequent value of a mentoring program, train mentors. Many people have not naturally developed the skills required for being a good mentor and thus require training in interpersonal communication.

5. Allow the mentor-protégé pair to work together on a trial or preparatory basis for a brief period. This gives them the opportunity to get acquainted and resolve logistical problems such as scheduling conflicts. After this trial period, it's important to review the roles, responsibilities, expectations, and goals of the association.

6. Monitor, evaluate, and make adjustments over the duration of the mentoring relationship.

7. Encourage protégé independence. The mentor must guide the protégé to become more and more independent and self-reliant.

SOURCE: Adapted from Newby, T. J., & Heide, A. (1992). The value of mentoring. *Performance Improvement Quarterly*, 5.4, 2–15.

mentoring
A developmentally oriented relationship between senior and junior colleagues or peers that involves advising, role modelling, sharing contacts, and giving general support.

Mentoring.   **Mentoring** is a developmentally oriented relationship between senior and junior colleagues or peers. Mentoring relationships, which can occur at all levels and in all areas of an organization, generally involve advising, role modelling, sharing contacts, and giving general support. Mentoring can be either voluntary and informal or involuntary and formal. Informal mentoring is generally more effective than mentoring done solely as a formal responsibility,[39] though there are situations in which a formal mentoring program may be the better choice.

Mentoring has been found to make a real difference in careers, with executives who were mentored early in their careers tending to make more money at a younger age and more likely to follow a career plan than those who were not mentored. For mentors, particularly those nearing retirement, the mentoring role can offer new challenges and reignite enthusiasm and motivation.

There are, it should be noted, some problems with this kind of development program. Female employees are often reluctant to initiate a relationship with a potential male mentor because such an appeal may be misconstrued as a sexual advance. And with the increasing attention being paid to sexual harassment in the workplace, male managers may be even more hesitant to take on a female protégé. Formal mentoring programs can help counter this reluctance. Formal programs may also offer advantages to visible minority employees.

Successful formal mentoring programs involve much more than simply bringing mentor and protégé together. See the Manager's Notebook entitled "A Short Course in Mentoring Management" for guidelines on how to increase the value of a mentoring program.[40]

While formal mentoring programs are more likely to be found at large companies, some small companies have developed more informal, but equally intensive, mentoring programs. Ed Fu, the owner of a growing computer consulting firm Fu Associates, takes a personal interest in training a select group of talented employees. He calls it "Fu-izing." Each new hire starts out working directly with a mid-level employee. After new hires have been on the job a couple of months, Fu chooses from among them designers to serve on projects for which he is the senior systems analyst.[41]

Coaching.   Employee *coaching* consists of ongoing, sometimes spontaneous, meetings between managers and their employees to discuss each employee's career goals and development. Working with employees to chart and implement their career goals enhances productivity and can spur a manager's own advancement. Then why do so many managers give short shrift to employee coaching? For one thing, in today's flatter organizations managers have more people under their supervision and less time to spend on developing each employee. For another, as we noted earlier, managers tend to view "employee development" as a buzz phrase unless top management clearly and strongly supports it. Finally, most managers are ill-prepared to coach employees and feel uncomfortable in the role.[42]

Coaching need not be the ordeal many managers think it is. The secret is to take advantage of what some HR consultants have called "coachable moments"—opportunities that occur in the midst of ongoing work for valuable, if brief, career counselling. Here are five common cues from employees that can open the door to coachable moments:

1. An employee demonstrates a new skill or interest.

2. An employee seeks feedback.

3. An employee expresses an interest in a change in the organization.

4. An employee is experiencing a poor job fit.

5. An employee mentions a desire for development opportunities.[43]

Job Rotation.   *Job rotation* involves assigning employees to various jobs so that they acquire a wider base of skills. Broadened job experience can give workers more flexibility to choose a career path. And, as we discussed in the previous chapter, employees can gain an even wider and more flexible experience base through cross-functional training.

In addition to offering more career options for the employee, job rotation results in a more broadly trained and skilled work force for the employer. However, job rotation programs have some disadvantages. They do not suit employees who want to maintain a narrow and specialized focus. From the organization's perspective, they can slow down operations as workers learn new skills. While the development benefits of job rotation may be high in the long run, firms should be aware of the intermediate costs.

Tuition Assistance Programs.   Organizations offer *tuition assistance programs* to support their employees' education and development. Tuition and other costs of educational programs (ranging from seminars, workshops, and continuing education programs to degreed programs) may be entirely covered, partially covered, or covered contingent upon adequate performance (such as grades) in the program.

A recent survey of educational reimbursement programs revealed that 43 percent of these plans reimbursed less than 100 percent of tuition. Typically, there is a fixed limit—such as 75 percent of tuition—for all courses. Some companies, however, vary the percentage of tuition funds reimbursed according to the relevance of the course to organizational goals. For instance, a business-book publishing company might encourage its editors to take professional courses related to the business, such as economics and marketing, by reimbursing these courses at 100 percent. However, if editors want to take courses on sign language interpretation, art history, or English literature, the company might reimburse only 50 percent of the tuition.

■ Special Issues in Career Development

We conclude this chapter by examining three special issues related to career development. The first concerns the particular components of a management development program, the second pertains to development issues specific to particular age groups, and the third to the management of your personal career.

■ Management Development

With the urgent need for Canadian companies to become more globally competitive, management development has taken on major importance and undergone a huge shift in emphasis. Historically, companies viewed management development purely as a means of bringing managers up to speed on fundamental management skills such as the basics of finance and marketing and techniques for supervising employees. A former professor comments that this approach is now "as outmoded as rear-wheel-drive V8-engine cars." Today companies are crafting executive education programs intended to teach the more intangible aspects of leadership. They are also using executive education to spur organizational change. For instance, an education program might be designed to transform a traditional organizational culture into one that emphasizes continuous improvement and total quality management.[44]

The general development issues we have already discussed also apply to the special case of management development. However, there are several types of programs

Assessing Management Potential.

Some companies ask outside consultants to evaluate their internal candidates for promotion. Here, psychologists at the Centre for Creative Leadership assess candidates' leadership skills through one-way glass.

that are specifically associated with the development of managers. Management development systems usually incorporate more than one of these programs.

♦ *Company schools.* Some large companies have their own separate "schools" for managers. CIBC, for example, has established its leadership centre in premises originally built as a luxury spa near King City, Ontario, and uses it for residential, management development programs for employees from across Canada. Company schools educate both current and potential managers in the corporate culture, management philosophy and skills, and methods of doing business.

♦ *University-based programs.* Many business schools offer education programs designed specifically for managers and executives. They include executive MBA programs that use innovative scheduling and a tailored curriculum; advanced management courses running two to four weeks (for example, Queen's University, the University of Western Ontario, the Banff School for Advanced Management, the University of British Columbia); postdegree certificate programs such as that offered by York University's Schulich School of Business; and a wide range of short courses on specific topics that are consistent with a just-in-time, focussed approach to training.

♦ *Management training.* We looked at general training programs in Chapter 8. Management training, whether provided in a company school, university business school, or (as is most often the case) a less formal setting, often utilizes special techniques. One such technique is the **case study method,** in which students do in-depth analyses of real-life companies. Another is **role-playing,** in which participants adopt the role of a particular manager placed in a specific situation—for instance, a manager who has to give a negative performance review to an employee. **Management games** are elaborate role-playing exercises in which multiple participants enact a management situation. For instance, the Centre for Creative Leadership conducts the Looking Glass simulation, in which 20 participants "manage" the Looking Glass Company over a three-day period. The participants interact with one another, both face-to-face and by phone, write memos and reports, and make decisions.

case study method

A business school teaching method in which students do in-depth analyses of real-life companies.

role-playing

A management development technique in which participants adopt the role of a particular manager placed in a specific situation.

management games

Elaborate role-playing exercises in which multiple participants enact a management situation.

The Centre for Creative Leadership
www.crl.org

▤ Development Through the Life Cycle

As we discussed in Chapter 4, age is a source of diversity in organizations. Career development programs, like all other human resource initiatives, need to be flexible enough to deal with employees at different stages of life.

Younger Employees.   Younger employees starting their careers have different development needs than do middle-aged employees or employees who are approaching retirement. For instance, the group of approximately 50 million people who are approaching or in their 20s and early 30s—the so-called baby busters— have a different attitude toward work and its significance for their lives than older people do. "The quality of working life as a career objective is far higher on the priority list and is a more important selection criterion than in the past," says Eleanor Haller-Jorden, founder of the Paradigm Group, an international human resources consulting firm. This attitude may stem from the experience of looking for work in a recessionary economy, in which monetary rewards are lower. Also important to baby busters is quality of family life. In a recent survey, 62 percent of the 25- to 35-year-old respondents cited family-related issues as their single most important concern over the next three years.[45]

One Canadian company that has tapped the enthusiasm of a youthful work force is Rocky Mountain Bicycle of Delta, British Columbia. A company that grew from a family bike shop to sales in 1995 of $12 million, Rocky Mountain, with slogans like "total commitment—no compromise," sounds like a success story to rival the fabled development of the Macintosh computer at Apple, where a group of true believers launched a major revolution in the concept of computing. Unfortunately, Rocky Mountain had a close call with financial disaster and required the intervention of someone with management and financial expertise to put the company on solid footing. Youthful energy and commitment needed to be melded with the discipline of solid management to sustain this company, which has gained stability and sustained quality and received a nod from *Mountain Bike Magazine* in 1995 for its "mountain bike of the year."[46]

Whether or not a company can offer these kinds of policies, managers would do well to follow certain guidelines in supervising and developing younger workers:

◆ Do not treat younger employees as children. Instead, empower them and request them to contribute to the organization as adults. At exemplary companies, for instance, younger employees are involved in decision making, allowed to develop and implement new ideas, and encouraged to take calculated risks.

◆ Spend a lot of time early on with younger employees, keeping them informed, including them in meetings, taking them out to lunch, and generally showing them the ropes. Making younger workers participants in the company's mission can increase loyalty in an age group in which job hopping is the norm.

◆ Don't assume that a baby buster has the same values or point of view as older workers. For example, traditionalists—members of the World War II generation—are very loyal to their jobs and see work as a key part of their identities. The same goes for the baby boom generation (those born between 1946 and 1964), many of whom became workaholics in the 1980s.

Middle-Aged Employees.   While younger employees are learning the ropes and trying on new experiences for size, many baby boomers are feeling stymied in their careers. With the elimination of whole layers of management in many companies in the 1980s and 1990s, employees caught between youth and old age are facing a new type of midlife crisis. These midlifers may be competing without much hope against 30 other employees for the same promotion, but fear to leave the company because of the tight job market. This unanticipated and unwanted levelling of careers is known as **plateauing.** A typical reaction to this dilemma is that of a 46-year-old geologist who had spent 11 years with a major Alberta oil company when the industry suddenly collapsed. Instructed to fire half of her close-knit team of 12 geologists, she began to fear getting the axe herself. In the weak oil market job hopping wasn't an option, and she recalls, "I felt trapped. I would come home and go to bed earlier and earlier so I wouldn't have to think about my job." Eventually, this woman adopted a more philosophical "what will be, will be" attitude.[47]

Some companies are taking measures to reinvigorate their diminished and demoralized ranks of midlife management employees. These measures include additional training, lateral moves, sabbaticals, and compensation based on people's contribution and skills rather than on the job they hold. We discuss the new types of compensation plans in Chapters 10 and 11, but here's how one organization offers its employees a change of pace:

After 13 years of paperwork and writing proposals in the equal employment opportunity and customer billing offices at Alagasco, a utility company, Thomas L. Wilder Jr. was looking for a change. ... Wilder ... traded his suit and tie for company overalls and a hard-hat. For six months he worked on Alagasco's construction crew, repairing gas lines

David versus Goliath.

Jennifer Wiebe and Tessa Lowinger, two teenagers from Squamish, B.C., disliked the working conditions of the McDonald's where they worked and they decided to do something about it. In doing so, they made history by successfully organizing the first unionized McDonald's in Canada. Their actions run counter to the stereotypes of a disengaged younger generation.

Rocky Mountain Bicycle
www.rocky-mountain.com

plateauing

The unanticipated and unwanted levelling of careers due to the elimination of layers of management through corporate restructuring.

and digging ditches. ... Newly returned to the air conditioning, Wilder says he feels "refreshed and a lot less bored." ... So far Alagasco has reassigned 75 of its 1,300 employees, some to the United Way, others to summer job programs for disadvantaged youth.[48]

Older Employees.   As middle-aged employees struggle to keep their careers afloat, older workers face employment-related decisions such as whether to retire, whether to return to the work force after retirement, and if so, whether to do so on a part-time or full-time basis. Although there has been a gradual trend toward early retirements, there is great variability around that lowering average. There are strong reasons to anticipate that increasing numbers of older workers will want to stay attached to the labour force later into their lives. Increasingly, employers will see many as a source of trained and dedicated employees, at the same time as the supply of younger workers decreases. Jobs that are not physically demanding (which comprise a growing proportion of jobs) will provide a constructive outlet for the increasingly healthy older population. And, importantly, as the demographic pressures on retirement income systems grow, pension plans are increasingly likely to provide financial incentives for not leaving early.

Older workers will remain an important part of the employment landscape in the years to come. Roughly 25% of the work force will be 55 years old or older during the next two decades. The following suggestions can help managers supervise an older work force effectively.[49]

◆ *Provide flexible work schedules and part-time jobs.* Many older workers do not want a full-time job, but do wish to remain in the work force and to continue to build their retirement income entitlements. Restructuring a job into a part-time position may make the difference between losing and retaining the valuable experience of older workers.

◆ *Making training relevant to older workers.* Older workers want to learn and are just as capable of learning as other employees. However, older workers may have a greater need to see the direct relevance of the training they're receiving. McDonald's, as an illustration, has initiated a McMasters program that provides training in a hands-on mode geared to the learning strengths of older workers.

◆ *Sensitize managers and other workers to older employees.* Younger managers may be uncomfortable directing older workers. Also, other employees may have negative stereotypes about older workers and their capabilities. This kind of training deals with the myths as well as the real differences between older workers and other employees, and provides managers and other employees with an opportunity to ask the questions.

◆ *Tailor career opportunities.* Some older workers are satisfied with a part-time job and limited responsibility, while others want a challenge or a change from what they have been doing in the past. As with any group of employees, the best result is to fit the person to the job situation to the extent that the needs of the organization permit.

◆ *Ask older workers to consider being mentors.* Career paths for many employees "plateaued" several years before they retire. This need not be a negative situation, since many employees want to make a contribution even when the prospects of promotion are low. By legitimizing and honouring the mentoring that such experienced workers can provide to younger employees, the organization can benefit from both the wisdom that is passed on and from the fully engaged older employee who has the opportunity to play a new and valued role.

▣ Self-Development

When an employer does not routinely offer development programs, it is essential that employees work out their own development plan. Employees who neglect to do this risk stagnation and obsolescence.

Figure 9–7 lists a set of suggestions to help employees enhance their own development and increase their opportunities for advancement. The development suggestions focus on personal growth and direction, while the advancement suggestions focus on the steps that employees can take to improve their promotability in the organization.

Development	Advancement
1. Create your own personal mission statement. 2. Take responsibility for your own direction and growth. 3. Make enhancement your priority, rather than advancement. 4. Talk to those in positions to which you aspire and get suggestions on how to proceed. 5. Set reasonable goals. 6. Make investment in yourself a priority.	1. Remember that performance in your function is important, but interpersonal performance is critical. 2. Set the right values and priorities. 3. Provide solutions, not problems. 4. Be a team player. 5. Be customer-oriented. 6. Act as if what you're doing makes a difference.

Figure 9–7 Suggestions for Self-Development

SOURCE: Advancement suggestions adapted from Matejka, K., & Dunsing, R. (1993). Enhancing your advancement in the 1990s. *Management Decision*, 31, 52–54.

Development Suggestions.   The development suggestions in Figure 9–7 are based on the assumption that the organization does not offer development programs. However, these suggestions are relevant even when the company provides development activities.

1. *Create your own personal mission statement.* Like an organizational mission statement, a *personal mission statement* should indicate the business and role you would like to be in.[50] You should see the statement as changeable over time, not a commandment to which you must blindly adhere regardless of situational or personal factors.

   The process of developing the statement may be more important than the actual statement that results because it can reveal personal values and preferences you may not have realized you have. Once completed, the mission statement should help you set your strategic direction, clarify your priorities, and avoid investing time and energy in pursuits that are not instrumental to achieving your mission.

2. *Take responsibility for your own direction and growth.* You should not place all of your hopes in a company-provided development program. Things change, and steps in a career path can be eliminated as a result of downsizing or reorganizing. Organizations may also eliminate or replace development programs. Such changes could be devastating for people who placed their future entirely in the hands of their organization.

3. *Make enhancement, rather than advancement, your priority.* Organizational flattening and downsizing mean that there will be fewer opportunities for advancement in the coming years. Even today direct upward paths to desired higher-level positions are rare. It is best to accept this reality and search for opportunities to broaden your skills in the short term. Enhancing your skills in the short run should lead to advancement in the longer run.

4. *Talk to those in positions to which you aspire and get their suggestions on how to proceed.* People who are currently in the kind of job you desire can give you valuable insight into what the job is really like and what you must do to make it to that level. Talking to people is also a good way of networking and keeping your name on people's lips.

5. *Set reasonable goals.* As with any major undertaking, it is best to set reasonable goals along the way to your ultimate goal. Breaking your career aspiration into smaller, more manageable goals can help you take the necessary steps toward accomplishing your ultimate goal. It is important to make these minigoals reasonable and achievable. Expecting too much too soon can lead to disillusionment and frustration.

6. *Make investment in yourself a priority.* Your self-development activities might involve self-study, attending workshops and seminars, and interviewing executives and other professionals. When multiple demands are made on your time and attention, it is easy to neglect self-development activities. It's important to remind yourself that these activities are actually investments in yourself and your future, and that no one else is likely to make those investments for you. Place a high priority on your self-development activities.

Advancement Suggestions.   The advancement suggestions in Figure 9–7 focus on the steps you can take to improve your chances of being considered for advancement. The development suggestions are fundamental and provide the necessary base, but the advancement suggestions provide the necessary attitudes and organizational presence.

Images of Career Progress.

Traditionally, a successful organizational career was one in which an individual rose swiftly to the top. Today, while upward movement is still important, successful careers have more in common with the task of the climbers in the photo — teamwork, flexibility, a willingness to move laterally, and focussed attention on the job at hand.

1. *Remember that performance in your function is important, but interpersonal performance is critical.* Advancing in an organization requires adequate interpersonal skills. The abilities to communicate (both one-on-one and to groups), to collaborate, to listen, to summarize, and to write concise reports and memos are essential to being considered a viable candidate for advancement.

2. *Set the right values and priorities.* Your worth to an organization increases after you have discovered what the values and priorities of the organization are and aligned yourself with them. Some organizations, for example, place a high value on collaboration and teamwork, while others emphasize independence and individual contribution. Aligning your own behaviour with the organization's values and priorities improves your chances for advancement.[51]

3. *Provide solutions, not problems.* Nobody likes to hear complaints. So, rather than voicing complaints and pointing out problems, take some time to think issues through and offer potential solutions. You'll be perceived as a much more valuable member of the organization.

4. *Be a team player.* You should not try to steal the limelight for the accomplishments of your work group. Rather, you should try to shine the spotlight on the group's efforts. When you do, you'll be viewed as a facilitator rather than a grandstander. However, you should be sure that those responsible for evaluating your performance are aware of your personal accomplishments. One way to balance these concerns is to refuse to seek public praise for your performance, but not be afraid to call attention to your successes when appropriate.

5. *Be customer-oriented.* Always keep in mind that anyone with whom you have an exchange is your "customer." Whether these interactions are internal or external, understanding and satisfying customer needs should be a top priority. When you take a customer-oriented approach to your job, the organization will recognize you as a high-quality representative who can be expected to accomplish things.

6. *Act as if what you're doing makes a difference.* A sure way to be overlooked for advancement is to display an apathetic or negative attitude toward work. Not all tasks or projects to which you're assigned will spur your interest, but if you approach these activities with a positive attitude and the good of the organization in mind, others will see you as a contributor and a solid corporate citizen.

Summary and Conclusions

What Is Career Development?   Career development is an ongoing organized and formalized effort that focusses on developing enriched and more capable workers. It has a wider focus, longer time frame, and broader scope than training. Development must be a key business strategy if an organization is to survive in today's competitive and global business environment.

Challenges in Career Development.   Putting a career development program in place, management needs to determine (1) who will be responsible for development, (2) how much emphasis on development is appropriate, and (3) how the development needs of a diverse work force will be met.

Meeting the Challenges of Effective Development. Career development is a continuing cycle of three phases: an assessment phase, a direction phase, and a development phase. Each phase is an important part of developing the work force.

In the assessment phase, employees' skills, values, and interests are identified. These assessments may be carried out by the workers themselves, by the organization, or by both. Self-assessment is often done through career workbooks and career-planning workshops. Organizational assessment is done through assessment centres, psychological testing, performance appraisal, promotability forecasts, and succession planning.

The direction phase involves determining the type of career that employees want and the steps they must take to make their career goals a reality. In this phase workers may receive individual counselling or information from a variety of sources, including a job-posting system, skills inventories, career paths, and career resource centres.

The development phase involves taking actions to create and increase employees' skills and promotability. The most common development programs are mentoring, coaching, job rotation, and tuition assistance programs.

Special Issues in Career Development.   Management development is a high priority in today's intensely competitive business environment. Organizations employ company schools, university-based programs, and management training programs to provide employees with the skills they need to be effective managers.

Career development programs must be flexible enough to deal with employees at different stages of the life cycle. Younger employees place great importance on quality of work life and on having time off for family life. Midlife employees are subject to plateauing, the unanticipated and unwanted levelling of careers that is the outgrowth of corporate restructuring and downsizing. Many older workers have entered or remained in the work force; managers need to be aware of their scheduling and training needs.

In situations where the employer does not routinely offer development programs, employees must take an active role in their own development. To do otherwise is to risk stagnation and obsolescence.

Key Terms and Concepts

assessment centre, 268
assessment phase, 266
career development, 262
career path, 271
career workbooks, 266
career-planning workshops, 266
career resource centre, 271
case study method, 276
coaching, 274
development phase, 273

direction phase, 269
dual-career couple, 265
individual career counselling, 270
interest inventory, 267
job-posting system, 270
job rotation, 275
management games, 276
mentoring, 274
personal mission statement, 279
plateauing, 277

promotability forecast, 268
psychological testing, 268
role-playing, 276
skills assessment exercises, 267
skills inventory, 271
succession planning, 268
tuition assistance program, 275
values clarification, 268

Discussion Questions

1. Retention of top talent is a critical element in the strategy of today's leaner organizations. How can career development activities contribute to retention?

2. How would you go about determining your current strengths and weaknesses?

3. Today's organizations are flatter and offer fewer opportunities for advancement. How do you think careers should be developed in this kind of an organizational environment?

4. In a recent survey of 925 male and female MBAs, it was found that "traditional" married men—those who have children and whose wives don't work—earn on average 20 percent more per year than family men with children and employed wives. Yet only 21 percent of the managers surveyed said they were in this type of traditional family structure. By contrast, 39 percent are in post-traditional family units, and these workers express greater satisfaction with their careers. What challenges do these "post-traditional" family units pose to company career development plans? How can companies meet these challenges?

5. People who adopt a "careerist" strategy focus on career advancement through political machinations rather than excellent performance Experts have pointed out four ways in which workers try to influence superior's opinions of them: favour doing (doing a favour for a superior to win support); opinion conformity (agreeing with the superior to build trust); flattery (to appeal to vanity or insecurity); and self-presentation (deliberate attempts to influence through dress, deportment, values, and attitudes expressed). In what other ways might employees try to influence their superiors' opinions of them? How can managers assess subordinates' sincerity? What criteria should be used in making a promotion decision?

6. Companies use various tactics to encourage managers to make employee development a top priority. At one company, a prestigious award worth $3,000 is given to those managers who contribute strongly to their unit's profitability, who assist the career development of at least three people, and who have excellent records as mentors of diverse employee groups. Winners gain companywide recognition as well as the financial reward. What do you think of this policy of tying financial rewards to people development? What are some other ways that companies can hold managers accountable for developing those they supervise?

Check out our Companion Website at: **www.prenticehall.ca/gomez** for a selection of self-study questions, key terms and concepts, updated Weblinks to related Internet sites, newsgroups, CBC video updates, and more.

MiniCase 1   *Go Abroad to Get Ahead*

Gary Ellis works at Medtronic, a major producer of pacemakers and other medical devices. Gary had advanced quickly at Medtronic and everyone recognized him as someone on the management fast track. Why, then, did Medtronic ship him off to Brussels to head the company's European operations? Because global experience is increasingly part of the fast track at Medtronic and other corporations. Medtronic's CEO believes that living and working abroad for several years will be a prerequisite for successful executives in the future.

While on his assignment in Europe, Gary quickly gained a great deal of management experience. He had to confront a variety of situations and effectively deal with a wide assortment of people, including factory managers, labour leaders, and government ministers. After a couple of years

Medtronic needed a corporate comptroller back at head office and—you guessed it—Gary got the job.

Discussion Questions

1. Overseas assignments were once considered career-ending experiences, but they're now viewed as a very useful, perhaps essential, step in the development of a managerial career. However, the risk still exists that managers will be forgotten once they've been shipped overseas. What steps can managers take to minimize this risk and keep abreast of developments back home?

2. Global experiences may be a key career development experience that leads to advancement. How could you go about landing an overseas assignment for yourself? What qualities do you think a manager needs to be successful abroad?

SOURCE: Adapted from Loeb, M. (1995). The real fast track is overseas. *Fortune,* 132, 129.

MiniCase 2   *A Résumé on the Screen*

One of the supreme on-the-job fears is having your boss come into your office while your résumé is up on the computer screen. Of course employees shouldn't conduct job-hunting activities during office hours. But should they always keep their outside job-hunting efforts secret from their employers? What happens when companies find out about concealed efforts to search for opportunities outside the company walls? The fallout can range from awkwardness and tension to firing, as this incident shows:

... Though he kept his quest secret, a job search nearly cost Christopher Hunt his post as credit manager for MLC Financial, a medical-equipment leasing company. ... A potential employer told MLC about Mr. Hunt's search.

The division president became angry and wanted to fire Mr. Hunt for disloyalty. MLC had spent "a lot of time and effort to bring me up to speed," says Mr. Hunt, " . . . but I had every right to look around." He escaped the axe after his immediate supervisor pleaded with the division

president. Mr. Hunt says he quit anyway a month later to take a credit director's job that paid 15 percent more.

Discussion Questions

1. Do you think companies should encourage employees to tell them about their efforts to seek employment elsewhere or do you think they should punish employees whose job-hunting activities come to light? Explain your answer.

2. MLC's division head believed that Hunt's job search revealed disloyalty. What career development tactics could MLC have deployed to retain Hunt and win his loyalty?

3. Many of the companies discussed in this chapter have internal career resource centres in which employees can discuss their career plans with professional career counsellors. Should these discussions be kept confidential or should they be made known to employees' immediate supervisors? How do you think companies can employ the services of career counsellors to meet both individual and organizational needs?

SOURCE: Reprinted from Lublin, J. S. (1993, July 28). Managing your career: A good boss may even help you find a greener pasture. *The Wall Street Journal,* B1.

Case 1

Family versus Career—and a Company Caught in the Middle

Dave and Nora live in the Vancouver area, where Dave works for a major software company. He is very motivated to put in whatever time and effort are needed to complete tasks and projects successfully. Top management recognizes his contributions as important and his prospects at the company are excellent.

Nora has been married to Dave for five years and knows how devoted he is to his career. Both of them want to start a family and agree that Vancouver isn't where they want to raise their children. Nora, feeling that she can't wait forever to have kids, has been pressuring Dave to find a job in a smaller town.

Understanding Nora's concerns, Dave made a couple of discreet phone calls and was soon asked in for an interview by a company located in a town in Alberta. Dave didn't know what to say when the company made him an offer. The job pays less than his present job and offers fewer opportunities for advancement, but the area is the kind of environment he and Nora want. He knows Nora is thrilled at the prospect of the move, yet he can't help feeling sad. How can he simply walk away from all he has invested in his career at his present company? Maybe there is more to life than his career, but he is already depressed and he hasn't even quit yet.

When Dave told his boss, Terri, about the new job offer, Terri was shocked. Dave is a central figure in the company's plans for the next couple of years, and his expertise is indispensable on a couple of important projects. Terri feels that Dave has blindsided the company. Things will be a mess for a long time if he leaves. But what can the company do to keep him if money isn't the issue?

Critical Thinking Questions

1. What preventive measures could Dave's company have taken to avoid the crisis it is faced with? What can the company do now?
2. Should Dave's company involve Nora in any of its attempts to retain Dave? How?
3. Should Dave's company implement any career development programs after this crisis passes? What kind would you recommend? Why?

Cooperative Learning Exercises

4. Ask students who have seen someone in their family leave a job because of dual-career or family issues to describe the circumstances to the class and address what the organization could have done to avoid losing the person.
5. Besides a husband or wife, who else can have a significant influence on a person's career decisions? Brainstorm the possibilities with your partner or team and share your ideas with the class. How might the organization deal with these people?

Case 2

Stuck at the Bottom

Sam has been an employee at Consumer Electronics (CE) for three years. He has worked in the warehouse since his first day with CE and has seen most of his co-workers get promoted to sales and beyond. Consumer Electronics has a promotion-from-within policy. All of the current sales staff started working in the warehouse. Before they moved into sales, though, most of them took courses at a local community college in sales and marketing, and some even took courses in electronics repair and maintenance. The company does not formally require such courses of its sales people and does not reimburse them for their tuition costs.

Sam does not think he needs these courses. He has tinkered with electronic devices since he was in elementary school, so he is sure the electronics courses would be a waste of time. Further, he worked in sales at a furniture retailer for a year and a half before he got this job and was the top seller during his last quarter there. He feels he is qualified for a sales job right now.

When he was given the opportunity to work on the loading dock, Sam turned it down because it was still a warehouse job. He also applied for higher-level jobs in the company but never got them. He had hoped to be a sales manager by now, but here he is, still in the warehouse. Now he finds it hard to care much about his job or the organization, and keeps wondering if he will be fired.

Critical Thinking Questions

1. What do you think Consumer Electronics should do about Sam's career aspirations?
2. If you were Sam's supervisor, what would you say to him and what would you do?
3. If you were a consultant to Consumer Electronics, what advice would you give top management about the company's lack of a formal development program for employees?

Cooperative Learning Exercises

4. At least part of the problem appears to be that Sam isn't taking responsibility for his own development and advancement. With your partner or group, identify how Sam can do more to advance his own career. Select the best ideas generated and share them with the class.
5. Do you think it's possible for all people to learn the skills necessary to develop and advance themselves? Or is this an area in which some people excel and others don't? Have the class choose sides on this issue and select teams to debate the question.

VideoCase

Men and Women at Work

Most of us have spent our entire lives in frequent contact with people of both sexes, in family situations, in school, socially, and at work. It is reasonable to assume that neither men nor women, as categories of people, are strangers to us.

As we have seen in previous chapters, the demographics of the work force have changed quite remarkably during the past two or three decades, most notably in the increased presence of visible minorities and especially in the growth of women's participation in paid employment. The implications of these changes for human resource management have been quite dramatic: pay equity, family-friendly HR policies of various kinds, human rights legislation, and so forth. Many of these issues have been organized around how the employer should treat people, so far as the terms and conditions of employment (recruiting, hiring, promoting, paying) are concerned.

There is an even more basic HR issue to deal with when people work with others who belong to groups different from their own—how to deal with their sense of difference. This requirement is especially important when employees encounter members of these groups and need to work with them as if the differences among us (gender, race, religion, national origin, etc.) had no relevance to the working relationship. Even with the best will in the world, this is not always an easy task for people. We have all been socialized by our experience. For example, if you ask one person to describe another person, they will often mention sex, age, physical proportions (tall/short, thin/heavy), apparent race or ethnicity, physical attractiveness (or its opposite), accented speech (if noticeably different), and other traits. Although these attributes are properly "out-of-bounds" in terms of how people are to be treated as employees or fellow workers, they are often characteristics that most of us do notice in other people.

The idea that women, religious minorities, people of non-European ancestry, or other individuals who fall outside the stereotypic "white male" group can be regarded as inferior or less worthy is (thankfully) unacceptable to the vast majority of Canadians. However, this consensus does not automatically lead to easy and productive relations among individuals from significantly different backgrounds. The employer's task in creating an effective, cohesive organization often includes assisting employees to deal constructively with the obstacles these differences can create in workplace relations.

Discussion Questions

1. To what extent should employees be expected to adapt to an organization's culture, as opposed to having the culture change to accommodate the individuals who become part of it? Is this a matter in which an employer should intervene, or should the employees be allowed to work it out informally? (Do you think the answer to this question is likely to differ between people who are "white males" and those who are not?)

2. What workplace issues are most likely to be affected by the sense of difference (sex, race, etc.) that people bring with them to the workplace? What makes these issues important or sensitive?

3. What do employers need to do to effectively intervene in relations among different groups within their work force, to decrease friction and increase employees' capacity to work effectively together?

Video Resource: Men/Women, *Venture* (March 20, 1994).

Managing Compensation

After reading this chapter, you should be able to deal more effectively with the following challenges:

1 Identify the compensation policies and practices that are most appropriate to a firm.

2 Weigh the strategic advantages and disadvantages of different compensation options.

3 Establish a job-based compensation scheme that is internally consistent and linked to the labour market.

4 Understand the difference between a compensation system in which employees are paid for the skills they use and one in which they are paid for the job they hold.

5 Make compensation decisions that comply with the legal framework.

Salaries, commissions, bonuses, profit sharing, share ownership programs—compensation takes many forms. While direct compensation is not the only part of an employee's total compensation package, it is the largest component. Money is not the only thing that motivates employees, but it has been shown to be an important motivator. Employees work harder and are more dedicated to their jobs when they perceive a relationship between their contributions and their pay.

Sigma Technologies is a medium-sized biotechnology firm specializing in genetic engineering. The firm was founded in 1982 by a university professor, Dr. Nazir Muhammad, who left academia to start a new company in a promising young field. The venture has been a resounding success, with Sigma's stock price increasing one hundredfold over its original value and its number of employees reaching 350. Muhammad is still the chief executive officer (CEO) of Sigma and continues to be actively involved in all hiring and pay decisions. He repeatedly tells his line managers that Sigma "will pay whatever it takes to hire the best talent in the market."

During the past year Muhammad has noticed an erosion in Sigma's "family atmosphere" and an increase in the number of disgruntled employees. Despite the generous compensation Sigma provides to its employees, pay appears to be a major concern. There have been three pay-related complaints during the past week alone, and Muhammad suspects this is only the tip of the iceberg. The first complaint came from a computer programmer who has been with Sigma for five years. She is upset that another programmer was recently hired at a salary 15 percent higher than hers. Muhammad explained that such starting salaries are necessary to attract top experienced programmers from other firms, but that Sigma can't afford to raise its present programmers' salaries. The second complaint came from a software engineer who feels that Sigma's best technical people—the lifeblood of a biotechnology firm—are discriminated against in pay because supervisors (who, in his words, are often "failed engineers") receive 30 percent more pay. The third complaint was filed by an administrative assistant who has been with Sigma from the start. She is angry that janitors are getting more money than she is, and Muhammad's explanation that it is difficult to hire and retain reliable people who are willing to clean up and dispose of dangerous chemicals has failed to placate her.

Sigma's experience raises several important questions that firms face in designing and administering compensation programs. Among these questions:

♦ Who should be responsible for making salary decisions?

♦ Should pay be dictated by what other employers are paying?

♦ Given limited resources, should a company pay more to attract employees from other firms without raising the salaries of present employees?

♦ What types of activities should be rewarded with higher salaries?

♦ What criteria should be used to determine salaries?

♦ Which employee groups should receive special treatment when scarce pay resources are allocated?

The way a firm handles these and other compensation-related questions is likely to have a direct impact on its ability to attract, retain, and motivate employees. It will also have a direct bearing on the extent to which labour costs detract from or contribute to business objectives and profitability.

Managers need to understand the important issues related to the design and management of a compensation system. In the first part of this chapter, we define the components of compensation and present the nine criteria used in developing a compensation plan. Next, we describe the process of designing a compensation plan. We conclude the chapter with a discussion of the legal and regulatory influences on employee compensation.

What Is Compensation?

As Figure 10–1 shows, an employee's **total compensation** has three components. The relative proportion of each (known as the *pay mix*) varies extensively by firm.[1] The first and, in most firms, largest element of total compensation is **base compensation,** the fixed pay an employee receives on a regular basis, either in the form of a salary (for example, a weekly or monthly paycheque) or as an hourly wage. The second component of total compensation is **pay incentives,** programs designed to reward employees for good performance. These incentives come in many forms (including bonuses and profit sharing) and are the focus of Chapter 11. The last component of total compensation is the category of *employee benefits,* sometimes called *indirect compensation.* Benefits encompass a wide variety of programs, including pensions, dental plans, legally mandated payments, and paid holidays. The costs of benefits account for roughly 30 percent of total employment costs.[2] A special category of benefits called *perquisites,* or "perks," are available only to employees with some special status in the organization, usually upper-level managers. Common perks are a company car, a special parking place on company grounds, and company-paid country club membership fees. Chapter 12 discusses benefit programs in detail.

Compensation is the single most important cost in most firms. Personnel costs are as high as 60 percent of total costs in certain types of manufacturing environments, and even higher in some service organizations (for example, direct pay and benefits combined frequently account for 80 percent and more of the operating budgets of community colleges and universities). This means that the effectiveness with which compensation is allocated can make a significant difference in gaining or losing a competitive edge. For instance, a high-technology firm that provides generous compensation to managerial and marketing personnel yet underpays its research and development staff may find that it has lost its ability to innovate because competitors have pirated away its best talent. Thus *how much* is paid and *who* gets paid what are crucial strategic issues for the firm; they affect the cost side of all financial statements and determine the extent to which the firm realizes a low or high return on its payroll dollars.[3]

Building Managerial Skills: Designing a Compensation System

An employee's paycheque is certainly important for its purchasing power. In most societies, however, the amount of money an individual earns also serves as an indicator of power and prestige and is tied to feelings of self-worth. In other words, compensation affects a person economically, sociologically, and psychologically.[4] For this reason, mishandling the compensation-allocation process is likely to have a strong negative impact on employees and, ultimately, on the firm's performance.[5]

The wide variety of pay policies and procedures available to organizations presents managers with a two-pronged challenge: to design a compensation system that (1) enables the firm to achieve its strategic objectives and (2) is moulded to

total compensation
The package of quantifiable rewards an employee receives for his or her labours. Includes three components: base compensation, pay incentives, and indirect compensation/benefits.

base compensation
The fixed pay an employee receives on a regular basis, either in the form of a salary or as an hourly wage.

pay incentive
A program designed to reward employees for good performance.

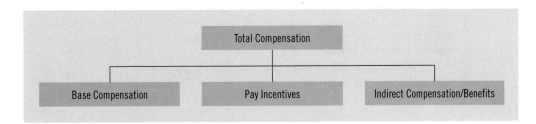

Figure 10–1 The Elements of Total Compensation

the firm's unique characteristics and environment.[6] We discuss the criteria for developing a compensation plan in the sections that follow and summarize these options in Figure 10–2. Although we present each of these as an either/or choice for the sake of simplicity, in reality most firms institute policies that fall somewhere between the two poles.

Internal versus External Equity

Fair pay is pay that employees generally view as equitable. There are two forms of pay equity. **Internal equity** refers to the perceived fairness of the pay structure within a firm. **External equity** refers to the perceived fairness of pay relative to what other employers are paying for the same type of labour.

In considering *internal versus external equity*, managers can use two basic models: the distributive justice model and the labour market model.

The Distributive Justice Model

The *distributive justice model of pay equity* holds that employees exchange their contributions or input to the firm (skills, effort, time, and so forth) for a set of outcomes. Pay is one of the most important of these outcomes, but non-monetary rewards like a company car may also be significant. This social-psychological perspective suggests that employees are constantly comparing (1) what they bring to the firm to what they receive in return and (2) comparing this input/outcome ratio with that of other employees within the firm. Employees will think they are fairly paid when the ratio of their inputs and outputs is equivalent to that of other employees whose job demands are similar to their own.

Some employees compare their input/outcome ratio to that of employees in other firms but most compare themselves to their peers in the same organization. From this perspective, then, the compensation system's key task is to ensure that salaries and wage rates are set so that employees perceive a fair input/outcome balance within the firm and, to a lesser extent, outside it.

internal equity

The perceived fairness of the pay structure within a firm.

external equity

The perceived fairness in pay relative to what other employers are paying for the same type of labour.

1. **Internal versus External Equity** Will the compensation plan be perceived as fair within the company, or will it be perceived as fair relative to what other employers are paying for the same type of labour?

2. **Fixed versus Variable Pay** Will compensation be paid mainly on a fixed basis—through base salaries—or will it fluctuate depending on such pre-established criteria as performance and company profits?

3. **Performance versus Membership** Will compensation emphasize performance and tie pay to individual or group contributions, or will it emphasize membership in the organization—logging in a prescribed number of hours each week and progressing up the organizational ladder?

4. **Job versus Individual Pay** Will compensation be based on how the company values a particular job, or will it be based on how much skill and knowledge an employee brings to that job?

5. **Egalitarianism versus Elitism** Will the compensation plan place most employees under the same compensation system (egalitarianism), or will it establish different plans by organizational level and/or employee group (elitism)?

6. **Below-Market versus Above-Market Compensation** Will employees be compensated at below-market levels, at market levels, or at above-market levels?

7. **Monetary versus Non-Monetary Awards** Will the compensation plan emphasize motivating employees through monetary rewards like pay and share options, or will it stress non-monetary rewards such as more interesting work and job security?

8. **Open versus Secret Pay** Will employees have access to information about other workers' compensation levels and how compensation decisions are made (open pay), or will this knowledge be withheld from employees (secret pay)?

9. **Centralization versus Decentralization of Pay Decisions** Will compensation decisions be made in a tightly controlled central location, or will they be delegated to managers of the firm's units?

Figure 10–2 The Nine Criteria for Developing a Compensation Plan

The Labour Market Model.   According to the *labour market model of pay equity,* which was developed by labour economists, the wage rate for any given occupation is set at the point where the supply of labour equals the demand for labour in the marketplace (W_1 in Figure 10–3). In general, the less employers are willing to pay (low demand for labour) and the lower the pay workers are willing to accept (high supply of labour) for a given job, the lower the wage rate for that job.[7]

The actual situation is a great deal more complicated than this basic model suggests, however. People base their decisions about what jobs they are willing to hold on many more factors than pay. The organization's location and the job's content and demands are just two of these factors. Moreover, the pay that an employer offers is based on many factors besides the number of available people with the skills and abilities to do the job. These factors include historical wage patterns, the presence or absence of unions, and internal organizational politics. A complete exploration of this topic is beyond the scope of this book. However, the basic point of the labour market model is that external equity is achieved when the firm pays its employees the "going rate" for the type of work they do.[8] A firm cannot stray too far in either direction from the market wage. If it offers pay much below the going rate, it may find itself unable to attract and retain qualified workers; if it pays much more than the going rate, it may be unable to charge competitive prices for its product because its labour costs are too high.

Balancing Equity.   Ideally, a firm should try to establish both internal and external pay equity, but these objectives are often at odds. For instance, universities sometimes pay new assistant professors more than senior faculty who have been with the institution for a decade or more,[9] and on occasion firms pay recent engineering graduates more than engineers who have been on board for several years.[10] This occurs when demand increases sharply for candidates with certain specific qualifications.

You may find this startling and wonder why the senior employees acquiesce instead of leaving and competing for higher-paying positions elsewhere. Senior faculty are usually tenured, which means they would give up a great deal of job security if they went to another university. Further, both professors and engineers work in fields where the knowledge base is constantly changing, making more recent graduates (who are more likely to be aware of new developments in their field) somewhat more valuable employees.

Many firms have to determine which employee groups' pay will be adjusted upward to meet (or perhaps exceed) market rates and which groups' pay will remain at or under market. This decision is generally based on each group's relative importance to the firm. For example, marketing employees tend to be paid more in firms that are trying to expand their market share and less in older firms that have a well-established product with high brand recognition.

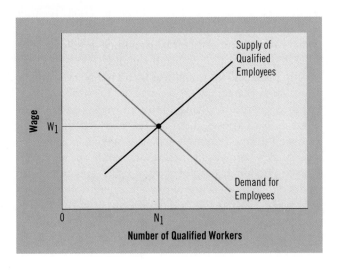

Figure 10–3 The Labour Market Model

In general, emphasizing external equity is more appropriate for newer, smaller firms in a rapidly changing market. These firms often have a high need for innovation to remain competitive and are dependent on key individuals to achieve their business objectives.[11] Much of the relatively new high-technology industry fits this description. A greater emphasis on internal equity is more appropriate for older, larger, well-established firms. These firms often have a mature product, employees who plan to spend most of their career with the firm, and technology and jobs that don't change often. Much of the utilities industry fits this description.

Fixed versus Variable Pay

Noranda
www.noranda.com

Firms can choose to pay a high proportion of total compensation in the form of base pay (for example, a predictable monthly paycheque) or in the form of variable pay that fluctuates according to some pre-established criterion. Traditional pay practices in many organizations have used fixed compensation (i.e., wages or salaries set in terms of hourly, weekly, or monthly rates) for virtually all employees except senior management and sales force employees. However, such practices are no longer standard. Many Canadian major employers including Royal Bank, Noranda, Magna International, Inco, and Sun Life are aggressively introducing or expanding the use of incentive pay at lower levels of the organization.[12]

There is a great deal of variation in the way firms answer the *fixed versus variable pay* question. According to a survey conducted by Ernst and Young, variable pay constituted 5.7 percent of base salary for hourly workers, 6.4 percent for professional and technical employees, 10.2 percent for middle management, and 17.2 percent for senior management.[13] This compares with 20 percent in Japan. However, the range is huge in both countries—from zero percent up to 70 percent. For select employee groups (such as sales), variable pay can be as high as 100 percent.[14]

As we discuss in the next chapter, variable compensation takes many forms, including individual bonuses, team bonuses, profit sharing, and share ownership programs. The higher the proportion of variable pay, the more *risk sharing* there is between the employee and the firm. This means a trade-off for employees between income security and the potential for higher earnings.[15]

Fixed pay is the rule in the majority of organizations largely because it reduces the risk to both employer and employee. However, variable pay can be used advantageously in smaller companies, firms with a product that is not well established, companies with a young professional work force that is willing to delay immediate gratification in hopes of greater future returns, firms supported by venture capital, organizations going through a prolonged period of cash shortages, and companies that would otherwise have to institute layoffs because their revenues are volatile.

Although smaller companies such as B.C.-based Quadra Logic Technologies can use employee ownership via share options to their advantage during periods of rapid growth when cash rewards are difficult to provide,[16] employee ownership is not limited to such situations. Companies listed on the Toronto Stock Exchange with employee ownership plans showed significantly higher growth and profitability than companies without such plans.[17]

Employee ownership is geared to giving the employees a stake in the success of the organization, but it also exposes them to the risks that the employer faces. Unless employees are well informed about negative as well as positive possibilities, downturns in business success can result in serious morale problems.

It is not uncommon to encounter employee ownership initiatives as a response to crisis. While not an incentive in the same sense as a share option for a successful company, employee buyouts, such as the one that occurred at the Pine Falls, Manitoba, paper mill once owned by Abitibi-Price, provide the motivational foundation needed to attempt to launch a turnaround.[18] Perhaps the highest-profile

success story of this kind recently is the dramatic turnaround at Algoma Steel in Sault Ste. Marie, Ontario, which returned to strong profitability from the brink of financial collapse in the early 1990s.

Not all variable pay plans work out well for employees, however.

■ Performance versus Membership

A special case of fixed versus variable compensation involves a choice between performance and membership.[19] A company emphasizes performance when a substantial portion of its employees' pay is tied to individual or group contributions and the amount received can vary significantly from one person or group to another. The most extreme forms of *performance-contingent compensation* are traditional piece-rate plans (pay based on units produced) and sales commissions. Other performance-contingent plans use awards for cost-saving suggestions, bonuses for perfect attendance, or merit pay based on supervisory appraisals. All these options are provided on top of an individual's base pay (see Chapter 11).

Firms that emphasize *membership-contingent compensation* provide the same or a similar wage to every employee in a given job, as long as the employee achieves at least satisfactory performance. Employees receive a paycheque for logging in a prescribed number of hours of work per week. Typically, salary progression occurs by moving up in the organization, not by doing the present job better.

The relative emphasis placed on *performance versus membership* depends largely on the organization's culture and the beliefs of top managers or the company's founder. The notable sustained success of 3M is attributed by its CEO to the managerial value that "human beings are endowed with the urge to bring into being something that has never existed before ... [therefore] rewards have to be tied directly to successful innovation ... the worst thing to do with [innovators] is to base their rewards on how well they fit in with some preconceived management mould."[20] It is an understatement to say that 3M's encouragement of innovation has paid off. In what has become a legend in the field of product development, one of its chemists developed the immensely popular adhesive Post-it® Notes after getting tired of having bookmarks fall out of his hymnal at church. It took a year of tinkering to develop the final product, but 3M provided the chemist with the time to tinker and a handsome bonus for the final result.[21]

Most companies that emphasize performance in setting pay tend to be smaller than 3M. They are usually characterized by fewer management levels, rapid growth, internal competition among people and groups, readily available performance indicators (see Chapter 7), and strong competitive pressures.[22]

■ Job versus Individual Pay

Most traditional compensation systems assume that in setting base compensation a firm should evaluate the value or contributions of each job, not how well the employee performs it.[23] Under this system, the job becomes the unit of analysis for determining base compensation, not the individual(s) performing that job. This means that the minimum and maximum values of each job are set independent of individual workers, who must be paid somewhere in the range established for that job. For instance, an unemployed Ph.D. in chemistry may accept a job as a janitor and do an outstanding job of keeping the building clean

Performance-Contingent Compensation.

Clothing manufacturers around the world have traditionally paid their employees on piece-rate plans. Workers receive a specific amount for each piece produced.

and well organized. Yet he may be paid $6.85 an hour—not because he doesn't deserve more, given his credentials and janitorial performance, but because this is the maximum hourly pay set for this job. He can get paid more only by being promoted, and this could take years.

Rather than basing pay on a narrowly defined job, managers may choose to emphasize an individual's abilities, potential, and flexibility to perform multiple tasks in setting his or her pay. The chemistry Ph.D., for example, may be offered a job at $40 per hour because he can do many things that are as necessary to the organization as cleaning, such as helping in the lab and drafting reports. In this type of **knowledge-based pay** or **skilled-based pay** system, employees are paid on the basis of the jobs they *can* do or the talents they have that can be successfully applied to a variety of tasks and situations.[24] Thus the more hats an individual can wear, the more pay he or she will receive. Employees' base compensation increases as they become able to perform more duties successfully. The results of a review of current research on competency-based pay plans (CBPPs) show that employer interest in the concept is high, but adoption of such plans has been cautious for several reasons: complexity, cost, and the potential conflicts with the norms of seniority or merit, which are strongly ingrained.[25]

While the traditional job-centred system of pay is still predominant, more and more firms are opting for an individualized knowledge-based approach. Proponents argue that knowledge-based pay provides greater motivation for employees, makes it easier to assign workers on a moment's notice to where they are most needed, reduces the costs of turnover and absenteeism because other employees can assume missing employees' duties, and provides managers with much more staffing flexibility. Critics, however, maintain that a skill-based system may lead to higher labour costs, loss of labour specialization, greater difficulty in selecting applicants because the qualifications are less specific, and a chaotic workplace where "the left hand doesn't know what the right hand is doing."[26]

How, then, should managers approach the *job versus individual pay* option? Research suggests that neither approach is universally preferable; the better choice depends on the prevailing conditions at the firm. A job-based pay policy tends to work best in situations where:

◆ Technology is stable

◆ Jobs don't change often

◆ Employees do not need to cover for one another frequently

◆ Much training is required to learn a given job

◆ Turnover is relatively low

◆ Employees are expected to move up through the ranks over time, and

◆ Jobs are fairly standardized within the industry.

The automobile industry fits most of the preceding criteria. In contrast, individual-based compensation programs are more suitable when:

◆ The firm has a relatively educated work force with both the ability and the willingness to learn different jobs

◆ The company's technology and organizational structure change frequently

◆ Employee participation and teamwork are encouraged throughout the organization

◆ Opportunities for upward mobility are limited

◆ Opportunities to learn new skills are present, and

◆ The costs of employee turnover and absenteeism in terms of lost production are high.[27]

Individual-based pay plans are common in manufacturing environments that rely on continuous-process technologies.[28]

knowledge-based pay or skill-based pay

A pay system in which employees are paid on the basis of the jobs they can do or talents they have that can be successfully applied to a variety of tasks and situations.

Elitism versus Egalitarianism

Firms must decide whether to place most of their employees under the same compensation plan—an **egalitarian pay system**—or to establish different compensation plans by organizational level and/or employee group—an **elitist pay system.** For example, in some firms only the CEO is eligible for share options. In other companies even the lowest-paid worker is offered share options. Some companies offer a wide menu of pay incentives only to specific employee groups (such as salespeople), while others make these available to most employees. Magna International, the car-parts manufacturer, has seen companywide profit sharing as a definitive element in its culture since it began. Ten percent of pre-tax profits are distributed to employees in a program that became enshrined in its corporate charter.[29] When the company does well, everyone does well. The profit-sharing plan awards the same percentage to all employees, from the top to the bottom.[30]

The *egalitarianism versus elitism* choice is important because it creates an impression of what it takes to succeed in the firm and the type of work managers value. A traditional organizational hierarchy is reinforced by compensation plans and perquisites that vary with one's place in the hierarchy.[31] For instance, in one large computer firm, average compensation was perfectly correlated with the floor on which one worked in corporate headquarters: the higher the floor, the higher the pay. In addition, there were four dining rooms in the building and employees could use only the one assigned to them; an observer could immediately tell a person's rank (and prestige level) by where he or she had lunch.

The trend in recent years has been toward more egalitarian compensation systems.[32] Why? A company that has fewer differences between employee levels and fewer compensation plans, allows employees to increase their earnings without moving into management, and keeps status-related perquisites to a minimum, enjoys distinct benefits. The most significant of these are a focus on joint-task accomplishment, more consultation between subordinates and supervisors, and better cooperation among employees.

Nonetheless, both systems have their advantages and disadvantages. Egalitarianism gives firms more flexibility to deploy employees in different areas without having to change their pay levels. It can also reduce barriers between people who need to work closely together. Elitist pay structures tend to result in a more stable work force because an employee's potential to move up through the company depends to a great extent on how long that person stays with the firm.

Elitist compensation systems are more prevalent among older, well-established firms with mature products, a relatively unchanging market share, and limited competition. Egalitarian compensation systems are more common in highly competitive environments, where firms frequently take business risks and try to expand their market share by continually investing in new technologies, ventures, and products.

Below-Market versus Above-Market Compensation

The *below-market versus above-market compensation* decision is crucial for two reasons.[33] First, the pay received by employees relative to alternative employment opportunities directly affects the firm's ability to attract workers from other companies. Pay satisfaction is very highly correlated with pay level, and low pay satisfaction is one of the best predictors of employee turnover. Second, the choice has an important cost component. The decision to pay above market for all employee groups allows the firm to hire the "cream of the crop," minimize voluntary turnover, and create a climate that makes all employees feel they are part of an elite organization. This has traditionally been the choice for "blue chip" firms like IBM Canada and Procter & Gamble. However, few companies can

egalitarian pay system

A pay plan in which most employees are part of the same compensation system.

elitist pay system

A pay plan in which different compensation systems are established for employees or groups at different organizational levels.

A Question of Ethics

Some people argue that it is wrong for CEOs to earn multimillion-dollar salaries while some of their employees are earning the minimum wage or even being laid off. Some suggest that a firm's top earner should earn no more than 20 times what the lowest-ranked employee earns. What do you think?

Proctor & Gamble
www.pg.com

afford such a policy. Instead, most firms recognize the importance of certain groups explicitly by paying them above market, and cover these costs by paying other groups below market. For example, many high-tech firms compensate their R&D workers quite well while paying their manufacturing employees below-market wages.

In general, above-market pay policies are more prevalent among larger companies in less competitive industries (like utilities) and among companies that have been performing well and therefore have the ability to pay more. In addition, companies starting up in some overseas areas must consider paying above-market wages to retain workers. Demi Lloyd found this out the hard way when she and her husband set up DD Traders, Inc., a buying agency for Christmas decorations in Hong Kong, and within six months experienced 100 percent turnover in staff. Since Hong Kong's unemployment rate was historically below two percent, employees had the upper hand. To attract and retain the best and most experienced workers, Lloyd found she had to offer salaries 10 to 20 percent above the market levels.[34] Unions, which we discuss in detail in Chapter 15, also contribute to above-market pay. Unionized workers receive approximately 10 to 20 percent higher wages than similar non-unionized workers do.[35]

At-market wages are typical in industries that are both well established and highly competitive (for example, grocery store and hotel chains). Firms paying below market tend to be small, young, and non-unionized. They often operate in economically depressed areas and have a higher proportion of women and minorities in the work force. Growing firms making risky business decisions that leave them short of cash may also offer a lower base salary relative to the market combined with greater incentives (such as stock and bonuses) to minimize labour costs.

Monetary versus Non-Monetary Rewards

One of the oldest debates about compensation concerns *monetary versus non-monetary rewards*. Unlike cash or payments that can be converted into cash in the future (such as shares or a retirement plan), non-monetary rewards are intangible. Such rewards include interesting work, challenging assignments, and public recognition.[36]

Many surveys have shown that employees rank pay low in importance. For example, in one large-scale survey only two percent of respondents declared that pay is a very important aspect of a job.[37] This finding should be viewed with skepticism, however, because what people say to pollsters is often out of sync with how they act. Because greed is stigmatized, most people are reluctant to admit that pay is important to them. As two well-known commentators note, pay "may rank higher than people care to admit to others—or to themselves. In practice, it appears that good old-fashioned cash is as effective as any reward that has yet been invented."[38]

Most HRM researchers and practitioners agree that pay symbolizes what the organization values and signals to employees what activities it wants to encourage. For instance, research-oriented universities gear pay to the number of papers a faculty member has published in leading academic journals. One result: teachers at these universities spend a great deal of time writing papers for publication.

Organizations face a choice concerning how much emphasis to place on money and how much to place on other rewards such as high job security. Real estate companies are well known for the extent to which brokers depend on sales commissions for their income; some have used an explicit strategy of trying to recruit the highest-producing brokers by giving them much higher than industry-standard percentages of the commissions generated. In comparison, major firms in other industries such as financial services and manufacturing, while not ignoring financial incentives, have utilized wages and salaries augmented by indirect compensation as the mainstay of their compensation package to attract and retain employees, and to reinforce their performance.

In general, companies that emphasize monetary rewards want to reinforce individual achievement and responsibility, while those that emphasize non-monetary rewards prefer to reinforce commitment to the organization. Thus a greater emphasis on monetary rewards is generally found among firms facing a volatile market with low job security, those emphasizing sales rather than customer service, and those trying to foster a competitive internal climate rather than long-term employee commitment. A greater reliance on non-monetary rewards is usually found in companies with a relatively stable work force, those that emphasize customer service and loyalty rather than fast sales growth, and those that want to create a more cooperative atmosphere within the firm.[39]

It should also be noted that in the midst of an economic recession or a downturn in company profits, some companies offer non-monetary rewards as a way to retain employees for whom getting a new job is the only way to get a raise in pay. Financially squeezed by the recession of the early 1990s, some companies developed creative non-monetary ways to reward employees. For instance, to avoid a brain drain of their scientists, some high-technology companies set up a technical track to let scientists advance without taking on the managerial tasks they dislike. Other companies provided flexible work arrangements, overseas transfers, or educational sabbaticals.[40]

■ Open versus Secret Pay

Firms vary widely in the extent to which they communicate openly about their compensation levels or even compensation practices. At one extreme, some firms require employees to sign an oath that they will not divulge their pay to co-workers; the penalty for breaking the oath is termination. At the other extreme, every employee's pay is a matter of public record. Many organizations come down somewhere in between on the *open pay versus secret pay* issue: they do not publish individual data but they do provide information on pay and salary ranges.

Open pay has two advantages over secret pay.[41] First, limiting employees' access to compensation information often leads to greater pay dissatisfaction because employees tend to overestimate the pay of co-workers and superiors. In other words, when compensation is secret, people tend to feel more underpaid than they really are. Second, open pay forces managers to be more fair and effective in administering compensation because bad decisions cannot be hidden and good decisions can serve as motivators to the best workers.

But open pay has a downside. First, it forces managers and supervisors to be prepared to defend their compensation decisions publicly. As we will see later in this chapter, personal judgements play a major role in deciding who gets paid what in any pay system. Regardless of good-faith attempts to explain these judgements, it may be impossible to satisfy everyone (even those who are doing very well may feel that they should be doing better). Second, the cost of making a mistake in a pay decision increases when pay is open, and this may prevent managers from being more innovative in the way they spend compensation dollars. Third, to avoid time-consuming and nerve-wracking arguments with employees, managers may eliminate pay differences among subordinates despite differences in performance levels. This, in turn, may lead to turnover of the better performers, who feel underpaid.

So, despite its potential benefits, open pay is not appropriate for every organization. Recent research suggests that greater pay openness is more likely to be successful in organizations with extensive employee involvement and an egalitarian culture that engenders trust and commitment.[42] This is because open pay can foster perceptions of fairness and greater motivation only in a climate that nurtures employee relations. In more competitive climates, it may unleash a destructive cycle of conflict and hostilities that is difficult to stop.

▇ Centralization versus Decentralization of Pay Decisions

Organizations must decide where pay decisions will be made. In a centralized system, pay decisions are tightly controlled in a central location, normally the human resources department at corporate headquarters. In a decentralized system, pay decisions are delegated deep down into the firm, normally to managers of each unit. What are the advantages of *centralization versus decentralization of pay decisions*?

Centralized pay is more appropriate when it is cost effective and efficient to hire compensation specialists who can be located in a single place and made responsible for salary surveys, benefits administration, and record keeping.[43] If the organization faces frequent legal challenges, it may also be prudent to centralize major compensation decisions in the hands of professionals. In addition, companies tend to centralize these functions during periods of decline to control expenses.

There are some potential negative consequences of too much centralized control. A centralized system maximizes internal equity, but does not handle external equity (market) concerns very well. Thus large and diverse organizations are better served by a decentralized pay system. Also, as more and more companies try to build stronger links between pay and performance, one of the first things they realize is that one department—typically HR—can't make all the compensation decisions effectively. In 1991, Sun Life introduced an approach it calls a "prism" strategy, characterized as "grass-roots" and "bottom-up." The emphasis is on teamwork, involvement, and continuous improvement to become more responsive to customer needs. Teams of employees, having created an approved mission statement and plan, are measured on results and share the financial gains attributable to their performance. Rewards have ranged from $200 to $2,000; some 1,400 of Sun Life's 3,500 employees are involved in approved prism strategies, and more sites are under development. The employer is enthusiastic about the response to the program.[44]

The Manager's Notebook, "Checklist for Planning a New Way to Pay," lists some crucial questions that managers should consider when helping to devise a new compensation program.[45]

Summary. Compensation is a complex topic that has a significant impact on the success of an organization. You may be feeling a bit overwhelmed at this point by the number of decisions that managers need to make in designing and implementing a compensation system. In practice, however, the nine issues we have discussed are not independent of one other. For instance, if circumstances dictate that paramount attention be given to external equity, then decisions on the other issues will follow from that. Pay for the job (as opposed to the individual) will be necessary because the job is the basis of the external comparison and market wages are by definition associated with external equity. Monetary rather than non-monetary rewards will probably be used because money is the usual measure of external equity. And, as we have just seen, external equity is easier to manage in a decentralized system.

In short, the good news is that there are not as many separate compensation systems as the nine options might suggest. The bad news is that none of these options is a simple either/or decision. Rather, each pair of criteria defines two end points on a continuum, with many possibilities between them.

Manager's Notebook

Checklist for Planning a New Way to Pay

◆ Are we currently able to attract the calibre of employees we need in our work unit?
◆ What are the strengths and deficiencies of our current salary program?
◆ In what areas are my needs as supervisor not being met? Are these shortfalls due to the compensation program design?
◆ What components of the program seem to be out of sync with my understanding of our compensation philosophy and program objectives? Does this mean we need to replace these components or can we fix them?
◆ Are we communicating to employees appropriately? Do they understand our objectives and the program's rationale? Can we fine-tune the program to correct the message?

SOURCE: Excerpted from Risher, H. (1993, January–February). Strategic salary planning. *Compensation and Benefits Review*, 46–50.

One final note: we will discuss the role of unions in Chapter 15. However, it is important to note here that compensation policies that apply to a unionized work force are subject to negotiation and bargaining. Thus managers in union shops are often severely restricted in what they can and cannot do with regard to compensation issues.

■ Compensation Tools

For the past 100 years, companies have used numerous techniques to decide who should get paid what. The goal of all these tools is to produce pay systems that are equitable and that allow the firm to attract, retain, and motivate workers while keeping labour costs under control. Despite their diversity, compensation tools can be grouped into two broad categories, depending on the unit of analysis used to make pay decisions: job-based approaches and skill-based approaches.

The first category, *job-based approaches,* includes the most traditional and widely used types of compensation programs.[46] These plans assume that work gets done by people who are paid to perform well-defined jobs (for example, secretary, book-keeper). Each job is designed to accomplish specific tasks (for example, typing, record keeping) and is normally performed by several people. Because all jobs are not equally important to the firm and the labour market puts a greater value on some jobs than on others, the primary objective of a compensation system is to allocate pay so that the most important jobs that command the highest earnings in the labour market are paid the most.

A simplified example of a typical job-based pay structure appears in Figure 10–4. It shows the pay structure of a hypothetical large restaurant with 87 employees performing 18 different jobs. These 18 jobs are grouped into six *pay grades,* with pay levels ranging from $6.85 an hour for jobs in the lowest grades to a maximum of $42 an hour for the job in the highest grade (chef). Employees are paid within the range established for the grade at which their job is classified. Thus a dishwasher or a busperson would be paid between $6.85 and $7.50 an hour (Grade 1).

The second type of pay plan, the *skill-based approach,* is far less common. It assumes that workers should be paid not according to the job they hold, but rather by how flexible or capable they are at performing multiple tasks. Under this type of plan, the greater the variety of job-related skills workers possess, the more they would be paid. Figure 10–5 shows a simplified example of a skill-based approach that could be used at the same hypothetical restaurant as an alternative to the job-based approach depicted in Figure 10–4. Workers who master the first set of skills (Block 1) receive $7 an hour; those who learn the skills in Block 2 (in addition to those in Block 1) receive $9.00 an hour; those who acquire the skills in Block 3 (in addition to those in Blocks 1 and 2) are paid $13.50 an hour; and so on.

In the sections that follow, we discuss these two major types of compensation programs in greater depth. Because compensation tools and pay plans can be very complex, we avoid many of the operational details, focussing instead on these programs' intended uses and their relative strengths and weaknesses. Excellent sources that provide step-by-step procedures of how to implement such programs are available elsewhere.[47]

■ Job-Based Compensation Plans

There are three key components of developing job-based compensation plans: achieving internal equity, achieving external equity, and achieving individual equity. Figure 10–6 summarizes how these are interrelated and the steps involved in each component. The majority of larger Canadian firms rely on this or a similar scheme to compensate their work force.[48]

	Jobs	Number of Positions	Pay
GRADE 6	Chef	2	$27.50–$42.00/h
GRADE 5	Manager	1	$14.50–$28.00/h
	Sous-Chef	1	
GRADE 4	Assistant Manager	2	$9.00–$15.50/h
	Lead Cook	2	
	Office Manager	1	
GRADE 3	General Cook	5	$7.50–$11.00/h
	Short-Order Cook	2	
	Assistant to Lead Cook	2	
	Clerk	1	
GRADE 2	Server	45	$7.00–$8.50/h
	Hostess	4	
	Cashier	4	
GRADE 1	Kitchen Helper	2	$6.85–$7.50/h
	Dishwasher	3	
	Janitor	2	
	Busperson	6	
	Security Guard	2	

Figure 10–4 Pay Structure of a Large Restaurant Developed Using a Job-Based Approach

Skill Block	Skills	Pay
5	• Create new items for menu • Find different uses for leftovers (e.g., hot dishes, buffets) • Coordinate and control work of all employees upon manager's absence	$31.00/h
4	• Cook existing menu items following recipe • Supervise kitchen help • Prepare payroll • Ensure quality of food and adherence to standards	$22.50/h
3	• Schedule servers and assign workstations • Conduct inventory • Organize work flow on restaurant floor	$13.50/h
2	• Greet customers and organize tables • Take orders from customers • Bring food to tables • Assist in kitchen with food preparation • Perform security checks • Help with delivery	$9.00/h
1	• Use dishwashing equipment • Use chemicals/disinfectants to clean premises • Use vacuum cleaner, mop, waxer, and other cleaning equipment • Clean and set up tables • Perform routine kitchen chores (e.g., making coffee)	$7.00/h

Figure 10–5 Pay Schedule of a Large Restaurant Designed Using a Skill-Based Approach

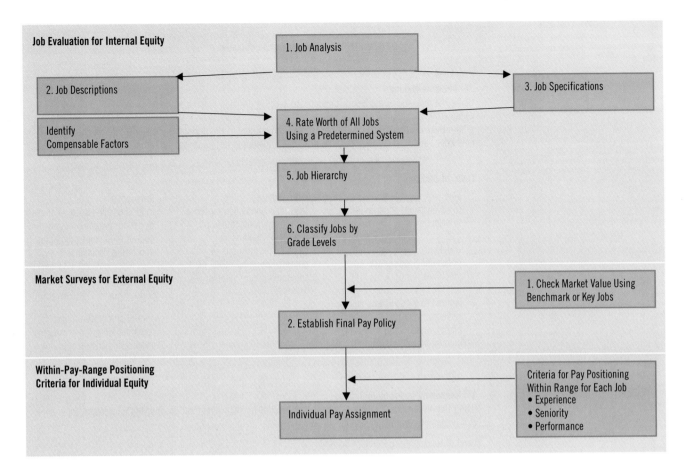

Figure 10–6 The Key Steps in Creating Job-Based Compensation Plans

Achieving Internal Equity: Job Evaluation.   The first six steps in determining job-based compensation are designed to assess the relative value or contribution of different jobs (*not* individual employees) to an organization. This six-step process, referred to as **job evaluation,** is intended to provide a rational, orderly, and systematic judgement of how important each job is to the firm. Its ultimate goal is to achieve internal equity in the pay structure.

Step 1: Conduct job analysis.   As we discussed in Chapter 2, **job analysis** is the gathering and organization of information concerning the tasks, duties, and responsibilities of specific jobs. In this first step in the job-evaluation process, information is gathered about the duties, tasks, and responsibilities of all jobs being evaluated. Job analysts may use personal interviews with workers, questionnaires completed by employees and/or supervisors, and business records (for example, cost of equipment operated and annual budgets) to study the what, how, and why of various tasks that make up the job. Sample items from a commonly used job analysis questionnaire, the *Position Analysis Questionnaire,* appear in Figure 10–7. For each question, the job analyst considers what is known about the job and decides which of the five descriptions is most appropriate.

Step 2: Write job descriptions.   In the second step in the job-evaluation process, the job analysis data are boiled down into a written document that identifies, defines, and describes each job in terms of its duties, responsibilities, working conditions, and specifications. This document is called a **job description.** (You will recall this from Chapter 2.)

Step 3: Determine job specifications.   **Job specifications** consist of the worker characteristics that an employee must meet to perform the job successfully.

job evaluation
The process of evaluating the relative value or contribution of different jobs to an organization.

job analysis
The gathering and organization of information concerning the tasks and duties of specific jobs.

job description
A written document that identifies, defines, and describes a job in terms of its duties, responsibilities, working conditions, and requirements.

job specification
A prerequisite that an employee must meet to perform a job successfully.

Mental Processes

Decision Making, Reasoning, & Planning/Scheduling

36. Decision Making

Using the response scale below, indicate the level of decision making typically involved in the job, considering the number and complexity of the factors that must be taken into account, the variety of alternatives available, the consequences and importance of the decisions, the background experience, education, and training required, the precedents available for guidance, and other relevant considerations.

Level of Decision

1 Very limited
(e.g., decisions such as those in selecting parts in routine assembly), shelving items in a warehouse, cleaning furniture, or handling automatic machines)

2 Limited (e.g., decisions such as those in operating a wood planer, dispatching a taxi, or lubricating an automobile)

3 Intermediate
(e.g., decisions such as those in setting up machines for operation, diagnosing mechanical disorders of aircraft, reporting news, or supervising auto service workers)

4 Substantial
(e.g., decisions such as those in determining production quotas or making promoting and hiring decisions)

5 Very substantial
(e.g., decisions such as those in approving an annual corporate budget, recommending major surgery, or selecting the location for a new plant)

37. Reasoning in Problem Solving

Using the response scale below, indicate the level of reasoning required in applying knowledge, experience, and judgement to problems.

Level of Reasoning in Problem Solving

1 Very limited
(use of common sense to carry out simple or relatively uninvolved instructions, e.g., hand assembler or mixing machine operator)

2 Limited
(use of some training and/or experience to select from a limited number of solutions the most appropriate action or procedure in performing the job, e.g., sales clerk, electrician apprentice, or library assistant)

3 Intermediate
(use of relevant principles to solve practical problems and to deal with a variety of concrete variables in situations where only limited standardization exists, such as that used by supervisors or technicians)

4 Substantial (use of logic or scientific thinking to define problems, collect information, establish facts, and draw valid conclusions, such as that used by petroleum engineers, personnel directors, or chain store managers)

5 Very substantial (use of logical or scientific thinking to solve a wide range of intellectual and practical problems, such as that used by research chemists, nuclear physicists, corporate presidents, or managers of a large branch or plant)

Figure 10–7 Sample Items from Position Analysis Questionnaire

SOURCE: Purdue Research Foundation, West Lafayette, IN 47907-1650. Used with permission.

These prerequisites are drawn from the job analysis, although in some cases they are legally mandated (for example, plumbers must have a plumbing licence). Job specifications are typically very concrete in terms of necessary years and type of prior work experience, level and type of education, certificates, vocational training, and so forth. They are usually included on job descriptions.

Step 4: Rate worth of all jobs using a predetermined system. After job descriptions and job specifications are finalized, they are used to determine the relative value or contributions of different jobs to the organization. This job evaluation is normally done by a three- to seven-person committee that may include supervisors, managers, HR department staff, and outside consultants. Several well-known evaluation procedures have evolved over the years, but the *point factor system* is used by the vast majority of firms.[49]

The point factor system uses **compensable factors** to evaluate jobs. Compensable factors are work-related criteria that the organization considers most important in assessing the relative value of different jobs. One commonly used compensable factor is knowledge. Jobs that require more knowledge (acquired either through formal education or through informal experience) receive a higher rating, and thus more compensation. While each firm can determine its own compensable factors, or even create compensable factors suitable to various occupational groups or job families (clerical, technical, managerial, and so on), most firms adopt compensable factors from well-established job-evaluation systems. Two point factor systems that are widely accepted are the *Hay Guide Chart Profile Method* and the *MAA National Position Evaluation Plan* (formerly known as the NMTA point factor system). The Hay Method, which is summarized in Figure 10–8, uses three compensable factors to evaluate jobs: know-how, problem solving, and accountability. The MAA (NMTA) plan has three separate units: Unit I for hourly blue-collar jobs; Unit II for clerical, technical, and service positions; and Unit III for exempt supervisory, professional, and management-level positions. The MAA (NMTA) plan includes 11 factors divided into four broad categories (skill, effort, responsibility, and job conditions). The Unit I plan is summarized in Figure 10–9.[50]

In both systems each compensable factor is assigned a scale of numbers and degrees. The more important factors are given higher point values, while factors of less importance are assigned lower values. For instance, as Figure 10–10 on page 303 shows, the highest possible points under the MAA (NMTA) system are for experience, with each degree of experience worth 22 points. The value of the other two MAA (NMTA) skill factors is 14 points per degree. All other factors are worth either five or 10 points per degree.

compensable factors

Work-related criteria that an organization considers most important in assessing the relative value of different jobs.

KNOW-HOW

Know-how is the sum total of every kind of skill, however acquired, necessary for acceptable job performance. This sum total, which comprises the necessary overall "fund of knowledge" an employee needs, has three dimensions:

- ● Knowledge of practical procedures, specialized techniques, and learned disciplines.
- ●● The ability to integrate and harmonize the diversified functions involved in managerial situations (operating, supporting, and administrative). This know-how may be exercised consultatively as well as executively and involves in some combination the areas of organizing, planning, executing, controlling, and evaluating.
- ●●● Active, practising skills in the area of human relationships.

PROBLEM SOLVING

Problem solving is the original "self-starting" thinking required by the job for analysing, evaluating, creating, reasoning, and arriving at conclusions. To the extent that thinking is circumscribed by standards, covered by precedents, or referred to others, problem solving is diminished and the emphasis correspondingly is on know-how.

Problem solving has two dimensions:

- ● The environment in which the thinking takes place.
- ●● The challenge presented by the thinking to be done.

ACCOUNTABILITY

Accountability is the answerability for an action and for the consequences thereof. It is the measured effect of the job on end results. It has three dimensions:

- ● Freedom to act—the degree of personal or procedural control and guidance.
- ●● Job impact on end results.
- ●●● Magnitude—indicated by the general dollar size of the area(s) most clearly or primarily affected by the job (on an annual basis).

Figure 10–8 Hay Compensable Factors

SOURCE: Courtesy The Hay Group, Boston, MA.

Skill

1. *Knowledge.* Measures the level of learning or equivalent formal training applied in a given type of work.
2. *Experience.* Measures the amount of time usually needed before being able to perform a job's duties with no more than normal supervision.
3. *Initiative and ingenuity.* Indicates the extent to which independent judgement and decision making are exercised on the job.

Effort

4. *Physical demand.* Measures how much and how often duties include lifting heavy materials, moving them, and working in difficult positions.
5. *Mental attention or visual demand.* Measures how much fatigue occurs from work that is visually or mentally intense, concentrated, and exacting.

Responsibility

6. *Equipment or process.* Measures the damage to equipment or process that would probably result from error or carelessness.
7. *Material, product, or service quality.* Refers to losses that would likely occur through spoilage, waste, and negligence in processing, inspection, testing, or delivery of service.
8. *Safety of others.* Measures the extent to which a job involves protecting others from injury or health hazards.
9. *Work of others or as a member of quality/process team.* Refers to the extent of responsibility for assisting, instructing, or directing others or involvement in quality or process teams that affect other operations within the company.

Job Conditions

10. *Working conditions.* Measures the degree of exposure to such elements as dust, heat, noise, or fumes.
11. *Hazards.* Concerns the risk of injury from materials, tools, equipment, and locations that remains even after protective and safety measures have been taken.

Figure 10–9 MAA National Position Evaluation Plan's 11 Compensable Factors (Unit I—The Manufacturing, Maintenance, Warehousing, Distribution, and Service Positions)

SOURCE: MAA (formerly NMTA) National Position Evaluation Plan.

This scale allows the evaluation committee to assign a number of points to each job on the basis of each factor degree. For example, using the MAA (NMTA) table in Figure 10–10, let's assume that job X is rated at the fifth degree for physical demand (50 points), equipment or process (25 points), material or product (25 points), safety of others (25 points), and work of others (25 points); at the fourth degree for mental or visual demand (20 points), working conditions (40 points), and hazards (20 points); at the second degree for experience (44 points); and at the first degree for knowledge (14 points), and initiative and ingenuity (14 points). The total points for this job across all 11 MAA (NMTA) compensable factors is thus 302.

job hierarchy

A listing of jobs in order of their importance to the organization, from highest to lowest.

Step 5: Create a job hierarchy.   The four steps described thus far produce a **job hierarchy,** a listing of jobs in terms of their relative assessed value (from highest to lowest). Figure 10–11 illustrates a job hierarchy for office jobs in a typical large organization. Column 1 of the figure shows the total points assigned to each job in descending order. These range from a high of 300 for customer service representative to a low of 60 for receptionist.

Step 6: Classify jobs by grade levels.   For the sake of simplicity, most large organizations classify jobs into grades as the last step in the job-evaluation process. Traditional compensation systems with 20 or more grades, or "bands," can be reduced to as few as five grades. The use of "broad-banding" at Canadian General Electric was part of a sweeping set of organizational changes introduced in 1992. One of the major benefits for the company was that broad-banding removed employees' preoccupation with their grade level, and allowed them to become more open to the need for acquiring particular skills to support the new organizational design.[51] Typically, the job hierarchy is reduced to a manageable number of grade levels with the assigned points used to determine where to set up dividing lines between grades. This resembles the process used by a professor converting the total-points earned in a course into grades of A+, A, B+, C, C+, and so on. For example, column 2 in Figure 10–11 shows how the hierarchy of 18 clerical jobs is

Factor Degree	1st Degree	2nd Degree	3rd Degree	4th Degree	5th Degree
Points Assigned to Factor Degrees					
Skill					
1. Knowledge	14	28	42	56	70
2. Experience	22	44	66	88	110
3. Initiative and Ingenuity	14	28	42	56	70
Effort					
4. Physical Demand	10	20	30	40	50
5. Mental or Visual Demand	5	10	15	20	25
Responsibility					
6. Equipment or Process	5	10	15	20	25
7. Material or Product	5	10	15	20	25
8. Safety of Others	5	10	15	20	25
9. Work of Others	5	10	15	20	25
Job Conditions					
10. Working Conditions	10	20	30	40	50
11. Hazards	5	10	15	20	25

Figure 10–10 MAA National Position Evaluation Plan: Points Assigned to Factor Degrees
SOURCE: MAA (formerly NMTA) National Position Evaluation Plan.

	1 Points	2 Grade	3 Weekly Pay Range
Customer Service Representative	300	5	$700–$900
Executive Secretary/Administrative Assistant	298		
Senior Secretary	290		
Secretary	230	4	$630–$770
Senior General Clerk	225		
Credit and Collection	220		
Accounting Clerk	175	3	$600–$675
General Clerk	170		
Legal Secretary/Assistant	165		
Senior Word Processing Operator	160		
Word Processing Operator	125	2	$545–$600
Purchasing Clerk	120		
Payroll Clerk	120		
Clerk-Typist	115		
File Clerk	95	1	$490–$550
Mail Clerk	80		
Personnel Clerk	80		
Receptionist	60		

Figure 10–11 Hierarchy of Clerical Jobs, Pay Grades, and Weekly Pay Range for a Hypothetical Office

divided into five grade levels. All jobs in a given grade are judged to be essentially the same in terms of importance because the points assigned to each are very close in number.

Other job-evaluation systems are the *ranking system* (in which the evaluation committee puts together a hierarchy of job descriptions from highest to lowest based on an overall judgement of value); the *classification system* (in which the committee sorts job descriptions into grades, as in the federal civil service job classification system); *factor comparison* (a complex and seldom-used variation of the point and ranking systems); and *policy capturing* (in which mathematical analysis is used to estimate the relative value of each job based on the firm's existing practices).

Two key aspects of our discussion so far should be kept in mind. First, job evaluation is performed internally and does not take into account the wage rates in the marketplace or what other firms are doing. Second, job evaluation focusses only on the value of the tasks that make up each job, not the people performing them. The MAA (NMTA) booklet distributed to all employees whose jobs are evaluated under that system makes this very explicit: "The plan does not judge anyone as an individual; it does not rate anyone's ability to perform a job. It [evaluates] each job according to a simple set of [compensable] factors ... that are applied in exactly the same way to all jobs."[52]

Achieving External Equity: Market Surveys.

To achieve external equity, firms often conduct *market surveys*. The purpose of these surveys in most job-based compensation systems is to determine the pay ranges for each grade level. An organization may conduct its own salary surveys, but most purchase commercially available surveys. Consulting firms conduct literally hundreds of such surveys each year for almost every type of job and geographical area.

Why spend time and money on internal job evaluations when market data can be used to determine the value of jobs? There are two reasons. First, most companies have jobs that are unique to the firm and therefore cannot be easily matched to market data.[53] For instance, the job of "administrative assistant" in Company Y may involve supporting top management in important tasks (for example, making public appearances for an executive when he or she is not available), while in Company Z it may involve only routine clerical duties. Second, the importance of a job can vary from firm to firm. For example, the job of "scientist" in a high-tech firm (where new-product creation is a key to competitive advantage in the market) is usually far more important than in a mature manufacturing company (where scientists are often expected only to perform routine tests).

Using market surveys to link job-evaluation results to external wage/salary data generally involves two steps: benchmarking and establishing a pay policy.

benchmark job or **key job**

A job that is similar or comparable in content across firms.

Step 1: Identify benchmark or key jobs.

To link the internal job-evaluation hierarchy or grade level to market salaries, most firms identify **benchmark** or **key jobs**—that is, jobs that are similar or comparable in content across firms—and check salary surveys to determine how much these key jobs are worth to other employers. The company then sets pay rates for non-key jobs (for which market data are *not* available) by assigning them the same pay range as key jobs that fall into that grade level.

An example will help here. Let's say five of the jobs in our office example in Figure 10–11 are identified as key. (These are briefly described in Figure 10–12.) The company purchases a salary survey for office workers in the area showing both average weekly pay and the 25th, 50th, and 75th percentiles in weekly pay for these key jobs. For example, Figure 10–13 shows that 25 percent of the customer service representatives in organizations included in the survey earn $550 per week or less, 50 percent earn $700 or less, and 75 percent earn $900 or less. The average weekly salary in the area for this job is $680. The company uses these market data to assign a pay range for all jobs that were evaluated at the same grade level as the key job of customer service representative—in this case, executive secretary and senior secretary. But first it needs to establish a pay policy.

pay policy

A firm's decision to pay above, below, or at the market rate for its jobs.

Step 2: Establish a pay policy.

Because market wages and salaries vary widely (look again at Figure 10–13), the organization needs to decide whether to lead, lag, or pay the going rate (which is normally defined as the midpoint of the wage/salary distribution in the survey). A firm's **pay policy** is determined by how it chooses to position itself in the pay market. The hypothetical firm shown in

CUSTOMER SERVICE REPRESENTATIVE—Establishes and maintains good customer relations and provides advice and assistance on customer problems.

CREDIT AND COLLECTION CLERK—Performs clerical tasks related to credit and collection activities; performs routine credit checks, obtains supplementary information, investigates overdue accounts, follows up by mail and/or telephone to customers on delinquent payments.

ACCOUNTING CLERK—Performs a variety of routine accounting clerical work such as maintaining journals, subsidiary ledgers, and related reports according to well-defined procedures or detailed instructions.

WORD PROCESSING OPERATOR—Operates word processing equipment to enter or search, select, and merge text from a storage device or internal memory for continuous or repetitive production of copy.

CLERK-TYPIST—Performs routine clerical and typing work; follows established procedures and detailed written or oral instructions; may operate simple types of office machines and equipment.

Figure 10–12 Sample Benchmark Jobs for Office Personnel

SOURCE: 1994 AMS Foundation *Office, Secretarial, Professional, Data Processing and Management Salary Report.* AMS Foundation, 550 W. Jackson Blvd., Suite 360, Chicago, IL 60661.

Benchmark Jobs	Weekly Pay Percentile			Weekly Pay Average
	25th	50th	75th	
1. Customer Service Representative	$550	$700	$900	$680
2. Credit and Collection Clerk	$550	$630	$770	$635
3. Accounting Clerk	$520	$600	$675	$600
4. Word Processing Operator	$530	$545	$600	$550
5. Clerk-Typist	$460	$490	$550	$480

Figure 10–13 Market Salary Data for Selected Benchmark Office Jobs

Figure 10–11, for example, decided to set a pay policy pegging the minimum pay for each grade to the 50th percentile and the maximum pay to the 75th percentile in the market (see column 3 of Figure 10–11). Some firms use more complex methods to achieve the same objective.[54]

Achieving Individual Equity: Within-Pay-Range Positioning Criteria.   After the firm has finalized its pay structure by determining pay ranges for each job, it must perform one last task: assign each employee a pay rate within the range established for his or her job. Companies frequently use previous experience, seniority, and performance appraisal ratings to determine how much an employee is to be paid within the stipulated range for his or her job. The objective of this last step, *within-pay-range positioning criteria,* is to achieve individual equity. **Individual equity** refers to fairness in pay decisions for employees holding the same job.

individual equity

The perceived fairness of individual pay decisions.

Evaluating Job-Based Compensation Plans.   As we noted earlier, job-based compensation programs are widely used by employers. The major benefit of such systems is that they appear to be rational, objective, and systematic, all features that minimize employee complaints. They are also relatively easy to set up and administer. However, these programs have several significant drawbacks, specifically:

◆   Job-based compensation plans do not take into account the nature of the business and its unique problems. For example, jobs are harder to define and change more rapidly in small, growing companies than in larger, more stable companies (such as those in the insurance industry). Heavy reliance on job-evaluation procedures and surveys assumes a universal perspective that may not be relevant to the firm, and may even be detrimental.

◆ The process of establishing job-based compensation plans is much more subjective and arbitrary than its proponents suggest. These plans may provide a façade of objectivity to cover what is essentially a series of judgement calls.

◆ Job-based systems are less appropriate at higher levels of an organization, where it is more difficult to separate individual contributions from the job itself. At managerial and professional levels, the employee helps define the job. To force people to conform to a narrowly defined job description robs the organization of much-needed creativity.

◆ As the economy has become more service-oriented and the manufacturing sector has continued to shrink, jobs have become more broadly defined. As a result, job descriptions are often awash in generalities. This makes it more difficult to evaluate the relative importance of jobs.

◆ Job-based compensation plans tend to be bureaucratic, mechanistic, and inflexible. Once an internal pay structure is put in place, it is difficult to change. Thus firms cannot easily adapt their pay structures to a rapidly changing economic environment, such as that faced by the automobile industry in the 1980s and 1990s. In addition, because they rely on fixed salary and benefits associated with each level in the hierarchy, these plans tend to result in layoffs to save on costs during economic downturns. Japanese firms, which rely less on job-based compensation plans and often provide 20 to 30 percent of their employees' pay in variable form, have greater flexibility to absorb the economy's ups and downs.

◆ The job-evaluation process is a *systematic* one in which organizations attempt to apply consistent criteria to the jobs being performed. However, job evaluation is not and cannot be *scientific* in determining the value of jobs, since value is ultimately a human assessment. The relatively high weights frequently given to physical demands and risks and to hierarchical level, and the lower weights assigned to job requirements for interpersonal and nurturing behaviours, can be seen as reflecting a cultural bias that values "male" roles more highly. Whether or not one is persuaded that this bias in job evaluation schemes has much influence, the Ontario Pay Equity legislation, by using male-dominated and female-dominated positions as the focus of its regulations, underscores the importance of gender-based roles as an influence in the pay gap between men and women.

◆ Wage and salary data obtained from market surveys are not definitive. After adjusting for job content, company size, firm performance, and geographic location, differences ranging from 35 to 300 percent in the pay of identical jobs within the same industry are not uncommon.[55] One researcher has concluded: "Clearly, the pay practices of firms in the same industry are often widely divergent.... No doubt, this means that employers, on the basis of a carefully selected survey sample, can justify widely divergent pay practices (a point frequently ignored when competitive pay is analysed and discussed)."[56]

◆ In determining internal and external equity, it is the employees' perceptions of equity that count, not the assessments of job-evaluation committees and paid consultants. Job-based compensation plans assume that the employer can decide what is equitable for the employee. Because equity is in the eye of the beholder, this approach may simply rationalize an employer's pay practices rather than compensate employees according to their contributions.

Despite all these criticisms, job-based compensation plans continue to be widely used, probably because there are no alternative systems that are both cost efficient and generally applicable. Skill-based pay, which we describe a little later in this chapter, offers an alternative approach, but it is costly and its uses are limited.

Suggestions for Practice.   Rather than dismissing job-based compensation plans completely, it is more realistic to take steps to reduce the potential problems associated with them. In developing a job-based pay plan, the firm should take the following recommendations into account:

◆ *Think strategically in making policy decisions concerning pay.* Tools are a means to an end, not an end in themselves. For example, it may be in the firm's best interests to design a certain number of jobs very broadly and flexibly. The firm may also find it advantageous to pay at the top of the market for critical jobs that are central to its mission and at the low end of the market for jobs it considers less critical. In short, the firm's business and HR strategy should drive the use of compensation tools rather than the other way around.

◆ *Secure employee input.* Employee dissatisfaction will be reduced to the extent that employees have a voice in the design and management of the compensation plan. A simple, straightforward way to solicit employee input is to use computers. Computer-assisted evaluation systems allow employees to describe their jobs in a way that can be synthesized, displayed, rearranged, and easily compared. This approach offers two benefits. First, it gives employees a chance to describe what they do. This tends to improve the acceptability of job-evaluation results (although it does not eliminate the need for evaluative judgements to develop a job hierarchy). Second, it offers a very inexpensive way to update job descriptions and to incorporate these changes into the system regularly (for example, yearly).

◆ *Increase each job's range of pay while expanding its scope of responsibility.* For instance, instead of setting the difference between the low and high end of the pay range at 15 percent on average, the firm might increase the difference to 50 percent. This approach, commonly called *job banding,* entails replacing narrowly defined job descriptions with broader categories (bands) of related jobs. Job banding allows the firm to cut back on the number of job titles and permits employees to receive a substantial pay raise without having to change jobs within the firm. Banding has three potential benefits. First, it gives the firm more flexibility because jobs are not narrowly defined. Second, during periods of slow growth, the firm can reward top performers without having to promote them through an organizational hierarchy. Third, the firm may save on administrative costs because with banding there are fewer layers of staff and management. For more details on how one company instituted a successful job banding system, see the Issues and Applications feature entitled "Banding at Fine Product: A Boost in Competitive Advantage."

◆ *Conduct pay equity audits periodically to ensure that the gender composition of a job does not affect its position in the hierarchy or in the interpretation of salary survey data.* Several procedures have been suggested for accomplishing this.[57] One approach uses computer-generated data to examine the extent to which job-evaluation results reflect differences in job content rather than the proportion of women in a given job.[58]

◆ *Expand the proportion of employees' pay that is variable (bonuses, shares plans, and so forth).* Variable pay programs provide the firm with the flexibility to reduce costs without resorting to layoffs. A large firm may prevent thousands of layoffs by devoting as little as 10 percent of an employee's pay to a variable pay pool that rewards workers during good times and serves as a "shock absorber" for the company during bad times when it must be withheld or reduced.

◆ *Establish dual career ladders for different types of employees so that moving into management ranks or up the organizational hierarchy is not the only way to receive a substantial increase in pay.* In some situations, such as in a large organization with multiple business units and several layers of management, a tall job hierarchy is appropriate; in others, a relatively flat hierarchy with much room for salary growth (based, for instance, on performance and seniority), makes more sense. Figure 10–14 is an example of a dual career ladder.

■ Skill-Based Compensation Plans

Unlike job-based compensation plans, skill-based compensation plans use skills as the basis of pay.[59] All employees start at the same pay rate and advance one pay level for each new skill they master.[60]

Three types of skills may be rewarded. Employees acquire *depth skills* when they learn more about a specialized area or become expert in a given field. They can acquire *horizontal* or *breadth skills* when they learn more and more jobs or tasks within the firm, and *vertical skills* when they acquire "self-management" competence, such as scheduling, coordinating, training, and leadership. This skill-based pay has been adopted by a wide range of industries, such as telecommunications (Nortel), insurance (Manulife and Guardian Insurance), natural resources (Shell Canada), and utilities (Ontario Hydro). Although still used by only a minority of employers, skill-based (or "competency-based") compensation is growing rapidly in its use, and fits particularly well with the trend to flatter, more flexible and team-based organizations.

Nortel
www.nortel.com

Shell Canada
www.shell.ca

Figure 10–14 Example of a Dual Career Ladder

Traditionally, jobs higher on the organizational chart receive greater compensation than those below. In contrast, the dual career ladder illustrated here shows that certain valuable employees can receive greater compensation than managers to whom they report.

SOURCE: LeBlanc, P. (1992). Banding the new pay structure for the transformed organization. *Perspectives in Total Compensation,* 3(8). American Compensation Association, Scottsdale, AZ. Used with permission of the author, Peter V. LeBlanc, of Sibson & Company.

Band	Managerial	Individual Contributor
13	President	
12	Executive Vice-President	
11	Vice-President	Executive Consultant
10	Assistant Vice-President	Senior Consultant
9	Director	Consultant
8	Senior Manager	Senior Adviser
7	Manager	Adviser
6		Senior Specialist
5		Specialist
4		Senior Technician
3		Senior Administrative Support, Technician
2		Administrative Support, Senior Manufacturing Associate
1		Clerical Support, Manufacturing Associate

Banding at Fine Products: A Boost in Competitive Advantage

Fine Products, Inc., a highly profitable consumer products company, found itself faced with increasing competition from lower-cost producers and consumer demand for greater product variety. An executive task force identified the company's compensation system for managers and professionals as a major impediment to dealing with these competitive challenges. Separate pay programs for different employee groups promoted a feeling of "class distinction"; workers could obtain significant pay increases only by moving up through a hierarchy of 20 levels; and a large number of job titles with narrow salary ranges prevented effective teamwork. In addition, managers were being rewarded for "empire building" rather than performance because their pay was linked to the number of people reporting to them. To solve these problems the company implemented a broad-banding system, reducing the company's overloaded job structure to six broadbands and collapsing many managerial and professional job titles. For example, the company collapsed 13 separate plant, regional, and production manager job titles down to four jobs with increased responsibility. The pay differential between bands was set at approximately 30%, with the range within each band set at approximately 90% (from $28,500 to $54,500 for "Band C," for instance).

Fine Products' new compensation system has given it the competitive advantage it needed. Broader salary bands have offered more room to reward sustained contributions, skills acquisition, and effective involvement in task force or project team assignments. The decreased emphasis on job levels has encouraged employees to make cross-functional moves to jobs that were at the same or a lower level in the old system. The new program has also facilitated job flexibility and cross-training because the broad bands can accommodate workers' current pay levels. Only a significant increase in an employee's accountability now justifies moving that employee to a new band.

SOURCE: Based on Haslett, S. 91995, November/December). Broadbanding: A strategic tool for organizational change. *Compensation and Benefits Review,* 40–43. Reprinted by permission of the publisher. American Management Association, N.Y. All rights reserved.

Skill-based pay offers several potential advantages to the firm.[61] First, it creates a more flexible work force that is not straitjacketed by job descriptions specifying work assignments for a given job title. Second, it promotes cross-training in which team members learn to do one another's jobs, thus preventing absenteeism and turnover from disrupting the work unit's ability to meet deadlines. Third, it calls for fewer supervisors, so management layers can be cut to produce a leaner organization. Fourth, it increases employees' control over their compensation because they know in advance what it takes to receive a pay raise (learning new skills).

Skill-based pay does pose significant risks to the organization. First, it may lead to higher compensation and training costs that are not offset by greater productivity or cost savings. This can happen when many employees master many or all of the skills and thus receive a higher wage than they would under a job-based pay rate. Second, unless employees have the opportunity to use all the skills they've acquired, they may become "rusty." Third, when employees hit the top of the pay structure, they may become frustrated and leave the firm because they have no further opportunity to receive a pay raise. Fourth, attaching monetary values to skills can become a guessing game unless external comparable pay data are available. Finally, skill-based pay may become part of the problem it is intended to solve (extensive bureaucracy and inflexibility) if an elaborate and time-consuming process is required to monitor and certify employee skills. In one large manufacturing firm, for example, skill-based pay has led to a civil-service-type system (the epitome of bureaucracy, in many people's eyes) that requires employees to furnish work samples and take paper-and-pencil tests and oral exams to qualify for pay associated with higher skills.

In short, skill-based pay is no panacea. To avoid cost overruns, perceptions of unfairness, and a highly regimented system, managers must carefully fit a skill-based pay system into their entire human resource strategy. For example, to justify the additional training expenditures associated with skill-based pay, human resource development should receive high priority in the firm's strategic plan. Such programs are more likely to work in organizations staffed with employees who are interested in learning multiple jobs rather than in beating the game to receive higher pay.

One final observation about skill-based pay: This is the pay system that many new and small businesses use by default. An entrepreneur who needs additional help hires people because of what they can do. Those who can do more things are more valuable to a growing business. Because flexibility is crucial for continued growth, flexible employees are more highly valued and paid accordingly. When a business is fairly new, of course, there is no formalized system relating specific skills to specific compensation values. However, at some point before too many employees are added, the company must systematize its compensation structure. It is then that the design issues described earlier become critical.

■ The Legal Environment and Pay System Governance

The legal framework of human resource management is an important consideration in the design and administration of compensation systems. Nearly nine of 10 people employed in Canada work for employers regulated by provincial legislation; the remainder work in federally regulated employment. Although statutes in various jurisdictions frequently differ in some specific provisions, there are clear common patterns. Compensation in Canada is generally shaped by three major categories of legislation: employment standards legislation, legislation geared to prevent unfair discrimination, and income tax legislation.

■ Employment Standards

Employment standards legislation exists in all jurisdictions. Such legislation sets parameters in a number of employment matters. The overall intent of employment standards legislation is to establish *minimum* standards of treatment for workers. In areas such as hours of work, standard wages and overtime rates, and paid holidays and vacations, floors on payments and ceilings on expectations are set.

Issues Subject to Regulation.   The ***Canada Labour Code*** (which applies to federally regulated employment such as airlines, banks, and the federal civil service) and the various provincial labour standards acts all specify a minimum wage, make some provision for a maximum number of hours of work, mandate minimum standards for overtime pay, specify the minimum amount of paid vacation, the number and dates of paid holidays, and several other issues. The various laws differ in their details. For example, as of March 1998, the minimum wage in Newfoundland was $5.05 per hour while in British Columbia it stood at $7.15,

Canada Labour Code
labour.hrdc-drhc.gc.ca/labour/
labstand/toc.html

Canada Labour Code

Federal legislation that regulates employment practices and standards in enterprises under federal jurisdiction.

some 33 percent higher. And within a jurisdiction, some occupational groups are treated differentially by these laws. For example, minimum wages are in some cases lower for younger workers (Alberta and Ontario: students under 18), or wage parameters may be framed differently for workers in certain occupations or industries (e.g., bartenders, seasonal agricultural workers, residential caretakers).

Employee Groups Covered by Employment Standards: Comparison with the United States.
Managerial and often professional employees are generally not covered by the minimum wage and maximum hours of work provisions of the law, nor by the overtime pay regulations that are standard elements of labour standards legislation. It is important to be aware that the legal environment in these matters in the United States is framed primarily by federal legislation, the *Fair Labor Standards Act,* which draws a clear, if elaborate distinction between employees not covered by the *Act*, widely referred to as "exempt" employees, and those who are covered ("non-exempt"). In contrast, there is no single exempt/non-exempt distinction that applies throughout Canada. Parallel specifics in Canadian employment standards legislation typically refer to "exclusions" of certain employee categories. Exactly which employees are excluded and for which aspects of the law varies from one jurisdiction to the next. For example, Ontario's act does not apply to people participating in work-experience programs and substantial portions of the act do not apply to qualified professionals (lawyers, doctors, engineers, architects, teachers, etc.), students employed in recreation industries, domestic servants, home-workers, and others. Lists of exclusions for other provinces are generally similar, but not identical. The significance of these lists of exclusions for Canadian employers is the necessity of knowing specifically which regulations apply to them.

Effects of Minimum Wage.
Employment standards legislation has been a subject of academic and political debate for decades. Those who favour minimum wages being set at a relatively high level generally see such regulation as protecting the wages of people whose earnings are at the bottom of the income spectrum. To illustrate this view, consider that an individual earning a "high" minimum wage of $7.15 per hour (the 1998 rate in British Columbia), would earn $14,000 in a year if he or she worked a full 2,000 hours. In many Canadian locations, such an income would not be sufficient to provide a family income that is above the poverty line. The need for a reasonable "floor" on earnings therefore persuades some observers that high minimum wages are an important social policy measure.

Those who oppose high minimum wages cite the fact that many industries, particularly those that employ lower-skilled workers in a global economy, tend to migrate to parts of the world where labour costs are low. Their claim is that high minimum wages "kill" jobs and lead to unnecessarily high levels of unemployment. Their preference is to allow the market to set wage levels and to allow individuals to accept or reject those jobs. They also suggest that high minimum wages lead to a pattern of wages described as *pay compression,* a situation in which the lowest-paid employees' compensation is too high by market standards and thus employees in more demanding jobs make only slightly more than the minimum because of market forces. If pay compression is severe or protracted, it can lead to morale problems and high turnover.

Lower Minimum for Some.

In some jurisdictions, occupations where employees normally receive tips are subject to lower minimum wages than are other occupations.

Overtime.   Once employees have worked a certain number of hours in a day (typically, eight) or in a week (40, 44, or 48, depending on jurisdiction), employers are required to pay employees at a higher minimum rate. In most cases the rate is 1.5 times their regular hourly rate, although in some provinces (Newfoundland and Nova Scotia) it is 1.5 times the *minimum wage*. Mandatory overtime premium pay, combined with regulations on the maximum number of hours an employee can work without requiring special arrangements with the government regulator, creates a situation where employers cannot require employees to work excessive hours, if the employees are covered by the legislation. Despite the overtime pay required, however, many employers still choose to use overtime extensively. While more expensive than regular hourly rates, overtime provides employers with flexibility to meet varying workloads, and it enables the employer to avoid the hiring, training, and fixed benefits costs of hiring additional staff.

◼ Legislation to Reduce Unfair Treatment

Two major forms of legislation motivated by the intent to reduce unfair discrimination affect compensation practices.

Human Rights Legislation.   All Canadian jurisdictions have human rights codes. These codes prohibit discrimination against people (in employment, among other activities) on the basis of certain personal attributes. Although the lists of proscribed categories are not uniform across all jurisdictions, all codes include sex, race/ethnicity/origin, marital status, and religion/creed as unacceptable reasons for discrimination. If a person is paid less because of gender, race, religion, or other prohibited criteria, the employer has violated the human rights code. However, demonstrating that the reason for paying the person less was discrimination and not a difference in qualifications, length of service, or performance is often difficult. It is clear from experience that unfair discrimination cannot be eliminated through human rights procedures alone. The persistence of disparities in pay among various groups of employees has led to other kinds of legislation, including pay equity laws. In 1998, a tribunal established by the Canadian Human Rights Commission ruled on a pay-equity appeal launched by federal public servants some 12 years earlier. The precise cost of the award at the time it was rendered was estimated to be between $2 billion and $6 billion. The federal government has decided to appeal the ruling, but the implications are clear: persistent underpayment of women can result in substantial unexpected costs for an employer that is found to be in violation.

Pay Equity.   The goal of equitable treatment of employees has led to several forms of legislation. In employment matters, generally, equity legislation has identified women, visible minorities, people with disabilities, and aboriginal people as groups deserving special protection and support. Where employment equity laws apply, they affect groups in their work rather than in their pay. However, since having a job and being promoted to more senior levels of responsibility both affect pay, employment equity has an important indirect effect on pay. Specific pay fairness laws differ from employment equity legislation in that pay fairness laws focus specifically on pay and generally on male–female differences. The purpose of these laws is to reduce unjustified pay differences between men and women. It is clear that women, on average, earn considerably less than men. Commonly accepted estimates are that women working full time earn, on average, 73 cents for each dollar earned by the average male working full time.[62] It is also generally accepted that only some of that difference in men's and women's earnings can be attributed to legitimate reasons such as the occupations people work in, their qualifications (including amount and type of experience), their length of service, and their performance. Twenty percent of the gap between men and women is estimated to be the result of discrimination.

Legislated attempts to eliminate the unwarranted part of that difference began with the requirement that there be equal pay for equal work. All Canadian jurisdictions have equal pay laws, either as separate legislation or as part of human rights codes. The standard in equal pay laws was that people doing the same job are legally entitled to the same pay, although variations in pay were allowed for differences in such considerations as performance and length of service. The impact of such laws has been limited, although they did help to establish clearly that the notion of paying women less *because* they are women is not acceptable. The limited impact of equal pay laws came from the fact that women and men tend to work in different occupations. For example, clerical workers and elementary school teachers are two groups that tend to be predominantly female; construction and maintenance occupations tend to be male.

The legislated standard is evolving from "equal pay for equal work" to "equal pay for work of equal value." This latter standard, generically termed **comparable worth,** is much more complicated to implement. This is particularly true in the case of the federal legislation, which specifies the principle but not the procedures to determine the extent of pay inequality. The difficulties stem from the need to compare jobs that have dissimilar content, such as a cook and a building maintenance employee. Legislated pay equity has gained prominence in the past 10 years, although there is great variability in current legislation. Ontario, Quebec, the federal jurisdiction, Prince Edward Island, Nova Scotia, and Manitoba have taken a variety of approaches. Ontario places the greatest onus on employers (in both the public and the private sectors) by requiring that employers take initiatives to identify and reduce the inequities that they identify. The verdict on the overall effect of pay equity legislation is still out. It is clear that the process will take time, and that there are significant administrative costs as well as payroll adjustment costs in complying with pay equity laws. Overall costs and benefits stemming from this legislation are yet to be assessed.

comparable worth

A pay concept or doctrine that calls for comparable pay for jobs that require comparable skills, effort, and responsibility and have comparable working conditions, even if the job content is different.

Woman's Work

As more women move into jobs traditionally filled by men, the issue of comparable worth has entered the spotlight.

■ Revenue Canada

The income tax system in Canada, administered by Revenue Canada, affects how much of an employee's earnings he or she keeps. The tax regulations also affect how benefits are treated for tax purposes, as will be discussed in Chapter 12. The law requires the employer to withhold and submit to the government a portion of employees' earnings to meet the employees' federal and provincial income tax obligations.

The tax laws change with almost every budget, either in the rates of taxation imposed, the tax treatment of various benefits, or both. An employer needs to understand the obligations imposed by income taxation, both to comply with the law, and to ensure that pay policies take advantage of whatever opportunities exist to provide cost-effective and attractive compensation under the law. The general trend over recent years has been to reduce the range of benefits (e.g., group life insurance) that can be provided without the value of the benefit being added to the employee's taxable compensation. However, such policies as dental and supplemental medical coverage present cost-effective alternatives for employers. This is a constantly changing area of human resource management, one for which specialized legal and benefits consultation and advice can be of great value.

Summary and Conclusions

What Is Compensation?　Total compensation has three components: (1) base compensation, the fixed pay received on a regular basis; (2) pay incentives, programs designed to reward good performance; and (3) benefits or indirect compensation, including health insurance, vacations, and perquisites.

Designing a Compensation System.　An effective compensation plan enables the firm to achieve its strategic objectives and is suited to the firm's uniqueness as well as to its environment. The pay options that managers need to consider in designing a compensation system are: (1) internal versus external equity, (2) fixed versus variable pay, (3) performance versus membership, (4) job versus individual pay, (5) egalitarianism versus elitism, (6) below-market versus above-market compensation, (7) monetary versus non-monetary rewards, (8) open versus secret pay, and (9) centralization versus decentralization of pay decisions. In all situations, the best choices depend on how well they "fit" between business objectives and the individual organization.

Compensation Tools.　There are two broad categories of compensation tools: job-based approaches and skill-based approaches. The typical job-based compensation plan has three components. To achieve internal equity, firms use job evaluation to assess the relative value of jobs throughout the firm. To achieve external equity, they use salary data on benchmark or key jobs obtained from market surveys to set a pay policy. To achieve individual equity, they use a combination of experience, seniority, and performance to establish an individual's position within the pay range for his or her job.

Skill-based compensation systems are more costly and more limited in use. Skill-based pay rewards employees for acquiring depth skills (learning more about a specialized area), horizontal or breadth skills (learning about more areas), and vertical skills (self-management).

The Legal Environment and Pay System Governance.　The major federal laws that govern compensation practices are in three areas: employment standards, which establish minimum wages, maximum hours of work, overtime premiums, paid holidays and paid vacations; protection from discrimination, in the form of human rights laws, equal-pay and pay equity legislation; and income tax legislation, which specifies how much tax employers are to withhold and the taxable status of indirect forms of compensation such as benefits. Unlike the United States, where such legislation is mainly federal, Canada's legal environment varies from one jurisdiction to the next in many of the specifics of its laws, although the general pattern of the legislated requirements is similar in many respects.

Key Terms and Concepts

base compensation, 287
below-market versus above-market compensation, 293
benchmark job or key job, 304
Canada Labour Code, 309
centralization versus decentralization of pay decisions, 296
classification system, 303
comparable worth, 312
compensable factors, 301
depth, horizontal/breadth, and vertical skills, 307
distributive justice model of pay equity, 288
egalitarian pay system, 293
egalitarianism versus elitism, 293
elitist pay system, 293
employee benefits or indirect compensation, 287
external equity, 288
factor comparison, 303
fair pay, 288

fixed versus variable pay, 290
Hay Guide Chart Profile Method, 301
individual equity, 305
internal equity, 288
internal versus external equity, 288
job analysis, 299
job banding, 307
job-based approach, 297
job description, 299
job evaluation, 299
job hierarchy, 302
job specifications, 299
job versus individual pay, 292
knowledge-based pay or skill-based pay, 292
labour market model of pay equity, 289
MAA (NMTS) National Position Evaluation Plan, 301
market surveys, 304
membership-contingent compensation, 291
minimum wage, 311

monetary versus non-monetary rewards, 294
open versus secret pay, 295
pay compression, 310
pay grade, 297
pay incentive, 287
pay mix, 287
pay policy, 304
performance-contingent compensation, 291
perquisite, 287
point factor system, 301
policy capturing, 304
Position Analysis Questionnaire, 299
ranking system, 303
risk sharing, 290
skill-based compensation plan, 297
total compensation, 287
within-pay-range positioning criteria, 305

Discussion Questions

1. Some employers have a policy of selectively matching external offers to prevent employees from leaving the organization. What are the pros and cons of such a policy? Explain.

2. Seventeen years ago a brash young engineer in a large chemical company handed her boss a four-page list of the promotions she expected to gain every two years as she rose through the ranks. She hoped for a vice-presidency eventually, which would put her only half-a-dozen rungs below chairman at this title-stingy company. The engineer has held nine jobs so far, but the last three have kept her at the director's level. The company is restructuring and this talented 48-year-old woman is getting discouraged. What kind of non-monetary rewards can the company offer to keep her from leaving?

3. One observer argues that external equity should always be the primary concern in compensation, noting that it attracts the best employees and prevents the top performers from leaving. Do you agree?

4. Should employees be paid primarily on the basis of the job they hold or according to their work performance?

5. For jobs in much of the public sector, compensation is based on job-evaluation systems. Several of these evaluation systems award high points, and thus high pay, for decision making, but their definition of "decision" can be controversial. For instance, one sign language interpreter told a legislative committee that she had to make four decisions at the same time in her work, but under her jurisdiction's evaluation system, these types of decisions did not count. By emphasizing decision making, how might such a job-evaluation system affect the management style of government department heads? Do you agree with those, like the sign language interpreter, who argue that job evaluation is unfair? What are its advantages and disadvantages?

6. Recall the woman in question 2 who has been stuck at the director's level for several years. She is one of the few female engineers in the company, and she just found out through the grapevine that a male engineer at her rank is getting paid 25 percent more than she is. How would you determine whether the pay difference between the male and the female engineer is legitimate?

Take it to the Net

Check out our Companion Website at: **www.prenticehall.ca/gomez** for a selection of self-study questions, key terms and concepts, updated Weblinks to related Internet sites, newsgroups, CBC video updates, and more.

MiniCase 1   *Success at Talisman: More Than Luck*

Talisman Energy, a 600-employee firm, has implemented a team-based organizational design with a compensation system intended to reinforce job performance. There is a goal-setting process that includes relating departmental goals to overall corporate goals, and then "cascading" these goals to branches and smaller groups. At all stages of goal setting, there is a dialogue that is intended to ensure that goals of larger and smaller units are aligned and that they are clearly understood.

The compensation system uses a base component and a variable component; the extent to which employees earn the variable element depends on attaining predetermined goals and on adding value to the organization. The variable pay component is large enough that it represents pay that is "at risk" rather than being seen as an add-on. At higher salary bands, a greater proportion of the pay is "at risk." The range of variable pay is from nothing to (at most) double the target amount. Begun in 1993, the plan met a mix of enthusiasm and skepticism about whether there really was a realistic upside to the variable component, and concern about significant pay being at risk. After three years of healthy company performance and payouts, the skepticism seems to be waning.

➤

Discussion Questions

1. Talisman indicates the following to be among their compensation goals: aligning programs to business needs, structure and culture; attracting and retaining required skills in a competitive marketplace; supporting the shared responsibility of job enrichment, growth and development; and reducing fixed costs and increasing flexibility within cash flow means. How does the program described help to accomplish those ends? Is the program more relevant to some of these goals than to others?

2. What reaction do you think Talisman would experience if payouts declined because the company encountered competitive pressures that reduced its profitability?

SOURCE: Skrzypinski, L. (1996, February 26). The many faces of team incentives: Skepticism waning for "at-risk" design. *Canadian HR Reporter*, 14. Used with permission of *Canadian HR Reporter*, MPL Communications Inc. Copyright 1996.

MiniCase 2   *Aetna Finds Strength In Fewer Numbers— of Job Descriptions*

Like many large firms, Aetna Life and Casualty Company has always relied on a highly stratified job-classification system in which everything, from salary levels and promotional opportunities to job descriptions and supervisory responsibilities, is connected to job class. "You know your job class, you know everything," explains Aetna's director of base-salary development.

Since it became a diversified financial services company, Aetna has been operating in a fast-changing and increasingly competitive business environment. But its employees are not accustomed to responding to market changes unless new tasks are written into their job descriptions. Since the old job-classification system isn't working in the new climate, Aetna is in the process of changing it. The company now defines work by the actual functions performed, gives information on market compensation levels to managers, and lets them make pay decisions based on an individual's performance. Major skills and competencies needed by employees are being identified and grouped into a broad job-family structure. With fewer job levels, employees may no longer be able to rely on promotions to get ahead. Instead they will earn bonuses for performing better. When Aetna completes this process, it expects to have just 200 job families instead of 7,000 job descriptions covering its 42,000 employees.

Discussion Questions

1. How would you describe Aetna's new system in terms of the following compensation criteria: laid out in this chapter: job-based versus individual pay, centralized versus decentralized pay decisions?
2. Why does Aetna think that having broad rather than narrow job classifications is a motivating force? What kind of employees do you think will do best under the new system?

SOURCE: Adapted from Caudron, S. (1993, June). Master the compensation maze. *Personnel Journal*, 64B–640. Copyright June 1993. Reprinted with permission of *Personnel Journal*, ACC Communications, Inc., Costa Mesa, CA (714) 752–1883; all rights reserved..

Case 1

Scott Paper—A Miracle or a Hoax?

After less than two years as CEO of Scott Paper, in 1996 Albert J. Dunlap, nicknamed "chainsaw Al," walked away with nearly $100 million in salary, bonus, stock gains, and other perks. Kimberly-Clark (which recently purchased Scott Paper) had agreed to pay Dunlop and a corps of his loyal lieutenants an extraordinary $41 million in the most lucrative noncompete agreement ever crafted in U.S. business. Dunlap alone got $20 million in exchange for his agreement not to work for a rival for five years, while five senior executives pocketed $4.2 million each.

Critics argue that Dunlap and other former Scott Paper executives were being rewarded for doing all the wrong things.

Soon after taking over, critics say, Dunlap's team began making moves that suggested their time horizons weren't very long. In late 1994, Scott's R&D budget was slashed in half, to about $35 million, and 60% of the R&D was eliminated. At the request of Dunlap's team, the marketing department began to generate weekly volume forecasts rather than monthly reports.

The cost cutters didn't go after just R&D, according to detractors. They also forbade managers from being involved in community activities because that would take away from their business duties. They banned memberships in industry organizations that allowed managers to network with competitors. They also scrapped a yearly event at which Scott met with its leading suppliers to improve relationships and get better prices. As a result of these policies, several communities lost a generous corporate citizen—especially in the Philadelphia area, where the company was headquartered from its founding in 1879 until 1995. Before moving the world headquarters to Boca Raton, Florida—just after buying an $18 million house there—Dunlap eliminated all corporate gifts to charities, even reneging on the final $50,000 payment of a $250,000 pledge to the Philadelphia Museum of Art. More than 11,000 of Scott's employees (71% of headquarters staff, 50% of managers, 20% of hourly workers) lost their jobs during Dunlap's brief tenure.

Scott's earnings more than doubled during Dunlap's tenure as CEO, but critics claim Dunlap engineered these illusory gains to maximize his pay and that of his close colleagues. They argue that Dunlap cut plenty of muscle along with the fat, pumping up short-term results at the expense of long-term health and destroying employees' commitment to the firm. To bolster their claim, Dunlap's critics point out that Scott actually lost market share in the three major product fields (paper towels, bathroom tissue, and facial tissue) during Dunlap's tenure.

Critical Thinking Questions

1. What problems may arise when pay is based on "objective" performance results?
2. What are some of the pros and cons of Scott's compensation policies for top managers and executives? Are these attuned to Scott's goal of increasing profits and competitiveness in an increasingly crowded market? Explain.
3. Under Dunlap's leadership, Scott's stock rose 22.5%, making shareholders very happy. Many financial experts believe that maximizing shareholders' welfare must be a corporation's overriding objective in a free market economy. Do you agree that managers' pay should be closely tied to the pursuit of this goal? Explain.

Cooperative Learning Exercise

4. Students divide into groups of five. Some groups are asked to defend Dunlap's actions at Scott Paper, while other groups are asked to argue the opposite side. The instructor will play the role of moderator in an open debate.

SOURCE: Byrne, J. A., and Weber, J. (1996, January 15) *Business Week*, 44–49; Reinhard, B. (1995, July 19), Scott CEO reaps millions from turnaround merger. *Palm Beach Post* (Internet site); and Reinhard, B. (1995, July 20). Scott's second quarter earnings triple to record $145.5 million. *Palm Beach Post* (Internet site).

Case 2

An Academic Question?

Provincial University is a medium-sized university with 21,000 students and 1,200 faculty members. The College of Business Administration is the largest one on campus, with 8,000 students and 180 faculty members. For the past few years, the dean has had to deal with a large number of disgruntled faculty who complain that they are underpaid relative to newly hired faculty. Many of the complainants are senior tenured professors who refuse to engage in committee activities beyond the minimum service requirements and who are seldom in their offices because they feel aggrieved. They teach six hours a week, spend two hours in the office, and

then disappear from campus. Recently, the head of the college's faculty council compiled some statistics and sent these to the dean, demanding "prompt action to create more equity in the faculty pay structure." The average salary statistics are shown in the accompanying table.

The dean replied that he has little choice but to make offers to new faculty that are competitive with the market and that the university will not provide him enough funds to maintain equitable pay differences between new and current faculty or between higher and lower ranks.

Rank	1982		1988	
	New Hires	Current	New Hires	Current
Full professors	$42,300	$46,500	$65,800	$58,800
Associate professors	$35,150	$40,750	$54,600	$50,400
Assistant professors	$25,200	$28,000	$47,000	$42,000
Rank	1994		Now	
	New Hires	Current	New Hires	Current
Full professors	$95,200	$78,400	$110,600	$86,800
Associate professors	$86,800	$71,400	$102,500	$85,400
Assistant professors	$72,800	$67,200	$ 85,000	$82,600

➤

Critical Thinking Questions

1. Based on the data collected by the faculty council, name three compensation problems that exist at Provincial University.
2. Is the dean's explanation for decreased pay differences by rank and/or seniority justifiable?
3. How would you suggest the dean deal with disgruntled senior faculty who feel underpaid?

Cooperative Learning Exercise

4. A group of six faculty members have come to see the dean to express their dissatisfaction with pay compression at the College. All six represent current faculty: two are assistant professors, two are associate professors, and two are full professors. Students divide into groups of seven and role-play this situation as the dean attempts to deal with the pay complaints raised by the faculty. The dean doesn't have the money to correct the pay compression problem, yet he can't afford to alienate the faculty.

chapter 11

Rewarding Performance

After reading this chapter, you should be able to deal more effectively with the following challenges:

1 Recognize individual and group contributions to the firm by rewarding high performers.

2 Develop pay-for-performance plans that are appropriate for different levels in an organization.

3 Identify the potential benefits and drawbacks of a particular pay-for-performance system and choose the plan that is most appropriate for a particular firm.

4 Understand how the components of an executive compensation package motivate executives to make decisions that are in the firm's best interests.

5 Weigh the pros and cons of different compensation methods for sales personnel and design an incentive plan that is consistent with the firm's marketing strategy.

6 Design an incentive system to reward excellence in customer service.

A job well done. The positive psychological effects of recognition for a job well done are substantial. For this reason, many companies offer their employees not only annual raises and bonuses, but also prizes and awards ceremonies.

Century Telephone Company bases its employees' annual pay raises on how well they perform their job duties. For the past 10 years, these "merit raises" have averaged 4.5 percent of base pay. About two years ago the HR department conducted an employee attitude survey. One of its most striking findings: more than three-fourths of employees felt that pay raises and performance were unrelated. In response, top managers asked the HR staff to determine if pay raises were indeed based on performance (as required by policy) or on some other unrelated factors. Surprisingly, the data showed that employees were right: supervisors rated more than 80 percent of their workers as "excellent," and there was only minimal differentiation in the percentage raises received by individual employees.

Top management concluded that supervisors were equalizing performance ratings and raises, sidestepping their responsibility to reward employees on the basis of performance.

To remedy this situation, Century instituted a new procedure a year ago to reward the best performers. Under this new system, supervisors must distribute employee performance ratings as follows: excellent (top 15%), very good (next 20%), good (next 20%), satisfactory (next 35%), marginal or unsatisfactory (lowest 10%). Pay raises are pegged to these performance classifications, with employees at the top receiving at least a 10-percent raise and those at the bottom receiving nothing.

Shortly after the system was put in place, it became obvious that something had gone wrong. A large number of employees complained that they could not understand how or why their performance had "dropped" compared with the previous year. Many believed that favouritism played a big role in who received what amount of pay increase. Irate employees hounded their supervisors, who in turn complained to their superiors that increased tension was poisoning interpersonal relationships and interfering with the work unit's overall performance.

The experience of Century Telephone (a real company here given a fictitious name) shows what can happen when well-meaning attempts to motivate employees with pay incentives backfire. Nonetheless, the use of pay incentives is clearly on the upswing. In a report by N. Winter Consulting, 70 percent of 84 Canadian companies surveyed paid incentives to employees at all levels, based on predefined performance targets.[1] According to a survey by Ernst and Young, between 1992 and 1996, variable pay as a proportion of overall pay increased significantly. For middle and senior management, it doubled; for professional and technical employees, the average proportion of pay that was variable tripled (from 2.8% to 7.7%); and for hourly and clerical employees, the average went from less than two percent to nearly six percent.[2]

In this chapter we discuss the effective design and implementation of pay-for-performance systems. First, we address the major challenges and pitfalls facing managers in their attempts to link pay and performance. Second, we offer a set of general recommendations to deal with these challenges. Third, we describe specific types of pay-for-performance programs and analyse the advantages and disadvantages of each and the conditions under which each is most appropriate. We conclude the chapter with a discussion of unique pay-for-performance plans for two important employee groups: executives and sales personnel.

▉ Pay for Performance: The Challenges

Most employees believe that those who work harder and produce more should be rewarded. If employees see that pay is not distributed on the basis of merit, they are more likely to lack commitment to the organization, decrease their level of effort, and look for employment opportunities elsewhere.[3]

In Chapter 10, we examined the process of classifying jobs into hierarchies. Jobs at the top of the hierarchy contribute more to the organization and, therefore, receive higher compensation than jobs at the bottom of the hierarchy. In this chapter, we are concerned with how effectively employees within the same job classification perform their job. **Pay-for-performance systems**, also called **incentive systems**, reward employee performance on the basis of three assumptions:[4]

1. Individual employees and work teams differ in how much they contribute to the firm—not only in what they do, but also in how well they do it.

2. The firm's overall performance depends to a large degree on the performance of individuals and groups within the firm.

3. To attract, retain, and motivate high performers and to be fair to all employees, a company needs to reward employees on the basis of their relative performance.

These assumptions seem straightforward and acceptable. However, it is widely recognized that incentive systems can create negative consequences for firms. Thus, before talking about specific types of pay-for-performance plans, we will discuss eight challenges facing organizations that want to adopt an incentive system to stimulate higher levels of performance. (For a brief summary of the theoretical foundations for incentive pay, see the Appendix at the end of this chapter.)

▉ The "Do Only What You Get Paid For" Syndrome

To avoid the charge that pay is distributed on the basis of subjective judgements or favouritism, pay-for-performance systems tend to rely on objective indicators of performance.[5] This may lead some managers to use whatever "objective" data are available to justify pay decisions because doing so lets them explain judgement calls to subordinates. Unfortunately, the closer pay is tied to particular performance indicators, the more employees tend to focus on those indicators and neglect other important job components that are more difficult to measure. Consider the following examples:

◆ In some school systems where teachers' pay has been linked to students' scores on standardized tests, teachers spend more time helping students do well on the tests than helping them understand the subject matter. As one expert has noted, "When you interview the teachers, they tell you they would like to teach other things, but they feel they have to teach to the test [because] they are afraid that a poor showing by their pupils will result in negative evaluations for themselves or their schools."[6]

◆ Many brokerage houses pay more than 50 percent of a broker/analyst's compensation in the form of commissions generated on the stocks they pick. This sometimes leads analysts to push stocks that pay the highest commissions, even if these are a poor investment for clients. This potential conflict of interest has exposed brokerage houses to significant legal risks and, in some cases, costly court settlements in favour of customers.

◆ Several airlines faced a substantial increase in the number of "no shows" after instituting a policy in which reservation agents were compensated partly on the number of reservations they booked.

◆ Division managers rewarded for cutting costs often resort to tactics that lead to short-term savings or profits (for example, postponing equipment maintenance, laying off employees, and reducing capital investments). These tactics often hurt the company in the long run.

pay-for-performance system or incentive system

A system that rewards employees on the assumptions that: (1) individual employees and work teams differ in how much they contribute to the firm; (2) the firm's overall performance depends to a large degree on the performance of individuals and groups within the firm; and (3) to attract, retain, and motivate high performers and to be fair to all employees, the firm needs to reward employees on the basis of their relative performance.

■ Negative Effects on the Spirit of Cooperation

The experiences of Century Telephone Company clearly show that pay-for-performance systems may provoke conflict and competition in the organization while discouraging cooperation.[7] For instance, employees may withhold information from a colleague if they believe that it will help that person get ahead. Those who are receiving less than they feel they deserve may try to get back at those who are receiving more, perhaps by sabotaging a project that the more highly rewarded employees are working on or by spreading rumours to damage their reputations. Internal competition may set off rivalries that lead to quality problems or even cheating.

■ Lack of Control

As we noted in Chapter 7 employees often cannot control all of the factors affecting their performance. Some examples of factors that are beyond an employee's control are the supervisor, performance of other work group members, the quality of the material or product the employee is working with, working conditions, and the amount of support from management.[8] For instance, the sales generated by a particular salesperson may be more a function of the territory than of the person's sales ability. Linking pay to performance in such a situation is inequitable and demoralizing.

■ Difficulties in Measuring Performance

As we saw in Chapter 7, assessing employee performance is one of the thorniest tasks a manager faces, particularly when the assessments are used to dispense rewards.[9] At the employee level, the appraiser must try to untangle individual contributions from those of the work group while avoiding judgements based on a personality bias (being a strict or a lenient rater), likes and dislikes, and political agendas. At the group or team level, the rater must try to isolate the specific contributions of any given team when all teams are interdependent.[10] The appraiser experiences the same difficulties in attempting to determine the performance of plants or units that are interrelated among themselves and with corporate headquarters. In short, accurate measures of performance are not easy to achieve and tying pay to inaccurate measures is likely to create problems.

■ Psychological Contracts

Once implemented, a pay-for-performance system creates a psychological contract between the employee and the firm.[11] A *psychological contract* is a set of expectations based on prior experience, and it can be very resistant to change. Several factors account for this resistance: fear of the unknown, perceived threats to self-interest, distrust of management, and the existence of powerful groups within the firm that prefer to do things as they've been done in the past.

Breaking a psychological contract can have damaging results. For instance, when a computer products manufacturer changed the terms of its pay-for-performance program three times in a two-year period in response to changes in its financial conditions, the result was massive employee protests, the resignation of several key managers, and a general lowering of employee morale.

Two other problems may arise with respect to the psychological contract. First, because employees feel entitled to the reward spelled out in the pay-for-performance plan, it is difficult to change the plan even when conditions call for a change. Second, it is sometimes hard to come up with a formula that is fair to diverse employee groups.

■ The Credibility Gap

Employees often do not believe that pay-for-performance programs are fair or that they truly reward performance, a phenomenon called the *credibility gap*.[12] Some studies indicate that as many as 75 percent of a typical firm's employees question the integrity of pay-for-performance plans.[13] If employees do not consider the system legitimate and acceptable, it may well have negative rather than positive effects on their behaviour. For instance, merit pay for teachers has been contemplated as a way of improving educational outcomes, but the merit pay systems that have been tried have generally received low marks from teachers. In one pilot outsiders sat in on classes three times a year to review teachers' performance. Teachers complained that the reviews were subjective and that bad teachers just cleaned up their act for the evaluation.[14]

■ Job Dissatisfaction and Stress

Pay-for-performance systems may lead to greater productivity but lower job satisfaction.[15] Some research suggests that the more pay is tied to performance, the more the work unit begins to unravel and the more unhappy employees become.[16] The Issues and Applications feature describing what happened at Lantech illustrates how incentives can raise stress along with productivity.

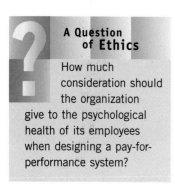

A Question of Ethics

How much consideration should the organization give to the psychological health of its employees when designing a pay-for-performance system?

■ Potential Reduction of Intrinsic Drives

Pay-for-performance programs may push employees to the point of doing whatever it takes to get the promised monetary reward, in the process stifling their talents and creativity. Thus an organization that puts too much emphasis on pay in attempting to influence behaviours may reduce employees' *intrinsic drives* and suffer subtle but important losses—for example, there may be a narrowed work focus and less innovation. One expert argues that the more a firm stresses pay as an incentive for high performance, the less likely it is that employees will engage in activities that benefit the organization (such as overtime and extra special service) unless they are promised an explicit reward.[17]

■ Building Managerial Skills: Meeting the Challenges of Pay-for-Performance Systems

Properly designed pay-for-performance systems present managers with an excellent opportunity to align employees' interests with those of the organization. The following recommendations can help to enhance the success of performance programs and avoid the pitfalls we just discussed.

■ Link Pay and Performance Appropriately

piece-rate system

A compensation system in which employees are paid per unit produced.

There are few cases in which managers can justify paying workers according to a pre-established formula or measure. Traditional **piece-rate systems,** in which workers are paid per unit produced, represent the tightest link between pay and performance. Many piece-rate systems have been abandoned because they tend to give rise to the kinds of problems discussed earlier, but there are situations in which piece-rate plans are appropriate. The primary requirement is that the employee have complete control over the speed and quality of the work. For example, it is appropriate to pay typists for the number of pages they type *if* they can work at their own pace. However, most typists should not be paid on a piece-rate basis because they often have other responsibilities (for example, handling telephone calls) and are subject to constant interruptions.

■ Use Pay for Performance as Part of a Broader HRM System

Pay-for-performance programs are not likely to achieve the desired results unless complementary HRM programs are implemented at the same time. For instance, per-

formance appraisals and supervisory training usually play a major role in the eventual success or failure of a pay-for-performance plan. As we saw in Chapter 7, performance ratings are often influenced by factors other than performance, such as like or dislike of an employee, halo error, and legal pressures. Since a defective appraisal process can undermine even the most carefully conceived pay plan, supervisors should be rigorously trained in correct rating practice.

Poor staffing practices can also damage the credibility of a pay-for-performance program. For instance, if employees are hired because of their political connections rather than for their skills and abilities, other employees will get the message that good performance is not that important to the organization.

■ Build Employee Trust

Even the best-conceived pay-for-performance program can fail if managers have a poor history of labour relations or if the organization has a cutthroat culture. Under these conditions, a pay-for-performance plan may make matters worse because employees are not likely to attribute the rewards received to good performance, but rather to chance or good impression manage-

Issues and Applications

Incentives That Backfired: The Case of Lantech

Lantech, a small machinery manufacturer learned through firsthand experience how incentive plans can backfire:

> Incentive pay encourages workers to improve quality, cut costs, and otherwise enhance the corporate good. Right? Well, that's the way it's supposed to work. In the real world, pay for performance can also release passions that turn workers into rival gangs, so greedy for extra dollars they will make another gang's numbers look bad to make their own look good. Such was the experience of Pat Lancaster, the chairman of Lantech. . . . To his dismay, Lancaster discovered that the lust for bonus bucks grew so overheated and so petty that one of his workers tried to stiff a competing division for the toilet paper bill.

> "Incentive pay is toxic," says Lancaster, "because it is so open to favouritism and manipulation."

> At one point, each of the company's five manufacturing divisions was given a bonus determined by how much profit it made. An individual worker's share of the bonus could amount to as much as 10% of his or her regular pay. But the divisions are so independent, it was very difficult to sort out which division was entitled to what profits. "That led to so much secrecy, politicking, and sucking noise that you wouldn't believe it," says CEO Jim Lancaster, Pat's son. For example, the division that built standard machines and the one that added custom design features to those machines depended on each other for parts, engineering expertise, and such. So inevitably the groups clashed, each one trying to assign costs to the other and claim credit for revenues.

> "I was spending 95% of my time in conflict resolution instead of on how to serve our customers," recalls Pat. The division wrangled so long over who would get charged for overhead cranes to haul heavy equipment around the factory floor that Lantech couldn't install those useful machines until 1992, several years later than planned. At the end of each month, the divisions would rush to fill orders from other parts of the company. Such behaviour created profits for the division filling the order but, unfortunately, generated piles of unnecessary and costly inventory in the receiving division. Some employees even argued over who would have to pay for the toilet paper in the common restrooms.

> So Lantech has finally abandoned individual and division performance pay, and relies instead on a profit-sharing system in which all employees get bonuses based on salary. Furious passions have subsided, and the company is doing just fine now, says the senior Lancaster.

SOURCE: Reprinted from Nulty, P. (1995, November 13). Incentive pay can be crippling. *Fortune*, 235.

ment. If a pay-for-performance program is to have any chance of succeeding, managers may have to make major changes in the organization's climate in order to build employee trust.

Building trust can be a tall order, particularly in companies where cynicism rules. Managers should answer these questions from their employees' perspective:

◆ Does it pay for me to work longer, harder, or smarter?

◆ Does anyone notice my extra efforts?

If the answers are no, managers need to go all out to show that they care about employees as individuals and are aware of the work they do. Even more important, they need to keep employees informed and involved when making any management or compensation plan changes.[18]

■ Promote the Belief That Performance Makes a Difference

Because of the problems noted earlier, managers may shy away from using pay to reward performance.[19] However, unless an organization creates an atmosphere in which performance makes a difference, it may end up with a low-achievement organizational culture. In a sense, then, pay-for-performance systems are the lesser of two evils because without them, performance may drop even lower.[20]

■ Use Multiple Layers of Rewards

All pay-for-performance systems have advantages and disadvantages. For instance, bonuses or pay raises given to individual employees are more motivating than some other incentives because they allow employees to see how their personal contributions led to a direct reward. At the same time, though, they tend to create more internal competition, which leads to less cooperation. Bonuses given to teams or work units promote cooperation (because they foster a sense of common interest), but they also prevent individual employees from linking the reward to their own efforts, and thus reduce the reward's motivational impact.

Since all pay-for-performance systems have positive and negative features, providing different types of pay incentives for different work situations is likely to produce better results than relying on a single type of pay incentive. With a multiple-layers-of-rewards system, the organization can realize the benefits of each incentive plan while minimizing its negative side effects. For example, 3M Canada utilizes a range of performance-related payment schemes to reinforce corporate goals. With a heavy reliance on innovation and new products, it provides a dual ladder career system for scientists so that they can receive increasing pay and perquisites otherwise limited to managerial careers, while remaining basic researchers. 3M also encourages its researchers to spend 15 percent of their time on projects of their own design, and has a range of internal awards and grant programs to encourage excellence from all employees, not just those with technical or research programs. Another program available to most employees is termed Partici-Pay, in which employees commit two percent of their annual pay, receiving nothing if 3M Canada's results for the year are poor, but up to three times their investment when there is a good year.[21]

■ Increase Employee Involvement

An old saying among compensation practitioners is: "Acceptability is the ultimate determinant of success in any compensation plan." When employees do not view a compensation program as legitimate, they will usually do whatever they can to subvert the system—from setting maximum production quotas for themselves to shunning co-workers who receive the highest rewards and accusing supervisors of favouritism. The best way to increase acceptance is to have employees participate in the design of the pay plan.[22] Employee involvement will result in a greater understanding of the rationale behind the plan, greater commitment to the pay plan, and a better match between individual needs and pay-plan design.[23]

Royal Bank, with some 50,000 employees, utilizes a suggestion system with significant employee incentives attached to suggestions that has led to service improvements and cost reduction. In one typical year, there were over 8,500 suggestions received, and a total of $178,000 was paid out. One of the larger awards was $25,000, split between two employees for their idea of how to streamline computer backup procedures and substantially reduce equipment requirements. Schneider Corporation, the Kitchener, Ontario-based food products company, has had a suggestion system for years, but has used it more intensively since the company adopted a continuous improvement program. Schneider now awards incentives equal to 10 percent of the first year's savings to a maximum of $5,000 for an individual or $7,500 for a team. In one recent year, some 3,000 suggestions were received, an average of more than one for each of the company's 2,500 employees.[24]

Schneider Corporation
www.theschneidercorp.com

Employee participation in designing the plan is not the same as employee dispensation of the rewards. Managers should still control and allocate rewards because employees may not be able to separate self-interest from effective pay administration. Managers can, however, solicit employee input in reward-allocation decisions by instituting an appeal mechanism that allows employees to voice their complaints about how rewards have been distributed. Such a mechanism is likely to enhance the perceived fairness of the system, particularly if a disinterested third party acts as an arbitrator and is empowered to take corrective actions.[25] A good appeals system may also save the organization large sums of money by helping it avoid the costly legal fees and penalties in back pay that often result when disputes are resolved through litigation.

■ Use Motivation and Non-Financial Incentives

This chapter focuses on financial awards, which are managers' biggest concern in administering incentive plans. However, non-financial rewards can be used effectively to motivate employee performance. One of the most basic facts of motivation is that people are driven to obtain the things they need or want. While pay is certainly a strong motivator, it is not an equally strong motivator for everyone. Some people are more interested in the non-financial aspects of their work.

Non-financial rewards may be public and private praise, honorary titles, and expanded job responsibilities. Even if it is impossible to provide a financial reward for a job well done, many employees appreciate overt recognition of excellent performance.

■ Types of Pay-for-Performance Plans

A firm may use a variety of approaches to reward performance. As Figure 11–1 shows, pay-for-performance plans can be designed to reward the performance of the individual, team, business unit or plant, entire organization, or any combination of these. All these plans have advantages and disadvantages, and each is more effective in some situations than in others. Most organizations are best served by using a variety of plans to counterbalance the potential drawbacks of any single plan.

■ Individual-Based Plans

At the most micro level, firms attempt to identify and reward the contributions of individual employees. *Individual-based pay plans* are the most widely used pay-for-performance plans in industry.[26]

Unit of Analysis			
Microlevel		*Macrolevel*	
Individual	**Team**	**Business Unit/Plant**	**Organization**
Merit pay	Bonuses	Gainsharing	Profit sharing
Bonuses	Awards	Bonuses	Stock plans
Awards		Awards	
Piece rate			

Figure 11–1 Pay-for-Performance Programs

SOURCES: Welbourne, T. M., & Gómez-Mejía, L. R. (1991). Team incentives in the workplace. In M. L. Rock & L. A. Berger (1991). *The compensation handbook,* 236–247. New York: McGraw-Hill.

merit pay

An increase in base pay, normally given once a year.

bonus program or lump-sum payment

A financial incentive that is given on a one-time basis and does not raise the employee's base pay permanently.

award

A one-time reward, usually given in the form of a tangible prize.

expectancy theory

A theory of behaviour holding that people tend to do those things that are rewarded.

Of the individual-based plans commonly used, merit pay is by far the most popular; its use is almost universal.[27] **Merit pay** consists of an increase in base pay, normally given once a year. Supervisors' ratings of employees' performance are typically used to determine the amount of merit pay granted. For instance, subordinates whose performance is rated "below expectations," "achieved expectations," "exceeded expectations," and "far exceeded expectations" may receive 0%, 3%, 6%, and 9% pay raises, respectively. Once the merit pay increase is given to an employee, it remains a part of that employee's base salary for the rest of his or her tenure with the firm (except under extreme conditions, such as a general wage cut or a demotion).

Individual **bonus programs** (sometimes called **lump-sum payments**) are similar to merit pay programs but differ in one important respect. These financial incentives are given on a one-time basis and do not raise the employee's base pay permanently. Bonuses tend to be larger than merit pay increases because they involve lower risk to the employer (the employer is not making a permanent financial commitment). Bonuses can also be given outside the annual review cycle when employees achieve certain milestones (for example, completing a challenging project early and under budget) or offer a valuable cost-saving suggestion.

Awards, like bonuses, are one-time rewards, but tend to be given in the form of a tangible prize, such as a paid vacation, a TV set, or a dinner for two at a fancy restaurant.

Perhaps the oldest and most extreme individual-based pay incentive is the piece-rate system we discussed earlier. The piece-rate system is less often used today because it does not fit with the greater interdependencies in modern production processes, rapid technological changes, and the increased emphasis on quality and service rather than on raw quantity.[28]

Advantages of Individual-Based Pay-for-Performance Plans.

There are four major advantages to individual-based plans:

◆ *Performance that is rewarded is likely to be repeated.* **Expectancy theory,** a widely accepted theory of motivation, is often used to explain why higher pay leads to higher performance. People tend to do those things that are rewarded. Since money is an important reward to most people, then where a strong performance-pay linkage exists, individuals tend to improve their work performance.[29] In other words, because employees value money as a reward, they will work harder to achieve or exceed a performance level if they believe that they will receive money for doing so.

◆ *Individuals are goal-oriented, and financial incentives can shape an individual's goals over time.* Every organization is interested not only in the level at which employees perform but also in the focus of their efforts. A pay incentive plan can help make employees' behaviour consistent with the organization's goals.[30] For instance, if an automobile dealer has a sales employee who sells a lot of cars, but whose customers rarely return to the dealership, the dealer might implement a pay incentive plan that gives a higher sales commission for cars sold to repeat buyers. This plan would encourage the sales staff to please the customer rather than just sell the car.

◆ *Assessing the performance of each employee individually helps the firm achieve individual equity.* An organization must provide rewards in proportion to individual efforts. Individual-based plans do exactly this. If individuals are not rewarded, high performers may leave the firm to join a company that values their contributions or they may reduce their performance level to make it consistent with the payment they are receiving.

◆ *Individual-based plans fit in with an individualistic culture.* National cultures vary in the emphasis they place on individual achievement versus group achievement (see Chapter 17). According to work done by Dutch scholar Geert Hofstede, a number of national cultures, of which Canada's is one, place strong emphasis on individualism. (To the surprise of very few observers, the United States registered the most individualistic orientation.) Canadians and others who value individualism expect to be rewarded for their personal accomplishments and contributions. Such an orientation makes pay-for-performance policies potentially very powerful influences because the policies fit with the culturally based expectations of employees.

In contrast, the Japanese don't tend to reward the performance of individual employees. "It's against their ethic," says a consultant with Tasa, Inc., which has conducted executive searches for North American offices of many Japanese concerns.[31] While thinking in terms of national cultural patterns can be misleading when assessing *individuals* (it can be a form of stereotyping), such patterns can be important when devising policies that will be applied to *large numbers of people* who have been shaped by one or another particular national culture.

Disadvantages of Individual-Based Pay-for-Performance Plans.

Many of the pitfalls of pay-for-performance programs are most evident at the individual level. Two particular dangers are that individual plans may (1) create competition and a lack of cooperation among peers and (2) sour working relationships between subordinates and supervisors. And because many managers believe that below-average raises are demoralizing to employees and discourage better performance, they tend to equalize the percentage increases among employees, regardless of individual performance. This, of course, defeats the very purpose of an incentive plan.

Pink Cadillac, Plush Velvet Seats.

Mary Kay Ash, founder of Mary Kay Cosmetics, knows how to motivate her salespeople. She gives them prizes and recognition, not just cash. These Mary Kay sales directors drive the company's coveted pink Cadillacs. Mary Kay's Cadillac fleet includes over 6,500 cars and is worth more than $100 million.

Mary Kay Cosmetics
www.marykaycosmetics.com

Other disadvantages of individual-based plans include the following:

◆ *Tying pay to goals may promote single-mindedness.* Linking financial incentives to the achievement of goals may lead to a narrow focus among employees and the avoidance of important tasks, either because goals are difficult to set for these tasks or because their accomplishment is difficult to measure at the individual level. For instance, if a grocery store sets a goal of happy and satisfied customers, it would be extremely difficult to link achievement of this goal to individual employees. Individual-based plans have a tendency to focus on goals that are easy to measure even if these goals are not very important to the organization. They also tend to encourage people to "play it safe" by choosing to accomplish more modest goals instead of riskier goals that are harder to achieve.

◆ *Many employees do not believe that pay and performance are linked.* Although practically all organizations claim to reward individual performance, it is difficult for employees to determine to what extent their companies really do so. As we saw in Chapter 7, many managers use the performance appraisal process for reasons other than accurately measuring performance.[32] So it should come as no surprise that many surveys over the past three decades have found that up to 80 percent of employees do not see a connection between personal contributions and pay raises.[33] The beliefs underlying this perception, many of which have proved very resistant to change, are summarized in Figure 11–2.

◆ *Individual pay plans may work against achieving quality goals.* Individuals rewarded for meeting production goals often sacrifice attention to product quality. Individual-based plans also work against total quality management programs that emphasize teamwork since they generally do not reward employees for helping other workers or coordinating work activities with another department.

◆ *Individual-based programs promote inflexibility in some organizations.* Because supervisors generally control the rewards, individual-based pay-for-performance plans promote dependence on supervisors. Thus these plans tend to prop up traditional organizational structures,[34] which makes them particularly ineffective for firms trying to reorganize to take a team approach to work.

◆ Performance appraisal is inherently subjective, with supervisors evaluating subordinates according to their own preconceived biases.

◆ Regardless of the appraisal form used, rating errors are rampant.

◆ Merit systems emphasize individual rather than group goals, and this may lead to dysfunctional conflict in the organization.

◆ The use of a specified time period (normally one year) for the performance evaluation encourages a short-term orientation at the expense of long-term goals.

◆ Supervisors and employees seldom agree on the evaluation, leading to interpersonal confrontations.

◆ Increments in financial rewards are spaced in such a way that their reinforcement value for work behaviours is questionable. For example, becoming twice as productive now has little perceived effect on pay when the employee must wait a whole year for a performance review.

◆ Individual merit pay systems are not appropriate for the service sector, where many people in Canada work. In knowledge-based jobs (such as "administrative assistant"), it is even difficult to specify what the desired product is.

◆ Supervisors typically control a rather limited amount of compensation, so merit pay differentials are normally quite small and therefore of questionable value.

◆ A number of bureaucratic factors that influence the size and frequency of merit pay (for example, position in salary range, pay relationships within the unit and between units, pay compensation, and budgetary limitations) have little to do with employee performance.

◆ Performance appraisals are designed for multiple purposes (training and development, selection, work planning, compensation, and so forth). When a system is used to accomplish so many objectives, it is questionable whether it can accomplish any of them well. It is difficult for the supervisor to play the role of counsellor or adviser and evaluator at the same time.

Figure 11–2 Factors Commonly Blamed for the Failure of Individual-Based Pay-for-Performance Systems
SOURCE: Balkin, D. B., & Gómez-Mejía, L. R. (Eds.). (1987). *New perspectives on compensation*, 159. Englewood Cliffs, NJ: Prentice Hall.

Conditions Under Which Individual-Based Plans Are Most Likely to Succeed.
Despite the challenges they present to managers, rewards based on individual performance can be highly motivating. Individual-based pay-for-performance plans are most likely to be successful under the following conditions:

◆ *When the contributions of individual employees can be accurately isolated.* Although identifying any one person's contributions is generally difficult, it is more easily done for some jobs than for others. For instance, a strong individual incentive system can work well with salespeople because it is relatively easy to measure their accomplishments in a timely manner. In contrast, research scientists in industry are generally not offered individual-based performance incentives because they typically work so closely together that individual contributions are hard to identify. In addition, the value of their achievements is usually not known until well after they have completed their work.

◆ *When the job demands autonomy.* The more independently employees work, the more it makes sense to assess and reward the performance of each individual. For example, the performance of managers of individual stores in a large retail chain like The Gap can be rated fairly easily, whereas the performance of the human resource director in a large company is much more difficult to assess.

◆ *When cooperation is less critical to successful performance or when competition is to be encouraged.* Practically all jobs require some cooperation, but the less cooperation needed, the more successful an individual-based pay program will be. For example, less employee cooperation is expected of a stockbroker than of a pilot in a military squadron.

■ Team-Based Plans

In an attempt to increase the flexibility of their work forces, a growing number of firms are redesigning work to enable employees with unique skills and backgrounds to tackle common projects or problems together. For instance, Amdahl Canada's 140 employees are organized into two units each headed by a customer service manager, one group dealing with the greater Toronto area, and the other with customers elsewhere in Canada. Within each group, there are teams of seven or eight members, each coordinated by a team leader. This team leadership role can shift among members of the group and carries with it a premium of five percent of base pay. Teams receive bonuses if they exceed targets in three performance areas: budgeted expenses, revenues, and customer satisfaction. If they exceed targets in all three areas, the bonuses earned for the first two areas are doubled. Teams can allocate bonuses among team members to acknowledge differences in individual contribution.[35] Nadine Winter, an established compensation consultant, has identified team incentives as one compensation trend that may qualify as a "best practice" if it is congruent with the culture, goals, and management priorities of an organization.[36]

Team-based pay plans normally reward all team members equally based on group outcomes. These outcomes may be measured objectively (e.g., completing a given number of team projects on time or meeting all deadlines for a group report) or subjectively (e.g., using the collective assessment of a panel of managers). The criteria for defining a desirable outcome may be broad (e.g., being able to work effectively with other teams) or narrow (e.g., developing a patent with commercial applications). As in individual-based programs, payments to team members may be made in the form of a cash bonus or in the form of non-cash awards such as trips, time off, or luxury items.

Low on Calories, Big on Bonuses.

A team of young managers at Yoplait yogurt has built the company into a thriving business by setting even tougher goals for themselves than their parent company set for them. When the team exceeded these goals, its managers collected bonuses of $30,000 to $50,000, about half their annual salaries.

Advantages of Team-Based Pay-for-Performance Plans.

When properly designed, team-based incentives have two major advantages.

Yoplait
www.yoplait.com

♦ *They foster group cohesiveness.* To the extent that team members have the same goals and objectives, work closely with one another, and depend on one another for the group's overall performance, team-based incentives can motivate group members to behave and think as a unit rather than as competing individuals. In this situation, each worker is more likely to act in a way that benefits the entire group.[37]

♦ *They facilitate performance measurement.* A number of studies have shown that performance can be measured more accurately and reliably for an entire team than for individuals.[38] This is true because less precise measurement is required when an individual's performance does not need to be identified and evaluated in relation to others in a group.

Disadvantages of Team-Based Pay-for-Performance Plans.

Managers need to be aware of potential pitfalls with team-based plans. These are:

♦ *Possible lack of fit with individualistic cultural values.* Because most North American workers expect to be recognized for their own personal contributions, they may not react well to an incentive system in which their individual efforts take a back seat to the group effort, with all team members rewarded equally. On the other side of the coin, individual incentives are likely to fail in societies with a collective orientation. The Japanese, for example, are far less comfortable with individual risk than Canadians or Americans are. Nonetheless, in a striking display of cultural insensitivity, many U.S. companies have introduced high-risk individual incentives to their Japanese subsidiaries in the belief that cash motivates everyone and that Japanese workers will love these plans once they get used to them. These plans have generally failed.[39]

♦ *The free-riding effect.* In any group, some individuals put in more effort than others. In addition, ability levels differ from one person to the next. Those who contribute little to the team—either because of low effort or limited ability—are free riders.

When all team members (including free riders) are rewarded equally for a group outcome, there are likely to be complaints of unfairness. (Think what would happen in a classroom study group if the same grade were given to all group members.) The end result may be conflict rather than the cooperation the plan was intended to foster, with supervisors having to step in to judge who is contributing what.[40] Supervisory intercession, of course, negates the worth of team-based incentives and may produce a very negative climate of accusation and infighting.

To minimize the free-riding effect, some companies have been adjusting pay incentives to encourage individual performance within teams. One major high-tech company sets annual base pay raises on performance reviews by a team coach and three peers chosen by the employee. All team members can also receive up to 20% of base pay as a team bonus. Another employer created wider differences in base salaries after employees in a 200-member team demanded greater recognition of their individual performances.[41]

◆ *Social pressures to limit performance.* Although group cohesiveness may motivate all team members to increase their effort and work to their full potential—both positively through encouraging a supportive team spirit and negatively through reproaching those who don't carry their share of the weight—it can also dampen team productivity. When the labour relations climate is hostile, workers do not trust managers or fear layoffs, or the firm has a history of broken promises (for example, managers have raised the standards required to obtain the reward), group dynamics may result in the setting of artificial performance limits. When commercial airline pilots want to express a grievance, for instance, they sometimes agree among themselves to fly "by the book." This means that they follow every rule without exception, leading to an overall work slowdown. This is a very effective strategy because the airline can hardly complain publicly that its pilots are following the rules. Group dynamics may also encourage team members to try to beat the game—cheating to get the reward, for instance—as a way to get back at management.[42]

◆ *Difficulties in identifying meaningful groups.* Before they decide how to distribute rewards based on team performance, managers must define a *team*.[43] Coming up with a definition can be tricky because various groups may be highly interdependent, making it difficult to identify which ones did what. Also, a person may be a member of more than one team, and teams may change members frequently. For instance, while the editor of the book you are reading now is a member of the editorial team, she works closely with the production team (to produce the book), the art team (to develop the art program and design), the photo team (to research and get permission to reprint the photos in this book), the marketing team (to make the book meet its audience's expectations and demands) and, finally, the sales force (to sell the book to your instructor and provide customer service.).

◆ *Intergroup competition leading to a decline in overall performance.* A team may become so focussed on maximizing its own performance it begins to compete with other teams. The results can be quite undesirable. For instance, the manufacturing group may produce more units than the marketing group can possibly sell, or the marketing group may make sales commitments that manufacturing is hard pressed to meet on schedule.

Conditions Under Which Team-Based Plans Are Most Likely to Succeed.   While managers need to be aware of the potential disadvantages of team-based plans, they should also be on the lookout for situations conducive to their successful use. Such plans are likely to be successful under the following circumstances:

◆ *When work tasks are so intertwined that it is difficult to single out who did what.* This is often the case in research and development labs, where scientists and engineers work in teams. It is also the case with firefighter crews and police units, which often think of themselves as one indivisible entity and develop very close ties.

◆ *When the firm's organization facilitates the implementation of team-based incentives.* Today many organizations are reorganizing to take a team approach to work. In these organizations team-based incentives are more appropriate than individual-based incentive systems. Team-based incentives are appropriate when:

1. *There are few levels in the hierarchy, and teams of individuals at the same level are expected to complete most of their work with little dependence on supervisors or upper management.* Both public-sector and private-sector organizations that have had to lay off workers to maintain efficiency and profitability have found that teamwork becomes a necessity. For example, Ontario Hydro implemented a new organizational structure in 1993 with the purpose of becoming more accountable, businesslike, and responsive to customers. Its reorganization and workforce reductions have led to compensation schemes (for senior management and some business units) such as competency-based pay and broad-band salary structures, both of which facilitate the flexibility needed in team-based work.[44]

2. *Technology allows for the separation of work into relatively self-contained or independent groups.* This can be done more easily in a service unit (such as a telephone repair crew) than in a large manufacturing operation (such as a traditional automobile assembly line).

3. *Employees are committed to their work and are intrinsically motivated.* Such workers are less likely to shirk responsibility at the expense of the group, so free-riding is not a serious concern. Intrinsic motivation is often found in not-for-profit organizations whose employees are emotionally committed to the organization's cause.

4. *The organization needs to insist on group goals.* In some organizations this is a paramount need. For example, high-tech firms often find that their research scientists have their own research agendas and professional objectives—which are frequently incompatible with those of the firm or even their peers. Team-based incentives can focus such independent-minded employees' efforts on a common goal.[45]

♦ *When the objective is to foster entrepreneurship in self-managed work groups.* Sometimes, to encourage innovation and risk taking among employee groups, a firm will give certain groups extensive autonomy to perform their task or achieve certain objectives. This practice is often referred to as *intrapreneuring* (a term coined by Gifford Pinchot, who published a book with that title in 1985). Intrapreneuring means creating and maintaining the innovation and flexibility of a small-business environment within the confines of a large bureaucratic structure.[46] In an intrapreneuring environment, management often uses team-based incentives as a hands-off control mechanism that allows each group to assume the risk of success or failure, as entrepreneurs do.

The formation of self-managed teams and the use of team-based pay plans are not limited to large companies. When The Published Image, a custom newsletter publisher with 26 employees, experienced extremely rapid growth at the expense of low quality, low employee morale, and high turnover, the firm's founder, Eric Gershman, decided on a radical reorganization. To combat employees' belief that their job was to please the boss instead of the customer, he divided employees into four largely autonomous teams, each with its own clients and staff of sales, editorial, and production workers. Published Image managers-turned-coaches field questions and rate the teams for timeliness and accuracy. A monthly score of 90 or higher entitles team members to biannual bonuses, which can add up to 15 percent of their base pay.[47]

■ Plantwide Plans

Plantwide pay-for-performance plans reward all workers in a plant or business unit based on the performance of the entire plant or unit. Profits and stock prices are generally not meaningful performance measures for a plant or unit because they are the result of the entire corporation's performance. Most corporations have multiple plants or units, which makes it difficult to attribute financial gains or losses to any single segment of the business. Therefore the key performance indicator used to distribute rewards at this level is plant or business unit efficiency, which is normally measured in terms of labour or material cost savings compared to an earlier period.

Plantwide pay-for-performance programs are generally referred to as **gainsharing** programs because they return a portion of the company's cost savings to the workers, usually in the form of a lump-sum bonus. Three major types of gain-

gainsharing
A plantwide pay-for-performance plan in which a portion of the company's cost savings is returned to workers, usually in the form of a lump-sum bonus.

Scanlon Plan Associates
www.scanlonassociates.org

sharing programs are used. The oldest is the *Scanlon Plan,* which dates back to the 1930s. It relies on committees of employees, union leaders, and top managers to generate and evaluate cost-saving ideas. If actual labour costs are lower than expected labour costs over an agreed-upon period (normally one year), the difference is shared between the workers (who, as a group, usually receive 75 percent of the savings) and the firm (which usually receives 25 percent of the savings). A portion of the savings may also be set aside in a rainy day fund.

The second gainsharing program, the *Rucker Plan,* uses worker-management committees to solicit and screen ideas. These committees are less involved and simpler in structure than those used by the Scanlon Plan. But the cost-saving calculation in the Rucker Plan tends to be more complex because the formula encompasses not only labour costs but also other expenses involved in the production process.

The last type of gainsharing program, *Improshare* ("*Im*proved *pro*ductivity through *shar*ing"), is a relatively new plan that has proved easy to administer and communicate. First, a standard is developed—based on either studies by an industrial engineering group or some set of base-period experience data—that identifies the expected number of hours required to produce an acceptable level of output. Any savings arising from production of this agreed-on output in fewer than the expected hours are shared between the firm and the workers.

Although gainsharing plans have been associated most frequently with private sector manufacturers, public-sector employers and those producing less tangible products are developing their own adaptations of gainsharing. SaskPower and IBEW, the union representing a significant portion of its work force, had been experiencing rather polarized labour relations. As a way forward, company and union began exploring through various informal and educational interventions how they could attempt to find win/win solutions to some of the issues between them. The result has been the emergence of mutual gains bargaining, a process characterized by SaskPower's vice-president of HR, Keven Mahoney, as one where "you throw the issue on the wall and hammer the issues instead of each other."[48]

Salomon Smith Brothers
www.salomonsmithbarney.com

While gainsharing is often associated with people at the top of the organization (that is, those with profit responsibility) and the rank and file, it can work just as well with employees in the middle. Salomon Brothers, the international investment firm, had long been heaping bonuses on its traders and investment bankers when it decided to use a program called Teamshare to reinvent its crucial back-office support organization. Salomon's 505 support staff members, including about 17 managers who make over $130,000 a year, now get to keep 10 percent of the savings they generate through cost-cutting measures. Under this program, the annual bonus for an accountant whose salary is $80,000 could be as much as $8,000.[49]

Advantages of Plantwide Pay-for-Performance Plans.

The primary rationale for gainsharing programs can be traced to the early work of Douglas McGregor,[50] a colleague of and collaborator with Joseph Scanlon, founder of the Scanlon Plan. According to McGregor, a firm can be more productive if it follows a participative approach to management—that is, if it assumes that workers are intrinsically motivated, can show the company better ways of doing things if given the chance, and enjoy being team players.

In contrast to individual-based incentive plans, gainsharing does not embrace the idea that pay incentives motivate people to produce more. Rather, gainsharing suggests that cost savings result from treating employees better and involving them intimately in the firm's management. The underlying philosophy is that competition between individuals and teams should be avoided, that all workers should be encouraged to use their talents for the plant's common good, that employees are willing and able to contribute good ideas to the firm, and that the financial gains generated when those ideas are implemented should be shared with employees.

Gainsharing plans can provide a vehicle to elicit active employee input and improve the production process. They can also increase the level of cooperation across workers and teams by giving everyone a common goal to work toward. Another advantage of gainsharing plans is that they are subject to fewer measurement difficulties than individual- or team-based incentives. Because gainsharing plans do not require managers to sort out the specific contributions of individuals or interdependent teams, it is easier both to formulate bonus calculations and to achieve worker acceptance with these plans.

Gainsharing plans have been lauded not only for increasing organizational productivity but also for improving quality in manufacturing firms that previously relied on individual-incentive or piece-rate plans. When Tech Form Industries, a producer of tubular exhaust systems, realized that its individual-based incentive plans were driving quality—and its business—down the tubes, it discontinued its piece-rate system and, with employee involvement, developed a companywide gainsharing plan. Within three years returns of defective products went down by 83 percent, direct labour hours spent on repairs decreased by 50 percent, and grievances declined by 41 percent. The transition from an individual-based incentive system to gainsharing required many steps, the first of which was negotiating salary packages with the union that were at least comparable to the piecework plan.[51]

Disadvantages of Plantwide Pay-for-Performance Plans.

Like all other pay-for-performance plans, plantwide gainsharing programs may suffer from a number of difficulties, among them:

♦ *Protection of low performers.* The free-rider problem can be very serious in plants where it is difficult for workers to see the impact of their individual contributions and where rewards are spread across a large number of employees. Because so many people work together in a plant, it is less likely that peer pressure will be used to bring low performers into the fold.

♦ *Problems with the criteria used to trigger rewards.* Although the formulas used to calculate bonuses in gainsharing plans are generally straightforward, four problems may arise. First, once the formula is determined, employees may expect it to remain the same forever. A too-rigid formula can become a management straitjacket, but managers may not want to risk employee unrest by changing it. Second, improving cost savings will not necessarily improve profitability because the latter depends on many uncontrollable factors (such as consumer demand). For example, an automobile production facility can operate at high efficiency, but if it is producing a car that is in low demand, that plant's financial performance will not look good. Third, when gainsharing is first instituted, it is easier for inefficient than for efficient plants or business units to post a gain. This is because opportunities for dramatic labour-cost savings are much higher in the less efficient units.[52] Thus gainsharing programs may seem to penalize already-efficient units, which can be demoralizing to those who work in them. Fourth, there may be only a few labour-saving opportunities in a plant, and since these may be quickly exhausted once the gainsharing plan goes into effect, further gains will be difficult to achieve. The inability to achieve results can also be demoralizing.

♦ *Management-labour conflict.* Many managers feel threatened by the concept of employee participation. When the gainsharing program is installed, they may be reluctant to give up their authority to committees, creating conflict and jeopardizing the program's credibility. Second, only hourly workers are included in most of these plans. The exclusion of salaried employees may foster hard feelings among them.

Conditions Favouring Plantwide Plans.

A number of factors affect the successful implementation of gainsharing programs.[53] These are:

♦ *Firm size.* Gainsharing is more likely to work well in small to mid-size plants, where employees can see a connection between their efforts and the unit's performance.

♦ *Technology.* When technology limits improvements in efficiency, gainsharing is less likely to be successful.

◆ *Historical performance.* If the firm has multiple plants with varying levels of efficiency, the plan must take this variance into account so that efficient plants are not penalized and inefficient plants rewarded. It is difficult to do this where there are scanty historical records. In these cases, past data are an insufficient basis for establishing reliable future performance standards, making it difficult to implement a gainsharing program.

◆ *Corporate culture.* Gainsharing is less likely to be successful in firms with a traditional hierarchy of authority, heavy dependence on supervisors, and a value system that is antagonistic to employee participation. Gainsharing can be used effectively in a firm that is making the transition from a more autocratic to a more participative management style, but it is doubtful that it can successfully lead the charge as a stand-alone program.

◆ *Stability of the product market.* Gainsharing is most appropriate in situations where the demand for the firm's product or service is relatively stable. Under these circumstances, historical data may be used to forecast future sales reliably. When demand is unstable, the formulas used to calculate bonuses may prove unreliable and force management to change the formula, which is likely to lead to employee dissatisfaction. For example, increases in total output that occur as efficiency improves may create an inventory surplus that cannot be absorbed by the market. When this happens, management may have little money to distribute or, even worse, may have to lay off employees as a cost-cutting measure.

■ Corporatewide Plans

The most macro type of incentive programs, *corporatewide pay-for-performance plans,* reward employees based on the entire corporation's performance. The most widely used program of this kind is **profit sharing,** which differs from gainsharing in several important ways:[54]

profit sharing

A corporatewide pay-for-performance plan that uses a formula to allocate a portion of declared profits to employees. Typically, profit distributions under a profit-sharing plan are used to fund employees' retirement plans.

◆ In a profit-sharing program, no attempt is made to reward workers for productivity improvements. Many factors that affect profits (such as luck, regulatory changes, and economic conditions) have little to do with productivity, and the amount of money employees receive depends on all of these factors.

◆ Profit-sharing plans are very mechanistic. They make use of a formula that allocates a portion of declared profits to employees, normally on a quarterly or annual basis, and do not attempt to elicit worker participation.

◆ In the typical profit-sharing plan, profit distributions are used to fund employees' retirement plans. As a result, employees seldom receive profit distributions in cash. (This deferral of profit-sharing payments is commonly done for tax reasons.) Profit sharing that is distributed via a retirement plan is generally viewed as a benefit rather than an incentive. Some companies do have profit-sharing programs that are true incentives, however. At Celestica, the high-technology components manufacturer that was spun off from IBM Canada, it is possible for staff to earn bonuses of up to 30 percent of their base pay.[55]

employee share ownership plan (ESOP)

A corporatewide pay-for-performance plan that rewards employees with company shares, either as an outright grant or at a favourable price that may be below market value.

Like profit sharing, **employee share ownership plans (ESOPs)** are based on the entire corporation's performance—in this case, as measured by the firm's share price. ESOPs reward employees with company shares, either as an outright grant or at a favourable price that may be below market value. Employers often use ESOPs as a low-cost retirement benefit for employees because share contributions made by the company are non-taxable until the employee redeems the shares. Employees whose retirement plans are based on ESOPs are exposed to risk, however, because the price of the company's shares may fluctuate as a result of general stock market activity or mismanagement of the firm. ESOPs exist across Canada, but are perhaps most easily accommodated legally in British Columbia, with tax credits equal to 20 percent of earnings up to $2,000 a year ($10,000 in a lifetime) available to top employees. Well-run ESOPs align the interests of workers with founding owners, and have been credited with major contributions to organizational success.[56]

Advantages of Corporatewide Pay-for-Performance Plans.   Corporatewide pay-for-performance plans have several advantages, a number of which are economic rather than motivational. These are:

◆ *Financial flexibility for the firm.* Both profit sharing and ESOPs are variable compensation plans: their cost to the firm is automatically adjusted downward during economic downturns. This feature allows the firm to retain a larger work force during a recession. In addition, these plans allow employers to offer lower base compensation in exchange for company shares or a profit-sharing arrangement. This feature gives the firm "float," or flexibility to direct scarce cash where it is most needed. ESOPs may also be used to save a foundering company—one whose cash is running low or is in an otherwise vulnerable position. Algoma Steel, Spruce Falls, Inc. (a paper mill), and Canadian Pacific Express and Transport have all used ESOPs successfully in such circumstances.[57]

◆ *Increased employee commitment.* Employees who are part owners of the firm are more likely to identify themselves with the business and increase their commitment to it. Many consider the sharing of profits between the firm's owners and workers as a just distribution of income in a capitalistic society.

◆ *Tax advantages.* Deferred profit-sharing plans, including those used to purchase shares in the company, provide a tax advantage for the employees so long as they retain their holdings in the form of shares. Although such plans have the direct effect of reducing tax revenues, defenders suggest that the advantages of such plans (in the form of increased productivity and especially in the form of the dynamism associated with rapidly growing entrepreneurial firms that may not otherwise be able to attract and retain excellent staff) more than offset the costs involved.

Disadvantages of Corporatewide Pay-for-Performance Plans.   Like all other pay-for-performance programs, corporatewide plans have their drawbacks:

◆ *Employees may be at considerable risk.* Under profit-sharing or ESOP plans, workers' financial well-being may be threatened by factors beyond their control. Often workers are not fully aware of how much risk they are taking by staying with the firm because the factors affecting profits or share prices can be very complex. The more reliant long-term employees are on these programs for savings (for their children's university tuition, their own retirement, or some other purpose), the more vulnerable they are to the firm's fate.

◆ *Limited effect on productivity.* Because the connection between individual goal achievement and firm performance is small and difficult to measure, corporatewide programs are not likely to improve productivity. They should, however, reduce turnover if seniority strongly affects how much an employee is entitled to under the plan.

◆ *Long-run financial difficulties.* Both profit sharing and ESOPs often appear painless to the company in the short run, either because funds are not paid out to employees until retirement or because employees are paid in "paper" (company shares). This illusion may induce managers to be more generous with these types of compensation than they should be, leaving future management generations with less cash available, lower profits to distribute to investors, and a firm that has decreased in value.

Conditions Favouring Corporatewide Plans.   A number of factors influence the successful implementation of corporatewide pay-for-performance plans:

◆ *Firm size.* Although they may be used at firms of any size, profit sharing and ESOPs are the plans of choice for larger organizations, in which gainsharing is less appropriate.[58]

◆ *Interdependence of different parts of the business.* Corporations with multiple interdependent plants or business units often find corporatewide plans most suitable because it is difficult to isolate the financial performance of any given segment of the corporation.

◆ *Market conditions.* Unlike gainsharing, which requires relatively stable sales levels, profit-sharing and ESOP programs are attractive to firms facing highly cyclical ups and downs in demand for their product. The structuring of these incentives helps the firm cut costs during downturns. (This is why these programs are often called "shock absorbers.") Employees are not affected by these fluctuations in short-term earnings because most profit-sharing benefits are deferred until retirement.

◆ *The presence of other incentives.* Because corporatewide pay-for-performance plans are unlikely to have much motivational impact on individuals and teams within the firm, they should not be used on their own. When used in conjunction with other incentives (for example, individual and team bonuses), corporatewide programs can promote greater commitment to the organization by creating a sense of common goals, partnership, and mission among managers and workers.

■ Designing Pay-for-Performance Plans for Special Employee Groups

Executives and salespeople are normally treated very differently than most other types of workers in pay-for-performance plans. Because pay incentives are an important component of these employees' total compensation, it is useful to examine their special compensation programs in some detail. It is also useful to examine how companies are rewarding excellence in customer service—a key source of competitive advantage today.

■ Executives

Is anyone's work worth $27.4 million a year? That's how much Robert Gratton, CEO of Power Financial Corporation, earned in 1997 when you combine his salary, bonuses, and the surrender of stock options. While a smaller figure than the highest compensation paid CEOs in the United States (where CEOs' pay is at least double in equivalent after-tax income in Canada), the amount Gratton received is equivalent to over $9100 per hour, assuming a 50-week year and 60 hours per week—or over $150 per minute for every minute he was running the company.[59]

The average total compensation for CEOs of major Canadian corporations in 1997 was equivalent to U.S.$440,000, about half of the $901,000 for U.S. CEOs but about 10% higher than Japanese CEOs.[60] Canada, and especially the United States, have much higher ratios of CEO pay to average worker pay than Japan does.[61]

A variety of plans are used to link executives' pay to firm performance, and there is little agreement on which is best. The disagreement is only heightened by the huge sums of money involved and the weak or inconsistent correlation between executive earnings and firm performance.[62]

Salary and Short-Term Incentives. As indicated in the statistics just reviewed, large public Canadian companies provide base salaries that account for about 47 percent of total compensation, an average of $375,000. Executives' bonuses are usually short-term incentives linked to short-term company objectives. On average, CEOs receive an amount equal to 59 percent of their salary in the form of short-term bonuses. A 1993 ruling from the Ontario Securities Commission that senior executives' compensation must be made public (for companies whose shares are traded on the TSE) was followed by a subsequent requirement that the rationale for payment levels be provided. Such rulings have opened executive compensation in large Canadian companies to greater scrutiny than has historically been the pattern. Early results indicate that there is great variability, both in what the criteria are and in how clearly employers have been able to articulate them. Figure 11–3 indicates some examples of pay packets for Canadian CEOs.

Two major concerns are often expressed regarding executives' annual bonuses. First, because executives are likely to maximize whatever criteria are used to determine their bonuses, they may make decisions that have short-term payoffs at the expense of long-term performance. For instance, long-term investments in research and development may be crucial to the firm's success in introducing new products over time. Yet if bonus calculations treat such investments as costs that

Ontario Securities Commission
www.osc.gov.on.ca

Company	Industry	CEO	Total Compensation*
Alcan	Mining	Jacques Bougie	$ 2,632,489
Bank of Montreal	Financial Services	Matthew Barrett	$ 4,194,994
Bombardier	Transportation Mfg.	Laurent Beaudoin	$ 2,507,227
George Weston	Food, Retailing	Galen Weston	$ 7,652,755
CanWest Global	Broadcasting	Israel (Izzy) Asper	$ 2,177,524
Magna	Auto parts	Donald Walker	$ 4,058,580
Midland Walwyn	Brokerage	Robert Schultz	$ 3,370,348
Newcourt Credit	Financial Services	Steven Hudson	$ 2,254,671
Power Corporation	Financial	Robert Gratton	$ 27,395,123
TrizecHahn Corp	Property Devel.	Peter Munk	$ 2,813,480

*Total compensation includes salary, bonuses, housing and other allowances, benefits from incentive and retirement schemes and the exercise of stock options.

Report on Business Magazine
http://www.robmagazine.com/
top1000/other/ceo_headless.htm

Figure 11–3 Cash Compensation Paid to Selected Canadian CEOs (1997)

SOURCE: *Report on Business Magazine,* July 1998.

reduce net income on the balance sheet, executives may be tempted to scale back R&D investment. Second, many bonus programs represent salary supplements that the CEO can expect to receive regardless of the firm's performance. This practice is likely to become less frequent in larger companies because of the Ontario Securities Commission's requirements for disclosure of senior executives' pay.

The almost automatic payment of lavish bonuses to top executives has led to much resentment among middle managers. One vice-president and financial analyst at a major bank expressed a common middle-management frustration: "It disturbs me when someone on high dictates that no matter how hard you work or what you do, you're only going to get a 6% increase, and if you don't like it, you can take a hike. Yet whatever they've negotiated for themselves—10%, 20%, or 30%— is a different issue from the rest of the staff."

Corporate profitability and increased share values have become associated with cost reductions, including pay freezes, rollbacks, and workforce reductions during the 1990s. This had led to the paradox of senior executives receiving healthy bonuses and other compensation in companies where rank-and-file employees have seen their incomes curtailed.

Long-Term Incentives.   Most executives also receive long-term incentives, either in the form of equity in the firm (share-based programs) or a combination of cash awards and shares. The primary criticism of long-term incentive plans is that they are not very closely linked with executive performance. There are three reasons for this. First, even executives themselves rarely know the value of the equity they own in the firm[63] because it depends on such hard-to-make assumptions as the price of the stock at redemption. Second, the executive is likely to have very little control over the value of a company's stock (and thus the worth of the executive's own long-term income) since share prices tend to be highly volatile. (This can work to the executive's benefit or detriment. Magna's Stronach was able to take advantage of the resurgence of the North American auto industry, which amplified the recovery of his firm's competitiveness in the auto-parts sector. On the other hand, executives in many companies, who had been lent money to buy shares in their companies during the periods of overheated stock markets, found themselves in a difficult position when share values fell precipitously.) Third, designing long-term incentive plans involves many judgement calls, and these are not always addressed in a manner consistent with achieving the firm's long-term strategic objectives. The major questions that firms should address in designing executive long-term programs are listed in Figure 11–4.

It is interesting that stock options for executives are almost unheard of in Asia and most parts of Europe. In fact, the countries most admired for their long-term

1. How long should the time horizon be for dispensing rewards?
2. Should length of service be considered in determining the amount of the award?
3. Should the executive be asked to share part of the costs and, therefore, increase his or her personal risk?
4. What criteria should be used to trigger the award?
5. Should there be a limit on how much executives can earn or a formula to prevent large unexpected gains?
6. How often should the awards be provided?
7. How easy should it be for the executive to convert the award into cash?

Figure 11–4 Key Strategic Pay Policy Questions in the Design of Executive Long-Term Income Programs

SOURCE: Gómez-Mejía, L. R., & Balkin, D. B. (1992). *Compensation, organizational strategy, and firm performance,* 225. Cincinnati, OH: South-Western.

business vision—Germany and Japan—do not have any long-term financial incentives for CEOs.[64]

There are some patterns of difference in executive pay. One general pattern is that CEOs of subsidiaries of foreign-owned multinationals tend to earn less than do the CEOs of large Canadian-based multinationals, partly because the Canadian companies need to attract and retain executives to provide strategic leadership in a global competitive market.

perquisites ("perks")

Non-cash incentives given to a firm's executives.

Perks.   In addition to cash incentives, many executives receive a large number of **perquisites** or **"perks."** These may keep the executive happy, but they are seldom linked to business objectives. They are also an easy target of criticism for those who feel that executive compensation is already excessive.

There are no easy answers to these criticisms. Executive compensation will probably always be more an art than a science because of all the factors that must be considered and each firm's unique conditions. Nonetheless, it is safe to say that an executive compensation plan is more likely to be effective if: (1) it adequately balances rewarding short-term accomplishments with motivating the executive to consider the firm's long-term performance; (2) the incentives provided are linked to the firm's overall strategy (for example, fast growth and risky investments versus moderate growth and low business risks); (3) the board of directors can make informed judgements about how well the executive is fulfilling his or her role; and (4) the executive has some control over the factors used to calculate the incentive amount.[65]

■ Salespeople

Sales professionals, working with the marketing staff, are responsible for bringing revenues into the company. There are several reasons that setting up a compensation program for salespeople is so much different from setting up compensation programs for other types of employees.[66]

♦ The spread in earnings between the lowest- and highest-paid salesperson is usually several times greater than the earnings spread in any other employee group within the company.

♦ The reward system for salespeople plays a supervisory role because these employees generally operate away from the office and may not report to the boss for weeks at a time.

♦ Perceptions of pay inequity are a lesser concern with this group than with others because few employees outside the company's marketing organization have knowledge of either sales achievement or rewards.

♦ Sales compensation is intimately tied to operating business objectives and strategies.

♦ The performance variation among salespeople tends to be quite large. Most organizations rely on a relatively few stars to generate most of the sales.

◆ The salesperson generally works alone and is personally accountable for results.

◆ Accurate market data on pay practices and levels are extremely difficult to find for salespeople, and commercial salary surveys are usually unreliable.

Sales professionals may be paid in the form of *straight salary* (with no incentives), *straight commission* (in which all earnings are in the form of incentives), or a *combination plan* that mixes the two. Straight salary is most appropriate when maintaining good customer relations and servicing existing accounts are the key objectives, with increased sales a secondary goal. Straight commission is most appropriate when the key objective is to generate greater sales volume through new accounts. Only one-quarter of all firms use either a straight-salary or straight-commission method. Three-quarters use a combination of the two, though the relative proportion of salary versus incentives varies widely across firms.[67]

As the Manager's Notebook shows, all three sales compensation methods have their pros and cons. The main criterion that should determine the type of plan chosen is overall marketing philosophy, which is derived from the firm's business strategies.[68] If increased sales is the major goal and these sales involve a one-time transaction with the customer with little expectation of a continuing relationship, then a greater proportion of incentives in the pay mix is appropriate. If customer service is crucial and the sales representative is expected to respond to clients' needs on a long-term basis, then greater reliance on straight salary is appropriate. For example, used-car salespeople are often paid in the form of straight commission, while sales representatives for highly technical product lines (which often require extensive customer service) tend to be paid on straight salary.

Manager's Notebook

Salary? Commission? Or Both?

Straight-Commission Sales Compensation Plan

Advantages
◆ Effective for generating new accounts
◆ Sales force is highly motivated to sell the product
◆ High performers' contributions are recognized with pay
◆ Sales representatives become entrepreneurial and require minimal supervision
◆ Selling costs are efficiently controlled
◆ Plan administration is simple

Disadvantages
◆ Sales volume is emphasized over profits
◆ Customer service may be neglected
◆ Sales representative may overstock the customer
◆ Offers less economic security to sales force
◆ Provides less direct control over sales force
◆ Top-performing sales representatives may outearn other employees, including executives
◆ Possible resistance to changes in sales territories
◆ Possible focus on products that require the least effort to sell

Straight-Salary Sales Compensation Plan

Advantages
◆ Secure income
◆ Sales force is willing to perform non-selling activities
◆ Plan administration is simple
◆ Sales force is less likely to overstock customers
◆ Low resistance to change in sales territories
◆ Low employee turnover rates
◆ Sales force treated as salaried professionals

Disadvantages
◆ Low motivational impact
◆ Difficult to attract or retain top sales performers
◆ More sales managers are needed to provide supervision
◆ Sales representatives may focus on products that require least effort to sell

Combination Sales Compensation Plan

Advantages
◆ Incorporates advantages of both straight-salary and straight-commission plans
◆ Recognizes both selling and non-selling activities with pay
◆ Can offer both economic security and monetary incentives to sales representatives
◆ Greater variety of marketing goals can be supported with plan

Disadvantages
◆ Plan is more complicated to design
◆ Sales force may become confused and try to accomplish too many objectives
◆ Plan is more difficult and costly to administer
◆ Sales representatives may receive unanticipated windfall earnings

■ Rewarding Excellence in Customer Service

More and more companies are using special incentive systems to reward and encourage better customer service. Amdahl Canada, mentioned earlier in this chapter, has initiated team-based incentives. IBM Canada has put all employees on variable pay, with part of each employee's annual bonus based on customer satisfaction.[69] The SHARE program at CP's Royal York Hotel makes customer service standards a make-or-break constraint that must be satisfied before other performance achievements will trigger the employee ownership incentive.[70] Doug Pinder of Calgary-based Dino Rossi Footwear Inc. has created an innovative bonus plan designed to reward staff for customer relations excellence. Retail sales staff fill out daily forms on which they indicate what they've done to provide service. They accrue points for writing down customer names and sizes, jobs or professions, and clothing preferences, sending thank-you cards and making follow-up phone calls. A customer thank-you note is weighted heavily. Bonus dollars are determined by point totals.[71]

A recent survey revealed that some 35 percent of respondents factor customer service into their formula for determining incentive payments, and that another third were considering doing so. Common measures of customer satisfaction used to determine incentive payments are customer surveys, records of on-time delivery of products and services, and numbers of complaints received.[72]

Summary and Conclusions

Pay-for-Performance: The Challenges.   Pay-for-performance (incentive) programs can improve productivity, but managers need to consider several challenges in their design and implementation. Employees may be tempted to do only what they get paid for, ignoring those intangible aspects of the job that are not being explicitly rewarded. Cooperation and teamwork may be damaged if individual merit pay is too strongly emphasized. Individual merit systems assume that the employee is in control of the primary factors affecting his or her work output, an assumption that may not be true. Individual performance is difficult to measure, which makes merit decisions difficult. Pay incentive systems can be perceived as an employee right and can be difficult to adapt to the organization's changing needs. Many employees do not believe that good performance is rewarded. Emphasizing merit pay can place employees under a great deal of stress and lead to job dissatisfaction. Finally, merit pay may actually decrease employees' intrinsic motivation.

Meeting the Challenges of Pay-for-Performance Systems.   To avoid the problems sometimes associated with pay-for-performance systems, managers should: (1) link pay and performance appropriately, (2) use pay for performance as part of a broader HRM system, (3) build employee trust, (4) promote the belief that performance makes a difference, (5) use multiple layers of rewards, (6) increase employee involvement, and (7) consider using non-financial incentives. Employee participation in the design of the plan can enhance its credibility and long-term success.

Types of Pay-for-Performance Plans.   Incentive programs are classified according to the organizational level used to measure performance. At the individual level,

merit pay (which becomes part of base salary) and bonuses (given on a one-time basis) determined via supervisory appraisals are most common. Bonuses and awards are also used. At the next level, team-based plans reward the performance of groups of employees who work together on joint projects or tasks, usually with bonuses and non-cash awards. At the level of the plant or business unit, gainsharing is the program of choice. Gainsharing rewards workers based on cost savings, usually in the form of a lump-sum bonus. At the fourth and highest level of the organization—the entire corporation—profit sharing and employee share ownership plans (ESOPs) are used to link the firm's performance with employees' financial rewards. Both plans are commonly used as retirement funds.

Designing Pay-for-Performance Plans for Special Employee Groups.   Two employee groups, top executives and sales personnel, are normally treated very differently than most other workers in pay-for-performance plans. Short-term annual bonuses, long-term incentives, and perks may be used to motivate executives to make decisions that are in the best interests of shareholders and that help the firm meet its long-term strategic goals. Sales employees are revenue generators, and their compensation system is normally used to reinforce productive behaviour. A reliance on straight salary for salespeople is most appropriate in situations where maintaining customer relations and servicing existing accounts are the key objectives. A heavy reliance on straight commission is most appropriate if the firm is trying to increase sales. Most firms use a combination of the two plans. In today's globally competitive marketplace, many firms are also using incentive programs to reward customer service.

Key Terms and Concepts

award, 326
bonus program or lump-sum payment, 326
combination plan, 339
corporatewide pay-for-performance plans, 334
credibility gap, 322
employee share ownership plan (ESOP), 334
expectancy theory, 326

free-riding, 329
gainsharing, 331
Improshare, 332
individual-based pay plans, 325
intrinsic drive, 322
merit pay, 326
pay-for-performance system or incentive system, 320
perquisites ("perks"), 338
piece-rate system, 322

plantwide pay-for-performance plans, 331
profit sharing, 334
psychological contract, 321
Rucker Plan, 332
Scanlon Plan, 332
straight commission, 339
straight salary, 339
team-based pay plans, 329

Discussion Questions

1. This chapter identifies three assumptions underlying pay-for-performance plans. Do you believe these assumptions are valid?

2. How can a pay-for-performance system increase the motivation of individual employees and improve cooperation at the same time?

3. One observer notes that "the problem with using pay as an incentive is that it is such a powerful motivational weapon that management can easily lose control of the situation." Do you agree? Why or why not?

4. This chapter discusses certain conditions under which individual-based pay-for-performance plans are most likely to succeed. Can you think of specific jobs, occupations, or types of organizations where such a system is likely to be successful?

5. An insurance company compensates its work teams by awarding an annual bonus based on three factors: productivity, customer satisfaction, and quality of work. In one of its teams, four members came up with a way to speed up claims payments that, in turn, boosted customer satisfaction and productivity and also satisfied quality goals. In this situation, is a bonus for the entire team justified? How can the insurance com-

pany make sure that free riders (low performers) don't benefit from the productivity of others in the group, and that those who do the most work will be rewarded appropriately?

6. Both plantwide and corporatewide pay-for-performance plans have advantages and disadvantages. If you were asked to decide which of these plans to adopt at your company, what factors or type of information would you need to consider? Explain.

7. Incentive systems for top executives are often criticized for filling the pockets of these individuals, with little benefit (and sometimes even negative results) to shareholders and the company in general. Using the latest annual listing of the highest-paid executives from the *Report on Business* magazine, pick five CEOs and try to determine which CEO gave shareholders the most for his or her pay and which company did the best relative to the CEO's pay.

8. A customer survey for Landmark Company reports that people don't trust what sales representatives say about their firm's products. How might you use the compensation system to help change this negative image?

Check out our Companion Website at: **www.prenticehall.ca/gomez** for a selection of self-study questions, key terms and concepts, updated Weblinks to related Internet sites, newsgroups, CBC video updates, and more.

MiniCase 1 — *At Battelle, R&D Means Royalties and Development*

A research scientist for a large pharmaceutical corporation develops and patents a successful new drug that produces $100 million in revenue during its first year in the market. The executives of the division receive large cash bonuses and the salespeople enjoy windfall commissions, but the scientist walks away with a $500 honorarium.

Contrast this scenario, a common one at many companies, with what happens at Battelle Pacific Northwest Laboratory. At Battelle, researchers develop technologies that the company then licenses to private industry. The company receives licensing fees for the technology, as well as royalties on any products using it. Key researchers share a pool of funds worth 10 percent of gross royalties or other proceeds derived from the licensing fees. On average, four to six employees share royalties on any given technology patent, and in the last three years key contributors have received approximately $200,000 through the royalty program. There is a catch, though. Employees don't receive royalties unless they're still at Battelle when the technology achieves commercialization. After that, royalties continue even if the employee leaves the company.

Discussion Questions

1. What do you feel are the advantages and disadvantages of rewarding technology developers or research scientists with royalties from the sale or licensing of products they develop?
2. Do you think there would be any difference in team dynamics between Battelle and a company where researchers work together to develop a product without getting a share in the profits? Explain.

SOURCE: Adapted from Caudron, S. (1993, September 6). *Share the wealth*, 45–46.

MiniCase 2 — *New Incentives at Aetna Canada*

During the 1980s, employees were accustomed to receiving substantial increases in pay, partly because inflation was pushing prices and wages up and partly because of the salary-plus-increase form of merit pay that was widely in use. Raises of eight percent to 12 percent were not unusual for exemplary employees. The 1990s have presented a different environment, featuring low inflation and an increased emphasis on "at-risk" pay for performance, and not only at executive levels. Aetna Life Insurance of Canada has introduced an Employee Performance Sharing Plan for rank-and-file employees that will allow an award of 1.5 percent of base salary if the company meets overall profit targets, another 1.5 percent if the division meets its goals, and an additional one percent for non-managerial staff if they exhibit outstanding performance as individuals (only 25 percent of the employees can be awarded this last amount).

The result is that an employee earning $35,000 would be eligible for a maximum of $1,400.

Discussion Questions

1. What kind of issues do you think a company like Aetna Canada has to deal with when moving from the compensation environment of the 1980s to the kind of system described above?
2. Aetna introduced a provision that even if the corporate or the divisional goals were not met, the individual awards would still be available. Why do you think they did this? Is it a good policy?
3. What is your assessment of the fact that no more than 25 percent of the employees can receive the individual award? Why did Aetna do it? How are employees likely to respond to this provision?

SOURCE: Kinross, L. (1994, February 28). Inventive incentives for employees. *Canadian HR Reporter*, 8–9. Used with permission of *Canadian HR Reporter*, MPL Communications Inc. Copyright 1994.

Case 1

Loafers at Interlake Utility Company

Interlake Utility Company provides electrical power to a district with 50,000 households. Pamela Johnson is the manager in charge of all repair and installation crews. Each crew consists of approximately seven employees who work closely together to respond to calls concerning power outages, fires caused by electrical malfunctions, and installation of new equipment or electric lines. Fourteen months ago Johnson decided to implement a team-based incentive system in which an annual bonus would be provided to each crew that met certain performance criteria. Performance measures included such indicators as average length of time needed to restore power, results of a customer satisfaction survey, and number of hours required to complete routine installation assignments successfully. At the end of the first year, five crews received an average cash bonus of $12,000 each, with the amount divided equally among all crew members.

Soon after Johnson announced the recipients of the cash bonus, she began to receive a large number of complaints. Some teams not chosen for the award voiced their unhappiness through their crew leader. The two most common complaints were that the teams working on the most difficult assignments were penalized (because it was harder to score higher on the evaluation) and that crews unwilling to help out other crews were being rewarded.

Ironically, members of the crews that received the awards also expressed dissatisfaction. A surprisingly large number of confidential employee letters from the winning teams reported that the system was unfair because the bonus money was split evenly among all crew members. Several letters named loafers who received "more than their share" because they were frequently late for work, took long lunches and frequent smoking breaks, and lacked initiative. Johnson is at a loss about what to do next.

Critical Thinking Questions

1. What major issues and problems concerning the design and implementation of pay-for-performance systems does this case illustrate? Explain.
2. Are team-based incentives appropriate for the type of work done by Johnson's crews?
3. Might it be desirable to use a combination of team-based and individual incentives at Interlake Utility Company? How might such a plan be structured?

Cooperative Learning Exercises

4. Students form pairs. One student takes the role of Pamela Johnson, the other the role of an HRM consultant Johnson has hired to help her decide what to do next. Role-play the meeting between the two in which Johnson explains what has happened and the consultant reacts.
5. The class divides into groups of five students each. One of the students takes the role of a consultant hired by Pamela Johnson to help her decide what to do and the remaining four students take the roles of line workers, each from a different crew. The consultant is gathering information from the crews about how they feel about the bonus system and what changes they would like to see.

Case 2

Too Good to Be True: You Get What You Pay For

During the late 1980s and early 1990s, Hong Kong was the star of Bausch & Lomb's (B&L's) international division, often racking up annual growth of 25% as it rocketed to about $100 million in revenues in the mid-1990s.

Trouble was, in recent years, some of the reported sales were fake. Under heavy pressure to maintain its phenomenal record, the Hong Kong unit would pretend to book big sales of Ray-Ban sunglasses to distributors in Southeast Asia. But the goods would not be shipped. Rather, staffers were instructed to send the goods to an outside warehouse in Hong Kong. Later, some of B&L's sales managers would try to persuade distributors to buy the excess. Some of the glasses were also funnelled into the *grey market*; buyers could profit by reselling them in Europe or the Middle East, where wholesale prices were higher. But Hong Kong began to have trouble keeping up its juggling act. Tipped off by falling revenues and soaring receivables—since no one was paying for many of the glasses booked as sales—B&L sent a team of auditors to Hong Kong. The auditors discovered significant irregularities, including half a million pairs of sunglasses stashed in a warehouse.

Investigation revealed that these events were hardly isolated. They were also evident in many other B&L locations. Dan Gill, GEO of B&L, managed by the numbers. "Each year, the top executives would agree on what number they wanted

to make," recalls Harold O. Johnson, the longtime head of the contact lens unit. "The numbers would be divided out by operating units and then assigned. The president would come to me and say, "Here's your number." Once the goals were set, Gill and other top executives rarely accepted excuses for shortfalls; even Gill's backers agree that "making the numbers was key." This was often accomplished at the expense of sound business practice or ethical behaviour. B&L's operating units gave customers extraordinarily long payment periods and threatened to cut off distributors unless they took on huge quantities of unwanted products. Some also shipped goods before customers ordered them and booked the shipments as sales. The compensation system, which emphasized sales growth and de-emphasized customer satisfaction, played a major role in B&L's troubles. The compensation signals from the top down led some to cut corners, several former managers say. As a result, some divisional managers began using tactics that were costly for the company but which maximized reported earnings and thus their own bonuses.

Critical Thinking Questions

1. Bausch & Lomb's intense focus on the bottom line and quarterly results is hardly unique. Many of corporate America's most successful companies have a similar focus. What do you think went wrong at B&L? Explain.

➤

2. Some experts believe that managerial incentives should be exclusively based on the price of the company's stock because it is determined by the "invisible hand" of the market and can't be manipulated (unlike reported earnings, which can be manipulated, as described above). Do you agree? Why or why not?

Cooperative Learning Exercises

3. The class divides into groups of six members each. Each group prepares a series of recommendations to change B&L's culture to prevent the problems described in this case. The groups will then debate their recommendations in front of the class, with the instructor serving as moderator.

4. Students form into groups of three and spend about five minutes brainstorming the advantages and disadvantages of linking top management's pay to accounting performance measures (such as sales growth, earnings, total revenues, and the like), and then about five minutes brainstorming the advantages and disadvantages of linking top executives' pay incentives to the price of the company's stock. Does either of these plans emerge as clearly superior?

SOURCES: Barnathan, J. (1995, October 23). *Business Week*, 78–92; Reuters News Service (1996; April 23), Bausch & Lomb, Inc. absolves executives in probe; Maremont, M., and DeGeorge, G. (1995, October 23). Money laundering in Miami? *Business Week*, 89.

Appendix to Chapter 11

AN OVERVIEW OF WORK MOTIVATION THEORIES

(Note: The following is a brief overview of work motivation theories. Readers interested in greater detail will find it in any standard text in organizational behaviour.)

The purpose of a theory is to describe, explain, and predict. Because we generally conceive of human performance as depending on capability and motivation, work motivation has received a great deal of attention. Unlike a person's capability, which depends on natural ability and time-consuming training, motivation is usually seen as the determinant of employee work performance that can be increased or decreased most quickly and dramatically by employer actions.

Most theories of work motivation, including those that underlie the discussion in Chapter 11, have a common assumption—*hedonism*. This term refers to the notion that people (like other organisms) seek pleasure and avoid pain. Where the many theories part company is when it comes to the identifying *what* objects or experiences provide pleasure (or pain) and *how* those influences actually work. The "what" question has been answered by what will be categorized in this summary as **content models** of motivation; the "how" question has been answered by what will be categorized as **process models** of motivation.

Content models. The question of what motivates people has provided philosophers, historians, the writers of great literature and any reflective person with a rich and endless topic. Motivation has been studied using non-human subjects (rats, pigeons, dogs, primates) by focussing on physiological motives (hunger, thirst, etc.). The extent of deprivation (e.g., how many calories an animal had been allowed in the previous 24 hours) was used as an indicator of the level of motivation. One of the obvious limitations to this as a way of thinking about *human* motivation was that it accounted for too little of the full range of human experience. In fact, it also failed to account for quite a bit of animal behaviour.

One of the first observers to make systematic observations about the complexity of human motivation was Abraham Maslow, who suggested that human motives ("needs") were organized hierarchically. That is, *physiological* needs such as food, water, sleep, and freedom from pain were basic and would dominate behaviour if there were serious deficiencies in those areas. When these needs were not pressing, *safety* needs (an environment free from threats) would be a strong influence. If both physiological and safety needs were reasonably satisfied, *social* needs (love, affection, social acceptance) would emerge as important. When these first three needs categories were relatively satisfied, Maslow suggested that *esteem* needs (being well regarded by others) and ultimately *self-actualization* needs (realizing one's potential, personal growth) would become important influences on behaviour.

Maslow's model has been influential even though some of the specific elements in his model have not been sustained by research. A more recent formulation by Clayton Alderfer has categorized human motives under the headings "existence," "relatedness," and "growth." Although there is a priority among these (existence needs dominate when they are strong), Alderfer's model includes the possibility of linkages among the three levels such that frustration of growth needs can lead to greater emphasis by the person on existence or relatedness needs. Other content theorists saw people as varying significantly in the patterns of their higher order needs, rather than sharing essentially the same hierarchy. David McClelland, for example, focussed on *need for achievement, need for affiliation,* and *need for power* as explaining important differences in work behaviour.

The important implication of these content theorists is that employee motivation responds to a variety of influences. People are not motivated solely by financial outcomes. They are also strongly influenced by social dynamics in the work place–the norms of work groups can support (or oppose!) employer performance objectives. In addition, employees can be influenced by job design through the opportunity for growth, achievement and increased self-esteem. Financial incentives can be important as motivating influences, but as Chapter 11 illustrates, there also are important non-monetary motivators.

Process models.   Employers can more easily influence *extrinsic* rewards (pay, promotion, praise) than *intrinsic* rewards (liking a job's content, personal growth, self-esteem). Process models have tended to emphasize extrinsic rewards. **Expectancy theory** is perhaps the dominant process model. Stated in its simplest terms, expectancy theory predicts that people will do what they *perceive* to be in their own best interest. The value of expectancy theory for a practising manager comes in a slightly expanded version of that statement. The perceived *chain* of causation ($E \rightarrow P \rightarrow V$, see below) is a useful summary. The elements of this chain or path include:

a. The value of the ultimate reward offered for successful performance, referred to as *valence (V)*. The issue for the practitioner is whether the reward (pay, promotion, etc.) is highly valued by the people to whom it is being made available.
b. The perceived likelihood that successfully accomplishing the task [*performance (P)*] will lead to the reward.
c. The perceived likelihood that *effort (E)* will be sufficient to accomplish the level of performance required to earn the reward.

The point of expectancy theory is, quite simply, that there must be a clearly perceived causal path between exerting effort and gaining a desired reward. This chain can break down if (1) the person does not perceive him- or herself to be capable of achieving the needed performance through his or her efforts, (2) the person does not perceive that performance will necessarily trigger the reward(s) being used, or (3) the person does not put a high value on the reward(s) on offer. Problems that could trigger a breakdown at "1" could include poor training, poor job design, and inappropriate supervision. A breakdown at "2" usually results from a reward system that is poorly designed or implemented so that employee performance that is supposed to lead to rewards, doesn't. Effective performance appraisal is one of the keys to avoiding such problems. The breakdown at "3" usually involves either misreading what is important to an employee (e.g., more money versus having a more flexible schedule) or offering a reward that is the right kind, but too small to have much value (e.g., a $15 bonus for a productivity suggestion). And, since expectancy is based on employee *perception*, poor communication about any of these linkages can cause a reduction in innovation. Expectancy theory can help shed light on other motivational issues, once we accept that employees attach valence to many things. For example, an incentive plan may be well designed but ineffective if the employee's peers become hostile to a "rate buster"–more money is desirable, but the loss of a friendly environment may well have an offsetting negative valence.

While expectancy theory portrays employee motivation as goal oriented, **equity theory** portrays people as striving for a *balance* between their work inputs (or contributions) and their outcomes (rewards). Inputs typically include effort, education, training, experience, and so forth, while outcomes include extrinsic rewards (pay, benefits, perquisites) and intrinsic/social rewards (job title, status, nature of the job). While there is a version of equity theory that asserts that this standard of fairness is intuitive, the more common formulation is that of J. Stacy Adams, who suggested that people determine what is fair by observing the treatment of others around them. Adams' view is that people who perceive that they are *under-rewarded* compared others will be motivated to either *in-*

crease outcomes or reduce inputs, to restore the balance. This fits with common sense – if you are overworked compared to the work and rewards of others, you may well feel justified in backing off, and not working so hard. The other imbalance, where you are *over-rewarded,* leads to working harder according to Adams' model. *Research suggests that underpayment leads to a stronger reaction than overpayment.* The main implication of this finding is that poorly designed or poorly implemented pay-for-performance policies may have a negative effect on motivation because those who are poorly treated (underpaid) will respond more than those who are overpaid.

Performance-based pay can be very effective, but work motivation theories and research serve us well because they flag the fact that economic motives are only one factor of the many that shape human behaviour in organizations. *How* economic rewards in combination with other motives influence employee behaviour makes simplistic motivational prescriptions almost always wrong.

chapter 12

Designing and Administering Employee Benefits and Services

After reading this chapter, you should be able to deal more effectively with the following challenges:

1 Understand the significance of employee benefits to both employers and employees.

2 Design a benefits package that supports the firm's overall compensation strategy and other HRM policies.

3 Distinguish between a defined benefit retirement plan and a defined contribution retirement plan, and recognize the situations in which each plan is most appropriate.

4 Explain how publicly funded health care and various supplemental health programs offered by employers relate to each other and to the funding of health care expenses in Canada.

5 Develop cost containment strategies for the different types of employee benefits.

6 Understand the administrative complexities of providing a full array of benefits to a company's work force, and suggest ways to deliver benefits effectively.

7 Recognize the HR department's key role in keeping accurate records of employee benefits and informing employees about their benefits.

Rest, relaxation, rejuvenation. Employers provide their employees with paid vacations to give them time away from the stresses and strains of the daily work routine. Vacation time is an important benefit that allows employees to recharge themselves psychologically and emotionally, helping them sustain a high level of performance.

Today's HR managers are faced with a number of challenges that did not exist a decade ago. One of these challenges is to develop strategies to manage the rapidly increasing costs of employee benefits. Although health care costs have received a great deal of attention, the costs of many other benefits, particularly dental insurance and long-term disability insurance, have also been on the rise. At the same time, benefits remain crucial to attracting, retaining, and motivating employees.

The following examples give some idea of the many ways employers are managing benefits in difficult times. In some cases, employers are:

◆ *Cutting benefits wherever they can.* Although the first line of attack on health benefits costs seems to be intensified communication with employees to get them to use their benefits in a less prodigal way, 80% of those surveyed thought they would be introducing flexible benefits as a cost-containment measure, 77% plan to increase employee contributions, 81% plan to increase annual deductibles, and 59% will allow people to opt out of extended health care programs.[1]

◆ *Providing more flexible benefits.* In early 1995, the e-mail at Canada Trust was busy with some 14,000 employees constructing their own benefits packages. Employees are all given core disability insurance and an allocation of pre-tax dollars that they can spend in a number of ways. "Employees tend to use their benefits without thinking—it's seen as an entitlement. Now they're faced with a fixed amount of money to spend on benefits and a requirement to budget for some of those things. ... What they have to do now is rethink the entire benefits offering, and buy it back," says Vic Clive, assistant VP, compensation and benefits.[2]

Offering benefits that give employees a sense of security while containing costs might seem to be contradictory objectives. The challenge for managers and HR professionals is to work in tandem to (1) give employees meaningful benefits choices that match their needs, (2) keep the costs of those benefits under control, and (3) see that employees are up to date on their benefits so that they know how to use them effectively.

HRM on the Web

http://www.hdrc.drhc.gc.ca/
common/home.shtml

HDRC (Human Resources Development Canada) National Internet Site, home page

With respect to benefits, the quick links on this page to the pages dealing with Income Security Programs such as CPP and to Employment Insurance provide quick and authoritative answers, many of the practical and important issues that arise with employee benefits.

In this chapter we will examine benefits in detail. We will begin with a broad overview of the significance of employee benefits and the relationship of benefits to the rest of the compensation package. Second, we will examine strategies for designing benefits packages. Next, we will describe the scope and significance of two categories of employee benefits programs: legally required benefits and voluntary benefits. Finally, we discuss some important issues in benefit administration.

An Overview of Benefits

In the previous two chapters, we have focused on direct compensation—payments to employees in the forms of wages, salaries, commissions, bonuses, profit sharing, and the like. This chapter focuses on **indirect compensation**—payments in two basic forms: benefits (contingency-based payments to employees) and employee services (payments in kind rather than in monetary form).

indirect compensation

Payments made to employees either on a contingency basis (benefits) or as payments in kind (services).

The Importance of Employment Income.   The vast majority of Canadians derive their livelihood from employment. Most people depend on a paycheque (their own or that of someone else in their household) for economic viability. For that reason, most of us are vulnerable to an interruption in our employment-based income and, as a result, many employee benefits are attempts to reduce the economic risks that we face.

Lives can be seriously disrupted, economically and otherwise, by interruption in income or by unanticipated expenses. Many forms of indirect compensation are mandated by law, while others are the result of voluntary employer initiatives. Because there is such a wide range of specific benefits, it is useful to put them into an overall context. What follows is an overview of the principal financial risks Canadians face, which are reflected in employee benefits programs. As Figure 12–1 illustrates, three of every 10 compensation dollars is spent on indirect compensation. Of the indirect compensation paid, slightly more than a third is for time not worked, a similar amount is spent voluntarily by the employer for a range of benefits, and roughly a quarter is for legally mandated (statutory) benefits.

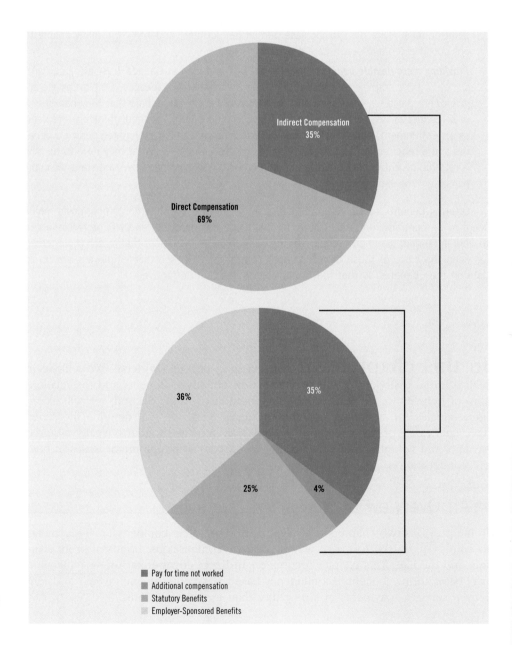

Figure 12–1 Forms of Compensation Spending

SOURCE: KPMG. (1994). *Nineteenth survey of benefits costs in Canada, Table 9.*

Interruption of Income and Related Benefits.   Employment income can be interrupted by a number of circumstances, which are met with a range of legal and voluntary programs:

Unemployment.   Employers are required by law to make *Employment Insurance (EI)* contributions, as are employees. If you lose your job, you qualify for payments (based on your earnings and length of employment) that replace part of what you would have earned. A few employers also provide *supplementary unemployment benefits (SUBs),* which increase income levels closer to what an employee would receive if on the job. SUB programs are usually the result of collective bargaining. Employment Insurance benefits last less than a year, at the longest. In addition, *severance payments* are required in most cases where an employee is not being dismissed for cause.

Illness or injury.   If you are unable to work because of illness or injury, several benefits programs may be available. If the illness or injury is work-related, Workers' Compensation (a government-mandated and employer-funded program) provides medical treatment, partial income replacement, and rehabilitation services. In addition, many employers provide *short-term disability* and/or *long-term disability (LTD) insurance* on a voluntary basis. In addition, Employment Insurance provides short-term income replacement in the case of disabling injury or illness, while the Canada (or Quebec) Pension Plan (CPP or QPP) provides long-term disability benefits to plan contributors that continue (if necessary) until a person is eligible for retirement benefits.

Time off work.   Employers are required to provide paid statutory holidays and annual vacations for most employees, especially those working full time. This legal obligation is often augmented by more generous voluntary vacation entitlements offered to longer-service employees.

Retirement.   Retirement can be made mandatory at age 65. With life expectancy at birth well beyond 75 in Canada for both men and women, it is clear that not having sufficient income during the post-employment period is potentially a serious problem. In Canada there are three main sources for retirement incomes.

◆ *Government* programs include the Canada (or Quebec) Pension Plan as well as the recently integrated *Old Age Security (OAS)* program and *Guaranteed Income Supplement (GIS)*.

◆ *Employers* often sponsor *private pension plans,* funded either by the employer or a combination of employer and employee contributions. Pension payments reflect contributions made on behalf of an employee and tend to be larger for high-income, long-service employees.

◆ *Individuals* must also include their own savings and investments as sources of income. The legislation that created *Registered Retirement Savings Plans (RRSPs)* allows individuals to deduct plan contributions from their taxable income and shelter the investment income in their RRSPs from taxation.

Death.   An employee who dies doesn't need income, but if he or she has dependants, they are often affected financially as well as emotionally by the death. Financial death benefits and survivor pensions are provided by the CPP/QPP. In addition, many employers offer *group life insurance,* frequently linked to an employee's salary (payments range from one to three times the annual amount).

The social value of employee benefits.   In all these cases, the legislated and voluntary programs result in *benefits* that replace at least some of the income a person would earn through employment. These benefits serve two related purposes in society:

1. At the micro level (the individual and his or her family), income replacement allows people at least a temporary reprieve so that they do not quickly use up their savings or find themselves having to sell their home or other major possessions to generate income to live on. Usually, income replacement is partial, and if re-employment is not achieved fairly quickly, some adjustments in spending patterns may be required. However, income replacement benefits provide time for adjustment and orderly transitions.

2. At the macro level (overall economic activity), income replacement benefits provide something of a shock absorber for the economy, taxing employers and employees more heavily when the economy is strong, and maintaining a certain level of buying power in the economy that would otherwise disappear in the troughs of the business cycle. These public policy issues are one reason that governments have legislated extensively in employee benefits matters.

The Risk of Large Expenses and Related Benefits.   If a person or a household loses their customary income, there is an obvious problem. On the other hand, anyone can have a similar problem with *no* loss of income if he or she incurs large unexpected expenses. In Canada, one of the major financial risks—health care—is publicly funded, which means that the risk is shared collectively across the population. (In the United States, by contrast, uninsured medical costs have caused financial chaos in many otherwise financially stable households.) In addition to physician and hospital costs, there are other significant medical costs (particularly medications) that are not fully covered by government programs. These costs lead many employers to provide *supplementary health insurance* that often includes prescription medications, out-of-country coverage, ambulance and other transportation services, physiotherapy, and upgrades in hospital accommodation. Dental and vision care costs are also insured by some employers' benefits programs. Such insurance covers costs incurred by the employees and often by the employees' dependants.

Protection from income interruptions and unexpected expenses reduces employee vulnerability, and therefore such benefits are attractive to many employees. However, such programs are a major expense—a fact that has led many employers to examine the benefits they provide in order to reduce costs or get greater value from benefits spending.

Employee Services.   Human resources, unlike other factors of production, can't be physically separated from the people providing them. Employee services are provided to enhance the quality of employees' personal or work lives. Such services make working for a particular organization more attractive to many employees. They also yield other productivity-related payoffs for employers, such as reducing employee stress, increasing fitness, or helping employees integrate family and employment responsibilities. The range of possible employee services is very broad, but all share one characteristic: rather than putting money directly into employees' hands, services are provided (fitness clubs, counselling, meal or clothing subsidies, and the like) at reduced costs.

■ Why Indirect Compensation?

Indirect compensation—benefits and employee services—is more complicated to administer than direct pay. Compared with direct compensation, indirect compensation allows employees *less flexibility* in how the money paid to them, or paid on their behalf, is spent. In a market-based economy, economic logic suggests putting money into employees' hands and letting them choose what they most want to do with it. Despite this, spending on benefits has increased dramatically. Why? There are three main reasons:

1. *Governments require that employers be involved in many benefits programs.* Minimum vacation requirements and statutory holidays, Employment Insurance, Workers' Compensation, and the Canada Pension Plan are *not* optional. All of these programs are under increasing financial pressures; employer contributions to them have risen, and are likely to continue increasing.

2. *Indirect compensation is an important part of competing in the labour market.* Employees value benefits and services. For many people, benefits are an indicator of overall employer practices—a good benefits package is a mark of a good employer. In addition, many people welcome the fact that they don't have to assume a very complicated set of decisions completely on their own. Employers, especially if unionized, are under pressure to match the benefits offered by other employers. During the 1950s, '60s, and early '70s, collective agreements in the private sector were a major factor in the expansion of benefits programs. Even if an employer is non-unionized, the presence of a unionized competitor can have a similar effect. (Dofasco, the non-unionized Hamilton steel company, has long had a policy of monitoring unionized Stelco's pay and benefits in setting their own compensation policy.) Once a benefit is added, completely withdrawing it is difficult for reasons of employee morale, although employers often introduce copayment and deductible changes for cost control.

3. *Cost advantages.* Employers can, in some cases, get more "bang for their buck" by using indirect compensation. There are two mechanisms that can make it less expensive to provide benefits and services directly rather than let employees purchase them on their own.

   (a) *Group-based plans can be cheaper on a per person basis.* For example, an insurance company sells one group policy rather than hundreds or thousands of individual policies, reducing sales and administration costs. This also reduces the need to assess clients individually because risk-based premiums can be set on the basis of the overall population. The fact that an employer with hundreds or thousands of employees is "shopping" for coverage gives the employer greater expertise and more bargaining power with insurance companies than is the case for individuals.

   (b) *Some benefits and services—the list tends to shrink with each federal budget—are not taxable as income.* In essence, these benefits (e.g., supplementary medical and dental insurance) and services (e.g., career or financial counselling) are often cheaper for the employer to provide than for the employee to purchase directly, since the employee would be using after-tax dollars.

■ The Role of the (Non-HR) Manager

More than almost any other issue addressed in this text, benefits programs are designed and controlled by an organization's human resources department. Nonetheless it is important that *all* managers be familiar with benefits programs for day-to-day as well as strategic reasons:

◆ *Benefits are important to employees.* For example, if one of a manager's employees has a child that has a medical problem requiring expensive medication, the medical coverage available is something the manager should understand, as well as whom in the organization to contact for the technical detail on the extent of coverage and on making a claim.

◆ *Benefits can be a powerful recruiting tool.* Managers at companies that offer attractive benefits can use this advantage to help recruit high-quality applicants for job openings.

◆ *Certain benefits play a part in managerial decisions.* Some benefits, such as vacations and holidays, family and medical leaves, and sick days, influence the scheduling of work and managerial planning. Managers need to be aware of those provisions to effectively manage work schedules.

◆ *Benefits are important to managers.* Managers need to be aware of their own benefits options. Some decisions, especially those having to do with retirement plans, have long-term consequences. For example, whether to put additional retirement savings into the company pension plan or to invest them in an RRSP often requires clear understanding of those plans, as well as of one's own career plans.

■ Basic Terminology

Before we proceed further, it is useful to define some basic terms that appear throughout this chapter.

contributions

Payments made for benefits coverage contributions for a specific benefit. These may come from employer, employee, or both.

copayments

Payments made to cover insured expenses (such as for prescription medications) that are split between the insurance company and the insured employee.

deductible

An annual out-of-pocket expenditure that an insurance policyholder must make before the insurance plan makes any reimbursements.

flexible or **cafeteria benefits**

A benefits program that allows employees to select benefits they need most from a menu of choices.

◆ **Contributions** are the sources of funding for a benefit. All benefits are funded by contributions from the employer, from the employee, or from both. As an example, vacations are an employer-provided benefit; that is, the payment of wages and benefits during the vacation period comes from the employer. CPP premiums, and often employer-sponsored pension plans, involve contributions by both employer and employee. (In addition to employer–employee monies, some legally required benefits, such as Employment Insurance, may also tap general government revenues for special programs.)

◆ **Copayments** covering various insured expenses, such as major dental restorations (crowns, bridges, etc.), are often split between the employee and the employer's insurance company. The split can vary widely, from 50–50 to 80–20. In the latter case, a $600 bill for a new crown would be paid with $480 from the insurance company and $120 from the employee.

◆ **Deductible.** This is an annual out-of-pocket amount that must be paid before additional insured costs are absorbed by the insurance company. If the copayment example above also had a $400 deductible, the crown would cost the employee ($400 + 0.2 [$200]), or $440, with insurance covering the other $160. A second crown within the same year—subject only to copayment provisions—would cost the employee only $120.

◆ **Flexible benefits** programs, also called **cafeteria benefits** programs, allow employees to select the benefits they need most from a menu of choices. Unlike employers who try to design a one-size-fits-all benefits package, employers who adopt a flexible benefits program recognize that their employees have diverse needs that would best be met by differing benefits programs. For example, a 25-year-old single employee with no dependants is likely to prefer an extra week of vacation to child care benefits. A 30-year-old employee with a working spouse and small children is more likely to see child care benefits as more valuable, and may be willing to forego the extra vacation time. A 50-year-old employee may well take a benefit of the same value in the form of an additional contribution to his or her company pension account. Flexible benefits are described in greater detail later in this chapter.

■ Growth of Benefits and Services in Canada

Types of Benefits.   Benefits programs respond to the desire of people to be protected from interruptions to their income and their desire to protect themselves from unexpected large expenses, as we have seen. These objectives are met by a combination of legally defined benefits and benefits provided voluntarily by employers. The design of voluntary programs must take the legally required elements into account.

The benefits available to employees can be grouped into the following categories:

Legally required benefits.   Employers are generally required to make payments to (1) the Canada Pension Plan (or Quebec Pension Plan), (2) Employment Insurance, and (3) Workers' Compensation. Statutory holidays and basic vacation entitlements for full-time employees are also set by law. There are further examples of legally mandated pay for time not worked, such as "call-in" pay and overtime premiums. In addition, (unpaid) leaves of absence for pregnancy and adoption oblige employers to keep jobs open for employees in those circumstances.

Voluntary benefits programs. Employers often choose to provide benefits over and above the set that are mandated by law. The major voluntary benefits programs are:

◆ *Health insurance.* Canada's publicly funded health system does not cover all medical costs. Health insurance provided by employers can cover prescription medications, various therapies not covered by the publicly funded system, dental and vision care.

◆ *Retirement.* Employers can provide various forms of retirement income through pension plans, deferred profit sharing, and other vehicles.

◆ *Insurance.* Insurance plans protect employees and their dependants against income loss due to disability or death.

The Financial Dimensions of Benefits Programs.

In historical terms, indirect compensation has become an important element of employment cost structures only recently. However, over 30 cents of every compensation dollar is now being spent on benefits of various kinds.[3] (Refer back to Figure 12–1.) This proportion has been stable for over a decade, but it has remained so because employers have reduced coverage through copayments, deductibles, and other measures to deal with the otherwise increasing costs in medical and dental coverage. Without such measures, the costs for voluntary health benefits would have increased 30 percent in one recent three-year period during which the costs for dental care would have increased 43 percent.[4] A major catalyst in this development was the economic environment of World War II. In the United States, wage controls imposed by law during the war posed a challenge for employers competing for workers in a seller's market. The use of benefits (non-wage payments) avoided violating the intended anti-inflationary limits. These rather minor supplements, termed "fringe" benefits to suggest their inconsequential nature, have now grown to be very significant costs for employers and/or taxpayers throughout much of the industrialized world.

Differences between public and private sectors.   Public-sector employers spend an amount equal to 49 percent of their (direct) payroll on indirect compensation, compared with 35 percent in the private sector. The distribution among forms of indirect compensation in the two sectors, as well as in the two groups combined, is presented in Figure 12–2. Private-sector employers place relatively greater emphasis on statutory benefits and employer-sponsored benefits, while public-sector employers spend a greater fraction on vacations and other time off.

Disability issues.   The term "stress" has become a fixed part of people's vocabulary during the past two decades—the slang expression "stressed out" needs little elaboration for most people. What was once regarded as an "inability to cope" is now understood in terms of the situation that creates the stress. Still, it is a

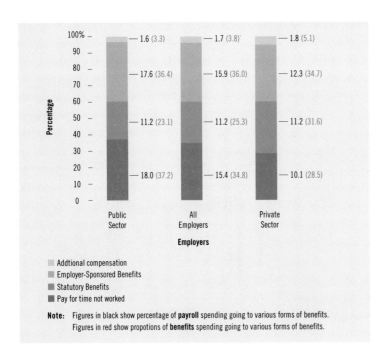

Figure 12–2 Mix of Benefits Spending by Sector

SOURCE: KPMG. (1994). *Nineteenth survey of benefits costs in Canada,* Table 9.

condition with few universally obvious symptoms. Gordon Stainton, human resources manager at Oakville, Ontario-based Procor Ltd., which sells and leases rail
cars, puts it this way: "If only they would look sick. It would be a lot easier to accept if they had blood pouring out of their bodies." While sympathetic to the truly
distressed, Stainton expresses concern for the potential use of stress-based disability
as a de facto early retirement scheme. "Unless we do something, [stress leaves] are
going to become the condition of choice."[5]

There is evidence that such concerns are justified. A recent comprehensive report covering some 35 group-disability insurers, produced by Mercantile and General Reinsurance, reviewed the outcomes of mental and nervous disability claims,
which constituted nearly one in five disability claims. One rather startling finding
was that new group-plan mental and nervous cases increased 31 percent while total disability claims increased just 1.6 percent.[6] Disability premiums are closing the
gap on extended health as the most expensive insurance offered as an employee
benefit.[7] (See Figure 12–3.)

Benefits Canada
www.benefitscanada.com

Cost concerns.   According to *Benefits Canada,*[8] the three most pressing issues
facing insurers' clients (that is, employers) are:

1. *Cost containment.* The Royal Bank of Canada no longer pays the entire cost of dependent health care. With some 50,000 employees, the bank has trimmed their reimbursement for extended health benefits from 80 percent to 70 percent, and has made "enhanced"
   coverage available as an option to employees on a 50–50 copayment basis. McMaster
   University's employees' drug coverage has been revamped, with a smaller reimbursement
   for dispensing fees and the use of a "smart card" to avoid delays in reimbursement. The
   card also permits the employer to build a benefits-use database at the same time.[9]
2. *Taxation of benefits.* At various times prior to the announcement of federal budgets there
   has been concern that the tax status of health insurance benefits would be changed. Groups
   such as the Canadian Dental Association have lobbied vigorously against the change.[10]
3. *Cost-shifting from the public to the private sector.* In one survey, nine of 10 respondents
   indicated that changes in public health care spending were important influences in their
   assessment of their employer-sponsored programs.[11]

Health care benefits are an area of particular concern because they are large,
and rising. The Employer Committee on Health Care—Ontario (ECHCO), a group
of 31 major employers with a total employment of 350,000 people, an annual
payroll of $14.9 billion, and health care spending of $700 million, produced a
document reflecting a desire to enhance employee well-being *and* contain costs.
Their action plan calls for:

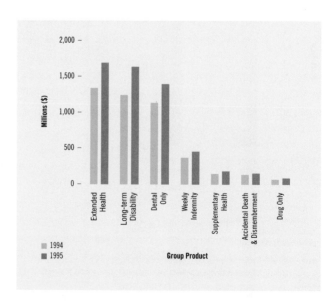

Figure 12–3 Long-Term Disability
Leads the Way
SOURCE: Rising to the challenge.
(1996, May). *Benefits Canada,* 36.

◆ More information and education for payers, patients, providers and the health care community

◆ Streamlining and coordinating services

◆ Illness prevention and the promotion of good health.[12]

Prescription medications play a particularly significant role in their assessment of escalating costs, leading to recommendations for physician prescribing guidelines.[13] In a similar move, the Public Service Health Care Plan has recently been changed so that substitution of generic drugs for more expensive brand names became mandatory, unless the physician specified "no substitutions."[14] A series of measures, some of which can be used in combination, have been identified that are estimated to have the potential of reducing insured drug expenses by substantial amounts (estimated savings in parentheses):

1. A specified formulary of medications, chosen for their medicinal value and cost (4%)

2. Generic substitution (as with the federal program, mentioned above—4% to 6%)

3. Use of preferred providers, that is, selected pharmacies with lower dispensing fees (4% to 9%)

4. Mail-order drug facilities with discounted dispensing fees and mark-ups (8% to 10%)

5. Drug utilization review programs that assess early and late refills and potential drug interactions (5% to 6%).[15]

Health accounts (see the Issues and Applications feature on health accounts) are another initiative aimed at controlling health care benefits costs.

Benefits and Non-Standard Work.

The benefits status of part-time employees and others who work but who are not full-time employees is an important matter, given the increasing role of non-standard work arrangements. From 1976 to 1994, part-time work climbed from 11 to 17 percent of the employed work force. During the early 1990s, the number of Canadians working in temporary positions increased 21 percent, the number holding multiple (typically, part-time) jobs increased 49 percent, and the number of people reporting themselves to be self-employed increased 34 percent.[16] Government-mandated programs such as the Canada/Quebec Pension Plan and Employment Insurance require employer and employee contributions for many non-standard work situations. However, voluntary benefits such as extended health insurance, dental insurance, disability plans, and pensions are frequently not available to part-time or temporary employees.

Part-time employment.

Employers are generally required to make contributions to government-mandated employment benefits, but only in Saskatchewan is there a legislative requirement to provide prorated benefits. The

---

Manager's Notebook

Health Accounts Becoming Popular as Costs Rise

Ottawa—The Conference Board of Canada recently reported that businesses are becoming increasingly worried by the rising costs of their benefit plans due to hefty increases in the cost of prescription drugs, private hospital rooms, and other health care expenses. The report noted that the cost of prescription drugs had risen 9.5 percent between 1990 and 1991, and semi-private hospital rooms in Ontario had risen 20 percent since 1988.

Employers looking to shave overall benefit costs are finding health care spending accounts an attractive concept. Employers allocate a set amount for each employee to use and can set amounts by type of employee. This allows employers to ensure that the benefit levels are maintained for certain employee groups (executives, for example) while overall expenses are cut. The contribution is tax deductible for the employer and tax free for the employee (except in Quebec). The plans may not work as a complete replacement for group plans, but they can help to cap or limit expenses and to allow employees greater flexibility in where they spend their health care dollars.

Tax rules define what medical expenses are eligible under health care spending accounts for tax-free status; the list is far greater than most group plans, including such items as orthodontics, cosmetic dentistry and surgery, medically prescribed weight-loss or smoking-cessation drugs, birth control pills, and fertility treatments. The health care accounts can also be used to "top up" payment on expenses that surpass the maximum limit of the group plan.

To get tax-deductible status, health care spending accounts must meet Revenue Canada's rules for "private health services plans," or PHSPs. PHSPs have a written agreement, like an insurance contract, between the employer and the employee. The employer commits to reimburse the employee for expenses related to an uncertain occurrence. The employer credits the employee with X hundreds or thousands of dollars each year. If the employee doesn't use the allocation, it is carried forward up to 12 months—then the employee loses that allocation.

The health care account can also be set up for only a certain group of employees, usually executives. Or, different rules can be set up for different classes of employees. The plans can even be set up on an individual basis, allowing employers to distribute individual health perks as they desire.

SOURCE: *Human Resources Management in Canada*, Report Bulletin 150, pp. 3–4. Copyright Carswell Thomson Professional Publishing.

1995 legislation attempts to address some of the concerns in a province where part-timers represent one-fifth of the work force, and almost half of them wanted but were unable to find full-time work.[17] The bill extended coverage to some 4,600 employees, of a total 66,000 employees working part time. The legislation exempts full-time employees working a part-time job, contract workers, and full-time students.[18] One of the unexpected complaints about the bill has come from some of the part-timers who are covered—their take-home pay is reduced because some benefits require employee contributions, and there is no provision in the legislation to allow them to opt out.[19]

The Saskatchewan experience has drawn a great deal of attention, given the small number of people affected. Employer resistance was criticized by Saskatchewan Federation of Labour president Barb Byers, who thinks it sends the wrong message to employees: "People will realize that they're seen as disposable and will come in and get what they can and get out. It's not good to have a continuously changing work force, and it's not good for productivity."[20]

The issues are important. Aside from providing benefits to a broader range of people, one intended outcome of the legislation is to remove some of the incentive to replace full-time with part-time workers. In doing so, there may be some inadvertent pressure on "good" employers who offer benefits: by forcing them to offer them to an increasing number of employees, it increases the cost advantage to other employers who offer very few benefits to any of their employees. To date, employers in other jurisdictions have looked to alternatives to benefits for part-timers, rather than include them in the full range of benefits. Merck Frosst Canada, Inc. of Kirkland, Quebec, provides one day of pay for every 22nd day worked, and Pacific Coach Lines of Vancouver provides part-time employees a 10-percent premium on their gross pay. However, Henry Toby, an associate with Morris and Mackenzie Inc. of Toronto suggests that "... insurers, unless they want to see dwindling numbers of premiums coming in for full-time employees, will have to modify their stances as to minimum allowable hours."[21]

Merck Frosst Canada
www.merckfrosst.ca

Self-employment. It's an exaggeration to say that "everyone" is going freelance these days, but the numbers are up sharply, up from 10 to 15 percent in the 1990s. A self-employed person is not eligible for Employment Insurance, although contributions to the Canada Pension Plan are required. However, the medical, dental, disability and other benefits often provided by medium- and large-sized employers clearly aren't there. There are alternatives to expensive individual coverage, however. Insurers have provided group-coverage rates for self-employed professionals such as doctors, lawyers, accountants, and engineers through their professional associations, for some time. As larger numbers of people become self-employed, insurance companies will be assessing whether other groups will be offered similar arrangements. Insurers are more willing to deal with larger associations that are well established and have a marketing plan to minimize their risks.[22]

The Issue: Too Much of a Good Thing?

Competition is increasingly international. Tariff and non-tariff barriers have dropped, and the combined influence of microelectronics and telecommunications has effectively shrunk the world so that international standards of price and quality are applied more and more widely to Canadian organizations. Organizations need strategies to meet these standards, strategies that involve change. Inevitably, this means change for employees. The demand for some skills increases while that for other skills declines. Employment patterns shift—occupationally, from one industry to another, and from one region to another. Most employee benefits are designed to buffer people from financial trauma, but some employers have raised concerns about whether the level and design of benefits provide so much protection that it is counter-productive for the economy.

Some employers are concerned that the costs associated with employee benefits make it difficult to compete with other jurisdictions where comparable payroll taxes (Canada Pension Plan, Workers' Compensation, Employment Insurance) and general taxation levels that support social programs are lower. They see such employment-specific taxes as "job-killers" because they raise the direct and administrative costs of hiring full-time employees and lead to increased use of overtime, more contingent workers, and greater substitution of technology for people. A Bank of Canada analyst has suggested that sharply increased payroll taxes during the early 1990s had the effect of reducing employment levels by one percent, or some 130,000 jobs.[23] Other observers suggest the patterns of income replacement programs that have been devised over the years have resulted in people staying attached to industries and occupations that would not be viable without those programs, slowing the change to new industries and jobs while placing an economic drag (via taxes) on the whole economy. Although the issue is relevant to both large and small employers, small businesses are particularly sensitive to payroll taxes. The Ontario Restaurant Association indicates that payroll taxes represent 11.6 percent of payroll costs and about 3.7 percent of gross industry sales in a sector where margins are quite thin. Jonathan Muir, tax manager with a Toronto accounting firm, has noticed a small-business trend to using independent contractors: "There's no incentive for hiring."[24]

Individuals and communities who see rapid change as a threat to their skills, their incomes, and their overall way of life see income replacement benefits as crucial, and are understandably dubious about the unrestrained "invisible hand" of the marketplace. However, few people, even those who favour activist government policies, would suggest that current programs need no improvement.

As citizens, as managers, and through industry and professional associations, you will find yourself engaged in the ongoing debate about public policy in the area of legally mandated benefits. As you will see in the remainder of this chapter, the HR issues attached to benefits are among the most expensive and contentious introduced in this text.

Bank of Canada
www.bank-banque-canada.ca

■ Benefits Strategies

To design an effective benefits package, an employer needs to align its benefits strategy with its overall compensation strategy. The benefits strategy requires making decisions in three areas: benefits mix, benefits amount, and flexibility of benefits. These choices provide a blueprint for the design of the benefits package.

■ The Benefits Mix

The **benefits mix** is the complete package of benefits that an employer chooses to offer its employees. There are at least three issues that should be considered when making decisions about benefits mix: the total compensation strategy, organizational objectives, and the characteristics of the work force.[25]

The total compensation strategy issue corresponds to the below-market versus above-market compensation decision that we discussed in Chapter 10. The employer must choose the market in which it wants to compete for employees and then must provide a benefits package attractive to the people in that market. In other words, management tries to answer the questions: Who are my competitors for employees? and What kinds of benefits do they provide?

For example, a high-technology company may want to attract people who are risk takers and innovators. The firm's management may decide not to institute a company-sponsored pension plan because their recruiting and retention targets are for people in their 20s, most of whom are not interested in retirement and most of whom realistically expect to work for a number of organizations during their

A Question of Ethics

Most larger employers provide some sort of pension system for employees. Do you think that employers are ethically obliged to do this? Would your answer be affected by the strength or weakness of the organization's financial condition?

benefits mix
The complete package of benefits an employer offers its employees.

career. Apple Computer, once an upstart challenger to IBM, chose not to offer retirement benefits because management did not think this would attract the entrepreneurial employees it wanted.[26]

The objectives of the organization also influence the benefits mix. If the organization's culture is one that minimizes the differences between rank-and-file employees and senior management, the benefits mix should be similar for all employees. If the organization is growing and needs to limit turnover, particular care needs to be taken to ensure that the benefits package reflects what employees are looking for.

Finally, the characteristics of the work force must be considered when choosing the benefits mix. If the firm's work force consists largely of young female employees, it is likely that child care benefits and generous maternity leaves would be highly valued. A highly educated work force will probably appreciate extensive consultation over benefits-mix questions. A unionized work force, particularly in manufacturing industries, is likely to emphasize security-related benefits such as pensions and disability insurance.

■ Benefits Amount

The *benefits amount choice* governs the percentage of the total compensation package that is allocated to benefits compared with other components (base pay and variable pay). It is an extension of the fixed-versus-variable pay decision covered in Chapter 10. Once management determines the "envelope" available for benefits, it can establish a benefits budget and decide on the level of funding for each part of the benefits program. Decisions can then be made about the funding of each program, and the role of copayments, deductibles, and caps in allocating the costs of the benefits between employer and employees. These decisions require sophisticated analysis, and most employers benefit from specialized expertise when making the basic design decisions about benefits programs.

A company that focusses on providing job security and long-term employment opportunities is likely to place a strong emphasis on benefits and devote a larger portion of its compensation budget to benefits. There is quite a bit of variation by industry. The amount spent on benefits in hospitals and other public sector health care organizations is 50 percent of the amount spent on direct compensation; in broadcasting, communications, and publishing, the figure is 41 percent; in banking and financial institutions, about 30 percent; and in hospitality, tourism, and recreation, about 24 percent.[27]

■ Flexibility of Benefits

The *flexibility of benefits choice* is concerned with the degree of freedom employers give employees to tailor the benefits package to their personal needs. This choice extends the centralization-versus-decentralization of pay decision described in Chapter 10. Some organizations have a relatively standardized benefits package that offers few options, if any. This system makes sense in smaller organizations or in those that have fairly homogeneous work forces—for example, a law or accounting firm. Such firms can design benefits for the "typical" employee and serve most of the work force reasonably well. However, the changing and increasingly varied demographics of the Canadian work force, particularly the dramatic increase in employed women including those with young children, have led to an increasing *variety* in employee needs. The "typical" employee often is as artificial a notion as the "average Canadian," which means that decentralized or flexible benefits are increasingly appropriate.

■ Legally Required Benefits[28]

■ The Canada/Quebec Pension Plan

Canada Pension Plan (CPP).   The CPP is a federally administered plan that provides retirement income and other benefits, including benefits to spouses and dependent children, in the event of an individual's death. It also provides disability pensions to people covered by the plan who become unable to work prior to normal retirement age. The CPP is a contributory plan (i.e., both employers and employees are required to make contributions), and its benefits are allocated to individuals on the basis of their contributions. Contributions are also required from most self-employed people. The CPP is designed to be self-funding, without the use of general government revenues.

Quebec Pension Plan (QPP).   The QPP applies to people employed in the province of Quebec. It was initiated in 1966 (as was the CPP), is administered by the Quebec Pension Board (*Régie des rentes du Québec*), and invests its funds with the *Caisse de dépôt et placement du Québec*. It is a separate entity from the CPP but has very similar provisions in terms of contributions, benefits, and rules. For our purposes, the two programs are sufficiently similar that we will focus on the CPP for the sake of simplicity.

Contributions and Coverage.   All persons who are 18 or older and are engaged in pensionable employment must have or must apply for a Social Insurance Number (SIN). This identifier is used to track contributions to the CPP by the individual and by his or her employer(s). Only a small number of employment situations are exempt from mandatory contributions, including casual workers (grass cutters, baby-sitters) and certain migratory workers in agriculture and other such occupations. Employees and employers each contribute a percentage—3.3 percent each, as of 2000, growing to 5.05% each in 2016—of an employees' *contributory earnings*, an amount that has an upper limit ("Year's Maximum Pensionable Earnings"). Maximum annual employer and employee contributions stand at $1,068.80 in 1998. Contributions are deductible from income for both employer and employee. Employer contributions are not a taxable benefit.

CPP Benefits.   Benefits are payable to CPP contributors (or their survivors) in the event of the contributor's retirement, disability, or death. *Retirement benefits* are based on the level of contributions and the length of time a person has contributed. To receive retirement benefits, a person must apply some six months before the time he or she wishes benefits to begin, which may as early as age 60 (at which point the individual would receive a pension amount equal to 70 percent of age 65 entitlement) or as late as age 70 (130 percent of the age 65 pension amount). A person may continue to work after beginning to receive CPP retirement benefits, but contributions cease and no increases in CPP pension amounts result from earnings received after CPP payments commence. *Disability benefits* are payable after a four-month waiting period to individuals who have made contributions in two of the previous three years (or five of the previous 10) and who incur a disability, severe enough to impair their ability to earn, that is expected to continue for a prolonged period. Monthly payments comprise the sum of a flat rate, an amount equal to 75 percent of (imputed) retirement benefits, and a flat-rate amount for each dependent child. *Death benefits* are (relatively small) lump sums paid to a contributor's estate or heirs. A monthly pension is payable to a surviving spouse (formal or common-law); the amount is higher if the spouse is over

Canada/Quebec Pension Plan

A program administered either federally or by the Quebec government, funded by employer and employee contributions and providing retirement and disability income replacement to individuals who have contributed as employees or as self-employed persons.

65 or has dependent children. A spouse under 35 with no dependent children receives no survivor benefits until age 65. All benefits are indexed annually to adjust for changes in the cost of living. CPP benefits must be included in the recipient's taxable income.

■ Workers' Compensation

workers' compensation

A collection of similar mandatory, employer-funded provincial programs that provide partial income replacement and rehabilitation services to employees who become injured or ill on the job.

Objectives. The primary objective of **workers' compensation** is to return employees to work by providing medical care, income support, and rehabilitation. Workers' compensation is the responsibility of the provincial and territorial governments. It provides assistance to employees (and their dependants) who suffer job-related accidents or industrial diseases, in three ways:

1. Financial payments to make up for lost compensation, because of death or disabilities (whether partial or total, and whether temporary or permanent)
2. Financial provision for required medical care not otherwise provided by government health systems
3. Rehabilitation services to assist the employee to regain employability.

Origins. Workers' compensation (WC) was developed to deal with the economic hardships that result from a person's becoming unable to work because of job-related illness or injury. Prior to WC, the employee's legal option was to sue the employer if the employee thought that the employer was responsible. (If the employee was responsible, then there was no legal recourse.) As a practical matter, the costs and time involved made legal proceedings an ineffective solution in most cases.

A Question of Ethics

Employees receive WC rights in exchange for losing the right to sue an employer. Because the maximum awards are less than what a non-employee might win in a negligence lawsuit, should employees be able to sue in cases where clear and flagrant negligence has been demonstrated by an employer?

WC as "No-Fault" Insurance. Workers' Compensation is, in effect, a form of "no-fault" insurance. Paid for by employer premiums with *no* employee contributions, WC effectively removes the employee's right to sue the employer for negligence. In place of the right to sue, to be eligible for WC benefits employees need only demonstrate that the injury or illness is, in fact, work related. There is no requirement to demonstrate that the employer was negligent or otherwise at fault in order for an employee to be eligible for WC benefits.

Workers' compensation is administered by Workers' Compensation Boards, constituted under legislation specific to each province and territory. Premiums paid toward WC funding are deductible as business expenses for the employer and are not imputed as income for employees. Payments made to employees under workers' compensation are (effectively) not treated as taxable income.

Variations in WC. Like other employment legislation emanating from provincial jurisdictions, there is some variation among WC programs across Canada. Generally, however, payments for lost income and death benefits are computed on the basis of the extent of the disability and employee earnings at the time of the event, subject to some maximum amount. There is considerably more variation within provinces in certain provisions of workers' compensation legislation. The premiums charged to employers are a function of their industry, and in some jurisdictions the claims record ("experience rating") of particular employers may be used to modify the payments required. One of the emerging issues with workers' compensation is the attempt to control costs. Changes passed into law in Ontario, effective in 1998, included reduction of benefits from 90% to 85% of pre-injury net average earnings, the exclusion of chronic mental stress as an insured condition, and the replacement of the Workers 'Compensation Board with the Workplace Safety and Insurance Board.[29]

■ Employment Insurance

Employment Insurance (EI) in Canada—known as *Un*employment Insurance (UI) until 1996 legislation—is the responsibility of the federal government, unlike many employment matters that are in provincial jurisdictions. Employment Insurance initially covered only termination or layoff, but a 1971 amendment to the legislation expanded it to cover such situations as sickness, injury, pregnancy, and adoption. In addition, the EI program has been used to provide extended (longer duration) benefits in regions of Canada with unusually high unemployment, and to provide funds for various training and job-creation programs. The development of EI over the years has changed its emphasis from being strictly a short-term income replacement program to an approach that includes a wider range of social and economic objectives. The costs and objectives of this program are a matter of continuing discussion and evolution. In 1996, the Human Resources Development Minister, Lloyd Axworthy, submitted a number of amendments, one of which was to change the name of the program to "Employment Insurance." HR management requires ongoing adjustment to the legal and regulatory environment, and the changes to EI provide an instructive example of such change.

Employment Insurance (EI)

A program mandated by the federal government and paid for with (required) employer and employee contributions, to provide income replacement payments for employees who lose their jobs.

Funding.   Employment Insurance is funded primarily through the mandatory contributions of employers and employees for all employees working more than 15 hours or earning more than 20 percent of the "maximum weekly insurable earnings," although the federal government has provided funds from general tax revenues for special programs. Some 95 percent of employees are covered by EI; self-employed persons are not covered. Rates and benefits are adjusted from time to time. Employee assessments are approximately 2.70 percent of earnings, up to a maximum of $39,000 per year; employer contributions are set at up to 3.78 per-cent of that amount, dependent on whether employers have a wage loss replacement plan.[30] Because some regions and industries consistently take more out of EI than they contribute while others have the reverse pattern, there has been some suggestion that an experience rating or other mechanism be found to rebalance the program.[31]

Unemployment Benefits.   Regular EI benefits are payable, after a specified waiting period, to employees who have had an interruption of earnings either through termination or layoff. Benefits of 55 percent of the individual's average weekly insured earnings are paid to employees who have been employed for at least 22 weeks (or as few as 14, in high unemployment regions) during the preceding year. Benefits are payable for at least 14 weeks, and may be paid for as long as 45 weeks in regions of high unemployment. EI premiums paid by the employee are treated as non-refundable tax credits, and any benefits received are treated as taxable income. Employer premiums are deductible as a business expense and are not imputed to employees as taxable income.

Fighting to preserve our future.

Many Canadians have fought long and hard to preserve the Canada Pension Plan (CPP), Canada's publicly funded pension system. Public concerns in recent years about the future of the plan resulted in the federal government announcing significant changes to the system, to ensure the future of the plan.

Special benefits for sickness or maternity/parental reasons are paid at the same rate as regular benefits, but the qualifying period is 20 weeks, regardless of location. Sickness benefits are payable for a maximum of 15 weeks, as are maternity benefits. Parental benefits of up to 10 weeks are available for biological or adoptive parents.

■ Absence from Work Entitlements

On what the sales clerk referred to as "one of our T-shirts with an 'attitude'" was printed the following: "Never confuse having a career with having a life." Many people do find a great deal of satisfaction in their work, but few would agree that that's all there is to life. Several legal requirements reflect the legitimate need of employees to be away from work with pay, for a variety of reasons.

Vacations.   Paid vacations are a standard feature of employment standards laws. After a year of employment, entitlements of two weeks are common. The need to be away from work for an extended period for rest or recreation, and to be able to afford being away, is the ideal embedded in this obligation. In effect, mandatory paid vacations represent roughly a four percent premium on an employee's regular rate of pay.

Statutory Holidays.   For full-time employees who work prior to and after a statutory holiday, a paid day off is generally required. Employees who work on statutory holidays are typically entitled to a premium (overtime) rate of pay.

Other Reasons for Absence.   There are other situations in which employees are legally entitled to be away from work, although the employer's obligation is limited to treating them as continuing employees (that is, to take them back at the end of specified periods of absence). By far the most universal and widely used reason for absence is *pregnancy/maternity leave,* typically a 17-week entitlement. Parental and adoption entitlements from 8 to 18 weeks have been implemented, in most cases as an extension of the same logic used for pregnancy and maternity. The employer is not obliged to pay people during such absences, but Employment Insurance does provide partial income replacement (after a waiting period) for maternity and adoption situations.

■ Voluntary Benefits

■ Health Insurance

Canada Health Act

Federal legislation that requires provincial health plans to meet certain medical and administrative requirements, thereby providing a minimum uniform level of physician and hospital services to Canadians.

Canada Health Act (1984).   Canada does not have a national health insurance plan as such. However, the *Canada Health Act* (1984) does require that a series of interlocking provincial programs meet certain coverage and administrative standards to qualify for (substantial) federal government financial contributions, effectively providing an assured minimum level of service across the country. Employer-provided health insurance is offered in the context of these public programs. Figure 12–4 briefly sketches what is and is not covered by most government health plans in Canada.

Employer-Funded Extended Health Care Plans.   Clearly, those medical costs not covered by government programs can represent substantial expenses, and it is in these areas that employers often provide additional coverage. The typical approach is to cover many of these expenses through a single *major medical* or *extended health care program.* Major elements of these programs are usually (1) uninsured hospital expenses, (2) medical expenses (services) excluded from provincial plans, (3) prescription medications (reimbursement or "pay-direct"), and (4) vision and hearing care plans. Various cost-containment tactics have been developed to inhibit unnecessary use of such benefits, including:

Provided by Government Programs	Not Provided by Most Government Programs
Medically required services provided by physicians and other qualified health professionals	Extra cost of semi-private or private (preferred) accommodation in hospital
Standard ward accommodation and meals in hospital	Third-party medical examinations for employment, insurance, camp medicals, telephone advice
Laboratory and diagnostic procedures	Private-duty nursing
Drugs and medications administered in hospital	Out-of-country expenses in excess of provincial levels
Hospital facilities (i.e., operating rooms)	Vision and dental care
	Cosmetic surgery
	Prescription drugs and medications

Figure 12–4 Medical Services In Canada

Source: Adapted from McPherson, D. L., & Wallace, J. T. (1994, October). Employee benefit plans. *Human Resources Management in Canada,* 45,023–45,024. Copyright Carswell Thomson Professional Publishing.

♦ *Coordinating benefits,* that is, ensuring that benefits payable under one spouse's benefits plan are not also claimed under the other spouse's plan

♦ *Excluding some services* (e.g., cosmetic surgery) or products (e.g., non-prescription medications)

♦ *Implementing deductibles,* that is, a threshold expense level that must be passed before costs are insured

♦ *Implementing co-insurance,* under which employees must pay a certain percentage of all claimed expenses

♦ *Establishing caps,* or a maximum level of payment, either annually (e.g., $250 per person for vision care) or over an employee's lifetime ($2,500 per person for orthodontic services).

Income Tax Implications.   In provinces where the public health care system is supported in part by premiums paid by employers and/or employees, such premiums are included in the employee's taxable income. With respect to extended (i.e., voluntary) health care plans, employee contributions are not deductible from income, although they do qualify as "medical expenses" for tax purposes. Employer contributions are deductible as a business expense, but such payments are not imputed as taxable income for employees; any benefits received by employees under the plans are not taxable.

International Comparisons.   Although recent budget cuts in various jurisdictions have increased concerns over the future of health care, most Canadians have been generally enthusiastic about their health care system. Many are aware that we spend less of our GDP per capita on health care than does the United States. However, ours is not an inexpensive system by international standards, as you can tell from Figure 12–5. Many European countries spend 10 to 20 percent less than Canada.

Dental Insurance and Vision Care.   *Dental care* is unavailable through publicly funded programs for the vast majority of Canadians. As a result, dental care is a very popular employee benefit, especially for employees with dependent children. Dental associations and insurers have classified services into three areas: basic preventative diagnostics and restorative services, major restorations (crowns and bridges), and orthodontic services. Because the costs of the latter two categories can be substantial, they are frequently subject to maximum payments and copayments. *Vision care* benefits typically reimburse employees for the costs of glasses and contact lenses. In most jurisdictions, the professional fees for examination and approved medical treatment of vision problems are covered by government-funded programs. The tax treatment of dental plans and vision care is similar to the treatment of other elective health care plans.

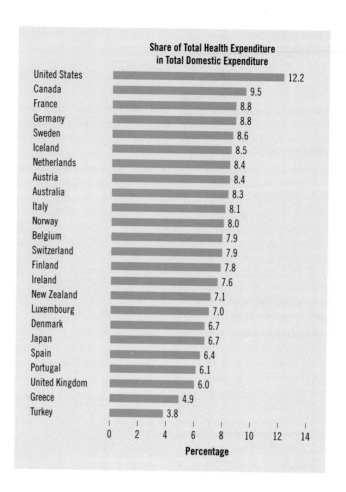

Figure 12–5 Health Spending in Various Countries
SOURCE: OECD. (1993). *OECD health systems: facts & trends, 1960–1991.* Vol. 1. Paris: OECD.

■ Retirement Benefits

After retiring, people have three main sources of income: government programs such as the Canada/Quebec Pension Plan and OAS/GIS payments, personal savings and assets, and retirement benefits from their employer(s). The consensus of experts is that government programs alone are not adequate for most people, and are most unlikely to provide increased payments in the future. Personal assets and employer-based retirement programs will be increasingly important, especially as increasing life expectancies extend the period for which retirees need income. Already the sums of money in private plans are very large. Defined benefit plans (discussed in more detail below) still account for the largest amount by far—some $384 billion—but other forms of retirement savings are also formidable: group RRSPs account for some $11.4 billion in assets; defined contribution pension assets, $10.4 billion; and deferred profit sharing, $1.4 billion.[32]

An important service that the HR department can provide to employees is *pre-retirement counselling*. Although often directed to employees within 10 or 15 years of retirement, such counselling is increasingly appropriate for younger employees. Pre-retirement counselling sessions give financial information to employees about their retirement benefits so that they can plan their retirement years accordingly. The earlier employees learn of their prospects, the more opportunity they have to take action to make sure their retirement needs are met.[33] A benefits specialist can answer such questions as:

◆ What will my total retirement income be when CPP is added to it?

◆ Will my retirement income be taxed, and by how much?

◆ Would I be better off taking a retirement allowance in lump-sum form or as an annuity?

◆ What would the tax effects be if I had other income from investment or self-employment?

◆ How much longer do I need to work for the company in order to be eligible for retirement benefits, and how much of a penalty do I pay in terms of reduced pension if I retire early?

Company pension plans that are properly registered with Revenue Canada allow employee contributions to be deducted when employees calculate their taxable income each April. Registered pension plans don't permanently exempt that money from income taxes, but it is taxed only when pension benefits are paid. The combination of deferring taxes on contributions (plus the investment income they generate) and then paying tax on income levels that are typically lower than during prime earning years creates a real advantage for most people.

Revenue Canada
www.rc.gc.ca

Regulation of Company Pensions in Canada.

In addition to specific pension-related legislation, the laws that shape pension regulation in Canada include the *Income Tax Act,* employment standards legislation, labour law, and family law. Of the roughly 16,000 registered pension plans in Canada in one recent year, 94 percent were regulated by provincial legislation. The detailed technical aspects of pensions are beyond the scope of our discussion, but the following elements of pensions are regulated in virtually all jurisdictions:

◆ Plan membership and eligibility

◆ Employer contributions

◆ Vesting of funds to members (the conditions under which the employee is entitled to contributions made on his or her behalf)

◆ Locking in of retirement savings into the plan until the employee reaches an age that entitles him or her to a pension

◆ Portability of funds into and out of plans when employees change employers

◆ Mandatory survivor benefits for spouses

◆ Disclosure of information

◆ Duties of administrators and others.[34]

Revenue Canada determines whether contributions to a plan are given preferential treatment. Tax reform in 1990 integrated the rules for pension plan contributions with other retirement vehicles, such as Registered Retirement Savings Plans (RRSPs) and deferred profit-sharing plans (DPSPs) to attempt to put the different vehicles on the same plane when it comes to allowable limits for tax-sheltered contributions.[35]

Defined Benefit Plans.

A **defined benefit plan** is one that promises to pay the plan member a fixed dollar amount of retirement income based on a formula that takes into account the average of the employee's best (usually last) three to five years of earnings prior to retirement. The pension amount is also affected by years of service. The formula might be two percent of a person's average income over those "best" years for each year of service, to a maximum of 30 years. The resulting pension from such a formula would be 60 percent of the best earnings. These plans are most frequently found at medium-sized and large employers.

defined benefit plan
A pension plan in which retirement benefits are defined by a formula based on length of service and income levels, usually during the latter years of employment.

Defined Contribution (or "Money Purchase") Plans.

A **defined contribution plan** is a pension plan in which the commitment from the employer is to make certain contributions. For example, an employer may make contributions equal to (say) five percent of an employee's gross pay each pay period. Often—in contributory plans—employees put some of their own money into the plan. At the time of retirement, the funds contributed on an employee's behalf along with the investment earnings on those funds are used to purchase an annuity or other approved financial vehicle, which then pays a regular income to the retired employee.

defined contribution plan
A pension plan in which the contributions by employer and employee are specified, but the pension benefits received depend on the total accumulated on an individual's behalf, with no guarantees of specific amounts.

Other related money purchase plans include group RRSPs and deferred profit-sharing plans. Together, they accounted for some $30 billion in assets in 1995. Group RRSPs have recently become more flexible, allowing members to elect early pensions—"life income funds"—facilitating early retirement as soon as age 55.

Because securities markets can be volatile and investment managers have varying levels of success, there is greater uncertainty about the pension amount that an employee will receive with a defined contribution plan, compared with a defined benefits plan. Of 159 employers surveyed in 1990, 80 percent reported shifting investment decisions to employees or sharing those decisions with them, in recognition of the risks involved.

The Shift to Defined Contribution Plans.   Employers can no longer rely on traditional defined benefits plans to the extent that they have previously. The rapid increase in part-time and contract workers, and the increasing tendency to multiple-employer careers make money purchase plans appropriate in a growing number of situations. Larger organizations will be attracted by the increased flexibility and lower cost of money purchase plans. Smaller organizations can provide coverage at levels that would be unlikely if defined benefits plans were the only option. Even the smallest employers can benefit from offering tax credits at source through a group RRSP—and employer contributions to the group plan or to deferred profit-sharing plans can be used as performance incentives.

RRSPs and Other Retirement Income Vehicles.   The *Registered Retirement Savings Plan (RRSP)* is a retirement savings vehicle that allows individuals to save and invest money, with tax advantages to provide the incentive to do so. Money invested in RRSPs is deducted from income in the year contributions are made, and the investment earnings on that money are also not taxable while the money is in the plan. This allows individuals some of the same benefits available to participants in pension plans, and the large number of Canadians who work for small employers or who change employers frequently during their career have the opportunity to amass retirement income that would otherwise be missing.

■ Insurance Plans

A variety of insurance plans can provide financial security for employees and their families. Two of the most valued company-provided insurance benefits are life insurance and long-term disability insurance.

Life Insurance.   Basic *term life insurance* pays a benefit to the designated survivors of a deceased employee. The typical benefit is from one to three times the employee's annual income. In most cases, company-provided term life insurance policies cover workers only while they are employees. Companies with flexible benefits may allow employees to purchase additional coverage. An employee who is the only source of income for the household could require up to five years' coverage to provide an adequate amount of insurance.

Long-Term Disability Insurance.   Employees who experience a serious injury (for example, an automobile accident) may be disabled and unable to work for an extended period, sometimes permanently. These employees and their families need replacement income during such a period. Workers' compensation does not provide any benefits for disabilities caused away from work, and the Canada Pension Plan provides only very modest levels of payment.

Long-term disability (LTD) insurance provides replacement income to disabled employees who cannot fulfill their essential job duties. An employee is eligible to receive disability benefits, typically after six months or more. Benefits usually range from half to two-thirds of an employee's salary.[36] Employees away from work for less than the length of time before LTD begins are usually covered under sick leave policies (discussed later in this chapter). In some cases, short-term disability insurance is provided on either an elective or a universal basis. The combination of CPP disability payments and LTD (where provided) can result in relatively complete restoration of lost income.

■ Paid Time Off

Sick Leave and "Personal" Days.

Sick leave provides full pay for short-term absences due to illness, or other short-term disability to do the job. Absence from work occurs for several reasons. Most frequently, the reason employees give is illness. Most employers allow employees a certain number of days of absence without loss of income, in recognition of the fact that illness is not completely avoidable and that it may be counter-productive to have migraine-suffering or flu-ridden, feverish employees trying to work rather than taking a day or two in bed to recover. Sick leave can be abused. The excuse of "illness" sometimes is a misrepresentation that is used to avoid loss of pay or potential disciplinary steps. Statistics Canada research found that absence had increased from an average of 8.6 days in the mid-1980s to 9.3 days a decade later, about an eight percent increase. Behind this overall change is the fact that illness and disability absences had *decreased* from 6.7 days to 6.1 days, but that time lost for family reasons increased from 1.9 days to 3.3.[37] (The increased presence of dual-career households is clearly a contributing factor to this trend.) Recognizing that there are acceptable reasons for absence other than illness, ranging from medical appointments to family responsibilities, some employers provide for one to three "personal days" each year, which employees need not justify in terms of illness.

One issue that arises with the provision of sick leave is the tendency for some employees to see it as an entitlement. Companies that want to limit lost productivity and worker replacement costs associated with unscheduled absences are getting tougher about sick leave. Some require medical documentation for even brief absences. Other employers have tried aggressive but less invasive methods to "reward" employees who do not use their full allotment of sick leave days, such as allowing them to convert some fraction of unused sick leave to additional vacation time.[38]

The HR unit should monitor and control sick leave to minimize sick leave abuse. A variety of policy initiatives can be considered:

◆ Set up a *wellness plan* that monetarily rewards employees who do not use their full allotment of sick leave days.

◆ Establish flexible work hours so that employees can take care of some personal business during the week without having to be gone for an entire day, thereby decreasing their need to use sick leave for those purposes.

◆ Reward employees with a lump sum at their retirement or when they leave the organization.

◆ Allow employees to take two or three personal days during the year. This encourages employees to recognize and respect the difference between personal days and sick leave, rather than have some misuse of sick leave come to be regarded as normal and accepted.

Vacations.

Employers provide paid vacations to give their employees time to get away from the stresses and strains of the daily work routine and to reward them for service to the organization. Vacation time allows employees to recharge themselves psychologically and emotionally and can lead to improved job performance.[39] Many employers increase employees' paid vacation entitlement beyond the legal minimum, usually on the basis of length of service. Vacation entitlements of four, six, and even eight weeks, along with growing company-sponsored pensions, can create a strong incentive for medium- and long-service employees to stay with an employer.

Figure 12–6 is an international comparison of the annual number of paid vacation days that employees receive after one year's service. Canadian employees (like those in Japan and the United States) average about 10 days—effectively, two weeks—of paid vacation. Most European countries offer considerably more, with France at five weeks and Austria and Sweden at six weeks.

A benefit that a small but increasing number of Canadian employers offer to employees—and one limited historically to university academics—is *sabbatical leave*, an extended period of paid time off. (Sabbaticals can be thought of as "vacations with a purpose.") Some school boards have negotiated with teachers to opt for a "four-over-five" arrangement, which allows teachers to spread pay for four years over five, with the fifth year being free of work responsibilities.

Maternity Benefits. Statistics Canada indicates that the percentage of women on maternity leave who received EI benefits plus another form of compensation during their absence from work increased from eight percent in 1981 to 17 percent in 1991. The extent and duration of these benefits vary. Calgary-based Gulf Canada, for example, provides a top-up to 100 percent of regular earnings during the first six weeks of the 27 weeks they award for maternity leave. Big V Pharmacies of London, Ontario, covers (at 100 percent of earnings) the two-week waiting period before EI benefits commence. AT&T Global Information Systems of Mississauga, Ontario, tops up salaries for six weeks (to a maximum top-up of 35 percent of earnings), a move they made in order to become consistent with AT&T (who had acquired them); that made it easier for career mobility within the parent company.[40]

Other Paid Time Off. There are other occasions when some employers elect to provide paid time off that may be important to individual employees, although these constitute a relatively small portion of overall employment costs. Jury duty is a citizen's obligation, when called, and many employers will continue paying employees while they are away from work although there is no legal requirement that they do so. In many environments, non-productive activities such as breaks and clean-up occur during paid time, either voluntarily or through collective agreements. And there are some union contracts that require payment for scheduled work, even on occasions when there is no work to be done.

Figure 12–6 Annual Number of Vacation Days in Various Countries for Employees with One Year of Service

SOURCE: Reprinted, by permission of publisher, from Matthes, K. (1992, May). In pursuit of leisure: employees want more time off. *HR Focus*, 7. © 1992. American Management Association, New York. All rights reserved.

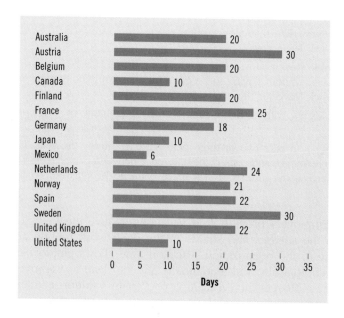

Employees receiving paid time off usually use it for their own benefit. However, some employees appreciate the opportunity to make a contribution to their community, and employers often wish to make similar contributions. When the two correspond, there are possibilities for innovative programs, such as McKinsey and Company's pro-bono work for the National Ballet of Canada, the Canadian Opera Company, and the Shaw Festival; Procter & Gamble's donation of a full-time employee as administrative assistant to the Alliance for a Drug-Free Canada; and Bell Ontario's topping up of employees' salaries while they're on leave at non-profit or charitable organizations.[41]

Whether paid or made up on an informal basis, flexible scheduling on such occasions as March break can pay off for employers. Carol Dale, who works for Freeway Ford Sales in Toronto, says that the assurance that something will be worked out makes a big difference. "I know I'm lucky—extremely. By the same token, I think they've gotten more than they bargained for. I give 150 percent. I get the same respect that I give."[42] Reservists in the Canadian Forces are receiving more generous treatment from a number of employers since the formation of the Canadian Forces Liaison Council in 1992. The number of companies having a reserve leave policy has increased from as few as 20 to over 1,200.[43]

Severance Pay.   While not typically thought of as a benefit, the severance pay some companies give to employers who have been laid off is also a form of paid time off. An individual whose employment is terminated, but not for cause, is entitled by statute to certain notice or pay in lieu of notice, as discussed in Chapter 3. The common-law precedents for wrongful dismissal provide additional legal guidance for minimum severance or notice amounts. The various inducements offered as part of reorganization and downsizing processes constitute an important (and expensive) employee benefit, even though they are not awarded to continuing employees. The average amount of severance paid has decreased from six months in 1992 to three months in 1994.[44]

Combining Roles.

Employment standards legislation in every Canadian jurisdiction permits female employees unpaid leave for at least 17 weeks in the final stages of pregnancy and after the birth of a child, and Employment Insurance provides partial income replacement for as much as 15 weeks.

McKinsey and Company
www.mckinsey.com.au/html/globe/index.htm

Canadian Forces Liaison Council
www.vcds.dnd.ca/vcds/cres_cdt/cflc/intro_e.asp

■ Benefits and the Smaller Employer

Employers provide additional benefits to employees to compete in the labour market, and because it can be a more cost-effective way of providing certain forms of compensation. Generally, the size of an employer is an indicator of the likelihood of voluntary benefits packages. However, of the over 900,000 businesses that existed in Canada in 1993, 97 percent had fewer than 50 employees. There are no overall statistics on how many of these offer benefits packages, but many do, and others appear to be considering the option. Some offer them through larger associations; for example, Fredericton's Blaine Thomas Travel Service works though the local Chamber of Commerce. Another example is AirTindi Ltd. of Yellowknife, Northwest Territories. Air Tindi, a regional air carrier, has from 50 to 70 employees depending on the season and has offered a benefits package since 1988, extending coverage to seasonal as well as year-round employees. Terry Arychuk, operations manager, comments, "Offering benefits makes working here appealing to employees. Because of our location, we need something to entice pilots to stay."[45]

■ Employee Services

The other form of indirect compensation, aside from benefits, is *employee services.* Employee services compensate employees by providing direct services or by subsidizing the costs of goods or services that employees receive. Employees are paid in kind rather than in cash. Generally, these services are not treated as taxable income. This allows employers to provide these services more cheaply than if employees were paid additional compensation that would necessitate their using after-tax dollars for the same results. Figure 12–7 lists some well-known employee services and subsidies. These include child care, health club memberships, subsidized company cafeterias, and discounts on company products.

Companies are taking a fresh look at employee services and their value to those who select them. One criticism of many forms of employee services (for examples, sponsoring employee athletic teams) and subsidies has been that often they are used by a very small portion of the work force, and therefore have little general value in HR management. What this view overlooks is the symbolic value of these programs. People who never use them still see them as a reflection of a company that cares, and some services, such as financial counselling, may be like insurance—employees may not wish to make a "claim," but they are glad it is there in case they need it. For years, employers offered these programs somewhat tentatively. Now, many are looking to such programs as cost-effective ways of enhancing compensation packages to attract and retain good employees.

Other companies offer more unconventional services to their workers. As the demographics of Canada change, increasing attention is being paid to the "sandwich generation," those who have personal responsibilities for both children and aging parents. According to the Vanier Institute, "If you are a woman, you can expect to spend 18 years of your life helping an aging parent and 17 years caring for children."[46] The growing numbers of dual-career households means that this statement increasingly applies to men as well as women.

The sandwich generation is a phase of life that many people pass through, not a distinct group like the baby boomers. An increasing number of employees will be in this situation as baby boomers move into their fifties. Delayed marriages and a tough labour market for young people will lead to more children remaining in the parental home, and increasing life expectancy will mean larger numbers of older Canadians. For example, the Bank of Montreal provides a range of resources and tools to help employees balance their work and personal lives, including counselling, information on child care and elder care, and noon-hour "lunch and learn" sessions on a range of related topics.[47]

Companies that decide to offer child care services have several options. The most expensive is an on-site child care centre, if the employer both provides the

Vanier Institute
www.familyforum.com/vanier/
index.htm

Figure 12–7 **Selected Benefits and Services That May Provide Tax Advantages**

SOURCE: Henderson, R. (1989). *Compensation management,* 443. Englewood Cliffs, NJ: Prentice Hall.

1. Charitable contributions
2. Counselling
    Financial
    Legal
    Psychiatric/psychological
3. Tax preparation
4. Education subsidies
5. Child adoption
6. Child care
7. Elder care
8. Subsidized food service
9. Discounts on merchandise
10. Physical awareness and fitness programs

11. Social and recreational opportunities
12. Parking
13. Transportation to and from work
14. Travel expenses
    Car reimbursement
    Tolls and parking
    Food and entertainment reimbursement
15. Clothing reimbursement/allowance
16. Tool reimbursement/allowance
17. Relocation expenses
18. Emergency loans
19. Credit union
20. Housing

space and pays a substantial portion of the operating costs. *Child care consortiums* are an alternative that overcomes some of the difficulties of on-site care—limited space, zoning, being distant from a child's school or home or other parent's place of work. Consortiums involve the partnering of two or more organizations, with a formal agreement, to support a common facility. The extent and nature of the support can vary, with employees paying reduced fees based on their employer's contributions. One such arrangement was struck in 1986 between Global Communications, Sony Canada, and the North York Board of Education, which had space available in one of its schools. Harlequin Enterprises joined the consortium a year later.[48] A recent Revenue Canada ruling has made employer-subsidized day care more attractive—the subsidies are tax deductible for the employer but are not treated as a taxable benefit for the employee.[49] Other child care options include establishing a child care referral service for working parents, as well as providing flexible scheduling to accommodate family routines. Because child care is expensive, employers (who sometimes pay as much as 50 to 75 percent of the cost) are undertaking a major financial commitment.[50]

On-Site Child Care.

An increasingly popular employee service offered by some organizations is on-site child care, or (when more than one employer participates) creation of an off-site child care consortium. In Canada, employer subsidies for child care are tax deductible for the company and are not considered a taxable benefit for the employees.

Sony Canada
www.sony.com

Building Managerial Skills: Administering Benefits

We conclude this chapter by examining two critical issues in the administration of employee benefits: the use of flexible benefits and the importance of communicating benefits to employees. Included is a discussion of a third important issue in contemporary benefits administration: the provision of same-sex benefits. The HR department usually takes the lead in administering employee benefits, but managers need to help communicate options to employees, provide advice occasionally, keep records of absences and vacations, and know when to involve the HR department in a benefits-related decision.

Flexible Benefits

As we have seen, employees have different benefits needs, depending on a number of factors: age, marital status, whether their spouse works and has benefits coverage, and the presence and ages of children in the employee's household. A flexible benefits program allows employees to choose from a selection of such employer-provided benefits as vision care, dental care, extended health care, additional life insurance coverage, long-term disability insurance, child care, elder care, more paid days of vacation, legal services, and additional contributions to various vehicles for retirement income. The idea of flexible benefits has been around for at least three decades (it was initially referred to as "cafeteria-plan" benefits). The popularity of flexible benefits has increase recently because of two forces—the increasing diversity of the work force, and the advent of inexpensive computing that makes the complex record keeping feasible at an acceptable cost. The roll-call of flexible benefits employers in Canada includes a diverse group: American Express Canada, Nortel, McDonald's Restaurants of Canada, and Du Pont Canada, among others. The fullest form of flexible benefits, where employees get dollars or credits to spend as they please, is found in roughly 100 companies, representing some 15 to 20 percent of the largest Canadian employers, according to benefits expert Bob McKay of Hewitt Associates.[51]

American Express
www.americanexpress.com

Types of Flexible Benefits Plans. The three most popular flexible benefits plans are *modular plans, core-plus-options plans,* and *flexible spending accounts.*[52]

Modular plans consist of a series of different bundles of benefits or different levels of benefits coverage for different subgroups of the employee population. For example, module A might be the basic package paid for entirely by the employer. It would contain only the most essential benefits and would be designed for single employees. Module B might include all of A plus such additional benefits as family coverage under the extended health insurance plan, dental care, and child care. This module might be designed for married employees with young children and could require contributions from both employer and employee.

Core-plus-options plans consist of a core of essential benefits and a wide array of other benefits options that employees can add to the core. The core is designed to provide a base level of economic security for employees, and usually includes a basic extended health insurance plan, life insurance, long-term disability insurance, pension plan contributions, and a vacation allotment above statutory minimums. Core-plus-options plans give employees "benefits credits" that entitle them to "purchase" additional benefits that they value. In most cases, employees all receive the same number of credits and may use them to purchase higher levels of coverage in the core package or to purchase non-core benefits such as child care subsidies or dental care.

Flexible spending accounts are individual employee accounts funded by the employer, the employee, or both. Employees "pay" for the combination of benefits from their accounts. There is some provision in this approach to convert from direct compensation to indirect, and the reverse. A narrower use of this notion is the health care expense account from which employees can allocate employer dollars to vision care, reducing insurance deductibles, or upgrading dental coverage or the like. For money not used for health care, roughly three in five employers surveyed by Hewitt Associates allowed employees to take the money as cash, and the same proportion allowed them to place the funds in a group RRSP.[53]

Challenges with Flexible Benefits. Flexible benefits offer employees the opportunity to tailor a benefits package that is meaningful to them at a reasonable cost to the employer. However, they do pose some challenges to benefits administrators:

1. *Adverse selection.* This problem occurs when enough employees use a specific benefit more than the average employee does. Intensive use of a benefit can drive up its cost and force the employer either to increase spending on benefits or reduce the amount of coverage it provides. For example, employees who know they will need expensive dental work may select a dental care option instead of some other benefit. Or, employees who know they have a high probability of an early death (due to a health condition such as high blood pressure or diabetes or even a terminal condition such as cancer) may choose extra life insurance coverage. In both cases, the cost of the insurance coverage will eventually be driven up because more benefits will be paid to these individuals.

   Benefits administrators can deal with the adverse selection problem by placing restrictions on benefits that are likely to result in adverse selection problems. For instance, the company might require a successfully passed physical exam from those applying for higher life insurance coverage. They can also bundle a broad package of benefits together into modules to ensure greater employee participation and a more balanced utilization of each benefit.[54]

2. *Employees who make poor choices.* Sometimes employees make a poor choice of benefits and later regret it. For example, an employee who selects additional vacation days instead of long-term disability insurance is likely to regret this choice if he or she experiences a long-term illness that exceeds the accumulated amount of sick leave available. Benefits administrators can manage this problem by (1) establishing core benefits that minimize an employee's risks and (2) communicating benefits choices effectively so that employees make appropriate choices.

3. *Administrative complexity.* A flexible benefits program is difficult to administer and control. Employees must be kept informed of changes in the cost of benefits, the coverage of benefits, and their utilization of benefits. They must also be given the opportunity to change their benefits selection periodically. In addition, the potential for errors in record keeping is high. Fortunately, computer software packages can help the HR department manage the record-keeping aspect of flexible benefits programs. Benefits consultants can assist HR staff in selecting and installing these software programs.

For details on some other ways to control the costs of benefits, see the Manager's Notebook entitled "Eight Ways to Save a Bundle on Benefits."

■ Benefits Communication

Benefits communication is a critical part of administering an employee benefits program. Many employees in organizations with excellent benefits packages are poorly informed about the value of these benefits and are likely to underestimate their value.[55] The two major obstacles to effective benefits communication are (1) the increasing complexity of benefits packages and (2) employers' reluctance to devote enough resources to explain benefits to employees.

Traditionally, benefits have been communicated via a benefits handbook that describes each benefit and its level of coverage, or via a group meeting held during new-employee orientation. In today's dynamic world of employee benefits, however, more sophisticated communications media, such as videotaped presentations and computer software that generates individualized benefits statements, are needed and affordable. Here are a few approaches being taken by employers to inform employees about their employee benefits:[56]

> **Manager's Notebook**
>
> ## Eight Ways to Save a Bundle on Benefits
>
> Thousands of dollars can be saved by administering the basics of benefits well. Here are eight practical ways to save big benefit dollars:
>
> **1.** Grant vacation and personal time on a pro rata basis (for example, one day of vacation per four weeks worked) instead of giving employees lump-sum amounts at the beginning of a year to be used by the end of that year. This can prevent employees from using a full year's vacation quota in their first three months of employment and then resigning.
>
> **2.** Enforce use of vacation time with a "use it or lose it" policy. Don't allow the time to accrue indefinitely.
>
> **3.** Companies that give new hires a probationary period might consider not granting health care benefits until the probationary period is over.
>
> **4.** Use a no-fault absence approach to counter sick time abusers. Under a no-fault system, the reason for an unscheduled absence is irrelevant. After a specified number of unscheduled absences, formal discipline occurs, leading up to termination.
>
> **5.** Reward employees for wellness. Rewards might include granting bonuses when an employee reaches the ideal cholesterol count or paying for health club memberships.
>
> **6.** Pay employees a bonus if they find errors in benefits bills.
>
> **7.** Demand employee utilization data from health and dental carriers. Information is power, and utilization data help identify underutilized services that, if managed properly, will lower the company's costs.
>
> **8.** Consider offering long-term disability coverage no higher than 60% of salary. Lowering the benefit payment from 66.67% to 60%, for instance, can significantly reduce the premium.
>
> SOURCE: Adapted from Markowich, M. M. (1992, October). 25 ways to save a bundle. *HRMagazine*, 48–57. Reprinted with the permission of *HRMagazine* (formerly *Personnel Administrator*), published by the Society for Human Resource Management, Alexandria, VA.

◆ A major financial services organization implemented flexible benefits with the objective of containing costs. By clearly communicating the 75%–25% split to which they were committed, the employer created a "no surprises" environment in which benefits were valued more highly, and not seen as an entitlement.

◆ A high-tech company, determined to gain flexibility of choice and contain costs, engaged in an intensive communication program to change employee behaviour with respect to frequency of claims and purchasing of medications. Combined with a copayment scheme, this got the message across.

◆ An insurance company opted for a core-plus-options flex plan and cost sharing with employees to convey the message of value to their employees.

Figure 12–8 lists some of the ways a company can keep its employees informed about their benefits or answer questions about coverage under a specific benefits program.

Colourful Flyers or Newsletters
Can be mailed to employees' homes so they can read them at leisure.

Payroll Stickers or Posters
Pique employees' curiosity, and are especially good for calling attention to an enrollment period.

Wallet Cards
Provide important numbers, such as a toll-free employee assistance program number.

Audio-Visual Presentations
Slides and videos that present concepts in an upbeat fashion can ensure that employees at different locations receive the same information.

Toll-Free Number
Lets employees call to enroll in a benefits program or hear automated information about these programs 24 hours a day.

Computer Software Package
Allows employees to play "what if" scenarios with their benefits. For example, they can determine the amount that will be deducted from their paycheques if they enroll in medical plan A as opposed to plan B, or how much money they would save by age 60 if they contribute 6% a year to their RRSP.

SOURCE: Adapted from Families and Work Institute, 1992. Reprinted by permission.

Figure 12–8 Selected Methods of Employee Benefits Communication

■ Same-Sex Benefits

As discussed in Chapter 3, human rights protection with respect to sexual orientation has become a high-profile benefits issue. The issue is whether homosexual employees in long-standing relationships should be treated as spouses with respect to insurance and pension benefits.

The Case for Same-Sex Benefits.   The essential points of the argument for *same-sex benefits* are the following: (1) Many benefits programs provide payments or insurance coverage for dependants of the employee, typically the employee's spouse and dependent children. (2) Legally, an established common-law ("marital") relationship between partners of the opposite sex provides the same claim of spousal relationship for benefits eligibility as does a formal marriage. (3) Under human rights legislation, sexual orientation is a prohibited basis for discrimination in most Canadian jurisdictions, the exceptions being Alberta, Newfoundland, Prince Edward Island, and the Northwest Territories. (And, in the case of Alberta, a 1998 Supreme Court decision effectively amended Alberta's code to include protection on the basis of sexual orientation.) The argument that has been made successfully in some legal venues is that a long-standing homosexual relationship is indistinguishable from a heterosexual common-law relationship, and that the homosexual partner (and his or her children, if part of the household) are therefore entitled to be treated as spouse and dependants of the employee.

Complications from the *Income Tax Act.*   This interpretation legitimizes an extended definition of "immediate family." However, until recently, the actions needed for HR compliance were obstructed by the *Income Tax Act.* The Act determines whether the expenses of providing a pension benefit is a tax-deductible expense for the employer. In the *Act* the definition of spouse was someone of the opposite sex. Plans that provided benefits to same-sex spouses could not be registered and contributions were not given favourable tax treatment.[57] Employers caught between the human rights obligations and the tax laws were advised to set up parallel or optional coverage provisions to accommodate both legal obligations. However, with the addition of sexual orientation to *the Canadian Human Rights Act* in 1996, the basis for a legal resolution was laid.

In May 1998, a decision of the Ontario Court of Appeal in favour of two female employees with female partners (*Rosenberg v. Canada*) found that the provisions of the Income Tax Act that limited the definition of "spouse" to being a person of the opposite sex were discriminatory. The decision of the federal government not to appeal to the Supreme Court of Canada effectively requires that the definition of "spouse," at least insofar as it is used with respect to registered pensions, include same sex spouses. While Revenue Canada has initially indicated that it will not extend this definition to RRSP and RRIF contributions, the apparent consensus among high courts and governments suggests that same-sex spousal treatment may well become uniform across the full range of benefits where spousal relations are a defining element.[58]

Summary and Conclusions

An Overview of Benefits.   Benefits and services constitute indirect compensation of employees. Benefits have grown dramatically during the past few decades and now constitute roughly 30 percent of all compensation costs. People depend on employment income, and most benefits program spending either protects people from the interruption of employment earnings or from extraordinary expenses. Indirect compensation exists for three main reasons: to comply with legal requirements, to compete in the labour market, and to capture cost advantages based on group coverage or taxation policies.

Benefits Strategies.   The design of benefits packages should be aligned with the business's overall compensation strategy. The benefits strategy requires making choices in three areas: (1) benefits mix, (2) benefits amount, and (3) flexibility of benefits.

Legally Required Benefits.   Federal and provincial laws require that employers provide for and financially contribute to the Canada (or Quebec) Pension Plan, Employment Insurance (formerly Unemployment Insurance), and workers' compensation. As well, employers must provide certain amounts of paid time off work, including statutory holidays and minimum vacation periods. These benefits form the core of the individual employee's benefits package. Employers should take legally required benefits into account in the design and administration of voluntary benefits.

Voluntary Benefits.   Canadian employers elect to provide a wide and varied array of benefits to their employees. Health care, disability insurance, and retirement income plans are the three most expensive items. Basic health care (physician services and hospital expenses) is provided by taxes and, in some cases, employer assessments. Extended health care, dental care, and vision care are popular benefits. Retirement benefits provided through pension plans take two primary forms: defined benefits plans and defined contribution plans (sometimes known as money purchase plans). Although the assets tied up in defined benefit plans are far greater than those in defined contribution plans, there seems to be a shift toward defined contribution plans, to meet the changing employment market and to give employees greater autonomy. Insurance plans (life and disability) address the concerns of employees in providing protection for their dependants. Both publicly funded programs that provide disability (CPP, WC) and employer-sponsored disability insurance programs have seen a rapid increase in utilization since the beginning of the 1990s. Paid time off over and above the legal minimums and various employee services represent important—although less expensive—ways employers can articulate their understanding of the employment relationship.

Administering Benefits.   Two important issues involving benefits administration are the use of flexible benefits and communicating benefits to employees so that they understand the significance of their benefits and how to use them. Although the administration of employee benefits is likely to be performed by a HR specialist, managers need to understand their organizations' benefits package well enough to help communicate benefits information, and to keep appropriate records.

Key Terms and Concepts

Discussion Questions

1. How might increasing the diversity of the work force affect the design of employee benefits packages in large companies?

2. Canadian law mandates CPP, EI (formerly UI), and Workers' Compensation. Employment standards require certain levels of paid vacation. Yet, some employers provide many other benefits—extended health coverage, life and disability insurance, pensions, and so forth. Why do so many employers provide benefits that they are not compelled to provide?

3. As the cost of health care increases, the publicly funded health system continues to look for ways to save money. What pressures do you see building on employer-sponsored health insurance? What measures should employers be taking to deal with these pressures?

4. What is the difference between defined benefit pensions and defined contribution pensions? Why are the latter gaining in popularity?

5. How can flexible benefits help control benefits costs? What other measures are available for an employer attempting to control such costs, and are there any drawbacks with their use?

6. In what ways are employee benefits good for the economy? In what ways can they be detrimental to the economy?

Check out our Companion Website at: **www.prenticehall.ca/gomez** for a selection of self-study questions, key terms and concepts, updated Weblinks to related Internet sites, newsgroups, CBC video updates, and more.

MiniCase 1   *A Pension for Choice*

"I don't remember—when I was 25—ever thinking I was going to live to retire," says Jackie Kot, pension manager for AT&T (Canada) Inc. "There's so much interest in retirement at a younger age now."

The company's retirement education was previously event driven, "but it's going to be ongoing, especially now since we have a defined contribution plan—now everyone is responsible for their own pension."

Her company and two other AT&T units—AT&T Global Information Solutions and AT&T Global Information systems IS—are moving toward integrating their HR functions. Last year they all introduced similar pension plans along with employee investment education. AT&T Global Information Solutions has launched an education program that resulted in dramatic changes in employee behaviour regarding pension investments.

"Our associates didn't fully understand the plans that were in place," says Stephen Liptrap, pension manager for AT&T GIS. "We needed more two-way communication. Everyone is different in terms of their life needs. We wanted to give them more choice and flexibility and to educate them so they could take more responsibility."

The company (1,500 employees, 80 locations) has had a defined benefit plan and an RRSP plan (deferred profit sharing) since 1984. Employees could always choose between GICs or fixed-income instruments or equities, but they were having trouble deciding where to invest. So AT&T worked with its U.S. counterpart and investment managers to develop specific investment strategies, packaged in a program called "Benefits Built for You."

The four investment strategy options (and the percentage of the employees that chose them) are:

◆ Conservative: GICs managed by an investment company: (7%)

◆ Moderately cautious: GICs, bonds, and equities: (29%)

◆ Moderate: 50% bonds and 50% equities (20% foreign): (33%)

◆ Aggressive: 75% equity (20% foreign) and 25% bonds: (31%)

There are distinct investment managers for each component, plus an overall plan administrator.

Discussion Questions

1. A great deal of emphasis is now being placed on employee responsibility in the administration of pensions and other benefits. What are the reasons behind this change?

2. Are employers that give employees a great deal of choice likely to be well liked for these changes? What will employees appreciate? What changes may make them unhappy?

3. What kinds of education and orientation are required for success in introducing the kind of change AT&T has undertaken?

SOURCE: Czarnecki, A. (1995, April 25). Pension education: Who's doing it? *Canadian HR Reporter*, 13. Reprinted with permission of MPL Communications Inc.

MiniCase 2   *Classroom Meets Boardroom*

After Trish Sailer drops her children off at school in the morning, an elevator whisks her to work—12 floors above the classroom.

Sailer's son and daughter are two of the 65 students this year in Canada's first workplace school. AGT Limited, the privately owned Alberta telephone company and the largest subsidiary of TELUS Corporation, teamed up with the Calgary Board of Education to launch the on-site school on the ground floor of the AGT office tower in downtown Calgary. The public elementary school, offering classes from kindergarten (ECS) to grade three, has a curriculum identical to that of elementary schools throughout the city.

Called the "workplace school" thus far—an official name is forthcoming—its doors are open not only to children of AGT employees but to those of other Calgary companies. The only difference: AGT employees had a month jump-start on school registration. As it turns out, about half the students' parents work at AGT, the other half in a variety of nearby businesses.

Discussion Questions

1. Although this is the first workplace school in Canada, many employers are getting involved in supporting child care and other aspects of employees' family lives. What are the benefits to the parents/employees? From an employer's viewpoint, is this a good idea, or does it divert attention, energy and resources to the few at the expense of the larger number of employees for whom the benefit doesn't have relevance?

2. Is this kind of program consistent with the theme within many benefits programs that encourage employers to take greater responsibility for themselves? What message is the employer sending with such a program?

3. What are the advantages and disadvantages of employers getting closely involved with the local school system?

SOURCE: McCallum, T. (1995, November). *Human Resources Professional*, 12–15.

Case 1

Freedom (?) 55

The barrage of layoffs and general stressfulness of work has many people fantasizing about getting a "package" and taking off. Here are some facts that need to be considered in such a decision:

◆ The average Canadian man of 55 can expect to live another 22 years, and the average woman another 27 years.

◆ There is every indication that the prevalence of buy-outs and early retirement packages will diminish over the next decade or two, and that programs such as the CPP may increase the age at which people are entitled to a full pension from 65 to 67 or even 69, to redress the payer-recipient imbalance resulting from the "baby bust" that followed the "baby boom."

◆ Actuaries are suggesting that, in addition to government pensions, private pensions, and individual savings, retirement incomes should include a fourth component: earnings from work.

What is becoming clear is that not only is the nature of work changing, from working in full-time jobs for one or a few employers from end-of-school until 65th birthday to a much more varied prospect, but that the nature of retirement also is changing. The notion of leaving the world of work for the last third of life is becoming less desirable and less feasible.

Critical Thinking Questions

1. What kind of career strategy and retirement advice would you give to a person who is now 25 years old? 40 years old? 55 years old? Explain.
2. What kinds of conflict or controversy do you expect to see as the realities of people needing to continue longer in the work force becomes clear? Who will see themselves as being treated unfairly by these developments, and why?

Cooperative Learning Exercise

3. In small groups, role-play a focus group in a company providing feedback to the HR unit on how the employer's benefits program will need to be revised as the company prepares to make retirement optional until age 68. Choose roles from varied age and skill-set groups within the organization.

Case 2

Managing Sick Leave at Northfield Homes

Northfield Homes is a regional business providing upscale residence and assisted living arrangements for seniors. At six different locations, complexes that consist of apartments with minimal kitchens and a large common dining room form one part of the facility, with a separate (but connected) building providing nursing home accommodation. Clients who live in the apartments have priority options on nursing home spaces if they need to make such a move. There is a large staff of caregivers, from health care aides to medical personnel and administrative staff. The staff of 800 represents a major part of Northfield's operating costs, and Peter Hanson, the Human Resources Director, is looking for ways to reduce benefits expenses as part of an overall cost-control initiative.

One benefit that Peter believes is used inefficiently is sick leave. Under Northfield's current sick leave policy, employees earn one day off per month. Sick leave accumulates as long as the employee works for Northfield. When employees leave, however, they forfeit their accrued sick leave. In 1994, the average number of days absent for illness was six days. Northfield needed to have sufficient staff so that such absences could be covered. The employee benefits coordinator, Mary Rasmussen, had organized informal focus groups to discuss a range of issues—one of the insights was that perhaps half the sick leave taken was by employees who were dealing with job-related stress.

Peter asked Mary to develop some recommendations for reducing sick leave costs. After much discussion with her staff,

Mary submitted the following three recommendations, all in use at one or more other employers in the area.

◆ A "use it or lose it" plan that prevents employees from accumulating sick days beyond one year. At the end of the year, employees forfeit all unused sick leave days.
◆ A requirement that employees obtain a doctor's note for each sick day taken. The note must indicate that the employee was too sick to perform the job on the day in question.
◆ A "wellness pay" incentive program that rewards employees who do not use any of their sick leave days with a bonus of $300 and recognition in the employee newsletter.

Mary thinks that all these plans would prove cost effective, but warns Peter that each has some disadvantages.

Critical Thinking Questions

1. Which of the three recommendations for managing sick leave would be most appropriate for Northfield Homes?
2. Might one or more of these approaches encourage employees to go to work when they are sick? If so, should Northfield be concerned about the effect of this on the health of their clients?

Cooperative Learning Exercise

3. With a partner or a small group, try to develop a better approach to managing sick leave at Northfield Homes. What criteria could be used to judge whether your group's sick leave policy is effective in cutting costs?

VideoCase

What We Owe Each Other

Countries are cohesive to the extent that they perceive that they share common cause. In historical terms, many countries look to military events to provide an outline of the definitive events in their formation and identity. Americans, for example, would quickly cite their revolution against England, their Civil War of the mid-19th century, and their rise to super-power status during the 20th century (as reflected in their roles during WWI and WWII) as historical events that speak to who they are. European history and national identities are dense with wars, alliances, and colonial activity, and there are parallel examples from all corners of the world.

Canada is somewhat different. While Canadians have been involved in warfare, their involvement was generally as part of the British Empire or (more recently) the Commonwealth. The current public perception of Canada's armed forces is much more centred on Canada's frequent responsibilities in peacekeeping roles.

Canada's sense of common causes has woven in a great deal of emphasis on the role of government in assuring basic living standards–Social Assistance ("welfare"), Old Age Security, the Canada (or Quebec) Pension Plan, Employment (formerly Unemployment) Insurance, Workers' Compensation, and tax-paid health care programs. This collection of programs is sometimes referred to as the "social safety net." These programs have become increasingly expensive as the range of benefits and beneficiaries have expanded and as the age profile of the population has changed. Public debt has prompted political choices to curtail spending on many of these programs. Because most people look to their work as their basic source of income, reductions in government spending on income security and health care implicitly raise the question of what such a shift means for employers.

Discussion Questions

1. Why do you think that recent responses to the increased costs of social safety net programs have emphasized spending reductions rather than increases in taxes and contribution rates to cover the increased costs?

2. What overall impact do you think the reduction in tax-based programs will have on the expectations employees have of employers?

3. Should employers attempt to design insurance and other benefit programs that "pick up the slack" from areas in which governments are spending less? Explain the advantages and disadvantages of such an undertaking.

Video Resources: "Social Reform," *Prime Time Magazine* (February 6, 1995) and "Pension Pax," *Prime Time Magazine* (March 14, 1995).

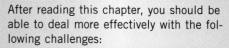
Developing Employee Relations and Communications

After reading this chapter, you should be able to deal more effectively with the following challenges:

1 Understand how employee relations can contribute to business goals.

2 Describe the three types of programs that can be used to facilitate employee communications.

3 Explain the various appeals procedures available to employees to challenge management actions.

4 Understand the significance of employee assistance programs in helping employees deal with personal problems that may interfere with job performance.

5 Be aware of some of the technological innovations in employee communications that allow managers to disseminate information more quickly and how information dissemination may influence an organization's employee relations.

Their job's a picnic. Good employee relations involve making employees feel like valued members of the organization. As part of their employee relations program, many companies hold annual picnics and holiday parties. Pictured here is the annual summer picnic of the Prentice Hall Business Publishing team—the people who worked with the authors of this text to edit, produce, and distribute the textbook you are now reading.

Nancy is a customer service manager for a copier company. She started about four years ago as a customer service representative. In her position she occasionally came into contact with a customer who would "hit" on her or make a rude comment, but she was always able to handle those situations. Usually, a diplomatic brush-off was enough. Now, however, she faced a situation that she did not know how to handle.

It all began six months ago when she was promoted to her current position. She supervises 20 customer service reps, and rarely makes a direct call on a customer. She really likes the job and the company, and hopes to be promoted further. The problem is her boss. Steve was largely responsible for her promotion and Nancy feels indebted to him. But after about two months, she realized that his attention to her was not only work related. He began to tell her about his marriage problems and commented that he found her very attractive. After all the help he had given her, Nancy hesitated to tell him directly that she wasn't interested in him romantically. But after he started sending flowers and asking her out, she finally asked him to stop.

That didn't work. In fact, things got much worse. Steve's requests became more direct, and now they had threats attached. Specifically, he told her that if she did not begin a relationship with him, he would not only not recommend her for any further promotions, he would try to get her terminated. Nancy felt trapped. She knew that Steve was well liked by his colleagues, and she was afraid that if she complained about him to his boss, she would only lose her job faster.

Then she read in the monthly newsletter about the company's employee relations program. One of the purposes of the program was to give employees confidential access to an employee relations specialist who could help them resolve interpersonal problems on the job. Nancy called the confidential hotline and set up an appointment with a counsellor. Nancy was looking forward to explaining her dilemma to someone who was impartial and in a position to help her.

Dealing successfully with a problem like Nancy's requires effective employee relations—the subject of this chapter. First, we explore the roles of managers and employee relations specialists and describe how they should work together to coordinate an employee relations program. Next, we present a model of how communication works and explore specific policies that give employees access to important company information and provide feedback to top managers. Finally, we examine some programs for recognizing employees' individual and team contributions to company goals.

■ The Roles of the Manager and the Employee Relations Specialist

Good *employee relations* involve providing fair and consistent treatment to all employees so that they will be committed to the organization's goals. Organizations with good employee relations are likely to have a human resource strategy that places a high value on employees as stakeholders in the business. Employees who are treated as stakeholders have certain rights within the organization and can expect to be treated with dignity and respect. For example, service sector companies such as the banks are clearly dependent on their human resources to make them effective. The Bank of Montreal, recently ranked first in human resources by the *Report on Business*' "most respected" poll, has committed to programs that would allow their employees to balance multiple commitments to work, family, and community. These goals had high priority for President Tony Comper, who said: "... If they're on my agenda, they're going to be on the agenda of all levels of management at the bank."[1] To implement this kind of employee relations philosophy, managers must listen to and understand what employees are saying and experiencing, keep them informed about what management is planning to do with the business, and tell them how those plans may affect their jobs. Employees, on their side, should have the freedom to air a grievance about management decisions. There may be good reasons for not changing the decision, but management should at least listen to grievances.

Effective employee relations require cooperation between managers and **employee relations representatives.** Employee relations specialists are members of the HR department who act as internal consultants to the business. They try to ensure that company policies and procedures are followed and advise both supervisors and employees on specific employee relations problems. **Employee relations policies** are designed to provide channels to resolve such problems before they become more serious.

For example, an employee whose supervisor has denied her request for two weeks' vacation (to which she is entitled according to the employee handbook) may ask the employee relations representative to speak to her supervisor and clarify why she is being denied her preferred vacation time. A supervisor may request assistance because he suspects that one of his subordinates has an alcohol abuse problem that is affecting job performance. In both these cases, the employee relations representative will try to resolve the problem within the letter and spirit of the appropriate employment policy, while carefully balancing the interests of the supervisor, the employee, and the company.

Employee relations representatives may also develop new policies that help maintain fairness and efficiency in the workplace. The client in this situation may be a top manager requesting assistance in drafting a new policy on smoking in the workplace or the hiring of employees' spouses and other relatives.

◼ Developing Employee Communications

Many companies have found that the key to a sound employee relations program is a *communication channel* that gives employees access to important information and an opportunity to express their ideas and feelings. When supervisors are familiar with employment policies and employees are aware of their rights, there is less opportunity for misunderstandings to arise and productivity to drop.

Because corporations are very complex, it is necessary to develop numerous communication channels to move information up, down, and across the organization structure. IBM, for instance, provides many communication channels that allow employees and managers to speak to each other and share information. Whether it's the mechanics of HR policy or the broad issues of organizational culture and goal sharing, multiple channels need to be used. In 1992, the senior management of Lennox Industries (Canada) went through a visioning process that helped them define their direction for the next three years. Communication with Lennox employees used a cross-functional employee council to translate these goals into specific terms. The council produced a communiqué on the mission statement, and later produced mugs and T-shirts with the new logo. The following year, management sent all employees a personalized letter that summarized the company's business objectives. They also put together a four-minute video of interviews with factory workers discussing the importance of the company's mission statement.[2]

---

employee relations representative

A member of the HR department who ensures that company policies are followed and often consults with both supervisors and employees on specific employee relations problems.

employee relations policy

A policy designed to communicate management's thinking and practices concerning employee-related matters and prevent problems in the workplace from becoming more serious.

Lennox Industries (Canada)
www.icgti.org/open/mplace/
Lennox/index.htm

Types of Information

Two forms of information are sent and received in communications: facts and feelings. *Facts* are pieces of information that can be objectively measured or described. Examples are the cost of a computer, the daily defect rate in a manufacturing plant, and the size of the deductible payment of the company-sponsored health insurance policy. Recent technological advances have made factual information more accessible to more employees than ever before. Facts can be stored in databases and widely distributed to employees by networks of personal computers.

Feelings are employees' emotional responses to the decisions made or actions taken by managers or other employees. Managers who implement decisions must be able to anticipate or respond to the feelings of the employees who are affected by those decisions. If they cannot or do not, the plan may fail. For example, a university changed its health insurance coverage without consulting the employees affected by the change. When these employees learned of their diminished coverage, they responded so negatively that the manager of employee benefits resigned. (The health insurance policy was subsequently changed to be more favourable to the employees.)

One instance in which a company must be especially careful of employees' feelings is when the company is restructuring or downsizing and laying off a considerable portion of its work force. A production employee at a large manufacturing firm remembers how top management kept issuing memos that said, in effect, "we're doing fine, we're doing fine," and then suddenly announced that profits were falling and there would be layoffs. Survivors of the layoff were shocked and hurt and became highly distrustful of management.[3]

Organizations need to design communication channels that allow employees to communicate facts and feelings about specific aspects of their job. In many cases, these channels must provide for face-to-face communication because many feelings are conveyed non-verbally. Employees cannot write on a piece of paper or record on a computer database their complex emotional reactions to an announced restructuring that they fear may cost them their jobs.

How Communication Works

Figure 13–1 is a simple representation of the communications process within an organization. Communication starts with a *sender* who has a message to send to the *receiver*. The sender must encode the message and select a *communication channel* that will deliver it to the receiver. In communicating facts, the message may be encoded with words, numbers, or digital symbols; in communicating feelings, it may be encoded as body language or tone of voice.

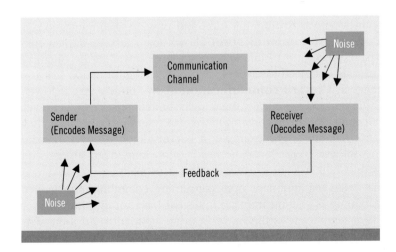

Figure 13–1 The Communications Process within an Organization

Some communication channels are more appropriate than others for sending certain messages. For example, *memos* are usually not very effective for sending information that has a lot of feeling in it. A more effective channel for conveying strong emotions is a meeting or other form of face-to-face communication.

Communication is not effective unless the receiver is able to *decode* the message and understand its true meaning. The receiver may misinterpret a message for many reasons. For example, the message may be filled with technical jargon that makes it difficult to decode, the receiver may misinterpret the sender's motives for sending the message, or the sender may send a message that lends itself to multiple interpretations.

Because of the strong possibility of miscommunication, important communications should include opportunities for *feedback* from the receiver. This way the sender can clarify the message if its true meaning is not received. In addition, noise in the sender's or receiver's environment may block or distort the message. Noise is anything that disrupts the message: inaccurate communication by the sender, fatigue or distraction on the part of the receiver, or actual noise that distorts the message (other people talking, traffic, telephone ringing). Very often it is information overload. For example, if the receiver receives 65 memos in one week, she may not read the most important one very carefully because she is overwhelmed by the barrage of paper.

Communication is important, but there are times when communication problems are not the result of technical flaws in encoding, decoding, or transmission. Rather, communication fails because there is deliberate obstruction or distortion. The cliché, "knowledge is power," suggests a cynical, "political" approach to communication. Such a calculating approach—"editing" what you hear or see before you pass it on, withholding information that might be damaging to your interests and so forth—will always be present in organizations, at least to some extent. However, it is important to realize that many employees who would otherwise be open and loyal to the organization may behave differently if they feel insecure or threatened.

Communications that provide for feedback are called *two-way communications* because they allow the sender and receiver to interact with each other. Communications that provide no opportunity for feedback are *one-way*. Although ideally all communications should be interactive, this is not always possible in large organizations, where large amounts of information must be distributed to many employees. For example, top executives of large companies do not usually have the time to speak to all the employees they need to inform about a new product about to be released. Instead, they may communicate with the employees via a memo or report. In contrast, top executives at small businesses have much less difficulty communicating with their employees.

Downward and Upward Communication.

Employee relations specialists help to maintain both downward communication and upward communication in an organization. **Downward communication** allows managers to implement the decisions they have made and to influence employees lower in the organizational hierarchy. It can also be used to disperse to employees information that is controlled by top managers. **Upward communication** allows employees at lower levels of the organization to communicate their ideas or feelings to higher-level decision makers. Unfortunately, many organizations erect serious barriers in their upward communication channels. For example, it is considered disloyal in many companies for an employee to go "over the head" of an immediate supervisor and communicate with a higher-level executive about a problem.

One final but very important note concerning communication in general: The Canadian economy is shifting from an industrial base to an information base. This revolution is as significant as the move from an agrarian to an industrial economy over a century ago. In an industrial economy, production processes are the focus of concern. In an information economy, communication (the production and transmission of information) is the focus. How information is communicated, both internally

downward communication
Communication that allows managers to implement the decisions they have made and to influence employees lower in the organizational hierarchy.

upward communication
Communication that allows employees at lower levels of the organization to communicate their ideas and feelings to higher-level decision makers.

and externally, is becoming more and more important to organizational success. There are a number of companies that illustrate how central information is to wealth creation, particularly in the software industry. Software, with virtually no distinguishing physical properties, is close to being pure information. Microsoft—founded and headed by Bill Gates, who is currently the wealthiest man in North America—is familiar to almost everybody. However, the more dramatic reality is the many thousands of people whose careers and livelihoods are grounded in this industry.

■ Building Managerial Skills: Facilitating Effective Communications

Working with supervisors and managers, employee relations representatives can facilitate effective communications by developing and maintaining three types of programs: information dissemination, employee feedback, and employee assistance.

■ Information Dissemination

Information is a source of power in organizations. In traditional top-down hierarchical organizations, top managers zealously guard information as their special preserve. But the information age has forced many businesses to forge a new set of rules. Today organizations depend more and more on knowledge workers to produce their product or service. **Knowledge workers** (for example, programmers, writers, educators) transform information into a product or service and need large amounts of information to do their jobs effectively. For these workers, the dissemination of information throughout the organization is critical to providing high-quality service and products to all of the organization's customers.

Information dissemination involves making information available to decision makers, wherever they are located. Because they are better informed, employees who have access to abundant information are more likely to feel empowered and are better able to participate in decision making. Information dissemination also helps managers adopt more participative leadership styles and work configurations, leading to greater employee involvement and, ultimately, to better-quality employee relations.

The most important methods of disseminating information to employees are employee handbooks, written communications, audiovisual communications, electronic communications, meetings, and informal communications.

The Employee Handbook. The *employee handbook* is probably the most important source of information that the HR department can provide. It sets the tone for the company's overall employee relations philosophy,[4] informing both employees and supervisors about company employment policies and procedures and communicates an employee's rights and responsibilities. The handbook lets employees know that they can expect consistent and uniform treatment from supervisors on issues that affect their job or status in the company. It also tells supervisors how to evaluate, reward, and discipline their employees. It can protect supervisors and the company from making uninformed and arbitrary decisions that may hurt the morale of the work force or lead to litigation from an angry employee.

Employee handbooks contain information on such issues as employee benefits, performance evaluation, employee dress codes, employment of family members, smoking, probationary employment periods, drug-testing procedures, family leave policies, sexual harassment, discipline procedures, and safety rules.[5] Handbooks need to be updated annually to reflect the current legal environment and to remain consistent with the company's overall employee relations philosophy.

Recent court interpretations in some U.S. states have suggested that employee handbooks may constitute an implied contract between employer and employee that restricts the employer's freedom to discharge an employee without just cause. To avoid such restrictive interpretations by the courts, employers should include

knowledge worker

A worker who transforms information into a product or service.

information dissemination

The process of making information available to decision makers, wherever they are located.

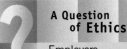

A Question of Ethics

Employers sometimes attempt to establish limits for employee behaviour off the job. Even if there aren't formal rules about drinking or other "frowned upon" behaviours, the expectations that "our people don't do that" can be communicated in a variety of ways, along with the knowledge that transgressions may hurt a person's chances for promotion or other preferment. Is it ethical for employers to attempt to control what people do off the job?

at the end of their handbooks a disclaimer stating that employees can be discharged for any reason or no reason and that the handbook does not constitute an employment contract.[6] Some firms have even gone further to protect themselves. They ask all new employees to sign an employee handbook acknowledgment form that states they have received the handbook, will refer to it for company rules, regulations, and policies, and understand that it is in no way a contract. Figure 13–2 shows a sample employee handbook acknowledgement form.[7] Not surprisingly, such practices have been controversial because the legal protection they provide the employer also tends to undermine the goodwill the handbook was designed to foster between employees and management.

Still, employee handbooks can help prevent or solve problems in the work force. Figure 13–3 shows how a firm might communicate an enlightened nepotism policy through its employee handbook. (**Nepotism** is the practice of favouring relatives over others in the workplace.) The policy communicated in Figure 13–3 protects the rights of family members but balances those rights with the company's need to avoid conflicts of interest that could affect the efficiency of its business.

In family-owned businesses where owners often groom sons or daughters or other family members to take over the company, nepotism is taken for granted. In these situations, the question becomes: How much nepotism is okay? It is not uncommon for the company owners to put their progeny in positions of power for which they are ill prepared and grant them pay, titles, and privileges denied to more experienced or qualified company employees. Naturally, this antagonizes non-family employees. Family business consultants Craig E. Aronoff and John L.

nepotism

The practice of favouring relatives over others in the workplace.

TJP LTD. EMPLOYEE HANDBOOK ACKNOWLEDGEMENT FORM

This employee handbook has been given to _____

on (date) _____

by _____ (title) _____

Employee's effective starting date _____

Employee's pay period _____

Employee's hours and work week are _____

Welcome to TJP Ltd. Below are a list of your benefits with their effective date:

Benefit		Effective Date
Hospitalization (semi-private room)	_____	_____
Life insurance	_____	_____
Retirement	_____	_____
Vacation	_____	_____
Sick leave	_____	_____
Holidays	_____	_____
Personal days	_____	_____
Bereavement	_____	_____
Workers' compensation	_____	_____
Your first performance appraisal will be on	_____	_____

I understand that my employee handbook is for informational purposes only and that I am to read and refer to the employee handbook for information on employment work rules and company policies. TJP Ltd. may modify, revoke, suspend or terminate any and all policies, rules, procedures and benefits at any time without prior notice to company employees. This handbook and its statements do not create a contract between TJP Ltd. and its employees. This handbook and its statements do not affect in any way the employment-at-will relationship between TJP Ltd. and its employees.

(Employee's signature) _____

(Date) _____

Figure 13–2 Sample Employee Handbook Acknowledgement Form

SOURCE: Adapted, by permission of publisher, from Brady, T. (1993, June). Employee handbooks: contracts or empty promises? *Management Review,* 34. © 1993. American Management Association, New York. All rights reserved.

NEPOTISM POLICY

Section 1. Family Member Employment. The Company considers it an unlawful employment practice regarding a member of an individual's family working or who has worked for the Company to:

a. Refuse to hire or employ that individual;

b. Bar or terminate from employment that individual; or

c. Discriminate against that individual in compensation or in terms, conditions, or privileges of employment.

Section 2. Conflict of Interest. The Company is not required to hire or continue in employment an individual if it:

a. Would place the individual in a position of exercising supervisory, appointment, or grievance adjustment authority over a member of the individual's family, or in a position of being subject to the authority that a member of the individual's family exercises; or

b. Would cause the Company to disregard a bona fide occupational requirement reasonably necessary to the normal operation of the Company's business.

Section 3. Member of an Individual's Family. Member of an individual's family includes wife, husband, son, daughter, mother, father, brother, brother-in-law, sister, sister-in-law, son-in-law, daughter-in-law, father-in-law, aunt, uncle, niece, nephew, stepparent, or stepchild of the individual.

Figure 13–3 Sample Nepotism Policy Statement from an Employee Handbook

SOURCE: Adapted from Decker, K. H. (1989). *A manager's guide to employee privacy: Policies and procedures*, 231–232. New York: Wiley.

Ward recommend that family members meet the following three qualifications before making the family business a permanent career:

◆ Get an education appropriate for the job sought.

◆ Work three to five years outside the family business.

◆ Start in an existing, necessary job and honour precedents for pay and performance.[8]

Written Communications.   There are many other forms of written communication besides the employee handbook. *Memos* are useful for conveying changes in policies or procedures that are not reflected in the employee handbook. For example, when there is a change in coverage of a specific type of medical procedure, the affected group of employees can be notified by written memo. In addition, financial reports should be disseminated to employees so they are knowledgeable about the company's performance. Shareholders are routinely given this information, but employees should receive it too because it is an important source of feedback on their aggregate performance.

One activity for which the HR department is very likely to have direct responsibility is the production and distribution of an employee newsletter. The *newsletter* is usually a short monthly or quarterly publication designed to keep employees informed of important events, meetings, and transitions in jobs and to provide inspirational stories about employee and team contributions to the business (Figure 13–4). Newsletters help foster community spirit in a company or unit by keeping everybody informed about what others are doing. The advent of desktop publishing packages for personal computers has made newsletter production and distribution feasible for even the smallest of companies. For example, Valley-lab, a medical instruments manufacturer, started a newsletter to inform its employees about quality improvements made by various employee teams under its total quality management program.

Two important components for work teams in a TQM program are ongoing information about rivals and feedback on their own performance from managers.[9] Some managers use a simple bulletin board to post ongoing team performance data and comparisons with outside competitors or other teams within the company.

Figure 13–4 Sample Employee Newsletter

SOURCE: VIACOM, Inc. and design by the Barnett Group, Inc.

Audiovisual Communications.   New technologies have made it possible to disseminate information that goes beyond the printed word. Visual images and audio information are powerful communication tools. The widespread use of videocassette recorders (VCRs) in the home has made it feasible for companies to distribute videotapes to employees when they need to convey important information. As we saw earlier in the chapter with the example of Lennox Industries' campaign to imbue employees with the corporate mission, the VCR's accessibility and ease of use means that important messages can distributed to people who would have a difficult time getting together at a single time or place. Major announcements of change requiring careful and complete presentation, such as reorganizations or layoffs, new products, or changes in key management positions, can be communicated with a minimum of distortion.

A recent technological advance, **teleconferencing,** allows people with busy schedules to participate in meetings even when they are a great distance away from the conference location (or each other). Through video cameras and other sophisticated equipment, teleconferencing makes it possible for employees at remote locations to interact with other people at a meeting just as if they were seated with them in the conference room. One four-hour video conference that keeps five people off an airplane and out of hotels and restaurants could save a company at least $5,000.

Take the example of Frank Addison, President of Addison Travel Marketing in Vancouver. Scheduled for a tutorial meeting with some marketing students in New Brunswick, he drove not to the airport but to an office in downtown Vancouver and did the session over a high-capacity phone line video link. In British Columbia, BC Tel has combined forces with the Coast Hotel chain to provide a dedicated high-end video conference service between five provincial locations. At roughly $1,000 for a two-hour conference, it rarely takes more than two people who would need to travel from out-of-town locations to break even on the travel costs, let alone the time saved for often expensive managerial and professional employees.[10]

With systems ranging in price from $20,000 to $40,000, however, the costs of videoconferencing are still prohibitive for many companies. Fortunately, advances in computers and phone networks may soon make it possible to equip desktop computers with a camera and videoconferencing circuit board for as little as $1,000 to $1,500. Besides making videoconferencing more affordable, desktop systems promise to make the technology less intimidating to managers and employees.[11]

teleconferencing

The use of audio and video equipment to allow people to participate in meetings even when they are a great distance away from the conference location or each other.

Teleconferencing.

Teleconferencing allows people at remote locations to interact with other meeting participants just as if they were seated with them in a conference room. One four-hour video conference that keeps five people off an airplane and out of hotels and restaurants could save a company $5,000.

Electronic Communications.   Advances in electronic communications have made interactive communications between sender and receiver possible even when they are separated by physical distance and busy schedules. With **voice mail,** an employee can avoid the unpleasant experience of playing "telephone tag" with busy managers and instead leave a detailed voice message for them. The sender can also transmit a prerecorded voice mail message to all individuals within a telephone network in the company. For example, an executive can send a personalized greeting to a large group of employees. In addition, the receiver can leave different voice mail messages for different types of callers by creating a menu of messages for various individuals. Voice mail can also be used strategically by companies engaged in quality management efforts. Nortel, when it launched its flexible benefits program, avoided the traditional seminar approach. Instead, it sent an information package home to each employee so that they could work through it on their own time, and discuss it with their spouse. By dialling a 1-800 number, employees could have their inquiries answered. Not only could they obtain information on the flex-plan policies, but they could also get up-to-date information on all their benefits, from vacation days to pensions.[12]

Like any technology, voice mail has some drawbacks. Many people still dislike having a machine answer their calls. And this machine has plenty of potential for misuse. People often use it to screen calls, avoiding callers they don't want to talk to by pretending they're not there. This is fine in private life, but screening too many calls at the office can create problems for companies. The following guidelines can help managers cut down on abuses of the voice mail system:[13]

voice mail

A form of electronic communication that allows the sender to leave a detailed voice message for a receiver.

B.C. Tel
www.bctel.net

◆ *Limit message capacity.* To discourage long-winded voice mail messages, set the individual message capacity for 60 seconds.

◆ *Don't leave people in limbo.* Sometimes it's necessary to screen calls. For instance, an editor negotiating a contract with an author may not want to talk to the agent until she has her terms and strategy ready. However, screening doesn't mean letting people leave innumerable messages and not getting back to them for five or six days. To prevent the screening habit, some companies have a policy stipulating that answering machines cannot be on when employees are in their offices.

◆ *Don't use voice mail as a crutch.* Senders who are supposed to phone someone with unpleasant news should not wait until the person is out to lunch so they can leave the message on voice mail.

◆ *Make sure everyone understands the system.* This includes temporary employees, people from other departments, and new hires.

◆ *Respect the caller.* Employees who will be away from the office on business, or on vacation and not checking their messages, should leave a message for the callers telling them how to reach a colleague who is taking their calls.[14]

electronic mail (E-mail)

A form of electronic communication that allows employees to communicate with each other via electronic messages sent through personal computer terminals linked by a network.

Electronic mail, or **E-mail,** allows employees to communicate with each other via written electronic messages sent through personal computer terminals linked by a network. E-mail is a very fast way to convey important business results or critical events to a large number of employees.[15] It also permits the sharing of large databases of information among employees and even members of different organizations. E-mail has made it possible for professors at different universities (for example, McGill and UBC) to collaborate on research studies, write manuscripts, and share data as quickly as if they were working next door to each other at the same university. Interorganizational electronic communication is likely to increase significantly in the coming years, thanks to the Internet. For more details on how the Internet works and the opportunities it offers for improved HRM services, see the Issues and Applications feature entitled "Opportunities Galore on the Internet."

Despite its many advantages, E-mail has created some challenging problems for managers. E-mail can be written quickly and transmitted instantly to large numbers of people. Rather than solving communications problems, poorly utilized E-mail can quickly clog and slow the process, because people need to read them. Many E-mail messages have no value or relevance. As a work-flow mechanism, E-mail simply automates a manual process and turns it into a network broadcast storm versus a paper blizzard. Microsoft's Bill Gates (among many others) has taken to utilizing a software program, called a "bozo filter,"

Issues and Applications

Opportunities Galore on the Internet

The Internet, a worldwide network of linked computers that allows people to exchange text, data, and graphics, provides many opportunities for enhanced communication. Many organizations have developed home pages on the World Wide Web (a part of the Internet with multimedia capabilities) that offer a wealth of information about the organization's products and services.

For example, many universities are now listing the details of their educational programs on the Internet to attract students from other countries.

The Internet offers many opportunities for improved HRM services. New businesses post résumés on an online Internet site that employers can access as they seek to fill positions. For example, Actors Pavilion provides a Web site on which actors can post their résum´s and photographs, which can be downloaded by casting directors who are seeking actors to fill parts in films, plays, or commercials.

The Net offers a variety of newsgroups, "virtual communities" of people who share professional or personal interests. Newsgroup subscribers converse on an Internet "party line" that makes the content accessible to all group members. The HRNet newsgroup, sponsored by the Academy of Management's Human Resource Management Division, has over 3,000 members, mostly academics and HRM practitioners. A practitioner may post a question about an HRM practice that the company is considering, such as a casual dress code, and quickly get feedback from other members of the HRNet who have experience with casual dress codes. Such information can be invaluable when it comes time to make the final decision.

SOURCES: Sprout, A. (1995, November 27). The Internet inside your company. *Fortune,* 161–168; Kirkpatrick, D. (1995, May 1). As the Internet sizzles, online services battle for stakes. *Fortune,* 86–96; and Grusky, S. (1996, February). Winning résumé. *Internet World,* 58–64.

that automatically culls mail from other than a pre-selected list of senders. Other control techniques include limiting the number of messages an account will store and returning surplus messages to senders.

Firms that set up E-mail systems with the idea of boosting productivity are sometimes dismayed to find they are actually *lowering* productivity because the systems are not being used properly. Technology and management consultant Ira Chaleff recommends the following guidelines for storing and retrieving information productively:

◆ Establish an E-mail improvement team to develop protocols and procedures for getting the most out of the system.

◆ Create electronic files for messages that need to be saved and organize them in subject folders for quick retrieval.

◆ Set up a common folder or electronic bulletin board to which senders can route reports and memos intended for general distribution. This can save considerable system space and time.[16]

◆ Shut off the computer beep that alerts the receiver to incoming messages to prevent constant interruptions of work.

◆ Do not send all kinds of documents through E-mail. Regular interoffice mail should be used most of the time; the bureaucratic tendency to upgrade most messages to "certified" and "confidential" should be avoided.

The thorniest problem that managers confront with E-mail requires consultation with HR professionals. This is the tendency of employees to view their E-mail messages as private property, sacrosanct from employer inspection. This assumption can lead them to use E-mail to communicate about off-hours activities or to spread rumours, misinformation, and complaints speedily throughout the organization. Some managers have been shocked to find "gripe-nets" formed by disgruntled workers who use E-mail to sabotage managers' plans.[17] For these reasons, employers sometimes decide to monitor their employees' E-mail. Although employees resent this as an invasion of their privacy, E-mail is not private communication in a legal or practical sense.

According to lawyer Jeffrey Goodman, employers should take two steps with regard to E-mail and the potential for litigation:[18]

1. Encourage employees to draft E-mail messages with the same discretion they would use when drafting interoffice correspondence or memos. Inform employees that all E-mail messages relating to an employee that could be relevant will have to be produced in future employment litigation. Inform them that "deleted" E-mail messages remain in the system and can be recovered.

2. Create and enforce a policy that E-mail messages are erased in a logical and prompt manner and do not build up in the system. Messages about an employee that could be relevant to future litigation must be printed and placed in the employee's personnel file. Neither the company's E-mail system nor its shared drives should be used as an electronic filing system.

Multimedia technology has potential applications in many areas. One is employee training programs (see Chapter 8). For example, pilots can develop aviation skills on a multimedia flight simulator without the risks of learning while actually flying. Many textbooks now offer multimedia disks that help students learn skills and apply information they have learned from the text. Such programs can contain voice and video clips and ask the student to make decisions based on a menu of choices. After making the choice, the student can see the outcome on the video.

Another application of multimedia technology is in telecommuting, a trend that is already changing the face of companies across the nation. More and more employees are working with employer-equipped computer systems and faxes in their home or in office "hotels" away from the employer's permanent location. The

multimedia technology
A form of electronic communication that integrates voice, video, and text, all of which can be encoded digitally and transported on fibre optic networks.

Five Keys to Managing Telecommuters

Telecommuting must be carefully planned. The following suggestions can make managing telecommuters a little easier:

◆ Select telecommuters with care, considering the work habits of the employee and the type of work involved. People who are not very self-motivated may not be able to manage their time well at home.

◆ Maintain schedules and make sure telecommuters stick to deadlines. While it's okay for telecommuters to work off-hours, they should be available for consultation when the company needs them.

◆ Make sure the technology works. Without the right compatibility between employers' and telecommuters' computer systems, there will be delays in communication and traffic tie-ups on the electronic highway.

◆ Have home-based workers come in to the office on a regular basis so they can attend meetings and interact with managers. This not only keeps these employees in the flow but also helps combat their feelings of isolation.

◆ Don't discriminate against telecommuters. These employees should receive the same pay, benefits, and promotion opportunities as in-house employees.

SOURCES: Based on Caudron, S. (1992, November). Working at home pays off. *Personnel Journal*, 40–49; Broadwell, L. (1993, August). Long-distance employees. *Small Business Reports*, 44–48; and *Information Management Forum* (1993, February). Telecommuting: Pros and cons. An insert in *Management Review*, 3.

accompanying Manager's Notebook, "Five Keys to Managing Telecommuters," addresses the managerial implications of this new workplace development.

Meetings.   Formal meetings are opportunities for face-to-face communication between two or more employees and are guided by a specific agenda. Formal meetings facilitate dialogue and promote the nurturing of personal relationships, particularly among employees who may not interact frequently because they are separated by organizational or geographic barriers.

Meetings take place at different organizational levels. For example, staff meetings allow managers to coordinate activities with subordinates in their units. Division or corporate meetings involve issues that have a larger impact, and may include managers or employees from all divisions across the corporation. Task force meetings may be called to discuss specific goals such as a change in marketing strategy or compensation policies.

It has been estimated that managers and executives spend as much as 70 percent of their time in meetings.[19] Poorly managed meetings can be a colossal waste of time that lower a company's productivity. Think about what it might cost for several highly paid executives to spend three hours at a meeting without accomplishing their objectives—and then multiply that amount by 260 workdays a year. Yet meetings don't have to be a necessary evil. Here are some guidelines for making meetings more productive:

1. Decide whether it's even necessary to hold a meeting. If a matter can be handled by a phone call or memo, don't schedule a meeting.

2. Make meeting participation match the meeting's purpose. For instance, if a meeting is being held for the purpose of sharing information, a large group might be appropriate. For a problem-solving session, a smaller group is usually more productive.

3. Distribute a carefully planned agenda before the meeting. This will provide participants with purpose and direction and give them a chance to plan their own contributions.

4. Choose an appropriate meeting space and time. It's difficult for people to accomplish much when they're crowded into a small room with notepads balanced on their laps. But holding a meeting in a room that's too large may encourage participants to spread out and not develop the necessary cohesion. Timing is crucial, too. At meetings scheduled in the hour before lunch, attendees may be listening to their own stomachs growl rather than to their colleagues. Some managers like to schedule meetings in the morning, when people are more alert. To encourage promptness, they set a time that is not exactly on the hour—such as 10:10 instead of 10:00 A.M.

5. Close with an action plan in the case of a problem-solving or policy-setting meeting and follow up with a memo outlining what happened at the meeting and what steps need to be taken.[20]

Skillful management of the dynamics among meeting participants is even more important than logistics. It is inevitable that some participants will attempt to dominate the proceedings with either helpful or negative contributions. Meeting leaders must strive to establish an atmosphere in which everyone feels at ease—one in which differences of opinion are encouraged and treated with respect.

Further clouding the air in the conference room are gender differences. Women often complain that they find it difficult to get, and hold, the floor in meetings with male colleagues. Sociolinguist Deborah Tannen has found that women and men have different communication styles that lead to misunderstandings both at work and at home.[21] Cultural differences also crop up in the meeting room. An American manager visiting a foreign company might find herself in a meeting that little resembles the ones in her home company. In a North American business meeting, the focus tends to be on action. In contrast, the objective of Japanese business meetings is to gather information about a subject or to analyse data before planning action, while in Italy meetings are often a crucial way for managers to demonstrate their authority and power.[22]

In addition to scheduled formal meetings with specific work-related goals, managers can use informal types of meetings to build personal relationships between employees. In some organizations, the socializing that was once relegated to the water cooler, the company picnic, and the holiday party has become more frequent and more embedded in the work cycle. The microelectronics industry has found, led by the California sensibilities of Silicon Valley, that regular Friday afternoon social get-togethers turn out to be a good opportunity for people from different departments and from different ranks within the organization to share information that would not otherwise be available. The practice of trying to reduce formality along with the social distance that inhibits communication has started to show up as "casual Fridays," where normal business attire gives way to T-shirts and casual pants. One survey suggested that two-thirds of the employers who responded offer at least occasional casual days, among them Toronto-based publisher Harlequin Enterprises.

Retreats.   Another type of meeting that has gained popularity with a number of Canadian businesses in recent years is the *retreat*. The company takes a group of employees to a relaxing location such as a mountain lodge or an oceanside resort, where they mix business with recreational activities like golf, tennis, or sailing. Some retreats are designed to develop creative ideas for long-term planning or for implementing changes in business practices. Others, such as the outdoor adventures organized by Outward Bound, encourage employees to develop new interpersonal skills by involving them in risk-taking activities such as climbing a mountain or whitewater rafting, where they are forced to be interdependent. These intense shared experiences can foster mutual appreciation among co-workers. A retreat can also be an excellent way of turning around a reputation for poor employee relations. One medium-sized law firm used this kind of meeting to improve relations between partners and (junior) staff lawyers. All of the firm's members spent two days at a mountain lodge talking in small groups about ways to improve their relationships with each other. These discussions brought into the open many touchy issues that had been simmering. In the retreat setting, the firm's members could deal with them constructively.

Outward Bound
www.outwardbound.ca

Retreats can also serve a crucial role in addressing serious structural and process problems within an organization. When recent graduate Paul Hallson was offered a position as a programmer with a particular branch of the Ontario Ministry of Municipal Affairs, he was delighted. His enthusiasm collided with an unhappy reality.

> From the first day, it was clear that I had come to a bizarre environment. People didn't talk to one another—except to shout. At one point, a vicious argument broke out over the photocopier, which was next to my workstation. Later the window beside me rattled. It had been hit by the computer print-out report that one staff member had thrown at another. I remember sitting at my desk and thinking, 'What have I gotten myself into?' It was awful.[23]

The long turnaround project undertaken by a new manager included an off-site retreat at Collingwood. Key to its success was the fact that the sessions were organized by non-management members of the unit and led by them—a process that signifi-

They Heard It through the Grapevine.

The grapevine is a powerful informal communications network in most organizations. Open-office set-ups, in which workers sit in cubicles or workstations rather than fully enclosed offices, are particularly conducive to fostering informal relationships among workers.

informal communications

Also called "the grapevine." Information exchanges that occur informally among employees, without a planned agenda.

management by walking around (MBWA)

A technique in which managers walk around and talk to employees informally to monitor informal communications, listen to employee grievances and suggestions, and generally build rapport and morale.

employee feedback program

A program designed to improve employee communications by giving employees a voice in policy formulation and making sure that they receive due process on any complaints they lodge against managers.

cantly helped to reduce the skepticism and cynicism that had become such a dominant part of the unit's culture. Employees began to see that change for the better was possible, and—partly because of a one-day Outward Bound experience—began to get past the barriers of distrust. Action plans followed the retreat and, even though some of them did not work as anticipated, the goodwill that began to grow through the retreat allowed the plans to be reworked. The consensus is that the unit has come an "amazingly long way."

In addition to using retreats to air important issues, many family businesses use them to set up a family council, an organizational and strategic planning group whose members regularly meet to decide values, policy, and direction.

Informal Communications.   Sometimes called the "grapevine," **informal communications** consist of information exchanges that occur informally among employees without a planned agenda. Many informal communications take place among employees who form friendships or networks of mutual assistance at the water fountain or in the hallway, company cafeteria, offices, or parking lot. Informal communications pass along information that is usually not available through more formal communication channels—for example, the size of upcoming merit pay increases, who is in line for a big promotion, who has received an outside job offer, and who has gotten a low performance evaluation and is upset about it.

Informal communications can be the source of creative ideas. One regional telecommunications company has designed a new research facility to take advantage of the benefits of informal communication. The architect designed "breakout rooms" and hallways to optimize spontaneous interactions between technicians and scientists so that informal groups could brainstorm together to solve technical problems and generate ideas.

When organizations allow too much information to be communicated informally, there is a good chance that it will be distorted by rumour, gossip, and innuendo. The result may be poor employee morale and poor employee relations. To guard against this, the HR department and managers need to monitor informal communications and, when necessary, clarify them through more formal channels. One effective way to monitor informal communications is through **management by walking around (MBWA).** MBWA, championed by Tom Peters and Robert Waterman in their book *In Search of Excellence,* is a management technique in which the manager walks around the company so that employees at all levels have an opportunity to offer suggestions or voice grievances. This management style is used to build rapport with employees and monitor morale at IBM and many other companies.

▓ Employee Feedback Programs

To provide upward communications channels between employees and management, many organizations offer **employee feedback programs.** These programs are designed to improve management–employee relations by (1) giving employees a voice in decision making and policy formulation and (2) by making sure that they receive due process on any complaints they lodge against managers. The HR department not only designs and maintains employee feedback programs but is also expected to protect employee confidentiality in dealing with sensitive personal issues. HR personnel are also charged with ensuring that subordinates are not subject to retaliation from angry managers.

The most common employee feedback programs are employee attitude surveys, appeals procedures, and employee assistance programs. Here we discuss the first two kinds of programs, which are intended to resolve work-related problems. Employee assistance programs (EAPs), which are designed to help employees resolve personal problems that are interfering with their job performance, are discussed later in this chapter.

Employee Attitude Surveys.   Designed to measure workers' likes and dislikes of various aspects of their jobs, **employee attitude surveys** are typically formal and anonymous. They ask employees how they feel about the work they do, their supervisor, their work environment, their opportunities for advancement, the quality of the training they received, the company's treatment of women and minorities, and the fairness of the company's pay policies. An excerpt from an employee attitude survey is reproduced in Figure 13–5. The survey responses of various subgroups can be compared to those of the total employee population to help managers identify units that are experiencing poor employee relations and give them the attention they need.

Making specific improvements in employee relations can avert acts of sabotage or labour unrest (such as strikes, absenteeism, and turnover) that are directly attributable to strains between subordinates and managers. For example, in analysing attitude survey data, one chain of retail stores found that employees at one store had much lower levels of satisfaction with their jobs than did the employees at any other store in the chain. The chain's top managers immediately realized this was the same store that had experienced several serious acts of sabotage. Instead of retaliating against employees, corporate management set out to solve supervision problems at the store with training and mediation.

employee attitude survey

A formal anonymous survey designed to measure employee likes and dislikes of various aspects of their jobs.

To what extent are you satisfied with...				
	Highly Satisfied		Satisfied		Highly Dissatisfied
1. my pay and bonus	1	2	3	4	5
2. my benefits – overall	1	2	3	4	5
3. my chance to get a promotion or a better job	1	2	3	4	5
4. having a sense of well-being on the job	1	2	3	4	5
5. the respect and recognition I receive from management	1	2	3	4	5
6. my job security	1	2	3	4	5
7. the morale of my division	1	2	3	4	5
8. the degree of responsibility and autonomy I have in doing my work	1	2	3	4	5
9. the opportunity to have my ideas adopted	1	2	3	4	5
10. working with highly talented and capable people	1	2	3	4	5
11. inter-divisional cooperation and communication	1	2	3	4	5

Figure 13–5 Excerpt from an Employee Attitude Survey

SOURCE: Goodrich & Sherwood Company, 521 Fifth Avenue, New York, NY 10175. Used with permission.

To manage an employee attitude survey effectively, managers should follow three rules. First, they should tell employees what they plan to do with the information they collect and then inform them about the results of the survey. There is no point in surveying opinions unless the firm intends to act on them. If it doesn't, or can't, employees will see the survey as an empty exercise. Second, managers should use survey data ethically to monitor the state of employee relations, both throughout the company and within employee subgroups (such as women, accountants, or newly hired workers), and to make positive changes in the workplace. They should not use the information they collect to fire someone (for example, a supervisor whose workers are unhappy) or to take away privileges. Finally, to protect employee confidentiality and maintain the integrity of the data, the survey should be done by a third party, such as a consulting firm.

Appeals Procedures.   Providing a mechanism for employees to voice their reactions to and challenge management decisions will enhance employees' perception that the organization has fair employment policies. Organizations without an effective set of **appeals procedures** increase their risk of litigation, costly legal fees, and back-pay penalties to employees who use the courts to obtain justice.[24] Effective appeals procedures give individual employees some control over the decisions that affect them and serve to identify managers who are ineffective or unfair.

Some of the most common management actions appealed by employees are:

◆ The allocation of overtime work

◆ Warnings for safety rule violations

◆ The size of merit pay increases

◆ The specification of job duties

◆ The employer's reimbursement for medical expense claims filed by employees

◆ Performance evaluations.

Managers may choose from several different types of appeals procedures that vary in formality.[25] The most informal is an *open-door program*. While the specifics of these programs vary from company to company, the common theme is that all employees have direct access to any manager or executive in the organization. IBM's reputation as an employer, in Canada and throughout IBM's worldwide operations, has been much admired and imitated. At IBM, an employee can walk into the office of any manager other than his or her direct supervisor (up to and including the CEO) and ask for an opinion on a complaint or any other problem worrying the employee. The manager consulted must conduct a fair investigation into both sides of the issue and provide an answer within a specified period of time. For example, an employee who is dissatisfied with his or her performance evaluation may seek a second opinion from another manager. The open-door policy has two major benefits: it makes employees feel more secure and committed to IBM, and it makes managers less likely to act arbitrarily.

Like the open door policy, a *speak-up program* is informal and flexible. It differs in that it prescribes specific steps for the employee to take in bringing a work problem to management's attention. CIGNA, a financial services and insurance company, has a speak-up program called Speak Easy that guarantees employees access to higher levels of management, but normally only after they bring their problems to the attention of their immediate supervisor (Figure 13–6).

The grievance panel and the union grievance procedure are the most formal mechanisms used by organizations to handle employee complaints. *Grievance panels* are used in a number of non-unionized firms. They are composed of the complaining employee's peers and managers other than the employee's direct manager. The grievance panel conducts an investigation into the grievance brought before it. Grievance panels are typically the last step in the appeal process for a complaint that could not be resolved by other procedures. For example, Honeywell's griev-

appeals procedures

Procedures that allow employees to voice their reactions to management practice and to challenge management decisions.

CIGNA
www.cigna.com

Speak Easy

Speak Easy is a special program that gives you the opportunity to talk to management about work-related concerns. Speak Easy, with the support of CIGNA Corporation management, ensures an open line of communication and guarantees a timely response.

Through the Speak Easy Program, you may want to:

- Comment on your treatment as an employee;
- Describe a specific situation that is affecting your performance or the way you feel about your job.

Management wants to hear what you have to say …. so Speak Easy.

Hear's how the program works:

Phase I. This is the first and most direct way to raise issues about your job or work situation. Go to your supervisor or manager and ask to talk over problems or questions. He or she is committed to listen and give you a fair and honest answer.

But if your supervisor or manager disagrees, cannot correct the situation, or is unwilling to change an earlier decision, Phase I offers you another step.

At your request, your supervisor will arrange interview(s) with additional levels of your management, including the top company official of your department or location. You will be invited to present your concerns, and every effort will be made to resolve your issue.

Phase II. Phase II has been designed for privately raising the matters not resolved in Phase I. You may be unhappy with the course of action taken or feel the matter is too touchy to go through your supervisor. Phase II will give you another audience—someone not directly involved in the situation. But it's important to note that this phase is normally **not a replacement for Phase I employee/management discussions.**

In Phase II of the program, your issues will be kept strictly confidential and reviewed impartially by the Speak Easy Coordinator. Only the coordinator will know your identity if you choose.

All you do is pick up a Speak Easy envelope located in holders throughout your office and fill in the pertinent information…. Then, drop the completed form and envelope in the mail. You can expect a prompt response from the coordinator, so long as your signature, home address and phone number are on the form. Otherwise, you cannot be contacted and advised of the results of the coordinator's review.

If, for some reason, the review cannot be continued without revealing your name, the coordinator will tell you. It will be your decision or not to continue.

Please remember the sole responsibility of the Speak Easy Coordinator is to make sure that your situation is dealt with fairly and equitably.

Phase III. This is the final step if you still aren't completely satisfied with the decision. This phase gives you direct access to the Head of your Operating Group or Staff Organization.

If after using Phases I and II, you are not satisfied with the decision about your situation, you may send a Speak Easy form or a letter fully stating the issue to the Head of your Operating Group or Staff Organization with a copy to your Speak Easy Coordinator.

The situation will be immediately reviewed and you will be informed promptly of the final resolution of your appeal. If the review supports the previous opinions or decisions, these will be upheld; if not, the prior decision will be modified.

Figure 13–6 Excerpt from CIGNA's Speak Easy Brochure

SOURCE: Excerpt from CIGNA's "Speak Easy" Brochure. Reprinted with permission of the CIGNA Corporation..

ance panel, called the Management Appeals Committee, is asked to resolve a grievance only if solutions have not been found at earlier steps involving, first, the employee's supervisor and, second, the employee relations representative.

The *union grievance procedure* is the appeals procedure used by all employees working under a union contract. Like the grievance panel procedure, it entails multiple steps leading to a final and binding last step with a neutral decision maker called an arbitrator. The union grievance procedure is an important feature of labour contracts, and we will explain it in greater detail in Chapter 15.

Organizations should use a mixture of appeals procedures. For instance, a company might implement an open-door policy to deal with fairly simple problems that can be resolved quickly (such as determining whether an employee violated a safety rule). Next, it might institute an employee assistance program to deal with sensitive problems that involve an employee's privacy (such as a terminal illness). Finally, it might set up a grievance panel to examine complex problems affecting employee relations within a group or organizational unit (such as the definition of a fair production quality standard).

■ Employee Assistance Programs

employee assistance program (EAP)

A company-sponsored program that helps employees cope with personal problems that are interfering with their job performance.

Employee assistance programs (EAPs) help employees cope with personal problems that are interfering with their job performance, such as alcohol or drug abuse, domestic violence, elder care, AIDS and other diseases, eating disorders, and compulsive gambling.[26] Organizations with EAPs publicize the programs to employees and assure them that their problems will be handled with confidentiality. When an employee's personal problem interferes with job performance, the individual is considered a *troubled employee*.[27] In a typical company about 10 percent of the total employee population at any given time is troubled.

Figure 13–7 shows some of the symptoms of a troubled employee. A troubled employee generally behaves inconsistently in terms of attendance, quality of work, attention to detail, and concern for personal appearance. A great deal of the person's energy is devoted to coping with a personal crisis that he or she may want to keep secret from the company. Until the personal problem is resolved, the employee will be in emotional and/or physical pain and the company will be deprived of the full benefit of his or her skills. It is therefore in the interests of both the troubled employee and the employer to resolve the problem.

Four steps are involved in the operation of an EAP (Figure 13–8):

1. The first step is identifying troubled employees and referring them for counselling. About half of all referrals are self-referrals made by employees who realize they are in a crisis and need help, but want to keep their problem confidential. The other half are made by supervisors who observe some of the symptoms of a troubled employee. When job performance is deficient, the EAP referral is usually linked to the company's discipline procedure—it may be the last step taken before the employee is dismissed. Employees have the right to refuse to participate in the EAP, but refusal may mean termination if the problem is having a significant negative impact on work. In fact, though, many employees appreciate the company's willingness to help them through EAP counselling.

2. The second step after referral is a visit with an EAP counsellor, who interviews the employee to help identify the problem. In the case of a complex personal problem like alcohol abuse, employees may strongly deny that it is a problem, insisting rather that the surface problem is merely the symptom of their real problem, such a faltering marriage or an insensitive boss. The counsellor, however, is trained to identify the real problem and arrange for treatment.

1. Excessive absenteeism patterns: Mondays, Fridays, days before and after holidays
2. Unexcused absences
3. Frequent absences
4. Tardiness and early departures
5. Altercations with co-workers
6. Causing other employees injuries through negligence
7. Poor judgement and bad decisions
8. Unusual on-the-job accidents
9. Increased spoilage and breaking of equipment through negligence
10. Involvements with the law—for example, a DWI (driving while intoxicated) conviction
11. Deteriorating personal appearance

Figure 13–7 Symptoms of a Troubled Employee

SOURCE: Adapted from Filipowicz, C. A. (1979). The troubled employee: Whose responsibility? *Personnel Administrator, 24*(6), 8. Reprinted with the permission of *HRMagazine* (formerly *Personnel Administrator*) published by the Society for Human Resource Management, Alexandria, VA.

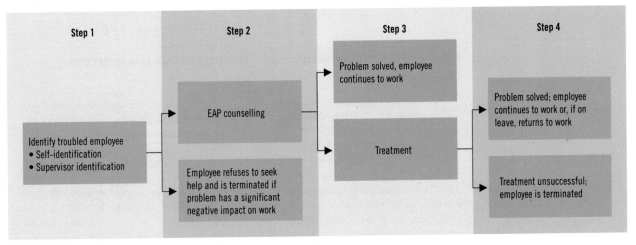

Figure 13–8 An Employee Assistance Program

3. The third step is to solve the problem. Sometimes the EAP counsellor is able to help the employee do this in a short time (three sessions or fewer). For example, an employee in financial difficulty may need only short-term counselling in how to manage personal finances. Some problems, however, take longer to resolve. For these, the EAP counsellor will send the troubled employee to an outside agency equipped to provide the necessary treatment. Because the EAP provides financial assistance for this treatment, the counsellor will try to find a service that best fits the employee's needs and is also cost-effective. For example, an EAP counsellor who determines that an employee needs treatment for alcoholism must decide if the employee should receive inpatient residential treatment, receive outpatient treatment, or attend Alcoholics Anonymous (AA) meetings.[28] Inpatient residential treatment is expensive. The other two alternatives cost much less.

4. The fourth and final step depends on the outcome of the treatment. If the employee has been placed on leave and the treatment has been successful, the employee is allowed to return to work. In some cases, treatment does not require the employee to take a leave of absence; the employee remains on the job while being treated and continues after treatment has been successfully concluded. If the treatment is unsuccessful and the difficulty continues to disrupt the employee's work performance, the employer usually terminates the employee.

EAPs can help employees suffering from the heightened stress resulting from restructuring or downsizing that has arisen in many Canadian companies. Continual downsizing at Labatt Breweries was taking its toll on the survivors: "Symptoms of burnout spread like the flu."[29] Labatt spent an average of $500 per employee on a voluntary course in goal setting and balancing work, family, and personal time. This kind of "wellness program" is much less common than the traditional crisis-driven EAP offered by over half of major Canadian employers. Proactive programs—weight control, smoking cessation, and physical fitness—are offered by perhaps a quarter of all employers, but have increased significantly during the past decade. At Labatt, the wellness initiative helped, but the company also looked at the other side of the equation, reviewing work load and job design. The Issues and Applications feature entitled "Pre-emptive Assistance for Employees in High-Stress Circumstances" takes a look at CIBC's attempts to help employees deal with the demands of managing their own careers, as well as a few examples of other attempts to alleviate a problem in its early stages.

EAPs contribute to effective employee relations because they represent a good-faith attempt by management to support and retain employees who might otherwise be dismissed because of poor performance. The annual cost per employee of an EAP runs about $45 to $60.[30] However, employers gain financial benefits that outweigh their out-of-pocket expenses for EAPs in terms of savings on employee turnover, absenteeism, medical costs, employment insurance rates, workers' compensation rates, accident costs, and disability insurance costs. One study showed that the rate of problem resolution for EAPs is about 78 percent.[31]

Issues and Applications

Pre-emptive Assistance for Employees in High-Stress Circumstances

Each year the Canadian Imperial Bank of Commerce (CIBC) sends thousands of its managers to its leadership training centre for an intensive, week-long self-development course. The 1994 plan involved 4,000 managers with a budget of $11.8 million—roughly $3,000 per person. This happened within the broader context of infrastructure support for employees, which emphasized the manager as coach and the employee as the player responsible for career development. The bank made sure that all jobs were posted internally on E-mail and voice-mail systems, and also devised a complete evaluation system for identifying employee skills. A career guide indicating competencies required for various positions and typical career progressions provided the third leg of the stool on which this employee responsibility initiative was based.

Other employers have taken other approaches. A multimedia company has retained a shiatsu massage therapist to visit and provide massages for employees on the job; a retailer offers lunch-time yoga classes, and another employer facilitates support groups for employees dealing with teenaged children. When it comes to stress-related problems, early intervention is key because stress is cumulative. A divorce or a new assignment may be the trigger that prompts inappropriate and ineffective behaviour. In many cases, however, the event is disruptive because of the broader mix of stresses the individual is experiencing, and the strength or weakness of his or her coping skills—not simply a single traumatic event.

SOURCES: Nolan, C. (1996, March). Stressed to the max: Lending a hand. *Benefits Canada*, 32; Schilder, J. (1994, August). The new Darwinian workplace. *Human Resources Professional*, 9–11.

CIBC
www.cibc.com

■ Employee Recognition Programs

Companies operating in global markets need employees to continuously improve the way they do their jobs so the company can remain competitive. Employees are more likely to share their ideas for work improvements when managers give them credit and recognition for their contributions. **Employee recognition programs** can enhance effective employee relations by communicating to all employees that the organization cares about their ideas and is willing to reward them for their efforts. The HR department can help here by developing and maintaining formal employee recognition programs such as suggestion systems and recognition awards.

employee recognition program
A program that rewards employees for their ideas and contributions.

■ Suggestion Systems

A *suggestion system* is designed to solicit, evaluate, and implement suggestions from employees, and then reward the employees for worthwhile ideas.[32] Although the reward is often monetary, it does not have to be. It might instead be public recognition, extra vacation time, a special parking spot, or some other benefit. Suggestion systems have been successfully introduced in such widely varied environments as hospitals, universities, government, and private-sector companies such as the Royal Bank and Schneider's Corporation, a food products company based in Kitchener, Ontario.

Managers should adhere to three guidelines when designing a suggestion system. They should:

◆ Use a suggestion evaluation committee to evaluate each suggestion fairly and provide a reasonable explanation to employees why their suggestions have been rejected.

◆ Implement accepted suggestions immediately and give credit to the suggestion's originator. The company newsletter can be used to recognize publicly employees whose suggestions have resulted in improvements.

◆ Make the value of the reward proportional to the suggestion's benefit to the company.

Suggestion systems, long a part of U.S. business, have become more popular globally in recent years. For example, Japanese companies have successfully gathered numerous suggestions from their employees, resulting in significant improvements in their products (including automobiles).

■ Recognition Awards

Recognition awards give public credit to people or teams that make outstanding contributions to the organization. These people or teams may become role models for others in the organization by communicating what behaviours and accomplishments the company values. Fast-food giant McDonald's of Canada, like many other service-intensive organizations, has an Employee of the Month Award that is posted for both customers and employees to see. Royal Bank's suggestion system has resulted in modest cash awards in many cases, but has paid as much as $25,000 in response to the value of a particular creative and valuable suggestion.

McDonald's of Canada
www.mcdonalds.com/
surftheworld/north/canada/
index.html

The recognition of teams and people who make important quality contributions is an important component of a total quality management (TQM) program. The recognition awards associated with TQM can be either monetary or non-monetary.

A recognition award can be initiated by a manager or by an internal customer of an individual or a team, with nominees evaluated by a recognition and awards committee. To emphasize that quality improvement should be continuous, there should be no limit on the number of times that a person or team can receive a recognition award.

A recognition award should be a celebration of the team's or individual's success that encourages all organization members to work toward the organization's goals.[33] Recognition awards that focus attention on team or individual accomplishments include:

◆ A company-paid picnic to which all team members and their families are invited.

◆ T-shirts, coffee mugs, or baseball caps with a team insignia encouraging team commitment.

◆ A company-paid night on the town (such as dinner at a nice restaurant or tickets to a concert or sports event) for an employee and his or her spouse.

◆ A plaque engraved with the names of individuals or teams that have made outstanding contributions.

Recognition reward programs can serve purposes other than providing positive feedback to employees. One hotel rewarded employees who made outstanding contributions with a free night's stay at the hotel. Not only was this a valued prize, but it also gave employees the chance to view their organization from the customer's perspective. Management hoped that this experience would prompt new suggestions for improving customer service.

Summary and Conclusions

The Roles of the Manager and the Employee Relations Specialist.
Good employee relations involves providing fair and consistent treatment to all employees so that they will be committed to the organization's goals. The backbone of an effective employee relations program is the manager, who is expected to evaluate, reward, and discipline employees in line with the company's employee relations philosophy. Employee relations representatives from the HR department ensure that employment policies are being fairly and consistently administered within the company. They often consult with both supervisors and employees on specific employee relations problems.

Developing Employee Communications.
To develop effective employee relations, a company needs communication channels to move information up, down, and across the organization. Effective communications in an organization involve (1) a sender who encodes the message, (2) a communication channel that transmits the message, (3) a receiver who decodes the message, and (4) provisions for feedback because noise in the environment may distort the message's true meaning.

Facilitating Effective Communications.
Working with supervisors and managers, employee relations representatives can facilitate effective communications by

developing provisions for (1) information dissemination, (2) employee feedback, and (3) employee assistance programs.

Information dissemination involves making information available to decision makers, wherever they are located. This is especially important in organizations that expect all employees to participate actively in decision making and to make suggestions for quality improvements. Employee handbooks, written communications, audiovisual communications, electronic communications, meetings, and informal communications are some of the choices available for disseminating information to employees.

Employee feedback programs are designed to improve communications by giving employees a voice in decision making and policy formulation and making sure they receive due process on any complaints they make concerning management decisions. Two programs that

the HR department can establish to solicit employee feedback are (1) employee attitude surveys and (2) appeals procedures.

Employee assistance programs are designed to help employees whose emotional or psychological troubles are affecting their work performance. The employee is given the opportunity and resources to resolve the problem. Successful resolution of personal problems benefits both the employer and the employee.

Employee Recognition Programs. Employee recognition programs can enhance communications and employee relations by recognizing and rewarding employees who make important contributions to the organization's success. Recognition programs often use suggestion systems and recognition awards. The rewards given to individuals or teams may be monetary or non-monetary.

Key Terms and Concepts

Discussion Questions

1. List three ways the HR department can contribute to positive employee relations in a company.

2. Employee privacy has been called "the workplace issue of the 1990s." What kinds of dilemmas have the new technologies created regarding employee privacy? What other kinds of problems have the new technologies created in employee relations and communications and how might managers deal with them?

3. Bob Allenby's company handbook states that employees will be fired only if they violate the company's listed reasons for termination. Bob is fired, yet his conduct did not match any of the reasons outlined in the handbook. He has decided to file a lawsuit against his company for wrongful dismissal. Can an employee handbook be considered an employment contract, and if so, is Bob's company liable in this case? What can HR specialists do to protect a company against such lawsuits?

4. What are the advantages and disadvantages of telecommuting employees, from the employer's perspective?

5. Why do employees not take suggestion systems seriously in some companies? What can management do to improve the credibility of its employee suggestion system?

6. Shelly Wexler tells her supervisor, Rob Levine, that having to care for her aging mother is forcing her to leave work early and is making her increasingly "stressed out." While Rob refers her to the company's EAP, he also tries to convince her to put her mother in a home for the aged and even gives her some information about nursing homes in the area. Do you think Rob is just showing ordinary concern for his employee or do you think he is overstepping managerial boundaries? Discuss the supervisor's role in implementing an EAP. Should a supervisor try to diagnose an employee's personal problem? Why or why not?

7. Do you think most employees have reservations about using an appeals procedure such as an open-door policy? What can managers do to convince employees that the available procedures are fair and effective?

Check out our Companion Website at: **www.prenticehall.ca/gomez** for a selection of self-study questions, key terms and concepts, updated Weblinks to related Internet sites, newsgroups, CBC video updates, and more.

MiniCase 1 — *McDougal, Littel & Company: A Publisher Opens Its Books—and Teaches Employees How to Read Them*

Many companies talk about sharing financial information with employees, but McDougal, Littel, a publisher of educational materials, has gone a step further. To help them understand the monthly financial reports it distributes, it sends all of its 300 employees to a day-long accounting class and a customized seminar that explains a year's worth of company financials. And because any kind of training needs to be reinforced, the company holds monthly budget meetings that all 40 managers are required to attend but that are also open to everyone else in the company. "This is to reinforce the notion that the company financials are not a secret," stresses the company's controller.

The financial lessons are paying off. A case in point: When several inventory control managers were preparing a quarterly budget meeting, they grew concerned that the distribution centre was spending $13,000 to store excess inventory in an outside facility, so they devised a way to use their existing warehouse space better by timing the purchasing of materials to keep inventory down. Other payoffs: More sales reps are booking lower air fares by taking advantage of Saturday night stayovers, and customer service reps are questioning expensive priority mail shipments.

Discussion Questions

1. How do you think that sharing financial information affects employer–employee relations at McDougal, Littel?
2. Can you think of situations in which a company should withhold financial information from its employees?
3. Do you think knowledge of the company's financial situation is enough to motivate employees to trim costs? Given what you learned about variable pay plans in Chapter 12, what type of compensation system do you think McDougal, Littel has?

SOURCE: Adapted, by permission of publisher, from Livingston, A. (1993, November). There are no secrets here. *Small Business Report*, 9–13. © 1993. American Management Association, New York. All rights reserved.

MiniCase 2 — *Walking the Talk*

London, Ontario, is home to 3M Canada. The famous multinational corporation, of which 3M Canada is a part, is a $15-billion business that has sustained a remarkable record for consistent profitability. Creativity is important to 3M—one of its self-imposed rules is that 30 percent of annual revenues must come from products that are less than four years old. 3M has devoted much of its resources to bringing out the creative potential in its employees. It is not a matter of simply taking a "made-in-USA" formula and imposing it across the board. Canadian innovations, as well as those from operations elsewhere, have been adopted by the parent company at sites around the globe. A prime example is 3M's new Brockville, Ontario, plant. After more than three years of planning, this tape manufacturing facility features such innovations as shop-floor employees conducting the entire process of employee selection—work values assessment, paper-and-pencil tests for problem-solving ability, and a work-sampling format for team skills assessment—not just interviewing, as is the (innovative) practice at most 3M facilities. This major assignment of responsibility to rank-and-file employees reflects the extensive use of small work teams at this plant, even for staff tasks such as quality control, logistics, scheduling, shipping, and receiving. Work teams at Brockville are given power and responsibil-

➤

ity. Their rewards are pride—and a share of the cost savings their creativity generates.

Discussion Questions

1. This particular innovation was done at a new plant. Do you think it would have been easier or more difficult to make the same changes in an existing facility? What communications issues would have had to be considered at an existing facility?

2. Does 3M have an advantage in launching a program such as the one described here, compared with an employer whose approach in the past has been traditional (innovation assigned to engineers and to R&D)? If this were a new direction for the company, compared with an extension of an established culture, what additional communications challenges would the company face?

3. What importance do you attach to the fact that there were both intrinsic rewards (responsibility, decision-making authority) and extrinsic rewards (a share in the cost savings resulting from employees' work)? How is this a communications issue?

SOURCE: Zeidenberg, J. (1996, June). HR and the innovative company. *Human Resources Professional*, 12, 14–15.

Case 1

Casual Dress at Digital Devices

Digital Devices designs and manufactures custom integrated circuits for electronic consumer products such as pocket pagers, electronic calculators, and cellular phones. Based on the results of an employee attitude survey, the company's top executives decided to implement a casual dress code policy for Digital employees. Management announced the casual dress policy in the employee newsletter and in an e-mail message sent to all employees. The policy stated simply that employees are encouraged to come to work in casual clothes except on days when they have meetings with clients (on those days, appropriate business attire is required).

There are several advantages of casual dress for both the company and employees. Casual dress improves employee morale by reducing status barriers that tend to separate managers (who are likely to wear suits) from nonmanagement personnel. There is likely to be better communication and collaboration throughout the organization when status barriers are reduced. Casual dress is a good recruiting tool for top technical people, who tend to be young engineering graduates who want to work in a progressive company with a "fun" atmosphere. Employees also like that fact that casual dress is more comfortable and saves them money—they don't have to buy more expensive business clothes or use dry cleaning services to main the clothing.

Six months after the casual dress policy was announced, Sharon Greene, Digital's manager of human resources, noticed that the casual dress policy was a mixed blessing. Several unanticipated problems cropped up with employees' misuse of the policy, including the following:

◆ Some employees try to test the limits of casual dress. Computer programmers have come to work in T-shirts displaying their favourite rock groups, such as the Grateful Dead, that many have references to drug use or sexual innuendoes that may offend other employees or clients.

◆ Employees' behaviour has become more casual, and in phone conversations with clients they often refer to customers or prospects as "buddies." This casual style has resulted in some complaints to the sales manager.

◆ The HR department is now referred to as the "fashion police" because it is expected to uphold dress standards when employees wear inappropriate dress (tank tops, bicycle shorts, jeans with holes in them, and so on). This new role has undermined some of HR's credibility.

Greene is now contemplating ways to improve the casual dress policy at Digital Devices.

Critical Thinking Questions

1. Do you think Digital Services should abandon its casual dress policy? Why or why not?

2. Suppose that Digital decides to revise its casual dress policy. Should the revised policy list approved types of clothing and unacceptable types of clothing so that employees know exactly what they can and cannot wear to work? Are there any potential problems with this approach?

3. How should the company communicate the revised casual dress policy to its employees?

Cooperative Learning Exercises

4. The class divides into groups of four or five students each. Each group develops a new casual dress code policy for Digital Devices. One representative of each group presents the group's recommended policy to the class. Other students and the instructor may ask questions or comment on the features of each group's policy.

Case 2

Was the Loader Loaded?

Bill Slater is the operations manager of a distribution centre for a national auto-parts retailer. The distribution centre has 65 employees, mostly inventory clerks, truck loaders, and forklift operators.

Slater suspects that Phil McCoy, one of the truck loaders, has a drinking problem, and he is concerned that this problem could lead to an accident and/or hurt the morale of the other loaders, all of whom work in teams. Slater is considering a confrontation with McCoy before the problem turns into a disaster.

Slater's suspicion about McCoy arose from McCoy's behaviour both at work and off the job. Slater and some of the distribution centre's other employees usually go out for drinks on Fridays after work to celebrate the end of the week. Slater has noticed that McCoy drinks as many as four or five bottles of beer on Fridays, while Slater and the others drink no more than two. McCoy, normally a quiet man, becomes loud and animated at these get-togethers. One Friday night, McCoy made some critical comments about Slater's leadership style, indicating that Slater is not a very good listener.

The incident that convinced Slater he must deal with McCoy immediately happened just yesterday. McCoy had come to work with his hair uncombed and a day's growth of stubble on his face. When Slater greeted McCoy on the loading dock, McCoy's words were so slurred that his response was barely understandable. Later that day, Kathy Jaworski, one of the other loaders on McCoy's loading team, told Slater that she saw at least six empty beer cans in the back seat of McCoy's car as she passed it in the company parking lot that morning.

Critical Thinking Questions

1. Do you think Slater should confront McCoy about his drinking problem? Or should he let it go until something serious happens?
2. How convincing is the evidence that McCoy has a drinking problem?
3. What advice would an employee relations representative be likely to give Slater about handling this problem?

Cooperative Learning Exercises

4. One student plays the role of Slater and another the role of McCoy at a meeting Slater has set up to confront McCoy with the evidence of his drinking problem. The class should evaluate Slater's effectiveness at this meeting. What has he done well? How could his effectiveness in this situation be improved?
5. One student plays Slater and another an employee relations representative to whom Slater has gone for advice about how to handle the situation described in the case. What specific advice would be appropriate in this situation?

14

Respecting Employee Rights and Managing Discipline

After reading this chapter, you should be able to deal more effectively with the following challenges:

1 Understand the origins and the scope of employee rights and management rights.

2 Explain why the HR department must balance management's rights and employees' rights when designing employment policies.

3 Understand the master-servant relationship and distinguish it from employment at will.

4 Distinguish between progressive discipline procedures and positive discipline procedures.

5 Apply fair standards to a case of employee misconduct and justify the use of discipline.

6 Manage difficult people who challenge their supervisors with such problems as poor attendance, low performance, insubordination, and substance abuse.

7 Avoid disciplinary actions by taking a proactive and strategic approach to human resource management.

A Problem Employee?
Managers need to be trained to recognize the symptoms of troubled employees and potential disciplinary problems. In addition to dealing with drug- and alcohol-related problems in the workplace, managers must often confront employees who exhibit poor attendance, insubordination, or poor performance.

All employees have rights that are based on laws, company employment policies, and traditions. These rights lead to expectations about how managers should treat workers. Employers also have rights that support their authority and what they can expect from their employees. Sometimes these two sets of rights conflict. For example, an employer's right to ensure high-quality service for its customers by listening in on telephone conversations between customers and customer service representatives may conflict with employees' perceived rights to privacy.

Also consider the following situations:

◆ A collective agreement gave an employer leave to grant "other leave with pay" at the employer's discretion. Several Jewish employees grieved the employer's refusal to grant such leave for absence on the holy days Rosh Hashanah and Yom Kippur on the basis that the contract also had a "no discrimination article." The employer did allow the employees to be absent with pay, but charged the time against vacation entitlements. The grievance was resolved at arbitration, in favour of the employer.

◆ Weavexx, a British Columbia company, recruited a top-notch salesman who had a history—not uncommon in the industry—of moving from company to company. Concerned that he might quit his job, they asked him to make a commitment until retirement, which he did. After five months on the job, the employer concluded that the arrangement was not working out and let the salesman go. After several months of unemployment, the employee found another position elsewhere at lower pay. Because of the terms of his hiring, he received a "wrongful hiring" settlement of some 11 years' compensation, in excess of $400,000.[1]

◆ GM Canada has extended Awareline, a program already in use in U.S. operations in Canada. Awareline—a program staffed on contract by non-GM employees (to preserve confidentiality) that allows employees to report anonymously concerns of potential criminal wrongdoing by company management, supervisors, or employees—has met intense opposition from the Canadian Auto Workers (CAW). Buzz Hargrove, CAW president, characterizes this as an attempt to turn workers against each other and "... reveals an insulting attitude to the work we do, and an arrogant disregard for the problems workers face."[2]

These examples illustrate the potential conflict between an employer's priorities and employees' expectations about the limits of their obligations to their employer and what the employer "owes" them. The HR department can help here by (1) developing and enforcing policies that inform employees of their rights and responsibilities and (2) making managers aware of their employees' rights and managers' obligations to employees. But it is the manager who is on the front line. Managers who respect employees' rights are more likely to have subordinates with higher levels of morale and job satisfaction than managers who ignore these rights. Besides being good management practice, respecting employees' rights also lessens the likelihood of a costly grievance procedure or lawsuit.

In this chapter, we examine employee rights and employee discipline. These two issues are closely related to the quality of employee relations (discussed in the previous chapter). Organizations with effective employee relations ensure that their managers respect employees' rights and use fair and consistent discipline procedures.

First, we examine the concepts of employee rights, management rights, and the master-servant relationship that governs non-unionized employment. Second, we explore some challenges that managers encounter in balancing employee rights with their own rights and duties. Next, we discuss employee discipline and offer some suggestions for managing difficult employees. We conclude by examining how the HR department can support managers with proactive policies that minimize the need for disciplinary procedures.

■ Employee Rights

right

The ability to engage in conduct that is protected by law or social sanction free from interference by another party.

A **right** is the ability to engage in conduct that is protected by law or social sanction free from interference by another party, such as an employer. For example, employees have the legal right to form a union with co-workers. It is illegal for an employer to discourage employees from exercising their right to form a union by withholding pay increases from those who support the union.

The extent of legally grounded *employee rights* has increased substantially over the past two decades, particularly in the area of protection from discriminatory employer behaviour. In addition to changes in legislation, court decisions have broadened and refined the common law protections in such matters as wrongful dismissal.

The notion of individual rights in Canada has been heightened since the patriation of the Constitution in 1982, which included a *Charter of Rights and Freedoms,* the employment effects of which have been strongest in public-sector employment. Until the enactment of the *Charter,* the foundation for legal rights of individual Canadians was the common law—the accumulated precedents of the courts. This arrangement contrasts quite sharply with the United States, where the *Bill of Rights*—the first 10 amendments to the U.S. Constitution—explicitly defined the rights of (U.S.) citizens and shaped a political culture in which much public discourse invokes the language of "rights."

It is important to be sensitive to differences in usage of the term "rights" in the employment context. Figure 14–1 groups rights into three categories about which managers should be knowledgeable: statutory rights, contractual rights, and other rights.

■ Statutory Rights

statutory right

A right established by legislation.

Some employee rights, called **statutory rights,** derive from specific legislation. Employees are protected by human rights codes against unfair discrimination in employment based on sex, age, race, religion, and other grounds. In some jurisdictions, women, visible minorities, aboriginal people, and people with disabilities have the additional expectation that employers will initiate proactive policies to ensure that these groups receive full consideration in hiring, promotion, and other HR decisions. Pay equity legislation requires employers to take steps to redress inequitable payment of women compared with men. (Refer to Chapters 3 and 4.)

Another area in which employees have legally defined rights is protection from unsafe or unhealthy working conditions. Not only are employers obliged by omnibus health and safety legislation (as well as a great variety of industry-specific legislation) to provide a safe work environment; the law in most jurisdictions allows employees to refuse unsafe work without retribution from the employer (see Chapter 16).

Statutory Rights	Contractual Rights	Other Rights
◆ Protection from discrimination	◆ Employment contract	◆ Ethical treatment
◆ Safe working conditions	◆ Union contract	◆ Privacy (limited)
◆ Right to form unions	◆ Implied contracts/ employment policies	◆ Free speech (limited)

Figure 14–1 Categories of Employee Rights

Employees in most employment settings have the right to organize and join a union. Labour relations legislation in Canada compels employers to allow employees to engage in such activities without being subject to penalty or harassment. (See Chapter 15.) Labour Relations Boards, by defining what are and are not fair labour practices, regulate the behaviour of employers and employees during the organizing period, in bargaining, and in disputes over the interpretation of collective agreements.

Canada Labour Relations Board
home.istar.ca/~clrbccrt

■ Contractual Rights

As the term implies, **contractual rights** are based on the law of contracts. A **contract** is a legally binding agreement or promise between two or more competent parties.[3] A breach of contract, in which one of the parties does not comply with the terms of the agreement, is subject to legal remedy.

Both employers and employees have rights and obligations to each other when they enter into a contract. An **employment contract** spells out in explicit detail the terms of the employment relationship for both the employee and the employer. In general, such contracts state that the employee is expected to work competently over a stipulated period of time and that the employer is expected to provide a mutually agreed upon amount of pay, as well as specific working conditions for the employee, over this time period. At one time, very few people had explicit, written employment contracts. Professional athletes, authors, actors, and a few others fell into this category. In recent years there has been a significant increase in contract work. Some senior managers work on a contract basis that may include elaborate compensation and termination provisions. Large numbers of more junior employees are also being hired on written contracts, which typically specify the length of employment period. Fixed-term contracts are especially attractive to employers because they do not obligate to provide them ongoing employment; no financial obligations continue beyond the term of the contract. Contracts can be renewed by mutual agreement, and contract employees sometimes work for an employer on consecutive contracts for an extended period. However, employers who wish to avoid commitments to a full-time work force, and therefore renew employment contracts repeatedly, will often find that government agencies deem these people effectively to be employees and will impose the obligations on employers (notice of termination, employee benefits) that they would have with regular employees.

The provisions of the employment contract afford the employee a right to job security and are, at least theoretically, negotiated individually. We say "theoretically" because there are cases in which contracts are so similar as to be standard. For some high-profile jobs, such as top-level executives, the contract will not follow the standard pattern and will, in fact, be negotiated individually. An employee under contract may be fired for reasons other than non-performance, but he or she is then entitled to compensation for the life of the contract. For executives, this typically amounts to several years of pay and benefits.

A significant percentage of employees in the Canadian labour force (around 37 percent of non-agricultural workers) are covered by *union contracts*, which protect groups of unionized workers. Union contracts do not provide as much job security for workers as individually negotiated employment contracts do, but they do provide some job security through the recognition of seniority and union grievance procedures. Seniority provisions protect the jobs of the most senior workers through the "last in, first out" layoff criterion that is commonly written into the union contract (see Chapter 6). Union grievance procedures subject all disciplinary actions (including dismissal) to **due process,** which requires a fair investigation and a showing of just cause to discipline an employee who has not performed according to expectations. An arbitrator who is empowered to decide discipline and rights cases can restore the job rights and back pay of an employee who has made a claim of **wrongful dismissal** (dismissal for reasons that are either illegal or contrary to the contract).

contractual right

A right based on the law of contracts.

contract

A legally binding promise between two or more competent parties. Breach of contract is subject to legal remedy.

employment contract

A contract that spells out in explicit detail the terms of the employment relationship for both employee and employer.

due process

Equal and fair application of a policy or law.

wrongful dismissal

Termination of an employee for reasons that are either illegal or contrary to the contract.

Not all contracts are written. If two parties mutually agree to terms, even if they are spoken and not written, a formal contract may exist. Obviously, it is better and clearer to have written agreements—misunderstandings are much less unlikely, and disputes can be resolved with less energy. A mutual understanding of the kind described here means that the parties have entered an *implied contract*. Comments from a manager to an employee at the time of hiring such as, "So long as you do your work well, you'll have a job here," have been treated as increasing an employer's obligation to provide job security.

Employee handbooks can be another source of implied employment contracts if they offer job security. In addition, when an employee handbook or employment policy makes a distinction between "probationary" and "permanent" employees, the courts have held that employers are promising continued employment to workers who successfully complete the probationary period and become permanent employees.

■ Other Rights

Some "rights" have little or no legal foundation, but still play a significant role in the employment relationship. The notion of what is fair is one that has been very important in shaping legal frameworks for employment (see Chapter 3). But the idea of what is fair has an influence beyond simply those specifics included in statutes. Employment is one of the most important relationships in the lives of adults, and employees' behaviour is influenced by whether they see themselves as being treated fairly. Employees often believe they have certain rights, and react negatively when employers appear to violate those rights.

As we saw in Chapter 12, the employment relationship involves considerably more than simple wages or a salary in exchange for a certain number of hours of unthinking compliance with the boss's orders. Organizations are looking for more—creativity, commitment, teamwork, problem solving, the assumption of responsibility. Employees are looking for more, as well, including being treated fairly and with respect.

These elaborate employment relationships are governed by what can be thought of as a *psychological contract*—a mutually understood and accepted set of expectations that employers and employees have of each other. Employers who meet the "terms" of the contract are more likely to find that their employees are willing to fulfill employer expectations. In contrast, employers who violate the terms of the contract often find that their employees consider themselves no longer obligated to do the extra things that are key to making an organization work well. Whether people quit, look to unionization for protection, or simply refuse to expend the extra energy, the result of violating implicit employee rights can be damaging.

Ethical conduct builds employee trust and confidence—knowing the values and standards that shape decisions lets people "buy in" because management has committed itself. One way of sealing the psychological contract as it applies to ethical issues is to develop and publicize a code of ethics. The Issues and Applications feature entitled "Ethics—More Than Skin Deep" sketches a variation of the notion of a formal code, one that has been remarkably influential.

Managers and supervisors can influence their companies' climate of fairness and ethical behaviour by the tone they set for employees in their work units. Specifically, managers and supervisors should:

◆ Take actions that develop trust, such as sharing useful information and making good on commitments.

◆ Act consistently so that employees are not surprised by unexpected management actions or decisions.

◆ Be truthful and avoid white lies and actions designed to manipulate others by giving a certain (false) impression.

◆ Demonstrate integrity by keeping confidences and showing concern for others.

◆ Meet with employees to discuss and define what is expected of them.

◆ Ensure that employees are treated equitably, giving equivalent rewards for similar performance and avoiding actual or apparent special treatment of favourites.

◆ Adhere to clear standards that are seen as just and reasonable—for example, neither praising accomplishments out of proportion nor imposing penalties disproportionate to offences.

◆ Demonstrate respect toward employees, showing openly that they really care about employees and recognize their strengths and contributions.[4]

Privacy. Certain aspects of employee privacy are subject to legislation. For example, the widespread use of computerized databanks raised sufficient

Issues and Applications

Ethics—More Than Skin Deep

The Body Shop is recognized as being a leader in raising issues of ethics in business. Employers have taken a wide range of approaches to establishing ethical standards—some emphasize codes while others include ethical dimensions in performance appraisals. What has been discovered is that, regardless of implementation, ethics are not an added program or policy, but rather must permeate the organization's culture. The following sketch of the Body Shop provides a sense of what that can mean.

There's an expression often heard at the offices of Body Shop Canada: Dig deep into the obvious. It explains perfectly how the company keeps its ethical environment alive, says President Margot Franssen. Create a workplace that cares about your employees; they will in turn take care of the company, Franssen explains simply. "They'll make sure that what they do reflects well on the company." An interna-

tional retail phenomenon recognized for its ethical philosophy and practices and its commitment to social and environmental issues, [one of] the Body Shop's most recent awareness and fundraising campaign[s] was entitled "In the Name of Love—Stop the Violence Against Women Now."

According to Sean Quinn, head of the Body Shop's Social Inventions Department, "We [the Body Shop] can have sales of $100 million while taking a stand on animal testing, human rights protection, and environmental conservation, the three main criteria against which all our activities are measured. This success demonstrates that profits can be made and principles maintained."

SOURCES: Goodson, L. (1996, February/March). Doing the right thing. *Human Resources Professional,* 21–22; McCallum, T. (1994, October). Taking the high road. *Human Resources Professional,* 21–23.

concern about the use of Social Insurance Numbers (SINs) as employee ID numbers that the practice is now prohibited. This prohibition seeks to limit the ways in which personal information provided for income tax or CPP purposes might be combined with other data. Employers are also limited in the kinds of personal information they can collect from applicants and employees with respect to matters that may compromise human rights protection (see Chapter 3). The civil courts also offer recourse for a former employee who is defamed by a previous employer who is providing a reference. This possibility has led many employers, when asked for a reference, to provide only the barest confirmation of employment dates and positions held—effectively increasing the individual's privacy.

However, there are many privacy issues where what is legal may exceed what many employees find to be acceptable. For example, it is legally permissible for the employer to search employees' worksite premises, including going through an employee's E-mail directories and inspecting the contents of lockers and filing cabinets. Many employees would feel angry and violated by such legal acts, unless a clear case had been made for the necessity of such practices. For employees who deal with highly valuable products (large amounts of cash, jewellery, negotiable securities) or with highly sensitive information, the presence of controls, inspections, background checks and so forth make sense and are easily accepted. On the other hand, closed-circuit cameras trained on washroom doors to determine the frequency and duration of time away from work or unannounced supervisory eavesdropping on phone conversations are (actual) examples that have proven much harder to defend as reasonable. In general, personal privacy should be respected unless there is compelling reason to intrude.

Freedom of Expression. As citizens, Canadians have broad freedom of expression. As employees, some limits exist. Every employee has a *fiduciary duty* to the

Subject to Search.
In an attempt to reduce theft and enhance employee safety, some employers actively assert their right to inspect lockers and other areas as a deterrent to illicit activities.

employer, an obligation that implies loyalty and avoiding conflicts of interest. There is a potential tension between the role of citizen in a democracy and the role of employee in a hierarchical organization. For example, you might have strong convictions about the damage caused by urban sprawl, but find yourself working for an organization that has decided to take a "cheap land and tax holiday" package from an outlying suburb rather than enlarge and refurbish their current city location. While as a citizen you can speak up in many forums, there are very few hard and fast rules that govern how vocal you—the employee—can be, inside or outside the organization, about your convictions as they apply to your employer's relocation plans.

It is legal to discipline an employee—and dismiss him or her in the most serious cases—for acts that negatively affect the operation, reputation, or management of the organization. The reasons for such discipline may include not only what an employee does (dishonesty, careless work, safety infractions, etc.), but also what a person writes or says. As we saw in the Chapter 13, effective human resource practices include mechanisms that give employees a legitimate way to voice their views, such as "speak-up" programs, suggestion systems, and employee surveys. The likelihood that employees will use unacceptable ways to express criticism is reduced when there are legitimate means available to them. However, employees—particularly those whose jobs include representing the organization to customers, suppliers, or the media—do have a responsibility to not act in a way that damages the organization.

Some groups of employees, such as unionized workers or civil servants, can use grievance or appeal procedures to protect themselves from arbitrary or disproportionate disciplinary actions. In other settings the limits to such discipline are set mainly by the judgement and integrity of the management involved—the principal exceptions being human rights infractions or wrongful dismissal litigation.

Employers need to strike a balance in issues of privacy and freedom of expression. It is naive to ignore the potential damage that dishonest or thoughtless employees can cause by compromising the organization's interests. Control of sensitive information and discipline for unacceptable behaviour make sense. However, policies and practices that communicate distrust and violate employees' personal dignity can undermine the employment relationship. Employees who "do the right thing" because they believe in it rather than because they fear punishment for infractions contribute more—and they require much less "policing."

■ Management Rights

The rights of the employer, usually called **management rights,** can be summed up as the right to run the business and to retain any profits that result. In Canada, management rights are supported by property laws, common law, and the values of a capitalistic society that accepts the concepts of private enterprise and the profit motive.[5] The shareholders and owners who control a firm through their property rights delegate to managers the authority to run the business.

Management rights include the right to manage the work force and the rights to hire, promote, assign, discipline, and dismiss employees. Management's right to direct the work force is moderated by the right of employees (at least those who have not signed an employment contract) to quit their jobs at any time. Thus it is in management's interest to treat employees fairly.

Management rights are influenced by the rights of groups who have an interest in decisions made in the workplace. For example, managers have the right to hire the employees they wish to hire, but this right is affected by human rights legislation that prevents the employer from discriminating on the basis of certain applicant characteristics (age, race, sex, and so on). Further, managers have the right to set pay levels for their employees, but the presence of a union labour contract with a pay provision requires managers to pay employees according to the contract's terms.

Management rights are often termed *residual rights* because they consist of the remaining rights that are not affected by contracts or laws that represent the interests of employees or other parties (such as a union).[6] According to the residual rights perspective, managers have the right to make decisions that affect the business and the work force except where limited by laws or contract provisions.

■ Master-Servant Relationship

As we saw in Chapter 3, the common law backdrop for employment in Canada is the **master-servant relationship.** The essence of this legal doctrine is that, in the absence of a formal contract specifying a particular term of employment, employment is an ongoing relationship. This is not to suggest that employment is seen as a permanent (lifetime) arrangement, but rather that an employer wishing to dismiss an employee is obliged to provide the employee with reasonable notice of termination. (Employers who wish an employee to leave immediately may provide pay for the notice period in lieu of notice.) As we have seen in Chapter 6, employment standards legislation requires certain minimum notification periods, depending on the length of service. Longer notice periods are also required by statute when large numbers of employees are being laid off or dismissed within a short period of time. However, these statutory minimum notices (or "payments in lieu") are often shorter than the courts would prescribe under master-servant common law when employees lose their jobs through wrongful dismissal.

> **master-servant relationship**
> A common law doctrine that specifies the obligations between employer and employee.

Wrongful Dismissal.   If an employer terminates the employment relationship in the absence of a formal employment contract or a collective agreement, the termination can be either "for cause" or it is legally construed to be a "wrongful dismissal." The difference can be significant: an employee dismissed for cause is not entitled to any payments beyond the point at which he or she is informed of the dismissal, while employees wrongfully dismissed are entitled to substantial monetary benefits.

Dismissing an employee for cause is possible, but "cause" is not easily established. The legal standard of proof that must be met is, as in other civil cases, "the balance of probabilities." This is an easier standard than "beyond a reasonable doubt," which is required for convictions on criminal charges. But the onus is still on the employer to make the case. The following behaviours are generally considered to constitute cause:[7]

◆ Fraud, dishonesty, forgery, assault or other serious offence occurring in the course of employment.

◆ Gross insubordination, refusal to obey (legal) orders of superiors, excessive absenteeism.

◆ Persistent and demonstrable poor performance.

According to a comprehensive study of wrongful dismissal suits in Canada, misconduct was claimed by the employer in roughly two-thirds of the cases and incompetence in the other third. Employers succeeded about 40 percent of the time when they claimed dishonesty, theft, and "frailty of character"—substance abuse; abusive behaviour toward co-workers, customers and the public; and off-duty conduct. Employers succeeded 54 percent of the time when the issue was insubordination, and 65 percent when the issue was conflict of interest or competing with the employer. Poor performance is often the reason employers would like to invoke more frequently. The fact that they don't may result from the fact that the success rate for this basis for dismissal is only about 25 percent.[8] In order to substantiate in court that poor performance is the basis (cause) for dismissal, an employer must be able to demonstrate:

1. that the performance problems have been documented and have been brought to the attention of the employee (usually through a documented performance appraisal),

2. that the employee has been given the opportunity to improve, and

3. that, after a reasonable period of time, the performance problems have not been rectified.

If there is an indication that the pattern of performance has persisted over a long period with no documented record of communicating the unacceptability to the employee, the employer will be seen as having condoned this level of performance, and will find it difficult to establish cause. This combination of needing to act quickly in response to poor performance, needing to communicate and provide the opportunity for improvement, and needing to be able to document these circumstances has led to relatively few dismissals for cause where cause was poor performance.

The amount of notice (or payment in lieu of notice) a former employee can be awarded for wrongful dismissal varies with a number of factors, primarily the employee's age, length of service, level of position, degree of specialization, probable difficulty in securing a similar position, and level of compensation.[9] In general, higher levels of any of those criteria (other factors being equal) will result in higher awards. Many wrongful dismissal suits do not go to court because lawyers for the employer and the dismissed employee can negotiate a settlement, knowing the likely court outcomes well enough to avoid incurring court costs. Figure 14–2 provides examples of negotiated wrongful dismissal settlements.

Constructive Dismissal. Under the master-servant common law doctrine, employers cannot *unilaterally* change an employee's job responsibilities and authority in a way that repudiates the contract between employer and employee. To do so may result in what is called *constructive dismissal.* An employee upon whom such changes have been forced can, under certain circumstances, sue the employer for a form of wrongful dismissal. The employee must be able to demonstrate:[10]

1. that there has been a fundamental alteration of the terms of the employment contract,

2. that the alteration is sufficient to imply the employer's intention to repudiate the contract,

3. that the alteration can be established objectively (and not only in the perception of the employee), and

4. that some employer-initiated alterations are possible without triggering a finding of "constructive dismissal."

A case that was resolved in an Alberta court in 1992 (*Wilkinson v. T. Eaton Company*) provides an illustration of constructive dismissal. The employee had worked for a long period (1949–90) as a secretary. In 1990, she was advised that she would be required to work on the sales floor full time. She had advised her manager numerous times that she would feel ill at ease dealing with people in a sales situation. She refused the sales position, left the organization, and was successful in her suit for constructive dismissal. At one time, an employee suing for constructive dismissal was advised to quit, and then sue, in order to avoid the appearance of condoning the change. Since 1989, court precedents indicate that employees may have an obligation to remain in the new position to mitigate the damages involved unless the salary has been changed, the working conditions are substantially different, the work is demeaning, or if there are personally acrimonious relationships. The secretary in this case was not obliged to accept the new assignment, even temporarily, because the court determined that she should not be compelled to do something of which she was incapable.[11]

Formal contracts and collective agreements provide slightly different contexts for termination. A *formal employment contract* usually specifies a term of employment, makes some provisions for procedures if either party wants to terminate the arrangement before the end of the term, and may provide a process for renewing or extending the contract. One issue that is sometimes part of formal contracts for senior management or professional employees is a restraint on their ability to work for a competitor or to go into direct competition with the employer,

Position	Age	Length of Service (Years)	Annual Salary	Length of Severance (Months)	Method of Payment
Senior Executives					
President	45	13	$400,000	24	Lump
President	53	8	$250,000	18	Salary Cont'd*
Sr. Vice-President	53	28	$250,000	18	Salary Cont'd
Exec. Vice-President	51	30	$260,000	36	Lump
Vice-President, Finance	37	8	$160,000	15	Lump
General Manager	52	16	$108,000	12	Lump
Chief Operating Officer	48	6	$95,000	12	Lump
General Manager	55	12	$90,000	16	Salary Cont'd
Senior Management					
Executive Director	45	1	$86,000	6	Salary Cont'd
Vice-President, Sales	43	22	$84,000	13	Lump
Director, Human Resources	37	13	$81,500	18	Lump
Corporate Controller	48	7	$75,000	9	Salary Cont'd
Director, Info. Systems	52	3.5	$70,000	9	Lump
Project Manager	33	10	$70,000	8	Lump
Director, Underwriting	46	29	$68,000	13	Lump
Director, Marketing Sales	57	7	$65,000	7	Lump
Middle Management					
Manager, Technical Services	42	11	$61,500	1	Salary Cont'd
Manager, Corporate Affairs	44	3	$60,000	4	Lump
Maintenance Manager	43	7	$58,000	4	Lump
Nurse Manager	49	3	$56,000	6	Salary Cont'd
Store Manager	46	21	$53,000	12	Lump
Credit Manager	52	17	$51,500	10	Salary Cont'd
Manager, Administration	53	30	$50,000	19	Salary Cont'd
Manager, Training	40	2	$45,600	3	Lump
Supervisory/Technical					
Sales Representative	42	21	$38,500	18	Salary Cont'd
Supervisor, Customer Service	46	18	$37,500	12	Salary Cont'd
Accounting Supervisor	43	3	$37,000	4	Lump
Programmer/Analyst	32	3	$36,500	3	Lump
Production Scheduler	51	11	$34,000	9	Lump
Supervisor, Quality Assurance	33	13	$32,500	9	Lump
Benefits Supervisor	28	10	$31,000	7	Lump
Clerical/Administrative Non-Union Hourly					
Traffic Coordinator	36	13	$29,200	8	Lump
Secretary	38	10	$29,300	5	Lump
Janitor	53	16	$26,600	8	Lump
Distribution Clerk	28	3	$25,100	4	Lump
Shipper	30	5	$25,000	4	Lump
Accounts Receivable Clerk	23	3	$24,500	2	Lump
Customer Service Rep	46	23	$23,000	15	Lump
Computer Operator	33	1	$22,500	2	Lump
Professionals/Other					
Partner, Audit	37	16	$114,000	9	Salary Cont'd
Law Partner	54	27	$100,000	24	Lump
Medical Doctor	53	22	$98,000	12	Lump
Pilot	49	17	$83,000	12	Lump
Nurse	58	24	$65,000	15	Salary Cont'd
Architect	35	6	$60,000	4	Salary Cont'd
Consultant	48	4	$60,000	4	Salary Cont'd
Priest	50	24	$18,000	6	Salary Cont'd

*Settlement paid at same rate as if the employee were still on the job.

SOURCE: Bullock, Kathy M. (1994). Termination of employment, Table 75-2. *Human Resources Management in Canada.* (pp. 75, 023–75, 024). Copyright Carswell Thomson Professional Publishing.

Figure 14–2 Examples of Severances Offered and Accepted by Terminated Employees

even if they have left the initial employer. The strength of the legal force of this fiduciary obligation is determined by:

1. whether the employee held a key executive position in the business,

2. whether the employee's decision-making powers made the employer's business vulnerable to the employee's discretion, and

3. how "specific" and how "ripe" was the employee's opportunity that was usurped for his/her own benefit.[12]

Collective agreements may have a wide variety of job-security and layoff procedures, as well as grievance mechanisms for testing justification of termination or other punitive measures an employer wants to impose. The remedies for dismissal without cause available under collective agreements are more extensive than the remedies under master-servant common law. Wrongful dismissal under common law can result in financial compensation for the employee, but other remedies are not available. Collective agreements, in contrast, are enforced through a grievance arbitration process. An arbitrator making a finding of dismissal without just cause can impose a financial settlement and can also order such remedies as letters of recommendation or apology and the reinstatement of an employee in his or her job.[13]

Other National Jurisdictions.   The common law doctrine that has formed the legal backdrop for employment in the United States is *employment at will.* This legal concept was introduced as an attempt to put employer and employee on an equal footing: since there was little to prevent an employee from leaving with scant or no notice, employment at will allowed employers to terminate employment at any time for any cause. In reality, this arrangement did not create a level playing field: an employer letting an employee go without notice generally has much more impact on an employee than an employee who quits abruptly has on the employer. Employment at will is still used, but the doctrine has been tempered by U.S. court decisions at the state level, especially over the past 10 years. These decisions, although varied, have limited employer options for three types of reasons: public policy exceptions (such as an employee refusing to violate professional ethics or filing a legitimate claim such as workers' compensation against the employer); situations in which there were judged to be implied contracts; and situations where the courts have found a lack of good faith or fair dealing on the part of the employer. The effect of such rulings is to move the overall standard slightly in the direction of the master-servant doctrine. Whatever the differences between Canada and the United States, it is possible to terminate an employee in either jurisdiction, although the costs may be greater in Canada. In Japan and in some European countries, it is very difficult to dismiss an employee, even when the case is clear. For example, a multinational pharmaceutical company with operations in Sweden wanted to fire an alcoholic employee who had not responded to treatment programs and other company-paid assistance. It took two years to get the man off the payroll, during which time he came to work drunk, was often incoherent, and annoyed co-workers. In some other European jurisdictions, the only allowed basis for immediate dismissal is criminal behaviour.[14]

■ Employee Rights Challenges: A Balancing Act

Three workplace issues are particularly challenging to managers and HR professionals because they involve balancing the legitimate, but competing interests of employers and employees. The issues are: (1) random drug testing, (2) electronic monitoring, and (3) whistleblowing.

■ Random Drug Testing

The practice of random drug testing pits management's obligation to protect the safety of employees and customers against an employee's expectation that his or her privacy will be respected. *Random drug testing* screens employees for indications of drug use, without suspicion or cause. In that sense it is like the police radar unit parked beside the highway—the assessment is made unexpectedly and the fact that it exists is intended to be a deterrent. Random drug testing typically involves the analysis of a urine specimen provided by the employee.

The use of drug testing for employee selection decisions was discussed in Chapter 5, and many of the general observations made there about employee drug testing also apply to the testing of current employees. However, there are three issues about drug testing of current employees, when legally permitted, that deserve attention.

1. If drug testing is used, should it be done randomly, or only when there is reason to believe that a problem may exist? Random testing has the advantage of being impersonal, and therefore may be easier for employees to accept—"it's not me they suspect, it's just that 'my number came up'." However, for random testing to be accepted as legitimate, the rationale for testing at all must be articulated so that the need is clear. If employees aren't convinced that a completely drug-free work force is essential to organizational performance and safety, they may well resent the intrusiveness of random testing. The risk with testing only where there are reasons for concern is that singling someone out for testing can be perceived as—and may sometimes be—a form of supervisory harassment.

2. If the rationale for testing is based mostly on concern for safety, should all employees be subject to random testing, or should testing be limited to those in safety-sensitive positions? How an employer handles this issue refers back to the first question. An argument for drug testing made on the basis of safety is more likely to be accepted if the employees subject to testing occupy demonstrably high-risk occupations. Only a broader rationale would support testing throughout the entire work force.

3. Is testing required as a basis for being "in business"? For organizations that support amateur athletes in international competition, there is no question about the requirement for elaborate testing regimes for athletes. In more mundane enterprises—for example, long-distance trucking—Canadian trucking firms are indirectly required to test drivers who drive loads into the United States, where such testing has become mandatory.

Designing a random drug-testing policy poses numerous challenges. HR professionals can assist managers in dealing with these issues. For example:

◆ How should employees who test positive be treated? Some jurisdictions, such as Ontario and the federal jurisdiction, have defined dependence on alcohol or other drugs to be a disability. Therefore, taking immediate disciplinary action based on a positive test is deemed to be unfair discrimination. Where such laws pertain, an employer must provide opportunity for the employee to stop using the substance—and should also consider support strategies such as those provided by EAPs. If, after given such an opportunity to improve, an employee fails to show results, only then can discipline or dismissal be considered legal options.

◆ Sometimes drug-testing procedures generate a false-positive outcome. If an employee tests positive for a legitimate reason, such as using a prescription drug, how can the employer ensure that the employee is not charged with using illegal drugs? How can an employer protect employees from false positives in general?

◆ What can managers do to maintain security over urine specimens provided for the drug test so that they are free from adulteration designed to alter the results without violating the employee's privacy rights?

Drug testing via urinalysis has limitations as a technique to ensure safety that are particularly important. First, a positive test is not an indication of impairment at the time the specimen is provided—the metabolites that are detected may be the residue of substances that entered the person's body days or even weeks ago. Second, the time required to process the specimens does not allow taking someone off the job on the spot. (Alcohol breath tests are not subject to these limitations.)

Fortunately, there is an alternative to drug testing that shows promise as a means to determine whether an individual is impaired. Performance tests that score reaction time, visual judgement and hand-eye coordination have been developed that allow an employer to tell whether an employee is physically capable of doing his or her job—quickly (within a matter of a few minutes), accurately, and at low cost.[15] These tests are, in essence, specially designed computer games. Some employers use them as a required start-of-shift procedure. Their strengths are speed and their non-intrusive nature. In addition, they identify impairment that may be caused by other conditions, such as illness or fatigue.

■ Electronic Monitoring

Some estimates indicate that the cost of employee theft, including cash, inventory, and fixed assets, is $20 billion per year.[16] Management consultant KPMG conducts regular surveys of companies to ask about their experience with fraud. Typically, slightly over half the organizations report that they have been defrauded during the previous year. In 1998, the average loss per organization was $1.3 million— and some 55 percent of the frauds reported were attributed to managers and employees of the organization. Typically, frauds involving non-managerial employees occur in such areas as expense account claims, petty cash, and kickbacks. Managers involved in fraud are more likely to have been engaged in conflicts of interest and phantom vendor schemes. Fraud is not a uniquely Canadian problem: one British study suggested that corporate theft in the United Kingdom has reached a level that is equal to doubling the corporate tax rate, while in the United States employee theft represents an annual loss estimated to be between (US)$40 billion and (US)$200 billion.[17]

Companies are attempting to fight these various forms of theft by using electronic surveillance devices to monitor their employees. To eavesdrop on employees, they use hidden microphones and transmitters attached to telephones and tiny fish-eye video lenses installed behind pinholes in walls and ceilings. Many companies also peek at their employees' E-mail or listen to their voice-mail messages. In a survey published by *Macworld* magazine, over 21 percent of respondents said they have "engaged in searches of employee computer files, voice mail, electronic mail or other networking communications." Most said they were monitoring work flow or investigating thefts or espionage.[18]

The increased sophistication of computer and telephone technology now makes it possible for employers to use electronic means for tracking employee job performance—for example, to count the number of keystrokes an employee makes on a computer terminal or determine how many reservations a travel agent books in a given time period.[19] This more pervasive use of electronic monitoring has raised concerns not only about employee privacy but also about the dehumanizing effect that such relentless monitoring can have on employees. Many employees whose work is being tracked electronically feel that monitoring takes the human element out of their work and causes too much stress. One recent study comparing monitored and non-monitored clerical workers showed that 50% of monitored workers felt stressed, compared with 33% of non-monitored workers; and that 34% of monitored workers lost work time because of stress-induced illness, compared with 20% of non-monitored workers.[20]

Some companies have re-examined their employee-monitoring programs and decided to pull the plug. Federal Express decided to discontinue a telephone monitoring system tracking 43,000 customer service employees because management felt that quality was being sacrificed to productivity. After Fed Ex began monitoring packages instead of people, productivity remained high and employee satisfaction increased.[21] In 1990 Nortel renounced the practice of secret electronic mon-

A Question of Ethics

You discover that your supervisor has been billing the company for business trips that he never took. When you ask him about it, he says this is common practice throughout the company, the other department heads do the same thing, and corporate headquarters has set reimbursement rates so low that employees have to do this to be fairly reimbursed. What should you do?

Macworld
www.macworld.com

Using Electronic Monitoring to Help Employees.

Here, a senior agent at an auto rental company provides direct monitoring, taking turns with a new employee (who had asked for help), responding to calls, giving her pointers on style and technique.

itoring of employee voice, video, and data communications.[22] Yet, given the increasing computerization of many job functions, electronic monitoring promises to become more, not less, widespread. The key for employers will be to put the technology to work *for* the employees rather than *against* them. Employees are most likely to see electronic monitoring as legitimate when management uses it to control theft.

To use electronic monitoring devices to control theft while not intimidating or invading the privacy of honest employees (who make up the majority of the work force), managers should:

◆ Make employees aware of any electronic surveillance devices that are being used to monitor their behaviour. Secret monitoring should be avoided, except with specific individuals whom managers have reason to believe are stealing from the company. In those cases, management should obtain a court order to perform the secret surveillance.

◆ Find positive uses for electronic monitoring devices that are beneficial to employees as well as to the employer. Monitoring devices can be used to provide feedback on employee performance, a practice that has been accepted as a valuable training tool.

◆ Develop a systematic anti-theft policy and publicize it throughout the company. Also establish other practices to discourage theft, such as reference checks, pencil-and-paper honesty or integrity tests that screen out employees who are likely to behave dishonestly, and internal controls that control the use of cash (accounting controls), merchandise (inventory controls), computers and databases (computer security controls), and company trade secrets (security badges and clearance procedures).

■ Whistleblowing

Whistleblowing occurs when an employee discloses illegal, immoral, or illegitimate practices under the control of the employer to persons or organizations that may be able to take corrective action.[23] Whistleblowing can result in effective solutions, but can also disrupt the organization's operations.

Whistleblowing is risky because managers and other employees often deal harshly with the whistleblower. One observer found that "... the overwhelming majority of whistleblowers indeed pay a heavy price for reporting of wrongdoing."[24] Statistics from the United States suggest that four out of five whistleblowers reported harassment as a result of their actions, three out of five lost their jobs, one in six lost their home, and one in 10 attempted suicide. Corporate whistleblowers have often been perceived to be "little more than snitches and malcontents who deserve to be treated as social pariahs."[25] For example:

◆ Ross Grey, at one time a vice-president at Standard Trustco Ltd., was dismissed from his job as a result of his having "blown the whistle" on illegal activities at the company. The company claimed that he had participated in the illegal activities. He filed a suit for wrongful dismissal.[26]

◆ In 1992, John Drennan, a senior engine inspector for Pratt and Whitney Canada, reported a problem with tiny cracks in engines leaving his overhaul shop to the Department of National Defence, for which the work was being done. He was fired and, like Grey, launched a wrongful dismissal suit.[27]

◆ When Margot O'Toole, an MIT scientist, exposed fabricated research data for a scientific article written by Nobel laureate David Baltimore, she lost her job. It took five years before she was vindicated when Baltimore admitted that his research was flawed.[28]

◆ A manager at MCA, a large entertainment conglomerate, suspected some executives of ordering large shipments of free record albums for recipients not entitled to them. He notified his supervisor three times of a possible kickback scheme. Instead of receiving thanks, he was fired, ostensibly for not performing his job adequately.[29]

Dealing with whistleblowers involves balancing an employee's right to freedom of expression with the legitimate expectations of the employer that the authority of the management system be respected and that the organization's reputation not

whistleblowing

Employee disclosure of illegal, immoral, or illegitimate practices under the control of the employer to persons or organizations that may be able to take corrective action.

be damaged by inappropriate employee behaviour. Unlike public sector employees in the United States, there is no omnibus protection for whistleblowers in Canada. Some employers have established internal channels for allegations of wrongdoing, and unionized employees have some protection in the grievance system. As Figure 14–3 indicates, a potential whistleblower should have good documentation of the evidence of wrongdoing before disclosing it to others. The whistleblower should also be prepared to deal with employer retaliation and have a contingency plan, which may include lining up another job in case the worst happens.

Despite all these risks, employees have used whistleblowing to call their employer to account for a wide range of conduct that they perceived to be improper. Thus employers must confront the reality that many outsiders—from regulators to auditors and prosecutors—may seek to hold them accountable for wrongdoing. For this reason some companies have realized that it is in their best interests to establish a policy on whistleblowing that encourages people to reveal misconduct internally instead of exposing it externally. This way they can avoid negative publicity and all the investigative, administrative, and legal actions associated with it.[30] Figure 14–4 lists some of the most important elements of an effective whistleblowing policy. Probably the most important is support by top management, including the chief executive officer. Other important elements of a whistleblowing policy are provisions for the whistleblower to remain anonymous initially and to be protected from retribution.

■ Building Managerial Skills: Disciplining Employees

Managers have traditionally recognized the need to control and change employees' behaviour when it does not meet their expectations. *Employee discipline* is a tool that managers have relied upon to communicate to employees that they need to change a behaviour to meet established standards. For example, some employees are habitually late to work, ignore safety procedures, neglect the details required for their job, act rude to customers, or engage in unprofessional conduct with co-workers. Employers should be aware that there is a possibility of being found criminally liable for illegal actions of employees—an eventuality that can be made less likely by notifying police promptly when employee crime is discovered and assisting in the investigation. Employers should also clearly communicate, via employee orientation, training, and codes of conduct, that even attempted crimes are a basis for immediate dismissal. They should further examine the reward system to ensure that employees are not induced into illegal activities because of the organization's rewards and penalties.[31] Employee discipline entails communicating the unacceptability of such behaviour to the employee along with a warning that specific actions will follow if the employee does not change the behaviour.

Figure 14–3 Dos and Don'ts for Whistleblowers

SOURCE: Adapted from Hamilton, J. (1991, June 3). Blowing the whistle without paying the piper. *Business Week*, 139.

DO make sure your allegation is correct. Something may look fishy but be allowable under a technicality you don't understand.

DO keep careful records. Document what you've observed—and your attempt to rectify the problem or alert a supervisor. Keep copies outside the office.

DO research on whether your jurisdiction provides protection for whistleblowers. It may require that you follow special procedures.

DO be realistic about your future. Talk to your family and make sure you're prepared for a worst-case scenario, which can include loss of job, severe financial burdens, and blacklisting in your field. Even if you're not fired, you may be treated with suspicion by colleagues and management.

DON'T assume a federal or provincial law will protect you. Legal protection for private sector workers is often inadequate and varies widely from province to province. Most federal protections cover only government workers.

DON'T run to the media. You may be giving up certain rights or risking a defamation suit. Check with a lawyer before contacting any reporters.

DON'T expect a windfall if you're fired. Although some provinces allow punitive damages, you may be eligible only for back pay and reinstatement—in a place you probably don't want to work anyway.

1. Develop the policy in written form.

2. Seek input from top management in developing the policy, and obtain approval for the finished work.

3. Communicate the policy to employees using multiple media. Inclusion in the employee handbook is not sufficient. Active communication efforts such as ethics training, departmental meetings, and employee seminars will increase awareness of the policy and highlight the company's commitment to ethical behaviour.

4. Provide a reporting procedure for employees that does not require them to go to their supervisor first. Instead, designate a special office or individual to hear initial employee complaints. Streamline the pro-cess and cut the red tape. Make it easy for employees to use the procedure.

5. Make it possible for employees to report anonymously, at least initially.

6. Guarantee employees who report suspected wrongdoing in good faith that they will be protected from retaliation by any member of the organization. Make this guarantee stick.

7. Develop a formal investigative process and communicate to employees exactly how their reports will be handled. Use this process to investigate all reported wrongdoing.

8. If the investigation reveals that the employee's suspicions are accurate, take prompt action to correct the wrongdoing. Employees will quickly lose confidence in the policy if disclosed wrongdoing is allowed to continue. Whatever the outcome of the investigation, communicate it quickly to the whistleblowing employee.

9. Provide an appeals process for employees dissatisfied with the outcome of the initial investigation. Provide an advocate (probably from the HR department) to assist the employee who wishes to appeal an unfavourable outcome.

10. Finally, a successful whistleblowing policy requires more than a written procedure. It requires a commitment from the organization, from top management down. This commitment must be to create an ethical work environment.

Figure 14–4 Developing an Effective Whistleblowing Policy

SOURCE: Adapted from Barrett, T. & Cochran, D. (1991). Making room for the whistleblower. *HRMagazine,* 36(1), 59. Reprinted with the permission of *HRMagazine* (formerly *Personnel Administrator*) published by the Society for Human Resource Management, Alexandria, VA.

Employee discipline is usually performed by supervisors, but in self-managed work teams employee discipline may be a team responsibility. At one food distribution centre, some 120 warehouse employees are divided into five teams, each of which has a serious-misconduct committee. The committee handles employee discipline and makes recommendations to management, including counselling and even dismissal. Management usually adopts the committee's recommendations. Serious-misconduct committees often generate creative solutions, and termination has rarely been needed.[32] One reason team-based organizations work well in many situations is that the teams are self-regulating, with unacceptable behaviour dealt with by informal methods.

Employee and employer rights may come into conflict over the issue of employee discipline. Sometimes employees believe they are being disciplined unfairly. In such situations, a company's human resource management staff may help sort out disputed rights. This HR contribution is particularly valuable because it can enable the employee and the supervisor to maintain an effective working relationship with each other.

Two different approaches to employee discipline are widely used: (1) progressive discipline and (2) positive discipline. In both these disciplinary approaches, it is necessary that supervisors discuss the behaviour in question with their employees. Managers almost invariably find it difficult to confront an employee for disciplinary purposes. Reasons for their discomfort include not wanting to be the bearer of bad news, not knowing how to get started on a discussion that may make an employee feel humiliated, and fear that the discussion will get out of control. The Manager's Notebook entitled "Ten Steps for Effective Disciplinary Sessions" offers some guidelines that should make it easier for managers to handle an admittedly distasteful task.

■ Progressive Discipline

The most commonly used form of discipline, progressive discipline consists of a series of management interventions that give employees opportunities to correct their behaviour before being discharged. **Progressive discipline** procedures are

progressive discipline

A series of management interventions that give employees opportunities to correct undesirable behaviours before being dismissed.

Ten Steps for Effective Disciplinary Sessions

1. Determine whether discipline is called for. Is the problem an isolated infraction or part of a pattern?

2. Have clear goals for the discussion with the poor performer. Many times a manager meets with an employee to discuss a performance problem, but by the end of the session, the employee still has no clear idea of the manager's expectations for improvement. Managers need to be specific; they should not rely on indirect comments.

3. Hold the discussion in private. Anyone who has ever witnessed a public reprimand knows full well that it embarrasses not only the employee but his or her co-workers as well. The result: the manager loses the trust and respect of all who observe the public reprimand.

4. Be calm. A manager who approaches a performance discussion calmly is more likely to remain objective and undistracted by irrelevant problems.

5. Time the discussion carefully. The manager who at 8 a.m. announces a 2:30 p.m. meeting is likely to destroy most of the employee's day. If the problem isn't obvious, the employee will spend the intervening time worrying about what is wrong. Conversely, if the problem is obvious, the employee will have plenty of time to prepare defensive arguments.

6. Prepare effective opening remarks. To make sure the meeting is effective, a manager needs to be absolutely confident about his or her opening remarks. These should be thought out in advance, even rehearsed.

7. Avoid beating around the bush. Too much small talk at the beginning will actually raise the employee's anxiety level rather than getting the employee to relax.

8. Ensure two-way communication. The most helpful disciplinary meeting is a discussion, not a lecture; a manager can't get to the bottom of a performance problem if the employee isn't allowed to speak. The objective of the meeting, after all, is to come up with a solution, not to berate the employee.

9. Establish a follow-up plan. The agreement to a follow-up plan is crucial in both the progressive and positive disciplinary procedures. It's particularly important to establish the time frame in which the employee's behaviour is to improve.

10. End on a positive note. This may be a time for the manager to emphasize the employee's strengths so that the employee can leave the meeting believing that the manager—and the company—wants him or her to succeed.

SOURCE: Adapted from Day, D. (1993, May). Training 101: Help for discipline dodgers. *Training & Development*, 19–22. Copyright May 1993, the American Society for Training and Development. Reprinted with permission. All rights reserved.

warning steps, each of which involves a punishment that increases in severity the longer the undesirable behaviours persist.[33] If the employee fails to respond to these progressive warnings, the employer is justified in discharging the individual.

Progressive discipline systems usually have three to five steps, although a four-step system is the most common. Minor violations of company policy involve using all the steps in the progressive discipline procedure. Serious violations, sometimes referred to as *gross misconduct,* can result in the elimination of several steps and sometimes even begin at the last step, which is dismissal. Examples of gross misconduct are assaulting a supervisor and falsifying employment records. Most applications of discipline, however, involve minor rule infractions such as violating a dress code, smoking at an inappropriate time or place, or being habitually late. These minor violations can be corrected through supervisory interventions that apply early steps in the progressive discipline procedure. Figure 14–5 shows more examples of minor and serious violations.

A four-step progressive discipline procedure includes the following steps:

1. *Verbal Warning*

An employee who commits a minor violation receives a verbal warning from the supervisor and is told that if this problem continues within a specific time period, harsher punishment will follow.

2. *Written Warning*

The employee violates the same rule within the specified time period and now receives a written warning from the supervisor. This warning goes into the employee's records. The employee is told that failure to correct the violation within a certain time period will result in more severe treatment.

3. *Suspension*

The employee still fails to respond to warnings and again violates the work rule. The employee is now suspended from employment without pay for a specific amount of time and receives a final warning from the supervisor indicating that dismissal will follow upon violating the rule within a specified time period.

4. *Dismissal*

The employee violates the rule one more time within the specified time period and is dismissed.[34] Figure 14–6 illustrates how an employer would use progressive discipline with an employee who has a pattern of unexcused absences from work.

For infractions that fall between the categories of minor violation and serious violation, one or two steps in the procedure are skipped. These infractions are usually handled by supervisors, who give the employees an opportunity to correct

Minor Violations	Serious Violations
◆ Absenteeism	◆ Drug use at work
◆ Dress code violation	◆ Theft
◆ Smoking rule violation	◆ Dishonesty
◆ Incompetence	◆ Physical assualt upon a supervisor
◆ Safety rule violation	◆ Sabotage of company operations
◆ Sleeping on the job	
◆ Horseplay	
◆ Tardiness	

Figure 14–5 Categories of Employee Misconduct

1. Verbal Warning

The employee has an unexcused absence from work. He receives a verbal warning from the supervisor and is told that if he takes another unexcused absence within the next month, harsher punishment will follow.

2. Written Warning

Two weeks after the verbal warning from his supervisor, the employee takes another unexcused absence. He now receives a written warning that if he fails to correct his absenteeism problem within the next two months, more severe treatment will follow. This warning goes into his personnel files.

3. Suspension

Six weeks later the employee fails to show up for work for two consecutive days. This time he is suspended from work without pay for one week. He also receives a final warning from his supervisor that if he has another unexcused absence within three months after his return from suspension, he will be terminated.

4. Discharge

Two weeks after his return from suspension, the employee does not show up for work. Upon his return to work the following day, he is discharged.

EXIT

Figure 14–6 Four Steps in a Progressive Discipline Procedure

the behaviour before discharging them. For example, two employees get into a fistfight at work, but there are mitigating circumstances (one employee verbally attacked the other). In this situation, both employees may be suspended without pay and warned that another such violation will result in dismissal.

▮ Positive Discipline

In many situations punishment does not motivate an employee to change a behaviour. Rather, it only teaches the person to fear or resent the source of punishment—that is, the supervisor. This emphasis on punishment in progressive discipline may encourage employees to deceive their supervisor rather than correct their actions. To avoid this outcome, some companies have replaced progressive discipline with **positive discipline**, which encourages employees to monitor their own behaviours and assume responsibility for the consequences of their actions.

Positive discipline is similar to progressive discipline in that it too uses a series of steps that increase in urgency and severity until the last step, which is dismissal. However, positive discipline replaces the punishment used in progressive discipline with counselling sessions between employee and supervisor. These sessions focus on getting the employee to learn from past mistakes and initiate a plan to make a positive change in behaviour. Rather than depending on threats and punishments, the supervisor uses counselling skills to motivate the employee to change. Rather than placing blame on the employee, the supervisor emphasizes collaborative problem solving. In short, positive discipline alters the role of a supervisor from adversary to counsellor.

To ensure that supervisors are adequately prepared to counsel employees, companies that implement positive discipline must see that they receive appropriate

positive discipline

A procedure that encourages employees to monitor their own behaviours and assume responsibility for the consequences of their actions.

training either from the company's own human resource department or from outside professional trainers. Union Carbide began using positive discipline at several of its plants by having managers attend a two-day training program to gain complete familiarity with positive discipline policies and practices and build the skills and self-confidence they need to use it effectively. Because Union Carbide had long used a progressive discipline approach, a key element of the training is helping managers abandon their tendency to respond to performance problems in a punitive way. They also receive training in documenting their discussions specifically, factually, and defensibly.[35]

A four-step positive discipline procedure starts out with a first counselling session between employee and supervisor that ends with a verbal solution to the problem that is acceptable to both parties. If this solution does not work, the supervisor and employee meet again to discuss why it failed and to develop a new plan and timetable to solve the problem. At this second step, the new agreed-upon solution to the problem is written down.

If there is still no improvement in performance, the third step is a final warning that the employee is at risk of being dismissed. Rather than suspend the employee without pay (as would happen under progressive discipline), this third step gives the employee some time to evaluate his or her situation and come up with a new solution. In doing so, the employee is encouraged to examine why earlier attempts to improve performance did not work. Some companies even give the employee a "decision-making day off" with pay to develop a plan for improved performance.[36]

Managers often resist this aspect of positive discipline because they feel that it rewards employees for poor performance. Some suspect that employees intentionally misbehave to get a free day off. According to the employee relations director of Union Carbide, which uses a paid decision-making day off as part of its procedure, this isn't so. The company believes a paid day off is more effective than the unpaid suspension used in progressive discipline procedures because (1) workers returning from an unpaid suspension often feel anger or apathy, which may lead to either reduced effectiveness on the job or subtle sabotage; (2) paying the employee for the decision-making day off avoids making the employee a martyr in the eyes of co-workers and turning what was an individual problem into a group problem; and (3) paying for the decision-making day off underscores management's "good faith" toward the employee and probably reduces the chances the employee will be able to win a wrongful dismissal suit if he or she is eventually terminated.[37]

Failure to improve performance after the final warning results in dismissal, the fourth step of the positive discipline procedure. Incidents of gross misconduct (such as theft) are treated no differently under a positive discipline procedure than under a progressive discipline procedure. In both systems, theft will most likely result in immediate dismissal.

In addition to the costs of training managers and supervisors in appropriate counselling skills and approaches, progressive discipline has another drawback. Counselling sessions require a lot of time to be effective, and this is time that both the supervisor and employee are not working on other tasks. Nonetheless, positive discipline offers considerable benefits to both employees and managers. Employees prefer it because they like being treated with respect by their supervisors. Counselling generally results in a greater willingness to change undesirable behaviours to conform to company policy than discipline does. Supervisors prefer it because it does not demand they assume the role of disciplinarian. Counselling makes for better-quality working relationships with subordinates than discipline does. In addition, under a system of positive discipline, managers are much more likely to intervene early to correct a problem.

Finally, positive discipline can have positive effects on a company's bottom line, as evidenced at Union Carbide. Studies in five of the company's facilities have shown an average decline in absenteeism of 5.5 percent since the company switched from punitive to positive discipline procedures. Moreover, in one unionized facility at the company, disciplinary grievances processed went down from 36 in one year to eight in the next. Since Union Carbide executives estimate that taking an employee complaint through all steps of the grievance procedure (short of arbitration) costs approximately $400 at this facility, the switch in discipline procedures saved the company over $11,000 per year.[38]

Administering and Managing Discipline

Managers must ensure that employees who are disciplined receive due process. In the context of discipline, due process means fair and consistent treatment. If an employee challenges a disciplinary action under human rights legislation or a union grievance procedure, the employer must prove that the employee engaged in misconduct and was disciplined appropriately for it. Thus supervisors should be properly trained in how to administer discipline. Two important elements of due process that managers need to consider in this area are (1) the standards of discipline used to determine if the employee was treated fairly and (2) whether the employee has a right to appeal a disciplinary action.

Basic Standards of Discipline

Some basic standards of discipline should apply to all rule violations, whether major or minor. All disciplinary actions should include the following procedures at a minimum:

◆ *Communication of rules and performance criteria.* Employees should be aware of the company's rules and standards and the consequences of violating them. Every employee and supervisor should understand the discipline policies and procedures fully. Employees who violate a rule or do not meet performance criteria should be given the opportunity to correct their behaviour.

◆ *Documentation of the facts.* Managers should gather a convincing amount of evidence to justify the discipline. This evidence should be carefully documented so that it is difficult to dispute. For example, time cards could be used to document tardiness; videotapes could document a case of employee theft; the written testimony of a witness could substantiate a charge of insubordination. Employees should have the opportunity to refute this evidence and provide documentation in self-defence.

◆ *Consistent response to rule violations.* It is important for employees to believe that discipline is administered consistently, predictably, and without discrimination or favouritism. If they do not, they will be more likely to challenge discipline decisions. This does not mean that every violation should be treated exactly the same. For example, an employee with many years of seniority and an excellent work record who breaks a rule may be punished less harshly than a recently hired employee who breaks the same rule. However, two recently hired employees who break the same rule should receive the same punishment.

The **hot-stove rule** provides a model of how disciplinary action should be administered. The rule suggests that the disciplinary process is similar to touching a hot stove:

1. Touching a hot stove results in immediate consequences. Discipline should also be an immediate consequence that follows a rule infraction.

2. The hot stove (by glowing red) provides a warning that one will get burned if it is touched. Disciplinary rules should clearly inform employees of the consequences of breaking rules.

3. A hot stove is consistent in administering pain to anybody who touches it. Disciplinary rules should be applied to all.[39]

hot-stove rule

A model of disciplinary action: discipline should be immediate, provide ample warning, and be consistently applied to all.

The Just Cause Standard of Discipline

In cases of wrongful dismissal, arbitrators require the employer to prove that an employee was discharged for *just cause*. This standard, which is written into union contracts and into many non-union companies' employment policies and employee handbooks, can be summarized into seven questions that must be answered in the affirmative for just cause to exist.[40] Failure to answer "yes" to one or more of these questions may indicate that the discipline was arbitrary or unwarranted.

1. *Notification*

   Was the employee forewarned of the disciplinary consequences of his or her conduct? Unless the misconduct is very obvious (for example, theft or assault), the employer should make the employee aware, either verbally or in writing, that he or she has violated a rule.

2. *Reasonable Rule*

   Was the rule the employee violated consistent with safe and efficient operations? The rule should not jeopardize an employee's safety or integrity in any way.

3. *Investigation Prior to Discipline*

   Did managers conduct an investigation into the misconduct before administering discipline? If immediate action is desirable, the employee may be suspended pending the outcome of the investigation. If the investigation reveals no misconduct, all of the employee's rights should be restored.

4. *Fair Investigation*

   Was the investigation fair and impartial? Fair investigations allow the employee to defend himself or herself.

5. *Proof of Guilt*

   Did the investigation provide substantial evidence or proof of guilt? Management needs to be able to meet the "balance of probabilities" standard.

6. *Absence of Discrimination*

   Were the rules, orders, and penalties of the disciplinary action applied evenhandedly and without any discrimination? It is not acceptable for managers to go from lax enforcement of a rule to sudden rigorous enforcement of that rule without notifying employees that they intend to do so.

7. *Reasonable Penalty*

   Was the disciplinary penalty reasonably related to the seriousness of the rule violation? The employer should consider related facts, such as the employee's work record, when determining the severity of punishment. There might be a range of penalties for a given rule infraction that depend on the length and quality of the employee's service record.

The Right to Appeal Discipline

Sometimes employees believe they have been disciplined unfairly, often because they feel their supervisors have abused their power or are biased in dealing with individuals whom they like or dislike. For a disciplinary system to be effective, employees must have access to an appeal procedure in which others (who are perceived to be free from bias) can examine the facts of the disciplinary action. As we discussed in the previous chapter, good employee relations requires establishing appeals procedures employees can use to voice their disagreement with managers' actions. For challenging disciplinary actions, two of the most useful appeals procedures are the open-door policy and the use of employee relations representatives. These two methods are attractive because of their flexibility and their ability to reach quick resolutions.

■ Building Managerial Skills: Managing Difficult Employees

Thus far we've focused on the challenges of administering discipline. We now turn to some common problems that managers are likely to encounter. All the problems we discuss here—poor attendance, poor performance, insubordination, and substance abuse—often lead to disciplinary actions. Managing the discipline of difficult employees requires good judgement and common sense.

■ Poor Attendance

The problem of poor attendance includes absenteeism and/or tardiness. Poor attendance can become a serious problem that leads to dismissal for just cause. If poor attendance is not managed properly, employee productivity can decline and group morale can suffer as those with good attendance habits are forced to increase their efforts to compensate for people who shirk their responsibilities.

Sometimes employees are absent or tardy for legitimate reasons—for example, sickness, child care problems, inclement weather, or religious beliefs. Managers should identify those employees who have legitimate reasons and treat them differently than they treat those who are chronically absent or tardy.

When disciplining an employee for poor attendance, managers need to consider several factors:

◆ *Is the attendance rule reasonable?* Attendance rules should be flexible enough to allow for the emergencies or unforeseen circumstances that most employees experience from time to time, including religious or cultural holidays celebrated by a diverse work force. Most companies deal with this issue by showing leniency when an employee gives notice that he or she is sick or experiencing an emergency. For instance, an increasingly likely emergency for many employees is providing care for an aging parent. Some companies require documentation, such as a doctor's note, in support of the incident.

◆ *Has the employee been warned of the consequences of poor attendance?* This could be particularly important when an employee is unaware of how much time flexibility is possible in reporting to the job.

◆ *Are there any mitigating circumstances that should be taken into consideration?* Sometimes special circumstances need to be considered. These circumstances include work history, length of service, reason for absence, and likelihood of improved attendance.[41]

Managers should be aware of patterns of poor attendance within a work unit. Systemic absenteeism or tardiness may be a symptom of job avoidance. Employees may dread coming to work because co-workers are unpleasant, the job has become unchallenging, they are experiencing conflicting demands from job and family, or supervision is poor. A disciplinary approach is not the best way to deal with this type of absenteeism. It would be better for the manager or company to look for ways to change the work environment. Possible solutions to job avoidance are redesigning jobs and, when the problem is widespread, restructuring the organization.

For employees whose absences are due to overwhelming family demands, flexible work schedules or permission to work at home (telecommuting) may be desirable. Flexible work schedules are gaining popularity in many companies, including the Bank of Montreal, Hewlett-Packard (Canada) Ltd. of Mississauga, Ontario, and BC Systems Corporation in Victoria, B.C., where there is a target of some 40 percent of the head office staff telecommuting part time.[42]

■ Poor Performance

Every manager must deal with employees who perform poorly and do not respond to coaching or feedback aimed at improving their performance. In most cases, the performance appraisal (see Chapter 7) can be used to turn around poor performers by helping them develop an action plan for improvement. Sometimes, however, the poor performance is so serious that it requires immediate intervention. Consider the following situations:

◆ A restaurant manager receives daily complaints from angry customers about the quality of one server's service.

◆ A partner's poor interpersonal skills affect his working relationships with the other two partners in his firm. The firm is now failing to meet its goals because of the severe conflicts and disruptions instigated by this one person.

These examples suggest a glaring need for progressive or positive discipline procedures. If any of these employees failed to make improvements in performance after receiving some warnings or counselling, dismissal would be justified.

Companies and managers should follow three guidelines when applying discipline for poor performance:

1. The company's performance standards should be reasonable and communicated to all employees. Job descriptions can be used for this purpose.

2. Poor performance should be documented and poor performers should be told how they are not meeting the expected standards. One source of documented evidence can be the pattern of the performance appraisals given to the employee over a period of time.

3. Managers should make a good-faith attempt to give employees an opportunity to improve their performance before disciplining them.

Sometimes poor performance is the result of factors beyond the employee's control. In these cases, managers should avoid using discipline except as a last resort. For example, an employee may be unable to perform at expected standards because of incompetence. An *incompetent employee* (one who is lacking in ability, not effort) may be given remedial training (see Chapter 8) or transferred to a less demanding job rather than dismissed. An incompetent employee's poor performance may be the result of a flaw in the organization's selection system that caused a poor match between the employee's skills and the job requirements.

Some organizations use a *probationary employment period* (a period of time that allows the employer to dismiss an employee without elaborate procedures) to weed out incompetent employees early. Probationary employment periods typically last one to three months. In Europe, where permanent employment is more common, many companies insist on a six-month trial period as part of the employment contract. However, this policy can present a problem when recruiting executives, who, understandably, want to be guaranteed a permanent position before leaving their current job.

It is not only inappropriate but also illegal to use discipline to correct poor performance when an employee has a physical or cognitive disability. Human rights codes that protect people with disabilities also impose the expectation that employers make reasonable accommodation to enable such employees to perform the job. This may include redesigning the job or modifying policies and procedures. For example, an employee who is diagnosed with a terminal illness may request a change from a full-time job to a part-time job or one with a more flexible work schedule in order to obtain medical treatment. Human rights commissions, which regulate how employers respond to the needs of disabled employees, would probably consider this a reasonable request, so failure to make such an accommodation could lead to legal sanctions.

Unfortunately, many myths hinder firms' undertaking steps to provide reasonable accommodation. One myth is that reasonable accommodation always involves prohibitive expense. Actually, accommodation is not necessarily costly, and more often than not, the money spent to accommodate an individual with a disability is minor compared with the cost of litigation. Samsonite Corporation has employed deaf production workers for years. The only accommodation necessary—beyond a positive attitude and the willingness of many employees to learn some sign language—has been the use of lights in the production area in addition to the standard beepers that alert employees to the presence of forklift trucks.[43]

◼ Insubordination

The willingness of employees to carry out managers' directives is essential to a business's effective operations. **Insubordination,** which involves an employee's refusal to obey a direct order from a supervisor, is a direct challenge of management's right to run the company. Insubordination also occurs when an employee is verbally abusive to a supervisor. The discipline for insubordination usually varies according to the seriousness of the consequences of the insubordination and the presence or absence of mitigating factors. Mitigating factors include the employee's work history and length of service and whether the employee was provoked by a supervisor's verbal abuse.

To justify disciplining an employee for insubordination, managers should document the following: (1) The supervisor gave a direct order to a subordinate, either in writing or orally; and (2) the employee refused to obey the order, either by indicating so verbally or by not doing what was asked. The discipline for a first insubordination offence ranges from applying the first step of the progressive discipline procedure to immediate suspension or dismissal.

Two exceptions allow an employee to disobey a direct order: legitimate safety concerns and being asked to commit an illegal act. Most Canadian jurisdictions now have health and safety legislation that allows employees to refuse what they consider to be unsafe work (see Chapter 16). A process, which varies among jurisdictions, is specified by which the situation is investigated and a determination is made of whether a safety justification exists. The employee is shielded from disciplinary action so long as the initial refusal was made in good faith. An employer cannot legally compel an employee to engage in illegal activities. In some cases, such as under Ontario's 1994 Environmental Bill of Rights, an employee can do more than refuse—employees are protected if they decide to report their employer because they perceive the employer to be guilty of an environmental offence.

Because the penalties for insubordination are severe, companies should create internal systems and cultures (open door policies, appeal systems) that allow employees to appeal charges of insubordinate behaviour. The penalties to companies for refusing to hear an employee's reasons for insubordination can be severe. Managers should be sure that insubordination charges are not being used to protect their own illegal or unethical behaviour. For instance, a supervisor who charges an employee with insubordination may be attempting to force out someone who objects to the supervisor's illegal behaviour. Companies that ignore such signs of trouble may find that what was originally a small problem has escalated into a very difficult and/or expensive situation.

◼ Alcohol-Related Misconduct

Employees' use of alcohol presents two separate challenges to managers. First, there is the challenge of managing an employee who is an alcoholic. Second, there is the challenge of managing an employee who uses alcohol or is intoxicated on the job. Each of these employees should be disciplined differently.

insubordination
Either refusal to obey a direct order from a supervisor or verbal abuse of a supervisor.

Sign of the Times.

Many companies have found the costs of hiring people with disabilities low and the benefits high. Several studies show that people with disabilities have significantly lower turnover rates than people without disabilities. A willingness by managers and co-workers to learn sign language has helped several firms attract and retain deaf workers.

Alcoholic employees are generally viewed sympathetically because alcoholism is an illness and medical treatment is the generally accepted remedy for it. However, as we mentioned in the previous chapter, some alcoholic employees have a strong denial mechanism that prevents them from admitting they are alcoholics. Others may not view them as alcoholics either because alcoholism is often masked by such behavioural symptoms as poor attendance. Thus a supervisor may perceive an alcoholic employee as someone who has an attendance or performance problem rather than an alcohol problem and discipline the employee accordingly. Organizations that have employee assistance programs give employees the opportunity to visit a counsellor as the last step in progressive discipline prior to discharge. This is where the alcoholism may finally be discovered and the employee referred to an alcohol rehabilitation facility.

Sometimes employees claim to be alcoholic to cover up their misconduct. If the EAP counsellor determines that the individual is not an alcoholic, the discipline procedure is the appropriate managerial response to the problem.

Using alcohol on the job and coming to work intoxicated are both considered serious misconduct and can lead to harsh discipline. Organizations that have job-related reasons to restrict alcohol use at work or working "under the influence" should have clearly stated and reasonable policies. For example, it is reasonable to restrict the alcohol use, on or off the job, of heavy equipment operators at a construction site. It is more difficult to forbid a sales representative to drink alcohol when entertaining a prospective client at a lunch.

The best way to prove that an employee has come to work intoxicated is to administer a blood-alcohol content test. A supervisor can ask an employee to submit to this test if there is a reasonable suspicion that the individual is intoxicated. Supervisors may suspect an individual is intoxicated if he or she engages in unusual behaviour (e.g., talking particularly loud or using profanity), has slurred speech, or has alcohol on the breath.

A first intoxication offence may result in suspension or dismissal because of the potential for damage to the employer that an alcohol-impaired employee can create. An example of the potential risks some employers face from alcohol-impaired employees is the grounding of the oil tanker *Exxon Valdez* in 1989 just off the coast of Alaska, an accident that resulted in a massive oil spill. A blood-alcohol test indicated that the ship's captain was impaired at the time; clean-up costs topped $1 billion. Imperial Oil's aggressive posture on impairment (see Chapter 5, Minicase 1) was, in part, a response to this event.

◼ Illegal Drug Use and Abuse

Drug use and abuse by employees also presents a serious challenge to managers. "Drug use" refers to any use of prohibited substances such as marijuana, heroin, and cocaine as well as illegal use of prescription drugs such as Valium. The problems associated with drug use are very similar to those associated with the use of alcohol. The primary difference is that the use of illegal drugs is prohibited by law and is socially unacceptable, while the use of alcohol in moderation is socially acceptable.

We examined the specifics of drug-use detection systems earlier in this chapter, and we will address the health aspects of drug use in Chapter 16. Here we note only that drug use is often masked by symptoms such as inattention and unexplained absences. Managers who suspect that drug use or addiction is the source of a performance problem should refer the employee to EAP counselling if the organization has such a program. Simultaneously, they should document performance problems and begin disciplinary procedures. These will prove valuable should it be necessary to terminate the employee because of failure to overcome the substance abuse problem after counselling and treatment.

■ Preventing Discipline with Human Resource Management

By taking a strategic and proactive approach to the design of human resource management systems, managers can eliminate a substantial amount of employee discipline. HR programs designed to use employees' talents and skills effectively reduce the need to resort to discipline to shape employee behaviour. In this section we briefly revisit some of the functional areas of HR we discussed in earlier chapters to show how each can be designed to prevent problem employees.[44]

■ Recruitment and Selection

By spending more time and resources on recruiting and selection, managers can make better matches between individuals and the organization.

◆ Individuals can be selected for fit in the organization as well as the job. The practice of choosing applicants who have career potential in the company decreases the likelihood that employees will exhibit performance problems later in their career with the organization.

◆ Checking references and gathering background information on applicants' work habits and character are useful preliminaries to making a job offer.

◆ Multiple interviews that involve diverse groups in the company can reduce biases that lead to poor hiring decisions. When women, minorities, peers, and subordinates, as well as senior people, are involved in the interviewing process, companies stand a better chance of obtaining an accurate portrait of the applicant.

■ Training and Development

Investing in employees' training and development now saves a company from having to deal with incompetence or workers whose skills are soon obsolete.

◆ An effective orientation program communicates the values important to the organization to all employees (especially the new ones). It also teaches employees what is expected from them as members of the organization. These insights into the company can help employees manage their own behaviour better.

◆ Training programs for new employees can reduce skill gaps and improve competencies.

◆ Retraining programs can be used for continuing employees whose skills have become obsolete. For example, employees may need periodic retraining on word processing software as the technology changes and more powerful programs become available.

◆ Training supervisors to coach and provide feedback to their subordinates encourages supervisors to intervene early in problem situations with counselling rather than discipline.

◆ Career ladders can be developed to give employees incentives to develop a long-term commitment to the organization's goals. When employees know that the organization has a long-term use for their contributions, they are more likely to engage in acts of good citizenship with their co-workers and customers.

■ Human Resource Planning

Jobs, job families, and organizational units can be designed to motivate and challenge employees. Highly motivated workers seldom need to be disciplined for inadequate performance.

◆ Jobs should be designed to utilize the best talents of each employee. It may be necessary to build some flexibility into job designs to put an employee's strengths to best use. One way companies are creating greater job flexibility is through *job banding*. Discussed in Chapter 10, this system replaces traditional narrowly defined job descriptions with broader categories, or bands, of related jobs. By putting greater variety into jobs, job banding makes it less likely that employees will feel so underchallenged or bored that they start avoiding work through absences or tardiness. Job banding has been implemented successfully by companies including GE Canada, Nortel, and Ontario Hydro.[45]

◆ Job descriptions and work plans should be developed to communicate effectively to employees the performance standards to which they will be held accountable.

■ Performance Appraisal

Many performance problems can be avoided by designing effective performance appraisal systems. An effective performance appraisal system lets people know what is expected of them, how well they are meeting those expectations, and what they can do to improve on their weaknesses.

◆ The performance appraisal criteria should set reasonable standards that employees understand and over which they have some control.

◆ Supervisors should be encouraged by their managers to provide continuous feedback to subordinates. Many problems can be avoided with early interventions.

◆ Performance evaluations for supervisors should place strong emphasis on their effectiveness at providing feedback and developing their subordinates.

◆ Employee appraisals should be documented properly to protect employers against wrongful dismissal or discrimination suits.

■ Compensation

Employees who believe that rewards are allocated unfairly (perhaps on the basis of favouritism) are likely to lose respect for the organization. Worse, employees who believe that pay policies do not recognize the value of their contributions are more likely to withhold future contributions to even the score.

◆ Pay policies should be perceived as fair by all employees. Employees deserve rewards for their contributions. It is important to explain to them the procedures used to establish their compensation level.

◆ An appeal mechanism that gives employees the right to challenge a pay decision should be established. Employees who can voice their frustration with a pay decision through a legitimate channel are less likely to engage in angry exchanges with supervisors, co-workers, or customers.

Summary and Conclusions

Employee Rights. In the employment relationship, both employees and employers have rights. Employee rights fall into three categories: statutory rights (protection from discrimination, safe work conditions, the right to form unions), contractual rights (as provided by employment contracts, union contracts, employment policies), and other rights (the rights to ethical treatment, privacy, and freedom of expression).

Management Rights. Employers have the right to run their business and make a profit. These rights are supported by property laws, common law, and the values of a society that accepts the concepts of private enterprise and the profit motive. Management rights include the right to manage the work force and to hire, promote, assign, discipline, and dismiss employees. Another important element is the master-servant common law doctrine that determines the extent of notice an employee is entitled to in cases of wrongful dismissal. In

the United States, the common law standard has been "employment at will," which allows employers to dismiss employees without cause or notice. There are three key exceptions to the employment-at-will doctrine: public policy exceptions, implied contracts, and lack of good faith and fair dealing.

Employee Rights Challenges: A Balancing Act. Sometimes the rights of the employer and employees are in conflict. For example, a random drug-testing policy can create a conflict between an employer's responsibility to provide a safe workplace and employees' rights to privacy. HR professionals need to balance the rights of the employee with those of the employer when designing policies that address emerging workplace issues such as drug testing, electronic monitoring of employees, and whistleblowing.

Disciplining Employees. Managers rely on discipline procedures to communicate to employees the need to change a behaviour to meet established standards. There are two approaches to discipline. The progressive discipline procedure relies on increasing levels of punishment leading to discharge. The positive discipline procedure uses counselling sessions between supervisor and subordinate to encourage the employee to monitor his or her own behaviour. Both procedures are designed to deal with forms of misconduct that are correctable.

Administering and Managing Discipline.   To avoid organizational conflict and potential litigation, managers must administer discipline properly. This entails ensuring that disciplined employees receive due process. Managers need to be aware of the standards used to determine if an employee was treated fairly and whether the employee has a right to appeal disciplinary action. For a disciplinary system to be effective, an appeal mechanism must be in place.

Managing Difficult Employees.   It is often necessary to discipline employees who exhibit poor attendance, poor performance, insubordination, or substance abuse. Managing the discipline process in these situations requires a balance of good judgement and common sense. Discipline may not be the best solution in all cases.

Preventing Discipline with Human Resource Management.   Discipline can often be avoided by a strategic and proactive approach to HRM that anticipates behavioural problems. A company can avoid discipline by recruiting and selecting the right employees for current positions as well as future opportunities, by training and developing workers, by designing jobs and career paths that best utilize people's talents, by designing effective performance appraisal systems, and by compensating employees for their contributions.

Key Terms and Concepts

collective agreement, 418
constructive dismissal, 416
contract, 411
contractual right, 411
due process, 411
employment contract, 411
employee discipline, 422
employee rights, 410
employment at will, 418
fiduciary duty, 413
formal employment contract, 416

gross misconduct, 424
hot-stove rule, 427
implied contract, 412
incompetent employee, 430
insubordination, 431
job banding, 433
just cause standard of discipline, 428
management rights, 414
master-servant relationship, 415
positive discipline, 425
probationary employment period, 430

progressive discipline, 423
psychological contract, 412
random drug testing, 419
residual rights, 415
right, 410
statutory right, 410
union contract, 411
whistleblowing, 421
wrongful dismissal, 411

Discussion Questions

1. Why have managers needed to place greater emphasis on employee rights in recent years?

2. Do employers have rights? If so, what are these rights?

3. A manager for a Kingston, Ontario, branch of Canada Trust is suing her employer for wrongful dismissal because she declared personal bankruptcy, largely the result of joint debts resulting from her husband's personal bankruptcy. Canada Trust has a written policy statement that indicates employees are expected "to manage your personal affairs and finances prudently and to be conservative with your use of indebtedness." Her job performance was not at issue—an appraisal two months previous had shown her to be average or above average in all areas—and the company, which offered her 21 weeks' severance, said it was not dismissing her for cause. Is this a case of wrongful dismissal? Do you think the employer is justified in the decision to terminate this employee? Why?

4. Mr. Neudorf, a manager and four-year employee for Sun Valley Co-Op, Ltd. in Manitoba, reacted negatively when a new general manager issued a hiring directive that Neudorf regarded to be another act stripping him of authority. He responded with a memorandum that was personally derogatory in which he refused to carry out the directive. The general manager terminated Neudorf after reading the memo. Do you think Neudorf, who sued for wrongful dismissal, would be successful in this case? What additional information would you seek to test your answer? Explain.

5. Compare and contrast the progressive and positive discipline procedures.

6. Total Recall Corporation has developed a camouflaged video surveillance system, called Babywatch, designed for parents who are concerned about the quality of child care they are receiving from their babysitters. The small inconspicuous device operates under low light and is capable of recording up to five hours of video and audio material. Do you think that parents using this system secretly would be invading the baby-sitter's privacy, or do you think they have a legitimate reason for monitoring the baby-sitter?

7. Should an employer always use the just cause criterion as the basis for disciplinary actions? Explain.

8. What alternatives to electronic monitoring could an employer use to effectively control employee theft?

Check out our Companion Website at: **www.prenticehall.ca/gomez** for a selection of self-study questions, key terms and concepts, updated Weblinks to related Internet sites, newsgroups, CBC video updates, and more.

MiniCase 1 — Co-Workers and the Company: Where Does Responsibility Lie?

An employee of a Newfoundland grocery store was involved in a dispute with store management in 1989. She was suspended for insubordination, but, after writing to the store's head office, she was reinstated with pay for the week she had been off work. From that point onward, she claims that supervisors harassed her about discrepancies in her cash receipts and treated her more strictly than her peers. She contended that the continual pattern of mistreatment meant that she could no longer work effectively at the store. She was successful in her suit for constructive dismissal.

Discussion Questions

1. Why do you think that the employee won in court?
2. Assume that the harassment had not come from supervisory personnel, but from other employees. Do you think the employer should still be held responsible—and bear the costs of constructive dismissal? Explain.
3. How can employers protect against being found liable for constructive dismissal? What general advice would you give?

SOURCE: *Human Resource Management in Canada.* (1995, January). Report Bulletin 143, p. 5. Copyright Carswell Thomson Professional Publishing.

MiniCase 2 — Just Curious

A manager with British Columbia Television Broadcasting Systems was very familiar with the organization's computing environment. One day he accessed a file containing all the organization's employees and their salary information—and copied it to his own computer. The employee spent several lunch hours ranking the employees' salaries from highest to lowest. He did not release salary information to anyone else. The employer learned of this and dismissed the manager for cause. Working under the jurisdiction of the *Canada Labour Code,* an adjudicator was appointed to evaluate the manager's claim of an unjust dismissal. After considering the evidence, the adjudicator reinstated the manager, pointing to three considerations:

◆ There was no indication that the employer or any third party was harmed.
◆ There was no indication that the manager used the information for his own gain.
◆ There were no written policies about access or use of computerized information.

Discussion Questions

1. Do you agree with the adjudicator's finding?
2. What steps should the organization take in order to prevent a recurrence of this or similar undesirable access to computer files?

SOURCE: Skippen, J. (1995, September). Employees and computer security: Clear policies are important. *Human Resources Professional,* 12–14.

Case 1

A Loose Cannon at Lakeland University

Kate Murphy, the chair of the Marketing Department at Lakeland University, and Carl Wharton, the dean of the College of Business Administration, have scheduled a meeting to discuss Professor Vladimir Badenov. Lakeland University is a large university with a prominent faculty noted for its excellence in research. Professor Badenov is one of the top schol-

➤

ars on the faculty; his research is highly respected and widely cited. However, because of his outrageous behaviour, Badenov is regarded as a "loose cannon" both by his colleagues and the administration.

Professor Badenov has embarrassed and intimidated Chairwoman Murphy during faculty meetings by interrupting her with loud and boisterous comments that make it impossible for her to run the meeting. Badenov has told graduate students not to work with one junior faculty member because he is a "loser" and does bad research. He has sent hundreds of E-mail messages to colleagues in different universities complaining that Dean Wharton is incompetent because Wharton would not provide funds for Badenov's trip to Paris to present a research paper. A faculty member who makes the mistake of offending Professor Badenov usually receives a barrage of obscenities in response. Badenov's antics have hurt the morale at the College of Business Administration. Most faculty members go out of their way to avoid him.

Professor Badenov is a full professor with tenure. At Lakeland, a tenured professor cannot be dismissed for any reason other than "moral turpitude," which is usually defined as "base or depraved acts." The administration does not regard his outrageous conduct as coming under these headings. Tenure is intended to protect freedom of expression, but some faculty members treat it as a licence to be disruptive without fear of retribution. Both Murphy and Wharton agree that something must be done about Professor Badenov's conduct.

Critical Thinking Questions

1. What are the likely consequences of doing nothing about Professor Badenov's conduct?
2. The administration cannot discharge Professor Badenov because he is protected by tenure. What kind of discipline could be used to discourage him from being a "loose cannon"?
3. Do you consider Professor Badenov's behaviour unethical? How can a professional who behaves unethically be discouraged from mistreating his or her colleagues?

Cooperative Learning Exercise

4. In small groups, develop an action plan that describes what the chair should do when a faculty member engages in disruptive behaviour. What conduct would justify the discharge of a tenured faculty member?

Case 2

The No-Smoker Policy at Health Unlimited

Health Unlimited is a store that sells health foods to the general public. It offers organically grown produce, meat that is raised without chemical additives, vitamins, and a health food restaurant with a salad and sandwich bar. As a condition of employment, each employee is required to sign a statement that he or she is a non-smoker and will not smoke either at work or away from work. Smoking at any time is considered a violation of this no-smoker policy and is enforced with immediate dismissal. The company justifies this policy by saying that smokers are sick or absent for reasons of illness more often than non-smokers. In addition, the extended health plan the employer provides is less expensive because employees are guaranteed to be non-smokers. Many of the store's customers and employees are as adamantly opposed to smoking as the company is.

Lisa DeMarco is the produce manager of Health Unlimited. She was an ex-smoker at the time of her initial employment. In recent months, though, because she is experiencing stress over her separation from her husband, Lisa has started smoking again. She restricts her smoking to off-duty hours away from the market. However, one of Lisa's co-workers spotted her smoking in a local bar and informed the store's manager, Ellen Guidry.

The next day Guidry confronted Lisa, who admitted to smoking and explained her situation. Ellen said she was sorry, but the no-smoker policy had to be enforced. She had no recourse but to discharge Lisa immediately. Lisa felt that her discharge was not fair because she was honest with her boss and had a good work record. She also believed she deserved some consideration for the difficulties she was going through in her personal life.

Critical Thinking Questions

1. Is it legal for a business to institute a no-smoking policy that restricts smoking during off-duty hours as well as at work? If legal, is such a policy ethical?
2. How can a company enforce a no-smoker policy during an employee's off-duty time?
3. Do you think Ellen treated Lisa fairly by discharging her for violating the no-smoker policy? Should the mitigating circumstances Lisa cited have entered into Ellen's decision? How would you have handled this case?

Cooperative Learning Exercise

4. In a small group, discuss why it is difficult to discipline employee off-duty conduct. Develop some general guidelines that managers should use to decide when and how to discipline employees' off-duty conduct.

15

Working with Organized Labour

After reading this chapter, you should be able to deal more effectively with the following challenges:

1 Understand why employees join unions.

2 Describe labour relations in Canada, and explain how labour relations differ in other parts of the world.

3 Identify labour relations strategies and describe how they affect operational and tactical labour relations decisions.

4 Describe the three phases of the labour relations process: union organizing, collective bargaining, and contract administration.

5 Explain how the union grievance procedure works and why the supervisor's role is critical in achieving sound labour relations with a union.

6 Identify the ways in which a union can affect a company's entire pattern of human resource management, including its staffing, employee development, compensation, and employee relations policies.

Labour actions span the spectrum of white- and blue-collar occupations. In September 1998, Air Canada pilots began a strike to press their demand for higher wages and improved working conditions. The 13-day strike inconvenienced travellers and businesses around the world. Most collective agreements are reached without strikes or lockouts, but the possibility of work (and pay) stoppages provides the incentive for both parties to take negotiations seriously.

Labour unions generate strong emotional responses from people. For some, unions are an anathema—an obstructive and costly intrusion into the management of an organization. For others, unions are the institutions that have protected workers from exploitative and abusive treatment by employers, and that have provided the leadership and political muscle that has led to progressive legislation in employment and broader social issues.

In Canada today there are still strong opinions, but there is also a general acceptance that unions will be part of the employment relationship in many organizations—some 38 percent of the non-agricultural work force is unionized. The issue today is often whether unions and employers can find ways of constructively resolving the issues between them. Those who do find the way often do more than survive—they flourish. Consider the following example:

In 1990, CBET, the CBC station in Windsor, Ontario, was closed by CBC because of a $108-million budget shortfall. The station lost some 85 positions and the news arm was reduced to three reporters and two camera operators whose main function was feeding stories to Toronto for redistribution as part of a southwestern Ontario programming package. Local residents were enraged by the reduction in local coverage.

By 1995, officials from news stations around the world were coming to investigate a new innovative news production at the station. What had happened? (The reason was *not* the restoration of previous funding.) CBC had been looking for ways of getting news service back to places like Windsor, but at a lower cost. After selecting Windsor as a test bed for the new approach, eight months of intensive negotiation ensued with NABET (the National Association of Broadcast Employees and Technicians) and the Canadian Media Guild. The result was an historic pact that allowed CBC management to introduce cost-cutting technology and to allow video journalists to combine reporting and video tasks—an arrangement that crossed traditional union boundaries.

By the time CBET went on the air again in October 1994, reopening with 23 positions (plus the five who had been in place for skeleton operations), it was a news station unlike any other in Canada or the United States. The station uses the latest non-linear editing machines and the Avid Airplay system, a disk (not tape) format that increases flexibility and eliminates many maintenance activities. The improvements in the station have not only made CBET economically viable, but have helped increase quality so that the station has achieved a healthy 36 share in BBM ratings of the adult viewer market.[1]

HRM on the Web

http://www.clc-clc.ca/ eng-index.html

Canadian Labour Congress

The Canadian Labour Congress is the primary national association of labour unions, with member unions representing approximately 2.3 million employees. Whether or not an employee is unionized, this site is useful because it reflects how organized labour represents itself to the general public and especially how the labour movement "frames" issues of public policy (including labour law) as it is discussed within its own ranks.

In this chapter we explore the labour-management relationship between employers and unions. We begin by examining why employees join unions and why many employers prefer the workplace not to be unionized. Since it is impossible to understand contemporary labour issues outside the context of economic and labour history, we then briefly review the historical origins of labour unions in Canada. Next, we discuss the role of the manager in labour relations and outline the major legislation that governs labour relations issues. This is followed by a description of the current status of labour relations in Canada, the United States, and some other countries. We then examine labour relations strategies available to employers and explore the rules and procedures that govern union activities. Finally, we address the impact of unions on other HR practices.

■ Why Do Employees Join Unions?

union

An organization that represents employees' interests to management on such issues as wages, work hours, and working conditions.

A **union** is an organization that represents employees' interests to management on such issues as compensation, hours of work, and working conditions. Employees participate in administering the union through *election of union officials* and support the union financially through *union dues*. (Many contracts include provision for dues check-offs—dues deducted from paycheques and transferred to the union.) The right to form and participate in unions is protected by law. The law also requires employers whose workers belong to recognized ("certified") bargaining units to confer with the union on various employment issues.

Generally, employees seek union representation because they (1) are dissatisfied with certain aspects of the job, (2) feel that they lack influence with management to effect certain changes, and (3) see unionization as a way of pursuing their interests and solving their problems.[2] If managers listen to employees, give their concerns legitimacy and consideration, and treat employees fairly, employees are less likely to organize or to join unions. In contrast, a management that ignores employees' interests and treats employees poorly is more likely to have a union to deal with.

There have been several explanations for the development of unionism over the past century—explanations that still have relevance, to varying degrees. Early observers emphasized competition among economic classes, pointing out that capitalism resulted in workers' no longer owning the tools of production and suggesting that unions provide a way for workers to protect and enlarge their share of what the economy produced. Automation and the replacement of employees with technology is an issue that figures in many discussions of today's economy; but this was also an issue during the 1920s and the Great Depression of the 1930s. Industrialization had by then proceeded to the point where it was clear that many people would depend on employment in industry. Unions emerged, according to more recent observers, as a response to the wide range of vulnerabilities to which workers are subject in industrialized economies—including job insecurity, deskilling of jobs, wage reductions, health and safety risks, and arbitrary treatment by managers.

Employer Preferences.   Employers usually prefer a non-unionized work force. The reasons are straightforward: unions exist to protect employees' interests against management decisions that are seen as damaging. Thus, unions seek mechanisms to limit managerial discretion. Under collective agreements, wages are set, seniority often becomes an entrenched criterion for promotion or layoffs, and binding work rules are drafted—meaning that management can be compelled to justify disciplinary or other decisions through the grievance process. From an employer's perspective, unions typically are seen to cause higher costs, reduce decision-making flexibility, and create a competing source of influence within the workplace.

■ The Origins of Canadian Labour Unions[3]

Unions have not always had the legal standing they have today, although they were present in Canada as early as the War of 1812. Local unions began emerging first in New Brunswick and Nova Scotia between 1812 and 1859 in the shipping, shipbuilding, and lumbering industries. Other groups organizing unions included printers, shoemakers, and tailors in centres such as Toronto, Hamilton, and Montreal. However, until 1872, the *Combines Act* made unions illegal, and it wasn't until the mid-1940s—with the passage of an Order-in-Council *(P.C. 1003)*—that the rights of workers to organize and bargain collectively were fully recognized on a national basis.

The notion that unions constitute an improper restraint on trade is based on a conception of employment as a private relationship that either party—employer or employee—is free to terminate if they find it unsatisfactory. In practice, of course,

Guide to Canadian Labour History Resources
www.nlc-bnc.ca/services/ esource2.htm

employers usually have considerably more power than individual employees. A large manufacturer such as Stelco, for example, rarely misses an individual employee who leaves as much as the individual is affected by leaving his or her job. Large employers have significant influence on communities as well as individuals. Any of Canada's resource-based communities (e.g., those dominated by mining or forestry) clearly illustrate that point. Even large urban centres are sometimes dominated by a particular industry—for example, base metal mining in Sudbury, steel production in Hamilton, and the huge GM complex in Oshawa. The power of employers that is based on the dependence of individuals and communities has historically been the context in which dangerous work conditions and exploitative human resource practices have been found, influences that were important in prompting the formation of unions.

The passing of the *Trade Unions Act* and the *Criminal Law Amendment Act* in 1872 was the result of labour unionism's quest for legal legitimacy. That legislation gave unions protection from charges of being a "criminal conspiracy." The formation of the Toronto Trades Assembly in 1871—a group that comprised some 15 local unions—was one of the developments that led to this change. This body, which later unsuccessfully attempted to become a national organization, was the result of the first of a number of attempts to expand union organizations into larger social and political instruments. Figure 15–1 presents an historical sketch of union developments in Canada.

The Canadian labour movement is an important dimension of the social and economic development of this country during the past 125 years. This development has been examined by historians and labour relations scholars. There are two dimensions to this history that we will consider: (a) the factionalism that characterized the development of unions in Canada, and (b) the influences of union development in the United States on Canadian unionism and collective bargaining. (Although the first international unions to appear in Canada were based in Britain, American unions began to appear as early as the 1860s and had a much more pervasive influence.)

From Figure 15–1 it is possible to get a sense of the forces at work in the Canadian labour movement. One of the main dynamics is the relationship between the influences of the labour movement in the United States and the pull of Canadian nationalism. Both inclusive unions, such as the Knights of Labour and One Big Union, and federations of unions, such as the Trades and Labour Congress (TLC), were strongly connected with U.S.-based organizations or movements. Yet the nationalist pull found a voice within these groups as well as in the early Canadian Federation of Labour and the Canadian Congress of Labour (CCL). In addition, the dynamics of unions within Quebec—including the strong role of the Catholic church until 1949—created a union movement there that developed separately from both the labour movement in the United States and also the movement in the rest of Canada. The founding of the Canadian Labour Congress in 1956, following the merger of the AFL and CIO in the United States in 1955, marked the beginning of a period in which jurisdictional disputes among unions diminished. It was also a period during which the Canadian labour movement increasingly established an internally cohesive structure, parallel to that of organized labour in the United States, but much less subordinate to it.

There have been many influences that have caused divisions within the labour movement in Canada. Some, such as the rivalry between *craft unions* (skilled trades) and the *industrial unions* (semi-skilled and unskilled workers), were important in the United States as well. The expulsion of the CIO from the AFL in the late 1930s and the jurisdictional feuds that continued for the next two decades washed over the border and saw the spinning off of the CCL from the TLC. Canada's small population and large land mass meant that regional differences, often correlated with differences in industries, would play a role in union relations. Some unions, such as those associated with the TLC, tended to follow the dictums of

Canadian Federation of Labour
www.infobahn.mb.ca/cfofl

Knights of Labour (1875–1910)

- founded in Philadelphia in 1869
- organized in craft or mixed local unions that combined to form district assemblies
- first local Canadian assembly in 1875 (Hamilton); by the late 1880s there were 250 assemblies in Canada
- grew rapidly in Quebec; laid groundwork for later Catholic unions (Canadian and Catholic Confederation of Labour [CCCL]), succeeded by Confederation of National Trade Unions (CNTU)
- lack of common denominators (trade or industry) contributed to eventual demise
- lasted longer in Canada than in U.S.

Trades and Labour Congress (TLC) (1886–1956)

- loose federation of craft unions
- strong emphasis on exclusive jurisdiction
- similar to and influenced strongly by the American Federation of Labor (AFL) in the U.S.
- political activism was relatively low, followed Samuel Gompers's business unionism philosophy
- unions grew rapidly and the TLC was the main labour federation during the 1902–1920 period
- membership stagnated during 1920s, decreased during 1930s
- a purge in the AFL (U.S.) in 1938 of industrial union members led to similar action in Canada

Canadian Federation of Labour (CFL) (1908–1927)

- a first attempt at an indigenous Canadian federation, wanted to become independent from AFL
- nationalist, but limited success due to lack of organizing skills and the affinity of Quebec unions for a separate Catholic trade union movement

One Big Union (1919–1956)

- grew out of the emergence of socialist labour organizations in western Canada and western U.S. in the early 1900s; sprang to prominence in 1919
- an industrial union movement (in contrast to the craft orientation of the AFL/CFL)
- did not initiate, but was a significant part of the Winnipeg General Strike of 1919
- caused some alarm because of its radicalism; internal dissension and opposition from government authorities led to rapid decline
- folded into the Canadian Labour Congress when it was formed in 1956

Canadian Congress of Labour (CCL) (1940–1956)

- in 1938 in the U.S., the Congress of Industrial Organizations (CIO), a group of industrial (not craft) unions, were expelled from the AFL
- the TLC was pressured by AFL to do the same thing in Canada; it did so in 1939, reluctantly, and the CCL was formed
- focussed on organizing mass production industries; grew rapidly
- suffered from internal divisions: nationalist versus CIO linkages, ideologies (communist versus non-communist orientation) in post-WWII era
- demonstrated that a Canadian trade union federation could be independent of the U.S.-based "international" unions, yet benefit from their resources

Canadian Labour Congress (CLC) (1956–present)

- the AFL and CIO merged in the U.S. in 1955, ending an extended period of rivalry and jurisdictional conflicts
- the TLC (a federation of mostly craft unions) and the CCL (primarily industrial unions) merged to form the CLC
- although facilitated by the AFL-CIO merger, the Canadian federation was independent; has frequently taken stands contrary to AFL-CIO

Labour Unions in Quebec

- 1921–1960: Canadian and Catholic Confederation of Labour (CCCL); the only church-based union in North America; emphasized French and Catholic priorities as well as economic issues
- post-WWII: union movement became more secular and increasingly independent of the Church, the main event being the asbestos strike of 1949, which signalled the end of the strong ties between the provincial government (under Duplessis) and the Church
- 1960–present: Confederation of National Trade Unions (CNTU) (or Confédération des syndicats nationaux [CSN])—name change of the CCCL reflecting the completion of secularization of the federation. Other major Quebec union federations: Quebec Federation of Labour (QFL), Quebec Teachers' Corporation

Figure 15–1 Trade Union Movements in Canada

SOURCE: Adapted from Craig, Alton W. J., and Solomon, Norman A. (1996). *The System of Industrial Relations in Canada* (5th ed.). Toronto: Prentice Hall Canada.

"business unionism," while others (One Big Union and some units of the CCL) were quite political in their orientation. The Quebec union movement, strongly influenced by the Catholic church until after World War II, developed within a frame of reference that was different because of its orientation to the French language and the culture of francophone Quebec. As a result, the development of unionism in Canada has had to contend with a wide range of factional influences.

■ The Role of the Manager in Labour Relations

The manager is on the front line in all labour-management relations. However, when a union represents a group of employees in a company, managers need a staff of specialists who can represent management's interests to the union. These **labour relations specialists,** who are often members of the HR department, help resolve grievances, negotiate with the union over changes in the collective agreement, and provide advice to top management on a labour relations strategy.

Still, it is managers who bear the major responsibility for day-to-day labour-management relations, so it is important that they understand workplace issues associated with unions. First, as we noted earlier, unions generally take hold only in firms where employees are dissatisfied with their jobs, and managers have a great deal to do with how employees perceive their work environment. Second, where there is a union, managers are responsible for the day-to-day implementation of the terms of the labour agreement. The more effectively they carry out this responsibility, the less time the company will spend resolving labour conflicts. Third, managers need to have a basic understanding of labour law so that they do not unintentionally create a legal liability for the company. Well-meaning managers can very easily do something illegal if they do not have a general understanding of the law. Finally, individual managers are often asked to serve on committees to hear grievances that union members bring against the company. A manager who understands general labour issues will be better prepared to hear and decide those cases.

In this text we have generally saved the discussion of legal issues until later in the chapter. However, because the nature and function of unions are so dependent on legislation, we will look at the specifics of that legislation first.

labour relations specialist
Someone, often a member of the HR department, who is knowledgeable about labour relations and can represent management's interests to the union.

■ The Legal Context of Labour Relations

Labour relations are governed by the same pattern of legislative jurisdictions as are many other aspects of employment, such as employment standards: the federal government regulates roughly 10 percent of employers and the provincial jurisdictions the other 90 percent. The result can be somewhat complicated in provincially regulated industries for organizations that operate in more than one province. While the laws are similar in many basic provisions, the steady flow of minor and major amendments requires that an HR professional keep up to date.

Legitimacy of Unions Established.   Historically, the *Trade Unions Act* and the *Criminal Law Amendment Act* of 1872 (precipitated by an 1871 strike by printers in Toronto and modelled over legislation in Great Britain) signalled the legal permissibility of unions. The former law established that the purposes of a trade union "were not unlawful merely because they were in restraint of trade," and the latter permitted peaceful picketing. These laws, however, did not require employers to recognize or negotiate with the unions.

Initial Legislative Frameworks.   For the period between this initial permissive legislation and the late 1930s, the major legislative change was the *Industrial Disputes Investigations (IDI) Act* of 1907, which required disputing parties to appear before a conciliation board, prohibiting strikes or lockouts until the board handed down a report. This federal legislation applied to a number of key industries such as public utilities, mining, transportation, and communication. A court challenge (the "Snider Case") resolved in 1925 had the effect of limiting the federal jurisdiction to a narrow range of industries. However, by 1932 all provinces except Prince Edward Island had passed legislation that made the federal law applicable to labour disputes within their jurisdictions. In 1937, various provinces began to elaborate labour legislation, but the advent of World War II had the effect of shifting authority back to the federal government under provisions of the *War Measures Act.*

P.C. 1003 and the Influence of the Wagner Act.
The most important of several Orders-in-Council during World War II was *P.C. 1003,* passed in 1944, better known as the Wartime Labour Relations Regulations. *P.C. 1003* combined principles from the landmark U.S. legislation—the *Wagner Act* (formally, the *National Labor Relations Act*) of 1935—with a two-stage conciliation process for settling contract negotiation impasses. The *Wagner Act* was designed to protect employees' rights to form and join unions and to permit employees to engage in activities such as strikes, picketing, and collective bargaining. It established the National Labor Relations Board (NLRB) that would:

1. administer *certification processes* to determine whether employees wanted to be represented by a particular organization, and

2. prevent and remedy unlawful acts called *unfair labour practices,* specifically: (a) interference with an employee's right to join a union, (b) domination of a labour union, (c) discrimination against an employee for engaging in union activities, (d) dismissal or otherwise penalizing an employee for filing charges under the Act, and (e) refusal to bargain with the certified union representing the employees.

The Canadian law, *P.C. 1003,* established a Wartime Labour Relations Board (WLRB), which had parallel responsibilities to the NLRB. This law was, in essence, Canada's national policy until the end of the war. The mandatory conciliation process reflects a slightly different philosophy from the U.S. legislation, where government was cast as referee and the parties were left largely to their own devices to negotiate a resolution to their differences. The conciliation process provided for mandatory use of a neutral third party: first, an individual conciliator, and subsequently, a conciliation board. An impasse not resolved through conciliation could then legally proceed to a strike or lockout. However, strikes and lockouts were not legally permitted during the term of a contract; a grievance process ending in binding arbitration, even if not explicit in the contract, was assumed. Most of these basic provisions still exist in most Canadian jurisdictions.

Post-War Labour Relations.
Unlike the United States, where labour relations were and are governed by federal legislation, Canada decentralized labour legislation after World War II because of provincial pressure to do so and the precedent of the Snider Case. The post-war federal legislation, the 1947 *Industrial Relations Disputes Investigations (IRDI) Act,* which sustained most of the provisions of *P.C. 1003,* therefore applied to only about 10 percent of the work force. Some provinces (Ontario, Nova Scotia, and Manitoba) enacted legislation similar to IRDI. Alberta and British Columbia adopted some of *P.C. 1003,* while Saskatchewan and Quebec enacted their own legislation. Throughout the 1950s, the wartime legislation provided the basic framework for labour relations in Canada. Since the early 1960s, innovation and variability have increased. And although public policy has generally supported the legitimacy of unions, the specifics of labour relations law continue to be contentious.

Basic Legal Issues.
There is consensus among Canadian jurisdictions about who can be represented by a union in dealing with a private sector employer: those

excluded are employees dealing with confidential industrial relations matters and those who are employed in a managerial capacity. While supervisors can join unions under the *Canada Labour Code* and in Manitoba, and while taxi drivers and other nominally independent contractors are allowed to organize in some jurisdictions, such variations are relatively minor.

There is a wide range of issues covered by labour legislation, but there are four that together provide a basic sense of how the legal framework functions.

1. *Recognition of a union.*

    (a) *Determining the unit.*   To form a union, it is necessary to determine which workers would be part of the bargaining unit. The initiative for this is with the workers or the union seeking to organize and represent them. The labour relations board, having been informed of the proposed bargaining unit, provides the employer and individual employees a chance to voice their views before determining which employees are to be included. The primary criterion is which set of workers shares a "community of interests" in matters such as work allocation, hours, conditions of work, and compensation.

    (b) *Certification.* The question of whether a union will be certified can be determined via voluntary recognition by the employer or through a demonstration of employee support. Within a specified time period, employee support must reach a certain threshold (ranging from 25 percent to 50 percent) of employees "signed up" in order to apply for certification. Certification results either from a high sign-up rate or a secret ballot, varying by jurisdiction. Decertification is possible, although it usually occurs through the replacement of one union with another rather than reverting to non-union status.

2. *Contract negotiation.* Once there is a recognized bargaining agent, employer and union are obliged to bargain in good faith. The traditional domain of these negotiations is compensation, hours of work, and "working conditions"—a broad category of work rules, job security, and other matters. Once the interests of the parties are resolved, a contract or *collective agreement* is drafted to reflect the arrangements arrived at. If the parties find themselves unable to agree, the strike or lockout weapons can be used by the union or the employer, respectively. Conciliation and, in some jurisdictions, mediation and supervised membership votes are mandatory before a legal strike or lockout may occur. Strikes or lockouts are ultimately resolved through negotiation and ratification of the new agreement by a vote of the members of the bargaining unit. One contentious issue about strikes is whether replacement workers can be hired to replace those on strike. Quebec law prohibits use of such workers, and British Columbia law limits their use. In general, strikers are legally entitled to reinstatement once the strike is resolved. There is no guarantee that all striking workers will be recalled immediately, and in some jurisdictions they may not be assured that they will return to the same job. By going on a legal strike, a worker is not seen as having abandoned his or her job. In contrast, replacement workers ("scabs," to union members) generally have little protection or legal claim to employment once a strike is resolved—and also might well find it difficult to work with those they displaced during the strike.

3. *Contract interpretation.*   All contracts must contain clauses that forbid strikes and lockouts during the life of collective agreements. Contract language can be subject to dispute, however, and there is therefore also a requirement that a grievance process, ending in arbitration if needed, be part of collective agreements. Even where such language does not appear in the contract, legally it is assumed to exist.

4. *Jurisdictional disputes.*   Although it is a much less pervasive issue in practice than the first three, there are still cases where competing unions claim representational jurisdiction for certain classes of workers, particularly in the construction trades. Curiously enough, the structure of these unions is such that the highest authority is actually the Washington, D.C.-based National Joint Board of AFL-CIO union representatives and four contractors' associations.[4]

Public-Sector Employees.   Public-sector workers in Canada are highly unionized. However, the use of strikes or lockouts to pursue a contract is not uniformly available. With the exception of Ontario, provincial government employees are not allowed to strike, the rationale being the harm such strikes cause the public. The right to strike in the broader public sector (schools, hospitals, municipal employees,

Keeping in Touch with the Workers.

To maintain open contact with local union members, representatives from the national office of each labour union visit the workplace periodically.

etc.) has been steadily extended over the past two decades. Some employees, such as police and firefighters, are frequently denied the right to strike and have their contract disputes resolved through binding arbitration. Even where the right to strike exists, various provisions requiring some employees to remain on the job are made to prevent the interruption of "essential services."

The federal jurisdiction's labour relations law is found in Part 5 of the *Canada Labour Code,* and applied to employees in:

◆ air transport, aircraft and airports,

◆ radio and television broadcasting,

◆ banks,

◆ federal Crown corporations,

◆ all extra-provincial shipping and services (e.g., longshoring, stevedoring),

◆ inter-provincial and international transportation and telecommunications services, and

◆ specified industries declared to be of interest to Canada or of two or more provinces (e.g., grain elevators, feed warehouses, uranium mining and processing).

The right to strike (and the right to lock out) exists for employees covered by federal law, although strikes that have caused large-scale disruption in the economy, such as in rail transportation or among dock workers in major ports, have frequently resulted in legislated solutions, often including binding arbitration.

Employees of the federal government are covered by the *Public Staff Relations Act* of 1967. This law allows unionization and bargaining over compensation, hours and other conditions of employment. At an early stage in contract negotiations, the union is given the option of choosing strike/lockout or compulsory arbitration as a means of resolving differences if a negotiated contract is not concluded.

▌Labour Relations in Canada

Labour relations in Canada have been shaped by domestic events and by international influences—from the United States in particular, as we have seen in the preceding discussion of union origins. In the following discussion, those matters or patterns that have influenced both Canada and the United States are referred to as "North American."

By and large, North American unions have accepted the legitimacy of capitalism and have sought a complementary legitimacy for unions as representatives of workers' interests. This observation is more true today than in earlier years of this century, when socialism and communism appeared to growing numbers of people as a constructive alternative to the social and economic problems of unrestrained capitalism. In Europe, unions became institutionalized parts of the political system, with "labour" parties contesting elections. North American unions took a more pragmatic approach, particularly in the United States. There are several key factors that characterize North American labour relations, in particular: (1) business unionism, (2) unions structured by job, (3) a focus on collective bargaining, (4) collective agreements, (5) adversarial union-management relations, and (6) the growth of unions in the public sector.

Business Unionism

Placing a high priority on protecting and improving the economic welfare of union members is the essence of business unionism. **Business unionism** focusses on "bread-and-butter" issues such as wages, benefits, and job security. This limited focus has led to less emphasis on broader political issues or on the employer's business strategies than is found in some international jurisdictions. When it comes to politics, business unionism is best summed up in the advice of AFL leader Samuel Gompers earlier in this century: "Reward your friends, punish your enemies." The implied corollary is, "but don't make a permanent commitment to any political party." Business unionism is not an absolute, even in the United States where for many years there was consistent support for the Democratic Party by organized labour. In Canada, unions and elective politics have had closer ties. The overlap between religion, politics, and organized labour was a significant influence in Quebec until well after World War II. Socialist and communist political movements were influential in many unions during the early part of the 20th century, especially during the Great Depression. Today, the New Democratic Party is typically identified as the party of labour in contemporary Canadian politics. The NDP has defined itself as representing more than simply a unionist constituency, but core membership and financial support have always included organized labour. Business unionism is reinforced by labour legislation that identifies compensation, hours of work, and working conditions as appropriate issues for collective agreements to resolve.

business unionism
A form of unionism that focusses on improving workers' economic well-being.

Unions Structured by Type of Job

Comparing North American unions with those in other parts of the industrialized world, there is a greater tendency in North America to form unions by type of job. Truck drivers are often organized by the Teamsters; teachers' unions are attached to provincial unions of teachers; auto workers belong to locals of the Canadian Auto Workers (CAW). This pattern of national or provincial unions with local affiliates at various employers tends to create a pattern of local unions looking after day-to-day issues, with the provincial or national union emphasizing strategic issues and orchestrating negotiating strategies. This pattern has some variations. The more highly skilled trades—the "craft" unions in the old TLC until the 1956 merger—have a narrower focus (e.g., carpenters and joiners), while the industrial unions, such as the CAW, have traditionally emphasized including as many workers from a particular employer as possible. The tensions that once existed between these approaches have largely abated since the creation of the CLC and the CNTU.

Focus on Collective Bargaining

Unions and management are the dominant players in the Canadian labour relations system. Generally, government takes a neutral role, allowing the players to make the rules that govern their particular workplace and attempting to facilitate the process through compulsory conciliation prior to legal strikes or lockouts. The mechanism of choice for developing these rules is collective bargaining. Under a **collective bargaining** system, unions and management negotiate with each other to develop the work rules under which union members will work for a stipulated period of time, usually two or three years. **Work rules** include any terms or conditions of employment, including pay, work breaks and lunch periods, vacation, work assignments, and grievance procedures.

collective bargaining
A system in which unions and management negotiate with each other to develop the work rules under which union members will work for a stipulated period of time.

work rules
Any terms or conditions of employment, including pay, work breaks and lunch periods, vacation, work assignments, and grievance procedures.

Unions that are legally elected by workers in Canada act as the sole representative of those workers' concerns to management. While unions may compete for recognition, once one is recognized, employees cannot choose to be represented by another union while the certification of the existing bargaining agent is in effect.

■ Collective Agreements

collective agreement

A union contract that spells out the conditions of employment and work rules that affect employees in the unit represented by the union.

The product of collective bargaining is a **collective agreement** that spells out the conditions of employment and the work rules that affect employees in the unit represented by the union. Because both parties enter the contract voluntarily, it can be used to enforce the terms agreed to. Violations are addressed through grievances that, if not resolved at an early stage, go to an arbitrator whose binding award can be enforced by the courts. For example, an employee who is fired in contravention of the contract can be reinstated by an arbitrator and have that reinstatement legally enforced.

Collective agreements are an important feature of the labour relations system in Canada. Most terms of employment can be negotiated. However, it is not generally permissible for a collective agreement to set terms that violate employment standards legislation, such as setting a wage rate below the minimum wage, setting a standard work week longer than the maximum number of hours allowed, or agreeing to eliminate payment premiums for working on statutory holidays. It also is not legal to agree to arrangements that violate legal human rights or employment equity standards.

Social and economic policy in Canada, including publicly funded health services, has been influenced by the labour movement as well as by many other politically influential groups. While not as pervasive a presence in Canada as in (say) Germany or Sweden, the legislation of benefits and working conditions is noticeably greater in Canada than in the United States.

■ The Adversarial Nature of Labour-Management Relations

The labour laws in all Canadian jurisdictions are based on the expectation that, for many issues, management and unions will find themselves in adversarial roles. This sense that some topics are in fact "win/lose" issues has led to rules designed to resolve these differences.

There are in labour relations parallels to the justice system, which pits the Crown against an accused or a plaintiff against a defendant. The justice system depends on rules to channel the contest and on judge and/or jury to determine what is fair. In labour relations, the same importance is attached to procedural rules, so that the antagonism is channelled via negotiations or grievance processes in a predictable manner. "Interest" disputes (negotiating a collective agreement) can lead to strikes, lockouts, or arbitration. Justice here is determined by the bargaining power and skill of the two parties (or their persuasiveness, if the result is determined by an arbitrator). When a contract is in effect, grievance resolution is limited to an bipartite administrative process that ends, if unresolved, in the hands of an arbitrator. From the data presented in Figure 15–2, the fact that unions are an established force in the workplaces of Canada, either through their bargaining or their indirect influence, is difficult to dispute.

The face of unionism has changed dramatically behind the relatively stable overall density of union membership. (Membership density is the ratio of unionized employees to all paid employees.) In 1967, union density among employed men was over 40 percent, while the figure for women was about 16 percent. In 1997, the sexes are approaching parity in union density, with men just over 32 percent and women at almost 30 percent. The stereotype of a union member as a male with modest education working in primary (agriculture and resource extraction) or secondary (manufacturing) sectors is quite at odds with the reality of the late 1990s.

	Union membership	Union density* Both sexes	Men	Women
			%	
	'000			
1967	2,056	33.2	40.9	15.9
1972	2,355	31.9	37.9	21.4
1977	2,785	31.2	37.4	22.6
1982	2,997	31.0	37.8	24.0
1987	3,614	32.0	36.0	27.0
1992	3,803	33.2	36.1	29.8
1997**	3,547	31.1	32.4	29.6

* Union density is the ratio of the number of employees who belong to a union to the number of paid employees.

**Average for the January-to-September 1997 period.

Figure 15–2 Union Membership and Density by Sex, 1967–1997

SOURCE: Statistics Canada, "Perspectives on Labour and Income," Catalogue No. 75–001, page 46.

The 1997 statistical portion of union members indicates that while blue-collar occupations have union densities of roughly 40 percent, white-collar occupations are approaching 30 percent. Union densities for employees with post-secondary diplomas or degrees are over 35 percent, compared to 26 percent for employees with less education. Accompanying and partially accounting for these patterns is the fact that union densities in the public sector are much higher (over 77 percent) than those in the private sector (about 22 percent).[5]

Organized labour is also an advocate for employees in the broader public debate about social policy. Unions in this venue are not necessarily in opposition to specific employers, although employers often take contrary positions to unions. Much of the legal framework for human resource management bears the imprint of these contesting points of view. Unions have generally advocated for increased minimum wages, shorter standard work weeks, better pensions, improved support for health care, improvements in workers' compensation, generous unemployment insurance, and so forth. Employers, understandably, are sensitive to the cost implications of these programs and frequently resist them. It is impossible to speculate exactly what "might have been" if unions and employers had not played the advocacy roles they have played, but it is safe to say that pay, benefits, hours, and working conditions in Canada would certainly be different than they are. Thus, the adversarial roles are not limited to contract negotiation and administration.

■ The Growth of Unions in the Public Sector

The general pattern of growth of Canadian union membership was relatively slow until World War II (20 percent of the non-agricultural work force in 1942), followed by a period of rapid union growth, driven first (throughout the 1950s) by widespread unionization of the mass production industries. This phase was followed by growth resulting from the legalization of public sector unionization and the right to strike during the 1960s and 1970s. The proportion of the non-agricultural work force that was unionized rose to 38.5 percent in 1980, and has since remained at just under that level—the figure for 1994 was 37.5 percent. The mix of public and private sector unionization during the past two decades shifted toward public sector organizations. (See Figure 15–3.)

During the past decade, the three largest unions in Canada were public-sector unions. Among the 10 largest unions, public-sector unions comprise over one million members, compared with roughly 750,000 members for private-sector unions.

Union	Membership	Public/Private
1. Canadian Union of Public Employees	412,200	Public
2. National Union of Public and General Employees	307,600	Public
3. Public Service Alliance of Canada	171,100	Public
4. United Food and Commercial Workers International Union	170,000	Private
5. National Automobile, Aerospace and Agricultural Implement Workers Union of Canada	170,000	Private
6. United Steelworkers of America	161,200	Private
7. Communications, Energy and Paperworkers Union of Canada	143,000	Private
8. International Brotherhood of Teamsters, Chauffeurs, Warehousemen and Helpers of America	95,000	Private
9. Social Affairs Federation Inc.	94,700	Public
10. School Boards Teachers' Federation	75,000	Public

Figure 15–3 The Largest Unions in Canada, 1993

SOURCe: Adapted from Craig, Alton W. J., and Solomon, Norman A. (1996). *The System of Industrial Relations in Canada* (5th ed.). Toronto: Prentice Hall Canada. Table 5.3. Toronto: Prentice Hall Canada.

When the top 20 unions were tallied, the number of members for the public and private sectors were 1.3 million and 1.05 million, respectively. Clearly, public sector unions play a very significant role in the Canadian labour movement.[6]

Public-sector unions no longer represent the source of growth they once did. Budgetary constraints at all levels of government have led to reductions in the work force not only among government employees, but throughout the broader public sector—in education, health care, and social services. Between 1989 and 1996, public-sector employment decreased by 38,000; in the private sector, goods-producing employers employed 75,000 fewer people, while service-producing organizations—many of them small businesses—increased employment by 1,195,000.[7]

◼ Labour Relations in Other Countries

Labour relations systems vary from country to country because unions mean different things in different countries. In Canada labour relations involves collective bargaining and collective agreements, but in Sweden and Denmark it involves national wage setting, in Japan it involves enterprise unions that cooperate with company management, in the United Kingdom it involves union affiliation with the Labour Party, and in Germany it involves union representation on the company's board of directors.[8] Unions not only represent a large portion of the labour force in most industrialized countries other than the United States, but are also important factors in the labour relations systems of many of those countries.

Figure 15–4 compares union membership both in numbers and as a percentage of the labour force in 12 industrialized countries, including Canada. Union membership as a percentage of the labour force is higher in most European countries, with Denmark and Sweden having, respectively, 88 percent and 95 percent of their workers represented by unions. Although unionism declined in the U.K. in the 1980s, British unions still represented 51 percent of the work force in 1989, one and a half times as many as in Canada and three times the proportion in the United States. More recent data suggest that Canada may be one of very few countries where union densities are increasing, while a sharp decline may be under way in the United Kingdom (see Figure 15-4). Even in Japan, whose firms frequently seek to avoid unions when they locate factories in North America, 25 percent of workers were unionized as of 1990.[9]

Year	Canada	United States	Aust-ralia	Japan	Den-mark	France	Ger-many	Italy	Nether-lands	Sweden	Switzer-land	United Kingdom
	Number (thousands)											
1955	1,268	16,802	1,802	6,286	861	2,554	7,499	5,536	1,221	1,722	663	9,738
1960	1,459	17,049	1,912	7,662	987	2,594	7,687	3,908	1,354	1,879	728	9,835
1965	1,589	17,299	2,116	10,147	1,075	2,914	7,986	4,011	1,462	2,161	783	10,325
1970	2,173	21,248	2,331	11,605	1,170	3,549	7,958	5,530	1,524	2,552	795	11,187
1975	2,884	22,361	2,833	12,590	1,359	3,882	8,623	7,707	1,710	3,053	887	12,026
1980	3,397	20,095	2,956	12,369	1,793	3,374	9,261	9,005	1,789	3,413	904	12,947
1985	3,666	16,996	3,154	12,418	2,034	2,944	9,324	8,861	1,540	3,762	882	10,821
1990	4,031	16,740	3,422	12,265	2,034	—	—	—	1,426	—	892	—

Year	Canada	United States	Aust-ralia	Japan	Den-mark	France	Ger-many	Italy	Nether-lands	Sweden	Switzer-land	United Kingdom
	Percent of Total Civilian Wage and Salary Employees											
1955	31	33	64	36	59	21	44	57	41	62	32	46
1960	30	31	61	33	63	20	40	34	42	62	33	45
1965	28	28	46	36	63	20	38	33	40	68	32	45
1970	31	30	43	35	64	22	37	43	38	75	31	50
1975	34	22	48	35	72	23	39	56	42	83	35	53
1980*	35 (36)	22 (22)	47 (48)	31 (31)	86 (76)	19 (18)	40 (36)	62 (49)	41(35)	88 (80)	35 (31)	56 (50)
1985	36	17	47	29	92	17	40	61	34	95	32	51
1990	36	16	43	25	88	—	—	—	28	—	31	—
1994*	(38)	(16)	(35)	(24)	(76)	(9)	(29)	(30)	(26)	(91)	(27)	(34)

Figure 15–4 Union Membership in Selected Countries, 1955–1990
SOURCE: Chang, C., and Sorrentino, C. (1991, December). Union membership statistics in 12 countries. *Monthly Labor Review*, 48; Employment Outlook, July 1998.

*Union densities, a slightly different statistic, are reported for 1980 and 1994 by Akyeampong, Ernest B. in "A statistical portrait of the trade union movement" in *Perspectives on Labour and Income*, Winter 1997 (page 53). Statistics Canada, Catalogue no. 75-001-XPE.

■ How Unions Differ Internationally

One analysis of unionism around the globe suggests that unions in different countries have different priorities.[10] Unions in different nations can be classified according to whether they emphasize economic issues, political issues, neither, or both. As we have seen, Canadian unions place very strong emphasis on economic issues, particularly pay, benefits, and (more recently) job security. Compared with unions in other countries, Canadian unions place much less emphasis on political issues, although the loosely coupled links with the NDP place Canadian unions somewhere between the U.S. model (strict "business unionism") and European approaches where Labour parties contest elections. Canadian unions and union leaders are involved in political life, but their involvement tends to be less ideological than pragmatic. That is, political involvement is just another means to address economic concerns.

At the other end of the spectrum, unions in France tend to be much more politically involved and less concerned with economic issues. The two largest labour confederations in France have clear political orientations, and one is also religiously oriented. Strikes in France tend to focus on political change as the primary means of protecting or improving conditions for union members.

Finally, Swedish unions provide an example of labour organizations that have a high degree of economic and political involvement. Swedish trade unions are often represented on governmental commissions in addition to actively representing their workers in economic affairs.[11]

Givebacks from the French.

In recent years, increased international competition has forced many Canadian unions to accept layoffs and other givebacks. The same is now happening in Europe. Here, French workers protest against proposed cuts in their pensions.

work councils

Committees composed of both worker representatives and managers, with responsibility for the governance of the workplace.

codetermination

The process of representing workers on a corporation's board of directors; used in Germany.

enterprise union

A labour union that represents workers in only one large company rather than in a particular industry; used in Japan.

Toyota Motor Company
www.toyota.com

We now turn our attention to two labour relations systems that have achieved high productivity and cooperation between unions and management: those of Germany and Japan.

■ Labour Relations in Germany

German law requires that all corporations involve workers in decisions at both the plant and the corporate level. This system is sometimes called *industrial democracy*. As practised in Germany, industrial democracy means workers are represented at the plant level in work councils and at the corporate level through codetermination.

Work councils, committees composed of both worker representatives and managers, have responsibility for the governance of the workplace. They are involved in operational decisions, such as the allocation of overtime, the discipline and discharge of workers, the hiring of new workers, and training.[12] At the plant level, work councils make many decisions on which unions would bargain with management in Canada. German unions focus on bargaining across industries on such issues as wages, rather than on bargaining within an industry, as is typical in North America.

Codetermination involves worker representation on a corporation's board of directors. In Germany, workers are well represented on boards of directors because it is assumed that labour and capital should form a partnership in governing the enterprise. With one-third to one-half of their boards of directors representing workers, German companies are likely to give employees' needs a high priority.[13] (The other members of the board represent the shareholders.) Not surprisingly, this feature of the German labour relations system has fostered a spirit of cooperation between workers and managers. For the German economy, the results have been fewer strikes and higher productivity. For workers, the results have been both greater responsibility and greater security. For example, IG Metall, the nation's largest union, has taken the lead on a number of important issues instead of merely reacting to company proposals. The union's group-work policies, the product of nearly two decades of research and activism, are designed to protect workers from layoff or transfer to lower-paying jobs. The program emphasizes retraining and gives employees real decision-making power. In 1988 work councils at all Volkswagen plants adopted the IG Metall program.[14]

■ Labour Relations in Japan

Japan has developed a successful labour relations system characterized by a high degree of cooperation between unions and management. A key factor in this success has been the Japanese enterprise union. The **enterprise union,** which represents Japanese workers in large corporations such as Toyota, Toshiba, and Hitachi, organizes the workers in only one company. This practice ensures that the union's loyalty will not be divided among different companies. The enterprise union negotiates with management with an eye on the company's long-term prosperity. This labour relations system was long reinforced by large Japanese corporations' offer of lifelong employment, which allowed Japanese workers to feel secure and unthreatened by changes in technology or job characteristics.[15]

The traditional lifelong employment policy has encouraged cooperation between the enterprise union and management. Many Japanese executives started their careers as union members right out of school, advanced to a leadership position in the union, and then got promoted into management, all within the same company. This type of labour relations system leads to close personal relationships among managers, union leaders, and workers that would be impossible under the more adversarial North American labour relations system. Because the enterprise union's legitimacy is unchallenged by management, there is a degree of trust and respect between the union and management in Japan that would be unthinkable in North America. This fact helps to explain the behaviour of Japanese executives who cooperate with a union in Japan but try at all costs to avoid unionization in their North American plants.

Unfortunately, there are signs that the labour relations systems in both Germany and Japan are in danger. In Germany, high labour costs for the average factory worker (Can$36 per hour versus Can$21 per hour, using a U.S. comparison) and the economic cost of unification with East Germany are forcing employers to drive harder bargains with unions. Competition in global markets has led to downsizings in some of Germany's largest companies and has strained labour relations. For example, Daimler-Benz, Germany's largest industrial company, has reduced its work force by 70,000 jobs and announced the expansion of a new plant in the southern United States, where labour costs are much lower than in Germany.[16] And in Japan, a closer look at life-long employment policies shows that they have always been restricted to the largest companies, applied only to men, and end at age 55. NTT, Japan's giant telecommunications company, announced in 1996 plans to reduce its work force by 45,000 jobs, a quarter of its total number of employees. Nissan, the auto maker, is planning to lay off 7,000 of its workers and close one of its auto assembly plants.[17]

Labour Relations Strategy

A company's **labour relations strategy** is its management's overall plan for dealing with unions. As Figure 15–5 shows, a company's labour relations strategy sets a tone for its relationship with the union that can range from open conflict to labour-management cooperation.

The most important strategic choice affecting a company's labour relations strategy is management's decision to accept or to avoid unions.[18]

labour relations strategy
A company's overall plan for dealing with labour unions.

Union Acceptance Strategy

Under a **union acceptance strategy,** management chooses to view the union as its employees' legitimate representative and accepts collective bargaining as an appropriate mechanism for establishing workplace rules. Management tries to obtain the best possible collective agreement with the union, and then governs employees according to the contract's terms. The labour relations policy shown in Figure 15–6 is an example of a union acceptance strategy.

A union acceptance strategy is likely to result in labour relations characterized by labour-management cooperation or working harmony. For example, Molson Breweries determined in the early 1990s that it needed to go beyond the traditional employer-union relationship in dealing with its 4,500 brewing, packaging, and trades employees. Contracts at the enterprise level included contract language designed to

union acceptance strategy
A labour relations strategy in which management chooses to view the union as its employees' legitimate representative and accepts collective bargaining as an appropriate mechanism for establishing workplace rules.

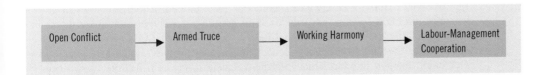

Figure 15–5 Types of Labour-Management Relations
SOURCE: Mills, D. O. (1989). *Labor-management relations*, (4th ed.), 222. New York: McGraw-Hill.

Our objective is to establish a labour policy that is consistent and fair. The purpose is to develop an agreeable working relationship with the union while retaining our full management rights. The rationale behind our labour relations policy is consistency, credibility, and fairness to union representatives and the workers who are in the union. In order to make our policy effective, the Company will:

◆ Accept union representation of employees in good faith, provided the union represents the majority of our employees;

◆ Maintain the right of management to manage;

◆ Adopt procedures by which top management continuously supports the positions of its representatives in implementing the firm's policies and practices in the area of industrial relations;

◆ Enforce disciplinary policies in a fair, firm, and consistent manner;

◆ See to it that union representatives follow all Company rules except those from which they are exempted under specific provisions of the labour contract;

◆ Handle all employee complaints fairly, firmly, and without discrimination;

◆ See that every representative of management exercises a maximum effort to follow Company policies fairly and consistently; and

◆ See to it that all decisions and agreements pertaining to the present contract are documented in writing.

Figure 15–6 Labour Relations Policy

SOURCE: (1990). *The company policy manual*, 332. New York: Harper Business Division of HarperCollins Publishers.

Molson Canada
www.molson.com

Chrysler Canada
www.chrysler.com

facilitate these partnerships, "[to] establish an enabling framework within which an organizational system can be sustained that will ensure an efficient and competitive operation and provide meaningful work and job satisfaction of employees." In many agreements, this led to the formation of joint steering committees to oversee employee participation initiatives such as project teams' job redesign and training activities. Such initiatives are difficult in a relationship that has long had a traditional adversarial flavour, but Molson is convinced that there is no alternative but to make the Molson Workplace Change process work.[19] Chrysler Canada is another organization where traditional union-management relationships have given way to new relationships—the new "deal" is not based on job security but rather on "You give us creative effort and we'll give you the opportunity to use it." The Windsor Assembly Plant has shown the results of the change in terms of quality and customer satisfaction, reduced injury rates, and half the number of grievances.[20]

Here are some other examples of union acceptance strategies:

◆ Ault Foods' representatives, expressing regret that labour legislation seems to be predicated on adversarial relationships, indicate that today's organizations often ask (unionized) employees to manage activities and give instruction to other employees. Their approach to managing has been to share information widely, fostering a collaborative environment. In one case, a plant that was losing money and also required some environmental upgrading was turned around through a combination of corporate investment and use of pension surpluses to offset the costs of environmental modifications.[21]

◆ Inglis invested $38 million in revising its Cambridge, Ontario, appliance plant into a state-of-the-art "cellular" manufacturing facility—one in which employees work in cells (self-managed teams) of seven to 10 members, each trained in the principles of group dynamics, problem solving, and quality. The employees are represented by the Communication, Energy and Paperworkers Union of Canada (CEP). CEP's administrative vice-president for the Ontario Region, Glenn Pattinson, cites Inglis's approach as a model. "Our union worked hand-in-hand with management to create a flexible work force."[22]

◆ Zehr's Markets, a grocery chain, and the union representing their employees (the United Food and Commercial Workers) jointly manage a training centre to upgrade and broaden employee skills. Workers' promotability has increased.[23]

As inspiring as these examples are, cooperation does not always guarantee success. In the second example above (Inglis), the employer promised not to close the factory as long as productivity stayed at or above a specified level. While there was disclosure of information and employees were happier and productivity improved, the improvements were not large enough and the plant was closed in 1994.[24]

Unions have had much less success in organizing small employers. Fewer than 10 percent of workers in small firms are organized, compared with some 44 percent of eligible employees in organizations employing more than 500 people.[25] Small organizations, especially those managed by their owners, tend to have a personal style of management. This often creates an informal culture in which the grievances that can lead to organizing are dealt with in an immediate or personal way. This is not always a constructive way, however—owner-operators with autocratic tendencies have been known to take a "my way or the highway" posture when complaints are raised. Not all owner-operators are good managers, and employees in smaller organizations often make less money and receive fewer benefits than they would in larger organizations. The presence of the owner-manager makes organizing difficult, and the small size of such employers often makes it less attractive for unions to approach workers.

This does not mean that unions are ignoring smaller employers. In Ontario, for example, the size of a newly certified (non-construction) bargaining unit dropped from 46.5 employees to 35 employees in the early 1990s—a decrease of 25 percent.[26] This change reflects the changes in the structure of the economy. Larger employers are shedding workers, and the net growth in employment is attributable to smaller firms. If unions are to grow, they must organize smaller workplaces. The Manager's Notebook entitled "Eight Ways to Attract a Union" provides a tongue-in-cheek set of guidelines that is particularly relevant to smaller employers.

> **A Question of Ethics**
>
> One strategy for suppressing union activity is to ask certain workers to report to management any union organizing activities that are taking place at the company. Is this legal? Is it ethical? Do you think it is good management practice? Why or why not?

▓ Union Avoidance Strategy

Management selects a **union avoidance strategy** when it fears the union will have a disruptive influence on its employees or fears losing control of its workers to a union. Managements that choose a union avoidance strategy are likely to be, at best, in an armed truce with unions and, at worst, in open conflict with them. (Refer back to Figure 15–5.)

There are two different approaches to union avoidance: union substitution and union suppression.[27] Which approach a company pursues usually depends on the values of top management.

union avoidance strategy
A labour relations strategy in which management tries to prevent its employees from joining a union, either by removing the incentive to unionize or by using hardball tactics.

Union Substitution.   In the **union substitution** approach, also known as the **proactive human resource management** approach, management becomes so responsive to employees' needs that it removes the incentive for unionization. Using this approach, many employers—including steel maker Dofasco, who uses unionized Stelco for reference; auto-parts giant Magna International, which has formalized an employee charter to ensure comprehensive dispute resolution[28]; and such small organizations as Alberta's County of Lacombe school board, which benchmarked and bettered the pay of unionized employees in the adjacent County of Ponoka[29]—have avoided unionization and have developed a reputation as being good places to work. All these companies have instituted a number of policies that lead to employees' feeling generally satisfied with their jobs and their ability to participate in management decisions. Some of the policies used by companies that take this union substitution approach are:

union substitution/proactive human resource management
A union avoidance strategy in which management becomes so responsive to employees' needs that it removes the incentives for unionization.

◆ Job security policies that protect the jobs of full-time workers. Among these are a policy that subcontracted, temporary, and part-time workers must be discharged before permanent employees can be laid off.

Manager's Notebook

Eight Ways to Attract a Union

Union drives start when owners and managers lose touch with employees and their needs. Labour lawyers and entrepreneurs who have fenced with unions offer these typical symptoms of a company on the road to unionization.

1. Retain poor employees who are habitual troublemakers. Experienced labour lawyers say it is those employees with the worst records who are usually the first to go to a union organizer. That's after they've already made the workplace unpleasant for good employees.

2. Discharge employees abruptly and without explanation. Firing employees must be done through graduated steps that are well reasoned, well documented, and offer assistance to correct poor performance. You don't want employees wondering who's next. Notes one entrepreneur, "Tyranny is not an effective way to avoid a union."

3. Spend money on expansion without raising salaries. This doesn't mean that you need to give everyone a raise. But take time to explain the situation. Perhaps the upgrades are necessary to protect jobs. But be prepared to set a date when raises may be expected.

4. Pay new employees as much as your old ones. Recognize length of service. Use salary, scheduling, and priority for vacant positions as rewards for loyal employees.

5. Let wages fall behind the going rate. Keep track of what competitors and similar industries in your region are paying. Upgrade salaries when necessary, and talk to your employees if you can't keep up.

6. Decrease the level of benefits your offer, or ask employees to fund more of the costs of benefits. This is asking for trouble. Don't cut costs on the backs of your employees and their families.

7. Don't worry about opportunities for promotion. Recognize service and delegate authority. If employees feel stagnant, it may be time for a new training program.

8. Trust in growth. Many entrepreneurs believe human resources problems will disappear as the company grows. You see this when managers ignore legitimate problems such as harassment or shift assignments. More often, it's a subtle message that builds as a company becomes preoccupied with new facilities or new markets. Your best policy is to communicate—and that means showing that your door is open and you're truly listening.

SOURCE: Unions: They're back! (1995, October/November). *Profit: The Magazine for Canadian Entrepreneurs,* 40–43.

- Promoting-from-within policies that encourage the training and development of employees.
- Profit-sharing and employee stock ownership plans (see Chapter 12) that share the company's success with its employees.
- High-involvement management practices that solicit employee input into decisions.
- Open door policies and grievance procedures that try to give workers the same sense of empowerment that they would have under a collective agreement.[30]

Union Suppression.   Management uses the **union suppression** approach when it wants to avoid unionization at all costs. Under this approach, management employs hardball tactics, which may be legal or illegal, to prevent the union from organizing its workers or to get rid of a union.

Although it is technically possible for employees to decertify a union or for the union to lose its certification for violations of labour relations laws, legislation in many Canadian jurisdictions makes it relatively difficult and time-consuming to do. Employers who want to dislodge a union have many tools, legal and otherwise, at their disposal; so to prevent union-busting, the hurdle for decertification is purposely set high. As a result, employers who wish to resist unionization use other means. One is to make it difficult for the new union to negotiate a first contract. Failure to negotiate a first contract can lead to decertification proceedings. Employers who use this tactic may be flirting with charges of unfair labour practices (in some jurisdictions, a first contract may be imposed by arbitration).

For employers that have established unions in place, the weapons available to weaken the union's power include contracting out (which increases flexibility and eliminates a certain number of union positions) and use of replacement workers. As mentioned earlier, use of replacement workers is illegal in British

union suppression

A union avoidance strategy in which management uses hardball tactics to prevent a union from organizing its workers or to get rid of a union.

Columbia and Quebec, and was illegal in Ontario until 1995 legislation repealed that provision. However, where replacement workers are allowed, a process of attrition can take place that can eventually erode the union's capacity to influence the employer. One high-profile example of this approach is the protracted strike at Irving Oil's main refinery in Saint John, New Brunswick. The strike began in May 1994 when the employer locked out the unionized employees. Key issues were the employer's demands for increased flexibility in job descriptions and the number of hours worked before overtime was to be paid. By January 1996, the union had rejected five versions of the company's offer. By using replacement workers and permitting striking employees to return to work (some 50 to 70 did, crossing their own union's picket lines), Irving declared its intention to proceed without the union, and ignore the strike.[31] The strike was finally resolved when the workers accepted a revised company offer and returned to worked in September 1996. However, this did not take place until labour mediator Innis Christie had issued an arrest warrant for the plant manager due to the employer's refusal to attend mediation proceedings. The Irving strike was generally viewed in New Brunswick as being important symbolically because of the widespread corporate operations of various Irving companies in that province. While the contract finally arrived at would be scant justification for the costs borne by the strikers, the fact that there is a contract and a union in place may well be important in the overall success or failure of the union suppression policy adopted by this employer.

In general, the union suppression approach is a higher-risk strategy than the union substitution approach and for that reason is adopted less frequently. Hardball tactics to suppress unions at all costs not only entail legal risks but can also come back to haunt management.

■ Building Managerial Skills: Managing the Labour Relations Process

Now that you have some grounding in the history of management-labour relations and relevant law, as well as a sense of the current state of labour relations and corporate strategies in this area, we can examine the specific components of the labour relations process. As Figure 15–7 shows, there are three phases of labour relations that managers and labour relations specialists must deal with on the job: (1) union organizing, in which employees exercise their right to form a union; (2) collective bargaining, in which union and management representatives negotiate a collective agreement; and (3) contract administration, in which the collective agreement is applied to specific work situations that occur daily.

■ Union Organizing

Union organizing takes place when employees work with a union to form themselves into a cohesive group. The key issues that managers confront in a union organizing campaign are union solicitation, pre-election conduct, and the certification election.

Union Solicitation.   Before a union can be certified as a bargaining agent, it must demonstrate that it has the support of the employees who are to be represented. This interest is demonstrated by getting employees to sign authorization cards and, where deemed necessary, to cast a secret ballot. Labour relations boards in Canadian jurisdictions vary in the percentage of the members in the bargaining unit (from 25 percent in Saskatchewan to 50 percent in Newfoundland and Prince Edward Island) who need to sign up before certification can be applied for. The sign-up process is required to show that there is sufficient interest in unionization to justify consideration. In most jurisdictions, the boards have the authority to certify a union without an election if there is clear evidence that at least 50 or 55 percent of the affected employees support unionization. (Alberta and recently, Ontario—like the United States, but unique in Canada—require a vote, regardless of the percentage signed up.)

Since most employers are not inclined to make it easy for a union to organize, unions often find that they need to approach employees carefully. Usually, unions

Figure 15–7 The Three Phases of the Labour Relations Process

first approach employees believed to be sympathetic to unionization, sometimes visiting them at their homes to explain and discuss the idea. This is a time-consuming process and usually gives way to a public campaign once a core of supporters is established. Soliciting interest via flyers (distributed as people enter or leave the workplace), face-to-face contacts, and holding meetings open to employees are usually part of the campaign. Employers are legally prohibited from active interference with, or discipline of, employees who show an interest in unionization. However, they are under no obligation to facilitate the process by allowing work time or company premises to be used for union organizing purposes.

Once a union has a sufficient number of cards signed and submitted to the labour relations board, under *regular certification,* the board will define the appropriate bargaining unit (which must include employees) and either certify the union or conduct a secret vote to determine that the union has support. It is useful to note that roughly four out of five certifications are the result of membership cards alone—that is, only about 20 percent of certifications are the result of a vote.[32] For those regular certification processes that do involve a secret vote, the conduct of union and management leaders should allow employees free exercise of their right to vote for or against representation.

There is an alternative mechanism for certification—the *prehearing vote*—that has recently been introduced in most Canadian jurisdictions. It is intended to be used in what one board chair described as "sticky situations"—for example, where there are indications that the employer is using unfair labour practices to avoid unionization. A vote is conducted before any hearing into the composition of the bargaining unit; the ballots are sealed until after the hearing. The intent is to prevent a campaign of intimidation from eroding the actual support for the union prior to a secret ballot being held. The ballots are unsealed only after a determination has been made as to which employees are in the proposed bargaining unit—theirs are the votes that are counted.

This process of certification is different from that in the United States, where the National Labor Relations Board requires an election after the collection of the required percentage of authorization cards for certification. The American certification process has been cited as one of the reasons for lower levels of unionization in the United States than in Canada—the time leading up to the election permits employers to engage in activities, both legal and in some cases illegal (threats, inducements, intimidation), that erode support for the union.[33] Such illegal conduct in most Canadian jurisdictions would result in automatic certification of the union and the imposition of a first collective agreement by the labour relations board or, possibly, by an appointed arbitrator.[34]

Certification Vote.   The labour relations board supervises the certification election, determining who is eligible to vote and counting the ballots. The voting is done by secret ballot, and the outcome is determined by majority vote. In Newfoundland, New Brunswick, Quebec, and Manitoba, the union must get 50 percent or more of all members in the bargaining unit. In other jurisdictions, the standard is 50 percent of those *voting*.

If the union receives the required majority, it becomes the certified bargaining agent for all the unit's employees. This means that it becomes the exclusive agent for both union and non-union employees in collective bargaining with the employer.

■ Collective Bargaining

If union organizing results in certification, the next step in the labour relations process is collective bargaining, which results in a collective agreement. Most collective agreements last for two to three years, after which they are subject to renegotiation.

Four of the most important issues related to collective bargaining are bargaining behaviour, bargaining power, bargaining topics, and impasses in bargaining. In all these areas, managers must monitor their behaviour carefully.

Bargaining Behaviour.   Once a union is certified by the labour relations board for that jurisdiction as the bargaining agent for a unit of employees, both management and the union have a duty to bargain with each other in "good faith." Refusing to bargain in good faith is subject to labour relations board sanctions. The following may be treated as examples of not bargaining in good faith:

◆ Failure to meet or unwillingness to meet with the other party.

◆ Suppression of information—the parties must present rationales for their various bargaining demands, although the other side is not obliged to accept such rationales.

◆ Reneging on commitments made or introducing new demands late in the process.

◆ Illegal demands, such as result in violations of human rights legislation.

In general, *good faith bargaining* means treating the other party reasonably even when disagreements arise. To show good faith, management should develop different proposals and suggestions for negotiating with the union instead of simply rejecting all union proposals.

Bargaining in Good Faith.
Employers and employees have different interests. Good faith bargaining can lead to mutually agreeable arrangements in the workplace.

Bargaining Power.   In collective bargaining sessions, both parties are likely to take opening positions that favour their goals while indicating that they are prepared to make some concessions to reach a satisfactory outcome. In other words, the parties select initial positions that leave them some room to negotiate. For example, on the topic of pay raises, the union may initially ask for eight percent but be willing to go as low as five percent. Management may initially offer the union two percent but be willing to go as high as six percent.

At which point will the parties reach agreement, five percent or six percent? The party that understands how to use its bargaining power will probably be able to achieve settlement closer to its initial bargaining position. *Bargaining power* is one party's ability to get the other party to agree to its terms. If management has greater bargaining power than the union, it will likely get the union to agree to a five percent pay increase.

An important aspect of a party's bargaining power is how it is perceived by the other party. Each party can engage in behaviours that shape the other party's perceptions. Management that acts in a powerful and intimidating manner may influence the union to make additional concessions. However, aggressive posturing by management may backfire and cause union negotiators to make fewer concessions. The 1995 rail strike had a number of manufacturers, including Ford of Canada, rethinking the savings of just-in-time (JIT) production techniques. Although such techniques have resulted in substantial savings, they make the manufacturer vulnerable to disruptions—estimates put Ford's excess costs during the strike at $90 million.[35] The threat of disruption in a highly interdependent production process has the effect of increasing the union's bargaining power.

Parties in negotiations have several tactical alternatives. Two modes of bargaining are available in pursuit of a collective agreement: distributive bargaining and integrative bargaining.[36]

Distributive Bargaining.   **Distributive bargaining** is an approach to bargaining that assumes that the issues are similar to "fixed-sum games"—if one party gains a benefit, it is because the other party loses that same amount. Unions that understand distributive bargaining will attempt to convince management that they

? A Question of Ethics

Suppose at a prebargaining meeting between the company's negotiating team and top management it is decided that the company will give up to a 4% raise. When negotiations start, however, the lead management negotiator states that the company cannot afford more than a 2% raise, and will go no higher. Is this ethical behaviour? What if the situation were reversed and it was the union negotiator who stated an absolute minimum demand, knowing that the union membership will accept less? Would that be ethical?

distributive bargaining
A approach to collective bargaining that treats the issues as fixed-sum ("win/lose") matters in which one party gains only at the expense of the other.

are willing and able to sustain a long strike that will severely damage the company's profits and weaken the company's position against its competitors. Managements that perceive the necessity of distributive bargaining will try to convince the union that the employer can sustain a long strike much better than union members, who will have to survive without their paycheques.

Thus, when parties perceive the issues at hand to be win/lose, fixed-sum matters, bargaining becomes a matter of bargaining power and the willingness to use it. Bargaining power depends fundamentally on the economics of the situation—from the employer's vantage, are the workers crucial to production, can they be replaced, and can the employer pass additional costs along in the form of increased prices? (When utility companies—e.g., long-distance phone services—were regulated monopolies, unions representing their employees had greater power than when these companies faced competition, because the employer could compensate for pay increases by raising utility rates.) From the union's point of view, can the union sustain a long strike? Bargaining power is also shaped by the expertise of the negotiators and the management of perceptions about the willingness of employees to strike or the management to lock out employees. Distributive bargaining is more likely when the issues are inherently win/lose, and when there is a history of abrasive and distrustful relations, even if a more constructive approach to bargaining is possible.

integrative bargaining

A approach to collective bargaining that treats the issues as variable-sum (potentially, "win/win," "win/lose," or "lose/lose") matters in which the outcome actually achieved depends on mutual trust and problem solving.

Integrative Bargaining.   **Integrative bargaining** is an approach to bargaining that assumes the issues are more like a "variable-sum game"—where, depending on the approach taken by the parties, both can gain or both can lose. This is the approach that assumes there is a "win/win" situation that can be found, but also acknowledges that one or both sides can be "losers" if the bargaining is not done effectively. Bargaining takes the form of problem solving rather than competition.

While integrative approaches seem commendable, the main challenge in trying to use integrative bargaining is the realization that it doesn't apply to all issues. Work rules, job descriptions, and similar matters often can benefit from an integrative approach. Wage rates and vacation entitlements are more likely to be "fixed-sum" issues. Employers and unions that have a mutual track record of integrity and civility are more likely to be able to identify matters where integrative approaches will work, and to use them. A mutual commitment to use integrative approaches where possible may also allow some of the tougher "bread-and-butter" issues to be examined in a more comprehensive way—a good example are the expenses involved in benefits programs: flexible benefits (see Chapter 12) often allow employees choices that let them tailor benefits to their needs while employers can introduce policies such as deductibles, copayments and "health accounts" that help them control costs. The employer's overall labour relations strategy therefore plays a major role in determining its approach to bargaining. Employers with a union acceptance strategy are more likely to mix integrative and distributive bargaining, while those with a union avoidance strategy are more likely to focus solely on distributive bargaining.

Bargaining Topics.

Bargaining topics can be grouped into three categories: basic, elective, and illegal. In the United States, a legal distinction is made between basic ("mandatory," in U.S. law) and elective ("permissive") topics. In Canadian jurisdictions, that distinction is not present.

Basic bargaining topics include wages, hours, and employment conditions. These are the topics that both union and management consider fundamental to the organization's labour relations, and are explicitly part of virtually all collective agreements. Some examples of each of these basic topics are shown in Figure 15–8.

"Compensation" can mean any type of compensation, including base pay rates, pay incentives, health insurance, and retirement benefits. "Hours" can mean anything to do with work scheduling, including the allocation of overtime and the

Compensation	Hours	Employment Conditions
Base pay rates	Overtime	Layoffs
Overtime pay rates	Holidays	Promotions
Retirement benefits	Vacation	Seniority provisions
Health benefits	Shifts	Safety rules
Travel pay		Work rules
Pay incentives		Grievance procedures
		Union shop
		Job descriptions

Figure 15–8 Basic Bargaining Topics

amount of vacation time granted. "Employment conditions" can mean almost any work rule that affects the employees represented by a union. These include grievance procedures, safety rules, job descriptions, and the bases for promotions.

Elective bargaining topics may be negotiated if the parties mutually agree, but such topics are not standard features of most collective agreements. Elective bargaining topics include provisions for union members to serve on the company's board of directors and benefits for retired members of the union. For example, in the recessionary economy of the early 1990s, some unions swapped wage concessions for equity in the company and a stronger voice in how it is run. It is possible for employers to reach individual arrangements with employees that may not be sanctioned by a collective agreement. The range of issues that can be bargained is quite diverse—consider the following examples:

Simon Fraser University
www.sfu.ca

◆ In one case, Simon Fraser University agreed to allow an employee to perform all his employment duties from home via computer. The union representing the employee argued that the employer had no right to schedule work at an employee's home. The British Columbia Court of Appeals agreed that the employer could not *unilaterally* schedule work at home, but that a mutually agreed-upon arrangement with an employee did not require consent from the union.[37]

◆ Another illustration shows that issues that seem mundane to outsiders can have practical and symbolic importance in specific circumstances. The contract negotiated between the Toronto Transit Commission and its transit workers in early 1996 included the normal hard bargaining over economic issues (employees got a one percent raise) and the clothing that could be worn to work—shorts were added as an optional part of the employees' uniform in hot weather.[38]

Toronto Transit Commission
www.city.toronto.on.ca/ttc/index.htm

Illegal bargaining topics may not be part of negotiations or collective agreements. Examples include demands that would result in policies or practices that are illegal under other statutes such as employment standards, human rights, or health and safety legislation. It is also illegal to attempt, in negotiations, to bargain jurisdictional matters (e.g., which employees in which unions, or which bargaining units, get assigned to certain organizational work) or to interfere in internal union matters such as selection of representatives or disciplining of members. However, it should be stressed that it is not *illegal* to engage in hard bargaining, including the use of harsh language and insults.

Impasses in Bargaining.   A collective agreement cannot be finalized until the bargaining representatives on both sides of the table go back to their organizations and obtain approval of the contract. Unions ask their members to vote on the agreement—a majority of union members is required to approve it. Management's negotiating team may need approval from the company's top executives, but usually has received authorization to make the offer on which the union votes. If the parties cannot agree on a tentative agreement, they may reach an *impasse* in bargaining.

One of the key differences between U.S. and Canadian labour relations law is the emphasis placed on third-party mechanisms in Canada. In Canada, before an impasse in bargaining can become a *legal* strike or lockout, compulsory conciliation must (and mediation sometimes may) take place. In some situations, such as those concerning police or other employees who cannot legally strike, compulsory binding arbitration is the mechanism for resolving differences that have not been resolved in negotiations.

Compulsory Conciliation. One feature of Canadian legislation since the federal *Industrial Disputes Investigations Act* of 1907 is the use of compulsory conciliation. If a contract has expired and either party believes that negotiations are unlikely to resolve the issues, a conciliation officer (usually a full-time employee of a labour department) may be requested to meet with the parties. After engaging in fact finding with the parties, the conciliator may conclude that there is in fact an impasse. Upon determining that there is an impasse, the conciliator may either recommend that a conciliation board be impanelled (which is rarely done) or file a report indicating that conciliation is unlikely to resolve the dispute. Because the conciliator is required to be strictly neutral, he or she is limited in the substantive interventions that can be made.

Having been through conciliation, the union and employer are in a position to engage in a strike or lockout. If the impasse persists because the parties have taken rigid positions, a strike may result. Mediation—an optional intervention, in some legislation—provides for a more wide-ranging intervention than does conciliation. Mediators are trained in conflict resolution techniques and are sometimes able to improve communication between the parties so that the impasse is resolved. Although mediation is available, it is not mandatory for most bargaining situations.

The Effect of Third-Party Intervention. For purposes of our discussion, it is useful to see the point in the process at which collective agreements are reached. Using bargaining units of 500 or more where contracts were negotiated in 1990, we find:

- ♦ 56% were resolved prior to any third-party involvement.
- ♦ 19% were resolved during the process of contact with a conciliator or conciliation board, or in bargaining that followed that contact.
- ♦ 12% were resolved during the process of mediation.
- ♦ 5% were settled through arbitration.
- ♦ 8% resulted in work stoppages (strikes or lockouts) before an agreement was reached.

Employers and unions resort to strikes or lockouts in roughly one in 12 cases. When one considers that only slightly over half of all negotiations are settled without third-party involvement, it appears that conciliation and mediation in particular are highly effective. The statistics tend to overstate the effectiveness of third-party intervention somewhat, because "going to conciliation" is often a ritual part of hard bargaining and is necessary to get to a legal strike position. Nonetheless, the use of third-party involvement is an important distinguishing feature of Canadian labour relations.

Strikes. Strikes are a way of applying economic pressure to employers. By withholding services and through picketing the premises of the employer, unions attempt to get employers to agree to their terms. Employers have a complementary option—the lockout—once the conciliation process is completed. Lockouts occur less frequently but still can be useful for employers, especially those with multiple locations facing rotating strikes or other pressure techniques such as "working to rule," in which the workers disrupt operations but are still earning most of their regular pay. The lockout allows the employer to force the issue by denying these options to the union. One problem with strikes or lockouts is that they raise the stakes for the parties—once the work stoppage has begun, it is difficult to go back to work without "winning" something. Experienced negotiators understand this and will often use this dynamic to reach an agreement at the "eleventh hour."

Striking union members receive no wages or benefits until they return to work, although they may draw some money from the union's strike fund, which is set up to give a small allowance to cover the striking members' basic expenses. However, a long strike may exhaust the strike fund, putting pressure on the union to make concessions in order to get its members back to work. The strike puts pressure on the employer, and also on the employees. Strike activity in Canada has varied significantly during the past two decades. In the late 1960s through the mid-1970s, Canada lost a greater proportion of work to strikes than any country other than Italy. The peak was 1976, in which roughly 11.5 million person-days of work were lost to strikes and lockouts, 0.53 percent of estimated working time for the year. The level has steadily declined, although the level of unionization has not changed substantially, so that in 1994, the number of days lost was 1.5 million, which represented 0.06 percent of potential working time.

Management also faces significant strike costs. A strike can force a company to shut down operations and lose customers. Strikes in the public-sector operations such as mass transportation, health care or schools can create strong pressure on the management and also on the elected officials who are alternately responsible. In a highly competitive market such actions may plunge the company into bankruptcy. Despite the negative outcomes sometimes associated with strikes, they are an important feature of the collective bargaining process. With the dramatic reduction in time lost to strikes, the impact of the strike weapon might seem small. Time lost to occupational health and safety reasons is considerably greater (see Chapter 16). Even more working time is lost because of the common cold than because of strikes.[39] However, without the potential for strikes, there would not be the same strong incentives for employers and unions to resolve their differences and come to an agreement about major features of the employment relationship. Arbitration is useful where public safety concerns make a work stoppage unacceptable. In some cases, such as the rail strike in 1995, arbitration is imposed via legislation. The strike and lockout provide an incentive to find common ground, and a negotiated settlement arrived at under those circumstances is more likely to be accepted as legitimate by the parties than one imposed from outside.

Strikes can occur in several circumstances. The only situation in which a strike is legally permitted is the one discussed above—the **economic strike.** Another type of strike, called the **wildcat strike,** is (ostensibly) a spontaneous work stoppage that occurs during the term of a valid contract—a work stoppage not initiated or usually approved by union leadership because it violates the contract. Wildcat strikes typically occur when workers are angered by a disciplinary decision or other decisions that are triggered by an incident in a highly sensitive area, such as seniority violations or contracting out. This type of strike is intended to draw management's attention to an issue that is sufficiently important to the employees involved that they are willing to violate the no-strike provisions of the contract—and risk the disciplinary penalties that may result—in order to bring the matter to a head. The preferred method of resolving disputes between unionized workers and management is the grievance procedure.

economic strike

A strike that takes place when there is an impasse in negotiations to reach a collective agreement.

wildcat strike

A spontaneous work stoppage that occurs during the term of a contract, usually the result of a management decision that employees deem provocative.

■ Contract Administration

The last phase of labour relations is contract administration, which involves application and enforcement of the collective agreement in the workplace. Disputes occasionally arise between labour and management over such issues as who should

grievance procedure

A systematic step-by-step process designed to settle disputes regarding the interpretation of a collective agreement.

union steward

An advocate responsible for representing an employee's case to management in a grievance procedure.

arbitration

The last step in a grievance procedure. The decision of the arbitrator, who is a neutral individual selected from outside the firm, is binding on both parties.

be promoted or whether an employee has abused sick leave privileges. The steps to be taken to resolve such disputes are spelled out in the collective agreement.

The mechanism preferred by most unions and managements to settle disputes is the grievance procedure. A **grievance procedure** is a systematic step-by-step procedure designed to settle disputes regarding the interpretation of the collective agreement.

Although employees may attempt to settle their grievances through such alternatives to the grievance procedure as an open door policy or a meeting with an employee relations representative in the HR department (see Chapter 13), grievance procedures under union contracts have two significant advantages for employees that no other HRM program can provide:

1. The grievance procedure provides the employee with an advocate responsible for representing the employee's case to management. This representative is called the **union steward.** Under any other system used to handle grievances, the employee is represented by someone who is either a manager or an agent of management. Such people obviously cannot be entirely dedicated to the employee's position.

2. The last step in the grievance procedure is **arbitration,** a quasi-judicial process that is binding on both parties. Arbitration can be provided by a single arbitrator, a permanent umpire, or a tripartite panel. The tripartite panel includes a union nominee, a management nominee, and a neutral chair selected by the two other members. Although once the most common form of arbitration, tripartite panels are now used less frequently than single arbitrators.

Steps in the Grievance Procedure.

Most union grievance procedures have three or four steps leading up to arbitration, the final step. Figure 15–9 illustrates a four-step union grievance procedure. Usually a time limit is set for resolution of the grievance at each step. Later steps in the procedure require more time than earlier steps, and the degree of formality increases with each step. Because the grievance procedure is both time-consuming and distracts several people from their regular job duties, it is generally advantageous for the company to try to solve disputes at as early a stage as possible.

The key to an effective grievance procedure is training supervisors to understand the collective agreement and to work with union stewards to settle grievances at the first step. The labour relations staff in the HR department can make an important contribution here by training and consulting with supervisors.

The first step of the grievance procedure is taken when an employee with a grievance tells the union steward about the dispute. In our example in Figure 15–9, the employee must make the dispute known to the supervisor and/or the steward within five working days of its occurrence. The steward refers to the collective agreement to determine if the grievance is valid and, if it is, tries to work with the employee's supervisor to settle it. The grievance may or may not be put in writing. Most grievances (about 75%) are settled at this first step.

If the dispute cannot be resolved at this first step, the grievance is put into writing, and, in our example, the department or plant manager and a union official (such as the union's business representative) have an additional five working days to resolve the issue. At this second step, a formal meeting is often held to discuss the grievance.

If the second step is unsuccessful at resolving the grievance, the parties move on to the third step. This usually involves both a corporate manager (for example, the company's director of labour relations) and a local and national union representative. In our example, the collective agreement gives these persons 10 days to respond to the grievance. Grievances that have the potential to set precedents affecting employment policy may get "kicked up" to this level because it is inappropriate for plant supervisors or managers to settle them. For example, a grievance concerning production standards may have widespread implications for all workers if a corporatewide collective agreement is in effect. Because the third

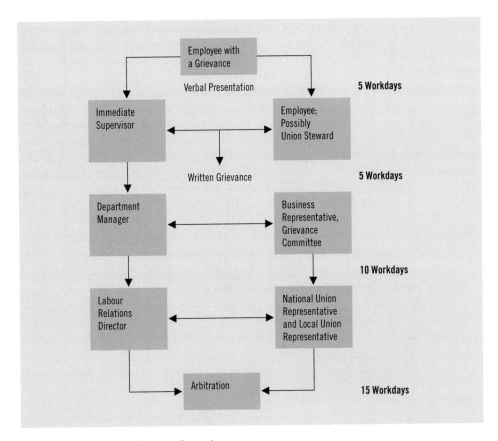

Figure 15–9 A Union Grievance Procedure

SOURCE: Adapted from Allen, R., & Keavany, T. (1988). *Contemporary labor relations* (2nd ed.), 530. Reading, MA: Addison-Wesley.

step is the last step prior to arbitration, it is management's final opportunity to negotiate a settlement with the union. It is common for management to try to "cut a deal" with the union at this step.

The final step of the grievance procedure is arbitration. Only about one percent of grievances get as far as arbitration; the rest are settled at the earlier steps. Both parties select the arbitrator, before whom the union and management advocates present their case and evidence at a hearing with a quasi-judicial format. The arbitrator then examines the evidence and makes a ruling. Most arbitrators also write an opinion outlining their reasoning and the sections of the collective agreement that influenced their decision. This opinion can serve as a guideline for dealing with similar disputes in the future. The arbitrator's decision is final and binding on both parties.

Recent Supreme Court of Canada rulings have expanded the authority of arbitrators in disputes arising from situations in which collective bargaining agreements are in place. In 1995, the Court found that disputes between an employer and an employee arising out of the interpretation, application, administration, or violation of the collective agreement were the exclusive jurisdiction of the arbitration process—parallel lawsuits between employer and employee were dismissed. The Court also found that arbitrators have the right to hear *Charter of Rights* claims and award remedies when allegations arise out of collective agreements, broadening the scope of cases arbitrators may hear.[40]

Types of Grievances.   Employees initiate two types of grievances. The first is a *contract interpretation grievance* based on union members' rights under the collective agreement. If the contract's language is ambiguous, this type of grievance may go to arbitration for clarification. For example, suppose that a collective agreement allows workers two 10-minute coffee breaks per day. If management decides it would be more efficient to eliminate coffee breaks and orders employees to stop taking them, employees may file a contract interpretation grievance to get this privilege restored.

The second type of grievance involves employee discipline. In such cases, the grievance procedure examines whether the employee in question was disciplined for just cause, and management has the burden of proof. An important aspect of these cases is determining whether the disciplined employee received due process. For minor infractions, management is expected to give employees the opportunity to correct their behaviour via the progressive discipline procedure (verbal warning, written warning, suspension, discharge). For more serious charges (such as theft), management must provide strong evidence that the discipline was warranted.

Benefits of Union Grievance Procedures.   Union grievance procedures provide benefits to both management and employees. Specifically:

◆ The grievance procedure protects union employees from arbitrary management decisions; it is the mechanism for organizational justice.

◆ The grievance procedure helps management quickly and efficiently resolve conflicts that could otherwise fester and lead to greater problems, either in the form of wildcat strikes or other "sabotage," or lead to a much more complicated negotiation when the current contract expires.

◆ Management can use the grievance procedure as an upward communications channel to monitor and correct the sources of employee dissatisfaction with jobs or company policies.

■ The Impact of Unions on Human Resource Management

A union can significantly alter a company's HRM policies because of its bargaining power, which is supported by labour law. In the absence of a union, management is more likely to develop HRM policies based on the principle of efficiency. For example, a non-unionized company is more likely to adopt a meet-the-market pay policy because the market wage is the most efficient way to allocate labour costs (see Chapter 10). But when a union enters the picture, management must develop policies that reflect the preferences of the majority of workers who are represented by the union.[41] In this case, management is more likely to adopt an above-the-market pay policy when it settles with the union because union members have strong preferences for higher wages. In this section, we look at the changes in staffing, employee development, compensation, and employee relations practices that are likely under unionization.

■ Staffing

seniority

An employee's length of service either in a specific position or with an employer.

Under a collective agreement, job opportunities are allocated to individuals on the basis of seniority. **Seniority** is the length of time a person works for an employer. In a unionized company, promotions, job assignments, and shift preferences are given to the employee with the most seniority in the unit.[42] Layoffs in unionized firms are almost always governed according to the last in, first out rule (see Chapter 6).[43]

Work rules tend to be less flexible in a unionized workplace because they are likely to be formalized in the labour agreement. When labour relations are adversarial, collective agreements are more likely to have inflexible work rules written into them. When labour relations are more cooperative, work rule specifications may purposely be left out of the contract. In certain industries, this gives management the flexibility to adjust to the rapidly changing technological requirements of producing a product or service. The major strike in the rail industry in 1995 is a classic example of the conflict that can emerge when flexibility has not been achieved. Some 20,000 employees of CP Rail, Canadian National Railways, and Via Rail Canada had achieved the eight years of service that allowed them to be assured work in their region. An illustration of the problems this caused, according to CP Rail spokesman B.C. Scott, was the 260 shop craft employees who were paid to sit at home in Montreal while CP Rail was required to hire new workers to do similar work in Western Canada.[44] The railways won considerable flexibility through an arbitrated settlement, including removal of the employment security provisions for recent hires, a six-year cap on security for those who have it, and a requirement that CN employees accept employment anywhere in the CN system.[45] Increasingly, unions and companies are finding ways to meld the understandable interest employees have in secure jobs with the employers' need for flexibility.

In the absence of a union, the employer is more likely to allocate job opportunities to employees on the basis of merit.[46] In most cases, merit is determined by a supervisor's judgement of the employee's performance. Supervisors in a non-unionized workplace have more power and influence because of their authority to reward employees' efforts with promotions, attractive job assignments, and preferred work schedules. Layoff decisions in non-unionized firms are more likely to take both merit and seniority into consideration. Finally, work rules are often more flexible in a non-unionized firm, because the employer is not tied to a contract and is therefore not required to justify to employees any changes made in the way work is done. In non-unionized firms it is management alone that determines the most efficient way to produce a product or service and deliver it to the customer. Managers in non-unionized firms also decide whether to have experts (such as engineers) improve work methods or to delegate that responsibility to employee problem-solving teams.

■ Employee Development

In unionized companies, the uses of performance appraisal are very limited because the appraisal data usually come from the supervisor, a source that many unions find problematic. Unions tend to balk at using performance appraisal as the basis for making pay and staffing decisions. If performance appraisal is done at all for union employees, it is used simply to provide some feedback on their performance. In a non-unionized workplace, however, the performance appraisal is likely to have a broad set of uses for HR decisions. It is used to determine pay raises, promotions, job assignments, career planning, training needs, and layoff or discharge.[47]

Unionized firms tend to retain their employees longer than non-unionized firms do.[48] There are a few reasons for the lower quit rates in unionized firms. First, unionized employees are more likely to express their dissatisfaction through the grievance procedure, so this channel may become an alternative to quitting. Second, unionized firms on average pay their employees a higher wage, which may make it more difficult for them to find an equally high-paying job if they leave. The higher employee retention rates at unionized companies provide an incentive for those companies to make greater investments in training because they can expect a longer payback on their training investment.[49]

Unions themselves have become far more interested in worker training and development in recent years. The food industry has created a special body, the Canadian Grocery Producers Council, with seed money from the federal government to develop training programs and standards for workers. The council includes some 181 companies and nine food worker unions, including the United Food and Commercial Workers International Union. The council has identified six training priorities with training scheduled to begin in September 1996.[50] Fred Pomeroy, an officer of the Communications, Energy and Paperworkers Union, in commenting

United Food and Commercial Workers International Union
www.ufcw.org

Canadian Grocery Producers Council
www.globalx.net/hrd/council/grocere.html

on workplace change, indicated that the debate within union circles of *whether* unions should participate in work reorganization has shifted to *how and under what conditions* should unions be involved. The common sentiment has become that management is too important to be left up to owners and their professional managers. When it comes to training, Pomeroy writes, "Training issues are central to workplace change. A union role needs to be built in."[51]

■ Compensation

A company experiences an increase in total compensation costs when a union organizes its employees. On average, union employees earn 10 to 20 percent higher wages than comparable non-unionized employees.[52]

The presence of a union also affects the company's policy on pay raises. Unionized firms are likely to give across-the-board pay raises to employees based on market considerations and avoid using merit pay plans.[53] Across-the-board pay plans are often based on **cost-of-living adjustments (COLAs)** that are tied to statistical inflation indicators. Unions prefer across-the-board pay raises to merit pay plans because they see the latter as undermining union solidarity by encouraging employees to compete against one another to win higher pay increases. Furthermore, unions are often skeptical of the fairness of merit pay increases because of the potential for favouritism on the part of supervisors (see Chapter 7). Unions apply this same logic to the use of individual pay incentives such as lump-sum bonuses. In contrast, non-unionized firms tend to use merit pay to encourage competition and recognize their top performers.

Unions are less likely to object to group pay incentives because group plans (such as gainsharing or profit sharing) tend to reinforce group cohesion. Each of the Big Three automakers has negotiated a profit-sharing plan. It is not unusual to find gainsharing plans in both union and non-unionized companies.[54] However, non-unionized firms generally have more flexibility to use both individual and group pay incentives to reward different types of work outcomes.

Unions have generally influenced employers to offer a more valuable benefit package to each employee.[55] Through collective bargaining, they have been able to negotiate packages with a broader array of benefits than non-unionized workers receive.

In unionized firms the employer pays for most benefits, while in non-unionized firms employer and employee share the costs.[56] Although unionized employers face the same rising health care costs, unions have used collective bargaining to persuade many of them to pursue alternative cost-saving methods such as managed health care, second opinions, and audits.[57]

In terms of retirement benefits, unions have been able to provide more security for employees by influencing employers to adopt a defined benefit plan, which provides a fixed amount of income to employees upon retirement.[58] Non-union employers are more likely to adopt a defined contribution plan, if they offer a pension plan at all. The trend toward defined contribution plans—where employers contribute, but make no commitment to the specific value of the pension to be received—is likely to be resisted by unions representing employees who work where defined benefit plans are currently in place. Even defined benefit plans can be contentious—recently the Canadian Media Guild sued Canadian Press for reducing contributions to the pension plan by almost half because less money was required to provide benefits to employees.[59]

■ Employee Relations

The union is an empowerment mechanism that gives employees a voice in the development of work rules that affect their jobs. The collective agreement gives employees specific rights. Non-performance by the employer of an employee right guaranteed in the contract can be remedied under the grievance procedure. For

---

cost-of-living adjustment (COLA)

Pay raises, usually made across the board, that are tied to statistical inflation indicators.

example, an employee overlooked for promotion may file a grievance and be reconsidered for the promotion if the contract stipulates that the employee has a right to that promotion.

Non-unionized employers tend to document their employees' basic rights in an employee handbook (see Chapter 13). However, employee handbooks provide fewer employee rights than collective agreements do. In fact, many of them contain only general guidelines and specifically state that supervisors may need to make exceptions to the written policy from time to time. For example, employees may have the right to bid on a promotion posted on a job board, but the handbook usually states that management reserves the right to determine which employee will ultimately get the job.

The appeals mechanism that a non-unionized employer is most likely to use is the open-door policy.[60] Unlike the grievance procedure, which is administered by both the union and management, the open-door policy is controlled by management. It gives management the opportunity to resolve an employee's complaint while balancing both parties' interests. The only recourse open to employees who are unhappy with the resolution of a complaint under the open-door policy is to find legal counsel and go to court to obtain justice—an option more employees are pursuing every year. Under the union grievance procedure, it is much less likely that an employee will take a case to court because judges are usually unwilling to challenge the results of arbitration.

Summary and Conclusions

Why Do Employees Join Unions? Employees seek representation from a union because they (1) are dissatisfied with certain aspects of their job, (2) lack influence with management to make the needed changes, and (3) see the union as a solution to their problems.

Labour unions became legal organizations in 1872, but it was not until 1944 with the passage of *P.C. 1003* that the general outlines of contemporary labour law took shape. The development of the union movement in Canada was characterized by the strong influences from labour relations developments in the United States and factionalism within the Canadian movement rooted in region, industry, political philosophy, and influence of the Catholic church on unionism in Quebec.

Managers strongly affect how employees perceive the work environment and thus whether they will be susceptible to unionization. Managers must possess enough knowledge of basic labour law to (1) avoid creating a legal liability for the company, (2) implement the terms of labour agreements fairly and impartially, and (3) hear and resolve employee grievances.

The Legal Context of Labour Relations. The legal context for labour relations varies slightly because provincial jurisdictions account for nine out of 10 employees. The *Industrial Disputes Investigations (IDI) Act* of 1907 established a federal presence in labour relations that was limited by the courts in 1925. Most provinces modelled their statutes on the federal law, but by the late 1930s were beginning to elaborate their legislation. Canada's entry into World War II consolidated authority for labour relations with the federal government, which passed *P.C. 1003* in 1944, a legal framework that incorporated major features of the U.S. *Wagner Act* and incorporated the Canadian emphasis on third-party involvement in contract negotiation impasses. Since World War II there has been a reversion to provincial jurisdictions, but there are similarities in most jurisdictions in the basic labour relations issues including union recognition, contract negotiation, and contract interpretation and administration.

Labour Relations in Canada. Labour relations in Canada are characterized by (1) business unionism, (2) unions structured by type of job, (3) a focus on collective bargaining, (4) the use of collective agreements, (5) the adversarial nature of labour-management relations, and (6) the growth of unions in the public sector.

Labour Relations in Other Countries. The labour relations systems of two of North America's key global competitors, Germany and Japan, have achieved a greater degree of cooperation between unions and management than the North American system has. The German system uses work councils and codetermination to involve workers in decisions at all levels of the organization. In Japan, enterprise unions have worked closely with companies for the mutual benefit of both parties. Some believe that economic pressures are straining labour-management relations in these countries in the 1990s.

Labour Relations Strategy.   A labour relations strategy is a company's overall plan for dealing with unions. Companies that choose a union acceptance strategy view unions as their employees' legitimate representatives and accept collective bargaining as an appropriate mechanism for establishing workplace rules. Companies that choose a union avoidance strategy use either union substitution or union suppression to keep unions out of the workplace.

Managing the Labour Relations Process.   The labour relations process has three phases: (1) union organizing, (2) collective bargaining, and (3) contract administration. In the union organizing phase, management must confront the issues involved with union solicitation, pre-election conduct, and the certification process. In the collective bargaining phase, union and management representatives negotiate workplace rules that are formalized in a collective agreement. The contract administration phase starts after the collective agreement is settled and deals with day-to-day administration of the work-place. The key feature of the contract administration phase is the grievance procedure, a step-by-step process for settling employee disputes about contract interpretations or disciplinary actions. Since every aspect of the labour relations process is highly regulated, managers must be careful to operate within the boundaries of the relevant laws.

The Impact of Unions on Human Resource Management.   The impact of a union on the way a company manages its human resources is significant. Management can expect that virtually every major area of HRM will be affected by the union. In a unionized workplace, staffing decisions will be heavily influenced by seniority rather than by merit. Employee development programs are affected in that individually focussed performance appraisals are severely curtailed, while training programs are emphasized. Unionized employees tend to receive larger compensation and benefits packages. Finally, the employee relations process in a union shop is by definition highly structured.

Key Terms and Concepts

arbitration, 464
bargaining power, 459
basic bargaining topics, 460
business unionism, 447
certification process, 444
codetermination, 452
collective agreement, 448
collective bargaining, 447
contract interpretation grievance, 465
cost-of-living adjustment (COLA), 468
craft union, 441
distributive bargaining, 459
economic strike, 463
election of union officials, 440

elective bargaining topics, 461
enterprise union, 452
grievance procedure, 464
good faith bargaining, 459
illegal bargaining topics, 461
industrial democracy, 452
Industrial Relations and Disputes Investigations (IRDI) Act, 443
industrial union, 441
integrative bargaining, 460
labour relations specialist, 443
labour relations strategy, 453
P.C. 1003, 444
prehearing vote, 458
Public Staff Relations Act, 446

regular certification, 458
seniority, 466
Trade Unions Act, 441
unfair labour practices, 444
union, 440
union acceptance strategy, 453
union avoidance strategy, 455
union dues, 440
union steward, 464
union substitution/pro-active human resource management, 455
union suppression, 456
wildcat strike, 463
work council, 452
work rules, 447

Discussion Questions

1. Why have labour and management tended to treat each other as adversaries?

2. What factors are encouraging unions and management to adopt more cooperative strategies today?

3. Why do managers have to be careful about what they say to employees in the period before certification takes place?

4. What is the role of the manager in the grievance process? How does this role affect the success of a company's labour relations policies?

5. How can management's collective bargaining tactics be influenced by the company's labour relations strategy? Provide examples.

6. What are some advantages and disadvantages of a strike from management's perspective? From the union's perspective?

7. What, in your opinion, is the most significant impact of a union on the management of human resources? Explain.

8. It is often said that "good pay and good management" are the keys to successful union avoidance. Spell out the kind of policies and practices companies should develop if they want to keep their workers from unionizing. Do you think the employee relations practices you've mentioned are less costly or more costly than working with unionized labour?

Check out our Companion Website at: **www.prenticehall.ca/gomez** for a selection of self-study questions, key terms and concepts, updated Weblinks to related Internet sites, newsgroups, CBC video updates, and more.

MiniCase 1   *Pipe Dream*

Consider the following story from a Toronto newspaper:

Nancy Eakins' dream turned into a nightmare.

Eakins is the first licensed plumber in the largest plumbers' local union—Local 46 of the United Association of Plumbers and Steamfitters, based in a sparkling new building at Warden and Eglinton Avenues.

In textbook terms, Eakins is a good plumber. She has Grade 13 (many plumbers have only Grade 10, the minimum requirement); she also has extra credentials, including a master plumber course that she is just completing.

But Eakins is a textbook case of sexual discrimination.

And she says she's not the only one. She's known half a dozen women who have dropped out of the plumbing trade, discouraged, she says, by an old boys' network that preserves jobs for its sons and brothers. ...

Eakins is not the sort to be deterred by a little prejudice. She's an adventurous woman, Toronto born and raised. She has travelled the world, slept on the beach in Bali, trekked through remote villages in India, dodged a coup in Venezuela. ...

She learned her trade the right way, studying hard and working on tough industrial construction sites, including three and a half years apprenticing at the Hospital for Sick Children. It was there, she says, where she was constantly harassed, delegated the most menial tasks, called "Molly Maid" over foremen's walkie-talkies, and made the butt of an endless stream of verbal digs, slurs and jokes. ...

When the strain became unbearable, she complained to Les Swan, the union shop steward who was also responsible for health and safety matters on the hospital job site. Swan ... was supportive of Eakins, although he now says he didn't realize how bad the situation was and that his response was inadequate.

That's about the only point on which Sean O'Ryan, the union's business manager, and Jack Cooney, the union's training coordinator, agree with Swan.

Swan ran unsuccessfully against O'Ryan in union elections last year. O'Ryan and Cooney suggest that Swan is trying to use Eakins's problems to undermine their leadership.

In an interview at union headquarters, O'Ryan was extremely aggressive, blaming Eakins and Swan for not properly informing union officials about harassment.

Eakins filed a human rights complaint, and negotiated an "Early Settlement Initiative" with the contractor, who didn't fight the case. The employer paid some $3,500 in lost wages—lost to stress—and agreed to employ her so that she could complete her apprenticeship period. Although she completed her apprenticeship, she subsequently was unable to find work. O'Ryan points to the 30 percent unemployment among union plumbers due to the building slump of the early 1990s, but Eakins is convinced that women such as herself are at an additional disadvantage.

Discussion Questions

1. It is clear, from Eakins' point of view, that the union did not provide her with the kind of support she thought she deserved. Do you agree? To the degree that her case was not given enough support, do you see it as a problem of rivalry between Swan and O'Ryan, or do you think there is bias against women in the union leadership as well as with some people on the job site where Eakins worked?

2. The protection of union members' rights is generally accomplished through grievance mechanisms. Eakins went to the human rights commission. The employer did not resist the claim. Does this option (the human rights alternative) provide a good safety valve for employees who think that their union is not treating them fairly?

3. O'Ryan and Cooney introduced the reporter to two female plumbers who had good things to say about the way they had been treated by the union. The reporter noted in her story that both of them had fathers who were members of the union, and in one case worked on the same job site as the daughter. Do you think that these family relationships are likely to have influenced the experience of these two women?

SOURCE: Steed, J. (1995, January 15). Pipe dream a nightmare. *The Weekend Star*, WS1, WS7. Reprinted with permission of The Toronto Star.

MiniCase 2   *1-800-Snitch*

In 1995, Maureen Kemptson-Darkes, GM Canada's president, wrote to employees, explaining the purpose of Awareline, a toll-free phone number that would allow employees to report events that they thought were inappropriate or damaging to the company. "We know that some individuals could be involved in unethical, illegal, or irresponsible acts," she wrote. "We hope you will receive and utilize this service for its intended purpose—to enable us to improve and strengthen our company."

Union officials warned that this "snitch" line (as they see it) would poison the working environment. Cooperation between GM and the union on a wide range of matters would become difficult, according to the president of the 16,000-member local of the Oshawa plant. The phone number is seen by the union as a move to intimidate and break the union's solidarity as they head into a bargaining year (1996), while to management it is "just another avenue for workers to raise issues."

Discussion Questions

1. Do you think this was a productive initiative for GM? What might they gain? What might they lose?

2. Do you think that, in general, employers should attempt to open as many communication channels with unionized employees as they can, even though the union might see this as an attempt to undercut its position as the representative of the employees?

3. Assuming that some employers might want to have some upward communication with unionized employees that wasn't filtered through the union, would it make any difference whether the employee communication was anonymous (like the 1-800 number) or should the employer require the employee to identify himself or herself?

SOURCE: Union fights snitch line. (1995, October 23). *Plant*, 2. Reprinted with permission of *Plant*, Canada's Industrial Newspaper/CP.

Case 1

Union Organizing at Sid's Market

Sid's Market is an upscale supermarket that caters to a clientele living in the prosperous suburbs of Vancouver. Although most of the supermarkets in the Vancouver area are unionized, Sid's Market has been able to avoid unions by matching unionized markets' pay and benefits. Sid Clark, founder and owner of Sid's, has told store manager Lee Shaw that one of her top priorities should be discouraging union organization at the market. Clark is convinced that if the store is unionized, it will lose its "family" environment and become a bureaucratic, impersonal market like the other major food chains in Vancouver.

Recently, Shaw became aware that the United Food and Commercial Workers (UFCW) union is attempting to organize Sid's Market. In trying to discourage the UFCW, she took the following actions to implement Sid's union avoidance strategy:

◆ She monitored all employees to make sure they were not soliciting for the union on company time. She disciplined two courtesy clerks who were wearing UFCW buttons on their clothing and told them to remove the buttons. Another courtesy clerk in the store was wearing a button that said "Go Grizzlies" in support of the Vancouver basketball team, but Shaw did not reprimand him.

◆ The UFCW wrote to Shaw and asked her to provide a list of the names and addresses of all the employees who work at Sid's Market. Shaw refused to do so.

◆ Shaw set up small group meetings of store employees on company time to explain why Sid's Market would be much better off without a union.

◆ Shaw instructed the market's security guards to ask the union organizers who are not employees at Sid's to stop handing out union literature to employees as they enter and leave the market. When the union organizers ignored this request, the guards escorted them off the market property and confiscated their literature.

A few weeks after these four incidents, Shaw received a letter from the Labour Relations Board indicating that the UFCW had accused Sid's Market of engaging in unfair labour practices designed to prevent employees from forming a union.

Critical Thinking Questions

1. Which of these four incidents is the Board most likely to view as unfair labour practices? Why?

2. Which of these four incidents is the Board not likely to consider unfair labour practices? Why?

3. What could Lee Shaw have done differently to operate within the law that governs union organizing activities?

Cooperative Learning Exercises

4. Students divide into groups of four to five. Assume that you are employees at Sid's Market. Would you support the formation of a union? Why or why not? Compare your reasons with those of other groups.

5. The class divides into six groups. Three of the groups identify reasons to support a union, with one group taking the perspective of employees, another the perspective of customers, and another the perspective of management. The remaining three groups identify reasons not to support the union, with each group taking one of the three different perspectives. Six students, one from each group, should debate the value of unions, with each maintaining his or her group's perspective, positive or negative.

Case 2

Rocky Mountain Hiring

Federal government budgetary reductions have had an impact throughout the greater public sector. Employees of Parks Canada who maintain highways, buildings, campgrounds or provide a range of other services have two choices: lose their jobs or come back on contract. According to Doug Martin, Alberta vice-president of the Public Service Alliance of Canada, some 600 employees have their jobs on the line. If they choose to come back, they have three years' work guaranteed, after which they must bid on their jobs with anyone else from the public. Special legislation will be introduced to exempt the newly reorganized Canada Heritage Department from provisions of labour relations and other laws that might otherwise block this change.

Critical Thinking Questions

1. What advantages, if any, accrue to the federal government during the first three years of this arrangement, assuming that salaries remain the same?

2. What kind of relationship do you think will develop between employees who take this option and those who remain Parks Canada employees working in conservation, environmental assessment, and public safety roles? Do you think there will be any change in the experience that users of the National Parks enjoy? Why?

3. What response(s) would you anticipate from the union?

Cooperative Learning Exercise

4. Form groups of four to six members. Assume you are members of the negotiating committee for the unit of Parks Canada employees to whom this change will apply. Half the group should be from the maintenance employee group, the rest from conservation and related positions. Prepare a bargaining strategy over this issue—what would you ask for, what would you hope to achieve, and what is the *least acceptable arrangement* that would not result in a bargaining impasse?

SOURCE: National parks workers can do same job as contractors. (1996, March 16). *Canadian Press Newswire.*

chapter 16

challenges

Managing Workplace Safety and Health

After reading this chapter, you should be able to deal more effectively with the following challenges:

1 Describe the extent of the employer's responsibility to maintain a safe and healthy work environment.

2 Explain the reasons for safety and health laws and the costs and obligations they impose on employers.

3 Identify the basic provisions of workers' compensation laws and health and safety legislation.

4 Develop an awareness of contemporary health and safety issues, including AIDS, violence against employees, workplace smoking, repetitive strain injuries, substance abuse, and hazardous materials.

5 Describe the features of safety programs and understand the reasons for and the effects of programs designed to enhance employee welfare.

Keeping employees safe on the job. Governments at the federal and provincial levels have passed legislation to regulate and improve workplace safety and health. Such measures range from requiring protective gear to dealing with hazardous substances to workers' compensation. Still, each year there are hundreds of deaths and many thousands of injuries on the job in Canada.

There are any number of reasons people may wish not to go to work—boredom, fatigue, a difficult boss, a workplace that is physically uncomfortable, a sense of being treated unfairly. However, for some people who have had personal experience with violence or who work where violent acts have occurred, there may be another reason—fear. A few actual examples:[1]

◆ A transit driver removes a passenger who refuses to pay a fare—and who punches him in the mouth.

◆ A cashier at a retail store is robbed at knifepoint and has difficulties with post-traumatic stress.

◆ An aide in a long-term care facility is punched in the side of the head by a resident.

◆ A taxi driver is attacked and robbed by five men, suffering injuries to his back and head.

Thankfully, these are not the everyday experiences of most employees, but for those who have ever been seriously hurt, the personal emotional impact will often last long after the physical injuries have healed. However, the problem of workplace violence is one dramatic tip of the iceberg of a broader and very serious workplace issue—one that affects hundreds of thousands of Canadians every year: the health and safety of employees. Although it is not written into the *Charter of Rights and Freedoms,* most people would agree with the philosophy expressed by G. Peter Robson, long-time occupational hygienist at Du Pont Canada: "Every worker has a right to go to work and to come home from work and not have suffered any adverse affects from being at work."[2]

Some health and safety issues make the headlines. Spills of radioactive material into the environment at nuclear power facilities, PCB spills, mine explosions, and major fires often call people's attention to the dangers faced by workers as well as the general public.

The crash of Valujet flight 592 into the Florida Everglades in 1997 illustrates the devastating consequences of paying insufficient attention to safety concerns. As companies strive to cut costs to remain competitive, the potential implications for safety in their products and services becomes an understandable concern.

Heightened public awareness of workplace safety issues has increased demands that organizations take measures to protect the public from industrial accidents and pollution resulting from their operations, and to provide a safe and healthy work environment for their employees. Creating a safe and healthy work environment goes beyond eliminating workplace accidents. Managers must also deal with a variety of occupational diseases and workplace problems that interfere with the normal functioning of the human body and that make work uncomfortable or unsafe. These range from environmental contaminants such as dust, radiation, chemicals, noise, and cigarette smoke to more specialized workplace problems like carpal tunnel syndrome (a painful hand injury that often affects data-entry personnel), stress-related health problems, and substance abuse. In addition, managers must create a workplace where employees can be reasonably certain they will be free from harm by co-workers or customers.

social responsibility

The practice in which a company
goes beyond legal requirements
and actively seeks to balance its
commitments—not only to its
investors, but also to its
customers, other businesses, and
the community or communities in
which it operates.

Organizations are, in fact, becoming more safety-conscious for three reasons. First, all Canadian organizations must comply with specific legal requirements to maintain employee safety and health.

Second, many companies have a genuine desire to treat employees humanely. They see workplace safety and health as part of their overall social responsibility. As we noted in Chapter 1, a company dedicated to the concept of **social responsibility** goes beyond legal requirements and actively seeks to balance its commitments—not only to its investors but also to its employees, other businesses, and the community or communities in which it operates. Social responsibility involves doing what is right and just with regard to employee welfare, not simply what is legally required.

Finally, organizations are becoming increasingly safety-conscious because they recognize that safe organizations are more effective organizations. Work-related accidents and illnesses have high economic and human costs. Failure to ensure workplace safety can increase an organization's direct costs by leading to a higher number of workplace accidents and thus to higher insurance premiums. Indirect costs may be incurred in the form of lower productivity and difficulties in recruiting and retaining employees. A safe and healthy work environment enhances the organization's image with the public and its customers, and helps to maintain employee commitment to the organization.

In this chapter we discuss workplace safety and health in detail. First, we deal with the legal issues of workplace safety and health by exploring management's legal obligations to fund a workers' compensation system and to provide a safe and healthy workplace. Next we present and discuss a variety of contemporary safety and health issues, including AIDS, violence in the workplace, smoking, cumulative trauma disorders, substance abuse and testing, and hazardous materials. Finally, we describe and evaluate programs designed to maintain employee safety and health.

■ Workplace Safety and the Law

Each year in Canada, hundreds of thousands of workers are injured on the job seriously enough to lose time from work. In the early 1990s, the average was 500,000 worker-days lost each year. The annual cost in 1996 of health and safety losses to the economy have been estimated in excess of $9.6 billion.[3] And even during the period of the early 1980s when union strike activity was considerably higher than it was in the 1990s, the number of days' work lost due to occupational injuries and illnesses was more than three times greater than the losses due to strikes and lockouts.[4]

The scale and nature of the occupational health and safety concern are summarized by two trends—one of which is encouraging, while the other is not. Comprehensive national statistics are not available because each jurisdiction collects its own data, with differing coverage and reporting conventions. However, Human Resources Development Canada does collect information from the workers' compensation authorities in each jurisdiction—statistics that reflect the experience of 65 to 100 percent of the work force, depending on the jurisdiction involved.[5] A summary of this experience is presented in Figure 16-1.

Human Resources
Development Canada
www.hrdc-drhc.gc.ca

It appears that the likelihood of experiencing an occupational injury is decreasing. During the period of 1971–1996, the number of fatalities per 100,000 workers has decreased from 12.8 to 5.5. The incident of injuries resulting in time-loss injuries increased during the early part of this period but decreased more substantially in the second half. As a result, although there were 4.3 time-loss injuries per 100 workers in 1971, the number had fallen to 3.1 per 100 workers by 1996. The incidence of all injuries decreased from 11 per 100 employees in 1976 to 6.5 per 100 in 1996. While these trends are encouraging, it remains that in 1996, 770 Canadian workers lost their lives due to work-related injuries and over 430,000 (a rate of almost one per minute, every day, 24 hours a day) were injured sufficiently to cause them to take at least one day off work for treatment and/or recuperation.[6]

Year	Injuries per 100 employees	Time-loss injuries per 100 employees	Workers Fatalities per 100,000 employees	Compensation Payments (in 1996 dollars) (000,000)
1971	11.0	4.3	12.8	$1,339
1976	10.2	4.6	9.2	2,177
1981	12.1	5.9	9.7	2,852
1986	10.3	5.8	7.3	4,181
1991	7.9	4.5	7.2	5,376
1996	6.5	3.1	5.5	4,913

Figure 16–1 Injuries and workers' compensation payments, 1971–1996

SOURCE: Human Resources Development Canada, (Occupational Injuries and Their Costs in Canada). Reproduced with the permission of the Minister of Public Works and Government Services Canada, 1999.

The second trend is the source of considerable concern. Total workers' compensation costs of occupational injury have increased (in 1996 dollars) from $1.34 billion in 1976 to $4.91 billion in 1996. This translates into a cost per worker employed (not per worker injured) of $413 in 1996, compared with $186 (1996 dollars) in 1976. In short, while the *incidence* of workplace injuries seems to be decreasing, using various measures, the cost is moving steadily in the other direction.[7] The nature of injuries/disabilities and recovery prospects play a significant role in this cost escalation.

To address the issues of occupational health and safety, numerous laws have been passed at both the federal and provincial levels. Many of these deal with the specific health and safety issues of a particular industry or occupation, such as mining or construction. There is, however, an overall framework of legislation that affects the broad range of employment settings. Legislation has had two specific aims with respect to worker health and safety. The first is the concern with the injured worker, ensuring that the worker receives income protection and rehabilitation (workers' compensation). The second objective is prevention of accidents and occupational illnesses in the workplace by establishing minimum safety standards and providing mechanisms for their enforcement. Canada differs from the United States in that there is no single piece of national legislation comparable to the U.S. *Occupational Safety and Health Act (OSHA)*. As with other areas of employment law (employment standards, labour relations) there is no one legislated standard, but rather jurisdictions (federal plus 10 provinces and two territories).

In addition to these two types of legislation designed to protect and compensate employees, other health and safety legislation is relevant to human resource management, although detailed discussion is beyond the scope of this chapter. Product safety legislation designed to protect consumers becomes a dimension of job performance for people producing those products. The transportation of dangerous goods is regulated to protect the general public—complying involves appropriate employee behaviours. The same is true of environmental pollution legislation. Figure 16–2 shows a sample of the legislation in one province—Ontario—having an effect on workplace safety.

■ Workers' Compensation

In the early 1800s, people injured on the job went without medical care unless they could afford to pay for it themselves and rarely received any income until and unless they could return to work. Employees who sued their employers for negligence had little hope of winning, for under common law the courts habitually ruled that employees assumed the usual risks of a job in return for their pay. In

Statute	Specific Hazard/Issue
Boiler and Pressure Vessels Act	boilers and pressure vessels
Building Code Act	construction and use of buildings
Construction Hoists Act	construction hoists
Elevators and Lifts Act	installation and use of elevators
Environmental Protection Act	discharge of pollutants
Act to Restrict Smoking in the Workplace	second-hand smoke

Figure 16–2 Examples of Province-Specific Legislation (Ontario) that Influences Workplace Health and Safety

addition, under the *doctrine of contributory negligence* employers were not liable for an employee's injuries when that employee's own negligence contributed to or caused the injury. And under the *fellow-servant rule,* employers were not responsible for an employee's injury when the negligence of another employee contributed to or caused the injury.

In the early years of the 20th century—after a host of workplace disasters—public opinion pressured several state legislatures in the United States to enact *workers' compensation* laws. The workers' compensation concept is based on the theory that work-related accidents and illnesses are costs of doing business that should be paid for by the employer and passed on to the consumer.[8] Workers' compensation became widely legislated in Canada as a provincial matter—Ontario's first workers' compensation law was passed in 1914.

The stated goals of the workers' compensation laws are:[9]

◆ Providing prompt and sure medical care to victims and income to both victims and their dependants.

◆ Providing a "no-fault" system in which injured workers can get quick relief without undertaking expensive litigation and suffering court delays. The victim need only demonstrate that he or she was an employee, was injured or became ill, and that the condition was attributable to work.

◆ Encouraging employers to invest in safety.

◆ Promoting research on workplace safety.

The Benefits of Workers' Compensation. Workers' compensation benefits compensate employees for injuries or illnesses occurring on the job. These benefits are:[10]

◆ *Total disability benefits.* Partial replacement of income lost as the result of a work-related total disability.

◆ *Impairment benefits.* Benefits for temporary or permanent partial disability, based on the degree and duration of the impairment. Injuries are classified as scheduled or non-scheduled. "Scheduled" injuries are those in which a body part (such as an eye or a finger) is lost; there is a specific schedule of payments for these injuries. "Non-scheduled" injuries are all other injuries (such as back injuries); these are dealt with on a case-by-case basis.

◆ *Survivor benefits.* In cases of work-related deaths, the worker's survivors receive a burial allowance and income benefits.

◆ *Medical expense benefits.* Workers' compensation provides medical coverage, if needed, over and above public health benefits.

◆ *Rehabilitation benefits.* Workers' compensation provides medical rehabilitation for injured workers, and many jurisdictions provide vocational training for employees who can no longer work at their previous occupation as the result of a job-related injury or illness.

Accident Reporting. All Canadian jurisdictions require employers to report accidents causing time-loss injury or occupational disease to their Workers' Compensation Board. This reporting is for the purpose of administering compensation and rehabilitation programs. (There are usually separate reporting requirements for specified accidents and illnesses under the occupational health and safety legislation.)

Problems with Workers' Compensation (WC).   The WC system has received considerable criticism from all sides. Many employers, especially smaller ones, claim that the costs of WC are a threat to their ability to compete. Costs have risen steadily over recent years, although some jurisdictions—Alberta, for example—have announced slight decreases.

Workers' compensation costs are increasing for a number of reasons. The growth in occupational illnesses, including stress and chronic problems attributed to various chemical substances in the work environment, represents a form of WC claim that is growing beyond what traditional experience would suggest. Medical costs, rehabilitation costs, and long-term disabilities have increased to the point where many WC systems face substantial unfunded liabilities, while others—Alberta, Saskatchewan, the Yukon, and the Northwest Territories—have avoided or eliminated their unfunded liabilities. Downwards adjustments in WC payments to claimants in Nova Scotia and Ontario may signal the way in which imbalance may be corrected over time.

The extent of the financial challenges faced by WC programs holds out the spectre of sharply increased costs to employers and/or taxpayers. In addition, the administrative procedures and costs are frequently a contentious matter. Employers' groups generally accept the concept of workers' compensation, but are often critical of the extension of the definition of an occupational illness or decisions that award benefits in marginal circumstances. A frequently mentioned condition when abuse of WC is discussed is back injuries. Back pain (some 27 percent of all claims) can be quite debilitating but is frequently difficult for a physician to assess independently, leading to the perception that some back injuries are either faked or exaggerated. The variability of benefits and assessments across jurisdictions is also an area of concern. An employer operating in more than one provincial jurisdiction has quite a bit to keep track of.

■ Laws to Reduce Workplace Injuries and Illnesses

Legal responsibilities for occupational health and safety are set by the provinces, the territories, and the federal government in their respective jurisdictions. The major statute(s) and the government instrument for administering the law are identified in Figure 16–3. As with any complex legal area, it is not possible to provide a detailed synopsis in the space available. However, the following overview provides (1) a sketch of some common features of health and safety legislation designed to reduce workplace accidents and injuries, (2) a discussion of the emphasis on the notion of shared responsibility for health and safety, including the widespread requirement for health and safety committees and the legal right to refuse work, and (3) a brief description of the enforcement practices of governments.

Common Patterns in Health and Safety Legislation.   Given the wide range of specific legislation, it useful to note that there are some common patterns in how health and safety legislation works in Canada.

1. A common feature of most legislation is a *general duty clause.* Such clauses have the effect of placing general responsibility on the employer to operate in such a way as not to endanger the health or safety of employees. This includes the duty to provide adequate information, training, and supervision to ensure worker safety and health. This clause supports specific elements of legislation that may omit a particular circumstance and indicates that operating safely is an employer's responsibility.

2. Duties are assigned to various parties in the employment relationship: employers, employees, supervisors, owners, contractors, and others. In Ontario, officers and directors are charged with taking reasonable steps to comply with the provisions of the *Occupational Health and Safety Act.* Discharging these duties is important, and the parties must be able demonstrate "due diligence" if their behaviour is challenged in court.

Jurisdiction	Legislation	Main Agency of Gov't Involved
Federal	Canada Labour Code, Part 2	Dept. of HR Development
Alberta	Occupational Health & Safety Act	Alta. Dept. of Labour
BC	Workers' Compensation Act; Workplace Act; Industrial Health & Safety Regulations; Factory Act; Mines Act	Workers' Compensation Board
Manitoba	Workplace Safety & Health Act	Ministry of Labour
New Brunswick	Occupational Health & Safety Act	Occupational Health & Safety Commission (a tripartite body)
Newfoundland	Occupational Health & Safety Act; Workers' Compensation Act	Dept. of Employment & Labour Relations
Nova Scotia	Occupational Health & Safety Act; Health Act; Occupational Health Regulations	Dept. of Labour & Manpower, Health & Safety Division
Ontario	Occupational Health & Safety Act	Min. of Labour
PEI	Occupational Health & Safety Act; Industrial Safety Regulations	Dept. of Labour, Occupational Health & Safety Division
Quebec	An Act Respecting Occupational Health & Safety; Environmental Quality Act; Quality of Work Environment (regulation); Workers' Compensation Act	Health & Safety Commission, Dept. of Social Development (a tripartite body)
Saskatchewan	Occupational Health & Safety Act; Occupational Health & Safety Regulations	Dept. of Labour, Occupational Health & Safety Division
Yukon	Occupational Health & Safety Act	Workers' Compensation, Health & Safety Board
NWT	Safety Act	Chief Safety Officer

Figure 16–3 Major Health and Safety Legislation in Canadian Jurisdictions

SOURCE: Robertson, D. (1994, November). Occupational health and safety (pp. 60, 044–60, 045). *Human Resources Management in Canada.* Copyright Carswell Thomson Professional Publishing.

3. Regulations that spell out the more general obligations of the parties are either part of the legislation, or (more frequently) are given force of law by the statutes, but usually do not have to be passed as specific legislation.

4. Health and safety legislation is given "legs" through several mechanisms:

   a. *Issuing regulations under the authority of the statute.* Provincial acts typically take the form of "enabling legislation." The statutes give governments wide latitude—often, the signature of the lieutenant-governor is all that is needed—to establish and change regulations as the government sees appropriate.

   b. *Enforcement procedures.* Inspectors may enter premises, conduct *workplace inspections,* issue orders for change, and initiate prosecutions under the terms of the legislation. The penalties for violations can be substantial: Ontario, for example, can levy fines of up to $25,000 on individuals and $500,000 on corporations.[11]

   c. *Referencing codes or standards.* By naming regulations or standards detailed elsewhere—for example, the CSA (Canadian Standards Association) standards for safety shoes, portable ladders, or other procedural codes—the legislation gives these standards legal leverage.

   d. *Setting out statutory rights.* This is perhaps the single factor that most differentiates Canadian law from the enforcement emphasis OSHA regime in the United States.

OSHA's emphasis on inspection and enforcement is reflected in the schedule of penalties presented in Figure 16–4. In contrast, Canadian law makes workers one of the parties responsible for workplace safety. Reflecting the active role envisioned for employees, workers in most Canadian jurisdictions have the right to refuse to do what they consider to be unsafe work and are protected in the exercise of that right. The law assigns authority to resolve such refusals to a process that involves worker-management committees at early stages. We examine the "right to refuse" in more detail below.

Employers and Employees: Shared Responsibility.   Canadian legislation in health and safety matters, as in labour relations, attempts to create an environment of shared responsibility. Although the government agencies can and do inspect workplaces, and do enforce the regulations of the various statutes, there is also an emphasis on employers and employees jointly taking responsibility for health and safety matters. Several jurisdictions specifically provide for a workplace safety representative who is authorized to call in inspectors and/or accompany them on their visits. All jurisdictions make provisions for two kinds of shared-responsibility activities: *health and safety committees* and the *right to refuse unsafe work.*

Health and Safety Committees.   Joint management-worker health and safety committees are mandatory under certain circumstances (e.g., depending on the size of the workplace, or the risk of exposure to biological or chemical hazards) in all jurisdictions except Alberta, Newfoundland, Prince Edward Island, and Quebec, where they may be required at the discretion of the relevant minister. These committees—which usually must have a membership of at least 50 percent workers—have varying responsibilities, including:

- meeting at a prescribed minimum frequency—typically, monthly or quarterly,
- making health and safety recommendations,
- making workplace inspections,
- participating in accident investigations,
- receiving suggestions and complaints from workers, and
- participating in the development of educational programs for the workplace.

The fact that these committees have legal foundations gives them legitimacy and also reflects the consensus that management and employees need to be involved in health and safety matters for such programs to be effective.

The Right to Refuse Unsafe Work.   The explicit legislation of the right to refuse unsafe work codifies what was theoretically possible under common law.

> **A Question of Ethics**
>
> Opponents of "big government" claim that excessive regulation of workplace safety hurts productivity and increases costs. They argue that in a free market economy employees should be responsible for their own health and safety—that they should be free to choose between taking a wage premium for hazardous work and accepting lower pay for safer work. If it were legal, would such a policy be ethical?

Violation	Description	Penalty
Other than serious violation	No direct relationship to job safety or health; probably not capable of causing death or serious physical harm.	Discretionary fine of up to $1,000 for each violation.
Serious violation	Serious probability death or serious injury could result and employer knew, or should have known, of the hazard.	Mandatory $1,000 penalty for each violation.
Willful violation	Intentionally or knowingly committing a violation.	Fine of up to $10,000 per violation. Possible criminal penalties.
Repeated violation	Reinspection reveals a substantially similar violation.	Fine of up to $10,000 per violation.
Failure to correct prior violation	Failure to correct a violation for which the company was previously cited.	Fine of up to $1,000 for every day the violation continues.

Figure 16–4 Penalties for Violations of OSHA Standards

SOURCE: U.S. Department of Labor, Occupational Safety and Health Administration. (1985). *All about OSHA* (rev. ed.). Washington, DC: U.S. Government Printing Office.

By providing the mechanism to refuse, the legislation has made clear how an employee can invoke the right and what the procedures are when such a refusal takes place. (In Alberta, the law actually *requires* that employees refuse dangerous work.[12]) So long as the refusal is done in compliance with the legal procedure, the employee is protected from disciplinary or other retribution by the employer. When first introduced, there was concern that this right would be abused by employees, either individually or (potentially) as part of a union campaign to put pressure on the employer over other issues. Happily, these concerns have not been realized in the broad patterns that have developed.

In general, the right to refuse work does not depend on the worker's ability to prove that a hazard exists—the standard that applies is having "reason to believe" that the situation is unsafe. There are certain exceptions to this right—some jurisdictions limit the right for certain occupations (e.g., firefighters, police officers) and many qualify it if the refusal has the effect of putting another employee in serious danger.

The procedures for exercising the right to refuse are spelled out. Usually, the refusal and the reasons for it are to be reported first to the person's immediate supervisor, followed by an inspection by the supervisor—typically accompanied by a worker representative. When the matter cannot be resolved internally, provision is usually made to involve an arbiter, typically from the government ministry involved. Other workers can be asked to do the task refused, but either the law or common sense (depending on jurisdiction) requires that the second worker be told of the refusal of the first.

Enforcement Procedures.   Enforcement of health and safety regulations is generally done through the authority granted to government-appointed inspectors. Inspectors can issue orders where there are violations of the statute. Their powers are wide-ranging—up to and including the shutting down of a machine, part of the operation, or the entire site. They may inspect because of an accident, a request on the part of workers or a health and safety committee, or on their own initiative.

Some enforcement and administration is triggered by required accident and occupational illness reporting. Failure to report is an offence that can result in charges and significant fines. Serious incidents are very likely to result in an inspection of the premises by government inspectors. Although there is some variability in detailed requirements, most require immediate notification of accidents causing death or critical injury, or where there have been explosions that caused or could have caused serious injury. In serious injury cases, employers are often required not to disturb the scene until it has been examined by inspectors. In addition, all jurisdictions other than British Columbia, Alberta, and the Northwest Territories require notification of the health and safety committee, typically by copy of the report submitted to the governmental authority.

Violations of health and safety laws leading to serious accidents and injuries incur a wide and sometimes unpredictable range of financial penalties. For example, one accident in British Columbia caused the death of a logger who was walking between log piles and was struck by the skidder (a piece of logging equipment). After pleading guilty to one of the 10 charges laid, the employer was fined $750. In contrast, the collapse of a derrick at a Toronto building site—the load of concrete had fallen to the ground, but there were no injuries—was deemed to be the result of employer safety violations and cost the employer $50,400.[13]

■Building Managerial Skills: Managing Contemporary Safety, Health, and Behavioural Issues

Effectively managing workplace safety and health requires far more than reducing the number of job-related accidents and injuries. In practice, managers must deal with a variety of practical, legal, and ethical issues, many of which involve a careful balancing of individual rights (particularly the right to privacy) with the needs of the organization (see Chapter 14). Because these issues often give rise to legal and ethical questions, HR professionals are frequently called upon to develop and implement policies to deal with them. Among the weightiest issues facing employers today are dealing with AIDS in the workplace, workplace violence, smoking in the workplace, cumulative trauma disorders, substance abuse and testing, and hazardous materials.

It is important to recognize that, in addition to these direct challenges in the safety and health arena, there is also the challenge of employee commitment to safety and health programs. Many organizations face the problem of employees ignoring and even being hostile toward safety and health measures. The reason: employees often view safety and health measures as intrusive and inefficient.

Commitment to safety and health programs can be generated by explaining to supervisors and others the rationale for the relevant safety and health practices. For example, it is important that everyone understand the cost of accidents to the organization. Further, the costs (such as fines) for violating safety and health standards should be clearly explained to employees at all levels. Once people understand the links between safety and health measures and the business's bottom line, resistance to safety and health measures should be largely removed. Of course, removing human resistance to any kind of program can be a difficult and delicate process that requires time and commitment.

Employers often inadvertently create safety problems. Safe operation sometimes takes more time—protective clothing makes movement more difficult, guards on the machines get in the way, and so forth. If first-level and middle management are under pressure to produce quickly, the "safety message" may not carry as much weight as it should. Including safety performance in the reward systems and performance appraisal is crucial to avoid cynicism and disregard for safety programs.

Statistics indicate that logging and other forestry occupations are among the most dangerous.

■ AIDS

Dealing effectively with workplace concerns that arise when an employee contracts acquired immunodeficiency syndrome (AIDS) will be one of the most important workplace health challenges during the next decade, at least. In the early 1980s AIDS was scarcely known, but 10 years later survey evidence began to indicate that a significant proportion of employers had one or more employees who were HIV positive.[14] Because the human immunodeficiency virus (HIV) can be present in an individual for an extended period—often several years—without causing illness, being HIV positive is not the same thing as having AIDS, although most people with HIV have eventually manifested AIDS symptoms. In North America, AIDS is most prevalent in the 25- to 44-year-old age group. This means that it is a health matter with which employers will increasingly be confronted as the spread of AIDS continues.

To date, employers have been slow to develop proactive programs dealing with AIDS. There are some exemplary employers, however, including BC Tel, Levi Strauss, and Sun Life's initiatives in their New York offices. Having AIDS or being HIV positive is included in the definition of a "handicap" under federal and many provincial human rights codes, and therefore creates a situation where employers cannot simply terminate employees, reassign them, or take other arbitrary action simply because they are discovered to be HIV positive or to be manifesting AIDS symptoms. As a result, the concepts of "reasonable accommodation" and "bona fide occupational requirements" (see Chapter 3) come into play. In 1993, Simon Thwaites was awarded $152,000 from the Canadian Armed Forces, which claimed

Levi Strauss
www.levi.com

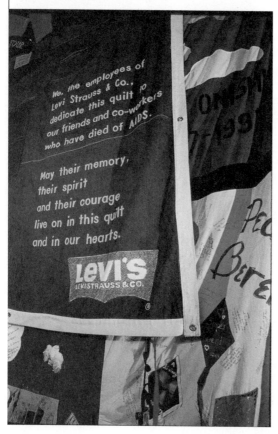

he had been fired because of a disability. Although the Armed Forces argued that his condition put him at risk if he were stationed in a remote location without necessary medical facilities, the Canadian Human Rights Tribunal found that the employer had neither demonstrated that it could not accommodate his condition nor that it had formally assessed the impact of his condition on his ability to perform his job.[15] In general, the fair and legal way of responding to AIDS is no different from responding to any other serious disease that affects employees.

The lack of a proactive AIDS policy in most organizations can be attributed to several causes—denial and the prevalence of stereotypes being two influential factors. The fear and anxiety that AIDS provokes—because it is incurable and inevitably fatal—makes it very disturbing to think about. Although treatments are increasingly effective at extending the life expectancy and quality of life of people living with HIV or AIDS (PHAs), contemplating an AIDS diagnosis is more disturbing for most people than the prospect of being diagnosed with cancer.

The devastating quality of the disease is compounded by the fact that homosexual men and users of illicit intravenously injected drugs are the subgroups of the North American population where the disease has spread most rapidly. However, AIDS is not a "gay disease." It has spread into the general population through heterosexual contact and through the use of contaminated blood products prior to effective screening. Yet the stigma attached to the disease has not disappeared, and the tendency toward denial is compounded for those who are neither gay nor injecting drugs.

The occupational health and safety issues surrounding AIDS come from the responses of people who work with PHAs. A recent survey by the U.S. Centers for Disease Control and Prevention found that 67 percent of respondents would have "some misgivings" about working with someone with AIDS, and 26 percent would feel "uncomfortable." While 90 percent of respondents said that HIV-positive employees should be treated like anyone else, many employers still do not have an explicit policy about AIDS in spite of the legal obligations mentioned earlier.[16] The issues in dealing with HIV-positive employees are several and sometimes difficult—confidentiality of information, the scope of accommodation (job assignments, provisions for absences or shortened work days), and the extent of medical benefits and long-term disability are but a few of the significant issues that should be addressed. It is important that there be a formal corporate policy. Such a policy should include at least two elements:

◆ The policy should outline how the company will respond to disclosure of the fact that an employee is HIV positive, or has progressed to the point at which AIDS symptoms occur.

◆ The company should make provisions to educate all employees about AIDS and the employer's policy.

The specific policies should be consistent with those dealing with other serious diseases, such as cancer. The policies should ensure confidentiality of medical information, and they should provide an indication that the employer will undertake accommodation measures. Education is most effective when it is done by knowledgeable presenters in formats (such as small groups) that allow employees to raise questions. The most important single fact for most employees to hear and accept is that the employer is fully committed to providing a safe and healthy working environment, and that they are not at risk from being near, touching, or having other normal workplace contact with people who are HIV positive.

The HR Manager's Role.   Companies must address many issues when developing and implementing an AIDS policy. Figure 16–5 outlines some of these issues, which tend to be complex and require many difficult and important decisions.

Because of the impact of AIDS on employee benefits and the need to deal with the potential for human rights violations when employment-related decisions are taken, the human resource manager's participation in formulating the AIDS policy is vital. In addition, the HR professional will likely be called on to facilitate the process of communicating the AIDS policy and to train employees and managers about the practical and legal issues involving employees with AIDS. See Minicase 2 at the end of this chapter for a look at how one company has taken a proactive approach to dealing with AIDS issues.

■ Violence in the Workplace

Most Canadians think of violence as a risk most likely encountered on a darkened street in the wrong part of town. Such places may indeed be dangerous, and most people try to avoid these circumstances. However, violence—happily, something most of us learn about primarily from second- or third-hand accounts—is more likely to be the act of someone the victim knows, and it is likely to occur in what we generally think of as safe places: the home and, increasingly, the workplace.

Statistics on workplace violence in Canada are sketchy. In 1994, the Workers' Compensation Board in British Columbia dealt with 1,235 violence claims. The number in Alberta was 726; in Nova Scotia, there were 512.[17] In 1993, the Ontario WC Board reported 1,341 cases.[18] Not every act of violence results in an injury, and like most kinds of physical assaults, only a very small percentage are actually reported—a 1990 study by CUPE (a public sector union) indicated that the level of reporting was less than five percent. The consensus is that violence is becoming a more widespread problem. Some sectors seem to be most affected. A study of WC-reported incidents in British Columbia found that the victims were overwhelmingly women—mainly nurses and health care workers—employed in long-term care facilities, acute-care hospitals, psychiatric hospitals, and group homes.

- Who is responsible for development and implementation of the policy?

- What are the objectives of the AIDS policy?

- What is covered under the AIDS policy?

- What rights will covered employees have, particularly in terms of workplace accommodation and confidentiality?

- What benefits will PHAs receive?

- Who is in charge of administering the policy?

- What kind of training should supervisors and managers have, particularly to prepare them to manage co-workers' concerns and fears?

- How does the company deal with job restructuring issues, accommodation, and requests for transfers by PHAs and co-workers?

- How and to what extent should the AIDS policy be communicated to employees?

- How should organizations deal with affected workers' productivity problems?

- How can organizations help PHAs cope by providing support and referral services?

Figure 16–5 Issues in the Development and Implementation of an AIDS Policy

SOURCES: Adapted from Fremgen, B., & Whitty, M. (1992, December). How to avoid a costly AIDS crisis in the organization. *Labor Law Journal*, 751–758. Smith, J. M. (1993, March). How to develop and implement an AIDS workplace policy. *HR Focus*, 15; and Stodghill, R. (1993, February). Why AIDS policy must be a special policy. *Business Week*, 3303, 53–54.

Such incidents accounted for about two-thirds of the total. A similar finding was found in an examination of Nova Scotia statistics, with slightly over 70 percent of all workplace violence WC claims occurring in health care and social services occupations.[19] In many of these cases the assailant was a patient or client.

There is another form of workplace violence that springs to mind when we hear the term: the disgruntled employee (or former employee), angry with the employer, boss or co-workers, appears at the workplace with a weapon and attacks. Such events do happen in Canada, but indications are that it occurs more frequently in the United States, which experiences 15 workplace murders a week,[20] and where ownership and use of firearms is more pervasive than in Canada. However, Canada is not immune to violent employee behaviour, as the following example indicates:

> An employee in a large manufacturing firm is known to have a temper and occasionally be violent. He tells his co-workers that a U.S. employee reported to have stormed into his workplace and to have shot several co-workers "had a good idea." When his supervisor criticizes the employee's work, the man punches the supervisor in the mouth.[21]

Because organizations include employee safety in the human resources portfolio, HR managers are often responsible for creating policies to avoid violence and for dealing with the aftermath when violent incidents occur. For a variety of reasons, dealing with workplace violence is challenging. Security is often difficult because many workplaces provide easy access to the general public. Security services ("guards") are often good at monitoring access to parking areas and dealing with non-aggressive intruders. Yet, the determined or belligerent individual may be difficult to exclude from the premises. Thankfully, most employees are not preoccupied with their physical safety. But that implicit confidence in their co-workers and in the general public they deal with makes it difficult to get them to take prudent violence-protection policies and practices seriously.

Another reason that dealing with employee violence is difficult is that it is usually hard to predict which employees will become violent. Often people give little indication of violent tendencies. Yet, in retrospect after a violent episode, seemingly insignificant events or actions may be identified that could have alerted managers and co-workers to the possibility of violence. It is important to realize that violence is usually the result of a combination of personal and situational factors, and that there are different levels of violence. Violence of a serious nature is more likely to occur where lesser violence has appeared, especially if incidents are not dealt with effectively by the employer. One view of workplace violence suggests the following categories of unacceptable aggressive behaviour. Tolerating some of these increases the likelihood of more frequent and serious incidents.

◆ *Least injurious:* (Malicious) gossip, rumours; swearing; verbal abuse; pranks; minor violations of company policy, occasional arguments with customers, co-workers, or supervisors.

◆ *Moderately injurious:* Property damage, vandalism; sabotage; pushing, fistfights; major violations of company policies; frequent arguments; theft.

◆ *Highly injurious:* Physical attacks and assaults; psychological trauma; anger-related accidents; rape; arson; murder.[22]

Workplace situations can lead to increased likelihood of aggressive or violent behaviour. Singly or in combination, these have a serious effect. (See Figure 16–6 for a list of 10 "triggers" for violent behaviour.)

To some degree, employers are in a "Catch-22" situation when they attempt to control workplace violence: If they exercise extreme diligence in investigating applicants' backgrounds, applicants may feel that their privacy is being unnecessarily compromised and, depending on the nature of the inquiries, human rights pro-

1. Poor management relations	6. Inconsistent rule enforcement
2. Strict hierarchy and rules	7. Ignoring cultural concerns
3. Employee harassment	8. Failure to address threats of violence
4. Vague demands	9. Overcrowded, unpleasant worksite
5. Ambiguous standards	10. Insufficient worksite security

Figure 16–6 Ten Triggers to Workplace Violence

SOURCE: Newton, E. (1996, February 26). Clear policy, active ear can reduce violence. *Canadian HR Reporter,* 16–17. Reprinted with permission of MPL Communications Inc.

tections could come into play (for example, marital status information gathered by inquiries about domestic violence).

What can organizations do to control workplace violence? Every organization should have a policy in place to prevent violence and to deal with such incidents when they occur. Top management should recognize that the potential for violence always exists and develop cross-functional teams to deal with violence effectively. The first step in this process is to identify organizational policies and practices that might contribute to the problem, such as the way change is planned and communicated, particularly regarding upsetting events such as downsizing, restructuring, and layoffs. Other practices that can lead to violence are employee disciplinary measures that are perceived to be unfair, and rigid rules and procedures that are poorly communicated or poorly implemented. The second step is to change the policies and procedures, where plausible, seeking employee input to increase the level of understanding for the rules. The third step is to develop programs such as employee assistance plans (EAPs) to help employees cope with work-related stress and change.

Over and above these process interventions, physical safety can be enhanced by such measures as extra lighting, video cameras, alarms, security guards, and parking lot escort services. Countering workplace violence may also entail:[23]

◆ Reviewing reported incidents of violence for indications of recurring problems.

◆ Training managers to identify troubled employees and get help for them.

◆ Creating contingency plans to deal with trauma arising from any violent incidents that do occur, including providing support and counselling to victims.

◆ Creating strong anti-harassment and progressive discipline policies, and removing troubled employees from the workplace. Care should be taken, however, in dealing with such people if termination is the course of action.

◆ Improving physical security and screening applicants for history of violent behaviour.

The HR Manager's Role.   HRM professionals play an important role at every step in the planning and administration of an anti-violence program. The HR manager's major responsibility is to be certain that selection policies include careful screening and reference checking so that the organization can avoid hiring applicants with a history of violent behaviour. The HR manager should also take the lead in enforcing fair treatment of employees. This includes training managers and supervisors to recognize performance problems, refer troubled employees for counselling before they become a problem, and apply progressive discipline procedures uniformly and consistently.

■ Smoking in the Workplace

Dramatic change has taken place over the past two decades with regard to the acceptability of smoking in public places. Increasing evidence of the health risks associated with second-hand or "side-stream" tobacco smoke has shifted the issue from whether it is inconsiderate of people to smoke where non-smokers will have to breathe in the smoke to the fact that it is injurious to be exposed to second-hand smoke. To date, the federal government, Ontario, and Newfoundland have enacted legislation that prohibits smoking in enclosed workplaces, subject to the employer's right to designate particular areas where smoking is permissible—Ontario allows up to 25 percent of the workplace to be so designated. In addition, Alberta and Prince Edward Island have recently enacted anti-smoking legislation for government workplaces. The health risks have led many employers to initiate smoking regulations—including total bans—on their own, even in jurisdictions where there is no specific legislation to date.

Not surprisingly, such policies are often unpopular with employees who smoke. In some cases of total smoking bans, trade unions have taken grievances to arbitration, but with limited success. In one case in Nova Scotia (Benz Ltd. [1993]), a total smoking ban was ruled *not* to be an unreasonable extension of management rights unless non-smokers were not affected by the smoking of co-workers and also where smokers can be easily accommodated, conditions that did not apply in this case. The arbitrator explicitly rejected the union's claim that the employer should be required to take any significant steps to accommodate the interests of smokers. And in Ontario, one arbitrator has ruled that an employer can unilaterally prohibit smoking, even though the collective agreement permits smoking in specific areas. It was found that the provincial legislation making the provision of designated smoking areas an employer *option* held precedence over the collective agreement.[24]

The patchwork of legislative and administrative/judicial precedents that affects many areas of human resource management is also a fact of life in the matter of smoking control. If anything, it is more fragmented, because municipalities have become important players in setting the rules. In general, management should anticipate that, eventually, smoking in the workplace will be severely limited or prohibited by law. Unless there is a way of completely segregating the ventilation systems used for smoking areas from non-smoking areas, the prudent course will be to move toward policies that eliminate tobacco smoke in the workplace.

Smoking policies have two other dimensions worth examining. First, is it enough simply to announce, explain, and enforce a new policy? Some employers have found that acceptance of new smoking policies, as is the case with other policies, increases with employee participation. Nordion International Inc., of Kanata, Ontario—a 400-employee company that produces radioscopes for the health care industry—has limited smoking since 1988, partly because of the nature of their business. In 1994, it was decided to make all indoor areas smoke-free and in the autumn of 1995, the entire site was made off limits for smoking. A 1994 employee meeting asked for suggestions on how to make the transition easier and resulted in the building of on-site, outdoor shelters for smokers. These shelters were converted to picnic areas with the 1995 decision. Employees and their spouses received a $400 subsidy that could be used to pay for a variety of smoking cessation programs. In all, the company spent some $16,000 on smoking cessation initiatives, not including the shelters.[25]

The other smoking issue, more contentious than the others, is the matter of whether smoking should be considered in employee selection. There are reasonable grounds to suggest that smokers, on average, are less productive, lose more time to illness (absence rates are 50 percent higher; work-related accidents 29 percent higher), and have 50 percent more medical claims than non-smokers.[26] However, should somebody be denied a job because he or she smokes? According to University of Toronto constitutional expert Peter Russell, there is nothing in the Canadian Constitution or *Charter of Rights and Freedoms* that would prohibit Canadian employers from imposing such a condition.[27] While there has been only one employee smoking complaint before the Canadian Human Rights Commission in 16 years (the complaint was thrown out by the Commission), the acceptance of drug and alcohol dependencies as "disabilities" in human rights cases suggests that dependence on nicotine (via smoking) may yet be broached as a human rights protection for smokers.

The HR Manager's Role.   It is clear that attitudes toward workplace smoking are rapidly changing as smokers become a shrinking minority and as employers become more concerned with the health-related costs of smoking and smoking-related liability claims by employees exposed to second-hand smoke. Controlling smoking-related costs and protecting the rights of non-smokers without violating the host of new anti-discrimination laws protecting smokers requires a careful balancing act. In this area the role of the human resource manager is multifaceted and may include:

◆ Providing assistance in the development of smoking policies that avoid conflict between smokers and non-smokers.

◆ Ensuring that non-smokers who are sensitive to smoke are accommodated.

◆ Utilizing available resources to help employees who want to quit smoking.

◆ Evaluating the costs of smoking and creating selection and benefits policies to deal with these costs.

Cumulative Trauma Disorders

A welder at Pratt & Whitney's aircraft engine plant in Longueil, Quebec, spends an average of four hours a day working upright with both hands over his head. When he gets home, he may notice numbness in his arms and an inability to grasp anything firmly. A bus driver for the city of Edmonton may traverse the city 30 times a shift, wrestling the vehicle through traffic and around turns. When she gets home, she may experience back pain and soreness in her wrists and arms.[28]

Both individuals are experiencing manifestations of musculoskeletal disorders variously know as repetitive strain injury (RSI) or cumulative trauma disorder (CTD). The fastest-growing occupational injury in the last decade has been repetitive motion injury or **cumulative trauma disorder (CTD).** CTD results from the repetitive movements common in many occupations, such as meat packing, assembly-line work, and computer data entry. There is growing recognition that video display terminals (VDTs) can cause CTDs.[29] VDTs have been associated with a host of vision problems collectively referred to as computer vision syndrome (CVS). Symptoms of CVS include blurred vision, headaches, light sensitivity, and after-images.[30] One of the more serious repetitive strain injuries is *carpal tunnel syndrome,* which occurs when ligaments in the hand force nerves against bone, causing a sharp pain sometimes described as being like a "sunburn on the inside." CTDs are taking an economic toll on Canadian business. Statistics Canada reported that for 1994, sprains and strains accounted for 190,000 of some 429,000 total time-loss injuries. The single most important source of these were body motion, accounting for 66,000 cases—most of them involving muscles, tendons and nerves in the neck, arms, shoulders, and upper back. This family of injuries includes tendinitis, bursitis, and carpal tunnel syndrome, and nearly all involve pain and inflammation to a joint due to damage to the joint of surrounding tissues. Accurate estimates of the precise costs are difficult to ascertain, but it is clear from data in all jurisdictions that the frequency is increasing. As an illustration, the WCB in Ontario reported an increase from 5,000 RSI claims to 6,300 over a four-year period, each one costing roughly $11,000 with 83 days of lost work per injury.[31] Canada is not alone in this pattern of increase. Evidence indicated that in the mid-1980s four percent of the U.S. work force suffered from motion injuries, and an estimated 185,000 new repetitive strain cases are reported each year. One expert estimates that CTDs will account for half of all workers' compensation cases by the end of the 1990s.[32] CTDs are not exclusively a North American problem. Australia has experienced dramatic increases in CTD cases and record numbers of workers' compensation claims, with as many as one-half of all office workers suffering problems.[33]

Ergonomic Designs.

This keyboard of this Apple Macintosh computer can be configured in several different ways to prevent carpal tunnel syndrome and other repetitive stress injuries.

cumulative trauma disorder (CTD)

An occupational injury that occurs from repetitive physical movements, such as assembly-line work or data entry. Also called *repetitive motion injury.*

The HR Manager's Role. HR managers can help control CTDs by developing policies to avoid some of the problems that lead to carpal tunnel syndrome and other cumulative trauma disorders. The initial focus of these policies might be on workplace **ergonomics,** the manner in which tools and equipment are designed and used. Properly designed workstations can greatly alleviate the problems associated with VDTs. Factors to consider in the design of workstations are comfortable and supportive chairs, detachable keyboards, antiglare filters on VDT screens, and adequate lighting. In addition, workstation characteristics need to be flexible. Workers come in different sizes and shapes, so it is important that they be able to customize the workstation to their size and individual preferences. Jobs and equipment can be redesigned and workers can be trained in proper techniques so that the kinds of repeated motion that cause a CTD can be avoided. Also, because psychological stress brought about by job pressures may contribute to a CTD, HR managers may want to investigate developing wellness programs (discussed in Chapter 12 and later in this chapter) to control stress.

> **ergonomics**
>
> The manner in which tools and equipment are designed and used.

Unlike most members of the HR department, managers are on the front line, working with employees vulnerable to CTDs. They need to stay alert to signs of problems and take corrective measures promptly. Sometimes the corrective measure is as simple as adjusting chair height or keyboard angle. At other times managers may need to consult with the HR department to devise more extensive ergonomic changes.

■ Substance Abuse and Testing

Drug abuse and alcoholism are major workplace problems. Estimates suggest that 12 percent or more of the work force has substance abuse problems.[34] In the United States, where drug testing is more frequently used as a hiring criterion by employers, the percentage of applicants testing positive for illegal substances ranges from five percent to 25 percent.[35] Substance abuse is an economic issue because employees who abuse drugs and alcohol exhibit lower productivity and higher absenteeism, on average. It is also a workplace safety issue because substance abusers file more WC claims and have accident rates as much as four times higher than non-abusers.[36] Dramatic accidents such as a 1991 subway crash in New York City where operator impairment was a key factor provide one face of this risk. More important, and more numerous by far in the aggregate, are the employees who are injured or killed singly or in abuse-caused workplace accidents.

Drug testing is controversial because of its intrusive nature (requiring urine or blood samples) and because tests used for substances other than alcohol indicate past use but not necessarily current impairment. The implicit assumption in drug testing is that any drug use is, de facto, abuse. While people who use no drugs are clearly not abusing them it is not clear that all users are abusers in the sense that their level and pattern of use interferes with their work. Employers do have a legitimate interest in whether employees are impaired on the job, but it is less clear that employers have a role in monitoring and controlling employee behaviour off the job without being able to demonstrate the connection to the employee's work-related responsibilities. Although the testing can be accurate, the less expensive tests are not always so, and even the best tests can register false-positive results under certain circumstances. As we have seen elsewhere (Chapters 3, 5, and 14), there are legal constraints on the use of drug testing. Substance dependence is treated as a handicap, and thus use of addictive substances can receive human rights protection. To deny employment preemptively or to base HR decisions on positive drug tests can be successfully challenged in many circumstances. The drug-testing policies that have been accepted have done so because they have provided support and time for employees to change their patterns.

In spite of the limitations of drug testing, there are legitimate safety concerns to be addressed. For some occupations (e.g., pilots, crane or forklift operators), safety concerns are such that drug testing that is part of an explicit, even-handed policy can be acceptable. The larger safety issue is impairment. Alcohol is the single largest source of substance-based impairment, and most drug testing does not address alcohol problems. Impairment can also result from fatigue or illness, neither of which can be identified by testing.

While drug testing may have some contribution to make to safety, behavioural screening devices (such as those described in Chapter 14) address the immediate and fundamental question, "Is this employee currently impaired—by any condition or influence—in a way that makes him or her unfit to undertake normal work responsibilities?" Impaired employees should not be allowed to attempt to work. Employers are legally permitted to send them to a physician for medical attention (if they are ill), send them home to get some rest (if they are severely fatigued), and apply some combination of discipline and EAP if the impairment is drug or alcohol based.

The HR Manager's Role.   HR managers are responsible for participating with other senior managers in the development of their organization's policies regarding substance testing and abuse. This participation includes making decisions about how substance testing will be used to screen applicants and how testing will be used with current employees. HR staff also develop plans for dealing with employees who have substance-abuse problems. These may range from ensuring fair disciplinary procedures to creating programs to counsel troubled employees.

Line managers who suspect an employee has a substance-abuse problem that is interfering with on-the-job performance should confront the employee with documented evidence of poor performance and explain that these performance problems will lead to disciplinary action, and ultimately dismissal, if the employee refuses to correct them. The manager should then offer the employee help in the form of referral to a confidential employee assistance program.

■ Hazardous Materials

Chemistry has been essential to industrial development in this century. From plastics to metallurgy to solvents and fuels, very few of the objects we currently use, wear, or live in would exist without the many new chemical substances developed during the 20th century. However—along with the unquestioned economic and technological benefits—these new substances have also created a wide range of risks. Product safety has become an important issue for consumers. (For example, officials of the federal government have advised that people take down and dispose of inexpensive PVC window blinds because of high lead levels—the lead is released as the plastic compound breaks down over time from exposure to sunlight.)

In the workplace, it is not only the products produced but also the substances used in the production process that can pose health and safety risks. The rate of technological innovation makes it difficult to keep regulations or other controls up to date. Toxicity data are unavailable for some 80 percent of chemicals that are used in commercial applications.[37] In terms of frequency of workplace injuries, chemical burns and poisoning placed second only to repeated trauma injuries to wrists and arms in 1993.[38]

Canada has addressed the problem of hazardous substances through legislation. *The Hazardous Products Act* of 1969 was amended in 1985, creating the *Workplace Hazardous Materials Information System (WHMIS)*. This federal legislation, applied as well through provincial law, requires:

♦ that suppliers of hazardous substances label all hazardous materials,

♦ that suppliers provide Material Safety Data Sheets (MSDSs) for all such products, and

♦ that employers provide training that will enable employees to recognize the WHMIS hazard symbols and understand the information in the MSDSs for materials they use or to which they are exposed.

The WHMIS hazard classes and logos are presented in Figure 16–7. These symbols quickly alert workers to the presence of a range of potentially dangerous materials: compressed gases, flammable and combustible materials, oxidizing materials, poisonous and infectious materials (subdivided into [a] those causing immediate and serious toxic side effects, [b] those causing other toxic effects, and [c] biohazardous infectious material), corrosive materials, and dangerously reactive materials.

The Material Safety Data Sheets are required to include the following information about hazardous materials:

◆ A listing and identification (via standard codes) of the hazardous ingredients.

◆ Identification of who prepared the material, and the date it was prepared.

◆ Full product identification: name, manufacturer, supplier, and intended product use.

◆ Physical data: e.g., physical state, odour and appearance, boiling and freezing points, vapour pressure and evaporation rates.

◆ Qualities as a fire or explosion hazard: flammability, how to extinguish, sensitivity to impact.

◆ Reactivity information: stability, listing of incompatible materials, hazardous decomposition products.

◆ Toxicological properties, specifying possible routes of entry into the body (skin contact, eye contact, inhalation, ingestion): effects of acute or chronic exposure, exposure limits, extent of evidence re: carcinogenicity, reproductive toxicity, mutagenicity.

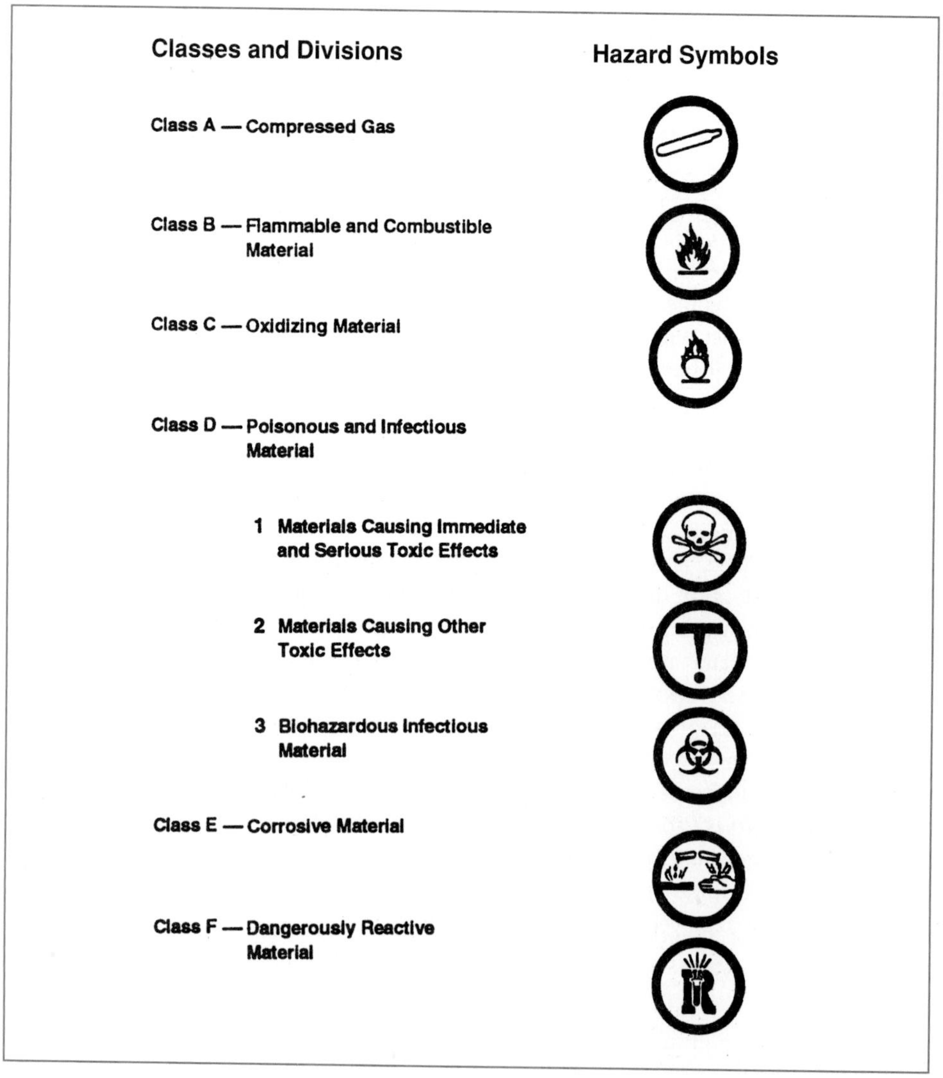

Classes and Divisions

Class A — Compressed Gas

Class B — Flammable and Combustible Material

Class C — Oxidizing Material

Class D — Poisonous and Infectious Material

   1 Materials Causing Immediate and Serious Toxic Effects

   2 Materials Causing Other Toxic Effects

   3 Biohazardous Infectious Material

Class E — Corrosive Material

Class F — Dangerously Reactive Material

Figure 16–7 WHMIS Hazard Symbols

◆ Preventative measures indicated: personal protective equipment (gloves, footwear, eye protection, respiratory protection), engineering controls, ventilation, enclosed process, leak and spill procedure, waste disposal, handling, storage, and shipping.

◆ First aid procedures for inhalation, ingestion, eye contact, skin contact, etc.

The HR Manager's Role.   According to a recent survey of occupational health and safety practitioners, controlling hazardous materials and keeping the WHMIS on track are very important issues. This is one of five issues rated as "very important" in these practitioners' jobs. Nearly three of four practitioners surveyed thought that WHMIS had improved workplace health and safety, and WHMIS training remains their top training priority.[39] Legislation requires annual reviews and refresher training (where needed). One of the results of this is a tendency to make training more job specific. Generic training via commercially available videos typically deals with the major classes of hazardous materials. The general content of such training materials makes it difficult to relate to specific worksite situations. Gwen Suchy of Lakeside Packers in Brooks, Alberta, saw the first round of WHMIS training as "so bloody boring" that workers often did not clearly understand the relevance of WHMIS to their immediate situation.[40] Some employers, such as the Royal Victoria Hospital in Montreal and the Calgary General Hospital, which have devised two-and-a-half-day training sessions for laboratory technicians, are finding it important and effective to go beyond the basic requirements. The main reason is that many chemicals fall into more than one WHMIS category and the worker has the onus of determining the appropriate handling and emergency procedures—a tedious and sometimes difficult process of reviewing MSDSs and applying the information to the quantities, concentrations, and environments in which the material will be used.[41]

◼ Safety and Health Programs

We have devoted most of the chapter thus far to discussing physical hazards in the workplace and their impact on both workers and the organization. However, there is another group of hazards that has major effects on workers, including stress, unsafe behaviours, and poor health habits. To cope with both types of hazards, companies often design comprehensive safety and health programs.

◼ Safety Programs

A safe working environment does not just happen; it has to be created, and that is not easy to do. The organizations with the best reputations for safety have developed deliberate, well-planned, and thorough safety programs. Concern for safety should begin at the highest level within the organization, and managers and supervisors at all levels should be charged with demonstrating safety awareness, held responsible for safety training, and rewarded for maintaining a safe workplace. Typically, however, the safety director and most safety programs are part of the human resource function. HR managers are often responsible for designing and implementing safety programs, as well as for training supervisors and managers in the administration of workplace safety rules and policies.

Effective safety programs share the following features:

◆ They include the formation of a safety committee and participation by all departments within the company. Employees participate in safety decisions, and management carefully considers employee suggestions for improving safety.

◆ They communicate safety with a multimedia approach that includes safety lectures, films, posters, and pamphlets.

◆ They instruct supervisors in how to communicate, demonstrate, and require safety, and they train employees in the safe use of equipment.

◆ They use incentives, rewards, and positive reinforcement to encourage safe behaviours. They reward employee complaints or suggestions about safety. They may also provide rewards (such as the safe driving awards given to truck drivers) to employees with exceptional safety records.

◆ They communicate safety rules and enforce them. They know that the law obligates employees to adhere to safety rules, and they are willing to use the disciplinary system to penalize unsafe work behaviour.

◆ They use safety directors and/or the safety committee to engage in regular self-inspection and accident research to identify potentially dangerous situations, and to understand why accidents occur and how to correct them.

Companies with comprehensive safety programs are likely to be rewarded with fewer accidents, fewer workers' compensation claims and lawsuits, and lower accident-related costs.

■ Employee Assistance Programs (EAPs)

Du Pont Canada
www.dupont.ca

burnout

A stress syndrome characterized by emotional exhaustion, depersonalization, and reduced personal accomplishment.

As we saw in Chapter 13, *employee assistance programs (EAPs)* are programs designed to help employees whose job performance is suffering because of physical, mental, or emotional problems. Originating in the 1940s in firms like Du Pont and Eastman Kodak as programs to treat alcoholism, EAPs now address a variety of employee problems ranging from drug abuse to marital problems. Roughly 50 percent of all Canadian employers offer EAPs.

Many organizations create EAPs because they recognize their ethical and legal obligations to protect not only their workers' physical health but their mental health as well. The ethical obligation stems from the fact that the causes of organizational stress—climate, change, rules, work pace, management style, work group characteristics, and so forth—are also frequently the causes of behavioural, psychological, and physiological problems for employees.[42] Ethical obligation becomes legal obligation when employees file workers' compensation claims for stress-related illnesses. In fact, much of the heightened concern about dealing with the consequences of workplace stress stems from the increasing incidence and severity of stress-related workers' compensation claims and their associated costs.[43] In Japan work-related stress has come to be seen as a deadly national problem, as the Issues and Applications feature entitled "Karoshi: Death by Overwork" describes. The Manager's Notebook titled "10 Ways That Managers Can Help Overworked Employees Reduce Stress" gives valuable pointers on preventing stress from turning into a serious health problem.

Stress often results in **burnout,** a syndrome characterized by emotional exhaus-

Issues and Applications

Karoshi: Death by Overwork

A lot of the stress that North American workers experience comes from overwork. After all, North Americans put in some 300 hours more on the job per year than the average European, and the average work week has increased in recent years. But Canadian workers are on the job several weeks less a year than the average Japanese worker.

Overwork in Japan is so prevalent that *karoshi,* or death by overwork, is now an officially recognized and documented ailment. *Karoshi* is attributed to the stress-induced pressures of overwork, and its symptoms include high blood pressure, fatigue, eating disorders, skin problems, and hair loss. The phenomenon of working oneself to death came to national attention in 1989, when a 48-year-old Osaka man dropped dead after working 15-hour days and hundreds of hours of overtime every year. Since then, the reported incidents of *karoshi* have steadily increased. There were 777 applications for compensa-

tion for *karoshi* in 1990, and the problem appears to be growing.

Karoshi is the most dramatic result of the hard-ball competition for jobs that prevails in many Japanese organizations. Indeed, this competition is so severe that many workers are afraid to take their vacations. With competitive pressures so intense, some Japanese politicians have concluded that the only solution is a legal one and have proposed legislation to compel workers to work fewer hours.

Meanwhile, *karoshi* is a real risk for many Japanese workers. One Japanese life insurance company surveyed 500 workers, each with more than 15 years' experience, and found that 80% wanted to sleep more, 70% felt stressed, almost half were constantly fatigued, and 42% feared that death from overwork would put a premature end to their careers.

SOURCE: Solomon, C. M. (1993, June). If you're feeling overworked, just think about how the Japanese feel. *Personnel Journal 72,* 58.

tion, depersonalization, and reduced personal accomplishment.[44] People who experience burnout may dread returning to work for another day, treat co-workers and clients callously, withdraw from the organization, and feel less competent in their jobs. Some of the factors that may lead to burnout include ambiguity and conflict regarding how to deal with various job-related issues and problems.[45] A lack of social support can aggravate these effects.

Burnout can lead to important negative consequences for the individual and for the organization. Mental and physical health can be negatively affected by burnout.[46] Mental health problems resulting from burnout can include depression, irritability, lowered self-esteem, and anxiety. Physical problems can include fatigue, headaches, insomnia, gastrointestinal disturbances, and chest pains. Organizational outcomes associated with burnout include turnover, absenteeism, and decrease in job performance.[47] In addition, increased drug and alcohol use has been found to be related to burnout.[48]

Many organizations perceive EAPs as being cost-effective solutions to performance, stress, and burnout problems from which all parties benefit. Although EAPs are expensive, many employers see them as investments, saving three to five dollars for every dollar spent.[49] The savings come from lower insurance costs, reduced sick time, and better job performance.

The success of EAPs depends on how well they are planned and implemented. There is also some evidence that they are more effective at dealing with certain types of problems than others. For instance, EAPs appear to be more effective at dealing with alcoholism than with drug addiction.[50]

Manager's Notebook

10 Ways That Managers Can Help Overworked Employees Reduce Stress

1. Allow employees to talk freely with one another. This not only reduces stress but also enhances productivity and problem solving.

2. Reduce personal conflicts on the job. To minimize conflicts: work with employees to resolve conflicts through communication, negotiation, and respect; treat employees fairly; and define job expectations clearly.

3. Give employees adequate control over how they do their work. Workers are more productive and better able to deal with stress if they have some control over how they perform their work.

4. Ensure that staffing budgets are adequate. Heavier workloads can increase illness, turnover, and accidents and decrease productivity. Therefore, a new project may not be worth taking on if staffing and funding are inadequate.

5. Talk openly with employees. Keep employees informed about bad news as well as good news. Give them opportunities to air their concerns.

6. Support employees' efforts. Workers are better able to cope with heavy workloads if managers are sympathetic, understanding, and encouraging. Listening to employees and addressing issues they raise is also helpful.

7. Provide competitive personal leave and vacation benefits. Workers who have time to relax and recharge after working hard are less likely to develop stress-related illnesses.

8. Maintain current levels of employee benefits. Workers' stress levels increase when their benefits are reduced. Employers must weigh carefully the savings gained from reducing benefits with the potentially high costs of employee burnout.

9. Reduce the amount of red tape for employees. Managers can lower burnout rates if they ensure that employees' time isn't wasted on unnecessary paperwork and procedures.

10. Recognize and reward employees for their accomplishments and contributions. Ignoring employees' accomplishments can lower morale and encourage talented and experienced employees to seek work elsewhere.

SOURCE: Adapted with permission from Solomon, C. M. (1993, June). Working smarter: How HR can help. *Personnel Journal, 72,* 54–64.

◼ Wellness Programs

As health care costs have skyrocketed over the last two decades, organizations have become more interested in preventive programs. Companies, recognizing that they can have an effect on their employees' behaviour and lifestyle off the job, are encouraging employees to lead healthier lives. They are also attempting to reduce health care costs through formal employee wellness programs. Where EAPs focus on *treating* troubled employees, **wellness programs** focus on *preventing* health problems. By the late 1980s, more than half of all U.S. business units with more than 50 employees were offering some type of wellness program,[51] and the trend seems to be accelerating.

A complete wellness program has three components:

◆ It helps employees identify potential health risks through screening and testing.

◆ It educates employees about such health risks as high blood pressure, smoking, poor diet, and stress.

wellness program

A company-sponsored program that focuses on preventing health problems in employees.

◆ It encourages employees to change their lifestyles through exercise, good nutrition, and health monitoring.

Wellness programs may be as simple and inexpensive as providing information about stop-smoking clinics and weight-loss programs or as comprehensive and expensive as providing professional health screening and multimillion-dollar fitness facilities.

The Canadian Approach. "Wellness" or health promotion programs have taken hold much more widely among U.S. employers than those in Canada. U.S. programs have been driven by the extent to which employers are affected by the health care expenses that employees incur. Since individuals in the United States are responsible for physician and hospitalization costs that are provided through public programs in Canada, the medical benefits programs provided by U.S. employers have much larger bills to pay. Measures that reduce those costs have major advantages for the employer—hence, "wellness" programs. Nonetheless, many Canadian employers are becoming involved in wellness promotions—some 25 percent of all Canadian employers are offering such programs as weight control, smoking cessation, stress management, and physical fitness. And the trend is upward, according to a Wyatt Company Survey of Group Benefits Plans.[52]

Labatt Breweries of Canada
www.labatt.com

In 1994, Labatt Breweries of Canada Ltd. introduced what was described as a "reverse EAP plan" for employees at its Toronto head office: an attempt to teach skills that would avoid burnout rather than deal with it after it had resulted in a work-related or domestic crisis. In the wake of extensive reorganization that saw four of every 10 employees relocated or laid off, the signs of burnout were everywhere. Labatt spent an average of $500 per employee on a voluntary course in goal setting and balancing work, family, and personal time. The program was more a course in changing attitudes than in managing stress. The results included an increased level of morale, and an openness to talking about stress in the workplace. And it was not just talk. The employer has taken measures to review job structure, assess workload, and make adjustments as necessary. Susan Laberee, the company's human resource director, says: "We can deal with the workload issue to make sure it's not required of you, but we've made it clear that if you choose to spend 12 or 15 hours in here every day, you're going to have to deal with the consequences in your own life."[53]

A Question of Ethics

Some feel that wellness and employee assistance programs should be evaluated on a cost-benefit basis and discontinued if it cannot be demonstrated that their benefits exceed their costs. Others feel that since companies create many of the stressful conditions that contribute to employee health problems, they are ethically bound to continue providing these types of programs. What do you think?

The combination of concerns for employee well-being and enlightened self-interest (i.e., reducing long-run costs) is likely to make Labatt and other Canadian employers offering wellness programs less the exception and more the rule. By the mid-1990s, health care costs in Canada were in excess of $70 billion and rising.[54] The increasing costs of advanced medical procedures and the aging population are colliding with the fiscal realities of government debt—the long-term implication is that, as governments search for ways to limit their role, increasing pressure will be placed on employers to assist employees via insurance or other means to absorb the expenses. To a certain extent, this is already occurring in workers' compensation where, in British Columbia for example, stress cases doubled within a four-year period. At one major insurance company, disability claims attributable to mental and nervous disorders (including stress) increased from 16 percent of claims to 26 percent in a five-year period, a change representing an "earthquake" for a disability insurer.[55] Some observers with a skeptical view of stress disabilities see them as the white-collar parallel of manual workers' lower back pain—an affliction often identifiable only by the person suffering it, and therefore an invitation to malingerers when income replacement is insured. Undoubtedly there is some abuse, but the rate of change and the heightened levels of uncertainty that characterize many organizations have created a very different workplace, one in which stress needs to be treated as the serious condition that it has become for growing numbers of employees.

Summary and Conclusions

Workplace Safety and the Law.

There are two sets of workplace safety laws: (1) workers' compensation, an employer-funded insurance system that operates at the provincial level, and (2) occupational health and safety legislation in each of Canada's 13 jurisdictions that mandates safety standards and procedures in the workplace.

Workers' compensation—which consists of total disability, impairment, survivor, medical expense, and rehabilitation benefits—is intended to ensure prompt and reasonable medical care to employees injured on the job, as well as income for them and their dependents. It also encourages employers to invest in workplace safety by requiring higher insurance premiums of employers with numerous workplace accidents and injuries.

Occupational health and safety legislation fixes employers with the responsibility to provide a safe and healthy working environment, comply with specific occupational and health standards, and keep records and submit reports. These laws also make health and safety in the workplace an employee responsibility, through the mandating of health and safety committees and by creating a legal right to refuse unsafe work. These laws are enforced by inspection and can result in significant fines when employers are found guilty of violations.

Contemporary Safety, Health, and Behavioural Issues.

The most significant safety, health, and behavioural issues for employers are AIDS, violence and smoking in the workplace, cumulative trauma disorders, substance abuse and testing, and hazardous materials. In all of these areas HR and line managers must deal with a variety of practical, legal, and ethical questions that often demand a careful balancing of individual rights (especially privacy rights) with the needs of the organization.

Safety and Health Programs.

Comprehensive safety programs are well-planned efforts in which management (1) carefully considers employee suggestions, (2) communicates safety rules to employees and enforces them, (3) invests in training supervisors to demonstrate and communicate safety on the job, (4) uses incentives to encourage safe behaviours, and (5) engages in regular self-inspection and accident research to identify and correct potentially dangerous situations.

Employee assistance programs (EAPs) are designed to help employees cope with physical, mental, or emotional problems (including stress) that are undermining their job performance.

Wellness programs are preventive efforts designed to help employees identify potential health risks and deal with them before they become problems.

Key Terms and Concepts

burnout, 494
carpal tunnel syndrome, 489
cumulative trauma disorder (CTD), 489
doctrine of contributory negligence, 478
employee assistance program (EAP), 494

ergonomics, 490
fellow-servant rule, 478
general duty clause, 479
health and safety committees, 481
impairment benefits, 478
medical expense benefits, 478
rehabilitation benefits, 478
right to refuse unsafe work, 481

social responsibility, 476
survivor benefits, 478
total disability benefits, 478
wellness program, 495
workers' compensation, 478
Workplace Hazardous Materials Information System (WHMIS), 491
workplace inspections, 480

Discussion Questions

1. What are the differences between the objectives of workers' compensation and the objectives of health and safety legislation?

2. What kinds of policies do you think would work best to prevent workplace violence?

3. Should current employees who test positive for drugs be fired? Why or why not?

4. If a job is potentially hazardous to the fetus of a pregnant employee, should it be legal for the company to restrict the job to men?

5. How can managers use the discipline system and the organization's reward system to encourage workplace safety?

6. How can managers use the discipline system and the organization's reward system to encourage workplace safety?

MiniCase 1 — *But You Look Fine*

There was a time when the notion of workers' compensation for office employees seemed superfluous, a protection for a few clumsy people who tripped over electrical wires or walked into open file drawers. No longer. The "light work" of office jobs can have some very serious physical consequences, as the following account indicates:

Lisa Doherty was in pain. But as the senior administrative assistant to the CEO of one of the largest manufacturing firms in Canada, she hadn't let anyone know about it. Lisa, a dedicated employee for the past 13 years, had been spending over 70 percent of her work day at a computer keyboard, either the old IBM that sits on her desk or the laptop she uses for frequent business trips. She had worked many hours of overtime without complaint, and had been a perfectionist about her job.

But several months ago, something started to go awry with Lisa's body. At first, she began to experience a tingling sensation in her right hand. A few weeks later she noticed that when she gripped a pen, or typed at her keyboard for an extended period of time, her right hand seemed weaker.

…

As the weeks dragged on, Lisa's symptoms intensified. She started to notice a constant ache in her mid-back and shoulders; soon both hands felt numb, and her forearms heavy. Lisa often experienced her right hand to be colder than her left, and she began to have difficulty with some of her routine daily chores. The tight feeling and pain in her upper back made it difficult for her to drive a car, cook meals, turn doorknobs, or even blow-dry her hair. Lisa continued to be a loyal employee, but it was an exhausting task.

For fear of being seen as desiring attention or wanting less of a workload, she confided only in her close friend. When Lisa began making mistakes at the keyboard, she visited her family doctor. Lisa's doctor sympathized with Lisa's problems, but could find nothing wrong on physical examination. He noted some tenderness in Lisa's forearms and suggested that she may have tendinitis, and possibly carpal tunnel syndrome. He told Lisa that most of her problems were due to stress. He prescribed some anti-inflammatory medication and suggested she report her problems at work, take a few weeks short-term disability, and receive an assessment at a local Workers' Compensation Board clinic. Exasperated, Lisa followed his instructions.

At the WCB clinic a nerve conduction test proved to be normal, ruling out carpal tunnel syndrome. Lisa was told to strengthen her forearms with light weights and to apply ice packs to her muscles. An ergonomist was asked to assess Lisa's workstation and to recommend appropriate remediation. Lisa's boss was as understanding as his workload allowed, and supported Lisa's application for a new workstation. He could not tolerate her being off work for more than one week, and he was pleased the WCB's recommendation that she return to full-time employment. Lisa had some symptom relief with treatment and rest, and physically she was deemed fit.

By the time Lisa had returned to work, the company had paid for her WCB treatments, six weeks' disability, a new workstation, and one month's medication (which she stopped because of gastrointestinal side effects). The day after Lisa returned to work, as she processed computer data on a business flight to Vancouver, her symptoms returned. For Lisa and her employer, the slide into the abyss of repetitive strain injury had begun. This abyss can eventually include assessment after assessment, diagnosis after diagnosis, and treatment after treatment—with multiple, unsuccessful attempts at work re-integration. Failed surgeries, inappropriate medication trials, and poorly thought out work modification may lead to the long-term disability of a competent and valued employee.

Discussion Questions

1. What are the physical dimensions of Lisa's job that contributed to her problem?
2. What are the job design factors that contributed to Lisa's problem?
3. What are the social and employee relations dynamics that contributed to Lisa's problem?
4. What could have been done to prevent the kind of problem Lisa developed? What steps might have allowed the problem to be addressed before it became what the authors describe as the "abyss" of RSI?

SOURCE: Tick, H., & Gilbert, M. (1996, June 17). Workplace RSI: A complex malady often misdiagnosed, mistreated. *Canadian HR Reporter,* 15–16, 23. Reprinted with permission of MPL Communications Inc.

MiniCase 2 — *Developing an AIDS Policy at Burroughs Wellcome*

Survey after survey has revealed that though the number of AIDS cases continues to increase, few large companies and virtually no small organizations have established formal AIDS policies. While top managers realize that AIDS could become a serious problem in their organization, most have no plan to deal with it. In contrast, management at Burroughs Wellcome realized early on that their corporate culture dictated a proactive stance toward the AIDS issue. They felt that Burroughs had the social responsibility to provide not only medical benefits but also support, compassion, and understanding to employees with AIDS.

In 1987 Burroughs became a pioneer when it announced that it would not discriminate against people with HIV/AIDS (PHAs)—that, on the contrary, it would provide such employees with health benefits and counselling. The company articulated a policy to educate *all* employees about the effects of AIDS and provided a mechanism to deal with safety questions. Burroughs used its own employees to prepare an educational video on AIDS. It also set up training sessions employing the video, educational brochures, and scientific and medical staff to train managers on how to deal with employees with AIDS. Burroughs feels that its program is responsible for the fact that the company has experienced no AIDS-related problems.

Discussion Questions

1. What can companies that fail to develop an AIDS policy expect when, for the first time, an employee reveals that he or she has the AIDS virus? Why must an AIDS policy stress education?

2. To what lengths should an organization go to help prevent employees from contracting HIV/AIDS? Should training include materials on "safer sex" or healthy lifestyles?

SOURCE: Adapted, by permission of publisher, from Bradley, J. (1990, February). Developing and implementing a policy on AIDS. *Management Review, 79*(2), 64. © 1990. American Management Association, New York. All rights reserved.

Case 1

A Crisis at Realgood Snack Foods

Joe Carriere, the director of human resources at Realgood Snack Foods, is sitting in plant manager Bill Stein's office stunned. Just 20 minutes ago the production supervisor, Max Jones, had been in Carriere's office describing what sounded like an employee revolt. Jones said that several people on his team had discovered this morning that a co-worker, Robert Carter, has AIDS. Not only were they refusing to work alongside Carter, they were also threatening to go "public" with the news that the company was allowing someone with AIDS to work on the assembly line.

Carriere knows that Realgood has a written policy on how to deal with an employee who has AIDS. His boss at headquarters mailed everyone a copy of the policy last year, but never said much about it. Carriere himself had never given much thought to the possibility that he would have to deal with an AIDS-related problem until today. He doesn't quite know why the line employees are so upset and wonders what he can do to mollify them.

The plant, one of several of Realgood's manufacturing facilities scattered across Canada, employs about 800 people engaged in manufacturing potato chips and corn chips. It is located in a medium-sized conservative community. The company was unionized several years earlier, so all production employees are union members. The relations between union and management are generally good, and the company offers pay somewhat above the area average and equally good benefits.

As Carriere sits in Stein's office, he remembers some of the facts that led to the present crisis. Carter is a good production worker who, up until a few months ago, had an excellent attendance record. Since August, however, he has missed work several times, with each episode lasting several days. Jones felt that the morale of Carter's work team had diminished considerably over the last two months, and part of

the reason was Carter's behaviour. Carter had recently become somewhat withdrawn and prone to anger easily. Additionally, some team members had begun to gripe about having to cover for his continued absences.

When Carter returned to work this morning from his most recent absence, he looked terrible. A member of his team asked him sarcastically, "What's wrong, Carter, you got AIDS?" The laughter abruptly died when Carter replied that, indeed, he did have AIDS. After several minutes of discussion, several team members came to Jones with their ultimatum.

Stein immediately realized the seriousness of the situation, particularly the employees' threat to go to the press. He is certain that the public will react to the disclosure by refusing to buy Realgood's products. As plant manager, he feels the only reasonable solution is to remove Carter from the work group. Since Carter's recent attendance has been poor and his behaviour hostile, Stein believes that it would save the company a lot of trouble simply to fire him and be done with it. He is looking to Carriere for advice on the best way to handle the situation.

Critical Thinking Questions

1. Based on what you know about this situation, could Realgood have done anything to prevent the employees' reaction to Carter's illness?

2. Can the employer fire Carter for his absences and angry behaviour? What might be the union's role in this issue?

3. Suppose that Carriere advises Stein to tell Jones to order the team members back to work and they refuse to go. What actions should management take?

4. Compare Realgood's legal obligations to its social responsibility in this situation. Is there a conflict between Stein's duty to Realgood's shareholders and the company's ethical obligation to Carter? How would you handle this situation if you were Carriere?

➤

Cooperative Learning Exercises

5. Students form into groups of four or five. Each group should develop a sample AIDS policy that meets the criteria described in the chapter and present it to the class.

6. Form into pairs to survey local organizations to see if they have developed formal AIDS policies. Each pair should go to one or two organizations and report back to the class. The class then discusses any common features found in these policies, especially in how they are communicated (e.g., to employees, or only to supervisors and managers) and whether or not they include AIDS education.

Case 2

More Than He Could Handle

The following account appeared in a recent HR publication:

Brian is the founding president of a high-tech manufacturing operation. The first several years of his tenure were spent in developing key products, which Brian (not his real name) and his team felt were ready for the global market. A lot rested on implementing their expansion plan, in which they had invested heavily.

The day after Brian publicly announced the global launch of their product line, his only son, 17, was arrested for selling drugs at his high school. The shock, along with the demands of the launch, led Brian to overreact, alienating his son. He first tried to conceal the incident from his senior team, but it quickly became evident to all involved that his worry over his son was interfering with the company's major strategic initiative.

The new HR director hired for the expansion had not yet implemented an EAP, but his previous experience led him to contact the president of an EAP firm he had used in the past. The EAP president also had an adolescent son, which struck a chord with the troubled executive. He began to take a more understanding approach to his son's difficulties, leading to a reconciliation that brought the entire family closer together. The son entered a rehabilitation program, and the family concentrated on supporting the treatment.

Brian took comfort in knowing that he did not have to face this personal problem alone. Counselling helped him balance the family issue and his work requirements, rather than sacrifice one for the other. At Brian's request, the counsellor also met with his executive team, to help them deal with their feelings about any disruption and work through any adjustments required to their original game plan.

Critical Thinking Questions

1. In small companies, access to EAP programs are more the exception than the rule. If there had been no EAP intervention in this case, what do you think would likely have happened?

2. Brian was, in some ways, atypical of senior executives because he was open to the suggestion that he might benefit from some EAP-style help. Why do you think senior executives are often reluctant to acknowledge difficulties arising from stress?

3. Would EAP services for senior managers be more likely to be used if integrated with annual checkups at company expense, or with wellness programs? Why or why not?

Cooperative Learning Exercise

4. Working in groups of three or four, identify and visit local EAP providers and two or three companies that provide EAP services to their employees. Determine the nature of the issues most frequently prompting EAP use, and whether different groups of employees are more or less likely to use these services.

SOURCE: Santa-Barbara, J. (1995, October 9). When work and family concerns collide. *Canadian HR Reporter*, 20. Reprinted with permission of MPL Communications Inc.

VideoCase

Competitiveness and the HRM Dimension

Most of us are familiar with the parable of the three blind men and the elephant, in which each man touches a different part of the animal's body (trunk, leg, etc.) and concludes very different things about the nature of the animal. The clear lesson is that you rarely understand the nature of something with only one perspective.

The same lesson applies to organizations—they can be thought of in many different ways. Owners and managers tend to think of organizations as "tools," as social inventions that are used to get things done. The language and the metaphors of management—job (or organizational) *design*, scientific management, chain of command, boss-subordinate relationships, information or control systems, specialization, coordination, efficiency—consistently reflect this notion that organizations exist to get things done, and therefore imply that employees and the jobs they do are to be justified and thought of in terms of the contribution they make to the elaborate tool we call a "company" (or a "plant," or a "firm"). In short, employees are typically seen as being part of a machine. The intensified competition and economic uncertainty in many sectors of the economy have increased the emphasis that many employers give to this perspective.

Employees often bring other perspectives. They do understand that a company needs to produce goods and/or services and sell them at a profit in order to be viable in the long run. But employees also see the organization that employs them as something they (the employees) have helped create—a moral/ethical sense of "ownership" regardless of whether they actually own any shares. Frequently employees perceive that the employer has drawn strength *from* the community as well as *contributing to* its well-being. To varying degrees, employees feel they should "own" the jobs that they do so long as they meet basic expectations of the employer—showing up for work, following directions, and performing at an "acceptable" level. For employees, their work is their economic lifeline as well as a social setting where they spend a significant part of their lives.

Discussion Questions

1. Downsizing can be either part of a proactive strategy—part of re-positioning the organization or getting out of certain segments that seem to be in decline—or reactive—a course of last resort to reduce operating budgets. What impacts does downsizing have on employees who "survive" the cuts? Are these unavoidable, or can the employer take actions that reduce the negative consequences? Does downsizing increase the "clout" of management with survivors ("I really have to do my best to be safe if there is another round." or decrease it through the bad feelings the survivor have toward their employer? Explain.

2. If an employer needs less absence or greater productivity from its work force in order to meet competitive standards, what are the main ways in which they can attempt to achieve those improvements? What role should careful monitoring of employee behaviour take in such initiatives? What role should electronic record-keeping and surveillance play? Explain.

Video Resources: "Downsizing Survey," *Venture* 643 (May 25, 1997), and "No Place to Hide," *Venture* 646 (June 15, 1997).

chapter 17

challenges

Meeting the International HRM Challenge

After reading this chapter, you should be able to deal more effectively with the following challenges:

1 Specify the HRM strategies that are most appropriate for firms at different stages of internationalization.

2 Identify the best mix of host-country and expatriate employees in international operations given the particular conditions facing a firm.

3 Explain why international assignments often fail and the steps a firm can take to ensure success in this area.

4 Reintegrate returning employees into the firm after they complete an international assignment.

5 Develop HRM policies and procedures that match the needs and values of different cultures.

Brave New World. Countries no longer conduct business in a vacuum; they face competition from all over the world. As firms expand their operations beyond their national borders, they encounter significant new challenges, among them cultural differences that affect the way they manage their human resources.

Historically international firms wanting to sell to the Canadian market often found it necessary to set up branch plants within Canada to avoid the steep tariffs that made imported goods expensive. The past two decades have seen rapid changes including the General Agreement on Tariffs and Trade (GATT), now superseded by the World Trade Organization, the Free Trade Agreement with the United States, and more recently the North American Free Trade Agreement (NAFTA). The following account demonstrates the ways in which things have changed.

> Several times a day at the IBM Canada plant in Bromont, Quebec, east of Montreal, a tractor-trailer arrives from an IBM plant in Burlington, Vermont, loaded up with microprocessor chips. Engineers and technicians, working in high-tech "clean" rooms, install the chips onto subassemblies that will ultimately serve to connect these components to the rest of the computer. Once packaged, the output of Bromont is shifted on to the next stage in IBM's production process, much going back to Burlington for installation in computers assembled there. There is no warehouse and no inventory in Bromont. As Doug Gregory, an IBM spokesman said, "We look at it as one long production line, 250 kilometres long, and it just happens to have an international border between one end and the other." IBM has reduced its worldwide payroll by some 40 percent in recent years, but Canada's two plants (the other being in Toronto) have survived—not to beat a tariff barrier, but because they demonstrated that they could deliver high quality at low cost. IBM Canada's Bill McClean, vice-president of manufacturing and development, puts it this way: "The 49th parallel is the least of my worries. This is a global business. The IBM company couldn't care whether it got this stuff from Canada or Hungary or Malaysia."[1]

Canada's history has been strongly influenced by the dynamics of international trade. The arrival of Europeans in North America resulted in large part from the pursuit of wealth to be found in new lands. Colonial settlements eventually grew to the point that, either through revolution (in 1776 in what became the United States) or through mutual arrangements (the *British North America Act of 1867*), independent countries emerged. The fur trade, as well as the mining and forestry industries, which have been central to Canadian economic development, were all predicated on export markets. As a result, Canada has always been embedded in international trading relationships. However, during Canada's first century, much of the country's economic policy with respect to manufacturing was shaped by the legacy of Sir John A. Macdonald who, as Canada's first prime minister, saw economic union with the United States as the major threat to Canada as a distinct political and cultural entity. His legacy was reflected in the building of the Canadian Pacific Railway and in a national policy of high tariffs, to nurture ties within Canada and deflect the economic pull of the United States.

The recent past has seen a significant shift in markets for Canadian manufactured goods. In 1981, Canadian manufacturers exported about 25 percent of what they produced. By the mid-1990s, that level had increased to 60 percent. About 50 percent of manufacturing jobs and profits derive from U.S. sales.

As a result of these trends, interprovincial trade is becoming less important as a part of overall economic activity.

The pattern of manufacturing sales is also reflected in the broader economy. For every dollar of goods and services sold by Quebec in 1981 to other parts of Canada, it sold 74 cents elsewhere in the rest of the world; by 1995 Quebec's "rest-of-the-world" figure had increased to $1.37. For British Columbia—always a more externally oriented economy—the 1981 figure was $1.87 but rose to $2.38 by 1995. For Ontario, the change has been the most dramatic: in 1981, domestic and international sales were almost equal, but by 1995 the figure was $2.25 of exports for every interprovincial dollar of sales, some $140 billion in total.

Whether Sir John A.'s misgivings about the political results of economic integration with the United States will ultimately be borne out is an intriguing question, yet to be answered. What has become undeniably clear is that Canada's economic future is one in which international standards will play an increasing and eventually a dominant role. Canadian organizations, like those in every country with an advanced economy, must meet international standards of quality, costs, innovativeness, and responsiveness to clients and customers. Both domestic and international business is at stake. Human resource management has a crucial role to play.

HRM on the Web

http://www.t-bird.edu/

Thunderbird School of International Management

This Web site provides access to Dom Pedro II International Studies Research Center, which is an outstanding source of international business and HR information. Thunderbird's home page provides links to files on more than 200 countries, as well as information on the European Union (EU) and the North American Free Trade Association (NAFTA). The sources of this information include economic reports, articles from international journals, and news clippings that pertain to business in many different countries and cultures.

The fortunes of most Canadian firms, large and small, are inextricably bound to the global economy. In this chapter we demonstrate how managers can effectively utilize HRM practices to enhance their firms' competitiveness in an era of international opportunities and challenges. First we cover the stages of international involvement, the challenges of expatriate job assignments, and ways to make those assignments more effective. We then discuss the development of HRM policies in a global context and the specific HR concerns of exporting firms.

■ The Stages of International Involvement

As Figure 17–1 shows, firms progress through five stages as they internationalize their operations.[2] The higher the stage, the more HR practices need to be adapted to diverse cultural, economic, political, and legal environments.

◆ In *Stage 1,* the firm's market is exclusively domestic. The high tariff environment that held sway during Canada's first century created many of these firms, which in many cases are too small to export efficiently to markets with larger-scale producers. With the liberalization of international trade, the number of manufacturers in this category has dwindled. Service-sector organizations are more likely to remain strictly Canadian, often because they specialize in services that require "local" expertise—law firms, consultants in legally defined areas such as pensions, and certain parts of the retail and hospitality industry are typical of firms less likely to pursue international expansion or sales.

◆ In *Stage 2,* the firm expands its market to include foreign countries, but retains its production facilities within domestic borders. HRM practices at this stage should facilitate exporting of the firm's products through managerial incentives, appropriate training, and staffing strategies that focus on the demands of international customers.

Many of Canada's resource-based companies (mining, forest products) have always been predicated on export markets. Abitibi-Price and MacMillan Bloedel sell newsprint around the world. Others have become dominant players in specific foreign markets—for example, McCain Foods Ltd. holds some 75 percent of the oven fries market in Germany and has a very strong presence in the frozen fries market in both the United Kingdom and France.[3]

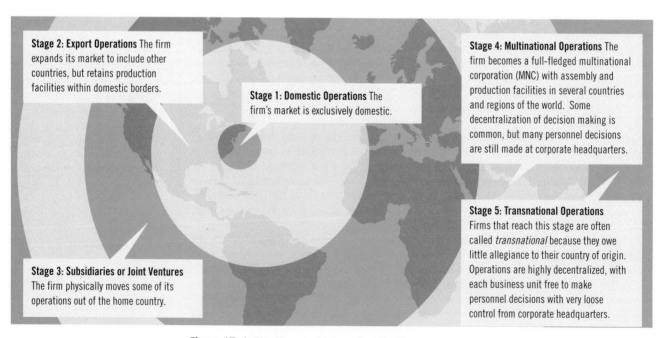

Figure 17–1 The Stages of Internationalization

◆ In *Stage 3,* the firm physically moves some of its operations out of the home country. These facilities are primarily used for parts assembly, although some limited manufacturing may take place. In other cases, companies license their technology to expand sales. Can-Eng Manufacturing, Canada's largest supplier of industrial furnaces, exports under licensing agreements with countries including Japan, Korea, Germany, and Brazil.[4] The foreign branches or subsidiaries tend to be under close control of corporate headquarters at this stage, and a high proportion of top managers are **expatriates** (employees who are citizens of the corporation's home country). HRM practices at Stage 3 need to focus on the selection, training, and compensation of expatriates, as well as on the development of personnel policies for local employees where the foreign facilities are located.

◆ In *Stage 4,* the firm becomes a full-fledged **multinational corporation (MNC),** with assembly and production facilities in several countries and regions of the world. Strategic alliances between corporations from different countries are becoming increasingly common. While there is usually some decentralization of decision making for firms at Stage 4, many personnel decisions affecting foreign branches are still made at corporate headquarters, typically by an international personnel department. In addition, foreign operations are still managed by expatriates. The United States has been a dominant economic force for most of this century, and many of the world's multinational corporations are based there. IBM, General Motors, Xerox, and many others are very familiar to Canadians. However, Canada is itself home to some significant multinationals, including Nortel, Noranda, Hiram Walker, Bombardier, and Alcan. HRM practices at these companies are quite complex because they must deal with large numbers of expatriates and their families in overseas assignments, and diverse ethnic and cultural groups in multiple countries. They must also facilitate the control of overseas subsidiaries from corporate headquarters.

◆ In *Stage 5,* the most advanced stage of internationalization, firms are often called **transnational corporations** because they owe little allegiance to their country of origin and have weak ties to any given country. Operations are highly decentralized; each business unit has the freedom to make personnel decisions with very loose control from corporate headquarters. The board of directors is often composed of people of different nationalities, and the firm tries hard to develop managers who see themselves as citizens of the world. These firms freely hire employees from any country. For example, Olivetti, the large Italian-based conglomerate, has an extensive "no frontiers" recruitment program to hire managers and professionals from around the world.

HRM practices at Stage 5 companies are designed to blend individuals from diverse backgrounds to create a shared corporate (rather than national) identity and a common vision. For instance, Gillette (which develops and manufactures personal care products) has developed an extensive program in which local personnel offices in 48 countries search for the best young university graduates who are single and fluent in English. The individuals selected are given six months of training in the home country, and those who come through this probationary period successfully travel to Gillette's headquarters to begin 18 months of training. Managers are routinely sent on one- to three-year assignments overseas to gain greater international exposure. In the words of Gillette's international personnel director, "The person we are looking for is someone who says, 'Today, it's Manila. Tomorrow, it's the U.S. Four years from now, it's Peru or Pakistan.' … We really work hard at finding people who aren't parochial and who want international careers."[5]

■ Determining the Mix of Host-Country and Expatriate Employees

Once a firm passes from the exporting stage (Stage 2) to the stage in which it opens a foreign branch (Stage 3)—either a **wholly owned subsidiary** (the foreign branch is fully owned by the home office) or a **joint venture** (part of the foreign branch is owned by a host country entity: another company, a consortium of firms, an individual, or the government)—it must decide who will be responsible for managing the unit. This decision is important because in most cases the

expatriate
A citizen of one country living and working in another country.

multinational corporation (MNC)
A firm with assembly and production facilities in several countries and regions of the world.

transnational corporation
A firm with operations in many countries and highly decentralized operations. The firm owes little allegiance to its country of origin and has weak ties to any given country.

wholly owned subsidiary
In international business, a foreign branch owned fully by the home office.

joint venture
In international business, a foreign branch owned partly by the home office and partly by an entity in the host country (a company, a consortium of firms, an individual, or the government).

investment required for plant and equipment is enormous, and the success of the foreign venture (like that of any other business) depends largely on who is in charge.

There are three basic approaches to managing an international subsidiary: ethnocentric, polycentric, and geocentric.[6]

ethnocentric approach

An approach to managing international operations in which top management and other key positions are filled by people from the home country.

◆ In the **ethnocentric approach** to managing international operations, top management and other key positions are filled by people from the home country. For instance, Fluor Daniel, Inc., has 50 engineering and sales offices on five continents and concurrent construction projects in as many as 80 countries at any given time. The firm uses a large group of expatriate managers, including 500 international HRM professionals who are involved in recruitment, development, and compensation worldwide and who report directly to a corporate vice-president. The vice-president himself is a roving expatriate who spends at least two months a year abroad supervising international operations.

polycentric approach

An approach to managing international operations in which subsidiaries are managed and staffed by personnel from the host country.

◆ In the **polycentric approach,** international subsidiaries are managed and staffed by personnel from the host country. Ford adopted this approach in its operations in Sonora, Mexico, where with one exception (a technical expert from the United States) all 2,000 employees are Mexican citizens.[7] Coca-Cola, which has been global for most of its 100-year history, currently operates in 160 countries, employing about half a million workers worldwide.

geocentric approach

An approach to managing international operations in which nationality is downplayed and the firm actively searches on a worldwide or regional basis for the best people to fill key positions.

◆ In the **geocentric approach,** nationality is deliberately downplayed and the firm actively searches on a worldwide or regional basis for the best people to fill key positions. Transnational firms (those in Stage 5) tend to follow this approach. For example, Electrolux (the vacuum cleaner company) has for many years attempted to recruit and develop a group of international managers from diverse countries. These people constitute a mobile pool of managers who are used in a variety of facilities as the need arises. Rather than representing a particular country, they represent the organization wherever they are. Most important to Electrolux is the development of a common culture and an international perspective, and the expansion of its international networks.[8]

Coca-Cola
www.coca-cola.com

As Figure 17–2 shows, there are both advantages and disadvantages to using local nationals and expatriates in foreign subsidiaries. Most firms use expatriates only for such key positions as senior managers, high-level professionals, and technical specialists. Because expatriates tend to be very costly (approximately a third of a million dollars per person per year), it makes little financial sense to hire expatriates for positions that can be competently filled by foreign nationals. In addition, many countries require that a certain percentage of the work force be local citizens, with exceptions usually made for upper management. In general, reliance on expatriates increases when:[9]

◆ *Sufficient local talent is not available.* This is most likely to occur in firms operating in developing countries. For instance, top managers of Falconbridge and Alcoa (both mining companies operating in Latin America and Africa) are almost always expatriates.

◆ *An important part of the firm's overall business strategy is the creation of a corporatewide global vision.* Some firms prefer to make subsidiaries part of an international network with a shared corporate identity. When this is the case, expatriates are used to link the organization's international subsidiaries. Too much reliance on locals can undermine this effort because their views and experiences tend to be more localized and they are generally more concerned with their own unit than with the organization as a whole.

◆ *International units and domestic operations are highly interdependent.* In some cases, the production process requires that all divisions of a corporation, both international and domestic, work closely with one another. This is particularly necessary when the output of one business unit is needed as an input by another business unit of the same company. The illustration of IBM's integration between Bromont, Quebec, and Burlington, Vermont, which opened this chapter, is a good illustration. Linking production processes generally calls for greater reliance on expatriate managers and specialists, who can bridge the gaps and tie the units of the organization together.

This policy is not necessary in corporations with primarily stand-alone operations with low interdependence across units. For instance, McDonald's Corporation operates in more than 50 countries; approximately 3,000 of its 12,000 restaurants are located overseas. The

Locals

Advantages	Disadvantages
• Lowers labour costs	• Makes it difficult to balance local demands and global priorities
• Demonstrates trust in local citizenry	
• Increases acceptance of the company by the local community	• Leads to postponement of difficult local decisions (such as layoffs) until they are unavoidable, when they are more difficult, costly, and painful than they would have been if implemented earlier
• Maximizes the number of options available in the local environment	
• Leads to recognition of the company as a legitimate participant in the local economy	• May make it difficult to recruit qualified personnel
• Effectively represents local considerations and constraints in the decision-making process	• May reduce the amount of control exercised by headquarters

Expatriates

Advantages	Disadvantages
• Cultural similarity with parent company ensures transfer of business/management practices	• Creates problems of adaptability to foreign environment and culture
	• Increases the "foreignness" of the subsidiary
• Permits closer control and coordination of international subsidiaries	• May involve high transfer and salary costs
• Gives employees a multinational orientation through experience at parent company	• May result in personal and family problems
	• Leads to high failure rate
• Establishes a pool of internationally experienced executives	• Has disincentive effect on local-management morale and motivation
• Local talent may not yet be able to deliver as much value as expatriates can.	• May be subject to local government restrictions

Figure 17–2 Advantages and Disadvantages of Using Local and Expatriate Employees to Staff International Subsidiaries

SOURCES: Locals: Adapted from Doz, Y., & Prahalad, C. K. (1986). Controlled variety: A challenge for human resource management in MNC. *Human Resource Management*, 21(1), 57; Expatriates: Adapted from Hamil, J. (1989). Expatriate policies in British MNNs. *Journal of General Management*, 14(4), 20.

primary involvement of corporate headquarters is to train restaurant managers from all over the world at McDonald's Hamburger University in Chicago. The company also has five international personnel directors who serve as internal consultants. Thus, although McDonald's demands strict product quality standards across countries, expatriates play a minor role in this process because each restaurant functions as a highly autonomous unit.

◆ *The political situation is unstable.* Corporations tend to rely on expatriates for top-management positions when the risk of governmental intervention in the business is high, when actual or potential turmoil within the country is serious, when the threat of terrorism exists, and when there has been a recent history of social upheaval in the country. Although expatriate top managers may increase tensions between nationalistic groups and a foreign firm, they do provide some assurance to the home office that its interests are well represented locally. Expatriates are also less susceptible to the demands of local political forces.

Most Western ventures in the new republics of Eastern Europe and the former Soviet Union are run by expatriates. The same is true in the few remaining communist countries, where political instability remains high.

◆ *There are significant cultural differences between the host country and the home country.* The more dissimilar the culture where the subsidiary is located to that of the home office (in terms of language, religion, customs, and so forth), the more important it is to appoint expatriates who can serve as interpreters or go-betweens for the two cultures. Since this boundary-spanning role demands much cross-cultural sensitivity, the MNC needs to select and carefully train individuals suitable for these positions. This may require considerable career planning.

McDonald's Hamburger University
www.mcdonalds.com/careers/ hambuniv/hambuniv.html

Researchers have identified nations and world regions where dissimilarities with Canadian culture are great and the expatriate needs exceptional skills to be successful. Cultural barriers are lowest in the United States, European countries, Australia, and New Zealand; mid-range in most of Latin America; and greatest in India, Pakistan, Southeast Asia, the Middle East, North Africa, East Africa, and Liberia.[10]

■ The Challenges of Expatriate Assignments

One of the most challenging tasks for any firm operating internationally is to manage its expatriate work force effectively. The statistics, unfortunately, are not encouraging. One of the main HR challenges in managing expatriate assignments is the rate at which they can fail. Failure is defined as a person's not serving the intended term of his or her foreign posting. The failure rate in the United States ranges from 20 to 40 percent. Canadians have a somewhat better track record—they have long had a strong international reputation for their combination of North American business education and experience, and for being better able to bridge cultures, especially between the United States and Europe.[11] (Unlike Americans who take assignments outside their home country, Canadians often leave without the strong sense that it is a temporary move. In fact, there are indications that during the 1990s, there has been something of a "brain drain" of Canadian professionals in information technologies, some of the best law-school graduates and executives who have moved to the United States and other international destinations.[12]) The difficulties that Americans—and Canadians, to a lesser extent—have had compares unfavourably with a failure rate of less than five percent for Japanese expatriates, according to a recent survey of 144 multinationals. One of the reasons cited for the difference is that Japanese expatriates receive far more orientation and language instruction than U.S. expatriates do. Another reason for their smooth adjustment overseas could be their tendency to take refuge in frequently large expatriate communities.[13]

Global Imperative.

Business organizations, both large and small, no longer have the option of ignoring international forces in their strategies. Deciding how to compete in other countries and at home always involves a human resources dimension.

Failures can be very expensive. Premature returnees cost U.S.$70,000 to U.S.$210,000 each in 1993 dollars, which translates into U.S.$2.7 billion per year in direct costs (to U.S. firms). The more intangible costs of failure in terms of business disruptions, lost opportunities, and negative impact on the firm's reputation and leadership are probably many times greater. In addition, the personal hardship on the people involved and their families, including diminished self-image, marital strife, uprooted children, lost income, and tarnished career reputation, can be substantial.[14]

■ Why International Assignments End in Failure

It is important to understand the reasons behind expatriates' high failure rates so that preventive measures can be taken. Six factors account for most failures, although their relative importance varies by firm.[15] These are career blockage, culture shock, lack of cross-cultural training, an overemphasis on technical qualifications, a tendency to use international assignments as a way to get rid of problem employees, and family problems.

Career Blockage.   Initially, many employees see the opportunity to work and travel abroad as exciting. But once the initial rush wears off, many feel that they have been forgotten by the home office and that their career has been sidetracked while their counterparts at home are climbing the corporate ladder. Statistics indicate that a very small portion of people sent on international assignment saw those assignments as essential to a career route to the top.[16] Many employers that use international postings give themselves high marks for career planning for their expatriate employees but, according to a recent survey by the Society for Human Resources Management, only 15 percent of the over 200 managers who responded assessed their firm's career planning for them as being sufficient.[17]

Culture Shock.   Many people who take international assignments cannot adjust to a different cultural environment, a phenomenon called **culture shock.** Instead of learning to work within the new culture, the expatriate tries to impose the home office's or home country's values on the host country's employees. This practice generally results in frustration and may trigger cultural clashes and misunderstandings that escalate until the expatriate decides to return home to more familiar surroundings—perhaps leaving a mess behind.

In his book *Going International,* consultant Lewis Griggs recounts the culture shock experienced by a female vice-president of a company doing business in Saudi Arabia. She was invited to dinner at the home of a Saudi businessman, and, upon entering the home, was escorted to a room set aside for women. Feeling that she was not being accorded proper respect as head of the American delegation, she joined the men in their dining room. Dinner and business discussion ended abruptly.

Firms can help employees avoid culture shock by using selection tools to choose employees with the highest degree of cultural sensitivity. However, research indicates that few companies are doing so. For example, only 18 percent of the companies in a recent survey use structured interviews; only 12 percent use candidate/spouse self-assessment; only 6 percent use psychological and cognitive testing, and only 2 percent use formal assessment centres.[18]

Lack of Predeparture Cross-Cultural Training.   Surprisingly, only about one-third of multinationals provide *any* cross-cultural training to expatriates, and those that do tend to offer rather cursory programs.[19] Often the expatriate and his or her family literally pack their bags and travel to their destination with only a passport and whatever information they could cull from magazines, tourist brochures, and the library. This is a recipe for trouble, as the following examples illustrate:

> One chief engineer, working in a petroleum plant in Bangladesh, insisted that one of his subordinates of his report to work the following morning (which was the Muslim holiday Eid) due to an emergency. Within one hour there was a walkout and the plant shut down. The Muslim employees, upon hearing the demand placed on their colleague, claimed that the engineer had insulted their religion.[20]

> I once attended a business meeting in Tokyo with a senior U.S. executive. The Japanese go through a very elaborate ritual when exchanging business cards, and the American didn't have a clue. She just tossed some of her business cards across the table at the stunned Japanese executives. One of them turned his back on her and walked out. Needless to say, the deal never went through.[21]

Overemphasis on Technical Qualifications.   The person chosen to go abroad may have impressive credentials and an excellent reputation in the home office for getting things done. He or she may seem like the natural choice to start a new international facility, to manage a subsidiary that needs tightening up, or to act as a troubleshooter when technical difficulties arise. Unfortunately, the same traits that led to success at home can be disastrous in another country unless cultural sensitivity is also part of the expatriate's personality and outlook. Consider the experience of one executive from a large electronics firm who spent only three months of what was supposed to be a two-year assignment in Mexico:

Society for Human Resources Management
www.shrm.org

culture shock
The inability to adjust to a different cultural environment.

> I just could not accept the fact that my staff meetings would always start at least a half hour late and that schedules were treated as flexible guidelines with much room to spare. Nobody seemed to care but me! I also could not understand how many of the first-line supervisors would hire their friends and relatives, regardless of competence. What I viewed as nepotism of the worst kind was seen by them as an honourable obligation to their extended families, and this included many adopted relatives or compadres who were not even related by blood.[22]

Prudential Relocation
www.prudential.com/prm

In a recent survey, 96 percent of respondents rated the technical requirements of a job as the most important selection criteria for international assignment, largely ignoring cultural sensitivity.[23] This outlook is a recipe for failure. In more enlightened companies, such as Prudential Relocation, nearly 35 percent of managers cite "cultural adaptability" as the most important trait for overseas success. Only 22 percent of Prudential managers cite technical skills as most important.[24]

Getting Rid of a Troublesome Employee.

International assignments may seem to be a convenient way of dealing with managers who are having problems in the home office. By sending these managers abroad, the organization is able to resolve difficult interpersonal situations or political conflicts at the home office, but at a significant cost to its international operations. Although the number of people in this category is difficult to assess, the "let's find an out-of-the-way place for So-and-So" syndrome is not unusual. The following true story was told to one of the authors:

> Joe and Paul were both competing for promotion to divisional manager. The vice-president in the corporate headquarters responsible for making the selection decision felt that Joe should be the one to get the promotion but that Paul would never be able to accept that and would actively try to undermine Joe's authority. Paul also had much support from some of the old-timers, so the only way to avoid the dilemma was to find a different spot for Paul where he could not cause any trouble. The vice-president came up with the idea of promoting Joe to divisional manager while appointing Paul as a senior executive at the Venezuelan subsidiary. Paul (who had seldom been out of the country and who had taken introductory Spanish in high school 20 years earlier) took the job. It soon became obvious that the appointment was a mistake. Two months after being assigned to the Venezuelan post there was a major wildcat strike attributed to Paul's heavy-handed style in dealing with the labour unions and he had to be replaced.

Family Problems.

The inability or unwillingness of the expatriate's spouse and children to adapt to life in another country is one of the most important reasons for failure. In fact, more than half of all early returns can be attributed to family problems.[25] Given the stress the employee usually experiences in trying to function in unfamiliar surroundings, trouble at home can easily become the proverbial straw that breaks the camel's back.

It is surprising that most firms do not anticipate these problems and develop programs to assist expatriates' families in adjusting to their new surroundings. One survey showed that while all married expatriates considered their spouse's opinion a very important factor in their decision whether to take an international assignment, fewer than a third felt that their company took this into account.[26] One expatriate's wife comments:

> A husband who is racked by guilt over dragging his wife halfway around the world, or distracted because she is ill-equipped to handle a foreign assignment, is not a happy or productive employee. ... Most women actually start out all right. The excitement quickly fades for a travelling wife, though, when her husband abandons her for a regional tour immediately upon arrival and she's left behind with the moving boxes and the responsibility of finding good schools. Or when she is left to hire servants to set up a household without knowing the language ... [Often] they are asked to jump off their own career paths and abandon healthy salaries ... just so that they can watch their self-esteem vanish somewhere over the international date line.[27]

The expectations of dual-career couples are another cause of failure in expatriate assignments. MNCs are increasingly confronted with couples who expect to work in the same foreign location—at no sacrifice to either's career. Yet one spouse usually has to sacrifice, and this often leads to dissatisfaction. When 10-year AT&T veteran Eric Phillips was asked to move to Brussels in 1991 to manage the company's sales of communication services in Europe, his wife, Angelina, had to give up her well-paying job as a market researcher. While the move represented a terrific career opportunity for Phillips, his wife recalls finding it very difficult to adjust.[28]

■ Difficulties upon Return

Although it is the failure of expatriates abroad that has received the most attention in research journals, a number of studies suggest that expatriates' return home may also be fraught with difficulties. It is estimated that 20 to 40 percent of returning expatriates (called *repatriates*) leave the organization shortly after returning home.[29] Four common problems that confront returning expatriates are likely to have a negative impact on their performance, career development, and commitment to the firm. These are their company's lack of respect for the skills they acquired while abroad, loss of status, poor planning for the expatriate's return, and reverse culture shock. This chapter's Manager's Notebook titled "Communicate to Repatriate" summarizes some of the practices that companies can use to counter these problems. We discuss these practices in greater detail later in this chapter.

Lack of Respect for Acquired Skills.   Many Canadian firms are still heavily oriented toward the domestic market. This is true even of many of those that have a long history of operating internationally. As a result, international experience is not highly valued. The expatriate who has gathered a wealth of information and valuable skills on a foreign assignment may be frustrated by the lack of appreciation shown by peers and supervisors at corporate headquarters. Some in the organization even see the expatriate as out of touch and dancing to a different set of drums, particularly if the international assignment lasted several years. According to recent data, only 12 percent of expatriates felt that their overseas assignment had enhanced their career development, and almost two-thirds reported that their firm did not take advantage of what they had learned overseas.[30]

Loss of Status.   Returning expatriates often experience a substantial loss of prestige, power, independence, and authority. This *status reversal* affects as many as three-quarters of repatriated employees.[31] It is common to respond to this situation with bitterness, as the following example illustrates:

> When I was in Chile, I had occasions to meet various ministers in the government and other high-ranking industry officials. Basically my word was the final one. I had a lot of latitude because the home office didn't really want to be bothered with what was happening in Chile and therefore was uninformed anyway. I made decisions in Chile that only our CEO would make

---

Manager's Notebook

Communicate to Repatriate

Companies that have relatively low repatriation failure rates attribute their success to intensive interactions with the individual and his or her family before, during, and after the international assignment. Here are some of the practices and programs that have been found to increase organizational commitment among expatriate employees:

◆ Advance career planning helps expatriates know what to expect when they return home. Management needs to sit down with HR professionals and the employee to lay out a potential career path before the employee is sent abroad.

◆ Mentors can make the expatriates feel they are vital members of the organization. At Nortel, for instance, senior managers and vice-presidents correspond regularly with expatriate employees and meet with them periodically either at the home office or on location. The reentry process is much easier for employees who do not feel they were forgotten while they were away.

◆ Opening global communication channels keeps expatriates up-to-date on organizational developments. Some companies do this through newsletters and briefings. And, of course, telecommunications technology enables expatriates to stay in constant touch with the home office through faxes and E-mail.

◆ Recognizing the contributions of repatriated employees eases their reentry. Repatriated employees whose accomplishments abroad are acknowledged are more likely to stay with the company.

SOURCE: Adapted from Shilling, M. (1993, September). How to win at repatriation. *Personnel Journal*, 40.

for the domestic operation. When I returned, I felt as though all the training and experience I had gotten in Chile was totally useless. The position I had seemed about six levels down as far as I was concerned. I had to get approval for hiring. I had to get my boss' signature for purchases worth one-tenth of the values of ones I approved in Chile. To say I felt a letdown would be a significant understatement.[32]

Poor Planning for Return Position.

Often management repatriates an employee with no idea of what position this person should hold in the home office. Uncertainties regarding their new career assignment may provoke much anxiety in returning employees. One survey suggests that more than half of expatriates were unaware of what job awaited them at home.[33] The following story is typical of returning expatriates:

I received a letter from the home office three months prior to the expiration of my assignment in Hungary (where I was responsible for a team of engineers developing a computerized system for handling inventories in four new joint ventures). I was told that I would be assuming the position of Supervisor of Technical Services in corporate headquarters. It sounded impressive enough. I was astonished to find out upon return, however, that I was given the honorary title of supervisor with nobody under my command. It smelled like a dead rat to me so I jumped ship as soon as I could.[34]

Reverse Culture Shock.

Most firms assume the returning expatriate will be happy to be back home. But this is not always true, particularly for those returning from extended international assignments. Living and working in another culture for a long time changes a person, especially if he or she has internalized some of the foreign country's norms and customs. Since much of this internalization occurs subconsciously, expatriates are usually unaware of how much psychological change they have undergone until they return home. It has been reported that as many as 80 percent of returning expatriates experience *reverse culture shock,* which sometimes leads to alienation, a sense of uprootedness, and even disciplinary problems.[35] One expatriate who had worked in Spain notes:

I began to take for granted the intense camaraderie at work and after hours among male friends. Upon returning . . . I realized for the first time in my life how [here] males are expected to maintain a high psychological distance from each other, and their extremely competitive nature in a work environment. My friendly overtures were often misperceived as underhanded manoeuvres for personal gain.[36]

Despite all these difficulties, many managers today are lining up for international assignments as companies gradually realize that employees with international experience under their belts are an asset in the global economy. One recent survey showed that most companies have increased their expatriate populations since 1989 and expect to increase or maintain that volume.[37] The "out of sight—out of mind" mentality that has long governed international assignments is being replaced at some companies by the notion that these assignments should be structured to enhance the firm's global efforts. For instance, Gerber Products, which is busily building markets in Latin America and Central and Eastern Europe, has announced that from now on, international assignments will be emphasized as part of normal career development for company executives. As a result, Gerber's country manager in Poland feels he has an edge over many of his colleagues. "My overseas experience sets me apart from the rest of the MBA bunch," he says. "I'm not just one of hundreds of thousands."[38]

Gerber Products
www.gerber.com

■ Building Managerial Skills: Enhancing the Effectiveness of Expatriate Assignments with HRM Policies and Practices

Although expatriate assignments will probably always be more problematic than domestic transfers, companies can minimize the chances of failure by putting in place a sensible set of HRM policies and practices that get to the root of the problems we've discussed. In this section we look at how selection, training, career development, and compensation policies can avoid some of these problems.

■ Selection

The choice of employee for an international assignment is a critical decision. Because most expatriates work under minimal supervision in a distant location, mistakes in selection are likely to go unnoticed until it is too late. To choose the best employee for the job, management should:

◆ *Emphasize cultural sensitivity as a selection criterion.* The firm should assess the candidate's ability to relate to people from different backgrounds. For instance, one large electronics manufacturing firm conducts in-depth interviews with the candidate's supervisors, peers, and subordinates, particularly those whose gender, race, and ethnic origin are different from the candidate's. Personal interviews with the candidate and written tests that measure social adjustment and adaptability should also be part of the selection process.

Cultural Sensitivity for Consumer Satisfaction.

Some companies need to make only language adjustments in packaging, signs, and logos when attempting to sell their products in international markets. Coca-Cola is exactly the same whether it is sold in Seattle or Moscow—except for the lettering on the bottle. McDonald's restaurants in Saudi Arabia, however, have also had to adjust their menus, ingredients, and hours of operation to suit Arab culture.

◆ *Establish a selection board of expatriates.* Some HRM specialists strongly recommend that all international assignments be approved by a selection board consisting of managers who have worked as expatriates for a minimum of three to five years.[39] This kind of board should be better able to detect potential problems than managers with no international background. For instance, an employee may express the desire to work in South America where "maids are cheap." This kind of remark may be regarded as inconsequential or humorous by the personnel director, but would probably raise a red flag among managers with international experience.

◆ *Require previous international experience.* While not always feasible, it is highly desirable to choose candidates who have already spent some time in a different country. Increasingly, knowledge of other countries and other cultures on a first-hand basis is becoming an important prerequisite for such postings. Michael Stern, a Toronto-based management consultant and columnist, contends that Canadians are often more "exportable" than their U.S. counterparts because they either know or see the value in other languages and are often less aggressive and therefore more adaptable.[40] Professional management education is also becoming more international in its focus—a good illustration is the International MBA offered by York University's Schulich

Coca-Cola
www.coca-cola.com

School of Business. Students completing this degree are required both to acquire a facility in a foreign language related to their region of interest and also to spend an extended period studying and, in many cases, working there.

◆ *Explore the possibility of hiring foreign-born employees who can serve as "expatriates" at a future date.* Japanese companies have been quite successful at hiring young foreign-born (non-Japanese) employees straight out of college to work in the home office in Japan. These recruits enter the firm with little experience and exposure to work in their host country, and thus are blank slates on which the Japanese multinational can write its own philosophy and values.[41] Some North American companies, such as Coca-Cola, have been following a similar practice for years.

◆ *Screen candidates' spouses and families.* Because the unhappiness of expatriates' spouses and family members plays such a large role in the failure of international assignments, some companies are screening candidates' spouses. Some employers attempt to assess the spouse's suitability for a foreign assignment. Others improve the odds of success by providing information and assistance in the transition, in the spirit of a realistic job preview. Among key issues, other than differences in language, culture and infrastructure (e.g., health care system), two of the most important issues are the possibility of the spouse's working and the educational requirements of school-age children. In addition, Procter & Gamble Canada, among other companies, attempts to establish social networks among the various expatriate families in a particular location. Price Waterhouse has set up a "host" program for relocated employees, pairing the new employee with one in the local operation who shares similar demographics (age, family structure).[42]

■ Training

The assumption that people everywhere respond in similar fashion to the same images, symbols, and slogans has often hurt North American advertisers offering their products in international markets. Consider the following examples:

◆ Some products and ads should never travel much farther than their country of origin. General Motors learned this lesson when it tried to introduce its Nova model into Spanish-speaking countries. The name of the car was frequently mispronounced "no-VAH," which means "doesn't go" in Spanish.

◆ In 1990 Procter & Gamble's commercial for Camay soap worked wonders in Europe but bombed in Japan. The image of a husband barging into the bathroom as his wife lathered up with Camay in the bathtub struck Japanese consumers as rude. P&G changed the commercial to show a European woman alone in a European-style bath, and now deems the ad a success in Japan.

◆ Choice Hotels now makes sure the suitcase it depicts in the German version of its international commercial is the hard-sided kind after discovering that, for Germans, a cloth suitcase conjures up images of job-seeking immigrants rather than upscale travellers.

◆ An international division of a North American airline translated its slogan, "Travel on leather," for the Latin American market. Unfortunately, the literal translation, *viaje en cuero*, means "travel naked." The advertisements had to be pulled.[43]

If these companies had given their expatriate executives appropriate cross-cultural training before their departure, these blunders would never have been committed. Cross-cultural training sensitizes candidates for international assignment to the local culture, customs, language, and government.[44]

Because insensitivity to the local culture can have severe financial consequences, cross-cultural training seminars are on the rise in global-minded companies. While these seminars cost $1,000 and upward per manager, many companies feel the expense is very minor compared to the huge cost of failed expatriate stints. For instance, despite massive cost-cutting moves at General Motors, the auto giant still spends nearly $500,000 a year on cross-cultural training. GM's general director of international personnel attributes the very low (less than one percent) premature return rate of GM expatriates to this training. The experience of one family transferred to Kenya by GM is typical. The family members underwent three days of cross-cultural training that consisted of a crash course in African political history, business practices, social customs, and non-verbal gestures. The family's two teenagers, who were miserable about moving to Africa, sampled Indian food (popular in Kenya) and learned how to ride Nairobi public buses, speak a little Swahili, and even how to juggle.[45]

Other cross-cultural training sessions are not custom-designed to address the cultural and political realities of a particular country but instead focus on giving executives the skills to deal with a wide range of people with different values. Motorola, for instance, has opened a special centre for cultural training at its headquarters, with the goal of making Motorola managers "transculturally competent."[46]

While all employees embarking on an international assignment would benefit from extensive training, economic sense dictates that the more rigorous and lengthy training be reserved for expatriates whose stay abroad will exceed one year and whose job assignment requires a good deal of knowledge of the local culture. Figure 17–3 shows three approaches to cross-cultural training. The least expensive type, the *information-giving approach*, lasts less than a week and merely provides indispensable briefings and a little language training. The *affective approach* (one to four weeks) focusses on providing the psychological and managerial skills the expatriate will need to perform effectively during a moderate-length assignment. The most extensive training, the *impression approach* (one to two months), prepares the manager for a long assignment with greater authority and responsibility by providing, for instance, field experiences and extended language training. Ideally, at least a portion of these training programs should be targeted to the expatriate's family. Although Figure 17–3 is concerned with predeparture training, it is also possible (indeed desirable) to use similar "decompression" training programs for returning expatriates to help them cope with reverse culture shock.

Length of Stay	Length and Level of Training	Cross-Cultural Training Approach
1–3 years	1–2 months+ High	**Impression Approach** Assessment centre Field experiences Simulations Sensitivity training Extensive language training
2–12 months	1–4 weeks Moderate	**Affective Approach** Language training Role-playing Critical incidents Cases Stress-reduction training Moderate language training
1 month or less	Less than a week Low	**Information-Giving Approach** Area briefings Cultural briefings Films/books Use of interpreters "Survival-level" language training

Figure 17–3 Three Approaches to Cross-Cultural Training

SOURCE: Adapted from Mendenhall, M., & Oddou, G. (1986). Acculturation profiles of expatriate managers: Implications for cross-cultural training. *Columbia Journal of World Business,* 78. Copyright 1986. *Columbia Journal of World Business.* Reprinted with permission.

■ Career Development

The expatriate's motivation to perform well on international assignment, to remain in the post for the duration of the assignment, and to be a high performer upon returning to the home office will depend to a large extent on the career development opportunities offered by the employer. At a minimum, successful career planning for expatriates requires the firm to do two things:

◆ *Position the international assignment as a step toward advancement within the firm.* The firm should explicitly define the job, the length of the assignment, and the expatriate's reentry position, level, and career track upon return. Companies with successful expatriate programs such as Dow Chemical and Arthur Andersen have practised this policy for years.

◆ *Provide effective support for expatriates.* To prevent expatriates from feeling isolated and disconnected, the home office should stay in touch with them regularly. Maintaining contact can be accomplished in a number of ways.[47] A popular method is the buddy system, in which a manager or mentor at the home office is appointed to keep in touch with the expatriate and to provide assistance wherever necessary. Another approach has the expatriate employee come back to the home office occasionally for assignments to foster a sense of belonging to the organization and to reduce re-entry shock. A third approach offers mini-sabbaticals in the home office at specified intervals (for example, for two weeks every six months) to keep the expatriate tuned in to current happenings and future plans at the corporate base. Some firms will pay for the expatriate's family to return home with him or her during this time.

Compensation

Firms can use compensation packages to enhance the effectiveness of expatriate assignments. However, compensation policies can also create conflict if locals comparing their pay packages to the expatriate's believe they are being treated unfairly.

Planning compensation for expatriates requires management to follow three important guidelines:

Corporate Resources Group
www.corpresgroupinc.com/
index.htm

◆ *Provide the expatriate with a disposable income that is equivalent to what he or she would receive at the home office.* This usually requires granting expatriate employees an allowance for price differences in housing, food, and other consumer goods. Allowances for children's schooling and the whole family's medical treatment may also be necessary. The best-known cost-of-living index for world locations is published by Corporate Resources Group, a Geneva-based consulting firm that surveys 97 cities worldwide twice a year. Using New York as a base of 100, Tokyo (at 171) and Osaka (at 157) are the most expensive cities in the world for expatriates, with Bombay (at 61) the least costly.[48] Maintaining income equality with the home office is not an exact science (for example, finding housing in Japan comparable to that available in Canadian suburbs is nearly impossible), but as a general rule, it is better to err on the side of generosity. See Figure 17–4 for a comparative list of housing costs in various cities around the world.

◆ *Provide an explicit "add-on" incentive for accepting an international assignment.* This incentive may take several forms. The company may provide a sign-on bonus prior to departure. Or it may offer the employee a percentage increase over his or her home base salary; the standard increase is 15 percent of the base salary.[49] Or it may provide a lump-sum payment upon successful completion of the foreign assignment. Some firms offer a combination of these incentives. Generally, the greatest incentives are reserved for the least desirable locations. For instance, multinationals hoping to lure Western managers to Eastern Europe, where poor air quality, political instability, and a shortage of quality housing make assignments unattractive, often offer packages that include company-paid housing, subsidized shipment of scarce consumer goods, up to four trips home a year, and weekend getaways to Western Europe.[50]

◆ *Avoid having expatriates fill the same jobs held by locals or lower-ranking jobs.* This is to prevent perceptions of inequity. Local employees tend to compare their pay and living standards to those of expatriates, and feelings of unfairness are more likely to surface if an expatriate at the same or lower rank than the local is receiving greater pay.

Location	Total Annual Housing Cost
Tokyo	$164,166
Hong Kong	117,562
Paris	99,507
London	71,332
Caracas	64,247
Frankfurt	64,004
Mexico City	62,230
Rio de Janeiro	53,049
Toronto	48,156
Chicago	40,130
Vancouver	33,308
Montreal	27,288

Figure 17–4 What It Costs to House Expatriates Worldwide

SOURCES: Runzheimer International, cited in Laabs, J. J. (1993, July). For your information. *Personnel Journal*, 16; Gouvernement du Québec. (1994, May). *Taxation of individuals and cost of living: Comparison between Montréal and various other North American cities* (p. 20).

Calculating compensation packages for expatriate employees is one of the most difficult tasks for multinationals developing an international work force.[51] Compensation used to be a relatively simple issue: low-level local hirees got paid in the local currency, while expatriate managers' pay was pegged to home-country salaries. However, in an era of dramatic corporate restructuring to cut costs, expatriate packages based on home-country salaries are increasingly being seen as too expensive. Moreover, as companies move into the later stages of internationalization, they work with a team of international employees operating out of the home office rather than just expatriates. As it has become more costly to maintain salary equity between these two groups of employees, more companies have been devising pay packages like the one created by Phillips Petroleum Company. When a British geophysicist first went abroad to work for Phillips in the mid-1970s, he was paid in dollars and his salary was equivalent to that of someone at home doing a similar job. Today, under Phillips' third-party nationals program, he gets the same housing allowance, home leave, and educational assistance for his children. However, his salary is now pegged to the more modest level at which he would be paid in his home country rather than to the U.S. salary for that job.

Still, many other companies are grappling with complicated issues of fairness as well. Some companies are opting to distinguish between expatriate pay packages and those for international managers. Seagram Spirits and Wine Group, for instance, has come up with an "international cadre policy" for those expatriates who work abroad permanently (as opposed to expatriates who will return to North America in the future). The package features a standardized cost-of-living adjustment and a global standard employee housing contribution that is the same regardless of location. For temporary expatriates, Seagram maintains what it terms a "pure expatriate" package that keeps people up to par with North American compensation standards.[52]

Seagram Spirits and Wine Group
www.seagram.com

■ Developing HRM Policies in a Global Context

Firms operating in multiple countries need to worry not just about meeting the special needs of expatriate employees and enhancing their performance but also about the design and implementation of HRM programs in diverse cross-cultural settings. One company that is widely viewed as exceptional in its achievement of a unified global HRM program—even with two-thirds of its employees working overseas—is Coca-Cola.

In many countries reliance on Western managerial practices is likely to clash with deeply ingrained norms and values.[53] For instance, the open-door style of management, which works well in a culture that readily accepts questioning of authority, will probably not work where such behaviour is considered unacceptable. Effectively meeting the multinational challenge requires a sophisticated HRM system that can be adapted to a variety of cultural conditions. In other words, rather than simply transferring abroad HRM practices that are based on the home country's social and cultural standards, managers should mould these practices to the cultural environment in which a particular facility is located. If there is too much inconsistency between a nation's culture and a company's HRM practices, the company is likely to face non-compliance at best, and acts of open hostility at worst.

◼ National Culture, Organizational Characteristics, and HRM Practices

"Culture is important to HRM practices." This statement may seem obvious, but its relevance may be lost in a country like the United States, where many of the best-known theories of management practice are firmly rooted in Western culture. Geert Hofstede, a Dutch professor, has spent the better part of his professional life studying the similarities and differences among cultures. He has concluded that there are five major dimensions to culture:

1. *Power distance,* the extent to which individuals expect a hierarchical structure that emphasizes status differences between subordinates and superiors.
2. *Individualism,* the degree to which a society values personal goals, autonomy, and privacy over group loyalty, commitment to group norms, involvement in collective activities, social cohesiveness, and intense socialization.
3. *Uncertainty avoidance,* the extent to which a society places a high value on reducing risk and instability.
4. *Masculinity/femininity,* the degree to which a society views assertive or "masculine" behaviour as important to success and encourages rigidly stereotyped gender roles.
5. *Long-term/short-term orientation,* the extent to which values are oriented toward the future (saving, persistence) as opposed to the past or present (respect for tradition, fulfilling social obligations).[54]

Although Hofstede's research has been criticized for being based largely on the experiences of employees working for only one company and for downplaying the importance of cultural differences within countries, other evidence suggests that five dimensions are a fair summary of cultural differences.[55] These dimensions have proved useful for examining how organizational characteristics and HRM practices respond to cultural factors. Most important, they provide clues regarding the general configuration of HRM strategies that are most likely to mesh with a particular culture's values. Figure 17–5 outlines the characteristics of cultures ranking high or low on each of Hofstede's dimensions, lists sample countries falling at each end of the spectrum, and summarizes the organizational features and HRM practices that work best at each end of the scale.

The information in Figure 17–5 has enormous implications for international firms. As businesses move out of their home countries and employ individuals with potentially very different cultural values, it is essential that corporations consider the inevitable clash between their "imported" HRM practices and the national culture.

As a general principle, *the more an HRM practice contradicts the prevailing societal norms, the more likely it will fail.* For instance, Hofstede describes management by objectives (MBO) as "perhaps the single most popular management technique 'made in the U.S.A.'"[56] because it assumes (1) negotiation between the boss and employee, or a not-too-large power distance; (2) a willingness on the part of both parties to take risks, or weak uncertainty avoidance; and (3) that both supervisors and subordinates see performance and its associated rewards as important. Because all three assumptions are prominent features of North American culture, MBO "fits" here. But in other countries—France, for example—MBO has generally run into problems because of cultural incompatibility:

Power Distance, Organizational Characteristics, and Selected Human Resource Practices

		Dominant Values	Sample Countries	Organizational Features	Reward Practices	Staffing/Appraisal Practices
POWER DISTANCE	**HIGH**	• Top-down communications • Class divisions seen as natural • Authoritarianism • High dependence on superiors • Power symbols • White-collar jobs valued more than blue-collar jobs	• Malaysia • Philippines • Mexico • Arab nations • Venezuela • Spain	• Centralization and tall organizational structures • Traditional line of command	• Hierarchical compensation system • Differences in pay and benefits reflect job and status differences; large differential between higher- and lower-level jobs • Visible rewards that project power such as a large office or company car	• Limited search methods in recruitment; emphasis on connections and "whom you know" • Few formal mechanisms of selection • Superior makes selection choice for his/her sphere of influence • Personal loyalty to superior is crucial trait for advancement • Social class and extended family may play a role in personnel decisions • Nepotism may be commonly practised • Formal appraisals lacking; more "verbal" or "psychological contracts" between supervisor and subordinate
	LOW	• Egalitarianism • Status based on achievement • Joint decision making • High value placed on participation • Low dependence on superiors • Disdain for power symbols • Hard work valued even if manual in nature	• The Netherlands • Australia • Switzerland • Sweden	• Flatter organizational structures • Decentralized control • Greater reliance on matrix-type networks • Great degree of worker involvement	• Egalitarian-based compensation systems • Small differences in pay and benefits between higher- and lower-level jobs • Participatory pay strategies (such as gainsharing) more prevalent	• Multiple search methods; extensive advertisement • Formalized selection methods "to give everyone a fair chance" • Superior constrained in making selection choices • Selection based on merit; loyalty to superiors deemphasized • Contextual non-job-related factors (such as social class) ignored • Nepotism viewed as conflict of interest and even unethical • Formal appraisals based on notion of joint planning, two-way feedback, and performance documentation

Individualism, Organizational Characteristics, and Selected Human Resource Practices

		Dominant Values	Sample Countries	Organizational Features	Reward Practices	Staffing/Appraisal Practices
INDIVIDUALISM	**HIGH**	• Personal accomplishment • Selfishness • Independence • Belief in individual control and responsibility • Belief in creating one's own destiny • Business relationship between employer and employee	• United States • New Zealand • Great Britain • Canada	• Organizations not compelled to care for employees' total well-being • Employees look after their own individual interests • Explicit systems of control necessary to ensure compliance and prevent wide deviation from organizational norms	• Performance-based pay • Individual achievement rewarded • External equity emphasized • Extrinsic rewards are important indicators of personal success • Attempts made to isolate individual contributions (i.e., who did what) • Emphasis on short-term objectives	• Emphasis on credentials and visible performance outcomes attributed to individual • High turnover; commitment to organization for career reasons • Performance rather than seniority as criterion for advancement • "Fitting in" deemphasized; belief in performance as independent of personal likes and dislikes • Attempts at ascertaining individual strengths and weaknesses and providing frequent feedback to employee
	LOW	• Team accomplishment • Sacrifice for others • Dependence on social unit • Belief in group control and responsibility • Belief in the hand of fate • Moral relationship between employer and employee	• Singapore • South Korea • Indonesia • Japan • Taiwan	• Organizations committed to high-level involvement in workers' personal lives • Loyalty to the firm is critical • Normative, rather than formal, systems of control to ensure compliance	• Group-based performance is important criterion for rewards • Seniority-based pay utilized • Intrinsic rewards essential • Internal equity guides pay policies • Personal needs (such as number of children) affects pay received	• Value of credentials and visible performance outcomes depends on perceived contributions to team efforts • Low turnover; commitment to organization as "family" • Seniority plays an important role in personnel decisions • "Fitting in" with work group crucial; belief that interpersonal relations are important performance dimension • Limited or no performance feedback to individual to prevent conflict and defensive reactions

➤

Figure 17–5 Cultural Characteristics and Dominant Values

SOURCE: This is an updated and expanded version of an earlier chart appearing in Gómez-Mejía, L. R., & Welbourne, T. (1991). Compensation strategies in a global context. *Human Resource Planning 14(1)*, 38.

Uncertainty Avoidance, Organizational Characteristics, and Selected Human Resource Practices

		Dominant Values	Sample Countries	Organizational Features	Reward Practices	Staffing/Appraisal Practices
UNCERTAINTY AVOIDANCE	**HIGH**	• Fear of random events and the unknown • High value placed on stability and routine • Low tolerance for am-biguity • Low risk propensity • Comfort in security, lack of tension, and lack of contradictions	• Greece • Portugal • Italy	• Mechanistic structures • Written rules and policies guide the firm • Organizations strive to be predictable • Management avoids making risky decisions • Careful delineation of responsibilities and work flows	• Bureaucratic pay policies utilized • Compensation programs tend to be centralized • Fixed pay more important than variable pay • Little discretion given to supervisor in dispensing pay	• Bureaucratic rules/procedures to govern hiring and promotion • Seniority an important factor in hiring and promotions • Government/union regulations limit employer discretion in recruitment, promotion, and terminations • Limited external hires • Limited use of appraisals requiring judgement
	LOW	• Unexpected viewed as challenging and exciting • Stability and routine seen as boring • Ambiguity seen as providing opportunities • High risk propensity • Tensions and contradictions spur innovation, discovery, and mastery of change	• Singapore • Denmark • Sweden • Hong Kong	• Less-structured activities • Fewer written rules to cope with changing environmental forces • Managers are more adaptable and tend to make riskier decisions	• Variable pay a key component in pay programs • External equity emphasized • Decentralized pay program is the norm • Much discretion given to supervisors and business units in pay allocation	• Fewer rules/procedures to govern hiring and promotions • Seniority deemphasized in personnel decisions • Employer provided much latitude in recruitment, promotion, and terminations • External hiring at all levels • Extensive use of appraisals requiring judgement

Masculinity/Femininity, Organizational Characteristics, and Selected Human Resource Practices

		Dominant Values	Sample Countries	Organizational Features	Reward Practices	Staffing/Appraisal Practices
MASCULINITY	**HIGH**	• Material possessions important • Men given higher power and status than women • Rigid gender stereotypes • Gender inequities in pay accepted as a given	• Austria • Mexico • Germany • United States	• Some occupations labelled as "male," others as "female" • Fewer women in higher-level positions	• Differential pay policies that allow for gender inequities • Tradition an acceptable basis for pay decisions • "Male" traits rewarded in promotions and other personnel decisions • Paternalistic benefits for women (such as paid maternity leave, day care, special work hours)	• De facto preferential treatment for men in hiring/promotion decisions into higher-level jobs (even if it is illegal) • "Glass ceiling" for women • Occupational segregation • Only small proportion of men supervised by women • "Male" traits (such as aggressiveness, initiative, leadership) highly valued in appraisals
	LOW	• Quality of life valued more than material gain • Men not believed to be inherently superior • Minimal gender stereo-typing • Strong belief in equal pay for jobs of equal value, regardless of workers' gender	• The Netherlands • Norway • Sweden • Finland • Denmark	• More flexibility in career choice for men and women • More women in higher-level jobs	• Jobs evaluated without regard for gender of job holders • Focus on work content rather than tradition to assess value of different jobs • Well-developed "equity goals" for pay determination • "Masculine" traits carry no special value for promotions and other personnel decisions • Few perks based on gender	• Gender deemphasized in hiring/promotion decisions for any job • More females in upper-level positions • Occupational integration between the sexes • Little stigma for men to be supervised by women • Appraisals not biased in favour of male-oriented characteristics

Long-Term/Short-Term Orientation, Organizational Characteristics, and Selected Human Resource Practices

		Dominant Values	Sample Countries	Organizational Features	Reward Practices	Staffing/Appraisal Practices
LONG-/SHORT-TERM ORIENTATION	**LONG-TERM**	• Future-oriented • Delayed gratification • Persistence • Long-term goals	• Japan • Hong Kong • China	• Stable organizations • Low employee turnover • Strong company culture	• Long-term rewards • Seniority as basis for pay • Managers rewarded for multi-year accomplishments • Reliance on qualitative measures to distribute rewards • No expectation of frequent pay adjustments	• Slow promotions • Promotions from within • High employment security • Minimal feedback • High emphasis on saving employees' face • High emphasis on coaching vs. evaluation • High investment in training and employee development

➤

Long-Term/Short-Term Orientation, Organizational Characteristics, and Selected Human Resource Practices					
LONG-/SHORT-TERM ORIENTATION	short-TERM	**Dominant Values** • Past- or present-oriented • Immediate gratification • Change course of action as necessary • Short-term goals	**Sample Countries** • United States • Indonesia	**Organizational Features** • Changing organization • High employee turnover • Weak company culture	**Reward Practices** • Short-term rewards • Recent performance as a basis for pay • Managers rewarded for annual accomplishments • Reliance on quantitative measures to distribute rewards • High expectation of frequent pay adjustments	**Staffing/Appraisal Practices** • Fast promotions • Internal and external hires • Low employment security • High appraisal feedback • Low emphasis on saving employees' face • High emphasis on evaluation vs. coaching • Low investment in training and employee development

Figure 17–5 continued

The high power distance to which the French are accustomed from childhood ultimately has thwarted the successful utilization of MBO as a truly participative process. ... The problem is not necessarily with MBO per se but the French managers ... who are unaware that they are trying to exert control through the implementation of the objectives of MBO almost by fiat.[57]

◼ Important Caveats

The effectiveness of an HRM practice depends on how well it matches a culture's value system. Even so, managers need to keep several caveats in mind.

◆ *"National culture" may be an elusive concept.* For this reason, managers should be careful not to be guided by stereotypes that hold some truth but may not apply to very many individuals in a culture. Stereotyping is a great danger in large, heterogeneous countries like Canada, where cultural differences are often huge, but it can also cause problems even in relatively homogeneous nations. For instance, West German firms hiring East German workers frequently found that the latter reacted negatively to incentive systems that had been used successfully with their West German counterparts despite the fact that the two groups shared the same language, ethnicity, and cultural background. The East Germans distrusted such incentive schemes, reported they felt manipulated by management, and shunned those workers who outproduced others.[58]

◆ *Corporate headquarters sometimes blame international personnel problems on cultural factors without careful study.* Often personnel problems have little to do with cultural values and much to do with poor management. For example, one company introduced individual incentives for R&D employees at its English subsidiary. This created intense conflict, lack of cooperation, and declining performance. Top managers blamed the strong role of labour unions in England for these disappointing results. In fact, a large amount of evidence indicates that individual-based incentives are counter-productive when the nature of the task requires extensive teamwork (as is the case in R&D). The outcome in this case had nothing to do with national culture.[59]

◆ *Hard data on the success or failure of different HRM practices as a function of national culture are practically non-existent.* This means that judgement calls, gut feeling, and some trial and error based on a fine-tuned cultural sensitivity and openmindedness are mandatory in international human resource management.

◆ *Different cultures often have very different notions of right and wrong.* In many cases, corporate headquarters may have to impose its own value system across multiple nations with conflicting value structures. For example, child labour is common in many Asian and African countries. The corporation may choose to avoid such practices on ethical grounds, but it must recognize that doing so can put it at a competitive disadvantage because local firms that have no qualms about using child labour will have lower labour costs.

A Question of Ethics

In some areas of the world business practices that are contrary to Western values—such as child labour, payment of bribes to government officials, and sex or race discrimination in hiring and promotion—are common. Should Canadian corporations and their expatriate representatives refuse to engage in such practices even if doing so would put the firm at a competitive disadvantage?

■ Human Resource Management and Exporting Firms

Our discussion so far has focused on larger firms with international facilities (that is, those in Stages 3–5 of internationalization). However, the practices we've discussed are also relevant to smaller firms that are interested solely in exporting their products. As we saw in the opening section of this chapter, Canadian firms, including smaller manufacturers, have turned increasingly to international markets as tariff barriers have fallen—both to take advantage of new opportunities and as a defensive response to the invasion of the relatively small Canadian market.

A number of studies have shown that the key impediments to exporting are (1) lack of knowledge of international markets, business practices, and competition and (2) lack of management commitment to generating international sales.[60] These impediments can be largely attributed to poor utilization of human resources within these firms rather than to external factors. There is some evidence that a company that clearly reinforces international activities in its HRM practices is more likely to fare better in its export attempts.[61] Reinforcing international activities in HRM practices requires a company to:

◆ Explicitly consider international experience when making promotion and recruitment decisions, particularly to the senior management ranks.

◆ Provide developmental activities designed to equip employees with the skills and knowledge necessary to carry out their jobs in an international context. Developmental activities that enhance a firm's ability to compete globally include (1) programs designed to provide specific job skills and competencies in international business, (2) opportunities for development and growth in the international field, and (3) the use of appraisal processes that explicitly consider international activities as part of performance reviews.

◆ Create career ladders that take into account short- and long-term international strategies.

◆ Design a reward structure that motivates key organizational players to take full advantage of the company's export potential. Reinforcing desired export-related behaviours is likely to increase commitment to foreign sales as managers devote greater attention to skill development, information gathering, and scanning the environment for international opportunities.

The decision to export will require CEOs and senior marketing personnel to spend significant time away from the office attending trade missions and shows and developing relationships with distributors and companies abroad. This means, particularly in small companies, that the staff back home must be empowered to make decisions regarding the running of the business, with the travelling CEOs and executives keeping in touch via phone or fax.

The process of making the right export connections and establishing relationships can be slow and painstaking, but for many small firms, patience has paid off. Many small firms limit themselves to the domestic market. However, some products and technologies virtually require "going international" to be economically viable. Robert Glegg, who graduated from McGill with degrees in engineering and business in the mid-1960s, has built up a water purification process that provides the ultra-high quality of water required for some industrial processes. His market is truly export oriented—some 96 percent of his sales are outside Canada, mostly in the United States but also in Europe, Asia, and Latin America.[62]

Summary and Conclusions

The Stages of International Involvement. Firms progress through five stages as they internationalize their operations: (1) domestic, (2) export, (3) subsidiary or joint venture, (4) multinational, and (5) transnational. The higher the stage, the more HR practices need to be adapted to diverse cultural, economic, political, and legal environments.

Determining the Mix of Host Country and Expatriate Employees. In managing its overseas subsidiaries, a firm can choose an ethnocentric, polycentric, or geocentric approach. Firms tend to rely on expatriates more when sufficient local talent is unavailable, the firm is trying to create a corporatewide global vision, international and domestic units are highly interdependent, the political situation is unstable, and there are significant cultural differences between the host country and the home country.

The Challenges of Expatriate Assignments.
An important part of international HRM is managing expatriate employees, both during their international assignments and when they return home. International assignments fail because of career blockage, culture shock, lack of predeparture cross-cultural training, an overemphasis on technical qualifications, the use of such assignments to get rid of troublesome employees, and family problems. Upon returning, expatriates may meet with a lack of respect for their acquired skills, a loss of status, poorly planned jobs, and reverse culture shock.

Enhancing the Effectiveness of Expatriate Assignments with HRM Policies and Practices.
To avoid problems in the international arena, a sensible set of HR policies should be put in place. In selecting people for international assignments, employers should emphasize cultural sensitivity, establish a selection board of expatriates, require previous international experience when possible, explore the possibility of hiring the foreign-born who can later serve as "expatriates," and screen candidates' spouses and families. Cross-cultural training programs of various lengths and levels of rigour can be implemented to prepare employees for their assignments. In terms of career development for expatriates, companies should position international assignments as a step toward advancement within the firm and provide support for expatriates. To avoid problems in the compensation area, companies should provide expatriates with enough disposable income and incentive bonuses, and avoid having expatriates fill the same or lower-ranking jobs than locals hold in the international operation.

Developing HRM Policies in a Global Context.
Rather than simply transferring abroad HRM practices based on the home country's social and cultural standards, managers should mould these practices to the cultural environments in which the international facilities are located. In general, the more an HRM practice contradicts prevailing societal norms, the more likely it will fail.

Human Resource Management and Exporting Firms.
Many firms have the potential to export profitably. A company that clearly reinforces international activities by (1) explicitly considering international experience in hiring decisions, (2) providing developmental activities to equip employees with international skills, (3) creating career ladders for internationally experienced employees, and (4) designing a reward structure that motivates employees to begin export activities is more likely to fare better in its export attempts.

Key Terms and Concepts

affective approach, 515
culture shock, 509
ethnocentric approach, 506
expatriate, 505
geocentric approach, 506
impression approach, 515
individualism, 518

information-giving approach, 515
joint venture, 505
long-term/short-term orientation, 518
masculinity/femininity, 518
multinational corporation (MNC), 505
polycentric approach, 506

power distance, 518
repatriates, 511
reverse culture shock, 512
status reversal, 511
transnational corporation, 505
uncertainty avoidance, 518
wholly owned subsidiary, 505

Discussion Questions

1. Why are so many North American firms operating international facilities? What major challenges are these firms facing from a human resource perspective?

2. How can HRM policies and practices facilitate international expansion? How can they hinder it?

3. Under what specific conditions would you recommend an ethnocentric, a polycentric, and a geocentric approach to staffing?

4. U.S. multinationals experience a much higher rate of early returns with their expatriate employees than European and Japanese MNCs do. What explains this difference? What HRM policies and procedures would you develop to reduce this problem?

5. Expatriates frequently complain that when they accept an international assignment they put their career on hold while their peers in the home office continue to climb the corporate ladder. To what would you attribute this perception? What recommendations would you make to change it?

6. Some people believe that North American multinationals should serve as vehicles for cultural change in developing countries by introducing "modern" HRM practices and instilling values (such as punctuality and efficiency) in the work force that are necessary for industrialization. Do you agree with this assertion? Explain.

7. The recent history of law and business ethics shows that, to remain competitive, some MNCs are willing to engage in bribery in foreign countries where bribes are the custom. Similarly, a few years back, many MNCs acquiesced in the policy of apartheid in South Africa, despite the fact that such behaviour would not be tolerated in Canada or the United States. Some argue that a multinational company should be able to use whatever HRM practices produce the most prof-its at the lowest costs, as long as these practices comply with the labour codes and laws of each country where the MNC operates. Do you agree or disagree? State your reasons.

8. Studies indicate that, generally, Canadian firms do not exploit international markets for their products as well as firms in other industrialized nations do. How can a firm use its human resources to change this disparity?

Take it to the Net

Check out our Companion Website at: **www.prenticehall.ca/gomez** for a selection of self-study questions, key terms and concepts, updated Weblinks to related Internet sites, newsgroups, CBC video updates, and more.

MiniCase 1   *A Long Way from Portage and Main*

John Agitt joined Imperial Oil in 1956. He thinks of Toronto as home, having moved there from Winnipeg as a student. His career since 1956 has been with Imperial and related companies. These details do not differentiate Agitt's career path from that of many other others. What follows, does.

Looking back on a recent month, he determined that he had spent one day in his office—the head office of Exxon Chemical International, of which he is president, in Brussels. He has another office—in Connecticut—but estimates that he travels 75 percent of the time, including a recent trip to Singapore and Bangkok. His career saw him rise during his first 20 years to become executive VP of Esso Chemical Canada (a division of Imperial). This current posting in Brussels, his second, has been in effect for the past four years; he has also been posted twice to New York. For Agitt, the travel involved is necessary and demanding, but stimulating, and he characterizes his position as "extremely challenging" and a "super job."

He sees the timing as having been just right for his personal circumstances. When the time came to take on the international postings, his children weren't young, and his wife was able to accompany him—two conditions he sees as essential, along with good health. Agitt is enthusiastic about the influence his international career created for his children: "They receive[d] an education that is better than it ever could be if they stayed in one place." His children, now grown, live in Italy, Spain, and Canada, but each Christmas finds the Agitt family gathering for a holiday together— a mobile celebration that has taken place in Singapore, Florida, Brussels, and London in recent years.

Discussion Questions

1. Senior responsibilities often do not accrue during the first few years of a career. As a result, international career paths such as Agitt's will tend to develop after children have gotten well into school. If employers start moving professional and technical people internationally at earlier stages of their career (when they are younger), what kinds of personal and family issues are they likely to face when they approach an employee about making the move to another country?

2. How are managerial careers for people starting out in the 1990s likely to differ from those starting out in the 1950s, with respect to the international dimension?

3. With the increased rates of corporate change (acquisitions, reorganizations, outsourcing, etc.), is it realistic today to assume that an "orderly" international career such as John Agitt's can be shaped through formal career development policies and programs? Explain.

SOURCE: Finlayson, J. (1990, Summer). Exotic assignments. *Imperial Oil Review*, 74(397), 30. Reprinted courtesy of *Imperial Oil Review*.

MiniCase 2   *Supporting Expatriates— at Arm's Length*

Dave Wilkin noticed the difference. Having just returned home to Ontario from his third international assignment for IBM, the administrative efficiency of the move was clearly better than during the previous two. Issues had been dealt with quickly, problems were resolved effectively, and the overall process was less bureaucratic. What could account for the change?

The answer was clear. IBM had retained an outside firm, Interlynx, to replace its own internal processes for managing expatriates' moves. Paul Cutler, Senior Partner at Interlynx, indicates that the combination of a growing number of people on international assignments and the fact that average length of stay has dropped (from 60 months to 33 months) has created an increased demand for these services. Even major international corporations like IBM have found it useful not to try to manage the process themselves. Services provided typically include:

◆ Meeting employee and spouse to discuss company policies, pay and benefits issues, taxation implications of the move, and similar matters.

◆ Dealing with realtors to manage sale or lease of real estate.

◆ Arranging for language instruction and cultural orientation.

◆ Setting up financial details.

◆ Arranging and handling paperwork for visas and work permits.

◆ Arranging for shipping of household goods.

◆ Working with third parties to arrange housing and provide transition support in the new location.

◆ Approving expenses.

◆ Acting as ombudsman for the employee.

Since an international transfer can cost $150,000 to $300,000, it is important that the transferred employee get through the transition process as smoothly as possible, to begin taking on his or her new assignment. Companies such as Interlynx, PHH Relocation Services, and Price Waterhouse's Expatriate Consulting Services not only can save money on the direct costs because of their relations with suppliers; they also ensure that the reason for the transfer—to put highly valued human resources in place—happens with the least delay and disruption.

Discussion Questions

1. If an employer uses a firm like Interlynx, what tasks are still left for the employer when it comes to managing expatriates?

2. Often, employees on international assignment will seek some kind of consideration not anticipated by the employer's policies, such as additional R&R travel. What effect do you think having a third party, such as those described above, would have on how those situations are handled? Explain.

3. Why do you think international assignments seem to be decreasing in length? How do you think this is likely to affect the willingness of people to accept these assignments, and their success when they return to Canada after the assignment?

SOURCE: Goodson, L. (1996, May). No excess baggage. *Human Resources Professional*, 21–23.

Case 1

Two Sides to Every Story

Four years ago Pressman Company entered into a joint venture with a Polish firm to manufacture a variety of plumbing supplies both for the internal Polish market and for export to neighbouring countries. Last week Pressman received the resignation of Jonathan Smith, an expatriate from the home office who nine months ago was appointed general manager of the Polish subsidiary for a four-year term. In the previous 39 months, two other expatriate general managers from the home office had also decided to call it quits long before their foreign

assignments expired. In addition, 13 of the 28 Canadian technicians sent to work in the Polish facility returned home early. George Stevens, a senior vice-president in corporate headquarters, estimates that these expatriates' resignations and early returns have cost the company at least $4 million in direct expenses and probably three times as much in lost production and delayed schedules.

When he heard rumours of widespread discontent in the work force and a threatened wildcat strike, Stevens decided to travel to the Polish facility to find out what was happening. In the course of interviewing five local supervisors and 10 workers with the help of a translator, he repeatedly heard three complaints: first, the Canadian managers and technicians thought they "knew it all" and treated their Polish counterparts with contempt; second, the Canadian employees had unrealistic expectations of what could be accomplished within the stipulated deadlines established at corporate headquarters; and third, Canadian employees were making three times more money than their Polish counterparts and enjoyed looking down their noses at locals by driving fancy cars, living in expensive homes, and hiring an army of maids and helpers.

When he arrived back in Canada, Stevens also interviewed Jonathan Smith and five of the technicians who returned early. Some common reasons for their early resignations emerged from these interviews. First, they described their Polish colleagues as "lazy" and "just doing the minimum to get by while keeping a close eye on the clock for breaks, lunches, and go-home time." Pushing them to work harder only provoked anger. Second, they indicated that the Polish workers and managers had a sense of entitlement with little intrinsic motivation and initiative. Third, they complained of loneliness and their inability to communicate in Polish. Finally, most reported that their spouses and children were homesick and longing to return to Canada after the first month or so. As he sits in his office, George Stevens is staring blankly out the window, trying to decide what to do.

Critical Thinking Questions

1. Based on what you have learned in this chapter, what do you think are the underlying problems in this Polish subsidiary of Pressman Company?

   How would you account for the sharp differences in the perceptions of the Polish locals and Canadian expatriates?

3. If you were hired as a consultant by Pressman Company, what steps would you recommend that Stevens take?

Cooperative Learning Exercises

4. Students form pairs. One student plays Stevens, the other an HRM consultant. Role-play the initial meeting between these two, with Stevens explaining the problems at the Polish plant and the consultant identifying the additional information that will be needed to get to the root of the difficulties and how this information might be collected.

5. Students form into groups of four or five. Each group's task is to make suggestions for the content of a training program for the next group of employees to be sent to Pressman's Polish plant. Besides information from this chapter, use principles you learned from Chapters 4 (Managing Diversity) and 8 (Training) to develop these programs. When the task is finished (approximately 20 minutes), a member from each group should present the group's recommendations to the class. How similar or dissimilar are the groups' recommendations? Why? Which recommendations are likely to be most effective?

Case 2

Are Culture-Specific Human Resource Policies a Good Idea?

Over the past 10 years, East Computer Company has grown from a domestic producer of IBM clones in Vancouver to a multinational company with assembly plants in four foreign locations. The company's personnel policies were developed five years ago, prior to East Computer's international expansion, by a task force headed by the vice-president for human resource management. The company's CEO has just appointed a new task force to examine the extent to which current domestic personnel policies can be "exported" to East's new international locations. The essential elements of these policies are the following:

1. All job openings are posted to allow any employee to apply for a position.

2. Selection is based on merit. Appropriate selection devices (for example, tests, structured interviews, and the like) are used to ensure proper implementation of this policy.

3. Nepotism is expressly forbidden.

4. Promotion from within is the norm whenever feasible.

5. Equal employment opportunities are available to all, regardless of sex, race, national origin, or religion.

6. Pay for various positions is established through a rational process that includes both job evaluation and market survey data.

7. There is equal pay for equal work, regardless of sex, race, national origin, or religion.

8. Goals are jointly set by supervisor and subordinate, with an annual formal appraisal session at which both parties have the chance to discuss progress toward goal achievement. This appraisal is used both to provide performance feedback to the employee and as a basis for merit pay decisions.

As a first step in evaluating these policies, the vice-president for human resource management classified the countries where East's facilities are located according to Hofstede's dimensions. She came up with the matrix at the bottom of this page.

You have been hired by East Computer Company to help management develop personnel policies for each of the four international facilities. Ideally, management would prefer to use the same policies that it uses in Canada to maintain consistency and reduce administrative problems. However, the vice-president for human resource management has made a strong case for "tailor-made" personnel policies that are suitable to the cultural environment of each facility.

Critical Thinking Questions

1. Given East Computer Company's present personnel policies, what problems is the company likely to face in each facility if it transports its domestic policies abroad?

2. How would you change or adapt each of the company's current personnel policies to better fit the cultural environment of each international facility?

3. What could go wrong if your recommendations are implemented? In other words, what warnings would you give to East's management along with your recommendations?

Cooperative Learning Exercises

4. Students break into groups of five. One student role-plays a consultant who is conducting an exercise to uncover possible problems in uniform application of the company's current policy. Each of the other four students takes the role of advocate for one of the four international locations. Each advocate should make an argument for or against keeping specific parts of East's existing HR policies.

5. Students form groups of four, with each group acting as the advocate for one of the four international locations. After deciding which policies to keep and which to change, a representative from each group presents the group's recommendations to the class. Following these brief presentations, the class discusses the costs and benefits of culture-specific human resource policies.

CULTURAL DIMENSIONS

Facility Location	Power Distance	Individualism	Uncertainty Avoidance	Masculinity	Long-Term Orientation
Australia	Low	High	Medium	Medium	Low
Mexico	High	Low	High	High	Medium
England	Low	High	Low	High	Low
Norway	Low	Medium	Medium	Low	High

VideoCase

Globalization and HRM

Market economies use mergers, acquisitions, and other forms of economic restructuring as some of the mechanisms for allocating investment funds to productive uses. Such activities have always had a certain degree of controversy attached to them in democratic states, because large corporations (where unregulated) can use mergers and acquisitions to gain a measure of monopoly power over the markets in which they operate. Government, in representing the public interest, attempts to provide protection from the potential acquisition and abuse of monopoly power. Some sectors of the economy in Canada have been operated as regulated monopolies; long-term examples include utility companies where technologies made it unfeasible to have competing providers in a single market. Sometimes activities such as education, garbage collection, and hospital care have been run as state (that is, government) operations. In other sectors, regulatory regimes, such as the Bank Act or combines legislation, have attempted to sustain an environment in which competition is a viable mechanism to assure consumers of choice, quality, and service.

So long as governments have retained the leverage to effectively regulate the actions of large organizations, the impact of financial restructuring, mergers, and the like on employment practices of employers has been an issue on which it is possible to legislate. However, when governments lose that leverage, the large corporations' inclination to protect themselves from competitive pressures are no longer checked by the structures or limits established by law and regulation.

Globalization is one of the primary factors reducing the regulatory leverage of governments in both the financial and non-financial sectors of the economy. The importance and the mobility of capital to modern economies is clear, and global financial markets have become an increasingly potent influence in national economies around the world. When provincial or national governments attempt to regulate what is effectively an international corporate/financial system, the international mobility of capital can limit the extent and forms of internal regulation that differentiate one jurisdiction from another. While the initial impact is on patterns of trade and investment, the implications for employment practices cannot be ignored.

Discussion Questions

1. What are the implications for human resources management in Canada of the growing internationalization of the economy?
   a. What new pressures will Canadian employers face?
   b. In what areas and in what directions are governments likely to change policies? Is it possible for legislation to move toward being more protective of Canadian workers (for example, employment standards, health and safety regulations, human rights issues, etc.), or are the laws more likely to move toward deregulation? Explain.

2. For an employer that wishes to remain competitive in an economic world that is becoming increasingly "borderless," what kinds of human resource strategies are most likely to support that goal? Develop recommendations and rationales in each of the following areas.
   a. Staffing
   ◆ The mix of permanent and contingent workers.
   ◆ Outsourcing tasks versus doing them in-house.
   b. Training and development
   ◆ The kinds of skills that an employer should "buy" from the external market, and the kinds of skills that should be created through internal training and development.
   ◆ The forms of career development that are appropriate.
   c. Compensation
   ◆ The mix of direct compensation and benefits that makes most sense.
   ◆ The usefulness of employee ownership and profit-based bonuses
   ◆ The usefulness of "creative" benefits such as sabbaticals or working to create employee-friendly corporate cultures.

Video Resources: "Bank Merger Reaction," *Venture* 676 (January 27, 1998).

Endnotes

Chapter 1

1. "The Future of GM." (1998, July 23). *The National* (CBC Television) transcripts. (Web site reference: **www.tv.cbc.ca/national/trans/T980723.html**); Milner, Brian. (1998, July 18). "Danger Ahead." (The Globe and Mail Web site **www.theglobeandmail.com**).

2. Butler, J. E., Ferris, G. R., & Napier, N. K. (1991). *Strategy and human resources management.* Cincinnati, OH: Southwestern; and Dyer, L. (1984). Linking human resources and business strategies. *Human Resource Planning, 7*(2), 79–84.

3. Bailey, B. (1991). Ask what HR can do for itself. *Personnel Journal, 70*(7), 35–39; Filipowski, D. (1991, June). Life after HR. *Personnel Journal,* 64–71.

4. Einhorn, B. (October 31) This tiger has a thorn in its paw. *Business Week,* 48.

5. *Plant.* (1994, October 3). Chrysler concentrates on change, 10, 24.

6. Statistics Canada, 1996 census data from Catalogues 93F0026XDB96004/5/6. Copyright 1996–1997

7. Taylor, C. (1995). Building a case for business diversity. *Canadian Business Review, 22*(1), 12–15.

8. Statistics Canada, *op cit.*

9. Forest, A. (1995). Labour legacy in question: Retelling the story of Order-in-Council PC 1003,1944. *Canadian Dimension, 29*(1). 29–32.

10. *Maclean's.* (1995, August 21). Women at work: A new study shows the continuing gender gap, 28–29.

11. *Occupational Health and Safety.* (1995, September/October). The aging work force: Shattering the myths and facing the realities associated with older workers, 28–37.

12. Gómez-Mejía, L. R. (1988). The role of human resources strategy in export performance. *Strategic Management Journal, 9*(3), 493–505.

13. Liberman, K. (1992). Speech to "The Flexible Workplace Conference." The Canadian Institute. Cited in Frank, T., 1994. Lero, D., & Johnston, K. (1990). *Integrating work and family responsibilities.* Ottawa: Statistics Canada, Population Studies Division.

14. Statistics Canada, based on 1996 census data from Catalogues 93F0027XDB96014 Copyright 1996–1997, 93F0030XDB96004. Copyright 1998–1999.

15. Doeringer, P. B., & Piore, M. J. (1971). Theories of low-wage labor workers. In L. G. Reynolds, S. H. Masters, & C. H. Moser (Eds.), *Readings in labor economics and labor relations,* 15–31. Englewood Cliffs, NJ: Prentice Hall; and Pinfield, L. T., & Berner, M. F. (1994). Employment systems: Toward a coherent conceptualization of internal labor markets. In G. Ferris (Ed.), *Research in Personnel and Human Resources Management, 12,* 50–81.

16. See, for example, De Meuse, K. P., & Tornow, W. W. (1990). The tie that binds has become very, very frayed. *Human Resource Planning, 13*(3), 203–213.

17. Salwen, K. G. (1994, February 8). Decades of downsizing eases stigma of layoffs. *The Wall Street Journal,* B1.

18. Marcus, S. (1991). Delayering: More than meets the eye. *Perspectives, 3*(1), 22–26.

19. Odom, M. (1994, February 23). Management guru preaches to choir. *The Arizona Republic,* E2.

20. McBride, H. (1994, January 25). How to lose freedom and gain the world. *The Globe and Mail,* B22.

21. Hackman, J. R. (1986). The psychology of self-management in organizations. In M. S. Pollack and R. O. Perloff (Eds.), *Psychology and work: Productivity change and employment,* 85–136. Washington, DC: American Psychological Association; and Walton, R. E. (1985). From control to commitment in the workplace. *Harvard Business Review, 63,* 77–84.

22. Booth, P. (1994). *Challenge and change: Embracing the team concept.* Ottawa: Conference Board of Canada.

23. Kapel, C. (1994, August). Master copy. *Human Resources Professional,* 17–18.

24. Parker, J. (1995, January 17). Truce tames chemical warfare. *The Globe and Mail,* B32.

25. Davison, D. (1994). Transformation to a high-performance team. *Canadian Business Review, 21*(3), 18–19.

26. Manz, C. C., & Sims, H. P., Jr. (1993). *Business without bosses: How self-managing teams are building high performance companies* (p. 1). New York: Wiley.

27. Quality. (1994, February). Encouraging individual responsibility.

28. Starke, F. A., & Sexty, R. W. (1995). *Contemporary management in Canada* (pp. 615–620). Toronto: Prentice Hall Canada.

29. Adapted from Fry, F. L. (1993). *Entrepreneurship: A planning approach.* St. Paul, MN: West.

30. Little, B. (1994, November 22). Statscan economists give nod to the little guys in the long-standing debate. *The Globe and Mail,* B1, B8.

31. Adapted from Schein, E. H. (1986). *Organizational culture and leadership.* San Francisco, CA: Jossey Bass.

32. Adapted from *Id.*

33. Drucker, P. F. (1993, October 21). The five deadly business sins. *The Wall Street Journal,* R2.

34. Odom, 1994.

35. *The Wall Street Journal.* (1994, February 11). Special report on telecommunications. B1.

36. Rothfeder, J. (1994, January). Dangerous things strangers know about you. *McCall's,* 88–94.

37. Schuler, 1989, p. 265.

38. Wilke, J. R. (1993, December 9). Computer links erode hierarchical nature of workplace culture. *The Wall Street Journal,* A10.

39. Walker, J. (1992). *Human resource strategy.* New York: McGraw Hill; Shiffman, B. (1991, March 3). Tougher tactics to keep out unions. *The New York Times,* 8.

40. Craig, A. J., & Solomon, N. A. (1996). *The system of industrial relations in Canada* (pp. 139–141). Toronto: Prentice Hall Canada.

41. Gupta, A. K., & Govindarajan, V. (1984). Business unit strategy, managerial characteristics, and business unit effectiveness at strategy implementation. *Academy of Management Journal, 27,* 25–41.

42. Balkin, D. B., & Gómez-Mejía, L. R. (1985). Compensation practices in high tech industries. *Personnel Administrator, 30*(6), 111–123.

43. Associated Press. (1994, March 3). Women win discrimination case against Honeywell after 17 years. *The Arizona Republic,* A17.

44. Pastin, M. (1986). *The hard problems of management: Giving the ethics edge.* San Francisco: Jossey Bass; Noe, R., Hollenbeck, J. R., Gerhart, G., & Wright, P. M. (1994). *Human resource management: Gaining a competitive advantage.* Homewood, IL: Austen.

45. Mathieu, J. E., & Zajac, D. M. (1990). A review and meta-analysis of the antecedents, correlates, and consequences of organizational commitment. *Psychological Bulletin, 108,* 171–194.

46. DeMont, Phillip. (1998). Nice guys can finish first. *Financial Post* (March 28).

47. Hom, P., & Griffeth, R. (1994). *Employee turnover.* Cincinnati, OH: Southwestern.

48. Campion, M. A., & McClelland, C. L. (1991) Interdisciplinary examination of the costs and benefits of enlarged jobs. *Journal of Applied Psychology, 76,* 186–198.

49. Southerst, J. (1992, October). There goes the future. *Canadian Business,* 98–105.

50. Bertin, O. (1994, March 15). Bombardier hits cruising speed. *The Globe and Mail,* B24.

51. Drucker, P. (1993, October 21). The five deadly business sins. *The Wall Street Journal,* R2.

52. Charles, J. (1995, March). Multiple exposures. *Benefits Canada,* 28–29.

53. Stewart, J. M. (1994, March/April). Future state visioning at National Rubber company. *Planning Review,* 20–24, 33.

54. Kapel, C. (1994, April). Variation is the theme: Organizations that value diversity glimpse profits in improved productivity. *Human Resources Professional,* 9–12.

55. Lilley, W. (1995, April). Banking on equity. *Report on Business Magazine,* 67–69.

56. Nelton, S. (1994, February). Put your purpose in writing. *Nation's Business,* 61–64.

57. Butler, J. E., Ferris, G. R., & Napier, N. K. (1991). *Strategy and human resources management.* Cincinnati, OH: Southwestern.

58. Mintzberg, H. (1990). The design school: Reconsidering the basic premises of strategic management. *Strategic Management Journal, 11,* 171–196.

59. Walker, J. (1992). *Human resource management strategy,* Chapter 1. New York: McGraw-Hill.

60. Mintzberg, H. 1990.

61. Brockner, J. (1992). The escalation of commitment to a failing course of action: Toward theoretical progress. *Academy of Management Review, 17*(1), 39–61; and Staw, B. (1976). Knee-deep in Big Muddy: A study of escalating commitment to a chosen course of action. *Organizational Behavior and Human Performance, 16,* 27–44.

62. See the following reviews: Dyer, L., & Holder, G. W. (1988). A strategic perspective of human resource management. In L. Dyer (Ed.), *Human resource management: Evolving roles and responsibilities.* Washington, DC: Bureau of National Affairs; and Gómez-Mejía, L. R., & Balkin, D. B. (1992). *Compensation, organizational strategy, and firm performance.* Cincinnati, OH: Southwestern.

63. Kerr, J. (1985). Diversification strategies and managerial rewards: An empirical study. *Academy of Management Journal, 28,* 155–179; Leontiades, M. (1980). *Strategies for diversification and change.* Boston: Little, Brown; and Pitts, R. A. (1974, May). Incentive compensation and organization design. *Personnel Journal, 20*(5), 338–344.

64. Bulkeley, W. M. (1994, March 1). Conglomerates make a surprising comeback—with a '90s twist. *The Wall Street Journal,* A1.

65. Gómez-Mejía, L. R. (1992). Structure and process of diversification, compensation strategy, and firm performance. *Strategic Management Journal, 13,* 381–397; and Kerr, 1985.

66. Farnam, A. (1994, February 7). Corporate reputations. *Fortune,* 50–54.

67. Porter, M. E. (1980). *Competitive strategy.* New York: Free Press; Porter, M. E. (1985). *Competitive advantage.* New York: Free Press; and Porter, M. E. (1990). *The competitive advantage of nations.* Boston: Free Press.

68. Miles, R. E., & Snow, C. C. (1978). *Organizational strategy, structure, and process.* New York: McGraw-Hill; and Miles, R. E., & Snow, C. C. (1984). Designing strategic human resources systems. *Organizational Dynamics, 13*(1), 36–52.

69. Montemayor, E. F. (1994). Pay policies that fit organizational strategy: Evidence from high-performing firms. Unpublished paper. East Lansing, MI: School of Industrial and Labor Relations, Michigan State University.

70. *Id.*

71. Smyrlis, L. (1995, February). MAC Closures fuels growth with training. *Canadian Plastics,* 18–20.

72. Pitts, G. (1992, June 20). Stepping on the quality ladder. *The Globe and Mail,* B20.

73. Burn, D. (1994, February). On-site training. *Canadian Plastics,* 29–30.

74. Miles & Snow, 1984, 1978.

75. Miles, R. E., Snow, C. C., Meyer, A. D., & Coleman, H. J. (1978). Organizational strategy, structure, and process. *Academy of Management Review, 3,* 546–562.

76. Gómez-Mejía & Balkin, 1992, p. 125.

77. For another example, see Corden, R., Elmer, M., Knudsen, J., Mountain, R., Rider, M., & Ross, W. (1994, March–April). When a new pay plan fails: The case of Beta Corporation. *Compensation & Benefits Review,* 26–32.

78. Jones, G., & Wright, P. (1992). An economic approach to conceptualizing the utility of human resource management practices. *Research in Personnel/Human Resources, 10,* 271–299; Schuler, R., & Walker, J. (1990, Summer). Human resources strategy: Focusing on issues and actions. *Organizational Dynamics,* 5–19; and Wright, P., & Snell, S. (1991). Toward an integrative view of strategic human resource management. *Human Resource Management Review,* 203–225.

79. Gómez-Mejía, 1994.

80. Bailey, B. (1991, July). Ask what HR can do for itself. *Personnel Journal,* 35–39.

Chapter 2

1. Gordon, J., & Wiseman, J. (1994). *Best plant practices: The human resource factor.* Montreal: McGill–Queen's University Press.

2. Mark, K. (1994, Spring). All in one go. *Canadian Business* (Special Technology Issue), 39–43.

3. Armstrong, L. (1994). Evolution to a team-based organization. *Canadian Business Review, 21*(3), 14–17.

4. McKenna, E. (1994, November). Dream teams. *Human Resources Professional,* 17–19.

5. How training primed the pump. (1993, November 16). *The Globe and Mail,* B26.

6. Thompson, A., & Strickland, A. (1993). *Strategic management* (7th ed.). Homewood, IL: Irwin.

7. Lorinc, J. (1994, October). Guerrilla in gray flannel. *Canadian Business, 67*(10), 94–109.

8. CIBC's radical makeover. (1994). *United States Banker, 104*(10).

9. Lawler, E. (1992). *The ultimate advantage.* San Francisco, CA: Jossey-Bass.

10. Kanebo, S. W. (1994, April 25). Pratt-Canada focuses on export markets. *Aviation Week and Space Technology, 140*(17), 24–25.

11. Air Canada saves jobs. (1993, April 15). *The Globe and Mail,* B3.

12. Auto plant's success proves Canadians can compete. (1993, February 1). *This Week in Business,* F13; CAMI's striking experiment. (1992, October 13). *The Globe and Mail,* B18; Trading places: Managers of the Japanese transplants are learning that the natives can teach them a thing or two about good management. (1992, March). *Report on Business Magazine,* 17–27.

13. Fulmer, W. E. (1989). Human resource management: The right hand of strategy implementation. *Human Resource Management, 12*(4), 6.

14. Hammer, M., & Champy, J. (1994, April). Avoiding the hottest new management cure. *Inc.,* 25–26.

15. Hammer, M., & Champy, J. (1993). *Reengineering the corporation.* New York: HarperCollins.

16. *Id.*

17. Greengard, S. (1993, December). Reengineering: Out of the rubble. *Personnel Journal,* 48B–48O; and Verity, J. (1993, June 21). Getting work to go with the flow. *Business Week,* 156–161.

18. Hammer & Champy, 1993.

19. *Id.*

22. Katzenback, J., & Smith, D. (1993, March–April). The discipline of teams. *Harvard Business Review,* 111–120.

23. Orsburn, J., Moran, L., Musselwhite, E., & Zenger, J. (1990). *Self-directed work teams.* Homewood, IL: Business One Irwin.

24. Katzenback & Smith, 1993.

25. Hoerr, J. (1989, July 10). The payoff from teamwork. *Business Week,* 56–62.

26. Palef, R. (1994, February). The team and me: Reflections of a design group. *Personnel Journal,* 48.

27. Hamill, J. (1994, Winter/Spring). Teamwork at Tremco: The transition from "naivete" to power. *PEM: Plant Engineering and Maintenance.*

28. Davison, D. (1994). Transformation to a high performance team. *Canadian Business Review, 21*(3), 18–19.

29. Kapel, C. (1994). Master copy. *Human Resources Professional, 11*(6),17–18.

30. Orsburn, Moran, Musselwhite, & Zenger, 1990.

31. Hoerr, 1989.

32. Parker, J. (1995, January 17). Truce tames chemical warfare. *The Globe and Mail,* B32.

33. Steers, R. (1984). *Introduction to organizational behavior* (2nd ed.). Glenview, IL: Scott, Foresman.

34. Herzberg, F. (1968, January–February). One more time: How do you motivate employees? *Harvard Business Review,* 52–62.

35. Lofquist L., & Dawis, R. (1969). *Adjustment to work: A psychological view of man's problems in a work-oriented society.* Englewood Cliffs, NJ: Prentice Hall.

36. Locke, E. (1968). Toward a theory of task motives and incentives. *Organizational Behavior and Human Performance, 3,* 157–189.

37. Pinder, C. (1984). *Work motivation.* Glenview, IL: Scott, Foresman.

38. Hackman, J., & Oldham, G. (1976). Motivation through the design of work: Test of a theory. *Organizational Behavior and Human Performance, 16,* 250–279.

39. Nadler, D. A., Hackman, J. R., & Lawler, E. E. (1979). *Managing organizational behavior.* Boston: Little, Brown.

40. *Id.*

41. Hackman, J. (1976). Work design. In Hackman, J., & Suttle, J. (Eds.). *Improving life at work,* 96–162. Santa Monica, CA: Goodyear.

42. Pastore, R. (1994, September 15). Leading by example. *CIO, 7*(21), 30–34.

43. Szilagyi, A., & Wallace, M. (1980). *Organizational behavior and performance* (2nd ed.). Santa Monica, CA: Goodyear.

44. Lawler, E. (1986). *High involvement management.* San Francisco, CA: Jossey-Bass.

45. Kapel, C. (1993). Shooting for the moon. *Human Resources Professional, 9*(1), 17–20.

46. Schilder, J. (1993). Secret agents. *Human Resources Professional, 9*(1), 23–25.

47. Lawler, 1992.

48. Geber, B. (1992, June). Saturn's grand experiment. *Training,* 27–35.

55. Cardy, R., & Dobbins, G. (1992, Fall). Job analysis in a dynamic environment. *Human Resources Division News,* 4–6.

56. *Id.*

57. Jones, M. (1984, May). Job descriptions made easy. *Personnel Journal,* 31–34.

58. Fierman, J. (1994, January 24). The contingent work force. *Fortune,* 30–36.

59. Flexible workstyles: In the future workplace, fewer workers will have full-time permanent jobs. (1995, March). *Canada and the World Backgrounder,* 20–24.

60. Castro, J. (1993, March 29). Disposable workers. *Time,* 43–47.

60. *Canadian Press Newswire.* (1995, June 28).

63. McCallum, T. (1995, June). The old "seven to three." *Human Resources Professional, 14*(4), 12–14.

64. Slofstra, M. (1994, August 16). A positive new image in the works. *Computing Canada, 20*(16), 27.

63. *Id.*

65. *The Economist.* (1994, April 23). Benetton: The next era, 68.

66. *Id.*

67. For information on a new twist on outsourcing, see Semler, R. (1993). *Maverick.* New York: Warner Books.

688. Pearce, J. (1993). Toward an organizational behavior of contract laborers: Their psychological involvement and effects on employee co-workers. *Academy of Management Journal, 36,* 1082–96.

69. Cost-cutting boosts SNC-Lavalin's results. (1994, March 28.) *ENR,* 26.

70. Graduates with work: Students are confident about work in the new economy. (1994, June 27). *Maclean's,* 34–36.

71. Denton, D. (1993, January–February). Using flextime to create a competitive workplace. *Industrial Management,* 29–31.

72. McCallum, 1995, 12–14.

73. Kavanaugh, M., Gueutal, H., & Tannenbaum, S. (1990). *Human resource information systems: Development and application.* Boston, MA: PWS-Kent.

74. Leonard, B. (1991, July). Open and shut HRIS. *Personnel Journal,* 59–62.

75. *Id.*

Chapter 3

1. B.C. Council of Human Rights. (1992) *Robert G. Henderson v. B.C. Transit.*

2. Smeenk, B. (1992, December). Bill 40 blues. *Human Resources Professional,* 8, 10; Smeenk, B. (1993, April). Policy palavers. *Human Resources Professional,* 9–11; Evaluating equity. (1993, November). *Human Resources Professional,* 7–12.

3. Human rights complaint costs Hydro $400,000. (1994, June). *Human Resources Management in Canada.* Report Bulletin 136 (pp. 5–6). Toronto: Prentice Hall Canada.

4. Worker hurt after drinking wins $2M from Nike. (1996, February). *Human Resources Management in Canada.* Report Bulletin 156 (pp. 6–7). Toronto: Carswell Business Publishing.

5. Employers liable for employee's criminal acts. (1995, August). *Human Resources Management in Canada.* Report Bulletin 150 (pp. 7–8). Toronto: Prentice Hall Canada.

6. CIBC fined $40,000 for wrongful dismissal. (1994, November). *Human Resources Management in Canada.* Report Bulletin 141 (pp. 5–6). Toronto: Prentice Hall Canada.

7. Geyelin, M. (1993, December 17). Age-bias cases found to bring big jury awards. *The Wall Street Journal,* B1.

8. Firm pays $300,000 in record racial harassment settlement. (1989, February). *Human Resources Management in Canada.* Report Bulletin 72 (pp. 1–2). Toronto: Prentice Hall Canada.

9. Oral statement costs employer $300,000. (1995, December). *Human Resources Management in Canada.* Report Bulletin 154 (pp. 6–7). Toronto: Carswell Business Publishing.

10. Employees owe notice too. (1996, February). *Human Resources Management in Canada.* Report Bulletin 156 (pp. 5–6). Toronto: Carswell Business Publishing.

11. Employers must turn over records to ESA. (1994, December). *Human Resources Management in Canada.* Report Bulletin 142 (p. 6). Toronto: Prentice Hall Canada.

12. Shouldice, L. (1995, November). Employment standards—Ontario. *Human Resources Management in Canada* (pp. 80,060-4–80,060-5). Toronto: Prentice Hall Canada.

13. Employees on strike still owed severance. (1996, January). *Human Resources Management in Canada.* Report Bulletin 155 (p. 7). Toronto: Carswell Business Publishing.

14. Directors' liability upheld—three owe $500,000. (1995, December). *Human Resources Management in Canada.* Report Bulletin 154 (p. 7). Toronto: Carswell Business Publishing.

15. Report Bulletin 192, *Human Resources Management in Canada.* (April, 1988). Alberta Human Rights Code to Be Read as Protecting Gays. 6-7. Carswell (Thomson Professional Publishing).

16. Discrimination endemic in recruitment, group says. (1988, May). *Human Resources Management in Canada*. Report Bulletin 63 (pp. 63.1–63.2). Toronto: Prentice Hall Canada.

17. Jain, H. J. (1995). Human rights: Issues in employment. *Human Resources Management in Canada* (pp. 50,020–50,021). Toronto: Prentice Hall Canada.

18. *Id*.

19. Jain, 1995, pp. 50,034–50,035.

20. $100,000 defence of BFOR fails. (1994, December). *Human Resources Management in Canada*. Report Bulletin 142 (p. 7). Toronto: Prentice Hall Canada.

21. Jain, 1995, p. 50,036.

22. *Id*.

23. MacKillop, M. (1995, October). Should eligibility for benefits be based on sexual orientation? *Human Resources Professional*, 16–17.

24. Canadian Human Rights Commission. (1985, July). *Harassment* (pamphlet).

25. Poor harassment policy may cost $120,000. (1995, March). *Human Resources Management in Canada*. Report Bulletin 145 (pp. 7–8). Toronto: Prentice Hall Canada.

26. *Annual Report* of the Canadian Human Rights Commission. (1998) (Web: http://www.chrc.ca/ar1997/).

27. Abella, R. (1984). *Equality in employment: A Royal Commission Report*. Ottawa: Supply and Services Canada.

28. Jain, 1998, p. 50,074.

29. Commission des droits de la personne. (1994). *1994 Annual Report*. Quebec.

30. Jain, H. (1994). An assessment of strategies of recruiting visible-minority police officers in Canada: 1985–1990. In R. C. McLeod & D. Schniederman (Eds.), *Police powers in Canada: The evolution and practice of authority*. Toronto: University of Toronto Press.

31. Cornish, M. (1986). *Equal pay: Collective bargaining and the law*. Ottawa: Minister of Supply and Services.

32. The progress of women. (1995, August 11). *The Globe and Mail*, A10.

33. McCarthy, Shawn. (1998, July 31), Ottawa inflating pay-equity costs, union says. Toronto: *The Globe and Mail*, A3.

34. Otten, L. A. (1994, April 15). People patterns. *The Wall Street Journal*, B1.

35. Ledvinka, J., & Scarpello, V. G. (1991). *Federal regulation of personnel and human resource management* (2nd ed.). Boston: PWS-Kent; and Twomomey, D. P. (1990). *Equal employment opportunity* (2nd ed.). Cincinnati, OH: South-Western.

36. Civil rights of 1991. (1991, November 11). *Employee Relations Weekly* (special supplement). Bureau of National Affairs.

37. Evans, S. (1994, March). Doing mediation to avoid litigation. *HR Magazine*, 48–51.

Chapter 4

1. Edwards, A. (1991, January). The enlightened manager. *Working Women*, 45–51 (p. 45).

2. Allport, G. W., & Odbert, H. S. (1933). Trait-names: A psycho-lexical study. *Psychological Monographs, 47*, 171–220.

3. Loden, M., and Rosener, J. B. (1991). *Work force America*, 18. Homewood, IL: Irwin.

4. Hartzler, M. (1992). *Making type work for you: A resource book*. Type Resources Inc.; and Dr. Hazel Rosin (1996). Personal communication.

5. Sullivan, L. (1995, June 19). RCMP dress code ruling supports effective policing. *Canadian HR Reporter*, 6.

6. Samuel, T. J. (1994). *Visible minorities in Canada: A projection*. Toronto: Canadian Advertising Foundation.

7. Harrison, B., & Marmar, L. (1994). *Languages in Canada*. Ottawa: Statistics Canada Catalogue No. 96-313E, 42.

8. *Religions in Canada*. (1993). Ottawa: Statistics Canada Catalogue No. 93-319, 1.

93. *A portrait of persons with disabilities*. (1994). Ottawa: Statistics Canada Catalogue No. 89-542E.

10. *Population projections for Canada, provinces and territories: 1993–2016*. (1994, November). Ottawa: Statistics Canada Catalogue No. 91-520, 3.

11. *Id.,* 4, 5.

12. Taylor, C. (1995, Spring). Building a business case for diversity. *Canadian Business Review, 22*(1), 12–15.

13. Cox, T. H., & Blake, S. (1991). Managing cultural diversity: Implications for organizational competitiveness. *Academy of Management Executives, 5*(3), 45–46.

14. Kanter, R.M. (1983). The *change masters*, 52. New York: Simon and Schuster.

15. Author's files.

16. Sheppard, C. R. (1964). *Small groups* (p. 118). San Francisco: Chandler.

17. Samuel, 1994.

18. Ignatieff, M. (1994?). *Blood and belonging: Journeys into the new nationalism*. Toronto: Viking Press.

19. Author's files.

20. How to manage a diverse work force. (1991, October). *American Banking Association Journal*, 122.

21. Pinkerton, J.P. (1995, November 23). Why affirmative action won't die. *Fortune*, 191–198.

22. Glass ceiling still intact. (1995, May). *Human Resources Professional*, 22.

23. *Women in the labour force* (1994 ed.). Ottawa: Statistics Canada, Catalogue No. 75-507E, Table 1.1, 10.

24. *Id.,* 5.

25. *Id*.

26. Women to watch. (1987, June 22). *Business Week*, 88.

27. Welcome to the woman-friendly company. (1990, August 6). *Business Week*, 53.

28. Baird, J. E., Jr., & Bradley, P. H. (1979, June). Styles of management and communications: A comparative study of men and women. *Communication Monographs, 46*, 101–110.

29. DePalma, A. (1991, November 12). Women can be hindered by lack of "boys" network. *Boulder Daily Camera* (Business Plus Section), 9.

30. Weiner, N. (1996, March 25). "Teasing" can lead to harassment complaints. *Canadian HR Reporter*, 15.

31. Bordo, H. (1995, February/March). Sex and the single HRM. *Human Resources Professional*, 22.

32. What to do about sexual harassment. (1995, January 30). *Canadian HR Reporter*, 10.

33. Canadian Human Rights Commission. (1991). *Harassment casebook: Summaries of selected harassment cases*. Ottawa: Minister of Supply and Services.

34. The aging workforce: Shattering the myths and facing the realities associated with older workers. (1995, September/October). *Occupational Health and Safety*, 28–37.

35. Loden. M., & Rosener, J. B., 1991, 55.

36. Muir, J. G. (1993, March 31). Homosexuals and the 10% fallacy. *The Wall Street Journal*, A13.

37. Harnden, L. H. (1993, September). AIDS awareness. *Human Resources Professional*, 23.

38. *A portrait of persons with disabilities*. (1995). Ottawa: Statistics Canada, Catalogue 89-542E, 5, 7.

39. Weber, J. (1988, June 8). Social issues: The disabled. *Business Week*, 140.

40. *A portrait of persons with disabilities*, 1995, Table 6.16, p. 57.

41. Oh Canada! Vive la diversité. (1996, April). *Human Resources Professional*, 26.

42. Samuel, T. J., 1994.

43. *Id*.

44. *Id*.

45. Hill, J. (1993, March). Sounding good: Accent reduction and voice training. *Human Resources Management in Canada,* 30-573–30-577.
46. Moyer, C. (1995, November). Diversity management: The bottom-line impact of an equitable employment system. *Human Resources Professional,* 21–22.
47. Lilley, W. (1995, April). Banking on equity. *Report on Business Magazine,* 67, 69.
48. Davies, D. (1993, April). Equity equations: Scrapping equity programs when profits are down doesn't add up. *Human Resources Professional,* 15.
49. Moyer, 1995.
50. *Id.*
51. Davies, 1993, 17.
52. Gleckman, H. T. S., Dwyer, P., Segal, T., & Weber, J. (1991, June 8). Race in the work place. *Business Week,* 50–63.
53. Stewart, T. A. (1991, December 10). Gay in corporate America. *Fortune,* 42–50.
54. Thomas, R. F. (1990, March/April). From affirmative action to affirming diversity. *Harvard Business Review,* 107–119.
55. Lee, M. (1993, September 3). Diversity training brings unity to small companies. *The Wall Street Journal,* B2, 3.
56. Knight, C. (1995, May 22). More female workers mean "family-friendlier" workplaces. *Canadian HR Reporter,* 6.
57. Spinks, N. (1996, April 6). Adventures in innovative childcare. *Canadian HR Reporter,* 12.
58. Goodstein, J. D. (1994). Institutional pressures and strategic responsiveness: Employer involvement in work-family issues. *Academy of Management Journal, 37*(2), 350–383.
59. Hammonds, K. H. (1991, April 15). Taking baby steps toward a daddy track. *Business Week,* 90–92.
60. Davies, 1993, 17.
61. *Id.*
62. Royal Bank agrees to increase hiring of the disabled. (1995, November). *Human Resource Management in Canada,* Report Bulletin 153, 8.
63. Davies, 1993, 17.
64. Reverse discrimination a myth, says human-rights chief Max Yalden. (1995, January 31). *Canadian Press Newswire.*
65. Wartzman, R. (1992, May 4). A Whirlpool factory raises productivity and pay of workers. *The Wall Street Journal,* A1.

Chapter 5

1. See, for example, Rothwell, W. J., & Kazanas, H. C. (1988). *Strategic human resources planning and management.* Englewood Cliffs, NJ: Prentice Hall; Bartholomew, D. J., & Forbes, A. F. (1979). *Statistical techniques for manpower planning.* Chichester, England: Wales; Heneman, H. G. III, & Sandver, M. G. (1977). Markov analysis in human resource administration: Applications and limitations. *Academy of Management Review, 2*(4), 535–542; and Burack, E. H., & Mathys, N. J. (1987). Human resource planning: A pragmatic approach to manpower staffing and development. Lake Forest, IL: Brace-Park.
2. Bowen, D. E., Ledford, G. E., & Nathan, B. R. (1991, November). Hiring for the organization, not the job. *Academy of Management Executive, 5* (4), 35–51.
3. Semler, R. (1993). *Maverick,* 169–177. New York: Warner Books.
4. Rynes, S. L. (1991). Recruitment, job choice, and post-hire consequences: A call for new research directions. *Handbook of industrial and organizational psychology* (2nd ed.), Vol. 2, 399–444.
5. Gunsch, D. (1993, September). Comprehensive college strategy strengthens NCR's recruitment. *Personnel Journal,* 58–62.
6. Yamamoto, T. (1993, October). Recruiting system badly designed, badly run, unlikely to change. *Tokyo Business Today,* 52–54.
7. Posner, B. G. (1990). Putting customers to work. *Inc., 12,* 111–112.
8. Chamie, N. (1995). *Why the jobless recovery.* Ottawa: The Conference Board of Canada, Report 154-95.
9. Klein, E. (1993, January–February). Heroes for hire. *D&B Reports,* 26–28.
10. Wanous, J. P. (1992). *Organizational entry* (2nd ed.). Reading, MA: Addison-Wesley.
11. Change costly for Laidlaw. (1994, November 24). *The Globe and Mail,* B15.
12. *Training & Development.* (1993, November). Catalysts for career development: Four case studies, 26–27.
13. Laabs, J. J. (1991, May). Affirmative outreach. *Personnel Journal,* 86–93.
14. Walker, J. W. (1990, December). Human resource planning, 1990s style. *Human Resource Planning,* 229–230.
15. Hunter, J. E., & Hunter, R. F. (1984). Validity and utility of alternative predictors of job performance. *Psychological Bulletin, 96,* 72–98; Hunter, J. E., & Schmidt, F. L. (1982). The economic benefits of personnel selection using psychological ability tests. *Industrial Relations, 21,* 293–308; and Schmidt, F. L., & Hunter, J. E. (1983). Individual differences in productivity: An empirical test of the estimate derived from studies of selection procedure utility. *Journal of Applied Psychology, 68,* 407–414.
16. Hunter & Hunter, 1984.
17. Muchinsky, P. M. (1979). The use of reference reports in personnel selection: A review and evaluation. *Journal of Occupational Psychology, 52,* 287–297.
18. Aamodt, M. G., Bryan, D. A., & Whitcomb, A. J. (1993). Predicting performance with letters of recommendation. *Public Personnel Management, 22,* 81–90.
19. Peres, S. H., & Garcia, J. R. (1962). Validity and dimensions of descriptive adjectives used in reference letters for engineering applicants. *Personnel Psychology, 15,* 279–296.
20. Russell, C. J., Mattson, J., Devlin, S. E., & Atwater, D. (1990). Predictive validity of biodata items generated from retrospective life experience essays. *Journal of Applied Psychology, 75,* 569–580.
21. Hunter, J. E. (1986). Cognitive ability, cognitive aptitudes, job knowledge, and job performance. *Journal of Vocational Behavior, 29,* 340–362.
22. Bounds, G.M., Dobbins, G.H., and Fowler, O.S. (1995), *Management: A Total Quality Perspective.* Cincinnati, Ohio: South-Western.
23. Harville, D.L. (1996). Ability test equity in predicting job performance work samples. *Educational and Psychological Measurement, 56,* 344–348.
24. Hogan, J. and Quigley, A. (1994). Effects of preparing for physical tests. *Public Personnel Management, 23,* 85–104.
25. McCallum, T. (1995, May). The science of selection. *Human Resources Professional, 12*(3). 9–12.
26. Guion, R. M., & Gottier, R. F. (1965). Validity of personality measures in personnel selection. *Personnel Psychology, 18,* 135–163.
27. Bernardin, H. J., & Beatty, R. W. (1984). *Performance appraisal: Assessing human behavior at work.* Boston: Kent.
28. Landy, F. J. (1989). The psychology of work behavior (4th ed.). Pacific Grove, CA: Brooks/Cole.
29. Guion & Gottier, 1965.
30. Kleiman & Faley, 1985.
31. Funder, D. C., & Dobroth, J. M. (1987). Difference between traits: Properties associated with inter-judge agreement. *Journal of Personality and Social Psychology, 52,* 409–418.
32. Digman, J. M. (1990). Personality structure: Emergence of the five-factor model. *Annual Review of Psychology, 41,* 417–440; and Goldberg, L. R. (1993). The structure of phenotypic personality traits. *American Psychologist, 48,* 26–34.
33. Barrick & Mount, 1991; Digman, 1990; Hogan, R. (1991). Personality and personality measurement. In M. D. Dunnette & L. M. Hough (Eds.), *Handbook of industrial and organization psychology* (2nd ed.), Vol. 1. Palo Alto, CA: Consulting Psychologists.
34. Barrick & Mount, 1991.
35. Bowen, Ledford, & Nathan, 1991.

36. Arvey, R. D., & Campion, J. E. (1982). The employment interview: A summary and review of recent research. *Personnel Psychology, 35,* 281–322; and Harris, M. M. (1989). Reconsidering the employment interview: A review of recent literature and suggestions for future research. *Personnel Psychology, 42,* 691–726.

37. Springbett, B. M. (1958). Factors affecting the final decision in the employment interview. *Canadian Journal of Psychology, 12,* 13–22.

38. Buckley, M. R., & Eder, R. W. (1988). B. M. Springbett and the notion of the "snap decision" in the interview. *Journal of Management, 14,* 59–67.

39. Campion, M. A., Pursell, E. D., & Brown, B. K. (1988). Structured interviewing: Raising the psychometric properties of the employment interview. *Personnel Psychology, 41,* 25–42.

40. Pursell, E. D., Campion, M. A., & Gaylord, S. R. (1980). Structured interviewing: Avoiding selection problems. *Personnel Journal, 59,* 907–912.

41. Wright, P. M., Licthenfels, P. A., & Pursell, E. D. (1989). The structured interview: Additional studies and a meta-analysis. *Journal of Occupational Psychology, 62,* 191–199.

42. Hunter & Hunter, 1984.

43. McCallum, 1995.

44. Warmke, D. L., & Weston, D. J. (1992, April). Success dispels myths about panel interviewing. *Personnel Journal,* 120–126.

45. Harris, 1989.

46. Kerr, J. (1982). Assigning managers on the basis of the life cycle. *Journal of Business Strategy, 2,* 58–65; Olian, J. D., & Rynes, S. L. (1984). Organizational staffing: Integrating practice with strategy. *Industrial Relations, 23,* 170–183; and Rynes, S., & Gerhart, B. (1990). Interviewer assessments of applicant "fit": An exploratory investigation. *Personnel Psychology, 43,* 13–35.

47. Chatman, 1989.

48. *Id.*

49. Rose, R. C., & Garrett, E. M. (1992, December). Guerrilla interviewing. *Inc.,* 145–147.

50. Pouliot, J. S. (1992, July). Topics to avoid with applicants. *Nation's Business,* 57–59.

51. Broadbent, D. (1994, Autumn). Recruitment using work simulations in groups. *Optimum,* 40–43.

52. McEvoy, G. M., & Beatty, R. W. (1989). Assessment centers and subordinate appraisals of managers: A seven-year study of predictive validity. *Personnel Psychology, 42,* 37–52.

53. Bender, J. M. (1973). What is "typical" of assessment centers? *Personnel, 50,* 50–57.

54. Lopez, J. A. (1993, October 6). Firms force job seekers to jump through hoops. *The Wall Street Journal,* B1, B6.

55. footnote '63' from 1st Canadian edition

56. Solomon, R., & Usprich, S. J. (1993, Winter). Employment drug testing. *Business Quarterly,* 7.

57. TD drug tests upheld. (1994, September/October). *Journal of the Addiction Research Foundation, 23*(5), 3.

58. *Canadian Press.* (1998, July 25). TD drug-testing policy wrong, court says. *The Globe and Mail,* A7.

59. Catch 22: Under Imperial Oil's revamped drug policy. (1994, November/December). *Journal of the Addiction Research Foundation, 23*(6), 12.

60. Sleep disorders linked to workplace disorders. (1994, November/December). *Occupational Health and Safety, 10*(6), 10–11.

61. Worries raised over on-the-job snooping by employers. (1994, July 5). *Canadian Press Newswire.*

62. Wessel, D. (1989, September 7). Evidence is skimpy that drug testing works, but employers embrace practice. *The Wall Street Journal,* B1 & B9.

63. Terris, W., & Jones, J. W. (1982). Psychological factors relating to employees' theft in the convenience store industry. *Psychological Reports, 51,* 1219–38.

64. Bernardin, H. S., and Cooke, D. K. (1993). Validity of an honesty

test in predicting theft among convenience store employees. *Academy of Management Journal, 36,* 1097–1108.

65. Budman, M. (1993, November–December). The honesty business. *Across the Board,* 34–37.

66. Rafaeli, A., & Klimoski, R. J. (1983). Predicting sales success through handwriting analysis: An evaluation of the effects of training and handwriting sample content. *Journal of Applied Psychology, 68,* 212–217.

67. Kleinmutz, B. (1990). Why we still use our heads instead of formulas: Toward an integrative approach. *Psychological Bulletin, 107,* 296–310.

68. Wanous, J. P., Reichers, A. E., & Malik, S. D. (1984). Organizational socialization and group development: Toward an integrative perspective. *Academy of Management Review, 9,* 670–683.

69. Breaugh, J. A. (1983). Realistic job previews: A critical appraisal and future research directions. *Academy of Management Review, 8,* 612–623.

70. Broadfoot, 1994.

71. Bragg, A. (1989, September). Is a mentor program in your future? *Sales & Marketing Management,* 54–63.

72. Jain, H. (1995). Human rights: Issues in employment. *Human Resources Management in Canada* (pp. 50,002–50,110). Toronto: Prentice Hall Canada.

73. *Id.*

Chapter 6

1. Papp, L. (1995, January 27). Hydro buyout gets lots of bites. *Toronto Star,* A14.

2. Mobley, W. H. (1982). *Employee turnover: Causes, consequences, and control.* Reading, MA: Addison-Wesley.

3. Forced retirement policy discriminatory, court rules. (1994, March). *Human Resources Management in Canada.* Report Bulletin 133, 6–7.

4. Job losses forcing earlier retirement—1994 data. (1995, September 9). *Canadian Press Newswire.*

5. Greying of the workforce: Report on a symposium. (1995, Spring). *Perspectives.* Ottawa: Statistics Canada Catalogue 75-001E, 34.

6. Axsmith, M. (1995). *1995 Canadian dismissal practices survey.* Toronto: Murray Axsmith.

7. Grant, P. B. (1991). The "open window"—Special early retirement plans in transition. *Employee Benefits Journal, 16*(1), 10–16.

8. Severance benefits shrink. (1995, April). *Human Resources Professional,* 20.

9. Civil servants scramble to get buyouts. (1995, July 15/17). *The Financial Post,* 3.

10. University slashed staff in record buyout. (1996, January 19). *Canadian Press Newswire.*

11. Age-old problem: Are LTD programs becoming early retirement schemes? (1995, September). *Benefits Canada,* 63–65; Study warns disability pensions a threat to CPP. (1995, December 22). *The Financial Post Daily,* 5.

12. Legault, A. (1993, December). Aging disgracefully. *Human Resources Professional,* 10–11.

13. Greying of the workforce, 1995.

14. Rail jobs can be axed: Federal arbitrators eliminate railways job-for-life contracts. (1995, June 15). *The Financial Post Daily,* 1, 2.

15. Fleet executives join staff in salary cuts: reduction not offset with perks. (1994, March 18). *The Globe and Mail,* B5.

16. Air Canada loses $326 million: Turnaround in operating profit keeps airline on road to financial respectability. (1994, February 19). *The Globe and Mail,* B20.

17. Paper workers pressed to help save mills: unions fear concession will spread. (1994, February 24). *The Globe and Mail,* B1, B10.

18. McCabe, D. (1993, December). Improvising the future. *Human Resources Professional,* 17.

19. Civil servants scramble to get buyouts. (1995, July 15/17). *The Financial Post,* 3.

20. McCabe, 1993.

21. Brockner, J., Grover, S., Reed, T. F., & DeWitt, R. L. (1992). Layoffs, job insecurity, and survivors' work effort: Evidence of an inverted-U relationship. *Academy of Management Journal, 35,* 413–425.

22. Ehrenberg, R. G., & Jakubson, G. H. (1988). *Advance notice provisions in plant closing legislation.* Kalamazoo, MI: W. E. Upjohn Institute for Employment Research.

23. Alexander, S. (1991, October 14). Firms get plenty of practice at layoffs, but they often bungle the firing process. *The Wall Street Journal,* B1.

24. Bunning, R. L. (1990). The dynamics of downsizing. *Personnel Journal, 69*(9), 69–75.

25. Alexander, 1991.

26. Brockner, J. (1992). Managing the effects of layoffs on survivors. *California Management Review, 34*(2), 9–28.

27. Reibstein, L. (1988, December 5). Survivors of layoffs receive help to lift morale and reinstate trust. *The Wall Street Journal,* 31.

28. O'Neil, H.M. and Lenn, D.J. (1995). Voices of survivors: words that downsizing CEOs should hear. *Academy of Management Executive,* 9(4), 23-34.

29. Noer, David M. (1993). *Healing the wounds: Overcoming the trauma of layoffs and revitalizing downsized organizations.* San Francisco, CA: Jossey-Bass.

30. Execs cite firing line as top stress factor. (1993, May). *Human Resources Professional,* 6.

31. Stewardson, J. (1992, October). Terminal affairs. *Human Resources Professional,* 17.

32. Communicating workplace change a necessity. (1995, April 15/17). *The Financial Post,* 27.

33. Sweet, D. H. (1989). Outplacement. In W. Cascio (ed.), *Human resource planning, employment and placement,* Washington, DC: Bureau of National Affairs.

34. Newman, L. (1988). Good bye is not enough. *Personnel Administrator, 33*(2), 84–86.

35. Axsmith, 1995.

36. Newman, 1988.

37. Sweet, 1989.

38. Gibson, V. M. (1991). The ins and outs of outplacement. *Management Review, 80*(10), 59–61.

39. Burdett, J. O. (1988). Easing the way out. *Personnel Administrator, 33*(6), 157–166.

40. Crofts, P. (1991). Helping people face up to redundancy. *Personnel Management, 23*(12), 24–27.

41. Rudolph, B. (1986, December 8). The sun also sets. *Business Week,* 60–61.

42. Borrus, A. (1987, April 6). Saying sayonara in a way that will save face. *Business Week,* 54.

Chapter 7

1. Carroll, S. J., & Schneir, C. E. (1982). *Performance appraisal and review systems: The identification, measurement, and development of performance in organizations.* Glenview, IL: Scott, Foresman.

2. Banks, C. G., & Roberson, L. 9 (1985). Performance appraisers as test developers. *Academy of Management Review, 10,* 128–142.

3. Cleveland, J. N., Murphy, K. R., & Williams, R. E. (1989). Multiple uses of performance appraisals: Prevalence and correlates. *Journal of Applied Psychology, 74,* 130–135.

4. Landy, F. J., & Farr, J. L. (1980). Performance ratings. *Psychological Bulletin, 87,* 72–107.

5. Bureau of National Affairs. (1975). Employee performance: Evaluation and control. *Personnel Policies Forum.* Survey No. 8. Washington, DC: Bureau of National Affairs.

6. Bernardin, H. J., & Klatt, L. A. (1986). Managerial appraisal systems: Has practice "caught up" to the state of the art? *The Personnel Administrator,* 79–86.

7. Odom, M. (1992, October 18). From tough to tender, firms reconsider employee appraisals. *The Washington Post,* H2.

8. Nunnally, J. C. (1978). *Psychometric theory.* New York: McGraw-Hill.

9. Bernardin, H. J., & Beatty, R. W. (1984). *Performance appraisal: Assessing human behaviour at work.* Boston, MA: Kent; Latham, G. P., & Wexley, K. N. (1981). *Increasing productivity through performance appraisal.* Reading, MA: Addison-Wesley; Miner, J. B. (1988). Development and application of the rated ranking technique in performance appraisal. *Journal of Occupational Psychology, 6,* 291–305.

10. Miner, 1988.

11. Cardy, R. L., & Sutton, C. L. (1993). *Accounting for halo-accuracy paradox: Individual differences.* Paper presented at the Annual Conference of the Society for Industrial and Organizational Psychology, 1993, San Francisco.

12. Harris, C. (1988). A comparison of employee attitudes toward two performance appraisal systems. *Public Personnel Management, 17,* 443–456.

13. Bernardin & Beatty, 1984.

14. *Id.*

15. Latham & Wexley, 1981.

16. Blood, M. R. (1973). Spin-offs from behavioural expectation scale procedures. *Journal of Applied Psychology, 59,* 513–515.

17. Harris, 1988.

18. Drucker, P. F. (1954). *The practice of management.* New York: Harper.

19. Cardy, R. L., & Krzystofiak, F. J. (1991). Interfacing high technology operations with blue collar workers: Selection and appraisal in a computerized manufacturing setting. *Journal of High Technology Management Research, 2,* 193–210.

20. Bernardin & Beatty, 1984.

21. See, for example, Smith, R. W. (1992, Fall). Moving managers to a higher plane of performance. *Business Forum,* 5–6.

22. Cardy, R. L., & Dobbins, G. H. (1994). *Performance appraisal: Alternative perspectives.* Cincinnati, OH: Southwestern Publishing Co.

23. Borman, W. C. (1979). Individual difference correlates of rating accuracy using behaviour scales. *Applied Psychological Measurement, 3,* 103–115.

24. Cardy, R. L., & Kehoe, J. F. (1984). Rater selective attention ability and appraisal effectiveness: The effect of a cognitive style on the accuracy of differentiation among ratees. *Journal of Applied Psychology, 69,* 589–594.

25. Thorndike, E. L. (1920). A constant error in psychological ratings. *Journal of Applied Psychology, 4,* 25–29.

26. Cooper, W. H. (1981). Ubiquitous halo. *Psychological Bulletin, 90,* 218–244.

27. Edwards, M. R., Wolfe, M. E., & Sproull, J. R. (1983). Improving comparability in performance appraisal. *Business Horizons, 26,* 75–83.

28. Bernardin, H. J., & Buckley, M. R. (1981). Strategies in rater training. *Academy of Management Review, 6,* 205–212.

29. Bernardin, H. J., & Pence, E. C. (1980). Rater training: Creating new response sets and decreasing accuracy. *Journal of Applied Psychology, 65,* 60–66; Cardy, R. L., & Keefe, T. J. (1994). Observational purpose and valuative articulation in frame-of-reference training: The effects of alternative processing models on rating accuracy. *Organizational Behaviour and Human Decision Processes 57,* 338–357.

304. Zajonc, R. B. (1980). Feeling and thinking: Preferences need no inferences. *American Psychologist 35,* 151–175.

31. Alexander, E. R., & Wilkins, R. D. (1982). Performance rating validity: The relationship between objective and subjective measures of performance. *Group and Organization Studies, 7,* 485–496.

32. Cardy & Dobbins, 1994.

33. Cardy, R. L., & Dobbins, G. H. (1986). Affect and appraisal: Liking as an integral dimension in evaluating performance. *Journal of Applied Psychology, 71,* 672–678.

34. Cardy & Dobbins, 1994.

35. Bernardin, H. J., & Walter, C. S. (1977). Effects of rater training and diary keeping on psychometric error in ratings. *Journal of Applied Psychology, 62,* 64–69; and Flanagan, J. C. (1954). The critical incident technique. *Psychological Bulletin, 51,* 327–358.

36. Flanagan, J. C., & Burns, R. K. (1957, September–October). The employee performance record: A new appraisal and development tool. *Harvard Business Review*, 95–102.

37. Day, D. (1993, May). Training 101: Help for discipline dodgers. *Training & Development*, 19–22.

38. Jacobs, H. (1993, October). The rating game. *Small Business Reports*, 21–25.

39. Adapted from Longenecker, C.O., Sims, H.P., Jr., and Gioia, D.A. Behind the mask.: The politics of employee appraisal. Copyright © by the Academy of Management. Reprinted by permission of the publisher. *Academy of Management Executive 1* (3), August 1987, 183–197.

40. Longenecker, Sims, & Gioia, (1987).

41. Cardy & Dobbins, 1993.

42. Cardy, R.L. and Dobbins, G.H. (1996). Total quality and the abandonment of performance appraisal: Taking a good thing too far? *Journal of Quality Management*, 1, 193–206.

43. Cardy, R.L. and Stewart, G.L. (1997). Quality and teams: Implications for HRM theory and research. In D.B. Fedor and S. Ghost (Eds.), *Advances in the management of organization quality*, 2, Greenwich, CT: JAI Press.

44. Landy & Farr, 1980.

45. Bernardin & Beatty, 1984.

46. Dobbins, G. H., Cardy, R. L., & Carson, K. P. (1991). Perspectives on human resource management: A contrast of person and system approaches. In G. R. Ferris & K. M. Rowland (Eds.), *Research in personnel and human resources management* (Vol. 9). Greenwich, CT: JAI Press; and Ilgen, D. R., Fisher, C. D., & Taylor, S. M. (1979). Consequences of individual feedback on behaviour in organizations. *Journal of Applied Psychology*, 64, 347–371.

47. Carson, K. P., Cardy, R. L., & Dobbins, G. H. (1991). Performance appraisal as effective management or deadly management disease: Two initial empirical investigations. *Group and Organization Studies*, 16, 143–159.

48. Kelly, H. H. (1973). The processes of causal attribution. *American Psychologist*, 28, 107–128.

49. Cascio, W. F. (1991). *Applied psychology in personnel management* (4th ed.). Englewood Cliffs, NJ: Prentice Hall.

50. Blumberg, M., & Pringle, C. D. (1982). The missing opportunity in organizational research: Some implications for a theory of work performance. *Academy of Management Review*, 7, 560–569; Carson, Cardy, & Dobbins, 1991; and Schermerhorn, J. R., Jr., Gardner, W. L., & Martin, T. N. (1990). Management dialogues: Turning on the marginal performers. *Organizational Dynamics*, 18, 47–59.

51. Blumberg & Pringle, 1982; and Rummler, G. A. (1972). Human performance problems and their solutions. *Human Resource Management*, 19, 2–10.

52. Booth, 1994, p. 11.

53. Rummler, 1972.

54. Longenecker, C. O., & Gioia, D. A. (1991, Fall). SMR Forum: Ten myths of managing managers. *Sloan Management Review*, 33(1), 81–90.

55. Evered, R. D., & Selman, J. C. (1989). Coaching and the art of management. *Organizational Dynamics*, 18, 16–33.

56. Schermerhorn, Gardner, & Martin, 1990.

Chapter 8

1. Adams, N. (1995). Lessons from the virtual world. *Training*, 32, 45–47.

2. Fitzgerald, W. (1992). Training versus development. *Training & Development*, 46, 81–84.

3. Bartz, D. E., Schwandt, D. R., & Hillman, L. W. (1989). Differences between "T" and "D." *Personnel Administrator*, 34, 164–170.

4. Rummler, G. A. (1972). Human performance problems and their solutions. *Human Resource Management*, 19, 2–10.

5. Cummings, J. (1993, February 15). Survey finds managers lack focus on training goals. *Network World*, 75.

6. Gordon, J., & Wiseman, J. (1995). *Best plant practices: The human resource factor*. Kingston, ON: Queen's University/IRC Press.

7. Muller, R. (1995, Spring). Training for change. *Canadian Business Review*, 22(1), 16–19.

8. Goldstein, I. L. (1986). *Training in organizations: Needs assessment, development, and evaluation* (2nd ed.). Monterey, CA: Brooks/Cole.

9. Mirabile, R. J. (1991). Pinpointing development needs: A simple approach to skills assessment. *Training & Development*, 45, 19–25.

10. Mager, R. F., & Pipe, P. (1984). *Analyzing performance problems: Or, you really oughta wana*. Belmont, CA: Lake and Rummler, 1972.

11. Mellow, J. A. (1994, Autumn). A strategized approach towards AIDS in the workplace: Experience at Sun Life. *Employee Relations Today*, 21(3), 139–338.

12. Nowack, K. M. (1991). A true training needs analysis. *Training & Development Journal*, 45, 69–73; and Phillips, J. J. (1983, May). Training programs: A results-oriented model for managing the development of human resources. *Personnel*, 11–18.

13. *Id*.

14. Mullaney, C. A., & Trask, L. D. (1992, October). Show them the ropes. *Technical & Skills Training*, 8–11.

15. Gupta, U. 1996, January 3. TV seminars and CD-ROMs train workers. The B1, B8. *Wall Street Journal*.

16. Hall, B. (1996). Lessons in corporate training: Multimedia's big payoff. *NewMedia*, 40–45.

17. Hughes, D. (1994, June 20). Production pace quickens at Mirabel. *Aviation Week and Space Technology 140*(25), 51–52.

18. Geber, B. (1990) Simulating reality. *Training*, 27, 41–46.

19. Middleton, T. (1992, Spring). The potential of virtual reality technology for training. *The Journal of Interactive Instructional Development*, 8–11.

20. Psotka, J. (1995). Immersive Training systems: Virtual reality and education and training. *Instructional Science*, 23. 405–431.

21. Swink, D. F. (1993). Role-play your way to learning. *Training & Development*, 47, 91–97.

22. Estabrooke & Foy, 1992.

23. Patterson, P. A. (1991). Job aids: Quick and effective training. *Personnel*, 68, 13.

24. Barker, P. (1994, February 2). A mobile way to reach the customer. *Computing Canada*, 20(3), 33.

25. All in one go. (1994, Spring). *Canadian Business*, 67, 39–43.

26. Challenger, J. E. (1993). Two or more for one: A new way of looking at employment. *Industry Week*, 242, 25.

27. Nilson, C. (1990). How to use peer training. *Supervisory Management*, 35, 8.

28. Filipczak, B. (1993, June). Frick teaches Frack. *Training*, 30–34.

29. Messmer, M. (1992). Cross-discipline training: A strategic method to do more with less. *Management Review*, 81, 26–28.

30. Santora, J. E. (1992, June). Keep up production through cross-training. *Personnel Journal*, 162–166.

31. Fyock, C. D. (1991). Teaching older workers new tricks. *Training & Development Journal*, 45, 21–24.

32. Bowen, D. E., Ledford, G. E., & Nathan, B. R. (1991). Hiring for the organization, not the job. *Academy of Management Executive*, 5, 35–51.

33. Goldstein, I. L. (1993). *Training in organizations* (3rd ed.). Pacific Grove, CA: Brooks-Cole.

34. Camp collegiality. (1994, December 12). *Maclean's*, 44–45.

35. Hartmann, C. R. (1994, January/February). Games to sharpen sales skills. *D&B Reports*, 43(1), 62.

36. Ames, L. (1991, July 21). An obstacle course, lessons in teamwork. *The New York Times*, WC 2.

37. Hequet, M. (1992, February). Creativity training gets creative. *Training*, 41–46.

38. *Training*. (1995). Vital statistics. 32: 55–66.

39. Burdett, J. O. (1994, Summer). A Sackett's Harbour weekend. *Business Quarterly*, 58(4), 60–70.

40. Wise, R. (1991). The boom in creativity training. *Across the Board, 28,* 38–42.

41. Solomon, C. M. (1990). Creativity training. *Personnel Journal, 69,* 65–71.

42. Wise, 1991.

43. Factory offers workers a second chance. (1995, June 2). *Canadian Press Newswire.*

44. Lund, L., & McGuire, E. P. (1990). *Literacy in the work force.* New York: The Conference Board.

45. McCarthy, J. P. (1992, September). Focus from the start. *HR Magazine,* 77–83.

46. Wanous, J. P. (1992). *Organizational entry* (2nd ed.). Reading, MA: Addison-Wesley.

47. Wanous, 1992.

48. *Id.*

Chapter 9

1. Leibowitz, Z. B. (1987). Designing career development systems: Principles and practices. *Human Resource Planning, 10,* 195–207.

2. *Id.*

3. Lilly, W. (1995, April). Banking on equity. *Report on Business Magazine,* 67–68.

4. Frank, T. (1994). *Canada's best employers for women.* Toronto: Frank Publications.

5. Gutteridge, T. B., Leibowitz, Z. B., & Shore, J. E. (1993). *Organizational career development: Benchmarks for building a world-class workforce.* San Francisco: Jossey-Bass.

6. Morgan, D. C. (1977). Career development programs. *Personnel, 54,* 23–27.

7. Gutteridge, T., & Otte, F. (1983). Organizational career development: What's going on out there? *Training and Development Journal, 37,* 22–26; Hall, D. T. (1986). An overview of current career development, theory, research, and practice. In D. T. Hall & Associates (Eds.), *Career development in organizations,* 1–20, San Francisco: Jossey-Bass; and Leibowitz, Z. B., & Schlossberg, N. K. (1981). Designing career development programs in organizations: A systems approach. In D. H. Montross & C. J. Shinkman (Eds.), *Career development in the 1980s,* 277–291, Springfield, IL: Charles C. Thomas.

8. Russell, J. E. A. (1991). Career development interventions in organizations. *Journal of Vocational Behavior, 38,* 237–287.

9. Koonce, R. (1991, January–February). Management development: An investment in people. *Credit Magazine,* 16–19.

10. Steele, B., Bratkovich, J. R., & Rollins, T. (1990). Implementing strategic redirection through the career management system. *Human Resource Planning, 13,* 241–263.

11. Tucker, R., & Moravec, M. (1992, February). Do-it-yourself career development. *Training Magazine,* 48–52.

12. *Id.*

13. Feldman, D. C., & Weitz, B. A. (1991). From the invisible hand to the gladhand: Understanding a careerist orientation to work. *Human Resource Management, 30,* 237–257.

14. Kalish, B. B. (1992, March). Dismantling the glass ceiling. *Management Review, 64;* and Hawkins, B. (1991, September 8). Career-limiting bias found at low job levels. *Los Angeles Times Magazine,* 33.

15. Advancing women in the workplace. (1993, September). *Training & Development,* 9–10.

16. Bourne, K. (1992). Companies offer career management for couples. *Journal of Compensation and Benefits, 7,* 32–36.

17. *Id.*

18. Bures, A.L., Henderson, D.M. Ma¥field, J., Mayfield, M., and Worley, J. (1995). The effects of spousal support and gender on workers' stress and job satisfaction: A cross-national investigation of dual career couples. *Journal of Applied Business Research, 12,* 52–58.

19. Scarpello, V. G., & Ledvinka, J. (1988). *Personnel/human resource management: Environment and functions.* Boston: PWS-Kent; and Russell, 1991.

20. Haskell, J. R. (1993, February). Getting employees to take charge of their careers. *Training & Development,* 51–54.

21. Anastasi, A. (1976). *Psychological testing* (4th ed.). New York: Macmillan.

22. Scarpello & Ledvinka, 1988.

23. Morgan, M. A., Hall, D. T., & Martier, A. (1979). Career development strategies in industry—Where are we and where should we be? *Personnel, 56,* 13–30.

24. Rocco, J. (1991, August). Computers track high-potential managers. *HR Magazine,* 66–68.

25. Russell, 1991.

26. McDougall, B. (1994, November). Succession. *The Financial Post Magazine,* 84–89.

27. Gutteridge, Leibowitz, & Shore, 1993.

28. Howard, A. (1986). College experiences and managerial performance. *Journal of Applied Psychology, 71,* 530-552.

29. Judge, T.A., Cable, D.M., Boudreau, J.W., and Bretz, R.D. (1995) An empirical investigation of the predictors of executive career success. *Personnel Psychology, 48,* 485–519.

30. Baehr, M.E. and Orban, J.A. (1989). The role of intellectual abilities and personality characteristics in determining success in higher—level positions. *Journal of vocational behaviour, 35,* 270–287.

31. Garrett, E. M. (1994, April). Going the distance. *Small Business Reports,* 22–30.

32. *Id.*

33. Russell, 1991.

34. Gutteridge, T. (1986). Organizational career development systems: The state of the practice. In D. T. Hall & Associates (Eds.), *Career development in organizations,* 50–94. San Francisco: Jossey-Bass.

35. Gutteridge, 1986.

36. Russell, 1991.

37. Author's personal communication with the Association, November 1998.

38. Women go online to crash through the glass ceiling. (1995, April 29/May 1). *The Financial Post,* C24.

39. Noe, R. A. (1988). An investigation of the determinants of successful assigned mentoring relationships. *Personnel Psychology, 41,* 457–479.

40. *Association Management.* (1993, May). Mentor program promotes opportunity for all, 166.

41. Rothman, H. (1993, April). The boss as mentor. *Nation's Business,* 66–67.

42. Kaye, B. (1993, December). Career development—Anytime, anyplace. *Training & Development,* 46–49.

44. *Id.*

44. O'Reilly, B. (1993, April 8). How executives learn now. *Fortune,* 52–58.

45. Solomon, C. M. (1992, March). Managing the baby busters. *Personnel Journal, 52,* 54–59.

46. Williamson, R. (1996, February 2). Bike maker makes rebound. *The Globe and Mail,* B8.

47. Bryant, M. (1990, August). When employees "plateau." *Business & Health,* 46–47.

48. Fierman, J. (1993, September 6). Beating the midlife career crisis. *Fortune,* 52–62.

49. Adapted from Solomon, G.L. (1995). Unlock the potential of your older workers. *Personnel Journal, 74,* 56–66.

50. Morrisey, G. L. (1992, November). Your personal mission statement: A foundation for your future. *Training & Development,* 71–74.

51. Matejka, K., & Dunsing, R. (1993). Enhancing your advancement in the 1990s. *Management Decision, 31,* 52–54.

Chapter 10

1. Milkovich, G. T., & Newman, J. M. (1993). *Compensation* (3d ed.). Homewood, IL: Irwin.

2. McPherson, D., & Wallace, J. T. (1990). Employee benefit plans. *Human Resources Management in Canada,* 45,003. Toronto: Prentice Hall Canada.

3. Gómez-Mejía, L. R., & Balkin, D. B. (1992a). The determinants of faculty pay: An agency theory perspective. *Academy of Management Journal 35*(5), 921–955.

4. Wallace, M. J., & Fay, C. H. (1983). *Compensation theory and practice.* Boston: PWS-Kent.

5. Wallace, M. J. (1991). Sustaining success with alternative rewards. In M. L. Rock & L. A. Berger (Eds.), *The compensation handbook.* New York: McGraw-Hill.

6. Carroll, S. J. (1987). Business strategies and compensation systems. In D. B. Balkin & L. R. Gómez-Mejía (Eds.), *New perspectives on compensation.* Englewood Cliffs, NJ: Prentice Hall; and Milkovich, G. T., & Broderick, R. F. (1991). Developing a compensation strategy. In M. L. Rock & L. A. Berger (Eds.), *The compensation handbook.* New York: McGraw-Hill.

7. Ehrenberg, R. G., & Smith, R. S. (1988). *Modern labor economics.* Glenview, IL: Scott, Foresman.

8. Wallace, M. J., & Fay, C. H. (1983). *Compensation theory and practice* (1st ed.). Boston: Kent Publishing Co., 41.

9. Gómez-Mejía & Balkin, 1992a.

10. Cascio, W. F. (1990). Strategic human resource management in high technology industry. In L. R. Gómez-Mejía & M. Lawless (Eds.), *Organizational issues in high technology management.* Greenwich, CT: JAI Press; and Kail, J. C. (1987). Compensating scientists and engineers. In D. B. Balkin & L. R. Gómez-Mejía (Eds.), *New perspectives on compensation.* Englewood Cliffs, NJ: Prentice Hall.

11. Gómez-Mejía, L. R., & Welbourne, T. M. (1988). Compensation strategy: An overview and future steps. *Human Resource Planning, 11*(3), 173–189.

12. Czarnecki, A. (1995, April 10). Incentive pay is moving down the ladder. *Canadian HR Reporter,* 17–18.

13. Knight, C. (1995, December 4). Variable pay will continue to gain ground in 1996. *Canadian HR Reporter,* 1–2.

14. Gómez-Mejía, L. R., & Balkin, D. B. (1992b). *Compensation, organizational strategy, and firm performance.* Cincinnati, OH: Southwestern.

15. Milkovich, G. T., Gerhart, B., & Hannon, J. (1991). The effects of research and development intensity on managerial compensation in large organizations. *Journal of High Technology Management Research, 2*(1), 133–150.

16. Reality cheques: Here's how some B.C. companies are starting to change the way they pay. (1994, February). *B.C. Business Magazine,* 28–38.

17. Employee share plans pay off, forum hears. (1995, October 14/16). *The Financial Post,* 16.

18. Paper money: Will an employee-owned mill survive in the newsprint game? (1994, June). *Manitoba Business,* 26–27.

19. Mahoney, T. A. (1989). Employment compensation planning and strategy. In L. R. Gómez-Mejía (Ed.), *Compensation and benefits.* Washington, DC: Bureau of National Affairs.

20. Lehr, L. W. (1986, Winter). The care and flourishing of entrepreneurs at 3M. *Directors and Boards,* 18–20.

21. Bylinsky, G. (1990, July 2). Turning R&D into real products. *Fortune,* 72+.

22. Lawler, E. E., III. (1991). Paying the person: A better approach to management. Unpublished technical report, Center for Effective Organizations, University of Southern California.

23. Wolf, M. G. (1991). Theories, approaches, and practices of salary administration. In M. L. Rock & L. A. Berger (Eds.), *The compensation handbook.* New York: McGraw-Hill.

24. Tosi, H., & Tosi, L. (1986). What managers need to know about knowledge-based pay. *Organizational Dynamics, 14*(3), 52–64; and Wallace, 1991.

25. St.-Onge, Sylvie. (1998, September), Competency-based pay plans revisited. *Human Resources Professional* , 29-34.

26. Dewey, B. J. (1994, Jan.–Feb.). Changing to skill based pay. *Compensation and Benefits Review,* 38–43; Ledford, L. W. (1991). The design of skill-based plans. In M. L. Rock & L. A. Berger (Eds.), *The compensation handbook.* New York: McGraw-Hill.

27. Gómez-Mejía & Balkin, 1992b.

28. Caudron, S. (1993, June). Master the compensation maze. *Personnel Journal,* 64B–64O.

29. Knight, 1995.

30. Laabs, J. (1992, November). Ben and Jerry's caring capitalism. *Personnel Journal,* 50–57.

31. Gómez-Mejía, L. R., Balkin, D. B., & Milkovich, G. T. (1990). Rethinking your rewards for technical employees. *Organizational Dynamics, 1*(1), 107–118; and Lawler, E. E., III. (1990). *Strategic Pay.* San Francisco: Jossey-Bass.

32. Lawler, 1991.

33. Fay, C. H. (1987). Using the strategic planning process to develop a compensation strategy. *Topics in Total Compensation, 2*(2), 117–129.

34. Lloyd, D. (1994, January 24). Manager's journal: Beating the Hong Kong hiring blues, *The Wall Street Journal,* A12.

35. Freeman, R. B. (1982). Union wage practices and wage dispersion within establishments. *Industrial and Labor Relations Review, 36,* 3–21.

36. Hambrick, D. C., & Snow, C. C. (1989). Strategic reward systems. In C. C. Snow (Ed.), *Strategy, organization design, and human resources management.* Greenwich, CT: JAI Press.

37. Associated Press. (1991, April 4). What matters to Americans. *Arizona Republic,* A7.

38. Seidman, W. L., & Skancke, S. L. (1989). *Competitiveness: The executive's guide to success.* New York: M.E. Sharpe.

39. Gómez-Mejía & Balkin, 1992b.

40. Weber, J. (1990, December 10). Farewell fast track: Promotions and raises are scarcer—So what will energize managers? *Business Week,* 192–200.

41. Lawler, 1990.

42. Gómez-Mejía & Balkin, 1992a.

43. Balkin, D. B., & Gómez-Mejía, L. R. (1990). Matching compensation and organizational strategies. *Strategic Management Journal, 11,* 153–169; and Carroll, 1987.

44. Czarnecki, 1995.

45. Caudron, S. (1993, June). Master the compensation maze. *Personnel Journal,* 64B–64O.

46. Kanin-Lovers, J. (1991). Job evaluation technology. In M. L. Rock & L. A. Berger (Eds.), *The compensation handbook.* New York: McGraw-Hill.

47. Milkovich & Newman, 1994; Rock, M. L., & Berger, L. A. (Ed.) (1991). *The compensation handbook.* New York: McGraw-Hill; and issues of *Compensation & Benefits Review* and *American Compensation Association Journal.*

48. Gómez-Mejía, Balkin, & Milkovich, 1990.

49. Milkovich & Newman, 1994.

50. Additional information on the criteria, conventions, interpretation, and application of the MAA (NMTA) plan can be obtained from MAA association offices.

51. Winter, N. (1995, December 18). Broad-banding: Who's using it and why? *Canadian HR Reporter,* 8, 11.

52. NMTA Associates. (1992). National position evaluation plan. Clifton, NJ, p. 3.

53. Lichty, D. T. (1991). Compensation surveys. In M. L. Rock & L. A. Berger (Eds.), *The compensation handbook.* New York: McGraw-Hill.

54. Milkovich & Newman, 1994; Rock & Berger, 1991.

55. Dunlop, J. T. (1957). The task of contemporary wage theory. In G. W. Taylor & F. C. Pierson (Eds.), *New concepts in wage determination.* New York: McGraw-Hill; Gerhart, B., & Milkovich, G. T. (1993).

Employee compensation: Research and practice. In M. D. Dunnette & L. M. Hough (Eds.), *Handbook of industrial and organizational psychology* (Vol. 3). Palo Alto, CA: Consulting Psychologists Press; and Treiman, D. J., & Hartmann, H. I. (Eds.). (1981). *Women, work, and wages: Equal pay for jobs of equal value.* Washington, DC: National Academy Press.

56. Foster, K. E. (1985, September). An anatomy of company pay practices. *Personnel, 66–72.*

57. See, for example, Hill, F. S. (1987). *Compensation decision making.* Hinsdale, IL: Dryden.

58. Gómez-Mejía, Page, & Tornow, 197.

59. Ledford, 1991.

60. Wallace, M. J. (1990). *Rewards and renewal: America's search for competitive advantage through alternative pay strategies.* Scottsdale, AZ: American Compensation Association.

61. Gupta, N., Ledford, G. E., Jenkins, G. D., & Doty, D. (1992). Survey based prescriptions for skill-based pay. *American compensation Association Journal, 1*(1), 48–59; Ledford, L. W. (1990). The effectiveness of skill-based pay. *Perspectives in total compensation, 1*(1), 1–4; Ledford, 1991; and Tosi & Tosi, 1986.

62. Statistics Canada, Catalogue 13-271-XPB.

Chapter 11

1. Incentive plans catching on. (1995, April). *Human Resources Professional,* 20.

2. Knight, C. (1995, December 4). Variable pay will continue to gain ground in 1996. *Canadian HR Reporter,* 1, 2.

3. Gerhart, B., & Milkovich, G. T. (1993). Employee compensation: Research and practice. In M. D. Dunnette & L. M. Hough (Eds.), *Handbook of industrial and organizational psychology* (Vol. 3). Palo Alto, CA: Consulting Psychologists Press.

4. Gómez-Mejía, L. R., & Balkin, D. B. (1992). *Compensation, organizational strategy, and firm performance.* Cincinnati, OH: South-Western.

5. Milkovich, G. T., Wigdor, A. K., Broderick, R. F., & Mavor, A. S. (Eds.) (1991). *Pay for performance: Evaluating performance appraisal and merit pay.* Washington, DC: National Academy Press.

6. *Boston Globe* (1992, October 16). Teaching to the test shortchanges pupils. Article appearing in the *Arizona Republic* (October 16), A4.

7. Pearce, J. L. (1987). Why merit pay doesn't work: Implications from organizational theory. In D. B. Balkin & L. R. Gómez-Mejía (Eds.), *New perspectives on compensation.* Englewood Cliffs, NJ: Prentice Hall.

8. Gabor, A. (1991). *The man who discovered quality.* New York: Time Books; Scholtes, P. R. (1987). *An elaboration on Deming's teachings on performance appraisal.* Madison, WI: Joiner Associates; and Walton, M. (1991). *Deming management at work.* New York: G. P. Putnam's Sons.

9. Lord, R. G. (1985). Accuracy in behavioural measurement: An alternative definition based on raters' cognitive schema and signal detection theory. *Journal of Applied Psychology, 70,* 66–71; Murphy, W., & Cleveland J. (1991). *Performance appraisal: An organizational perspective,* Boston: Allyn and Bacon; and Tsui, A. S., & Ohlott, P. (1988). Multiple assessment of managerial effectiveness: Interrater agreement and consensus in effectiveness models. *Personnel Psychology, 41,* 779–802.

10. Lawler, E. E. III, & Cohen, S. G. (1992). Designing a pay system for teams. *American Compensation Association Journal, 1*(1), 6–19.

11. Gómez-Mejía, L. R., & Welbourne, T. M. (1988). Compensation strategy: An overview and future steps. *Human Resource Planning, 11*(3), 173–189.

12. Hills, F. S., Scott, D. K., Markham, S. E., & Vest, M. J. (1987) Merit pay: Just or unjust deserts? *Personnel Administrator, 32*(9), 53–64; and Hughes, C.L. (1986). The demerit of merit. *Personnel Administrator, 31*(6), 40.

13. Kanter, R. M. (1987) The attack on pay. *Harvard Business Review, 65*(2), 60–67.

14. *Business Week* (1992, July 6), 38.

15. Schwab, D. P. (1974). Conflicting impacts of pay on employee motivation and satisfaction. *Personnel Journal, 53*(3), 190–206.

16. Gómez-Mejía & Balkin, 1992.

17. Deci, E. L. (1972). The effects of contingent and non-contingent rewards and controls on intrinsic motivation. *Organizational Behaviour and Human Performance, 8,* 15–31.

18. *Profit-Building Strategies for Business Owners* (1992, December), *22*(12), 23–24.

19. Greeley, T. P., & Oshsner, R. C. (1986). Putting merit pay back into salary administration. *Topics in Total Compensation, 1*(1), 14–30; and Smith, J. M., President of American Compensation Association. (1990, July 9). Interview appearing in the *Arizona Republic,* B-6.

20. Gómez-Mejía, & Balkin, 1992.

21. Perry, D. (1991, March). Reworking reward and recognition. *Human Resources Management in Canada,* 40,518–40,519. Toronto: Prentice Hall Canada.

22. Gómez-Mejía, L. R., Page, R. C., & Tornow, W. (1982). A comparison of the practical utility of traditional, statistical, and hybrid job evaluation approaches. *Academy of Management Journal, 25,* 790–809.

23. McAdams, J. L., & Hawk, E. J. (1992). Capitalizing on human assets through performance based rewards. *American Compensation Association Journal, 1*(1), 60–71.

24. Big payoff for employee suggestions. (1995, September 25). *Canadian HR Reporter,* 7.

25. Greenberg, J. (1990). Looking fair vs. being fair: Managing impressions of organizational justice. In L. Cummings & B. M. Staw (Eds.), *Research in organizational behaviour* (Vol. 2). Greenwich, CT: JAI Press.

26. Milkovich, G. T., & Newman, J. M. (1994). *Compensation* (3d ed.). Plano, TX: B.P.I.

27. Gómez-Mejía, L. R., & Balkin, D. B. (1989). Effectiveness of individual and aggregate compensation strategies. *Industrial Relations, 28,* 431–445.

28. Lawler, E. E. III. (1989). The strategic design of pay-for-performance programs. In L. R. Gómez-Mejía (Ed.), *Compensation and benefits.* Washington, DC: Bureau of National Affairs; and Lawler, E. E. III. (1990). *Strategic pay.* San Francisco: Jossey-Bass.

29. Mount, M. K. (1987). Coordinating salary action and performance appraisal. In D. B. Balkin & L. R. Gómez-Mejía, *New perspectives on compensation.* Englewood Cliffs, NJ: Prentice Hall.

30. Locke, E. A., Shaw, K., Saari, L. M., & Latham, G. P. (1981). Goal setting and task performance: 1969–1980. *Psychological Bulletin, 90,* 125–152.

31. Fuchsberg, G. (1990, April 18). Culture shock. *The Wall Street Journal,* R5:1.

32. See Longenecker, C. O., Sims, H. P., & Gioia, D. A. (1987). Behind the mask: The politics of employee appraisal. *Academy of Management Executive, 1,* 183–193, for appraisal issues; see Bartol, K. M., & Martin, D. C. (1989). Influences on managerial pay allocations: A dependency perspective. *Personnel Psychology, 41,* 361–378, for a discussion specific to pay decisions.

33. Hills et al., 1987.

34. Kanter, R. M. (1987).

35. Chrzan, C. (1996, February 26). The many faces of team incentives: Message worked but gate needed to control OT. *Canadian HR Reporter,* 15.

36. Winter, N. (1995, October 23). Compensation trends and fads: What are "best practices" anyway? *Canadian HR Reporter,* 6.

37. Lawler & Cohen, 1992.

38. Liden, R. C., & Mitchell, T. R. (1983). The effects of group interdependence on supervisor performance evaluations. *Personnel Psychology, 36,* 289–299.

39. Reynolds, C. (1992). Developing global strategies in total compensation. *American Compensation Association Journal, 1*(1), 74–85.

40. Albanese, R., & VanFleet, D. D. (1985). Rational behaviour in groups: The freeriding tendency. *Academy of Management Review, 10,* 244–255.

41. Henerman, F. and Von Hippel, (1995, November 28). Interview appearing in *the Wall Street Journal,* A1.

42. Gordon, D. M., Edwards, R., & Reich, M. (1982). *Segmented work, divided workers: The historical transformation of labor in the United States.* London: Cambridge University Press.

43. Mohrman, A. M., Mohrman, S. A., & Lawler, E. E. (1992). *Performance measurement, evaluation and incentives.* Boston: Harvard Business School.

44. Moorthy, M. (1996, February 26). The many faces of team incentives: Incentives grow as targets met. *Canadian HR Reporter,* 15.

45. Martell, K., Carroll, S. J., & Gupta, A. K. (1992). What executive human resource management practices are most effective when innovativeness requirements are high? In L. R. Gómez-Mejía & M. W. Lawless (Eds.), *Top management and effective leadership in high technology.* Greenwich, CT: JAI Press.

46. Pinchot, G. (1985). *Intrapreneuring.* New York: Harper & Row.

47. Selz, M. (1994, January 11). Testing self-managed teams, entrepreneur hopes to lose job. *The Wall Street Journal,* B1–B2.

48. Kapel, C. (1995, April). The feeling's mutual. *Human Resources Professional,* 9–13.

49. Tully, S. (1993, November 1). Your paycheck gets exciting. *Fortune,* 83–84.

50. McGregor, D. (1960). *The human side of enterprise.* New York: McGraw-Hill.

51. Ross, T. L., Hatcher, L., & Ross, R. A. (1989, May). The incentive switch: From piecework to companywide gainsharing. *Management Review,* 22–26.

52. Sullivan, J. F. (1988). The future of merit pay programs. *Compensation and Benefits Review, 20*(3), 22–30.

53. Gómez-Mejía & Balkin, 1992.

54. Florkowski, G. W. (1987). The organizational impact of profit sharing. *Academy of Management Review, 12,* 622–636.

55. Divide and conquer: The turnaround at IBM—Canada's manufacturing spinoff. (1994, December). *Canadian Business,* 113–116.

56. Taking the leap of faith in starting one's own business. (1995, October 28/30). *The Financial Post,* 14–15.

57. Mark, K. (1995, April). Buyout and the bottom line. *Human Resources Professional,* 17–19.

58. Cheadle, A. (1989). Explaining patterns of profit sharing activity. *Industrial Relations, 28,* 387–401.

59. *ROB Magazine,* July 1998. (Internet: http://www.robmagazine.com/top1000/other/ceo–headlegs.htm).

60. *Id.*

61. Average pay packet for CEOs $800,000, study shows (1995, September 15). *Canadian Press Newswire.*

62. Hyman, J. S. (1991). Long term incentives. In M. L. Rock & L. A. Berger (Eds.), *The compensation handbook.* New York: McGraw-Hill.

63. Crystal, G. S. (1988, June 6). The wacky, wacky world of CEO pay. *Fortune,* 68–78.

64. Reynolds, 1992.

65. Gómez-Mejía, L. R. (1994). Executive compensation. Chapter in Ferris, R. (6th ed.). *Advances in personnel/human resource management.* Cincinnati, OH: JAI Press, 25–50.

66. Gómez-Mejía & Balkin, 1992

67. *Id.*

68. Colletti, J. A. (1986). Job evaluation and pay plans: Field sales representatives. In J. Famularo (Ed.), *Handbook of human resources administration.* New York: McGraw-Hill; Colletti, J. A., & Cichelli, D. J. (1991). Increasing sales force effectiveness through the compensation plan. In M. L. Rock & L. A. Berger (Eds.), *The compensation handbook.* New York: McGraw-Hill; and Stanton, W. J., & Buskirk, R. H. (1987). *Management of the sales force* (7th ed.). Homewood, IL: Irwin.

69. McGugan, I. (1994, March). The new blue. *Canadian Business,* 35–36.

70. Clark, C. J. (1996, February 26). The many faces of team incentives: Safety, service are "make or break." *Canadian HR Reporter,* 15–16.

71. Breakin' all the rules: Competing in today's global economy means you have to step off the traditional marketing path and take real risks. (1995, June). *Profit,* 49–54.

72. Incentive pay focusses on quality. (1983, July). *HR Focus,* 15.

Chapter 12

1. Health benefits: Here and now. (1994, November). *Benefits Canada,* 27–31.

2. Charles, J. (1995, January). Some assembly required. *Benefits Canada,* 24–26, 28.

3. KPMG. (1994). *Nineteenth survey of benefits costs in Canada.* (Table 9.) Toronto: KPMG.

4. Benefits: Health down; incentives up. (1994, October). *Human Resources Management in Canada.* Report Bulletin 140, p. 1. Toronto: Prentice Hall Canada.

5. Nolan, C. (1996, March). Stressed to the max. *Benefits Canada,* 29–33.

6. *Id.*

7. Bak, L., & Dempsey, S. (1996, May). Rising to the challenge. *Benefits Canada,* 33–38.

8. *Id.*

9. Employees now sharing the burden of escalating health care costs. (1994, May 9). *Canadian HR Reporter,* 11.

10. Dentists fight health benefits tax. (1994, December). *Human Resources Management in Canada.* Report Bulletin 144, p. 1. Toronto: Prentice Hall Canada.

11. Health benefits: Here and now, 1994.

12. Knight, C. (1995, August 14). Employers address health care issues. *Canadian HR Reporter,* 1, 7.

13. *Id.*

14. Knight, C. (1996, January 12). Feds plan to reduce drug costs in public service. *Canadian HR Reporter,* 1.

15. Knight, C. (1995, October 9). Drug plan could save 40% of costs. *Canadian HR Reporter,* 1.

16. Krahn, H. (1995, Winter). Non-standard work on the rise. *Perspectives.* Statistics Canada Catalogue No. 75-001E, Table 1, p. 37.

17. Knight, C. (1995, March 27). Saskatchewan legislates benefits for part-timers. *Canadian HR Reporter,* 1.

18. Part timers get stat benefits in Saskatchewan. (1995, January). *Human Resources Management in Canada.* Report Bulletin 143, p. 4. Toronto: Prentice Hall Canada.

19. Nolan, C. (1996, February). Catch-32. *Benefits Canada,* 39–40.

20. Part-timers deserve benefits too. (1994, December). *Benefits Canada,* 11.

21. Question of the month: "What do you see as the future of benefits for part-time workers?" (1996, February). *Benefits Canada,* 17.

22. Felix, S. (1995, May). Benefits on the go. *Benefits Canada,* 21–23.

23. Payroll taxes blamed for job loss. (1995, August). *Human Resources Management in Canada.* Report Bulletin 150, p. 1. Toronto: Prentice Hall Canada.

24. Stokes, D. (1996, February 3). Tax burden leaves small players little incentive for hiring. *The Financial Post,* 45.

25. McCaffery, R. M. (1989). Employee benefits programs. In L. R. Goméz-Mejía (Ed.) *Compensation and benefits.* Washington, DC: The Bureau of National Affairs.

26. Lawler, E. E. III. (1990). *Strategic compensation.* San Francisco: Jossey-Bass.

27. KPMG, 1994.

28. A very useful overview of employee benefits in Canada, used as a reference throughout this chapter, is provided by McPherson, D. L., & Wallace, J. T. (1994, October), "Employee benefit plans," in *Human Resources Management in Canada.* Toronto: Prentice Hall Canada.

29. KPMG Canada website: http://www.kpmg.ca/abc/vl/update/ud9710.htm October 1997.

30. Rontiris, G. (1996, February/March). Brave new world. *Human Resources Professional,* 10–11.

31. Experience rating penalties for UI? (1995, May). *Human Resources Management in Canada.* Report Bulletin 147, pp. 1–2. Toronto: Prentice Hall Canada.

32. Spoils of battle. (1994, December). *Benefits Canada,* 29–31.

33. Wiley, J. L. (1993, August). Preretirement education: Benefits outweigh liability. *HR Focus,* 11.

34. Rules of the game: A primer on the laws and rules which govern why pensions plans look and act the way they do. (1995, March). *Benefits Canada,* 47.

35. *Id.*

36. DeCenzo, D. A., & Holoviak, S. J. (1990). *Employee benefits.* Englewood Cliffs, NJ: Prentice Hall.

37. Akyeampong, E. B. (1995, Spring). Missing work. *Perspectives.* Statistics Canada Catalogue 75-001E, pp. 13–16.

38. Kilborn, P. T. (1992, November 30). Abuse of sick leave rises and companies fight back. *The New York Times,* A12.

39. Matthes, K. (1992). In pursuit of leisure: Employees want more time off. *HR Focus,* 1.

40. Question of the month: Are you topping up your employees' maternity benefits? (1995, November). *Benefits Canada,* 13.

41. Goodson, L. (1992, December). Sweet charity. *Human Resources Professional,* 11–13.

42. With a little help... (1995, March 6). *Toronto Star,* C1, C2.

43. Romanow, P. (1995, May). Business and reservists. *Human Resources Professional,* 13–14.

44. Severance benefits shrink. (1995, April). *Human Resources Professional,* 20.

45. Question of the month: Do you have a benefits plan for your employees? (1995, October). *Benefits Canada,* 13.

46. Nolan, March 1996.

47. Question of the month: What benefits are you offering to help employees of the sandwich generation deal with eldercare and childcare? (1996, May). *Benefits Canada,* 13.

48. Bonanno, R. (1994, January 17). Childcare consortiums: The future of work-related childcare? *Canadian HR Reporter,* 10–11.

49. Employer-provided daycare may increase. (1996, February). *Human Resources Management in Canada.* Report Bulletin 156, pp. 2–3. Toronto: Prentice Hall Canada.

50. Henderson, R. (1989). *Compensation management.* (5th ed.). Englewood Cliffs, NJ: Prentice Hall.

51. Charles, 1995.

52. Fuchsberg, G. (1992, April 22). What is pay, anyway? *The Wall Street Journal,* R3.

53. Gordon, 1995.

54. McCaffery, R. M. (1992). *Employee benefit programs: A total compensation perspective.* (2nd ed.). Boston: PWS-Kent.

55. Wilson, M., Northcraft, G. R., & Neale, M. A. (1985). The perceived value of fringe benefits. *Personnel Psychology, 38,* 309–320.

56. Scott, W. (1995, June 19). *Canadian HR Reporter,* 19.

57. Nolan, C. (1995, December). Same-sex rights. *Benefits Canada,* 59–60.

58. KPMG Canada website: http://www.kpmg.ca:80/abc/vl/benefax/bfa9807b.htm July 1998.

Chapter 13

1. Lilley, W. (1995, April). Banking on equity. *Report on Business Magazine, 67,* 69.

2. Kapel, C. (1993, June). Brave new breeds. *Human Resources Professional,* 17–21.

3. Noer, D. M. (1993). *Healing the wounds: Overcoming the trauma of layoffs and revitalizing downsized organizations,* 103–104. San Francisco: Jossey-Bass.

4. Johnson, P. R., & Gardner, S. (1989). Legal pitfalls of employee handbooks. *SAM Advanced Management Journal, 54*(2), 42–46.

5. Hesser, R. G. (1991, July). Watch your language. *Small Business Reports,* 45–49.

6. Johnson & Gardner, 1989.

7. Brady, T. (1993, June). Employee handbooks: Contracts or empty promises? *Management Review,* 33–35.

8. Aronoff, C. E., & Ward, J. L. (1993, January). Rules for nepotism. *Nation's Business,* 64–65.

9. Lawler, 1992.

10. Screen to screen: Will video-conferencing ever overcome our human need for face-to-face meetings? (1995, September). *B.C. Business Magazine,* 35–39.

11. Flanagan, P. (1994, February). Videoconferencing changes the corporate meeting. *Management Review,* 7; and Bhargava, S. W., & Coy, P. (1991, November). Video-screen meetings: Still out of sight. *Business Week,* 162E.

12. Mark, K. (1995, October). Cost management via flexible benefits. *Human Resources Professional,* 7–9.

13. *Information Management Forum.* (1993, January). Voice mail or voice pony express, insert into *Management Review,* 3.

14. Weeks, D. (1995, February) Voice mail: Blessing or curse? *World Traveler,* 51–54.

15. Lawler, 1992.

16. Pearl, J. A. (1993, July). The E-mail quandary. *Management Review,* 48–51.

17. Crawford, M. (1993, May). The new office etiquette. *Canadian Business,* 22–31.

18. Goodman, J. (1996, June). The paperless chase. *Human Resources Professional,* 6–7.

19. Mintzberg, H. (1975, July–August). The manager's job: Folklore or fact. *Harvard Business Review 53,* 69–71.

20. Michaels, E. A. (1989, February). Business meetings. *Small Business Reports,* 82–88.

21. Interview of Deborah Tannen by L. A. Lusardi (1990, July). Power talk. *Working Woman,* 92–94.

22. Elashmawi, F. (1991, November). Multicultural business meetings and presentations. *Tokyo Business Today, 59*(11), 66–68.

23. McKay, S. (1995, May/June). Building morale: The key to successful change. *Nonprofit World,* 40–46.

24. Gómez-Mejía, L. R., & Balkin, D. B. (1992). *Compensation, organizational strategy, and firm performance.* Cincinnati, OH: Southwestern. 25. Aram, J. D., & Salipante, P. F., Jr. (1981). An evaluation of organizational due process in the resolution of employee/employer conflict. *Academy of Management Review, 16,* 197–204.

26. Kirrane, D. (1990). EAPs: Dawning of a new age. *HR Magazine, 35*(1), 30–34.

27. Filipowicz, C. A. (1979). The troubled employee: Whose responsibility? *Personnel Administrator, 24*(6), 5–10.

28. Carson, K. D., & Balkin, D. B. (1992). An employee assistance model of the health care management for employees with alcohol-related problems. *Journal of Employment Counselling, 29,* 146–156.

29. Charles, J. (1995, February). Life skills. *Benefits Canada.*

30. Cascio, W. F. (1991). *Costing human resources: The financial impact of behaviour in organizations* (Vol. 6) (3rd ed.). Boston: PWS-Kent.

31. Luthans, F., & Waldersee, R. (1989). What do we really know about EAPs? *Human Resource Management, 28,* 385—401.

32. Meyers, D. W. (1986). *Human resources management.* Chicago: Commerce Clearing House.

33. Orsburn, J. D., Moran, L., Musselwhite, E., & Zenger, J. H. (1990). *Self-directed work teams.* Homewood, IL: Business One Irwin.

Chapter 14

1. Canto-Thaler, J. (1996, June 3). Wrongful hiring? You bet—and it's a growth industry. *Canadian HR Reporter,* 13–14.

2. Gibb-Clark, M. (1995, September 21). "Snitch-line" called insult. *The Globe and Mail,* B5.

3. Davidson, D. V., Knowles, B. E., Forsythe, L. M., & Jesperson, R. R. (1987). *Business law* (2nd ed.). Boston, MA: Kent.

4. Sashkin, M., & Kiser, K. J. (1993). *Putting total quality management to work.* San Francisco, CA: Berrett-Koehler.

5. Holley, W. H., & Jennings, K. M. (1991). *The labour relations process* (4th ed.). Chicago, IL: Dryden.

6. Elkouri, F., & Elkouri, E. A. (1973). *How arbitration works* (3rd ed.). Washington, DC: Bureau of National Affairs.

7. Bullock, K. (1994, October). Termination of employment. *Human Resources Management in Canada* (p. 75,017). Toronto: Prentice Hall Canada.

8. Wagar, T. (1996, June). Wrongful dismissal: Perception vs. reality. *Human Resources Professional,* 8, 10.

9. Wagar, 1996, 75,020.

10. Gale, W. (1994, October). Dismissed, constructively? *Human Resources Professional,* 10–11.

11. *Id.*

12. Farson, M. (1994, August). All's fair... *Human Resources Professional,* 19–20.

13. Shouldice, L. (1995, May). Unjust dismissal provisions: Broad remedial options available to employees. *Human Resources Management in Canada* (pp. 80,519–80,524). Toronto: Prentice Hall Canada.

14. Utroska, D. R. (1992, November). Management in Europe. *Management Review,* 21–24.

15. Hamilton, J. O. (1991, June 3). A video game that tells if employees are fit for work. *Business Week,* 36; and Maltby, L. (1990).

16. Controlling employee theft. (1993, September). *CMA Management Accounting Magazine,* 16–19.

17. Snyder, N. H., & Blair, K. E. (1989). Dealing with employee theft. *Business Horizons, 32* (3), 27–34; Burn, D. (1994, October). An ounce of prevention. *Human Resources Professional,* 13–15; Avoid fraud in lean management. (1995, June). *Human Resources Management in Canada.* Report Bulletin 148 (p. 2). Toronto: Prentice Hall Canada.

18. *USA Today.* (1993, May 24). Bosses peek at E-mail, B, 1:2.

19. *Business Week.* (1990, January 15). Is your boss spying on you? 74–75.

20. See Garson, B. (1988). *The electronic sweatshop: How computers are transforming the office of the future into the factory of the past.* New York: Penguin Books; Piturro, M. (1989, May). Employee performance monitoring ... or meddling? *Management Review,* 31–33.

21. Coale, K. (1992, February 17). Northern Telecom sees, hears no "evil." *Infoworld,* 50.

22. Griffith, T. L. (1993, February). Teaching Big Brother to be a team player: Computer monitoring and quality. *Academy of Management Executive,* 7(1), 73–80.

23. Near, J., & Miceli, M. (1985). Organizational dissidence: The case of whistleblowing. *Journal of Business Ethics, 4,* 1–16.

24. Millan, L. (1994, June 20). Whistle blowers pay heavy price. *Canadian HR Reporter,* 1.

25. *Id.*

26. McHough, M. (1991, August 26). Blowing whistle on company can be risky venture. *The Financial Post,* 2.

27. Millan, L. (1994, June 20). Quebec whistle-blowing case raises need for legislation. *Canadian HR Reporter,* 1.

28. Hamilton, J. (1991, June 3). Blowing the whistle without paying the piper. *Business Week,* 138–139.

29. *Id.*

30. Boyle, R. D. (1990). A review of whistleblower protection and suggestions for change. *Labour Law Journal, 41*(12), 821–828.

31. Legault, A. (1993, July/August). Guilt by association? *Human Resources Professional,* 14–15.

32. Weinstein, S. (1992, September). Teams without managers. *Progressive Grocer,* 101–104.

33. Redeker, J. R. (1989). *Employee discipline.* Washington, DC: Bureau of National Affairs.

34. *Id.*

35. Osigweh, C., Yg, A. B., & Hutchison, W. R. (1989, Fall). Positive discipline. *Human Resource Management, 28*(3), 367–383.

36. Bryant, A. W. (1984). Replacing punitive discipline with a positive approach. *Pe nel Administrator, 29*(2), 79–87.

37. Osigweh et al., 1989.

38. *Id.*

39. Sherman, C.V. (1987). *From losers to winners.* New York; American Management Association.

40. Bureau of National Affairs. (1987). *Grievance guide* (7th ed.). Washington, DC: Bureau of National Affairs.

41. Redeker, 1989.

42. Do flexible work arrangements really lure and retain high-quality employees to an organization? (1995, February). *Benefits Canada,* 10.

43. Breuer, N. L. (1993, September). Resources can relieve ADA fears. *Personnel Journal,* 131–142.

44. Sherman, C. V. (1987). *From losers to winners.* New York: American Management Association.

45. Winter, N. (1995, December 18). Broadbanding: Who's using it and why? *Canadian HR Reporter,* 8.

Chapter 15

1. Windsor's enterprise going where no TV news station has gone before. (1995, April). *Broadcaster,* 12–14.

2. Brett, J. M. (1980). Why employees want unions. *Organizational Dynamics, 9,* 316–332.

3. For a more detailed discussion of unions and collective bargaining in Canada, the reader may wish to consult Craig, A. W. J., & Solomon, N. A. (1996), *The system of industrial relations in Canada* (Toronto: Prentice Hall Canada), which has informed this overview.

4. Craig, A. W. J., & Solomon, N. A. (1996). *The system of industrial relations in Canada* (5th ed.) (p. 230). Toronto: Prentice Hall Canada.

5. Akyeampong, Ernest B. (1997) Table 2 in A statistical portrait of the union movement. *Perspectives,* Winter 1997. Statistics Canada, Catalogue no. 75-001-XPE, 48–49.

6. Data presented in Craig, A. W. J., & Solomon, N. A., 1996, 184.

7. Jobs: Government cuts and corporate layoffs create a national mood of insecurity. (1996, March 11). *Maclean's,* 12–16.

8. Freeman, R. B. (1989). The changing status of unionism around the world. In W. C. Huang (Ed.), *Organized labor at the crossroads.* Kalamazoo, MI: W. E. Upjohn Institute for Employee Research.

9. Chang, C., & Sorrentino, C. (1991, December). Union membership statistics in 12 countries. *Monthly Labor Review,* 46–53.

10. Ofori-Dankwa, J. (1993). Murray and Reshef revisited: Toward a typology/theory of paradigms of national trade union movements. *Academy of Management Review, 18,* 269–292.

11. *Id.*

12. Mills, D. Q. (1989). *Labor-management relations.* New York: McGraw-Hill.

13. Wilpert, B. (1975). Research in industrial democracy and the German case. *Industrial Relations Journal, 6*(1), 53–64.

14. Hoerr, J. (1991, May–June). What should unions do? *Harvard Business Review,* 30–45.

15. Marsland, S. E., & Beer, M. (1985). Note on Japanese management and employment systems. In M. Beer and B. Spector (Eds.), *Readings in human resource management.* New York: The Free Press.

16. *The Economist.* (1996, February 10). Stakeholder capitalism: Unhappy families, 23–25.

17. *Id.*

18. Delaney, J. T. (1991). Unions and human resource policies. In K. Rowland and G. Ferris (Eds.). *Research in personnel and human resources management.* Greenwich, CT: JAI Press.

19. McKenna, L. (1995, Summer). Moving beyond adversarial relationships. *Canadian Business Review, 22*(2), 25–27.

20. Chrysler concentrates on change. (1994, October 3). *Plant,* 10, 24.

21. Kapel, 1996.

22. Davenport, C. (1993, December). Labour pains. *Human Resources Professional,* 13–15.

23. Griffin, R. W., Ebert, R. J., & Starke, F. A. (1996). *Business* (2nd ed.) (p. 262). Toronto: Prentice Hall Canada.

24. *Id.*

25. Size counts: Small isn't beautiful or even desirable, at least when it comes to business. (1995). *The Financial Post Magazine,* 54–56+.

26. *Id.*

27. Kochan, T. A., & Katz, H. C. (1988). *Collective bargaining and industrial relations.* Homewood, IL: Irwin.

28. Magna-mania: Resurrection of his on-the-brink auto parts empire didn't satisfy Frank Stronach, who plans growth and monuments with equal flair. (1995, August 12/14). *The Financial Post,* 12–13.

29. Goodbye CUPE: Ponoka school board employees vote to decertify. (1995, September 11). *Western Report,* 18.

30. Foulkes, F. (1980). *Personnel policies in large nonunion companies.* Englewood Cliffs, NJ: Prentice Hall.

31. The Irving way right for workers, company says. (1995, December 15). *Canadian Press Newswire.*

32. Craig & Solomon, 1996, 216.

33. Summers, C. W. (1991). Unions without majorities: The potentials of the NRLA. *Proceedings of the 43rd Annual Meeting of the IRRA.* Madison, WI: IRRA, p. 154.; Thomason, T. (1994, January). The effect of accelerated certification processes on union organizing success in Ontario. *Industrial and Labor Relations Review, 47*(2), 210–211.

34. Craig & Solomon, 1996, 217.

35. CP strike raises JITters. (1995, April). *Human Resources Management in Canada.* Report Bulletin 146 (p. 9). Toronto: Prentice Hall Canada.

36. Walton, B., & McKersie, R. (1965). *A behavioral theory of labor negotiations.* New York: McGraw-Hill.

37. Employer has right to homework agreement. (1994, August). *Human Resources Management in Canada.* Report Bulletin 138 (p. 9). Toronto: Prentice Hall Canada.

38. TTC workers get 1% raise and right to wear shorts. (1996, April). *Human Resources Management in Canada.* Report Bulletin 158 (p. 9). Toronto: Carswell.

39. Freeman, R. B., & Medoff, J. L. (1984). *What do unions do?* New York: Basic Books.

40. Arbitrators get more power under SCC decision. (1995, July). *Human Resources Management in Canada.* Report Bulletin 149 (pp. 6–7). Toronto: Prentice Hall Canada.

41. Freeman, R. B., & Medoff, J. L. (1979). The two faces of unionism. *The Public Interest, 57,* 69–93.

42. Abraham, K. G., & Medoff, J. L. (1985). Length of service and promotions in union and nonunion work groups. *Industrial and Labor Relations Review, 38,* 408–420.

43. Abraham, K. G., & Medoff, J. L. (1984). Length of service and layoffs in union and nonunion work groups. *Industrial and Labor Relations Review, 38,* 87–97.

44. Employment security at heart of CP strike. (1995, March). *Human Resources Management in Canada.* Report Bulletin 145 (p. 9). Toronto: Prentice Hall Canada.

45. Rail jobs can be axed: Federal arbitrators eliminate railways job-for-life contract. (1995, June 15). *The Financial Post Daily,* 1, 2.

46. Foulkes, 1980.

47. Bernardin, J., & Beatty, R. (1984). *Performance appraisal: Assessing human behavior at work.* Boston: Kent.

48. Abraham, K. G., & Farber, H. S. (1988). Returns to seniority in union and nonunion jobs: A new look at evidence. *Industrial and Labor Relations Review, 42,* 3–19; and Freeman & Medoff, 1984.

49. Bartel, A. P. (1989). *Formal employee training programs and their impact on labor productivity: Evidence from a human resources survey.* National Bureau of Economic Research Working Paper No. 3026.

50. Food firms start council to train workers. (1995, October 19). *The Financial Post Daily,* 13.

51. Pomeroy, F. (1995, Summer). Workplace change: A union perspective. *Canadian Business Review, 22*(2), 17–19.

52. Freeman, R. B. (1982). Union wage practices and wage dispersion within establishments. *Industrial and Labor Relations Review, 36,* 3–21.

53. Id.

54. Driscoll, J. W. (1979). Working creatively with a union: Lessons from the Scanlon Plan. *Organizational Dynamics, 8,* 61–80.

55. Freeman, R. B. (1981). The effect of unionism on fringe benefits. *Industrial and Labor Relations Review, 34,* 489–509.

56. Fosu, A. G. (1984). Unions and fringe benefits: Additional evidence. *Journal of Labor Research, 5,* 247, 254.

57. Gómez-Mejía, L. R., & Balkin, D. B. (1992). *Compensation, organizational strategy and firm performance.* Cincinnati: Southwestern.

58. Freeman, 1991.

59. Union sues CP over pension cuts. (1996, January). *Human Resources Management in Canada.* Report Bulletin 155 (p. 9). Toronto: Carswell.

60. Foulkes, 1980.

Chapter 16

1. The face of workplace violence. (1995, August 14). *Canadian HR Reporter,* 20.

2. Peter's principles: A profile of Lifetime Achievement Award winner Peter Robson. (1995, January/February). *Occupational Health and Safety,* 17.

3. Human Resources Development Canada (1998). Occupational Injuries and their Cost in Canada. Catalogue No. L2-38/1998-IN.

4. Robertson, D. (1994, November). Occupational health and safety. *Human resources management in Canada* (p. 60,017). Toronto: Prentice Hall Canada.

5. Human Resources Development Canada (1998). Occupational Injuries and their Cost in Canada. Catalogue No; L2-38/1998-IN.

6. Human Resources Development Canada (1998). Data from Table 1 in Occupational Injuries and their Cost in Canada. Catalogue No; L2-38/1998-IN.

7. Human Resources Development Canada (1998). Calcualted by author based on data from Table 1 in Occupational Injuries and their Cost in Canada. Catalogue No; L2-38/1998-IN.

8. Sherman, A. W., & Bohlander, G. W. (1992). *Managing human resources* (9th ed.), 398. Cincinnati, OH: Southwestern.

9. McCaffery, R. M. (1992). *Employee benefit programs: A total compensation perspective,* 57–58. Boston: PWS-Kent.

10. *Id.,* 59–60.

11. Robertson, 1994, 60,054.

12. Robertson, 1994, 60,057.

13. Canto-Thaler, J. E. (1995, September 11). Size of OHSA fines hard to predict. *Canadian HR Reporter,* 8.

14. American Society for Personnel Administration. (1987, October). Few companies have policies to cover employees with AIDS. *Resource, 6*(12), 6–7.

15. Bonanno, R. (1994, April 11). AIDS education rare in workplace. *Canadian HR Reporter,* 12–13.

16. Bureau of National Affairs. (1993, April 5). AIDS ranks as chief health concern of half of U.S. workers, survey says. *BNA Employee Relations Weekly, 11,* 4.

17. Newton, E. (1996, February 26). Clear policy, active ear can reduce violence. *Canadian HR Reporter,* 16–17; Pearson, G. (1995, August 14). Workplace violence: Incidence rises in health care, social services. *Canadian HR Reporter,* 19–20.

18. Looking out for trouble. (1995, March/April). *Occupational Health and Safety,* 34–37.

19. *Id.*

20. Newton, 1996.

21. *Id.*

22. Looking out for trouble, 1995.

23. Commerce Clearing House. (1993, December 20). Employers should take measures to minimize potential for workplace violence. *Ideas and Trends in Personnel, 317,* 201–208; and Thornburg, L. (1993, July). When violences hits business. *HR Magazine 38*(7), 40–45.

24. Arbitrators snuff out claims of injustice by smoking workers. (1995, September/October). *Canadian Occupational Safety,* 15–16+.

25. A tale of two smoking policies. (1996, May 6). *Canadian HR Reporter,* 2, 10.

26. Fry, E. H. (1990, November–December). Not smoking in the workplace: The real issue. *Business Horizons, 33*(6), 13–17; Marley, S. (1992, February 10). Employers pay when workers smoke: Study. *Business Insurance, 26*(6), 3, 22.

27. Smokers could get burned by employers. (1996, January 10). *The Financial Post Daily,* 1.

28. Lewis, J. (1996, February 12). Employers move to reduce RSI losses. *Canadian HR Reporter,* 20–21.

29. Matthes, K. (1992). A prescription of healthier offices. *HR Focus, 69,* 4–5.

30. Sheedy, J. E. (1992). VDTs and vision complaints: A survey. *Information Display: The Official Journal of the Society for Information Display, 8,* 20.

31. Lewis, 1996.

32. Horowitz, J. M. (1992, October 12). Crippled by computers. *Time,* 70–72; and Mallory, J., & Bradford, H. (1989, January 30). An invisible workplace hazard gets harder to ignore. *Business Week,* 92–93.

33. Kiesler, S., & Finholt, T. (1988, December). The mystery of RSI. *American Psychologist, 43,* 1004–15.

34. Pace, L., & Smits, S. (1989, April). Workplace substance abuse: A proactive approach. *Personnel Journal,* 84–88.

35. Anthony, W. P., Perrewe, P. L., & Kacmar, K. M. (1993). *Strategic human resource management,* 534–535. Fort Worth, TX: Dryden.

36. Murphy, B. (1989, Summer). Drug testing in the utility industry. *Management Quarterly,* 16–30.

37. Adler, T. (1989, May). Experts urge control of aerospace toxics. *APA Monitor,* 1.

38. Van Alpen, T. (1995, April 17). New epidemic in the workplace? *The Toronto Star,* B1, B3.

39. Current OH&S issues: A look at the six hottest topics. (1995, July/August). *Occupational Health & Safety,* 31–37.

40. *Id.*

41. Making WHMIS training relevant. (1995, July/August). *Occupational Health & Safety,* 38–41.

42. Fisher, C. D., Schoenfeldt, L .F., & Shaw, J. B. (1993). *Human resource management* (2nd ed.), 646–653. Boston: Houghton Mifflin; and Schuler, R. S., and Huber, V. L. (1993). *Personnel and human resource management* (5th ed.), 667–669. Minneapolis: West..

43. Thompson, R. (1990). Fighting the high cost of workers' comp. *Nation's Business, 78*(3), 28.

44. Maslach, C., & Jackson, S. E. (1981). The measurement of experienced burnout. *Journal of Occupational Behaviour, 2,* 99–113.

45. Gordes, C. L. & Dougherty, T. W. (1993) A review and integration of research on job burnout. *Academy of Management Review, 18,* 621–656.

46. Kahill, S. (1988). Symptoms of professional burnout: A review of the empirical evidence. *Canadian Psychology, 29,* 284–297.

47. Gordes & Dougherty, 1993.

48. Jackson, S. E., & Maslach, C. (1982). After effects of job-related stress: Families as victims. *Journal of Occupational Behaviour, 3,* 63–77.

49. Kirrane, D. (1990, January). EAPs: Dawning of a new age. *HR Magazine,* 34.

50. Anthony, Perrewe, & Kacmar, 1993, 535–536; and Pesternak, C. (1990, August). HRM update. *HR Magazine,* 24.

51. Hirsh, J. (1986, October 5). What's new in wellness programs? *The New York Times,* F19.

52. Life skills: The ultimate employer-sponsored benefit may be to encourage workers to get a life. (1995, February 17). *Benefits Canada,* 17.

53. *Id.*

54. The high cost of health: Will business be a partner in the solution? (1995, April). *CMA Management Accounting Magazine,* 12–14.

55. The stress mess: If you're an employer in B.C., not to mention a taxpayer, it's starting to cost you a bundle. (1995, December). *BC Business Magazine,* 20–27.

Chapter 17

1. Ip, G. (1996, July 6). The borderless world. *The Globe and Mail,* D1, D5.

2. Deans, C. P., & Kane, M. J. (1992). *International dimensions of information systems and technology.* Boston, MA: PWS-Kent.

3. Berkowitz, P. (1991, December). You say potato, they say McCain. *Canadian Business,* 44–48.

4. In hot pursuit of international markets. (1990, Summer). *Innovation,* 11–13.

5. Laabs, J. J. (1991, August). The global talent search. *Personnel Journal,* 39.

6. Dowling, P., & Welch, D. E. (1991). The strategic adaptation process in international human resource management: A case study. *Human Resource Planning, 14*(1), 61–69.

7. Rosemblum, K. (1992, February 6). Mexicanization of Ford plant: One American left at Sonora. *The Arizona Republic,* C6.

8. Hardy, L., & Barham, K. (1990). International management development in the 1990s. *Journal of European Industrial Training, 14*(6), 31.

9. Boyacigiller, N. (1990). Role of expatriates in the management of interdependence, complexity, and risk of MNNs. *Journal of International Business Studies,* 3rd quarter, 357–378.

10. Mendenhall, M., & Oddou, G. (1985). Dimensions of expatriate acculturation. *Academy of Management Review, 10*(1), 39–47.

11. Canada is increasingly becoming an exporter of business talent—Long. (1995, November 11/13). *The Financial Post,* 19.

12. So you want to move to the US, eh? (1996, January). *The Financial Post Magazine,* 30–37.

13. Oster, P. (1993, November). Why Japan's execs travel better. *Business Week,* 68.

14. Stephens, G. K., & Black, S. (1991). The impact of spouse's career-orientation on managers during international transfers. *Journal of Management Studies, 28*(4), 417–429; and Tung, R. (1988). *The new expatriates: Managing human resources abroad.* Cambridge, MA: Bellinger.

15. Gómez-Mejía, L. R., & Balkin, D. B. (1987). The determinants of managerial satisfaction with the expatriation and repatriation process. *Journal of Management Development, 6,* 7–18; Hamill, J. (1989). Expatriate policies in British multinationals. *Journal of General Management, 14*(4), 19–26; and Hixon, A. L. (1986, March). Why corporations make haphazard overseas staffing decisions. *Personnel Administrator,* 91–94.

16. Fuchsberg, G. (1992, January 9). As costs of overseas assignments climb, firms select expatriates more carefully. *The Wall Street Journal,* B1.

17. Rowland, M. (1993, December 5). Thriving in a foreign environment. *The New York Times,* Sect. 3, p. 17.

18. Swaak, R.A. (1995, September-October). Role of human resources in China. *Compensation and Benefits Review,* 39–46.

19. Dunbar, E., & Katcher, A. (1990, September). Preparing managers for foreign assignments. *Training and Development Journal,* 45–47.

20. Kim, W. C., & Mauborgne, R. A. (1987). Cross cultural strategies. *Journal of Business Strategy, 7*(4), 28–35 (p. 30).

21. *Fortune,* (1995, October 16). From the front, 225.

22. Personal interview conducted by authors.

23. Swaak, *op. cit.*

24. Dallas, S. (1995, May 15). Working overseas: Rule no. 1: Don't diss the locals. *Business Week,* 8.

25. Tung, 1988.

26. Ivancevich, J., & Baker, J. (1970). A comparative study of the satisfaction of domestic United States managers and overseas United States managers. *Academy of Management Journal 13*(1), 69–77.

27. Pascoe, R. (1992, March 2). Employers ignore expatriate wives at their own peril. *The Wall Street Journal,* A10.

28. Oster, P. (1993, November 1). The fast track leads overseas. *Business Week,* 64–68.

29. Oddou, G. R., & Mendenhall, M. E. (1991, January–February). Succession planning for the 21st century: How well are we grooming our future business leaders? *Business Horizons,* 26–35.

30. *Id.*

31. Gómez-Mejía & Balkin, 1987.

32. Oddou & Mendenhall, 1991, p. 29.

33. Gómez-Mejía & Balkin, 1987.

34. Personal interview conducted by authors.

35. Gómez-Mejía & Balkin, 1987.

36. Personal interview conducted by authors.

37. *CompFlash.* (1994, March). Expatriate numbers should continue to rise, 9.

38. Oster, P. (1993). The fast track leads overseas.

39. Hixon, 1986.

40. Burn, D. (1995, June). Crossing global bridges. *Human Resource Professional,* 9–11.

41. Bird, A., & Makuda, M. (1989). Expatriates in their own home: A new twist in the human resource management strategies of Japanese MNCs. *Human Resource Management, 28*(4), 437–453.

42. Successful executive relations depend on HR's attention to family concerns. (1993, October). *Canadian HR Reporter,* 6.

43. Barrett, A. (1995, April 17). It's a small business world. *Business Week,* 96–97.

44. Beamish, P. W., Killing, J. P., Secraw, D. J., & Morrison, A. J. (1994) *International Management.* Burr Ridge, FL: Irwin.

45. Lublin, J.S. (1992, August 4). Companies use cross-cultural training to help their employees adjust abroad. *The Wall Street Journal,* B1, B3.

46. Hagerty, B. (1993a, June 14). Trainers help expatriate employees build bridges to different cultures. *The Wall Street Journal,* B1, B3.

47. Kendall, D. W. (1981). Repatriation: An ending and a beginning. *Business Horizons, 24*(6), 21–25.

48. *The Wall Street Journal.* (1991, December 6). Expensive cities for expatriates, R1.

49. Fuchsberg, 1992.

50. Lublin, J. S. (1993, March 12). Jobs in Eastern Europe demand more goodies. *The Wall Street Journal,* B1.

51. Reynolds, C. (1994). *Compensation basics for North American expatriates.* Scottsdale, AZ: American Compensation Association.

52. Cook, M. (Ed.). (1993). *The human resources yearbook, 1993–1994 Edition,* 3.14–3.16.

53. *Business Week.* (1990, May 14). The stateless corporation, 98–105.

54. Hofstede, G. (1980). *Culture's consequences.* Beverly Hills, CA: Sage, and (1993). Cultural constraints in management theories. *Academy of Management Executive, 7,* 81–94.

55. Jaeger, A. (1986). Organization development and national culture: Where's the fit? *Academy of Management Review, 11*(1), 178–190.

56. Hofstede, 1980, p. 58.

57. Jaeger, 1986, p. 180.

58. Gómez-Mejía, L. R., & Welbourne, T. (1991). Compensation strategies in a global context. *Human Resource Planning, 14*(1), 38.

59. *Id.*

60. Cavusgil, T. S. (1984). Organizational characteristics associated with export activity. *Journal of Management Studies, 24*(1), 3–21.

61. Gómez-Mejía, L. R. (1988). The role of human resources strategy in export performance: A longitudinal study. *Strategic Management Journal, 9*(3), 493–505.

62. Mahood, C. (1994, April 12). Glegg makes splash abroad. *The Globe and Mail,* B1–B2.

Appendix I • HRM and Business Periodicals

The following is an annotated listing of general business publications and more specialized HRM publications. Many of these resources may prove helpful to you, not only in your study of HRM but also in your own career development. As we noted in the text, more and more companies are shifting career development responsibilities onto their employees, while providing them with tools for career planning. These tools can be the first in your career-planning toolkit.

General Business Periodicals

Across the Board. Conference Board. 845 Third Avenue, New York, NY 10022. Provides articles that present business topics in nontechnical terms. Articles range from discussions of general business issues to examinations of specific companies and industries.

Black Enterprise. Earl G. Graves Publishing Co. 130 Fifth Avenue, New York, NY 10011. *Black Enterprise* focuses on business, jobs, career potential, and financial opportunities as they relate to African, Caribbean, and African-American consciousness. Its annual list of the nation's top black businesses and financial institutions is considered an invaluable accounting of African-American business enterprises.

Business Week. McGraw-Hill, Inc. 1221 Avenue of the Americas, New York, NY 10020. The leading general business magazine, *Business Week* offers comprehensive coverage of the news and developments affecting the business world. It includes information on computers, finance, labor, industry, marketing, science, and technology.

Forbes. Forbes, Inc. 60 Fifth Avenue, New York, NY 10011. A general business magazine that celebrates capitalism. Short articles report on company activities, industry developments, economic trends, and investment tips. It also features the "Forbes 400," a yearly listing of the richest people in America.

Fortune. Time, Inc. Time & Life Building, Rockefeller Center, New York, NY 10020. *Fortune* reports on companies and industries, developments and trends. Its articles tend to be longer than those in other business magazines, and its frequent use of sidebars allows readers to learn more about corollary issues.

Harvard Business Review. Graduate School of Business Administration, Harvard University. Boston, MA 02163. This well-known product of Harvard Business School publishes articles in the areas of business and management. Topics include planning, manufacturing, and innovation. Each issue includes a case study.

Inc.: The Magazine for Growing Companies. Goldhirsch Group, Inc. 38 Commercial Wharf, Boston, MA 02110. *Inc.* is targeted to the person involved in managing new, small, or growing companies. Articles focus on entrepreneurial ventures, general business topics, and profiles of successful managers.

Journal of Business Ethics. Kluwer Academic Publishers. 101 Philip Dr., Norwell, MA 02061. This journal publishes scholarly articles dealing with the ethical issues confronted in business. It is clearly written, free of technical jargon, and contains articles on such topics as ethics and business schools, competitor intelligence, corporate executives, and disasters.

Management Review. American Management Association. 135 West 50th St., New York, NY 10020. This monthly publication describes management trends, techniques, and issues for middle- and upper-level managers in the corporate and public sector.

Nation's Business. U.S. Chamber of Commerce. 1615 H St. N.W., Washington, DC 20062. *Nation's Business* reports on current business activities and topics such as quality, entrepreneurship, and going public. It is directed mainly to entrepreneurs and small business owners and managers. Each issue contains a feature on issues affecting family businesses.

Small Business Reports. American Management Association. 135 West 50th St., New York, NY 10020. Articles in this monthly magazine tend to offer practical advice for small business owners and managers. However, topics are of interest to all business managers.

The Wall Street Journal. Dow Jones & Co., Inc. 200 Liberty St., New York, NY 10281. With a greater circulation than either *The New York Times* or *USA Today*, this comprehensive national newspaper offers in-depth coverage of national and international finance and business. A must for anyone interested in the business of business.

Working Woman. Working Woman, Inc. 230 Park Avenue, New York, NY 10169. Geared toward the white-collar career woman interested in advancing in her field. Articles focus on career advancement, management, communication skills, money management, and investment information. Features items on new technology, changing demographics, and profiles of successful businesswomen. Of special interest is the annual "Hottest Careers" issue featuring listings of up-and-coming occupations.

General Business Periodicals (Canadian)

Canadian Business. (Canadian Business Media Ltd.) Maclean Hunter Building, 777 Bay Street, Toronto, Ontario, M5W 1A7. This monthly magazine covers the full range of business and management issues and is written for a general and managerial audience.

Report on Business Magazine. (The Globe and Mail) 444 Front Street, Toronto, Ontario, M5V 2S9. This magazine is an extension of the "Report on Business" section of the *Globe*, and covers a full range of financial and managerial topics, often emphasizing the international aspects of business.

Regional business magazines. There are periodicals that reflect and report on business and political issues of both regional and national scope. The following is a sampling of such publications.
  a. *Atlantic Progress.* P.O. Box 428, Dartmouth, Nova Scotia, B2Y 3Y5. (E-mail: progress@istar.ca)
  b. *Manitoba Business.* (Canada Wide Magazines and Communications Ltd.) 8 Donald Street, Winnipeg, Manitoba, R3L 2T8.
  c. *Saskatchewan Business.* (Sunrise Publishing) 2213C Hanselman Court, Saskatoon, Saskatchewan, S7L 6A8.

Canadian Business Review. (Conference Board of Canada) 255 Smyth Road, Ottawa, Ontario, K1H 8M7. (WWW: http://ww.conferenceboard.ca) This publication presents conceptual and public policy-oriented articles related to business. It can be useful for the overviews and synthesis of issues discussed.

CCPA Monitor. (Canadian Centre for Policy Alternatives) #804-251 Laurier Avenue West, Ottawa, Ontario. (E-mail: ccpa@magi.com) This publication, produced 10 times a year, provides a broader range of perspectives on business and public policy issues than is typical of most of the business press.

HRM Periodicals

Compensation & Benefits Review. American Management Association. 135 West 50th St., New York, NY 10020. A specialized publication of the American Management Association, this journal contains four to six articles in each issue, covering compensation management and strategy and such diverse topics as job evaluation as a barrier to excellence and compensating overseas executives. One invaluable feature is its condensations of noteworthy articles appearing in other business publications.

Employee Relations Law Journal. Executive Enterprises, Inc. 22 West 21st St., New York, NY 10010. While geared toward attorneys specializing in employment law, in-house counsel, and HR executives, this journal contains practical advice that is not highly technical. Articles deal with such topics as personnel management techniques, legal compliance, and court cases, and such issues as sex discrimination, privacy in the workplace, and drug testing. Features up-to-date coverage of federal regulatory agency actions.

Employee Relations Weekly. Bureau of National Affairs. 1231 25th Street, N.W., Washington, DC 20037. This government publication covers such workplace issues as EEO developments, health and safety, pay and benefits, and policy and practices. Recent articles have touched on employee committees, domestic partner benefits, the Clinton administration's health-care plan, and sexual harassment. Useful for discussions of court cases relevant to employee relations.

HR Magazine. Society for Human Resource Management. 606 N. Washington St., Alexandria, VA 22314. Formerly called *Personnel Administrator,* this magazine offers in-depth coverage of all areas of HRM.

Labor Notes. Labor and Education Research Project. 7435 Michigan Avenue, Detroit, MI 48210. This workers' magazine is as critical of big labour as it is of management. It features nationwide coverage of such issues as contracts, ongoing negotiation, boycotts, working conditions, and problems confronting women and minority workers. Useful for its "shop-floor" view and as counterbalance to the management perspective.

Monthly Labor Review. Bureau of Labor Statistics. U.S. Department of Labor, Washington, DC 20402. The source for U.S. labour statistics. Each issue carries four in-depth articles on labour-related topics.

Organizational Dynamics. American Management Association. 135 West 50th St., New York, NY 10020. Articles deal with appraisal systems and management systems in general, as well as with other relevant aspects of systems administration.

Personnel Journal. 245 Fischer Ave. B-2, Costa Mesa, CA 92626. *Personnel Journal* covers the full range of issues in human resources. There is extensive coverage of current HR policies and practices at actual companies, and each article contains company vital statistics. *Personnel Journal* also sponsors the annual Optimas Awards, which spotlight companies with excellent HR initiatives in a variety of categories.

Public Personnel Management. Personnel Management Association. 1617 Duke St., Alexandria, VA 22314. Research articles useful to personnel administrators in public-sector personnel management. Typical subjects are recruiting, interviewing, training, sick leave, and home-based employment.

Supervisory Management. American Management Association, 135 West 50th St., New York, NY 10020. Within its concise 12-page format, this magazine contains numerous brief articles offering practical advice on such topics as building quality awareness, handling problem employees, and conducting effective meetings.

Training & Development. American Society for Training & Development. 1640 King St., Alexandria, VA 22313. The official magazine of ASTD, *Training & Development* is directed toward HR professionals and other managers. It covers both practical issues and trends in training and development, including such topics as how to make a training video, how to train workers to write more clearly, and the ins and outs of successful diversity training.

HR Publications (Canadian)

Human Resources Professional. Human Resources Professionals Association of Ontario. 2 Bloor Street West, Suite 1902, Toronto, Ontario, M4W 3E2. This magazine includes a large number of articles of interest to HRM readers anywhere in Canada, although there is an emphasis on Ontario in articles dealing with legal aspects of employment.

Canadian HR Reporter. 133 Richmond Street West, Toronto, Ontario, M5H 3M8. This bi-weekly publication contains a variety of articles and columns on the full spectrum of sub-fields within HRM. Its coverage is national and its format emphasizes relatively short, focused articles, often based on the experience of a specific employer or HRM policy.

Occupational Health and Safety Canada. (Southam Magazine and Information Group) 1450 Don Mills Road, Don Mills, Ontario, M3B 2X7.

Canadian Occupational Safety. (Clifford/Elliot Ltd.) Royal Life Centre, Suite 209, 277 Lakeshore Road East, Oakville, Ontario, L6J 6J3.

Benefits Canada. (Maclean Hunter Ltd.) 777 Bay Street, Toronto, Ontario, M5W 1A7.

Human Resources Management in Canada. (Carswell-Thomson Professional Publishing) One Corporate Plaza, 2075 Kennedy Road, Scarborough, Ontario, M1T 3V4. This is a combination reference and professional newsletter publication. Contained in two binders, there are applications-oriented reference sections on most major sub-functions within HRM and monthly "Report Bulletins" as well as feature articles on topical matters.

Relations Industrielles/Industrial Relations. (Département des rélations industrielles de l'Université Laval) Québec, Québec. G1K 7P4. (E-mail: relat.ind@rlt.ulaval.ca). This academic journal contains human resource and labour economics research, most of it specific to Canada. Articles are in French or English.

Company, Name, and Product Index

Subject Index

Key terms are shown in boldface type.

Total disability, 478
Total quality management (TQM)
　feedback, 389
　information about rivals, 389
　recognition, importance of, 403
　strategy, 50
　work flow analysis and, 52
Trainers, 240, 247
Training
　behaviour modelling, 254–55
　and career development, 26
　cost, 179
　cost effectiveness of, 234–36
　creativity, 249–50
　crisis, 252
　cross-cultural, 514–15
　cross-functional, 247
　customer service, 252, 253
　defined, 233
　difference between development and,
　　233–34
　diversity, 252
　effectiveness, 236
　experiential, 249
　leadership, 249
　literacy, 250–52
　management, 276
　off-the-job, 240–41
　on-the-job, 239–40
　performance deficits and, 234, 433
　skills, 244–46
　See also Presentation options
Training process
　development and conduct phase,
　　239–52
　evaluation phase, 252–54
　needs assessment phase, 237–38
Trait appraisal instruments, 207–8
Traits, 158
Transfer, of deficient worker, 238
Transnational corporations, 505
Tripartite panel, 464
Troubled employee, 400
Tuition assistance programs, 275
Turnover rate, 178
Two-factor theory, 56
Two-way communication, 386

U

Uncertainty avoidance, 518, 520
Unemployment, benefits, 351, 363
Union acceptance strategy, 453–55
Union avoidance strategy, 455–57
Union contracts. *See* Collective agreements
Union steward, 464
Union substitution, 455
Union suppression strategy, 456–57
Unions, 15
　certification, 445
　craft, 441, 447
　and electoral politics, 447, 451
　enterprise, 452–53
　European, 450–52
　factors for unionizations, 440
　grievance procedure, 398
　industrial, 441, 447
　Japanese, 452–53

legal standing, 443
membership, 448–50
North American, 441, 446–50, 447
organizing, 457–66
origins of labour movement, 440–43
public sector, 449–50
social and economic policy, influence
　over, 448, 449
and worker training, 467–68
See also Collective agreement; Collective
　bargaining; Labour relations; Labour
　relations strategy
Unit, 3
United Kingdom
　corporate theft, 420
　labour relations, 450
United States
　civil suits in illegal discrimination cases,
　　85
　compansation for CEOs, 336
　domestic market, 5
　employee theft, 420
　employment standards, 310
　equal opportunity law, 102–3
　health and safety, 477, 480–81
　labour relations, 441, 447, 451
　legal protection of homosexuals, 124
Universal concept of management, 115
University, and college recruitment, 151
Unsafe workplace, 431, 481–82
Unstructured interviews, 160
Upward communication, 386
　See also Employee feedback programs

V

Vacations, 90, 364, 369–70
Validity
　defined, 156
　of honesty tests, 164
　of personality tests, 158
Values assessment, 268
Verbal commitments, 85–86
Verbal warning, 424, 425
Vertical skills, 307
Violence, workplace, 485–86
Virtual reality (VR) training, 243–44
Visible minorities
　Gross Domestic Product, 113
　immigration, 126
　"outsider" group status, 129–30
　representation in federally regulated
　　employment, 99
Vision care, 22, 365
Voice mail, 391
Voluntary separation
　defined, 181
　quits, 181
　retirements, 182
　types of, 181–84

W

Wages
　lost, 97
　minimum, 88–90, 309–10
　union, 294, 468
Wagner Act (U.S.), 444
War Measures Act, 444

Wartime Labour Relations Board, 444
Wellness
　plan, 369
　programs, 495–96
Whistleblowing, 421–22
Wholly owned subsidiary, 505
Wildcat strike, 463
Within-pay-range positioning criteria, 305
Women
　communication style, 395
　economic role of, 12–13
　glass ceiling effect, 92, 116, 119
　as head of families, 119
　labour force participation, 5, 112
　occupational segregation, 102
　representation in federally regulated
　　employment, 99
　in senior management, 20
　social roles, 119–20
　in traditional occupations, 119
　union membership, 448
　victims of violence, 485
Work
　group perspective, 53–55
　hours, 90
　individual perspective, 55–70
　organizational perspective, 48–53
　simplification, 58–59
　specialization, 50
　standard week, 90
Work adjustment theory, 56
Work councils, 452
Work flow, 24, 25
　analysis, 51–52
　defined, 48
Work rules
　defined, 447
　flexibility, 466–67
Work teams. *See* Self-managed work teams;
　Teams
Work-sample tests, 157
Worker-requirements questions, 159
Workers' compensation, 351
　abuses, 479
　accidents reporting, requirement,
　　478–79
　benefits, 478
　jurisdictional variation, 362
　"no-fault" insurance, 362
　objective, 362
　origins, 362
　rising costs, 479
　See also Health and safety legislation
Workforce diversity. *See* Diversity
Workplace Harassment (Ontario Women's
　Directorate), 121
Workplace Hazardous Materials Information
　System (WHMIS), 491–92
Written warning, 424, 425
Wrongful dismissal, 85, 217, 411, 415, 418

Y

Yield ratios, 154
Yukon
　human rights code, 93
　pay equity, 102
　workers compensation system, 479

Photo Credits